The Routledge Handbook of
Applied Linguistics

The Routledge Handbook of Applied Linguistics serves as an introduction and reference point to key areas in the field of applied linguistics.

The five sections of the volume encompass a wide range of topics from a variety of perspectives:

- Applied linguistics in action
- Language learning, language education
- Language, culture and identity
- Perspectives on language in use
- Descriptions of language for applied linguistics

The 47 chapters connect knowledge about language to decision-making in the real world. The volume as a whole highlights the role of applied linguistics, which is to make insights drawn from language study relevant to such decision-making.

The chapters are written by specialists from around the world. Each one provides an overview of the history of the topic, the main current issues and possible future trajectory. Where appropriate, authors discuss the impact and use of new technology in the area. Suggestions for further reading are provided with every chapter. *The Routledge Handbook of Applied Linguistics* is an essential purchase for postgraduate students of applied linguistics.

James Simpson is a senior lecturer in the School of Education, University of Leeds.

Routledge Handbooks in Applied Linguistics

Routledge Handbooks in Applied Linguistics provide comprehensive overviews of the key topics in applied linguistics. All entries for the handbooks are specially commissioned and written by leading scholars in the field. Clear, accessible and carefully edited, *Routledge Handbooks in Applied Linguistics* are the ideal resource for both advanced undergraduates and postgraduate students.

The Routledge Handbook of Forensic Linguistics
Edited by Malcolm Coulthard and Alison Johnson

The Routledge Handbook of Corpus Linguistics
Edited by Anne O'Keeffe and Mike McCarthy

The Routledge Handbook of World Englishes
Edited by Andy Kirkpatrick

The Routledge Handbook of Applied Linguistics
Edited by James Simpson

The Routledge Handbook of Multilingualism
Edited by Marilyn Martin-Jones, Adrian Blackledge and Angela Creese

The Routledge Handbook of Second Language Acquisition
Edited by Susan Gass and Alison Mackey

The Routledge Handbook of Discourse Analysis
Edited by James Paul Gee and Michael Handford

The Routledge Handbook of Language Testing
Edited by Glenn Fulcher and Fred Davidson

The Routledge Handbook of Intercultural Communication
Edited by Jane Jackson

The Routledge Handbook of Translation Studies
Edited by Carmen Millán and Francesca Bartrina

The Routledge Handbook of Applied Linguistics

Edited by
James Simpson

Routledge
Taylor & Francis Group

LONDON AND NEW YORK

First published in paperback 2013
First published 2011
by Routledge
2 Park Square, Milton Park, Abingdon, OX14 4RN

Simultaneously published in the USA and Canada
by Routledge
711 Third Avenue, New York, NY 10017

Routledge is an imprint of the Taylor & Francis Group, an informa business

British Library Cataloguing in Publication Data
A catalogue record for this book is available from the British Library

Library of Congress Cataloging in Publication Data
The Routledge handbook of applied linguistics / [edited by] James Simpson. – 1st ed.
  p. cm.
  Includes index.
  1. Applied linguistics–Handbooks, manuals, etc. I. Simpson, James, 1967–
  P129.R68 2010
  418–dc22
  2010023814

ISBN: 978-0-415-49067-2 (hbk)
ISBN: 978-0-415-65815-7 (pbk)
ISBN: 978-0-203-83565-4 (ebk)

Typeset in Times New Roman
by Taylor & Francis Books

Contents

Contents

Contents

Tables and figures

Tables

Figures

Illustrations

Contributors

Svenja Adolphs is Professor in Applied Linguistics at the University of Nottingham, UK. Her research interests are in corpus linguistics and discourse analysis and she has published widely in these areas. Her books include *Introducing Electronic Text Analysis: A Practical Guide for Language and Literary Studies* (Routledge, 2006) and *Corpus and Context: Investigating Pragmatic Functions in Spoken Discourse* (John Benjamins, 2008). She has a particular interest in the development and analysis of multi-modal corpora of spoken English, and in the relationship between language-in-use, gesture, prosody, and context.

Elisabeth Ahlsén is Professor of Neurolinguistics at the SSKKII Interdisciplinary Centre of the University of Gothenburg. She is a speech and language therapist. Her main research areas are neurolinguistics, aphasiology, pragmatics, and embodied and multimodal communication.

Mona Baker is Professor of Translation Studies at the Centre for Translation and Intercultural Studies, University of Manchester; author of *In Other Words* and *Translation and Conflict*; Founding Editor of *The Translator*; and Vice-President of the International Association of Translation and Intercultural Studies.

Joe Barcroft is Associate Professor of Spanish and Second Language Acquisition at Washington University in St Louis, MO. His research focuses on second language vocabulary acquisition, lexical input processing, acoustic variability in language learning and processing, and the bilingual mental lexicon.

Judith Baxter is Reader in Applied Linguistics at Aston University. Her research interests are in language and gender, discourse analysis and the language of leadership. She is author of *Positioning Gender in Discourse* (2003), and *The Language of Female Leadership* (2010), both published by Palgrave Macmillan.

Mike Baynham is Professor of TESOL at the University of Leeds and co-convenor of the AILA Language and Migration Research network. He has research interests in migration narratives and edited *Dislocations/Relocations: Narratives of Displacement* (St Jerome Publishing, 2005) with Anna de Fina. He recently edited, with James Collins and Stef Slembrouck, *Globalization and Language Contact*, published by Continuum in 2009.

Selim Ben Said is Assistant Professor in the English Language and Literature Academic Group of the National Institute of Education, Singapore. His research interests include multilingualism, language policy and planning, and linguistic landscapes.

Aditi Bhatia is an Assistant Professor in the Department of English at the City University of Hong Kong. Her research interests include discourse analysis of political, professional and institutional contexts, in particular the discourses of terrorism and the environment. She has been published in international journals such as *Journal of Pragmatics* and *Discourse and Society*, and is currently engaged in an international project on collective argumentation in the climate change debate.

Vijay Bhatia is a Visiting Professor of English at the City University of Hong Kong. His research interests are: genre analysis; ESP and professional communication; simplification of legal and other public documents; cross-cultural and cross-disciplinary variations in professional genres. Two of his books, *Analysing Genre: Language Use in Professional Settings* and *Worlds of Written Discourse: A Genre-based View*, are widely used in genre theory and professional practice.

Simon Borg is Professor of TESOL in the School of Education, University of Leeds. His key areas of research and professional activity in applied linguistics and TESOL are teacher cognition, teacher education, professional development, teacher research, and research methods training. Full details of his work are available at http://www.education.leeds.ac.uk/people/staff/academic/borg/.

Suresh Canagarajah is Kirby Professor in Language Learning at the Pennsylvania State University. He teaches and publishes on bilingualism, literacy, and critical pedagogy. His *Resisting Linguistic Imperialism in English Teaching* (Oxford University Press, 1999) won MLA's Shaughnessy Award.

Jasone Cenoz is Professor of Research Methods in Education at the University of the Basque Country in San Sebastian/Donostia. She works on multilingualism and language acquisition in educational contexts. She is editor of the International Journal of Multilingualism. Her recent publications include a monograph on *Towards Multilingual Education* (Multilingual Matters, 2009) and an edited book on *The Multiple Realities of Multilingualism* (with Elka Todeva, Mouton de Gruyter, 2009).

Sarah Collins is a lecturer in communication at Manchester Medical School, University of Manchester. Her interdisciplinary research focuses on communication in healthcare consultations, and on developing applications for medical and nursing education.

Guy Cook is Professor of Language in Education at King's College London. He has published extensively on discourse analysis, applied linguistics, and language teaching. He was co-editor of *Applied Linguistics* (2004–9) and is Chair of the British Association for Applied Linguistics.

Kees de Bot is Professor at the University of Groningen, the Netherlands and University of the Free State, South Africa. His research interests focus on language development over the lifespan, in particular from a Dynamic Systems perspective.

David Deterding is an Associate Professor at the University of Brunei Darussalam. His book *Singapore English* was published by Edinburgh University Press in 2007, and he has papers on the pronunciation of various East Asian Englishes in *World-Wide English* and RP British English in *Journal of the International Phonetic Association*.

Nick C. Ellis is Professor of Psychology, Research Scientist in the English Language Institute, Professor of Linguistics, and Associate of the Center of the Study of Complex Systems at the University of Michigan. He serves as the General Editor of *Language Learning*.

John Field teaches psycholinguistics at the University of Reading and cognitive approaches to SLA at Cambridge University. He has a long-term commitment to making psycholinguistics more accessible within applied linguistics. His research interests lie in first and second language listening; his latest book is *Listening in the Language Classroom* (Cambridge University Press, 2008).

Thierry Fontenelle is currently Head of the General Affairs Department of the Translation Centre for the Bodies of the European Union in Luxembourg. He is also Past President of the European Association for Lexicography (EURALEX) and an Associate Editor of the *International Journal of Lexicography*. His books include *Turning a Bilingual Dictionary into a Lexical-Semantic Database* (Max Niemeyer Verlag, 1997) and, as editor, *Practical Lexicography: A Reader* (Oxford University Press, 2008).

Helen Fraser studied linguistics and phonetics at Macquarie University, Sydney, and the University of Edinburgh, then taught at the University of New England, Australia, from 1990–2008. Since 1998, a great deal of her research and practice has been focused on applied topics, especially second language pronunciation and forensic phonetics.

Ingrid Gogolin is Professor for Comparative and Intercultural Education at the University of Hamburg, Germany. Her research area concerns migration and multilingualism with special focus on the educational attainment and success of immigrant minority children in schools.

Durk Gorter is Ikerbasque Research Professor at the Faculty of Education of the University of the Basque Country in San Sebastian/Donostia, where he carries out work on multilingualism and minority languages in Europe. His two most recent edited books are *Linguistic Landscape: Expanding the Scenery* (with Elana Shohamy, Routledge, 2009) and *Multilingual Europe: Facts and Policies* (with Guus Extra, Mouton de Gruyter, 2008).

Roxy Harris is a member of the Centre for Language, Discourse and Communication at King's College London. He researches the links between language, power, ethnicity and culture. He is the author of *New Ethnicities and Language Use* (Palgrave Macmillan, 2006).

Nigel Harwood is a Senior Lecturer at the University of Essex. He has published articles on how pronouns and citations are used in academic prose and on taking a critical pragmatic approach to EAP. His main research interests are in the areas of academic writing, EAP, materials design, and corpus-driven pedagogy.

Agnes Weiyun He is an Associate Professor of Applied Linguistics and Asian Studies at Stony Brook University. She is the author of *Reconstructing Institutions* (Greenwood, 1998), co-editor of *Talking and Testing* (John Benjamins, 1998) and primary editor of *Chinese as a Heritage Language* (University of Hawaii Press, 2008).

Sara Howard is Professor of Clinical Phonetics in the Department of Human Communication Sciences at the University of Sheffield. She has published widely in the area of clinical phonetics and phonology and is currently President of the International Clinical Phonetics and Linguistics Association.

Richard Kern is Associate Professor of French and Director of the Berkeley Language Center at the University of California at Berkeley. He teaches courses in French language and linguistics, applied linguistics, and foreign language pedagogy. His research interests include foreign language learning, literacy, and relationships between language and technology.

Andy Kirkpatrick is Chair Professor of English as an International Language at the Hong Kong Institute of Education. His most recent book is *English as a Lingua Franca in ASEAN: The Multilingual Model* (Hong Kong University Press, 2010). He is also editor of *The Routledge Handbook of World Englishes*, published in 2010.

Claire Kramsch is Professor of German and Affiliate Professor of Education at the University of California at Berkeley. She is the author of *Context and Culture in Language Teaching* (Oxford University Press, 1993), *Language and Culture* (Oxford University Press, 1998) and *The Multilingual Subject* (Oxford University Press, 2009).

Diane Larsen-Freeman is Professor of Education, Professor of Linguistics, former Director and current Research Scientist at the English Language Institute, University of Michigan, Ann Arbor. She is also a Distinguished Senior Faculty Fellow at the SIT Graduate Institute in Brattleboro, Vermont. Her academic interests include second language acquisition/development, language teaching methodology, language teacher education, English grammar, and complexity theory.

Phoebe M. S. Lin is a Senior Research Fellow in the Department of Chinese, Translation and Linguistics at the City University of Hong Kong. Her recent research examines the prosody of English phraseology in a multimodal corpus of British academic speech. More generally, her research interests include corpus linguistics, lexical studies, English intonation, spoken discourse, psycholinguistics, and second/foreign language acquisition.

Carmen Llamas lectures in sociolinguistics in the Department of Language and Linguistic Science, University of York. She is co-editor of *The Routledge Companion to Sociolinguistics* (with Peter Stockwell and Louise Mullany, Routledge, 2007) and *Language and Identities* (with Dominic Watt, Edinburgh University Press, 2010).

Janet Maybin is a Senior Lecturer in Language and Communication at the Open University. Originally trained as a social anthropologist, she has written extensively for Open University courses on language, literacy and learning, and also researches and writes on children and adults' informal language and literacy practices.

Bonny Norton is Professor and Distinguished University Scholar in the Department of Language and Literacy Education, University of British Columbia, Canada. Her research addresses identity, language learning, critical literacy, and international development. In 2010, she was the inaugural recipient of the Senior Researcher Award by the Second Language Research SIG of the American Educational Research Association. Her website can be found at http://educ.ubc.ca/faculty/norton/.

Kieran O'Halloran is a Reader in Applied Linguistics at King's College, University of London. Publications include *Critical Discourse Analysis and Language Cognition* (Edinburgh University Press, 2003), *Applying English Grammar: Functional and Corpus Approaches* (with Caroline Coffin and Ann Hewings, Hodder Arnold, 2004) and *Applied Linguistics Methods: A Reader* (with Caroline Coffin and Theresa Lillis, Routledge, 2009).

Anne O'Keeffe, Senior Lecturer at Mary Immaculate College, University of Limerick, Ireland, has published *Investigating Media Discourse* (Routledge, 2006), *From Corpus to Classroom: Language Use and Language Teaching* (with Ronald Carter and Michael McCarthy, Cambridge University Press, 2007), *The Vocabulary Matrix* (with Michael McCarthy and Steve Walsh, Heinle, 2009) *Introducing Pragmatics in Use* (with Brian Clancy and Svenja Adolphs, Routledge, 2011). She has edited *The Routledge Handbook of Copus Linguistics* (with Michael McCarthy, Routledge, 2010).

Barry O'Sullivan is Professor of Applied Linguistics, and Director of the Centre for Language Assessment Research, Roehampton University, London. He has published widely in the area and has presented his work at conferences around the world. He is active in language testing globally, working with ministries, universities and examination boards.

Lourdes Ortega is Professor of Second Language Studies at the University of Hawai'i at Mānoa and serves as Journal Editor of *Language Learning*. Recent books are *Synthesizing Research on Language Learning and Teaching* (co-edited with John Norris, John Benjamins, 2006), *The Longitudinal Study of Advanced L2 Capacities* (co-edited with Heidi Byrnes, Routledge, 2008), and *Understanding Second Language Acquisition* (Hodder Arnold, 2009).

Luis Pérez-González is Senior Lecturer in Translation Studies at the Centre for Translation and Intercultural Studies, University of Manchester; author of numerous papers in scholarly journals and collected volumes on translation studies; and editor of the Features section of *The Interpreter and Translator Trainer*.

Michael Perkins is Emeritus Professor of Clinical Linguistics in the Department of Human Communication Sciences at the University of Sheffield. He has published numerous articles and books both in his specialism of clinical linguistics and in areas such as pragmatics, semantics and language development.

Sarah Peters is a Senior Lecturer and chartered health psychologist at the University of Manchester. Her research focuses on the communication of emotion and illness cognition within clinical settings, with a particular interest in managing and negotiating uncertainty.

Bojana Petrić is a Lecturer at the University of Essex. She has published papers on citations in student writing, students' conceptions of voice, contrastive rhetoric, plagiarism, writer identity, and English teacher identities. Her research interests include academic writing, EAP, and cultural and identity issues in the teaching/learning of English as a global language.

Celia Roberts is Professor of Applied Linguistics at King's College London. She works on the relationship between language and cultural processes in institutional settings and has a particular interest in the practical relevance and application of sociolinguistics to real world problems.

Frances Rock is Senior Lecturer in the Centre for Language and Communication Research at Cardiff University. She has worked on the language of arrest and detention, police interviews and calls for police assistance. She uses a broadly interactional sociolinguistic approach.

Hans-Jörg Schmid holds the Chair of English Linguistics at Munich University, Germany. He is author of *English Abstract Nouns as Conceptual Shells* (Mouton de Gruyter, 2000) and co-author of *An Introduction to Cognitive Linguistics* (2nd edn, Pearson Education, 2006) and has published in the areas of lexical semantics, word-formation, pragmatics and corpus linguistics.

Norbert Schmitt is Professor of Applied Linguistics at the University of Nottingham, and is interested in all aspects of second language vocabulary. He recently published a vocabulary research manual entitled *Researching Vocabulary* with Palgrave Press.

Elena Semino is Professor of Linguistics and Verbal Art in the Department of Linguistics and English Language at Lancaster University. Her books include *Cognitive Stylistics: Language and Cognition in Text Analysis* (co-edited with Jonathan Culpeper, John Benjamins, 2002), *Corpus Stylistics: Speech, Writing and Thought Presentation in a Corpus of English Writing* (with Mick Short, Routledge, 2004) and *Metaphor in Discourse* (Cambridge University Press, 2008).

Gretchen Sunderman is Assistant Professor of Spanish at Florida State University. Her research focuses on the bilingual mental lexicon, the role of individual differences in second language lexical processing, and second language vocabulary acquisition.

Rachel Sutton-Spence is Senior Lecturer in Deaf Studies at the University of Bristol. Her research and teaching are in the field of sign language, especially in creative signing in narratives, poetry and humour.

Michael Swan is a freelance writer specializing in English language teaching and reference material. His interests include descriptive and pedagogic grammar, cross-language influence, instructed and naturalistic second language acquisition, and the relationship between applied linguistic theory and language-teaching practice.

Thomas Tasker is a doctoral candidate at the Pennsylvania State University. He works within a CHAT framework to explore teacher learning through inquiry-based approaches to professional development.

Scott Thornbury is Associate Professor of English Language Studies at the New School, New York. His research interests include language teaching methodology and pedagogical language analysis.

Steven L. Thorne holds faculty appointments in the Department of Foreign Languages and Literatures at Portland State University (USA) and in the Department of Applied Linguistics at the University of Gröningen, the Netherlands. His research has examined social media, multiplayer online gaming, intercultural communication, and cultural-historical and usage-based approaches to second and foreign language development.

Amy B. M. Tsui is Pro-Vice-Chancellor and Vice President as well as Chair Professor of Language and Education at the University of Hong Kong. She has published eight books and numerous articles in the areas of conversation analysis, teachers' professional development, classroom discourse, and language policy.

Karin Tusting is Lecturer in Linguistics and Literacy Studies at the Department of Linguistics and English Language, Lancaster University. Her research draws on linguistic ethnographic methodologies to study literacy practices, with a particular interest in workplace practices and the impact of paperwork demands on people's lives and identities.

Friedrich Ungerer is Emeritus Professor of English Linguistics at the University of Rostock, Germany, but he has also taught at the Universities of Munich, Jena and Minneapolis. He is co-author of *An Introduction to Cognitive Linguistics* (2nd edn, Pearson Education, 2006) and has published on lexical concepts and their conceptual hierarchies, on emotion concepts and metaphors, and also on iconicity.

Nienke van der Hoeven holds degrees in English Language and Literature and Applied Linguistics. She teaches at the University of Gröningen Language Centre and her Ph.D. studies are in the area of language, cognition and ageing.

Theo van Leeuwen is Professor of Media and Communication and Dean of the Faculty of Arts and Social Sciences at the University of Technology, Sydney. He has published widely in the area of critical discourse analysis, social semiotics and multimodality. His books include *Reading Images: The Grammar of Visual Design* (with Gunther Kress, Routledge, 1996), *Speech, Music, Sound* (Palgrave Macmillan, 1999), *Multimodal Discourse: The Modes and Media of Contemporary Communication* (with Gunther Kress, Hodder Arnold, 2001), *Introducing Social Semiotics* (Routledge, 2005), *Discourse and Practice* (Oxford University Press, 2008), and *The Language of Colour* (Routledge, 2010).

Shigenori Wakabayashi is Professor of Applied Linguistics at Chuo University, Japan. He teaches courses in English language, theoretical and applied linguistics, and foreign language pedagogy. His research interests lie in generative approaches to first and second language acquisition, and psycholinguistics. He is a founding member and currently the secretary of the Japan Second Language Association (J-SLA).

Doris S. Warriner is an Assistant Professor of Applied Linguistics at Arizona State University. Her teaching and scholarship on experiences of language learning and displacement is informed by a critical perspective and focuses on questions of access and engaged participation among recently arrived immigrant and refugee families.

Ian Watt is a Professor of Primary and Community Care at the University of York, and a practising GP. His research interests include: communication and health care; effectiveness of health and healthcare interventions; and the dissemination of research evidence and professional behaviour change.

Lionel Wee is a Professor in the Department of English Language and Literature at the National University of Singapore. He is co-author of *Language Policy and Modernity* *in Southeast Asia* and *Style, Identity and Literacy: English in Singapore*, and author of *Language Without Rights.*

Bencie Woll is Professor of Sign Language and Deaf Studies at UCL and Director of the Deafness, Cognition and Language Research Centre. Her research and teaching interests embrace a wide range of topics related to sign language.

Lynne Young is an Associate Professor in the School of Linguistics and Language Studies at Carleton University, Ottawa, Canada. Her research has focused on SFL and CDA; more recently she has extended her studies into the related areas of Multimodality and Social Semiotics.

Acknowledgements

My sense of gratitude on the publication of this volume is deep, for its writing and editing has been a cooperative and collaborative process. First and foremost I wish to thank the contributors for their participation, and for their tolerance of my editorial efforts. I would also like to express my thanks to the following, who generously devoted their time and expertise to read, comment upon and otherwise help develop chapters in the volume: Richard Badger, Mike Baynham, Krystina Benson, Andrew Blake, David Block, John Callaghan, Lynne Cameron, Ron Carter, Michael Clyne, Caroline Coffin, Guy Cook, Melanie Cooke, Justine Coupland, Alice Deignan, Gibson Ferguson, John Flowerdew, Carmen Fought, Maria Luisa Garcia Lecumberri, Phil Graham, Johanna Gundlach, Naseem Hallajow, Roger Hawkins, Margaret Hearnden, Michael Hepworth, Encarna Hidalgo Tenorio, John Ingram, Alison Johnson, Clara Keating, Paul Kerswill, Martin Lamb, Diane Larsen-Freeman, Clare Mar Molinero, John Matthews, Melissa Moyer, Paul Nation, Kieran O'Halloran, Andreas Papapavlou, J. C. Pascual, Graeme Porte, Ben Rampton, John Rickworth, Celia Roberts, Penelope Robinson, Denise Santos, Stef Slembrouck, Ruth Swanwick, Jane Sunderland, Paul Thompson, David Thornton, Steve Walsh, Martin Wedell, Lydia White, Melinda Whong and Stephen Woulds. My advisory board – Ron Carter, Guy Cook, Diane Larsen-Freeman and Amy Tsui – have offered swift, sound and wise advice at all stages of the production of this *Handbook*, and I would like to thank them most sincerely. My colleagues in the School of Education, University of Leeds, and in particular Mike Baynham and Tom Roper have made every effort to enable me to work within and around institutional constraints at crucial points. Catherine Howarth and Louise Williams provided attentive assistance in preparing chapters for publication. Louisa Semlyen at Routledge, and her colleagues Sophie Jaques, Sam Vale Noya and Ursula Mallows, have been unstinting in their support. Finally, as always, to my wife Mary and my sons Joe, Daniel and Lucas I owe untold personal debts.

The publishers wish to thank *The Mirror*, 'Air protesters target travellers', 13 August 2007; by permission of *The Mirror*.

Introduction

Applied linguistics in the contemporary world

James Simpson

This *Handbook* is a reference work covering key topics in applied linguistics. Each chapter provides an accessible introductory overview of an area of the field. The book is intended for a diverse audience, but is firmly oriented towards newcomers: you, the reader, might be a researcher, a graduate student, an academic wanting to familiarize yourself with the field, or a indeed a language professional looking for a 'way in' to one of the many topics encompassed by applied linguistics.

Applied linguistics

Applied linguistics is the academic field which connects knowledge about language to decision-making in the real world. Generally speaking, the role of applied linguists is to make insights drawn from areas of language study relevant to such decision-making. In this sense applied linguistics mediates between theory and practice.

The origins of applied linguistics lie in the mid-twentieth century effort to give an academic underpinning to the study of language teaching and learning. Until at least the 1980s applied linguistics was most closely associated with the problems and puzzles surrounding language pedagogy, learning and acquisition. This focus is still prominent for many: it remains the most active area of applied linguistic enquiry, though the time is past when it could be considered the sole motivation for the field. As chapters in this volume demonstrate, applied linguistics concerns range from the well-established ones of language learning, teaching, testing and teacher education, to matters as disparate as language and the law, the language of institutions, medical communication, media discourse, translation and interpreting, and language planning. Applied linguistics engages with contemporary social questions of culture, ethnicity, gender, identity, ageing, and migration. Applied linguists adopt perspectives on language in use spanning critical discourse analysis, linguistic ethnography, sociocultural theories, literacy, stylistics and sociolinguistics. And applied linguistics draws upon descriptions of language from traditions such as cognitive linguistics, corpus linguistics, generative linguistics and systemic functional linguistics, among others.

Though this is an applied field and an interdisciplinary one, it is not fragmented. The distinctive identity of contemporary applied linguistics can be characterized both in conceptual terms and in terms of its scope and coverage.

The most widely cited definition of applied linguistics comes from Christopher Brumfit, who describes it as: 'the theoretical and empirical investigation of real-world problems in which language is a central issue' (1995: 27). Brumfit's definition is broad enough to encompass the range of areas of enquiry indicated above. It also firmly distinguishes applied linguistics from other related fields by making it problem-oriented. While language is, of course, fundamental to human life, and surrounds us, the problem orientation helps to delimit the field. That is, the motivation for applied linguistics lies not with an interest in autonomous or idealized language, as with understandings of linguistics which deal in linguistic universals: applied linguistics data is typically collected empirically in contexts of use. Nor is its concern with the entirety of 'language in use'. It is demarcated by its interest in how language is implicated in real-world decision-making.

Yet though the problem orientation helpfully bounds applied linguistics, the array of issues opened up by Brumfit's definition can still seem unconstrained, a point made often before. The main ramification is that practically everything in life poses a problem in which language is central: 'It is hard to think of any "real-world" problems', says Greg Myers (2005: 527), 'that do not have a crucial component of language use', for language is a central issue in most human endeavour. Hence a challenge for this volume is to present a view on the extent of the field. Readers will judge the success or otherwise of this, as I sketch out the sections and chapters below.

The scope of this volume

Each chapter in this volume focuses on a specific area of applied linguistics. The chapters share broadly the same format, covering a history of the area, a critical discussion of its main current issues, and an indication of its emergent debates and future trajectory. Where appropriate, authors discuss the influence of new technology in the area. Chapters conclude with a list of related topics in the volume. Each chapter has a section on further reading: a short annotated list of works which readers might consult for a more in-depth treatment of the area. Finally, bibliographical references appear at the end of each chapter, making them self-contained.

In a collection of such size and diversity, there will be aspects to regard critically. Some readers will doubtless disapprove of the way authors have examined a particular topic. Others will take issue with the organization of the volume. And others still will find that the inevitable gaps are insupportable. Clearly, and despite my intention to cover much ground, certain areas are not as fully dealt with as some might wish. Nonetheless, the five sections of the volume do group into broad themes: here I take each in turn to provide an outline.

Part I: Applied linguistics in action

'One is tempted to wonder', says Martin Bygate (2005: 570) 'what is so special about studying language within real-world problems if the only purpose is to use it as a stimulus for academic reflection.' The first section of this *Handbook* consists of chapters on a variety of applied linguistics topics which explain ways in which the study of language involves not only the description of real-world matters, but suggestions about how they can be addressed. Hence, in this section above all, the practical general relevance of applied linguistics is apparent, the issues with which it engages are to the fore, and the breadth of contemporary applied linguistics is reflected. Of the areas chosen, some are well-established sub-fields of applied linguistic study, while others have hitherto been considered independent or peripheral. Readers will realize that in this section, chapters would surely have proliferated, had space allowed.

A number of the chapters invoke globalization. Opening the book, *Language Policy and Planning* has a long history in terms of interventions into language practices, as Lionel Wee says, but a short one as an area of academic study. Wee examines the valuable contributions which applied linguistics can make in this difficult area. For Vijay Bhatia and Aditi Bhatia, *Business Communication* refers specifically to English business communication and English for Business Purposes. Positioning the area firmly in relation to the globalization of trade and commerce, they trace the development of an applied linguistics interest in business communication to sociolinguistically-informed English for Specific Purposes (ESP), genre analysis, and communication studies. Mona Baker and Luis Pérez-González adopt an ideologically critical stance towards their topic, *Translation and Interpreting*, noting its social relevance in globalized, postcolonial society.

For most chapters in the section, the influence of new technology is a crucial current concern. Thierry Fontenelle's chapter on *Lexicography* delves into the fascinating history of the subject. His focus then turns to pedagogical dictionaries for foreign language learners and bilingual dictionaries, and he brings us up to date with informed discussion of the influence of what he rightly terms 'the corpus revolution'. Also concerned with new technology is Anne O'Keeffe: her chapter on *The Media* discusses the applied linguistic interest in print and broadcast genres, and most recently, in what is broadly termed 'new media'.

Celia Roberts, in her chapter on *Institutional Discourse*, describes how institutions are held together by language, and how a study of the language of institutions can afford insights into the way they function. The primary focus of the related chapter, *Medical Communication*, as Sarah Collins, Sarah Peters and Ian Watt note, is the language practices surrounding the doctor-patient relationship, in consultations and other encounters. They attend to the increasing interest in cultural and linguistic diversity, and to the influence of new technology as the computer enters the relationship. *Clinical Linguistics*, explain Michael Perkins and Sara Howard in their foundational survey of the area, involves the study of how language and communication may be impaired. They point to its interdisciplinarity, its connections with social and medical sciences as well as linguistics. Kees de Bot and Nienke van der Hoeven present a cognitively oriented chapter on *Language and Ageing*, covering the effects of ageing on language use and cognitive processing.

Finally, in this section there are few areas where the practical nature of applied linguistics is more apparent than with *Forensic Linguistics*, which, as Frances Rock notes in her chapter, 'permits linguists to make positive contributions to the operation of law and thus society'.

Part II: Language learning, language education

Language learning and language education are at the historical heart and core of applied linguistics, a field with a commitment to mediating between theory and practice (Widdowson 1984). This obligation is clear in the study of language learning, which investigates the two-way relationship between the tangible practical experience of learners and teachers on the one hand, and more abstract perspectives on language and learning on the other. As Cook and Seidlhofer (1995: 10) suggest: 'Teachers like to have a sound theoretical underpinning for what they do: one which does justice to the complexity of language, language learners, language learning, and the social context in which these exist.' Applied linguists with an interest in language teaching will certainly find much of relevance beyond this section: other practically oriented and more theoretically oriented chapters will no doubt inform those involved in language teaching and learning. Inclusion of the topics in this section clears the ground for a considered reflection of the field for those professionals for whom language learning and teaching are their daily concern.

Language pedagogy is both fast-moving and at the same time subject to shifts of fashion which are confusing for novices and veterans alike. The three opening chapters provide an accessible basis for an informed understanding. The first chapter frames the section: Diane Larsen-Freeman writes about *Key Concepts in Language Learning and Language Education*. Lourdes Ortega's chapter on *Second Language Acquisition* and Scott Thornbury's on *Language Teaching Methodology* complement the opening chapter with, on the one hand, a focus on theory, and on the other, attention to practice.

The global relevance of applied linguistic concerns is greatly in evidence in this section. Richard Kern, in his chapter *Technology and Language Learning*, describes the purposes for which digital technology has been used in language learning, relating these to features of electronic discourse and the affordances of new technologies. Not least among these is the ability learners now have to engage with communication in a new language and culture. Simon Borg, in addressing the 'diverse global scope' of *Language Teacher Education*, stresses the connections between contexts of initial and continuing teacher education, regardless of the languages at issue or where the activity takes place. Ingrid Gogolin discusses the specific issues of *Bilingual Education* in an increasingly multilingual world.

Nigel Harwood and Bojana Petrić present an overview of *English for Academic Purposes*. They point out that although EAP relates to the very practical matter of assisting learners' study of English, research in the area has contributed to applied linguistic theory more generally. The chapter on *Language Testing*, by Barry O'Sullivan, likewise engages with the practical and the theoretical, including a treatment of validity and test validation, and critical discussion of emerging debates. Amy Tsui's chapter on *Classroom Discourse* explains how discourse analysis is employed to study a range of issues relating to language use in language classrooms.

Finally, in this section Agnes He discusses a view of language in which she considers it not as a body of knowledge but as semiotic resource. *Language Socialization* is concerned with how novices, who might be children, language learners, or new members of communities, are socialized to be competent members in the 'target culture' through language use, and how they are socialized to use language. This is an approach which provides a counterbalance in language pedagogy to more familiar understandings of the nature of language, its learning, and its use.

Part III: Language, culture and identity

Understanding language learning and use involves far more than an investigation of its formal properties. Chapters in this section give voice to the recognition that matters of culture and identity are intertwined with language use, and with knowledge about language. The applied linguistic concern with language in the social world entails an exploration of phenomena, connections and relationships from the micro to the macro scale – from language-related issues of individual identity to those of globalized society.

The study of culture and of identity runs as a thread through contemporary social sciences. The first two chapters of this section, presenting an applied linguistics exploration of the subjects, complement and to an extent contrast with each other. Claire Kramsch, in her chapter *Culture*, discusses the development of an interest in culture in applied linguistics. Bonny Norton's focus is on *Identity* and the individual. In each case, the authors argue against a conception of language as abstract and of language learning as a decontextualized skill.

Claire Kramsch maintains a position whereby language is viewed as cultural understanding. For Bonny Norton, the study of identity affords an insight into 'the relationship between the language learner and the larger social world'. Closely related concerns are the topics of the next two chapters. In her chapter on *Gender*, Judith Baxter discusses gender, ideology and identity from a sociolinguistic perspective. Roxy Harris's chapter is on *Ethnicity*, a much-neglected topic in applied linguistics, towards which he adopts a critical stance. The very particular issues relating to the description and use of the group of languages known as *Sign Languages* are the subject of the chapter which follows, by Bencie Woll and Rachel Sutton-Spence.

Globalization is the concern of the next chapters in the section. Language teachers of all stripes will find these chapters relevant and interesting, relating as they do to questions of differences between and within languages, the dominance of one language or variety of a language over others. The position and role of world languages, and the growth of English in particular, is a key applied linguistic concern which connects to English language learning, for example. Andy Kirkpatrick and David Deterding discuss the status, development and future of *World Englishes*. World languages are examined from a more critical perspective by Suresh Canagarajah and Selim Ben Said, in their chapter on *Linguistic Imperialism*.

Global society in the post-colonial age is characterized by international flows of people, bringing the issues of multilingualism and migration to the fore. In their chapter on *Multilingualism*, Jasone Cenoz and Durk Gorter note that 'a traditional monolingual view has seen multilingualism as a problem'. The alternative view which they outline considers it as 'a powerful resource for individuals and societies'. Migration is increasingly of interest to language professionals, for example those whose concern is with the teaching of a new language to migrants. The final chapter in this section, *Language and Migration* by Mike Baynham, presents a framework for its study.

Part IV: Perspectives on language in use

Language surrounds us: it is central to psychological and cognitive development, and to social contact, relationships and understandings; it pervades human life. Perspectives on the study of language in use are therefore by definition wide-ranging. The varied and intersecting chapters in this section examine approaches to the study of language use, language development in the brain and the mind, and language in society. The particular aspect of language in use that is the object of enquiry will bear on the view of language itself, and these chapters usefully develop the question of the complexity and multiplicity of what language *is*, and thus foreshadow the final section.

Guy Cook's chapter on *Discourse Analysis* opens the section. Cook reminds us that an interest in discourse analysis originated 'in an awareness of the inability of formal linguistics to account for how participants in communication achieve meaning'. As such, it has been highly influential in pushing the entire field of applied linguistics towards its current independent status. Cook ends on a quizzical note, however, contemplating the very identity of discourse analysis as a distinct area of study. Kieran O'Halloran writes on another significant and somewhat contested applied linguistic area, *Critical Discourse Analysis*, the investigation of how 'language use may be affirming and indeed reproducing the perspectives, values and ways of talking of the powerful, which may not be in the interests of the less powerful'.

Language development as it relates to individual neurological and psychological processes, and to the broader social context, is the focus of the following three chapters. Elisabeth Ahlsén notes that *Neurolinguistics*, the study of language and the brain, is a truly interdisciplinary pursuit, involving neuroscience, psychology, linguistics, speech pathology and biology. Its relevance to therapy in particular makes it an applied linguistic concern. In his chapter *Psycholinguistics*, John Field explores some familiar territory for applied linguistics, as he examines the cognitive processes at play in language use and acquisition. *Sociocultural and Cultural-Historical Theories of Language Development*, explain Steven Thorne and Thomas Tasker, view mental development as fundamentally constructed through 'engagement with cultural practices, artifacts, and milieus'. This understanding of language development stresses the relationship between an individual's development and 'the social and material conditions of everyday life, including those comprising formal instructional settings'.

Sociolinguistics – the topic of the chapter by Carmen Llamas – is itself a broad field of language study, and concerns language in social contexts, language change and variation, and the signalling and interpretation of meaning in interaction, all matters of central relevance and connection to applied linguistics. Janet Maybin and Karin Tusting write on *Linguistic Ethnography*, a fast-growing area which combines ethnography with linguistics and other strategies to investigate social processes. Perhaps because of its *emic* perspective and sensitivity to contextual features, linguistic ethnography is emerging as a key paradigm for investigating language in use in the world today. Doris Warriner adopts an approach to *Literacy* which also regards language and literacy practices as contextually situated. Such practices – as she says – can be seen not as problems but as resources 'which might be differentially valued and supported depending on situation, place, audience, and goals'. Finally in this section *Stylistics* is concerned with the description and interpretation of distinctive linguistic choices and patterns in general and in literary texts, as Elena Semino explains in her overview.

Part V: Descriptions of language for applied linguistics

At a time when applied linguistics was still establishing its identity as a field of study, debates emerged about whether 'applied linguistics' should in fact be properly thought of as 'linguistics applied' (Widdowson 1984). That is to say, how far should *linguistics* provide the basic principles upon which applied linguistics should draw? In the 'linguistics-applied' view, the theoretical foundations derive from linguistics: for proponents of this view, linguistic theories came first and were applied – and in the early days, were applied exclusively – to language teaching problems. In short, in the 'linguistics-applied' view there is no sense that applied linguistics needs its own theory, for the theories come from linguistics. (See Davies 1999: chapter 1, and Cook 2005, for discussions.) With the widespread acceptance of Brumfit's formulation – *the theoretical and empirical investigation of real-world problems* – the sanction for applied linguistics to develop its own models of description is now no longer contended. The central questions for theory therefore become, in Widdowson's words (1984: 22): 'how can *relevant* models of language description be devised, and what are the factors which will determine their effectiveness?' Part V presents descriptions of language for applied linguistics: in each case, authors discuss the concerns that might be addressed effectively with such models. It could be said that applied linguistics is in part defined by its approaches to the description of language: a field which is concerned with real-world decision-making characteristically makes use of empirically secured data and empirical research methods. Nonetheless, in an echo of earlier chapters, readers will note that no one description, model or view of language will suffice for all intentions: one's understanding of language will depend to an extent on one's particular concern of the time, and it is for readers to judge the relevance of these descriptions for their own purposes. As Widdowson notes (2003: 14), applied lingusitcs 'does not impose a way of thinking, but points things out that might be worth thinking about'.

The section opens with three chapters of importance to language teaching and learning, and certainly with broad general relevance. Michael Swan presents an overview of *Grammar* in its 'narrow sense', that is, morphology and syntax. This chapter is followed by that on *Lexis*, by Joe Barcroft, Gretchen Sunderman and Norbert Schmitt, who describe this as the area of language study where form and meaning meet. Speech, argues Helen Fraser in her chapter on *Phonetics and Phonology*, is best regarded as a complex (rather than a complicated) system; she outlines a theoretical approach to the study of speech that is relevant to practice – for example, to language teaching.

Svenja Adolphs and Phoebe Lin provide an overview of the data-driven study of language description that is *Corpus Linguistics*. The influence of corpus linguistics is undisputed: many authors of chapters in this volume describe how the insights gained by the study of machine-readable samples of real spoken and written language have transformed their own areas. In *Cognitive Linguistics*, as Hans-Jörg Schmid and Friedrich Ungerer put it in their chapter, 'knowledge about linguistic structures is explained with recourse to our knowledge about the world, and it is assumed that language both reflects and contributes to shaping this knowledge'.

The following three chapters present competing accounts of language description. Lynne Young, discussing *Systemic Functional Linguistics* (SFL), explains the view of language inspired by the work of Halliday: language as a social semiotic, a system of meaning-making embedded in social contexts of use. Shigenori Wakabayashi makes the case for the relevance of an area of language description frequently misunderstood as not relevant to applied linguistics – *Generative Grammar*. In some contrast, in *The Emergence of Language as a Complex Adaptive System*, Nick Ellis describes the emergent patternings of language, and how these are revealed when it is viewed as a complex system.

The final chapter in the volume, on *Multimodality*, connects linguistic to non-linguistic dimensions of meaning-making, as Theo van Leeuwen explains how language cannot be adequately understood without taking non-verbal communication into account.

References

Brumfit, C. J. (1995) 'Teacher professionalism and research', in G. Cook and B. Seidlhofer (eds) *Principles and Practice in Applied Linguistics: Studies in Honour of H. G. Widdowson*, Oxford: Oxford University Press.

Bygate, M. (2005) 'Applied linguistics: a pragmatic discipline, a generic discipline?', *Applied Linguistics* 26(4): 568–81.

Cook, G. (2003) *Applied Linguistics*, Oxford: Oxford University Press.

——(2005) 'Calm seas or troubled waters? Transitions, definitions and disagreements in applied linguistics', *International Journal of Applied Linguistics* 15(3): 282–302.

Cook, G. and Seidlhofer, B. (eds) (1995) *Principles and Practice in Applied Linguistics: Studies in Honour of H. G. Widdowson*, Oxford: Oxford University Press.

Davies, A. (1999) *An Introduction to Applied Linguistics: From Practice to Theory*, Edinburgh: Edinburgh University Press.

Myers, G. (2005) 'Applied linguists and institutions of opinion', *Applied Linguistics* 26(4): 527–44.

Widdowson, H. G. (1984) 'Models and fictions', in H. G. Widdowson (ed.) *Explorations in Applied Linguistics 2*, Oxford: Oxford University Press.

——(2003) *Defining Issues in English Language Teaching*, Oxford: Oxford University Press.

Part I
Applied linguistics in action

1

Language policy and planning

Lionel Wee

Introduction

Understood broadly as interventions into language practices, language policy and planning (LPP) has had a long and checkered history. As an academic discipline, however, LPP is relatively recent in origin, having gained momentum from the drives toward nationalism and nation building (Wright 2004: 8).

The focus of this overview is primarily on developments within LPP as an academic discipline. The modern history of this discipline can be described in terms of three main stages (Ricento 2000): (i) an initial stage of optimism in the 1960s and 1970s that the language problems of newly independent states could be solved via the implementation of rational and systematic procedures; (ii) a period of disillusionment in the wake of LPP failures (1980s and 1990s) that opened the way for a more critical and reflexive appreciation of the role that language and linguists play in society; and (iii) in the present period, a growing sense that LPP needs to be reconstituted as a multidisciplinary and politicized approach, since the issues it grapples with are complex and represent interests that can pervade multiple levels of social life, ranging from the individual to the state and across state boundaries as well.

A motif of this chapter is that it is worth viewing this history of LPP as a dynamic interplay between academic concerns, on the one hand, and political/bureaucratic interests, on the other. The benefit of such a perspective is that it provides us with a better awareness of the kinds of constraints faced by applied linguistics as it attempts to engage with 'real-world' language-related problems.

So, though it is the next section that specifically delves into the history of LPP, there is good reason, even as we move on to the later sections, to also keep in mind the challenges that arise when attempting to marry more intellectual understandings of language with the practical demands faced by both policy-makers and the people whose lived experiences are affected by socio-political decisions about language.

LPP: a relatively brief history

Developing nation-states, developing LPP

The emergence of LPP as a coherent field was closely tied to the fact that newly independent states in the postcolonial era (mainly Asian and African) were seen as in need of appropriate modernization and development programs. For these states, the concerns were multiple. There was often a desire to reclaim some essentialized national identity and a language that could be emblematic of this identity, as both were felt to have been lost (or least compromised) under colonial rule. The national identity and language, however mythical, usually had to be (re-) constructed in the context of an ethnolinguistically diverse populace.

Such a situation already carried the potential for inter-ethnic tensions as competing ethnic loyalties had to be measured against any proposed candidate for national language status. But since a significant legacy of the colonial rule was an educated elite class with affiliations towards the colonial language, this meant that in addition to the need to manage ethno-linguistic diversity, there was also the need to stem any potential conflict arising from class divisions. As a consequence, while it was essential that these states worked to forge some sense of national cohesion, it was equally imperative that they aimed to raise the general level of education and welfare amongst the citizenry.

The well-intentioned desire to contribute towards programs that could help cultivate national solidarity whilst also improving on standards of education and creating opportunities for economic growth led linguists to position themselves as expert consultants with the state as client. What this means is that LPP practitioners tended to see themselves as devising maxi-mally rational and efficient 'solutions' to the language 'problems' faced by these states (Haugen 1966; Kloss 1969; Rubin and Jernudd 1971). Thus, LPP was described by Das Gupta and Ferguson (1977: 4–6) as:

> those planned activities which attend to the valuation of language resources, the assign-ment of preferences to one or more languages and their functional ordering, and devel-oping the language resources and their use in a manner consistent with the declared objectives identified as planned targets … successful language planning, or degrees of it, can be understood in terms of the efficacy of planned policy measures as well as the target populations' propensity to comply with the public policies pertaining to language planning.

As a result of this desire to design programs that could contribute to public policy objectives, a series of technical concepts and distinctions were constructed that aimed to provide linguists with the theoretical vocabulary to systematically approach and diagnose LPP-related issues. Examples include:

(i) The idea of a *rational model* (Jernudd 1973), where alternative ways of tackling a problem were carefully compared before settling on the optimal choice. This approach assumed that LPP issues could be approached in terms of a cost-benefit analysis.

(ii) The distinction between *status planning* and *corpus planning* (Kloss 1969): the former was concerned with official decisions about the appropriate use of a language. The latter was concerned with developing the 'nuts and bolts' of language itself (its vocabulary, forms of pronunciation and syntax), so that a language could indeed serve its designated function.

(iii) The distinction between processes of language *selection*, *codification* of the selected language as standard or correct, *elaboration* of the language form where necessary, and *implementation* to ensure that the standards were properly adopted (Haugen 1966). These processes were typically understood to apply sequentially, so that LPP would be pursued in a manner that was organized and systematic.

And understandably, the preferred method for data gathering during this period was the sociolinguistic survey. Given that LPP practitioners were mostly working at the level of the state, the scale of the envisaged changes made the choice of survey a practical one, as far as the tracking of language attitude and use amongst a large population were concerned. Information gathered via the survey was also more amenable to quantification, and relative rates of success could then be presented in a manner that was digestible to policy-makers.

There is no disputing the fact that these concepts and distinctions, even today, continue to serve as valuable tools when thinking about LPP. This is because, at bottom, LPP involves making decisions about the desirability (or not) of promoting some language practices over others. And all such decisions require some appreciation of the possible relationships between forms of language and their uses, and the ways in which these relationships might be influenced.

What was problematic in this period, however, was the absence of a critical orientation that might have otherwise prevented a number of assumptions from going unquestioned, such as the notion that each nation-state would be ideally served by having just one national language; the concomitant implication that multilingualism is potentially problematic and ought to be minimized; and the belief that a developmental model designed for one societal context could be applied to another despite significant differences in socio-cultural and historical specificities.

As a consequence, these assumptions often guided the enthusiastic articulation of solutions designed along technocratic lines, when it would perhaps have been more helpful to ask if the framing of what counts as an LPP problem was itself in need of interrogation. I say 'perhaps' because, to be fair to these early attempts at LPP, it is not clear what kind of impact such a critical orientation – had one been present – would have had on decision-makers involved in the management of state objectives. There was always the possibility that in challenging or deconstructing a state's framing of problems, linguists could simply have found themselves deemed largely irrelevant to the needs of these newly independent states.

Looking within

By the 1980s and part of the 1990s, however, it became difficult to deny that many of the state-level LPP projects were failures: either the desired outcomes were not achieved, or worse, social and ethnic unrest continued to rise in many states despite the careful implementation of programs. LPP practitioners were then more reticent about acting as advisors to the state. As Blommaert (1996: 203) puts it:

> The grand projects in third world nations more or less disappeared during the 1980s, either because of manifest failure, or because of a lack of interest, resources, or political importance. Language planning experts reoriented their work away from the creation of policies and plans towards the implementation of experimental and mostly small-scale (nongovernmental) projects, and towards assessments of past experiments and current situations. The enthusiasm for language planning as an academic subject faded in the wake of the collapse of state systems and economies in the third world.

This withdrawal of LPP practitioners from the role of expert consultant was accompanied by an internal criticism of the field itself. In an incisive paper, Luke *et al.* (1990: 27) suggested that LPP had been overly concerned with maintaining a 'verneer of scientific objectivity' and had 'tended to avoid directly addressing larger social and political matters within which language change, use and development, and indeed language planning itself are embedded'. Luke *et al.*'s point is that by viewing LPP as an essentially technocratic process of efficiently administering resources so as to achieve specific goals, little consideration had been given to questions of how such processes might help sustain dominance and dependency relations between groups. In other words, by not adequately attending to the socially and politically contested nature of language, LPP initiatives, rather than solving problems, may in fact have simply exacerbated old problems or even created new ones.

In a similar vein, Tollefson (1991) introduced a distinction to characterize what he saw as two major approaches to LPP: the neoclassical and the historical-structural. The major differences between the neoclassical and the historical-structural approaches are as follows (from Wiley 1996: 115):

1 The unit of analysis employed: While the neoclassical approach focuses on individual choices, the historical-structural pays attention to relationships between groups.
2 The role of the historical perspective: The neoclassical is more interested in the current language situation; the historical-structural, in contrast, emphasizes the role of socio-historical factors.
3 Criteria for evaluating plans and policies: The neoclassical is primarily amoral in its outlook; policies are evaluated in terms of how efficiently they achieve their goals. The historical-structural is more sensitive to issue of domination, exploitation and oppression.
4 The role of the social scientist: Consistent with its amoral outlook, the neoclassical assumes that the social scientist must and can approach language problems in an apolitical manner. On the other hand, the historical-structural views political stances as inescapable so that 'those who avoid political questions inadvertently support the status quo'.

The neoclassical approach thus tends to emphasize the rational and individualistic nature of choices. As an illustration, individuals may choose to learn a new language because of certain perceived benefits such as access to better jobs. Or they may decide that the time and money spent on learning a new language may not be worth the potential benefits, and hence may not make the effort to expand their linguistic repertoire. Whatever the outcome, the neoclassical approach treats these as decisions that are freely and rationally made. But Tollefson emphasizes that we need to also ask questions like 'Why must that individual expend those particular costs? Why are those particular benefits rather than others available to that individual? What are the costs and benefits for other people in the community?' (Tollefson 1991: 32). These kinds of questions require attending to the socio-historical contexts and constraints inherited by individuals and *mutatis mutandis*, communities.

LPP in the 1960s and 1970s had tended to work within the neoclassical approach, where, as we have seen, language-related issues were treated as problems that could be rationally and logically solved by adopting the appropriate language policy. The individuals, families, or communities that were the targets of LPP were, by the same token, assumed to be likely to respond in a neoclassical fashion. Consequently, a major problem was that it had neglected to take into consideration the effects of socio-historical factors in constraining the nature of choices.

Tollefson's position is that the neoclassical approach had been all too dominant in LPP, and this state of affairs needed to be changed to show more sensitivity towards the historical-structural approach. This latter approach pays more careful attention to the kinds of interests that particular policies may serve. LPP that is informed by the historical-structural approach would then aim to 'examine the historical basis of policies and to make explicit the mechanisms by which policy decisions serve or undermine particular political and economic interests' (Wiley 1996: 32). This understanding of LPP would have the advantage of helping practitioners be more cognizant of the possibility that planning bodies involved in policy-making may reflect the interests of dominant political groups, and that this may work against any desire to achieve a broader and more equitable distribution of social and economic resources.

As a result of these critical reflections about the flaws and limitations of LPP, energies were instead directed more towards analyzing language-related decisions in a variety of spheres. In addition to those decisions initiated by governments (Pennycook 1994), there was stronger interest in schools (Corson 1989; Heller 1999), and in the workplace (Gee et al. 1996), and there was also a greater focus on the ways in which public debates about language are initiated, resisted or resolved (Blommaert 1999; Cameron 1995; Milroy and Milroy 1999). And perhaps paradoxically, the challenges involved in trying to better understand the complex and often conflicted nature of language in social life helped contribute to the invigoration of LPP.

Renewing LPP

In the present period, LPP has seen renewed interest and activity. A significant part of the excitement stems from the appreciation that linguists need not be apologetic about representing group-specific interests; they simply need to be clear about the nature of their involvement. Another reason for the excitement comes from the realization that LPP is even more complex than has been realized so far, and that if it is to be relevant as a field of applied linguistics, it will need to draw upon the insights of multiple disciplines.

Once it became understood that LPP is always going to be inextricably intertwined with the advancing of specific interests, linguists were able to engage in various LPP-related activities with a clearer appreciation of their roles and responsibilities. 'Scientific objectivity' no longer means being blind to class interests or political factionalism. Rather, it means being aware that by acting as expert consultant to a group, community, institution or state, a linguist has to be clear and comfortable with the goals of the client. Scientific objectivity, in this case, arises from the linguist utilizing his/her expert knowledge about sociolinguistic processes and the ways in which linguistic and non-linguistic variables interact, so as to better advise the client. This does not mean passively accepting a client's goals: it is possible to argue that a consultancy also opens up the opportunity for both the linguist and client to learn from each other. And this process of exchange may lead to an evaluation of the goals as well as a richer understanding of the social nature of language. For example, in their own experience with medical health professionals, Roberts and Sarangi (1999: 474) suggest that it might be useful to adopt a stance of 'joint problematization', where the emphasis is one of 'participatory and action-oriented research'. The advantage of this, as Roberts and Sarangi (1999: 498) point out, is that:

> In presenting findings in a non-conclusive way, social scientific researchers, including discourse analysts, can distance themselves from a problem-solver role by underscoring the fact that practical solutions are not in a one-to-one relationship with research-based

knowledge. In other words, knowledge generated through research needs to be recontextualized in a reflexive way by the practitioners.

In other cases, a linguist may have a very personal commitment towards specific community goals. This could because, having conducted fieldwork in a particular community, a linguist might form a strong attachment to that community and a desire to help improve its wellbeing. In such a case, the linguist is essentially acting as not just expert consultant, but also as advocate. One example is the Master-Apprentice Program that was developed by Leanne Hinton (see Hinton 1997) in 1992 in California. The program aims to prevent, as far as possible, the indigenous Native American languages from dying out. The program pairs master speakers (the tribal elders) with language learners in learning situations with relatively modest outcomes. Apprentices are not expected to develop the same level of fluency as the masters, since many of the masters themselves may have not used their own languages for quite some time. Rather, it is hoped that by the end of about three years, apprentices will be able to hold simple conversations. As Grenoble and Whaley (2006: 63) point out:

> The program does not attempt to revitalize speaker bases and make the target language a fully used system of communication in all aspects. Instead, it is a realistic, practical approach in situations of severe language attrition where it is most probably impossible to build a new speaker community.

The complexity (Spolsky 2004: 39ff) comes from the awareness that LPP can operate at units of varying sizes, including the individual, the family, the social group, the school, the state and the diasporic community. LPP also involves 'a wide range of linguistic and non-linguistic elements', such as age, ethnicity, education, economic progress, gender, religious beliefs, among many others. Furthermore, LPP is not limited to just named varieties of language ('English', 'Spanish', 'Malay') but can involve smaller bits of language (pronunciation, punctuation, word choice) and also bigger bits as well (forms of discourse). To make this complexity more tractable, LPP needs to consistently distinguish between the language practices of a community, language beliefs or ideology, and any efforts to modify or influence the practices (Spolsky 2004: 5). The first two components are always present in any community, since people will be using language for the conduct of activities, and people will also have various beliefs about language. The third component may not be present, since there may not be any actual efforts made to influence language practices. Under such circumstances, 'ideology operates as "default" policy' (Lo Bianco 2004: 750).

This appreciation that LPP must acknowledge the ideological basis of language practices has led to greater convergences with work coming from linguistic anthropology, since it is the latter that has contributed much to theorizing the processes by which language ideologies come to be formed. It should be clarified here that the anthropological notion of ideology is not to be simply equated with false beliefs. Rather, ideologies here refer to the specific social positions that individuals/communities/institutions all inevitably occupy, and which mediate the understanding of sociolinguistic facts. In other words, 'the very real facts of linguistic variation constrain what linguists and native speakers can persuasively say and imagine about them', but at the same time 'there is no "view from nowhere" in representing linguistic differences' so 'those representations, in turn, influence the phenomena they purport to represent' (Irvine and Gal 2000: 78–9).

Sensitivity to the contestable nature of language decisions has also meant a greater need to attend to variability and context when studying LPP. This in turn has led to a widening of the methods that might be considered useful to LPP. Because language ideologies are highly variable and context-dependent, data gathered via the analysis of narratives, ethnographic approaches, and historically sensitive comparisons (Heller 1999; Milani 2007; Pennycook 1998; Philips 2000, among others), all came to be considered relevant to the study of LPP, in addition to surveys. This is not to deny the value of larger scale statistical data, but such data are primarily 'synoptic' representations that abstract away from specific situational details (Bourdieu 1977: 107). They need to be complemented by richer understandings of the roles that actual language practices and the valuations accorded to them play in the lives of individuals and communities.

Paralleling this interest in ideology, Lo Bianco (2004: 743, italics in original) has suggested that in addition to corpus and status planning, LPP also needs to recognize *discourse planning*, which refers to:

> the influence and effect on people's mental states, behaviors and belief systems through the linguistically mediated ideological workings of institutions, disciplines, and diverse social formations. Although discourse is quintessentially dialogical, and by definition permits contest and negotiation, *planning* discourse refers to the efforts of institutions and diverse interests to shape, direct and influence discursive practices and patterns.

This suggestion that attention be paid to discourse planning is obviously entirely congruent with the call by Luke *et al.* that LPP needs to be more appreciative of the fact that there is no such thing as a purely objective or interest-free policy. All such initiatives represent specific agenda, covertly or otherwise (Shohamy 2006). A discourse orientation can thus highlight the ways in which problems are framed, the interests served in such framings, and the possibility of alternative framings (Lakoff 2004; Schön 1993).

Finally, works drawing together the insights of scholars with backgrounds in economics, political philosophy, political science, social theory, as well as linguistics, are slowly becoming more regularly produced (Brown and Ganguly 2003; Kymlicka and Patten 2004; Rappa and Wee 2006). This is a particularly important development that should be further encouraged, since it promises to benefit these contributing disciplines as well as enrich our understanding of LPP. For example, while linguists can hope to learn more about the political complexities that inevitably accompany language in social life, political theory, too, can grow from taking greater note of the complications posed by language, since linguistic diversity 'has received relatively little attention from political theorists' (Patten and Kymlicka 2004: 1). In fact, De Schutter (2007: 1) has pointed out that unless there is greater cross-disciplinary work, there is a danger that debates in political philosophy will end up 'steering its own independent course apart from existing debates over language policy'.

The developments described here are critical because they put LPP in a position to better handle a number of important challenges, and it is to a discussion of these challenges that we now turn.

Challenges for LPP

It would not be an overstatement to suggest that LPP is in fact gaining in practical importance and urgency because of the way the world is developing. As a branch of applied linguistics, there is much that LPP can do to make a contribution to debates and discussions about the role of language in a fast-changing and increasingly culturally complex world.

One significant challenge for LPP is to find ways of addressing multiculturalism. Much of the recent theorizing regarding multiculturalism and the politics of identity has come from philosophically inclined political or legal theorists (Benhabib 2002; Ford 2005; Kymlicka 1995; Taylor 1994) rather than linguists. While such theorizing is undoubtedly valuable, it is usually based on an 'outdated empirical understanding of the concept of language itself' and tends to be 'unaware of important sociolinguistic and other research on these matters' (De Schutter 2007: 3). Where LPP is concerned, the most prominent response has been to call for the adoption of language rights (May 2001; Phillipson and Skutnabb-Kangas 1995). The general motivation behind the proposal for language rights is to ensure that an identifiable group – usually a discriminated or stigmatized ethnic minority – is granted specific forms of protection and consideration on the basis of their associated language. The concept of language rights has had enormous appeal, finding a broad swathe of support amongst linguists, sociologists, political philosophers, policy-makers and community activists (Kymlicka 1995; May 2001; Phillipson and Skutnabb-Kangas 1995). However, this actually makes it all the more critical that language rights be subjected to careful scrutiny (Blommaert 2001; Stroud 2001). For example, while language rights may be useful as a short-term measure, it is not clear that they are tenable in the longer term. One reason for this is that there will be parties who have a vested interest in maintaining their (usually hard-won) language rights, and their motivations – such as the desire to cling to political power or to continue enjoying the benefits afforded by such rights – can be quite independent of how effective such rights may actually have been in dealing with discrimination. This means that LPP needs to better understand the pros and cons of language rights, and where necessary, explore alternative ways of responding to multiculturalism. This requires combining the insights of social and political theorists with a more sophisticated appreciation of the nature of language (Makoni and Pennycook 2007; see also discussion below).

The interest in multiculturalism and language rights gains further resonance because of complications posed by the commodification of language. As Budach *et al.* (2003: 604, upper case in original) point out:

> in a new world dominated by service and information economies, globalization engenders a seemingly paradoxical valuing of community and authenticity … In the new economy … the value of community and authenticity takes on a new shape in which COMMODIFICATION is central. At the same time, commodification provokes a potential uncoupling of language and community.

Speakers and communities are likely to be increasingly caught up in the contradictions between treating language as a mark of cultural heritage, and as a skill or resource to be used for socio-economic advancement. And this can have interesting repercussions on specific implementations of LPP. For example, in Singapore, the policy of multiracialism aims to guarantee equal status amongst the three official ethnic mother tongues: Mandarin (for the Chinese community), Malay (for the Malay community) and Tamil (for the Indian community). However, the state has recently argued that, in addition to heritage reasons, Mandarin should also be learned in order to take advantage of China's growing economy, thereby actively conceding that instrumental value is an important motivating factor in language choice. As a result, Mandarin is now becoming so popular that a growing number of non-Chinese parents want schools to allow their children to study the language. This new emphasis on Mandarin as a language commodity has led to concerns within the Chinese community that the language is being learnt for the 'wrong' reasons: the language is being treated less as an emblem of local ethnicity and more as an economic resource for conducting business negotiations with China. More generally, these developments potentially undermine the multiracial logic of the policy, since the equal status that all three mother tongues are supposed to enjoy is compromised by the fact that neither Malay nor Tamil can be claimed to enjoy the same level of economic cachet as Mandarin (Wee 2003).

Thus, another important challenge for LPP is to take better account of the fact that traditional notions of ethnicity and nation do not fit easily with the multilingual dynamics of late modern societies, which are increasingly characterized by a pervasive culture of consumerism (Baudrillard 1988; Bauman 1998), where 'people define themselves through the messages they transmit to others through the goods and practices that they possess and display' (Warde 1994: 878). In this regard, Stroud and Wee (2007) have suggested that the concept of sociolinguistic consumption should be given a more foundational status in language policy in late modernity, suggesting that this might offer a more comprehensive account of the dynamics of language choice and change.

Finally, one of the most pressing challenges facing the world today is that of global migration and the related issue of ensuring the wellbeing and dignity of individuals as they move across the globe in search of a better life. As many states work to accommodate the presence of foreign workers, asylum seekers and other newcomers within their territories, the need to come up with realistic and sensitive language policies will require the input of LPP specialists. If such input is absent, there is a danger that language policies may unfairly penalize the very people they were intended to help. Maryns (2005) provides one such example in her discussion of a young female from Sierra Leone seeking asylum in Belgium. Even though applicants are given the opportunity to declare what language they want to use for making their case, Maryns (2005: 300) notes that:

> Actual practice, however, reveals serious constraints on language choice, and these constraints are language-ideologically based: only monolingual standard varieties qualify for procedural interaction. This denial of linguistic variation leads to a denial of pidgins and creoles as 'languages in their own right.'

The effect of an ideology of monolingualism is to deny pidgins and creoles any legitimate presence in the asylum-seeking procedure despite the fact that for many asylum seekers, such mixed languages might constitute their most natural communicative codes. Thus, the move to a foreign country is not simply a shift in physical location; it is also a shift into a location where linguistic codes are differently valued. And the asylum seeker is expected to accommodate the foreign bureaucratic context despite the communicative problems this raises. Maryns (2005: 312) points out that:

> The asylum seeker has to explain her very complex and contextually dense case, addressing an official with different expectations about what is relevant and required in a bureaucratic-institutional context. The bureaucratic format of the interview and the time pressure under which the interaction takes place offer very little space for negotiating intended meanings.

In the particular case that Maryns observed, the female applicant's (2005: 313) 'intrinsically mixed linguistic repertoire' (West African Krio) was displaced by the bureaucracy's requirement that interviews and reports utilize only monolingual standards. The interview was conducted in English and a subsequent report written in Dutch, neither of which were languages that the applicant was comfortable with. As a result, details of the applicant's narrative were omitted or misunderstood, and the applicant had no opportunity to correct any inaccuracies. Thus, the state representatives officiating over asylum-granting procedures often conduct interviews with asylum seekers in contexts where the linguistic codes being used are not likely to be shared by those whose communicative needs are greatest. Notice that the problem here goes much deeper than making available different languages, such as Dutch, English, Xhosa or Bantu. It involves a general reluctance to treat certain codes as being *proper languages* in the first place because of their mixed heritage. On this basis, mixed codes become stigmatized and are automatically ruled out of official consideration despite the fact that these codes are precisely what might be needed in order for asylum seekers to gain a fair hearing.

Even when a migrant has been granted permission to stay, challenges to LPP remain. For example, most Western countries have assumed that migrants will assimilate into their new societies by learning the dominant language (and its associated culture). But this assumption is increasingly being challenged by the fact that 'the size of minority residential communities' makes it possible 'that many of their members will be able to live out their lives using only, or predominantly, the minority language', and also by the 'tendency of migrants to maintain closer and more regular connections with their countries of origin' (Ferguson 2006: 7).

The future of LPP

The closing observation in the previous section highlights an urgent need for LPP to start rethinking the ontological nature of language, and seriously evaluate the material implications. For too long, LPP has worked with a relatively convenient conception of language as a stable and identifiably bounded entity corresponding to established language names, despite being aware that this overlooks 'the problematic history of the construction of such languages' (Makoni and Pennycook 2007: 11).

Consider a brief example (from Makoni and Pennycook 2007: 9). Sir George Abraham Grierson's linguistic *Survey of India*, which was completed in 1928, had to face the problem of deciding on the boundaries between languages and dialects. To do this, Grierson openly admitted the need to invent language-names while ignoring the complexity of actual language use (1907: 350, quoted in Makoni and Pennycook 2007: 10):

> nearly all the language-names have had to be invented by Europeans. Some of them, such as Bengali, Assamese, and the like, are founded on words which have received English citizenship, and are not real Indian words at all, while others, like 'Hindostani', 'Bihari', and so forth, are based on already existing Indian names of countries and nationalities.

The significance of this is that 'these were not just new names for existing objects ... but rather the invention and naming of new objects. The naming performatively called the languages into being' (ibid.). This does not mean that LPP should dismiss language names as mere fiction. As a metalinguistic label, it very possibly orients the language practices and social evaluations of speakers towards each other, and conversely, towards those whom they might consider non-members of the group. But LPP needs to start being more attentive to the problematic ways in which specific language practices get categorized under particular labels (including that of *non-*language), and the attendant impact of such categorizations on the social trajectories of different individuals and communities.

Similar considerations apply to concepts such as community, identity, and practice (Heller 2008), which have for too long tended to be treated as 'stable and bounded' rather than 'shifting and dynamic'. These are concepts that figure, in one way or another, in LPP studies, and unless they are reconceptualized, LPP will continue to be encumbered by 'some of their built-in limitations in current confrontations with the way things are unfolding in the world around us, confounding our attempts to understand them' (2008: 505).

Concluding remarks

It is appropriate to end this chapter by returning to the theme of how LPP practitioners should engage policy-makers and the general public. The critical revaluation of concepts such as language, community and identity is part and parcel of the intellectual maturity of the field. But translating the insights gained by this maturity into relevant practical implications is a difficult enterprise. This is because there is an inevitable lag between the scholarly critique of concepts and the ways in which these are apprehended by the broader community. And if policy-makers and members of the public are still operating with less nuanced understandings of such concepts, these could make them less receptive to LPP initiatives that are grounded in more critical orientations.

This is not to say that linguists should be considered final arbiters of appropriate LPP initiatives (recall the reference to Roberts and Sarangi's notion of 'joint problematization'). But it does mean that linguists need to be more strategic about how they position themselves as participants in language ideological debates. Specifically, they need to ask how they can resist the pressure to oversimplify their own expert knowledge of language whilst still remaining relevant to the 'real' world.

Related topics

bilingual education; ethnicity; institutional discourse; language and migration language learning and language education; language testing; linguistic imperialism; multilingualism; world Englishes

Further reading

Blommaert, J. (ed.) (1999) *Language Ideological Debates*, Berlin: Mouton de Gruyter. (This edited collection provides an excellent overview of some of the processes by which public controversies and political debates around language come to be shaped.)
Cameron, D. (2000) *Good to Talk? Living and Working in a Communication Culture*, London: Sage. (Cameron's work presents a highly readable and insightful account of LPP – although this is not a term that is used in the book – in the call center industry and its connections to the broader global economy.)
Makoni, S. and Pennycook, A. (eds) (2007) *Disinventing and Reconstituting Languages*, Clevedon: Multilingual Matters. (This is an important book that reminds us of the need to rethink our assumptions about language and the implications for applied linguistics.)
Spolsky, B. (2004) *Language Policy*, Cambridge: Cambridge University Press. (Spolsky provides an invaluable introduction to key concepts in the study of LPP, conveying the complexities of the field in a highly accessible manner.)
Tollefson, J. W. (1991) *Planning Language, Planning Inequality*, London: Longman. (This is a theoretically rich and ethnographically sensitive book that gives a special focus to language education policies affecting migrants.)

References

Baudrillard, J. (1988) *Selected Writings*, Cambridge: Polity Press.
Bauman, Z. (1998) *Work, Consumerism and the New Poor*, Buckingham: Open University Press.

Benhabib, S. (2002) *The Claims of Culture: Equality and Diversity in a Global Era*, Princeton, NJ: Princeton University Press.

Blommaert, J. (1996) 'Language planning as a discourse on language and society: the linguistic ideology of a scholarly tradition', *Language Policy and Language Planning* 20: 199–222.

——(ed.) (1999) *Language Ideological Debates*, Berlin: Mouton de Grutyer.

——(2001) 'The Asmara Declaration as a sociolinguistic problem: reflections on scholarship and linguistic rights', *Journal of Sociolinguistics* 5(1): 131–42.

Bourdieu, P. (1977) *Outline of a Theory of Practice*, Cambridge: Cambridge University Press.

Brown, M. and Ganguly, S. (eds) (2003) *Fighting Words: Language Policy and Ethnic Relations in Asia*, Cambridge, MA: MIT Press.

Budach, G., Roy, S. and Heller, M. (2003) 'Community and commodity in French Ontario', *Language in Society* 32: 603–27.

Cameron, D. (1995) *Verbal Hygiene*, London: Routledge.

Corson, D. (1989) *Language Policy Across the Curriculum*, Philadelphia, PA: Multilingual Matters.

Das Gupta, J. and Ferguson, C. A. (1977) 'Problems of language planning', in J. Rubin, B. H. Jernudd, J. Das Gupta, J. A. Fishman and C. A. Ferguson (eds) *Language Planning Processes*, The Hague: Mouton.

De Schutter, H. (2007) 'Language policy and political philosophy', *Language Problems and Language Planning* 31(1): 1–23.

Ferguson, G. (2006) *Language Planning and Education*, Edinburgh: Edinburgh University Press.

Ford, R. T. (2005) *Racial Culture: A Critique*, Princeton, NJ: Princeton University Press.

Gee, J. P., Hull, G. and Lankshear, C. (1996) *The New Work Order: Behind the Language of the New Capitalism*, NSW, Australia: Allen and Unwin.

Grenoble, L. A. and Whaley, L. J. (2006) *Saving Languages*, Cambridge: Cambridge University Press.

Haugen, E. (1966) *Language Conflict and Language Planning: The Case of Modern Norwegian*, Cambridge, MA: Harvard University Press.

Heller, M. (1999) *Linguistic Minorities and Modernity*, London: Longman.

——(2008) 'Language and the nation-state: challenges to sociolinguistic theory and practice', *Journal of Sociolinguistics* 12(4): 504–24.

Hinton, L. (1997) 'Survival of endangered languages: The California Master-Apprentice Program', *International Journal of the Sociology of Language* 123: 177–91.

Irvine, J. T. and Gal, S. (2000) 'Language ideology and linguistic differentiation', in P. V. Kroskrity (ed.) *Regimes of Language: Ideologies, Polities and Identities*, Santa Fe, NM: School of American Research Press.

Jernudd, B. H. (1973) 'Language planning as a type of language treatment', in J. Rubin and R. Shuy (eds) *Language Planning: Current Issues and Research*, Washington, DC: Georgetown University Press.

Kloss, H. (1969) *Research Possibilities in Group Bilingualism*, Quebec: International Center for Research on Bilingualism.

Kroskrity, P. V. (ed.) (2000) *Regimes of Language: Ideologies, Polities, and Identities*, Santa Fe, NM: School of American Research Press.

Kymlicka, W. (1995) *Multicultural Citizenship: A Liberal Theory of Minority Rights*, Oxford: Clarendon Press.

Kymlicka, W. and Patten, A. (2004) *Language Rights and Political Theory*, Oxford: Oxford University Press.

Lakoff, G. (2004) *Don't Think of an Elephant! Know your Values and Frame the Debate*, Vermont: Chelsea Green.

Lo Bianco, J. (2004) 'Language planning as applied linguistics', in A. Davies and C. Elder (eds) *Handbook of Applied Linguistics*, Oxford: Blackwell.

Luke, A., McHoul, A. and Mey, J. L. (1990) 'On the limits of language planning: class, state, and power', in R. B. Baldauf, Jr and A. Luke (eds) *Language Planning and Education in Australasia and the South Pacific*, Clevedon: Multilingual Matters.

Makoni, S. and Pennycook, A. (2007) 'Disinventing and reconstituting languages', in S. Makoni and A. Pennycook (eds) *Disinventing and Reconstituting Languages*, Clevedon: Multilingual Matters.

Maryns, K. (2005) 'Monolingual language ideologies and code choice in the Belgian Asylum Procedure', *Language and Communication* 25: 299–314.

May, S. (2001) *Language and Minority Rights: Ethnicity, Nationalism, and the Politics of Language*, London: Longman.

Milani, T. M. (2007) 'Debating Swedish: Language Politics and Ideology in Contemporary Sweden', Ph.D. dissertation, Stockholm University.

Milroy, J. and Milroy, L. (1999) *Authority in Language*, 3rd edn, London: Routledge.

Patten, A. and Kymlicka, W. (2004) 'Introduction', in W. Kymlicka and A. Patten (eds) *Language Rights and Political Theory*, Oxford: Oxford University Press.

Pennycook, A. (1994) *The Cultural Politics of English as an International Language*, Harlow: Longman.

——(1998) *English and the Discourses of Colonialism*, London: Routledge.

Philips, S. U. (2000) 'Constructing a Tongan nation-state through language ideology in the courtroom', in P. V. Kroskrity (ed.) *Regimes of Language: Ideologies, Polities, and Identities*, Santa Fe, NM: School of American Research Press.

Phillipson, R. and Skutnabb-Kangas, T. (1995) 'Linguistic rights and wrongs', *Applied Linguistics* 16(4): 483–504.

Rappa, A. L. and Wee, L. (2006) *Language Policy and Modernity in Southeast Asia*, New York: Springer.

Ricento, T. (2000) 'Historical and theoretical perspectives in language policy and planning', in T. Ricento (ed.) *Ideology, Politics and Language Policies: Focus on English*, Amsterdam: John Benjamins, pp. 9–25.

Roberts, C. and Sarangi, S. (1999) 'Hybridity in gatekeeping discourse: issues of practical relevance for the researcher', in S. Sarangi and C. Roberts (eds) *Talk, Work and Institutional Order: Discourse in Medical, Mediation and Management Settings*, Berlin: Mouton de Gruyter.

Rubin, J. and Jernudd, B. H. (eds) (1971) *Can Language be Planned? Sociolinguistic Theory and Practice for Developing Nations*, Honolulu: University of Hawaii Press.

Shohamy, E. (2006) *Language Policy: Hidden Agendas and New Approaches*, London: Routledge.

Schön, D. A. (1993) 'Generative metaphor: a perspective on problem-setting in social policy', in A. Ortony (ed.) *Metaphor and Thought*, 2nd edn, Cambridge: Cambridge University Press.

Spolsky, B. (2004) *Language Policy*, Cambridge: Cambridge University Press.

Stroud, C. (2001) 'African mother-tongue programs and the politics of language: linguistic citizenship versus linguistic human rights', *Journal of Multilingual and Multicultural Development* 22(4): 339–55.

Stroud, C. and Wee, L. (2007) 'Consuming identities: language planning and policy in Singaporean late modernity', *Language Policy* 6: 253–79.

Taylor, C. (1994) 'The politics of recognition', in A. Gutmann (ed.) *Multiculturalism: Examining the Politics of Recognition*, Princeton, NJ: Princeton University Press.

Tollefson, J. W. (1991) *Planning Language, Planning Inequality: Language Policy in the Community*, New York: Longman.

Warde, A. (1994) 'Consumption, identity-formation and uncertainty', *Sociology* 28(4): 877–98.

Wee, L. (2003) 'Linguistic instrumentalism in Singapore', *Journal of Multilingual and Multicultural Development* 24(3): 211–24.

Wiley, T. G. (1996) 'Language planning and policy', in S. McKay and N. Hornberger (eds) *Sociolinguistics and Language Teaching*, Cambridge: Cambridge University Press.

Wright, S. (2004) *Language Policy and Language Planning: From Nationalism to Globalization*, Basingstoke: Palgrave Macmillan.

2

Business communication

Vijay Bhatia and Aditi Bhatia

Introduction

Business communication, as used in this chapter, refers to English business communication and English for Business Purposes (EBP), and represents a development that integrates three main areas of study. The first significant area is English for Specific Purposes (ESP), which draws its strength from linguistics, particularly from sociolinguistics, through the analyses of functional variation in language use, and curriculum studies. In fact, the ESP tradition can be considered an outcome of analysis of various forms of academic and disciplinary discourses within the framework of register analysis, and more recently, genre analysis (Swales 1990), which may be considered the second major area of study that has influenced business communication. The third main tradition, which has significantly influenced current thinking in business communication, is communication studies, which has several dimensions, some of which include organizational communication, management communication, and corporate communication, all of which are often grouped under professional communication. Unlike ESP, which draws its inspiration from language description, none of these rather different sub-areas of communication studies have been seriously influenced by studies in discourse and genre analysis until recently. Instead, they have traditionally drawn their strength from various communication theories. The focus in these individual dimensions of professional communication has been primarily on text-external factors, including context. It is interesting to note that of these major traditions, two at least, i.e. ESP and communication studies, developed almost independently of each other, and remained so for a long time, the latter focusing primarily on first language users, and the former targeting second or foreign language users. Register and genre analysis developed when the field of applied linguistics became seriously interested in all forms of academic and professional genres, including those associated with business contexts. However, in recent years, it has been taken more seriously by both the traditions, that is, ESP as well as communication studies, especially professional communication, management communication, organizational communication and, certainly business communication. This can be represented and summarized as follows (Figure 2.1):

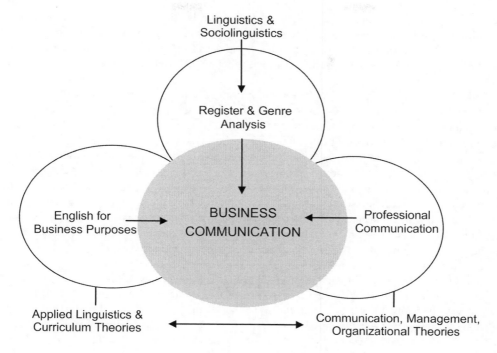

Figure 2.1 Dynamics of business communication: motivation and inspiration

We would now like to give more substance to this view of business communication as emerging from the recent works published in these three rather distinct areas of study and application. Let us begin with English for Business Purposes.

English for business purposes

Ever since English became the primary language of international business, research in the nature and function of what has come to be known as Business English has flourished. Approaches to course design and materials development in ESP in general, and English for Business Purposes in particular, have been overwhelmingly driven by descriptions of restricted uses of language, initially identified as register (Halliday *et al.* 1964) with emphasis on 'textualization', and then as discourse (Widdowson 1973) with emphasis on coherence and organization, and in more recent years, as genre (Swales 1990; Bhatia 1993), with emphasis on wider context and conventions of language use (see Bhatia 2004: 12 for a detailed account of the development of genre analysis). In the last two decades, genre analysis has become one of the most favoured approaches to the design of ESP syllabuses and materials.

ESP drew its inspiration from the work of Halliday *et al.* on functional variation in English, which put forward the notion that 'language varies as its function varies; it differs in different situations' (1964: 87). They pointed out that a variety of language distinguished according to its use was *register*. Halliday and his colleagues rightly indicate that register could be differentiated as sub-codes of a particular language on the basis of the occurrence of lexico-grammatical features of that register. Thus according to them, it was possible to characterize the register of business by identifying the use of an above-average incidence of a specific set of lexico-grammatical features in that register. Subsequently, there have been several studies identifying and describing typical characteristics of various academic and professional registers, such as scientific English, business English, and legal English. Originally, much of the work done on the functional variation in English focused on scientific English, particularly in academic settings.

English for Business Purposes (EBP), also known as Business English, became an independent area of study in the early 1990s, primarily as a consequence of the globalization of trade and commerce, which made it necessary for business people to move out of their home grounds and operate across territorial, linguistic, cultural as well as socio-political boundaries. This new business environment achieved further incentive through the massive influx of multimedia that seeped into the traditional business world, with the result that the business people found themselves operating in a vibrant international marketplace, which was so different from their more traditional base. Computer-mediated communication, in certain respects, was considered a sub-field of business communication; however, the blending of multimedia in the traditional business environment is deteriorating this distinction, as mediated communication 'is infused into nearly any business communication context, perhaps even coming to dominate certain areas as public relations' (Jackson 2007: 10).

This kind of merging of disciplinary boundaries also brought the predominantly American business communications research tradition into close contact with the EBP/ESP tradition, which was typically British and European (Dudley-Evans and St John 1998). There were obvious advantages in identifying and analysing ESP registers and using them as input for various kinds of ESP courses. Swales, referring to the early work of Halliday *et al.* (1964), further points out:

> [T]he 1964 'manifesto' offered a simple relationship between linguistic analysis and pedagogic materials … there was no strong emphasis on the need for practitioners to have … content knowledge of the fields or professions they were trying to serve … The early LSP practitioners were thus well equipped to carry out relatively 'thin' descriptions of their target discourses. What they principally lacked was a perception of discourse itself and of the means for analyzing and exploiting it – lacunae that were largely rectified by the 1980s.
>
> *(Swales 2000: 60)*

The inspiration for ESP courses continued to come from studies of functional analyses of subsets of English, which gradually developed as discourse analysis, and later in the 1980s as genre analysis. In more recent years the frameworks and methods of language description have become increasingly sophisticated, focusing more on context, rather than just the text. This has prompted investigations into variations in professional discourses, emphasizing genres and genre systems, mixing, embedding and bending of genres, further leading to critical examination of professional practices. Also, with the emphasis on text-task relationships, the focus shifted to the achievement of successful outcomes in professional activities, rather than just on the writing of a grammatically correct and acceptable text. Livesey (2002) puts emphasis on language not simply as an instrument or tool for accomplishing particular managerial objectives, but as the very means for expressing identity. He further says:

> Formal and surface features of texts are thus brought together with narratives of context derived by the authors from their study of historical materials. Both text and researcher are embedded in different cultural contexts, which constitute 'horizons' of meaning that are never precisely the same … Fusing the text's and the researcher's 'horizons', however,

leads to a creative-critical moment of understanding. This reveals the ideological meaning of particular texts and the sectional interests that they serve.

(Livesey 2002: 7–9)

Communication thus is not simply a matter of putting words together in a grammatically correct and rhetorically coherent textual form, but more importantly, it is a matter of having a desired impact on how a specifically relevant professional community views it and how the members of that community negotiate meanings in professional documents. In this sense, written communication is more than knowing the semantics of lexico-grammar; in fact, it is a matter of understanding why members of a specific business or disciplinary community communicate the way they do. This may require, among a host of other inputs, the discipline-specific knowledge of how professionals conceptualize issues and talk about them in order to achieve their disciplinary and professional goals. Often it is found that outsiders to a discourse or professional community are not able to follow what specialists write and talk about even if they are in a position to understand every word of what is written or said. Being a native speaker in this context is not necessarily beneficial if one does not have enough understanding of the more intricate insider knowledge, including conventions of the genre and professional practice. Widdowson (1998: 7) highlights this aspect of communicative efficiency when he indicates that genre analysis seeks to identify the particular conventions for language use in certain domains of professional and occupational activity. He further points out that it is a development from, and an improvement on, register analysis because it deals with discourse and not just text. It seeks to reveal how lexico-grammatical forms realize the conceptual and rhetorical structures, modes of thought and action, which are established as conventional for certain discourse communities. Genre analysis thus is about the conventions of thought and communication which define specific areas of professional activity.

Genre theory has thus become a favourite tool for the analysis of professional and academic discourses (Swales 1990; Bhatia 1993). In more recent years, genre theory has become increasingly multi-perspective (Bhatia 2004) through an integration of a number of different methodologies (Zhang 2007), such as textography (Swales 1998), interpretive ethnography (Smart 1998), corpus analysis (Pinto dos Santos 2002; Nelson 2006; Fuertes-Olivera 2007), participant-perspectives on specialist discourses (Louhiala-Salminen 1996; Locker 1999; Rogers 2000), cross-cultural and intercultural perspectives (Bilbow 1999; Gimenez 2001; Vergaro 2004; Planken 2005; Vuorela 2005), multimodal analysis (Brett 2000), and observation analysis (Louhiala-Salminen 2002), to name only a few. The implication for ESP/EBP thus is that text-based analyses within register or genre analysis have become increasingly inadequate in explaining and accounting for the typical use of language in various business contexts.

The other significant development in ESP and EBP was the analysis of the needs of the specialist group of ESP/EBP learners (Munby 1978; Chambers 1980; Jacobson 1986; Coleman 1988; Nickerson 1998). The rationale for needs analysis was that since ESP learners have a limited set of requirements for which they often use English as a second language, there was no use giving them extensive courses in all forms and functions of English, which can be time-consuming, difficult, and ineffective. It was possible to design short-term courses in the teaching of English to meet their specific needs more economically and effectively. In terms of teaching methodology, one of the typical characteristics of many of the EBP courses has been the appropriation and often integration of specific disciplinary approaches. In the case of EBP, for instance, one of the most useful and popular trends has been the use of the case study method, which many consider an integral part of all EBP programs (Westerfield 1989;

Esteban and Cañado 2004). Similarly, the role of new media and technology can hardly be overlooked.

Variations in business discourse

ESP has always been identified in terms of disciplinary variations, so that English for law, English for science and technology, English for marine engineering, etc., have been some of the successful and pragmatically effective labels. In recent years, ESP practitioners have been motivated to go a step further to investigate the role of sub-disciplinary variation in order to sharpen the focus in specific ESP courses. English for Business Purpose courses, for instance, have been further classified on the basis of variations in the use of language across sub-disciplines of business, that is, economics, marketing, management, and accountancy. The assumption that every discipline has its own repertoire of typical genres, which are unlikely to be used by members of other disciplinary or professional communities, seems to be well established in recent genre-analytical literature (Swales 1990; Bhatia and Candlin 2001; Bhatia 2004). This is due to the fact that each discipline has its own typical ways of constructing, interpreting, and using genres, defining membership characteristics of such communities, specifying and validating evidence to construct valid and acceptable arguments and make sustainable claims within their specific contexts (Bhatia 1999a; Hewings and Nickerson 1999; Hyland 2000). All these factors contribute to the determination of typical ways of thinking and behaving in specific disciplines or sub-disciplines. Assumptions of this kind may lead one to say 'He behaves like an accountant', or 'That's very typical of a marketing person.' Specialists within broad disciplines, such as law and accountancy, have a general affiliation to a professional community, and they generally operate rather distinctively within their own disciplinary frame. However, they may also create disciplinary conflicts within the general community of professionals, if they operate in an interdisciplinary context, which quite often is the case when in a business meeting we have an engineer, a lawyer, and an accountant. Just as it is true of such broad disciplines, to a somewhat more limited extent, it is also true of sub-disciplines, such as, accountancy, marketing, management, and economics (Bhatia 1999b). The sub-disciplinary distinctions across these areas may be as valid as the ones we see across major disciplinary cultures. To give more substance to this claim, we would like to refer to an extensive study of disciplinary variations in business education led by Bhatia and Candlin (2001). The main purpose of this study, which was undertaken by a group of researchers from five Hong Kong universities, was to determine the nature of the competing interdisciplinary discursive practices (modes of discourse and genre presentation, student and teacher expectations in interdisciplinary academic contexts, individual study patterns, patterns of assessment, etc.) in an attempt to understand the extent to which disciplinary specialists (both students and teachers) were aware of the subject-specific frames that underlie their practices, and also to what extent they were responsive to the interdisciplinary requirements of their students' communicative performance.

The findings of this study clearly established that there were some fundamental and pedagogically important sub-disciplinary differences that influenced the teaching and learning of academic discourses particularly relevant to EBP or business communication programmes. Although there were considerable overlaps in business discourses of various kinds, there were nonetheless distinctive generic characteristics, which were reflective of the requirements of the different sub-disciplines.

The study also revealed that there was an initial general perception on the part of many of the stakeholders that the tasks, such as projects, presentations, essays, reports, and other written assignments, case studies, and analysis of business situations that students had to carry out during their academic study were similar across different disciplines. The subject teachers had the impression that such tasks involved applying theory to the real world to solve a particular business-related problem; however, there were clearly significant disciplinary and sub-disciplinary differences, which represented different perspectives and hence warranted different approaches to business studies. The tasks in Accountancy were mostly calculations-based essays or reports, often emphasizing individual work and analytical skills, but de-emphasizing the application of theory. In Economics, on the other hand, there was a greater emphasis on theory, writing essays, drawing diagrams, and interpreting graphs; tasks often focusing on the 'real world' of supply and demand. In Management the tasks were frequently case studies, projects, or essays, with greater focus on definitions and on argument. In Finance the focus was also on calculation, but this was all done within the framework of case studies and essays. Finally, in Marketing there was a greater focus on projects, collaborative work, and applying theory to investigating the needs of customers, with some use of calculation. The distinctive character of such disciplinary tasks, as revealed in that study, is visually represented in Figure 2.2.

An interesting issue for us is to what extent these sub-disciplinary variations are likely to create academic problems for students in their academic study. Bhatia and Candlin (2001), in their study, raised this issue in their discussions with teachers and students. Teachers' views, in terms of disciplinary variation, and the ability of students to handle this within and across subject boundaries reflected interesting disparities. Many staff members commented that they were not actually aware of common concepts appearing in other disciplines and of being treated differently in terms of application/concept, etc., as subject teachers only prepared their own courses and did not generally collaborate with other subject teachers. Others felt that

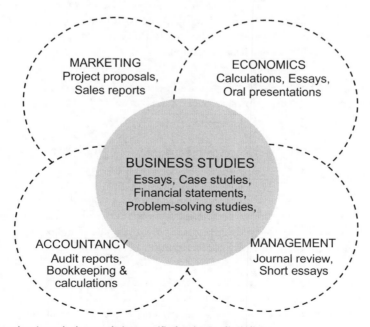

Figure 2.2 Academic task demands in specific business disciplines

there were no great differences across the demands of the different disciplines and students knew how to adjust from one to another. They speculated that students generally compartmentalized the subject and particular skills of a discipline, and probably did not carry skills, style or methods over to another discipline.

On the other hand, some teachers pointed out that the boundaries across sub-disciplines were not distinctive, and that students were sometimes confused about overlapping concepts. For example, it was easy for students to confuse the management concept of corporate strategy (the long-term overall aim of a company) with the marketing concept of strategy (marketing a product or service). There was a common perception that students in their initial years had problems in adapting from discipline to discipline as it required a lot of effort, and that no one actually explicitly pointed out the differences in disciplinary demands to them. However, some of them believed that as they progressed through the programmes, especially in the second and the final year, they started handling these differences in the language and terminology of various disciplines.

There are a number of ways these generic variations can be studied. The variations can occur within a specific domain, or across several domains. In order to handle domain-specific genres, Devitt (1991) proposed the notion of *genre set* to refer to a range of texts that a particular professional group produces in the course of their daily routine. She discussed the case of *tax accountants*, who in their daily work produced a limited range of generic texts, some of which might include various kinds of letters such as an opinion letter to the client, a response letter to the client, a letter to tax authorities, all of which are considered distinct, but at the same time intertextually linked to each other. The typical set of products resulting from these tasks formed a genre set. The genres comprising a set are individually distinct, but at the same time, intertextually linked. The texts from a particular genre set also display typical patterns found in similarly produced texts by other fellow professionals in the same field. This rather limited set of generic texts resulting from a narrowly defined professional activity represents the participation of only one side of the professional output. The professional activity might also involve a number of other participants from within or outside the profession, texts, or other semiotic constructs, but the concept of genre set seems to include one side of the professional practice. As Bazerman mentions,

> The genre set represents ... only the work of one side of a multiple person interaction. That is, the tax accountants' letters usually refer to the tax code, the rulings of the tax department in this case, the client's information and interests, and these references are usually presented in highly anticipatable ways appropriate to the genre of the letter, but the genre set is only the tax accountant's participations, as intertextually linked to the participations of the parties.
>
> *(Bazerman 1994: 98–9)*

To extend the concept of genre set in an attempt to account for the full set of genres, Bazerman (1994: 97) proposed the concept of *systems of genres*, which refer to all 'the interrelated genres that interact with each other in specific settings'. He pointed out:

> The system of genres would be the full set of genres that instantiate the participation of all the parties – that is the full file of letters from and to the client, from and to the government, from and to the accountant. This would be the full interaction, the full event, the set of social relations as it has been enacted. It embodies the full history of

speech events as intertextual occurrences, but attending to the way that all the intertext is instantiated in generic form establishing the current act in relation to prior acts.

(Bazerman 1994: 99)

The notion of a system of genres is thus a useful development on the earlier notion of genre set, and is a very useful tool to investigate intertextually and interdiscursively related text-genres embedded within a specific professional activity (see Bhatia 2004, 2008a, 2008b, 2010 for a detailed account). Generic versatility also functions in yet another way. Genres generally operate across disciplinary boundaries, so that we find a constellation of reporting genres of various kinds, some of which include newspaper reports, business reports, science reports, medical reports, police reports, technical reports, all of which display interesting generic similarities. However, it is also necessary to consider variations within a broad discipline.

For example, one may find interesting variation in business reports in terms of their sub-disciplinary frames. Some variations include:

- Investigation report (suggesting solutions for existing problems)
- Performance report (evaluating an individual product, service or activity)
- Progress or status report (reporting development as part of a project / activity)
- Process report (reporting on how-to aspects of projects or activities)
- Feasibility report (reporting on chances of failure or success of projects)
- Sales report (reporting on periodic sales figures, may include market analysis)
- Field trip report (recording business activities at various locations)
- Annual report (reporting on overall perspective on an organization)
- Audit report (indicating economic efficiency).

An interesting aspect of such variation is that just as it is possible to view individual genres as part of a specific disciplinary domain, it is equally possible to view some other aspects of these very genres displaying overlaps across a number of sub-disciplinary domains. Therefore, the reality of the situation can only be captured by a much more complex and perhaps dynamic picture displaying similarities as well as overlaps within and across disciplinary frames and discursive practices (Bhatia 1999a). It is thus possible for us to view any one of these reporting genres, business reports, for example, and identify similarities as well as distinctions across more specific realizations of this genre. Obvious examples will include sales reports, progress reports, project reports, audit reports, financial reports, and annual reports, to name a few. The differences between these are less discernible in terms of broad communicative purposes but more in terms of the nature of activity, task, or sub-domain they serve, but all of them are valid instances of business reports.

As mentioned in the beginning, although there was no direct relationship between the first two main dimensions, that is, communication studies and ESP, there have always been impressions of overlap between these in terms of their concerns, methodologies, materials and applications. Williams *et al.* (1984) regard these two traditions as two halves of a single profession, in that both were concerned with the teaching and learning of effective communication through English in business contexts.

Business communication

Business communication in its present form combines the strengths of both these traditions to look for effective and efficient ways of training uninitiated learners into the intricacies of business communication, both written as well as spoken. Bargiela-Chiappini and Nickerson (2002), introducing the special issue of *International Review of Applied Linguistics* (*IRAL*) on Business Communication, define it as talk and writing between individuals whose main work, activities, and interests are in the domain of business and who come together for the purpose of doing business, which usually takes place within a corporate setting, whether physical or virtual. The label 'Business Communication' thus seems to be best understood as a discipline integrating communication in business, including organizational and management contexts, and other ESP-based approaches to the teaching and learning of English for business purposes. Suchan and Charles (2006: 393) explain that the 'lack of a research identity' and the copious multi-disciplinarity is a consequence of the significantly different departments and schools, such as English, business and management, speech communications, and even information technology. They argue that:

> These different disciplinary homes result in our using theories, frameworks, and information sources that lack significant overlap. This lack of overlap contributes to the shapelessness of our field and makes it difficult for us to define to our stakeholders and ourselves the work we do and the value it provides.
>
> *(Suchan and Charles 2006: 393)*

However, interdisciplinarity across seemingly diverse disciplines must not be seen as undermining the contribution that each discipline makes towards a better understanding of the nature and function of communication in professional and corporate settings. It is, instead, recognition of the complex and dynamic nature of the discursive realities of the corporate world that are more accurately understood through multiple as well as complementary perspectives. Despite growing criticism that business communication research lacks a 'comprehensive theoretical grounding' (Shelby 1988: 13) and instead draws its findings from many different places, Rogers (2001: 16) argues that 'there are signs that we're growing more comfortable with our plurality, even beginning to acknowledge some of its value'. She also claims (2001: 15) that convergence is not an entirely foreign concept as far as business communication research is concerned, as academics in this discipline have been 'navigating multiple disciplines and diverse methods for some time now. In fact, our diversity in backgrounds, cultures, approaches, and institutions has become central to our identity.' The ability of business communication to draw from different fields only emphasizes its 'unique place at the intersection of business and communication' (Reinsch and Lewis 1993: 450). Similarly, Ulijn *et al.* emphasize the need for new approaches to the study of globalism, organizations, and communication. They rightly say that:

> multiparadigmatic approaches facilitate the work of scholars who find both value and disappointment in various theoretical perspectives but who understand the need to acknowledge and integrate multiple approaches in an effort to clarify complex and obscure human and organizational phenomena.
>
> *(Ulijn et al. 2000: 310–11)*

A special issue of *Management Communication Quarterly* (1996) demonstrates that there is a wide scope for dialogue and possible cross-fertilization across disciplines, even if some of them (e.g. organizational communication) are seen to be more dependent on a symbiotic relationship with the corporate world (Mumby and Stohl 1996).

In this context, it is interesting to note that Rogers (1998: 80), who has a background in management studies, in her discussion of national agendas in business communication found at least five key concerns. First, it was felt that teaching and research in business communication must go hand-in-hand, which has also been a main concern in ESP/EBP. Second, it was found that to enhance business practice, research must focus on authentic texts, which has also been a consistent argument in ESP/EBP ever since the 1970s. The third concern was that research must be multidisciplinary, just as ESP is. The fourth concern was that one must take into account research in cross-cultural communications and intercultural negotiations. Rogers concluded that language learning, linguistic analyses, and discourse patterns are some of the main areas of research and investigation. In her subsequent study, Rogers (2000) says that in text-based genre analyses there is a strong tendency to conceptualize communicative purposes in terms of the strategies of the speakers or writers, but she argues that such purposes cannot be fully understood without some understanding of how these purposes are interpreted by members of the specialist community, for which she recommends user-based analyses. Rogers (2000: 426) thus extends the boundaries of genre analysis to take it beyond the text to context and audience response, looking for the relevance of user-based analytical tools to analyze a small corpus of CEO presentations in the context of earning announcements. It is hardly surprising then that in much of Rogers' work we find a fine integration of not simply the two strands of Business Communication, that is EBP and Professional Communication, but also that of genre analysis. Similarly, Charles (1996: 20) makes a necessary attempt to fill in the gap between a contextual business approach and a linguistic text-based approach. Her work on business negotiations examines the particular ways in which the extra-linguistic 'business context shapes negotiation discourse, and thus creates a mutual interdependency'. Relatedly, Nickerson (1998), in her survey of the impact of corporate culture on non-native corporate writers working in a multinational and multilingual context, also adopted an inter-disciplinary approach which incorporated not only ESP research but also organizational theories that account for the general patterns of communication found within multinational corporations.

Yet another methodological procedure, which allows one to incorporate intercultural and cross-cultural variations in business communication, has, once again, its roots in both professional communication and ESP/EBP. Gimenez's study on cross-cultural business negotiations focuses on cross-cultural negotiations and communication styles, and he discovered that some of the 'cultural differences seemed to be overridden by the status-bound behaviour of the negotiators' (2001: 188). On the other hand, Vergaro (2004) undertook a contrastive study to investigate the rhetorical differences between Italian and English sales promotion letters, which are considered standardized, ritualistic or even formulaic. Her main concern was to explore how information was presented and what rhetorical strategies were used to obtain compliance by a given readership in a given culture. She used pragmatic and ethno-linguistic research by contrastively analyzing a corpus of authentic Italian and English business letters. Similarly, Planken (2005) studied how facework was used to achieve interpersonal goals in intercultural sales negotiations by undertaking linguistic analyses of 'rapport management', which, in a negotiation context, is aimed primarily, but not exclusively, at building a working relationship. Coming from the communication angle, Varner (2000) views intercultural communication differently from intercultural business communication. He mentions that in intercultural business communication the business strategies, goals, objectives, and practices become an integral part of the communication process and help create a new environment out of the synergy of culture, communication, and business. He further argues that:

as the study of culture is not an end in itself, so communication is not an end in itself. In intercultural business communication the communication has a business purpose. The channels, levels of formality, use of technology, content and style of delivery, are influenced by cultural and business considerations. The objectives of the business, the level of internationalization, the structure of organization, will help determine the intercultural business communication strategy.

(Varner 2000: 48–9)

Bhatia (2004, 2008a, 2010) argues that the study of conventional systems of genres (Bazerman 1994) often used to fulfil the professional objectives of specific disciplinary or professional communities may not be sufficient to understand the complexities of business communication. He argues that a comprehensive understanding of the motives and intentions of business practices is possible only if one goes beyond the textual constraints to look at the multiple discourses, actions and voices that play a significant role in the formation of specific discursive practices within the institutional and organizational framework. He develops the notion of 'interdiscursivity' as a function of appropriation of contextual and text-external generic resources within and across professional genres and professional practices. Devitt (1996: 611) argues that 'we need to find ways to keep genre embedded and engaged within context while also keeping our focus on learning about genre and its operations'. Devitt (2004: 188) also adds that 'to teach students the rhetorical and cultural significance of one genre will require teaching the significance of its genre set and the place of that genre within that set'. Similarly, Bremner (2008) favours a more comprehensive understanding of interdiscursive voices in any system of activity. He points out that genres are interconnected in wider systems of activity, and they influence each other in the system. He says that:

A key feature of intertextuality to consider, then, is that it is not simply a link between texts, but a phenomenon that helps shape other texts: as genres combine to achieve different goals, they contribute to the development of new genres as they are recontextualised (Linell, 1998). Thus the generic, linguistic and rhetorical choices that a writer makes will be influenced by the texts that precede or surround the text under construction, and will in turn have an effect on the final textual product.

(Bremner 2008: 308)

Louhiala-Salminen's (2002) work is also important in that, in order to look at the full potential of who contributed what in which context, she closely observed a business manager's professional practice in a Finnish multinational corporation by tape recording most of the discourse activities during the day, and accessing copies of all the written materials. She supplemented this data with interviews in order to understand some of the typical features of the discourse activities in a multinational corporation.

Concluding remarks

We have presented in this chapter the current view of business communication as a truly interdisciplinary area of study and application, which may be viewed as an integration not only of two of the rather distinct approaches to the teaching and learning of English used in the professions, that is ESP and professional communication studies, but also as seriously nurtured by multidimensional and multi-perspective analyses of systems of business genres (Bhatia 2004). We have also made an effort to point out that advances in the field of genre analysis, particularly the effort to go beyond the textual artefacts to investigate context of various kinds, including intertextuality as well as interdiscursivity, are crucial to a comprehensive understanding of business communication. Babcock and Du-Babcock (2001) nicely sum up the intercultural variables we have discussed in the preceding paragraphs, when they point out that:

> Language can be seen as the gateway to culture as it frames the nature of cultural exposure and contact as well as how information is filtered through the perceptual screens of all communicators … language shapes how international business communicators perceive cultural influences and cues in different communication zones as they engage in the international business communication process.
>
> *(Babcock and Du-Babcock 2001: 373–6)*

It may also be said at this stage that research in areas such as the relationship between discursive activities and professional practices in most disciplinary, professional and institutional contexts (Bhatia 2006, 2008a, 2008b) is still in its early stages, and a lot more work is needed before we can find convincing answers to the question that Bhatia (1993) raised, that is, 'why do most professionals use the language the way they do?' For instance, we still have no comprehensive understanding of 'what makes a novice accounting student into a good accountant', or 'how do we identify, train, and appraise a good manager, marketing executive, or a public relations expert?' One may also raise a number of other similar questions, such as the following:

- What is the role of language in the development of specialist expertise in a particular professional field?
- What are the core competencies that are needed to make a person a competent professional?
- Are these competencies teachable?, and
- Is it possible to assess the acquisition of such expertise?

Although we seem to be a long way from any kind of definite and convincing answers to some of these questions, and a lot more work is needed, we seem to be heading in the right direction.

To conclude, we would like to suggest a few directions in which research in the future is likely to go. In our view, there is a need to integrate English for Business Purposes with current research in business communication, as these are simply two sides of the same coin. This will also help us to have a more comprehensive view of business communication. In addition to this, the field of business communication can be enriched by integrating insights from and about business practices, which can and have, in recent genre analytical studies, been successfully undertaken with insightful conclusions. If we can continue to explore some of these perspectives, we feel that we will be very close to demystifying some of the hitherto hidden complexities associated with acquisition of specialist business and disciplinary competence.

Related topics

English for academic purposes; institutional discourse; language education; language learning

Further reading

Bargiela-Chiappini, F. and Nickerson, C. (eds) (2002) *Writing Business: Genres, Media and Discourse*, London: Longman. (A comprehensive account of business discourses in specific and yet diverse business contexts, integrating insights from discourse analysis and business practices.)

Bhatia, V. K. (2004) *Worlds of Written Discourse: A Genre-based View*, London and New York: Continuum. (This volume offers a genre analytical framework for the study of discursive and professional practices in a number of different business and disciplinary contexts.)

——(2006) 'Discursive practices in disciplinary and professional contexts', *Linguistic and Human Sciences* 2(1): 5–28. (This paper argues for an integrated view of management and discourse analytical theories for the study of business and other disciplinary practices.)

——(2008) 'Genre analysis, ESP and professional practice', *English for Specific Purposes* 27(2): 161–74. (This paper explores professional practices through discourse and genre analysis.)

Smart, G. (2006) *Writing the Economy: Activity, Genre and Technology in the World of Banking*, London: Equinox Publishing. (An engaging and well-researched analysis of an important banking institution.)

References

Babcock, R. D. and Du-Babcock, B. (2001) 'Language-based communication zones in international business communication', *Journal of Business Communication* 38(4): 372–412.

Bargiela-Chiappini, F. and Nickerson, C. (eds) (2001) *Writing Business: Genres, Media and Discourse*, London: Longman.

Bazerman, C. (1994) 'Systems of genres and the enhancement of social intentions', in A. Freedman and P. Medway (eds) *Genre and New Rhetoric*, London: Taylor & Francis.

Bhatia, V. K. (1993) *Analysing Genre: Language Use in Professional Settings*, Harlow: Longman.

——(1999a) 'Integrating products, processes, purposes and participants in professional writing', in C. N. Candlin and K. Hyland (eds) *Writing: Texts, Processes and Practices*, London: Longman.

——(1999b) 'Disciplinary variation in business English', in M. Hewings and C. Nickerson (eds) *Business English: Research into Practice*, Englewood Cliffs, NJ: Prentice Hall.

——(2004) *Worlds of Written Discourse: A Genre-based View*, London and New York: Continuum.

——(2006) 'Discursive practices in disciplinary and professional contexts', *Linguistic and Human Sciences* 2(1): 5–28.

——(2008a) 'Genre analysis, ESP and professional practice', *English for Specific Purposes* 27(2): 161–74.

——(2008b) 'Creativity and accessibility in written professional discourse', *World Englishes* 27(3): 319–26.

——(2010) 'Interdiscursivity in professional communication', *Discourse and Communication* 21(1): 32–50.

Bhatia, V. K. and Candlin, C. N. (eds) (2001) *Teaching English to Meet the Needs of Business Education in Hong Kong*. A project report to the SCOLAR Language Fund, Government of Hong Kong, published by the Centre for English Language Education and Communication Research, City University of Hong Kong.

Bilbow, G. T. (1999) 'Look who's talking: an analysis of "Chair-talk" in business meetings', *Journal of Business and Technical Communication* 12(2): 157–97.

Bremner, S. (2008) 'Intertextuality and business communication textbooks: why students need more textual support', *English for Specific Purposes* 27(3): 306–21.

Brett, P. (2000) 'Integrating multimedia into the business English curriculum: a case study', *English for Specific Purposes* 19(3): 269–90.

Chambers, F. (1980) 'A re-evaluation of needs analysis in ESP', *The ESP Journal* 1: 25–33.

Charles, M. (1996) 'Business communications: interdependence between discourse and the business relationship', *English for Specific Purposes* 15(1): 19–36.

Coleman, H. (1988) 'Analysing language needs in large organizations', *English for Specific Purposes* 7(3): 155–69.

Devitt, A. (1991) 'Intertextuality in tax accounting: generic, referential and functional', in C. Bazerman and J. Paradis (eds) *Textual Dynamics of the Professions*, Madison: University of Wisconsin Press.

——(1996) 'Genre, genres, and the teaching of genre', *College Composition and Communication* 47(4): 605–16.

——(2004) *Writing Genres*, Carbondale: Southern Illinois University Press.

Dudley-Evans, T. and St John, M. (1998) *Developments in English for Specific Purposes: A Multi-disciplinary Approach*, Cambridge: Cambridge University Press.

Esteban, A. A. and Cañado, M. L. P. (2004) 'Making the case method work in teaching business English: a case study', *English for Specific Purposes* 23(2): 137–61.

Fuertes-Olivera, P. A. (2007) 'A corpus-based view of lexical gender in written business English', *English for Specific Purposes* 26(2): 219–34.

Gimenez, J. C. (2001) 'Ethnographic observations in cross-cultural business negotiations between non-native speakers of English: an exploratory study', *English for Specific Purposes* 20: 169–93.

Halliday, M. A. K., McIntosh, A. and Strevens, P. (1964) *The Linguistic Sciences and Language Teaching*, London: The English Language Book Society and Longman Group.

Hewings, M. and Nickerson, C. (eds) (1999) *Business English: Research into Practice*, London: Longman/The British Council.

Hyland, K. (2000) *Disciplinary Discourses: Social Interactions in Academic Writing*, Harlow: Pearson Education.

Jackson, M. H. (2007) 'Should emerging technologies change business communication scholarship?' *Journal of Business Communication* 44(1): 3–12.

Jacobson, W. H. (1986) 'An assessment of the communication needs of non-native speakers of English in an undergraduate Physics lab', *English for Specific Purposes* 5(2): 173–87.

Livesey, S. M. (2002) 'Interpretive acts: new vistas in qualitative research in business communication', *Journal of Business Communication* 39(1): 6–12.

Louhiala-Salminen, L. (1996) 'The business communication classroom vs. reality: what should we teach today?' *English for Specific Purposes* 15(1): 37–51.

——(2002) 'The fly's perspective: discourse in the daily routine of a business manager', *English for Specific Purposes* 21(3): 211–31.

Locker, K. O. (1999) 'Factors in reader responses to negative letters: experimental evidence for changing what we teach', *Journal of Business and Technical Communication* 13(1): 5–48.

Mumby, D. K. and Stohl, C. (1996) 'Disciplining organizational communication studies', *Management Communication Quarterly* 10(1): 50–72.

Munby, J. (1978) *Communicative Syllabus Design*, Cambridge: Cambridge University Press.

Nelson, M. (2006) 'Semantic associations in business English: a corpus-based analysis', *English for Specific Purposes* 25(2): 217–34.

Nickerson, C. (1998) 'Corporate culture and the use of written English within British subsidiaries in the Netherlands', *English for Specific Purposes* 17(3): 281–94.

Pinto dos Santos, V. B. M. (2002) 'Genre analysis of business letters of negotiation', *English for Specific Purposes* 21(2): 167–99.

Planken, B. (2005) 'Managing rapport in lingua franca sales negotiations: a comparison of professional and aspiring negotiators', *English for Specific Purposes* 24(4): 381–400.

Reinsch, N. L. Jr and Lewis, P. V. (1993) 'Author and citation patterns for The Journal of Business Communication, 1978–92', *The Journal of Business Communication* 30: 435–62.

Rogers, P. S. (1998) 'National agendas and the English divide', *Business Communication Quarterly* 61(3): 80.

——(2000) 'CEO presentations in conjunction with earning announcements: extending the construct of organizational genre through competing values profiling and user-needs analysis', *Management Communication Quarterly* 13(3): 426–85.

——(2001) 'Convergence and commonality challenge business communication research', *Journal of Business Communication* 38(1): 14–23.

Shelby, A. N. (1988) 'A macro theory of management communication', *Journal of Business Communication* 25(2): 13–28.

Smart, G. (1998) 'Mapping conceptual worlds: using interpretive ethnography to explore knowledge-making in a professional community', *Journal of Business Communication* 35(1): 111–27.

Suchan, J. and Charles, M. (2006) 'Business communication research: past, present, and future', *Journal of Business Communication* 43(4): 389–97.

Swales, J. M. (1990) *Genre Analysis: English in Academic and Research Settings*, Cambridge: Cambridge University Press.

——(1998) *Other Floors Other Voices: A Textography of a Small University Building*, London: Lawrence Erlbaum Associates.

——(2000) 'Language for specific purposes', *Annual Review of Applied Linguistics* 20: 59–76.

Ulijn, J., O'Hair, D., Weggeman, M., Ledlow, G. and Hall, H. T. (2000) 'Innovation, corporate strategy, and cultural context: what is the mission for international business communication?', *Journal of Business Communication* 37(3): 293–317.

Varner, I. I. (2000) 'The theoretical foundation for intercultural business communication: a conceptual model', *Journal of Business Communication* 37(1): 39–57.

Vergaro, C. (2004) 'Discourse strategies of Italian and English sales promotion letters', *English for Specific Purposes* 23(2): 181–207.

Vuorela, T. (2005) 'How does a sales team reach goals in intercultural business negotiations? A case study', *English for Specific Purposes* 24(1): 65–92.

Westerfield, K. (1989) 'Improved linguistic fluency with case studies and a video method', *English for Specific Purposes* 8(1): 75–83.

Widdowson, H. G. (1973) 'An Applied Linguistic Approach to Discourse Analysis', Ph.D. thesis, University of Edinburgh.

——(1998) 'Communication and community: the pragmatics of ESP', *English for Specific Purposes* 17(1): 3–14.

Williams, R., Swales, J. and Kirkman, J. (1984) *Common Ground: Shared Interest in ESP and Communication Studies,* ELT Documents 117. Oxford: Pergamon Press in association with the British Council.

Zhang, Z. (2007) 'Towards an integrated approach to teaching business English: a Chinese experience', *English for Specific Purposes* 26(4): 399–410.

3

Translation and interpreting

Mona Baker and Luis Pérez-González

Introduction

Translation and interpreting are forms of linguistic mediation that involve rendering written or oral text from one language to another. As language-based activities that have practical implications, they are often seen as falling within the remit of applied linguistics. Following a brief introduction and historical survey of the field, this chapter focuses on some of the main issues that have interested both translation scholars and applied linguists in recent years. It does not engage with the use of translation in language teaching (for an authoritative overview of this issue, see Cook 2009).

Increased globalization, growing mobility of people and commodities, and the spread and intensity of armed conflicts in recent years have established translation and interpreting more firmly in the public consciousness. As both facilitators and beneficiaries of increased global interconnectedness, translators and interpreters have become important economic players in the services sector worldwide, with surveys forecasting an average annual business growth of 5–7.5 per cent between 2005 and 2010 (CSA 2004; EUATC 2005) and the global translation industry turnover expected to exceed €12 billion in 2010 (ABI 2002). Recent comparable reports on the interpreting industry estimate the global outsourced interpreting market at $2.5 billion, $700 million of which is generated by the burgeoning field of telephone interpreting (CSA 2008). At the same time, translators and interpreters have become more widely recognized as important political players, with their involvement in Kosovo, Iraq and Afghanistan in particular receiving widespread media attention.

Economic clout and political impact aside, the growing pervasiveness of translation and interpreting in all domains of private and public life has also heightened the need for a better understanding of their social relevance. Against the backdrop of the growing dominance of English as a lingua franca, translation and interpreting have become central to promoting cultural and linguistic diversity in the information society and in the development of multilingual content in global media networks and the audiovisual marketplace. They have also become central to the delivery of institutional agendas in a wide range of settings, from supranational organizations to judicial and healthcare services at community level. The importance of translation and interpreting as tools of empowerment is further evident in the emergence of new forms of intersemiotic assistive mediation; these include subtitling for the deaf and hard-of-hearing and audio description for the blind, both of which aim to facilitate access to information and entertainment for sensory-impaired members of the community.

Historical overview

The study of translation has a very long history, going back several centuries to scholars like Cicero, Horace and Jerome, all of whom commented extensively on strategies of translation (e.g. word-for-word versus sense-for-sense). But the academic study of translation and interpreting dates back only to the middle of the twentieth century. Initially focusing on short, often decontextualized stretches of text, much theorizing during the 1950s, 1960s and 1970s revolved around elaborating taxonomies of different types of equivalence that may hold between a source text and its translation. Largely understood as a semantic category in the 1950s, equivalence was first defined as

> a process by which a spoken or written utterance takes place in one language which is intended and presumed to convey *the same meaning* as a previously existing utterance in another language. It thus involves two distinct factors, a 'meaning', or reference to some slice of reality, and the difference between two languages in referring to that reality.
>
> *(Rabin 1958: 123, emphasis added)*

The notion of equivalence here is similar to that of synonymy, except that one applies to items in two different languages and the other to items in the same language. As a semantic category, the notion of equivalence is static – it is not dictated by the requirements of the communicative situation but purely by the semantic content of the source text.

Partly in response to developments within linguistics, which for a long time was the main source of theorization about translation, the treatment of equivalence as a semantic category soon came to be regarded as untenable. One of the first alternatives to be offered was a definition of equivalence not as a question of 'how close' a target text is to the same reality portrayed in the source text but rather as how close it comes to reproducing the *same effect* or response in the target readers. This approach originated with Bible translators: Nida (1964); Nida and Taber (1969); and Larson (1984). The idea of equivalent effect proved equally problematic, however, since no reliable way could be found for measuring effect in readers. Not only is it impossible to know how two people are likely to respond to a given text, but even the same reader will respond differently to the same text on different occasions. Some scholars later attempted to salvage something of the potential usefulness of the idea of 'equivalent effect' by limiting it to 'similarity' in a very immediate sense. For instance, Hervey and Higgins (1992: 23) suggest that the translator of a portion of a source text which makes the source reader laugh can attempt to produce a translation which makes its own reader laugh. As they themselves go on to explain, this is 'a gross reduction of the effects of a text to a single effect'.

An alternative which gained much ground in the 1970s and 1980s was *equivalence of function*. Scholars such as Reiss (1971) and House (1981) tried to categorize the range of possible textual functions or communicative purposes and suggest ways in which equivalence may be achieved in relation to the most prominent function in the source text. House's model of quality assessment, for example, draws on Halliday's notions of ideational and interpersonal functions and involves three steps: drawing a textual profile which characterizes the function of the source text, drawing a similar profile for the translated text, and comparing the two to identify any shifts in function. The result is a statement of the relative match of the two functional components (the ideational and interpersonal).

Apart from the obvious problems of defining a single function for a text, this approach is divorced from the realities of translation in that it assumes that the function of the target text has to be equivalent to that of the source text. But in the professional world it is common for clients to request rough translations which allow for a basic understanding of the content of source texts (e.g. contracts or judgments) but are not meant to serve an equivalent (regulatory or argumentative) function in the target context. In response to this challenge, new approaches emerged in the 1980s, particularly in Germany, which pointed out that the reasons for commissioning or initiating a translation are independent of the reasons for creating the source text. What matters, therefore, is the function of the translated text, not that of the source text. Equivalence here becomes a function of the commission accompanying a request for translation (Vermeer 1989b/2000). Scholars like Vermeer therefore talk of 'adequacy' with regard to the commission or purpose of translation, rather than equivalence, as the standard for judging target texts. Nord (1991) takes this further by suggesting that it is not the text itself that has a function – rather a text acquires its function in the situation in which it is received.

As can be seen from the development of thinking about equivalence, by the late 1980s studies of translation had begun to widen their scope of analysis considerably: they gradually moved outwards from the word to the sentence, to structures above the sentence, to the text as a unit of analysis, and finally to the text as a cultural artefact that functions in a specific context of situation. By then, too, the text had come to be seen as an instance of interaction that embodies the values a given culture attaches to certain practices and concepts. Cultural studies and literary theory in particular came to exercise considerable influence on the study of translation from this non-linguistic perspective (Venuti 1995; Hermans 1996; Tymoczko 1999). As far as linguistics is concerned, scholars of translation also began to draw on an expanding array of theoretical strands and fields – including but not limited to critical discourse analysis, pragmatics, sociolinguistics, conversation analysis, psycholinguistics and semiotics (Saldanha 2009). The work of Hatim and Mason (1990, 1997) proved extremely influential in widening the remit of linguistically informed studies of translation and interpreting, in particular by engaging with issues of ideology and positioning.

Corpus linguistics has provided a robust methodology for studying translation since the mid-1990s (Laviosa 2002). The application of corpus-based methodologies in translation studies uniquely involves comparing a computer-held corpus consisting exclusively of translated text and one consisting exclusively of non-translated texts (or utterances) produced *in the same language*. Such comparison aims to demonstrate the distinctive nature of translation as a genre in its own right by identifying recurrent patterns in the language produced by translators (Baker 1996; Laviosa 1998; Olohan 2003) and interpreters (Pérez-González 2006a). Baker (1993) first proposed that translation is subject to a set of constraints which inevitably leave traces in the language that translators produce: the fact that a translated text is constrained by a fully articulated text in another language, for instance, constitutes a major and unique constraint. This builds on the work of Frawley (1984), who suggested that the confrontation of source text and target language during the process of translation results in creating what he called a 'third code'. In other words, the language that evolves during translation and in which the target text is expressed is a kind of compromise between the norms of the source language and those of the target language. But corpus-based studies of translation go further, by suggesting that, for example, translators have a tendency to make explicit what is either implicit in the source text or would be implicit in a non-translated text in the same language. Along these lines, corpus-based studies undertaken by Burnett (1999) and Olohan and Baker (2000) have since revealed a much higher tendency to spell out the optional *that* in reporting structures in translated English text compared to non-translated English text belonging to the same genres. Similarly, Olohan (2003) found a noticeable tendency to avoid contractions (as in *won't* instead of *will not*) in translated vs non-translated English text.

Since the 1990s, many studies have focused on the role played by ideology and power in shaping translational behaviour. The extent to which translational behaviour lends support to or undermines the use of language as an instrument of ideological control is becoming a recurrent object of enquiry in studies informed by critical discourse analysis; Saldanha (2009) offers a detailed overview of such advances. Other research strands drawing on the social sciences attempt to account for the impact of mediators' view of the world on their translational behaviour by exploring the narratives to which they and their communities subscribe (Baker 2006). Such studies interrogate the way in which the professional conduct of translators and interpreters is negotiated against the backdrop of existing norms of translation as a social institution, and have challenged the widely held perception of translation and interpreting as routinized, uncritical activities.

Current research issues in translation and interpreting

Translation and interpreting as institutionalized and institution-building practices

Koskinen (2008: 17) argues that institutions, which she defines as forms of 'uniform action governed by role expectations, norms, values and belief systems', can be studied on different levels of abstraction. This section focuses on two types of institutional settings: local/national organizational systems and supranational bureaucratic cultures.

With increased globalization, migration and other forms of mobility, encounters between representatives of institutions and lay citizens requesting a range of services have come to be heavily mediated by interpreters and translators. Bilingual courtroom proceedings in English-speaking countries, for instance, are characterized by sophisticated use of questioning strategies by barristers; the effectiveness of such strategies is heavily dependent on the interpreters' mediation, as demonstrated in a number of studies (Berk-Seligson 1999; Hale 2001; Pérez-González 2006a). Recognizing the potential impact of interpreters on the judicial process, the legal profession has attempted to regulate the interpreters' role by means of codes of practice that require them to refrain from explicating or clarifying those elements which are deliberately left ambiguous, implicit or unclear in the counsel's original formulation. Similarly, interpreters involved in doctor-patient interaction and interviews of asylum seekers and political refugees are expected to align themselves with the interactional goals of their respective institutions, rather than with the individuals requiring institutional assistance. Interpreters have been shown to reinforce institutional discourses and agendas by enforcing certain interactional patterns, such as rigid question-answer exchanges that prevent political refugees from launching into a narrative of their personal tragedies while their asylum claims are being assessed (Jacquemet 2005), and by exercising their discretion in organizationally sanctioned ways. Medical interpreters, for example, tend to elicit from the patient and pursue issues that they regard as diagnostically relevant and excise those parts of the patient's response that contain subjective accounts of their concerns (Bolden 2000).

Despite ongoing efforts to limit the interpreter's latitude, work on institutional interpreting, including research informed by various strands of linguistic theories, has shown that even interpreters bound by the strictest codes of ethics often fail to provide the sort of straightforward, unedited renditions which their organizational co-interactants expect (Berk-Seligson

1999; Angelelli 2004). For one thing, lack of syntactic and semantic equivalence between languages, together with the stress under which interpreters operate, often lead them to inadvertently alter the tenor of the original utterance, for example by downgrading the suggestive and intimidating nature of key questions and statements. At the same time, even conference interpreters working in a highly formal context have been shown to depart from their canonical roles as conduits and speak in their own voice in order to defend themselves against charges of misinterpreting by other interactants wishing to use them as scapegoats (Diriker 2004). In the light of such findings, the overall field of interpreting studies, it has been argued, should refrain from 'comparing the propositional meaning of utterances and their interpretation' and seek instead to challenge the conceptualization of the role of interpreters as neutral conduits by describing 'the behaviour of all parties in terms of the set of factors governing the exchange' (Mason and Stewart 2001: 54). Such arguments have paved the way for the emergence and consolidation of dialogue interpreting, a distinct sub-field within interpreting studies which has enhanced the study of mediation in institutional settings. Dialogue interpreting approaches face-to-face encounters as three-way interactions, understood as a series of triadic exchanges between the institutional representative, the client and the interpreter (Mason 2001).

The power imbalance inherent in interpreter-mediated institutional encounters makes politeness theory an attractive framework to draw on. Interpreters occasionally need to mitigate the face-threatening acts of an interactant – for example, when a powerless speaker refuses or fails to comply with the requirements of the institutional representative. They also need to protect their own face, perhaps by distancing themselves from the contributions of one or more speakers. Such dialectics of interactional status and face-saving work has also been explored through investigations of turn-taking management and the use of hedging, downtoning or amplifying interactional devices. Here, Goffman's (1981) 'participation framework' has proved helpful (Wadensjö 1998; Roy 2000) and has also been applied in studies of sign language interpreting (Metzger 1999). Documented shifts in footing reveal the interpreters' alignments in relation to other interactants and highlight their role as institutional 'gatekeepers' (Wadensjö 1998). In managing the exchanges between lay people and institutional representatives, interpreters perform a range of repairing and bridging work required for a successful unfolding of the ongoing encounter. In the course of doing so, they often interpret selectively; indeed, medical interpreters have been found to offer their own answers to patients' questions without the physician necessarily being aware of it, thus acting as covert co-diagnosticians (Davidson 2000). Interpreters thus claim a participatory role for themselves 'as speaking agents who are critically engaged in the process of making meaningful utterances that elicit the intended response from, or have the intended effect upon, the hearer' (Davidson 2002: 1275). Ultimately, interactants, including the interpreter, realign themselves as required by the turn-by-turn unfolding of the conversation by exploiting the politeness and face-saving strategies available at each stage in order to maximize the effectiveness of the ongoing interview or interrogation.

Studies such as those discussed above have drawn attention to interpreters' active participation in the management of institutional interaction. At the same time, the vulnerability of interpreters to exercises of power by institutional representatives has received some attention from scholars interested in the workings of institutions that regulate the flow of asylum seekers and political refugees (Barsky 1996; Jacquemet 2005; Inghilleri 2007), from journalists reporting on the involvement of interpreters and translators in various wars (Levinson 2006; Packer 2007), and from professionals concerned about the welfare of interpreters operating in conflict zones (Kahane 2007). Interpreters working in the asylum system are often co-opted into the

Mona Baker and Luis Pérez-González

relevant institutional cultures and made to assume responsibilities that lie outside their canonical role, for example by participating in the evaluation of the asylum applicant's credibility, thus exacerbating their shifting perceptions of their own position as mediators within these structures of power. Similarly, interpreters working for the American troops in Iraq in the first decade of the twenty-first century were often assigned intelligence-gathering tasks that further alienated them from their local community and put their lives at greater risk (Packer 2007).

In addition to nationally based systems such as asylum, court and medical institutions, international organizations like the United Nations and the European Union also rely heavily on translators and interpreters. Indeed, they address their respective constituencies through translated and interpreted texts, such that 'in a constructivist sense, the institution itself gets translated' (Koskinen 2008: 22). One issue raised in the relatively small body of literature on international organizations available so far concerns efforts by these organizations to hide their translational character, and their subsequent effacement of the role played by translators and interpreters at different levels. On the one hand, translators' and interpreters' individual identities and contributions are diluted through the enforcement of collective workflow processes which serve to strengthen the public perception of the organizational voice. On the other hand, translators' and interpreters' ability to exercise their professional discretion is significantly restricted by means of institutional guidelines which seek to effect a gradual routinization and mechanization of translational behaviour and ensure that the language they produce 'functions seamlessly as part of the discourse' of the institution in question (Kang 2009: 144). Once again, despite the efforts of international organizations to develop translational cultures of their own, current research has identified a slippage between what translators and interpreters are officially expected or asked to do and what they actually do. This has been attributed to mismatches between institutional doctrine and 'interpreting habituses' (Marzocchi 2005) and to the growing impact of the economics of translation (i.e. time/costs factors), rather than socio-cultural policies, as the driving force behind institutional agendas (Mossop 2006). Mason ([2003] 2004: 481) also reports on the 'little uniformity of practice or evidence of influence of institutional guidelines on translator behaviour' that he found in his analysis of data from the European Parliament and UNESCO. His study suggests that institutional translators are responsible for numerous 'discoursal shifts', i.e. concatenations of small shifts in the use of transitivity patterns throughout the translated text, which result in attenuating or intensifying the message conveyed in the original text. Mason's contention that such discoursal shifts display traces of the ideologies that circulate in the translators' environment reinforces their interactional status as agents who are actively engaged in the production of institutional discourses, rather than simple mouthpieces whose role consists of consolidating 'habitualized' discourses through mechanistic practices of mediation.

Power, inequality, minority

Much of the current literature on translation and interpreting approaches cross-cultural encounters that involve an element of interlinguistic mediation as a space of radical inequality. Translators and interpreters mediating these encounters play a major role in asserting, questioning and sometimes forcefully resisting existing power structures. Viewed from this perspective, translation does not resolve conflict and inequality by enabling dialogue but rather constitutes a space of tension and power struggle in its own right. Casanova (2010), for example, examines translation as a factor in the struggle for legitimacy in the literary and political fields – a factor that participates in the consecration of authors and works, both nationally and internationally, and in the distribution and transfer of cultural capital. In her model, structural inequality evident in the imbalance between dominating and dominated languages and literatures reflects the struggle within any field in Bourdieu's terms. Inghilleri similarly draws on Bourdieu's notions of habitus, field, capital and illusio to demonstrate that interpreters working in the asylum system 'act within and are constituted by ... power-laden macro-structures ... that impact directly and indirectly on the interpreting activity' (2003: 261).

Growing interest in issues of power and inequality has naturally drawn attention to the role played by translation and interpreting in shaping the relationship between minority and majority groups in any society. Translation has always been a powerful instrument of the nation-state, not only in colonial and postcolonial contexts (Niranjana 1990; Dodson 2005) but also in the context of more modern, multicultural and multi-ethnic societies. Minority issues become particularly acute, with translation and interpreting acquiring increased significance, in diglossic situations, where the dominant, colonial or majority language inhabits and has monopoly on official, public life, and where the native language is relegated to the realm of the home, the casual, the ephemeral. Cronin (1998) was among the first to stress the urgency of exploring the effects of translation on various minority languages given their diminishing numbers across the world. He distinguishes between translation efforts that seek to obliterate the minority language by assimilating it to the dominant language and those which seek to retain and develop the minority language and resist its incorporation into the dominant language. Examples of the former abound in the Irish experience and are brought to life vividly in Brian Friel's *Translations* (Friel 1981), a play that depicts the process of anglicizing Ireland through the British Ordnance Survey in 1833. Examples of the latter include translation both from and into Welsh in many official contexts today, and translations undertaken from a wide range of prestigious literatures and languages into Scots in order to 'raise its status and establish its validity as a literary medium' (Corbett 1999: 3). Beyond the mere survival of the dominated language, translation into a minority language like Corsican is sometimes also 'a way of demonstrating a new confidence in [that] language and identity by acting *as if* it were a language of power' (Jaffe 1999: 264; original emphasis).

The deaf and hard-of-hearing are often treated as a minority group, and their interaction with the hearing community is seen as a site of power struggle in which translation and interpreting can play either an oppressive or empowering role. Those who are born deaf, in particular, generally do not acquire the majority language, or do not acquire it to native-speaker level, and because of their inability to hear they rely on interpreters throughout their life, and in a wide range of contexts. Improved access to interpreting services allows this particular minority group to participate more fully in various aspects of social life. It also improves their chances of advancing in their careers by using their own native, sign language in meetings and other face-to-face work encounters, rather than having to lip read, for instance. However, McKee (2003) warns that for various reasons to do with lack of cultural knowledge, issues of literacy, and the gap between the experience of the hearing interpreter and the deaf person, the mere provision of interpreting services can have a disempowering effect by creating an illusion of access or independence without necessarily putting the deaf person on an equal footing with their hearing co-interactants.

Translators and interpreters in the war zone

Scholars of translation have only recently begun to engage in a sustained manner with various aspects of the role and positioning of translators and interpreters in the war zone. Their focus has varied from an interest in the impact of interpreter and translator behaviour on other parties in the conflict, and the way they align or do not align with the institutions that employ them (Jacquemet 2005; Baker 2006; Salama-Carr 2007), to the impact of the war situation and proximity to violence on the interpreters and translators themselves (Maier 2007; Inghilleri 2008, 2009; Stahuljak 2010).

Drawing on narrative theory, Baker (2006) demonstrates how the discursive negotiation of competing narratives of wars and armed conflicts is realized in and through acts of translation and interpreting in the media, literature, scholarly articles, documentary film, political reports and Websites. Rafael (2007) argues that in the case of armed conflicts, interpreters can become particularly involved on the ground and find themselves occupying precarious positions, often exposed to extreme discursive violence and distrusted by the very same parties which deployed them as instruments of surveillance. He examines the tensions and indeterminacy inherent in the positions that translators and interpreters occupy in the context of various wars. Despite their essential function in fighting insurgents, he argues, locally hired interpreters are also feared as potential insurgents themselves. Distrust of local interpreters and translators in the context of colonial expansion and armed conflict is well documented historically. Niranjana (1990) notes that the colonial governor of India, William Jones, and his British administrators found it 'highly dangerous to employ the natives as interpreters, upon whose fidelity they could not depend' (1990: 774), and that their remedy for this state of affairs was to substitute local interpreters and translators with British ones. Takeda (2009) similarly reports that interpreters and translators of Japanese origin were not used in code-breaking work in the USA during the Second World War for security reasons, and that their non-Japanese colleagues were secretly instructed to monitor them and to ensure that they were translating and interpreting accurately. Stahuljak (2010) offers a more extended and specific account of interpreting in contemporary war zones, with reference to the war in Croatia in the early 1990s.

Research on the role of translators and interpreters in mediating armed conflict suggests that they typically assume a wide range of tasks that extend well beyond any canonical definition of their responsibilities and obligations. Based on interviews with British and French journalists who worked in Iraq following its invasion by US troops in 2003, Palmer (2007) confirms that interpreters often selected the individuals to be interviewed by the media representative and advised on whether it was safe or practical to travel to a particular place to secure an interview. Takeda (2009: 52) states that second-generation Japanese Americans recruited and trained by the US military during the Second World War 'translated captured enemy documents, interrogated Japanese prisoners of war, persuaded Japanese soldiers and civilians to surrender, and participated in propaganda activities'. Similar findings have emerged from the UK-based Languages at War Project, run by the University of Reading and the University of Southampton in conjunction with the Imperial War Museum.

Translation and interpreting in the globalized information society

Recent technological developments have made it possible to overcome spatial barriers and speed up the circulation of information. This 'de-materialization of space' (Cronin 2003) is responsible for the creation of supraterritorial readerships and audiences and accounts for the growing importance of instantaneity in the translation profession. Although these developments have strengthened the translation and interpreting industries in economic terms, the current literature on globalization has failed to engage meaningfully with the role that these forms of mediation play within the global deterritorialized space. As noted by Bielsa (2005), theorists of cultural globalization have tended to put a positive spin on the instantaneity of global flows and to assume uncritically that it allows a straightforward juxtaposition of cultures and spaces. The emphasis on the dynamics of instant circulation also glosses over the problematic reliance of users and viewers on content in English as a lingua franca. Translation scholars have sought to tackle the complexity of this situation, either by attempting to establish how the dominant lingua franca influences other languages via processes of translation and multilingual text production, or by exploring the way in which translation can serve as a strategy of resistance against the linguistic and cultural dominance of English.

Bennett (2007) examines the role of translation in strengthening the position of English as a lingua franca in academic discourse, and hence in configuring knowledge and controlling the flow and format of information. Referring to the discourse routinely employed by academics and academic translators as 'predatory', she describes some of its main principles as follows: the discourse has to be clear and coherent; the language must be impartial and objective; the text has to be hierarchically organized into sections with a clear introduction, development and conclusion; the prose must be lucid, economical and precise; vagueness and verbosity must be avoided; impersonal structures, including use of the passive and nominalized forms, are preferred; and material and existential processes tend to dominate, reflecting a preoccupation with statements of fact and descriptions of actions. Bennett draws on examples of Portuguese academic articles translated for publication in English to demonstrate the extent to which the ideological framework that informs the original articles is disrupted and replaced by a positivist structure inherent to English academic discourse. She concludes that translators' complicity in enforcing ideologies embedded in English academic discourse must be questioned since it can lead to the systematic destruction of rival forms of knowledge.

In studies conducted over the past decade, House (2004, 2008) explored the impact of English on a number of target languages more systematically by investigating the communicative norms operating in a wide range of texts translated from English and those operating in comparable texts written originally in the target language. In attempting to establish whether translation from English results in eroding the communicative norms of a target language, House assumes that, whether inadvertent or not, choices made in the course of translation either reinforce cultural diversity or participate in imposing Anglo-Saxon norms on other cultures under the guise of 'universality'. Although the studies conducted so far have not produced clear-cut evidence, they suggest that textual norms in languages other than English are likely to be adapted to Anglophone ones, 'particularly in the use of certain functional categories that express subjectivity and audience design' (House 2008: 87). Such adaptations include shifts from the ideational (message-oriented) to the interpersonal (addressee-oriented) function of language, from informational explicitness to inference-inducing implicitness, and from 'densely packed information to loosely linearized information' (House 2004: 49).

Another aspect of the interface between globalization and translation which has attracted growing scholarly attention is the impact of new information and communication technologies on the way we use and conceptualize language, including translational practices. The instantaneity of global flows resulting from technological advances is often an oppressive factor forcing translators to produce assignments within increasingly short response periods. According to Cronin (1998), technology-driven instantaneity generates pressure on translation to become a uniform, transparent medium of fluid exchange: as professionals struggle to translate more and faster, the communicative norms and specialized terminology of dominant languages are more likely to find their way into the target texts, thus gradually eroding the native resources. But the effects of technology can be more specific, particularly in the context of machine translation systems and translation memory tools. As Raley (2003) explains, machine translation technologies place particular emphasis on functionality and utilitarianism: reasonably accurate and functional draft translations are thus only feasible when the input is basic, and when both input and output are restricted in terms of style, vocabulary, figurative expression and content. Unsurprisingly, given its centrality to technological developments, English is the language which has most informed the design of input entry protocols in machine translation, thus further contributing to the growing hegemony of this language and its communicative norms. The privileging of English modes of expression in the context of machine translation, however, can also be resisted. As suggested by Raley (2003), the 'broken' English which makes up machine translation input and output lends itself to 'free' adaptation by native and non-native speakers alike. Ultimately, free adaptation can contribute to severing the link between English and specific geophysical spaces as well as undermining collective identities based on this link. Beyond machine translation as such, translation memory tools have also been found to impact our use of language in a number of ways. Translating in this environment, for instance, involves the mechanical segmentation of the source text into trans-lation 'units'. Translators are thus prompted to use the same number of segments in the target language, which often results in the erosion of cohesion resources and, more widely, a partial excision of the rhetorical element of language.

Technological advances have also stimulated interest in the diversity of resources that can be used to create texts. In addition to the spoken and written word, different semiotic modalities such as gestures, visuals and music are often co-deployed within a multimodal text to create meaning. Although the study of multimodal translational behaviour has traditionally focused on the subtitling and dubbing of films and other audiovisual broadcasts, attention is increas-ingly shifting towards new areas of multimodal mediation, often involving the transfer of meaning across semiotic modes. These include subtitling and interpreting for the hard of hearing and the deaf, as well as the audio description of films for the blind. Audio description consists of a spoken account of those visual aspects of a film which play a role in conveying its plot, rather than a translation of linguistic content (Pérez-González 2009).

Recent changes in the audiovisual landscape, including the development of digitization techniques and emergence of new patterns in the distribution and consumption of audiovisual products, have encouraged the emergence of interventionist practices such as 'fansubbing', whether for aesthetic or political reasons. Unhappy with the shortage and cultural insensitivity of commercial translations of their favourite audiovisual programmes and genres, networks of fans, known as fansubbers, produce their own subtitled versions which are then circulated globally through Internet-based channels. In order to allow their fellow fans to experience the cultural 'otherness' of the programme they are subtitling, these amateur translators exploit traditional meaning-making codes in a creative manner and criss-cross the traditional bound-aries between linguistic and visual semiotics in innovative ways. For example, they use 'head-notes' and written glosses at the top of the screen to expand or elaborate on the meaning of 'untranslatable' cultural references in the film dialogue; the cultural references in question still feature untranslated within the 'traditional subtitle' displayed simultaneously at the bottom of the screen. Fansubbers also favour the 'dilution' of subtitles within the image: technological developments allow them to display subtitles in unusual angles, perspectives and fonts which blend in with the aesthetics of the film, thus maximizing the viewer's enjoyment of the visuals (Pérez-González 2006b). Subtitling is also being increasingly appropriated by politically engaged groups without formal training in translation to undermine the socio-economic structures that sustain global capitalism. Pérez-González (2010) describes how these commu-nities of politicized 'non-translators' capitalize on the potential of networked communication to circulate translations of audiovisual content that would otherwise be only available in English. This interventionist engagement of activist communities represents a challenge to the control that media corporations have traditionally exerted over the distribution and reception of their news programmes: audiovisual content mediated by activists often takes on new resonances when displaced from the global circuits it was originally intended for and watched by a national audience with a specific take on what is reported.

Concluding remarks

The prevalence and pervasiveness of translation and interpreting in all areas of social interaction have important consequences for society as a whole, as this chapter has attempted to demonstrate. More specifically, their impact is also being felt in the academy. Translation and interpreting are increasingly being acknowledged as core areas of research. Rather than a subfield of linguistics or cultural studies, translation studies has become an interdisciplinary field in its own right. Its remit encompasses, extends and surpasses a range of issues with which other disciplines have traditionally engaged from different perspectives. As it continues to develop in the twenty-first century, many scholars now believe that its next and most consequential challenge is to shed its Eurocentric origins and prepare to embrace the variety of theoretical perspectives, experiences and traditions that the West's many 'others' have to offer. This challenge is already being undertaken, with a growing number of voices of non-Western scholars continuing to gain strength and calling into question much of our received wisdom in the field (Hung and Wakabayashi 2005; Cheung 2006; Bandia 2008; Selim 2009).

Related topics

corpus linguistics; critical discourse analysis; culture; discourse analysis; identity; institutional discourse; linguistic imperialism; medical communication; migration; multimodal communication; sign language; the media

Further reading

Baker, M. (ed.) (2010) *Critical Readings in Translation Studies*, Abingdon and New York: Routledge. (A thematically organized reader which prioritizes latest developments in the field rather than foundational texts and features detailed summaries of each article, follow-up questions for discussion and recommended further reading.)

Baker, M. and Saldanha, G. (eds) (2009) *The Routledge Encyclopedia of Translation Studies*, 2nd edn, Abingdon and New York: Routledge. (A standard reference in the field which features extended entries on core concepts, types of translation and interpreting and theoretical approaches, plus entries which summarize the history of translation in a wide range of Western and non-Western societies.)

Munday, J. (2012) *Introducing Translation Studies: Theories and Applications*, 3rd edn, London and New York: Routledge. (Munday provides a balanced and accessible overview of the main theoretical strands in the discipline, supported by illustrative case studies in different languages, suggestions for further reading and a list of discussion and research points.)

Pöchhacker, F. (2004) *Introducing Interpreting Studies*, London: Routledge. (A clear and comprehensive introduction to interpreting studies as an academic discipline, outlining its origins and development to the present day.)

Venuti, L. (2004) *The Translation Studies Reader*, 2nd edn, London and New York: Routledge. (A chronologically organized reader which focuses largely on foundational texts. Extended introductions to each section clearly outline the main trends during the relevant period.)

References

ABI (Allied Business Intelligence Inc.) (2002) *Language Translation, Localization and Globalization: World Market Forecasts, Industry Drivers and eSolutions*, USA. Available at: www.abiresearch. com/

Angelelli, C. (2004) *Re-visiting the Role of the Interpreter: A Study of Conference, Court and Medical Interpreters in Canada, Mexico and the United States*, Amsterdam and Philadelphia: John John Benjamins.

Baker, M. (1993) 'Corpus linguistics and translation studies. Implications and applications', in M. Baker, G. Francis and E. Tognini-Bonelli (eds) *Text and Technology: In Honour of John Sinclair*, Amsterdam: John Benjamins.

——(1996) 'Corpus-based translation studies: the challenges that lie ahead', in H. Somers (ed.) *Terminology, LSP and Translation: Studies in Language Engineering, in Honour of Juan C. Sager*, Amsterdam and Philadelphia: John Benjamins.

——(2006) *Translation and Conflict: A Narrative Account*, London and New York: Routledge.

Bandia, P. (2008) *Translation as Reparation: Writing and Translation in Postcolonial Africa*, Manchester: St Jerome Publishing.

Barsky, R. (1996) 'The interpreter as intercultural agent in convention refugee hearings', *The Translator* 2(1): 45–63.

Bennett, K. (2007) 'Epistemicide!: the tale of a predatory discourse', *The Translator* 13(2): 151–69.

Berk-Seligson, S. (1999) 'The impact of court interpreting on the coerciveness of leading questions', *Forensic Linguistics* 6(1): 30–56.

Bielsa, E. (2005) 'Globalisation and translation: a theoretical approach', *Language and Intercultural Communication* 5(2): 131–44.

Bolden, G. B. (2000) 'Toward understanding practices of medical interpreting: interpreters' involvement in history taking', *Discourse Studies* 2(4): 387–419.

Burnett, S. (1999) 'A Corpus-based Study of Translational English', M.Sc. Dissertation, Manchester: Centre for Translation Studies, UMIST.

Casanova, P. (2010) 'Consecration and accumulation of literary capital: translation as unequal exchange', translated from French by S. Brownlie, in M. Baker (ed.) *Critical Readings in Translation Studies*, Abingdon and New York: Routledge.

Cheung, M. (ed.) (2006) *An Anthology of Chinese Discourse on Translation*, vol. 1: *From Earliest Times to the Buddhist Project*, Manchester: St Jerome Publishing.

Cook, G. (2009) 'Foreign Language Teaching', in M. Baker and G. Saldanha (eds) *Routledge Encyclopedia of Translation Studies*, 2nd edn, Abingdon and New York: Routledge.

Corbett, J. (1999) *Written in the Language of the Scottish Nation: A History of Literary Translation into Scots*, Clevedon: Multilingual Matters.

Cronin, M. (1998) 'The cracked looking glass of servants: translation and minority languages in a global age', *The Translator* 4(2): 145–62.

——(2003) *Translation and Globalization*, London and New York: Routledge.

CSA (Common Sense Advisory Inc.) (2004) *Global Business Confidence Survey: Translation*, USA. Available at: www.commonsenseadvisory.com/

——(2008) *Telephone Interpretation*, USA. Available at: www.commonsenseadvisory.com/

Davidson, B. (2000) 'The interpreter as institutional gatekeeper: the social-linguistic role of interpreters in Spanish-English medical discourse', *Journal of Sociolinguistics* 4(3): 379–405.

——(2002) 'A model for the construction of conversational common ground in interpreted discourse', *Journal of Pragmatics* 34: 1273–300.

Diriker, E. (2004) *De-/Re-Contextualizing Conference Interpreting: Interpreters in the Ivory Tower?*, Amsterdam and Philadelphia: John Benjamins.

Dodson, M. S. (2005) 'Translating science, translating empire: the power of language in colonial North India', *Society for Comparative Study of Society and History* 809–35.

EUATC (European Union of Associations of Translation Companies) (2005) *The European Translation Industry. Facing the Future.* Available at: www.euatc.org/

Frawley, W. (1984) 'Prolegomenon to a theory of translation', in W. Frawley (ed.) *Translation: Literary, Linguistic, and Philosophical Perspectives*, London and Toronto: Associated University Press.

Friel, B. (1981) *Translations*, London: Faber and Faber.

Goffman, E. (1981) *Forms of Talk*, Philadelphia: University of Pennsylvania Press.

Hale, S. (2001) 'How are courtroom questions interpreted? An analysis of Spanish interpreters' practices', in I. Mason (ed.) *Triadic Exchanges: Studies in Dialogue Interpreting*, Manchester: St Jerome Publishing.

Hatim, B. and Mason, I. (1990) *Discourse and the Translator*, London and New York: Longman.

——(1997) *The Translator as Communicator*, London and New York: Routledge.

Hermans, T. (1996) 'The translator's voice in translated narrative', *Target* 8(1): 23–48.

Hervey, S. and Higgins, I. (1992) *Thinking Translation: A Course in Translation Method: French to English*, London and New York: Routledge.

House, J. (1981) *A Model for Translation Quality Assessment*, Tübingen: Gunter Narr.

——(2004) 'English as a lingua franca and its influence on other European languages', in J. M. Bravo (ed.) *A New Spectrum of Translation Studies*, Valladolid: Universidad de Valladolid.

——(2008) 'Global English and the destruction of identity?', in P. Nikolaou and M.-V. Kyritsi (eds) *Translating Selves: Experience and Identity between Languages and Literatures*, London and New York: Continuum.

Hung, E. and Wakabayashi, J. (eds) (2005) *Asian Translation Traditions*, Manchester: St Jerome Publishing.

Inghilleri, M. (2003) 'Habitus, field and discourse: interpreting as a socially situated activity', *Target* 15(2): 243–68.

——(2007) 'National sovereignty versus universal rights: interpreting justice in a global context', *Social Semiotics* 17(2): 195–212.

——(2008) 'The ethical task of the translator in the geo-political arena: from Iraq to Guantánamo Bay', *Translation Studies* 1(2): 212–23.

——(2009) 'Translators in war zones: ethics under fire in Iraq', in E. Bielsa and C. W. Hughes (eds) *Globalization, Political Violence and Translation*, Basingstoke: Palgrave Macmillan.

Jacquemet, M. (2005) 'The registration interview: restricting refugees' narrative performance', in M. Baynham and A. de Fina (eds) *Dislocations/Relocations: Narratives of Displacement*, Manchester: St Jerome Publishing.

Jaffe, A. (1999) 'Locating power: Corsican translators and their critics', in J. Blommaert (ed.) *Language Ideological Debates*, Berlin and New York: Mouton de Gruyter; reprinted in M. Baker (ed.) (2010) *Critical Readings in Translation Studies*, Abingdon and New York: Routledge.

Kahane, E. (2007) 'Interpreters in conflict zones: the limits of neutrality', *Communicate!* (AIIC's online journal). Available at www.aiic.net/ViewPage.cfm?page_id=2691

Kang, J.-H. (2009) 'Institutional translation', in M. Baker and G. Saldanha (eds) *Routledge Encyclopedia of Translation Studies*, 2nd edn, Abingdon and New York: Routledge.

Koskinen, K. (2008) *Translating Institutions*, Manchester: St Jerome Publishing.

Larson, M. (1984) *Meaning-based Translation: A Guide to Cross-language Equivalence*, Lanham, MD, New York and London: University Press of America.

Laviosa, S. (ed.) (1998) *L'approche basée sur le corpus/The Corpus-Based Approach*, special issue, *Meta* 43(4). Available at: www.erudit.org/revue/meta/

Laviosa, S. (2002) *Corpus-based Translation Studies: Theory, Findings, Applications*, Amsterdam and New York: Rodopi.

Levinson, C. (2006) 'Iraq's "Terps" Face Suspicion from Both Sides', *Christian Science Monitor*, 17 April. Available at: www.csmonitor.com/2006/0417/p01s01-woiq.html

McKee, R. (2003) 'Interpreting as a tool for empowerment of the New Zealand deaf community', in S. Fenton (ed.) *For Better or For Worse: Translation as a Tool for Change in the South Pacific*, Manchester: St Jerome Publishing.

Maier, C. (2007) 'The translator's visibility: the rights and responsibilities thereof', in M. Salama-Carr (ed.) *Translating and Interpreting Conflict*, Amsterdam: Rodopi.

Marzocchi, C. (2005) 'On a contradiction in the discourse on language arrangements in EU institutions', *Across Languages and Cultures* 6(1): 5–12.

Mason, I. (2001) *Triadic Exchanges: Studies in Dialogue Interpreting*, Manchester: St Jerome Publishing.

——(2003) 'Text parameters in translation: transitivity and institutional cultures', in E. Hajicova, P. Sgall, Z. Jettmarova, A. Rothkegel, D. Rothfuß-Bastian and H. Gerzymisch-Arbogast (eds) *Textologie und Translation*, Tübingen: Gunter Narr. Reprinted in L. Venuti (ed.) (2004) *The Translation Studies Reader*, 2nd edn, London and New York: Routledge.

Mason, I. and Stewart, M. (2001) 'Interactional pragmatics, face and the dialogue interpreter', in I. Mason (ed.) *Triadic Exchanges: Studies in Dialogue Interpreting*, Manchester: St Jerome Publishing.

Metzger, M. (1999) *Sign Language Interpreting: Deconstructing the Myth of Neutrality*, Washington, DC: Gallaudet University Press.

Mossop, B. (2006) 'From culture to business: federal government translation in Canada', *The Translator* 12(1): 1–27.

Nida, E. A. (1964) *Toward a Science of Translating, with Special Reference to Principles and Procedures Involved in Bible Translating*, Leiden: E. J. Brill.

Nida, E. A. and Taber, C. (1969) *The Theory and Practice of Translation*, Leiden: E. J. Brill.

Niranjana, T. (1990) 'Translation, colonialism and the rise of English', *Economic and Political Weekly*, 14 April: 773–9.

Nord, C. (1991) *Text Analysis in Translation,* Amsterdam and Atlanta, GA: Rodopi.

Olohan, M. (2003) 'How frequent are the contractions? A study of contracted forms in the translational English corpus', *Target* 15(1): 58–89.

Olohan, M. and Baker, M. (2000) 'Reporting that in translated English: evidence for subconscious processes of explicitation?', *Across Languages and Cultures* 1(2): 141–58.

Packer, G. (2007) 'Betrayed: the Iraqis who trusted America the most', *The New Yorker*, 26 March. Available at: www.newyorker.com/reporting/2007/03/26/070326fa_fact_packer

Palmer, J. (2007) 'Interpreting and translation for western media in Iraq', in M. Salama-Carr (ed.) *Translating and Interpreting Conflict*, Amsterdam and New York: Rodopi.

Pérez-González, L. (2006a) 'Interpreting strategic recontextualization cues in the courtroom: corpus-based insights into the pragmatic force of non-restrictive relative clauses', *Journal of Pragmatics* 38: 390–417.

——(2006b) 'Fansubbing Anime: insights into the butterfly effect of globalisation on audiovisual translation', *Perspectives: Studies in Translatology* 14(4): 260–77.

——(2009) 'Audiovisual translation', in M. Baker and G. Saldanha (eds) *Routledge Encyclopedia of Translation Studies*, 2nd edn, Abingdon and New York: Routledge.

——(2010) '*Ad-hocracies* of translation activism in the blogosphere: a genealogical case study', in M. Baker, M. C. Perez and M. Olohan (eds) *Text and Context: Essays on Translation and Interpreting in Honour of Ian Mason*, Manchester: St Jerome Publishing.

Rabin, C. (1958) 'The linguistics of translation', in H. Smith (ed.) *Aspects of Translation: Studies in Communication*, London.

Rafael, V. L. (2007) 'Translation in wartime', *Public Culture* 19(2): 239–46.

Raley, R. (2003) 'Machine translation and global English', *The Yale Journal of Criticism* 16(2): 291–313.

Reiss, K. (1971) *Möglichkeiten und Grenzen der Übersetzungskritik,* Munich: Hueber.

Roy, C. (2000) *Interpreting as a Discourse Process*, New York and Oxford: Oxford University Press.

Salama-Carr, M. (ed.) (2007) *Translating and Interpreting Conflict*, Amsterdam and New York: Rodopi.

Saldanha, G. (2009) 'Linguistic approaches', in M. Baker and G. Saldanha (eds) *Routledge Encyclopedia of Translation Studies*, 2nd edn, Abingdon and New York: Routledge.

Selim, S. (ed.) (2009) Nation and translation in the Middle East, special issue, *The Translator* 15(1).

Stahuljak, Z. (2010) 'War, translation, transnationalism: interpreters in and of the war (Croatia, 1991–92)', in M. Baker (ed.) *Critical Readings in Translation Studies*, Abingdon and New York: Routledge.

Takeda, K. (2009) 'War and interpreters', *Across Languages and Cultures* 10(1): 49–62.

Tymoczko, M. (1999) *Translation in a Postcolonial Context: Taming the Wild Irish*, Manchester: St Jerome Publishing.

University of Reading (n.d.) Languages at War Project. Available at: www.reading.ac.uk/languages-at-war/lw-home.aspx

Venuti, L. (1995) *The Translator's Invisibility*, London and New York: Routledge.

Vermeer, H. J. (1989b/2000) 'Skopos and Commission in Translational Action', in A. Chesterman (ed.) *Readings in Translation Theory*, Helsinki: Oy Finn Lectura Ab; reprinted in L. Venuti (ed.) *The Translation Studies Reader*, London and New York: Routledge.

Wadensjö, C. (1998) *Interpreting as Interaction*, London and New York: Longman.

4

Lexicography

Thierry Fontenelle

Introduction

Lexicography is an area of applied linguistics that focuses on the compilation of dictionaries (practical lexicography) as well as on the description of the various types of relations found in the lexicon (theoretical lexicography). It is neither a new science nor a new craft. Historians generally agree that the first dictionaries can be traced back to the explanations of difficult words inserted into Latin manuscripts in the Middle Ages. These glosses evolved into glossaries which were sorted alphabetically or thematically and, as Cowie (2009: 2) points out, came to fulfill a vital function in teaching and the transmission of knowledge. The use of Latin words to explain more difficult Latin ones foreshadowed monolingual dictionaries, with their headwords and definitions, while explanations of hard Latin words in Old English or Old French can be seen as a precursor of modern bilingual dictionaries.

Dictionaries are primarily compiled to meet practical needs. They are also cultural artifacts which convey a vision of a community's language. The tension between prescriptive and descriptive approaches has often made lexicographers uncomfortable, since, as Atkins and Rundell argue (2008: 2), many users perceive dictionaries as 'authoritative records of how people ought to use language'. Modern lexicography is more concerned with a descriptive approach where the lexicographer compiles a description of the vocabulary of a given speech community.

Robert Cawdrey's *A Table Alphabetical* (1604) is usually considered as the first printed monolingual English dictionary. However, the history of lexicography remembers Samuel Johnson's *Dictionary of the English Language* (1755) as the first modern and innovative dictionary of English. Johnson's dictionary reflected the need for a prescriptive and normative authority which would serve to establish a standard of correctness. In his 'Plan of a Dictionary of the English Language', addressed to Lord Chesterfield in 1747, Johnson discussed all the crucial issues which lexicographers are faced with, even today, when starting a dictionary project, ranging from inflectional and derivational morphology, to pronunciation and etymology. The representation of syntactic information (Johnson did not use the modern term 'subcategorization') attracted his attention when he pointed out that one 'dies of one's wounds while one may perish with hunger'. He stressed that 'every man acquainted with our language would be offended with a change of these particles'. Johnson's preoccupations are still at the heart of the creation of current dictionaries, especially learners' dictionaries. He was a radical thinker who was well ahead of his time and who managed to shed light on the nature of language and meaning, long before philosophers like Wittgenstein started addressing the crucial issue of word meaning. He asked many important questions which are still hotly debated in contemporary lexicography circles. He was aware of the need to establish clear criteria for selecting words to be included in dictionaries, or for distinguishing between general language and specialized terminology. The term 'corpus lexicographer' did not exist in 1755, but because he was the first to base his dictionary on authentic examples of usage, collected from the works of English authors, he was definitely a precursor of corpus lexicography.

A monument of English lexicography is undoubtedly Murray's *Oxford English Dictionary* (*OED*), whose final section was published in 1928. The original aim of the project, which started in 1879, was to produce a four-volume dictionary which would record the history of the English language from Anglo-Saxon times, using nearly two million citation forms to track the genesis and evolution of lexical items. Several supplements were published in the twentieth century (the first supplement appeared in 1933) and, today, the *OED* includes around 300,000 entries defining over half a million lexical items (Murray *et al*. 1933). The electronic version, which corresponds to the 20-volume integrated work, offers powerful search and browse functionalities which provide scholars with exciting vistas to research the history and evolution of the English language.

Historical dictionaries have been compiled for several other languages, such as for French, the prime example being the *Trésor de la langue française*, whose sixteen volumes are based on a huge corpus of millions of authentic citations from literary texts. It took nearly 150 years to compile the Dutch *Woordenboek der Nederlandsche Taal* (*WNT*), which, with its 40 volumes and 400,000 headwords, aims to provide an objective linguistic description of the vocabulary stock of that language. All these major historical dictionaries cover general-language words, but also dialectal, jargon and slang terms, as well as offensive and swear words which are more likely to be left out from general-purpose dictionaries.

The advent of learners' dictionaries

The vocabulary control movement

The most noticeable impact of lexicography on applied linguistics is probably related to the advent of learners' dictionaries, which has heavily influenced Anglo-Saxon lexicography. One of the chief weaknesses of native-speaker dictionaries is that the words used in definitions are often difficult to understand for non-native speakers, which means that these dictionaries do not meet the specific needs of second language learners. The history of monolingual learners' dictionaries can be traced back to the contributions of a number of key figures such as A. S. Hornby, Michael West and H. E. Palmer, who created the so-called 'vocabulary control movement' and can justifiably be seen as the founding fathers of applied linguistics (see also Cowie 2009 for more information about this major development). The leading figure of this movement, Harold Palmer, was interested in identifying the set of words which speakers use most frequently to communicate. After realizing that a high level of natural communication could be achieved by using a vocabulary of around 1,000 words, he worked with A. S. Hornby to produce *Thousand-Word English* (Palmer and Hornby 1938), a word list of initially 900 words which was intended to lighten the learning load of foreign students. Michael West took the vocabulary control idea further by developing a limited vocabulary of about 1,500 words which he used to write the definitions of his *New Method English Dictionary* (West and Endicott 1935). West's subsequent General Service List (1953), which includes frequency ratings for words in their particular senses as well as collocations and idioms, also definitely influenced the next generation of learners' dictionaries. The first edition of the *Longman Dictionary of Contemporary English*, a.k.a. *LDOCE* (Procter 1978) followed this tradition by using a controlled vocabulary of about 2,000 words to write the definitions, while, more recently, the *Macmillan English Dictionary for Advanced Learners*, *MEDAL* (Rundell 2007) uses a limited defining vocabulary of about 2,500 words. In *LDOCE1*, the words which do not belong to this set are printed in small capitals. Consider the definition of *mink*, where *weasel* and *carnivorous* are not part of the controlled vocabulary of this dictionary:

> **mink** *n* **1** [Wn1;C] a type of small WEASEL-like animal – see picture at CARNIVOROUS **2** [U] the valuable brown fur of this animal, often used for making ladies' coats

The vocabulary control movement therefore influenced the macrostructure of the dictionary. The list of words that are granted entry status is indeed significantly smaller than a native-speaker dictionary's macrostructure and rare and highly technical words are not likely to be included in learners' dictionaries.

The second edition of the Macmillan (*MEDAL*) dictionary (Rundell 2007) highlights the top 7,500 words which account for about 92 per cent of most texts. This distinction between high-frequency core vocabulary and less common lexical items reflects the distinction between receptive and productive vocabulary. In this dictionary, the core headwords are shown in red and are banded by frequency into three equal sets of 2,500 words each. This system is based upon research into vocabulary size, which has shown that learners need to be familiar with a fairly large number of lexical items to perform successfully at advanced level (see also Barcroft *et al.*'s chapter on *Lexis* in this volume for more details about vocabulary learning). Headwords that are part of the core vocabulary will therefore receive more extensive treatment and will provide users with more information in the form of additional examples, in-depth information about collocational and subcategorization preferences, frequent mistakes typically made by learners, etc.

The way definitions are written is also different from what can be found in dictionaries for native speakers. The use of a strictly controlled vocabulary facilitates the decoding task (understanding what a word means) and forces the lexicographer to resort to specific defining patterns or formulae. The following examples, excerpted from *LDOCE1*, illustrate patterns such as 'a person who' to define nouns denoting professions, or '(cause to)' and 'make or become', used to indicate that a verb participates in the so-called causative-inchoative alternation, which is typical of change-of-state verbs like *open*, *break*, *boil* or *increase*:

> **florist** *n a person who* keeps a shop for selling flowers
> **herbalist** *n* **1** *a person who* grows and/or sells HERBS, esp. for making medicine
> **shorten** v [T1; I0] to *make or become* short or shorter
> **develop** [T1; I0] to *(cause to)* grow, increase or become larger or more complete

Combining dictionaries and grammars

The examples in the preceding section illustrate the use of a feature which distinguishes learners' dictionaries from their unabridged counterparts for native speakers, namely a system of grammar codes designed to represent the types of syntactic environment in which a given lexical item can be inserted. The first learners' dictionaries owed much to Harold Palmer's pioneering work in the field of verb syntax. Palmer had experimented with various systems for accounting for verbal valency (i.e. the nature and number of complements a verb can take) before publishing his *Grammar of English Words* in 1938, which was the first learners' dictionary to contain a verb-pattern scheme. In this dictionary, each verb pattern was identified by means of a number code, and one or more codes were included in verb entries. Palmer heavily influenced A. S. Hornby in the 1930s and the latter took over this idea of using verb-pattern schemes in his *Idiomatic and Syntactic English Dictionary* (Hornby *et al.* 1942), which, in 1952, would become known as the *Advanced Learner's Dictionary of Current English*. Hornby improved on Palmer's presentation of verb patterns and started to arrange the patterns and illustrative examples in a series of tables where vertical divisions are made to correspond to the major structural elements of a pattern, for example, noun phrases corresponding to the Object in the pattern VP9 corresponding to 'Verb + Object + Past Participle'. In 1974, Hornby adopted the verb-complementation scheme of Quirk *et al.*'s *Grammar of Contemporary English*, grouping together verb patterns that had the same major function (e.g. the class of ditransitive verbs corresponded to Verb Patterns 11 to 21).

In addition to information on pronunciation, syllable division, compounds and irregular inflections, the first edition of *LDOCE* in 1978 proposed a systematic organization of grammatical categories and codes. The double articulation of the *LDOCE* table of grammar codes made it possible to represent the syntactic function of a given constituent class. The codes were made up of a capital letter, corresponding to word classes or parts of speech, followed by a number representing the type of environment in which a code-bearing item can be found. In the examples above, the letter T in the code T1 (in *shorten*) corresponds to a transitive verb and the number 1 indicates that this verb can be followed by one or more noun phrases. The letter I in I0 indicates that the verb can be used intransitively, 0 meaning that it need not be followed by anything. Other letters are used to denote ditransitive verbs (D), linking verbs (L), uncountable nouns (U), count nouns (C), etc.

Combining the letter and number information gives a very sound and systematic indication of the syntactic environment in which a word is used in a given sense. This double articulation was at the time an innovative feature. The similarity between the realizations of syntactic patterns described by codes like T5, D5 or U5 is reflected in the make-up of the codes themselves (the code-bearing lexical item is italicized in the examples below):

> [D5]: ditransitive verb with Noun Phrase followed by a that-clause: He *warned* her that he would come.
> [T5]: monotransitive verb with one that-clause object. I *know* that he'll come.
> [U5]: uncountable noun followed by a that-clause. Is there *proof* that he is here?

The three codes describe a pattern that includes a common element (a *that*-clause), a similarity which they reflect in their internal organization, since the three codes have [5] as second element. In 1978, this was a highly innovative approach, since the only major rival at the time – Hornby's *Oxford Advanced Learners' Dictionary* (1974) – relied upon unanalyzed codes such as VP9 (S + V + that) or VP11 (S + V + NP + that), which did not enable the user to figure out that the patterns included this common element.

As can be seen above, the system of grammar codes found in learners' dictionaries is designed to meet the encoding needs of users, especially non-native speakers of English, who need explicit guidance to produce grammatically and stylistically correct documents. This points to the dual function of dictionaries, which can be used for receptive use (to decode or understand a text), or for productive use (to encode a text).

Lumping vs splitting

One of the key questions in lexicography is the issue of word senses and polysemy. As noted by Kilgarriff (1997), dictionaries, which are frequently called upon to resolve disputes about meaning, must be clear and draw a line around a meaning, so that a use can be classified as on one side of the line or the other. Lexicographers are therefore under pressure to present sets of discrete, non-overlapping meanings for a word. Yet, when one examines corpus data and actual evidence of usage based upon collections of millions of words of authentic texts, one quickly realizes that these discrete, non-overlapping sets of senses are frequently a myth. Two key concepts to understand the dilemmas lexicographers regularly face are *lumping* (considering two slightly different patterns of usage as a single meaning) and *splitting* (which happens when the lexicographer separates slightly different patterns of usage into distinct meanings). Consider the following *LDOCE1* definition for the verb *shorten*, which illustrates the lumping strategy: one single definition captures two distinct types of subcategorization possibilities, an intransitive use and a transitive one:

shorten *v* to make or become short or shorter

The same lexical-semantic property is accounted for via the splitting strategy in the same dictionary for other verbs, like *addle*:

addle *v* 1 [T1; I0]   a: to cause (an egg) to go bad
                            b: (of an egg) to go bad

The advantage of splitting the different syntactic patterns is clear: *addle* indeed has a specific collocational preference for the noun *egg* used as a patient argument (the entity that changes state). The verb *shorten* does not exhibit specific collocational preferences, which makes it possible to lump all the relevant information into one single definition, the conjunction *or* in *make or become* indicating that the verb participates in two distinct syntactic constructions.

The question whether word senses exist at all is an important one. Dictionaries are based on a huge oversimplification which posits that words have enumerable, listable meanings which are divisible into discrete units. Yet, corpus linguistics and the systematic analysis of authentic evidence have shown that the concepts of polysemy and word senses are a lot more mysterious than we think. Some linguists prefer to talk about 'meaning potentials', which are 'potential contributions to the meanings of texts and conversations in which the word is used and activated by the speaker who uses them' (Hanks 2000). In this sense, dictionaries only contain lists of meaning potentials, while electronic corpora contain traces of meaning events. Word sense disambiguation therefore boils down to trying to map the one onto the other and it is crucial for lexicographers to devise systems to discover the contextual triggers that activate the components making up a word's meaning potential. Recent work on Corpus Pattern Analysis, CPA (Hanks and Pustejovsky 2005), to build up an inventory of syntagmatic behaviour that is useful for automatic sense disambiguation seems to be a promising attempt to contribute to the development of such systems.

Even if the existence of enumerable and listable meanings is an oversimplification, for practical purposes, lexicographers do divide polysemous words into numbered senses. Samuel Johnson was aware of this problem when he wrote that 'the shades of meaning … pass imperceptibly into each other; so that it is impossible to mark the point of contact' (1755: 5). However frequently meanings blur into each other, the lexicographer needs to sort them out and present them to the dictionary user in such a way that the information can be used to decode a text and to produce grammatically correct and natural sentences. The next section discusses the techniques used by today's lexicographers to address this issue.

Lexicography and corpus linguistics

The recent generation of learners' dictionaries owes a lot to the late John Sinclair's work on corpora at the University of Birmingham in the 1970s and 1980s. His research led to the publication of the COBUILD (Collins Birmingham University International Language Database) series of monolingual dictionaries. The first edition of *Cobuild* (Sinclair 1987) truly revolutionized the field of dictionary-making, to such an extent that all dictionaries nowadays claim to be 'corpus-based' and to provide a description of the English vocabulary based upon 'natural' or 'real' data. Yet, it might be objected that even the previous generation of dictionaries resorted to 'real' data. The main difference is that lexicographers of the pre-corpus era used to record their findings on slips of paper that they conscientiously kept in shoeboxes. They were primarily concerned with rare phenomena and weird contexts and combinations which had attracted their attention. It has been shown that such shoeboxes were excellent repositories of idiosyncratic descriptions which would be better found in historical dictionaries than in monolingual learners' dictionaries, whose task is primarily to capture the most frequent patterns of usage. Unfortunately, these shoeboxes frequently failed to record the prototypical uses of a word. Moreover, they usually included citations from well-respected literary texts only.

Another difference is that pre-corpus lexicographers had to rely on their own reading program and their encyclopedic skills. The advent of computers has now made dozens of millions of words available to them. The sorting functionalities provided by modern concordancers enable lexicographers to examine the right and left contexts of a given word with thousands of KWIC (Key-Word In Context) lines. Such concordances have now become the primary material they use. KWIC lines are tapped to identify the typical preposition used with a given adjective or verb, they reveal collocational preferences (preferred contexts), or show that a given word is used only, say, in non-assertive contexts (consider *budge*, which is used exclusively in negative contexts like 'the door wouldn't budge'), etc. Some linguists talk about colligational preferences, colligations being seen as a midway relation between grammar and collocation (Hoey 2005: 43). Colligation will, for example, include, in a verb, a marked preference for one particular form or use (e.g. passive or progressive form), or, in a noun, a marked preference for either the singular or plural form. Similarly, the marked preference for attributive position after a noun in the adjective *galore* ('there will be food galore at the party') will be described as a colligational preference that should be mentioned in a dictionary entry.

The following example illustrates the concept of KWIC line, in which a given word (the node) is centered in the middle of the table. A number of words to the right and left of the node are displayed. Most concordancers or corpus tools make it possible to sort such data on, say, the first word to the right or the first word to the left, which is a very effective means of discovering regular patterns in which the word can be found.

ordainements. 4. cysticercosis in	\<bovines,\> swine, sheep and goats when no
nged to grey in the case of	\<bovine\> meat or to ash grey in the case o
evel of concern surrounding	\<bovine\> spongiform encephalopathy (bse) a
disease was transmitted to	\<bovines\> through animal protein rations (
seminar on the diagnosis of	\<bovine\> spongiform encephalopathy (bse) c
a prohibition on the use in	\<bovine\> rations of meat meal and bonemeal
sease. the scientific facts	\<bovine\> spongiform encephalopathy is a tr
ransmitted via ingestion in	\<bovine\> rations of meat meal and bonemeal
is aspect. 2) the brains of	\<bovines\> which when alive have presented
inutes of the conference on	\<bovine\> spongiform encephalopathy held at
om in view of the spread of	\<bovine\> spongiform encephalopathy in that
ncrease in the incidence of	\<bovine\> spongiform encephalopathy in the
ou our information pamphlet	\<'bovine\> spongiform encephalopathy (bse)'
rmality which affects adult	\<bovines\> and culminates in death. it is c

As can be seen above, a word like *bovine* can readily be described as a noun (which can be pluralized – *bovines*) or as an adjective. Sorting the data on the first item to the right reveals that *bovine* is frequently found in multi-word entries like *bovine spongiform encephalopathy* (a.k.a. BSE) or in collocations like *bovine meat* and *bovine rations*.

Today, with the entire Web at the lexicographers' fingertips, one of the major problems which they face is no longer the scarcity of the data. Rather, the analysts are confronted with a wealth of data which, after a given threshold, can no longer be analyzed manually. A hundred KWIC lines are manageable. Five thousand lines cannot be read and 'digested' by any human being working under the time constraints imposed by publication deadlines. Yet, with corpora of hundreds of millions of words, most queries are likely to generate several thousand lines. Computational linguists have therefore collaborated with lexicographers to propose a number of statistical methods whose aim is precisely to help the latter separate the wheat from the chaff and identify central and typical usages. One such method relies on the concept of mutual information (MI), which is used to identify relations between words which occur more often than chance (Church and Hanks 1990; Church *et al.* 1994). MI values may be used in deciding whether a sequence of two words such as 'requested and' is more or less interesting than the sequence 'requested anonymity'. Lexicographers intuitively feel that the former sequence is linguistically (and lexicographically) uninteresting, while the latter combination probably deserves more attention and is a suitable candidate for inclusion in a dictionary (whether as an example of what one can typically *request* or as an example of which verb typically combines with *anonymity*). Intuition is not reliable, however, and cannot be readily tapped to discover that one typically requests anonymity, permission (to do something), political asylum, copies (of a document) or documents themselves. The very first applications in printed dictionaries can be found in the *Cobuild* dictionary (Sinclair 1987). Variations of MI scores were then adapted and refined, for instance by taking into account the relative frequencies of the words, because the original MI statistics unfortunately gave too much weight to low-frequency words. In more recent learners' dictionaries, such as *MEDAL* (Rundell 2007), the lexicographers have partnered with computational linguists who have developed techniques to 'summarize' the data extracted from corpora. The *MEDAL* team used the Sketch Engine (Kilgarriff *et al.* 2004), which produces 'word sketches', which can be seen as distinct collocate lists for subjects, direct objects, adjectives, Noun of Noun phrases, etc., extracted from a lemmatized and parsed corpus.

Word sketches provide an interesting synthesis of the grammatical and collocational environment in which lexical items can be inserted. The most salient and relevant collocations are displayed, exploiting MI and frequency statistics. The subject-of or object-of relations allow lexicographers to quickly identify typical predicates (*bank* is frequently found as the object of the verbs *burst*, *rob* or *privatize*). Words are automatically grouped as a function of the relation which links them to the node item, which facilitates the lexicographer's task of selecting examples and summarizing this into a dictionary entry. Of course, the ultimate analysis still requires lexicographical and linguistic interpretive skills, since nothing in the lists of collocates of *bank* generated by the sketch engine indicates that the verbs *burst* or *overflow* are linked to the 'river bank' sense while the object of the verbs *rob* or *privatize* is the 'financial institution' sense of *bank*.

The main advantage of such a tool is that it is nearly impossible to miss common and typical patterns and that the lexicographer has access to a treasure trove of pre-digested material to choose from. In *MEDAL2*, such collaboration between lexicographers and computational linguists has resulted in the creation of 'collocation boxes' which list common collocates of frequent words, as in the following entry:

> **campaign** 1 n
> Collocations
> Verbs frequently used with **campaign** as the object:
> *conduct, fight, launch, lead, mount, spearhead, wage*

One of the next steps will be to create tools that help lexicographers identify good examples and relevant lexical items whose collocates are worth including in a dictionary. This area of research is still in its infancy, but the results of preliminary investigations seem to be promising (Kilgarriff 2006).

The systematic inclusion of information about collocational preferences in dictionary entries testifies to the revival undergone by the study of multi-word units over the last twenty years. Much of this contemporary research into the distribution of phraseological units is based upon Sinclair's 'idiom principle', which states that language users have available to them a large number of semi-preconstructed phrases that constitute single choices, even though they might appear to be analyzable into segments (Sinclair 1991: 110). The idiom principle is generally opposed to the open-choice principle, which states that a large number of choices opens up and the only restraint is grammaticalness.

Learners' dictionaries now also increasingly benefit from the analysis of learner language and learner corpora. Most of these dictionaries now include specific sections that address writing issues, using typologies of frequent mistakes compiled on the basis of large learner corpora such as the *International Corpus of Learner English* (*ICLE*, Granger *et al.* 2002) or the *Cambridge Learner Corpus*. The second edition of the *MEDAL* dictionary (Rundell 2007) is a case in point, with its dozens of 'Get it Right' boxes which, at the level of individual entries, identify common errors, give examples from learner corpora and suggest the correct forms, as in the following:

> Contribute
> Get it Right!
> Don't use a verb in the infinitive after contribute. Use the pattern **contribute to doing something**:
> ✗ Technology has **contributed to improve** our lives.
> ✓ Technology has **contributed to improving** our lives.

✗ A positive aspect of education is that it **contributes to confirm** one's identity.

✓ A positive aspect of education is that it **contributes to confirming** one's identity.

You can also use the pattern **contribute to something**:

Technology has **contributed to improvements** in our lives.

The role of examples

One of the key questions in lexicography is what constitutes a good example to illustrate the meaning of a word and its lexical properties. Earlier dictionaries such as the *OED* or *Johnson's Dictionary*, as we saw above, mainly tapped literary texts and the best authors as sources of citations. The advent of computerized corpora like the HarperCollins Bank of English in the 1980s and 1990s and, more recently, the use of the Web as a corpus (Kilgarriff and Grefenstette 2003) have put hundreds of billions of words of texts at the linguist's disposal for language research, for the compilation of dictionaries, as well as for the development of natural language processing systems. The availability of examples does not mean that the lexicographer's task is made a lot easier, however. Twenty years ago, the controversy about the relative merits of authentic and invented examples was raging. The effectiveness of examples was discussed at length by applied linguists, who were trying to figure out whether the examples to be included in dictionaries should be excerpted from a corpus or invented by the lexicographer. Laufer (1992) showed that examples made up by lexicographers are sometimes pedagogically more beneficial for language learners than authentic ones. There is clearly a difference between interesting examples and authentic examples and it is essential that the user of the dictionary not be distracted with unintelligible examples. The key to the effectiveness of dictionary examples is for the compiler to select real, natural, typical, informative and intelligible sentences illustrating common usage and to resist the temptation to focus on abnormal and idiosyncratic usages. A lexicographer who would record untypical and abnormal usages in a dictionary would not do learners any favours. Atkins and Rundell (2008: 458–61) provide a series of clearly bad, uninformative and abnormal examples published in some contemporary dictionaries, a case in point being the idiom 'bring up the rear', illustrated by a totally uninformative although authentic example ('John brought up the rear'). The most efficient examples are probably those that are based upon corpus data and that have been carefully edited to remove the irrelevant portions that distract the user.

Definitions

Lexicographers are often judged by their ability to write definitions for dictionaries. Definitions are an essential component of monolingual dictionaries, since users tend to turn to dictionaries mainly to look up words in order to find out about their meanings. In most cases, dictionaries adopt the classical Aristotelian model of definitions based upon the distinction between *genus* (a superordinate word which locates the item being defined in the right semantic category) and *differentiae* (additional information which indicates what makes this item unique and how it differs from its cohyponyms, i.e. the other members of the same category). The difficulty is to choose a genus term that is neither too general nor too specific. In many cases, dictionaries tend to define by synonym and antonym. So, if, to quote Atkins and Rundell (2008: 414), the noun *convertible* is defined as 'car with a folding or detachable roof', *car* is the genus term and the differentia is the expression *with a folding or detachable roof*, which distinguishes a convertible from its cohyponyms *saloon*, *estate car* or *people carrier*.

Another strategy, introduced by the *Cobuild* lexicographers (Sinclair 1987), is to write longer definitions in which the definiendum (the word that is defined) is incorporated into the definition, which then takes the form of a full sentence. Consider the definition for the verb *capsize* in *COBUILD1*:

> capsize
> When you **capsize** a boat or when it **capsizes**, it turns upside down in the water.

Criticizing the over-use of parentheses to indicate likely objects and subjects, Hanks (1987) argues that the traditional conventions used in most modern dictionaries make definitions difficult reading for ordinary readers. *Cobuild*'s full-sentence definitions (FSDs) were considered a real revolution at the time, with a first part placing the word being explained in a typical structure (A brick is ... ; Calligraphy is ... – Hanks 1987: 117), and the second part identifying the meaning. In his discussion of the pros and cons of the traditional definitions, which are supposed to be substitutable in any context for the definiendum, Hanks stresses the importance of collocational and syntactic information and argues that full-sentence definitions make it possible to suggest much more easily whether collocates are obligatory, common but variable, or simply open. Selection preferences are easier to integrate into such definitions, Hanks claims, giving the example of an 'ergative' (causative-inchoative) verb like *fuse*, as in the following *COBUILD1* definition:

> 2 When a light or some other piece of electrical apparatus **fuses** or when you **fuse** it, it stops working because of a fault, especially because too much electricity is being used.

The revolution created by the introduction of full-sentence definitions attracted a lot of attention and certainly influenced other learners' dictionaries. However, *Cobuild*'s relatively dogmatic approach also attracted some criticism. Rundell (2006) explains why such defining conventions have not been adopted universally. He acknowledges that the FSD model works better than alternative models in a number of cases (for instance if a verb is nearly always used in the passive form, like *lay up*, a full sentence definition is clearly better – 'If someone is **laid up** with an illness, the illness makes it necessary for them to stay in bed'). The disadvantages of the FSD model cannot be ignored, however: the coverage of an FSD-based dictionary is reduced because these definitions are on average much longer than traditional definitions. The complexity of these longer definitions is also the source of a number of problems and can be challenging for learners. Pronoun references in *if*-definitions can be unclear, for instance, and the redundancy found in some long-winded structures is not always informative ('You use X to describe something that ... '). Rundell recommends using hybrid approaches and recognizes that FSDs work in some cases, but that, in many other cases, simplicity and economy are more adequate.

Bilingual dictionaries

A chapter on lexicography would not be complete without a section on bilingual dictionaries, given their importance in foreign language learning. Bilingual lexicography has also undergone significant changes over the last twenty years, thanks to the availability of multilingual corpora and to advances in the field of natural language processing, which now make it possible for lexicographers to identify the collocational patterns that help users match equivalents across languages.

Four major functions are generally assigned to bilingual dictionaries, depending on whether the user is using the dictionary to understand or translate a text written in the foreign language (L2) or in the first language (L1):

Reception in L2
Reception in L2 + production in L1
Production in L2
Reception in L1 + production in L2.

Most of the burning questions discussed above in the context of monolingual lexicography also apply to bilingual dictionaries. Should the lexicographer favour lumping or splitting strategies, for instance? Some other questions are more specific: should sense divisions be based upon the source language or the target language? It should indeed be realized that many bilingual dictionaries divide the semantic space of source items as a function of the target language. A word which is considered as monosemic in a monolingual dictionary may therefore be regarded as polysemic in a bilingual dictionary because the target language makes distinctions which are non-existent in the source language. Consider the entry for *croak* in the *Cambridge International Dictionary of English* (Procter 1995) below, which offers one definition to cover the general SOUND meaning (grammar codes appear between square brackets; e.g. [I] = intransitive use):

croak   [SOUND] *v* (of animals) to make deep rough sounds such as a FROG or CROW makes, or (of people) to speak with a rough voice because of a sore or dry throat. *I could hear frogs croaking by the lake.* [I] *'Water, water', he croaked.* [+ clause]

In comparison, a bilingual dictionary such as the *Collins-Robert Dictionary* (Atkins and Duval 1993) makes distinctions which are based solely on the existence of different potential translations:

croak 1 *vi* (a) *[frog]* coasser; *[raven]* croasser; *[person]* parler d'une voix rauque; (**grumble*) maugréer, ronchonner.

These examples point to the all-important nature of the metalinguistic indicators (*frog*, *raven*, *person*, *grumble*) in a good bilingual dictionary (see also Duval 1991; Béjoint and Thoiron 1996). Such dictionaries make use of collocates, subject labels, and various types of indicators to capture typical subjects or objects to provide foreign language users with as much information as possible about the semantic, syntactic and combinatory properties of lexical items.

Conclusion

It is not possible to discuss all aspects of lexicography as a branch of linguistics. In this article, we have focused on the applied linguistics features of dictionaries, which manifest themselves more clearly in pedagogical dictionaries for foreign language learners as well as in bilingual dictionaries. We deliberately excluded the very vibrant and active field of computational lexicography dealing with the construction of lexicons for natural language processing, which would be better suited for a handbook of computational linguistics and would deserve a chapter on its own. Building dictionaries is a time-consuming and costly activity that requires very special linguistic skills and lexical acquisition, the branch of lexicography that deals with the identification, acquisition and representation of lexicographically relevant facts in big corpora, is far from a trivial task. NLP researchers have been trying to construct very large lexicons for thirty years, first by trying to reuse existing machine-readable dictionaries like the *Longman Dictionary of Contemporary English*, then by exploiting large corpora and developing machine-learning techniques. The research in this field has allowed the creation of the WordNet lexical database, which combines a thesaurus and a dictionary and bridges the gap between traditional semasiological (word-to-meaning) lexicography and onomasiological (meaning-to-word) lexicons. WordNet is definitely not a pedagogical tool, but applied linguists have benefited from research in that field, with the development of production dictionaries designed to meet the encoding needs of learners, such as the *Longman Language Activator* (Summers 1993), the Word Routes series developed by Cambridge University Press (McCarthy and Walter 1994) or, more recently, the Macmillan thesaurus (Rundell 2007).

We have discussed several of the hot topics that are debated in lexicography circles, including the impact of the 'corpus revolution', which now allows lexicographers to compile dictionary entries on the basis of linguistic evidence extracted from corpora of hundreds of millions of words. Computers are good at counting and extracting patterns of usage, but condensing linguistic facts in an intelligible way and making sense of these masses of data to create reference works that are useful to language learners is still something for which lexicographers will always be needed for years to come.

Related topics

corpus linguistics; lexis

Further reading

Atkins, B. T. S. and Rundell, M. (2008) *Oxford Guide to Practical Lexicography*, Oxford: Oxford University Press. (A down-to-earth, step-by-step textbook on the making of dictionaries; an essential course for the training of lexicographers.)

Cowie, A. P. (ed.) (2009) *Oxford History of English Lexicography,* Oxford: Oxford University Press. (Two volumes that present the fullest account of the lexicography of English; covers general-purpose and specialized dictionaries, including the evolution of dictionaries aimed at foreign learners of English.)

Fontenelle, T. (2008) *Practical Lexicography: A Reader*, Oxford: Oxford University Press. (A collection of articles that have become classics in the field of lexicography; it covers topics hotly debated in lexicography circles: collocations and idioms, tools and methods, dictionary use, grammar and usage, word senses and polysemy, Johnson's Plan of a Dictionary, etc.)

Hartmann, R. R. K. and James, G. (1998) *Dictionary of Lexicography*, London: Routledge. (A useful resource to get definitions of terms used in dictionary making.)

Landau, S. (2001) *Dictionaries: The Art and Craft of Lexicography*, Cambridge: Cambridge University Press. (A classic volume recommended for anyone who wants to know what goes in to the production of a published dictionary.)

References

Atkins, B. T. S. and Duval, A. (1978) *Robert and Collins Dictionnaire Français-Anglais, Anglais-Français*, Paris: Le Robert/Glasgow: Collins.

——(1993) *Collins-Robert Dictionary*, Paris: Le Robert/Glasgow: Collins.

Atkins, B. T. S. and Rundell, M. (2008) *Oxford Guide to Practical Lexicography*, Oxford: Oxford University Press.

Béjoint, H. and Thoiron, P. (1996) *Les dictionnaires bilingues*, Aupelf-Uref, Duculot: Louvain-la-Neuve.

Church, K., Gale, W., Hanks, P., Hindle, D. and Moon, R. (1994) 'Lexical substitutability', in B. T. S. Atkins and A. Zampolli (eds) *Computational Approaches to the Lexicon*, Oxford: Oxford University Press.

Church, K. and Hanks, P. (1990) 'Word association norms, mutual information, and lexicography', *Computational Linguistics* 16(1): 22–9; reproduced in Fontenelle, T. (2008) *Practical Lexicography: A Reader*, Oxford: Oxford University Press.

Cowie, A. P. (ed.) (2009) *Oxford History of English Lexicography*, Oxford: Oxford University Press.

Duval, A. (1991) 'L'équivalence dans le dictionnaire bilingue', in F. J. Hausmann, O. Reichmann, E. Wiegand and L. Zgusta (eds) *Wörterbücher / Dictionaries / Dictionnaires. Ein internationales Handbuch zur Lexikographie / An International Encyclopedia of Lexicography / Encyclopédie internationale de lexicographie*, 3, Berlin and New York: De Gruyter; reprinted (in English) in Fontenelle, T. (2008) *Practical Lexicography: A Reader*, Oxford: Oxford University Press.

Granger, S., Hung, J. and Petch-Tyson, S. (eds) (2002) *Computer Learner Corpora, Second Language Acquisition and Foreign Language Teaching*, Language Learning and Language Teaching 6, Amsterdam and Philadelphia: John Benjamins.

Hanks, P. (1987) 'Definitions and explanations', in J. Sinclair (ed.) *Looking Up*, London: Collins.

——(2000) 'Do word meanings exist?', *Computers and the Humanities* 34 (1–2): 205–15; reprinted in Fontenelle, T. (2008) *Practical Lexicography: A Reader*, Oxford: Oxford University Press.

Hanks, P. and Pustejovsky, J. (2005) 'A pattern dictionary for natural language processing', *Revue Française de Linguistique Appliquée – Numéro spécial: Dictionnaires: nouvelles approches, nouveaux modèles*, December Vol. X(2): 63–82.

Hoey, M. (2005) *Lexical Priming: A New Theory of Words and Language*, London: Routledge.

Hornby, A. S., Cowie, A. P. and Windsor Lewis, J. (eds) (1974) *Oxford Advanced Learner's Dictionary of Current English*, 3rd edn, London: Oxford University Press.

Hornby, A. S. Gatenby, E. V. and Wakefield, H. (1942) *Idiomatic and Syntactic English Dictionary*, Tokyo: Kaitakusha.

Kilgarriff, A. (1997) 'I don't believe in word senses', *Computers and the Humanities* 31(2): 91–113; reprinted in Fontenelle, T. (2008) *Practical Lexicography: A Reader*, Oxford: Oxford University Press.

——(2006) 'Collocationality (and how to measure it)', in E. Corino, C. Marello and C. Onesti (eds) *Proceedings of the XIIIth EURALEX International Congress*, Turin: Università di Torino, pp. 997–1004.

Kilgarriff, A., Rychly, P., Smrž, P. and Tugwell, D. (2004) 'The sketch engine', in G. Williams and S. Vessier (eds) *Euralex 2004 Proceedings*, Lorient: University of Bretagne-Sud, pp. 105–16; reprinted in Fontenelle, T. (2008) *Practical Lexicography: A Reader*, Oxford: Oxford University Press.

Kilgarriff, A. and Grefenstette, G. (2003) 'Introduction to the special issue on the Web as corpus', *Computational Linguistics* 29(3): 333–48; reprinted in Fontenelle, T. (2008) *Practical Lexicography: A Reader*, Oxford: Oxford University Press.

Kilgarriff, A., Husak, M., McAdam, K., Rundell, M. and Rychl, P. (2008) 'GDEX: automatically finding good dictionary examples in a corpus', in E. Bernal and J. DeCesaris (eds) *Proceedings of the XIIIth EURALEX International Congress*, Barcelona.

Laufer, B. (1992) 'Corpus-based vs lexicographer examples in comprehension and production of new words', in *Euralex' 92 Proceedings*, University of Tampere, pp. 71–6; reprinted in Fontenelle, T. (2008) *Practical Lexicography: A Reader*, Oxford: Oxford University Press.

McCarthy, M. and Walter, E. (1994) *Cambridge Word Routes – Lexique Thématique de l'Anglais Courant*, Cambridge: Cambridge University Press.

Murray, J. A. H., Bradley, H., Craigie, W. A. and Onions, C. J. (eds) (1933) *The Oxford English Dictionary, Being a Corrected Reissue, with a Supplement* (*OED1*), 2nd edn, Oxford: Clarendon Press. Available at: www.oed.com

Palmer, H. E. (1938) *A Grammar of English Words*, London: Longmans, Green.

Palmer, H. E. and Hornby, A. S. (1938) *Thousand-Word English*, London: George Harrap.

Procter, P. (ed.) (1978) *Longman Dictionary of Contemporary English* (1987, LDOCE1, D. Summers (ed.), 2nd edn), Harlow: Longman.

——(1995) *Cambridge International Dictionary of English*, Cambridge: Cambridge University Press.

Rundell, M. (ed.) (2007) *Macmillan English Dictionary for Advanced Learners*, Oxford: Macmillan Publishers (2nd edn – *MEDAL*).

Rundell, M. (2006) 'More than one way to skin a cat: why full-sentence definitions have not been universally adopted', in E. Corino, C. Marello and C. Onesti (eds) *Proceedings of the XIIth EURALEX International Congress*, Turin: Università di Torino, pp. 323–38; Reprinted in T. Fontenelle (2008) *Practical Lexicography: A Reader*, Oxford: Oxford University Press.

Sinclair, J. (ed.) (1987) *Collins COBUILD English Language Dictionary*, London and Glasgow: Collins.

Sinclair, J. (1991) *Corpus, Concordance and Collocation*, Oxford: Oxford University Press.

Summers, D. (1993) *Longman Language Activator*, London: Longman.

Van Sterkenburg, P. (ed.) (2003) *A Practical Guide to Lexicography*, Amsterdam and Philadelphia: John Benjamins.

West, M. P. and Endicott, J. G. (1935) *The New Method English Dictionary*, London: Longmans, Green.

5

The media

Anne O'Keeffe

Historical overview of media discourse

'The media' is a very broad term, encompassing print and broadcast genres, that is anything from newspaper to chat show and, latterly, much more besides, as new media emerge in line with technological leaps. The study of 'the media' comes under the remit of media studies from perspectives such as their production and consumption, as well as their aesthetic form. The academic area of media studies cuts across a number of disciplines including communication, sociology, political science, cultural studies, philosophy and rhetoric, to name but a handful. Meanwhile, the object of study, 'the media', is an ever-changing and ever-growing entity. The study of 'the media' also comes under the radar of applied linguistics because at the core of these media is language, communication and the making of meaning, which is obviously of great interest to linguists. As Fairclough (1995a: 2) points out, the substantively linguistic and discoursal nature of the power of the media is a strong argument for analysing the mass media linguistically.

Central to the connection between media studies and studies of the language used in the media (media discourse studies) is the importance placed on ideology. A major force behind the study of ideology in the media is Stuart Hall (see, for example, Hall 1973, 1977, 1980, 1982). Hall (1982), in his influential paper, notes that the study of media (or 'mass communication') has had a chequered past. He charts its early years from the 1940s to the 1960s as being dominated by what he terms sociological approaches of 'mainstream' American behavioural science (Hall's emphasis). From the 1960s began the emergence of an alternative paradigm, a 'critical' one. In looking at ideology in the media, one is essentially taking a critical stance. As Hall puts it, 'the simplest way to characterise the shift from "mainstream" to "critical" perspectives is in terms of the movement from, essentially, a behavioural to an ideological perspective' (1982: 1).

An interesting example of a behaviourist-type study of the media is Horton and Wohl ([1956] 1979). Horton and Wohl were among the first to write about the way the media and media performers create the illusion of an interpersonal relationship between them and their audience. The concept of mediated (pseudo-)relations obviously has enormous relevance for the study of media discourse today in all its forms. Horton and Wohl referred to it as a 'para-social' relationship because it is based on an implicit agreement between the 'performer' and the audience that they will pretend the relationship is not mediated and is carried on as though it were face-to-face. In their study of the television chat show *The Johnny Carson Show* audiences, Horton and Wohl found that many viewers, in 1950s America, claimed that they 'knew' Johnny Carson better than their next-door neighbour. They also note the emergence of (marked words as in original):

> a new type of performer: quiz-masters, announcers, 'interviewers' in a new 'show-business' world – in brief, a special category of 'personalities' whose existence is a function of the media themselves. These 'personalities' usually, are not prominent in any of the social spheres beyond the media. They exist for their audiences only in the para-social relation.
>
> *(Horton and Wohl [1956] 1979: 186)*

This early study still has resonance for the study of media discourse today in that our relationship with media personae has, if anything, grown and deepened, compared with the days of Johnny Carson, and this is very much linked to how we use language in the creation, expression and maintenance of pseudo-intimate relationships (see O'Keeffe 2006).

Ideology has also had a major impact on the study of language in the media. O'Halloran (2010) explains that ideology is about looking at representations of aspects of the world which contribute to establishing and maintaining social relations of domination, inequality and exploitation. White (1997), for example, claims that by 'severely' circumscribing subjective interpersonal features in hard news reports, journalists can, through 'objective' language, purport to be neutral, essentially where formal language provides the veneer of neutrality. The dominant methodology which addresses this within media discourse studies is Critical Discourse Analysis (CDA), which we shall discuss further below. Van Dijk (2001: 352) offers the following definition of CDA:

> Critical discourse analysis (CDA) is a type of discourse analytical research that primarily studies the way social power abuse, dominance, and inequality are enacted, reproduced, and resisted by text and talk in the social and political context. With such dissident research, critical discourse analysts take an explicit position, and thus want to understand, expose, and ultimately resist social inequality.
>
> *(Van Dijk 2001: 352)*

In a later publication, van Dijk (2009), opting to use the term Critical Discourse Studies (CDS), brings further clarity to the notion of a critical approach to discourse studies in general, stating that it characterizes the orientation of the researcher rather than their method. CDS scholars are socio-politically committed to social equality and justice, he explains. This comes through in their research 'by the formulation of specific goals, the selection and construction of theories, the use and development of methods of analysis and especially in the application of such research in the study of important social problems and political issues' (van Dijk 2009: 63). Critical scholars are interested in the way 'discourse (re)produces social domination, that is the power abuse of one group over others, and how dominated groups may discursively resist that abuse' (ibid.). Van Dijk observes that critical studies of discourse are problem-led rather than discipline- or theory-oriented. Obvious examples of problems which relate to abuses of power and injustice are in relation to gender, race and class. As we will further discuss below (in the second and third sections), looking at ideological issues, or taking a critical stance, in relation to the study of media discourse, has proven to be very important to our understanding as consumers of mass media.

While CDA takes an ideological or critical stance in its approach to media discourse, other methodologies offer descriptive insights at the level of discourse and interaction. From the American tradition comes Conversation Analysis (CA), an approach which has its origins in ethnomethodology, a branch of sociology. In stark contrast to CDA, it is 'essentially grounded in surface data, without theoretical assumptions' (Lesser 2003). The area of Corpus Linguistics (CL), a relatively established area in its own right, is increasingly emerging in the study of language in the media (e.g. O'Keeffe 2002, 2003, 2005, 2006; Chang 2002; O'Halloran 2010). While CL can be purely descriptive and ideology-neutral, it can also work very well in tandem with critical approaches (see O'Halloran 2010, and O'Halloran, this volume). The added value of corpus linguistics in the study of media discourse is its ability to look at large amounts of media material (both written or spoken). Also, it allows researchers to make both qualitative and quantitative statements about the data.

Written versus spoken media discourse studies

Much study of language and the media over the years has focused on the written genres, particularly newspapers. This is largely because they are more readily available for analysis by virtue of being in written form compared with the ephemerality of spoken media discourse, which has to be recorded and then transcribed. The ease of recording and storage afforded by digital technology now means that there is much more scope for studies of spoken media discourse. However, the drudge of accurate transcription is still a barrier to research in the area.

Written media studies

Within the study of written media texts, there has been a growing body of quantitative and qualitative descriptive linguistic analyses by corpus linguists. Distinct registers, or genres, of media language are being examined using collections of empirical data. Biber *et al.* (1999), for example, identify the language of newspapers as one of the four major registers in all of the English language, along with spoken conversation, academic writing, and fiction. In their grammar of the English language, they profile syntactic patterns and lexico-grammatical usage across all four of these registers. This gives us a baseline for the use and frequency of language patterns in newspapers, against which other media-based findings can be compared and contrasted. Much attention is given to genre analysis (see Swales 1990) in the study of the language of newspapers. That is where the language used in print media is described in terms of what makes it different to other 'genres' of language, and in so doing linguists aim for a better understanding of generic characteristics. Toolan (1988) examines the language of press advertising. Other studies have examined sports reporting in newspapers (Wallace 1977; Ghadessy 1988; Bhatia 1993).

Many studies identify the mutually defining link between language variation and context (Halliday 1978; Leckie-Tarry 1995; Hasan 1996). Stubbs (1996) points out that texts encode representations of the world and so help to construct social reality. Thus textual analysis, he posits, is a vantage point from which to observe society. Other studies have looked at how different newspapers are socially stratified (see Bell 1991) and how this has an implication for the type of reality they construct for their respective readers. According to Hodge (1979: 157), 'newspapers only supply partial versions of the world and what they do present depends on what is expected of that newspaper'. In another study, Bell (1991) looked at one linguistic variable, determiner deletion in appositional naming expressions (e.g. 'Chairman of the board, Michael Milken' as opposed to non-determiner deletion: 'The chairman of the board, Michael

Milken') and found that the 'quality' US broadsheets such as the *Boston Globe*, *Washington Post*, *Hartford Courant*, and *New York Times* had a much lesser rate of determiner deletion than the popular press (i.e. tabloids). He concluded from this that the structure of determiner deletion reflects the social stratification of the papers in US print media.

According to Bell (1991), irrespective of what actually happens in real life, newspapers present their particular interpretations of events and so readers know in advance what they are buying. Along the same lines, McQuail (1994) claims that news content is moulded according to what journalists perceive the news public to find relevant and intrinsically interesting and he argues that the depiction of events in the print media is therefore inherently ideological. White (1997) asserts that hard news reports construct a model of social order and that events or situations that are construed as threatening to that social order are deemed newsworthy.

Spoken media

Studies of how the spoken media, especially television, have evolved show a fascinating move from the deferential host to the performer/public persona. The formality and rigidness of the early years of television were underpinned by varying state broadcasting controls and pre-scripted interviews and performances. Corner (1991) provides an insight into the evolution of the media interview, particularly within documentaries. He attributes the change and development in the mid- to late 1950s, where interviews became more immediate and natural, to the move towards on-location reality settings for the actual interviews. This development, he suggests, freed the programme makers from the limitations of studio treatments and, along with 'a newly democratic/populist sense of appropriate topics and framing', helped to construct 'naturalisms of behaviour and speech to exploit fully the possibilities for heightened immediacy and dynamism' (1991: 40).

Whale (1977) tells us that, until the 1950s, the broadcast interview was of little importance largely because until then broadcasting the spoken word was traditionally regarded as a matter of reading the printed word aloud. Moreover, statutory requirement for impartiality was strictly interpreted. As Dimbleby (1975: 214) noted, the interview was not yet:

> a means of extracting painful or revealing information; it did not test or challenge ideas, beliefs, attitudes and assumptions. The interviewer had not yet become an official tribune of the people, or prosecuting counsel, or chat-show host. His job was to discover some very simple facts: if he did more than that, it was chance not design. It was not thought proper to enquire (even gently) into private lives, or social problems.
>
> *(Dimbleby 1975: 214)*

Thus, as Wedell (1968) puts it, interviewers were little more than respectful prompters who fed the interviewees with soft soap questions in interviews that were often prearranged and lacking spontaneity (Day 1961). The broadcast interview was a set piece interaction in which the function of the interviewer was simply to provide a series of topic headings 'for the carefully prepared views of famous men and women designed to impart to their viewers or listeners' (Wedell 1968: 205). In the UK, the monopoly of deferential interviewing style prompted by the BBC and copied by many national broadcasting stations was undermined with the advent of Independent Television (ITV) in the mid-1950s. ITV producers took a looser interpretation of statutory obligations and brought more inquiry and investigation into news stories. This facilitated a more direct, searching and penetrating style of interviewing (Day 1961). Interviewers began to challenge and probe where previously they would have moved politely onto the next pre-arranged question. As a result, the news interview became a more flexible, lively, and influential instrument of journalistic inquiry, to the point where, for example, in the following extract, we see a serving British prime minister being challenged, contradicted and interrupted by his interviewer. The interview, in February 2003, was part of a special BBC *Newsnight* programme in the lead up to the invasion of Iraq. The interview, between then British Prime Minister, Tony Blair, and *Newsnight*'s presenter Jeremy Paxman, was held in front of a live public audience in Gateshead. In the later stages of the programme, the audience asked the prime minister questions. The transcript and video clip are available online.

[+ MARKS AN INTERRUPTED UTTERANCE]

JEREMY PAXMAN: And you believe American intelligence?

TONY BLAIR: Well I do actually believe this intelligence +

JEREMY PAXMAN: Because there are a lot of dead people in an aspirin factory in Sudan who don't.

TONY BLAIR: Come on. This intelligence is backed up by our own intelligence and in any event, you know, we're not coming to this without any history. I mean let's not be absurdly naïve about this+

JEREMY PAXMAN: Hans Blix said he saw no evidence of hiding of weapons.

TONY BLAIR: I'm sorry, what Hans Blix has said is that the Iraqis are not cooperating properly.

(6 February 2003. Full transcript and actual interview available at: http://news.bbc.co.uk/1/ hi/programmes/newsnight/2732979.stm)

As mentioned earlier, discourse studies of the spoken media are relatively few given how pervasive it has been in everyday life, especially since the 1950s. As we pointed out, the challenge of recording and transcribing the ephemeral word has been the central impediment. The bulk of studies undertaken in the area of spoken media discourse centre around the analysis of turn organization within a CA framework (see below). Clayman and Heritage (2002: 7), for example, set as their goal to 'examine the inner workings of the news interview in Anglo-American society'. In line with CA methodology, they contrast the rules of conversation with what happens during news interviews. In comparing British and American news interviews, they conclude that in spite of different developments due, in part, to differing laws about broadcasting in these two countries, the development of news interviews and their current state is remarkably similar. They also explain that the practices that they describe are 'shaped by the basic institutional conditions of broadcast journalism in Western democracies' (2002: 337).

Harris (1991) looks at political interviews and how politicians in particular respond evasively to questions in interviews. She finds that there is empirical evidence that politicians are evasive in political interviews especially when compared to responses with other non-politician respondents. She also notes that politicians are to a certain degree constrained by the syntax of the question and they are not free to ignore it with impunity. Blum-Kulka (1983) attempts to define the relationship between questions and answers in political interviews within the confines of different types of cohesion. Jucker (1986), in his study of news interviews, maintains that it is difficult to determine on syntactic grounds whether a politician has given a direct answer to a question. Clayman (1993) looks at how reformulations of interviewers' questions by the interviewee, as a preface to a response, can be used both to answer questions and to manipulate them and evade answering them in various ways, for example shifting the topical agenda, ignoring the second part of a two-part question, agreeing with some embedded proposition in the question without engaging with the main proposition, and so on. Carter and McCarthy (2002) tell us that conversation analysts, discourse analysts and pragmaticians have revealed much about the political interview and other broadcast interviews as genres, and have done so largely by comparing interviews with the social, pragmatic or structural norms of everyday mundane conversation. In this way, phenomena such as sequential organization, preference organization, turn-taking, topic management, opening and closure, etc. have been accurately described as indices of the unique generic configuration of the broadcast interview.

Apart from news interviews, radio chat shows and phone-ins have been the focus of various studies. Hutchby (1996a: 4) noted that many studies of talk radio fail to focus on the talk that actually takes place. Hutchby's analytical standpoint is firmly within the CA tradition. He points out that talk radio is a form of institutionalized interaction, where talk takes place within an organization, the broadcasting company, which has its own structure and stability (Hutchby 1996a: 7). Within the CA model, this structure and stability, as discussed by analysts such as Boden (1994) and Drew and Heritage (1992), propagates itself through talk and interaction. Hutchby's work focuses on *The Brian Hayes Show*, a daily show on London's LBC station (see Hutchby 1991, 1992, 1995, 1996a, 1996b, 1999).

Research methods and paradigms in media discourse

The dominant, though not exclusive, research method for the study of spoken language has been CA, while the study of written texts in the media has been dominated by studies of power and ideology within the research paradigm of critical discourse analysis (CDA).

Conversation analysis

CA focuses on the social organization of conversation, or 'talk-in-interaction', by a detailed inspection of tape recordings and transcriptions (ten Have 1986). Core to its inductive analysis of the structure of conversations are the following areas (see Richards *et al.* 1992):

1   How speakers decide when to speak during conversation, i.e. the rules and systematicity governing *turn-taking* (the turn-taking structure of casual conversation was delineated in the influential paper by Sacks *et al.* 1974).
2   How speaker turns can be related to each other in sequence and might be said to go together as *adjacency pairs* (for example, complaint + denial A: *You left the light on.* B: *It wasn't me.*).
3   How turns are organized in their local *sequential* context at any given point in an inter-action and the systematicity of these sequences of utterances (see Schegloff 1982).
4   How seemingly minor or mundane changes in *placement* within utterances and across turns are organized and meaningful (for example, the difference between the placement of a vocative at the beginning, mid or end point of an utterance; see Jefferson 1973).

The turn-by-turn analysis of CA has made it very applicable to the study of areas such as radio talk shows and phone-ins (for example, Hutchby 1991; Thornborrow 2001a, 2003b, 2001c; Rama Martínez 2003). Hutchby and Wooffitt (1998) point out that as far as CA is concerned, what characterizes interaction as institutional is not to do with theories of social structure but with the special character of speech exchange systems that participants can be found to orient to. Take for example this contrast between the canonical (or typical) sequence of turns in a telephone call between callers who have an unmarked relationship (that is, neither intimates nor strangers, Drew and Chilton 2000) from Schegloff (1986):

Canonical call opening between 'unmarked forms of relationships'

Summons-answer:	0. Phone rings	
	1. Answerer:	*Hello*
Identification-recognition:	2. Caller:	*Hello Jim?*
	3. Answerer:	*Yeah*
	4. Caller:	*'s Bonnie*
Greetings:	5. Answerer:	*Hi*
	6. Caller:	*Hi*
'How are you?' sequences:	7. Caller:	*How are yuh*
	8. Answerer:	*Fine, how're you*
	9. Caller:	*Oh, okay I guess*
	10. Answerer:	*Oh okay*
First Topic:	11. Caller:	*What are you doing New Year's Eve?*

Compare this with the call opening sequence presented by Whalen and Zimmerman (1987) as the typical sequence between strangers on an emergency phone line:

Call opening between strangers – Whalen and Zimmerman 1987 (after Hopper and Drummond 1992: 191)

Summons-Answer:	0. Phone rings	
	1. Answerer:	Mid-city Emergency
Business of Call:	2. Caller:	Um yeah. Somebody jus' vandalized my car.

Compare both of these with a call opening sequence in a radio phone-in show. Ostensibly, the participants are strangers:

Call opening from the *Brian Hayes Show* (a radio talk show broadcast on LBC radio, adapted from Hutchby 1991: 120–21)

Summons, identification & greeting:	1. Presenter: John is calling from Ilford good morning
Greeting, identification, & business of call:	2. Caller: h. good morning Brian (pause: 0.4).hh what I'm phoning up is about the cricket

What CA does powerfully is to show us typical patterns or sequences of turn organization and allows us see, by comparison, as Hutchby and Wooffitt (1998) put it, the special character of speech exchange systems that participants can be found to orient to. In the three extracts above we can see how, in institutional interactions, the turn sequences are attenuated (i.e. cut short). We can see that in the radio example, the typical call opening sequence is turned on its head when the 'answerer', that is the radio presenter in this case, conducts the summons, identification and greeting stage and the adjacent pair to this on the part of the caller is the reciprocation of greeting, identification and identification of the business of the call. This is all achieved in two turns compared with the canonical sequence which does not get to the business of the call until turn 11.

In this way, CA provides a research paradigm which has facilitated the detailed analysis of news interviews using natural conversation as a baseline for comparison. Heritage (1985), for example, compares questions-and-answer sequences in news interviews with casual conversation and courtroom interactions and finds that unlike casual conversation, it is possible to search through hours of courtroom and news interview interactions without encountering a single *mm hm*, *oh* newsmarker (see Jefferson 1984) or affiliative assessment. Instead, Heritage tells us, the interviews are conducted almost exclusively through chains of questions and answers, and in so doing, he claims, narratives are elicited step-by-step or opinions are developed and elaborated component-by-component.

Greatbatch (1988) profiles the turn-taking conventions of interviews using the baseline canonical framework provided by Sacks *et al.* (1974) as a comparison. He notes that interviewers and interviewees generally confine themselves, respectively, to turn-types recognizable as questions and answers. The interviewer does not normally engage in a wide range of responses that questioners normally engage in when they react to what they hear in a casual conversation (see Schegloff 1982; Jefferson 1984; Greatbatch 1986; Tottie 1991; McCarthy and Carter 2000; McCarthy 2002). Clayman (1991) looks in detail at news interview openings and concludes that they are highly organized so as to achieve institutional ends: (a) they mark the encounter from the outset as having been pre-assembled on behalf of the viewing audience, and (b) they set the agenda for the interview which is linked to newsworthy events in the world at large.

CA therefore has provided a very useful research paradigm for the study of media discourse by comparing its turn sequentiality with the canonical sequences of everyday conversation. The shortcoming of CA, however, is that it looks in detail at short sequences of interaction at turn level. CDA on the other hand is more focused on the recurring use of certain lexical items and how these are linked to ideology.

Critical discourse analysis

As discussed above, CDA brings a critical perspective to the study of media discourse. This involves the researcher taking a critical stance in respect of a media text. In applying a CDA framework, the researcher is not looking at the language in a neutral descriptive way, she/he is addressing fundamental issues of injustice and exposing how language has been used to sustain dominant ideologies. As O'Halloran (2010) puts it, CDA seeks to illuminate how language use contributes to the domination and misrepresentation of certain social groups.

CDA, it is argued, goes beyond academic inquiry. As van Dijk (1997: 22–3) explains, the 'ultimate goal is not only scientific, but also social and political, namely *change*'; or as O'Halloran (2010: 564) puts it, CDA is 'a form of social critique' which 'encourages reflection on social and cultural processes and their relationship with language use' (see also O'Halloran, this volume). Over the years, Fairclough has contributed much to the study of language and the media and has raised awareness as to its importance (see also Fairclough 1988, 1989, 1995b, 2000). According to Fairclough (2000: 158–9), CDA 'sees language as one element of a social practice ... this approach is particularly concerned with social change as it affects discourse, and with how it connects with social relations of power and domination'.

While CDA offers a powerful research framework, it often falls short as a research instrument because it can be overly qualitative. In other words, its assertions can be criticized on the basis of being overly interpretative or even subjective. However, this has been overcome by the use of corpus linguistics as a means of looking at language patterns across large amounts of media texts. By way of example, let's return to the BBC interview quoted from above, between Jeremy Paxman and Tony Blair. In this one short extract from the prime minister, we could make a statement about power and ideology based on the use of the pronoun *we* (marked in italic):

Tony Blair: The danger is that if *we* allow Iraq to develop chemical, biological, and nuclear weapons they will threaten their own region, there is no way that *we* would be able to exclude ourselves from any regional conflict there was there as indeed *we* had to become involved last time they committed acts of external aggression against Kuwait.

We could say that the prime minister appropriates the use of *we* to speak from the nation, in other words, he is positioning himself dominantly as the unified voice of Britain facing unanimously into war. We could extract many further examples to back up the above assertion but if we apply corpus linguistics, in tandem with CDA, we have a very powerful means of showing consistent use of language. We will return to this example below and apply corpus linguistic software to the interview.

Corpus linguistics

Corpus linguistics is essentially a research instrument which has application to many areas. It involves the principled gathering of spoken or written texts in electronic form to make a corpus. These can be explored using software which typically carries out the core functions of (1) word frequency counts, (2) key word calculations, and (3) key word in context (KWIK) searches (see Evison 2010; Scott 2010 and Adolphs and Lin, this volume, for an overview). For the purposes of the study of media discourse, it means that a researcher can address research questions over a large amount of data. The core functions of corpus software allow the researcher not only to look within the texts or transcripts but to compare these findings with other contexts. For example, the theme of evaluation, that is the expression of opinion (and ultimately stance), is one which has emerged strongly and is also linked to the use of more qualitative approaches to looking at media discourse through the use of corpora. Bednarek (2006a, 2006b) presents a corpus-based account of evaluation, which is based on 100 newspaper articles (a 70,000 word corpus), drawn from both tabloid and broadsheet media. Bednarek's work is quantitative and she provides detailed explanations and justifications of her framework of evaluation and bias in newspapers. O'Keeffe (2006) looks at over 200,000 words of transcripts from radio phone-ins, chat shows and political interviews from around the world.

Possibly the greater potential for CL, however, is in how it can complement other research frameworks. For example, O'Keeffe and Breen (2007), using over a corpus of 500,000 words of newspaper reports on child sexual abuse cases, over five years, conducted a content analysis and corpus-based lexiogrammatical analysis. The corpus-based component was able to provide consistent evidence for the findings from the content analysis component of the study. Carter and McCarthy (2002) show how CA and CL can work together when they look at one BBC radio interview with former British Prime Minister, Tony Blair, using a dual approach to its analysis. First, they apply the framework of CA in their analysis and subsequently they conduct corpus-based analysis on the same data. They conclude that the CA analysis shows that the interviewer and interviewee both adhere to and exploit the generic conventions of the interview in terms of turn-taking, topic management and participant relationships. The interviewer presses an agenda of getting the interviewee to commit to action; the interviewee, in turn, responds cohesively and coherently and yet avoids direct commitment to action and maintains his topical agenda without losing face (and with useful soundbites delivered along the way, which are likely to be extracted and quoted in subsequent national news bulletins). The application of corpus techniques to the transcript reveals much about the lexical environment, especially the semantic prosody of the high-frequency key words. Carter and McCarthy show how CA and corpus linguistics can complement each other and offer a more integrated way of understanding how conversational agendas are achieved when the two methods are used in combination than either of them can aspire to alone.

O'Halloran (2010) shows how CL can be a powerful complementary tool to CDA when he examines a set of texts over a six-week period in the British popular tabloid newspaper *The Sun* on the topic of the European Union (EU) expansion on 1 May 2004. The corpus he built consists of *Sun* texts in the six weeks prior to 1 May which contain the cultural keywords: '(im)migration', '(im)migrant(s)', 'EU' and 'European'. In all, the corpus comprises seventy-six texts, a total of 26,350 words, and is in chronological order from 20 March to 30 April 2004. O'Halloran is able to show, in a convincing and powerful way, how the language and ideology were intertwined in that period. For example, key words such as 'high unemployment', 'impoverished', 'poor' were linked to 'Eastern European' and were tied up with the presupposition that EU enlargement would mean that migrants would be a drain on social services, etc.

By way of further illustration, we return to the BBC public interview between Tony Blair and Jeremy Paxman. Above we looked at one extract from what the prime minister said and made claims about his use of the pronoun *we*. By saving the transcript of the interview as a plain text file and using concordance software to search for *we*, we can make the following empirically-based assertion and hence illustrate the complementarity of CDA and CL:

> *We* is used 49 times in the interview and 86 per cent of these are uttered by the Prime Minister to mean, 'we the people of Britain who are in favour of going to war'. As such, it shows a consistent dominant use of the pronoun to coercively position the people of Britain in line with the Prime Minister's stance on the justification of invading Iraq.

New media

The explosion of new media poses interesting challenges for the study of discourse in the media. Access to 'the media' used to be in the control of broadcasting companies. New media are there for the ordinary person to access as long as they have the technological know-how and the necessary hardware. Therefore, 'the media' is now much more 'our media'. The process of democratization means that lay people can access and 'broadcast' on new media such as the Internet and mobile phone technology, through Websites, blogs, wikis, tweets and text messages. In addition, the ever-expanding possibilities of virtual social networks mean that private personae can now co-exist in a public identity, within a shared social network. Such advances bring about new mediated participation frameworks (after Goffman 1981) and as a result mark another phase of change in how language is used. This change is revolutionary because of its democratized nature, and merits academic exploration.

Traditional definitions have mutated. We now see greater levels of intertextuality and a blurring of the lines between spoken and written media. Newspapers have Web and video links and sound clips, television news programmes have text on screen and Websites where you can 'chat'. Social network pages can link to clips for television, radio, newspapers as well as broadcast the mundane and minute from participants' daily lives, such as 'Going for a coffee', 'Oh no, time to wash the dog', 'Remind me never to go to a Whitney Houston concert again', and so on.

This kind of new order of things renders many old metaphors and frameworks anachronistic. In the literature, the accepted metaphor for audiences seemed to be 'overhearers' or 'eavesdroppers'. For example, Montgomery (1986: 428) refers to the audience as the 'overhearing recipient of a discourse' (see also Heritage 1985).

Now, with the advent of new media, audiences regularly voice their opinion and the traditional media of radio and television now regularly solicit text messages and tweets in real time during shows and report these back to the audience. As such, the television and radio audiences have been 'brought into the room' (or have brought themselves into the room) whereas before the hearing status of the audience in broadcast genres (such as radio phone-ins, TV chat shows, news interviews and so on) was for the most part ignored by analysts (see O'Keeffe 2006: ch. 3 for a detailed discussion).

Looking to the future

Because of the advent of new media, and the ever-changing nature of these, it is both an exciting and challenging time in the study of media discourse. There is a wealth of uncharted research territory. The arrival of 'the audience voice' into traditional media of television, radio and newpapers needs to be redefined and analyzed. The constructing of public identities on social networking sites, blogs and tweets, the creating and sustaining of these social networks, linguistically, also beg to be explored. However, the challenges remain. First, at a methodological level, the additionality of using CL to provide quantitative back-up to the qualitative approaches of CA and CDA needs to be reflected upon and scrutinized. Second, there needs to be a paradigm shift in terms of how we define communication within 'the new media'. In the old days, we could say that there were newspapers and there were readers or there were television or radio presenters and their audiences. The new democratized nature of things in the media begs for a new paradigm to encapsulate the changed dynamics, power structures, participation frameworks and discourses that are ever-emerging.

Related topics

CDA; corpus linguistics; discourse analysis

Further reading

Bednarek, M. (2006) *Evaluation in Media Discourse: Analysis of a Newspaper Corpus*, London: Continuum. (A corpus-based study of evaluation in newspapers based on a corpus of 100 newspaper articles comprising a 70,000 word corpus, from both tabloid and broadsheet media.)

Horton, D. and Wohl, R. R. (1956) 'Mass communication and para-social interaction: observations on intimacy at a distance', reprinted in G. Gumpert and R. Cathcart (eds) (1979) *Inter/Media: Interpersonal Communication in a Media World*, Oxford: Oxford University Press. (Given that this was written in the early days of television, it provides thought-provoking material that still has relevance to current-day studies of the media.)

O'Halloran, K. A. (2010) 'How to use corpus linguistics in the study of media discourse', in A. O'Keeffe and M. J. McCarthy (eds) *The Routledge Handbook of Corpus Linguistics*, London: Routledge. (An insightful illustration of the application of corpus linguistics to critical discourse analysis, using a corpus of articles from the UK newspaper, *The Sun*, as a case study.)

O'Keeffe, A. (2006) *Investigating Media Discourse*, London: Routledge. (A look at spoken media discourse using a combination of approaches including conversation analysis, discourse analysis and pragmatics in the exploration of a corpus of over 200,000 words of spoken media interactions.)

Stubbs, M. (1996) *Text and Corpus Analysis: Computer-assisted Studies of Language and Culture*, Oxford: Blackwell. (This book provides the ground-breaking framework for the computer-assisted analysis of texts and shows how corpus analysis can give insights into culturally significant patterns of language use.)

Anne O'Keeffe

References

Bednarek, M. (2006a) *Evaluation in Media Discourse. Analysis of a Newspaper Corpus*, London and New York: Continuum.

——(2006b) 'Evaluating Europe: parameters of evaluation in the British press', in C. Leung and J. Jenkins (eds) *Reconfiguring Europe: The Contribution of Applied Linguistics*, BAAL/Equinox (British Studies in Applied Linguistics).

Bell, A. (1991) *The Language of the News Media*, Oxford: Basil Blackwell.

Bhatia, V. K. (1993) *Analysing Genre: Language Use in Professional Settings*, London: Longman.

Biber, D., Johansson, S., Leech, G., Conrad, S. and Finegan, E. (1999) *Longman Grammar of Spoken and Written English*, Harlow: Pearson Longman.

Blum-Kulka, S. (1983) 'The dynamics of political interviews', *Text* 3(2): 131–53.

Boden, D. (1994) *The Business of Talk: Organizations in Action*, Cambridge: Polity Press.

Carter, R. A. and McCarthy, M. J. (2002) 'From conversation to corpus: a dual analysis of a broadcast political interview', in A. Sánchez-Macarro (ed.) *Windows on the World: Media Discourse in English*, Valencia: University of Valencia Press.

Chang, P. (2002) 'Who's behind the personal pronouns in talk radio? Cartalk: a case study', in A. Sánchez-Macarro (ed.) *Windows on the World: Media Discourse in English*, Valencia: University of Valencia Press.

Clayman, S. (1991) 'News interview openings: aspects of sequential organization', in P. Scannell (ed.) *Broadcast Talk*, London: Sage.

——(1993) 'Reformulating the question: a device for answering/not answering questions in news interviews and press conferences', *Text* 13(2): 159–88.

Clayman, S. and Heritage, J. (2002) *The News Interview: Journalists and Public Figures on the Air*, Cambridge: Cambridge University Press.

Corner, J. (1991) 'The interview as a social encounter', in P. Scannell (ed.) *Broadcast Talk*, London: Sage.

Day, R. (1961) *Television: a Personal Report*, London: Hutchinson.

Dimbleby, J. (1975) *Richard Dimbleby: A Biography*, London: Hodder and Stoughton.

Drew, P. and Chilton, K. (2000) 'Calling just to keep in touch: regular and habitual telephone calls as an environment for small talk', in J. Coupland (ed.) *Small Talk*, London: Longman.

Drew, P. and Heritage, J. (1992) *Talk at Work: Interaction in Institutional Settings*, Cambridge: Cambridge University Press.

Evison, J. (2010) 'What are the basics of analysing a corpus?', in A. O'Keeffe and M. J. McCarthy (eds) *The Routledge Handbook of Corpus Linguistics*, London: Routledge.

Fairclough, N. (1988) 'Discourse representation in media discourse', *Sociolinguistics* 17: 125–39.

——(1989) *Language and Power*, London: Longman.

——(1995a) *Media Discourse*, London: Edward Arnold.

——(1995b) *Critical Discourse Analysis*, London: Longman

——(2000) *New Labour, New Language*, London: Routledge.

Ghadessy, M. (1988) 'The language of written sports commentary: soccer – a description', in M. Ghadessy (ed.) *Registers of Written English: Situational Factors and Linguistic Features*, London and New York: Pinter

Goffman, E. (1981) *Forms of Talk*, Oxford: Basil Blackwell.

Greatbatch, D. (1986) 'Aspects of topical organization in news interviews: the use of agenda-shifting procedures by interviewees', *Media Culture and Society* 8: 441–5.

——(1988) 'A turn-taking system for British news interviews', *Language in Society* 17: 401–30.

Halliday, M. A. K. (1978) *Language as Social Semiotic: The Social Interpretation of Language and Meaning*, London: Edward Arnold.

Hall, S. (1973) 'Encoding and decoding in the media discourse', stencilled paper no.7, Birmingham, Centre for Contemporary Cultural Studies (revised as Hall 1980).

——(1977) 'Culture, the media, and the "ideological effect"', in J. Curran, M. Gurevitch and J. Woollacott (eds) *Mass Communication and Society*, London: Edward Arnold.

——(1980) 'Encoding/decoding', and 'recent developments in theories of language and ideology', *Culture, Media, Language*, London: Hutchinson.

——(1982) 'The rediscovery of "ideology": return of the repressed in media studies', in M. Gurevitch, T. Bennett, J. Curran and S. Woollacott (eds) *Culture, Society and the Media*, London: Methuen.

Harris, S. (1991) 'Evasive action: how politicians respond to questions in political interviews', in P. Scannell (ed.) *Broadcast Talk*, London: Sage.

Hasan, R. (1996) *Ways of Saying: Ways of Meaning*, London: Cassell.

Heritage, J. (1985) 'Analysing news interviews: aspects of the production of talk for an overhearing audience', in T. A. van Dijk (ed.) *Handbook of Discourse Analysis*, vol. 3: *Discourse and Dialogue*, London: Academic Press.

Hodge, R. (1979). 'Newspapers and Communities', in R. Fowler, B. Hodge, G. Kress and T. Trew (eds) *Language and Control*, London: Routledge/Kegan Paul.

Hopper, R. and Drummond, K. (1992) 'Accomplishing interpersonal relationship: the telephone openings of strangers and intimates', *Western Journal of Communication* 56: 185–99.

Horton, D. and Wohl, R. R. (1956) 'Mass communication and para-social interaction: observations on intimacy at a distance', reprinted in G. Gumpert and R. Cathcart (eds) (1979) *Intermedia – Interpersonal Communication in a Media World*, Oxford: Oxford University Press.

Hutchby, I. (1991) 'The organisation of talk on talk radio', in P. Scannell (ed.) *Broadcast Talk*, London: Sage.

——(1992) 'Confrontation talk: aspects of "interruption" in argument sequences on talk radio', *Text* 12(3): 343–71.

——(1995) 'Aspects of recipient design in expert advice-giving on call-in radio', *Discourse Processes* 19: 219–38.

——(1996) *Confrontation Talk: Arguments, Asymmetries, and Power On Talk Radio*, Mahwah, NJ: Lawrence Erlbaum Associates.

——(1999) 'Frame attunement and footing in the organisation of talk radio openings', *Journal of Sociolinguistics* 3: 41–64.

Hutchby, I. and Wooffitt, R. (1998) *Conversation Analysis: Principles, Practices and Applications*, Cambridge: Polity Press

Jefferson, G. (1973) 'A case of precision timing in ordinary conversation: overlapping tag-positioned address terms in closing sequences', *Semiotica* 9: 47–96.

——(1984) 'Notes of a systematic development of the acknowledgement token "yeah" and "mm mm"', *Papers in Linguistics* 17(2): 197–216.

Jucker, A. (1986) *News Interviews, A Pragmalinguistic Analysis*, Amsterdam: John Benjamins.

Leckie-Tarry, H. (1995) *Language and Context: a Functional Linguistic Theory of Register*, London: Pinter.

Lesser, R. (2003) 'When conversation is not normal: the role of conversation analysis in language pathology', in C. L. Prevignano and P. J. Thibault (eds) *Discussing Conversation Analysis: The Work of Emanuel A. Schegloff*, Amsterdam: John Benjamins.

McCarthy, M. J. (2002) 'Good listenership made plain: non-minimal response tokens in British and American spoken English', in R. Reppen, S. Fitzmaurice and D. Biber (eds) *Using Corpora to Explore Linguistic Variation*, Amsterdam: John Benjamins.

McCarthy, M. J. and Carter, R. A. (2000) 'Feeding back: non-minimal response tokens in everyday English conversation', in C. Heffer and H. Sauntson (eds) *Words in Context: A Tribute to John Sinclair on His Retirement*, Birmingham: ELR Discourse Monograph no. 18.

McQuail, D. (1994) *Mass Communication Theory*, London: Sage.

Montgomery, M. (1986) 'DJ talk', *Media, Culture and Society* 8: 421–40.

O'Halloran, K. A. (2010) 'How to use corpus linguistics in the study of media discourse', in A. O'Keeffe and M. J. McCarthy (eds) *The Routledge Handbook of Corpus Linguistics*, London: Routledge.

O'Keeffe, A. (2002) 'Exploring indices of national identity in a corpus of radio phone-in data from Irish radio', in A. Sánchez-Macarro (ed.) *Windows on the World: Media Discourse in English*, Valencia: University of Valencia Press.

——(2003) '"Like the wise virgins and all that jazz": using a corpus to examine vague language and shared knowledge', in U. Connor and T. A. Upton (eds) *Applied Corpus Linguistics: A Multidimensional Perspective*, Amsterdam: Rodopi.

——(2005) '"You've a daughter yourself?": a corpus-based look at question forms in an Irish radio phone-in', in K. P. Schneider and A. Barron (eds) *The Pragmatics of Irish English*, Berlin: Mouton de Gruyter.

——(2006) *Investigating Media Discourse*, London: Routledge.

O'Keeffe, A. and Breen, M. (2007) 'At the hands of the brothers: a corpus-based lexico-grammatical analysis of stance in newspaper reporting of child sexual abuse', in J. Cotterill (ed.) *The Language of Sexual Crime*, Basingstoke: Palgrave Macmillan.

Rama Martínez, M. E. (2003) *Talk on British Television: The Interactional Organisation of Three Broadcast Genres*, Vigo: Servicio de Publicacións da Universidade de Vigo.

Richards, J. C., Platt, J. and Platt, H. (1992) *Dictionary of Language Teaching and Applied Linguistics*, Singapore: Longman.

Sacks, H., Schegloff, E. A. and Jefferson, G. (1974) 'A simplest systematics for the organisation of turn-taking for conversation', *Language* 50(4): 696–735.

Schegloff, E. (1982) 'Discourse as interactional achievement: some uses of "uh huh" and other things that come between sentences', in D. Tannen (ed.) *Analysing Discourse: Text and Talk*, Washington, DC: Georgetown University Press.

——(1986) 'The routine as achievement', *Human Studies* 9: 111–52.

Scott, M. (2010) 'What can corpus software do?', in A. O'Keeffe and M. J. McCarthy (eds) *The Routledge Handbook of Corpus Linguistics*, London: Routledge.

Stubbs, M. (1996) *Text and Corpus Analysis: Computer-assisted Studies of Language and Culture*, Oxford: Blackwell.

Swales, J. (1990) *Genre Analysis*, Cambridge: Cambridge University Press.

ten Have, P. (1986) 'Issues in qualitative data interpretation', paper read at the International Sociological Association, XIth World Congress of Sociology, New Delhi, August 1986. Available at: www.pscw.uva.nl/emca/mica.htm

Thornborrow, J. (2001a) 'Authenticating talk: building public identities in audience participation broadcasting', *Discourse Studies* 3(4): 459–79.

——(2001b) 'Authenticity, talk and mediated experience', *Discourse Studies* 3(4): 391–411.

——(2001c) 'Questions, control and the organization of talk in calls to a radio phone-in', *Discourse Studies* 3(1): 119–43.

Toolan, M. (1988) 'The language of press advertising', in M. Ghadessy (ed.) *Registers of Written English: Situational Factors and Linguistic Features*, London: Pinter.

Tottie, G. (1991) 'Conversational style in British and American English: the case of backchannels', in K. Aijmer and B. Altenberg (eds) *English Corpus Linguistics*, London: Longman.

van Dijk, T. (1997) 'The story of discourse', in T. A. van Dijk (ed.) *Discourse as Structure and Process*, London: Sage.

——(2001) 'Critical discourse analysis', in D. Schiffrin, D. Tannen and H. Hamilton (eds) *The Handbook of Discourse Analysis*, Oxford: Blackwell.

——(2009) 'Critical discourse studies: a sociocognitive approach', in R. Wodak and M. Meyer (eds) *Methods of Critical Discourse Analysis*, London: Sage.

Wallace, W. D. (1977) 'How registers register: a study in the language of news and sports', *Studies in the Linguistic Sciences* 7(1): 46–78.

Wedell, E. G. (1968) *Broadcasting and Public Policy*, London: Michael Joseph.

Whale, J. (1977) *The Politics of the Media*, London: Fontana.

Whalen, M. R. and Zimmerman, D. H. (1987) 'Sequential and institutional context in calls for help', *Social Psychology Quarterly* 50(2): 172–85.

White, P. (1997) 'Death, disruption and the moral order: the narrative impulse in mass-media "hard news" reporting', in F. Christie and J. R. Martin (eds) *Genre and Institutions*, London: Cassell.

6
Institutional discourse

Celia Roberts

The development of the idea of 'institutional discourse'

Early theories

Institutions are held together by talk and texts both to maintain themselves and to exclude those who do not belong. The study of institutional discourses sheds light on how organisations work, how 'lay' people and experts interact and how knowledge and power get constructed and circulate within the routines, systems and common sense practices of work-related settings. 'Institutional discourse', therefore, spans many areas and this reflects the different theoretical backgrounds of those who have written about institutions.

These theorists can usefully be divided into those who look at the underlying processes that construct, maintain and give power to institutions and those who analyse the detailed conduct of how organisations work and interact with others. A fundamental notion of the institutional derives from a social constructivist view of reality in which all institutions are made up of shared habitual practices. Stable and enduring features are assembled through particular social settings:

> insitutionalisation occurs wherever there is a reciprocal typification of habitualised actions by types of actors.
>
> *(Berger and Luckmann 1967: 40)*

So the institution is brought about by the gradual sedimentation of repeated actions, which provide a common stock of cultural knowledge (Mumby and Clair 1997). Those 'in the know' are the professionals, experts and bureaucratic officials who assess people and problems according to this shared cultural knowledge.

The anthropologist Mary Douglas discusses how this knowledge is created and used to establish and maintain institutional life and bind society together: 'This is how ... we build institutions, squeezing each other's ideas into a common shape' (1986: 91). This squeezing is done through a process of building classifications which are then presented as natural and reasonable. Douglas argues that not only are organisations bound together by these classifications but they have a wider influence in maintaining social order. The feminist eth-nographer Dorothy Smith, taking a more overtly critical stance, also extends the notion of 'institutional' beyond the organisation to work outside formal contexts. Her notion of 'insti-tutional ethnography' encompasses the everyday world of women's work in supporting the home and family where this 'world' is 'organised by and sustains the institutional process' (1987: 166).

This notion of the 'institutional process' is not, therefore, tied to a particular organisation but is 'any relatively durable set of social relations which endows individuals with power, status and resources of various kinds' (Bourdieu 1991: 8). This complex of relations is what Smith calls 'the ruling apparatus':

> In contrast to such concepts as bureaucracy, 'institution' does not identify a determinate form of social organisation, but rather the intersection and co-ordination of more than one relational mode of the ruling apparatus.
>
> *(Smith 1987: 160)*

So institutional discourse covers both the objective and regulatory elements of any organised group of people, and also the wider set of ideologies and sets of relations which form this ruling apparatus.

Michel Foucault's work remains central to our understanding of institutional discourse. His historical studies of how institutions developed for discipline and punishment and for medicine are shaped by his theories of discourse. In 'The Order of Discourse' (1981) he describes how institutions both support powerful discourse (through pedagogy, books, labs, etc.) and in turn are supported by disciplines and codified ways of thinking. Institutions, he argues, try to organise and control the power of discourse and its 'great incessant and disordered buzzing' (1981: 68). They do this by regulating who is allowed to speak certain discourses and by the discursive policing which allows only certain discourses, including classification and metaphors, to be used at any one historical time.

But even more significantly, institutions are part of the wider discourse in which truth is conflated with knowledge. Foucault contrasts the ancient idea of truth as some eternal, innate, ritualised truth, one based on ritual and the authority of speakers, with a notion of truth based on empirical knowledge, systems of classification, codified knowledge and disciplines which produce their own truth, and so power, since they impose 'a certain position, a certain gaze and a certain function' (Foucault 1981: 56). The current focus on evidence-based practice and randomised control trials is an extreme form of this 'will to know' being equated with the 'will to truth'. The result of a clinical trial, for example, is treated not only as useful knowledge but as the truth of the matter. Institutions can use this over-arching truth/knowledge discourse to maintain themselves and increase their power. All the more so since this kind of 'truth' masks itself and the act of its production. We are unaware of 'the will to truth, that prodigious machinery designed to exclude' (1981: 58).

By contrast with these more abstract theories of institutional discourse, are those which deal with the conduct, text and talk of specific institutions. The most systematic literature in this area stems from the sociological tradition of Conversation Analysis (CA) which focuses on the detailed interactional processes of specific activities such as service encounters or proceedings in court. For example, in their wide-ranging overview of talk at work, Drew and Heritage (1992) describe 'institutional interaction' as task-oriented and involving at least one participant who represents a formal organisation:

talk-in-interaction is the principal means through which lay persons pursue various practical goals and the central medium through which the daily working activities of many professionals and organisational representatives are conducted. We will use the term 'institutional interaction' to refer to talk of this kind.

(Drew and Heritage 1992: 3)

The focus on talk in interaction grounds 'institutional discourse' in the social, the local and the organisational. Rather than addressing the underlying processes and discourses of an institution, these studies are concerned with the practical accomplishment of activities in socially competent ways. The pressure to be socially competent was brilliantly examined by Goffman in what he called 'total institutions' such as the asylum in which all aspects of everyday life are subject to a single authority (1961: 17).

Some of the different theoretical and empirical differences in approach are reflected in the debates around organisational discourse analysis and organisational discourse studies (Grant and Iedema 2005). Organisational discourse analysis based on sociolinguistic, pragmatic and CA theory uses technical linguistic analysis to look at how talk and text produce organisational life. Organisational discourse studies have emerged from management and organisational theory. Here discourse is treated as a rhetorical principle or set of arguments which challenge organisational stability.

So, discourse stretches from the micro-phenomena of pauses and prosody in the specific activities and the interactions of representatives of organisations to the orders and relations which are part of the 'ruling apparatus' (Smith 1987: 160), both in particular bounded institutions or, more generally, in everyday practices which are affected by and feed into the wider social order of such institutions as the family or the rule of law.

Institutional and professional settings and discourses

Most of the studies of institutional and workplace life involve professionals, and many studies include both 'institutional' and 'professional' discourse and use either as a cover term for both (Gunnarsson 2009). However, there are useful distinctions to be made between institutional and professional discourse (Sarangi and Roberts 1999). The latter is acquired by professionals as they become teachers, doctors, human resources personnel and so on. The notion of a profession is drawn from the concept of a vocation in which professed knowledge is learnt and used. Implied in the term is some notion of autonomy or freedom as a result of acquiring a body of knowledge through rigorous training. Professional discourse is a form of 'habitus' (Bourdieu 1991), a set of linguistic practices and conventionalised behaviour and values that the professional has to acquire mastery over.

Institutional discourse, by contrast, is formed both by the wider ideologies and relations of the ruling apparatus and, following Weber (1947) and the critical theorist Habermas (1979), is also characterised by rational, legitimate accounting practices which are authoritatively backed up by a set of rules and regulations, a bureaucracy (Sarangi and Slembrouck 1996) governing an institution. Unlike the professional's judgement based on their expertise, institutional representatives emphasise objectivity and rule-governed organisation. So, for example, in the medical setting, the diagnosis and agreed course of action or the clinicians' working up of narratives into a case are professional discourses but the gatekeeping functions of selection, assessment and training rely on institutional discourse. Indeed, increasingly professional concerns have to be cast in institutionally acceptable frames and institutional demands can be imposed on professional knowledge and practices.

So, in most settings, professionals are using both types of discourses, and it is the interplay of the two which is typical of organisational life. For example, record keeping has both professional and institutional functions (Garfinkel 1967). Cicourel (1981) shows that the recoding of patient information into abstract categories both relates to clinical treatment but also, institutionally, to the systematic organisation of patient care. At this level, the more abstract categories feed into the accounting practices and rules which construct the institution. Record keeping in medical (Cicourel 1981; Iedema 2003), educational (Mehan 1993), legal settings (Cicourel 1968) and other bureaucratic encounters (Sarangi and Slembrouck 1996) is an obvious activity where professional knowledge is recontextualised into a form where it can be institutionally managed.

Increasingly, professional discourses are laminated over by institutional discourses (Roberts and Sarangi 1999) as institutions act to maintain and defend themselves. This is particularly noticeable in the impact of the market economy discourses on specific services. These discourses are produced to maintain and manage such institutions as law, medicine and education within a model of late capitalism. For example, in British higher education, the professional discourses of learning and assessing and staff-student relationships are reworked, recontextualised, as institutional discourses of consumption and accountability (Fairclough 1993; Mautner 2005).

The distinction between professional and institutional discourse is also apparent in some of the 'frontstage' and 'backstage' work of professionals. Erving Goffman made the distinction between the 'performance' aspect of social life and the 'backstage' where this performance is knowingly contradicted (Goffman 1959). In institutional settings, the backstage is where professional knowledge is produced and circulated but also where staff and professional groups do the institutional work. Much of the frontstage work is between the expert and the lay client or applicant in service encounters in healthcare (Fisher and Todd 1983; West 1984; Heritage and Maynard 2006), social work (Hall 1997) or other bureaucratic settings (Collins 1987). Other frontstage work is even more clearly a performance, as in educational settings (Mehan 1979) or in legal settings (Atkinson and Drew 1979; Eades 2008). The backstage work is where, for example, care plans and records are discussed and made accountable, where decisions are ratified and the initial professional frontstage work is not so much contradicted, in Goffman's terms, but reshaped and reframed to fit into institutional categories (Agar 1985).

For this chapter, the discussion will be limited to those approaches and methodologies based on sociolinguistic, conversation analytic, ethnographic and micro-ethnographic methodologies from both descriptive and critical perspectives. The focus will be on specific activities where there is at least one institutional/organisational representative, rather than on wider institutional discourses of, for example, the media (Fairclough 1995; Richardson 2007; Mayr 2008), but we will also include studies where the analysis is informed by an understanding of these wider discourses that construct and control social and institutional life.

Major themes

Power and asymmetry

Institutional discourse cannot be uncoupled from powerful discourse, as Foucault's studies have shown, and institutional relations, ideologies and categories assume a hierarchy of knowledge, status and degree of belonging which produce asymmetrical interactions. Most studies of institutional discourse recognise its asymmetrical character, as these major themes illustrate. Typically these include: the degree of control over the content of talk; the allocation of turns; the special inferencing that experts have access to; the differential distribution of participation rights; and the very different impact that decisions have for the client or applicant (see below) (Drew and Heritage 1992; Thornborrow 2002). The asymmetrical nature of medical consultations has been widely studied to show these inequalities (Fisher and Todd 1983; West 1984; Mishler 1984).

The professional rarely has to exert raw power since their authority is acknowledged in the applicant's or patient's conduct. For example, in medical settings, studies show how patients are interrupted (Frankel 1984), do not challenge the health professional's decision or manage their explanations with the doctor's expertise in mind (Gill and Maynard 2006). The exercise of power and authority is also laminated over with language and bodily conduct which implies equality; for example in the 'conversational' mode of institutional talk where covert mechanisms of control are substituted for overt markings of power (Fairclough 1992). Talk becomes euphemised and cautious; for example, the 'little chat' describes a high-stakes gatekeeping interview and professional elicitations are embedded in seemingly casual conversation.

The simulation of equality and the euphemised talk (Bourdieu 1991) of institutional interaction illustrate the ways in which authority masks its own power. But these covert means are also sensitive to the social relations and alignments required in the moral conduct of face-to-face activities (Goffman 1959). Goffman's notion of 'footing' captures in its metaphor some of the delicate interactional footwork that has to be done by participants if they are to manage their professional or client identities, their roles and the moment-to-moment ways of relating to the other. For institutional representatives, their reputation, how they save 'face' and are sensitive to potential face loss in others, has to be managed within what is widely recognised as asymmetrical relations in most institutional interaction. Institutional talk takes on a special kind of asymmetry when both sides do not share the grounds for negotiating understanding, as is often the case with linguistic and socio-cultural differences between lay and expert participants (see the section on recent developments below).

Goal-oriented encounters

In comparing institutional talk to ordinary conversation, Drew and Heritage (1992: 21–4) suggest that its defining characteristic is that it is goal-oriented and that this, in turn, involves particular constraints on what is allowable, and special aspects of reasoning or inference. These goals may be more or less explicitly defined but they all have some element of what Agar calls 'diagnosis' (Agar 1985). For example, in emergency calls (Zimmerman 1992), the participants are clearly oriented to an urgent task and the institutional representatives' talk is highly scripted. By contrast, at the opening of an encounter between a family doctor and a patient, the routine is for the doctor to elicit some display of symptoms from the patient so that the goal of the consultation is clear, but the way in which it will then develop will depend upon local contingencies (Heath 1981). Home visits by a health visitor consist of several less well-defined goals (Heritage and Sefi 1992) and the purpose of the encounter is jointly negotiated over the course of the interaction.

Similarly, the constraints on contributions, while generally giving an interaction its institutional character, vary depending on the overall function of the event. Courtroom interaction (Atkinson and Drew 1979), prisoner rehabilitation training (Mayr 2004), police interrogations (Heydon 2005), police cautions (Rock 2007) and job interviews (see below) have clearly ritual and formal components which constrain turn-taking and what are allowable contributions.

Any one institutional encounter also entails 'special inferences' (Levinson 1979; Trinch 2003) drawn from both background knowledge and from the structural properties of the activity. This is well illustrated in Levinson's telling examples from courtroom testimony of a rape victim. Here the sequencing of the questions builds up a set of inferences to make what appears a natural argument for the jury that the victim's behaviour encouraged the defendant. The fact that the defence barrister has control over what topics are initiated and over the turn-taking system and that the young woman is positioned by these structural constraints means that she has no or little opportunity to challenge or rework the argument.

Gatekeeping and labelling

Most institutional and workplace encounters involve some sort of labelling and sorting process where people are checked through an invisible gate. In service encounters, 'the institutional representative uses his/her control to fit the client into the organisational ways of thinking about the problem' (Agar 1985: 153) and this may happen both frontstage and backstage. In studies of workplace settings, the labelling and sorting of people, information and arguments is distributed across many different groupings so that the decision-making process is hard to pin down to one event or encounter (Boden 1994).

The notion of gatekeeping implies the 'objective' assessment of applicants with a view to making decisions about scarce resources. These may be jobs, educational or training opportunities, housing and other social benefits and so on (Weber 1947). Ironically, these 'objective' procedures are in part a response to an increasingly ethnically and linguistically diverse society and yet studies of institutional discourse have shown how these very procedures tend to reproduce inequality:

> [G]atekeeping encounters are not a neutral and 'objective' meritocratic sorting process. On the contrary, our analysis suggests that the game is rigged, albeit not deliberately, in favour of those individuals whose communication style and social background are most similar to those of the interviewer with whom they talk.
>
> *(Erickson and Schultz 1982: 193)*

In their seminal study of educational counselling interviews, Erickson and Shultz show how decisions about students depend upon judgements of their 'performed social identity' (Erickson and Schultz 1982) as they are played out through the social and cultural organisation of the interaction. They identified two factors that were crucial in determining whether the counsellor's advice offered or closed down educational opportunities for students: one related to solidarity through shared membership of a group or community – co-membership – and the other to the interactional performance, in particular the rhythmic co-ordination of the interview. Lack of co-membership and conversational arhythmia led to less helpful and optimistic advice for students.

The relationship between language and the socio-cultural order, illustrated in this micro-ethnographic study, is particularly associated with John Gumperz and his studies of institutional responses to a linguistically diverse society (Gumperz 1982a, 1982b, 1992). Organisations have their own cultural practices, as the previous section has shown, and the gatekeepers tend to align to these ways of interacting since their own socio-cultural norms and styles of communicating are similar. There is a fit between their own ways of understanding and doing and the distinctive interests of the institution. However, where the lay participant brings to the interview different linguistic behaviour and socio-cultural knowledge, there is no easy fit and the social evaluation of the applicant is based on the uncomfortable moments and lack of alignment experienced by both sides. This can lead to less good advice or failure to secure a job or, in even more high-stakes encounters, as in asylum seeker interviews, deportation from a safe country to a dangerous one (Maryns 2006).

Gatekeeping decisions are interactionally produced but they are also the product of what Mehan calls the 'politics of representation'. This is the means by which various interested groups compete with each other over what is the correct, appropriate or preferred way of representing the particular slice of the world which is within the institutional gaze:

> Proponents of various positions in conflicts waged in and through discourse attempt to capture or dominate modes of representation. ... If successful, a hierarchy is formed, in which one mode of representing the world ... gains primacy over others, transforming modes of representation from an array on a horizontal plane to a ranking on a vertical plane.
>
> *(Mehan 1993: 241)*

These modes of representation include the technical jargon of institutions, the means of classifying and coding events and people and the way in which institutional representatives speak for the institution, for example, the use of 'we' rather than 'I' in patient-health care professional consultations. Linked to the notion of how lay stories can be fitted into institutional criteria, Mehan is interested in how categorical 'facts' and categories such as 'intelligence', 'special needs', 'deviance' emerge from the ambiguity of everyday life. Whereas many of the studies of institutional encounters focus on the formal face-to-face encounter, Mehan's ethnographic study of how children are considered for placement in special education programmes included observations and video recordings of frontstage settings (classrooms, testing rooms) and backstage ones such as teachers' lounges, referral committee meetings, and also interviews with parents and gatekeepers and reviews of student records.

With these different data types, Mehan illustrates how a general call for help from a classroom teacher becomes transformed into the more abstract and distant language of institutional discourse: from a schoolchild who 'needs help' into a 'learning disabled child'. Drawing on Habermas' distinction between the lifeworld and the systems world, Rick Iedema (2003) calls this process part of the new linguistic technologies in which power is simultaneously hidden and reinforced. Texts and modes of talking which are increasingly distant from active doing and saying become timeless and taken for granted. Power inheres in these increasingly abstract forms since only those in the know can fully understand their meanings. This depersonalised and distant institutional language is summed up by the critical anthropologist and social theorist Pierre Bourdieu as: 'impartiality, symmetry, balance, propriety, decency and discretion' (Bourdieu 1991: 130), and by his notion of 'euphemisation' in which uncomfortable judgements are masked by discreet language. The psychologist's role in labelling the child and deciding on what action to take over-rides the more contextual accounts from teachers and parents. So both the modes of representation and the interactional constraints imposed in such meetings ensure that institutional categories dominate and, in making decisions about ordinary people, the institution also looks after itself.

Methodologies and analytic frameworks

The studies discussed here share a common methodological interest. They reflect a social constructivist perspective in which small-scale routines and habits of institutional life are seen as feeding into wider social structures. They are also grounded in the observations, recordings and textual data of institutional activities, giving primacy to the fine-grained detail of these activities. Other studies, particularly of institutional written texts, use corpus linguistics.

Ethnographic studies

Some of the early ethnographies of the workplace stem from the tradition of the Chicago school where the focus on the observation of socially and culturally bounded worlds drew on methods of participant observation and interviews. Long periods spent within institutions provided insights not only into how they functioned as workplaces but also into the perspective of those who were regulated by them, for example, Goffman's account of 'total institutions' (Goffman 1961). More recent ethnographic work has combined detailed recordings of talk with a more traditional ethnography in educational settings (see the discussion above of Mehan 1993) and medical settings (Mishler 1984; Cicourel 1992; Atkinson 1995).

Sociolinguistics and linguistic ethnography

Early sociolinguistic studies were concerned with the relationship between language and context and how certain variables explain the nature of institutional interaction. However, increasingly, sociolinguists have drawn on ethnographic methods and on conceptual frameworks informed by social and critical theory, notably Foucault and Bourdieu (for example, Heller in French Canadian educational contexts [2006] and Gumperz in gatekeeping contexts [1992]). Interactional Sociolinguistics (IS), drawing on the ethnography of communication, pragmatics and conversation analysis (see below) has made gatekeeping encounters in linguistically diverse settings a special focus of interest (Gumperz 1982a, 1992). Gumperz and his associates (Gumperz 1999) link the CA methods of interactional analysis with a sociolinguistic understanding of a variety of communicative styles and relate situated interpretive processes to wider ideological discourses. This approach has recently been combined with extended ethnographic fieldwork to form a new hybrid methodology: linguistic ethnography (Rampton *et al.* 2007).

Conversation analysis

The most extensive and methodologically coherent studies of institutional talk are within CA. Drawing on Harvey Sacks' plea for an aesthetic of 'smallness and slowness' (Silverman 1999) the orthodox CA position is that the *how* of talk-in-interaction discovered through technical analysis must come before the *why*, and that the participants' orientation to what is happening should take priority over the analysts'. The interpretation of data depends on how participants display their understanding of the interaction rather than on any outside contextual information. Two edited collections (both already referred to), Drew and Heritage 1992 and Heritage and Maynard 2006, represent well CA methodology.

Discourse analysis and critical discourse analysis

Early discourse analysis (DA) used speech act theory to try to formulate rules for coherent discourse in institutional settings. However, the emphasis on rules for well-formed discourse underplayed the mutual negotiation of understanding and the active context creating function of interaction, which is the focus of CA and IS research. While Critical Discourse Analysis (CDA) maintains the focus on the detailed analysis of talk and text, it takes a radically different stance from the earlier studies and from CA. Detailed linguistic analysis is integrated with critical theory, drawing on Habermas, Foucault and Bourdieu to understand how institutional discourse serves to both reflect and construct unequal power relations. This understanding is designed to contribute to social change (Fairclough 1992; Caldas-Coulthard and Coulthard 1996; Sarangi and Slembrouck 1996; Wodak 1996; Iedema and Wodak 1999). However, CDA has been criticised for its over-reliance on social theoretical explanations, for overlooking sociolinguistics and for a lack of engagement with social actors.

Recent developments

The study of institutional discourse and its relation to other applied and sociolinguistic work is changing as a result of three main influences: theories of late modernity or postmodernism, new technologies, and globalisation; the latter two being aspects of what is referred to as new or fast capitalism. Postmodernity, while having an enormous impact on social theory, has tended to shift the sociolinguistic focus away from traditional institutional studies and more towards groups, styles and local communities where identity is assembled and displayed through a kaleidoscopic set of different conditions and affiliations (Bauman 1992). Relatively few studies of how such ideas affect institutions such as education have been carried out, but a notable exception is Rampton's analysis of urban classrooms (Rampton 2006).

In contrast, the impact of new technologies and global mobility on workplaces and institutional life is changing the landscape of institutional discourse studies. The globalisation of the market and the new digital technologies have created a 'new work order' (Gee et al. 1996) supported by the discourses of new or fast capitalism. The need to constantly change products and customise them to survive in the globalised market place has led to a restructuring of the workplace. There is an increased use of technologies, more multi-tasking at all levels, more flexibility required of workers as hierarchical structures are flattened, and workers are required to be more autonomous and self-regulating. The more textualised workplace has also created a 'new word order' (Farrell 2001) or 'wordforce' (Heller 2010) in which talk and text take on a new significance. However, new technologies that have helped to create the new work order have refocused linguists on the multimodality of everyday activities (Jewitt 2009). Language interacts with the texts and materialities of these new technologies which themselves facilitate new forms of language.

Many studies of workplaces have shown how routine activities are mediated by digital technologies (Suchman 1992; Goodwin 1995; Hindmarsh et al. 2006; Heath and vom Lehn 2008). There are new work genres, and new work and professional identities are constructed and negotiated through talk on the shopfloor (Hull 1997; Kleifgen 2001; Iedema and Scheeres 2003), health settings (Greatbatch et al. 1993; Cook-Gumperz and Messerman 1999) and in call centres (Cameron 2000; Heller 2002; Budach et al. 2003).

Changes in the nature of work itself have occurred at much the same time as global flows of people have begun to transform institutions and organisations. Early work on the impact of language diversity on institutions tended to focus on particular ethnolinguistic groups (Gumperz 1982a, 1982b; Goldstein 1997; Berk-Seligson 2002) and on clear demarcations of language use. Recent changes in migration and mobility have led to increasing situations of 'superdiversity' (Vertovec 2007) where no single ethnic group stands out but where employees are from many different backgrounds. Similarly, recent theorising about space, language and culture has raised questions about language choice and mix. Rather than language practices being determined unproblematically by specific domains, with, for example, a particular language used in one domain rather than another, they are more highly situated and dependent upon the context of the particular interaction, the institutional response to multilingualism and the mutual resources of the speakers (Blommaert *et al.* 2005; Blommaert 2007). This does not, however, mean that there is some free market in multilingualism, far from it. Particular languages, language varieties and indeed opportunity to use any talk at all are still regulated by overt and covert institutional practices and ideologies. 'In the workplace power is exercised precisely in those areas where language is most intense' (McCall 2003: 249).

Three examples illustrate some of these issues arising from the new work order and mobility from a critical perspective. The first one is based on the multilingual practices of a Belgian health clinic (Collins and Slembrouck 2006). It describes how local institutional economies adjust to a multilingual patient population. The linguistic ideologies of the institution permeate the decisions about how to respond to the 'language problem'. The preferred solution was to produce a multilingual consultation manual. However, after initial enthusiasm, it was found to be too unwieldy for situated communication. Collins and Slembrouck argue that this literacy solution had a strong institutional rationale behind it. A written text was thought to better regulate and control the consultation and eliminate the institutional unease felt about translation and, by transference, about the people who were the interpreters and translators. It was also a tangible product to show how the organisation had responded to multilingualism. So linguistic and institutional ideologies dominated over local, interactional solutions because alternatives such as more interpreters and more trust in them would invest linguistic minorities with relative power, status and competence.

The second example discusses the use of bilingual call workers in French Ontario. This is part of a growing literature that suggests there is a persistent gap between the official rhetoric of institutions and the policies on the ground in relation to multilingualism, and that linguistic ideology underpins both of them, either explicitly or implicitly. The official rhetoric that multilingualism is an asset was not played out in the local practices of the call centres. French bilingual speakers were excluded from the better paid bilingual jobs because of the commodification, standardisation, and codification of the dominant language, French (Budach *et al.* 2003). So the effect of globalisation in the new international call centres has local, exclusionary repercussions, even for bilingual and multilingual speakers, and shows that there is a linguistic market place (Bourdieu 1991; McCall 2003) which determines what counts as linguistic capital, what standards of linguistic acceptability are set and who is excluded by these linguistic and institutional ideologies.

The third and more extended example illustrates both some of the newer themes in institutional studies and those from the earlier studies. This example is from a series of studies on job interviews from both the English-speaking world and from Germany, the Netherlands and Scandinavia and draws, specifically, on two British studies on selection interviews for low-paid and junior management posts. Most of this research takes a critical stance, influenced by Gumperz's position that there is a communicative dimension to discrimination (Gumperz 1982a, 1982b, 1992) in which language and socio-cultural knowledge interact to produce and reproduce inequality.

The British research shows that it is not ethnicity per se that disadvantages minority ethnic groups in job interviews but a lack of socialisation into the norms and assumptions of this activity, since it is candidates who were born overseas, whatever their linguistic background, that fare less well (Roberts and Sarangi 1999; Roberts and Campbell 2005; Campbell and Roberts 2007). We argue that there is a 'linguistic penalty' experienced by this group. This penalty is faced by anyone who has not developed the 'linguistic capital' of the particular institutional sub-field of the job interview (Bourdieu 1991). The discourses required and the ability to move between and blend them into a convincing synthetic whole, interactionally construct the ideal candidate. The fact that this 'linguistic capital' is taken for granted by employers as a matter of individual competence or merely a question of adequate preparation masks its power in reproducing structural inequalities. Failed candidates 'just don't have the skills'.

In Britain, North America and other parts of the west, interviews are now routinely constructed around a competency framework that includes competencies such as team working, communications, customer focus, adaptability and flexibility. These reflect the discourses of the 'new work order' (Gee *et al.* 1996) discussed above. When there is no shared 'socially constructed knowledge of what the interview is about' (Gumperz 1992: 303), candidates cannot cue into the special inferences required to understand a competency question such as the following: 'right, what would you tell me is the advantage of a repetitive job?' So, despite attempts to make interviews culturally and ideologically neutral, current workplace ideologies leak into the interview at all points.

The interview also contains other inherent contradictions in its presentation as an objective sorting process (Linell and Thunquist 2003) since as a social encounter, it is shot through with subjectivities. Issues of personality, social class or ethnicity remain 'unmentionables' and are only conveyed implicitly (Komter 1991; Birkner 2004: 298), and yet personal liking and co-membership (Erickson and Schultz 1982) are at the hidden heart of decision-making.

The sequential organisation of the interview illustrates its fundamentally asymmetrical character and the role of the interviewer in the final decision-making. Candidates are routinely blamed for what is a joint production (Campbell and Roberts 2007). The interview is controlled almost entirely by the interviewers who govern the interactional norms, allocation of turns and speaking roles (Komter 1991; Birkner 2004). Unlike the evidence from earlier studies, gatekeepers are now drawn from minority backgrounds as well as from the white majority. The institution's response to more diverse institutional representatives is to require a script-like interaction in which set questions are asked and in which only certain answers are allowable and institutionally processable. Ironically, such script-like performances from gatekeepers produce an even more damaging linguistic penalty for those who lack the linguistic capital of the job interview (Roberts and Campbell 2005). So, the interview is not only a site for individual selection and the reproduction of inequality, it is also a site for the production and maintenance of institutional and social order. This order includes the defence of itself as an institution, and part of this defence is to present a public face of equal opportunity (Auer and Kern 2000; Makitalo and Saljo 2002).

The relationship between institutional discourse, globalisation, new technology and migration on a large scale has only just begun to be explored. There are still relatively few studies that examine the impact of the new work order on talk and text in institutions or the effect on social relations of working across distances in globalised organisations (Gunnarsson 2009). The work in ethnomethodology and conversation analysis on human-computer interaction has led to an increasing interest in the role of multimodality in workplace discourse (Hindmarsh *et al.* 2006, Heath and vom Lehn 2008). However, very little of the analysis of these changes to institutional and professional life has been framed by the profound change created by the global flows of people to wealthy countries (but see some exceptions, above). Future studies are likely to focus on how multilingualism interacts with other institutional changes. In particular, research is needed on how multilingualism and lingua franca regimes operate in specific organisations and whether new linguistic inequalities are produced. Within institutions, more research is needed on the impact of institutional and linguistic ideologies as exclusionary forces and, more widely, how the discourses that hold institutions together will manage the tension between being fair and accessible to all while maintaining their character as representative of the nation state in which they are established.

Summary

Institutional discourse is realised both in the objective, regulatory and accounting practices of any organisation or group of people organised through relations of power, and in the wider ideologies, means of classification and representation which create the 'ruling apparatus'. Studies of institutional life show how the depersonalised and distant discourse of the institution interacts with professional discourses to produce asymmetrical, goal-oriented and often exclusionary encounters where one version of reality prevails. Recent studies have begun to show the complex relationship between the new work order of globalised work practices, new technologies and the increasing mobility of people across the world. Despite the transformations resulting from the global market and the management of information, institutional practices and discourses still produce inequality.

Related topics

critical discourse analysis; linguistic ethnography

Further reading

Drew, P. and Heritage, J. (1992) *Talk at Work: Interaction in Institutional Settings*, Cambridge: Cambridge University Press. (Drawing very substantitally on conversation analysis, this edited collection examines some of the theoretical issues in institutional talk and analyses talk in a range of settings including health, the media and legal and workplace encounters.)

Mayr, A. (2008) *Language and Power: An Introduction to Institutional Discourse*, London: Continuum. (This takes a critical perspective on institutional discourse and analyses contexts which include prisons, the military, academia and the media.)

Sarangi, S. and Roberts, C. (eds) (1999) *Talk, Work and Institutional Order: Discourse in Medical, Mediation and Management Settings*, Berlin: Mouton de Gruyter. (An interdisciplinary approach to health, mediation and management settings is used to discuss the relationship between interactional and institutional orders.)

Thornborrow, J. (2002) *Power Talk: Language and Interaction in Institutional Discourse*, London: Longman. (Discourse, power and ideology are examined in several institutional settings including police and media interviews and the classroom.)

Wodak, R. (1996) *Disorders of Discourse*, London: Longman. (Using critical discourse analysis, this book looks at the barriers to communication in the coutroom, the school and the outpatient clinic.)

References

Agar, M. (1985) 'Institutional discourse', *Text* 5(3): 147–68.

Atkinson, M. and Drew, P. (1979) *Order in Court: The Organization of Verbal Interaction in Judicial Setting*, Cambridge: Cambridge University Press.

Atkinson, P. (1995) *Medical Talk and Medical Work: The Liturgy of the Clinic*, London: Sage.

Auer, P. and Kern, F. (2000) 'Three ways of analysing communication between East and West Germans as intercultural communication', in A. Di Luzio, S. Günthner and F. Orletti (eds) *Culture in Communication: Analysis of Intercultural Situations*, Amsterdam: John Benjamins.

Bauman, Z. (1992) *Intimations of Post-Modernity*, London: Routledge.

Berger, P. and Luckmann, T. (1967) *The Social Construction of Reality: A Treatise in the Sociology of Knowledge*, New York: Anchor Books.

Berk-Seligson, S. (2002) *The Bilingual Courtroom: Court Interpreters in the Judicial Process*, 2nd edn, Chicago: University of Chicago Press.

Birkner, K. (2004) 'Hegemonic struggles or transfer of knowledge? East and West Germans in job interviews', *Journal of Language and Politics* 3(2): 293–322.

Blommaert, J. (2007) 'Sociolinguistics and discourse analysis: orders of indexicality and polycentricity', *Journal of Multicultural Discourses* 2: 115–30.

Blommaert, J., Collins, J. and Slembrouck, S. (2005) 'Polycentricity and interactional regimes in "global neighborhoods"', *Ethnography* 6(2): 205–35.

Boden, D. (1994) *The Business of Talk: Organisations in Action*, Cambridge: Polity Press.

Bourdieu, P. (1991) *Language and Symbolic Power*, J. Thompson (ed.), G. Raymond and M. Adamson (trans.), Cambridge, MA: Harvard University Press.

Budach, G., Roy, S. and Heller, M. (2003) 'Community and commodity in French Ontario', *Language and Society* 32: 603–27.

Caldas-Coulthard, C. and Coulthard, M. (1996) *Texts and Practices: Readings in Critical Discourse Analysis*, London: Routledge.

Cameron, D. (2000) *Good to Talk? Living and Working in a Communication Culture*, London: Sage.

Campbell, S. and Roberts, C. (2007) 'Migration, ethnicity and competing discourses in the job interview: synthesising the institutional and personal', *Discourse and Society* 18(3): 243–71.

Cicourel, A. (1968) *The Social Organisation of Juvenile Justice*, New York: Wiley.

——(1981) 'Notes on the integration of micro- and macro-levels of analysis', in K. Knorr-Cetina and A. Cicourel (eds) *Advances in Social Theory and Methodology*, London: Routledge.

——(1992) 'The interpenetration of communicative contexts: examples from medical encounters', in A. Duranti and C. Goodwin (eds) *Rethinking Context: Language as an Interactive Phenomenon*, Cambridge: Cambridge University Press, pp. 291–310.

Collins, J. (1987) 'Conversation and knowledge in bureaucratic settings', *Discourse Processes* 10: 303–19.

Collins, J. and Slembrouck, S. (2006) '"You don't know what they translate": language contact, institutional procedure and literary practice in a neighbourhood health clinic in urban Flanders', *Journal of Linguistic Anthropology* 16(2): 249–68.

Cook-Gumperz, J. and Messerman, L. (1999) 'Local identities and institutional practices: constructing the record of professional collaboration', in S. Sarangi and C. Roberts (eds) *Talk, Work and Institutional Order: Discourse in Medical, Mediation and Management Settings*, Berlin: Mouton de Gruyter.

Di Luzio, A., Günthner, S. and Orletti, F. (eds) (2000) *Culture in Communication: Analysis of Intercultural Situations*, Amsterdam: John Benjamins.

Douglas, M. (1986) *How Institutions Think*, Syracuse, NY: Syracuse University Press.

Drew, P. and Heritage, J. (eds) (1992) *Talk at Work: Interaction in Institutional Settings*, Cambridge: Cambridge University Press.

Eades, D. (2008) *Courtroom Talk and Neo-colonial Control*, Berlin: Mouton de Gruyter.

Erickson, F. and Schultz, J. (1982) *The Counsellor as Gatekeeper: Social Interaction in Interviews*, New York: Academic Press.

Fairclough, N. (1992) *Discourse and Social Change*, Cambridge: Polity Press.

——(1993) 'Critical discourse analysis and the marketisation of public discourse: the universities', *Discourse and Society* 4: 133–68.

——(1995) *Media Discourse*, London: Arnold.

Farrell, L. (2001) 'The "new word order": workplace education and the textual practice of globalisation', *Pedagogy, Culture and Society* 9(1): 57–74.

Fisher, S. and Todd, A. (eds) 1983 *The Social Organization of Doctor-Patient Communication*, Washington, DC: Center for Applied Linguistics.

Foucault, M. (1981) 'The order of discourse', in R. Young (ed.) *Untying the Text*, London: Routledge/Kegan Paul.

Frankel, R. (1984) 'From sentence to sequence: understanding the medical encounter through micro-interactional analysis', *Discourse Processes* 7: 135–70.

Garfinkel, H. (1967) *Studies in Ethnomethodology*, Englewood Cliffs, NJ: Prentice Hall.

Gee, J. P., Hull, G. and Lankshear, C. (1996) *The New Work Order: Behind the Language of the New Capitalism*, St Leonards, NSW, Australia: Allen and Unwin.

Gill, V. and Maynard, D. (2006) 'Explaining illness: patients' proposals and physicians' responses', in J. Heritage and D. Maynard (eds) *Communication in Medical Care: Interaction between Primary Medical Care and Patients*, Cambridge: Cambridge University Press.

Goffman, E. (1959) *The Presentation of Self in Everyday Life*, New York: Doubleday.

——(1961) *Asylums: Essays on the Social Situation of Mental Patients and Other Inmates*, New York: Doubleday Anchor.

——(1981) *Forms of Talk*, Oxford: Blackwell.

Goldstein, T. (1997) *Two Languages at Work: Bilingual Life on the Production Floor*, Berlin: Mouton de Gruyter.

Goodwin, C. (1995) 'Seeing in depth', *Social Studies of Science* 25: 237–74.

Grant, D. and Iedema, R. (2005) 'Discourse analysis and the study of organisations', *Text* 25(1): 37–66.

Greatbatch, D., Luff, P., Heath, C. and Campion, P. (1993) 'Interpersonal communication and the human-computer interaction', *Interacting with Computers* 5(12): 193–216.

Gumperz, J. J. (1982a) *Discourse Strategies*, Cambridge: Cambridge University Press.

——(ed.) (1982b) *Language and Social Identity*, Cambridge: Cambridge University Press.

——(1992) 'Interviewing in intercultural situations', in P. Drew and J. Heritage (eds) *Talk at Work: Interaction in Social Settings*, Cambridge: Cambridge University Press.

——(1999) 'On interactional sociolinguistic method', in S. Sarangi and C. Roberts (eds) *Talk, Work and Institutional Order: Discourse in Medical, Mediation and Management Settings*, Berlin: Mouton de Gruyter.

Gunnarsson, B. (2009) *Professional Discourse*, London: Continuum.

Habermas, J. (1979) *Communication and the Evolution of Society*, T. McCarthy (trans.), London: Heinemann.

Hall, C. (1997) *Social Work as Narrative*, Basingstoke: Avebury.

Heath, C. (1981) 'The opening sequence in doctor–patient interactions', in P. Atkinson and C. Heath (eds) *Medical Work: Realities and Routines*, Aldershot: Gower.

Heath, C. and vom Lehn, D. (2008) 'Construing interactivity: enhancing engagement with new technologies in science centres and museums', *Social Studies of Science* 38: 63–96.

Heller, M. (2002) 'Globalization and the commodification of bilingualism in Canada', in D. Block and D. Cameron (eds) *Globalization and Language Teaching*, London: Routledge.

——(2006) *Linguistic Advances and Modernity*, London: Continuum.

——(2010) 'Language as a resource in the globalized new economy', in N. Coupland (ed.) *Handbook of Language and Globalization*, Oxford: Blackwell, pp. 349–65.

Heritage, J. and Maynard, D. (eds) (2006) *Communication in Medical Care: Interaction between Primary Medical Care and Patients*, Cambridge: Cambridge University Press.

Heritage, J. and Sefi, S. (1992) 'Dilemmas of advice: aspects of the delivery and reception of advice in interactions between health visitors and first-time mothers', in P. Drew and J. Heritage (eds) *Talk at Work: Interaction in Social Settings*, Cambridge: Cambridge University Press.

Heydon, G. (2005) *The Language of Police Interviewing: A Critical Analysis*, Basingstoke: Palgrave Macmillan.

Hindmarsh, J., Heath, C. and Fraser, M. (2006). '(Im)materiality, virtual reality and interaction: grounding the "virtual" in studies of technology in action', *Sociological Review* 54(4): 795–817.

Hull, G. (ed.) (1997) *Changing Work, Changing Workers: Critical Perspectives on Language, Literacy and Skills*, Albany, NY: State University of New York Press.

Iedema, R. (2003) *Discourses of Post-Bureaucratic Organization*, Amsterdam: John Benjamins.

Iedema, R. and Scheeres, H. (2003) 'From doing to talking work: renegotiating knowing, doing and talking', *Applied Linguistics* 24: 316–37.

Iedema, R. and Wodak, R. (1999) 'Organisational discourses and practices', *Discourse and Society* 10(1): 5–20.

Jewitt, C. (ed.) (2009) *Routledge Handbook of Multimodal Analysis*, London: Routledge.

Kleifgen, J. (2001) 'Assembling talk: social alignments in the workplace', *Research on Language and Social Interaction* 34(3): 279–308.

Komter, M. (1991) *Conflict and Co-operation in Job Interviews*, Amsterdam: John Benjamins.

Lemke, J. (2002) 'Travels in hypermodality', *Visual Communication* 3: 299–325.

Levinson, S. (1979) 'Activity types and language', *Linguistics* 17(5): 356–99.

Linell, P. and Thunquist, D. (2003) 'Moving in and out of framings: activity contexts in talks with young unemployed people within a training project', *Journal of Pragmatics* 35: 409–34.

McCall, C. (2003) 'Language dynamics in the bi- and multilingual workplace', in R. Bayley and S. Schecter (eds) *Language Socialization in Bilingual and Multilingual Societies*, Clevedon: Multilingual Matters.

Makitalo, A. and Saljo, R. (2002) 'Talk in institutional context and institutional context in talk: categories and situational practices', *Text* 22: 57–82.

Maryns, K. (2006) *The Asylum Speaker: Language in the Belgian Asylum Procedure*, Manchester: St Jerome Publishing.

Mautner, G. (2005) 'The entrepreneurial university: a discursive profile of a higher education buzzword', *Critical Discourse Studies* 2(2): 95–120.

Mayr, A. (2004) *Prison Discourse: Language as a Means of Control and Resistance*, Basingstoke: Palgrave Macmillan.

——(2008) *Language and Power: An Introduction to Insitutional Discourse*, London: Continuum.

Mehan, H. (1979) *Learning Lessons: Social Organization in the Classroom*, Cambridge, MA: Harvard University Press.

——(1993) 'Beneath the skin and the between the ears: a case study in the politics of representation', in S. Chaiklin and J. Lave (eds) *Understanding Practice*, Cambridge: Cambridge University Press.

Mishler, E. (1984) *The Discourse of Medicine: The Dialectics of Medical Interviews*, Norwood, NJ: Ablex.

Mumby, D. and Clair, R. (1997) 'Organizational discourse', in T. A. van Dijk (ed.) *Discourse Studies*, vol. 2: *Discourse as Social Interaction*, London: Sage.

Rampton, B. (2006) *Language in Late Modernity: Interaction in an Urban School*, Cambridge: Cambridge University Press.

Rampton, B., Maybin, J. and Tusting, K. (eds) (2007) 'Linguistic ethnography', special issue, *Journal of Sociolinguistics* 11(3): 575–716.

Richardson, J. (2007) *Analysing Newspapers: An Approach from CDA*, Basingstoke: Palgrave Macmillan.

Roberts, C. and Campbell, S. (2005) 'Fitting stories into boxes: rhetorical and textual constraints on candidate's performances in British job interviews', *Journal of Applied Linguistics* 2(1): 45–73.

Roberts, C. and Sarangi, S. (1999) 'Hybridity in gatekeeping discourse: issues of practical relevance for the researcher', in S. Sarangi and C. Roberts (eds) *Talk, Work and Institutional Order: Discourse in Medical, Mediation and Management Settings*, Berlin: Mouton de Gruyter.

Rock, F. (2007) *Communicating Rights: The Language of Arrest and Detention*, Basingstoke: Palgrave Macmillan.

Sarangi, S. and Roberts, C. (1999) 'The dynamics of interactional and institutional orders', in S. Sarangi and C. Roberts (eds) *Talk, Work and Institutional Order: Discourse in Medical, Mediation and Management Settings*, Berlin: Mouton de Gruyter.

Sarangi, S. and Roberts, C. (eds) (1999) *Talk, Work and Institutional Order: Discourse in Medical, Mediation and Management Settings*, Berlin: Mouton de Gruyter.

Sarangi, S. and Slembrouck, S. (1996) *Language, Bureaucracy and Social Control*, London: Longman.

Silverman, D. (1999) 'Warriors or collaborators: reworking methodological controversies in the study of institutional interaction' in S. Sarangi and C. Roberts (eds) *Talk, Work and Institutional Order: Discourse in Medical, Mediation and Management Settings*, Berlin: Mouton de Gruyter.

Smith, D. (1987) *The Everyday World as Problematic: A Feminist Sociology*, Boston: Northeastern University Press.

Suchman, L. (1992) 'Technologies of accountability: of lizards and airplanes', in G. Button (ed.) *Technology in Working Order: Studies of Work Interaction and Technology*, London: Routledge.

Thornborrow, J. (2002) *Power Talk: Language and Interaction in Institutional Discourse*, London: Longman.

Trinch, S. (2003) *Latinas' Narratives of Domestic Abuse: Discrepant Versions of Violence*, Amsterdam: John Benjamins.

Vertovec, S. (2007) 'Superdiversity and its implications', *Ethnic and Racial Studies* 30(6): 1024–54.

Weber, M. (1947) *The Theory of Social and Economic Organization*, M. Henderson and T. Parsons (trans.), Glencoe, IL: Free Press.

West, C. (1984) *Routine Complications: Troubles in Talk between Doctors and Patients*, Bloomington: Indiana University Press.

Wodak, R. (1996) *Disorders of Discourse*, London: Longman.

Zimmerman, D. (1992) 'The interactional organisation of calls for emergency assistance', in P. Drew and J. Heritage (eds) *Talk at Work: Interaction in Social Settings*, Cambridge: Cambridge University Press.

7

Medical communication

Sarah Collins, Sarah Peters and Ian Watt

Historical background

The main arena for medical communication can be most comprehensively viewed in terms of the doctor-patient relationship. The relationship between the patient and the doctor provides the foundations for establishing trust, rapport and understanding, explaining diagnoses, discussing prognoses, and negotiating treatment. The ways the doctor and patient use language to convey their perspectives determine how the patient's problem is understood, as well as shaping the relationship, which can have a therapeutic value in its own right.

Although there are earlier references to the nature and evolution of the relationship between patient and doctor, the 1950s saw the start of a growing body of cross-disciplinary work to develop theoretical underpinnings of the patient-professional relationship, to produce insights into uses of language in the healthcare consultation, and to engage professionals and the public in debates to promote 'good' consulting behaviours and to involve patients and enable their voices to be heard. Several strands of work developed in parallel: the therapeutic nature of the doctor-patient relationship (Balint 1957); consultation activities and doctors' consulting behaviours (Byrne and Long 1976); the concept of biopsychosocial medicine (Engel 1977); ethnographic observations of healthcare settings (e.g. Sudnow 1967).

Balint's (1957) work introduced the psychosocial element into understanding patients' problems. Drawing on psychotherapeutic principles, Balint turned doctors' attention to how listening to the patient and treating the patient's language as relevant, diagnostically and therapeutically, can significantly enhance medical practice.

Byrne and Long (1976) conducted a study of the primary care consultation, based on audio recordings of over 2,000 consultations. Their research was the first to detail the structure and delivery of the healthcare consultation. They identified six consultation phases: establishing a relationship; discovering the reason for a patient's attendance; conducting a verbal and/or physical examination; evaluating the patient's condition; detailing treatment or further investigation; and closing. Byrne and Long's analyses focused on doctors' statements and practices, and treated doctors' actions as causal. They were thus able to appraise the effectiveness of individual consultations, based on descriptions of how language is used and deployed by doctors. They observed, for example, that dysfunctional consultations tended to have less silence. They also found that the fourth phase of the consultation (evaluating the patient's condition) was accorded little attention by most doctors, who tended to move from examining the patient to detailing treatment 'with hardly a word to the patient en route' (Byrne and Long 1976: 50). Through their examination of doctors' language use, they identified a spectrum of consulting styles, from doctor-centred to patient-centred.

Sudnow (1967) conducted an ethnographic study of hospital practices in death and dying, in two different hospitals. His observations of the words and actions of hospital staff showed how death and dying is differently pronounced for patients according to individual and socio-demographic characteristics, and how a hospital's organisation impacted on forms of communication between staff, patients and their families. For example, Sudnow described how nurses approached the relative of a dying patient in such a way as to prepare them for what lay ahead and for meeting with the doctor, before any words were uttered. He recorded the words staff used to report a death to each other, and how their reports were differently phrased and pitched for relatives of the deceased. His identification of differential applications of terms such as 'dead on arrival', according to an individual's social characteristics, highlighted social inequalities in death and dying.

Understanding communication in healthcare consultations has evolved through a combination of disciplinary approaches and in response to particular societal expectations (e.g. what a patient wants from their doctor). Few of these early studies fall within the field of linguistics per se, but they all draw on language and communication to explain the complex processes housed within the doctor-patient relationship.

Main current issues

Since the 1980s, medical communication has developed as a field of research in its own right, as documented in numerous reviews (e.g. Ong *et al.* 1995; Stewart *et al.* 2003). This research has explored a range of communication features and dimensions to highlight their role in the delivery and uptake of healthcare. The predominant focus has been on the doctor-patient consultation in general practice.

Language and communication in the general practice consultation

Studies of the general practice consultation include empirical research into the details of language use and interaction and explorations of patients' and doctors' perceptions and experiences of their communication with one another, as well as conceptual studies of patient-centredness or shared decision-making.

Research employing conversation analysis has focused on particular consultation activities or phases. To give two examples, Heritage and Stivers (1999) identified features of doctors' 'on-line commentaries' during physical examinations. These can provide reassurance, justify a forthcoming diagnostic evaluation, and shape the patient's expectations towards a 'no-problem' explanation (i.e. one which does not require treatment or is not a particular cause for concern). Stivers (2005) described different formats in which doctors present treatment recommendations to patients, and showed that doctors who provide a specific, positive recommendation followed by a negative one are most likely to obtain patient acceptance when recommending a non-antibiotic treatment.

Discourse analytic studies of communication in consultations have addressed themes such as the place of the patient's narrative, the ways in which decisions are managed and negotiated, and cultural inferences and interpretations. Studies adopting a narrative-based approach

(Greenhalgh and Hurwitz 2004) have attended to how symptomatic information provided by a patient is contextualised through the 'story' they tell in the consultation. In hearing patients' stories, it is argued, doctors begin the cognitive processes of prediction, evaluation, planning and explanation, through the patient's words and the connections they make between symptoms, events and illness episodes. In research on decision-making, Elwyn *et al.* (1999) identified that consultations containing conflict about treatment for upper respiratory tract infection exhibited none of the ideological competencies of 'shared decision-making'. The authors argued that to address differences in understanding where the doctor and patient hold opposing views, further detailed empirical research, as well as revision of concepts of shared decision-making, are required. Roberts *et al.* (2005) explored how patients with limited English and culturally different communication styles consulted with doctors. Their analyses identified four categories of 'talk' contributing to misunderstandings: pronunciation and word stress; intonation and speech delivery; grammar, vocabulary and lack of contextual information; and style of presentation. In particular, they noted that the patient's style of self-presentation could lead to misunderstandings.

While much of the research on communication in the general practice consultation centres on the words used and how they are said, some specifically considers the relationship between verbal and non-verbal elements. For example, Ruusuvuori (2001) discriminated between 'patient-embodied' actions directed to the patient, and 'patient-inscribed' actions that draw on other information sources such as case notes, showing how doctors' movements away from or towards the patient can present problems for patients in determining whether the doctor is listening and can disrupt the flow of their talk. In paediatric primary care consultations, gaze direction has been noted to be one communication practice through which doctors' questions target either the child or the parent as respondent (Stivers 2001).

Other studies have employed observational, survey, interview and focus group data. These have explored patients' health and illness beliefs and doctors' responses to these (e.g. Britten *et al.* 2000), patients' views of patient-centredness (e.g. Little *et al.* 2001), doctors' views of shared decision-making (e.g. Elwyn *et al.* 2000) and concepts such as trust and empathy (Wright *et al.* 2004). Britten *et al.*'s (2000) study employed a combination of audio-recorded consultations and semi-structured interviews with patients and doctors to explore misunderstandings in prescribing. The fourteen categories of misunderstanding identified were all associated with a lack of patient participation in the consultation, and all carried potential or actual adverse outcomes, such as the patient deciding not to take a prescribed medicine. Britten *et al.* found that patients' preferences and expectations about medicines were rarely voiced in the consultations and doctors were unaware of the relevance of these for successful prescribing. Little *et al.*'s (2001) survey of patient-centredness demonstrated that patients valued communication and partnership most highly in consultations. Elwyn *et al.*'s (2000) exploration of doctors' views concerning shared decision-making, through focus groups, revealed doctors' ideological principles and consultation practices that added to existing models (e.g. Towle and Godolphin 1999): for example, participating doctors stressed the importance of portraying options *before* sounding out the patient's wishes for involvement in decision-making. Wright *et al.* (2004) interviewed patients with breast cancer and found that they valued trust in doctors' expertise above the communication skills that doctors are traditionally taught, such as demonstrating empathy. They gauged trust in terms of (among other features) doctors' displays of technical expertise, doctors 'being frank', and doctors who 'answered questions without hesitation'.

This research has been paralleled by conceptual and theoretical work on patient-centredness (Stewart 2001), patient participation (Coulter 2002) and shared decision-making (Towle and

Godolphin 1999). This reflects the shift from a paternalistic view of the patient to one in which the patient brings their expertise and knowledge to the consultation and in which shared decision-making can occur. Research has also identified how and to what extent these ideals are realised in practice. Studies have focused on the patient's role in decision-making, identifying strategies through which patients may get the most out of their consultations (Tuckett *et al.* 1985); on the ways patients interpret measures of their involvement (Entwistle *et al.* 2004); and on the variety of forms of patient participation (Collins *et al.* 2007).

When taken together, findings from these studies afford a view of the healthcare consultation in which different applications of language research combine to provide insights into the details of interaction and language use (word choice, phrasing of treatment options, non-verbal cues) as well as the expressed views and preferences of patients, their interpretations of the care they receive, and doctors' intentions and ideals. These observations of language and how it is employed in healthcare consultations build understanding of how the doctor-patient relationship, as the foundation of good medical practice, is established and maintained.

Extending the view beyond the general practice consultation

Research on the themes indicated above has extended to other types of healthcare consultation. This allows comparative research across different clinical settings and health professionals, to identify their unique and shared communication features. Studies in, for example, hospital settings consultations involving the patient and a carer/family member, nursing, pharmacy, physiotherapy and complementary and alternative medicine illustrate dimensions for further research and for extending our understanding of the healthcare consultation in general. The following are some examples.

Salter *et al.*'s (2007) study of pharmacists' home visits to the elderly revealed how, in that context, pharmacists' advice was generally ill-fitted and met with resistance. In a comparison of decision-making practices of GPs and hospital surgeons, Braddock *et al.* (1999) found that both groups infrequently had complete discussions of treatment decisions with patients. Coupland *et al.* (1994), in their study of doctor-patient communication in a geriatric outpatients' clinic, observed less division between medical and social talk than the literature generally suggests. Boundaries between social and medical topics were negotiated, and doctors frequently continued a social, conversational line, even when patients indicated readiness to move to the medical agenda. Beresford and Sloper (2003) used interviews and group discussions to document influences of chronic illness and parental involvement on adolescents' communication with doctors. They discovered how: the series of questions deployed by doctors to monitor the everyday management of an illness deterred adolescents from participating; talking with parents provided opportunities to rehearse concerns before presenting them to the doctor; through a sustained relationship with their doctor, adolescents could move beyond pretending about adherence to lifestyle or treatment regimens and talk openly about them. In complementary and alternative medicine research, randomised controlled trials have recently been conducted to explore whether the practitioner-patient relationship can enhance the effects of treatment. For example Kaptchuk *et al.*'s (2008) study with three participant groups (one receiving real acupuncture, one receiving sham acupuncture, and one receiving no acupuncture), revealed no therapeutic difference between the 'sham' and real acupuncture groups, suggesting that the process of receiving acupuncture may have its own, beneficial, placebo effect, and highlighting the therapeutic effects of communication and the patient-practitioner relationship.

Such studies indicate dimensions for comparison and further research: the ways doctors engage with patients in conversation as well as formal interaction, blurring distinctions between social and medical talk; how a planned policy intervention, such as pharmacists' home visits to the elderly, may be ill-fitted to certain healthcare contexts or professional roles; ways of isolating therapeutic effects of communication; and features of patient-doctor communication that promote or hinder patients' participation.

Cultural and linguistic diversity

Research exploring cultural and linguistic issues (see Roberts 2007 for a comprehensive discussion) has considered differences in cultural understandings of illness, the influences of multiple languages in a consultation, and how perceptions of race, education and social class shape doctor-patient communication.

In a review of research on culture and somatisation (the process by which psychological distress manifests in physical symptoms), Kirmayer and Young (1998) report that somatisation has been observed across all studied ethnocultural groups and societies, with significant cultural variations even where access to health services is relatively equitable. Patients' reports of bodily symptoms encode cultural models that supply patients with a vocabulary for describing symptoms, as well as a means of explaining them. One cultural difference concerns how distress is expressed. Kirmayer and Young (1998: 424) report that the idiom 'heart distress' among Iranians is a culturally prescribed way of talking about problems related to grief, and: 'Throughout the Middle East, references to the heart are commonly understood not just as potential signs of illness but as natural metaphors for a range of emotions.'

Research on consultations involving more than one language has explored the linguistic challenges that such consultations present, as well as highlighting features of language use that pertain to all healthcare consultations. Studies have shown how interpreters not only convey the meaning of the patient's words, but also how they are centrally involved in negotiating and achieving interactional goals with real consequences for the patient's care: for example the reporting of the patient's symptoms and the process of arriving at a diagnosis can be shaped by what the interpreter says and how they choose to present the patient's problem in medical and lay terms. For example, Davidson (2000) found that in consultations with English-speaking doctors, Spanish-speaking patients were left with concerns that were unaddressed; and Bolden (2000) found that the interpreter was oriented to achieving the goals of history-taking in what they perceived to be the most efficient manner, with the interpreter editing out information and words from the patient which the interpreter considered to be irrelevant. It has also been noted that where the patient and doctor speak different languages, patients have reported less than satisfactory interpersonal care, with or without an interpreter present (e.g. Ngo-Metzger *et al.* 2007). In such consultations, patients are more likely to have their comments ignored (Rivandeneyra *et al.* 2000), and in the absence of an interpreter, discussion of health promotion is limited (Ngo-Metzger *et al.* 2007).

Racial and ethnic disparities in quality of care for those with access to a healthcare system exist in the utilisation of diagnostic procedures and therapeutic interventions. One root cause of such disparity is variations in patients' ability to communicate their symptoms to a doctor who understands their meaning, expectations of care and adherence to lifestyle and medication regimes (van Ryn and Burke 2000). Stivers and Majid's (2007) study of doctors' questioning in consultations about routine childhood illnesses demonstrated a significant effect of parents' race and education on whether physicians select children to answer questions. Black children and Latino children of low-education parents were less likely to be selected to answer questions than their same-aged white peers, irrespective of their education.

Linguistic analysis as a diagnostic resource

A recent advance in applications of language research to medical communication concerns how language used by patients can serve as a diagnostic resource. In psychiatry, doctors depend on patients' language for diagnosis and treatment, but how words actually function in consultations to influence diagnostic reasoning and treatment decisions remains under-researched and is little understood (Fine 2006).

Schwabe et al. (2008) have identified features of patients' language that may be instrumental in differentiating between epileptic (ES) and non-epileptic seizures (NES). Patients with ES provide coherent accounts of individual seizures, relate subjective seizure experiences and use consistent metaphoric conceptualizations. Patients with NES tend not to volunteer subjective seizure symptoms, give accounts of their seizures that are difficult to understand and are inconsistent in their choice of metaphors.

A substantive and growing body of work on the use of language in diagnosis is research on communication disorders and language impairments (see Perkins and Howard, this volume).

The patient's illness experience

Increased emphasis on listening to the patient and understanding their perspective has invited reconsideration of how, through communication in the consultation, patients' perspectives can inform medical understanding: of particular diseases, of the nature of pain and how it may be described, and of connections between different symptoms.

One example is patients whose symptoms are not easily defined or explained according to physical pathology. Medically unexplained symptoms (MUS) not only present a cognitive challenge for the doctor, in making confident use of the label; they also pose a linguistic one, namely, how to explain and negotiate the 'unexplained'. Theoretical understanding of MUS initially led researchers to conceive of these problems as caused by an underlying psychological disorder (Lipowski 1988) or misattribution of psychological distress to physical causes (Kirmayer and Robbins 1991), with resultant interventions focused on addressing the patient's somatisation (e.g. Morriss et al. 2007). Applications of linguistics have led to more fruitful ways to understand MUS. Analyses of consultations have revealed complex interactions and negotiations whereby patients assert authority over their condition (Peters et al. 1998) to shape the consultation and its outcomes, securing referral to specialists (Salmon et al. 1999). A particular tension, played out through language use, has been highlighted, in which both patients and doctors use scientific discourse, but for different reasons: the doctor to maintain their distance and their expert stance, and the patient to engage the doctor (Chew-Graham et al. 2008). Furthermore, analysing patients' perceptions of their symptoms revealed that, rather than having unidimensional causal beliefs, individuals with MUS had a multifaceted understanding of their condition that recognised psychosocial factors (Peters et al. 2009). Patients' own rich illness models contrasted with their perceptions of doctors' more simplistic understanding. This led to patients' mistrust of their doctors, limiting the information they disclosed. Empathic responses to emotional cues appear critical for reassurance and building trust among patients with MUS (Epstein et al. 2007). This suggests that future interventions should focus not on reattribution of patients' understandings, but on developing doctors' awareness and communication responses to patients' needs, through linguistic approaches.

Influences of new technology

The influences of new technology on medical communication in recent years have been manifold: electronic patient records; use of email for consulting; phone-in consultations (such as NHS Direct, the UK's National Health Service telephone helpline) which guide the caller along particular routes according to their reason for calling; templates and aids for decision-making; and on-line communication, for example, for adolescents consulting about sexual health (Harvey *et al.* 2007).

The introduction of the computer into the consultation both hinders and promotes communication between patient and doctor, revealing interesting relations between non-verbal and verbal activity. For example, Hsu *et al.* (2005) observed that doctors' baseline communication skills (verbal and non-verbal) were amplified, positively or negatively, by the introduction of a computer to the consultation. In another study (Margalit *et al.* 2006), time spent gazing at the computer screen was inversely related to clinician engagement in psychosocial questioning and emotional responsiveness, and time spent typing was inversely related to the amount of dialogue between clinician and patient. McGrath *et al.* (2007) found that patients exploited silences created by the doctor's use of electronic patient records to ask questions.

Cultural models, broader discourses and media representations

While research on language and medicine has largely centred on examining the structure and content of the doctor-patient encounter, realms of communication that extend beyond the consultation and the doctor-patient relationship have also been investigated.

One example is Bell's (2009) study of cultural models of chemotherapy expressed in a cancer support group, showing how patients' understandings of chemotherapy diverge from biomedical models of treatment. Iedema's (2007) investigation of the discourse of hospital communication explores the complexities of the healthcare system and shows how health professionals are compelled to reinvent their communication strategies to manage changes in the system and their relationships with each other. Through textual discourse analysis of key policy documents and interviews with policy-makers and stakeholders, Shaw and Greenhalgh (2008) produced a critical assessment of how policy has shifted healthcare research away from independent enterprise towards a strategic resource and 'population laboratory' for large-scale clinical trials.

Research methods

As illustrated by the research referenced above, diverse methods have been employed to study various forms of medical communication. These include conversation analysis (e.g. Heritage and Maynard 2006), discourse analysis (e.g. Roberts *et al.* 2005) and coding schemes (e.g. Roter and Larson 2002); corpus linguistics (e.g. Harvey *et al.* 2007); surveys (e.g. Little *et al.* 2001); semi-structured interviews (e.g. Wright *et al.* 2004); focus groups (e.g. Bell 2009); observation and ethnography (e.g. Sudnow 1967); document analysis (e.g. Shaw and Greenhalgh 2008); and randomised controlled trials (e.g. Heritage *et al.* 2007).

Regardless of the methods employed, researching medical communication presents ethical dilemmas and sensitivities that shape the nature of the data collected as well as how it is analysed. Obtaining consent from prospective participants, positioning recording equipment in a clinic or patient's home, being party to a patient's experience of their illness and treatment: all these bring further insights. During data collection in a cancer drop-in centre, Watts (2008) reported how her position shifted from initiating contact with participants, asking direct questions, and doing the talking, to one in which participants chose the point of contact and topic of discussion, seeking her out to report how they were managing, often during times of crisis. (See Maybin and Tusting, this volume, for an overview of linguistic ethnography.)

Particular methods (or combinations of methods) may be more suited than others, in researching different aspects of medical communication. In using an individual method, Harvey *et al.* (2007: 772) argue that, in the study of adolescent health communication, corpus linguistics is a means of describing a 'distinctive "genre"' of messages about sexual health. 'Comparative keyword analysis', employed by Seale *et al.* (2006) in a study exploring gender differences in how patients talk about their cancer experience, represents a new use of software designed for corpus linguistic analysis, as a way of conducting comparative qualitative analyses of large data sets. One combination that has proved productive is conversation or discourse analysis of a recorded consultation, coupled with interviews exploring the participants' perspectives and/or measurement of consultation outcomes (e.g. Barry *et al.* 2001).

An important distinction concerns the different aims and effects of descriptive, as compared to evaluative, approaches to medical communication research. That is, is the purpose simply to describe what happens, or is the research being conducted with the aim of improving the quality of healthcare? The purpose inevitably shapes the choice of methods and hence the results. For example, in coding consultations, different schemes have been developed: some make assumptions, for example about what is 'good' or 'bad' communication (Hall *et al.* 1987); while others are not based on a particular premise and therefore allow testing of different theories (e.g. Salmon *et al.* 2006). Some, like the Patient Enablement Index (Mercer and Howie 2006) explicitly combine the use of a schema for research with evaluation of doctors' consultation skills.

Some studies highlight how the methods employed can allow unexpected findings and relations between themes to surface. For example, O'Riordan *et al.* (2008), in their study of 'likeable' patients, employed concordance software alongside interviews. Concordance analysis uncovered new themes: for example, the words 'time' and 'years' recurred frequently and revealed the importance of the ongoing nature of general practice for building relationships with patients.

Many studies involve forms of comparison: for example professional versus conversational talk; one disease setting, or professional culture, versus another; or patients' versus doctors' perspectives. Comparative studies have revealed points of difference and similarity that warrant further investigation: for example, distinctive features of doctors', versus nurses', communication with patients highlight the potential complement between their contributions, for multidisciplinary healthcare (e.g. Collins 2005).

Effects of language use and communication on healthcare outcomes

There is increasing recognition of how communication can influence healthcare outcomes. Communication can positively influence adherence to treatment (e.g. Dowell *et al.* 2002). Studies exploring socio-relational factors, such as patients' satisfaction and feelings of ease, show that greater consultation length and continuity of care are positively correlated with patients' satisfaction (Mercer and Howie 2006). In consultations where patients perceived that they found common ground with their doctor in decision-making there were significantly fewer referrals and investigations over the following two months (Stewart *et al.* 1997). Research has also shown how patients' recall and understanding of information may be influenced through communication; for example, Britten *et al.* (2000) noted that doctors could avoid misunderstandings by asking patients directly what they thought about taking medicines. In a randomised controlled trial, Heritage *et al.* (2007) found that, depending on the phrasing doctors employ to elicit patients' concerns, the patient may be more or less likely to mention what is troubling them.

Medical education

Recent developments in medical education have given prominence to the importance of communication training, pre- and post-qualification. This training is modelled on professional guidelines for good medical practice (General Medical Council 2003) that pay close attention to the communication competencies and standards required for maintaining caring relationships with patients. Clinician educators are now expected to bring knowledge of communication and related research, as well as medicine, to their teaching. Increasingly, communication training involves the patient's perspective, conveyed through actors (Spencer and Dales 2006) or patients as real-life informants (Muir 2007).

Medical communication curricula are increasingly informed by research. The content employed across the UK for consultation skills teaching is based on the Calgary-Cambridge framework (Kurtz *et al.* 2005) compiled from research into the consultation. The design of curricula has also been informed by the literature in taking an integrative view of the consultation (Stewart *et al.* 2003): one in which clinical, biomedical tasks are necessarily fused with patients' views and psychosocial aspects. Communication is treated as an integral component, as reflected in teaching communication skills during clinical placements and in examining communication alongside other clinical skills, with real patients.

Medical education is a growing field of research. Linguistic approaches are employed to inform analyses and to define areas for further study. For example, regarding assessment of communication skills, Roberts *et al.* (2003) video-recorded students' consultation performance in clinical exams and analysed these recordings to investigate the details of interaction that lead to students being assessed as 'good' or 'poor' communicators. They were able to show, through reference to a range of constituents, how stronger candidates were 'empathetic' (responding attentively and using joint problem-solving) and weaker candidates were 'retractive' (responding inappropriately and demonstrating insensitivity to patients' understandings). Humphris and Kaney (2001) devised a coding scheme to assess the development of students' communication throughout their training. Students' performance improved over a 17-month period, but their knowledge and understanding at initial assessment did not show the predicted association with subsequent communication skills performance. Analyses of doctors' postgraduate consultation skills assessments (Campion *et al.* 2002) have identified that doctors find 'explanation and planning' particularly challenging and generally under-perform in this area.

Conceptual understanding of medical communication is also being advanced. 'Cultural competency', for example, is taught in medical school curricula, but is difficult to define and is continually being revisited (e.g. Betancourt *et al.* 2003) as a consequence of increasing diversity and change in the ethnic and socio-demographic composition not only of patient populations, but also of doctor populations, in the UK and elsewhere.

Future trajectory and new debates

The application of linguistics to the study of medical communication offers exciting prospects and opportunities for new dialogues between disciplines.

Medical communication is a relatively new field of research, in which linguistic expertise has played a small part. Many areas remain under-researched, such as consultations involving different languages (Shaw and Ahmed 2004). Certain linguistic methods and approaches remain under-used; for example, dialect variation and linguistic accommodation could be employed to study professional cultures and communication practices across clinical settings.

There is much that linguistics can offer medical communication. For example, we can use linguistics to explore how the language we use to describe medical communication creates a particular impression or reality, such as in the term 'patient-centred care'. An understanding of linguistics can help us to challenge assumptions in medical communication practice: for example, does a consultation involving a relative stand in the way of communication with a patient? Or does their presence facilitate the patient's participation, and in what ways?

By the same token, there is much that medical communication can offer linguistics. Medical communication compels researchers to make language-based studies relevant to healthcare professionals' and patients' everyday experience. It is useful to consider, then, whether the ways we apply linguistics to medical communication do actually translate into practice, and what is relevant to professional and patient experience (Roberts and Sarangi 2003). For example, when it is advocated that health professionals 'integrate' and 'weave between' medical and patient perspectives (Stewart *et al.* 2003), how does this translate into the language of the consultation? While medical students are taught skills such as summarising, whether and how doctors use summaries in practice, and to what effect, remains unknown. And while particular phrasings may be suggested by research, Heritage *et al.* (2007), for example, propose that 'something else' in place of 'anything else' is more likely to elicit a patient's concerns in a consultation, 'something else' may be less natural to say, and may only elicit one of several concerns. We need, therefore, to develop means of observing and measuring the effects of such research, as it is applied in medical practice.

The medical consultation and the health professional-patient relationship are likely to come under new forms of scrutiny as systems of healthcare evolve and as research methods develop. Extension of analyses of the consultation into a wider sphere (e.g. nurse consultations; use of the Internet and email; consultations in different languages) not only reflects increasing complexities and degrees of specialisation in healthcare; it also has the potential to illuminate our understanding of medical communication in general.

From the point of view of research methods, there is likely to be continued refinement of existing methods and interfacing with other disciplines (Candlin and Candlin 2003). Comparative and longitudinal research, using combinations of methods, will enable further systematic and detailed exploration. This process may be facilitated by the availability of shared databases of interviews or recorded consultations with patients and health professionals (e.g. Field and Ziebland 2008), although these also bring ethical issues concerning maintenance of personal data and its use by a wider audience. Comparative research needs to accommodate ordinary conversation alongside medical encounters and other forms of professional and institutional communication, so that features of medical communication can be precisely located and comprehensively understood.

Finally, although the doctor-patient relationship is so central to healthcare and so dependent on language, it has been little studied: rather, it has been assumed to play a part and has provided the impetus for studies. New research directions, such as work on emotion in language use (e.g. Ruusuvuori 2007), offer promising insights into the nature of the patient-doctor relationship.

Sarah Collins, Sarah Peters and Ian Watt

Summary

This chapter reviews research concerning language use in medical communication. The doctor-patient relationship has provided the impetus for a broad range of studies investigating different dimensions of medical communication. Conceptual and empirical work has sought to describe the constituents of patient-centred approaches in healthcare delivery, at the level of individual words and actions in consultations, through to patient and health professional perspectives and experiences, and ideological and policy-driven discourses. Medical communication research has employed novel uses of linguistic methods of analysis. These applications of linguistics have led to further understanding of how healthcare is delivered to, and taken up by, patients, and are proving increasingly relevant to healthcare education and practice.

Related topics

clinical linguistics; culture; institutional discourse; linguistic ethnography

Further reading

Balint, M. (1957) *The Doctor, his Patient, and the Illness*, New York: International Universities Press. (This pioneering work focuses attention on the patient as a person in the consultation and on the importance of the patient's language.)

Heritage, J. and Maynard, D. W. (eds) (2006) *Communication in Medical Care: Interaction between Primary Medical Care and Patients*, Cambridge: Cambridge University Press. (This collection of studies in primary care illustrates the potential of applying detailed analyses of language use in interaction to the study of medical communication.)

Kurtz, S., Silverman, J. and Draper, J. (2005) *Teaching and Learning Communication Skills in Medicine*, 2nd edn, Oxford: Radcliffe Medical Press. (Kurtz *et al.* provide a comprehensive review of medical communication research, set within their internationally recognised framework for teaching consultation skills to doctors.)

References

Adolphs, S., Brown, B., Carter, R., Crawford, P. and Sahota, O. (2004) 'Applying corpus linguistics in a health care context', *Journal of Applied Linguistics* 1(1): 44–9.

Balint, M. (1957) *The Doctor, his Patient, and the Illness*, New York: International Universities Press.

Barry, C. A., Stevenson, F. A., Britten, N., Barber, N. and Bradley, C. P. (2001) 'Giving voice to the lifeworld. More effective, more humane care? A qualitative study of doctor-patient communication in general practice', *Social Science and Medicine* 53: 487–505.

Bell, K. (2009) '"If it almost kills you that means it's working!" Cultural models of chemotherapy expressed in a cancer support group', *Social Science and Medicine* 68: 169–76.

Beresford, B. and Sloper, P. (2003) 'Chronically ill adolescents' experiences of communicating with doctors: a qualitative study', *Journal of Adolescent Health* 33(3): 172–9.

Betancourt, J. R., Green, A. R., Carrillo, J. E. and Ananeh-Firempong II, O. (2003) 'Defining cultural competence: a practical framework for addressing racial/ethnic disparities in health and health care', *Public Health Reports* 118: 293–302.

Bolden, G. B. (2000) 'Toward understanding practices of medical interpreting: interpreters' involvement in history taking', *Discourse Studies* 2: 387–419.

Braddock, C. H., Edwards, K. A., Hasenburg, N. M., Laidley, T. L. and Levinson, W. (1999) 'Informed decision-making in outpatient practice: time to get back to basics', *Journal of the American Medical Association* 282(24): 2313–20.

Britten, N., Stevenson, F. A., Barry, C. A., Barber, N. and Bradley, C. P. (2000) 'Misunderstandings in prescribing decisions in general practice: qualitative study', *British Medical Journal* 320: 484–88.

Byrne, P. S. and Long, B. E. L. (1976) *Doctors Talking to Patients: A Study of the Verbal Behaviours of Doctors in the Consultation*, London: HMSO.

Campion, P., Tate, P., Foulkes, J. and Neighbour, R. (2002) 'Patient centredness in the MRCGP video examination: analysis of large cohort', *British Medical Journal* 325: 691–2.

Candlin, C. N. and Candlin, S. (2003) 'Healthcare communication: a problematic site for applied linguistics research', *Annual Review of Applied Linguistics* 23: 134–54.

Chew-Graham, C., Cahill, G., Dowrick, C., Wearden, A., Richardson, V. and Peters, S. (2008) 'Using multiple sources of knowledge to reach clinical understanding of chronic fatigue syndrome', *Annals of Family Medicine* 6(4): 340–8.

Collins, S. (2005) 'Explanations in consultations: the combined effectiveness of doctors' and nurses' communication with patients', *Medical Education* 39: 785–96.

Collins, S., Britten, N., Ruusuvuori, J. and Thompson, A. (2007) *Patient Participation in Health Care Consultations: Qualitative Perspectives*, Maidenhead: Open University Press.

Coulter, A. (2002) *The Autonomous Patient: Ending Paternalism in Medical Care*, London: The Stationery Office and Nuffield Trust.

Coupland, J., Robinson, J. D. and Coupland, N. (1994) 'Frame negotiation in doctor-elderly patient consultations', *Discourse and Society* 5(1): 89–124.

Davidson, B. (2000) 'The interpreter as institutional gatekeeper: the social-linguistic role of interpreters in Spanish-English medical discourse', *Journal of Sociolinguistics* 4(3): 379–405.

Dowell, J., Jones, A. and Snadden, D. (2002) 'Exploring medication use to seek concordance with "non-adherent" patients: a qualitative study', *British Journal of General Practice* 52: 24–32.

Elwyn, G., Edwards, A., Kinnersley, P. and Grol, R. (2000) 'Shared decision making and the concept of equipoise: the competences of involving patients in healthcare choices', *British Journal of General Practice* 50: 892–7.

Elwyn, G., Gwyn, R., Edwards, A. and Grol, R. (1999) 'Is "shared decision-making" feasible in consultations for upper respiratory tract infections? Assessing the influence of antibiotic expectations using discourse analysis', *Health Expectations* 2: 105–17.

Engel, G. L. (1977) 'The need for a new medical model: a challenge for biomedicine', *Science* 196: 129–36.

Entwistle, V., Watt, I., Gilhooly, K., Bugge, C., Haites, N. and Walker, A. (2004) 'Assessing patients' participation and quality of decision making: insights from a study of routine practice in diverse settings', *Patient Education and Counselling* 55: 105–13.

Epstein, R. M., Hadee, T., Carroll, J., Meldrum, S. C., Lardner, L. J. and Shields, C. G. (2007) '"Could this be something serious?": reassurance, uncertainty and empathy in response to patients' expressions of worry', *Journal of General Internal Medicine* 22(12): 1731–9.

Field, K. and Ziebland, S. (2008) '"Beyond the textbook": a preliminary survey of the uses made of the DIPEx Website (www.dipex.org) in healthcare education'. Available at: www.healthtalkonline.org/Teaching AndLearning (accessed 21 May 2009).

Fine, J. (2006) *Language in Psychiatry: A Handbook of Clinical Practice*, London: Equinox Publishing.

General Medical Council (2003) *Tomorrow's Doctors*, London: HMSO.

Greenhalgh, T. and Hurwitz, B. (eds) (2004) *Narrative Research in Health and Illness*, London: BMJ Books.

Hall, J., Roter, D. and Katz, N. (1987) 'Task versus socio-emotional behaviours in physicians', *Medical Care* 25: 399–412.

Harvey, K. J., Brown, B., Crawford, P., Macfarlane, A. and McPherson, A. (2007) '"Am I normal?" Teenagers, sexual health and the Internet', *Social Science and Medicine* 65: 771–81.

Heritage, J. and Maynard, D. W. (eds) (2006) *Communication in Medical Care: Interaction between Primary Medical Care and Patients*, Cambridge: Cambridge University Press.

Heritage, J. and Stivers, T. (1999) 'Online commentary in acute medical visits: a method of shaping patient expectations', *Social Science and Medicine* 49: 1501–17.

Heritage, J., Robinson, J., Elliott, M., Beckett, M. and Wilkes, M. (2007) 'Reducing patients' unmet concerns in primary care: the difference one word can make', *Journal of General Internal Medicine* 22(10): 1429–33.

Hsu, J., Huang, J., Fung, V., Robertson, N., Jimison, H. and Frankel, R. (2005) 'Health information technology and physician-patient interactions: impact of computers on communication during outpatient primary care visits', *Journal of the American Medical Informatics Association* 12(4): 474–80.

Humphris, G. M. and Kaney, S. (2001) 'Assessing the development of communication skills in undergraduate medical students', *Medical Education* 35: 225–31.

Iedema, R. (2007) *The Discourse of Hospital Communication: Tracing Complexities in Contemporary Health Organisations*, Basingstoke: Palgrave Macmillan.

Kaptchuk, T. J., Kelley, J. M., Conboy, L. A., Davis, R. B., Kerr, C. E., Jacobson, E. E. *et al.* (2008) 'Components of placebo effect: randomised controlled trial in patients with irritable bowel syndrome', *British Medical Journal* (online) 336(7651), doi: 0.1136/bmj.39524.439618.25.

Kirmayer, L. J. and Robbins, J. M. (1991) 'Three forms of somatization in primary care-prevalence, co-occurrence, and sociodemographic characteristics', *Journal of Nervous and Mental Disease* 179(11): 647–55.

Kirmayer, L. J. and Young, A. (1998) 'Culture and somatisation: clinical, epidemiological, and ethnographic perspectives', *Psychosomatic Medicine* 60: 420–30.

Kurtz, S., Silverman, J. and Draper, J. (2005) *Teaching and Learning Communication Skills in Medicine*, 2nd edn, Oxford: Radcliffe Medical Press.

Little, P., Everitt, H., Williamson, I., Warner, G., Moore, M., Gould, C. *et al.* (2001) 'Preferences of patients for patient centred approach to consultation in primary care: observational study', *British Medical Journal* 322: 1–7.

Lipowski, Z. J. (1988) 'Somatisation: the concept and its clinical application', *American Journal of Psychiatry* 145: 1358–68.

McGrath, J. M., Arar, N. H. and Pugh, J. A. (2007) 'The influence of electronic medical record usage on nonverbal communication in the medical interview', *Health Informatics Journal* 13(2): 105–18.

Margalit, R. S., Roter, D., Dunevant, M. A., Larson, S. and Reis, S. (2006) 'Electronic medical record use and physician-patient communication: an observational study of Israeli primary care encounters', *Patient Education and Counselling* 61(1): 134–41.

Mercer, S. W. and Howie, J. G. (2006) 'CQI-2 – a new measure of holistic interpersonal care in primary care consultations', *British Journal of General Practice* 56(525): 262–8.

Morriss, R., Dowrick, C., Salmon, P., Peters, S., Dunn, G., Rogers, A. *et al.* (2007) 'Exploratory randomised controlled trial of training practices and general practitioners in reattribution to manage patients with medically unexplained symptoms', *British Journal of Psychiatry* 191: 536–42.

Muir, F. (2007) 'Placing the patient at the core of teaching', *Medical Teacher* 29: 258–60.

Ngo-Metzger, Q., Sorkin, D. H., Phillips, R. S., Greenfield, S., Massagle, M. P., Clarridge, B. and Kaplan, S. H. (2007) 'Providing high-quality care for limited English proficient patients: the importance of language concordance and interpreter use', *Journal of General Internal Medicine* 222(Suppl. 2): 324–30.

Ong, L. M. L., de Haesa, C. J. M., Hoosa, A. M. and Lammes, F. B. (1995) 'Doctor-patient communication: a review of the literature', *Social Science and Medicine* 40(7): 903–18.

O'Riordan, M., Skelton, J. and de la Croix, A. (2008) 'Heartlift patients? An interview-based study of GP trainers and the impact of "patients they like"', *Family Practice* 25: 349–54.

Peters, S., Rogers, A., Salmon, P., Gask, L., Towey, M., Clifford, R. *et al.* (2009) 'What do patients choose to tell their doctors? Qualitative analysis of potential barriers for managing unexplained symptoms', *Journal of General Internal Medicine* 24(4): 443–9.

Peters, S., Stanley, I., Rose, M. and Salmon, P. (1998) 'Patients with medically unexplained symptoms: sources of patients' authority and implications for demands on medical care', *Social Science and Medicine* 46(4–5): 559–65.

Rivandeneyra, R. M. A., Elderkin-Thompson, V., Silver, R. C. and Waitzkin, H. (2000) 'Patient centeredness in medical encounters requiring an interpreter', *American Journal of Medicine* 108(6): 470–4.

Roberts, C. (2007) 'Intercultural communication in healthcare settings', in H. Kotthoff and H. Spencer-Oatey (eds) *Handbook of Intercultural Communication*, New York: Mouton de Gruyter.

Roberts, C., Moss, B., Wass, V., Sarangi, S. and Jones, R. (2005) 'Misunderstandings: a qualitative study of primary care consultations in multilingual settings, and educational implications', *Medical Education* 39(5): 465–75.

Roberts, C. and Sarangi, S. (2003) 'Uptake of discourse research in interprofessional settings: reporting from medical consultancy', *Applied Linguistics* 24(3): 338–59.

Roberts, C., Wass, V., Jones, R., Sarangi, S. and Gillet, A. (2003) 'A discourse analysis study of "good" and "poor" communication in an OSCE: a proposed new framework for teaching students', *Medical Education* 37: 1–10.

Roter, D. and Larson, S. (2002) 'The Roter Interaction Analysis System (RIAS): utility and flexibility for analysis of medical interactions', *Patient Education and Counselling* 46(4): 243–51.

Ruusuvuori, J. (2001) 'Looking means listening: co-ordinating displays of engagement in doctor-patient interaction', *Social Science and Medicine* 52: 1093–108.

——(2007) 'Managing affect: integration of empathy and problem solving in two types of medical consultation', *Discourse Studies* 9(5): 597–620.

Salmon, P., Humphris, G. M., Ring, A., Davies, J. C. and Dowrick, C. F. (2006) 'Why do primary care physicians propose medical care to patients with medically unexplained symptoms? A new method of sequence analysis to test theories of patient pressure', *Psychosomatic Medicine* 68: 570–7.

Salmon, P., Peters, S. and Stanley, I. (1999) 'Patients' perceptions of medical explanations for somatisation disorders: qualitative analysis', *British Medical Journal* 318: 372–6.

Salter, C., Holland, R., Harvey, I. and Henwood, K. (2007) '"I haven't even phoned my doctor yet." The advice giving role of the pharmacist during consultations for medication review with patients aged 80 or more', *British Medical Journal* (online) 334(7603), doi: 10.1136/bmj.39171.577106.55.

Schwabe, M., Reuber, M., Schöndienst, M. and Gülich, E. (2008) 'Listening to people with seizures: how can linguistic analysis help in the differential diagnosis of seizure disorders?' *Communication and Medicine* 5(1): 59–72.

Seale, C., Ziebland, S. and Charteris-Black, J. (2006) 'Gender, cancer experience and Internet use: a comparative keyword analysis of interviews and online cancer support groups', *Social Science and Medicine* 62: 2577–90.

Shaw, A. and Ahmed, M. (2004) 'Translating genetics leaflets into languages other than English: lessons from an assessment of Urdu materials', *Journal of Genetic Counselling* 13(4): 321–42.

Shaw, S. and Greenhalgh, T. (2008) 'Best research – for what? Best health – for whom? A critical exploration of primary care research using discourse analysis', *Social Science and Medicine* 66: 2506–19.

Skelton, J. R., Wearn, A. M. and Hobbs, F. D. R. (2002) '"I" and "we": a concordance analysis of how doctors and patients use first person pronouns in primary care consultations', *Family Practice* 19: 484–8.

Spencer, J. and Dales, J. (2006) 'Meeting the needs of simulated patients and caring for the person behind them', *Medical Education* 40: 3–5.

Stewart, M. (2001) 'Towards a global definition of patient centred care', *British Medical Journal* 322: 444–5.

Stewart, M. A., Brown, J. B., Donner, A., McWhinney, I. R., Oates, J. and Weston, W. (1997) *The Impact of Patient-Centred Care on Patient Outcomes in Family Practice*, Ontario: Thames Valley Family Practice Research Unit.

Stewart, M. A., Brown, J. B., Weston, W. W., McWhinney, I. R., McWilliam, C. L. and Freeman, T. R. (2003) *Patient-Centred Medicine: Transforming the Clinical Method*, 2nd edn, Oxford: Radcliffe Medical Press.

Stivers, T. (2005) 'Non-antibiotic treatment recommendations: delivery formats and implications for parent resistance', *Social Science and Medicine* 60(5): 949–64.

——(2001) 'Negotiating who presents the problem: next speaker selection in paediatric encounters', *Journal of Communication* 51(2): 252–82.

Stivers, T. and Majid, A. (2007) 'Questioning children: interactional evidence of implicit bias in medical interviews', *Social Psychology Quarterly* 70(4): 424–41.

Sudnow, D. (1967) *Passing On: The Social Organisation of Dying*, Englewood Cliffs, NJ: Prentice-Hall.

Towle, A. and Godolphin, W. (1999) 'Framework for teaching and learning informed shared decision making', *British Medical Journal* 319: 766–71.

Tuckett, D., Boulton, M., Olson, C. and Williams, A. (1985) *Meetings Between Experts: An Approach to Sharing Ideas in Medical Concultations*, London: Tavistock.

van Ryn, M. and Burke, J. (2000) 'The effect of patient race and socio-economic status on physician's perceptions of patients', *Social Science and Medicine* 50: 813–28.

Wass, V., Roberts, C., Hoogenboom, R., Jones, R. and van der Vleuten, C. (2003) 'Effect of ethnicity on performance in a final objective structured clinical examination: qualitative and quantitative study', *British Medical Journal* 326(7393): 800–3.

Watts, J. H. (2008) 'Emotion, empathy and exit: reflections on doing ethnographic qualitative research on sensitive topics', *Medical Sociology Online* 3(2): 3–14.

Wright, E. B., Holcombe, C. and Salmon, P. (2004) 'Doctors' communication of trust, care and respect in breast cancer: qualitative study', *British Medical Journal* 328: 864–9.

8

Clinical linguistics

Michael Perkins and Sara Howard

Introduction

Clinical linguistics involves the study of how language and communication may be impaired. In its narrowest and most applied sense it focuses on the use of linguistics to describe, analyse, assess, diagnose and treat communication disorders (e.g. Crystal 1981). However, it is also commonly taken to include the study of clinical language data in order to throw light on the nature, development and use of normal language and thus to contribute to linguistic theory (Ball *et al.* 2008). Indeed, it is sometimes only through the analysis of language breakdown that we become aware of hitherto unknown features of language structure and function, and this is part of the reason why the discipline has grown considerably over the last few decades.

The scope of clinical linguistics is broad, to say the least. No level of language organisation, from phonetics to discourse, is immune to impairment, with problems manifested in both the production and comprehension of spoken, written and signed language across the human lifespan. The subject matter of clinical linguistics is thus amenable to study through virtually all branches of linguistics, and various sub-specialisms have been accorded their own distinct labels such as 'clinical phonology', 'clinical pragmatics' and 'clinical sociolinguistics'. The fact that communication disorders may be manifested linguistically does not necessarily mean that they will always have a specifically linguistic cause, and thus if we are interested in explaining them fully we are inevitably drawn beyond linguistics to its interfaces with domains such as physiology, neurology, cognition and social interaction. One might thus define clinical linguistics as 'the study of communication disorders, with specific emphasis on their linguistic aspects (while not forgetting how these interact with other domains)'. This cross-disciplinary perspective is a key feature of clinical linguistics. Such a breadth of focus notwithstanding, establishing a clear causal link between behavioural symptoms and underlying deficits is not always easy. For example, there is disagreement with regard to whether specific language impairment (SLI) (a condition found in otherwise healthy children who have problems with syntax and/or phonology) is best attributed to underlying deficits in auditory perception, cognitive processing, a dedicated language module or some combination of all of these (see below for further discussion). Nevertheless, it is still possible to characterise the *linguistic* features of SLI precisely enough to be able to design assessments and remedial programmes. It is this key

Michael Perkins and Sara Howard

grounding in linguistics – and in particular the focus on linguistic *behaviour* – which distinguishes clinical linguistics from related fields such as neurolinguistics (see chapter by Ahlsén, this volume) and speech and language pathology, which accord primary importance to the underlying causes of communication disorders. This important distinction was first outlined by Crystal (1980) in terms of the 'behavioural' as opposed to the 'medical' model of language pathology.

A brief history of clinical linguistics

Our understanding of communication impairment has come a long way in the last hundred years. As late as the 1920s, Scripture (1923) was still attributing a particular variety of lisping to neurosis with a recommendation that it be treated using '[a]rsenic, quinine, strychnine, and other tonics, cold rubs, lukewarm or cold half-baths, sprays, moist packs, electrotherapy, massage, change of climate, and sea baths. ... ' (1923: 185). A major milestone in putting the study and treatment of communication disorders on a more scientific footing, based on the discipline of linguistics, was Roman Jakobson's *Kindersprache, Aphasie und allgemeine Lautgesetze* (Jakobson 1941) (later published in English as *Child Language, Aphasia and Phonological Universals* [Jakobson 1968]) which emphasised the importance of studying systematic patterns of similarity and contrast in clinical language data, and relating these to linguistic theory. The assumption that atypical speech or language, however deviant, must still be systematic and rule-driven – and thus amenable to analysis – has remained an article of faith among clinical linguists ever since Jakobson's work became more widely known in the 1970s.

Jakobson's influence is evident in publications from the early 1970s, particularly in the USA, UK and Scandinavia, though the development of clinical linguistics as a branch of applied linguistics was given a boost in the UK in particular by the publication of the *Quirk Report* (1972) which recommended that the training of speech therapists – whose exposure to linguistics had hitherto been largely restricted to phonetics – should be extended to embrace all levels of language organisation, and that 'the would-be practitioner of therapy, whether of speech or hearing, of reading or of writing must in future regard language as the central core of his basic discipline' (1972: 6.60). Gradually from the mid-1970s, former two-year diploma courses were superseded by 3–4 year bachelors degrees in speech and language therapy at a number of universities across the UK, which resulted in the emergence of a new generation of therapists who were not only more linguistically knowledgeable than their predecessors, but also had at their disposal an increasingly extensive linguistic toolkit for use in assessment, diagnosis and remediation. The linguists who were recruited to teach these students in turn became more knowledgeable about communication impairments, which in many cases influenced the subsequent direction of their linguistic research. The main driving force behind these developments in the 1970s and 1980s was David Crystal, who set up the first degree course in Linguistics and Language Pathology at Reading University in 1976. With his colleagues, Crystal developed an influential range of analytical procedures for 'profiling' the phonological, grammatical, semantic and prosodic characteristics of developmental and acquired communication disorders (Crystal *et al.* 1976; Crystal 1982). Versions of *LARSP* (*Language Assessment, Remediation and Screening Procedure*), the most widely used, are now available in many languages (Ball *et al.* forthcoming). A further milestone was the publication of *Clinical Linguistics* (Crystal 1981), which consolidated and defined the field. Although the term 'clinical linguistics' had appeared in print earlier (e.g. Baltaxe 1976), Crystal's book had the effect of according the term official status, as it were, with the result that clinical linguistics came to be more and more widely accepted as a distinct subdiscipline of linguistics. The first issue of the journal *Clinical Linguistics and Phonetics* (*CLP*) appeared in 1987, inviting submissions 'either applying linguistic/phonetic analytic techniques to clinical problems, or showing how clinical data contribute to theoretical issues in linguistics/phonetics' (Ball and Kent 1987: 2), thus acknowledging the reciprocal relationship between language pathology and linguistic theory. Although phonetics is often subsumed within 'clinical linguistics', inclusion of the term in the journal title deliberately acknowledged that prior to 1987 most research on communication disorders had concentrated on speech production and organisation, which has remained the case to the present day as we shall see below. Growing awareness of the inability of the International Phonetic Alphabet (IPA) to capture a whole range of articulatory distinctions found in impaired speech led to the development of a supplementary set of phonetic symbols called 'ExtIPA' (extended IPA) (Duckworth *et al.* 1990) which were officially recognised by the International Phonetic Association and incorporated in its *Handbook* (International Phonetic Association 1999). *CLP* became the official journal of the International Clinical Phonetics and Linguistics Association (ICPLA) which was founded in 1990 and has since raised the global profile of clinical linguistics through its conferences around the world.

Research methods in clinical linguistics

The linguistics tradition

Because of its inherent interdisciplinarity, clinical linguistics embraces a wide range of research methods, but the core of the discipline, with its roots in the earlier work of Jakobson and Crystal, tends to follow the qualitative research paradigms of mainstream linguistics. One strong tradition, typified by Crystal's language profiles (Crystal 1982), is that of linguistic fieldwork and language description. In the case of clinical linguistics, the 'field' is typically the speech and language therapy clinic but with an emphasis on naturalistic language data, wherever possible, which is audio- or video-recorded and transcribed. Analysis involves the identification of systematic patterns in the data, making use of either predetermined or ad hoc categories as appropriate. In both cases, but particularly in the latter, hypotheses are commonly reached inductively, then subsequently tested and revised by returning to the data iteratively. Because clinical intervention usually focuses on the individual, there is a strong tradition of individual case studies (e.g. Perkins and Howard 1995). However, larger diagnostic groups can also be identified based on their linguistic characteristics, and an increasing number of clinical language corpora are available in repositories such as CHILDES and TalkBank (http://talkbank.org/), as are increasingly sophisticated computational tools for their analysis, such as CLAN (MacWhinney 2000).

In addition to the data-driven, naturalistic corpus approach, which focuses on language behaviour and its products, the theory-driven generative perspective on language as knowledge is also reasonably well represented in clinical linguistics (for an overview, see Clahsen 2008). Over the years, various categories and concepts from generative grammar have been used to analyse deviant language patterns. For example, the difficulties experienced by many Broca's aphasics in understanding passive sentences and other constructions have been described in terms of the deletion of movement traces (Grodzinsky 2000) and some have tried to account for the problems shown by children with SLI in marking tense in terms of an 'extended optional infinitive' developmental stage (Rice *et al.* 1995). Evidence from clinical data – particularly the use of inflections – has in turn been used to inform theoretical debate.

Social sciences

Complementing the focus on the treatment of individuals, clinicians also need to be able to allocate each individual to one or more larger diagnostic groups whose nature and characteristics are established using the methods of the social sciences, and of psychology in particular. These typically involve either small or large group studies using both clinical populations and healthy controls in which hypotheses are tested through experimentation and the results submitted to statistical analysis. In such studies, a modular view of language and cognition is commonly assumed according to which language capacity is seen as an amalgam of discrete interacting components which may be differentially impaired. Within the experimental paradigm, linguistic competence is normally assessed through performance on one or more tests.

An alternative to the psychological approach, one which has been gaining ground in clinical linguistics in recent years, is that of ethnography, which sees communication as an integral feature of contextualised social action. Rather than targeting underlying linguistic and cognitive deficits, analytical methods such as conversation analysis (Wilkinson 2008) see communication impairment as a function of the way individuals orient to each other, and are based on fine-grained analysis of interaction, turn by turn, in usually non-contrived settings.

Medical sciences

Crystal's earlier strictures notwithstanding (see above), the 'medical model' is still alive and well within the broader discipline of clinical linguistics. It provides an essentially reductionist view of communication impairment in terms of underlying anatomical, physiological and neurological 'causes' which have become increasingly amenable to analysis through technological advances in research methods such as neuroimaging and genetic profiling (e.g. Monaco 2007).

Although a great deal of research in clinical linguistics continues to be carried out within a specific methodological paradigm, the inherent interdisciplinarity of the subject area generates an awareness of alternative approaches. At the most applied end of the discipline – i.e. clinical practice – speech and language therapists benefit from being trained to be at least familiar with research methods in each of the above areas, and are hopefully able to exercise a degree of creative eclecticism in the research they draw on in treating any given client.

Key issues in clinical linguistics

Phonetics and phonology

The phonetic characteristics of atypical speech may be captured through the use of speech instrumentation and phonetic transcription, both separately and in combination. Instrumental methods have been brought to bear on all the sub-systems of speech production. Electro-palatography, EMA (Electro-Magnetic Articulography) and ultrasound have each been used to explore aspects of articulator activity: tongue, lip and jaw movements and coordination (Cheng *et al.* 2007; Gibbon 2008). Atypical patterns of nasal resonance, airflow and pressure, as encountered in speakers with neuromuscular difficulties associated with dysarthria and in speakers with structural abnormalities linked to a history of cleft palate have been investigated using nasometry and aerodynamic techniques (Whitehill and Lee 2008). Laryngography and videofluoroscopy have provided techniques for gathering detailed and diverse information about vocal fold activity (Abberton and Fourcin 1997) and spectrography has a long history of application to a wide range of aspects of atypical speech production from an acoustic perspective (Kent 2003).

Clinical phonetic transcription ranges from broad phonemic approaches to characterising a speaker's segmental or phonemic sound systems, to those using narrow phonetic transcription in order to capture the fine phonetic detail of speech output in segmental and prosodic domains, together, sometimes, with supplementary information on voice quality and the ways in which gesture and gaze interact with the speech signal (see Müller 2006 for an account of this type of 'multi-layered' transcription). Clearly, a range of challenges and pitfalls faces anyone attempting to make a phonetic transcription of radically atypical speech production (Howard and Heselwood 2002), and objections have often been raised regarding its validity and reliability. Some of these objections have been met by the development of consensus methods where a final version is reached through discussion among two or more transcribers (Shriberg *et al*. 1984) and through careful critiques of the flawed methodological approaches which have sometimes been used to challenge the value of transcription (e.g. Cucchiarini 1996).

By combining perceptual and instrumental methods, researchers have also been able to explore the gap between what a speaker intends and what the listener perceives. A significant body of research has used acoustic and electropalatographic analysis to demonstrate clear and consistent articulatory differences made by a speaker for different segmental targets, which are not identified by the listener (e.g. Howard 1994; Weismer *et al*. 1981).

Compared with clinical phonetics, which has a pedigree dating back at least as far as Aristotle (Eldridge 1967), clinical phonology, which emerged in the 1960s and 1970s at the time when linguistic approaches generally were beginning to be applied to communication impairments, is a relative latecomer. Nonetheless, it has proved a hugely influential and creative force in clinical linguistics. Early phoneme and feature-based accounts of atypical sound systems gave way in the 1980s to the application of natural phonological process analysis to atypical speech production, particularly in developmental speech difficulties, with work by Ingram (1976) in the USA and Grunwell (1981) in the UK exerting a huge influence on phonological analysis in the clinical context which still endures today (see, for example, Dodd 2005). Current clinical phonological approaches are drawn from a healthy range of theoretical perspectives including optimality theory (Gierut and Morrisette 2005), non-linear approaches (Bernhardt and Stemberger 1998), gestural phonology (Hodson and Jardine 2009) and cognitive/usage-based phonology (Sosa and Bybee 2008), with accompanying debate about the status of phonological accounts of atypical speech data: are they merely extremely useful descriptive devices, or do they reflect actual psycholinguistic processes? Phonological accounts of speech impairment have shown, crucially, that they are not necessarily the product of articulatory constraints, but reflect difficulties with the organisation and use of sound segments in words, as shown in the data in Example 1, from a four-year-old child with phonological difficulties. Here we can see that although the child is clearly able to articulate all the alveolar and velar plosives found in English ([t], [d], [k] and [g]), he does not yet use them appropriately in real words: rather they have an atypical albeit context-conditioned and non-random distribution.

Example 1
DOG [gɒg] DAD [dæd] CAT [tæt]
CAKE [keɪk] GOAT [dəʊt] TAKE [keɪk]

The child in Example 2, on the other hand, has speech output which is related to a history of cleft palate. She makes use of subtle and inventive articulatory strategies to maximise phonological contrasts despite complex articulatory constraints which make the production of oral plosives and fricatives particularly challenging for her.

Example 2

| PIG | [ɒɾʔʰ] | CHAIR | [ʔjɛə] | DOWN | [ʔaʊɴ] |
| BIG | [mɪʔʰ] | JAM | [ʔjæm] | CUP | [ʔʊʔʰ] |

(from Howard 1993)

What these examples show is how systematic and patterned atypical speech output is. Clinical phonetic and phonological analysis demonstrates this convincingly, and can reveal the range of speaker strategies observable in individuals who struggle to make themselves intelligible. While such analyses have traditionally focused on single word production, recent research has pointed to the value of examining the phonetics and phonology of longer utterances, and in particular how connected speech processes and the organisation of words into longer prosodic domains also demonstrates consistent patterns and strategies which can be directly related to speaker intelligibility, where a speaker's intelligibility in single words may differ radically from their intelligibility in longer utterances (Howard 2007). Widening the focus of clinical phonetic and phonological investigations to consider connected speech behaviours in real conversational interaction may have considerable value both for our understanding of speech impairment and for intervention by speech and language pathologists.

Grammar and semantics

There is still considerable disagreement about the extent to which grammatical impairment results from malfunction within a self-contained grammatical *system*, which is the primary focus of mainstream linguistics, or else is a consequence of the way language is *processed* when it is produced and understood, and therefore inextricably linked with physiology and cognitive processes such as memory and attention. Thus the kind of structural anomalies evident in Example 3 (e.g. omission of obligatory clause and phrase elements and problems with agreement and pronominal case marking), spoken by a 51-year-old man with agrammatic aphasia, are seen by some as the direct consequence of damage to a language module, whereas others attempt to explain them as a secondary consequence of processing limitations. The latter view may assume the existence of a grammar module of some kind as part of the computational system, or else see grammar as entirely epiphenomenal – an emergent by-product of 'lexical selection and arrangement' (van Lancker 2001: 356).

Example 3
   and then yeah . well . waste of time . cos mother . here everyday . sit down you know . mm . go and . clean . forget about it . and then er . me said well rubbish that . rubbish . er . doctor come for me ['.' = a short pause]

(from Perkins and Varley 1996)

The same debate is also prevalent in research into specific language impairment (SLI) in children which is likewise seen as resulting from either a deficit in linguistic competence, a processing deficit in a specific area or a limitation in general processing capacity (Leonard 1998). A further dimension comes from the developmental nature of the disorder – i.e. to what extent is the gradual emergence of SLI either exclusively linguistic or influenced by non-linguistic factors, and what role is played by the developmental process itself? Some argue, for example, that the purported modular independence of linguistic and cognitive functions found in adults is not present – at least to such a large extent – in infants, and is largely a consequence of maturation. Thus, any early problems of a linguistic nature will impact on other processing areas, setting in train a complex chain of compensatory adaptations with knock-on effects for the whole organism (Karmiloff-Smith 1998). The initial trigger may even be entirely unrelated to language – for example, a problem with auditory processing or procedural memory (Tallal and Piercy 1973; Ullman and Pierpont 2005).

Although aphasia and SLI have attracted the most attention from clinical linguists because of the supposedly specifically linguistic nature of the impairment, they are in fact frequently accompanied by non-linguistic problems, and it would probably be more accurate to regard them as one end of a continuum of linguistic-cognitive disorders. At the other end are conditions such as Williams syndrome (WS) (sometimes described as the 'opposite' of SLI (Pinker 1999)), which is typified by cognitive impairments but preserved linguistic ability. Here too, though, research has shown that both expressive and receptive grammatical ability in WS is far from intact, and that in some ways it resembles that of second language learners (Karmiloff-Smith et al. 1997; Stojanovik et al. 2006).

With regard to semantics, clinical interest in this area has focused mainly on gaps in the lexicon, problems with lexical access (or 'word finding') and thematic roles. The first is illustrated by the fact that it is not uncommon to find individuals with aphasia who are unable to name members of specific semantic categories such as vegetables, fruit, body parts and tools (Caramazza 2000). This is sometimes seen as the direct consequence of a lack of conceptual knowledge, rather than as a purely semantic problem, as is evident in the fact that people with WS with poor visuo-spatial abilities, for example, may have difficulty understanding spatial expressions (Phillips et al. 2004). In many cases, though, there is clear conceptual understanding but an inability to retrieve a word and link it to its referent, as in Example 4 from a conversation involving P who has anomic aphasia.

Example 4
> T   can you tell me what you are wearing on your wrist? *[pointing to his watch]*
> P   it's er – *[sighs]* what I put on my hair on . er not my hair . er – *[tuts]* put it right er . *[sighs]* dear dear dear get it . I'll get it in a minute *[looks at watch and shakes his head]* it's not going through

Clinically oriented work on the syntax-semantic interface – commonly discussed in terms of argument structure, thematic roles and semantic functions – may prove particularly useful for extending our knowledge of semantics. Based on an analysis of language output in developmental and acquired language disorders, Black and Chiat (2008) argue for a level of semantic organisation in terms of 'event structure' which needs to include aspectual properties, causal and temporal relations between 'subevents' and relevant properties of participants such as sentience and animacy.

Pragmatics and discourse

In the clinical domain, pragmatics and discourse analysis have proved particularly helpful in characterising the communication difficulties manifested in conditions such as autism, traumatic brain injury (TBI) and right hemisphere brain damage (RHD), whose underlying causes are usually seen as being primarily neurological and cognitive, rather than linguistic. People with autism, for example, can find it difficult to work out precisely what others mean by what they say, as in:

Michael Perkins and Sara Howard

Example 5
    Adult: can you turn the page over?
    Child with autism: yes *[makes no move to turn the page]*

and individuals with TBI are known for wandering off topic – for example:

Example 6
    I have got faults and . my biggest fault is . I do enjoy sport . it's something that I've always done . I've done it all my life . I've nothing but respect for my mother and father and . my sister . and basically sir . I've only come to this conclusion this last two months . and . as far as I'm concerned . my sister doesn't exist

(from Perkins et al. 1995: 305)

The challenge for clinical linguists is to explain such behaviours in ways which are both theoretically coherent and practically useful. Extensive use has been made of constructs and concepts from pragmatic theories such as speech act theory, Gricean conversational implicature and relevance theory to characterise pragmatically anomalous communication, but although these provide a useful set of descriptive labels for assessment purposes (e.g. we could describe Example 5 in terms of a lack of illocutionary uptake on the part of the child or a failure to derive the adult's intended implicature), in explanatory terms we are still only scratching the surface. For example, how do we differentiate between symptoms and causes for remedial purposes?

The search for the neurological bases of pragmatic impairment has given rise to the relatively new subdiscipline of 'neuropragmatics' (Stemmer 2008) which, on the basis of lesion studies, attempts to identify specific areas of the brain responsible for pragmatically relevant cognitive activities. So, for example, our awareness of others' mental states (often referred to as 'theory of mind') has been linked to the right frontal lobe, social reasoning and empathy to the ventromedial frontal lobe and metamemory judgement to the prefrontal cortex.

An alternative, non-reductionist approach is to see pragmatic and discourse impairment as being located in the social space constituted by communicating dyads and groups, rather than being solely attributable to an underlying deficit within an individual. A number of studies using conversation analysis, for example, have shown that people with neurological and/or cognitive deficits who have been diagnosed as pragmatically impaired on the basis of formal assessments in laboratory conditions are still, nonetheless, capable of considerable pragmatic sophistication outside the constraints of the testing situation (e.g. Schegloff 2003). A related line of research, which gives equal weight to the contribution of the conversational partner, has demonstrated that in some cases the effect of some supposed deficit within an individual may be exacerbated – or alternatively 'neutralised' – at the level of the dyad by the actions of the interlocutor (Muskett *et al.* 2010).

One way of integrating these various different perspectives is to see pragmatic/discourse impairment not as some unitary condition uniquely caused by an underlying neurological or cognitive deficit within the individual, nor as being a purely socially construct, but instead as an epiphenomenal consequence of all of these. The so-called 'emergentist' account sees pragmatic and discourse problems as a by-product of the way in which neurological, cognitive, linguistic and even sensorimotor difficulties play out in dyadic or group interaction (Perkins 2008). Such an approach also acknowledges the fact that pragmatic impairment is not a unitary condition. Indeed the label has been applied to a wide array of disparate behaviours in addition to those already illustrated, such as problems with fluency, prosody, lexical selection, cohesion, eye contact, turn-taking, stylistic variation and sociolinguistic sensitivity (Perkins 2007). To make things even more complicated, pragmatically inappropriate behaviours by different individuals may appear superficially similar – and therefore be described and categorised in the same way – while having very different underlying causes.

A further complicating factor is that there may not necessarily be a direct relationship between behaviour and underlying cause. For example, Simmons-Mackie and Damico (1996) describe how the use of neologisms, stereotyped phrases and other atypical communicative devices by people with aphasia were seen by interlocutors as symptoms directly caused by the brain lesions which gave rise to the aphasia, whereas in fact they were used to signal discourse functions such as turn initiation and termination – and apparently unconsciously recognised as such by interlocutors. In other words, they proved to be an indirect creative pragmatic solution to the linguistic problems caused by the aphasia, rather than a direct consequence.

In conclusion, current research in clinical pragmatics suggests that pragmatic and discourse impairment are complex phenomenona which have disparate and multiple causes, typically involve compensatory adaptation, and may be best seen as the emergent consequence of interactions between linguistic and cognitive processing both within and between communicating individuals.

Recent, current and future trends

Although articles under the broad heading of clinical linguistics are published in a wide range of journals, a good way to get a feel for recent and current trends in the development of the discipline is to examine what has appeared in its key journal *Clinical Linguistics and Phonetics*. In 2002 David Crystal published a brief survey of all the articles published in *CLP* during its first fifteen years of publication (Crystal 2002). For this chapter we have surveyed articles appearing in the subsequent seven years from 2002 to 2008, using the same categories and analytical method as Crystal to enable a direct comparison. We will refer to 1987–2001 as period A, and 2002–8 as period B. One of the most striking developments is the increase in number of articles published: an average of twenty-four per year during period A compared with forty-seven per year during period B. This is partly a reflection of the gradual increase in the number of issues per year (1987: 2; 1988–96: 4; 1997–9: 6; 2000–5: 8; 2005–7: 10; 2007–8: 12) and also because more of these issues are now devoted to conference proceedings comprising shorter articles. Table 8.1 gives a breakdown of articles according to 'linguistic themes'.

Table 8.1 Articles published in *Clinical Linguistics and Phonetics* according to linguistic theme

Linguistic theme	% of articles 1987–2001	% of articles 2002–8
Phonetics	38	43
Phonology	29	19
Graphology	1	1
Grammar	9	13
Semantics	2	4
Discourse	8	6
Pragmatics	2	7
Sociolinguistics	1	2
Linguistic theory	1	0
Methodology	7	4

The predominant focus of the discipline is clearly on phonetics and phonology with only a slight decrease from 67 to 62 per cent between periods A and B, and a small shift away from phonology to phonetics, possibly reflecting an increasing interest in the more phonetically-grounded phonological approaches. In other areas the percentages are relatively small, but there is a marked increase in the number of articles on pragmatics, and a slight increase in those devoted to grammar. Semantics (which Crystal [2002: 489] describes as 'the Cinderella of clinical linguistics') remains relatively little studied, which is perhaps surprising given the strong focus on the lexicon in aphasiology research.

The primary focus on speech has been evident in clinical linguistics since its inception. For example, out of a retrospective collection of eighty-nine seminal articles on the discipline (Powell and Ball 2010) more than half (55 per cent) are on phonetics or phonology. The bias towards phonetics and phonology was difficult to avoid even in the recent *Handbook of Clinical Linguistics* (Ball *et al.* 2008) where the editors made a deliberate attempt to provide an even coverage of the whole discipline. 50 per cent of the book is devoted to phonetics and phonology and the rest to the whole of syntax, semantics, pragmatics, discourse and sociolinguistics. This is largely attributable to the fact that there are so many active sub-areas of clinical phonetics and phonology while the other areas tend to be less well explored.

There is a slight increase from period A to B in the number of articles with a primary focus on languages other than English (from 12 to 15 per cent), which reflects a healthy awareness of multilingual and crosslinguistic issues. However, of those articles which address either developmental or acquired communication disorders, the split between the two remains the same (60/40 in period A and 61/39 in period B). One final notable statistic in period B (but not analysed by Crystal for period A) is that 25 per cent of articles were studies of normal, rather than clinical, populations, which perhaps reflects the strong need for a better characterisation of typical language behaviour in order to better understand the atypical.

Looking to the future, a number of sub-areas within clinical linguistics are likely to prove particularly influential in the years ahead. Work in genetics and neuroscience, aided by technological advances in brain imaging, is currently transforming our understanding of developmental communication disorders and the way that language is represented in the brain. Linked to this is a growing interest in focusing on the interfaces between different areas of linguistic and cognitive functioning rather than on their properties in isolation – i.e. on their *associations* rather than their *dissociations*. A related growth area for the study of clinical populations is the way in which spoken language functions as an integral component of a multimodal signalling system together with other components such as gesture, posture and eye gaze, and the crucial role played by interlocutors and social context. Another expanding area of study which is helping to refine the distinction between universal and local properties of language is the way in which communication disorders vary across speakers of different languages, and how they may manifest differently in speakers of more than one language. Finally, although corpora of disordered language remain tiny compared to what is available for analysis in other areas of linguistics, they have the potential to play a key role in our understanding of communication disorders both within and across languages.

Summary

Clinical linguistics has grown extensively as a discipline over the last few decades. While focusing primarily on the linguistic and phonetic characteristics of communication disorders, it is typified by an awareness of other inter-linked areas of processing such as neurology, cognition and social interaction. This inherent multidisciplinarity is also evident in the variety of research methods used, including those not just from linguistics but also from the social and medical sciences. Because it is practically grounded in the need to understand and treat the problems of individuals with communication impairments, clinical linguistics has tended to make less use of the kind of narrowly focused, more idealised theorising found in much mainstream linguistics and to favour instead more functionally oriented approaches which are better geared towards meeting the needs of clinicians. Among its many achievements, clinical linguistics has demonstrated that it is possible to enhance our understanding of language structure and use through an awareness of how it can go wrong.

Related topics

neurolinguistics

Further reading

Ball, M. J., Perkins, M. R., Müller, N. and Howard, S. (eds) (2008) *Handbook of Clinical Linguistics*, Oxford: Blackwell. (The most comprehensive overview of clinical linguistics to date, with authoritative contributions from leading researchers in the field.)
Crystal, D. (1981) *Clinical Linguistics*, London: Whurr. (Despite its age, a very approachable and practically oriented account of the application of linguistics to speech and language disorders.)
Damico, J. S., Ball, M. J. and Müller, N. (eds) (2010) *The Handbook of Language and Speech Disorders*, Oxford: Wiley-Blackwell. (A linguistically informed overview of a comprehensive range of communication disorders.)
Perkins, M. R. and Howard, S. J. (eds) (1995) *Case Studies in Clinical Linguistics*, London: Whurr. (Case studies of a wide range of communication disorders showing how linguistic analysis can contribute to assessment, diagnosis and treatment.)
Powell, T. W. and Ball, M. J. (eds) (2010) *Clinical Linguistics: Critical Concepts in Linguistics*, London: Routledge. (A collection of many of the most important research articles in clinical linguistics from the last fifty years or so.)

References

Abberton, E. and Fourcin, A. (1997) 'Electrolaryngography', in M. J. Ball and C. Code (eds) *Instrumental Clinical Phonetics*, London: Whurr.
Ball, M. J., Crystal, D. and Fletcher, P. (eds) (2011) *Assessing Grammar: The Languages of LARSP*, Abingdon: Multilingual Matters.
Ball, M. J. and Kent, R. D. (1987) 'Editorial', *Clinical Linguistics and Phonetics* 1: 1–5.
Ball, M. J., Perkins, M. R., Müller, N. and Howard, S. (eds) (2008) *Handbook of Clinical Linguistics*, Oxford: Blackwell.
Baltaxe, C. A. M. (1976) 'Clinical linguistics', *Sixth California Linguistics Association Conference Proceedings*, San Diego, CA: San Diego State University.
Bernhardt, B. and Stemberger, J. (1998) *The Handbook of Phonological Development*, New York: Academic Press.
Black, M. and Chiat, S. (2008) 'Interfaces between cognition, semantics and syntax', in M. J. Ball, M. R. Perkins, N. Müller and S. Howard (eds) *Handbook of Clinical Linguistics*, Oxford: Blackwell.
Caramazza, A. (2000) 'The organization of conceptual knowledge in the brain', in M. S. Gazzaniga (ed.) *The New Cognitive Neurosciences*, 2nd edn, Cambridge, MA: MIT Press.
Cheng, H. Y., Murdoch, B. E., Goozee, J. V. and Scott, D. (2007) 'Physiologic development of tongue-jaw coordination from childhood to adulthood', *Journal of Speech, Language, and Hearing Research* 50: 352.
Clahsen, H. (2008) 'Chomskyan syntactic theory and language disorders', in M. J. Ball, M. R. Perkins, N. Müller and S. Howard (eds) *Handbook of Clinical Linguistics*, Oxford: Blackwell.
Crystal, D. (1980) *Introduction to Language Pathology*, London: Edward Arnold.

——(1981) *Clinical Linguistics*, London: Whurr.

——(1982) *Profiling Linguistic Disability*, London: Edward Arnold.

——(2002) '*Clinical Linguistics and Phonetics*' first 15 years: an introductory comment', *Clinical Linguistics and Phonetics* 16: 487–9.

Crystal, D., Fletcher, P. and Garman, M. (1976) *Grammatical Analysis of Language Disability*, London: Arnold.

Cucchiarini, C. (1996) 'Assessing transcription agreement: methodological aspects', *Clinical Linguistics and Phonetics* 10: 131–56.

Dodd, B. (2005) *The Differential Diagnosis and Treatment of Children with Speech Disorders*, London: Whurr.

Duckworth, M., Allen, G., Hardcastle, W. and Ball, M. (1990) 'Extensions to the international phonetic alphabet', *Clinical Linguistics and Phonetics* 4: 273–83.

Eldridge, M. (1967) *A History of the Treatment of Speech Disorders*, Edinburgh: Livingstone.

Gibbon, F. E. (2008) 'Instrumental analysis of articulation', in M. J. Ball, M. R. Perkins, N. Müller and S. Howard (eds) *The Handbook of Clinical Linguistics*, Oxford: Blackwell.

Gierut, J. and Morrisette, M. (2005) 'The clinical significance of optimality theory for phonological disorders', *Topics in Language Disorders* 25: 266–80.

Grodzinsky, Y. (2000) 'The neurology of syntax: language use without Broca's area', *Behavioral and Brain Sciences* 23: 1–71.

Grunwell, P. (1981) *The Nature of Phonological Disability in Children*, London: Academic Press.

Hodson, S. and Jardine, B. (2009) 'Revisiting Jarrod: application of gestural phonological theory to the assessment and remediation of speech sound disorder', *International Journal of Speech-Language Pathology* 11: 122–34.

Howard, S. J. (1993) 'Articulatory constraints on a phonological system: a case study of cleft palate speech', *Clinical Linguistics and Phonetics* 7: 299–317.

——(1994) 'Spontaneous phonetic reorganisation following articulation therapy: an electropalatographic study', in R. Aulanko and A. M. Korpijaakko-Huuhka (eds) *Proceedings of the 3rd Congress of the International Clinical Phonetics and Linguistics Association*, 1993, Helsinki, Department of Phonetics, University of Helsinki.

——(2007) 'The interplay between articulation and prosody in children with impaired speech: observations from electropalatographic and perceptual analysis', *Advances in Speech-Language Pathology* 9: 20–35.

Howard, S. J. and Heselwood, B. C. (2002) 'Learning and teaching phonetic transcription for clinical purposes', *Clinical Linguistics and Phonetics* 16: 371–401.

Ingram, D. (1976) *Phonological Disability in Children*, London: Edward Arnold.

International Phonetic Association (1999) *Handbook of the International Phonetic Association: A Guide to the Use of the International Phonetic Alphabet*, Cambridge: Cambridge University Press.

Jakobson, R. (1941) *Kindersprache, Aphasie und allgemeine Lautgesetze*, Uppsala, Sweden: Almqvist and Wiksell.

——(1968) *Child Language, Aphasia and Phonological Universals*, The Hague: Mouton.

Karmiloff-Smith, A. (1998) 'Development itself is the key to understanding developmental disorders', *Trends in Cognitive Sciences* 2: 389–98.

Karmiloff-Smith, A., Grant, J., Berthoud, I., Davies, M., Howlin, P. and Udwin, O. (1997) 'Language and Williams syndrome: how intact is "intact"?', *Child Development* 68: 246–62.

Kent, R. (ed.) (2003) *MIT Encyclopedia of Communication Disorders*, Cambridge, MA: MIT Press.

Leonard, L. B. (1998) *Children with Specific Language Impairments*, Cambridge, MA: MIT Press.

MacWhinney, B. (2000) *The CHILDES Project: Tools for Analyzing Talk*, 3rd edn, vol. 2: *The Database*, Mahwah, NJ: Lawrence Erlbaum Associates.

Monaco, A. P. (2007) 'Multivariate linkage analysis of specific language impairment (SLI)', *Annals of Human Genetics* 71: 660–73.

Müller, N. (ed.) (2006) *Multilayered Transcription*, San Diego, CA: Plural Publishing.

Muskett, T., Perkins, M. R., Clegg, J. and Body, R. (2010) 'Inflexibility as an interactional phenomenon: using conversation analysis to re-examine a symptom of autism', *Clinical Linguistics and Phonetics* 19: 379–92.

Perkins, M. R. (2007) *Pragmatic Impairment*, Cambridge: Cambridge University Press.

——(2008) 'Pragmatic impairment as an emergent phenomenon', in M. J. Ball, M. R. Perkins, N. Müller and S. Howard (eds) *Handbook of Clinical Linguistics*, Oxford: Blackwell.

Perkins, M. R., Body, R. and Parker, M. (1995) 'Closed head injury: assessment and remediation of topic bias and repetitiveness', in M. R. Perkins and S. J. Howard (eds) *Case Studies in Clinical Linguistics*, London: Whurr.

Perkins, M. R. and Howard, S. J. (eds) (1995) *Case Studies in Clinical Linguistics*, London: Whurr.

Perkins, M. R. and Varley, R. (1996) *A Machine-Readable Corpus of Aphasic Discourse*, University of Sheffield, Department of Human Communication Sciences/Institute for Language, Speech and Hearing (ILASH).

Phillips, C. E., Jarrold, C., Baddeley, A. D., Grant, J. and Karmiloff-Smith, A. (2004) 'Comprehension of spatial language terms in Williams syndrome: evidence for an interaction between domains of strength and weakness', *Cortex* 40: 85–101.

Pinker, S. (1999) *Words and Rules: The Ingredients of Language*, London: Weidenfeld and Nicolson.

Powell, T. W. and Ball, M. J. (eds) (2010) *Clinical Linguistics: Critical Concepts in Linguistics*, London: Routledge.

Quirk Report (1972) *Speech Therapy Services*, London: HMSO.

Rice, M. L., Wexler, K. and Cleave, P. (1995) 'Specific language impairment as a period of extended optional infinitive', *Journal of Speech and Hearing Research* 38: 850–63.

Schegloff, E. A. (2003) 'Conversation analysis and communication disorders', in C. Goodwin (ed.) *Conversation and Brain Damage*, New York: Oxford University Press.

Scripture, E. W. (1923) *Stuttering, Lisping and Correction of the Speech of the Deaf*, New York: Macmillan.

Shriberg, L. D., Kwiatkowski, J. and Hoffman, K. (1984) 'A procedure for phonetic transcription by consensus', *Journal of Speech and Hearing Research* 27: 456–65.

Simmons-Mackie, N. and Damico, J. (1996) 'The contribution of discourse markers to communicative competence in aphasia', *American Journal of Speech-Language Pathology* 5: 37–43.

Sosa, A. V. and Bybee, J. (2008) 'A cognitive approach to clinical phonology', in M. J. Ball, M. R. Perkins, N. Müller and S. Howard (eds) *The Handbook of Clinical Phonetics*, Oxford: Blackwell.

Stemmer, B. (2008) 'Neuropragmatics', in M. J. Ball, M. R. Perkins, N. Müller and S. Howard (eds) *Handbook of Clinical Linguistics*, Oxford: Blackwell.

Stojanovik, V., Perkins, M. R. and Howard, S. (2006) 'Linguistic heterogeneity in Williams syndrome', *Clinical Linguistics and Phonetics* 20: 547–52.

Tallal, P. and Piercy, M. (1973) 'Developmental aphasia: impaired rate of non-verbal processing as a function of sensory modality', *Neuropsychologia* 12: 83–93.

Ullman, M. T. and Pierpont, E. I. (2005) 'Specific language impairment is not specific to language: the procedural deficit hypothesis', *Cortex* 41: 399–433.

van Lancker, D. (2001) 'Is your syntactic component really necessary?' *Aphasiology* 15: 343–60.

Weismer, G., Dinnsen, D. and Elbert, M. (1981) 'A study of the voicing distinction associated with omitted, word-final stops', *Journal of Speech and Hearing Disorders* 46: 320–7.

Whitehill, T. L. and Lee, A. (2008) 'Instrumental analysis of resonance in speech impairment', in M. J. Ball, M. R. Perkins, N. Müller and S. Howard (eds) *The Handbook of Clinical Linguistics*, Oxford: Blackwell.

Wilkinson, R. (2008) 'Conversation analysis and communication disorders', in M. J. Ball, M. R. Perkins, N. Müller and S. Howard (eds) *Handbook of Clinical Linguistics*, Oxford: Blackwell.

9

Language and ageing

Kees de Bot and Nienke van der Hoeven

Introduction

This contribution presents an overview of work on language and ageing, with an emphasis on ageing and cognitive processing. First we sketch a short history of the field. Then some of the major issues with regard to theoretical and methodological approaches are discussed. The focus is on psycholinguistic approaches because most of the work has been done in this area. However, we also point out the need for a more social/sociolinguistic perspective, because ageing as a topic of research typically relates to the interaction between individuals and their environment. The study of ageing has recently become heavily influenced by developments in the field of neuroscience, in particular the use of new neuroimaging techniques that have allowed the extraction of fine-grained data on neural substrates of language and cognition.

A part of this contribution is devoted to specific aspects of multilingualism and their impact on the ageing process.

Language and ageing: a short history

The interest in language and ageing developed as an offshoot of research on language and dementia. One of the early studies that have inspired research was Irigaray's (1973) *Le langage des déments*. This is probably the first comprehensive study that focuses on the specifics of language in this population. This start in pathological language development has defined the perspective on language and ageing in the sense that the focus has been largely on deficits and decline. The typical design of studies in the 1980s was to take some aspect of language (word recognition, verbal fluency, narrative skills) and test groups of young and elderly participants on these aspects to show how the elderly group differed from the younger group. Sometimes several age groups were included, but in many studies the first year university students typical of psychological research formed the control group. In the meantime, some of the pioneers of research on cognitive aspects of ageing, such as Baltes and Schaie, had already moved on to a somewhat different approach, in which life-span development was stressed rather than specific characteristics of certain age groups. The main aim of life-span developmental psychology is to study development as a life-long process. This implies that there may be gains and losses at different ages, and that development is not necessarily unidirectional. What counts as growth or decline is largely dependent on an external and basically inter-subjective criterion. In their introduction to research methods in life-span developmental psychology, Baltes *et al.* (1977) define the goal of research from this perspective as follows: 'Life-span developmental psychology is concerned with finding models that are appropriate for the construction of a theory of ontogenetic change over various age changes' (1977: 88). The study of development over the life-span covers a wide range of topics, including cognitive development, perceptual and motor development, social development, personality development and developmental psychopathology (see Magnusson 1996, and Demetriou *et al.* 1998, for overviews). In the past, developments in these areas were treated as specialized subfields that had few connections, but in the last two decades the awareness of the interconnectedness of developments on different levels and in different subsystems has grown. In particular, the booming research on brain functions has made it clear that cognitive functions interact with neurological functions, but also with physical changes and changes in the environment. Not all functions and sub-systems develop in parallel; some support each other's growth or decline, while others are compensatory in nature. There is evidence for a task dependency of how individuals differ in development.

In life-span developmental psychology, the concept of 'major life events' has been propagated (Baltes *et al.* 1977; Braet and Verhofstadt-Denève 1998). This refers to events that have a significant impact on the course of life, such as going to school, getting a job, getting married, migration, but also accidents, loss of a friend or relative, losing one's job and so on. What makes an event a major life event is highly dependent on individuals' settings and characteristics: having a divorce may be the worst possible nightmare for one individual, with very negative effects on life, and the best thing that could have happened for someone else. For the study of language development, specific *language related major life events* may be relevant (de Bot 2009). Such language-related events may be insignificant on the larger scale of life, but very significant for the development of the language system. Going to a bilingual kindergarten, having a penfriend abroad, choosing a school profile which includes foreign languages, studying abroad, international school exchanges, migration, they may all be relevant. Again, the patterns will be highly individual.

A critical discussion of main current issues

One issue that continues to generate discussions is what 'ageing' actually means and whether there is sufficient ground to treat elderly people as a more or less homogeneous group with its own specific characteristics. The life-span perspective discussed earlier provides arguments against such an approach. Developmental processes are typically gradual and there is no clear demarcation of age groups. Of course, societal factors such as retirement and specific institutions for the elderly have led to social stratifications, in which the third age more or less starts with retirement. In this respect, the current discussion on raising the retirement age to 67 in several countries because of the financial crisis is interesting.

For the study of language and ageing there are no clear boundaries between age groups. There is no longitudinal research that is dense enough to show how different language skills develop over time. And even if such studies existed, they would probably show that some individuals show specific decline at the age of 60, while others maintain their full language potential well into their 80s. Language development may be fairly homogeneous in the early years of life, but individual differences become more important over time. Differences in occupation, study, interest, opportunity and health lead to highly individual tracks over time

(Ardila *et al.* 2000). The study of development over the life-span is extremely complex: findings from longitudinal studies appear not to lead to the same findings as cross-sectional studies, and designs have to take into account that cohorts may differ significantly even on a year-to-year basis, due to events such as wars, financial crises or changes in the educational system (Schrauf 2009).

In recent years a new perspective on development and accordingly language development has emerged that fits very well with the life-span perspective discussed earlier. For quite some time, van Geert (1994, 2008, 2009) has been arguing for a dynamic systems perspective on development. Dynamic systems are defined as systems in which variables affect each other's change over time. Over the last few years this perspective has been taken up by various researchers (Larsen-Freeman 1997; Herdina and Jessner 2002; Elman 2005; de Bot *et al.* 2007; Larsen-Freeman and Cameron 2008) to describe first and second language development. A full treatment of the dynamic perspective on language development is beyond the scope of the present contribution. Here, the approach taken by de Bot and Makoni in their 2005 book on language and ageing in multilingual settings is discussed briefly. Language development is seen as a dynamic process in which many variables interact over time and that is highly idiosyncratic: while general factors such as level of education and intelligence are likely to have an effect on the group level, they are at the same time likely to have differential effects on individuals, because these factors may interact in specific ways with other individual factors. For instance, a high level of education may have little effect in a setting of migration where that education is not recognized and the migrant has to turn to manual labour to make a living. In ageing, three types of change seem to take place: physical changes (loss of brain cells, changes in sight and hearing), psychological changes (decline of working memory and speed of processing) and social changes (attitudes to ageing, social changes due to retirement or placement in a home for the elderly). The dynamic aspect is that these different types of factors interact: physical changes will lead to psychological changes and social changes, but also the other way around. Leading an active life has a positive effect on physical health and cognitive functioning. Mental activity is likely to lead to more and better social contacts and more physical activity, which in turn enhance physical health. It is argued that language is part of this process: physical changes such as hearing loss may lead to a reduction of communicative interaction, which may lead to a decline in accessibility of linguistic elements, due to non-use. Being seen as old leads to changes in interactions with younger generations and accordingly to a loss of interest in issues outside the immediate environment. Changes in health, psychological functioning and social environment may lead to a negative spiral in which less and less language is used and the language used becomes simpler. This may lead to reduced interaction with the environment and decline in life satisfaction.

One of the most burning issues, in particular in Europe, is the development of an ageing immigrant population. In many countries labour migration in the second part of the twentieth century has led to the development of large populations of immigrants that, despite intentions to return to their country of origin, appear to stay on, mainly because their families are now in the host countries. A study by Warnes *et al.* (2004) on elderly immigrants in Europe shows that they are becoming a group with specific needs:

> They include some of the most deprived and socially excluded, and some of the most affluent and accomplished, but all to a greater or lesser extent are disadvantaged through an interaction between social policies and their 'otherness' by living in a foreign country.
> *(Warnes et al. 2004: 307)*

While in some host countries, such as Australia and Canada, immigrant communities have set up their own ethnically oriented care systems for the elderly (Clyne 1977), no such developments seem to take place in Europe.

With respect to language and ageing, very specific problems may arise for these immigrant populations. One phenomenon that is mentioned regularly but little supported by empirical research is the idea of language reversion: the idea that people return to their first language when they age (de Bot and Clyne 1989; Schmid 2002; Keijzer 2007). It seems quite logical that immigrants who retire in settings in which they predominantly use their first language will lose some of their skills in the second language. It may also be the case that neurological changes reverse the order of prominence of different languages in the brain. Hyltenstam and Stroud (1993) suggest that in pathological ageing (Alzheimer's disease) language reversion, or regression, to use their terminology, happens occasionally. It is unclear, however, whether reversion is a sign of decline or attrition or reflects limited acquisition. Several of the Dutch immigrants in Australia studied by de Bot and Clyne (1994) indicated that they learnt English to just beyond survival level and saw no reasons to continue using it, apart from interaction with their grandchildren.

Another hotly debated issue that is relevant to the discussion of language and ageing is the idea of a Cognitive Reserve (CR) as a buffer in cognitive ageing. CR has been defined as 'the ability of individuals to cope with advancing brain pathology through either a set of acquired skills or inherent properties' (Kramer et al. 2006: 68). Interesting evidence on the role of education in CR comes from the famous 'nun studies' (Snowdon 2003). In this study, the brains of nuns that had been active as teachers well into their 80s were examined post-mortem. The brains of some of the nuns were similar to those of Alzheimer patients, although the nuns had been functioning adequately till shortly before they died. This suggested that their life-long mental activity and accumulation of knowledge and cognitive skills had given them a reserve that prevented the emergence of signs of decline. It should be added that Kemper et al. (2001) found no evidence for CR specific for language skills based on the written diaries of the nuns involved. Still it is conceivable that with equal rates of cognitive decline, individuals with larger vocabularies and language registers will be able to adequately communicate longer than individuals with smaller or more restricted vocabularies. To what extent being bilingual or multilingual can be seen as part of the CR is unclear. The only evidence we have related to this is the groundbreaking work by Ellen Bialystok and her colleagues, which will be discussed in the next section.

Cognitive advantages of bilingualism in ageing

What makes the research carried out by Bialystok and her group fundamentally different from most previous studies on language and ageing is that it is not so much concerned with effects of age-related biological or cognitive change on language development, but rather with the reverse, i.e. the effects of multiple language use on cognitive development over the life-span. In previous research, Bialystok found that bilingualism enhances the development of control processes in children (for an overview, see Bialystok 2001). This advantage was explained by the assumption that bilingual children have more practice in exercising inhibitory control than their monolingual compeers. Since a second language can never be switched off, but remains constantly active when the other one is used (see, for example, Francis 1999), bilingual children seem to develop a mechanism that controls attention to the language which is currently being processed, and that inhibits the second language from interfering. This control mechanism might benefit multilingual children in other, non-linguistic, cognitive domains as well, which could explain the advantage they have over monolinguals in the development of executive control processes (see Bialystok *et al.* 2004). Bialystok *et al.* (2004) investigated whether such an advantage might continue in adulthood and old age, thus protecting bilingual adults from age-related decline in executive functions. They reported on three experiments involving a middle-aged (mean age = 40) and an elderly (mean age = 71) monolingual and bilingual (English/Tamil) group who performed the Simon task, i.e. a non-linguistic task requiring quick reactions to congruent and non-congruent information. The bilinguals, apart from being more efficient on both congruent and incongruent trials than the monolinguals, appeared to show a reduced Simon effect, that is, they showed less disruption from incongruent information, and older bilinguals also produced a smaller age-related increase in the Simon effect than monolinguals. Moreover, bilinguals responded more rapidly to conditions that placed greater demands on working memory, which implies that the positive effects of bilingualism are not restricted to inhibitory control, but that bilingualism may attenuate negative age-related effects on 'executive control functions generally' (Bialystok *et al.* 2004: 301).

To determine more accurately which executive control functions are affected by bilingualism, a second series of experiments was carried out, involving the antisaccade task (Bialystok *et al.* 2006). Here, participants have to resist the impulse to look at a target that appears suddenly to the left or right of their focal point, and instead turn their gaze in the opposite direction. In the first experiment, in which eye-movements were measured, there were no effects of ageing or bilingualism. However, in the second experiment the participants' reactions were measured by means of key presses, that is, for antisaccadic items participants had to press the key opposite to the side of their focal point where the item was presented; now, bilinguals responded faster than monolinguals, and this advantage increased with age. The unexpected differences between these findings suggest that the bilingual advantage might only 'manifest itself later on in processing [...], in responses that take longer to develop', and that the key press paradigm involves 'some degree of symbolic mapping between the stimulus complex and the appropriate response' and that lifelong bilingualism might 'facilitate this translation process' (Bialystok *et al.* 2006: 1352).

More recently, other groups of researchers have studied potential effects of bilingualism and executive control as well. Colzato and colleagues (2008) tested groups of young bilingual and monolingual adults on three tasks (stop signal, inhibition of return, and attentional blink) that tapped into different aspects of inhibitory control, and reported that bilinguals do not differ from monolinguals in active inhibition, but have acquired a better ability to 'select goal-relevant information from competing, goal-irrelevant information' (2008: 310). Costa *et al.* (2008) tested groups of young bilingual and monolingual adults in the attentional network task, which supposedly taps into three attentional networks: alerting, orienting and executive control. The bilinguals were not only faster, but also proved more efficient in the alerting and executive control networks. However, these studies were primarily concerned with the issue of whether and how bilingualism affects control functions, and particularly inhibition mechanisms, and did not involve elderly participants.

After testing healthy bilinguals, Bialystok and her colleagues carried out a study involving elderly participants suffering from dementia, the background being that certain 'lifestyle factors', for instance physical activity, high levels of education and occupation, and mentally stimulating leisure activities, may help to build up CR (see Kramer *et al.* 2006, and the discussion of this concept in the previous section). Bilingualism, which in earlier studies was found to enhance executive control in children and adults, might be an example of the complex mental activities contributing to CR, thus protecting older adults from dementia-related decline. The study by Bialystok *et al.* (2007) involved a group of 288 patients with cognitive complaints, 184 of whom were diagnosed with dementia; 91 of these were monolingual and 93 bilingual (with a variety of mother tongues). The data, derived from the Mini Mental State Examination (MMSE), were controlled for level of education and occupation. Although the level of education – one of the main factors supposed to enhance cognitive reserve – of the bilingual group was significantly lower than that of the monolingual group, the bilinguals appeared to show symptoms of dementia about four years later than the monolinguals. Moreover, for a period of four years after the first diagnosis, a subset of patients in the two groups received further MMSE tests. No group difference was found for the rate of decline, which implies that the factor bilingualism delays the onset of dementia by four years without a change in progression rate.

The findings about cognitive advantages of bilingualism have raised many questions concerning the variables that play a role in this effect: can these findings with early bilingualism be extended to later, and also to less complete learning and use of a foreign language? In the studies reported on above, the criteria used for bilingualism were rather high: in all studies, participants regularly used at least two languages, were fluent in their second language and had been bilingual from either early childhood (Bialystok *et al.* 2004, 2006), or at least from early adulthood (Bialystok *et al.* 2007: 460) onward. Another question is whether additional languages also provide additional advantages. In the study by Bialystok *et al.* on dementia (2007), no distinction was made between bilinguals and multilinguals. More recently, this distinction was focused on in a large epidemiological study by Kavé *et al.* (2008). In a group of the oldest Israeli-Jewish population (N = 814, mean age = 83), the experimenters tested by means of a cognitive-screening test and the MMSE whether the number of languages spoken by the participants predicted cognitive state. Multilingualism, it appeared, 'added to the prediction of cognitive state beyond the effect of all the other demographic variables' (2008: 76), i.e. age, gender, place of birth, age at immigration, and education. However, their study is limited by a lack of details on level of proficiency, frequency of language use and age of language acquisition. Another confusing factor is that, unlike in the studies by Bialystok, where bilingualism usually resulted from exterior circumstances, for some participants their multilingualism might reflect an innate talent for language learning. This might imply that it is not the *use* of multiple languages that offers protection from cognitive decline, but that 'an innate flexibility in using brain structures' (Kavé *et al.* 2008: 77) might be a common cause for multilingualism and lack of cognitive decline.

Strongly related to the question of which variables affect cognitive advantages of bilingualism, is the most fundamental question: what exactly is the mechanism responsible for these advantages? As we have seen, Bialystok defined this cognitive advantage as an enhanced development of executive control functions, most notably inhibitory processing, and attributed it to the training bilinguals have in keeping their languages apart. These executive functions are normally considered to be located in areas of the frontal cortex, which leads Bialystok to speculate that 'for bilinguals, control over executive functions develops earlier in childhood and declines later in adulthood', because the frontal cortex is 'a region of the brain that is the last to develop in childhood and the first to deteriorate with aging' (Bialystok 2007: 219–20). In a later article, Bialystok (2009) also speculates that possibly the same mechanism might be responsible for both the linguistic disadvantage bilinguals have over monolinguals, i.e. in lexical retrieval, and their advantage, i.e. in executive control functions, because the 'joint activation of the two competing language systems' leads to a conflict, which 'both compromises lexical access because each selection is more effortful and enhances executive control through its continuous involvement in language production' (Bialystok 2009: 7).

An essential notion for Bialystok's explanations is that, contrary to previous premises in cognitive psychology, there is 'a potential for change in the structure and function of cognitive processes', so that 'these processes can be modified by experience' (Bialystok 2007: 215; see also Reuter-Lorenz 2002). Green *et al.* (2006) examined whether the acquisition of additional languages may cause functional and structural brain changes, using voxel-based morphometry (a neuroimaging technique that measures differences in local concentrations of brain tissue by means of a voxel-wise comparison of multiple brain images; for a description see Ashburner and Friston 2000). They report that 'preliminary analyses indicate an area in the left parietal cortex that shows a significant effect of the number of languages spoken' (Green *et al.* 2006: 109). However, research by Mechelli and colleagues (2004), who found that there is an increase of grey matter density with language learning, but also a decline with the increase of age of onset of acquisition, makes it unclear whether 'the density is higher because the L2 has been used more over the years, or the density is higher in younger years and is maintained over time' (de Bot 2006: 129). This line of argument leads to an alternative explanation for the experience-dependent plasticity of the brain: synaptic pruning. After early childhood, which is characterised by a peak in synaptic density, synapses that are not being used are eliminated (see Chechik *et al.* 1997). This could imply that bilingualism does not cause an increase in grey matter, but rather that 'monolingualism leads to extensive pruning' (de Bot 2006: 130), that is, of the synapses that are not used for a second language.

Lastly, Green and his colleagues also discuss an individual case (Emil Krebs, who spoke more than 60 languages; see Amunts *et al.* 2004) to suggest that there might also be individual differences in brain structure that affect the language acquisition process. This evidence is by no means at odds with theories on multiple language use leading to functional and structural changes in the brain, as the relationship between language development, cognitive functioning and brain structures is dynamic, so that changes in all systems mutually affect each other. The implications of these recent research developments are manifold. First, the possibility that some people, by virtue of certain characteristics of brain structure, might be more suited for learning languages than others, is not altogether new, but might offer new challenges in the field of language teaching. Second, the accumulating evidence on cognitive advantages of bilingualism, and particularly on the protection it might offer against dementia, can only increase the importance of learning (multiple) languages, also in adulthood.

Language, ageing and identity

In the study of language and ageing a distinction can be made between a psycholinguistic perspective, which focuses on language processing or on language as a code, and a sociolinguistic approach, which focuses on the interaction between individuals and their environment. In the present contribution the emphasis has been more on the former than on the latter. This difference in emphasis does not reflect a difference in relevance, but is mainly caused by the scarcity of research on the sociolinguistic side. In the field of sociolinguistics there are two main lines of research: one of them focuses on the language used with and among elderly speakers (the so-called 'Elderspeak'), while the second, related one addresses the way elderly people express their identity in discourse.

There is a considerable body of research on the language used in interaction with elderly people. Three aspects in the discussion on Elderspeak, as it is generally called, are relevant here. The first one concerns the characteristics of the language used in communication with elderly people. The second aspect addresses the question as to what extent accommodation to perceived communicative problems of elderly people actually helps to make communication more effective, while the third one concerns the issue to what extent such adaptations of speech are valued by the elderly interactants. The language used with elderly people has been compared with the languages used with children (caretaker speech) and with foreigners (foreigner talk). It is characterized by a slow speech rate, exaggerated intonation, shortening and simplification of sentences, and use of highly frequent vocabulary (Kemper *et al.* 1995). But not all these adaptations appear to enhance either the quality of the interactions or the self-image of elderly people. In their evaluation study, Kemper and Harden conclude:

> providing semantic elaborations and reducing the use of subordinate and embedded clauses benefit older adults and improve their performance on the referential communication task, whereas reducing sentence length, slowing speaking rate and using high pitch do not. The use of short sentences, a slow rate of speaking, and high pitch resulted in the older adults' reporting more communication problems.
>
> *(Kemper and Harden 1999: 656)*

Apart from the counter-effectiveness of the wrong type of adaptations, the use of Elderspeak is not evaluated positively by all elderly people. Research by Ryan and her colleagues points to the fact that the kind of modifications used in Elderspeak are primarily based on 'negative expectations of incompetence and dependency ... (occurring) independently of actual functioning' (Ryan *et al.* 2000: 272).

The other main line of sociolinguistic research on ageing concerns the sociolinguistic and discursive perspective on different age phases. In her introduction to a special issue of the journal *Ageing and Society* (Coupland 2009), Coupland reviews the still limited set of research on this topic. She draws an interesting parallel with sociolinguistic research on gendered speech and notices that 'There is very little age-focused research that could, for example, bear comparison with the feminist perspectives that drove sociolinguistics forward during and after the 1970s.' (2009: 849). One of the seminal publications on this perspective on language and ageing is *Language, Society and the Elderly* by Coupland *et al.* (1991). The relative lack of interest generated by sociolinguistic ageing research may be a result of the fact that the qualitative research methods used in this field were considered to be at odds with the more controlled and experimental information processing paradigms that were prevalent in the 1990s. The contributions to the special issue of *Ageing and Society* show that the use of such methods yields highly relevant and informative perspectives on perceptions and views of ageing. They show that ageing is at least partly socially constructed, and that the micro-social and macro-social perspectives in the study of language and ageing should be connected: the macro-social definitions of ageing do not necessarily reflect micro-social, individual and local experiences of elderly people (Nikander 2009).

Future trajectory and new debates

In recent years interest in ageing and multilingualism has grown, due in part to the findings on cognitive advantages of multilingualism in ageing and dementia by Bialystok and colleagues, described above. The socio-economic impact of potential delays in the onset of dementia is so high, that it seems highly recommendable to extend the line of research begun by Bialystok: which types of bilingualism will bring about these positive effects, and can other types of attentional control offer this protection too? The work that has been done so far (Bialystok *et al.* 2004, 2007) has been carried out with participants who grew up with two or more languages. One of the intriguing questions that follow from this is whether these findings with 'early bilingualism' can be extended to later and less complete learning of a foreign language.

Views on education have also changed in the last few decades. The idea of a separate phase of life that is devoted to learning and that ends in the mid-20s at the latest has been replaced by what is generally referred to as 'lifelong learning'. The thinking behind this is that in a world that is changing quickly, yesterday's knowledge may not be sufficient for today. With respect to ageing, continuous learning is part of a strategy to keep elderly people mentally alert and active. Learning or relearning languages is seen as a relevant and effective way to keep the mind active. Van der Hoeven and de Bot (forthcoming) looked at differences between three age groups (students/middle-aged/elderly) in the learning and relearning of words in French as a foreign language. Their main finding was that there was no difference in relearning words between the three groups, but that in particular the oldest group had significant problems learning new words.

The influence of new technology: neuroimaging and media

There are two types of technology that are relevant for the topics dealt with in this contribution: the use of new neuroimaging techniques for the study of the brain structures involved in language use on the one hand, and the role of electronic media in the lives of the elderly on the other.

In the last few decades a range of new neuroimaging techniques have been developed to study information processing in the *in vivo* brain. A very useful overview of techniques used in cognitive neuroscience is provided by Kramer *et al.* (2006). In their introduction these authors warn against overoptimistic expectations with regard to what we might learn about cognitive processes through the use of such techniques: 'However, electrophysiological techniques do not lend themselves to the unambiguous localization of the sources of brain activity that support the multitude of perceptual, cognitive and action-based processes of interest to researchers who study aging' (2006: 57). *Grosso modo* there are three types of techniques: techniques aimed at finding out the locus of cerebral activity during the performance of specific activities (fMRI, PET), techniques measuring the timing of activities in specific parts of the brain (ERP) and techniques creating short temporally and spatially delimited virtual lesions (TMS). Optical imaging techniques using parameters of near-infrared light have been shown to combine the advantages of fMRI and ERP, since both the spatial and the temporal resolution are sufficient. This allows the gathering of data using one instrument/technique, which removes the problem of aligning data from separate techniques. The specific advantage of TMS is that it allows for the study of the role of different brain structures in processing. By temporarily 'switching off' specific parts of the brain, their contribution to a task can be studied. There are some problems in applying these techniques in studying elderly informants. Kramer *et al.* (2006: 62) warn against simplistic comparisons between younger and older individuals, since ageing may involve anatomical and physiological changes that may have an impact on the propagation of electrical and magnetic signals to the scalp.

While there are some studies using these techniques for the study of language skills in elderly populations (see Burke and Shafto 2008), this is only the beginning and unreplicated findings flourish. Still, there can be no doubt that the application of such techniques will in the end provide us with rich data on the link between brain structures and cognitive functioning.

Compared to the vast amount of research using neuroimaging techniques for the study of language functions in ageing, research on the impact of technology on language in ageing is relatively scarce, which does not imply, however, that the role actually played by technology here is insignificant as well. To start with, old age is often accompanied by a decline in acuity of the senses, notably hearing and sight. As some researchers have pointed out (see, for example, Baltes and Lindenberger 1997), such a decline is bound to affect cognitive performance as well: most notably, declines in speech perception can have their impact on language comprehension (see Schneider and Pichora-Fuller 2000). Moreover, data from the British Royal National Institute for Deaf People (www.rnid.org) suggest that age-related hearing decline (presbycusis) is the rule rather than the exception. RNID estimates that 71.1 per cent of over-70s in the UK suffer from some kind of hearing loss. The potential impact of technology such as hearing aids on language development in the elderly, and thus on their social functioning and well-being, can therefore hardly be overestimated. Likewise, although generally the impact of age-related decline in sight on elderly people's language use may be less significant, it should be noted that progress in ophthalmic treatments, particularly in cataract surgery, has made it possible for elderly people to, for instance, continue reading till a very old age.

Another technological development that has had an impact on language use by the elderly is the advent of the home computer, and in its wake the recent rise of the Internet. Whereas initially the elderly had less access to and knowledge of computers and the Internet than younger age groups – a phenomenon described as the generational digital divide – there is some evidence that older people are now catching up and showing increasing interest in computer and Internet use: for instance, in 2005, 22.4 per cent of people over 65 in the USA connected to the Internet, compared to 34.9 per cent in 2007 (data derived from the US Census Bureau). Whatever the reason may be for the closing of this generation gap – the effect of computer courses for the elderly, or of younger, computer-literate generations 'pushing up' – it seems that, as far as computers are concerned, in the future older generations will no longer be completely 'linguistically excluded' (see Harwood 2007: 245). Some research has focused on what the elderly use computers and the Internet for; it seems that apart from maintaining social networks, finding medical and other information, the elderly also seem to use the Internet for identity functions (Harwood 2004, 2007: 256). However, what is still lacking is research on how computer and Internet use by the elderly affects their language performance.

Last but not least, use of another technological device, the television, will no doubt have an impact on language performance by the elderly, too. However, here as well research has focused mainly on the use of this medium, as well as on how the elderly are portrayed in television programmes. However, there has also been some research on television-watching habits of the elderly in relation with potential effects of leisure-time activities on cognitive state. Lindstrom and colleagues report an association between increased television viewing in midlife and an increased risk of Alzheimer's disease in later life (Lindstrom et al. 2005). Fogel and Carlson (2006) report that in a group of 289 older women, soap operas and talk shows as favourite television programmes are associated with lower scores on cognitive tests. As yet, it seems much too early to draw any causal conclusions from these studies, as both watching television and having preferences for certain programmes might very well reflect a cognitive state instead of inducing it, by way of taking up time that could have been spent on more stimulating activities. Still, these studies might initiate a line of research that may also address the issue of the impact of elderly people's TV-watching habits on language performance.

Summarizing comments

In this chapter an overview is presented on language and healthy ageing with an emphasis on bilingualism. It is argued that we need to move from a deficit and medicalized perspective on ageing to a life-span and dynamic perspective in which language development is seen as a process that starts at birth and continues over the course of life. Language-related major life events will affect language development at different ages and some age-related physical changes will have an impact on both cognitive functioning and interaction with the social environment. A perspective based on dynamic systems theory provides some ways to understand how a multitude of factors play a role in language development over the life-span and how earlier stages continue to affect the present.

Critical issues in the study of language and ageing are the interest in individual differences in the study of development, the roles of cognitive reserve and of bilingualism as a potential part of that, and the specific problems relating to immigration and ageing.

Recent developments in neuroimaging techniques have been affecting the research field of cognitive processing, and studies including elderly populations are beginning to be published. Such studies will provide us with a better understanding of the role of different brain structures in language use and the timing of language processing over time and across individuals. A largely unexplored area is the role of various types of electronic media, ranging from television and radio to messaging and on-line spoken communication, with regard to language and ageing.

Related topics

clinical linguistics; language learning; multilingualism; neurolinguistics; psycholinguistics

Further reading

Burke, D. and Shafto, M. A. (2008) 'Language and aging', in F. I. M. Craik and T. A. Salthouse (eds) *The Handbook of Aging and Cognition*, New York: Psychology Press. (This is probably the most complete overview of research on language and ageing available at the moment. It is an excellent starting point for any study of this topic.)
Craik, F. and Bialystok, E. (2006) 'Cognition through the life-span: mechanisms of change', *Trends in Cognitive Sciences* 10(3): 131–8. (In this article the main findings on cognitive changes over the life-span, including the impact of multilingualism, are discussed. It also provides a cognitively based theoretical approach to change over time.)
de Bot, K. and Makoni, S. (2005) *Language and Aging in Multilingual Settings*, Clevedon: Multilingual Matters. (While the literature discussed in this book is beginning to be outdated, it continues to be the only book on this topic providing both information on models of multilingualism and empirical work on a number of different elderly populations.)
Harwood, J. (2007) *Understanding Communication and Aging*, Los Angeles, CA: Sage. (This book takes a broad perspective on language and education by focusing on the communicative aspects, including health care communication and the use of new media, rather than adopting the narrower focus on psycholinguistic skills typically found in the literature.)

References

Amunts, K., Schleicher, A. and Ziller, K. (2004) 'Outstanding language competence and cytoarchitecture in Broca's speech region', *Brain and Language* 89: 346–53.
Ardila, A., Ostrosky-Solis, F., Rosselli, M. and Gomez, C. (2000) 'Age-related cognitive decline during normal aging: the complex effect of education', *Archives of Clinical Neuropsychology* 15: 495–513.
Ashburner, J. and Friston, K. (2000) 'Voxel-based morphometry: the methods', *NeuroImage* 11: 805–21.
Baltes, P. and Lindenberger, U. (1997) 'Emergence of a powerful connection between sensory and cognitive functions across the adult life span: a new window to the study of cognitive aging?', *Psychology and Aging* 12: 12–21.

Baltes, P., Reese, H. and Nesselroade, J. (1977) *Life-span Developmental Psychology: Introduction to Research Methods*, Monterey, CA: Brooks/Cole Publishing Company.

Bialystok, E. (2001) *Bilingualism in Development: Language, Literacy and Cognition*, New York: Cambridge University Press.

——(2005) 'Consequences of bilingualism for cognitive development', in J. F. Kroll and A. M. B. de Groot (eds) *Handbook of Bilingualism, Psycholinguistic Approaches*, Oxford: Oxford University Press.

——(2007) 'Cognitive effects of bilingualism: how linguistic experience leads to cognitive change', *The International Journal of Bilingual Education and Bilingualism* 10(3): 210–23.

——(2009) 'Bilingualism: the good, the bad, and the indifferent', *Bilingualism: Language and Cognition* 12(1): 3–11.

Bialystok, E., Craik, F. and Friedman, M. (2007) 'Bilingualism as a protection against the onset of symptoms of dementia', *Neuropsychologia* 45: 459–64.

Bialystok, E., Craik, F., Klein, R. and Viswanathan, M. (2004) 'Bilingualism, aging, and cognitive control: evidence from the Simon task', *Psychology and Aging* 19(2): 290–303.

Bialystok, E., Craik, F. and Ryan, J. (2006) 'Executive control in a modified antisaccade task: effects of aging and bilingualism', *Journal of Experimental Psychology: Learning, Memory and Cognition* 12(6): 1341–54.

Braet, C. and Verhofstadt-Denève, L. (1998) 'Developmental psychopathology', in A. Demetriou, W. Doise and C. van Lieshout (eds) *Life-span Developmental Psychology*, Chichester: John Wiley.

Burke, D. and Shafto, M. (2008) 'Language and aging', in F. Craik and T. A. Salthouse (eds) *The Handbook of Aging and Cognition*, New York: Psychology Press.

Chechik, G., Meilijson, L. and Ruppin, E. (1997) 'Synaptic pruning in development: a computational account', *Neural Computation* 10: 1759–77.

Clyne, M. (1977) 'Bilingualism in the elderly', *Talanya* 4: 45–65.

Colzato, L., Bajo, M., van den Wildenberg, W., Paolieri, D., Nieuwenhuis, S., La Heij, W. and Hommel, B. (2008) 'How does bilingualism improve executive control? A comparison of active and reactive inhibition mechanisms', *Journal of Experimental Psychology: Learning, Memory and Cognition* 34(2): 302–12.

Costa, A., Hernández, M. and Sebastián-Gallés, N. (2008) 'Bilingualism aids conflict resolution: evidence from the ANT task', *Cognition* 106: 59–86.

Coupland, J. (2009) 'Discourse, identity and change in mid-to-late life: interdisciplinary perspectives on language and ageing', *Ageing and Society* 29: 849–61.

Coupland, N., Coupland, J. and Giles, H. (1991) *Language, Society and the Elderly*, Oxford: Blackwell.

de Bot, K. (2006) 'The plastic bilingual brain: synaptic pruning or growth? Commentary on Green *et al.*', in M. Gullberg and P. Indefrey (eds) *The Cognitive Neuroscience of Second Language Acquisition*, Malden, MA: Blackwell Publishing.

——(2009) 'Multilingualism and aging', in W. C. Ritchie and T. K. Bhatia (eds) *The New Handbook of Second Language Acquisition*, San Diego, CA: Elsevier.

de Bot, K. and Clyne, M. (1989) 'Language reversion revisited', *Studies in Second Language Acquisition* 11: 167–77.

——(1994) 'A 16-year longitudinal study of language attrition in Dutch immigrants in Australia', *Journal of Multilingual and Multicultural Development* 15: 17–28.

de Bot, K. and Makoni, S. (2005) *Language and Aging in Multilingual Societies: A Dynamic Approach*, Clevedon: Multilingual Matters.

de Bot, K., Verspoor, M. and Lowie, W. (2007) 'A dynamic systems theory approach to second language acquisition', *Bilingualism: Language and Cognition* 10: 7–21.

Demetriou, A., Doise, W. and van Lieshout, C. (1998) *Life-span Developmental Psychology*, Chichester: John Wiley.

Elman, J. (2005) 'An alternative view of the mental lexicon', *Trends in Cognitive Sciences* 8: 301–6.

Fogel, J. and Carlson, M. C. (2006) 'Soap operas and talk shows on television are associated with poorer cognition in older women', *Southern Medical Journal* 99: 226–33.

Francis, W. (1999) 'Cognitive integration of language and memory in bilinguals: semantic representation', *Psychological Bulletin* 125: 193–222.

Green, D. W., Crinion, J. and Price, C. J. (2006) 'Convergency, degeneracy and control', in M. Gullberg and P. Indefrey (eds) *The Cognitive Neuroscience of Second Language Acquisition*, Malden, MA: Blackwell Publishing.

Harwood, J. (2004) 'Relational, role, and social identity as expressed in grandparents' personal Web sites', *Communication studies* 55: 300–18.

——(2007) *Understanding Communication and Aging*, Los Angeles, CA: Sage.

Herdina, P. and Jessner, U. (2002) *A Dynamic Model of Multilingualism. Perspective of Change in Psycholinguistics*, Clevedon: Multilingual Matters.

Hyltenstam, K. and Stroud, C. (1993) 'Second language regression in Alzheimer's disease', in K. Hyltenstam and A. Viberg (eds) *Progression and Regression in Language: Sociocultural, Neuropsychological, and Linguistic Perspectives*, Cambridge: Cambridge University Press.

Irigaray, L. (1973) *Le langage des déments*, The Hague: Mouton.

Kavé, G., Eyal, N., Shorek, A. and Cohen-Mansfield, J. (2008) 'Multilingualism and cognitive state in the oldest old', *Psychology and Aging* 23(1): 70–8.

Keijzer, M. (2007) 'Last in First Out? An Investigation of the Regression Hypothesis in Dutch Emigrants in Anglophone Canada', Ph.D. Dissertation, Free University, Amsterdam.

Kemper, S., Vandeputte, D., Rice, K., Cheung, H. and Gubarchuk, J. (1995) 'Speech adjustments to aging during a referential communication task', *Journal of Language and Social Psychology* 14: 40–59.

Kemper, S. and Harden, T. (1999) 'Experimentally disentangling what's beneficial about elderspeak from what's not', *Psychology and Aging* 14: 656–70.

Kemper, S., Greiner, L., Marquis, J., Prenovost, K. and Mitzner, T. (2001) 'Language decline across the life span: findings from the nun study', *Psychology and Aging* 16: 227–39.

Kramer, A., Fabiani, M. and Colcombe, S. (2006) 'Contributions of cognitive neuroscience to the understanding of behavior and aging', in J. E. Birren, K. W. Schaie, R. P. Abeles, M. Gatz and T. A. Salthouse (eds) *Handbook of the Psychology of Aging*, New York: Academic Press.

Larsen-Freeman, D. (1997) 'Chaos/complexity science and second language acquisition', *Applied Linguistics* 18: 141–65.

Larsen-Freeman, D. and Cameron, L. (2008) *Complex Systems and Applied Linguistics*, Oxford: Oxford University Press.

Lindstrom, H. A., Fritsch, T., Petot, G., Smyth, K. A., Chen, C. H., Debanne, S. M. *et al.* (2005) 'The relationships between television viewing in midlife and the development of Alzheimer's disease in a case-control study', *Brain and Cognition* 58: 157–65.

Magnusson, D. (1996) *The Lifespan Development of Individuals: Behavioral, Neurobiological, and Psychosocial Perspectives*, Cambridge: Cambridge University Press.

Mechelli, A., Crinion, J. T., Noppeney, U., O'Doherty, J., Ashburner, J., Frackowiak, R. S. *et al.* (2004) 'Structural plasticity in the bilingual brain', *Nature* 431: 757.

Nikander, P. (2009) 'Doing change and continuity: age identity and the micro–macro divide', *Ageing and Society* 29: 863–81.

Reuter-Lorenz, A. (2002) 'New visions of the aging mind and brain', *Trends in Cognitive Sciences* 6(9): 394–400.

Royal National Institute for Deaf People (n.d.) *Statistics on age-related hearing loss, based on a member survey in 2005*. Available at: www.rnid.org.uk/information_resources/aboutdeafness/statistics/statistics.htm#age (accessed 29 October 2009).

Ryan, E., Kennaley, D., Pratt, M. and Shumovich, M. (2000) 'Evaluations by staff, residents, and community seniors of patronizing speech in the nursing home: impact of passive, assertive, or humorous responses', *Psychology and Aging* 15: 272–85.

Schmid, M. (2002) *First Language Attrition, Use and Maintenance. The Case of German Jews in Anglophone Countries*, Amsterdam and Philadephia: John Benjamins.

Schneider, B. A. and Pichora-Fuller, M. K. (2000) 'Implications of perceptual deterioration for cognitive aging research', in F. I. M. Craik and T. A. Salthouse (eds) *The Handbook of Aging and Cognition*, Mahwah, NJ: Lawrence Erlbaum Associates.

Schrauf, R. (2009) 'Longitudinal designs in studies of multilingualism', in K. de Bot and R. Schrauf (eds) *Language Development over the Life Span*, New York: Routledge.

Snowdon, D. (2003) 'Healthy aging and dementia: findings from the nun study', *Annals of Internal Medicine* 139(5 part 2): 450–4.

U.S. Census Bureau (2007) *Population Survey Report on Computer and Internet Use in the United States* (Tables 2 and 4: 'Reported Internet usage for individuals 3 years and older, by selected characteristics'). Available at: www.census.gov/population/www/socdemo/computer/2007.html (accessed 29 October 2009).

van der Hoeven, N. and de Bot, K. (forthcoming) 'Relearning in the elderly: age-related effects on the size of savings', *Language Learning*.

van Geert, P. (1994) *Dynamic Systems of Development: Change Between Complexity and Chaos*, New York: Harvester.

——(2008) 'The dynamic systems approach in the study of L1 and L2 acquisition: an introduction', *Modern Language Journal* 92(2): 179–99.

——(2009) 'A comprehensive dynamic systems theory of language development', in K. de Bot and R. Schrauf (eds) *Language Development Over the Life Span*, New York: Routledge.

Warnes, A. M., Friederich, K., Kellaher, L. and Torres, S. (2004) 'The diversity and welfare of older migrants in Europe', *Ageing and Society* 24: 307–26.

10

Forensic linguistics

Frances Rock

Introduction

Have you ever puzzled over the 'small print' on a mobile telephone contract or insurance agreement, trying to figure out how it relates to you? Have you ever clicked your consent to a Website's terms and conditions without having even glanced at them? Have you ever scrutinised a roadside parking restrictions sign and wondered where you stand – or park? If so, you have encountered the potentially unsettling effects of legal language. You can probably recall many more examples, as law pervades daily life. Language is integral to this; repeatedly we are told 'the law is a profession of words' (Mellinkoff 1963: vii) and 'our law is a law of words' (Tiersma 1999: 1). Yet many other aspects of social life also rely on words. What is so special about connections between language and law?

Language sets up law, defining offences, obligations and rights and presenting these for legal specialists and for members of society who decide whether to live by law's words or face consequences also stated in language. Legal language governs relationships between individuals, companies and institutions. Law is also conducted, enforced, indeed brought into existence through language. In police stations, courts and prisons, for example, law moves off the page and into people's lives through the collection and use of evidence in interviews, cross examinations and review panels, and through communication of legal outcomes which shape social relations in areas as wide-ranging as who lives with whom and who faces what punishment. All of this provides stimulating foci for descriptive linguistics particularly at the discourse level. However, such study also illuminates the law and the ways in which society conducts important parts of its operation, concerning life, death, pain, retaliation, retribution, harm and change. With this in mind, language study in the legal system is more than the study of an interesting artefact of itself. Rather, linguists who study legal systems potentially become involved in the working of those systems, moving beyond description by turning their observations into social commentary or even activism or intervention. So, here is one crucial reason why the observation that language is essential to law is more than just a platitude; the study of language in legal systems permits linguists to make positive contributions to the operation of law and thus society.

Language is also essential to law because of the frequency with which language becomes part of legally sanctioned activities. Offences are planned and executed through language, so audio records of alleged offences can become subject to linguistic analysis, as can written texts potentially produced by perpetrators. In civil and criminal law, acts of misrepresentation, persuasion, and deception can underpin such offences as bribery, defamation, perjury, blackmail, threatening, libel and slander, rendering them amenable to linguistic analysis (e.g. Shuy 2010). Here, linguists with specialisms ranging from phonetics to pragmatics can perform tasks as fundamental as informing decisions about whether an illegal activity has occurred.

The term *forensic linguistics* is hotly debated. For some, it denotes only the work of those who provide expert evidence on language for police investigations or court hearings. For these terminological purists, the forensic linguist is essentially a consultant for hire. For others, the term has a wider meaning which extends to examining courtrooms, particularly criminal ones, by analysing talk from lawyers and witnesses. Finally, increasingly the term is coming to have a wider application to denote research on all areas of legal activity from the language of legislation through police stations and even into prisons and out into the worlds of consumers, families and corporations. Other labels circulate, such as *language and law* (Levi 1994), *forensic English* (Philbrick 1949) and the more specialised *forensic discourse analysis* (Coulthard 1994) and *forensic phonetics* (e.g. Foulkes and French 2001), yet *forensic linguistics* has, particularly outside the USA, become an umbrella term for all forms of language-based research on matters legal. No doubt the exact scope of the area will continue to shift as scholars pursue new foci and new alignments with the *forensic linguistic* label. Societies' changing notions of legality and law's scope will also be an influence. For now, this chapter is organised around a distinction between expert witness work, in which language becomes evidence, and descriptive research on language within, and reaching out from, legal systems.

Main current issues

Forensic linguistics is so new that its history is still being written and so diverse that this history has been traced from several directions. For example, scholars observe roots of the sub-field in detailed descriptions of legal language (Tiersma 1999), in analyses of texts arising from early miscarriages of justice (Coulthard and Johnson 2007: 5) and in research on legal language in social settings (Danet 1990). These different histories illustrate the diversity and vitality of the sub-field from its inception and, conversely, the potential for it to be viewed as merely a rag-bag collection of potentially disparate activities.

Current research tests the bounds of the forensic linguistic enterprise. Thus, the main issues it now faces are wide-ranging and topical, spanning questions like 'How distinctive is each individual's writing style?', 'What makes language difficult to understand?', 'How do speakers exert power over each other and what does that achieve?', 'What is the effect of an interpreter on one-to-one interactions?', 'How are "facts" best extracted from children?', 'How should linguists present information to non-linguists?'. Each of these is a huge question. Answering requires recourse to many approaches to language study, and this chapter gives a flavour of how some approaches are applied in tasks and settings which relate to law.

Language and expertise

Someone has been threatened and police are trying to discover who made the threat (e.g. Labov 1988). Someone has apparently killed themselves, leaving a suicide note and detectives are trying to discover whether the note was genuine or the suicide really a murder (e.g. Chaski 2005). Someone has been arrested and interviewed and they claim that the resulting written police statement has been tampered with – the words attributed to them are not theirs (e.g. Coulthard 2002). All of these scenarios have attracted forensic linguists' attention, working for prosecution, defence or within police investigations. Linguists have also become involved in investigating more unusual situations, for example cheating (fraud) in a game show (French and Harrison 2004). Whilst these various criminal and civil matters appear disparate, forensic linguistic case work always involves the linguist being set an exercise to complete using analytic tools. If they cannot complete the exercise with the tools available to them, they should refer the case to another linguist who has access to different, apparently necessary resources (e.g. knowledge of an additional language or technique) or they should report that the exercise is not amenable to linguistic analysis. What differs across the casework examples above is the degree of frequency with which forensic linguistic practitioners encounter each type of problem. Questions of authorship, broadly 'who wrote this', are fairly established, as are questions such as 'Who said this?' for the forensic phonetician (see Fraser, this volume).

Authorship investigation, for example, receives extensive scholarly attention both from those who take casework in this area (e.g. Eagleson 1994) and from those (not necessarily different individuals) who seek to answer big questions about whether and how writers reveal something about who they are through their linguistic choices (e.g. Grant 2008). Such researchers use established notions around sociolinguistic variation, identities and stylistics to test novel ways of measuring texts for their potential to distinguish individuals. They examine authorship markers (Grant 2008) or style markers (McMenamin 2002: 115), in other words, features of language in use which might discriminate authors. A great many markers have been investigated at the levels of vocabulary, phrase choice, syntax, spelling and discourse, for example verb forms (Chaski 2001), *hapax legomena* (words occurring only once) (Woolls 2003: 106) and mean word or sentence length (Grant 2007: 11). Authorship scholars do not naively ask whether one speaker or writer produces language which is completely unique to them. Rather, using markers they address more subtle questions about degrees of difference between a closed set of authors or, commonly, about whether the author of a 'questioned' text or texts is the same person as the author of a set of 'reference texts' which have been assembled for the investigation with such issues as writers' purpose and genre in mind.

Some scholars take an essentially quantitative line, seeking to count multiple authorship markers (e.g. Chaski 2001; McMenamin 2002: 137–61); others are more qualitative, examining particular occurrences of marked features in detail (e.g. Coulthard 2002). Both approaches have attracted criticism; for example, whilst quantification can appear rigorous, that which considers neither sampling nor variation as a complex sociolinguistic phenomenon risks 'dangerous' conclusions (Grant 2007: 2). Some qualitative work risks assuming that an individual's idiolect will identify them with too much conviction (Kniffka 2007: 185). As McMenamin notes, 'sometimes the linguistic significance of an identified variable is not captured by counting' (2002: 131). He exemplifies through a case of a contested will. Violet Hussein, born in Japan, had grown up in Hawaii before moving to Alaska where she eventually passed away. Her will, leaving an estate of $1.6 million to her neighbours, was a standardised one, purchased from a stationery store, accompanied by letters to a friend named Kim whom no one knew or could find. Her siblings contested the will.

The deceased woman's known writings included many Creole language features such as mass nouns replacing count nouns (e.g. 'our deepest appreciation*s*') and an absence of number concord between subjects and particular verbs (e.g. 'all of them *was* tops') (McMenamin 2002: 134). Yet the questioned writings, 'the "Kim" letters', incorporated only one such feature; deletion (of, for example auxiliary *do* (e.g. 'He say he not want my money') and of plural markers (e.g. 'I tell you these thing') (2002: 132)). Aside from the predictable question about whether the questioned and known writings were sufficiently different to suggest a different author, the 'Kim' letters invited consideration of whether there is any variety of English which can be characterised by only one grammatical process, deletion, and thus whether the letters were more generally plausible. McMenamin proposed that the presence of only deletions suggested authorship by 'a dialect imitator who stereotypically views Creole-English as just standard-English-with-things-missing' (2002: 135). The judge in the case found in favour of the siblings and against the neighbours who had, he ruled, prepared or directed the preparation of the 'Kim' letters.

The presentation of information by expert witnesses interests both forensic linguistic practitioners whose concern is how to communicate their evidence (e.g. Storey-White 1997; French and Harrison 2007) and descriptive linguists conceptualising expert testimony as an artefact of courtroom procedure (e.g. Hobbs 2002). Evidential rules, specific to each jurisdiction, restrict what can be presented and how. For example, criteria arising from the case of *Daubert v. Merrow Dow Pharmaceuticals Inc.* (1993) apply in the USA. These criteria seek to establish the acceptability of expert evidence by asking whether a method has been generally accepted, tested and peer-reviewed with a known error rate established. This challenges, for example, qualitative researchers and those using new or adapted methods. Linguists can equip themselves for court by reading about other linguists' experiences (e.g. Lakoff 1986), courts' perspectives (Tiersma and Solan 2002) or by digesting information on how to be a forensic linguist, such as Shuy's 'nuts-and-bolts guide book' (2006: v).

Good expert witnesses ground their work in research and remain cautious about what they can do. Unfortunately, in the area of so-called 'language analysis' or 'linguistic identification' the potential for language to identify speakers does not necessarily receive such respect. Language analysis is employed, in principle, to investigate claims from those seeking refugee status or asylum upon arriving in a new country in search of the help and safety that they lost at home (Eades and Arends 2004: 179–80). Potential host countries have devised ways to 'test' asylum claims. Tests rest on the assumption that some aspect of the speech of an asylum seeker will indicate their origin. Whilst such a relationship between language variables and social variables could be seen as perhaps the most central tenet of sociolinguistics, the tests 'are increasingly raising concerns about over generalised and erroneous assumptions and practices involved' (Eades and Arends 2004: 180). In particular, the tests connect language straightforwardly to place, assuming that if one comes from place 'A' one will speak (only) variety 'X'. Thus reports are often 'linguistically naïve', suggesting that analysts do not understand linguistic processes such as variation within a variety, language change and code-switching (Eades 2005: 510). Eades exemplifies this through a typical excerpt from a report on an analysis, in this case disputing a claim to Afghanistan nationality:

> The applicant speaks Dari Hazaragi, which is spoken in central Afghanistan as well as in the Quetta area in Pakistan, with a Pakistani accent and … he uses several Iranian words which the analyst states are not used in Afghan Dari but which do feature in the Dari Hazaragi as it is spoken in Pakistan.

> *(Eades 2005: 510)*

Blommaert notes not only linguistic naivety but also naivety about the state of the world, specifically contemporary inter-relationships between dialects, languages, nations, nation states, geographic mobility, time and individuals (2009). He describes the experience of one young man whose sociolinguistic history, which passed through a number of locations and living arrangements, had created in him a linguistic repertoire which did not conclusively link him to any particular place in the way that immigration officials expected. He concludes that one's 'linguistic repertoire reflects a *life*, not just birth' and that 'if such a life develops in a place torn by violent conflicts and dislodged social and political relations, the image of someone being born and bred in one community with one language as his "own" is hardly useful' (2009: 424).

As well as form, content of asylum seeker accounts has also attracted linguists' attention. Maryns' case studies of Belgian procedures show how asylum seekers frequently come to believe that 'their account is not sayable in an institutional context', leading them to 'hide behind a constructed story which in many cases ... falls short as a consistent and reliable narrative' (2006: 314).

Describing the legal system: policing

Police interviews are typically face-to-face encounters during which a member of the public is questioned by one or more investigators. They aim to gather evidence concerning possible crimes. Understandably, interviews are traditionally divided according to whether the interviewee is a suspect or witness. However, for linguistic study it is more useful to divide them according to whether the interview is audio-recorded or not because this more directly influences researchers' work.

Interviews which are not audio-recorded, which I will discuss first, are transitory – for legal purposes they do not exist beyond the interview interaction itself. From these interviews then, the only record is a written statement which is produced during and through the interview. This dialogic text production process leads to a particular interaction between talk and text (Jönsson and Linell 1991). Komter used conversation analysis to examine this within an interview through which a Dutch police officer created a suspect's statement by typing onto a computer. She explored how talk interwove with typing which became 'a special type of turn' which typically followed suspect's talk, yet did not function as a spoken turn in this position would, holding the floor, for example (2006: 222). Turning to text production she noted that the typist-interviewer was 'informed' by the computer screen 'projecting what to ask and write next' (2006: 223). Thus the technology influenced both the form and content of interviews.

The data below show the influence of a different recording technology, pen and paper on a witness interview. This technology affords limited editorial opportunities once words reach the page so the officer leads the witness through the crime narrative repeatedly, eliciting more or different detail each time, only then marking the official statement sheet. This practice, described in detail in Rock (2001), conforms to contemporary officer training (e.g. Benneworth 2009). The excerpt below, from the final written statement, describes events preceding the killing of the witness' friend:

Excerpt 1: The written statement
We were all drinking and I drank about 2 pints of cider and some spirits. These were given to me by Colin.

How did this written text about drinking emerge through the spoken statement-taking session? Initially, the witness volunteered a fairly monologic account, including the following:

Excerpt 2: Initial rendition
I was with ur (.) one geezer called Col I go to- like I went to his house at first- James and Dave but wha- everyone knows him as David and urm drinking at (.) Colin's house (.) and that him- they all got a bit drunk and that

Here, in only the fourth turn of the interview, the witness mentions drinking. He does not explicitly state that he was drinking. This could be inferred from *drinking at* although the witness only specifies that other people *all got a bit drunk*. After a further six turns, the witness' initial account of the whole crime narrative ends. After some negotiation the officer begins a second, more meticulous, pass through the narrative which includes over 250 questions from him. Within this extended dialogic account, the officer raises the topic of alcohol:

Excerpt 3: Second rendition
89   P   how much had you had to drink?
90   W   about I'd had about (.) phhh say had about (.) about two pints (.) in his house
91   P   were you drink- what were you drinking
92   W   was urm (.) some side- bit of cider (.) bit of ur (.) what was it now urm (.) no
          what's it called not rum the other stuff (.) ur not whisky either (1.5) urm (.)
          stuff next ((to that)) next down from rum anyway (.) was spirits anyway
93   P   you was drinking spirits
94   W   yeah

Here, the witness states that he drank *two pints* of unspecified liquid. The officer's question (line 91) prompts elaboration including mention of both *cider* and *spirits*. *Cider* has made it into the statement but the officer does nothing to identify the stronger drink, simply accepting *spirits* in talk and in his written notes. *Spirits* potentially connotes plurality and suggests a more prominent interest in drinking strong alcohol than in alcohol appreciation than a specific label would. We cannot know whether the officer leaves this unresolved because of impatience, confusion or a deliberate attempt to make the witness appear more, or indeed, less drunk than he might otherwise.

They next return to alcohol after the officer has initiated a third rendition of the crime narrative which enables him to check his notes:

Excerpt 4: Third rendition
551   P   you were drinking in Col's house
552   W   yeah
… description of a man intervenes …
565   P   (3.6) OK you say you went- while you were there you drank about two pints
          of cider and spirits who gave you the drink
566   W   Colin

Here, the officer maintains topic control, initiating (line 551) and revisiting (565) discussion of alcohol and introducing the alcohol's source, asking *who gave you the drink*.

Finally, the officer begins drafting the statement, reading aloud as he writes (indicated in italics) and, through such devices as rising intonation, tag questions and pausing, checking accuracy. We re-join the interview as they discuss alcohol once more:

Excerpt 5: Fourth and final rendition
715   P   *we were all drinking* (6.7) *and I drank* (3.2) *about* (.) *three pints* (2.2) *of cider*
          (.) *and some spirits?*
716   W   yeh
717   P   (4.5) *these were given to me?* (6.7) *by Col?* (.) *is that right*

718   W   yeh
719   P   we'll say Colin we'll call him Colin yeh
720   W   yep

This short excerpt illustrates this witness' response to speech recording technologies, being typical of this phase of this interview. He does not seek the floor whilst the officer writes, as Komter's (2006) interviewee did during typing, rather he only speaks to answer questions. Typing and writing perhaps have different significance to interlocutors. Regarding text construction, turn 715 sees the officer transforming *two pints* which occurred throughout the previous excerpts into *three pints*. The fragment of written statement included at the beginning of this discussion incorporated *two* rather than *three* pints; it is unclear why this alternative count does not materialise in the statement given that this rendition facilitates statement-drafting. The witness' lack of comment on this miscalculation raises the question of power asymmetry, a phenomenon elegantly explored in witness interviews by Thornborrow (2002: 37–60) and suspect interviews by Haworth (2006), for example. When providing an uninterrupted account (excerpt 2), the witness used both the address terms *Col* and *Colin*. In excerpt 4, the officer uses the abbreviation *Col* and the witness selects more formal *Colin*. In line 719 the officer announces his decision to record in writing the witness' relatively formal address term *Colin*. This metalanguage is not dissimilar to the witness' clarification in excerpt 2 *everyone knows him as David*, yet the officer's words dictate the written text, while the witness' words did not, due to both the witness' words' position in the initial narrative and the role and asymmetrical status of each speaker.

Through talk, technology and text construction then, the officer selects *Colin*, introduces and specifies the witness' drinking and its source and selects levels of detail in referring to alcohol types. Whilst the written text appears to be a monologic account from the witness – as courtroom participants, who might ultimately use this statement, might assume – it has been influenced by the officer.

Turning now to interviews which are audio-recorded, these, like their non-audio-recorded counterparts, yield written statements. However, recordings themselves will be available to investigators and courts. This ensures that investigators can review complete, raw evidence if necessary and reduces the risk of foul play or error shaping the only record. Talk in audio-recorded interviews therefore has more potential legal importance than transitory, non-recorded talk; it has accordingly attracted more linguistic interest. One key characteristic of the prolific and revealing work on audio-recorded interviews is the use of multiple methods within single studies. Both Haworth (2006) and Heydon (2005), for example, combine conversation analysis and critical discourse analysis, demonstrating power and control being discursively constructed and managed.

Other work examines the impact of particular linguistic features in interview talk. Question form has attracted attention. Johnson, for example, combines corpus linguistic techniques with discourse analysis to scrutinise *so*-prefaced questions such as *So are you saying that all evening you had four pints?* (2002: 105). In interviews with children and adolescents *so*-prefaced questions allow interviewers to adopt the main storyteller role by providing means to 'construct, summarise and organise' accounts. In adult interviews *so*-prefacing can 'recapitulate, summarise and evaluate the interviewee's previous responses in a way that expects or assumes agreement' as in the example above where it combines with evaluative *all evening*. This can prove difficult for interviewees to challenge (2002: 108). Stokoe and Edwards show how *so*-prefaced turns can become part of a questioning strategy centring on 'silly questions', sometimes explicitly marked as such, for example, *it seems a silly question but did you have any excuse?* (2008: 101). Officers combine these with other strategies such as reformulation to make suspects' 'intentions and knowledge' explicit. More importantly, by presenting upshots innocuously, they establish intent by stealth (2008: 108). Interest in audio-recorded interviews has not been restricted to interviewers' activities. Examination of answers shows interviewees' potential to be manipulated but also their capacity to resist control even during extremely coercive questioning. This casts the police interview as 'a site of resistance and struggle, where each participant attempts to accomplish different goals and inhabits opposing roles, asking and demanding [on the part of officers] versus giving and resisting [from interviewees]' (Newbury and Johnson 2008: 231).

Language in police custody has also become an established focus as researchers have examined how rights are presented and explained there (e.g. Cotterill 2000; Gibbons 2001; Rock 2007). Similarly, telephone calls for emergency police assistance have attracted researchers' attention. In that setting, the mundane has been scrutinised by conversation analysts who have focussed on the detail of call openings and closings (e.g. Zimmerman 1992), and the fantastic has attracted discourse analysts who demonstrate how speakers accomplish complex interactional tasks (e.g. Tracy and Anderson 1999).

Work on specific policing settings such as interviews and emergency calls must be set against that which takes a very different stance. Broader-based studies have used such concepts as community of practice (Ostermann 2003; Rock 2005) and gendered identities (McElhinny 1998) to conceptualise policing as activity and workplace. These studies begin to consider how identities and practices underpin legal practitioners' activities.

Describing the legal system: courtroom language

Perhaps the most established focus of forensic linguistics in legal settings is the study of courtroom language – having relative longevity and thorough coverage. Two research themes have predominated. First, examining the intricacies of courtroom questioning between lawyers and witnesses, and second, the words delivered by judges to juries.

When non-lawyers speak in court, whether victims or defendants; claimants or plaintiffs; lay or expert witnesses, their words have the potential to sway decision-makers – jurors, magistrates and judges – in ways which lawyers alone simply cannot. However, talk is not merely delivered by those on the stand in whatever way they wish; rather, testimony is elicited through question and answer routines which, it has been argued, significantly influence perceptions of witnesses (e.g. Chang 2004) and constrain their contributions (e.g. Harris 1984; Woodbury 1984). As Philbrick observed back in 1949, 'lawyers speak to persuade' (1949: 3) and work such as Heffer's illustrates through corpora and discourse analysis that this necessitates 'counsel being "above all a strategist" seeking to coerce "the witness into answering in a certain fashion"' (2005: 95). This is subtle due to the multiplicity of courtroom narratives, which are multiple in being delivered by witnesses in combination, though not necessarily collaboration, with lawyers (e.g. Cotterill 2003).

Courtroom research has been particularly concerted around the discourse of rape trials (e.g. Ehrlich 2001; Trinch 2003; papers in Cotterill 2007). For example, Matoesian, using data from the trial of William Kennedy Smith, shows how:

- male and female trial participants are denied equal access to interactional resources which can naturalise domination of women;
- law is gendered through communicative practices which disadvantage female trial participants;

- evidential weight is manipulated through exaggeration or minimisation of particular details;
- representation and repetition in court, for example through reported speech, can accomplish strategic ends;
- audio-recordings of police interviews can be strategically introduced in ways which create oppression by manipulating constructions of reality.

(Matoesian 2001)

Ehrlich points out the potential of *why*-questions to allow witnesses to give relatively lengthy answers in court and thus co-construct a narrative with lawyers (2007: 460). She notes that through these questions lawyers provide space for their own witnesses to pre-empt possible criticism from opposing lawyers. Consider the following two examples from a series of Canadian trials centring on sexual assault and examining the witness' actions during the alleged attack:

Excerpt 6

| L | Why were you mentioning your boyfriend Allan? |
| W | Because, like I said, I felt like if he ever – if – it might prevent him from going beyond any more touching |

(Ehrlich 2007: 462)

Excerpt 7

| L | If you didn't want to give him a massage at that point in time, why did you touch his shoulders? |
| W | I was afraid that if I put up any more of a struggle that it would only egg him on even more, and his touching would be more forced |

(Ehrlich 2007: 463)

In excerpt 6, the lawyer's *why*-question allows the witness to present her actions as a strategy 'to discourage the accused's sexual advances' (2007: 460); presumably people who have boyfriends and draw attention to them do not wish to encourage the sexual advances of others. Excerpt 7, in contrast, sees the witness presented with an opportunity to explain why she did engage in conduct which might be construed as the prelude to more intimate activities. The witness' explanation draws on the notion that compliance might reduce the severity, intensity or ferocity of an attack so this *why*-question allows 'the complainant's actions to be revealed' not as a precursor to consensual sex but a strategy of resistance (Ehrlich 2007: 464).

As well as the subtle influence of lawyers' questions, testimony itself can say more than speakers might expect. Conley *et al*. (1978) have illustrated the influence of speech style, in Lakoff's (1975) sense, on jurors' perceptions of speakers on the stand. Their combination of courtroom observation and experimentation indicated how such features as hesitations, hedging and hypercorrection can alter such matters as perceived trustworthiness (Conley *et al*. 1978).

Moving to language delivered by judges to juries, we find a tradition of examining the difficulty or inadequacy of such language. Jury instructions (as they are known in the USA) or directions (the UK term) are intended to explain both general points of law and case-specific legal issues. Research here has been influenced by the psychological studies of Charrow and Charrow (1979). They hypothesised that particular linguistic constructions caused difficulty in jury instructions and that if these were removed, comprehensibility would improve.

Experiments supported their hypothesis. Subsequent research has devoted much attention to further specifying and testing linguistic characteristics which might cause, or perhaps index, difficulty in legal texts (e.g. Stratman and Dahl 1996; Tiersma 1999; Gibbons 2003) and to specifying how these relate to judges' words (e.g. Dumas 2000). Danet (1990), for example, identifies sources of *lexical complexity* including technical terms and formal register; *syntactic complexity* including passives and strange anaphora and *discoursal complexity* including poor signposting and uninformative headings. Dumas (2000) compares jurors to students taking unfamiliar, difficult courses as they must 'absorb new information, learn new procedures, and digest and use new standards quickly, with no time for reading, reviewing, or consulting'. She suggests that providing a 'roadmap, list or diagram' before a trial, indicating what is to come, might help them to assimilate and use knowledge (2000: 57–8). Some linguists have become involved in rewriting standardised jury instructions (e.g. Tiersma and Curtis 2008). There is an obvious potential role for scholars in identifying linguistic features associated with difficulty and working with legal personnel to eradicate them whilst retaining legal sense and effectiveness. Nonetheless, some sociolinguists have questioned whether there really exists a neat fit between the presence of 'difficult' features in texts and comprehension of those texts by real listeners and readers in context (e.g. Solomon 1996; Rock 2007).

Heffer (2005) moves away from a deficit model through which lay people are taken to be lacking an adequate grasp of professional codes. Instead he draws on Bruner's distinction between narrative and paradigmatic modes of discourse. Narrative mode in court is realised through a focus on 'action, intersubjectivity and cultural norms' and paradigmatic mode through abstractions which allow participants 'to form universal rules of conduct' (2005: 36). Using naturally occurring courtroom data and observation he demonstrates how judges giving directions in the abstract, paradigmatic mode shift to the more concrete narrative mode which jurors might expect (2005: 181). Jurors' decision-making processes in the jury room have also received attention where legislation permits. Jackson provides a useful summary (1995: 452–4).

Courtroom studies are not restricted to examining lawyer-witness and judge-jury exchanges. The influential openings and closings delivered by lawyers at the beginning and end of the evidential phase of a trial, for example, illustrate language's power to persuade, manage impressions, establish points of view and recontextualise (e.g. Hobbs 2003).

The legal system and its actors face many challenges in dealing equitably with, and explaining effectively to, lay people. However, in some circumstances, the legal system needs to work even harder to ensure justice, not only equality (Gibbons 2003: 202), for example, when attempting to meet the needs of child witnesses (e.g. Aldridge 2007). Lay participants who do not share the language of the police or courtroom also present challenges which are resolved, in the eyes of the legal system, by providing an interpreter. Yet this is not straightforward for any participant. Interpreters have an undeniably tough job. They listen and speak in two languages whilst simultaneously navigating discoursal and pragmatic obstacles like orienting to norms of interactional structure (e.g. turn-taking); managing politeness and self-presentation (e.g. facework); resolving potential ambiguities (e.g. implicature); and attending to speaker intentions (e.g. speech acts). As if this was not enough for one interactant to handle simultaneously, the legal interpreter has to do all of this in a stressful situation often without adequate breaks, whist being seen by all courtroom participants as a source of unreasonable delay (Hale and Gibbons 1999) and always on the side of the opposition (Morris 1999).

In both police interviews and courtrooms, interpreters potentially create or develop miscommunication (e.g. Berk-Seligson 2002; 2009). In court, furthermore, the interpreter's words might create in jurors' minds a particular impression of the speaker they are interpreting for

(e. g. Hale 2002). Additional sensitivity is needed when people from different cultures routinely enter the justice system, as they risk not getting the help they need if they appear more linguistically competent than they really are (e.g. Eades 2004).

The future trajectory of forensic linguistics

Contemporary forensic linguistics sees scholars applying their findings. Whilst this is inevitable in the case of experts, those working on legal settings have also taken up this challenge (e.g. Garner and Johnson 2006; Rock 2007: 245–61) or are considering doing so (e.g. Benneworth 2009: 565–6). Whilst this is not without risks (Rock 2007: 249) the chance that researchers might improve the operation of societal justice is worth pursuing.

Shuy has frequently stressed that to be a forensic linguist one must first be an excellent linguist (2006: ix). As he observes, 'there's no need to try to apply linguistics to any other area of life before you've first learned what it is that you have to apply' (2006: 3). This cannot be stated too strongly. One cannot investigate language in any setting or system without first understanding significant and sufficient aspects of phonetics, phonology, morphology, syntax, semantics, sociolinguistics, pragmatics, discourse and so on and without being willing to push the boundaries of one's knowledge according to the challenges presented by the data and contexts encountered. Indeed, study of legal settings gives the individual linguist ways to understand and develop their own knowledge and perspective on their discipline.

Summary

We have seen that methods are understood, devised and applied differently in relation to different forensic linguistic endeavours. Compare, for example, the activities of scholars of authorship and interviews. Yet there exist many connections within forensic linguistics; for example, analysts of courtrooms and interviews share an interest in power and control, and key principles such as variation and style underpin forensic activities as they do all language study.

This chapter has illustrated the diversity of the activities of those working as experts and those examining legal settings. Inevitably, much has been omitted, but readers who reflect on the ubiquity of language about law, noted at the beginning of this chapter, will understand the potential reach of this sub-field and the exciting, informative future it promises.

Appendix

Names and anonymisation
Speakers in excerpts are labelled with consistent abbreviations:

P   Police officer
W   Witness

All names and other potentially identifying details have been anonymised. Pseudonyms have been inserted in place of personal names for ease of reading.

Key
(.)   A micropause of 0.9 seconds or less.
(1.2) A pause of 1.0 second or more, the duration appearing within the brackets. In this case, for example, the pause lasted for 1.2 seconds.

-     Self correction or speaker breaking off.
(( ))   Unclear speech
?   Rising intonation

Related topics

classroom discourse; corpus linguistics; critical discourse analysis; discourse analysis; ESP and business communication; institutional discourse; linguistic ethnography; medical communication; phonetics and phonology; sociolinguistics

Further reading

The first two books listed below offer overviews of forensic linguistics; the first is a single-authored book, the second an edited collection of papers. The final two items go into more detail about particular issues, the first relating to expert witness work, the second to language and the legal system.

Gibbons, J. (2003) *Forensic Linguistics: An Introduction to Language in the Justice System.* Oxford: Blackwell. (An accessible introduction to the forensic linguistic enterprise.)
Coulthard, R. M. and Johnson, A. (eds) (2010) *Routledge Handbook of Forensic Linguistics,* London: Routledge. (Chapters by authors writing on their areas of specialism. Great coverage and a good introductory level.)
Solan, L. and Tiersma, P. (2004) 'Author identification in American courts', *Applied Linguistics* 25(4): 448–65. (A useful overview of issues around both author identification and the regulation of expert witnesses at the time of writing in the USA.)
Brennan, M. and Brown, R. (2004) *Equality Before the Law: Deaf People's Access to Justice,* Gloucestershire: Douglas McLean. (Valuable work on the particular challenges in a marginalised group's contact with the criminal justice system.)

References

Aldridge, M. (2007) 'The questioning of child witnesses: a comparison of the child's linguistic experience in the initial interview and in the courtroom cross-examination', in J. Cotterill (ed.) *The Language of Sexual Crime,* Basingstoke: Palgrave, pp. 113–51.
Benneworth, K. (2009) 'Police interviews with suspected paedophiles: a discourse analysis', *Discourse and Society* 5(5): 555–69.
Berk-Seligson, S. (2002) *The Bilingual Courtroom: Court Interpreters in the Judicial Process,* 2nd edn, Chicago: Chicago University Press.
——(2009) *Coerced Confessions: The Discourse of Bilingual Police Interrogations,* Berlin: Mouton de Gruyter.
Blommaert, J. (2009) 'Language, asylum and the national order', *Current Anthropology* 50(4): 415–41.
Chang, Y. (2004) 'Courtroom questioning as a culturally situated persuasive genre of talk', *Discourse and Society* 15(6): 705–22.
Charrow, R. and Charrow, V. (1979) 'Making legal language understandable: a psycholinguistic study of jury instructions', *Columbia Law Review* 79(5): 1306–74.
Chaski, C. (2001) 'Empirical evaluations of language-based author identification techniques', *International Journal of Speech, Language and the Law* 8(1): 1–65.
——(2005) 'Who's at the keyboard? Authorship attribution in digital evidence investigations', *International Journal of Digital Evidence* 4(1).
Conley, J., O'Barr, W. and Lind, E. (1978) 'The power of language: presentational style in the courtroom', *Duke Law Journal* 1375–99.
Cotterill, J. (2000) 'Reading the rights: a cautionary tale of comprehension and comprehensibility', *International Journal of Speech, Language and the Law* 7(1): 4–25.
——(2003) *Language and Power in Court: A Linguistic Analysis of the O. J. Simpson Trial,* Basingstoke: Palgrave Macmillan.

——(ed.) (2007) *The Language of Sexual Crime*, Basingstoke: Palgrave Macmillan.

Coulthard, R. M. (1994) 'Powerful evidence for the defence: an exercise in forensic discourse analysis', in J. Gibbons (ed.) *Language and the Law*, London: Longman.

——(2002) 'Whose voice is it? Invented and concealed dialogue in written records of verbal evidence produced by the police', in J. Cotterill (ed.) *Language in the Legal Process*, Basingstoke: Palgrave.

Coulthard, R. M. and Johnson, A. (2007) *An Introduction to Forensic Linguistics: Language in Evidence*, London: Routledge.

Danet, B. (1990) 'Language and law: an overview of fifteen years of research', in H. Giles and P. Robinson (eds) *Handbook of Language and Social Psychology*, London: Wiley.

Dumas, B. (2000) 'US pattern jury instructions: problems and proposals', *International Journal of Speech, Language and the Law* 7(1): 49–71.

Eades, D. (2004) 'Understanding aboriginal English in the legal system: a critical sociolinguistics approach', *Applied Linguistics* 25(4): 491–512.

——(2005) 'Applied linguistics and language analysis in asylum seeker cases', *Applied Linguistics* 26(4): 503–26.

Eades, D. and Arends, J. (2004) 'Using language analysis in the determination of national origin of asylum seekers: an introduction', *International Journal of Speech, Language and the Law* 11(2): 179–99.

Eagleson, R. (1994) 'Forensic analysis of personal written texts: a case study', in J. Gibbons (ed.) *Language and the Law*, London: Longman.

Ehrlich, S. (2001) *Representing Rape: Language and Sexual Consent*, London: Routledge.

——(2007) 'Legal discourse and the cultural intelligibility of gendered meanings', *Journal of Sociolinguistics* 11(4): 452–77.

Foulkes, P. and French, J. (2001) 'Forensic phonetics and sociolinguistics', in R. Mesthrie (ed.) *The Concise Encyclopaedia of Sociolinguistics*, Amsterdam: Elsevier.

French, P. and Harrison, P. (2004) 'R *v* Ingram, C. and Whittock, T.: the *Who Wants To Be a Millionaire* fraud trial', *International Journal of Speech, Language and the Law* 11(1): 131–45.

——(2007) 'Position statement concerning use of impressionistic likelihood terms in forensic speaker comparison cases', *International Journal of Speech, Language and the Law* 14(1): 137–44.

Garner, M. and Johnson, E. (2006) 'Operational communication: a paradigm for applied research into police call-handling', *International Journal of Speech, Language and the Law* 13(1): 55–75.

Gibbons, J. (2001) 'Revising the language of New South Wales police procedures: applied linguistics in action', *Applied Linguistics* 22(4): 439–69.

Grant, T. (2007) 'Quantifying evidence for forensic authorship analysis', *International Journal of Speech, Language and the Law* 14(1): 1–25.

——(2008) 'Approaching questions in forensic authorship analysis', in J. Gibbons and M. Turell (eds) *Dimensions of Forensic Linguistics*. Amsterdam: John Benjamins.

Hale, S. (2002) 'How faithfully do court interpreters render the style of non-English speaking witnesses' testimonies? A data-based study of Spanish–English bilingual proceedings', *Discourse Studies* 4(1): 25–47.

Hale, S. and Gibbons, J. (1999) 'Varying realities: patterned changes in the interpreter's representation of courtroom and external realities', *Applied Linguistics* 20(1): 203–20.

Harris, S. (1984) 'Questions as a mode of control in magistrates' courts', *International Journal of the Sociology of Language* 49: 5–28.

Haworth, K. (2006) 'The dynamics of power and resistance in police interview discourse', *Discourse and Society* 17(6): 739–59.

Heffer, C. (2005) *The Language of Jury Trial*, Basingstoke: Palgrave Macmillan.

Heydon, G. (2005) *The Language of Police Interviewing: A Critical Analysis*, Basingstoke: Palgrave Macmillan.

Hobbs, P. (2002) 'Tipping the scales of justice: deconstructing an expert's testimony on cross examination', *International Journal for the Semiotics of Law* 15: 411–24.

——(2003) '"Is that what we're here about?": a lawyer's use of impression management in a closing argument at trial', *Discourse and Society* 14(3): 273–90.

Jackson, B. (1995) *Making Sense in Law: Linguistic, Psychological and Semiotic Perspectives*, Liverpool: Deborah Charles.

Johnson, A. (2002) '*So* … ?: Pragmatic implications of *so*-prefaced questions in formal police interviews', in J. Cotterill (ed.) *Language in the Legal Process*, Basingstoke: Palgrave.

Jönsson, L. and Linell, P. (1991) 'Story generations: from dialogical interviews to written reports in police interrogations', *Text* 11(3): 419–40.

Kniffka, H. (2007) *Working in Language and Law: A German Perspective*, Basingstoke: Palgrave Macmillan.

Komter, M. (2006) 'From talk to text: the interactional construction of a police record', *Research on Language and Social Interaction* 39(3): 201–28.

Labov, W. (1988) 'The judicial testing of linguistic theory', in D. Tannen (ed.) *Linguistics in Context*, Norwood, NJ: Ablex.

Lakoff, R. (1975) *Language and Woman's Place*, New York: Harper and Row.

——(1986) 'My life in court', in L. Sutton (ed.) (1998) *In Her Own Voice: Collected Writings of Robin Tolmach Lakoff*, Oxford: Oxford University Press.

Levi, J. (1994) 'Language as evidence: the linguist as expert witness in North American courts', *Forensic Linguistics* 1(1): 1–26.

McElhinny, B. (1998) '"I don't smile much anymore": affect, gender and the discourse of Pittsburgh Police Officers', in J. Coates (ed.) *Language and Gender: A Reader*, Oxford: Blackwell.

McMenamin, G. (2002) *Forensic Linguistics: Advances in Forensic Stylistics*, London: CRC Press.

Maryns, K. (2006) *The Asylum Speaker: Language in the Belgian Asylum Procedure*, London: St Jerome Publishing.

Matoesian, G. (2001) *Law and the Language of Identity: Discourse in the William Kennedy Smith Rape Trial*, Oxford: Oxford University Press.

Mellinkoff, D. (1963) *The Language of the Law*, Boston: Little, Brown and Company.

Morris, R. (1999) 'The gum syndrome: predicaments in court interpreting', *Forensic Linguistics* 6(1): 6–29.

Newbury, P. and Johnson, A. (2008) 'Suspects resistance to constraining and coercive questioning strategies in the police interview', *International Journal of Speech, Language and the Law* 13(2): 213–40.

Ostermann, A. (2003) 'Communities of practice at work: gender, facework and the power of *habitus* at an all-female police station and a feminist crisis intervention centre in Brazil', *Discourse and Society* 14(4): 473–505.

Philbrick, F. (1949) *Language and the Law: The Semantics of Forensic English*, London: Macmillan.

Rock, F. (2001) 'The genesis of a witness statement', *Forensic Linguistics* 8(2): 44–72.

——(2005) '"I've picked some up from a colleague": language, sharing and communities of practice in an institutional setting', in D. Barton and K. Tusting (eds) *Beyond Communities of Practice: Language, Power and Social Context*, Cambridge: Cambridge University Press.

——(2007) *Communicating Rights: The Language of Arrest and Detention*, Basingstoke: Palgrave Macmillan.

Shuy, R. (2006) *Linguistics in the Courtroom: A Practical Guide*, Oxford: Oxford University Press.

——(2010) *The Language of Defamation Cases*, Oxford: Oxford University Press.

Solomon, N. (1996) 'Plain English: from a perspective of language in society', in R. Hasan and G. Williams (eds) *Literacy in Society*, London: Longman.

Stokoe, E. and Edwards, D. (2008) '"Did you have permission to smash your neighbour's door?" Silly questions and their answers in police–suspect interrogations', *Discourse Studies* 10(1): 89–111.

Storey-White, K. (1997) 'KISSing the jury: advantages and limitations of the "keep it simple" principle in the presentation of expert evidence to courts and juries', *Forensic Linguistics* 4(2): 280–6.

Stratman, J. and Dahl, P. (1996). 'Readers' comprehension of temporary restraining orders in domestic violence cases: a missing link in abuse prevention?', *Forensic Linguistics* 3(2): 211–31.

Thornborrow, J. (2002) *Power Talk: Language and Interaction in Institutional Discourse*, Harlow: Longman.

Tiersma, P. and Curtis, M. (2008) 'Testing the comprehensibility of jury instructions: California's old and new instructions on circumstantial evidence', *Journal of Court Innovation* 1: 231.

Tiersma, P. and Solan, L. (2002) 'The linguist on the witness stand: forensic linguistics in American courts', *Language* 78: 221–39.

Tiersma, P. (1999) *Legal Language*, Chicago: University of Chicago Press.

Tracy, K. and Anderson, D. (1999) 'Relational positioning strategies in police calls: a dilemma', *Discourse Studies* 1(2): 201–25.

Trinch, S. (2003) *Latinas' Narratives of Domestic Abuse: Discrepant Versions of Violence*, Amsterdam: John Benjamins.

Woodbury, H. (1984) 'The strategic use of questions in court', *Semiotica* 48: 197–228.

Woolls, D. (2003) 'Better tools for the trade and how to use them', *International Journal of Speech, Language and the Law* 10(1): 102–12.

Zimmerman, D. (1992) 'Achieving context: openings in emergency calls', in G. Watson and R. Seiler (eds) *Text in Context: Contributions to Ethnomethodology*, London: Sage.

Part II

Language learning, language education

11

Key concepts in language learning and language education

Diane Larsen-Freeman

Introduction

In this chapter, I identify key concepts in language learning and language education. Rather than attempting to compile a comprehensive inventory of concepts, undoubtedly limited by my own experience, I have chosen a generative, question-posing approach, one that I have made use of over the years to situate developments in the field. It is in answering these questions that the key concepts emerge, a process I will illustrate by offering a few answers to each question. In order to bring some coherence to my discussion, I will adopt a heuristic in the form of a triangle (Figure 11.1).

In the top angle of the triangle, there is the teacher, who does the teaching. In the lower left angle, there is the subject matter. In the case of language education, this has meant the language and usually the culture in which it is embedded. The lower right angle of the triangle refers to the language learners in the process of doing the learning. The triangle is situated within a context, broadly interpreted to mean any place, situation, or time in which language education takes place. For instance, it could be in a national context or a more local classroom context with a particular group of students at a particular period of time, etc. Contextual factors affect answers to the questions, as do the prevailing theories at a particular period of time. In other words, there are no absolute answers to these questions at any one time or over time, and I make no claim that more recent evolutionary phases are necessarily superior to those which preceded them. Yet, even though the questions have not always been explicit nor their answers absolute, in this chapter they provide a useful framework for identifying the key concepts in the evolution of language learning and education.

History

What is language? What is culture?

Languages have been taught and learned for centuries. Over the years, circumstances have differed, resulting in one or more of the angles of the triangle being more influential than the others. Even within a given angle, the questions have not always been accorded equal

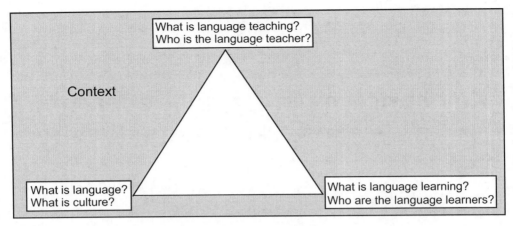

Figure 11.1 Questions related to key concepts in language learning and education

treatment. For instance, in defining the subject matter, language educators have sometimes stressed the inseparability of language and culture, and sometimes ignored treatment of culture altogether. The latter has been the case, for instance, given national needs during times of war because it has been assumed that explicit treatment of culture could be sacrificed in order to train proficient speakers and listeners of a 'strategic' language in as expeditious a manner as possible. Another example, this time with regard to the rise of English as an international language, has been the assumption that one can learn English for utilitarian purposes without becoming bicultural. However, for many applied linguists, language and culture are inextricable, where culture means the way that people express themselves and interpret the expressions of others as they share a social space and history (see Kramsch, this volume).

What then is language? Becker (1983: 219), a linguist, has written that 'Our "picture" of language is the single most important factor ... in determining the way we choose to teach it.' Of course, even if this is so, it is not always the individual teacher who defines language for pedagogical purposes. It is often the curriculum designer or materials developer who has more say. Still, the answers to the question have had a formative influence on language education, either directly through the textbook author's interpretation of language or the teacher's, sometimes tacit, assumption about its nature. After all, we teach something as we understand it ourselves.

Yet, Langacker's observation (1968: 3) of four decades ago still holds true:

> Despite its prevalence in human affairs, language is poorly understood. Misconceptions are legion, even among well-educated people, and not even professional linguists can claim to understand it fully. A person is radically mistaken to assume that the nature of language is self-evident or to conclude that we know all about a language just because we speak it.

Thus, the answer to the question 'What is language?' is by no means straightforward.

Cook and Seidlhofer (1995: 4) offer a number of answers to the question:

> Language is viewed in various theories as a genetic inheritance, a mathematical system, a social fact, the expression of individual identity, the expression of cultural identity, the

outcome of dialogical interaction, a social semiotic, the intuitions of native speakers, the sum of attested data, a collection of memorized chunks, a rule-governed discrete combinatory system, or electrical activation in a distributed network.

Their list is far from exhaustive (the authors do not claim otherwise). And, of course, these definitions are not all distinct in that several are implicationally related or apply to different levels of scale; nevertheless, it is easy to see even from this selective rendition that there is quite a range of views concerning language. Indeed, they are sufficiently distinctive to inform different approaches to language teaching and learning. For purposes of illustration, and because they are responsible more than any for pendulum swings in the field, let me now contrast two of Cook and Seidlhofer's characterizations of language: 'language as a rule-governed discrete combinatory system' and 'language as social fact'.

The former emanates from a formal or structural view of the language system. Its appearance on the modern scene can be traced to the writings of Saussure (1916), considered by many to be the founder of the discipline of linguistics. Interested in establishing linguistics as a science, Saussure chose to focus on the synchronic system of language, in particular *langue* (the abstract system of the shared code), as distinct from *parole* (the individual utterances of speech). Unpacking the definition 'language as a rule-governed discrete combinatory system', we see that language is a system, a system comprised of discrete segments: phonemes, lexemes, morphemes. These forms combine to make words, phrases, clauses, and sentences that comply with an established set of word order rules. Traditional, structural, descriptive, and generative linguistics have all adopted and contributed to this understanding of language. In language education, formal views are responsible for grammatical syllabi, in which linguistic structures are sequenced and graded according to increasing linguistic complexity. Formal views of language have also inspired pedagogical practices such as the use of inductive and deductive grammar exercises in which a grammar rule is discovered and practised, respectively.

It is not difficult to see that the view of language 'as a social fact' contrasts with a structural perspective. The social-fact view of language was propelled in part by Hymes' (1972) call for language education to move beyond linguistic competence to communicative competence: the knowledge of when and how to say what to whom. Focusing on language use, this view privileges language functions and meanings over language forms. Functions or speech acts such as promising, complaining, and inviting replace the structures of grammatical syllabi, and together with notions such as modality and temporality, make up notional-functional syllabi. Functional approaches to language have been realized in communicative language teaching approaches, widely practised these days.

In addition, a functional view of language includes how texts are organized to realize the meaning potential of language (Halliday 1978), stylistics or the distinctive patterns and choices people make when using language (Widdowson 1992), how different registers and genres are patterned (Swales 1990), how various conversational moves are structured (e.g., conversation openings and closings) (Sacks *et al.* 1974), how these are performed differently in different speech communities/cultures, the work of cross-cultural pragmatics (Blum-Kulka *et al.* 1989), and how the use of language differs across professional and academic contexts (Candlin and Candlin 2003).

In addition to endorsing communicative language teaching and notional-functional syllabi, then, a functional view also holds implications for teaching reading and writing and for realizing one's educational and professional/occupational ambitions. Of course, the dichotomy, formal versus functional, is an oversimplification, but I have evoked it to support my claim that it is important to understand the implications of a definition of language. Clearly, each

157

member of the dichotomy is far more complicated than first seems. Also, it is fair to say that most language educators attend to both forms and functions, although a satisfactory interface between the two has been elusive. While most people accept that ultimately the purpose of learning a language is to be able to communicate, the question of whether it is better to prepare students to communicate by having them build up a repertoire of lexical items and structures or by having them launch directly into communicating, however falteringly, has been at issue.

The problem with the former is that it leads to the inert knowledge problem. Students acquire a great deal of declarative knowledge or knowledge about language, but little by way of procedural knowledge, how to do things with language, especially when they attempt to use their knowledge for their own purposes outside of the classroom. The problem with a communication-first approach is that students speak and write with a great deal of inaccuracy. Moreover, a structural approach has the advantage of being compositional, in that the discrete pieces of language form natural syllabus units. On the other hand, dividing communication into discrete lessons is not easy, due to its protean nature (Larsen-Freeman and Freeman 2008). Even when communication is made divisible, say with inventories of functions and notions or language-use situations such as ordering food in a restaurant, opening a bank account, buying a bus ticket, etc., how to sequence units in a logical and pedagogically sound manner is not a straightforward matter.

Of course, as I have just written, many teachers teach their students both structures and how to communicate; however, even under these circumstances, by treating them separately in a given lesson, it is left to students to figure out how to apply their knowledge of grammar rules while communicating. One proposal that has been made to integrate the two includes focusing on structures, not by adopting a synthetic grammatical syllabus, but rather an analytic one (Wilkins 1976), where students engage in meaningful activities. During these, the teacher is encouraged to focus students' attention on form fleetingly, in a way that would not disrupt communication, e.g. by recasting or reformulating a student's error (Long 1991). Providing such 'negative evidence' is considered to be an important function of language teaching. Another proposal involves a procedural or usage-based approach to teaching grammar, 'grammaring' (Larsen-Freeman 2003), which calls for students to engage in dynamic, psychologically authentic practice, working not only on the form of grammar structures, but also on what they mean and when it is appropriate to use them. Gatbonton and Segalowitz's (1988) creative automatization is also a potential solution in that in their approach, it is patterns that are practised in meaningful communication, not grammar rules or structures.

I have chosen but two of the definitions from Cook and Seidlhofer's list: formal/structural and communicative/functional. I will not be able to venture further with the others on the list, let alone discuss views of language that are not represented there. However, one in the latter category that bears mentioning for its formative influence is the view that language serves the purpose of empowerment. Critical discourse analysts (Fairclough 1995) have pointed out that language is not a neutral medium of communication, which has led to a heightened sense of the political dimensions of language teaching and use (see chapter by Norton, this volume). One way that this view has been made manifest in language education is through a problem-posing approach, based on the work of Brazilian educator Paolo Freire. In a problem-posing approach, students are encouraged 'to perceive critically the way they exist in the world with which and in which they find themselves' (Freire 1970: 64). The goal of a such an approach is to help students to understand the social, historical, and cultural forces that shaped the context in which they live, and then to help empower students to take action and make decisions in order to gain control over their lives in that context. For instance, one pedagogical practice involves the selection of real-life issues from students' experience, the creation of short dialogues based upon these issues, and the engagement of students in an open-ended process of problem-solving.

What is learning? Who are the learners?

Turning now to the second angle of the triangle, we find the question 'What is learning?' Again, many answers to this question have been proffered. Certainly the most prominent answers in recent memory have been drawn from the theories of behaviourism, innatism, interactionism, and emergentism.

One version of behaviourism (Skinner 1957) has it that learning takes place through operant conditioning. There is no mental process involved; instead, learner behaviour is reinforced in order to condition a voluntary response to a particular stimulus. Key to this approach is the behavioural shaping, such as learning to make a new sound, that comes from selective reinforcement. Structuralists, such as Bloomfield (1942), had already introduced the idea that learning took place through habit formation. When language is construed as verbal behaviour, acquired through habit formation, it seems that the best way to learn a new language in the classroom is to 'overlearn' it – i.e. learners should practise the new patterns of the target language so thoroughly that they can choose the appropriate forms of the language while focusing their attention on the meanings they wish to express. Practices such as 'mimicry-memorization' (Bloomfield 1942) and pattern and dialogue practice (Fries 1945) became common.

Innatism entered the scene with Chomsky (1965). Chomsky questioned how it was possible for a child learning its native language to induce the rules necessary to produce grammatical sentences, given the impoverished input to which the child was exposed. There had to be, he reasoned, some innate faculty, a Language Acquisition Device (LAD) that guides the child in the language acquisition process. Without it, the child would generate countless hypotheses about the rules such that the induction problem would be insoluble, certainly within the time it normally takes a child to acquire his or her native language. Although the specifics of the LAD have changed over the years, perhaps the most productive contemporary description is that the LAD consists of innate general principles of language, which the child has to then but tune to the ambient language, said to involve a process of parameter-setting. Not much by way of pedagogical implications has followed from this position, but it has inspired considerable research in second language acquisition as researchers seek to establish the principles of a universal grammar (UG) and to discover whether they are still accessible during second language acquisition, in which case learners would then only have to learn to reset the parameters.

Chronologically, interactionism followed thereafter. Interactionists (e.g. Snow 1979) believe that it is not necessary to appeal to an innate LAD to explain the facts of language acquisition. They could instead be accounted for by looking closely at the interaction between the child and its caregivers, and the support the latter provides. For instance, even neonates engage in 'conversations' with their caretakers, with the latter making particular accommodations to facilitate language acquisition. The interactionist explanation has been extended to second language acquisition (Long 1996; Gass 1997). As native speakers and non-native speakers of the target language interact, language acquisition takes place, providing that native speakers accommodate non-native speakers, thereby making the input easier to comprehend (Krashen 1982).

In language education, a similar motivation applies to the use of meaning-based or task-based syllabi (Prabhu 1987; Willis 1996). The thinking goes: If communication is the end goal, why not make communication the means as well? Making communication the means calls for language students to engage in meaningful communication, such as using a map in order to give directions in the target language to some geographical point of interest. The goal is not to focus upon language forms or functions explicitly, but to solve some problem or to accomplish some task. Out of the interactions involved in performing the tasks, language is learned.

A more recent view of learning, inspired by seeing language from a complexity theory perspective (Larsen-Freeman 1997) as a complex adaptive system (Ellis and Larsen-Freeman 2009), has been called emergentism (Ellis and Larsen-Freeman 2006). Also rejecting the idea of the need to posit an innate LAD, emergentists argue instead that humans are well suited to perceive and to assimilate the patterns in the language spoken to them (and therefore the input is not as impoverished as Chomsky maintained). Emergentists have demonstrated that both children learning their native language (Goldberg 2006; Tomasello 2003) and adult learners learning a target language (Ellis and Larsen-Freeman 2009) can 'bootstrap' their learning by attending to frequently occurring form-meaning-use constructions in the language to which they are exposed. Learners build categories around frequent prototype exemplars, and from the categories extract the semantic and pragmatic information that allows them to analogize beyond the forms they have encountered. Frequent and reliably contingent form-meaning-use constructions are made more available to the learners through a social process of co-adaptation, an iterative process, with each interlocutor adjusting to the other over and over again (Larsen-Freeman and Cameron 2008). Emergentists (and connectionists) assert that this way of looking at learning finds empirical support in the architecture of the brain. With each new instance of meaningful language the learner encounters or uses, certain neural connections are strengthened and others atrophy, creating a dynamic, interconnected network of language-using patterns in memory (Larsen-Freeman and Cameron 2008).

Remaining in this angle of the triangle, but moving on to the question of 'Who are the language learners?', it should not be surprising that any answer to this question is multi-faceted as well. Certainly, even a cursory response to this question would include learners' ages, the native or other languages that they speak, and their individual differences. Taking these one at a time, starting with age, it was hypothesized by Eric Lenneberg (1964) that there is a critical period for language acquisition, usually ending around the time of puberty, after which a first language is no longer learned in a normal way. Most applied linguists accept that there is no absolute age threshold when the shift takes place, but they do point to the decrease in brain plasticity after puberty (or perhaps a bit earlier) to explain the apparent differences between the learning of languages by younger and older learners and the differential success of the latter. Of course, this hypothesis is not without controversy; nevertheless, it is difficult to argue that adult learners approach the challenge of learning another language in exactly the same way that children do, if only because the circumstances surrounding the learning are discrepant.

Furthermore, it is also well known that the native language that a learner speaks can make an impact on the way that the second language develops. This observation is supported by the Sapir-Whorf hypothesis, in which it is proposed that language determines thought. A more modest and more recent proposal, 'thinking for speaking', comes from Dan Slobin (1996). For Slobin, the native language does not determine thinking, but instead acts as a filter through which the world is perceived and registered. Even advanced second language learners, therefore, while otherwise producing accurate L2 utterances, may, at the same time, evidence L1 syntactic patterns. Brian MacWhinney (2006) attributes the L1 patterns cloaked in L2 words to the 'neural commitment' that L1 speakers have already made to their the native language. The neural connections made and strengthened over the years in the brain act as a deterrent to the acquisition of native-like L2 skills.

Of course, L1 language differences are embedded in L1 cultural differences, and these, too can have a profound effect on language education. To cite an obvious cultural difference with regard to language education, the way that languages are taught and mastered in Asia is much more text-and-memorization based than the way that it is taught elsewhere (Li 1998). Then, too, in many parts of the world, students are likely to expect, and even demand, that attention be given to grammar (Schultz 2001). Such differences have led certain applied linguists to warn against 'exporting' language teaching methods from Western countries to others (Holliday 1994).

It should also be noted that since its genesis, the subfield of SLA has adopted a bifurcated research agenda, which features both questions about the nature of the SLA process and about learners' differential success. There were four individual differences that were attested to influence language learners in 1976 (Schumann 1976), seventy-four in 1989 (Spolsky 1989) and now there are more likely over 100, as the list keeps growing. These factors are varied and range from innate language aptitude (Carroll 1963), to motivation (Gardner and Lambert 1972), to affective factors such as social attitudes toward the target language group (Gardner 1985), to learning style differences (Gardner 1983), to the preference for different learning strategies (Oxford 1989), to the circumstances of learning (i.e. as a second or a foreign language), and to the goals or needs of the learner.

To exemplify the last point, it is increasingly common to find heritage speakers in language classrooms these days. For these learners the language of the home is different from the ambient language and the language of the school. Nevertheless, heritage speakers have not had an opportunity to master their home language and so seek to do so through formal instruction. Having had some exposure to the language, at least in the language spoken around them, their needs are different from other learners who have no prior experience with the language they are studying. For instance, heritage speakers might understand the language, but not be able to speak it, or may be fluent orally (at least around certain topics), but not have developed literacy skills in the home language.

Such an observation underscores a critical issue in the field of language learning and language education: to what extent it is possible to make generalizations about learners apart from the circumstances of, and reason for, their learning? As Kramsch (2002: 4) has put it:

> It is no longer sufficient to talk about 'individual differences' in SLA against the backdrop of the universal learner. Difference and variation itself have moved to the center of language acquisition research. Variation becomes the primary given; categorization becomes an artificial construct of institutionalization and scientific inquiry.

It is common knowledge that there is a great deal of variation in L2 learner performance. Given the number of variables involved and the fact that they interact dynamically, influencing a learner in different ways at different times (for instance, motivation is not a steady state, but is characterized by ebbs and flows [Dörnyei 2009]), the question then becomes whether or not the variation is limitless and the experience of each individual learner unique. Perhaps if we are content to talk about tendencies, patterns, and contingencies, rather than absolute predictions and generalizations, then although individuals follow different trajectories in learning a second language, there may be some patterns that supersede the individual level (Larsen-Freeman 2006).

Another tension in the field of language learning has been the one between those who believe the learning process is essentially cognitive and individual, the learning by individuals of a mental grammar, and those who believe that learning is essentially a social enterprise (see, for example, Lafford 2007). Although most educators would again feel that both cognition and social interaction play a part, the important question of how they interface remains (Larsen-Freeman 2007).

What is teaching? Who are the teachers?

Visiting the final angle of the triangle, I begin with 'What is teaching?' As readers will have come to expect, there are different answers to this question as well. A traditional view of teaching has been characterized as 'knowledge transmission'. In this teaching-centred view, teachers are seen to be responsible for transmitting what they know to their students. These days it is common to be critical of a knowledge transmission view of teaching for the passive role it ascribes to language learners. Freire (1970: 72) has referred to knowledge transmission in terms of a banking metaphor: the teacher makes deposits of information into students who are to receive, memorize, and repeat them. However, knowledge transmission remains a common practice in many parts of the world. A skilled teacher's organization of knowledge can help students understand and remember what has been transmitted.

In contrast to knowledge transmission is a prominent alternative, student-centred, view of teaching, namely constructivism. The American philosopher of education John Dewey (1916) is generally considered to be the founder of constructivism. Like Freire, Dewey rejected approaches that construed learners as receptacles of the teacher's knowledge. In its place, Dewey believed that learning should be socially constructed and teaching meaningful, building on what students already know. This should be accomplished through active engagement with fellow students, the teacher, the world and by reflecting on these experiences. For this reason, a constructivist approach could also be called 'experiential'. Practices associated with this approach are procedures in which students are active thorough experimentation, problem-solving, and dialoguing. Students are also encouraged to reflect upon these experiences by talking about what they did and what understanding they came to.

Another answer to the question about language teaching comes from sociocultural theory, inspired by the Russian psychologist Lev Vygotsky. Vygotsky, in common with Freire and Dewey, saw the importance of social interaction in education. In fact, according to Vygotsky, it is through social interaction that higher order thinking emerges. The 'place' where this is most likely to be facilitated is in the 'zone of proximal development or ZPD', 'the distance between the actual developmental level [of the learner] as determined by independent problem-solving and the level of potential development as determined through problem solving under adult guidance or in collaboration with more capable peers' (Vygotsky 1978: 86). More capable peers (and teachers) aid or 'scaffold' learners in the ZPD, thus contributing a socially oriented rationale for interactive and collaborative pair and group work (Lantolf 2000).

It is a fact that each of the three approaches to teaching that I have briefly touched upon – knowledge transmission, constructivism, and socioculturalism – all confer different roles on language teachers. This is also true of the more narrowly-focused language teaching methods, positioning teachers across the spectrum from drill conductor and model (e.g. the Audio-Lingual Method) to facilitator and counsellor (e.g. Community Language Learning) (Larsen-Freeman 2000). While some say today's times call for us to move beyond methods, adopting post-method macro-strategies in place of prescribed and proscribed methodological practices (Kumaravadivelu 1994), the fact is that most teachers practise an eclectic form of teaching.

Work on teacher cognition has played an increasingly important role in helping us understand how teachers think and therefore the work of teaching (see Borg, this volume). For instance, in the language teaching field, Woods (1996) has demonstrated the importance of understanding the thinking process that underlies the decisions that teachers make moment by moment in conducting their lessons. Another widespread role ascribed to teachers and other professionals, ever since the publication of Schön's (1983) influential book, is that of 'reflective practitioner', someone who can detach oneself from experience, examine it, and learn from it (Richards and Lockhart 1994). This resonates with Allwright's (2003) 'exploratory practice'. Teachers are encouraged to experiment, to take risks, around some particular issue of interest in their teaching practice. They are then to step back and watch what happens. This set of procedures helps them to clarify issues around their own teaching practice and prevents it from going stale.

A recurring issue with which the field is sometimes called to contend is the widespread belief among non-professionals that if one can speak a language, one can teach it. This is known to be nonsense, although in truth little is known about the amount of training that is optimal or the way it should be distributed in teacher education programmes, i.e. the pre- versus in-service balance, with some arguing that a lengthy time spent on pre-service education before teacher-learners step into the classroom is not productive, and that at a minimum, learners of teaching should undergo a supervised teaching practicum (Bailey 2006).

Another issue that never seems to go away is the one regarding the speaker status of a tea-cher, i.e. native speaker or non-native speaker. While native speakers are preferred in many language education programmes, presumably for the model they provide and the access they have to intuitions about what is correct and how the language works, in actual fact, non-native speakers bring a great number of strengths to language teaching, not the least of which is that they are role models of successful learning themselves. Besides, if they speak the language of their students, they know the obstacles to acquisition and how to surmount them.

As I have visited each of the angles of the triangle, I have avoided suggesting that more recent developments have been superior to what preceded them. In fact, many of the educational developments, both old and new, are widely practised today. While it is true that one approach to language, teaching, and learning seeks to compensate for the perceived inadequacies of its predecessors, there is no perfect approach to language education, nor will there ever be (Prabhu 1990). Following from this premise and the recognition of learner differences, it is quite natural that language teachers would be eclectic. In fact, perhaps the most important role for a language teacher is that of mediator between the textbook/curriculum and the students, in order to address the multifarious and diverse needs of the present class.

Intersecting angles

This sequential treatment of the issues in the different angles suggests a more disjointed view of language education than is warranted. In truth, some of the most striking developments in the field have taken place at the intersection of the angles. Although I have already implicitly dealt with their connection in a few cases (e.g. the connection between a teacher and his or her conception of language; the connection between an interactionist perspective on SLA and task-based syllabi), I should also point out a few more overlaps between them to illustrate their interaction.

Language and learning

Answers to the question about language and about learning often come together in defining different language teaching methods. Another sector of the field at this intersection, which I have yet to introduce, is that of language assessment. From the ongoing assessment of language learning that teachers perform in order to decide on their next teaching move, to the design and administration of high-stakes language proficiency tests to certify language skills and general proficiency, assessing the language that has been learned is a major force in language education. While standardized tests have typically made use of indirect measures of language proficiency, such as multiple-choice tests, more and more direct measures, such as oral proficiency interviews, are being employed these days (see O'Sullivan, this volume).

To facilitate comparisons of language proficiency among individuals and between different systems of qualifications, the Common European Framework of Reference was developed. Through it, individuals can self-report or be assessed at certain levels defined by what they can do in another language. It is also important to recognize that individuals do not have complete and separate competences of the languages they have knowledge of (Cook 2002). As a result, the Council of Europe (2001) has developed the European language portfolio, a document in which learners can record their individual language and cultural experiences.

Language and teaching

A recent example of the intersection between language and teaching is one in which language teaching materials are informed by linguistic corpora, large databases of spoken utterances and written materials/texts, which can be mined with computer search engines to reveal language patterns. The patterns reveal collocations or conventionalized sequences for particular lexical items. The way that we express meaning in language is not through stringing together individual words, but rather is in the form of phrasal units and lexicalized stems that become conventionalized over time with use (see Adolphs and Lin, this volume).

Learners and language

The learner's age is often the deciding factor as to what type of language is studied. Many younger learners these days are being taught language through content. In content and language integrated learning (CLIL) or content-based language teaching, the language is the vehicle through which other school subjects are learned. This approach has often been adopted with the needs of immigrant children in mind. It is thought that postponing children's education in other subjects while they learn the language of instruction might be detrimental to their overall education. However, these days CLIL is being implemented in some countries, Spain and the Netherlands, for example, as a way to integrate English into the curriculum of all children.

The focus of instruction for older students is frequently different. Their reason for studying a language is often due to a particular goal, which results in their study of language for a specific occupational, technical, or academic purpose.

Context

One aspect of the figure that I have yet to discuss is the role of context, which can mean many things, not the least of which is the physical locale – where the language learning/education has taken place.

Much of the language learning in the world, although by no means all, takes place in classrooms, though this may be changing with the possibility of more autonomous learning, aided by technological advancements (see below). For example, in a new study conducted in

Austria, it was reported that 15 per cent of Austrians older than fifteen have learned one or more foreign languages outside of high school or university in the last ten years. However, in many parts of the world, classes are very large, and as much for classroom management as for promoting language acquisition, much of the work is done individually in a written form or in whole group choral responses. Although some SLA research has found that learning in and outside of the classroom is similar in certain respects (e.g. Felix 1981), others have found this not to be true in the case of the type of errors learners commit, for example (Pica 1983). Through language immersion programmes and study abroad opportunities, students can receive intensive experiences with language, which compensates for the slow progress and incomplete acquisition of many who study languages exclusively in the classroom.

Political pressures present in the context can also be influential. For instance, whereas bilingual education used to be a popular way to help students acquire another language while maintaining their heritage language and not falling behind in other subject matter, it has been considered a politically unpopular educational option in some circles and has been abolished in certain states of the USA. Then, too, whereas multilingualism is prevalent in many parts of the world and the plurilingualism of individuals promoted, increasing globalization has given rise to 'utilitarian' language teaching, and the dominance of a few languages, especially English as an international language of trade, commerce, technology, and science.

Also playing a contextual role are national language policies. One striking example of this is the termination of Russian language programmes in countries that formerly comprised the Soviet Union. For instance, Tajikistan has drafted a new law banning the use of Russian and other minority languages in advertisements, business papers, and government documents. Since the dissolution of the Soviet Union, students are being instructed in other modern languages, primarily English. Closely related to which languages are promoted in language policies is the matter of language ideology or the beliefs that people hold about language. For instance, Lippi-Green (1997) calls attention to the bias that exists towards an abstract, homogeneous standard language, which becomes what is taught despite the fact that there is a great deal of variation in actual language use outside the classroom.

Future trajectory

With the migration of the world's population on the rise, one of the current and likely to be future issues is how to support the complex needs of students being taught and expected to learn through a language that is not their native tongue (Bailey *et al.* 2008). General education teachers are increasingly expected to teach language to students from diverse backgrounds. At the same time, second language teachers are expected to support these students' learning across the curriculum. This demand is pushing the field of second language teaching to redefine its knowledge base and professional competencies.

A not unrelated issue confronting language educators these days is the fact that many of the world's languages are endangered. Whereas language policies in some countries have brought certain languages, such as Irish Gaelic, back from the brink, the rate at which other languages are dying out is worrisome. Concerted efforts to teach these languages must be made, or they will be lost forever.

Another related issue is which language to teach. As I have indicated earlier, English is the current favourite due to the global economy, but perhaps in the future it will be Chinese, as clearly Chinese is spoken by far more native speakers than English, although English currently surpasses all other languages in the number of people who speak it non-natively (Graddol 2006). Its dominance has led to concern for linguistic/cultural imperialism (Phillipson 1992)

165

(see Canagarajah and Ben Said, this volume). There are those, however, who point out that there need not be a hegemonic standard English, given that many varieties of world Englishes exist, moulded by the influences of (usually) post-colonial contexts in which they are spoken natively (see Kirkpatrick and Deterding, this volume). For other researchers, English has already become an international lingua franca and is therefore not owned by native speakers of English at all. As such, it may evolve a grammar and a sound system that is distinctive from native dialects, but which is somehow easier to acquire, while facilitating intercultural communication, often among non-native speakers of English with each other (Jenkins 2000; Seidlhofer 2001). Of course, questions of which language to teach and whose language it is do not involve English exclusively. Teachers of all languages wrestle with this issue. For example, Arabic instructors have to choose which dialect of spoken Arabic to teach, as the dialects vary substantially from one another and from the modern written standard.

A final issue that I will point to is the ambivalence to the study of other languages that exists in some circles. Perhaps, not surprisingly, the ambivalence is often most manifest in English-speaking countries. Also, not surprisingly, interest in other languages picks up during times of national crisis, when the government laments not having speakers of particular languages, deemed 'strategic'. Under those circumstances, there is a big infusion of government funding to encourage the teaching of certain languages, such as under the recent National Strategic Languages Initiative in the United States. At other times, when the perceived crisis is over, the level of funding is not sustained and the study of other languages languishes. Perhaps an exception to this trend is the US government's continuing sponsorship of Language Resource Centers, sited at universities throughout the country. All these centres have Websites, many of which offer language teaching materials and other resources, especially helpful in the case of the less commonly taught languages.

Another example of the ambivalence towards the study of other languages is what is currently taking place in the UK. It is now compulsory for children in primary schools in England to be taught a foreign language (this will be the case from 2010), but at the same time it is no longer mandatory for pupils to study a language beyond the age of fourteen. This move has led to plummeting numbers of students taking a modern language at GCSE. It seems the government is sending a mixed message.

Technology

There are three major ways that technology and language learning/education have interfaced in modern times. They are computer-mediated contact with other languages/cultures, the use of corpora to inform language teaching materials (and methods), and Internet-delivered language instruction. I will touch upon each of these in turn (see Kern, this volume).

Computer-mediated contact has meant that learners can engage with other learners of the same language or even with native speakers of the language they are studying. This might take the form of students' interacting in chat rooms or outside of class in online discussions with classmates. It has been found that such contact encourages the production of more language on the part of students, especially ones who might be more reticent to participate in face-to-face discussion in class. Of course, often the exchanges take the form of writing, not speech, although with increased bandwidth and such programmes as Skype, spoken interaction is possible. The opportunity for students to make contact with others in chat rooms and social networking sites has a positive influence on student motivation. Students who do not see the point of learning a foreign language find interacting with someone who speaks the other language very motivating. It should be pointed out, though, that conventional wisdom has it that the best approach is a blended one, involving both face-to-face and distance/computer-mediated interaction.

Every day one learns about a new corpus being developed. Each corpus acts as a database for written or transcribed oral language, which can be used to inform language teaching materials. Access to corpora comprising millions of words of text, makes it easy to discern usage patterns, which traditional grammars and descriptions of language have missed. For example, 'bordered on' can have a geographic reference, but it is used more often in reporting an undesirable situation, e.g. 'bordering on arrogance' (Schmitt 2009). In addition, students themselves are being taught to search corpora when they have their own question about collocates and connotations and context.

I think it is fair to say that the Internet has not yet delivered on its promise to make language education accessible to millions who would otherwise be denied it, especially in chronically understaffed language teaching situations. For example, the demand for English in China and the increasing popularity of the study of Chinese elsewhere has led to a national shortage of English teachers in China and a worldwide shortage of Chinese language teachers. However, technology may provide at least a short-term solution. One of the items making the headlines recently was an announcement from National Taiwan University that it will develop a worldwide online Mandarin Chinese teaching project.

Another advantage of Web-based instruction is that it provides access to languages that might not be offered locally. For instance, earlier this year, the University of California–Los Angeles (UCLA), went live with its Web-based instructional programmes in Azeri and the Iraqi dialect of Arabic. This development allows UCLA to send language instruction to other campuses of the University of California system, and in turn to receive instructional programmes in Danish, Filipino, Khmer, and Zulu from the University of California, Berkeley, which may present a partial solution to the problem of keeping robust the less commonly taught, even endangered, languages.

Chapter summary

In this chapter, I have highlighted some of the issues in language learning and education, without making the chapter one lengthy list (although it may still seem so to readers). In place of a list, I have offered readers what I have found to be a useful heuristic for organizing developments in the field, namely a set of questions. As I have considered a few answers to each, I have looked briefly at different definitions of language, theories of learning, individual learner factors, approaches to language teaching, and roles of language teachers. In some cases, I have discussed the pedagogical implications that have been informed by the answers to the questions. The truth is that the questions, which have yielded different answers in different places at different times, have implications for language education, though no question-and-answer or combination of questions and answers will produce a satisfactory solution for all times and places, due to local social, political, and economic factors, the uniqueness of individual language learners and instructional contexts, ever-new research findings, and the theoretical commitments educators make.

Although the areas of language learning and language education intersect, there remain some uneasy fits as well, such as the perennial one between structural and functional approaches. There is also some ebb and flow among the general populace, at least in some countries of the world, in the interest accorded modern language study. With the economic climate that globalization has engendered, often it is the international languages that do attract students, the result being that languages that are spoken by fewer speakers are becoming increasingly endangered. Although technology is not likely to resolve every issue, it does promise increased accessibility to language instruction for those who have the technological wherewithal, the access, and the computer literacy to take advantage of such instruction. It also may provide the means to keep some of the less commonly taught languages vital.

Related topics

Due to the broad coverage in this chapter, many of the other chapters in this volume are related. I have drawn attention to some of these already. Perhaps, though, the chapters that most complement this one are Scott Thornbury's chapter on methodology and Lourdes Ortega's chapter on second language acquisition.

Further reading

Larsen-Freeman, D. and Anderson, M. (2011) *Techniques and Principles in Language Teaching*, 3rd edn, Oxford: Oxford University Press. (This third edition explores a number of language teaching methods and methodological innovations by offering readers analyses of classroom lessons in terms of their philosophical underpinnings and the activities that are practised.)
Long, M. and Doughty, C. (eds) (2009) *The Handbook of Language Teaching*, Malden, MA: Blackwell. (The chapters in this handbook span a number of topics in the field, with each covering research findings on core issues.)
Spolsky, B. and Hult, F. (eds) (2008) *The Handbook of Educational Linguistics*, Malden, MA: Blackwell. (This volume contains forty-four chapters, featuring reviews of many areas of educational linguistics, including a section on research-practice relationships.)

References

Allwright, D. (2003) 'Exploratory practice: rethinking practitioner research in language teaching', *Language Teaching Research* 7(2): 113–41.
Bailey, F., Burkett, B. and Freeman, D. (2008) 'The mediating role of language in teaching and learning: a classroom perspective', in B. Spolsky and F. Hult (eds) *The Handbook of Educational Linguistics*, Malden, MA: Blackwell.
Bailey, K. M. (2006) *Language Teacher Supervision*, Cambridge: Cambridge University Press.
Becker, A. L. (1983) 'Toward a post-structuralist view of language learning: a short essay', *Language Learning* 33: 217–20.
Bloomfield, L. (1942) *Outline Guide for the Practical Study of Foreign Languages*, Baltimore: Linguistic Society of America.
Blum-Kulka, S., House, J. and Kasper, G. (eds) (1989) *Cross-cultural Pragmatics: Requests and Apologies*, Norwood, NJ: Ablex.
Candlin, C. N. and Candlin, S. (2003) 'Healthcare communication: a problematic site for applied linguistics research', *Annual Review of Applied Linguistics* 23: 134–54.
Carroll, J. (1963) 'Research on teaching foreign languages', in N. Gage (ed.) *Handbook of Research on Teaching*, Chicago: Rand-McNally.
Chomsky, N. (1965) *Aspects of the Theory of Syntax*, Cambridge, MA: MIT Press.
Cook, G. and Seidlhofer, B. (eds) (1995) *Principle and Practice in Applied Linguistics*, Oxford: Oxford University Press.
Cook, V. (2002) *Portraits of the L2 User*, Clevedon: Multilingual Matters.
Council of Europe (2001) *Common European Framework of Reference for Languages: Learning, Teaching and Assessment*, Cambridge: Cambridge University Press.
Dewey, J. (1916) *Democracy and Education*, New York: Macmillan.
Dörnyei, Z. (2009) *The Psychology of Second Language Acquisition*, Oxford: Oxford University Press.
Ellis, N. and Larsen-Freeman, D. (2006) 'Language emergence: implications for applied linguistics, introduction to the special issue', *Applied Linguistics* 27: 558–89.

——(2009) 'Constructing a second language: analyses and computational simulations of the emergence of linguistic constructions from usage', special issue, *Language Learning* 59, issue supplement s1: 90–125.

Fairclough, N. (1995) *Critical Discourse Analysis: The Critical Study of Language*, Boston: Addison Wesley.

Felix, S. (1981) 'The effect of formal instruction on second language acquisition', *Language Learning* 31: 87–112.

Freire, P. (1970) *Pedagogy of the Oppressed*, New York: Herder and Herder.

Fries, C. C. (1945) *Teaching and Learning English as a Foreign Language*, Ann Arbor, MI: University of Michigan Press.

Gardner, H. (1983) *Frames of Mind: The Theory of Multiple Intelligences*, New York: Basic Books.

Gardner, R. (1985) *Social Psychology and Second Language Learning: The Role of Attitudes and Motivation*, London: Edward Arnold.

Gardner, R. and Lambert, W. (1972) *Attitudes and Motivation in Second Language Learning*, Rowley, MA: Newbury House.

Gass, S. (1997) *Input, Interaction, and the Development of Second Languages*, Mahwah, NJ: Lawrence Erlbaum Associates.

Gatbonton, E. and Segalowitz, N. (1988) 'Creative automatization: principles for promoting fluency within a communicative framework', *TESOL Quarterly* 22: 473–92.

Goldberg, A. (2006) *Constructions at Work: The Nature of Generalization in Language*, Oxford: Oxford University Press.

Graddol, D. (2006) *English Next*, London: The British Council.

Halliday, M. A. K. (1978) *Language as Social Semiotic: The Social Interpretation of Language and Meaning*, London: Edward Arnold.

Holliday, A. (1994) *Appropriate Methodology and Social Context*, New York: Cambridge University Press.

Hymes, D. (1972) 'On communicative competence', in J. B. Pride and J. Holmes (eds) *Sociolinguistics: Selected Readings*, Harmondsworth: Penguin Books.

Jenkins, J. (2000) *The Phonology of English as an International Language*, Oxford: Oxford University Press.

Kramsch, C. (ed.) (2002) *Language Acquisition and Language Socialization: Ecological Perspectives*, London: Continuum.

Krashen, S. (1982) *Principles and Practice in Second Language Acquisition*, Oxford: Pergamon.

Kumaravadivelu, B. (1994) 'The postmethod condition: emerging strategies for second/foreign language teaching', *TESOL Quarterly* 28: 27–48.

Lafford, B. (ed.) (2007) 'Second language acquisition reconceptualised? The impact of Firth and Wagner (1997)', *The Modern Language Journal* 91, Focus Issue.

Langacker, R. (1968) *Language and its Structure: Some Fundamental Linguistic Concepts*, New York: Harcourt Brace and World.

Lantolf, J. P. (ed.) (2000) *Sociocultural Theory and Second Language Learning*, Oxford: Oxford University Press.

Larsen-Freeman, D. (1997) 'Chaos/complexity science and second language acquisition', *Applied Linguistics* 18: 141–65.

——(2000) *Techniques and Principles in Language Teaching*, 2nd edn, Oxford: Oxford University Press.

——(2003) *Teaching Language: From Grammar to Grammaring*, Boston: Heinle/Cengage.

——(2006) 'The emergence of complexity, fluency, and accuracy in the oral and written production of five Chinese learners of English', *Applied Linguistics* 27: 590–619.

——(2007) 'Reflecting on the cognitive-social debate in second language acquisition', *Modern Language Journal* 91: 771–85.

Larsen-Freeman, D. and Cameron, L. (2008) *Complex Systems and Applied Linguistics*, Oxford: Oxford University Press.

Larsen-Freeman, D. and Freeman, D. (2008) 'Language moves: the place of "foreign" languages in classroom teaching and learning', *Review of Research in Education* 32: 147–86.

Lenneberg, E. (1964) 'The capacity for language acquisition', in J. Fodor and J. Katz (eds) *The Structure of Language*, Englewood Cliffs, NJ: Prentice Hall.

Li, D. (1998) '"It's always more difficult than you plan and imagine." Teachers' perceived difficulties in introducing the communicative approach in South Korea', *TESOL Quarterly* 32: 677–703.

Lippi-Green, R. (1997) *English with an Accent*, London: Routledge.

Long, M. (1991) 'Focus on form: a design feature in language teaching methodology', in K. de Bot, R. Ginsberg and C. Kramsch (eds) *Foreign Language Research in Cross-cultural Perspective*, Amsterdam and Philadelphia: John Benjamins.

——(1996) 'The role of the linguistic environment in second language acquisition', in W. C. Ritchie and T. K. Bhatia (eds) *Handbook of Second Language Acquisition*, San Diego, CA: Academic Press.

MacWhinney, B. (2006) 'Emergentism: use often and with care', *Applied Linguistics* 27: 729–40.

Oxford, R. (1989) *Language Learning Strategies: What Every Teacher Should Know*, Boston: Heinle/Cengage.

Phillipson, R. (1992) *Linguistic Imperialism*, Oxford: Oxford University Press.

Pica, T. (1983) 'Adult acquisition of English as a second language under different conditions of exposure', *Language Learning* 33: 465–97.

Prabhu, N. S. (1987) *Second Language Pedagogy*, Oxford: Oxford University Press.

——(1990) 'There is no best method–why?' *TESOL Quarterly* 24: 225–41.

Richards, J. C. and Lockhart, C. (1994) *Reflective Teaching in Second Language Classrooms*, Cambridge: Cambridge University Press.

Sacks, H., Schegloff, E. A. and Jefferson, G. (1974) 'A simplest systematics for the organization of turn-taking for conversation', *Language* 50(4): 696–735.

de Saussure, F. (1916) *Cours de linguistiques générale*, W. Baskin (trans.) (1959) as *Course in General Linguistics*, New York: Philosophical Library.

Schmitt, N. (2009) 'What language models must explain', presentation at the Conference of the American Association of Applied Linguists, March 2009, Denver.

Schön, D. A. (1983) *The Reflective Practitioner: How Professionals Think in Action*, London: Temple Smith.

Schultz, R. (2001) 'Cultural differences in student and teacher perceptions concerning the role of grammar instruction and corrective feedback. USA–Colombia', *Modern Language Journal* 85: 244–57.

Schumann, J. (1976) 'Second language acquisition research: getting a more global look at the learner', special issue, *Language Learning* 4: 15–28.

Seidlhofer, B. (2001) 'Closing a conceptual gap: the case for a description of English as a lingua franca', *International Journal of Applied Linguistics* 11: 133–58.

Skinner, B. F. (1957) *Verbal Behavior*, Acton, MA: Copley Publishing Group.

Slobin, D. (1996) 'From "thought and language" to "thinking for speaking"', in J. J. Gumperz and S. C. Levinson (eds) *Rethinking Linguistic Relativity*, New York: Cambridge University Press.

Snow, C. E. (1979) 'The role of social interaction in language acquisition', in A. Collins (ed.) *Children's Language and Communication: Proceedings of the 1977 Minnesota Symposium on Child Development*, Hillsdale, NJ: Lawrence Erlbaum Associates.

Spolsky, B. (1989) *Conditions for Second Language Learning*, Oxford: Oxford University Press.

Swales, J. (1990) *Genre Analysis*, Cambridge: Cambridge University Press.

Tomasello, M. (2003) *Constructing a Language: A Usage-based Theory of Language Acquisition*, Cambridge, MA: Harvard University Press.

Vygotsky, L. S. (1978) *Mind in Society: The Development of Higher Psychological Processes*, Cambridge, MA: Harvard University Press.

Widdowson, H. G. (1992) *Practical Stylistics*, Oxford: Oxford University Press.

Wilkins, D. A. (1976) *Notional Syllabuses*, Oxford: Oxford University Press.

Willis, J. (1996) *A Framework for Task-based Learning*, Harlow: Pearson Longman.

Woods, D. (1996) *Teacher Cognition in Language Teaching*, Cambridge: Cambridge University Press.

12

Second language acquisition

Lourdes Ortega

Introduction

The field of Second Language Acquisition (SLA) is a branch of applied linguistics that has a history extending over half a century. It investigates the human capacity to learn additional languages during late childhood, adolescence, or adulthood, once the first language, in the case of monolinguals, or the first languages, in the case of bilinguals and multilinguals, have been acquired. SLA researchers strive to shed light on four overarching questions:

1　How do humans learn additional languages after they have learned their first?
2　In what ways is the learning of an additional language different from the learning of languages for which exposure is available from birth, and in what ways might it be similar?
3　What factors contribute to the variability observed in rates and outcomes of additional language learning?
4　What does it take to attain advanced language and literacy competencies in a language that is learned later in life?

SLA shares its interest in explaining human language development with two other fields, both of which study first language acquisition from the womb to right before children enter school. These are Bilingual First Language Acquisition (BFLA), which examines language development among infants and children when they grow up surrounded by two or more languages from birth (De Houwer 2009), and First Language Acquisition (FLA), also known as Child Language Acquisition, which investigates how infants and children learn their first language when they grow up surrounded by one language only (Clark 2003).

The differences in focus between these two fields and SLA are important. First, in the fields of bilingual and monolingual first language acquisition, infants and toddlers are investigated at the critical point in life when they are discovering human language, as instantiated in the specific language(s) that their carers happen to speak to them. By contrast, all participants in SLA studies will already be relatively mature users of at least one language, often more. Their existing language competencies will influence their learning of the language that is being added to their repertoire. Second, at the point of first language acquisition, infants and toddlers must develop socially and conceptually in tandem with developing linguistically. On the other hand, adults, adolescents, and even children as young as four or five, can be expected to bring to the task already relatively sophisticated and increasingly fine-tuned social and conceptual structures. Finally, BFLA and FLA researchers typically assume naturalistic conditions of language learning, because infants and toddlers learn language by being surrounded by meaningful language use and in the absence of instruction. SLA researchers, on the other hand, investigate language learning in any possible context, ranging from naturalistic acquisition within a non-instructional community (e.g. a neighbourhood, a church group, the workplace, or during regular schooling that happens to occur in a new language), to formal instruction of various kinds (e.g. tutorials or self-access; second, foreign, or heritage language classrooms; or classroom-engineered immersion settings), and often a combination of the two. This being so, instruction is an important area of study in SLA (see Larsen-Freeman, this volume).

SLA theories in historical perspective

Scholars have written about how people learn second languages and how to best teach foreign languages since ancient times. When in the late 1960s SLA emerged as a formal research community, it did so shaped by these long-standing interests in language learning and teaching. Additional influences came from more specific developments in the field of FLA, which at the time had been transformed by a process of theoretical renewal in reaction against the prevailing behaviourist view of language acquisition and had begun to yield exciting empirical findings about how children who grow up monolingual learn their mother tongue (e.g. Brown 1973).

The awakenings of SLA: interlanguage

The years 1967 and 1972 mark the publication of two seminal papers by Pit Corder and Larry Selinker that are often associated with the awakenings of the field because of the importance of the arguments they put forth. At an empirical level, they called to question the dominant practice of contrastive analysis, which looked for acquisition answers in the exhaustive comparison of the linguistic inventories of the language pairs involved in the learning task, the first language and the target language. Instead, Corder (1967) and Selinker (1972) argued researchers must turn for evidence to the actual language produced by learners as they try to communicate in the target second language (L2). This meant examining the 'errors' learners produce not as something to be pre-empted or remedied but as objects of study that hold great value for understanding L2 acquisition. At the theoretical level, the behaviourist view of language acquisition as mere habit formation was rejected and replaced by a novel conceptualization of acquisition as creative construction. For the first time, learners were viewed as active and rational agents who engaged in the discovery of underlying L2 rules. They formed hypotheses about the language, tested them, and employed a number of cognitive and social strategies to regulate their learning. These developments made interlanguage investigations during the 1970s and 1980s increasingly more focused on cognitive and psycholinguistic aspects of acquisition. Nevertheless, a few SLA researchers also working within the interlanguage tradition turned their attention to exploring the potential of quantitative sociolinguistic theories of variation for the study of L2 development (e.g. Tarone 1988).

Once the foundations of interlanguage as a novel and distinct object of inquiry were laid out, there was a justification for the need for a field that would investigate additional language development in its own right. After these beginnings, several broad phases can be distinguished in the history of SLA. The narrative depiction of orderly historical trends that follows below is only a convenient shorthand that undoubtedly obscures more complicated developments.

From first theories to the cognitive and linguistic emphases of the 1990s

By the early 1980s, the first attempt at a formal theory of L2 acquisition was mustered in the United States by Stephen Krashen (1985). Known as the Monitor Model, this theory became (and has remained) popular with language teachers. In a nutshell, Krashen proposed that: (a) the core ingredient of additional language learning is meaningful, comprehensible input; (b) the processes of additional language acquisition are implicit and subconscious and any explicit and conscious processes that may be summoned in the classroom can only help careful monitored performance but will have little effects on true language knowledge or on spontaneous performance; and (c) the main obstacles to additional language learning for adults stem from affective inhibitions. Despite its popularity, already in the mid-1980s the Monitor Model was evaluated as being too metaphorical to lend itself to proper empirical investigation. The strongest critiques were levelled by SLA scholars who were well versed in skills acquisition theory from the field of psychology (e.g. McLaughlin 1987), and also by scholars who had begun applying Universal Grammar theory from the field of linguistics to the disciplinary SLA project (e.g. Gregg 1984). In both cases, the criticisms also served to carve intellectual spaces for these newer kinds of SLA theories.

Thus, as the 1980s came to a close, the SLA research community had already developed several theoretically distinct proposals for explaining L2 acquisition. One view (Krashen 1985) was that L2 acquisition occurs within dimensions defined largely by input and affect and operating mostly at the unconscious level. Another position (McLaughlin 1987) held that learning an additional language is a complex, cognitive process similar to any other human learning (cooking, playing chess, riding a bike, thinking mathematically, knowing history); as such, it involves great amounts of experience aided by attention and memory and it must include the development of sufficient declarative knowledge about the language and sufficient deliberate practice to eventually support fully automatic use of language. A third view (White 1989) was that the mental grammar of second language learners must be explained by the relative contributions of two forces that guide tacit language knowledge formation and that are independent from other cognitive operations, and even relatively independent from surrounding ambient experience, namely abstract knowledge of Universal Grammar (which the human species is endowed with at birth) and more specific knowledge of a given first language (which is imprinted in the mind of language users during the critical years of learning a first language or languages).

Particularly during the 1990s, these varied SLA research efforts were strengthened to the point of cohering into what looked like one of two dominant approaches. A cognitive-interactionist prism (Larsen-Freeman and Long 1991) was strongly influenced by Swiss psychologist Jean Piaget and easily accommodated within it the interlanguage research tradition as well as the skills acquisition theory. It called for the examination of L2 acquisition as the sum contributions of learner-internal factors, such as attention and memory, and learner-external factors, such as the interactions offered to learners in the target language and the quality of any formal instruction they might seek. By contrast, a formal linguistic SLA prism (Hawkins 2001; White 1989) was strongly influenced by US linguist Noam Chomsky and flourished out of the strides made by this linguistic theory during the late 1980s. This research programme sought to tease out the degree to which Universal Grammar knowledge, knowledge stemming from the first language, or a combination of the two, guided the construction of mental L2 grammars. These two traditions have enjoyed continuity at both empirical and theoretical levels up to the present day, thus leading to considerable accumulation of disciplinary knowledge in the areas to which they have been applied.

The fate of other foundational SLA work, by comparison, appeared less promising. SLA researchers' interest in Krashen's Monitor Model had quickly waned. Likewise, the quantitative sociolinguistic forays into SLA heralded by a few interlanguage researchers (e.g. Tarone 1988) had seemingly remained of interest to only a minority in the field. It would take a few more years for the field to return to their important argument that language learning is fundamentally social.

Theoretical expansions: socioculturalism and emergentism

Already in the mid-1990s, however, two new theoretical forces joined the field and began new SLA traditions that soon would grow enormously in vitality. One is the study of L2 acquisition through the sociocultural theory of mind developed by Russian psychologist Lev Vygotsky, a contemporary of Piaget, and led in SLA by James Lantolf (Lantolf 1994). The other is the application of the usage-based, emergentist family of theories developed in cognitive science and initiated in SLA by Nick Ellis (1996) and Diane Larsen-Freeman (1997). The coexistence of the two better established approaches with the two young but bold newcomers created epistemological tension and led to the gradual articulation of differences.

On the one hand, the two psychologically oriented approaches, cognitive-interactionist and sociocultural, consider the learner's mind and the surrounding environment as essential dimensions of inquiry, but they differ radically in their position as to how the two should be investigated. For the cognitive-interactionist approach (well synthesized by Larsen-Freeman and Long 1991), mind and environment are analytically separable, and the influences stemming from one or the other should be isolated as learner-internal and learner-external factors, so that then their interactions can be investigated. This position is also known as interactionism in the first language development literature (see Bohannon and Bonvillian 2009). Mechanisms that explain how the linguistic data available in the surrounding external environment are used for internally driven learning invoke cognitive constructs such as *noticing*, when new features of language become available, even if most fleetingly, for conscious recognition. Environmental constructs of importance include *negotiation for meaning*, when interlocutors edit and reformulate their own and each other's language as they strive to make themselves understood, and *negative feedback*, when interlocutors wittingly or unwittingly offer potential evidence that a language choice may not be sanctioned by the speech community. By contrast, for the Vygotskian sociocultural approach (first synthesized at book length by Lantolf and Thorne 2006), mind is irrevocably social, and therefore it can only be investigated holistically in the unfolding process of social action and interaction. The construction of new knowledge (including knowledge of an additional language) arises in the social plane and gradually becomes internalized psychologically by the individual. Mechanisms that explain how new linguistic knowledge and capable behaviour come about invoke social processes such as *mediation* of activity by language through *private speech* (audible speech directed to the self), *social speech* (speech by more expert others with the aim to help regulate action by novices), and *inner speech* (inaudible speech directed to the self for self-regulation). Another important construct related to learning is the *zone of proximal development*. This refers to an emergent quality of collaborative social action by which knowledge that by itself would be above the current competencies of one or more of the participants becomes momentarily attainable through joint context-sensitive collaboration, thus potentially being available for individual, independent use at a later point.

The formal linguistic approach and the emergentist approach to SLA, too, exhibit key differences amidst critically intersecting interests. Both are vested in explaining language development as part of cognitive science, but they clash in their incompatible assumptions about what human language is and about the relative contributions that nature and nurture make to its development. Formal linguistic SLA researchers (Wakabayashi, this volume) adhere to radical nativism, modularity, and rule-based representationism. That is, they believe language is a biologically given faculty unique to the human species (*nativism*), operating independently from other cognitive faculties used to learn and process other kinds of knowledge (*modularity*), and encoded as a system of abstract rules of the sort that have been described in formal linguistic grammars (*rule-based representationism*). In sharp contrast, emergentist, usage-based SLA researchers (Ellis, this volume) are empiricist, generalist, and associationist. In other words, they hold that language in each individual emerges out of massive amounts of experience with the linking of form and meaning through language use that is driven by the species' social need to communicate (*empiricism*), enabled by simple memory and attention processing mechanisms that are the same as employed for all other cognitive functions (*generalism*), and self-organized out of the human brain's unique capacity to implicitly and mandatorily tally the statistical properties and contextual contingencies of the linguistic input they experience over a lifetime (*associationism*).

SLA after the social turn

The tensions briefly outlined above were only the tip of the iceberg of a wider social turn (Block 2003) which continued to gain momentum in the late 1990s. Not only Vygotskian socioculturalists (e.g. Pavlenko and Lantolf 2000) but also many other scholars from the wider field of applied linguistics criticized the SLA research community for investigating L2 acquisition in a-social and decontextualized ways (e.g. Firth and Wagner 1997).

The crisis fuelled by the social turn has left the field richer in theories and approaches. Among the most important new contributors, we find less cognitively and more socially minded approaches that have undertaken the task to re-specify in social terms all key elements in the SLA equation. Thus, if Vygotskian SLA already beginning in the mid-1990s offered a re-specification of *cognition* as fundamentally social (Thorne and Tasker, this volume), since then other SLA theories have contributed formal ways of studying additional language learning as social in terms of grammar, oral interaction, learning, and sense of self. Specifically, *grammar and language* are theorized as social in systemic functional linguistics for SLA (Young, this volume); *oral interaction* is redefined as social in conversation analysis as well as in other discourse approaches to additional language learning (Hellermann 2008; Young 2009); *learning* itself is understood as social in language socialization (He, this volume); and *sense of self* is reconceptualized as irrevocably social in identity theory (Norton, this volume).

Key themes in SLA research

Many themes have attracted attention in SLA, of which I have selected five that I consider to be fundamental areas of SLA inquiry.

Age: what are the effects of an early or a late start?

The question of age is perhaps the most investigated, debated, and misunderstood of all research areas in SLA, most likely because of its extraordinary theoretical and educational importance. No researcher denies that starting age greatly affects the eventual success of additional language learning. Success, naturally, is in the eye of the beholder, and we must not forget to ask: *Who is to judge success: the researcher, the teacher, one of many stakeholders in the life of the additional language user, or the user him- or herself?* When success is strictly understood in linguistic terms as determined by researchers, then it is an empirically established fact that people who begin learning an additional language by naturalistic immersion very early in life tend to attain high levels of linguistic competence, often (but not always) similar to others who begin learning the same language at birth. By comparison, people who begin learning an additional language later in life, and particularly any time after the end of adolescence, exhibit much greater variability in their levels of linguistic attainment. In addition, the majority (although not all) of late-starting language users will develop functional abilities in the new language that are different from and seemingly less proficient than the functional abilities of others who begin learning the same language at birth.

What is hotly debated and remains without a definitive research answer is what precisely explains the observed age effects. Proponents of the critical period hypothesis (e.g. Abrahamsson and Hyltenstam 2009) believe that the explanation is biological, in that they posit a maturational, time-locked schedule after which it is no longer possible to learn a language in exactly the same ways and to exactly the same high degrees of competence as any individual does between birth and age three or four. Sceptics of the critical period hypothesis (e.g. Hakuta 2001), on the other hand, point at alternative, non-biological reasons for the attested age effects, all of which are related to the many differences in experience (linguistic and non-linguistic) between infants and adults. For one, it may be that a later start leads to differential results because one or more other languages have been learned so well already (Flege 1999). This argument warrants careful consideration, given that late starters and early starters alike are usually compared to people who grew up by birth with only one language and therefore exhibit monolingual competence. Yet, monolingual competence cannot be expected to be identical to multilingual competence (Cook 2008). It may also be that the diverging linguistic competencies we observe at increasingly older starting ages are reflective of the varied social, educational, and emotional complications as well as the varied demands on time and pursuits that come with adult life, compared to the more uniform and restricted lives that infants and toddlers lead before they enter school.

The age debate has been further complicated in recent years by research conducted in foreign language contexts, where the availability of input is severely limited (e.g. two or three hours a week of foreign language study, in many school systems). Under such conditions, and when results have been evaluated at the point of high school graduation, beginning a couple of years earlier or later during elementary or middle school made no sizable overall difference (Muñoz 2008). As Muñoz notes, the empirical evidence accumulated from foreign language contexts suggests that age is confounded with another variable that must always be evaluated when interpreting critical period and age-related SLA studies: the quantity and quality of the ambient input.

Crosslinguistic influences stemming from already known languages

A second important theme in SLA research is how previously known languages, and particularly the mother tongue, influence the process of learning an additional language. Both strategically and unknowingly, learners rely on their first language and on other languages they know in order to accomplish something that is as yet unknown to them in the second language. In their comprehensive appraisal of this domain, Jarvis and Pavlenko (2008) identify several noteworthy insights from accumulated research. One is the realization that cross-linguistic phenomena can slow down the pace of learning in cases of language areas where negative transfer occurs, but also accelerate learning and facilitate development in many areas where positive transfer occurs (e.g. for language pairs that are typologically or genetically related and whose lexicons contain many helpful cognates, as in Spanish-English *creatividad* = *creativity*). Second, similarities in a given language pair can often lead to greater learning difficulties than differences do (e.g. in the case of false friends, as when assuming that the words *actualmente* in Spanish and *actually* in English mean the same thing). A third well-attested finding is that crosslinguistic influences are not linearly related to proficiency; instead, different areas of the languages of the individual can result in interactions at some levels of proficiency and not others.

The influence that the mother tongue has on the construction of the new grammar is also an important area of research for scholars who work with formal linguistic theories (Wakabayashi, this volume). However, their goals are different from those of most of the research surveyed by Jarvis and Pavlenko (2008). SLA formal linguistic researchers aim to tease out the differences in the initial and end states of grammar knowledge that obtains when one language is learned by birth, on the one hand, and when a second language is added later in life, on the other. A number of theoretical positions are considered empirically plausible, which are contained within two extremes. At the one extreme, full access to Universal Grammar is proposed and the influence of the L1 is believed to be minimal. This position assumes that first and second language acquisition are fundamentally similar in nature. At the other extreme, no access to Universal Grammar is posited during L2 acquisition and the L1 is afforded a central position in the construction of the L2 grammar. That is, after learning the first language from birth by recourse to Universal Grammar, any subsequent language learning is thought to be accomplished through the more detailed knowledge structures instantiated by the particular first-language grammar that is known already, and by resorting to processing mechanisms that are fundamentally different (Bley-Vroman 2009) from those employed by the infant learning a language or languages from birth to the pre-school years.

Environment and cognition: what are their contributions to additional language learning?

From the beginnings of the field, much SLA research has focused on human interactions and the discourse strategies in them that bring about potentially useful opportunities for learning. We know a great deal about how linguistically mature interlocutors can facilitate additional language learning by rewording their messages through simplifications and elaborations, by asking for clarifications and expansions, and by using language that is appropriate, interesting, and yet slightly above the level of their interlocutors (Long 1996). From socioculturally oriented studies of the environment for SLA, we also know that many additional language learners are actively involved in their own learning processes, both regulating challenges and maximizing learning opportunities as they seek environmental encounters (Brouwer and Wagner 2004; Donato 1994; Kinginger 2004). Finally, we also know that interaction is not a panacea, and that learning opportunities may not be actualized at all when interlocutors are not invested in communicating with each other, when they are antagonistic or, even worse, prejudiced, or (ironically) when they are so emotionally and intellectually engaged in communication that their attention glosses over the formal details of what is new to them in the L2.

Much SLA research since the mid-1990s has investigated issues related to memory, attention, and awareness and how they constrain what can be learned of the additional language, particularly through interaction and formal instruction. While it is clear that the more deliberate attention L2 users pay to new language, the more they learn (Schmidt 1995), it is also clear that much of a new language is learned via implicit attentional processes of extraction of meaning-form correspondences and their associated frequencies and distributions of occurrence (Ellis, this volume). More recently, SLA researchers have turned to the study of the properties of the linguistic data afforded by the environment, often using tools from corpus analysis, and how these properties are processed for learning by the cognitive architecture. Progress in this area will no doubt accelerate in coming years under the impulse of usage-based, emergentist perspectives, since they place the lion's share of acquisition with the statistical and form-and-meaning properties of the input as these interact with the learner's attentional capacities. There is already firm empirical support, for example, that language features that are highly frequent in the input are acquired earlier by L2 learners, provided that they are also phonologically salient and semantically prototypical (e.g. argument structure in Ellis and Ferreira-Junior 2009).

Three approaches to explaining variability of L2 learning across individuals

It has always been noted that adolescents and adults who learn an additional language present a daunting landscape of variability in terms of rates, processes, and outcomes by the time they (or the researchers who investigate them) can say they are 'done' with L2 learning. This issue of variability across individuals has been investigated from three perspectives.

The perspective with the longest tradition is known as *individual differences research* and draws on social psychological constructs and methods (see Dörnyei 2005). This research is quantitative and correlational, and it assumes multiple causal variables interacting and contributing together to explaining variation systematically. We know from SLA research on individual differences that people differ in how much of a gift they have for learning foreign languages and that this natural ability can be measured with precision via language aptitude tests. In general, we can expect aptitude scores and achievements scores (e.g. end-of-course grades, teacher evaluations, and even proficiency scores) to pattern together by about 16 to 36 per cent overlap. Motivation is another source of individual difference that has been investigated particularly energetically by SLA researchers over the years, and several theories have shed light on different qualities of motivation that are important in sustaining and nourishing learning efforts, including integrative motivation, self-determined motivation, and motivation guided by the positive concept of an L2-speaking self (see Dörnyei 2005).

A second perspective that can help explain individual variability is *socio-dynamic* and draws from complexity theory and dynamic systems theory, which are recent approaches within the emergentist family of SLA theories. As Larsen-Freeman and Cameron (2008) note, in the socio-dynamic approach all research is made to be centrally and primarily about variability. Indeed, variability is thought to be an inherent property of the system under investigation and increased variability is interpreted as a precursor for some important change in the system as well. This novel perspective calls for the use of new analytical methods that are quantitative, as in the traditional perspective, but also innovatively different because they are stochastic and non-causal, that is, based on probabilistic estimations that include the possibility of random variations and fluctuations tracked empirically over time (Larsen-Freeman and Cameron

2008). The new variability-centred framework can be applied to any area of SLA, from inter-language data (e.g. Verspoor *et al*. 2008) to the study of aptitude and motivation (e.g. Dörnyei 2010).

A third approach to variability across individuals contrasts sharply with the previous two in taking a *qualitative, sociocultural, and critical* perspective towards the problem at hand. As Norton and Toohey (2001) explain, in this perspective constructs such as motivation, aptitude, and other individual differences are reconceptualized as stemming from the interplay between people's understanding of themselves in the world and the constraints, material and symbolic, that their worlds afford them. These understandings are dialectically shaped by the hopes and aspirations of individuals and by the power structures of the societal milieus that they inhabit. Thus, there is a constant struggle between societal structure and individual agency. Structural dimensions include the socioeconomic power and the histories of settlement of each speech community in a given geography, as well as the naturalized ideologies and worldviews that construct certain attributes (e.g. ethinicity, race, language, culture) as desirable or undesirable. In terms of language learning, specifically, such structural forces shape the symbolic power of the languages in contact within a given social context, for example, Spanish and English in the United States (Valdés 2005) or Spanish, Catalan, and English in Catalonia (Pujolar 2010). They also shape the degree to which an L2 user may be viewed as a legitimate speaker of the language with the right to be heard by others (Norton Peirce 1995), or the roles and identities that are made available to them in their surrounding collective discourses (McKay and Wong 1996). Agency, on the other hand, is the relative power that people can garner as they respond to structural forces in their lives and to the positionalities of their contexts (Norton Peirce 1995; Pavlenko and Lantolf 2000). Agency may allow people to negotiate for themselves, through and in their new language, other desired roles and identities and to gain some access to symbolic and material resources that are mediated by their being a user of the additional language. When the structural and agentive sources of variability are investigated in these ways, we gain unique and much improved insights into how and why people learn or do not learn an additional language.

The role of instruction in SLA

People learning an additional language often seek formal instructional experiences to aid themselves in the process. Answers to what constitutes best language teaching practices have been sought by researchers who specialize in classroom SLA or instructed SLA (Ellis 2005; Lightbown and Spada 2006; Long and Doughty 2009). This sector of the SLA community has directed its efforts towards investigating theoretical questions, of which two seem particularly salient: the integration of form and meaning and the gauging of ideal degrees of explicitness in instructional options.

The question of how best to integrate form and meaning in language instruction has received great attention in instructed SLA. When instruction is designed with the exclusive goal of facilitating the learning of new forms out of context, it is clear that the results are unsatisfactory because the grammar that is understood (e.g. in traditional grammar teaching) or the stock of structures that are memorized (e.g. in audiolingual methods) do not suffice to make students into sophisticated and fluent language users. Conversely, when instruction is designed with the sole concern to surround learners with L2 input clothed in meaningful and interesting content in the new language, it has been shown that the results also fall short of the ideal, because much formal linguistic detail seems to be missed and not learned. This obser-vation is true notwithstanding strong benefits in comprehension, academic learning, and motivation (e.g. in bilingual immersion programmes designed for majority speakers) and despite deceptively fluent learning of the nuts-and-bolts of basic oral language (e.g. in majority-language-only submersion conditions typically inflected upon minority speakers). Different solutions to the question of form-meaning integration are currently investigated, including focus-on-form instruction, task-based language learning, content-based learning, and genre-based language curricula (see chapters in Long and Doughty 2009). The extent to which instructional efforts should be more explicit or more implicit is another central theoretical question in instructed SLA. At a broad level, it appears that instruction that is designed to present language or to directly summon learners to pay attention to language leads to more tangible results, at least in terms of post-test gains (Norris and Ortega 2000). However, we need much more nuanced answers as to what really constitutes degrees of 'explicitness' or 'implicitness' in L2 instruction (Ellis and Sheen 2006) and under what conditions and in what contexts a continuum of options might be successful.

In the end, beyond these efforts at elucidating the types and qualities of instruction that are most conducive to supporting L2 development, it is clear from interlanguage findings accumulated over half a century that with the aid of formal instruction of some kind the developing L2 repertoire can go further, and does so faster, than when L2 users are left to their own devices (Ortega 2009).

Looking into the future

Some research trends, already initiated by SLA scholars in recent years, hold particular promise for the future. First, more SLA researchers are becoming interested in not only the areas of language traditionally investigated the most (grammar, lexis, and phonology, and to a lesser extent pragmatics) but also in novel areas such as L2 gestures, conceptual structures, literacy, discursive practices, and identities (see Jarvis and Pavlenko 2008; Lantolf and Thorne 2006; Young 2009). Second, we are likely to see more in-depth investigation of the multiple directions in which all the languages known by an individual interact, for example, as seen in transfer from the L2 to the first language or from the L2 to a third language (Jarvis and Pavlenko 2008). This trend will hopefully fuel greater recognition by SLA researchers that crosslinguistic influences cannot be seen as a monocausal, monodirectional affair involving privileged knowledge of the mother tongue. Third, more SLA researchers will hopefully explore the actual empirical consequences of acknowledging that additional language learning is fundamentally about learning to become a bilingual or a multilingual and, therefore, about developing multicompetence (Cook 2008), a kind of linguistic competence that is not isomorphic with the competence of a monolingual user. Finally, we are likely to see an expansion of the learner populations studied by SLA researchers, a trend that has already begun, with some researchers representing a variety of theoretical standpoints currently investigating additional language acquisition by younger children (e.g. Haznedar and Gavruseva 2008), heritage learners (e.g. Montrul 2010; Valdés 2005), and youth with low alphabetic print literacy (e.g. Tarone *et al.* 2009).

We can expect that much SLA research will continue to engage with the details of how language competencies are acquired and how language development proceeds, and for this researchers will continue to employ quantitative tools and language analytical techniques that are typically employed in linguistically and psycholinguistically oriented studies of BFLA and FLA as well. A particularly fruitful area for growth in this regard will be the compilation and analysis of learner corpora (e.g. Granger 2009). Assuming that increasingly more SLA researchers will be able to secure training in the methodologies of the cognitive sciences, we may see a burgeoning of SLA studies that probe knowledge of how the brain works as it processes and acquires language by employing methods such as millisecond-sensitive behavioural measures involving reaction times and eye tracking, brain imaging techniques (e.g. functional magnetic resonance imaging and event related potentials), and computational modelling. Particularly important will also be to develop expertise in new graphic and stochastic-quantitative analyses that have been offered by dynamic systems and complexity theories affiliated with the usage-based, emergentist family of SLA theories (Larsen-Freeman and Cameron 2008; Verspoor *et al.* 2011).

On the other hand, given the great expansion of the theoretical landscape that has been brought about by the social turn, other methodologies drawn from qualitative and mixed methods repertoires are likely to become particularly useful for the investigation of SLA problems that are conceptualized as social. Thus, for instance, case study research (Duff 2008), has been a methodology fruitfully employed from the beginning of the field and might again become a preferred choice for SLA researchers in the future. Other qualitative methodological options that are likely to be vigorously used in the future include the microgenetic method employed in Vygotskian SLA, the specific methodologies developed for conversation analysis, and critical ethnographic and critical discourse methodologies tapped by identity theorists and language socialization scholars.

Conclusion

The field of SLA investigates the acquisition of an additional language after the first language or languages have been already learned in life. As such, it seeks to explain human language development by older children, adolescents, and adults across a wide variety of naturalistic, instructed, and mixed contexts. With a history extending over half a century that has been marked by strong influences from language teaching, psychology, and monolingual first language acquisition, SLA continues to be a most porous and interdisciplinary field. Today, it harbours a notable diversity of epistemological approaches. Four theoretical approaches showed tremendous vitality by the close of the twentieth century: cognitive-interactionist, formal linguistic, Vygotskian sociocultural, and usage-based emergentist SLA. SLA in the twenty-first century exhibits novel intellectual influences spurred by the social turn and by new interdisciplinary connections with bilingualism, psycholinguistics, education, anthropology, and sociology. These newer influences have led to the crafting of SLA theories that offer a social re-specification of many SLA interests.

By definition, factors that are specific to SLA inquiry and of central importance in understanding L2 acquisition include the varying *age* at which the additional language begins to be learned and used; the influence exerted by *knowledge of previous languages*, including the language or languages previously acquired from birth and other previously learned additional languages; and the possible contributions of *formal instruction* of various kinds recruited in support of L2 learning. Other factors of equal central importance are common to the study of any kind of human language development, notably the relative contributions of *environment* and *cognition* to the processes of acquisition and the psychological and social sources of the large *individual variability* observed in additional language learning. Although a shared interest with fields that focus on any kind of language acquisition, the investigation of environment, cognition, and individual variability presents unique challenges for SLA researchers. By the time (younger and especially older) people begin acquiring an additional language, they already know a lot about language, about the world, and about themselves; knowing so much both confers advantages and complicates things. Furthermore, life is likely to take each adolescent or adult along multifarious and divergent paths, where the make-up of languages they are exposed to, the educational structures within which they might obtain instruction in and about those languages, and the things they want to (or have to) do with them are radically heterogeneous and variable. These variations in surrounding linguistic, educational, social, and agentive affordances are at the heart of the challenges SLA researchers must contend with as they describe and explain additional language learning.

Related topics

generative grammar; identity; language emergence; language learning and language education; language socialization; multilingualism; sociocultural theory; systemic functional linguistics

Further reading

de Bot, K., Lowie, W. and Verspoor, M. (2005) *Second Language Acquisition: An Advanced Resource Book*, London: Routledge. (An accessible overview of SLA from a dynamic systems perspective.)
Doughty, C. J. and Long, M. H. (eds) (2003) *The Handbook of Second Language Acquisition*, Malden, MA: Wiley-Blackwell. (An advanced resource with chapters by experts on most central SLA topics.)
Ellis, R. (2008) *The Study of Second Language Acquisition*, 2nd edn, Oxford: Oxford University Press. (An encyclopedic and comprehensive survey of the field.)
Herschensohn, J. (2007) *Language Development and Age*, New York: Cambridge University Press. (An original treatment of the topic of age from a formal linguistic SLA perspective.)
Ortega, L. (2009) *Understanding Second Language Acquisition*, London: Hodder Arnold. (A research-oriented but accessible introduction to SLA.)

References

Abrahamsson, N. and Hyltenstam, K. (2009) 'Age of L2 acquisition and degree of nativelikeness: listener perception versus linguistic scrutiny', *Language Learning* 59: 249–306.
Bley-Vroman, R. (2009) 'The evolving context of the fundamental difference hypothesis', *Studies in Second Language Acquisition* 31: 175–98
Block, D. (2003) *The Social Turn in Second Language Acquisition*, Washington, DC: Georgetown University Press.
Bohannon, J. N. I. and Bonvillian, J. D. (2009) 'Theoretical approaches to language development', in J. B. Gleason and N. B. Ratner (eds) *The Development of Language*, Boston: Allyn and Bacon.
Brouwer, C. E. and Wagner, J. (2004) 'Developmental issues in second language conversation', *Journal of Applied Linguistics* 1(1): 29–47.
Brown, R. (1973) *A First Language: The Early Stages*, Cambridge, MA: Harvard University Press.
Clark, E. V. (2003) *First Language Acquisition*, New York: Cambridge University Press.
Cook, V. (2008) 'Multi-competence: black hole or wormhole for second language acquisition research?', in Z. Han (ed.) *Understanding Second Language Process*, Clevedon: Multilingual Matters.
Corder, S. P. (1967) 'The significance of learners' errors', *International Review of Applied Linguistics* 5: 161–70.
De Houwer, A. (2009) *Bilingual First Language Acquisition*, Bristol: Multilingual Matters.
Donato, R. (1994) 'Collective scaffolding in second language learning', in J. P. Lantolf and G. Appel (eds) *Vygotskian Perspectives to Second Language Research*, Norwood, NJ: Ablex.
Dörnyei, Z. (2005) *The Psychology of the Language Learner: Individual Differences in Second Language Acquisition*, Mahwah, NJ: Lawrence Erlbaum Associates.
——(2010) 'The relationship between language aptitude and language learning motivation: individual differences from a dynamic systems perspective', in E. Macaro (ed.) *Continuum Companion to Second Language Acquisition*, London: Continuum.

Duff, P. A. (2008) *Case Study Research in Applied Linguistics*, New York: Routledge.

Ellis, N. C. (1996) 'Sequencing in SLA: phonological memory, chunking, and points of order', *Studies in Second Language Acquisition* 18(1): 91–126.

Ellis, N. C. and Ferreira-Junior, F. (2009) 'Construction learning as a function of frequency, frequency distribution, and function', *Modern Language Journal* 93: 370–85.

Ellis, R. (2005) 'Principles of instructed language learning', *System* 33: 209–24.

Ellis, R. and Sheen, Y. (2006) 'Re-examining the role of recasts in second language acquisition', *Studies in Second Language Acquisition* 28: 575–600.

Firth, A. and Wagner, J. (1997) 'On discourse, communication, and (some) fundamental concepts in SLA research', *The Modern Language Journal* 81: 285–300.

Flege, J. E. (1999) 'Age of learning and second-language speech', in D. P. Birdsong (ed.) *Second Language Acquisition and the Critical Period Hypothesis*, Hillsdale, NJ: Lawrence Erlbaum Associates.

Granger, S. (2009) 'The contribution of learner corpora to second language acquisition and foreign language teaching: a critical evaluation', in K. Aijmer (ed.) *Corpora and Language Teaching*, Amsterdam: John Benjamins.

Gregg, K. (1984) 'Krashen's monitor and Occam's razor', *Applied Linguistics* 5: 79–100.

Hakuta, K. (2001) 'A critical period for second language acquisition?', in D. B. J. Bailey, J. T. Bruer, F. J. Symons and J. W. Lichtman (eds) *Critical Thinking About Critical Periods*, Baltimore, MD: Paul Brookes Publishing.

Hawkins, R. (2001) *Second Language Syntax: A Generative Introduction*, Malden, MA: Blackwell.

Haznedar, B. and Gavruseva, E. (eds) (2008) *Current Trends in Child Second Language Acquisition: A Generative Perspective*, Amsterdam: John Benjamins.

Hellermann, J. (2008) *Social Actions for Classroom Language Learning*, Clevedon: Multilingual Matters.

Jarvis, S. and Pavlenko, A. (2008) *Crosslinguistic Influence in Language and Cognition*, Mahwah, NJ: Lawrence Erlbaum Associates.

Kinginger, C. (2004) 'Alice doesn't live here anymore: foreign language learning and identity reconstruction', in A. Pavlenko and A. Blackledge (eds) *Negotiation of Identities in Multilingual Contexts*, Clevedon: Multilingual Matters.

Krashen, S. D. (1985) *The Input Hypothesis: Issues and Implications*, London: Longman.

Lantolf, J. P. (ed.) (1994) 'Sociocultural Theory and Second Language Learning', special issue, *Modern Language Journal* 78(4).

Lantolf, J. P. and Thorne, S. L. (2006) *Sociocultural Theory and the Genesis of Second Language Development*, New York: Oxford University Press.

Larsen-Freeman, D. (1997) 'Chaos/complexity science and second language acquisition', *Applied Linguistics* 18: 141–65.

Larsen-Freeman, D. and Cameron, L. (2008) *Complex Systems in Applied Linguistics*, New York: Oxford University Press.

Larsen-Freeman, D. and Long, M. H. (1991) *An Introduction to Second Language Acquisition Research*, New York: Longman.

Lightbown, P. M. and Spada, N. (2006) *How Languages are Learned*, 3rd edn, Oxford: Oxford University Press.

Long, M. H. (1996) 'The role of the linguistic environment in second language acquisition', in W. C. Ritchie and T. K. Bhatia (eds) *Handbook of Second Language Acquisition*, New York: Academic Press.

Long, M. H. and Doughty, C. J. (eds) (2009) *Handbook of Second and Foreign Language Teaching*, Malden, MA: Wiley-Blackwell.

McKay, S. L. and Wong, S.-L. C. (1996) 'Multiple discourses, multiple identities: investment and agency in second-language learning among Chinese adolescent immigrant students', *Harvard Educational Review* 66: 577–608.

McLaughlin, B. (1987) *Theories of Second Language Learning*, London: Edward Arnold.

Montrul, S. A. (2010) 'How similar are adult second language learners and Spanish heritage speakers? Spanish clitics and word order', *Applied Psycholinguistics* 31: 167–207.

Muñoz, C. (2008) 'Symmetries and asymmetries of age effects in naturalistic and instructed L2 learning', *Applied Linguistics* 29: 578–96.

Norris, J. M. and Ortega, L. (2000) 'Effectiveness of L2 instruction: a research synthesis and quantitative meta-analysis', *Language Learning* 50: 417–528.

Norton, B. and Toohey, K. (2001) 'Changing perspectives on good language learners', *TESOL Quarterly* 35: 307–22.

Norton Peirce, B. (1995) 'Social identity, investment, and language learning', *TESOL Quarterly* 29(1): 9–31.

Ortega, L. (2009) 'Sequences and processes in language learning', in M. H. Long and C. J. Doughty (eds) *Handbook of Second and Foreign Language Teaching*, Malden, MA: Wiley-Blackwell.

Pavlenko, A. and Lantolf, J. P. (2000) 'Second language learning as participation and the (re)construction of selves', in J. P. Lantolf (ed.) *Sociocultural Theory and Second Language Learning*, Oxford: Oxford University Press.

Pujolar, J. (2010) 'Immigration and language education in Catalonia: between national and social agendas', *Linguistics and Education* 21: 229–43, doi:10.1016/j.linged.2009.10.004.

Schmidt, R. (1995) 'Consciousness and foreign language learning: a tutorial on the role of attention and awareness in learning', in R. Schmidt (ed.) *Attention and Awareness in Foreign Language Learning*, Honolulu, HI: National Foreign Language Resource Center.

Selinker, L. (1972). 'Interlanguage', *International Review of Applied Linguistics* 10: 219–31.

Tarone, E. (1988) *Variation in Interlanguage*, London: Edward Arnold.

Tarone, E., Bigelow, M. and Hansen, K. (2009) *Literacy and Second Language Oracy*, Oxford: Oxford University Press.

Valdés, G. (2005) 'Bilingualism, heritage language learners, and SLA research: opportunities lost or seized?', *Modern Language Journal* 89: 410–26.

Verspoor, M., de Bot, K. and Lowie, W. (eds) (2011) *A Dynamic Approach to Second Language Development: Methods and Techniques*, Amsterdam: John Benjamins.

Verspoor, M., Lowie, W. and van Dijk, M. (2008) 'Variability in second language development from a dynamic systems perspective', *Modern Language Journal* 92: 214–31.

White, L. (1989) *Universal Grammar and Second Language Acquisition*, Philadelphia, PA: John Benjamins.

Young, R. (2009) *Discursive Practice in Language Learning and Teaching*, Malden, MA: Wiley-Blackwell.

13

Language teaching methodology

Scott Thornbury

Introduction

The choice as to the best, or the most appropriate, or the most effective, way of teaching a language is 'a clear and classic applied linguistic problem' (Cook 2003: 38), with important implications not just for classroom teaching, but for materials and curriculum design, for teacher education, and for educational policy-making in general. The way that teachers address this problem in their classroom teaching constitutes their *methodology*:

> Methodology can be characterized as the activities, tasks, and learning experiences selected by the teacher in order to achieve learning, and how they are used within the teaching/learning process.
>
> *(Richards 1990: 11)*

Methodology, then is the *how* of teaching. But also implicated are the *what*, the *why* and the *who*. That is, teachers' choices of activities, tasks, and learning experiences will be influenced by their (implicit or explicit) theories of language and of learning, as well as by their assessment of the requirements, learning styles and abilities of their learners. These choices in turn may be constrained by the curricular demands of their institution, such as its syllabus and learning objectives, by the teaching materials and technologies available, by the backwash effect of any tests or examinations that the students may be expected to take, by the local educational culture, and by the teachers' own training and experience.

More often than not, the methodological choices will themselves be pre-specified, and enshrined in the form of a *method*. 'A language teaching method is a *single* set of procedures which teachers are to follow in the classroom. Methods are usually based on a set of beliefs about the nature of language and learning' (Nunan 2003: 5, emphasis added). Likewise, Kumaravadivelu (2006) uses *method* 'to refer to established methods conceptualised and constructed by experts in the field', and methodology 'to refer to what practicing teachers actually do in the classroom in order to achieve their stated or unstated teaching objectives' (2006: 84).

Even so, in order to achieve their stated objectives, teachers may still select a method 'off the shelf' as it were, thereby blurring the distinction between what experts have conceptualized, and what the teacher actually does. This is especially the case where the materials that are used themselves instantiate a specific method. Hence, the distinction between methodology and method is not always clear-cut, and any discussion of methodology must take into account the notion of method, and the way that this notion has been represented in the literature. In tracking these representations, it is useful to think of the history of methodology less as a history of individual methods than as the recycling of a relatively small set of 'big ideas'. In what follows, both the methods and their underlying principles will be reviewed, with special reference to the teaching of English. Developments in the teaching of other languages have generally followed a parallel track.

Methods: a brief history

Reformers

The history of methodology is typically construed as both evolutionary and revolutionary: a process of gradual development and improvement, marked by occasional radical upheavals as existing orthodoxies are discredited and supplanted. Two such radical departures were the late nineteenth-century Reform Movement and the Communicative Approach, nearly a century later. Both developments represented a reaction away from a status quo perceived as being out of touch with learners' needs, and out of synch with educational reality. The dominant educational paradigm that the Reform Movement challenged was *grammar-translation*, an approach to modern language teaching that was modelled entirely on the teaching of the classics, and whose defining procedures were explicit rule statements and translation of written sentences. There could be no greater contrast than Palmer's (1921) statement of the basic principles of his 'Oral Method' – a precursor of the Direct Method – defined as

> learning to use a foreign language … almost entirely without reading, with little or no writing, without studying a systematized and formal theory of the language-structure, and without any unnecessary recourse to the mother-tongue as a vehicle for instruction.
>
> *(Palmer 1921: 12)*

Direct method classes typically revolved around extended teacher-led question-and-answer sequences (called *conversations*) that provided a context for new language items. The use of pictures and actions further reinforced the development of associations between referents and their linguistic realizations, unmediated by translation. In seeking to apply principles of psychology, such as habit formation, to language teaching, while at the same time devising pedagogically appropriate descriptions of language, Palmer and his forbears – most notably Sweet (1899) and Jespersen (1904) – prefigured the advent of applied linguistics as a recognized discipline.

Structuralists

In fact, the first use of the term 'applied linguistics' in relation to methodology is attributed to Charles Fries in the 1940s. The linguistics that Fries applied were structuralist (e.g. Fries 1952) and provided the ingredient that had been missing from earlier direct method courses: a systematic (hence gradable) description of sentence structures (or patterns). But otherwise, the methodology underlying what came to be known as audiolingualism was not very different from Palmer's, relying as it did on the induction of rules from examples, and on mimicry and memorization. The fundamental principle underlying the methodology continued to be habit-formation, realized by means of a range of different types of pattern-practice drills. It was only in the 1960s that the behavioural psychology of Skinner (1957) was enlisted to vindicate such practices, as well as to underpin research into programmed learning and the use of such technological innovations as the language laboratory.

The effect on methodology of Chomsky's theory of generative grammar (1957; 1965) was perhaps less revolutionary, and less the death-blow to audiolingualism, than is sometimes claimed. For a start, by the 1960s audiolingualism was already losing adherents, not least because of its failure to deliver (Rivers 1964). The focus on sentence-patterns at the expense of connected text, and on imitation at the expense of creativity, were seen as serious impediments to second language fluency. Also, the belief that learners' errors are caused mainly by mother tongue interference, and can be predicted through contrastive analysis, was yielding to the view that errors may in fact be developmental, and evidence of systematic hypothesis testing (Corder 1967; Selinker 1972). One (relatively short-lived) response to these developments, known as *cognitive code learning* (Carroll 1966), promoted a more intellectual, problem-solving approach, the chief legacies of which have been a greater tolerance for error, and an acceptance of the value of explicit rules of grammar. But, in the end, while relaxing the proscription on talking about grammar, Chomsky's transformational grammar had little effect on teaching. As Brumfit and Johnson commented, 'After all, the most it can offer is alternative strategies for teaching grammar – new ways of teaching the same thing' (1979: 3).

Natural and humanist approaches

Of greater impact than his linguistics, arguably, was Chomsky's claim that 'language acquisition is based on the child's discovery of what from a formal point of view is a deep and abstract theory – a generative grammar of his language' (1965: 58). The assumption that this deep and abstract theory could be triggered into life simply by exposure to the target language underlay what have been termed *comprehension approaches* (Winitz 1981). Both the *natural approach* (Krashen and Terrell 1983) and *total physical response* (Asher 1977) assume that language acquisition follows a predetermined path, and that, given the right conditions, this 'natural' route can be reactivated for second language acquisition. These conditions include the provision of *comprehensible input* (Krashen 1981) during a 'silent period' and in a state of low anxiety. Both approaches enlist direct method-type procedures, such as actions and pictures, in order to ensure comprehensibility of input; at the production stage error correction is avoided, in the interests of encouraging meaningful communication.

The emphasis on positive affective factors and their facilitative role in learning derives from another psychological tradition that achieved prominence in the 1960s and 1970s: the humanist psychology associated principally with the work of Carl Rogers (1969) and Abraham Maslow (1968), and promoted through the writings of Moscowitz (1978) and Stevick (1980). Humanistic education prioritizes personal growth and self-realization, goals which are achieved when learners are invested affectively as well as intellectually in the learning process. A number of language teaching methods that prioritized such principles emerged in close succession in the decades that followed the demise of audiolingualism. These included *the silent way* (Gattegno 1972), *community language learning* (Curran 1976) and *suggestopedia* (Lozanov 1978). While the methods themselves never became mainstream, humanistic principles have permeated more orthodox practices, in the form, for example, of an emphasis on learner-centredness and self-directed learning, a philosophy that, in turn, nourished the learner autonomy movement of the 1980s and 1990s (Holec 1980). More recently, the humanistic tradition has absorbed certain 'new age' training approaches, such as neuro-linguistic programming (NLP), and the theory of multiple intelligences (Gardner 1983).

The functional tradition

Running in parallel to these developments, the different strands that were to intertwine and combine to give rise to the communicative approach were gathering strength. The use of situations to contextualize the structural patterns described by Fries and (on the other side of the Atlantic) by Hornby (1954), became a distinctive feature of classroom materials in Britain in the mid-twentieth century. As well as providing a stimulus for elicitation, the use of situations to contextualize grammar items obviated the need for explanation or translation. Situational presentations, incorporated into the PPP model of lesson design (Byrne 1976), in which new patterns are first presented, then practised at degrees of decreasing control, before free production is allowed, came to be known as *situational language teaching* and proved remarkably enduring.

The arguments underlying the use of situations date back to the anthropological tradition in linguistics that underpinned the work of J. R. Firth, whose emphasis on context, meaning, and use was in sharp distinction to structuralism. Further developed by Firth's followers, this functionalist paradigm gathered strength, especially in Britain and Europe, and was reinforced by the speech act theory of Austin (1962), the sociolinguistics of Labov (1972), Halliday's functional grammar (1973), and Wilkins' notional syllabus (1976), effecting a major revision in learning goals and in methodology, and culminating in what came to be known as the *communicative approach*. Put simply, there was a marked shift away from a concern for what language *is* (and the way it is represented in the mind) to a concern for what language *does* (and the way it operates in the world).

The 'big idea' that fuelled the communicative approach, and which gave it its name, was Hymes' (1972) notion of *communicative competence* – the knowledge 'when to speak, when not, and as to what to talk about with whom, when, where, in what manner' (1972: 277). By redefining the scope of language learning in terms more extensive than Chomsky's restricted notion of linguistic competence, Hymes (and subsequently Canale and Swain [1980]) prompted a major re-evaluation of curriculum objectives, so as to include sociolinguistic and strategic, as well as grammatical, goals. Concurrently, the growing demand both for English for Specific Purposes (ESP) and for English as a Second Language (ESL) was encouraging course designers to specify learning objectives – and to assess their achievement – in terms of language *use*, rather than usage (Widdowson 1978). Accordingly, syllabuses were reconfigured to include communicative *functions* and semantic *notions* rather than (or alongside) grammatical structures, and the terms *skills* and *strategies* surfaced repeatedly in the literature.

Communicative methodology

This redefinition of goals had a knock-on effect in terms of methodology: the focus on communicating *messages* – as opposed to rehearsing structural patterns – created the need for activities that encouraged some kind of meaningful exchange, as in *information-gap* tasks, and, in order to practise functional language, *role plays* and *simulations* became standard practice. And since communicative competence implies the capacity to communicate one's meanings irrespective of formal accuracy, *fluency* was prioritized, reinforcing the trend towards incorporating less-controlled production activities within the PPP format. For similar reasons, the use of *authentic* reading and listening materials was promoted, and classroom procedures for minimizing the difficulties of these – such as the use of skimming and scanning strategies – became commonplace. The first mainstream coursebook to embody these principles was the 'Strategies' series (e.g. Abbs *et al.* 1975).

More radically, some scholars, such as Allwright, were arguing that, 'if communication is THE aim, then it should be THE major element in the process' (1979: 167, emphasis in original). A much-cited attempt to implement this 'strong form' of CLT was the Communicational Teaching Project, better known as the Bangalore Project (Prabhu 1987), whose syllabus consisted entirely of a succession of tasks, and was the forerunner of what became known as the *task-based approach*, or *task-based language teaching* (TBLT). Various versions of TBLT have been proposed (e.g. Willis 1996; Ellis 2003), with greater or lesser degrees of explicit language focus, but all subscribe to the basic principle of 'learning by doing', a principle that also underpins the *whole language* movement in North America (Freeman and Freeman 1992). Nevertheless, task-based learning, while attracting considerable theoretical interest, has not been widely adopted, partly due to the perception that it requires sophisticated classroom management skills as well as a high degree of target language proficiency on the part of the teacher (Ellis 2003).

Moreover, the selection and grading of syllabus objectives that are semantic and procedural, rather than structural, has proved a challenge to course designers. EFL contexts are typically too heterogeneous to provide accurate predictions of learners' communicative needs. Attempts to base syllabuses on word frequency data, now more readily available thanks to developments in corpus linguistics, were short-lived (Willis and Willis 1988). A lexical focus was also urged by Lewis (1993), who argued that the distinction between vocabulary and grammar was an artificial one. Despite being promoted as an 'approach', Lewis's recommendations were absorbed into mainstream courses mainly in the form of a greater emphasis on lexical 'chunks' and formulaic language.

A creative compromise was to interweave several strands – grammatical, lexical, and functional – into one integrated course design (e.g. Swan and Walter 1984), thereby offering a more comprehensive blueprint for communicative competence. Even so, the problem of how to grade semantic categories, compared to the relative ease with which structures can be graded, meant that multilayered syllabuses of this type tended to privilege form over function as the main organizational criterion. By 1986, with the publication of (the notionally communicative) *Headway Intermediate* (Soars and Soars), the grammatical syllabus had all but reasserted itself. In a sense, a focus on grammar within a communicative framework had already been sanctioned in Littlewood's (1981) model of lesson design, which proposed a sequence of activities from pre-communicative to communicative, with 'structural activities' included in the former. Effectively, this was the old PPP model by another name. It seemed that not a lot had changed since the situational courses of the 1970s, the main differences being the greater use of authentic (or 'semi-authentic') texts, more skills work generally, and a greater range of production activities, including role plays and information-gap tasks, in which meaning is 'negotiated' (Long 1983).

Communicative learning theory

One reason for such caution may have been the fact that the communicative approach had been fuelled by developments at the level of language description, but there had been no concomitant developments in learning theory (apart, perhaps, from Krashen's (1985) *Input Hypothesis*) and hence no real stimulus to rethink methodology. At most, there was an underlying assumption that using language in meaningful and communicative ways would better prepare learners for authentic language use outside the classroom.

One theoretical model that arrived in time to fill the gap took the form of cognitive learning theory. Anderson's ACT theory (1983) of skills acquisition, for example, vindicated the use of communicative activities as a means by which declarative knowledge is proceduralized through successive stages of practice (Johnson 1996). Information-processing models made a similar distinction between controlled and automatic processes (McLaughlin 1987) and helped suggest ways that task variables could be calibrated for different outcomes, such as accuracy, fluency and complexity (Skehan 1998). More recently, constructivist and sociocultural learning theories, aligned with the work of Bruner and Vygotsky, respectively, have provided a socially grounded rationale for the use of interactive and collaborative pair- and groupwork tasks, in which learning is jointly constructed, and progresses through stages of 'other-regulation' to 'self-regulation' (van Lier 1996; Lantolf 2000; see also Thorne and Tasker, this volume).

A logical development of the 'deep-end', task-based paradigm has been to blend, or to merge, language teaching with content teaching. A forerunner of this integrated approach was the immersion model practised in Canada from the 1960s, in which school subjects were taught entirely in French to students whose home language was English. Subsequently, a whole spectrum of different content-plus-language models has emerged, differentiated by the degree to which they incorporate explicit language instruction, and the extent to which they are integrated into the curriculum. These include *content-based instruction* and what is now generally know in Europe as CLIL (*content and language integrated learning*). In CLIL classes, curricular subjects and language are taught in conjunction, with attention being allocated to either content or language as demanded. Graddol identifies CLIL as being 'a significant curriculum trend in Europe' (2006: 86) but adds that 'CLIL is difficult to implement unless the subject teachers are themselves bilingual' (ibid.). Nevertheless, CLIL may represent the true descendant of the 'strong' version of the communicative approach.

Meanwhile, the 'weak' form of the communicative approach (which is essentially a more evolved form of situational language teaching) is generally considered to be the dominant methodological paradigm. Richards and Rodgers note that 'the general principles of Communicative Language Teaching are today widely accepted around the world' (2001: 151), while for Harmer, 'the Communicative approach has left an indelible mark on teaching and learning' (2007: 71). Shortly, we will examine the nature of that indelible mark. But first of all some caveats.

Methods: the issues and options

Beyond the 'methods narrative'

The foregoing historical outline obscures two important facts. The first: changes in methodology have not happened uniformly nor in unison. For long periods of time different methods functioned in parallel, and still do. As Larsen-Freeman notes: 'In some parts of the world, certain older language teaching methods, such as the Grammar-Translation Method, have endured for years. Similarly, the Direct Method has been preserved in particular commercial language teaching enterprises, such as the Berlitz Schools' (2000: 177). By the same token, features of different methods have often been combined to create methodological blends and fusions, an eclectic strategy that is probably more widespread than is acknowledged, and as such serves to blur the distinctions between one method and another. As Corder observed, some time back, 'The development of language-teaching methods ... has in fact been empirical rather than theory-directed. [...] The fact seems to be that teachers have "followed their noses" and adopted a generally eclectic approach to teaching methods' (1973: 135–6).

The second point to note is that, as Kelly long ago demonstrated, the history of methods might more accurately be characterized, not as a linear progression, but as cyclical: 'Old approaches return, but as their social and intellectual context are changed, they seem entirely new' (1969: 396). Likewise, Pennycook (1989), in a critique of the 'method construct', notes that

> while it is clear that language teaching has undergone many transformations over the centuries, a thorough examination of the past suggests that these changes have represented different configurations of the same basic options rather than some linear, additive progress towards the present day, and that these changes are due principally to shifts in the social, cultural, political, and philosophical climate.
>
> *(Pennycook 1989: 608)*

What, then, are these 'basic options', and in what ways might they be differently configured? Before attempting to answer this question, it is important to distinguish between at least two 'levels' of options. In his landmark historical study, Kelly (1969) argued that methodological choices are contingent on higher-level decisions at the level of principles and beliefs: 'Matter, methods, and media relate ultimately to the provenance of ideas' (1969: 3). According to this view, a method is one of a set of possible practical implementations of choices made at the level of ideology.

Beliefs and practices as dimensions of method

A similar two-tier constructional principle underlies more recent explorations in method analysis, such as Richards and Rodgers (2001), who observe that 'in describing methods, the difference between a philosophy of language teaching at the level of theory and principles, and a set of derived procedures for teaching a language, is central' (2001: 19). Accordingly, their model for method analysis incorporates both the *approach*, 'the level at which assumptions and beliefs about language and language learning are specified' (ibid.), and the actual classroom *procedures* by means of which the approach is implemented. A third strand, the *design*, roughly parallels Kelly's category of *matter*, where decisions about syllabus and materials are instantiated.

More recently, Richards and Schmidt have identified the following broad areas, beliefs about which, they argue, serve to distinguish methods:

(a) the nature of language
(b) the nature of second language learning
(c) goals and objectives in teaching
(d) the type of syllabus to use
(e) the role of teachers, learners, instructional materials
(f) the activities, techniques and procedures to use.

(Richards and Schmidt 2002: 330)

The historical account we have sketched demonstrates how these choices are configured differently for different methods, according to where each method positions itself in relation to a number of key parameters, or *dimensions*. The notion of dimensions draws on the work of Stern (1983, 1992), who in turn built on earlier work in the area of 'methodics' (Halliday *et al.* 1964; Mackey 1965), including the method feature analysis undertaken by Krashen and

Seliger (1975). Stern identified three 'central issues of language learning' (1983: 400), from which he derived three dimensions, each representing a continuum of strategic and procedural choices. These he labelled the *intralingual-crosslingual dimension*, the *analytic-experiential dimension*, and the *explicit-implicit dimension*. Expanding on these options so as to be able to map them on to the six domains identified by Richards and Schmidt (2002, above), and updating them in the light of recent educational, theoretical and ideological developments, we find at least ten dimensions to the concept of method:

The nature of language

- **the formal vs functional dimension:** the method construes language as a structural system, internalized as formal operations or rules, vs the method construes language as 'meaning potential', internalized as a system of semantic choices.

The nature of second language learning

- **the analytic vs experiential dimension:** the method prioritizes formal instruction and intentional learning, vs the method seeks to replicate naturalistic, informal, experiential, or incidental learning processes.

Goals and objectives in teaching

- **the product vs process dimension:** the method focuses on the teaching and assessing of pre-specified linguistic goals, vs the method aims at developing and assessing the learner's capability for language learning and use.
- **the accuracy vs fluency dimension:** the method aims at achieving formal accuracy, particularly of grammar, vs the method aims at achieving communicative fluency, particularly at the level of discourse.

The type of syllabus to use

- **the systems vs skills dimension:** the syllabus is organized according to linguistic criteria (e.g. grammar, phonology), vs the syllabus foregrounds language skills or competences.
- **the segregated vs integrated dimension:** the target language is taught apart from other subjects in the curriculum, vs the target language is integrated into other curricular content.

The role of teachers, learners, instructional materials

- **the cognitive vs affective dimension:** the method prioritizes mental effort and cognitive processing, vs the method prioritizes affective and holistic engagement.
- **the transmissive vs dialogic dimension:** teaching is viewed as the transmission of discrete units of knowledge, vs teaching is viewed as an interactive process in which knowledge is collaboratively constructed.

The activities, techniques and procedures to use

- **the deductive vs inductive dimension:** the method favours the explicit presentation of rules (e.g. of grammar), vs the method expects or invites learners to discover the rules for themselves.
- **the cross-lingual vs intralingual dimension:** the method acknowledges and exploits the learner's L1, vs the method rejects or discourages a role for the L1.

The first thing to note is that there is considerable correlation across these dimensions. For example, a method that adopts a functional view of language is likely to articulate its goals in terms of communicative fluency. Likewise, an analytic approach to language learning is likely to be realized in a transmissive teaching style. Thus, grammar-translation might be described as being heavily weighted towards the 'left-hand' end of each dimension: it assumes a formal view of language, and promotes both an analytic learning style and a transmissive teaching style, where intellectual effort, rather than affective engagement, is encouraged, and where cross-lingual activities (i.e. translation) are prominent. By contrast, task-based learning, of the type advocated by Prabhu (1987) occupies points at the other end of the spectrum.

Methodology: new debates

Beyond methods, towards appropriate methodology

The discussion so far has assumed that the concept of method is unproblematic and that methods are stable phenomena that can be described and classified in terms of their distinctive features. Recent developments in methodology have challenged that assumption. Referring to what he called 'the break with the method concept', Stern (1983) declared that 'several developments indicate a shift in language pedagogy away from the single method concept as the main approach to language teaching' (1983: 477). One such development was the failure, on the part of researchers, to find any significant advantage in one method over another. This was partly due to difficulties in operationalizing the concept of method, but also because of the complexity of variables involved. And, as has already been noted, the way that methods are actually implemented in classroom settings suggests that there is as much diversity within a given method's application as there is across methods. As Chaudron notes, 'teachers of supposedly different methodological persuasions in fact acknowledge quite diverse and overlapping behaviors in classroom practice' (1988: 8). He adds that comparison studies 'have rarely involved reliable, controlled observation of the classroom behaviors supposedly accompanying the methods under investigation' (ibid.).

Moreover, recognition of the huge range of contextual variables that impact on second language learning has challenged the notion of a single monolithic method, particularly one that is generated apart from the context in which it is implemented. This view has given rise to the notion of *appropriate methodology* (Holliday 1994), particularly in relation to the design of large-scale curriculum projects for non-BANA (British, Australian, and North American) contexts. Holliday warned that

> there is a grave danger of teachers and curriculum developers ... naively accepting BANA practice as superior, and boldly carrying what are in fact the ethnocentric norms of particular professional-academic cultures in English language education from one context to another, without proper research into the effect of their actions.
>
> *(Holliday 1994: 102)*

Kramsch and Sullivan (1996) and Canagarajah (1999) show how imported methods are customized, and tailored to local conditions – a case not so much of appropriacy as of *appropriation*. And in a much-cited paper in 1990, Prabhu argued that there can be no one method, but that individual teachers should fashion an approach that accords uniquely with their 'sense of plausibility'.

Disaffection with the method concept has also been fuelled by a general rejection of the notion that social change and improvement can be effected through the strict application of scientific method. The last decades of the last century witnessed a challenge to 'scientism' in the social sciences, a challenge associated with the advent of postmodernism and its rejection of the idea of universalist, objective knowledge. Allied with the view is that methods are never disinterested, but serve the dominant power structures in society, leading to 'a de-skilling of the role of teachers, and greater institutional control over classroom practice' (Pennycook 1989: 610). Such a view represents what might be called a 'critical turn' in methodology, whose proponents seek to redress social, cultural and/or linguistic inequalities, and to (re)instate the learner's agency and autonomy while, at the same time, wresting power, control, and authority away from the traditional stakeholders, such as examining bodies, publishers, education ministries and universities. To this end, methodology – as instantiated in methods, textbooks, examinations, official dictates, and so on – has been viewed with distrust, if not outright hostility (see Canagarajah and Ben Said, this volume).

This combination of factors has prompted a number of scholars to announce the 'death of method' (Allwright 1991) and to herald what is known as the *postmethod condition* (Kumaravadivelu 1994). Kumaravadivelu argues that, rather than subscribe to a single set of procedures, postmethod teachers should adapt their approach in accordance with local, contextual factors, while at the same time being guided by a number of *macrostrategies* that are 'derived from the current theoretical, practical, and experiential knowledge base' (Kumaravadivelu 2006: 69). Two such macrostrategies, for example, are 'Maximise learning opportunities' and 'Promote learner autonomy'. In a similar spirit, Allwright (2003) proposes an alternative to method called Exploratory Practice, predicated on the view that teachers can become their own researchers 'so that working for understanding is *part of* the teaching and learning, not extra to it' (2003: 127). More recently, the learners themselves have been enlisted as active partners in this developmental framework (Allwright and Hanks 2009).

Nevertheless, and in spite of the claims of the postmethodists, the notion of *method* does not seem to have entirely disappeared. In the on-line advertising for language courses, for example, the term *method* occurs frequently, collocating with adjectives such as *unique, effective, new* and *modern*. It seems that – in the public mind, at least – the method concept is alive and well. This is a view supported by Bell (2007) who interviewed a number of teachers on the subject, and concluded: 'Methods, however the term is defined, are not dead. Teachers seem to be aware of both the usefulness of methods and the need to go beyond them' (2007: 143).

Some scholars, such as Larsen-Freeman (2000), actively promote the concept of method as a useful heuristic device in teacher development, on the grounds that 'methods serve as a foil for reflection that can aid teachers in bringing to conscious awareness the thinking that underlies their actions' (2000: ix) and that, moreover, 'a knowledge of methods is part of the knowledge base of teaching' (ibid.)

On the other hand, Akbari (2008) suggests that, in many EFL contexts, the concept of method has been replaced by the *textbook* as the primary knowledge base for teaching. This is perhaps not surprising, given the global marketing of textbooks. As Kumaravadivelu notes, 'Because of the global spread of English, ELT has become a global industry with high economic stakes, and textbook production has become one of the engines that drives the industry' (2003: 255). And, arguably, one that drives and perpetuates the methodology – a methodology that has been characterized as being one in which, despite a nominal allegiance to the communicative approach, 'the textbook represents all types of issues and all types of discourse as not requiring much thought or action beyond the decision as to the appropriate grammatical structure – everything is reducible to form' (Grady 1997: 9).

A significant development in recent years has been the integration of new technologies into coursebook design and content delivery. Whereas twenty years ago the only accompanying aids might have been a set of classroom cassettes, nowadays coursebooks have audio CDs and video DVDs, CD-ROMs, dedicated Websites including downloadable podcasts, interactive whiteboard software, and test-generating software (although the extent to which teachers are taking advantage of these resources has yet to be properly evaluated). Moreover, the exponential growth of Web-based facilities such as social networking sites, blogs, wikis, and simulated environments, has fuelled the rapid development of on-line teaching and learning resources such that the hegemony of print materials is being seriously challenged (see also Kern, this volume). Inevitably, perhaps, there has been a reaction away from an over-reliance on materials and technology, and theories of language socialization (e.g. Kramsch 2002) have been invoked to argue for 'a pedagogy of bare essentials' (Meddings and Thornbury 2009).

Research into methodology

The shift away from a preoccupation with methods in favour of a concern for methodology, and the way that this is realized in actual classroom practice, has opened up new directions in classroom research, particularly in the area of classroom observation (Allwright 1988; van Lier 1988). If, according to the definition we started out with, methodology indeed comprises 'the activities, tasks, and learning experiences selected by the teacher in order to achieve learning, and how they are used within the teaching/learning process' (Richards 1990: 11), then it suggests that a primary research goal might be to identify what these activities, etc., are and to track the ways that they are used. Attempts to do this have involved both quantitative and qualitative methods of data collection and analysis.

Interaction analysis, discourse analysis, and conversation analysis are three related methodologies that, in conjunction with classroom observation, have been used as a means of obtaining objective and quantitative data as to what really goes on in classrooms. In interaction analysis, researchers typically employ a checklist of categories in order to capture and code observable classroom behaviours, especially the interactions between teachers and learners, and between the learners themselves. Discourse analysts and conversation analysts share an interest in fine-grained analyses of classroom talk, the former – following Sinclair and Coulthard (1975) – ascribing specific functions to different utterances (such as *initiation*, *response* and *follow-up*), and mapping these on to a hierarchically structured system of 'ranks'.

Often working in the sociocultural tradition, researchers have looked at the way learners co-construct learning during the performance of tasks (Bygate *et al.* 2001; Ellis 2003), and at how teachers structure and 'scaffold' teacher-learner talk in order to maximize learning opportunities (Jarvis and Robinson 1997; McCormick and Donato 2000; see also Tsui, this volume). In an extended study of classroom talk, Johnson (1995) uses an eclectic methodology to demonstrate how 'the patterns of classroom communication depend largely on how teachers use language to control the structure and content of classroom events' (1995: 145). Likewise, Walsh (2006), using a 'variable approach to investigating L2 classroom interaction' (2006: 55), including discourse analysis, identifies four 'modes' of classroom interaction, each with its distinctive discourse features, which provides a framework for self-evaluation and teacher development.

An ethnographic approach to classroom research 'attempts to interpret behaviours from the perspective of the participants' different understandings rather than from the observer's or analyst's supposedly "objective" analysis' (Chaudron 1988: 14–15). Rather than apply predetermined categories to the observation data, the researcher (who may also be a participant) simply describes, and draws connections between, classroom processes, 'not as these processes are depicted in methodology texts and position papers, but as they are experienced and understood by language learners and teachers' (Bailey and Nunan 1996: xi). As an example, Toohey (1998) in a longitudinal study, showed how certain classroom practices had a prejudicial effect on the few ESL children in a class of mainly Anglophone children. McDonough and Chaikitmongkol (2007) use a portfolio of research tools, including observations, interviews, and learning notebooks, to track teachers' and learners' reactions to a task-based EFL course over a twelve-month period. A more recent development, but one consistent with an ethnographic approach, is the use of ecological research models (van Lier 2004) which 'regard the educational context as a complex, messy system' (2004: 204). Ecological approaches 'situate' language classrooms in their particular contexts; critical approaches to classroom research (Pennycook 1994) do the same, but foreground the view that 'all knowledge production is situated in a particular social, cultural, and political context' (1994: 693). Canagarajah (1999), for example, shows how learners in periphery contexts resist the cultural, political and educational values enshrined in materials from 'the centre'.

Summary

This brief survey of research into language teaching methodology demonstrates how much more complex the situation is than a traditional 'methods' view of teaching might suggest. Classrooms are indeed 'complex, messy systems' that resist neat classifications. Factoring in the huge range of context variables – centre vs periphery; EFL vs ESL; child vs adult; native-speaker teacher vs non-native speaker; public vs private sector education; on-line vs face-to-face; integrated vs segregated curriculum; and so on – produces a situation that would seem to defy any attempts to define a set of core principles for language teaching. At the same time, walking into a language classroom in any part of the world, the visitor will be struck by just how much is shared across all these different contexts. Testimony to this fact is that, more than ever, teachers from different contexts regularly exchange experiences and beliefs about their teaching in on-line discussion groups or, directly, at conferences. They are trained in the same or similar methods, use the same or similar textbooks, read the same or similar teachers' guides, and use the same downloadable resources from the Internet. They also encounter the same or similar constraints in their local teaching contexts, and work at overcoming them using similar strategies. Language teaching methodology seeks to identify and describe these global commonalities while at the same explaining and vindicating diversity at the local level.

Related topics

classroom discourse; language learning and language education; language teacher education; technology and language learning

Further reading

Harmer, J. (2007) *The Practice of English Language Teaching*, 3rd edn, London: Pearson. (This remains the classic manual for teacher training courses which subscribe to a communicative approach, and now has an accompanying DVD.)
Kumaravadivelu, B. (2003) *Beyond Methods: Macrostrategies for Language Learning*, New Haven, CT: Yale University Press. (The writer lucidly outlines the rationale and design features of a post-method methodology.)

Larsen-Freeman, D. (2000) *Techniques and Principles in Language Teaching*, 2nd edn, Oxford: Oxford University Press. (This is a very readable overview of a range of teaching methods with blow-by-blow descriptions of how they might be implemented in practice.)

Richards, J. and Rodgers, T. (2001) *Approaches and Methods in Language Teaching*, 2nd edn, Cambridge: Cambridge University Press. (This is an updated version of a core text, describing methods in terms of their underlying principles as well as their surface practices.)

References

Abbs, B., Ayton, A. and Freebairn, I. (1975) *Strategies: Integrated English Language Materials*, London: Longman.

Akbari, R. (2008) 'Postmethod discourse and practice', *TESOL Quarterly* 42: 641–52.

Allwright, D. (2003) 'Exploratory practice: re-thinking practitioner research in language teaching', *Language Teaching Research* 7(2): 113–41.

——(1991) *The Death of Method*, Working Paper 10, The Exploratory Practice Centre, University of Lancaster.

——(1988) *Observation in the Language Classroom*, London: Longman.

——(1979) 'Language learning through communication practice', in C. J. Brumfit and K. Johnson (eds) *The Communicative Approach to Language Teaching*, Oxford: Oxford University Press.

Allwright, D. and Hanks, J. (2009) *The Developing Language Learner: An Introduction to Exploratory Practice*, Basingstoke: Palgrave Macmillan.

Anderson, J. R. (1983) *The Architecture of Cognition*, Cambridge, MA: Harvard University Press.

Asher, J. (1977) *Learning Another Language through Actions: The Complete Teacher's Guide Book*, Los Gatos, CA: Sky Oaks Productions.

Austin, J. L. (1962) *How to Do Things with Words*, Oxford: Clarendon Press.

Bailey, K. M. and Nunan, D. (eds) (1996) *Voices from the Language Classroom*, Cambridge: Cambridge University Press.

Bell, D. M. (2007) 'Do teachers think that methods are dead?', *ELT Journal* 61: 135–43.

Brumfit, C. J. and Johnson, K. (1979) 'The linguistic background', in C. J. Brumfit and K. Johnson (eds) *The Communicative Approach to Language Teaching*, Oxford: Oxford University Press.

Bygate, M., Skehan, P. and Swain, M. (2001) *Researching Pedagogic Tasks: Second Language Learning, Teaching and Testing*, London: Longman.

Byrne, D. (1976) *Teaching Oral English*, Harlow: Longman.

Canagarajah, A. S. (1999) *Resisting Linguistic Imperialism in English Teaching*, Oxford: Oxford University Press.

Canale, M. and Swain, M. (1980) 'Theoretical bases of communicative approaches to second language teaching and testing', *Applied Linguistics* 1: 1–47.

Carroll, J. B. (1966) 'The contributions of psychological theory and educational research to the teaching of foreign languages', in A. Valdman (ed.) *Trends in Language Teaching*, New York: McGraw-Hill.

Chaudron, C. (1988) *Second Language Classrooms: Research on Teaching and Learning*, Cambridge: Cambridge University Press.

Chomsky, N. (1965) *Aspects of the Theory of Syntax*, Cambridge, MA: MIT Press.

——(1957) *Syntactic Structures*, The Hague: Mouton.

Cook, G. (2003) *Applied Linguistics*, Oxford: Oxford University Press.

Corder, S. P. (1973) *Introducing Applied Linguistics*, Harmondsworth: Penguin.

——(1967) 'The significance of learners' errors', *International Review of Applied Linguistics in Language Teaching* 5: 161–70.

Curran, C. A. C. (1976) *Counseling-learning in Second Languages*, Apple River, IL: Apple River Press.

Ellis, R. (2003) *Task-based Language Learning and Teaching*, Oxford: Oxford University Press.

Freeman, Y. S. and Freeman, D. E. (1992) *Whole Language for Second Language Learners*, Portsmouth, NH: Heinemann.

Fries, C. C. (1952) *The Structure of English*, New York: Harcourt, Brace and Co.

Gardner, H. (1983) *Frames of Mind: The Theory of Multiple Intelligences*, New York: Basic Books.

Gattegno, C. (1972) *Teaching Foreign Languages in Schools: The Silent Way*, 2nd edn, New York: Educational Solutions.

Graddol, D. (2006) *English Next*, London: British Council.

Grady, K. (1997) 'Critically reading an ESL text', *TESOL Journal* 6(4): 7–10.

Halliday, M. A. K. (1973) *Explorations in the Functions of Language*, London: Edward Arnold.

Halliday, M. A. K., McIntosh, A. and Strevens, P. (1964) *The Linguistic Sciences and Language Teaching*, London: Longman.

Harmer, J. (2007) *The Practice of English Language Teaching*, 3rd edn, London: Pearson.

Holec, H. (1980) *Autonomy and Foreign Language Learning*, Strasbourg: Council of Europe.

Holliday, A. (1994) *Appropriate Methodology and Social Context*, Cambridge: Cambridge University Press.

Hornby, A. S. (1954) *Guide to Patterns and Usage in English*, London: Oxford University Press.

Hymes, D. (1972) 'On communicative competence', in J. Pride and J. Holmes (eds) *Sociolinguistics: Selected Readings*, Harmondsworth: Penguin Books.

Jarvis, J. and Robinson, M. (1997) 'Analysing educational discourse: an exploratory study of teacher response and support to pupils' learning', *Applied Linguistics* 18: 212–28.

Jespersen, O. (1904) *How to Teach a Foreign Language*, London: George Allen & Unwin.

Johnson, K. (1996) *Language Teaching and Skill Learning*, Oxford: Blackwell.

——(1995) *Understanding Communication in Second Language Classrooms*, Cambridge: Cambridge University Press.

Kelly, L. G. (1969) *25 Centuries of Language Teaching*, Rowley, MA: Newbury House.

Kramsch, C. (ed.) (2002) *Language Acquisition and Language Socialization: Ecological Perspectives*, London and New York: Continuum.

Kramsch, C. and Sullivan, P. (1996) 'Appropriate pedagogy', *ELT Journal* 50: 199–212.

Krashen, S. D. (1985) *The Input Hypothesis: Issues and Implications*, New York: Longman.

——(1981) *Second Language Acquisition and Second Language Learning*, Oxford: Pergamon.

Krashen, S. D. and Seliger, H. W. (1975) 'The essential contributions of formal instruction in adult second language learning', *TESOL Quarterly* 9: 173–83.

Krashen, S. D. and Terrell, T. D. (1983) *The Natural Approach: Language Acquisition in the Classroom*, Oxford: Pergamon.

Kumaravadivelu, B. (2006) *Understanding Language Teaching: From Method to Postmethod*, Mahwah, NJ: Lawrence Erlbaum Associates.

——(2003) *Beyond Methods: Macrostrategies for Language Learning*, New Haven, CT: Yale University Press.

——(1994) 'The postmethod condition: (E)merging strategies for second/foreign language teaching', *TESOL Quarterly* 28: 27–48.

Labov, W. (1972) 'The study of language in its social context', in J. B. Pride and J. Holmes (eds) *Sociolinguistics: Selected Readings*, Harmondsworth: Penguin Books.

Lantolf, J. P. (ed.) (2000) *Sociocultural Theory and Second Language Learning*, Oxford: Oxford University Press.

Larsen-Freeman, D. (2000) *Techniques and Principles in Language Teaching*, 2nd edn, Oxford: Oxford University Press.

Lewis, M. (1993) *The Lexical Approach*, Hove: Language Teaching Publications.

Littlewood, W. (1981) *Communicative Language Teaching*, Cambridge: Cambridge University Press.

Long, M. (1983) 'Native speaker/non-native speaker conversation and the negotiation of meaning', *Applied Linguistics* 4: 126–41.

Lozanov, G. (1978) *Suggestology and Outlines of Suggestopedy*, New York: Gordon and Breach.

McCormick, D. E. and Donato, R. (2000) 'Teacher questions as scaffolded assistance in an ESL classroom', in J. K. Hall and L. S. Verplaetse (eds) *Second and Foreign Language Learning through Classroom Interaction*, Mahwah, NJ: Lawrence Erlbaum Associates.

McDonough, K. and Chaikitmongkol, W. (2007) 'Teachers' and learners' reactions to a task-based EFL course in Thailand', *TESOL Quarterly* 41: 107–32.

Mackey, W. F. (1965) *Language Teaching Analysis*, London: Longman.

McLaughlin, B. (1987) *Theories of Second Language Learning*, London: Edward Arnold.

Maslow, A. (1968) *Towards a Psychology of Being*, New York: Van Nostrand Reinhold.

Meddings, L. and Thornbury, S. (2009) *Teaching Unplugged: Dogme in English Language Teaching*, Peaslake: Delta Publishing.

Moscowitz, G. (1978) *Caring and Sharing in the Foreign Language Class*, Cambridge, MA: Newbury House.

Nunan, D. (ed.) (2003) *Practical English Language Teaching*, New York: McGraw-Hill.

Palmer, H. (1921) *The Oral Method of Teaching Languages*, Cambridge: Heffer.

Pennycook, A. (1994) *The Cultural Politics of English as an International Language*, Harlow: Longman.

——(1989) 'The concept of method, interested knowledge, and the politics of language teaching', *TESOL Quarterly* 23: 589–618.

Prabhu, N. S. (1990) 'There is no best method – why?', *TESOL Quarterly* 24: 161–76.

——(1987) *Second Language Pedagogy*, Oxford: Oxford University Press.

Richards, J. (1990) *The Language Teaching Matrix*, Cambridge: Cambridge University Press.

Richards, J. and Rodgers, T. (2001) *Approaches and Methods in Language Teaching*, 2nd edn, Cambridge: Cambridge University Press.

Richards, J. and Schmidt, R. (eds) (2002) *Dictionary of Language Teaching and Applied Linguistics*, 3rd edn, Harlow: Longman.

Rivers, W. (1964) *The Psychologist and the Foreign Language Teacher*, Chicago: University of Chicago Press.

Rogers, C. (1969) *Freedom to Learn: A View of What Education might Become*, Columbus, OH: Charles E. Merrill.

Selinker, L. (1972) 'Interlanguage', *International Review of Applied Linguistics in Language Teaching* 10: 219–31.

Sinclair, J. M. and Coulthard, R. M. (1975) *Towards an Analysis of Discourse: The English Used by Teachers and Pupils*, Oxford: Oxford University Press.

Skehan, P. (1998) *A Cognitive Approach to Language Learning*, Oxford: Oxford University Press.

Skinner, B. F. (1957) *Verbal Behavior*, New York: Appleton-Century-Crofts.

Soars, J. and Soars, L. (1986) *Headway Intermediate*, Oxford: Oxford University Press.

Stern, H. H. (1992) *Issues and Options in Language Teaching*, Oxford: Oxford University Press.

——(1983) *Fundamental Concepts of Language Teaching*, Oxford: Oxford University Press.

Stevick, E. (1980) *Teaching Languages: A Way and Ways*, Rowley, MA: Newbury House.

Swan, M. and Walter, C. (1984) *Cambridge English Course, 1*, Cambridge: Cambridge University Press.

Sweet, H. (1899, 1964) *The Practical Study of Languages*, Oxford: Oxford University Press.

Toohey, K. (1998) '"Breaking them up, taking them away": ESL students in grade 1', *TESOL Quarterly* 32: 61–84.

van Lier, L. (2004) *The Ecology and Semiotics of Language Learning: A Sociocultural Perspective*, Dordrecht: Kluwer Academic.

——(1996) *Interaction in the Language Curriculum: Awareness, Autonomy and Authenticity*, Harlow: Longman.

——(1988) *The Classroom and the Language Learner*, Harlow: Longman.

Walsh, S. (2006) *Investigating Classroom Discourse*, London: Routledge.

Widdowson, H. (1978) *Teaching Language as Communication*, Oxford: Oxford University Press.

Wilkins, D. A. (1976). *Notional Syllabuses*, London: Oxford University Press.

Willis, J. and Willis, D. (1988) *Collins COBUILD English Course*, London: Collins.

Willis, J. (1996) *A Framework for Task-based Learning*, Harlow: Pearson Longman.

Winitz, H. (ed.) (1981) *The Comprehension Approach to Foreign Language Instruction*, Rowley, MA: Newbury House.

14

Technology and language learning

Richard Kern

Introduction

The relationship between technology and language learning begins over 5,000 years ago with the development of writing. Using clay tablets and reed styluses, Mesopotamian scribes used writing chiefly for accounting purposes, but pedagogy had its place too. Archaeological findings include lexical lists – thematically organized groupings of Sumerian words for professions, places, trees, wooden objects, leather objects, stones, fish, and so on – which scribes used to teach the conventions of the cuneiform writing system to their apprentices (Green 1986).

Racing through millennia, through the use of wax tablets and papyrus rolls in Ancient Greece, through parchment manuscripts in medieval times, we come to the form of technology that has without question had the greatest impact on language learning: the printed book. Books could be perused in nonlinear fashion, and were therefore well suited for reference use and autonomous study. Once they become affordable through mass production, they altered the relationship between learner and teacher. With knowledge and standards transmitted by print, teachers were no longer necessarily the ultimate source of all knowledge and came increasingly to be viewed as interpreters of books (Kelly 1976).

In the last 150 years, the phonograph, radio, film, tape recorders, television, and the computer have all played their role in language learning. Computer technology, because it incorporates and remediates all of the foregoing media, and because it has become so integrated into people's daily lives in industrialized societies, will be the focus of this chapter. But it should be borne in mind that the questions and issues raised are usually not just pertinent to computers but relate to technological support in general. Similarly, debates about the primacy of teachers versus technologies in teaching are not new. Despite the cries of doomsayers who believe that computers will replace teachers, teachers in the digital age are as essential as ever in helping students to make and interpret meaning in a new language and culture.

A unique and defining feature of digital technology is that it combines previous media which were traditionally displayed in their own specific medium and format (e.g. paper, vinyl, magnetic tape, cellulose) and represents text, image, sound, and video with a common underlying data structure encoded in zeros and ones, allowing unprecedented integration and manipulability of media. These changes in the material infrastructure of media, by allowing rapid electronic transfer, have been accompanied by social changes as well. Information and communication technologies have made it possible for us to make contact with people, images, ideas, and information from around the world faster and more cheaply than ever before. The rapid spread of participatory tools and sites facilitating social networking, interactive game playing, collaborative writing and editing, and multimodal production provide opportunities for new kinds of social encounters, new kinds of communities, and new kinds of learning environments.

We will begin our exploration of the topic by outlining some common metaphors of technology and language learning.

Metaphors of technology and language learning

Digital technology has been used for a wide range of purposes related to language teaching and learning. We can roughly categorize these uses in terms of three metaphors: computer as tutor, computer as tool, and computer as medium.

The 'tutor' metaphor implies that the computer is simulating a teacher in some way, such as when computers are used to present material (e.g. grammar, vocabulary, or cultural informa- tion – see Vlugter *et al.* 2009 as an example), to provide language practice (such as exercises in pronunciation, writing, listening or reading), to analyze learners' language performance and provide feedback (see Meurers 2009), or to test learners' knowledge of language and culture (see Chapelle and Douglas 2006). Voice interactive programs involving automated speech recognition and text-to-speech synthesis can also simulate communicative interaction (Holland and Fisher 2007) and chatbots (i.e. automated conversational agents) have been explored as learning resources (Coniam 2008; Sha 2009). Although research on tutorial applications has been dwarfed in recent years by work in electronically mediated communication, this area holds significant promise for developing learners' conscious knowledge of the language, for enhancing listening and reading comprehension, and for improving pronunciation (Hubbard and Siskin 2004).

The 'tool' metaphor puts the focus on individual learner capabilities and cognitive goals and needs. In this role, computers (via the Internet) provide learners ready access to a wide variety of written, audio, and visual materials relevant to the language and culture being studied. Such materials include news media, film clips and videos (some with closed captions or subtitles), radio and television broadcasts, special interest Websites, blogs, advertisements, and realia. The Internet also provides reference and research tools such as search engines, online diction- aries, grammar and style checkers, and audio waveform analysis. Corpus analysis and con- cordancing (see Adolphs and Lin, this volume), providing insight into the real-world contexts in which words and collocations occur across various genres, registers, and language varieties (including learner language) has been an increasingly researched area (see, for example, Braun *et al.* 2006; Belz and Vyatkina 2008). Finally, automated writing assessment tools (Warschauer and Grimes 2008) and the use of mobile devices such as iPods, cellphones, and personal digital assistants for language learning purposes (e.g. Schmidt 2008; Abdous *et al.* 2009; Pachler *et al.* 2010) are recent tool-oriented developments to watch in the coming years.

The computer as 'medium' metaphor emphasizes the communicative agency of language learners, who express themselves and interact with other people 'through' the computer. Learners can use computers to engage in a wide variety of communicative practices – some- times in instructional contexts, but often not. The 'medium' metaphor is by far the broadest in scope and includes work in computer-mediated communication (Danet and Herring 2007; Herring 1996), social networking (Alemán and Wartman 2009), and network-based language teaching (Warschauer and Kern 2000). Specific applications of the computer-as-medium metaphor will be described in the following section.

The tutor, tool, and medium metaphors relate more to functional uses of computers than to software applications, since applications may appeal to more than one metaphor. For example, using a word processor to write to a foreign pen pal (medium) may well involve the use of search function, online thesaurus, font selection and formatting commands (tool). If the software checks grammar and spelling automatically and signals errors to the learner, it then becomes a kind of tutor. Some of the most ambitious technology-based language learning projects, for example Gilberte Furstenberg's *À la rencontre de Philippe*; *Dans un quartier de Paris*; and *Cultura* (Furstenberg and Levet 1999, Furstenberg *et al.* 2001, Furstenberg *et al.* 1993) integrate elements relating to each of the three metaphors.

These three metaphors of technology interact with three metaphors of language learning. The first, associated with psycholinguistic, information processing approaches to language acquisition (see Field, this volume), metaphorically frames the learner as a computer that receives and processes language input in order to generate rules and verbal output. The second, associated with discourse analytic and anthropological approaches to language socialization (Ochs and Schieffelin 2008), frames the learner as an apprentice who uses language and behaviour to enter and participate in a community of practice, and who further learns language and behaviour by virtue of that participation (see He, this volume). A third, emergent metaphor of language ecology attempts to encompass the full complexity of the relationships and processes involved in learning to live in one or more languages and cultures (Kramsch 2002; Kramsch, this volume).

At first glance, the learner as computer metaphor would seem to map neatly onto the 'tutor' and 'tool' metaphors of technology, with the learner as apprentice metaphor corresponding to the 'medium' metaphor of technology. However, in practice, one finds that such mappings are not so tidy since all three technology metaphors can be applied in various permutations to both language acquisition and socialization metaphors (e.g. studying input/uptake in online exchanges, or learner socialization in computer-assisted tutorials). The ecology metaphor – because it focuses specifically on relationships between learners and their environments (including non-human artefacts such as computers) – has become particularly appealing for those who work in the area of technology and language learning (e.g. Lam and Kramsch 2003; van Lier 2003).

Features of electronically mediated communication

To elaborate on the 'medium' metaphor outlined above, electronically mediated communication (EMC) is often categorized as synchronous or asynchronous. Synchronous modes include text chat, instant messaging, Voice over Internet Protocol (e.g. Skype), videoconferencing, online games, MOOs, and virtual worlds (e.g. Second Life). Asynchronous modes include email, bulletin boards, forums, wikis, blogs, SMS texting, social networking sites (e.g. Facebook, MySpace). The synchronous/asynchronous distinction is not always clear cut, however, and often is determined more by the user than by the interface. For example, email or a Facebook page can be used 'synchronously' like instant messaging if the communicating parties are online at the same time. Conversely, instant messaging can be used 'asynchronously' like email if the user allows messages to collect and does not respond. In any event, none of the written modes is truly synchronous since messages are sent after being composed, rather than keystroke by keystroke (as was the case for the earliest texting systems). An important question (to be explored below) is whether the 'medium' or interface in these environments is really as neutral as is often thought and to what extent it becomes a social actor interacting with human actors (Latour 2005).

Although EMC has recently become increasingly speech- and video-mediated, the bulk of EMC is still currently written via keyboard. Written EMC ranges along a continuum from 'product'-oriented forms resembling paper-based writing (e.g. Websites, most email) to more 'process'-oriented interactive discourse (e.g. instant messaging, chat) that shares many features of speech (Baron 2000). Blogs and wikis would be variably placed along the continuum, depending on the nature of the writing. On the product-oriented end of the continuum, messages are composed as wholes before being 'released' to their reader(s). On the process-oriented end, utterances may be more fragmentary, and multiple participants can communicate spontaneously and simultaneously (even contributing comments at the same moment). In the face of quick flurries of messages, some users will break up a single message into segments sent over several turns in order to maintain a quick interactive rhythm and to keep their place and visibility in the exchange. Communicative motivation or purpose tends to vary along the continuum as well: the 'product' end is biased toward information exchange, whereas the 'process' end is biased toward social contact.

The interactive and fragmentary nature of chat and instant messaging make them seem somewhat speech-like. However, unlike spoken communication, the binary on/off nature of the medium does not allow backchannelling ('uh-huh', 'right', shaking of head, etc.) from a partner while one is communicating. This is symptomatic of the reality that EMC is a 'leaner' overall medium than face-to-face communication in the sense that information is communicated principally in textual form, whereas in face-to-face communication auditory, tactile, olfactory as well as visual channels operate in parallel – allowing eye contact, context perception, gestural and prosodic information – all of which enrich communication (Herring 1996). The relative leanness of EMC creates a different dynamic from that of spoken communication, and this difference may well be significant for language learning contexts that are exclusively EMC-based (e.g. tandems or 'key-pal' projects).

In some respects, however, less is more. In the case of instant messaging and email, for example, the text-only channel minimizes intrusiveness and affords the possibility of avoiding or delaying communication, and this is no doubt one reason why people often prefer instant messaging or email to a face-to-face meeting or a telephone call.

Another significant difference between EMC and spoken communication is that most (but not all) forms of written EMC leave an enduring trace, allowing them to be searched, sorted, reviewed, forwarded, and recontextualized. This has potential benefits for language learning in that exchanges can be mined for vocabulary, structures, discourse markers, and so on, but it also raises issues of privacy (see Erickson 1999).

Genre and register in EMC

Genres have to do with purposes of language use. They establish norms of interaction by codifying the respective roles of readers/listeners and writers/speakers and the relationships between them, and by setting corresponding parameters of appropriateness for language use. Narrative, lecture, conversation, discussion, report, interview, explanation, poem, are all examples of genres. Because genres are fundamentally social phenomena they most often vary across cultures.

As should be clear from the previous section, EMC is not a genre. Rather, its various modes (email, blogs, forums, etc.) can be linked to a range of genres, some of which are specific to the technological medium (e.g. SMS texting), some not (e.g. memoranda). Knowledge of genres gives learners a sense of organization beyond the sentence and paragraph level and allows them to make connections between social purposes, interactions they observe or participate in online, and what they learn in their language classes. On the other hand, mismatches of genres can render intercultural communication problematic (e.g. Kramsch and Thorne 2001; Hanna and de Nooy 2009).

Just as EMC is too broad to be linked to a single genre, it also cannot be tied to any particular register. Registers are varieties of language that relate to features of situational context. Halliday (1978) describes situational context in terms of 'field' (what is taking place), 'tenor' (who is taking part), and 'mode' (channel of communication). The EMC mode (email, blog, chat, etc.) thus plays a role in influencing linguistic form, but it is not the only factor involved; the particular social and cultural contexts, purposes, and demands of a given act of communication will always influence the particular form it takes. Within the mode of 'email', for example, one finds chatty, conversational messages as well as formal administrative communications.

From a teaching perspective, many instructors note that learners' language use in EMC environments is often less correct, less complex, less coherent than the language they use in their ordinary written assignments. Herring (2001) points out that non-standard features are generally not due to inattentiveness or not knowing the standard forms, but are often deliberate choices to minimize typing effort, to imitate speech or sounds, or to be inventive. Warner's (2004) work on language play corroborates this view by showing how learners of German used code-mixing in their synchronous chat sessions. Crystal (2006) adds that simplification (e.g. omission of prepositions, copulas, auxiliary verbs) is not just a matter of typing economy but likely represents dialect features, reflecting the pressure to accommodate many diverse group members. Sometimes accommodations go beyond simplification and become multilingual hybrid forms (Bloch 2004; Lam 2004).

Such tendencies in online discourse create tensions for teachers intent on helping their students develop proficiency in standard forms of language. Because language learners may not have any intuitions about what constitutes standard versus non-standard forms, they may end up learning the non-standard forms rather than the standard ones (Crystal 2006). From a pedagogical standpoint, this raises the issue of teaching students how to discern among standard, non-standard, and hybrid uses and how to use different registers appropriately in different communicative contexts.

But the interplay between EMC and language use may be even more subtle. As mentioned earlier, the electronic medium is often thought of as a neutral conduit. In the following section we will look critically at this assumption.

Mediation in EMC

Etymologically, the words 'medium' and 'mediate' have to do with being in the middle. What is 'in the middle' in online communicative interaction? Certainly language – writing in text-based EMC and speech/gesture/facial expressions/postures in audiovisual EMC. But that language and body language is in turn mediated materially by some kind of interface. The hardware and the software, the core of the interface, can be familiar or unfamiliar to the users, and this can make a difference in how communication unfolds. Hardware and software can also introduce time lags and distortions (sometimes without users' awareness) as well as noise and connection problems – all of which can affect communication. A technologically induced time lag, for example, might be interpreted by the receiver as meaningful hesitation on the part of the writer (and the writer, not aware of the time lag, might not know what to make of a response that attributed hesitation to him).

But, as in all acts of communication, the physical spaces, the temporal contexts, the cultural contexts, and the activity frames in which people communicate are also mediators. The difference is that these are more often out of sight and out of mind in EMC environments than in face-to-face communication. When these dimensions are closely aligned with participants' expectations or mental models, communication is facilitated; when they are not, confusion or misinterpretations may occur. An email riddled with typographical errors might lead me to attribute carelessness or ignorance to the author if I envision him or her writing at home on a desktop computer. But if I know he or she is on a crowded bus, typing into an iPhone while being jostled by other passengers I will read with a great deal more tolerance. The problem is that one usually doesn't know. The more the channel allows users to manage the 'mutual monitoring possibilities' of interaction (Jones 2004), the more agency they have to shape what counts as context, but even in videoconferencing environments participants' understanding of the other's context is often more illusory than real.

As suggested earlier, the mediational qualities of EMC environments will influence genre and register conventions. Consider, for example, Burbules's (2006) interrogation of the relationship between computers and the 'discussion' genre:

> are we more likely to debate contentiously or criticize when we cannot see our partners in online dialogue; are we more or less likely to disclose personal confidences when we feel safe behind a certain level of distance and anonymity; are we more or less likely to trust our partners in conversation … ? The space of online communication, like any other, is not neutral and shapes the form and content of what is said or written within it: Dynamic and flexible as these channels are, they have specific features – such as synchrony or asynchrony – which privilege certain voices, perspectives, and ways of communicating.
>
> *(Burbules 2006: 117)*

What is 'in the middle' is therefore not a clear conduit, but a dynamic ecology of complex human and technological relationships and interactions, which has the potential to transform both the human and the technological participants.

Hutchby (2001) takes up this issue in his study of conversation mediated by the telephone and by Internet Relay Chat. 'To what extent', he asks, 'are we "technologized" conversationalists? … or from the opposite angle, how far may we as competent conversationalists be configurers of the communicative properties of these technologies?' (2001: 7). To address these questions, Hutchby adopts what he calls a 'relational' perspective (cf. the ecology metaphor described above), drawing on Gibson's (1986) notion of 'affordances'. Technologies may be designed to serve particular functions, but end users establish their own relationships to them, making use of technologies in ways that suit their purposes, regardless of the designer's intention. Hutchby uses the terms 'design-features' and 'features-in-use' to characterize this intended vs actualized distinction (cf. de Certeau's (2002) notions of 'strategy', 'tactics' and 'making do'). Hutchby illustrates with the example of the telephone, which, despite being marketed as a business tool for men and as a household management tool for women, was quickly transformed by telephone users into a tool for social chatting.

Lamy and Hampel (2007) discuss the cyclical nature of this human-technological mutual 'shaping' and give an example from blogging: whereas blogs began as 'Web logs' (i.e. personal journals uploaded to the Web – a re-mediation of a long-standing human practice), they were quickly transformed (i.e. by human creativity) into a range of genres such as video logs (vlogs), photoblogs, niche blogs, research blogs, corporate blogs, and legal blogs (blawgs), all of which blend users' personal interests, social purposes, and subject matter knowledge.

These, in turn, become resources for future technological/social innovations, and the cycle continues.

Mediation is a fact of life in all forms of technology use. Although it is not always obvious, its effects are nevertheless powerful. Consequently, we are wise to follow Lamy and Hampel's (2007) advice that mediation 'needs to be foregrounded in any examination of the learning process where computers are involved' (2007: 47).

Instructional and non-instructional applications

Technology affords an ever-widening array of uses for language teaching (see Blake 2008; Chun 2008; Kern *et al*. 2008 for recent overviews). This section will focus on three major areas of current interest in the field: distance and blended learning, intercultural online encounters, and community participation (forums, games, and virtual worlds).

Distance and blended learning

Distance learning involves taking courses without physical presence in a classroom, and is the modern equivalent of correspondence courses. The traditional form of distance learning is by video teleconference, in which the instructor meets with students at various sites at specified times. Internet-based distance learning is often more flexible and many learner activities can be done according to learners' schedules, allowing them to self-pace, which fosters learner autonomy. In recent years the number of distance learning programmes has mushroomed, and most are now Internet-mediated. In the USA, more than 3.9 million students took one or more online courses in the fall 2007 term, and this was a 12 per cent increase over the previous year (Allen and Seaman 2008).

'Blended' or 'hybrid' learning environments typically involve a distance learning component but also traditional face-to-face teaching (and sometimes out-of-class learning). As online and self-directed learning components have become more common in foreign language teaching, blended learning is increasingly becoming the norm in university level courses.

The use of multimedia (Jewitt and Kress 2003; Mayer 2005) together with EMC is exemplified in courses such as *Spanish Without Walls* (Blake and Delforge 2007), *Arabic Without Walls* (Shiri 2004; see Figure 14.1), and languages taught at the Open University. EMC is essential to such courses, as it allows interaction and feedback between learner and teacher as well as among learners. However, Blake (2005) underlines the importance of training for both instructors and students in dealing with the idiosyncrasies of audiographic EMC, such as time lags, overlapping turns, knowing when to write and when to speak, and so on.

For more on distance learning, see Hauck and Stickler (2006) as well as Holmberg *et al*. (2005), and White (2003, 2006).

Online intercultural encounters

School pen pal exchanges and even multimedia exchanges have existed since at least the 1920s, when Célestin Freinet established the Modern School Movement in Europe. With the development of the Internet, such exchanges have gained an unprecedented immediacy. An increasing trend in language teaching is the development of long-distance collaborations involving two or more classrooms, usually in different countries. Often referred to as tele-collaboration, these international partnerships generally place an emphasis on culture in language use and learning.

Figure 14.1 Arabic Without Walls
Source: http://uccllt.ucdavis.edu/aww/info.html

One of the best known and most long-standing projects is *Cultura* (http://Web.mit.edu/french/culturaNEH/2006s/index.html). Developed in the late 1990s by Gilberte Furstenberg and her colleagues at MIT, *Cultura* is a set of online modules designed to encourage language learners from different countries to engage in dialogue about the concepts, values, beliefs and attitudes that undergird their respective cultures and language use (Furstenberg *et al.* 2001). The idea is not to transmit culture, but to problematize it by juxtaposing materials, interpretations, and responses to interpretations. In addition to working extensively with a wide variety of texts, questionnaires, images, and films, students 'meet' in an online forum that gives them time to read, think, and formulate their answers to their correspondents' questions. Their discussion of these questions leads to new questions, feeding an ongoing cycle of reflection, discussion, and further reflection.

A number of studies have found promising results regarding the viability of online encounters for developing intercultural competence and understanding (e.g. Kinginger 2000; Meskill and Ranglova 2000; von der Emde and Schneider 2003). Other studies show, however, that intercultural contact in and of itself does not necessarily lead to cultural understanding. Learners' language ability, linguistic style, academic cultures, and institutional and cultural characteristics can affect their negotiation of meaning and cultural understanding (Belz 2002; 2003; Belz and Müller-Hartmann 2003; O'Dowd and Ritter 2006). More subtle, yet significant factors are differences in communicative medium and communicative genres. For example, Ware (2005) found that the asynchronous discussion tool she used in a German-American telecollaborative exchange contributed (because of delayed response time and no consequences for dropping topics) to a disengagement she calls 'missed communication'. Kramsch and Thorne (2001) question the very premise that the kind of communication found in intercultural EMC exchanges fosters intercultural understanding. In their analysis of a conflictual French-American email exchange, they propose that a clash in cultural frames and communicative genres, not just linguistic misunderstandings, is what hindered the students' ability to

Figure 14.2 Student screen from videoconferencing session in French using Skype

establish common ground for cross-cultural understanding. What needed to be negotiated, they argue, 'was not only the connotations of words … but the stylistic conventions of the genre (formal/informal, edited/unedited, literate/orate), and more importantly the whole discourse system to which that genre belonged' (2001: 98).

In a recent and very promising development, online encounters have begun to incorporate Web-based videoconferencing, allowing participants to see and hear one another (Figure 14.2). Whereas written EMC exchanges are mediated by words, symbols, and their timing and layout, desktop videoconferencing adds voice, gesture, gaze, movement, and images of a physical setting framed by a Webcam. The advantages and constraints of combining audio, video, and text in online exchanges are explored in Develotte *et al.* (2008); Jauregi and Bañados (2008); Kern (2008); and O'Dowd (2006).

In sum, intercultural EMC studies indicate that just putting people together to communicate does not ensure cultural understanding, which depends on a negotiation of differences in genres, interaction styles, local institutional cultures, and culture more broadly. When designing exchanges for language learning purposes, teachers or researchers on both sides therefore need to determine how they will make students aware of this broad range of potential differences and what kinds of opportunities for negotiation they will provide.

Community participation (forums, games, and virtual worlds)

The Internet offers a wide range of opportunities for learners to participate in various sorts of online communities. Three that we will consider here are discussion forums, games, and virtual worlds.

Discussion forums are a potential gold mine for language learning, since learners can become involved in discussions in the target language on any conceivable topic of interest – thereby capitalizing on any areas of personal expertise they might have and boosting their motivation and degree of engagement. Although some forums are specifically designed for language learners and teachers (e.g. Simpson 2005), most are not. This poses potential risks to learners, who are attempting to enter into discussion with 'real people' who may have little patience for those who are still learning the language.

To date, the use of forums destined for the general public has appeared only rarely in the literature on language learning (e.g. Wanner 2008), but a collection of case studies by Hanna and de Nooy (2009) provides excellent coverage of this important topic. Underscoring the importance of communicative genres, they show that the ease with which learners enter into discussion with native speakers can be deceptive, precisely because what constitutes the genre called 'discussion' is not universal but varies across cultures (and across mediums, as we saw in the section on mediation above). In the context of online forums, Hanna and de Nooy show that politeness and linguistic accuracy prove to be much less important than a willingness to be socialized into the discourse rules of a particular online community. This means we must understand communicative competence as a relative construct, shaped by the conditions and constraints of particular communicative contexts.

Computer-mediated games provide a different kind of environment for language learning. Largely through the work of James Gee (2003), video games have gained educational respect-ability in recent years. Thorne (2008) considers the affordances of massively multiplayer online games (MMOGs), which have become immensely popular. Because players need to collabo-rate with other players in order to achieve certain goals, communication plays a central role. According to Thorne, MMOG players, who come from around the world and can number in the thousands at any given time, 'must learn to negotiate complex scenarios, be socialized into culturally specific discourse formations, and be capable of negotiating play in real-time with game-driven characters as well as other co-present gamers' (2008: 317). Analyzing the written interaction of two players (one American, one Russian) in *World of Warcraft*, Thorne shows how players can be exposed to, and can appropriate, elements of a new language.

O'Brien and Levy (2008) developed their own virtual reality game in which German stu-dents needed to assemble clues (from spoken or written commands, conversations between characters, radio and TV broadcasts, cellphone messages, and signs) to find the mayor of Salzburg's missing daughter. Students reported that the game was more favourable for devel-oping listening skills than other aspects. The authors argue that students' virtual world experience may enhance their awareness of the target culture, but primarily in terms of cultural products rather than practices.

Similar in certain respects to gaming is participation in virtual worlds such as Second Life; Open Life; Active Worlds; or There. These are multimedia simulated 3-D environments in which one navigates (walking, jumping, or flying) by means of a user-configurable online avatar. 'Speaking' to other avatars or to bots (resident robots) is usually done in writing (with cartoon-style speech bubbles appearing above avatars' heads), although voice chat has recently become the default mode in some environments. Unlike games, the 'content' of virtual worlds is mostly created by users themselves with the tools and infrastructure provided by the com-pany that has designed the product. Meeting and interacting with other people (i.e. their ava-tars), acquiring virtual goods, and designing one's own custom environment are the chief activities in these environments. Given the essentially social nature of these worlds, and the widely international provenance of their 'residents', many teachers and researchers see them as exciting sites for language learning. To date, however, little research has been done in this area.

Deutschmann *et al.* (2009) assessed the affordances of Second Life for developing the oral/aural abilities of their graduate students. To their surprise, they learned that the limited expressive qualities of the avatars was actually beneficial, since students reported they had to focus more on 'the speaking and listening aspects of language' (2009: 210). They also found that focused role-play tasks that worked well in the classroom were not successful in Second Life, perhaps because of the distraction of dealing with the interface (the 'human-machine' part of communication), which reduced attention to the 'human-human' communication (2009: 223).

Consequently, Deutschmann *et al.* recommend that teachers train students in the particular technical and social dimensions of the virtual world environment before launching into learning tasks.

Future directions

As the use of digital technologies continues to expand in the coming years, teachers and researchers may wish to consider the following points.

First, as text-only environments become increasingly multimodal with image, voice, and sound, our resources for expressing culture and representing ourselves online expand correspondingly. More than ever, we need to remain attuned to the subtle interactions between medium, genre, register, and culture so that students can be prevented from jumping to facile conclusions about 'the' way that their correspondents think, feel, express themselves, and so on. The broader the variety of modes of communication, the richer students' interpretive base will be, but teachers need to consider how the different groups involved relate to the electronic medium itself as a cultural tool of communication, in order to better understand how cultures of use might affect intercultural communication.

Second, on a related note, we will need more critical explorations of how culture is understood in online environments. In the case of games and virtual worlds, whose culture is expressed? Is there only the simulational (and commercial) computer culture? In the case of online exchanges, terms such as cross-cultural, intercultural, and transcultural have been used rather interchangeably, and the task of educators will be to refine the terms and develop viable methodologies and theories for examining issues of (pluri)cultural representation, identification, and contact in online contexts.

Third, because online environments are partly shaped by the cultures of their inhabitants, ethnographic research is of key importance. Miller and Slater (2000) advocate what they call a 'comparative ethnographic' approach that centres on the dynamics of objectification, mediation, normative freedom, and positioning.

To effectively study such dynamics, a great deal more longitudinal research is needed (e.g. Chen 2006; van Deusen-Scholl 2008). Tracking language learning through year-long or multi-year studies helps mitigate, for example, concerns about how the novelty of technology might affect learner outcomes. Furthermore, longitudinal studies provide a more adequate basis for understanding how language learning might transfer across skill areas, as researchers are more able to track students across multiple contexts of use.

Fourth, we need to be open to novel ways of integrating multiple ways of learning – some classroom-based and some not related to formal instruction. 'School' versus 'home' uses of computers is becoming a meaningless distinction, and some of the richest learning environments may not be at all 'pedagogical' in purpose (e.g. forums). At the same time, teachers must be wary of co-opting learners' established online practices by pedagogizing them.

Finally, given the rapid evolution of technologies and the fluidity of communicative environments, teachers face increasingly complex decisions related to teaching with technology. Success in technology-mediated projects has been repeatedly shown to depend largely on teachers' efforts in coordinating learners' activities, structuring language and content, and helping learners to reflect critically on language, culture, and context. But keeping on top of project goals, activity/task design, technology interface, and the management of often complex logistical realities is challenging, and flexibility is a key asset. Teachers also need to know how technology can constrain as well as enhance their students' language use and know when it is better *not* to use computers.

Summary

Millennia old, the relationship between technology and language learning has never been as complex or as interesting as it is today. The accelerating diffusion of digital media and wireless networks, together with the increased naturalization of EMC, promises that technology-supported language learning will remain a critical area for teaching and research.

This chapter began by considering 'tutor', 'tool' and 'medium' metaphors of computer use in relation to the learning metaphors of acquisition, socialization, and ecology, suggesting that the ecology metaphor, despite and because of its complexity, deserves special attention in future research.

The broad area of electronically mediated communication was described as a process-product continuum of modes, with process-oriented modes biased toward social contact and product-oriented modes biased toward information exchange. The notions of genre and register were discussed in relation to standard and non-standard language forms in EMC, and mediational factors (e.g. mode, interface, setting) were considered with regard to their interaction with genre and communication. A central point was that the communicative medium (book, cell-phone, chat, email, etc) is not neutral but it does not determine the characteristics, purposes, and contours of communication by itself. Rather, it does so in interaction with cultural factors. Technologies are therefore not just a matter of hardware and media; they are intrinsically bound to culturally embedded beliefs, habits, and procedures.

Three categories of instructional (and non-instructional) applications of technology to language learning (distance/blended learning, online exchanges, and community participation) were then presented, with examples from the research literature, followed by a few thoughts about future directions in technology and language learning and the crucial importance of teachers to students' learning.

Related topics

classroom discourse; corpus linguistics; language and culture; language learning and language education; language socialization; language teacher education; language teaching methodology; multimodality; psycholinguistics; SLA

Further reading

Belz, J. A. and Thorne, S. L. (eds) (2006) *Internet-mediated Intercultural Foreign Language Education and the Intercultural Speaker*, Boston, Heinle IV, New York: Routledge. (A four volume set on CALL that introduces critical concepts and reprints some of the most influential scholarship in the field over the past twenty-five years.)

Chapelle, C. A. (2003) *English Language Learning and Technology: Lectures on Applied Linguistics in the Age of Information and Communication Technology*, Amsterdam: John Benjamins. (A thought-provoking series of essays on the interplay between technology and applied linguistics, on how second language acquistion theory can help inform technology-based language learning practices, and how technology can be used as a tool for applied linguistics research.)

Goodfellow, R. and Lamy, M.-N. (eds) (2009) *Learning Cultures in Online Education*, London: Continuum. (A collection of empirical case studies of online learning communities in diverse international contexts that highlights the importance of cultural identities, linguistic practices, affect/emotion/play, and technology as a social actor.)

Hubbard, P. (ed.) (2009) *Computer Assisted Language Learning: Critical Concepts in Linguistics, vols I–IV*, New York: Routledge. (A four-volume set on CALL that introduces critical concepts and reprints some of the most influential scholarship in the field over the past twenty-five years.)

Richard Kern

Magnan, S. S. (ed.) (2008) *Mediating Discourse Online*, Amsterdam: John Benjamins. (An excellent collection of essays and research studies generally taking an ecological approach to issues of collaboration, speech and writing, narrative, identity, voice, and the ethics of researching online interaction.)

References

Abdous, M., Camarena, M. M. and Facer, B. R. (2009) 'MALL technology: use of academic podcasting in the foreign language classroom', *ReCALL* 21: 76–95.

Alemán, A. M. M. and Wartman, K. L. (2009) *Online Social Networking on Campus: Understanding What Matters in Student Culture*, London: Routledge.

Allen, I. E. and Seaman, J. (2008) *Staying the Course: Online Educaiton in the United States, 2008*, Needham, MA: Sloan Consortium.

Baron, N. S. (2000) *Alphabet to Email: How Written English Evolved and Where it's Heading*, London: Routledge.

Belz, J. A. (2002) 'Social dimensions of telecollaborative foreign language study', *Language Learning and Technology* 6: 60–81.

——(2003) 'Linguistic perspectives on the development of intercultural competence in telecollaboration', *Language Learning and Technology* 7: 68–99.

Belz, J. A. and Müller-Hartmann, A. (2003) 'Teachers as intercultural learners: negotiating German-American telecollaboration along the institutional fault line', *Modern Language Journal* 87: 71–89.

Belz, J. A. and Vyatkina, N. (2008) 'The pedagogical mediation of a developmental learner corpus for classroom-based language instruction', *Language Learning and Technology* 12: 33–52.

Blake, R. (2005) 'Bimodal CMC: the glue of language learning at a distance', *CALICO Journal* 22: 497–511.

Blake, R. and Delforge, A. (2007) 'Online language learning: the case of Spanish without walls', in B. Lafford and R. Salaberry (eds) *The Art of Teaching Spanish: Second Language Acquisition from Research to Praxis*, Washington, DC: Georgetown University Press.

Blake, R. J. (2008) *Brave New Digital Classrooms: Technology and Foreign-Language Learning*, Washington, DC: Georgetown University Press.

Bloch, J. (2004) 'Second language cyber rhetoric: a study of Chinese L2 writers in an online USENET group', *Language Learning and Technology* 8(3): 66–82.

Braun, S., Kohn, K. and Mukherjee, J. (2006) *Corpus Technology and Language Pedagogy: New Resources, New Tools, New Methods*, New York: Peter Lang.

Burbules, N. C. (2006) 'Rethinking dialogue in networked spaces', *Cultural Studies – Critical Methodologies* 6: 107–22.

Chapelle, C. A. and Douglas, D. (2006) *Assessing Language Through Computer Technology*, Cambridge: Cambridge University Press.

Chen, C.-F. E. (2006) 'The development of email literacy: from writing to peers to writing to authority figures', *Language Learning and Technology* 10: 35–55.

Chun, D. (2008) 'Computer-mediated discourse in instructed environments', in S. S. Magnan (ed.) *Mediating Discourse Online*, Amsterdam: John Benjamins.

Coniam, D. (2008) 'Evaluating the language resources of chatbots for their potential in English as a second language', *ReCALL* 20: 98–116.

Crystal, D. (2006) *Language and the Internet*, 2nd edn, Cambridge: Cambridge University Press.

Danet, B. and Herring, S. C. (eds) (2007) *The Multilingual Internet: Language, Culture, and Communication Online*, Oxford: Oxford University Press.

de Certeau, M. (2002) '"Making do": uses and tactics', in *The Practice of Everyday Life,* Berkeley: University of California Press.

Deutschmann, M., Panichi, L. and Molka-Danielsen, J. (2009) 'Designing oral participation in second life: a comparative study of two language proficiency courses', *ReCALL* 21: 206–22.

Develotte, C., Guichon, N. and Kern, R. (2008) '"Allo Berkeley? Ici Lyon … Vous nous voyez bien?" Étude d'un dispositif de formation en ligne synchrone franco-américain à travers les discours de ses usagers', *ALSIC* 11: 129–56.

Erickson, T. (ed.) (1999) Special issue of the *Journal of Computer Mediated Communication* on persistent conversation, (4)4.

Furstenberg, G. and Levet, S. (1999) *Dans un quartier de Paris*, New Haven, CT: Yale University Press.

Furstenberg, G., Levet, S., English, K. and Maillet, K. (2001) 'Giving a virtual voice to the silent language of culture: the CULTURA project', *Language Learning and Technology* 5: 55–102.

Furstenberg, G., Murray, J. H., Malone, S. and Farman-Farmaian, A. (1993) *A la rencontre de Philippe*, New Haven, CT: Yale University Press.

Gee, J. P. (2003) *What Video Games have to Teach Us About Learning and Literacy*, New York: Palgrave Macmillan.

Gibson, J. J. (1986) *The Ecological Approach to Visual Perception*, Hillsdale, NJ: Lawrence Erlbaum Associates.

Green, M. W. (1986) 'Archaic Uruk Cuneiform', *American Journal of Archaeology* 90: 464–6.

Halliday, M. A. K. (1978) *Language as Social Semiotic: The Social Interpretation of Language and Meaning*, Baltimore: University Park Press.

Hanna, B. E. and de Nooy, J. (2009) *Learning Language and Culture via Public Internet Discussion Forums*, Basingstoke: Palgrave Macmillan.

Hauck, M. and Stickler, U. (2006) 'What does it take to teach online?', *CALICO Journal* 23: 463–75.

Herring, S. C. (ed.) (1996) *Computer-mediated Communication: Linguistic, Social and Cross-cultural Perspectives*, Amsterdam: John Benjamins.

Herring, S. C. (2001) 'Computer-mediated discourse', in D. Schiffrin, D. Tannen and H. E. Hamilton (eds) *The Handbook of Discourse Analysis*, Malden, MA: Blackwell.

Holland, V. M. and Fisher, F. P. (eds) (2007) *The Path of Speech Technologies in Computer Assisted Language Learning: From Research Toward Practice*, London: Routledge.

Holmberg, B., Shelley, M. and White, C. (eds) (2005) *Distance Education and Languages: Evolution and Change*, Clevedon: Multilingual Matters.

Hubbard, P. and Siskin, C. B. (2004) 'Another look at tutorial CALL', *ReCALL* 16: 448–61.

Hutchby, I. (2001) *Conversation and Technology: From the Telephone to the Internet*, Cambridge: Polity Press.

Jauregi, K. and Bañados, E. (2008) 'Virtual interaction through video-Web communication: a step towards enriching and internationalizing language learning programs', *ReCALL* 20: 183–207.

Jewitt, C. and Kress, G. (2003) *Multimodal Literacy*, New York: Peter Lang.

Jones, R. H. (2004) 'The problem of context in computer-mediated communication', in P. LeVine and R. Scollon (eds) *Discourse and Technology: Multimodal Discourse Analysis*, Washington, DC: Georgetown University Press.

Kelly, L. G. (1976) *Twenty-five Centuries of Language Teaching*, Rowley, MA: Newbury House.

Kern, R. (2008) 'Literacy and technology in French language teaching: issues and prospects', in D. Ayoun (ed.) *Studies in French Applied Linguistics*, Amsterdam: John Benjamins.

Kern, R., Ware, P. D. and Warschauer, M. (2008) 'Network-based language learning and teaching', in N. van Deusen-Scholl and N. H. Hornberger (eds) *Encyclopedia of Language and Education*, 2nd revised edn, vol. 4, Heidelberg: Springer.

Kinginger, C. (2000) 'Learning the pragmatics of solidarity in the networked foreign language classroom', in J. K. Hall and L. S. Verplaetse (eds) *Second and Foreign Language Learning Through Classroom Interaction*, Mahwah, NJ: Lawrence Erlbaum Associates.

Kramsch, C. (2002) 'Introduction: "How can we tell the dancer from the dance?"', in C. Kramsch (ed.) *Language Acquisition and Language Socialization: Ecological Perspectives*, London: Continuum.

Kramsch, C. and Thorne, S. L. (2001) 'Foreign language learning as global communicative practice', in D. Block and D. Cameron (eds) *Globalization and Language Teaching*, London: Routledge.

Lam, E. (2004) 'Border discourses and identities in transnational youth culture', in J. Mahiri (ed.) *What They Don't Learn in School: Literacy in the Lives of Urban Youth*, New York: Peter Lang.

Lam, W. S. E. and Kramsch, C. (2003) 'The ecology of an SLA community in a computer-mediated environment', in J. Leather and J. van Dam (eds) *Ecology of Language Acquisition*, Dordrecht: Kluwer Academic.

Lamy, M.-N. and Hampel, R. (2007) *Online Communication in Language Learning and Teaching*, Basingstoke: Palgrave Macmillan.

Latour, B. (2005) *Reassembling the Social: An Introduction to Actor-network-theory*, Oxford: Oxford University Press.

Mayer, R. E. (ed.) (2005) *The Cambridge Handbook of Multimedia Learning*, Cambridge: Cambridge University Press.

Meskill, C. and Ranglova, K. (2000) 'Curriculum innovation in TEFL: a study of technologies supporting socio-collaborative language learning in Bulgaria', in M. Warschauer and R. Kern (eds) *Network-based Language Teaching: Concepts and Practice,* Cambridge: Cambridge University Press.

Meurers, W. D. (ed.) (2009) Special issue of *CALICO Journal* on the automatic analysis of learner language, (26)3.

Miller, D. and Slater, D. (2000) *The Internet: An Ethnographic Approach*, Oxford: Berg.

O'Brien, M. G. and Levy, R. M. (2008) 'Exploration through virtual reality: encounters with the target culture', *Canadian Modern Language Review* 64: 663–91.

O'Dowd, R. (2006) 'The use of videoconferencing and email as mediators of intercultural student ethnography', in J. A. Belz and S. L. Thorne (eds) *Computer-mediated Intercultural Foreign Language Education,* Boston: Heinle and Heinle.

O'Dowd, R. and Ritter, M. (2006) 'Understanding and working with "failed communication" in telecollaborative exchanges', *CALICO Journal* 23: 623–42.

Ochs, E. and Schieffelin, B. B. (2008) 'Language socialization: an historical overview', in P. A. Duff and N. H. Hornberger (eds) *Encyclopedia of Language and Education*, 2nd edn, vol. 8: *Language Socialization*, Heidelberg: Springer.

Pachler, N., Bachmair, B. and Cook, J. (2010) *Mobilelearning: Structures, Agency, Practices*, New York: Springer.

Schmidt, J. (2008) 'Podcasts as a learning tool: German language and culture every day', *Die Unterrichtspraxis/Teaching German* 41: 186–94.

Sha, G. (2009) 'AI-based chatterbots and spoken English teaching: a critical analysis', *Computer Assisted Language Learning* 22: 269–81.

Shiri, S. (2004) *Arabic Without Walls*, Davis, CA: University of California Consortium for Language Learning and Teaching.

Simpson, J. (2005) 'Learning electronic literacy skills in an online language learning community', *Computer Assisted Language Learning* 18: 327–45.

Thorne, S. L. (2008) 'Transcultural communication in open Internet environments and massively multiplayer online games', in S. S. Magnan (ed.) *Mediating Discourse Online*, Amsterdam: John Benjamins.

van Deusen-Scholl, N. (2008) 'Online discourse strategies: a longitudinal study of computer-mediated foreign language learning', in S. S. Magnan (ed.) *Mediating Discourse Online,* Amsterdam: John Benjamins.

van Lier, L. (2003) 'A tale of two computer classrooms: the ecology of project-based language learning', in J. Leather and J. van Dam (eds) *Ecology of Language Acquisition*, Dordrecht: Kluwer Academic.

Vlugter, P., Knott, A., McDonald, J. and Hall, C. (2009) 'Dialogue-based CALL: a case study on teaching pronouns', *Computer Assisted Language Learning* 22: 115–31.

von der Emde, S. and Schneider, J. (2003) 'Experiential learning and collaborative reading: literacy in the space of virtual encounters', in P. Patrikis (ed.) *Reading Between the Lines: Perspectives on Foreign Language Literacy*, New Haven, CT: Yale University Press.

Wanner, A. (2008) 'Creating comfort zones of orality in online discussion forums', in S. S. Magnan (ed.) *Mediating Discourse Online*, Amsterdam: John Benjamins.

Ware, P. D. (2005) '"Missed" communication in online communication: tensions in a German-American telecollaboration', *Language Learning and Technology* 9(2): 64–89.

Warner, C. N. (2004) 'It's just a game, right? Types of play in foreign language CMC', *Language Learning and Technology* 8(2): 69–87.

Warschauer, M. and Grimes, D. (2008) 'Automated essay scoring in the classroom', *Pedagogies* 3: 22–36.

Warschauer, M. and Kern, R. (eds) (2000) *Network-based Language Teaching: Concepts and Practice*, Cambridge: Cambridge University Press.

White, C. (2003) *Language Learning in Distance Education*, Cambridge: Cambridge University Press.

——(2006) 'Distance learning of foreign languages', *Language Teaching* 39: 247–64.

15

Language teacher education

Simon Borg

Introduction

This chapter examines key contemporary themes in the field of language teacher education (henceforth LTE), focusing specifically on the initial preparation and continuing professional development of second (L2) and foreign language (FL) teachers. My scope is broad, and the analysis that follows is not determined by a concern for particular languages, types of teachers and learners, teacher education programmes or geographical contexts. In fact, highlighting the diverse global scope of LTE – and the need for greater connections among its various sectors – is one of my goals here.

Brief history

As a field of activity, LTE does not have a long formal history; Schulz's (2000) review of articles about FL teacher development published in the *Modern Language Journal* between 1916 and 1999 suggests that methodology courses for FL teachers in the USA were available in the 1920s. The first teacher training course for EFL (English as a foreign language) teachers, however, only started in London in 1962 (Haycraft 1988). These courses were the precursors of the Certificate level TESOL (Teaching English to Speakers of Other Languages) qualifications that exist today in the form of Cambridge ESOL's CELTA and Trinity's Cert. TESOL (see Howatt and Widdowson 2004: 246, for a brief comment on the emergence of these courses).

The 1960s also witnessed the emergence of applied linguistics as a field, and 'with it came a body of specialized academic knowledge and theory that provided the foundation of the new discipline. This knowledge was represented in the curricula of MA programs, which began to be offered from this time' (Richards 2008: 159). On such programmes, professional development as a language teacher largely entailed becoming familiar with the latest theory and research in applied linguistics; it was assumed that such knowledge would enhance teachers' classroom practices.

Early in the 1980s, teacher training emerged as a priority in the work of the Council of Europe (see Trim 2007 for a historical account of modern language teaching in Europe). It is not clear how the work on LTE being done in continental Europe and that in the UK and USA interfaced at this time.

As a field of inquiry (i.e. one which is systematically researched and theorized), it is only in the last twenty years that LTE has emerged. In 1990, Richards and Nunan (1990: xi) wrote that

> the field of teacher education is a relatively underexplored one in both second and foreign language teaching. The literature on teacher education in language teaching is slight compared with the literature on issues such as methods and techniques for classroom teaching. Few of the articles published in the last twenty years are data-based, and most consist of anecdotal wish lists of what is best for the teacher.
>
> *(Richards and Nunan 1990: xi)*

The publication this extract comes from was a landmark in the development of LTE as a field. First, it acknowledged the limited empirical basis of LTE and stressed the need to address this. Second, this text argued for a new view of the education of language teachers, which it summarized as follows:

- a movement away from a 'training' perspective to an 'education' perspective and a recognition that effective teaching involves higher-level cognitive processes, which cannot be taught directly;
- the need for teachers and student teachers to adopt a research orientation to their own classrooms and their own teaching;
- less emphasis on prescriptions and top-down directives and more emphasis on an inquiry-based and discovery-oriented approach to learning (bottom-up);
- a focus on devising experiences that require the student teacher to generate theories and hypotheses and to reflect critically on teaching;
- less dependence on linguistics and language theory as a source discipline for second language teacher education, and more of an attempt to integrate sound, educationally based approaches;
- use of procedures that involve teachers in gathering and analyzing data about teaching.
  (Richards and Nunan 1990: xii)

These perspectives on LTE have been developed through a number of publications since; some early ones were Wallace (1991), Flowerdew *et al.* (1992) and Richards and Lockhart (1994). More recent contributions which have extended our understandings of what it means to become, be and develop as a language teacher are Freeman and Richards (1996), Richards (1998a), Tedick (2005), Grenfell (1998 – in the context of MFL – Modern Foreign Languages – in the UK), Johnson (2000), Johnson (1999), Johnson and Golombek (2002), Tsui (2003), Woods (1996), Borg (2006b), Farrell (2008b), Malderez and Wedell (2007), Bailey (2006), Johnson (2009) and the collection of thirty chapters on LTE in Burns and Richards (2009). Many of these sources which pre-date 2000 were reviewed in Crandall (2000), who identified four trends characterizing the LTE literature in the 1990s. These were:

- a shift from transmission, product-oriented theories to constructivist, process-oriented theories of learning, teaching, and teacher learning;
- efforts ... to transform teaching through a focus on situated teacher cognition and practice and the development of concrete, relevant linkages between theory and practice throughout the teacher education programme;

- a growing recognition that teachers' prior learning experiences play a powerful role in shaping their views of effective teaching and learning and their teaching practices;
- a growing concern that teaching be viewed as a profession (similar to medicine or law) with respect for the role of teachers in developing theory and directing their own professional development through collaborative observation, teacher research and inquiry, and sustained inservice programmes.

(Crandall 2000: 34–6)

This list and that above from Richards and Nunan (1990) overlap in certain respects; together they provide a summary of key themes in LTE in the 1990s. As we will see below, these themes continue to be of relevance today.

The analysis I present in the remainder of this chapter derives predominantly from literature on LTE published since 2005. This is not to suggest that material that predates this period is no longer valuable; as noted above, seminal work in the field stems from the 1990s. It has, though, been reviewed and discussed elsewhere (Richards 1998b, 2008, Crandall 2000, Borg 2003, Freeman 2002). I will thus focus here on more recent work in the field of LTE.

Volume of LTE research

It is clear from the available literature that a substantial body of work exists in relation to TESOL teacher education. In other areas of LTE the picture, however, varies. In the teaching of English language learners in the USA, for example, research interest in teacher education is a recent phenomenon (see the review in Lucas and Grinberg 2008), while the context of English as an additional language (EAL) in the UK would not seem to be characterized by any formal process of teacher preparation itself (Franson 2007), let alone a body of research examining this process. Also in the UK, a rapidly evolving ESOL context has in recent years witnessed increased LTE activity (see Morton *et al.* 2006 for a review of this work). MFL teacher education in the UK, at both primary and secondary level, does not seem to have been extensively researched (but see Hunt *et al.* 2005), while language teacher education in continental Europe has been the focus of projects supported by the Council of Europe and the European Commission (e.g. Kelly and Grenfell 2005) and also of some research articles (e.g. Garrido and Alvarez 2006; Ruiz 2008). FL teacher education in the USA has also been the subject of a number of recent journal articles (e.g. Antenos-Conforti 2008; Bateman 2008; Bell 2005; Geyer 2008; Pearson *et al.* 2006). The diversity of LTE is a theme I want to continue emphasizing, and the varying levels of research activity in the different domains noted here continues to support this point. One other point I want to stress further is the general lack of connections across the LTE sector as a whole. Lucas and Grinberg (2008) is an example of this; they present a thorough review of research on the preparation of non-specialist (in a language teaching sense) classroom teachers to support English language learners in the USA; the review is thoroughly grounded in mainstream teacher education literature yet makes no reference to key work in the field of TESOL teacher education generally or to the UK ESOL sector.

In addition to this general survey of the volume of research available in different areas of LTE, I assessed the prevalence of LTE research by examining the contents pages of six applied linguistics journals for the period 2005–9. Table 15.1 presents the results of this analysis.

These figures indicate that, between 2005 and 2009, less than 10 per cent of the articles in the journals analyzed focused on LTE. This suggests that LTE, while an established domain of enquiry, still lags far behind language learning and language teaching as core areas of research interest.

Table 15.1 LTE literature in six journals, 2005–9

Journal	Volumes	Total articles	LTE articles	%
Applied Linguistics	26(1)–30(2)	141	5	3.5
Foreign Language Annals	38(1)–42(2)	177	19	10.7
Language Teaching Research	9(1)–13(3)	90	16	17.8
Modern Language Journal	89(1)–93(2)	225	14	6.2
System	33(1)–37(2)	180	15	8.3
TESOL Quarterly	39(1)–43(1)	212	24	11.3
Total		1,025	93	9.1

Current issues in LTE

I will now provide concise commentaries on six themes which currently characterize LTE.

Teacher cognition

Teacher cognition is concerned with understanding what teachers think, know, and believe, and how these relate to what teachers do (see Borg 2006b). Writing about LTE, Johnson (2006: 235) claims that in the past forty years 'many factors have advanced the field's understanding of L2 teachers' work, but none is more significant than the emergence of a substantial body of research now referred to as teacher cognition'. As noted earlier, contemporary views of LTE acknowledge teachers as active, thinking decision-makers whose actions are influenced by the unobservable cognitive (and affective) dimension of teaching. Teacher cognition is also a fundamental element in teacher learning; drawing on constructivist theories of learning, it is now accepted in LTE that how and what teachers learn is shaped in no small way by their prior experience, knowledge and beliefs. Such views (and hence teacher cognition) are also central to contemporary sociocultural perspectives on LTE (Johnson 2009), which are based on the view that 'teachers' prior experiences, their interpretations of the activities they engage in, and, most important, the contexts within which they work are extremely influential in shaping how and why teachers do what they do' (Johnson 2006: 236). For all the above reasons, understanding teacher cognition is now recognized as a central part of understanding what it means to be, become and develop as a teacher. It is also accepted that the design and implementation of teacher education initiatives will be more effective when these are based on and take account of the cognitions teachers – whether pre-service or in-service – have. An analysis of contemporary research on LTE demonstrates the central standing a concern for teacher cognition has; among the ninety-three articles referred to in Table 15.1, those examining aspects of teacher cognition formed the largest single group; specific issues examined, for example, are teachers' perceptions of errors (Hyland and Anan 2006) and teachers' (and students') perceptions of effective FL teaching (Brown 2009).

The knowledge base for LTE

As Graves (2009) explains, the knowledge base of language teaching – i.e. what teachers need to know – has been traditionally divided into two separate domains – knowledge of language and knowledge of teaching. Current thinking in the field conceptualizes the knowledge base for LTE in much more complex terms. Heavily influenced by work in education generally (e.g. Shulman 1986), LTE now recognizes that teachers require several types of knowledge.

Richards (1998a), for example, proposes a scheme made up of six types of knowledge (theories of teaching, teaching skills, communication skills, subject matter knowledge, pedagogical reasoning and decision-making skills, and contextual knowledge). One feature of such contemporary typologies is the inclusion of knowledge which is internal to and created by teachers (e.g. personal theories and beliefs). This contrasts with views of the knowledge base for teaching which see it exclusively in terms of external knowledge which teachers must acquire and then apply.

Also, whereas different types of teacher knowledge were previously conceived of separately in LTE, contemporary thinking in the field argues for the need to develop in teachers an integrated knowledge base which they can deploy effectively in the classroom. Thus, for example, Morton *et al.* (2006: 38) conclude that LTE 'should recognise the complexities of what constitutes "subject knowledge" in language teaching, and how it is inseparable from "teaching knowledge" and involve participants in activities which capture the fusion of content and process typical of language teaching'.

These advances in how the knowledge base for LTE is conceptualized have not been reflected in LTE practices globally. Writing about the education of language teachers in K-12 settings in the USA, Tedick (2009: 265) argues that 'foreign language preservice teachers ... are left to their own devices to make the connections as they take courses in literature or phonology', suggesting that the dichotomies between subject matter and pedagogy referred to above continue to present a challenge to the effective education of language teachers.

Arguments originally put forward by Freeman and Johnson (1998) and since developed further (e.g. Freeman and Johnson 2005) critique conceptualizations of the knowledge base for LTE which are rooted in disciplinary traditions of linguistics and second language acquisition and which assume that learning to teach equates to the acquisition and transfer of knowledge from such disciplines. Without negating the value of such knowledge for teachers, Freeman and Johnson have argued that LTE needs to be grounded in the study of the activities of teaching itself and the social context in which they occur, and that a recognition of the teacher as a learner of language teaching is central to this process (see Johnson 2009 for an extended account of this position).

Knowledge about language

Linked to the previous theme, one aspect of teacher knowledge that has attracted specific research attention is teachers' knowledge about language. The papers in Bartels (2005) share a concern for different types of knowledge about language; collectively they demonstrate both the relevance of such knowledge to the work of language teachers, as well as some of the problems that can arise when teachers need to apply to pedagogical contexts theoretical knowledge acquired in the context of teacher education (see, for example, Bigelow and Ranney 2005). These themes are reprised in Bartels (2009), who also makes suggestions for the kinds of LTE practices which would make it more likely for teachers to use knowledge about language acquired through teacher education in their teaching (e.g. linking the analysis of such knowledge to real-life problems in classrooms). Andrews (2007) examines in detail teacher language awareness (TLA) – teachers' knowledge and understandings of language systems – and argues that 'the possession of an adequate level of TLA is an essential attribute of any competent L2 teacher' (2007: ix). More recently, with reference to FL teacher education in the USA, Lantolf (2009: 270) has also argued 'that foreign language (FL) teacher education programs need to (re)invest in courses designed to enhance the depth and breadth of explicit knowledge of the target language (TL) of their graduates'. While, as noted above, there is evidence that improved knowledge about language can enhance teaching, it is also important to remember the point made above that such knowledge alone – when divorced from knowledge about teaching and knowledge about learners – will not guarantee effective classroom practice.

In terms of empirical research, there is not much evidence of recent work on teachers' knowledge about language and its use in teaching. More research is needed into how knowledge about language can be developed through LTE in ways that enable teachers to use it productively to support learning.

Reflective practice

Reflective practice is another recurrent theme in contemporary LTE literature. Seminal thinking in relation to reflection stems from the work of Dewey (1933) and Schön (1983), while in LTE the notion was popularized by Wallace (1991). A number of definitions of reflection have been put forward (see the discussion in Korthagen 2001) but in essence, being reflective involves teachers in an on-going process of critically examining their beliefs and practices with a view to becoming aware of and enhancing them. While different perspectives on reflection exist, 'most teacher educators would argue that reflection is an essential tool in professional development' (Burton 2009: 300).

Farrell (2007b) discusses how reflective practice can be promoted in LTE and outlines several strategies which can support reflective practice, such as action research, journal writing, and teacher study groups. The use of technology in promoting reflective practice among language teachers has also emerged an area of research interest (e.g. Lord and Lomicka 2007; Pellerin 2008). In the European context, a concern for reflection is evident in the development of the EPOSTL, the European Portfolio for Student Teachers of Languages (for a description, see Burkert and Schweinhorst 2008).

Although the positive impact of reflection on teachers' knowledge and attitudes has been demonstrated (e.g. Kabilan 2007), evidence that reflection leads to better quality language teaching and learning is generally hard to locate. In his review of literature, Akbari (2007) concludes that 'there is little evidence that engaging teachers in reflection will result in higher student achievement and better teacher performance' (2007: 198). Such critical perspectives on reflection are valuable. In fact, my view on reflection is that the positive rhetoric in the literature is insufficiently grounded in the realities that language teachers work in, and a closer empirical analysis of these realities is required before reflective practice can become a viable global strategy for LTE (especially in in-service contexts). Some insights into teacher resistance to reflection are presented in Moon and Boullón (1997) while more recently A'Dhahab (2009) has shown that when language teachers are required (without adequate guidance or obvious purpose) to engage in reflective writing they complete the task mechanically, treating it as an administrative requirement which makes no contribution at all to their professional development.

The practicum

The practicum is a period of practice teaching in real classrooms that is a typical element in initial LTE programmes. In a practicum, teacher candidates are usually supervised – i.e. they are observed while teaching and receive feedback on their performance; the practicum is also normally assessed. The practicum can have range of goals (Gebhard 2009 lists eight), though primary amongst these is providing teachers with opportunities to develop their practical skills and pedagogical reasoning by working in a real classroom.

Periodic studies of the practicum in LTE settings have appeared (e.g. Johnson 1992; Numrich 1996) though this area is not characterized by an extensive research base. Much has been written on the subject of the supervision of language teachers generally – (see the discussion in Bailey 2006) but this often perpetuates assumptions about appropriate practices (e.g. that non-directive supervision is preferable to directive supervision) rather than interrogating such views empirically. Having said that, there have been some recent examples of research focusing on aspects of the practicum in LTE. Farrell (2007a) examined the experience of a student teacher who failed the practicum, while Farrell (2008a) and Smith and Lewis (2009) studied the perspectives of the practicum of student teachers and mentors respectively. Luk (2008) studied reflective writing in the context of the practicum, while a paper which explores how the practicum may actually limit language teacher learning is Ong'Ondo and Borg (2011).

The practicum involves various processes which we currently know little about. The transfer issue is an important one, in terms of how the learning that takes place on the practicum influences what teachers do once they become qualified teachers (some earlier LTE research, e.g. Spada and Massey 1992, suggested that transfer may sometimes be very limited but this is not an issue that has been widely studied). The nature of the triadic relationship among student teachers, university supervisors and school-based mentors, and how this relationship shapes teacher learning on the practicum, are also issues we know little about. More specifically, more research on the role of mentors in LTE is required (see Hobson *et al.* 2009 for a review of international literature on mentoring beginning teachers).

Teacher research

The last contemporary theme in LTE I will comment on here is teacher research, which is the process through which teachers systematically investigate aspects of their own professional practices with a view to enhancing, first, their understanding of these and, subsequently, the quality of their work. In the context of LTE, teacher research is seen to have the potential to contribute in many ways to teacher professional development (see, for example, Jones 2004; Nunan 1989). A number of publications in LTE have also appeared which provide evidence of teachers researching their own contexts and of the learning they derive from this process (e.g. Borg 2006a; 2008; Mitchell-Schuitevoerder and Mourão 2006; Burns and Burton 2007). The positive rhetoric in the literature on teacher research, though, obscures the fact that it remains a minority activity in the field of language teaching. It is important, from a LTE perspective, to consider the reasons for this, as a better understanding of them can enable teacher educators to approach the task of promoting language teacher research more feasibly. Work on language teachers' perceptions of research (Borg 2007a, 2009; Reis-Jorge 2007) and on the challenges language teachers wanting to do research face (Allison and Carey 2007) is important here as it provides insights into factors which may oppose engagement in this activity by teachers. Teacher educators in LTE can benefit from an awareness of such factors (see Borg 2007b for a discussion of this issue). For example, language teacher educators must be aware that making teacher research happen – especially in in-service contexts – involves much more than ensuring teachers have the technical competence to do research, and invokes a range of psychological, social, institutional, commercial and political considerations. These factors are, unfortunately, often overlooked in discussions of teacher research as a strategy for LTE. Much work has been done in mainstream education on ways of promoting and supporting teacher research (e.g. Sharp 2007; Davies *et al.* 2007) and LTE could benefit from a greater awareness of this literature. Borg (2010) provides a comprehensive review of the literature on language teacher research engagement.

Other themes

I will comment very briefly on three additional themes in LTE which merit further attention:

- *Teacher educator development.* Who are the teacher educators in LTE? How do they become language teacher educators? What skills and knowledge do they need? Wright and Bolitho (2007), Malderez and Wedell (2007) and Waters (2005) provide valuable experience-based insights into being a language teacher educator; empirical studies of these issues though are lacking.
- *Novice teachers.* What is the nature of the transition from student teacher to practising teacher? What impact does the first year have on teachers' subsequent careers? These are just two examples of questions relevant to an understanding of novice language teachers. Farrell (2008b) adds to early work on this theme (e.g. Pennington and Richards 1997) but research here remains limited (but see also Ruohotie-Lyhty and Kaikkonen 2009 for another study of relevance, and *TESOL Quarterly* 46(3), Special Issue on Novice Professionals in TESOL).
- *Teacher expertise.* The work of Tsui (2003, 2005) has made a central (though largely solitary) contribution to our understandings of what it means to develop expertise in language teaching. These understandings remain, however, incipient.

Future directions

There are two key messages I want to stress as a result of the above review of issues in LTE.

Enhancing cross-sector links

LTE as a field is immense in scope, spanning multiple and diverse international sites, socio-political contexts, teacher education programme structures, teacher educator backgrounds, and prospective and practising teacher profiles. While this scope means that each LTE context, such as primary MFL in the UK, or the teaching of ELLs in the USA, will have its unique concerns, it also presents excellent opportunities for shared knowledge development and practical advancement on a global scale. Having surveyed work across a range of LTE sectors, my first point here is that these opportunities for cross-sector links are not being exploited. There will be clear pragmatic reasons for this. However, it is clear that innovative work being conducted in particular LTE sectors may be of value to the field generally. This applies conceptually, empirically, and in more practical terms. It would seem that a review of LTE literature which looked globally at thinking, research, and practice would be an invaluable resource for language teacher educators. The production of such a review, placing it in the context of what is known about mainstream teacher education generally, therefore, is my first suggestion for future work in LTE. The analysis I have presented here merely hints at the potential that a much larger and more systematic analysis of issues across LTE worldwide could have.

Strengthening the empirical base

My second concluding point here is that in empirical terms LTE remains undeveloped. A number of concerns signalled in the mainstream teacher education literature are also being addressed in LTE (e.g. concerns with professional development and with the practicum). However, we are not in a position to provide confident research-based answers to many of the key questions that challenge language teacher educators. The vast pool of accumulated practical experience that language teacher educators around the world possess is undeniably valuable. If we are to make progress with some of the most pressing questions we face as a field, though, we also require systematic programmes of both qualitative and quantitative research, with scope for replications across different contexts, and which collectively will provide a knowledge base which can inform the continuing development of LTE as a field. Each of the key LTE themes I discussed above is in need of detailed specific study. Also, despite advances in this respect, LTE can also benefit from a greater awareness of the research being conducted in teacher education more generally. Readers here are referred to Cochran-Smith and Zeichner (2005), Darling-Hammond and Bransford (2005) and Cochran-Smith *et al.* (2008), which focus on the US context. Substantial work on mainstream teacher education has also been conducted in Europe, as exemplified in a report by the European Trade Union Committee for Education (ETUCE/CSEE 2008). Internationally, the OECD has also contributed to teacher education policy, most recently in its Teaching and Learning International Survey (TALIS) project. The first results from this project (drawing on responses from nearly 74,000 lower secondary school teachers) were released in mid-2009 (OECD 2009).

The issue of the impact of LTE is also one that has to date attracted limited empirical attention: what difference does LTE make to teachers and to their learners? There has been some limited debate of the relationship between teacher learning and student learning in LTE (Freeman and Johnson 2005; Borg 2006b; Andrews 2007), but Schulz's (2000) conclusion on reviewing eighty-five years of literature on FL teacher education in the USA applies today to LTE generally: 'our progress (i.e., any documented, measurable impact on quality, quantity, or both) in the area of teacher development has been disappointingly small'. Research in mainstream teacher education suggests that relationships between teacher education and student learning are difficult to study (Kwang *et al.* 2007); however, this is a challenge which confronts us as a field and which awaits a systematic response.

Thus, the development of systematic programmes of focused research is the second suggestion for the future I want to make here. An increase in the volume of high quality LTE research would justify the creation of an international journal dedicated solely to such work. Given the levels of LTE research activity I have noted here, though, such an exercise is at present not viable, though it is positive to note the continued periodic publication of special topic issues of leading journals dedicated to LTE (e.g. in 2010, *Language Teaching Research* vol. 14(3)).

Summary

The purpose of this chapter was to provide a critical overview of the field of language teacher education (LTE). I started by noting the global and varied scope of LTE, followed by a brief comment on the relatively recent history of LTE as a field of inquiry. An analysis of research published in six applied linguistics journals suggested that research outputs relevant to LTE were not currently particularly high. The limitations of the existing research base in LTE were highlighted in the core of the chapter, where key themes suggested in the current literature were discussed. For each theme, the discussion concluded that strong evidence in relation to central aspects of LTE is lacking and that widely accepted ideas in the field, while supported by experience, require empirical support too. Research from TESOL dominates LTE generally, though I did apply myself here to the task of surveying work from the range of LTE sectors identified earlier in the chapter. In terms of taking the field forward, I ended with two suggestions. One is the need for an international cross-sector review of what is known about LTE;

the second called for the development and implementation of systematic programmes of LTE research on a broad range of fundamental issues.

Related topics

key concepts in language learning and language education; language teaching methodology

Further reading

Andrews, S. (2007) *Teacher Language Awareness*, Cambridge: Cambridge University Press. (An analysis of the value to teachers of an awareness of language systems.)

Borg, S. (2006) *Teacher Cognition and Language Education: Research and Practice*, London: Continuum. (A review of research on language teachers' beliefs and knowledge and the methods used in such research.)

Burns, A. and Richards, J. C. (eds) (2009) *The Cambridge Guide to Second Language Teacher Education*, Cambridge: Cambridge University Press. (A collection of overviews of key themes in the field of L2 teacher education.)

Cochran-Smith, M. and Zeichner, K. (eds) (2005) *Studying Teacher Education: The Report of the AERA Panel on Research and Teacher Education*, Mahwah, NJ: AERA/Lawrence Erlbaum Associates. (A review of research on initial teacher education in the USA.)

Johnson, K. E. (2009) *Second Language Teacher Education: A Sociocultural Perspective*, London: Routledge. (An analysis of the implications of sociocultural theory for the practice of second language teacher education.)

References

A'Dhahab, S. M. (2009) 'EFL teachers' perceptions and practices regarding reflective writing', in S. Borg (ed.) *Researching English Language Teaching and Teacher Development in Oman*, Oman, Muscat: Ministry of Education.

Akbari, R. (2007) 'Reflections on reflection: a critical appraisal of reflective practices in L2 teacher education', *System* 35(2): 192–207.

Allison, D. and Carey, J. (2007) 'What do university language teachers say about language teaching research?', *TESL Canada Journal* 24(2): 61–81.

Andrews, S. (2007) *Teacher Language Awareness*, Cambridge: Cambridge University Press.

Antenos-Conforti, E. (2008) 'How far is Georgia?: New Jersey's teachers of Italian evaluate their preparation', *Foreign Language Annals* 41: 542–61.

Bailey, K. M. (2006) *Language Teacher Supervision*, Cambridge: Cambridge University Press.

Bartels, N. (ed.) (2005) *Applied Linguistics and Language Teacher Education*, New York: Springer.

Bartels, N. (2009) 'Knowledge about language', in A. Burns and J. C. Richards (eds) *The Cambridge Guide to Second Language Teacher Education*, Cambridge: Cambridge University Press.

Bateman, B. E. (2008) 'Student teachers' attitudes and beliefs about using the target language in the classroom', *Foreign Language Annals* 41: 11–28.

Bell, T. R. (2005) 'Behaviors and attitudes of effective foreign language teachers: results of a questionnaire study', *Foreign Language Annals* 38: 259–70.

Bigelow, M. and Ranney, M. (2005) 'Pre-service ESL teachers' knowledge about language and its transfer to lesson planning', in N. Bartels (ed.) *Applied Linguistics and Language Teacher Education*, New York: Springer.

Borg, S. (2003) 'Teacher cognition in language teaching: a review of research on what language teachers think, know, believe, and do', *Language Teaching* 36(2): 81–109.

——(2006b) *Teacher Cognition and Language Education: Research and Practice*, London: Continuum.

——(2007a) 'Research engagement in English language teaching', *Teaching and Teacher Education* 23(5): 731–47.

——(2007b) 'Understanding what teachers think about research', *The Teacher Trainer* 21(2): 2–4.

——(2009) 'English language teachers' conceptions of research', *Applied Linguistics* 30(3): 355–88.

——(2010) 'Language teacher research engagement', *Language Teaching* 43(4): 391–429.

Borg, S. (ed.) (2006a) *Language Teacher Research in Europe*, Alexandria, VA: TESOL.

——(2008) *Investigating English Language Teaching and Learning in Oman*, Oman, Muscat: Ministry of Education.

Brown, A. V. (2009) 'Students' and teachers' perceptions of effective foreign language teaching: a comparison of ideals', *Modern Language Journal* 93(1): 46–60.

Burkert, A. and Schweinhorst, K. (2008) 'Focus on the student teacher: the European Portfolio for Student Teachers of Languages (EPOSTL) as a tool to develop teacher autonomy', *Innovation in Language Learning and Teaching* 2: 238–52.

Burns, A. and Burton, J. (eds) (2007) *Language Teacher Research in Australia and New Zealand*, Alexandria, VA: TESOL.

Burns, A. and Richards, J. C. (eds) (2009) *The Cambridge Guide to Second Language Teacher Education*, Cambridge: Cambridge University Press.

Burton, J. (2009) 'Reflective practice', in A. Burns and J. C. Richards (eds) *The Cambridge Guide to Second Language Teacher Education*, Cambridge: Cambridge University Press.

Cochran-Smith, M., Feiman-Nemser, S., McIntyre, J. D. and Demers, K. E. (eds) (2008) *Handbook of Research on Teacher Education: Enduring Questions in Changing Contexts*, New York: Routledge/Association of Teacher Educators.

Cochran-Smith, M. and Zeichner, K. (eds) (2005) *Studying Teacher Education: The Report of the AERA Panel on Research and Teacher Education*, Mahwah, NJ: AERA/Lawrence Erlbaum Associates.

Crandall, J. A. (2000) 'Language teacher education', *Annual Review of Applied Linguistics* 20: 34–55.

Darling-Hammond, L. and Bransford, J. (2005) *Preparing Teachers for a Changing World*, San Francisco: Jossey-Bass.

Davies, P., Hamilton, M. and James, K. (2007) *Maximising the Impact of Practitioner Research: A Handbook of Practical Advice*, London: NRDC.

Dewey, J. (1933) *How We Think*, Buffalo, NY: Prometheus Books.

ETUCE/CSEE (2008) *Teacher Education in Europe*, Brussels: ETUCE/CSEE.

Farrell, T. S. C. (2007a) 'Failing the practicum: narrowing the gap between expectations and reality with reflective practice', *TESOL Quarterly* 41(1): 193–202.

——(2007b) *Reflective Language Teaching: From Research to Practice*, London: Continuum.

——(2008a) '"Here's the book, go teach the class": ELT practicum support', *RELC Journal* 39: 226–41.

Farrell, T. S. C. (ed.) (2008b) *Novice Language Teachers: Insights and Perspectives for the First Year*, London: Equinox.

Flowerdew, J., Brock, M. and Hsia, S. (eds) (1992) *Perspectives on Second Language Teacher Education*, Hong Kong: City Polytechnic.

Franson, C. (2007) 'Challenges and opportunities for the teaching profession: English as an additional language in the UK', in J. Cummins and C. Davison (eds) *International Handbook of English Language Teaching*, New York: Springer.

Freeman, D. (2002) 'The hidden side of the work: teacher knowledge and learning to teach', *Language Teaching* 35(1): 1–13.

Freeman, D. and Johnson, K. E. (1998) 'Reconceptualizing the knowledge-base of language teacher education', *TESOL Quarterly* 32(3): 397–417.

——(2005) 'Towards linking teacher knowledge and student learning.', in D. Tedick (ed.) *Second Language Teacher Education: International Perspectives*, Mahwah, NJ: Lawrence Erlbaum Associates.

Freeman, D. and Richards, J. C. (eds) (1996) *Teacher Learning in Language Teaching*, Cambridge: Cambridge University Press.

Garrido, C. and Alvarez, I. (2006) 'Language teacher education for intercultural understanding', *European Journal of Teacher Education* 29: 163–79.

Gebhard, G. (2009) 'The practicum', in A. Burns and J. C. Richards (eds) *The Cambridge Guide to Second Language Teacher Education*, Cambridge: Cambridge University Press.

Geyer, N. (2008) 'Reflective practices in foreign language teacher education: a view through micro and macro windows', *Foreign Language Annals* 41: 627–38.

Graves, K. (2009) 'The curriculum of second language teacher education', in A. Burns and J. C. Richards (eds) *The Cambridge Guide to Second Language Teacher Education*, Cambridge: Cambridge University Press.

Grenfell, M. (1998) *Training Teachers in Practice*, Clevedon: Multilingual Matters.

Haycraft, J. (1988) 'The first international house preparatory course: an historical overview', in T. Duff (ed.) *Explorations in Teacher Training: Problems and Issues*, London: Longman.

Hobson, A. J., Ashby, P., Malderez, A. and Tomlinson, P. D. (2009) 'Mentoring beginning teachers: what we know and what we don't', *Teaching and Teacher Education* 25(1): 207–16.

Howatt, A. P. R. and Widdowson, H. G. (2004) *A History of ELT*, Oxford: Oxford University Press.

Hunt, M., Barnes, A., Powell, B., Lindsay, G. and Muijs, D. (2005) 'Primary modern foreign languages: an overview of recent research, key issues and challenges for educational policy and practice', *Research Papers in Education* 20: 371–90.

Hyland, K. and Anan, E. (2006) 'Teachers' perceptions of error: the effects of first language and experience', *System* 34(4): 509–19.

Johnson, K. E. (1992) 'Learning to teach: instructional actions and decisions of preservice ESL teachers', *TESOL Quarterly* 26(3): 507–35.

——(1999) *Understanding Language Teaching: Reasoning in Action*, Boston, MA: Heinle and Heinle.

——(2006) 'The sociocultural turn and its challenges for second language teacher education', *TESOL Quarterly* 40: 235–57.

——(2009) *Second Language Teacher Education: A Sociocultural Perspective*, London: Routledge.

Johnson, K. E. (ed.) (2000) *Teacher Education*, Alexandria, VA: TESOL.

Johnson, K. E. and Golombek, P. R. (eds) (2002) *Teachers' Narrative Inquiry as Professional Development*, New York: Cambridge University Press.

Jones, J. F. (2004) 'The many benefits of a research component in English language teacher education: a case study', *Prospect* 19(2): 25–38.

Kabilan, M. K. (2007) 'English language teachers reflecting on reflections: a Malaysian experience', *TESOL Quarterly* 41(4): 681–706.

Kelly, M. and Grenfell, M. (2005) *European Profile for Language Teacher Education. A Frame of Reference*. Available at www.lang.soton.ac.uk/profile/index.html (accessed 20 April 2010).

Korthagen, F. A. J. (2001) *Linking Practice and Theory: The Pedagogy of Realistic Teacher Education*, Mahwah, NJ: Lawrence Erlbaum Associates.

Kwang, S. Y., Duncan, T., Silvia, W. Y., Scarloss, B. and Shapley, K. L. (2007) *Reviewing the Evidence on How Teacher Professional Development Affects Student Achievement*, Washington, DC: U.S. Department of Education, Institute of Education Sciences, National Center for Education Evaluation and Regional Assistance, Regional Educational Laboratory Southwest.

Lantolf, J. P. (2009) 'Knowledge of language in foreign language teacher education', *Modern Language Journal* 93(2): 270–4.

Lord, G. and Lomicka, L. (2007) 'Foreign language teacher preparation and asynchronous CMC: promoting reflective teaching', *Journal of Technology and Teacher Education* 15: 513–32.

Lucas, T. and Grinberg, J. (2008) 'Responding to the linguistic reality of mainstream teachers: preparing all teachers to teach English language learners', in M. Cochran-Smith, S. Feiman-Nemser, J. D. McIntyre and K. E. Demers (eds) *Handbook of Research on Teacher Education: Enduring Questions in Changing Contexts*, New York: Routledge/Association of Teacher Educators.

Luk, J. (2008) 'Assessing teaching practicum reflections: distinguishing discourse features of the "high" and "low" grade reports', *System* 36(4): 624–41.

Malderez, A. and Wedell, M. (2007) *Teaching Teachers: Processes and Practices*, London: Continuum.

Mitchell-Schuitevoerder, R. and Mourão, S. (eds) (2006) *Teachers and Young Learners: Research in Our Classrooms*, Canterbury: IATEFL.

Moon, J. A. and Boullón, R. (1997) 'Reluctance to reflect: issues in professional development', in D. Hayes (ed.) *In-Service Teacher Development: International Perspectives*, London: Prentice Hall.

Morton, T., Maguire, T. and Baynham, M. (2006) *A Literature Review of Research on Teacher Education in Adult Literacy, Numeracy and ESOL*, London: NRDC.

Newman, M. and Hanauer, D. (2005) 'The NCATE/TESOL teacher education standards: a critical review', *TESOL Quarterly* 39(4): 753–64.

Numrich, C. (1996) 'On becoming a language teacher: insights from diary studies', *TESOL Quarterly* 30(1): 131–53.

Nunan, D. (1989) *Understanding Language Classrooms*, New York: Prentice Hall.

OECD (2009) *Creating Effective Teaching and Learning Environments: First Results from TALIS*. Available at www.oecd.org/dataoecd/17/51/43023606.pdf (accessed 20 April 2010).

Ong'Ondo, C. O. and Borg, S. (2011). '"We teach plastic lessons to please them": the influence of supervision on the practice of English language student teachers in Kenya', *Language Teaching Research* 14(3): 509–28.

Pearson, L., Fonseca-Greber, B. and Foell, K. (2006) 'Advanced proficiency for foreign language teacher candidates: what can we do to help them achieve this goal?', *Foreign Language Annals* 39: 507–19.

Pellerin, M. (2008) 'The use of electronic journaling to support and promote the concept of reflective practice with pre-service language teachers', *Technology and Teacher Education Annual* 6: 3894–9.

Pennington, M. C. and Richards, J. C. (1997) 'Reorienting the teaching universe: the experience of five first-year English teachers in Hong Kong', *Language Teaching Research* 1(2): 149–78.

Reis-Jorge, J. M. (2007) '"Teachers" conceptions of teacher-research and self-perceptions as enquiring practitioners: a longitudinal case study', *Teaching and Teacher Education* 23(4): 402–17.

Richards, J. C. (1998a) *Beyond Training*, Cambridge: Cambridge University Press.

——(1998b) 'The scope of second language teacher education', in J. C. Richards (ed.) *Beyond Training*, Cambridge: Cambridge University Press.

——(2008) 'Second language teacher education today', *RELC Journal* 39(2): 158–77.

Richards, J. C. and Lockhart, C. (1994) *Reflective Teaching in Second Language Classrooms*, Cambridge: Cambridge University Press.

Richards, J. C. and Nunan, D. (eds) (1990) *Second Language Teacher Education*, Cambridge: Cambridge University Press.

Ruiz, E. M. (2008) 'Analysis of the system of practicum in Spanish universities', *European Journal of Teacher Education* 31(4): 339–66.

Ruohotie-Lyhty, M. and Kaikkonen, P. (2009) 'The difficulty of change: the impact of personal school experience and teacher education on the work of beginning language teachers', *Scandinavian Journal of Educational Research* 53(3): 295–309.

Schön, D. A. (1983) *The Reflective Practitioner: How Professionals Think in Action*, London: Temple Smith.

Schulz, R. A. (2000) 'Foreign language teacher development: MLJ perspectives 1916–99', *Modern Language Journal* 84(4): 496–522.

Sharp, C. (2007) *Making Research Make a Difference. Teacher Research: A Small-Scale Study to Look at Impact*, Chelmsford: Flare.

Shulman, L. S. (1986) 'Those who understand: knowledge growth in teaching', *Educational Researcher* 15(2): 4–14.

Smith, M. K. and Lewis, M. (2009) 'The language teaching practicum: perspectives from mentors', *Teacher Trainer* 23: 5–8.

Spada, N. and Massey, M. (1992) 'The role of prior pedagogical knowledge in determining the practice of novice ESL teachers', in J. Flowerdew, M. Brock and S. Hsia (eds) *Perspectives on Second Language Teacher Education*, Hong Kong: City Polytechnic.

Tedick, D. (ed.) (2005) *Second Language Teacher Education: International Perspectives*, Mahwah, NJ: Lawrence Erlbaum Associates.

Tedick, D. J. (2009) 'K-12 language teacher preparation: problems and possibilities', *Modern Language Journal* 93(2): 263–7.

Trim, J. L. M. (2007) *Modern Languages in the Council of Europe 1954–1997*, Strasbourg: Language Policy Division, Council of Europe.

Tsui, A. B. M. (2003) *Understanding Expertise in Teaching: Case Studies of ESL Teachers*, Cambridge: Cambridge University Press.

——(2005) 'Expertise in teaching: perspectives and issues', in K. Johnson (ed.) *Expertise in Second Language Learning and Teaching*, Basingstoke: Palgrave Macmillan.

Wallace, M. J. (1991) *Training Foreign Language Teachers: A Reflective Approach*, Cambridge: Cambridge University Press.

Waters, A. (2005) 'Expertise in teacher education: helping teachers to learn', in K. Johnson (ed.) *Expertise in Second Language Learning and Teaching*, Basingstoke: Palgrave Macmillan.

Woods, D. (1996) *Teacher Cognition in Language Teaching*, Cambridge: Cambridge University Press.

Wright, T. and Bolitho, R. (2007) *Trainer Development*. Available at: www.lulu.com/content/554846

Simon Borg

Language teacher education Websites

The Teacher Trainer journal. Available at www.tttjournal.co.uk

Standards for the preparation of ESL educators in the USA (see also Newman and Hanauer 2005). Available at http://www.tesol.org/advance-the-field/standards/tesol-ncate-standards-for-p-12-teacher-education-programs

Language teacher cognition bibliography. Available at http://www.education.leeds.ac.uk/people/staff/academic/borg/

16

Bilingual education

Ingrid Gogolin

Introduction

Bilingual education is a highly controversial matter. The debates surrounding the subject of bilingualism and bilingual education are deeply rooted in historical and political traditions. The first section of this chapter gives a historical outline of these traditions, focussing on the fact that the controversy took on a special significance with the emergence of the 'classical' nation state (Hobsbawm 1990). The notion of nation as developed in the eighteenth and nineteenth centuries gave rise to the idea that a state – and with it all inhabitants – is 'normally' monolingual. Since then, the idea of monolingualism in a whole country or territories in a country has been one of the key characteristics of the classical European concept of 'nation'.

This historical perspective sets the frame for the development of practice as well as evaluation of and research on bilingual education models. The second section presents a range of models which have been established under the label of 'bilingual education' in recent years. A critical discussion about the research which has been undertaken in this field, namely on the question of effects and effectiveness of 'bilingual education', is presented in the third section.

Historical perspective: nation state and monolingualism

There has long been an air of controversy surrounding the subject of bilingualism and bilingual education. On one hand, the bilingual personality is subject to admiration and respect. On the other hand, bilingualism is regarded with critical distance or even mistrust. In historical French reference works, the word 'bilingüe' is considered synonymous with 'cleft tongue' as well as 'split personality'.

The ambivalence of the notion of bilingualism took on a special significance with the emergence of the historical idea that a 'normal' nation is monolingual. In the era of the founding and establishment of the European – or 'classical' – concept of nation the debate about the inseparability of the people's language and the state erupted. Younger concepts which can for example be found in post-colonial nation states differ considerably from this, namely with respect to their linguistic constitutions (Alexander 2003). In any case, the European example is fundamental for historical as well as current debates on bilingual education, and influences the set of arguments which are used, especially with respect to power relations, often intrinsic in these debates.

According to the classical concept, monolingualism of a whole country or territories in a country is one of the key characteristics of a well-functioning and 'sound' nation state. Information about the language (or languages) a person lives in therefore signified not only a matter of language usage, but also the allegiance to a ('my') country. The official language of the nation mutated to the 'mother tongue' of its constituents. The use of the 'correct' language in the sense of the language of the nation has since then implied solidarity with the community of all those living in the respective nation.

Johann Gottlieb Fichte was one of the important philosophers to introduce the notion that the bonds between nation and language are inseparable. Later on, arguments like this are transferred into a consensus culture (Gramsci 1984): not only 'the bourgeoisie' but also 'the working class' identify themselves with the idea of the monolingual nation as the 'regular case'. Fichte pointed to the 'naturalness' of this for the architecture of a nation (or of territories within it):

> What speaks the same language, that is from the first and apart from all human contrivance united by mere Nature with a multitude of invisible ties, [...] it belongs together and is by nature one and an indivisible whole.
>
> *(Fichte 1896: 259)*

Statements like this introduced into the debate the recourse to a common bond, anchored in Nature itself, between an individual, her/his state, and consequently its language. This has developed into one of the reality-shaping myths since the close of the eighteenth century (Hobsbawm 1990).

In the nineteenth century these ideologies or myths were strengthened in nations based on this idea by argumentation as well as by their spread in discourse about the best and most appropriate functional systems for societal institutions – such as education, public administration and the judiciary – and by their assimilation into the individual's self-identity. Eric Hobsbawm (1990) characterized the nineteenth century as the era of *inventions* that are the source of the power of nationalism.

Recourse to such history (or rather histories) and their myths ensures they are strengthened – and transferred in a *common sense*. The myth of monoligualism as 'normality' is today inscribed in societal structures as well as the self-conception of individuals in the classical nation states: their *monolingual habitus* (Gogolin 1994, 2006). It appears in the structures of public institutions, most notably the education system, but also in the regulation of everyday social matters. As an illustration I present a section from a widely read pedagogical reference book of the nineteenth century in which the interplay of arguments is apparent:

> The unity of a state and specifically of the a culture of a state [requires] – merely because of the community of interests and to ensure all those belonging to it participate in its benefits, advantages and rights – that the language of those who take an eminent position of leadership due to education in general or through industriousness, trade, the arts and science should become the common language of all inhabitants ...
>
> *(Schubert 1873: 599)*

The argument that it is best to live in just one language because it benefits not only society but also the individual becomes, then, only logical. To illustrate this, I present another example from a pedagogical reference book, but in this case dating from the early twentieth century. Eduard Blocher, a Swiss theologian and campaigner for the status of German in Switzerland, contributed to Wilhelm Rein's ten-volume *Encyclopdia of Pedagogy* (*Encyklopädisches Handbuch der Pädagogik*) of 1910. In his entry on 'bilingualism' he argues that it can be beneficial only in terms of its 'usefulness', for example, for the work of interpreters or in cross-border business relations. Generally, however, his view is that bilingualism is burdened with disadvantages; that it means a danger to the physical, mental and spiritual development of the child:

> One disadvantage is the immense amount of time and mental energy needed to maintain and achieve bilingualism. [...] Another disadvantage is dulling and weakening of the innate sense of language. Here there are of course enormous differences depending on aptitude, education and environment. When all damage of a linguistic nature has been overcome, cognitive processes still show some traces of bilingualism. [...] To summarize, the disadvantages, which do not all need to occur in the same person, are greater expenditure of time and energy at the expense of other work, weakening of the innate sense of language due to mutual interference of the two languages, uncertainty how to express oneself, mixing of languages, lack of active vocabulary, loss of intellectual community with monolinguals, i.e. with the vast majority of countrymen.
>
> *(Blocher 1910: 667–9)*

The idea of 'subtractive bilingualism' shimmers through this point of view, as it was presented in reflections about bilingualism in the 1980s (e.g. Skutnabb-Kangas 1984).

In retrospect, the successful career of monolingualism as a feature of the individual's self-conception as well as that of the nation state was ratified by the societal and technical developments of the time. The Enlightenment and the French Revolution had initiated the emergence of a civic public sphere. Access to a common language thus meant at the same time inclusion and participation. The Industrial Revolution, and specifically the invention of print, made it possible to standardize languages as well as circulate the standardized versions among a large number of people. Systems of general education in the sense that they addressed every child (or at least every male child) were founded and allowed access to the common language in its standardized form. Initially, the creation of monolingualism was one of the necessary prerequisites for the development of democracies in today's sense.

The ambiguity of this development relates to the fact that the notion of nation developed into nationalistic concepts in the course of the nineteenth century. Participation in the civic public sphere was no longer considered a universal human right as it was initially conceptualized, but an exclusive right of the acknowledged member of a state, the citizen. The focus on functional aspects of language as tools for communication and participation were increasingly accompanied, if not replaced, by the connotation of language use as an expression of solidarity and loyalty with 'emperor, people and fatherland' – as it was expressed in late nineteenth-century Germany.

This development brings the close interconnection between language and power to the surface. The creation of a 'common language' inevitably meant the exclusion of other languages in a nation state from the privilege of commonness – or the creation of language minorities. Since the middle of the nineteenth century (in German-speaking areas, but elsewhere as well at different times) the existence of language minorities within countries has repeatedly led to disputes about *individual* versus *community* versus *common* language. Not only did aggressive state activities give rise to such disputes, as in the prohibition of the public use of languages and their exclusion from the education system, but so also did more peaceful manifestations of human mobility: namely migration processes.

Again, Germany can serve as an example, namely the industrialized Ruhr area. Many Polish-speaking people from East Prussia, but also Slovenians, Italians and people from other countries migrated to the Ruhr at the end of the nineteenth century, mostly in order to find work in the mines. Traces of this migration are obliterated in the German language today; they can still be found in the names of the offspring – provided their forebears did not make use of the offer by the authorities to Germanize names in order to erase anything reminiscent of a foreign origin. In such historical-political constellations the need for regulation of language issues grows – as, for example, was the case in Prussia, where several laws were enacted in reaction to migration and the foreign languages which immigrants brought with them. The central feature of these laws was prohibition of the use of these languages in public, as exemplified by the Prussian 'Business language law' of 1876, a 'Court language law' of 1877, and a piece of legislation from 1908 governing the language use in clubs and associations. At such points in history, public institutions of education were always the object of interest and regulation; in Prussia at the turn of the nineteenth century a number of ordinances were issued that, depending on the region, highly restricted or prohibited the use of the immigrants' languages in schools (see, for an overview, Krüger-Potratz 2005).

All classical nation states, at one point or the other in their histories, experienced processes of aggressive assimilation of linguistic minorities, be it in their own state territories or in the course of conquest – including the fact that more or less generous exceptions were made for certain languages which were provided with exclusive privileges (as was the case since the twentieth century for Sorbian or Danish in Germany, or for Frisian in the Netherlands, and so called lesser used languages in many states; see Hogan-Brun and Wolff 2003). Since the 1990s, the European Charter for Regional and Minority Languages (Council of Europe 1992) provides protection for autochthonous minority languages since they are considered as elements of the European cultural heritage. The claims for linguistic minority rights are in essence elementary struggles for participation and inclusion, and access to power in a society (Bourdieu 1991).

Although often forgotten or neglected, this historical development sets the framework for the controversies which play out around bilingual education in the present day. Any attempt at a scientific analysis of bilingual education cannot ignore the historical tradition surrounding the topic. This is especially true because similarities with earlier events and arguments appear repeatedly in revivals of the controversy as well as in a number of the arguments presented. If scientific dispute related to bilingualism is not to degenerate into mutual criticism of opposing ideologies, the history of the controversy must be well understood.

Types of bilingual education

As it is the case with the term 'multilingualism' (see Cenoz and Gorter, this volume), the term 'bilingual education' is broadly used in applied linguistics – but with a considerable range of connotations. Cenoz and Gorter state that the different ways 'multilingualism' is used are linked at least to three sources of variability: the individual versus social dimension, the number of languages involved, and the level of proficiency in the different languages. With regard to the number of languages involved, the term multilingualism implies 'multiple' languages; it usually refers to two or more. In contrast with this, the term 'bilingualism' is used when referring to 'two languages' – although 'bilingualism' is frequently used in cases where more than two languages are involved.

As this chapter focuses on bilingual education, the term 'bilingualism' is used when referring specifically to models or types of education which explicitly label themselves as bilingual. This may be independent from the number of languages involved as represented by the addressees of such education, but in general the intentional education or teaching programmes focus on two languages.

In line with the historical development as outlined above, bilingual education models have mostly been established as exceptions to a rule of 'regular' education – which was designed in a monolingual modus. Bilingual education schemes have usually been established to serve the needs or demands of certain groups in societies, not for societies as a whole. This again is different in the education systems of younger, mostly post-colonial nations. In parts of India or in some African states, South Africa for example, trilingual schooling was established in which children are taught in their home language first, plus the language of the region and a supraregional language, for example, English or French. Where they have been established, these models replace former post-colonial systems in which the children are taught in their home language at the beginning of their school careers, but after a foundation phase the teaching completely shifts to usually English or French as the language of instruction. This very specific constellation is conventionally not considered as 'bilingual education' (see Heugh 1995; Hornberger and Corson 1998; Agnihotri 2006).

The establishment of bilingual education models in classical nation states with two or more national languages, such as Canada, Belgium or Switzerland, seems to be an exception to the rule. In these countries, children are normally taught (at least one of) the other national language(s) at school. This can be organized as foreign language teaching: at a certain point in the school curriculum, the other national language is introduced to the curriculum as a subject. More ambitious are the so-called *immersion models*. Probably the best known and influential of these are the French immersion models in Canada (see Allen 2004; Statistics Canada 2005). Whereas English education models in Canada offer French as a subject, usually from grade 4, in the French immersion models all teaching (except English language and arts) to children in Anglophone school districts is provided in French. The models are established in different ways in nine Canadian provinces. Early immersion programmes begin in either kindergarten or grade 1; middle immersion programmes start midway through elementary school; and still others begin in the later grades. Attendance of immersion programmes varies by the type of programme. In the year 2000 for example, only 21 per cent of the students enrolled in French immersion in Nova Scotia had been attending immersion before grade 4, whereas about 80 per cent of the 15-year-olds enrolled in Manitoba, Saskatchewan and Alberta had started in early immersion programmes.

Statistical data show that the French immersion models in general led to high performance of the participating students in reading (Allen 2004; OECD 2006). However, it is not evident that the bilingual education model as such is the causal factor for its success. In analyses of the socio-economic background and the cultural capital (i.e. the forms of knowledge, skills and education of a person, Bourdieu 1979) of children participating in French immersion models, it turns out that they are highly self-selective (Statistics Canada 2005). The parents of immersion students are from higher socio-economic backgrounds, and are more likely to have a high cultural capital (postsecondary education) than the average school population. A higher proportion of girls enrol in immersion programmes, and as girls generally show better performance in language than boys, this distorts the results on 'average success'.

Consequently, more research is needed on the factors which result in the academic success of French immersion models. Nevertheless, their success story has inspired a number of imitators in many countries, including Australia, England, Scotland, elsewhere in Europe, and the

USA. The numbers and types of models change quickly; overviews can be found in Wikipedia under the headword 'bilingual education'. We find so-called two-way or dual immersion models which usually aim at helping children from immigrant minorities to catch up with the majority language. In theory, these models should be composed of 50 per cent bilingual children and 50 per cent monolinguals. Both languages are taught from the beginning, and a variety of academic subjects is taught in each of the languages. On the other hand, we find transitional bilingual education. Here, all the teaching takes place in the first language of the children in the beginning. The second (or majority) language is gradually introduced, at first in language as a subject only, then after some time also in other content areas. The aim of such models is to support the acquisition of the second (or majority) language and to prepare their transition to monolingual mainstream classes (Cummins 2003).

The Canadian model has been transferred to a number of different contextual conditions, and alterations have been made to the programmes – and not surprisingly, the 'successor models' have not necessarily been proven to lead to the academic success of their pupils. This is unremarkable, as the wholesale transfer of education models to new contexts is rarely successful (Seidel and Shavelson 2007; Slavin 2008). This also suggests that bilingual education models have to be highly adaptive to the particular conditions and requirements of the learners they address.

Irrespective of this, the Canadian French immersion models are emblematic of the fact that the establishment of bilingual education models always relates to specific power relations which accompany their instigation. On one hand, bilingual education is a privilege for specific elites, for example, for the children of diplomats during their stays abroad, or the children of employees of supranational agencies (e.g. the so-called European schools in a number of European cities where EU institutions are established), or the children of executive staff posted abroad (e.g. the Japanese schools in some European cities) – or, as it turns out in practice, in the Canadian French immersion models. In these cases, the models are either designed or emerge in practice as accessible to more affluent (and perhaps urban) communities, and they are used as strategies of social distinction (Bourdieu 1986). In the case of these bilingual education models, the effectiveness or appropriateness of bilingual education is hardly ever questioned. It is taken for granted that the learners from affluent backgrounds profit from bilingualism and bilingual education. Very little research has been carried out about the effects of such models, the evaluations in the Canadian case being an exception.

On the other hand, bilingual education models have been established to serve the needs of less privileged groups. This can be autochthonous minorities which, mostly after a period of struggle, were granted an education system matching their own perceived needs. These might also be minorities which have emerged as an effect of the change of borders after a war, an invasion or a treaty. In recent times the most frequent grounds for the development of bilingual models is immigration.

Immigration leads to language communities of varying sizes within the territory of a majority language. Bilingual education models have been established mostly in the service of larger immigrant communities. But size is not the only motivation. Another relevant factor is the access of a community to the power structures in either the country of origin or the country of residence. Examples of the establishment of bilingual models irrespective of the size of a language community are schools which are sponsored and supervised by the governments of the countries of origin. Usually such models emerge on the basis of bilateral agreements between the respective country of origin and the country of residence, allowing for the establishment of schools for their own constituents living abroad. A typical example for this are bilingual models in some German cities: they consist of 'regular' schools which offer bilingual programmes in immigrant minority languages. The teachers of these programmes are paid by and work under the supervision of their home countries, for example, Turkey, Spain, or Italy. The administration of the models is carried out in close cooperation with the regular German school inspectorate and the consulates of the respective country (see Gogolin *et al.* 2007).

A wide range of bilingual education models for immigrant minorities, nevertheless, has been established by countries of residence. It is mainly the latter type of model which is subject to controversies about its appropriateness and effectiveness – and consequently, the subject of research. It seems that in the case of privileged groups there is no doubt about the usefulness of bilingual education, whereas in the case of less privileged groups such doubts are justified per se. Jim Cummins, author of a number of major works on bilingual education, has brought this difference to attention; he introduced the notions of *additive* versus *subtractive* bilingualism for its description and pointed to the power relation in its background: In a situation of well-being, bilingualism is presented as a means of enrichment for an individual, whereas in underprivileged situations the individual seems to run a risk by being bilingual (Cummins 2000).

Another typology of bilingual education models relates to the ways in which educational programmes are organized and designed. As a general rule – with some, mostly historical exceptions – bilingual education refers to models in which both languages are used for teaching parts of the content matter. Beyond this general feature, the models can be organized in a broad range of different approaches. Differences relate to the amount of teaching hours in both languages – some models provide equal amounts of time for both languages concerned, others dedicate only a few teaching hours to one of the two languages. Also the sequence in which both languages are introduced to the curriculum differs – some models start with both languages at the same time, whereas others start with one language and introduce the second language gradually. Other differences can be found with respect to the duration of education in both languages; some models cover only one or two years of schooling, whereas others provide bilingual education throughout the whole of primary and even into secondary schooling.

Finally the overall goals of the models can differ. Whereas it is a common characteristic of all bilingual education models to give learners access to reading and writing in both languages concerned, the aims of this vary.

On one hand, in so-called language maintenance programmes, the aim can be to produce fluent and balanced bilingualism – or even more than that, to provide the entire curriculum in both languages. This kind of model has been established in particular for autochthonous minorities in areas with quite stable bilingual speech communities, but some attempts have also been made with respect to immigrant minority communities. Literacy in these models can be taught in parallel or consecutively. It is normally the case that the teachers involved are themselves bilingual in the languages concerned.

On the other hand, and very widespread, are the so-called transitional models of bilingual education. In the majority of cases, these models address immigrant minority students. They are based on the assumption that it is an advantage for children who grow up bilingually to develop their 'first language' – the family language – up to a certain level before the child is confronted with education in a further language. An influential theoretical assumption was the threshold hypothesis (Cummins 1979: 155), indicating that 'transfer' between the two languages is a positive feature for language development. This hypothesis is in educational practice and in research often misunderstood as a dictum, that a minimum command of the 'first language' is necessary in order to learn a second language successfully (see, for example, Stanat and Christensen 2006).

This general idea can already be found in historical beliefs and observations of the effects of language development. In the early nineteenth century, renowned pedagogues such as Moritz

Diesterweg (Diesterweg 1836) formulated as an 'uncontested methodical rule' that teaching has to follow the 'nature' of learning: the unknown has to be based on the known, the abstract on the tangible. With respect to language education this basic principle would demand that a second language should not be offered to the learner before the 'essence and forms' ('ihr Wesen und ihre Formen überhaupt' – 1836: 161) of the 'mother tongue' are indubitably acquired – as these are the indispensable prerequisite for learning – and learning in – a second language. If a new language were brought to a learner too early, 'obscurity and confusion' ('Unklarheit und Verwirrung') would be the inevitable effect. Diesterweg considered language development as a stepwise process, and at every step 'the mind of the learner can only be occupied with one [task]' (1836: 165).

The main and resilient argument of the threshold hypothesis today focuses on the interrelatedness of both languages in the repertoire of a speaker; the current research question is whether and under which conditions a positive transfer from one language to the other can be expected (Cummins 2003; 2008). Whereas this consensus has been reached in research, the misunderstood version of the threshold hypothesis is still 'common sense' for many supporters of transitional bilingual education models, especially for those which were established in order to facilitate the acquisition of the second language, generally the language of the majority. Especially in 'transitional' models it is a common feature that the amount of teaching hours of the two languages involved are reversed in the course of the schooling. At the beginning, the majority of teaching hours is dedicated to the first language or mother tongue of the children, and only few hours are dedicated to the second language. The balance of teaching hours changes gradually until most hours are taught in the second language. If transitional models are established in primary education, the shift usually takes place after the foundation period of schooling.

A variation on these models – with some borrowing from the principles of French immersion – has been established with respect to some immigrant minority languages: the 'two-way immersion' models. In these cases, the addressees of bilingual education are bilingual children (from autochthonous or immigrant minorities) as well as monolingual children; usually a composition of 50 per cent of learners from each group is recommended. In practice – at least in the European versions of such models – this is hardly ever achieved. Two reasons can be responsible for this: first, these models are often situated in multilingual areas, with the result that students may be bilingual, but represent other home languages than the partner language which is taught in the bilingual model. And second, the prestige of the languages involved in the model plays a role. Schools offering models with less prestigious languages face the possibility that monolingual parents will refuse to choose them for their children.

The curricula of such bilingual models show the tendencies of transitional models, as gradually more teaching hours are dedicated to the main language of schooling. In any case, the second or partner language is normally not reduced to mere language teaching, but will also be used for teaching one or more subject areas.

Another variety is bilingual education as an innovative approach in the context of foreign language education. Here, the second or partner language involved is not any learner's home language, but a foreign language for all students. This is known as 'Content and Language Integrated Learning' (CLIL; see Thornbury, this volume). In these models, a common foreign language – very often English or French in European states – is first introduced as a subject to the students. After a short period in which a certain level of proficiency is reached, the language teaching is combined with the teaching of another subject, such as history or science. This is based on the assumption that the results of language learning are more sustainable if content other than language itself is simultaneously acquired with language skills (e.g. http://ec.europa.eu/education/languages/language-teaching/doc236_en.htm).

Transitional bilingual education has played a prominent role in political and scientific debates on the effects of bilingual education. The most prominent debates have taken place in the USA. The fierce arguments around this issue resulted in the abolition of bilingual education in the states of Arizona and California (Ricento 2003). The political struggle also gave rise to a new critical examination of research on the effects and effectiveness of bilingual education. The following section will present the most important arguments and results of this research.

Effects and effectiveness of bilingual education

The majority of research studies on the effects and effectiveness of bilingual education have been carried out in Canada and the USA, including a number of meta-analyses of this research. An important state-of-the-art review of bilingual education research was initiated by the Social Science Research Centre Berlin (see Söhn 2005). Two examples of contributions to this endeavour will illustrate the research as well as the nature of dissent in the debates: a synthesis of research on the effects on reading instruction by Slavin and Cheung (2005) and a 'rebuttal' of former meta-analysis studies by Rossell and Kuder (2005). The presentation of these studies as examples will show that proponents and opponents of bilingual education shed light on different aspects of the research results. Moreover, both sides have in common that they accuse the other of being biased at best, and at worst, of arguing ideologically. This points to the fact that the 'bilingualism controversy' cannot be resolved by mere 'empirical' argument. The historical tradition in which it is embedded – which was explained in the first sections of this chapter – is always intrinsic to the debates. In the end, a decision about the value or importance of bilingual (or multilingual) education is generally – explicitly or implicitly – related to a normative basis. If, in principle, the value of bilingual education is determined by the point of view that the proficiency in *both* languages counts; the evaluation and judgement of the 'success' or 'effectiveness' of bilingual education models will turn out differently from approaches in which only the results in *one* language, namely the majority language, count as yardstick.

In the first example of meta-analysis presented here, Slavin and Cheung (2005) base their synthesis on research focusing on the effects of education models on reading skills of (mainly Hispanic) bilingual students in the USA. They use the method of 'best evidence synthesis' (Slavin 1986), taking into account consistent, unbiased information from experimental studies on English-only reading programmes and bilingual programmes. This strategy does not only re-analyse quantitatively (by effect sizes), but also takes narrative information on the observed models into consideration. The authors include all studies written in English about effects on reading skills which met a minimum methodological standard.

Before discussing the general results of their approach, the authors give a detailed insight into the characteristics of every programme included in their analysis, and thus provide a picture of the differences in approach which can be found under the heading of 'bilingual education' vs. 'English only' models. This leads them to conclude that adequate research on effects of models would most probably have to be carried out with methodological repertoires different from those which had been applied until then. Irrespective of the limitations of their own approach, they come to the conclusion that in 12 out of 17 studies in their review, effects favouring bilingual approaches can be found. Five studies showed no effect. None of the studies showed effects in favour of English immersion, that is to say, English monolingual approaches (Slavin and Cheung 2005: 31). The authors stress that the positive effects of bilingual education models do *not* relate to transitional bilingual models; the results were in favour of 'paired bilingual models' which introduce both languages in a correlated and continuous way. Yet the authors conclude that their analysis does not shed light on the question of whether the language of instruction is the causal factor of positive effects – or if it is a more general outcome of the quality of instruction. They conclude that more research and better evidence is needed – and they plead for an end to ideologically driven rather than empirically driven debates on the issue (2005: 34).

The second example is a study carried out by Rossell and Kuder (2005). These authors take an opposing stance, suggesting that positive effects of bilingual education models cannot be found. In their approach, the authors discuss earlier meta-analysis in the light of their 'background political bias' which led to the exclusion of studies 'on other grounds' than methodological evidence (2005: 45). They then clarify their view that 'bilingual' outcomes of educational models are not the focus of their own approach:

> It is indisputable and uncontroversial that a Spanish speaking child taught to read and write in Spanish will do better in Spanish than will a Spanish speaking child taught to read and write in English. What is controversial is the notion that a Spanish speaking child taught to read and write in Spanish will do better in English [...] and so that is the only outcome we examine or have ever examined.
>
> *(Rossell and Kuder 2005: 46)*

The authors present the quality criteria which they used for inclusion of studies into their sample and introduce their own methodological statistical approach for re-analysis, based on statistical methodology only. Moreover, the studies in their analysis were not focused on reading skills only, but included scores in reading, language and mathematics.

In the further course of their article, the authors themselves critique a number of critical reviews of their own earlier studies, pointing out that these reviews did not respect the criteria which were originally applied but introduced new criteria which Rossell and Kuder did not agree with. They then present on their part critical reviews of different studies – carried out by Slavin, Cheung and other co-authors, and by Greene (e.g. Greene 1997) – indicating methodological or theoretical inappropriateness. On the basis of their review, Rossell and Kuder qualify all conclusions testifying to the positive effects of bilingual education models as inappropriate or irrelevant.

In the last parts of their contribution, Rossell and Kuder present a re-analysis of their own earlier research, restricting the studies included in the sample to projects which were carried out for no less than a school year. They come to the conclusion that their new approach does not lead to any revision of former findings. The best programmes, according to their analysis, are structured immersion – i.e. English only – programmes. They state that the more first language education children receive, the lower is their achievement in the second language, namely English. The authors admit that 'a little bit of native tongue instruction does not hurt and might help if the first language is Spanish' (Rossell and Kuder 2005: 69). But they stress, however, that 'structured immersion' programmes – English only programmes with specific additional support – are the most successful. The authors conclude that the best approach to educating second language learners cannot be identified by meta-analysis or similar research: 'There is too much disagreement over what constitutes scientific research and too little specific research' (2005: 73). They nevertheless insist on their finding that structured immersion is the best approach for second language learners. In any case they claim that Spanish bilingual education would not be a disaster if the Spanish language were taught in a limited amount of time and if the idea that the first language must be mastered before a child is instructed in the second language were discarded in bilingual approaches.

What can we learn about the effects and effectiveness of bilingual education from the contributions to the 'bilingualism controversy' presented above?

First: a consensus has been reached about the effects or effectiveness of one specific group of bilingual education models: the transitional bilingual education models. These models are not supported by empirical research. Whereas supporters of the models are still found in the public sphere, in particular among lobbyists from minority groups, there is no evidence in empirical academic work that they are appropriate for the education of second language learners. A second consensus could possibly be reached through further research concerning the question of inclusion of first language instruction in the curriculum. The open question here is related to the amount of instruction in the first language, taking as a starting point the assumption that a limited number of lessons ('a little bit') could be supportive for the language development of bilingual learners. There is some evidence from studies on literacy development of learners who have first contact with the second or third language in older age, namely as adults, that it is beneficial for them to be taught literacy in their expert languages first, then to transfer those literacy skills to the next language they learn (see Klein and Dimroth 2005; Tarone *et al.* 2009). Among the supporters of bilingual education models we find a further consensus, indicating that bilingual education can only have positive effects if both languages are taught in a coordinated and balanced way.

Second: the examples show that the answer to the question of what bilingual education may or may not offer is not least dependent on the interests behind the research. As illustrated above, the question of what is gained from bilingual education can be defined by the criterion of the advantage it offers for acquisition of the *second* language. Rossell and Kuder (2005) or Esser (2006) stress that the question of bilingualism per se is irrelevant. What is relevant is the effect of teaching (in) the first language on mastery of the second. A different perspective is taken by such authors as Slavin and Cheung (and others; see, for example, the contributions by Bialystok, Auer, Anstatt and Tracy in Gogolin and Neumann 2009). Here, the acquisition of *both* languages of a bilingual individual is taken into account. The yardstick in these approaches is sufficient mastery of first *and* second language, or to be more precise, no disadvantage for the second language and at least access to literacy in the first language. The bilingualism controversy as carried out in the presented research is clearly related to a normative perspective with respect to the question: what counts as relevant and valuable language competence for a person living in two languages?

Outlook: bilingual education in a multilingual world

Societies of today and the future, and in particular their urban centres, are irreversibly typified by diversity in linguistic, cultural and social terms. Vertovec's framework of *super-diversity* offers a theoretical starting point for studying this diversity. Super-diversity refers to the dynamic interplay of linguistic, cultural and social phenomena which exceeds the magnitude and present understanding of complexity in societies. Vertovec refers to the growing complexity of social and cultural constellations in societies, which becomes obvious by observing the features of recent immigrations. An 'increased number of new, small and scattered, multiple-origin, transnationally connected, socio-economically differentiated and legally stratified immigrants' build the immigrant communities (not only) in urban areas. (Vertovec 2007: 1024).

Within such a framework, it is obvious that bilingual education models can open up possibilities for education in very specific, clearly defined linguistic constellations of learners, and in these constellations – provided that the concept and practice of teaching is of good quality – serve learners' needs. If the creation of bilingual individuals is the aim, positive effects can be expected: as is stressed in the overview of the research results presented in the project of the Social Science Research Center Berlin (Söhn 2005), none of the methodologically acceptable studies lead to the result that bilingual models (if they offer both languages) harm acquisition of the second language, but they provide access to two languages within the identical amount of time in which monolingual models are successful.

In any case, the linguistic reality of present and future society points to the fact that bilingual education is only one possible approach to educational achievement and success in super-diverse constellations. Further development and research is necessary, taking the multitude of the linguistic architecture of societies into account. Moreover, the conventional categories of mono-, bi- or multilingualism as descriptors of individual proficiency or social position are increasingly in question, as are the widely held understandings of linguistic development. These include, for instance, the normative notion of a sequence of languages acquired in the linguistic development of a person, and described by concepts such as 'first' or 'second' language. In this normative view a simultaneity of contact situations with different languages appears as an exceptional case, whereas it is in fact the reality in contemporary urban centres. The concept of super-diversity may allow for a change of perspective: towards the development of adequate and appropriate models of research on, as well as teaching of, languages in the complex social environments of today's societies.

Related topics

language and ageing, language and migration; language policy and planning; multilingualism; second language acquisition

Further reading

Baker, C. (2006) *Foundations of Bilingual Education and Bilingualism*, 4th edn, Clevedon: Multilingual Matters. (Key features of the book are the detailed presentation of different bilingual education models, their organizational structures and aims. Pros and cons of bilingual education and mainstreaming of bilingualism are discussed.)
Cummins, J. (2000) *Language, Power and Pedagogy: Bilingual Children in the Crossfire*, Clevedon: Multilingual Matters. (In this volume, the historical and political context of the debates around bilingualism and education is presented and discussed.)
García, O. and Baker, C. (2007) *Bilingual Education: An Introductory Reader*, Clevedon: Multilingual Matters. (The volume offers a selection of articles which present experience with bilingual education models, not only from Canada and the USA but also from a range of European countries.)
Gogolin, I. and Neumann, U. (eds) (2009) *Streitfall Zweisprachigkeit: The Bilingualism Controversy*, Wiesbaden: VS Verlag. (The volume offers a selection of papers which discuss the (dis-)advantages of bilingual education from different disciplinary perspectives, such as sociology, psycholinguistics, sociolinguistics and educational research.)
Kramsch, C. (2009) *The Multilingual Subject*, Oxford: Oxford University Press. (The book takes the perspective of individual bi- or multilingual learners into account, focusing on the question of how learners' attitudes and experience influence their approaches to language learning and to possible outcomes.)

References

Agnihotri, R. K. (2006) 'Identity and multiliguality: the case of India', in A. B. M. Tsui and J. W. Tollefson (eds.) *Language Policy, Culture, and Identity in Asian Contexts*, Mahwah, NJ: Lawrence Erlbaum Associates.
Alexander, N. (2003) *An Ordinary Country: Issues in the Transition from Apartheid to Democracy in South Africa*, New York: Berghahn Books.

Allen, M. (2004) 'Reading achievement of students in French immersion programs', *Educational Quarterly Review* 9(4): 25–30.

Blocher, E. (1910) 'Zweisprachigkeit. Vorteile und Nachteile', in W. Rein (ed.) *Encyklopädisches Handbuch der Pädagogik*, Bd 10, Langensalza: Hermann Beyer & Söhne.

Bourdieu, P. (1979) 'Les trois états du capital culturel', *Actes de la Recherche en Sciences Sociales* 30: 3–6.

——(1986) *Distinction: A Social Critique of the Judgement of Taste*, London: Routledge/Kegan Paul.

——(1991) *Language and Symbolic Power*, Cambridge: Polity Press.

Council of Europe (1992) *European Charter for Regional or Minority Language*, Strasbourg (European Treaty Series no. 148).

Cummins, J. (1979) 'Cognitive/academic language proficiency, linguistic interdependence, the optimum age question and some other matters', *Working Papers on Bilingualism* 19: 121–9.

——(2000) *Language, Power and Pedagogy, Bilingual Children in the Crossfire*, Clevedon: Multilingual Matters.

——(2003) 'Bilingual education', in J. Bourne and E. Reid (eds) *Language Education: World Yearbook of Education 2003*, London and Sterling: Kogan Page.

——(2003) 'Bilingual education: basic principles', in J.-M. Dewaele, A. Housen and L. Wei (eds) *Bilingualism: Beyond Basic Principles*, Clevedon: Multilingual Matters.

——(2008) 'Total immersion or bilingual education? Findings of international research promoting immigrant children's achievement in the primary school', in J. Ramseger and M. Wagener (eds) *Chancenungleichheit in der Grundschule. Ursachen und Wege aus der Krise*, Wiesbaden: VS Verlag.

Diesterweg, A. (1836) 'Über die Methodik des Sprachunterrichts', in E. Langenberg (ed.) *Adolph Diesterwegs ausgewählte Schriften*, 2nd edn, vol. 1, Frankfurt am Main: Verlag Moritz Diesterweg.

Esser, H. (2006) *Migration, Sprache und Integration*, Berlin: Arbeitsstelle Interkulturelle Konflikte, AKI-Forschungsbilanz 4.

Fichte, J. G. (1896) *Reden an die deutsche Nation* (1807/8). Mit Fichtes Biographie sowie mit erläuternden Anmerkungen versehen von Theodor Vogt. Langensalza: Hermann Beyer & Söhne.

Gogolin, I. (1994) *Der monolinguale Habitus der multilingualen Schule*, Münster: Waxmann.

——(2006) 'Linguistic habitus', in K. Brown (ed.) *Encyclopedia of Language and Linguistics*, 2nd edn, Oxford: Elsevier.

Gogolin, I., Neumann, U. and Roth, H.-J. (2007) *Bericht 2007, Abschlussbericht über die italienisch-deutschen, portugiesisch-deutschen und spanisch-deutschen Modellklassen*, Universität Hamburg. Available at: http://www2.erzwiss.uni-hamburg.de/institute/interkultur/Bericht_2007.pdf (accessed 28 April 2010).

Gramsci, A. (1984) 'Notes on language', *Telos* 59: 127–50.

Greene, J. P. (1997) 'A meta-analysis of the Rossell and Baker review of bilingual education research', *Bilingual Research Journal* 21: Spring and Summer.

Heugh, K. (1995) 'Disabling and enabling: implications of language policy trends in South Africa', in R. Mesthrie (ed.) *Language And Social History: Studies in South African Sociolinguistics*, Claremont: David Philip Publishers.

Hobsbawm, E. J. (1990) *Nations and Nationalism Since 1780: Programme, Myth, Reality*, Cambridge: Cambridge University Press.

Hogan-Brun, G. and Wolff, S. (eds) (2003) *Minority Languages in Europe: Status, Frameworks, Prospects*, Basingstoke: Palgrave Macmillan.

Hornberger, N. H. and Corson, D. (eds) (1998) *Encyclopedia of Language and Education*, vol. 8: *Research Methods in Language and Education*, Dordrecht and Boston: Kluwer Academic.

Klein, W. and Dimroth, C. (eds) (2005) *Spracherwerb*, Stuttgart: Metzler.

Krüger-Potratz, M. (2005) *Interkulturelle Bildung: Eine Einführung*, Münster: Waxmann.

OECD (ed.) (2006) *Where Immigrant Students Succeed: A Comparative Review of Performance and Engagement in PISA 2003*, Paris: OECD.

Ricento, T. (2003) 'The discursive construction of Americanism', *Discourse and Society* 14: 611–37.

Rossell, C. H. and Kuder, J. (2005) 'Meta-murky: a rebuttal to recent meta-analyses of bilingual education', in Arbeitsstelle Interkulturelle Konflikte und gesellschaftliche Integration (ed.) *The Effectiveness of Bilingual School Programmes for Immigrant Children*, Berlin: WZB discussion papers.

Schubert, F. W. (1873) 'Unterrichtssprache', in K. A. Schmidt (ed.) *Encyklopädie des gesammten Erziehungs- und Unterrichtswesens*. Bearb. von einer Anzahl Schulmänner und Gelehrten unter Mitw. von Prof. Dr. Palmer und Prof. Dr. Wildermuth. Bd 9. Gotha: Besser.

Seidel, T. and Shavelson, R. J. (2007) 'Teaching effectiveness research in the past decade: the role of theory and research design in disentangling meta-analysis research', *Review of Educational Research* 77: 454–99.

Skutnabb-Kangas, T. (1984) *Bilingualism or Not: The Education of Minorities*, Clevedon: Multilingual Matters.

Slavin, R. (1986) *Educational Psychology: Theory and Practice*, Boston: Pearson Education.

——(2008) 'Perspectives on evidence-based research in education: what works? Issues in synthesizing educational program evaluations', *Educational Researcher* 37(1): 5–14.

Slavin, R. E. and Cheung, A. (2005) 'A synthesis of research on language of reading instruction for English language learners', in Arbeitsstelle Interkulturelle Konflikte und gesellschaftliche Integration (ed.) *The Effectiveness of Bilingual School Programmes for Immigrant Children*, Berlin: WZB discussion papers.

Söhn, J. (2005) *Zweisprachiger Schulunterricht für Migrantenkinder Ergebnisse der Evaluationsforschung zu seinen Auswirkungen auf Zweisprachigkeit und Schulerfolg (AKI-Forschungsbilanz 2)*, Berlin: Arbeitsstelle Interkulturelle Konflikte.

Stanat, P. and Christensen, G. (2006) *Where Immigrant Students Succeed*, Paris: OECD.

Statistics Canada. (2005) *French Immersion 30 Years Later*, Ottawa: Statistics Canada.

Tarone, E., Bigelow, M. and Hansen, K. (2009) *Literacy and Second Language Oracy*, Oxford: Oxford University Press.

Vertovec, S. (2007) 'Super-diversity and its implications', *Ethnic and Racial Studies* 30(6): 1024–54.

17

English for academic purposes

Nigel Harwood and Bojana Petrić

What is EAP?

English for Academic Purposes (EAP) 'is usually defined as teaching English with the aim of assisting learners' study or research in that language', but is also a 'theoretically grounded and research informed enterprise' (Hyland 2006: 1). Ideas about the nature of language, learning, and teaching all impact on the theory and practice of EAP (Basturkmen 2006). Hence, the roles and responsibilities of the EAP practitioner are manifold: 'needs assessor, specialized syllabus designer, authentic materials developer, and content knowledgeable instructor, capable of coping with a revolving door of content areas relevant to learners' communities' (Belcher 2006: 139).

EAP instruction takes place with a range of learners, in a variety of contexts: (i) in higher education settings in English-speaking countries; (ii) in settings where English has official status and is used as a medium of instruction; (iii) in settings where certain school/university subjects are wholly or partly taught in English (e.g. medicine); and (iv) in settings where all tertiary education is taught in the L1, but English is recognized as an important additional language for study, and where certain learning materials and texts can only be found in English (Dudley-Evans and St John 1998: 35). Although EAP is traditionally associated exclusively with tertiary education, this perception is being eroded, with a recent special issue of *Journal of English for Academic Purposes* devoted to EAP in secondary education (see Johns and Snow 2006). EAP should not be exclusively associated with the non-native speaker of English either: the increasingly diverse student population means that some native speakers will lack the necessary academic communication skills (Hyland 2006).

EAP, together with English for Occupational Purposes (EOP), is a branch of English for Specific Purposes (ESP). Depending on the type of academic subject matter, EAP can be further divided into more specific sub-types, e.g. English for Medicine or English for Engineering. However, as Flowerdew and Peacock (2001) argue, the distinction between EAP and EOP is not always straightforward as many aspects of EAP are aimed at preparing students for their future careers in their disciplines. For instance, an English for Engineering course will typically cover both skills necessary for academic study (EAP), such as reading engineering textbooks and writing assignments, but also skills for engineers, such as writing technical reports, which can be classified as EOP. Flowerdew and Peacock (2001: 12) suggest that EAP should be subdivided into 'EAP designed to help students with their studies and EAP directed towards professional preparation'. While both EAP and EOP are carried out at the university, their goals are different in orientation in that the former is purely academic while the latter has a vocational dimension.

History of EAP

The origins of EAP can be traced back to the 1960s, when a growing interest in language as a means of communication, language variability in context and functions of specialized languages prepared the ground for the emergence of EAP (Flowerdew and Peacock 2001). However, equally important were various non-linguistic factors that led to the need for EAP, such as the rise of English as a global language.

Stages in the development of EAP

According to Dudley-Evans and St John (1998), the development of ESP (which includes EAP) can be divided into four stages: (i) register analysis, (ii) rhetorical and discourse analysis, (iii) study skills, and (iv) needs analysis. It is, of course, overly simplistic to see these stages as discrete; they overlap and elements of each stage continue to influence thinking in the field today, albeit to a greater or lesser extent.

Register analysis

The primary goal of register analysis was to identify the grammatical and lexical features occurring more frequently in scientific English than in general English; hence the term 'lexicostatistics' (Swales 1988). The assumption was that this information could then serve as a basis for syllabus and textbook design. Indeed, some of the first EAP textbooks were developed on the basis of the findings of register analysis (see Swales 1988, and Dudley-Evans and St John 1998 for more detail). However, it was realized that teaching the grammatical and lexical items found to be highly frequent in scientific English did not necessarily make learners successful users of scientific English. Seminal work from this period, together with a helpful commentary, can be found in Swales (1988). The more recent developments of academic corpora and sophisticated computer-based methods of analysis have renewed the interest in registers, as discussed in the section on corpora below.

Rhetorical and discourse analysis

The early 1970s brought a growing realization that linguistic analysis needed to take into account patterns above the sentence or utterance level (Swales 1988). Studies from this period focus on textual structure, discourse patterns and rhetorical functions of scientific discourse with the aim of providing practitioners with information on authentic language use in whole texts (Hutchinson and Waters 1987). Textbooks based on this work feature material on functions of scientific discourse, such as description and classification (e.g. Jordan 1990).

Study skills

In line with the focus on communicative skills in general ELT in the late 1970s, greater importance was given to the skills the learner needed in order to function effectively in academic environments. A typical project exemplifying the type of EAP work in this period is the University of Malaya ESP Project. Having identified reading skills as the most relevant to students studying in Malay but using literature in English, project participants developed a series of teaching materials specifically addressing various sub-skills needed for efficient reading of academic texts (Dudley-Evans and St John 1998; Swales 1988).

Needs analysis

EAP instruction is concerned with preparing students to work effectively within their academic environment. Given the diversity of the profile of EAP students and their learning situations, and due also to the limited duration of EAP courses, needs analysis is seen as the 'cornerstone' of EAP, since it helps determine 'the *what* and *how* of a course' (Dudley-Evans and St John 1998: 121). Although needs analysis had played a role in ESP from the 1960s, it was in the late 1970s and early 1980s that it became one of its central concepts. The publication of Munby's (1978) volume gave an impetus to the debate about different types of needs and procedures to establish them. The rise of needs analysis can be seen as a reaction against an exclusive focus on descriptions of language use in target situations of earlier periods, and a shift towards considering the learner as the centre of the teaching/learning process (Dudley-Evans and St John 1998). West (1994) offers a comprehensive survey of early work in needs analysis. As one of the major pillars of ESP, needs analysis continues to attract scholars' attention, as will be discussed in more detail in the third section below.

EAP today

All of the stages described above continue to influence contemporary approaches to EAP, as is apparent from contributions to the journals in the field: *English for Specific Purposes* and *Journal of English for Academic Purposes*. In the sections that follow, we identify salient topical issues and areas of research. Current debates are set against a backdrop of unprecedented growth in EAP across the globe in response to the increasing numbers of international students at universities in English-speaking countries, and the establishment of programmes taught in the medium of English in non-English speaking countries worldwide (see, for instance, Coleman 2006). That EAP is now a truly global field can be seen from the many national and international publications and conferences on EAP, and the establishment of EAP research groups worldwide (e.g. the City University of Hong Kong, CERLIS in Italy, KIAP in Norway, GRAPE and INTERLAE in Spain, and the University of Michigan's English Language Institute in the United States).

Current issues in EAP

General vs specific EAP

Blue (1988) distinguished between English for General Academic Purposes (EGAP) and English for Specific Academic Purposes (ESAP), EGAP being academic English skills, language, and activities relevant for students studying in any field, and ESAP being relevant for students in certain fields only. For instance, instruction in how to compile bibliographies, take notes, and listen to lectures could be covered in an EGAP syllabus, while ESAP would focus on discipline-specific requirements, such as writing a chemistry lab report.

An important debate is how general or specific EAP pedagogy should be, Spack (1988) being an advocate of EGAP, and Hyland (2002) of ESAP where possible. Arguments can be put forward in favour of both approaches, and in favour of a judicious general-specific combined approach. EGAP may appeal where student populations and fields of study are diverse, and where EAP teachers have little time or resources to design subject-specific programmes, since the challenges of researching, designing, and implementing as many appropriate programmes as are needed can be formidable (see Basturkmen 2003; Belcher 2006; Hyland 2006 for further discussion). Furthermore, in many contexts communication/cooperation between EAP teachers and content lecturers may be poor, thus preventing teachers from learning what is required of students entering various departments across their university. EGAP is also more economical, with one class for all, rather than several discipline-specific ESAP classes. On the other hand, as we shall see below, much recent EAP research has revealed that academic discourse varies from discipline to discipline, making a case for teaching students in discipline-specific classes. In addition, learners may find an ESAP class more relevant and motivating, because it directly relates to their field of study.

In reality, decisions about specificity are often constrained by national or institutional bodies, which do not always take as much account of research findings in the field as they should. In addition, these bodies may prescribe an EGAP approach when EAP teachers know very little about content lecturers' demands, but, as Basturkmen (2003) argues, in order to make such a course truly relevant for students' needs, research to identify generic and transferable academic skills relevant to all will still be required.

Cooperation between EAP teachers and subject teachers

We have seen in the discussion about EGAP and ESAP above that cooperation between EAP and subject teachers is an important issue. Dudley-Evans and St John (1998) talk of three levels of cooperation between the EAP teacher and subject teachers, each with an increasing level of interaction: cooperation, collaboration and team teaching. Cooperation involves information gathering from the subject department about tasks, syllabi, and other information useful for EAP course design. Collaboration involves the EAP teacher and the subject teacher working together in order to develop the EAP course in support of the subject course. Team teaching involves the two parties teaching together in the classroom. Those studies conducted to date (e.g. Barron 2002; Dudley-Evans 2001) reveal that factors impacting on the level of cooperation include the institutional context, differences in teaching methodologies and philosophies, the low status of the EAP teacher in some contexts, and related issues of power.

Needs analysis and rights analysis

Needs analysis 'underlies syllabus design, materials development, text selection, learning goals and tasks, and, ultimately, evaluation of students and course or program success' (Carkin 2005: 87). However, the meaning of 'needs' has been much debated (see Belcher 2006; Hutchinson and Waters 1987; Long 2005; West 1994), and there is much discussion about whose needs EAP teachers should take into account and the instruments teachers should use to conduct needs analyses (e.g. Jordan [1997] lists 14 different methods). Whereas it was the language 'expert' who traditionally identified needs (see Munby 1978), more recent approaches have recommended that a number of parties should have a say, including teachers, education authorities, and other stakeholders (e.g. parents, sponsors), as well as the learners themselves. In Hyland's (2006: 73) words, needs analysis must recognize 'learners' goals and backgrounds, their language proficiencies, their reasons for taking the course, their teaching and learning preferences, and the situations they will need to communicate in'. Hence Benesch (2001) prefers to speak of *rights analysis* rather than needs analysis, emphasizing the importance of giving the learners a say about what they are taught. For a summary of recent criticisms of needs analysis, see Basturkmen (2006: 19–20).

Critical EAP

Drawing on the teachings of Paulo Freire and writings on critical pedagogy in the education literature (e.g. Giroux 1988), the critical EAP movement is concerned with social justice, change, and empowerment of the EAP learner, who may feel the requirements of content lecturers are unclear – or unfair. It is concerned with '**critiquing** existing educational institutions and practices, and subsequently **transforming** both education and society' (Hall 2000: 3, emphasis in original. See also Benesch 2001; Canagarajah 2002b; Pennycook 1999). Since critical pedagogy is sometimes associated with political activism, some teachers (and learners) may feel such a pedagogy has little relevance to the EAP classroom (cf. Johns 1993; Johnston 1999). One powerful criticism that has been levelled at critical EAP is its tendency to theorize, rather than to offer implementable classroom activities (Johnston 1999). However, Benesch (2001) has offered both theory and practice, describing how critical EAP can provide students with 'strategies for challenging the way things are', as well as describing critical teaching activities and materials.

Both Benesch (2001) and Hyland (2006) point out that there are many types of critical EAP, with some types being less concerned with (political) transformation than others (cf. Allison 1996; and Harwood and Hadley 2004, who distinguish between 'pragmatic' and 'critical' approaches to EAP). So, as Benesch (2001) notes, critical EAP is nothing if not *locally appropriate*, addressing the learners' concerns in any given class.

Genre analysis

The concept of 'genre' is much discussed (see Johns 2008; Swales 1990, 2004). Hyland (2004: 4) offers the following accessible definition: 'Genre is a term for grouping texts together, representing how writers typically use language to respond to recurring situations'. Genres are characterized by their 'communicative purposes' as well as by their patterns of 'structure, style, content and intended audience' (Swales 1990: 58). John Swales' move analysis (e.g. 1981, 1990, 2004) is a particularly influential type of genre analysis, with 'move' referring to a section of the text which is seen to perform a specific communicative function. Swales famously demonstrated how writers of research articles can use their introductions to create a research space, identifying a gap in research community knowledge which they proceed to fill. A wide range of academic spoken and written genres has been investigated using move analysis. Some researchers have analyzed research articles in their entirety in a range of disciplines, including biochemistry (Kanoksilapatham 2007) and medicine (Nwogu 1997). Others have focused on specific parts of the research article, such as introductions (Samraj 2002a) and conclusions (Yang and Allison 2003). Still others have focused on other genres, such as the Ph.D. thesis (e.g. Bunton 2005).

As Johns *et al.* (2006) point out, however, a study of genre involves more than the words of the speaker or writer, encompassing 'the complexities of texts, contexts, writers and their purposes, and all that is beyond a text that influences writers and audiences' (2006: 247). Hence so-called ethnographic genre analyses have supplemented textual analysis with interviews with writers and speakers (and their audiences) and a wider investigation into the context in which the texts under study are produced. One such ethnographic genre analysis was conducted by Samraj (2002b), who found that the 'contextual layers' in which the writing/speaking is produced, such as the given course, task, and field of study, can impact on the genre's form.

Contrastive rhetoric

The field of contrastive rhetoric is over forty years old, and has grown in sophistication (see Connor 2002), telling us much about the differences in comparable texts across languages and cultures. Some studies compare non-native writing and speaking with comparable outputs by native authors, while others compare equivalent genres written in different languages. Although our focus in this chapter is on English academic discourse rather than equivalents in other languages, comparisons of an equivalent genre across languages may well enhance understandings of what the English language version requires. For instance, in a comparison of economics papers written in English by Finnish and Anglo-American academics, Mauranen (1993) found that English writers used more text-organizational devices (e.g. 'however'). She argues that this finding reveals differences in the two writing cultures, with English being more reader-oriented, i.e. more concerned with guiding the reader through text, and Finnish being more writer-oriented and implicit. She also notes the impact of educational factors, i.e. the differences in the writing instruction in the two writing cultures. While English writing manuals encourage the use of text-organizational devices, Finnish manuals advise writers against using such 'unnecessary' words. Additional contrastive studies of written genres include Martín-Martín and Burgess (2004) and Sanderson (2008) on the research article, Feng (2008) on grant proposals and Salager-Meyer et al. (2007) on academic book reviews. There have also been a few contrastive studies of spoken genres, including Schleef (2009), who compared German and American lectures and seminars across different disciplines.

Corpora and EAP

Computer corpora, that is, electronically stored databases of authentic spoken and/or written text (see Sinclair 2004), have led to important insights about the linguistic and rhetorical features of EAP spoken and written genres. By examining large amounts of academic speech and writing, corpus studies enable us to take 'an evidence-based approach' (Hyland 2006: 58) to EAP. Corpora provide the student and teacher of EAP with many different insights, including information about how frequent any given words/phrases are; the lexico-grammatical patterns which surround these words/phrases; and the text's keywords, i.e. those which are unusually frequent. Spoken and written academic discourse, and different spoken and written academic genres, can then be compared. As Hyland (2006) argues, perhaps the most noteworthy impact of corpora as far as EAP is concerned is the highlighting of the variation across different genres and disciplines, as we shall see below. There is a growing number of spoken and written corpora of academic English available, such as the British Academic Written English corpus (BAWE), the British Academic Spoken corpus (BASE), and the Michigan Corpus of Academic Spoken English (MICASE).

Inter-disciplinary differences

Corpora reveal much about how academic writing differs across the disciplines. For instance, Hyland (2000) analyzed expressions of praise and criticism in 160 book reviews from eight different disciplines. He found that book reviews in the sciences, such as engineering, contain more instances of praise than criticism, while those in the social sciences, such as sociology, tend to be more critical. Many corpus-based studies have focused on specific linguistic features, such as the function and frequency of imperatives (Swales *et al*. 1998).

There have also been studies of spoken academic language which highlight disciplinary differences, such as Simpson-Vlach's (2006) research on linguistic items in MICASE. Inter-disciplinary differences in spoken academic discourse have been investigated in lectures, with Thompson (2006) contrasting the language of lectures in the disciplines of economics and philosophy in the BASE corpus.

Intra-disciplinary differences

A less studied aspect of EAP focuses on how speech and writing can differ in *the same* discipline, although evidence of variations in generic structure within a discipline was noted as early as Swales (1981). Harwood (2006) found striking differences in the frequency of personal pronouns in political scientists' journal articles and he therefore interviewed the writers in an attempt to account for these discrepancies. The interviewees' different beliefs about (in)appropriate pronoun use can partly be explained by looking at the type of research they carry out, i.e. qualitative versus quantitative. Another recent study of intra-disciplinary differences is Ozturk (2007), which reports variations in the structure of research article introductions within applied linguistics.

Studies of academic speech and writing

A number of corpus studies have compared and contrasted linguistic features in academic speech and writing, notably the work done by Douglas Biber and colleagues (e.g. Biber 2006). Biber's multi-dimensional analysis methodology involves quantitatively and qualitatively analyzing large corpora of texts and identifying and describing a range of linguistic features contained in these texts. It shows how markedly speech and writing in general, and university language in particular, varies across registers.

Other studies contrasting academic speech and writing include Carter-Thomas and Rowley-Jolivet (2008), who have shown that the functions and frequencies of *if*-conditionals vary across written and spoken academic genres. This study compares *if*-conditionals in a corpus of three genres in the discipline of medicine: research articles, conference presentations, and editorials, with *if*-conditionals occurring almost four times as often in conference presentations as in research articles.

Learner corpora

Learner corpora, that is, collections of speech and writing by learners of English, are particularly useful for EAP (see Granger 2002). A number of studies have compared corpora of native and non-native student writing, noting differences in the frequency of certain linguistic features (e.g. Ädel 2008; Granger 1998; Hinkel 2002), thereby identifying language that the learners in question use significantly more or less often than native speaker counterparts, or misuse. A good example of a learner corpus study is Hyland and Milton's (1997) study of native and non-native students' use of epistemic modal language, which showed that the non-native writers relied on a more restricted set of items than their native speaker counterparts. There are also striking differences in the frequency of certain items: *appear*, for instance, is found thirty-three times more often in the native writers' corpus.

Corpora and EAP textbooks and teaching materials

Corpora have also been useful for identifying discrepancies between academic discourse and its representation in EAP textbooks (see Harwood 2005; Paltridge 2002). For instance, several studies which focus on modal verbs conclude that EAP textbooks and style guides are not only failing to teach the full repertoire of modal language, they are also failing to teach a number of items that learners would find most useful (Holmes 1988; Hyland 1994; Römer 2004). The textbooks are also providing misleading explanations for some of the language they do teach. However, some EAP textbook writers are now exploiting both spoken and written corpus data in their instructional materials (e.g. Feak *et al.* 2009; Swales and Feak 2000; and see Harwood 2010). Another encouraging development has seen teachers and researchers getting EAP learners themselves to consult corpora (Gavioli 2005; Lee and Swales 2006).

Academic vocabulary

Academic vocabulary is defined as words frequently occurring in academic but not other kinds of texts, words such as 'subsequent' or 'component' (Coxhead and Nation 2001). The most well-known list of academic vocabulary is the Academic Word List (AWL) (Coxhead 2000), which is based on an analysis of a 3,500,000-word corpus of academic English, consisting of a variety of academic texts covering arts, science, law and commerce. Knowing which words occur frequently in academic texts is very useful for EAP course and materials designers, as it enables them to prioritize lexical items to be taught, especially in contexts where general EAP classes are held for students from a variety of disciplines. Indeed, vocabulary teaching materials have been developed on the basis of the AWL (e.g. Schmitt and Schmitt 2005).

However, the AWL has recently been criticized by Durrant (2009) and Hyland and Tse (2007), who show that academic vocabulary varies across disciplines. It is timely, therefore, that researchers have started developing discipline-specific wordlists in a variety of fields and sub-fields, such as engineering (Mudraya 2006) and medicine (Wang *et al.* 2008). However, at this stage, there is still much work to be done on pedagogical applications of these findings.

Lexical bundles

There has been much research focused on identifying and analyzing recurrent linguistic items which feature in academic speech and writing, with various labels used to describe this phenomenon, such as 'lexical bundles' (Biber *et al.* 2004; Hyland 2008). Cortes (e.g. 2004) defines lexical bundles as sequences of three or more words that frequently occur in a particular register, such as *is likely to* and *these results suggest that*, both of which feature in academic writing. Cortes and Hyland have found important differences in how lexical bundles are used across disciplines and by student and expert writers. Focusing on writing in history and biology, Cortes (2004) demonstrates that biologists use a wider variety of bundles than historians, and that many of the bundles used frequently by academics are seldom used by students in the same fields. Another noteworthy study of lexical bundles in writing is Hyland (2008), while Nesi and Basturkmen (2006) have also studied lexical bundles, but in lectures, as opposed to writing.

Li and Schmitt's (2009) study of lexical bundles is particularly relevant to EAP teachers, since the focus is on acquisition rather than description. Li and Schmitt chart a Chinese M.A. student's use of written bundles over a year. Textual analysis of the student's phrases is complemented by interviews to investigate how the phrases were learned. Longitudinal studies of acquisition of salient language for EAP should prove useful in informing teachers and materials writers how much can be learned (and how), as will Jones and Haywood's (2004) account of promoting and assessing the effectiveness of the teaching of lexical bundles.

Academic lectures

Some of the research on lectures focuses on the language used (e.g. Lindemann and Mauranen 2001; Simpson-Vlach 2006). For instance, Crawford Camiciottoli (2007) identifies a wide range of discourse structuring expressions used by lecturers (e.g. *What I'm going to talk about today*; *We'll come back to that later*), and rightly argues that this type of research should enable EAP materials writers to better prepare learners for lectures by developing more authentic class-room activities to simulate lecture discourse. Thompson's study (2003) is notable because it focuses not only on organizational patterns in lectures, but also on lecturers' intonation. Thompson also contrasts her findings with information given on lecture organizational patterns and intonation in EAP textbooks, showing that the textbook material is potentially misleading. Other studies try to determine salient linguistic features of lectures that aid or hinder non-native understanding (e.g. Chaudron and Richards 1986; Flowerdew and Tauroza 1995). For instance, Jung (2006) focuses on contextualization markers which 'signal how learners should interpret the incoming information' (2006: 1929), showing that when these markers are absent, L2 learners more frequently misunderstand what is said. Other studies adopt a psycholinguistic perspective, attempting to assess the impact of working memory on non-natives' note-taking (e.g. Faraco *et al.* 2002).

Writing for international publication

Much of the work discussed above concerns university students and student genres, such as lectures and essays set by lecturers for assessment. However, another current area of EAP research concerns the dominant position of English in international scholarship and increasing pressure on scholars worldwide to publish in English. This has led to a growing body of research on writing for international publication in English (for a review of this work, see Uzuner 2008). Major themes in this literature include the difficulties multilingual scholars experience when writing for international publication and the strategies they employ to overcome them (Belcher 2007; Burrough-Boenisch 2003; Canagarajah 2002a, 2002b; Flowerdew 2001; Li and Flowerdew 2007; Lillis and Curry 2006).

Future directions for EAP research

We now identify several areas where further research is needed to enhance the knowledge base of EAP.

The efficacy of EAP

Master (2005) points to the lack of well-designed empirical research focused on the efficacy of EAP instruction: does EAP work? If there are two EAP programmes running, which leads to the better learning outcomes? Some of the work in this area includes Storch and Tapper (2009), a study of the impact of a postgraduate EAP writing course in Australia, and Robinson *et al.*'s (2001) experimental study of the effectiveness of teaching oral discussion skills using three different methods, one of a few studies which compare and contrast different pedagogical approaches to EAP.

EAP teacher training

In some parts of the world, institutions ask ELT teachers to teach EAP without providing specialized training. A discussion of the nature of such training has largely been neglected to date. Notable exceptions include a volume on teacher training for teaching languages for specific purposes (Howard and Brown 1997) and articles by Boswood and Marriott (1994), who describe an ESP teacher training course for experienced ELT teachers, Jackson (1998), who argues for the use of case studies in ESP teacher training, and Chen (2000), who reports on self-training through action research.

EAP, second language acquisition, and teaching materials

Basturkmen (2006) comments, 'ESP has not been much concerned with the debates and issues emerging in recent years in the field of second language acquisition' (2006: 5). Hence, as Hyland (2006) argues, 'Many EAP courses still lack a theoretical or research rationale and textbooks continue too often to depend on the writer's experience and intuition rather than on systematic research' (2006: 5). Basturkmen (2006) makes a step in this direction by exploring the links between EAP and SLA theories of language learning, such as information processing.

Ethnographies, academic literacies, and deeper understandings of EAP contexts

A case can be made for the need for EAP research to focus more heavily on 'processes and contexts' (Belcher 2006). The focus has often been on textual description, given the 'time sensitive nature of most ESP needs analysis, curriculum development, and the very real-world needs of learners', all of which has meant 'the more time-consuming investigations of processes and contexts' may have been somewhat neglected (2006: 149). However, there have been a number of landmark qualitative case studies documenting both native and non-native students' difficulties, particularly with writing, in university contexts (e.g. Casanave 2002; Leki 2007; Spack 1997). A related body of literature has focused on the process of academic enculturation (e.g. Casanave and Li 2008; Prior 1998). Another group of researchers associated with (critical) ethnographic research is 'academic literacies' scholars, who seek to 'go beyond texts', in Connor's (2004) words, and to gain insights into the contexts in which texts are produced and the actors who produce them, rather than limiting themselves to textual analysis (see Lillis and Scott 2007 for a survey of work conducted to date in this field).

Descriptions of language use

It will be apparent from this review that more work has been carried out on written than spoken academic discourse to date. New recording technologies and advances in corpus linguistics will enable more sophisticated analyses of spoken genres. One potentially exciting area is multimodal analysis, providing insights into sound and image, as well as text (see Kress 2010). One area where applications of multimodal analysis may be useful is the analysis of university lectures, which increasingly combine lecturer talk with textual, audio and visual material projected on the screen. Multimodal analysis of Web-mediated communication, common in today's workplaces, may also be of relevance to EAP.

EAP in dialogue with other fields

Many salient issues for EAP teachers and researchers are also of interest to scholars in other fields such as education and sociology, and EAP could benefit from adopting and adapting knowledge from a wider disciplinary base. For instance, there has been much interest in citation in academic writing by EAP researchers, but also by information scientists and sociologists of knowledge. Recent work (Harwood 2009; Hyland 2003; Petrić 2007) has drawn on all three areas, and a similar multidisciplinary approach could be usefully applied in EAP more generally.

Summary

The purpose of this chapter was to introduce the field of English for Academic Purposes. We began by defining EAP before providing an overview of its history and focussing on a number of pertinent current issues, including how specific EAP should be, whether and to what extent EAP and subject teachers should collaborate, different approaches to needs analysis, and how the developments in genre analysis, contrastive rhetoric and corpus-based work inform EAP pedagogy. The diversity of the directions for future research that we identify reflects the vibrancy of the field.

Related topics

corpus linguistics; ESP and business communication; lexis

Further reading

Basturkmen, H. (2007) *Ideas and Options in English for Specific Purposes*, Mahwah, NJ: Lawrence Erlbaum Associates. (This book explores the theories about language, learning and teaching in ESP, discussing major issues from the perspectives of theoretical background, recent research and practical applications, which is followed by questions and ideas for projects and suggestions for further reading.)

Dudley-Evans, T. and St John, M.-J. (1998) *Developments in English for Specific Purposes: A Multi-Disciplinary Approach*, Cambridge: Cambridge University Press. (This practical book provides a good introductory survey of major issues in ESP, including a separate chapter on EAP, with numerous illustrative examples, tasks for discussion and analysis, excerpts from textbooks, tests and other materials, an answer key for self-study purposes, and suggested readings for each chapter.)

Flowerdew, J. and Peacock, M. (2001) *Research Perspectives on English for Academic Purposes*, Cambridge: Cambridge University Press. (The twenty-five chapters in this book, written by leading figures in EAP, provide a comprehensive survey of major issues in EAP from a research perspective, focusing on research problems, methods, findings and their practical applications in various contexts.)

Hyland, K. (2006) *English for Academic Purposes: An Advanced Resource Book*, Abingdon: Routledge. (This useful resource book contains twelve units on salient issues in EAP today, each with excerpts from research articles and discussion and research tasks, as well as a useful glossary and suggestions for further reading for each topic.)

——(2009) *Academic Discourse: English in a Global Context*, London: Continuum. (Written in accessible language, this introductory book offers an overview of academic genres in the area of research, university instruction, student writing and popular science.)

References

Ädel, A. (2008) 'Metadiscourse across three varieties of English: American, British, and advanced-learner English', in U. Connor, E. Nagelhout and W. V. Rozycki (eds) *Contrastive Rhetoric: Reaching to Intercultural Rhetoric*, Amsterdam: John Benjamins.

Allison, D. (1996) 'Pragmatist discourse and English for academic purposes', *English for Specific Purposes* 15: 85–103.

Barron, C. (2002) 'Problem-solving and EAP: themes and issues in a collaborative teaching venture', *English for Specific Purposes* 22: 297–314.

Basturkmen, H. (2003) 'Specificity and ESP course design', *RELC Journal* 34: 48–63.

——(2006) *Ideas and Options in English for Specific Purposes*, Mahwah, NJ: Lawrence Erlbaum Associates.

Belcher, D. D. (2006) 'English for Specific Purposes: teaching to perceived needs and imagined futures in worlds of work, study, and everyday life', *TESOL Quarterly* 40: 133–56.

——(2007) 'Seeking acceptance in an English-only research world', *Journal of Second Language Writing* 16: 1–22.

Benesch, S. (2001) *Critical English for Academic Purposes: Theory, Politics, and Practice*, Mahwah, NJ: Lawrence Erlbaum Associates.

Biber, D. (2006) *University Language: A Corpus-based Study of Spoken and Written Registers*, Amsterdam: John Benjamins.

Biber, D., Conrad, S. and Cortes, V. (2004) 'If you look at … : lexical bundles in university teaching and textbooks', *Applied Linguistics* 25: 371–405.

Blue, G. (1988) 'Individualising academic writing tuition', in P. Robinson (ed.) *Academic Writing: Process and Product. ELT Documents 129*, London: Modern English Publications and the British Council.

Boswood, T. and Marriott, A. (1994) 'Ethnography for specific purposes: teaching and training in parallel', *English for Specific Purposes* 13: 3–21.

Bunton, D. (2005) 'The structure of PhD conclusion chapters', *Journal of English for Academic Purposes* 4: 207–24.

Burrough-Boenisch, J. (2003) 'Shapers of published NNS research articles', *Journal of Second Language Writing* 12: 223–43.

Canagarajah, A. S. (2002a) *A Geopolitics of Academic Writing*, Pittsburgh, PA: University of Pittsburgh Press.

——(2002b) *Critical Academic Writing and Multilingual Students*, Ann Arbor: University of Michigan Press.

Carkin, S. (2005) 'English for academic purposes', in E. Hinkel (ed.) *Handbook of Research in Second Language Teaching and Learning*, Mahwah, NJ: Lawrence Erlbaum Associates.

Carter-Thomas, S. and Rowley-Jolivet, E. (2008) '*If*-conditionals in medical discourse: from theory to disciplinary practice', *Journal of English for Academic Purposes* 7: 191–205.

Casanave, C. P. (2002) *Writing Games: Multicultural Case Studies of Academic Literacy Practices in Higher Education*, Mahwah, NJ: Lawrence Erlbaum Associates.

Casanave, C. P. and Li, X. (2008) *Learning the Literacy Practices of Graduate School: Insiders' Reflections on Academic Enculturation*, Ann Arbor: University of Michigan Press.

Chaudron, C. and Richards, J. C. (1986) 'The effect of discourse markers on the comprehension of lectures', *Applied Linguistics* 7: 113–27.

Chen, T.-Y. (2000) 'Self-training for ESP through action research', *English for Specific Purposes* 19: 389–402.

Coleman, J. A. (2006) 'English-medium teaching in European higher education', *Language Teaching* 39: 1–14.

Connor, U. (2002) 'New directions in contrastive rhetoric', *TESOL Quarterly* 36: 493–510.

——(2004) 'Intercultural rhetoric research: beyond texts', *Journal of English for Academic Purposes* 3: 291–304.

Cortes, V. (2004) 'Lexical bundles in published and student disciplinary writing: examples from history and biology', *English for Specific Purposes* 23: 397–423.

Coxhead, A. (2000) 'A new academic word list', *TESOL Quarterly* 34: 213–38.

Coxhead, A. and Nation, P. (2001) 'The specialized vocabulary of English for academic purposes', in J. Flowerdew and M. Peacock (eds) *Research Perspectives on English for Academic Purposes*, Cambridge: Cambridge University Press.

Crawford Camiciottoli, B. (2007) *The Language of Business Studies Lectures: A Corpus-based Analysis*, Amsterdam: John Benjamins.

Dudley-Evans, T. (2001) 'Team-teaching in EAP: changes and adaptations in the Birmingham approach', in J. Flowerdew and M. Peacock (eds) *Research Perspectives on English for Academic Purposes*, Cambridge: Cambridge University Press.

Dudley-Evans, T. and St John, M.-J. (1998) *Developments in English for Specific Purposes: A Multi-Disciplinary Approach*, Cambridge: Cambridge University Press.

Durrant, P. (2009) 'Investigating the viability of a collocation list for students of English for Academic Purposes', *English for Specific Purposes* 28: 157–69.

Faraco, M., Barbier, M. and Piolat, A. (2002) 'A comparison between notetaking in L1 and L2 by undergraduate students', in S. Ransdell and M. Barbier (eds) *New Directions for Research in L2 Writing*, Dordrecht: Kluwer Academic.

Feak, C. B., Reinhart, S. M. and Rohlck, T. N. (2009) *Academic Interactions: Communicating on Campus*, Ann Arbor: University of Michigan Press.

Feng, H. (2008) 'A genre-based study of research grant proposals in China', in U. Connor, E. Nagelhout and W. V. Rozycki (eds) *Contrastive Rhetoric: Reaching to Intercultural Rhetoric*, Amsterdam: John Benjamins.

Flowerdew, J. (2001) 'Attitudes of journal editors to nonnative speaker contributions', *TESOL Quarterly* 35: 121–50.

Flowerdew, J. and Peacock, M. (2001) 'Issues in EAP: a preliminary perspective', in J. Flowerdew and M. Peacock (eds) *Research Perspectives on English for Academic Purposes*, Cambridge: Cambridge University Press.

Flowerdew, J. and Tauroza, S. (1995) 'The effect of discourse markers on second language comprehension', *Studies in Second Language Acquisition* 17: 435–58.

Gavioli, L. (2005) *Exploring Corpora for ESP Learning*, Amsterdam: John Benjamins.

Giroux, H. A. (1988) *Schooling and the Struggle for Public Life: Critical Pedagogy in the Modern Age*, Minneapolis: University of Minnesota Press.

Granger, S. (1998) *Learner English on Computer*, London: Longman.

——(2002) 'A bird's-eye view of learner corpus research', in S. Granger, J. Hung and S. Petch-Tyson (eds) *Computer Learner Corpora, Second Language Acquisition and Foreign Language Teaching*, Amsterdam: John Benjamins.

Hall, G. (2000) 'Local approaches to critical pedagogy: an investigation into the dilemmas raised by critical approaches to ELT', *CRILE Working Paper* 48, Lancaster University.

Harwood, N. (2005) 'What do we want EAP teaching materials for?', *Journal of English for Academic Purposes* 4: 149–61.

——(2006) '(In)appropriate personal pronoun use in political science: a qualitative study and a proposed heuristic for future research', *Written Communication* 23: 424–50.

——(2009) 'An interview-based study of the functions of citations in academic writing across two disciplines', *Journal of Pragmatics* 41: 497–518.

——(ed.) (2010) *English Language Teaching Materials: Theory and Practice*, Cambridge: Cambridge University Press.

Harwood, N. and Hadley, G. (2004) 'Demystifying institutional practices: critical pragmatism and the teaching of academic writing', *English for Specific Purposes* 23: 355–77.

Hinkel, E. (2002) *Second Language Writers' Text: Linguistic and Rhetorical Features*, Mahwah, NJ: Lawrence Erlbaum Associates.

Holmes, J. (1988) 'Doubt and certainty in ESL textbooks', *Applied Linguistics* 9: 21–44.

Howard, R. and Brown, G. (eds) (1997) *Teacher Education for Languages for Specific Purposes*, Clevedon: Multilingual Matters.

Hutchinson, T. and Waters, A. (1987) *English for Specific Purposes: A Learning-Centred Approach*, Cambridge: Cambridge University Press.

Hyland, K. (1994) 'Hedging in academic writing and EAP textbooks', *English for Specific Purposes* 13: 239–56.

——(2000) *Disciplinary Discourses: Social Interactions in Academic Writing*, Harlow: Longman.

——(2002) 'Specificity revisited: how far should we go now?', *English for Specific Purposes* 21: 385–95.

——(2003) 'Self-citation and self-reference: credibility and promotion in academic publication', *Journal of the American Society for Information Science and Technology* 54: 251–9.

——(2004) *Genre and Second Language Writing*, Ann Arbor: University of Michigan Press.

——(2006) *English for Academic Purposes: An Advanced Resource Book*, London: Routledge.

——(2008) 'As can be seen: lexical bundles and disciplinary variation', *English for Specific Purposes* 27: 4–21.

Hyland, K. and Milton, J. (1997) 'Qualification and certainty in L1 and L2 students' writing', *Journal of Second Language Writing* 6: 183–205.

Hyland, K. and Tse, P. (2007) 'Is there an "academic vocabulary"?', *TESOL Quarterly* 41: 235–53.

Jackson, J. (1998) 'Reality-based decision cases in ESP teacher education: windows on practice', *English for Specific Purposes* 7: 151–67.

Johns, A. M. (1993) 'Too much on our plates: a response to Terry Santos' "Ideology in composition: L1 and ESL"', *Journal of Second Language Writing* 2: 83–8.

——(2008) 'Genre awareness for the novice academic student: an ongoing quest', *Language Teaching* 41: 237–52.

Johns, A. M., Bawarshi, A., Coe, R. M., Hyland, K., Paltridge, B., Reiff, M. J. and Tardy, C. (2006) 'Crossing the boundaries of genre studies: commentaries by experts', *Journal of Second Language Writing* 15: 234–49.

Johns, A. M. and Snow, M. A. (2006) 'Introduction to special issue: academic English in secondary schools', *Journal of English for Academic Purposes* 5: 251–3.

Johnston, B. (1999) 'Putting critical pedagogy in its place: a personal account', *TESOL Quarterly* 33: 557–65.

Jones, M. and Haywood, S. (2004) 'Facilitating the acquisition of formulaic sequences: an exploratory study in an EAP context', in N. Schmitt (ed.) *Formulaic Sequences: Acquisition, Processing and Use*, Amsterdam: John Benjamins.

Jordan, R. R. (1990) *Academic Writing Course: Study Skills in English*, 3rd edn, Harlow: Pearson Education.

——(1997) *English for Academic Purposes: A Guide and Resource Book for Teachers*, Cambridge: Cambridge University Press.

Jung, E. H. (2006) 'Misunderstanding of academic monologues by nonnative speakers of English', *Journal of Pragmatics* 38: 1928–42.

Kanoksilapatham, B. (2007) 'Rhetorical moves in biochemistry research articles', in D. Biber, U. Connor and T. A. Upton (eds) *Discourse on the Move: Using Corpus Analysis to Describe Discourse Structure*, Amsterdam: John Benjamins.

Kress, G. (2010) *Multimodality*, London: Routledge.

Lee, D. and Swales, J. M. (2006) 'A corpus-based EAP course for NNS doctoral students: moving from available specialized corpora to self-compiled corpora', *English for Specific Purposes* 25: 56–75.

Leki, I. (2007) *Undergraduates in a Second Language: Challenges and Complexities of Academic Literacy Development*, Mahwah, NJ: Lawrence Erlbaum Associates.

Li, J. and Schmitt, N. (2009) 'The acquisition of lexical phrases in academic writing: a longitudinal case study', *Journal of Second Language Writing* 18: 85–102.

Li, Y. and Flowerdew, J. (2007) 'Shaping Chinese novice scientists' manuscripts for publication', *Journal of Second Language Writing* 16: 100–17.

Lillis, T. and Curry, M. J. (2006) 'Professional academic writing by multilingual scholars: interactions with literacy brokers in the production of English-medium texts', *Written Communication* 23: 3–35.

Lillis, T. and Scott, M. (2007) 'Defining academic literacies research: issues of epistemology, ideology and strategy', *Journal of Applied Linguistics* 4: 5–32.

Lindemann, S. and Mauranen, A. (2001) '"It's just real messy": the occurrence and function of *just* in a corpus of academic speech', *English for Specific Purposes* 20: 459–75.

Long, M. L. (2005) 'Methodological issues in needs analysis', in M. H. Long (ed.) *Second Language Needs Analysis*, Cambridge: Cambridge University Press.

Martín-Martín, P. and Burgess, S. (2004) 'The rhetorical management of academic criticism in research article abstracts', *Text* 24: 171–95.

Master, P. (2005) 'Research in English for specific purposes', in E. Hinkel (ed.) *Handbook of Research in Second Language Teaching and Learning*, Mahwah, NJ: Lawrence Erlbaum Associates.

Mauranen, A. (1993) 'Contrastive ESP rhetoric: metatext in Finnish-English economics texts', *English for Specific Purposes* 12: 3–22.

Mudraya, O. (2006) 'Engineering English: a lexical frequency instructional model', *English for Specific Purposes* 25: 235–56.

Munby, J. (1978) *Communicative Syllabus Design*, Cambridge: Cambridge University Press.

Nesi, H. and Basturkmen, H. (2006) 'Lexical bundles and discourse signalling in academic lectures', *International Journal of Corpus Linguistics* 11: 147–68.

Nwogu, K. N. (1997) 'The medical research paper: structure and functions', *English for Specific Purposes* 16: 119–38.

Ozturk, I. (2007) 'The textual organisation of research article introductions in applied linguistics: variability within a single discipline', *English for Specific Purposes* 26: 25–38.

Paltridge, B. (2002) 'Thesis and dissertation writing: an examination of published advice and actual practice', *English for Specific Purposes* 21: 125–43.

Pennycook, A. (1999) 'Introduction: critical approaches to TESOL', *TESOL Quarterly* 33: 329–48.

Petrić, B. (2007) 'Rhetorical functions of citations in high- and low-rated master's theses', *Journal of English for Academic Purposes* 6: 238–53.

Prior, P. A. (1998) *Writing/Disciplinarity: A Sociohistoric Account of Literate Activity in the Academy*. Mahwah, NJ: Lawrence Erlbaum Associates.

Robinson, P., Strong, G., Whittle, J. and Nobe, S. (2001) 'The development of EAP oral discussion ability', in J. Flowerdew and M. Peacock (eds) *Research Perspectives on English for Academic Purposes*, Cambridge: Cambridge University Press.

Römer, U. (2004) 'A corpus-driven approach to modal auxiliaries and their didactics', in J. Sinclair (ed.) *How to Use Corpora in Language Teaching*, Amsterdam: John Benjamins.

Salager-Meyer, F., Alcaraz Ariza, M. A. and Pabón, M. (2007) 'The prosecutor and the defendant: contrasting critical voices in French- and English-written academia book reviews', in K. Fløttum (ed.) *Language and Discipline Perspectives on Academic Discourse*, Newcastle: Cambridge Scholars Publishing.

Samraj, B. (2002a) 'Introductions in research articles: variations across disciplines', *English for Specific Purposes* 21: 1–17.

——(2002b) 'Texts and contextual layers: academic writing in content courses', in A. M. Johns (ed.) *Genre in the Classroom: Multiple Perspectives*, Mahwah, NJ: Lawrence Erlbaum Associates.

Sanderson, T. (2008) 'Interaction, identity and culture in academic writing: the case of German, British and American academics in the humanities', in A. Ädel and R. Reppen (eds) *Corpora and Discourse: The Challenges of Different Settings*, Amsterdam: John Benjamins.

Schleef, E. (2009) 'A cross-cultural investigation of German and American academic style', *Journal of Pragmatics* 41: 1104–24.

Schmitt, D. and Schmitt, N. (2005) *Focus on Vocabulary: Mastering the Academic Word List*, London: Longman Pearson.

Simpson-Vlach, R. (2006) 'Academic speech across disciplines: lexical and phraseological distinctions', in K. Hyland and M. Bondi (eds) *Academic Discourse Across Disciplines*, Bern: Peter Lang.

Sinclair, J. (2004) *How to Use Corpora in Language Teaching*, Amsterdam: John Benjamins.

Spack, R. (1988) 'Initiating ESL students into the academic discourse community: how far should we go?', *TESOL Quarterly* 22: 29–52.

——(1997) 'The acquisition of academic literacy in a second language: a longitudinal case study', *Written Communication* 14: 3–26.

Storch, N. and Tapper, J. (2009) 'The impact of an EAP course on postgraduate writing', *Journal of English for Academic Purposes* 8: 207–23.

Swales, J. (1981) *Aspects of Article Introductions*, Birmingham: Language Studies Unit, University of Aston.

——(1988) *Episodes in ESP*, Hemel Hempstead: Prentice Hall International.

——(1990) *Genre Analysis: English in Academic and Research Settings*, Cambridge: Cambridge University Press.

——(2004) *Research Genres: Explorations and Applications*, Cambridge: Cambridge University Press.

Swales, J., Ahmad, U. K., Chang, Y. Y., Chavez, D., Dressen, D. and Seymour, R. (1998) 'Consider this: the role of imperatives in scholarly writing', *Applied Linguistics* 19: 97–121.

Swales, J. M. and Feak, C. B. (2000) *English in Today's Research World: A Writing Guide*, Ann Arbor: University of Michigan Press.

Thompson, P. (2006) 'A corpus perspective on the lexis of lectures, with a focus on economics lectures', in K. Hyland and M. Bondi (eds) *Academic Discourse Across Disciplines*, Bern: Peter Lang.

Thompson, S. E. (2003) 'Text-structuring metadiscourse, intonation and the signalling of organisation in academic lectures', *Journal of English for Academic Purposes* 2: 5–20.

Uzuner, S. (2008) 'Multilingual scholars' participation in core/peripheral academic communities: a literature review', *Journal of English for Academic Purposes 7:* 250–63.

Wang, J., Liang, S.-I. and Ge, G.-C. (2008) 'Establishment of a medical academic word list', *English for Specific Purposes* 27(4): 442–58.

West, R. (1994) 'Needs analysis in language teaching', *Language Teaching* 27: 1–19.

Yang, R. and Allison, D. (2003) 'Research articles in applied linguistics: moving from results to conclusions', *English for Specific Purposes* 22: 365–85.

18

Language testing

Barry O'Sullivan

Overview

In this chapter I will present a broad overview of what I see as the critical issues currently engaging language testers. Limitations of space mean that the overview can be neither comprehensive nor in-depth. Nevertheless, I hope it encourages you to continue to explore this fascinating area.

Brief history of language testing

The Chinese included a significant language element in their Imperial Examination system which was used to identify suitable candidates for the empire's bureaucracy and lasted for over 1,500 years before its demise in 1905. Within a few years of this the first standardised test of language (actually of handwriting) was developed at Teachers College, Columbia University by Thorndike (1911). The methodology followed by Thorndike was soon replicated by Hillegas (1912) who devised the first standardised test of English composition. The development of the multiple choice format by Kelly (1915) revolutionised the newly emerging discipline. The linking of standardisation to this new methodology offered the opportunity, for the first time, for mass testing.

In 1913, the University of Cambridge Local Examinations Syndicate (UCLES) introduced the first formal test of English as a foreign language, the Certificate of Proficiency in English (CPE). The CPE was heavily influenced by Sweet's *The Practical Study of Languages: A Guide for Teachers and Learners* (1899) and was aimed at overseas learners who wished to study at UK universities. In the same year, the Association of Modern Language Teachers of the Middle States of Maryland set up a special committee to explore the potential for mass testing of modern languages. The so-called 1913 Committee recognised the need for the curriculum to drive the learning environment though they saw practical limitations to the direct testing of speaking and thus began the move from direct to standardised tests in the USA.

As language learning and teaching became an industry, more and more tests emerged on both sides of the Atlantic, each essentially following the tradition of testing which dominated its place of origin. The early post-World War II tests that were developed in the UK by

UCLES (such as the First Certificate in English) followed very much in the footsteps of the CPE, while the Test of English as a Foreign Language (TOEFL), which was introduced by Educational Testing Services (ETS) in the USA in 1964, was based on what Spolsky (1998) has called the psychometric-structuralist approach which had developed over the previous half century in the USA.

The TOEFL was a significant test in that it was the first major test of English for specific purposes and the first major international test – the earlier CPE and FCE were essentially general language tests and never really reached the same scale of population as achieved by the TOEFL, though they were to become major international tests in their own right by the late 1980s. By this time testing had begun to change, with a growing awareness of the need for domain-specific examinations built on the pioneering work of Swales (1971 for example) and others on the theory and practice of English for specific purposes (ESP). The TOEFL/FCE comparability study (Bachman *et al.* 1995) marked the high point of the psychometric-structuralist driven tests. Despite its flaws, the study had a major impact on the attitude of UK-based examination boards towards measurement (by which I mean the psychometric qualities of their examinations). By the end of that decade, most examination boards had begun to focus on the issue of accuracy (often referred to, mistakenly, as 'reliability' – a technical term which refers only to the internal consistency of a test paper), though the emphasis in the UK was always on content.

The main current issues in language testing

The nature of validity

At around the same time as Galton (1879) was championing the early use of more scientific methods of measurement in the UK, Edgeworth (1888: 600) began to explore the accuracy of subjective measurement, noting that 'the observations of the senses are blurred by a fringe of error and margin of uncertainty'. He went on to propose a procedure for computing test error based on 'that part of the Calculus of Probabilities which is known as the Theory of Errors'. Within less than two decades, Spearman (1904) wrote what Brennan (2001: 297) saw as the paper that 'launched measurement as a distinct field of inquiry'.

The growth of the testing industry in the USA in the early part of the twentieth century saw a significant rise in interest in the quality of the examinations being developed and by the middle of the century, the notions of validity and reliability (evidence that a test is measuring the trait or ability its developer claims to be its focus and the accuracy of this measure respectively) had been established (e.g. Cronbach and Meehl 1955; Loevinger 1957). At this time, criterion (comparison with other measures or descriptions of language), content (the actual content of the test in relation to a hypothesised model of language ability) and construct (i.e. the trait or ability being tested) were seen as distinct types of validity with developers typically establishing evidence of just one. Cureton (1950) and later Loevinger (1957) reconceptualised validity, setting the scene for others (particularly Messick 1975, 1980) to develop the unitary conceptualisation of validity which remains dominant to this day.

Test validation

While applied linguists have for some time recognised the multi-componentiality of language ability, efforts by language testers have yet to establish evidence of an interaction between the various components hypothesised to comprise this ability. Even the most promising of the models proposed as the basis of language tests (Bachman 1990) has failed to provide a meaningful basis for developing language tests, though Saville and Hargreaves (1999) adapted the model which they describe as 'supporting' the Cambridge ESOL examinations. McNamara (2003: 468) in particular has criticised Bachman's model as being 'essentially psychological' with no reference to the social context of language use, a view shared by Kramsch (1986, 1998), Young (2000) and Chalhoub-Deville (2003). O'Sullivan and Weir (2011) support this view, adding that:

> Bachman's model offered an impressive theoretical model of CLA, albeit with limitations in both its cognitive and social dimensions, which was potentially useful for academics in testing research, but it suffered in terms of its suitability for use as an operational framework by language testing practitioners.

The underlying theory of validity that drove Bachman's attempt to apply practices from educational measurement to language testing was provided by his interpretation of the work of Messick. Messick was the most influential of a group of theorists who argued that *construct* was central to any validity argument and that all other kinds of evidence should be regarded as contributing to our understanding of this construct. He also argued that validity could only be established through a systematically presented argument composed of evidence from a variety of sources, including the traditional elements such as criterion and content, while taking into consideration the social consequences of test use.

However, while the language testing community has long accepted the importance of the work of Messick and scholars such as Kane (1992), Mislevy *et al.* (2002, 2003) and Chapelle *et al.* (2008) have grappled with his ideas, they have been unable to offer an operational specification for test validation. The cognitive and social aspects of language which had been highlighted by O'Sullivan (2000a) were instrumental to the development by O'Sullivan and Weir of a validation framework for speaking in the early 2000s. This work was built upon by Weir

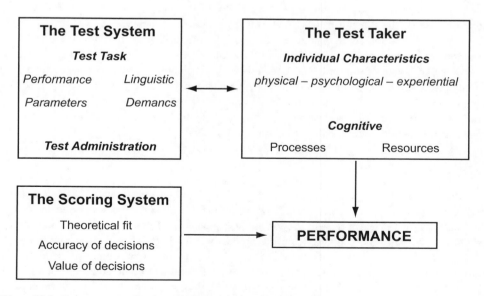

Figure 18.1 A reconceptualisation of Weir's socio-cognitive framework

(2005) to include all four skills. Detailed descriptions of the elements of the model can be found in Weir (2005).

In their most recent paper on the subject, O'Sullivan and Weir (2011) have begun to move away from the original model to a position taken by O'Sullivan over the past number of years. The reconceptualisation of the model suggested in this paper (presented here for the first time as Figure 18.1) suggests that the model should be reduced to three basic elements. These elements are briefly described in Table 18.1. The real strength of this model of validation is that it comprehensively defines each of its elements with sufficient detail as to make the model operationalisable and while much work is still needed to finalise this model (and in truth it may never be fully finalised), it has already been shown to offer a useful and practical approach to test development and validation (see O'Sullivan and Weir 2011).

Professionalisation

As language testing has developed over the past few decades it has grown into a clearly defined area of academic study in its own right, with a number of journals dedicated to the area (e.g. *Language Testing*, *Assessing Writing*, *Language Assessment Quarterly*). One result of this has been to broaden the appeal of the area so that its study has become an international affair. Examples of this can be seen in the growth of national and international associations such as the European Association for Language Testing and Assessment (EALTA) and the International Association of Language Testers (ILTA) and conferences such as the Language Testing Research Colloquium (international) and the Language Testing Forum (UK). At these events, it is not uncommon to have papers delivered on topics of current interest in a number of international contexts.

As these fora have emerged, the number of applied linguistics and English language teaching programmes that include language testing has grown across the world at undergraduate, postgraduate and research level. Together, these have prompted a growth in an awareness of the professional responsibilities of members of the profession and in the level of professionalism expected of test developers and researchers. Codes of Practice (from ILTA and EALTA for example) and of Ethics (again from ILTA) to help guide these practices.

However, there is still some disjuncture between the practice of testing and the theoretical discussions of academics. This has held back the profession, for example in the way academic theorists make apparently impractical demands of practitioners while at the same time not fully understanding that the realities of test development and practice perhaps require theories that are more operational in nature. While the approach to validation described above goes some way to meeting this requirement, it may well be that future developments can only happen with the cooperation of theorists and practitioners.

Localisation

Localisation refers to the recognition by developers of factors of the context and the test-taker which can impact on test performance. The importance of taking the context and test-taker into consideration is clearly seen in the validation framework (Table 18.1). If this model is to drive test development, we should begin the process by clearly defining the test taking population in terms of the three sets of characteristics (physical, psychological and experiential). We then turn to the ability we are attempting to test. At this point we should consider not only the details of language ability that will be our focus, but also the likely cognitive processing required for successful completion of the test. This of course means defining success – will it

Table 18.1 Model details

The test-taker

Individual characteristics	Physical	Includes things such as age and gender as well as both short-term ailments (such as cold, toothache, etc.) and longer-term disabilities (e.g. dyslexia, limited hearing or sight, etc.).
	Psychological	Includes things like memory, personality, cognitive style, affective schemata, concentration, motivation and emotional state.
	Experiential	Includes education (formal and informal) as well as experience of the examination and factors such as target language country residence.
Cognitive	Processes	Cognitive and metacognitive processing.
	Resources	Relates to knowledge of content and to language ability.

The test system

Test task	Performance parameters	These are parameters such as timing, preparation, score weighting, knowledge of how performance will be scored, etc.
	Linguistic demands	This refers to the language of the input and the expected language of the output and can also include reference to the audience or interlocutor where appropriate.
Test administration	Security	Refers to systems that are put in place to ensure the security of the entire administrative process.
	Physical organisation	Refers to room setup, etc.
	Uniformity	Systems to ensure that all administrations of the test are the same.

The scoring system

	Theoretical fit	The way in which test performance is assessed must fit with the conceptualisation of the ability being tested. This goes beyond a key or rating scale to inform the philosophical underpinning of rater and examiner selection, training and monitoring.
	Accuracy of decisions	Encapsulates the old idea of reliability, though broadening this to include all aspects of the psychometric functioning of a test.
	Value of decisions	This relates to criterion-related evidence such as comparison with measures such as teacher estimates, other test scores, performance standards such as the CEFR.

refer to answering a set of questions correctly (irrespective of how) or will it mean using a set of cognitive processes in such a way as to generate responses or performances that reflect 'real life' language use? The latter approach is the basis of the approach to validation suggested here, while the former typifies much past and current language testing practice.

This suggests that a test designed with no specific candidature in mind is unlikely to offer an appropriate measure of the language abilities required for a given context. For example, a university in the Middle East would be better served building the professional capacity to develop and validate its own exit test rather than rely on tests such as the International English Language Testing System (IELTS) or TOEFL Internet-based test (iBT) as these are designed to offer measures within a relatively narrow range of ability (likely to be beyond that of the current population) based on language needs identified in a very different context (i.e. university life in the UK or USA respectively). If international tests are to be used outside of their original specified domain then they really should be validated for such usage. This is rarely done; witness the use of IELTS for purposes other than which it was developed, discussed below.

Of course, tests developed for use in a local context are subject to the same requirements of consistency and accuracy as their international counterparts. While this can prove a challenge to institutions embarking on a development project, it should be noted that the figures published by large-scale international examination boards are typically based on very large and linguistically diverse populations. Since the estimates we use to establish consistency are affected by both number of items and range of candidate ability, it may well be that local developers are setting themselves unrealistic targets of consistency. Indeed, if international tests were administered to the same population as a local test it might well be the case that the difference in consistency is negligible, or at least significantly lessened.

As language testing becomes more professional and as levels of expertise grow and spread, there is increasingly less and less difference between local and international tests. This change has led to the final issue to be discussed here, that of fragmentation of the language testing industry.

Fragmentation

There has been evidence for some time now that the language testing industry is fragmenting. Not so long ago, test users looked almost exclusively to a handful of test providers in the USA and the UK. Nowadays, there are many more providers with a range of tests offering very different approaches. One interesting example of this is the Test of Interactive English (TIE – www.tie.ie) from Ireland. Here, test-takers first prepare a project on a self-selected topic, then read a self-selected book and finally follow a current news story (TV or newspaper). These activities are recorded in a logbook and form the basis of the test. While the format of the test is likely to limit its scope to that of a *niche* test, as candidates would need to attend a language school which takes the test as a focus for its courses, it is interesting to see how a non-traditional approach can result in a format that is radically different to that offered by major international developers. The test was originally designed to meet the needs of learners at a Dublin-based language school but its appeal has spread in recent years.

The tests provided by major international developers account for just a small (though important) proportion of the assessment carried out across the world, since the vast majority of language testing is classroom (i.e. learning domain) based (please note that I use the words testing and assessment interchangeably in this chapter though I recognise that some readers will have views as to the distinct meaning of each term). The type of testing and assessment carried out in this domain cannot be seen as adding to the fragmentation of the language testing industry. However, as educators gain more knowledge of how testing and assessment fits into the learning system, see Poehner (2008) on *dynamic assessment*, the perception that more locally appropriate assessment systems are needed grows.

Appropriacy, of course, has many guises. One rarely discussed aspect relates to the high cost of international examinations. In many emerging economies, this cost serves to disenfranchise a large proportion of the population. Abad Florescano *et al.* (2011) describe a project at the Universidad Veracruzana in which a set of affordable tests were developed specifically for less-well-off Mexican learners who were in a catch-22 situation in which they needed a recognised English language qualification to get a good enough job to be able to afford the English language qualification to get the job!

Fragmentation has both positive and negative effects. On the positive side, as the market fragments there are opportunities for developers who focus on very specific domains and contexts to offer tests that more closely fit the requirements of test users who are not looking to international work, travel or study situations. TIE is a good example of such a test. On the other hand, there are serious issues emerging regarding the issue of test quality, and in particular test level. Recent evidence from common European Framework of Reference (CEFR) linking projects (where developers attempt to establish an empirical link between their tests' cut scores and a specific CEFR level or levels) suggest that different developers interpret the CEFR levels differently and therefore the resultant tests cannot be shown to be at the level they purport to be (O'Sullivan and de Jong 2010).

Emerging debates

In this section I will outline some of the emerging debates in the area of language testing.

Assessment literacy

In the same way that test specifications are written with different audiences in mind (Alderson *et al.* 1995), different test stakeholders need to ensure that they have sufficient knowledge to support decisions they will be called on to make in their stakeholder role. Examples of what I mean include the test-taker, who is likely to be more concerned with the demands of the test than with its technical attributes. This latter level of knowledge is more appropriate for policy makers if they are to accredit tests that are suitable for purpose. An example of this is the recent discussion on the selection of English language tests for prospective students at UK-based colleges. Existing state bodies, such as the Qualifications and Curriculum Development Agency (QCDA) – whose remit it is to accredit examinations for use in the UK – appear unable to perform their role due to a critically inadequate level of assessment literacy. We can say essentially the same thing about almost all test stakeholders, and because of this it falls to language testing professionals to deliver stakeholder-specific information and training across society.

One of the key contributions made by Messick was his conceptualisation of the importance of social consequence to the valid use of tests in specific contexts. One aspect of test consequence is the misuse of tests by governments and institutions. Though I do not like to single out particular tests, I feel we should at this point focus on the IELTS, which was developed at Cambridge ESOL in the early 1980s as a tool to assess the language proficiency of students who were not native speakers of English and who wished to enter the United Kingdom to study. Two versions of the test are available, academic (for those who wish to study at tertiary level) and technical (for those pursuing non-academic training). Though the test was developed and validated with the above contexts in mind, the IELTS Website currently includes the claim that

> IELTS is a secure, valid and reliable test of real-life ability to communicate in English for education, immigration and professional accreditation.
>
> *(IELTS 2010)*

The lack of any information in the public domain regarding the validation of the IELTS for these additional uses and the implication that neither the government departments who recognise the IELTS for use (in contexts for which it was never intended) nor the developers (who are aware of this issue) perceive any need for the publication of this information speaks volumes for the need for greater levels of assessment literacy among test users.

The practice of making extravagant claims concerning the potential for tests to be used in contexts for which they were never intended is not, of course, limited to the IELTS. An even more obvious offender is the Test of English for International Communication (TOEIC), developed by ETS. The TOEIC is supported for its primary use by a sparse body of published research and is extremely limited in the language and contexts of language use it attempts to assess, yet it confidently claims that it is '[T]he global standard for measuring English language skills for business'.

Technical aspects

Stakeholders are beginning to understand more about the relevance of evidence-driven indicators of the level of language tests, thanks to some considerable extent to the influence of the CEFR and the Council of Europe's Manual for linking tests to the CEFR (Council of Europe 2003, 2009). Though the idea that test level is important has been recognised in the world of educational measurement for some time, it is really quite new to language testing. For example, if we look to Bachman's seminal work of 1990, there is no reference at all to either level or standards, nor is it mentioned in more recent leading language testing texts (e.g. Alderson *et al.* 1995; Brown 1996; Weir 2005). Test developers in Europe and beyond have tended to look to the CEFR when establishing evidence of the level of their products, though other standards such as the Canadian and Australian benchmarks have also been used as the basis of establishing test level. Developers are expected to establish this evidence using a systematic set of procedures in such a way as to ensure that the claims made are robust and transparent. The procedures set out in the Council of Europe's manual (2009) have been widely used, though not without criticism (O'Sullivan 2010).

One significant issue with the CEFR and other standards is the lack of sufficient detail necessary to adequately define a level for the purposes of test development, though interesting work has been done to date on the English Profile Project (EPP – www.englishprofile.org/) to identify specific features of language used at particular CEFR levels using advanced search engines and large corpora comprised of previously graded learners' written language (see Hawkins and Buttery 2009). However, even here there is some cause for concern as it is not certain that the levels identified by the EPP researchers truly reflect the CEFR levels. Recall the reference above to the growing debate on the interpretation of level by different test developers (O'Sullivan and de Jong 2010). The only way to fully assuage the concerns of testers across Europe is to broaden the scope of the corpora – in other words, use samples of learner language from a variety of different learning and assessment contexts.

Test theorists have got to come to terms with the need to consider level as a central aspect of development and validation. While I have set out a theoretical framework here (Table 18.1) and would suggest that level needs to be considered in each of the three aspects, much work is needed in the coming years to explore the practical delivery of tests developed with this model as a basis.

Assessment practice

There has been considerable growth in the use of English language tests for young and very young learners, in fact Khalifa *et al.* (2010) reported a population of 300,000 candidates for Cambridge ESOL's Young Learners English examinations. The majority of tests that exist tend to consist of a set of low-level tasks (in terms of cognitive load), the format of which reflects the more 'adult' or 'young adult' populations of the examination board's more traditional products. There are few examples of good practice in the area, though there has been one notable exception. This was an innovative test (entitled *The Stolen Elephant*) devised for 9-year-olds in Norway, in which the candidates were presented with a mystery in the form of a comic book. The apparent focus of the activity was to solve the mystery, though in doing so learners had to respond to a series of tasks; see Hasselgren (2000) for more details of this fascinating project.

While much excellent work has been done over the past decade on the discrete testing of grammar (in particular see Purpura 2004) we are still a long way from an empirically based model of grammar progression for learners. It should be recognised that such a progression is likely to be limited to suggesting rather than defining a pathway of progression. Projects using learner corpora, such as the EPP, aim to broaden our understanding of the receptive and productive skills and knowledge of language learners, and it is through this kind of work that researchers are beginning to discover the criterial differences between learners at different levels of language ability.

Corpus-based research on the nature and structure of spoken language has led to some exciting and potentially influential findings with regard to both grammar and fluency. Carter and McCarthy's (2006) grammar of spoken language pointed to a new understanding of the way in which we use language in different types of discourse. Recent research by McCarthy (2005) into the nature of fluency, suggests that we should also revisit the way in which this aspect of spoken language is assessed. McCarthy sees fluency in interactive discourse as being co-constructed by the participants in the interaction, an idea reflected in the concerns of McNamara (1997) who argued that meaning in interactive discourse emerges through the combined input of the interlocutors. The implication of these issues is that the discourse elicited from any individual is likely to be significantly affected by their interlocutor, suggesting that it could well change significantly in interactions with different interlocutors.

One of the arguments made in support of the paired format in tests of spoken language is that it facilitates the elicitation of a broader range of language functions than the interview format. While this is certainly the case (see O'Sullivan *et al.* 2002), the fact that variation in candidate performance due to affective reactions to the interlocutor-related (O'Sullivan 2000a, 2000b, 2002; O'Loughlin 2002), the format (Berry 2007) and the task topic (van Moere 2008) suggests that the format itself is essentially unstable. This instability, when considered in tandem with tester's questionable understanding of language accuracy and fluency (i.e. ignoring discourse type) and the co-constructed nature of interactive discourse, suggests that we should be extremely wary of using the paired or group format in our high stakes tests of speaking in the way we currently use the format. This might involve:

- the abandonment of the format entirely, though this will clearly result in a narrowing of the construct and a corresponding limitation to the generalisability of the test, or
- a review of how we use different tasks, for example we should consider using each task to evaluate separate aspects of a candidate's language; see Upshur and Turner's (1999) task-specific scales for example, though I am suggesting that we need different definitions of grammar and fluency depending on the discourse type.

Technology and language testing

I will initially focus on reviewing the impact of technology to date with regard to test design, development and delivery. Finally, I will briefly look at where technology is likely to have the most significant effect over the coming years.

Test design

One significant impact of new technology when it was first used by test developers was to limit the type of test tasks and items to those whose responses could be automatically read and transferred to datasets. However, as the technology improves, we are beginning to see a new generation of technology-driven tests (e.g. the Pearson Test of English) which are attempting to use technology in new ways. While the actual content of these new tests remains quite traditional, the fact that performance is assessed automatically by machine is certainly both innovative and controversial.

Automated assessment of writing has been the focus of intense research and interest since Page's (1968) Project Essay Grader (PEG). The current Pearson engine for assessing writing is based on an application of Latent Semantic Analysis (LSA), described by Landauer *et al.* (2004: 5214) as 'one of a growing number of corpus-based techniques that employ statistical machine learning in text analysis'. This (and other) automated scoring systems allow for what is known as a 'person-free' assessment of the written performance of learners and test-takers. Given the subjective and idiosyncratic of human ratings (see the work of Lumley (2005) and O'Sullivan (2008) who explored the nature of rating in tests of writing and the impact of interlocutor-related variables in testing speaking respectively), it is difficult to ignore the claims made by advocates of these automated systems, particularly when they report very similar outcomes to those of human raters but with much higher consistency (see, for example, Foltz *et al.* 2000). Clearly, we need to investigate the issue of human versus automated rating to understand better its impact on test validity.

Test development

Technology has also begun to find its way into the test development process. While we have used item banks for some years now (an item bank is a database of test items which have been tagged for things like difficulty, focus and descriptive data; see Vale [2007] for an overview), more recently, test developers have turned to the Web to access materials (e.g. reading and listening texts) as well as accessing Web-based research platforms.

I will use a case study to illustrate the point. When developing the vocabulary paper for the British Council's International Language Assessment (ILA), I used the online British National Corpus (BNC) as well as Tom Cobb's excellent *Compleat Lexical Tutor* Website. The combination of these two resources made it possible to develop an item type in which a set of words of a known frequency level were selected for a task that engaged the candidates in identifying both a synonym and a frequently occurring collocation for each word. Since the words to be matched with a target word were meant to occur less frequently than the target, the writing of the task would have been incredibly tedious without instant access to resources which allowed me to both check for frequency of all words and also identify the most frequently occurring collocation for that word.

Test delivery

Perhaps the most obvious change brought about by technology has been the development of computer adaptive tests (Davey and Pitoniak 2007). An adaptive test selects items from a bank in which the focus and difficulty of the items have been stored. Depending on the responses of the candidate on an initial group of items, another set of items are presented that are either harder or easier than the originals. This process continues until the candidate's responses stabilise on a set of items of a particular difficulty. Each test will differ in terms of specific content and in terms of time taken, as candidates will respond in different ways to the item sets.

In terms of the scoring of written responses, we have already seen how automated scoring is becoming a reality, and have also seen the introduction of technology to the scoring of hand-written responses. While some major examination boards have been exploring the feasibility of managing scripts online (and by this I mean they scan the original, save it as a PDF file, make it available online to raters for scoring and collect the score data also online), there is one excellent example of how such a system can be developed and sustained over time. The example I am referring to is the system devised for the CEPA English test in the United Arab Emirates. In operation now for several years, the CEPA system is an excellent example of what can be achieved with the intelligent use of technology; see Brown and Jaquith (2011).

Other changes have included the delivery of tests of speaking using computer technology (again see the Pearson Test of English in which the test performances are scored automatically) and the broader move towards the delivery of computer-assisted tests (where the actual test is a traditional stand-alone paper one, with only the delivery system changing from the traditional pen-and-paper) across more and more learning contexts.

The future?

Current approaches to the automated assessment of speaking are, like the *Ordinate Technology* that drives the Pearson Test of English, based on statistical predictions of performance based on word recognition, as well as locating and evaluating 'relevant segments, syllables and phrases in speech'. The system 'then uses statistical modelling technologies to assess the spoken performance' (Pearson 2007: 6). While the system appears to offer a significant advancement in automated scoring, it is still basically indirect in nature, and as such can only ever offer an estimate of ability. Voice recognition has come a long way over the past two decades, though it is still far from ready to allow for full comprehension even with training – though the training time has been greatly reduced under experimental conditions (the Human Languages Technology group at IBM is currently engaged in a broad range of research activities including natural language, speaker recognition and real-time translation of broadcast news). So, at some point in the not too distant future, we may be able to broaden the application of automated scoring of speaking to include automated direct measures of performance. However, even here there will be some issues related to the co-construction of discourse and meaning, suggesting that technology will continue to struggle with interactive dialogic communication.

Test developers urgently need to look at what computer-delivered tests can add to our understanding of the reading construct. In the absence of new item or task types, we need, for example, to consider things such as expeditious reading. Testing this using the pen-and-paper format is fraught with difficulties, owing not least to the lack of consistency shown by invigilators, though it is clear that the move to computer delivery should allow us to far more easily test this aspect of reading as we have full control over timing (for reading and responding to items).

On a slightly different note, I would like to end this section by referring to the continued impact on test development and validation practice of the Common European Framework of Reference for Languages (CEFR). The publication of the CEFR by the Council of Europe (2001) was followed by a set of suggested procedures for establishing evidence of a link between a test and a specific CEFR level (Council of Europe 2009). While this has been criticised (see, for example, Kantarcıoğlu et al. in press; O'Sullivan in press) it has been influential in leading thinking on the importance of standards in test development and theory.

The combination of factors discussed in this chapter, such as professionalisation, localisation and the CEFR have begun to change the face of testing. Nowadays, it is much more difficult to convince the education authorities in places such as Hungary that a test is valid for use in their jurisdiction than it is to get the same sanction for the UK.

Summary

Things are changing in language testing. Ever since Bachman (1990) presented his model of language ability and demonstrated how this could be used to support a language test which was designed to reflect the then current thinking in educational measurement, a new level of professionalism has emerged, with a growing worldwide cadre of scholars and practitioners with a level of technical expertise that far exceeds that of their predecessors. As testing knowledge spreads, people are beginning to realise that for *good* testing to happen, the domain to which it applies must be taken into consideration when interpreting the validation argument that accompanies it.

The implication here is that examinations are only of value if they are designed to be used in a specific domain. Until now, administrators and policy makers have argued, with a lot of success and some justification, that no local test could match the international examinations for quality. No longer. Nowadays, there are many examples of excellent local examinations in which the knowledge of the local domain (culture, language, society, etc.) contributes significantly to the format and contents of the test.

The process of *professionalisation* has led, over time, to one of test *localisation*. The latter process is the most significant current development in language testing, as it is based on the assumption (correct in my view) that in almost all circumstances, local tests are more likely to allow us to make more valid assumptions about test-takers than non-test-taker-specific competitors. While this has always been the case, the level of professionalism amongst local testers has begun to change dramatically (just look at the country of origin of most Ph.D. candidates in the USA and the UK over the past decade – you will find that they are almost all from places other than the USA and the UK).

All this has led to *fragmentation* in the language testing industry. There are still a number of big players, but they are competing for a limited (though large) market, which is defined by a small number of very specific domains – international business and country-specific higher education. As local expertise matures and confidence in localised solutions grows, this market will become ever more focused and local tests will begin to dominate specific markets.

Related topics

Since language testing builds on the research carried out across the areas of applied linguistics and SLA, almost any chapter in this volume will add insight for the test developer. In particular I would like to highlight the following chapters: corpus linguistics; English for academic purposes; language and culture; language learning and language education; psycholinguistics; SLA; technology and language learning

Further reading

Khalifa, H. and Weir, C. J. (2009) *Examining Reading: Research and Practice in Assessing Second Language Reading, Studies in Language Testing 29*, Cambridge: Cambridge University Press. (An excellent look at the testing of reading by a leading examining board and an equally interesting exemplification of Weir's (2005) validation framework for reading.)
Martyniuk, W. (ed.) (2010) *Relating Language Examinations to the Common European Framework of Reference for Languages: Case Studies and Reflections on the Use of the Council of Europe's Draft Manual*, Cambridge: Cambridge University Press. (A good overview of the sort of research and development work being undertaken across the world with regard to the CEFR and standard setting.)
O'Sullivan, B. (ed.) (2011) *Language Testing: Theories and Practices*, Basingstoke: Palgrave Macmillan. (A set of papers which offer a useful overview of the area, highlighting many of the issues discussed here.)

References

Alderson, J. C., Clapham, C. and Wall, D. (1995) *Language Test Construction and Evaluation*, Cambridge: Cambridge University Press.
Bachman, L. F. (1990) *Fundamental Considerations in Language Testing*, Oxford: Oxford University Press.
Bachman, L. F., Davidson, F., Ryan, K. and Choi, I. C. (1995) *An Investigation into the Comparability of Two Tests of English as a Foreign Language: The Cambridge-TOEFL Comparability Study*, Cambridge: Cambridge University Press.
Berry, V. (2007) *Personality Differences and Oral Test Performance*, Frankfurt: Peter Lang.
Brennan, R. L. (2001) 'An essay on the history and future of reliability from the perspective of replications', *Journal of Educational Measurement* 38(4): 295–317.
Brown, A. and Jaquith, P. (2011) 'The development and validation of an online rater training and marking system: promises and pitfalls', in B. O'Sullivan (ed.) *Language Testing: Theories and Practices*, Basingstoke: Palgrave Macmillan.
Brown, J. D. (1996) *Testing in Language Programs*, Upper Saddle River, NJ: Prentice Hall Regents.
Cambridge ESOL (2010) 'What is IELTS?' Available at: www.ielts.org/institutions/about_ielts.aspx (accessed 11 March 2010).
Carter, R. and McCarthy, M. (2006) *Cambridge Grammar of English: A Comprehensive Guide*, Cambridge: Cambridge University Press.
Chalhoub-Deville, M. (2003) 'Second language interaction: current perspectives and future trends', *Language Testing* 20(4): 369–83.
Chapelle, C. A., Enright, M. K. and Jamieson, J. (2008) *Building a Validity Argument for the Test of English as a Foreign Language*, New York: Routledge.
Council of Europe (2001) *Common European Framework of Reference for Languages: Learning, Teaching, Assessment*, Cambridge: Cambridge University Press.
——(2003) *Relating Language Examinations to the Common European Framework of Reference for Languages: Learning, Teaching, Assessment (CEF). Manual: Preliminary Pilot Version*. DGIV/EDU/LANG 2003, 5. Strasbourg: Council of Europe, Language Policy Division.
——(2009) *Relating Language Examinations to the Common European Framework of Reference for Languages: Learning, Teaching, Assessment: Manual*, Strasbourg: Council of Europe, Language Policy Division.

Cronbach, L. J. and Meehl, P. E. (1955) 'Construct validity in psychological tests', *Psychological Bulletin* 52: 281–302.

Cureton, E. E. (1950) 'Validity', in E. F. Lindquist (ed.) *Educational Measurement*, Washington, DC: American Council on Education.

Davey, T. and Pitoniak, M. J. (2007) 'Designing computerised adaptive tests', in S. M. Downing and T. M. Haladyna (eds) *Handbook of Test Development*, New York: Routledge.

Edgeworth, F. Y. (1888) 'The statistics of examinations', *Journal of the Royal Statistical Society* 1888: 599–635.

Educational Testing Services (2010) *TOEIC: Test of English for International Communication*. Available at: www.ets.org/toeic/ (accessed 18 April 2010).

Florescano, A. A., O'Sullivan, B., Chavez, C. S., Ryan, D. E., Lara, E. Z., Martinez, L. A. S., Macias, M. I. M., Hart, M. M., Grounds, P. E., Ryan, P. R., Dunne, R. A. and de Jesus Romero Barradas, T. (2011) 'Developing affordable "local" tests: the EXAVER project', in O'Sullivan, B. (ed.) *Language Testing: Theories and Practices*, Basingstoke: Palgrave Macmillan.

Foltz, P. W., Gilliam, S. and Kendall, S. A. (2000) 'Supporting content-based feedback in online writing evaluation with LSA', *Interactive Learning Environments* 8(2): 111–29.

Galton, F. (1879) 'Psychometric experiments', *Brain* 2: 149–62.

Hasselgren, A. (2000) 'Assessment of English ability in Norwegian schools', *Language Testing* 17 (2): 261–77.

Hawkins, J. A. and Buttery, P. (2009) 'Using learner language from corpora to profile levels of proficiency: insights from the English Profile Programme', in *Studies in Language Testing: The Social and Educational Impact of Language Assessment*, Cambridge: Cambridge University Press.

Hillegas, M. B. (1912) *A Scale for the Measurement of Quality in English Composition by Young People*, New York: Teachers College Press.

Jaquith, P. (2010) 'Time trials: an investigation of rater speed as a factor', Paper Presented at the Language Testing Research Colloquium, Cambridge.

Kane, M. T. (1992) 'An argument-based approach to validity', *Psychological Bulletin* 112(3): 527–35.

Kantarcıoğlu, E., Thomas, C., O'Dwyer, J. and O'Sullivan, B. (2010) 'The cope linking project: a case study', in W. Martiynuik (ed.) *Relating Language Examinations to the Common European Framework of Reference for Languages: Case Studies and Reflections on the Use of the Council of Europe's Draft Manual*, Cambridge: Cambridge University Press.

Kelly, F. J. (1915) *Kansas Silent Reading Test*, Topeka: Kansas State Printing Plant.

Khalifa, H., Ffrench, A. and Papp, S. (2010) 'The CEFR: its virtues and shortcomings when teaching and assessing young learners', Paper Presented at the Language Testing Research Colloquium, Cambridge.

Kramsch, C. (1986) 'From language proficiency to international competence', *Modern Language Journal* 70(4): 366–72.

——(1998) *Language and Culture*, Oxford: Oxford University Press.

Landauer, T. K., Laham, D and Derr, M. (2004) 'From paragraph to graph: latent semantic analysis for information visualization', *PNAS* 101(Suppl. 1): 5214–19.

Loevinger, J. (1957) 'Objective tests as instruments of psychological theory', *Psychological Reports, Monograph Supplement* 3: 635–94.

Lumley, T. (2005) *Assessing Second Language Writing: The Rater's Perspective*, Frankfurt: Peter Lang.

McCarthy, M. J. (2005) 'Fluency and confluence: what fluent speakers do', *The Language Teacher* 29(6): 26–8.

McNamara, T. (1997) '"Interaction" in second language performance assessment: whose performance?', *Applied Linguistics* 18(4): 446–66.

——(2003) 'Looking back, looking forward: rethinking Bachman', *Language Testing* 20(4): 466–73.

Messick, S. (1975) 'The standard program: meaning and values in measurement and evaluation', *American Psychologist* 30: 955–66.

——(1980) 'Test validity and the ethics of assessment', *American Psychologist* 35: 1012–27.

Mislevy, R. J., Steinberg, L. S. and Almond, R. G. (2002) 'Design and analysis in task-based language assessment', *Language Testing* 19(4): 477–96.

——(2003) 'On the structure of educational assessments', *Measurement: Interdisciplinary Research and Perspectives* 1(1): 3–62.

O'Loughlin, K. (2002) 'The impact of gender in oral proficiency testing', *Language Testing* 19(2): 169–92.

O'Sullivan, B. (2000a) 'Towards a Model of Performance in Oral Language Tests', Ph.D. thesis, University of Reading.

——(2000b) 'Exploring gender and oral proficiency interview performance', *System* 28(3): 373–86.

——(2002) 'Learner acquaintanceship and oral proficiency test pair-task performance', *Language Testing* 19(3): 277–95.

——(2008) *Modelling Performance in Oral Language Testing*, Frankfurt: Peter Lang.

——(2010) 'The city and guilds communicator examination linking project: a brief overview with reflections on the process', in W. Martyniuk (ed.) *Relating Language Examinations to the Common European Framework of Reference for Languages: Case Studies and Reflections on the Use of the Council of Europe's Draft Manual*, Cambridge: Cambridge University Press.

O'Sullivan, B. and de Jong, J. (2010) 'Interpreting the CEFR: are examination boards telling the same story?' Paper presented at the annual meeting of the British Association for Applied Linguistics Aberdeen, September.

O'Sullivan, B., Weir, C. J. and Saville, N. (2002) 'Using observation checklists to validate speaking-test tasks', *Language Testing* 19(1): 33–56.

O'Sullivan, B. and Weir, C. J. (2011) 'Language testing = validation', in B. O'Sullivan (ed.) *Language Testing: Theories and Practices*, Basingstroke: Palgrave Macmillan.

Page, E. B. (1968) 'The use of the computer in analyzing student essays', *International Review of Education* 14: 210–25.

Pearson (2007) PTE academic automated scoring, March 2009. Test documentation. Available at: www.pearsonpte.com/SiteCollectionDocuments/AutomatedScoringUK.pdf (accessed 5 May 2010).

Poehner, M. E. (2008) *Dynamic Assessment: A Vygotskian Approach to Understanding and Promoting L2 Development*, New York: Springer.

Poehner, M. E. and Lantolf, J. P. (2005) 'Dynamic assessment in the language classroom', *Language Teaching Research* 9(3): 1–33.

Purpura, J. (2004) *Assessing Grammar*, Cambridge: Cambridge University Press.

Saville, N. and Hargreaves, P. (1999) 'Assessing speaking in the revised FCE', *ELT Journal* 53(1): 42–51.

Spearman, C. (1904) 'The proof and measurement of association between two things', *American Journal of Psychology* 15: 72–101.

Spolsky, B. (1978) 'Language testing: art or science?', in G. Nickel (ed.) *Language Testing*, Stuttgart: HochschulVerlag.

Swales, J. (1971) *Writing Scientific English*, London: Thomas Nelson.

Test of Interactive English (2010) Test Website. Available at: www.tie.ie/index.htm (accessed 27 April 2010).

Thorndike, E. L. (1911) 'A scale for measuring the merit of English writing', *Science* 33: 935–8.

Upshur, J. A. and Turner, C. (1999) 'Systematic effects in the rating of second-language speaking ability: test method and learner discourse', *Language Testing* 16: 82–111.

Vale, D. (2007) 'Computerised item banking', in S. M. Downing and T. M. Haladyna (eds) *Handbook of Test Development*, New York: Routledge.

van Moere, A. (2008) 'Group Oral Tests: How Does Task Affect Candidate Performance and Test Scores?' Unpublished Ph.D. Thesis, Lancaster University, UK.

Weir, C. J. (2005) *Language Testing and Validation: An Evidence-Based Approach*, Basingstoke: Palgrave Macmillan.

Young, R. F. (2000) 'Interactional competence: challenges for validity', Paper Presented at the Language Testing Research Colloquium, Vancouver, Canada (March).

19

Classroom discourse

Amy B. M. Tsui

This chapter provides an overview of the emergence of classroom discourse research as a field of study, the major issues addressed, how the field has developed over time, its future development and the challenges it faces. The paradigm shift in theories of learning and its impact on classroom discourse research is highlighted. The term 'classroom discourse', as used in the chapter, encompasses linguistic as well as non-linguistic elements of discourse that occur in the classroom. The discussion focuses on second language (L2) and foreign language (FL) classroom research, and makes reference to first language (L1) classroom research only when it impacts on the latter.

History

Research on classroom discourse began in the early 1950s in the field of teacher education. It was initially motivated by the search for an 'objective' evaluation of classroom teaching through obtaining a factual record of pedagogical events which could, in turn, provide student teachers with feedback on their teaching competence. The evaluation and feedback focused on aspects of teacher behaviour related to learner performance. In order to achieve these objectives, tools for systematic observation of classroom interaction were proposed. One of the first and most widely adopted tools was Flanders' Interaction Analysis Categories (FIAC) (Flanders 1960). FIAC classifies classroom talk into teacher talk and student talk. Teacher talk is further categorized according to whether the teacher is exerting direct or indirect influence on students' behaviour, whereas student talk is further categorized into predictable and unpredictable responses. This kind of analysis provides an overall picture of the teaching patterns that occur in a lesson in terms of the proportions of teacher talk and student talk, direct and indirect teacher influence, and the types of student behaviour elicited by various teacher behaviours. Subsequent to FIAC, a large number of observation instruments were generated in the 1970s and 1980s, for teacher self-analysis and self-improvement.

Studies of L2/FL classroom teaching began in the 1960s, driven by the need to evaluate the effectiveness of the various FL teaching methodologies, with the aim of identifying the 'best' methodology. For example, the Pennsylvania Project set out to demonstrate the superiority of the audiolingual method over the traditional approach. The inconclusive findings, however, pointed to the problematic nature of the basic tenets of these studies (Allwright 1988). It was generally agreed that efforts to establish the superiority of one teaching methodology over another represented a simplistic view of classroom teaching processes and were unlikely to yield meaningful results. The aim of classroom-centred research, it was argued, should not be to prescribe the best method to teachers but to provide them with a detailed account of classroom teaching processes that focused on teaching styles, rather than teaching methods, and highlighted the relationship between teacher behaviour and learner achievements. Subsequently, classroom research shifted its focus from prescription to description. One could, however, argue that the intent was still largely prescriptive because the aim was to identify effective teaching styles that would lead to positive learning outcomes (Allwright 1988). Inspired by the work on systematic classroom observation in general education, a number of descriptive systems for L2/FL classrooms were proposed. FIAC was particularly influential because of its focus on the verbal behaviours of teachers and students. One of the earliest and most influential tools for L2/FL classroom observation tools was Moskowitz's Foreign Language Interaction (FLint), which extended FIAC to include interactional features characteristic of FL classrooms, such as the use of English (i.e. L1) instead of the target FL by the teacher (Moskowitz 1967).

Apart from general education research, L2 classroom discourse research was also influenced by L1 classroom discourse research that began in the 1960s as part of the *language across the curriculum* movement in Britain. The movement drew attention to the important role of language in education and a number of studies were conducted on L1 content classrooms. Particularly influential was the work of Barnes (1969) on the types of teacher questions (*open* versus *closed*; *pseudo* versus *genuine*), the types of learner responses elicited, the types of learner-talk (*exploratory* versus *final draft*) and the mental processes reflected by learner-talk.

Tools for teacher training purposes based on Flanders' work proliferated in the 1970s and 1980s, despite reservations about the underlying assumption of the causal relationship between teacher behaviour and learner achievement (Rosenshine 1970). During this period, descriptive systems proposed from alternative perspectives were also drawn on for analyzing L2/FL classroom discourse. One influential system was that proposed by Bellack *et al.* (1966), which aimed to understand how language was used to structure the classroom learning environment. Bellack *et al.*'s conception of classroom interaction as constituted by a finite set of pedagogical *moves*, namely structuring, soliciting, responding, and reacting, has been widely drawn on for analyzing the organization of classroom discourse. Another highly influential descriptive system was that proposed by Sinclair and Coulthard (1975) in their search for a descriptive model for the grammar of spoken discourse. Adopting Bellack *et al.*'s notion of *moves*, they provided a comprehensive account of all verbal elements of classroom discourse, and proposed a model of spoken discourse based on Halliday's categories of grammar (1961) in which discourse units, namely *acts*, *moves*, *exchanges*, and *transactions*, are organized in a hierarchical manner. The basic unit of organization in classroom discourse is the *exchange*, which consists of *initiating*, *responding*, and *follow-up moves* (IRF). Although this descriptive system was linguistically rather than educationally motivated, it has been widely adapted for the analysis of classroom discourse. A third influential system was that proposed by Fanselow (1977) for both teacher training and research purposes. Building on the work of Bellack *et al.*, Fanselow proposed an elaborate descriptive system, FOCUS (Foci for Observing Communications Used in Settings), which provides an account of five characteristics of a communicative event: source, medium, use, content, and pedagogical purpose. Fanselow maintained that this instrument would enable teachers, teacher trainers, supervisors and researchers to use a common language to provide a similar account of the same communicative event in both teaching and non-teaching settings.

The shift from a prescriptive to a descriptive orientation in classroom discourse analysis in the 1970s and 1980s resulted in more exploratory and explanatory investigations. Since then, considerable attention has been given to raising teachers' awareness of their own language use and how it affects learning opportunities (see, for example, Walsh 2006). (For an excellent review of classroom observation and descriptive instruments, see Allwright 1988.)

L2 classroom discourse studies conducted in the 1970s and 1980s focused mainly on the observables (i.e. what can be observed) in the classroom. By the late 1980s and early 1990s, it became clear that studies of the observables needed to be illuminated by the unobservables that also shaped classroom discourse. Researchers suggested that learners' participation in the classroom could be affected by their learning styles, psychological states, cultural backgrounds, and beliefs about classroom behaviour (Allwright and Bailey 1991; Tsui 1996). For example, studies of Asian learners' participation in multi-ethnic classrooms showed that they are, in general, less willing to volunteer answers and they take fewer turns than their non-Asian counterparts (Johnson 1995), and their observable behaviours are partly shaped by their cultural values and learning styles (Duff 2002). Similarly, the way in which teachers pose questions and provide feedback, and the kind of interaction they engage in with learners, is shaped by their conceptions of teaching and learning, and their lived experiences of classroom events.

Recognizing the importance of the unobservable dimensions of classroom discourse put into question the adequacy of descriptive tools that are *etic* (non-participant) in perspective and typically do not take context into account. Consequently, research methodologies in neighbouring disciplines have been appropriated. In particular, ethnographic approaches have become widely adopted. The most characteristic form of ethnographic research involves the researcher participating, overtly or covertly, in people's lives for an extended period of time, 'watching what happens, listening to what is said, asking questions – in fact, collecting whatever data are available to throw light on the issues that are the focus of the research' (Hammersley and Atkinson 1995: 1). However, as it is not always practicable to be a participant researcher, most classroom research aims to obtain an *emic* (participant) perspective on classroom processes through the collection of a variety of qualitative data, such as lesson plans, teachers' and learners' journals, interviews, and stimulated recall conducted with teachers and learners, in addition to recording classroom discourse data. Data on the wider educational and sociopolitical contexts that are relevant to the research focus are also collected and referenced in the interpretation of classroom discourse data, such as educational policy, school curriculum, the socioeconomic background of learners, and school culture (van Lier 1988; Johnson 1995; Bailey and Nunan 1996). Ethnomethodology, specifically Conversation Analysis (CA), has also been adopted to analyze classroom discourse data. For example, Seedhouse (2004) adopted a CA approach to the analysis of classroom discourse and pointed out that, similar to contexts in conversation, contexts in the classroom are not static throughout the whole lesson but fluid and mutually constructed by participants in the moment-to-moment development of the discourse (see also Markee 2008). He proposed a model in which classroom discourse data can be analyzed at three levels of context: micro discourse, L2 classroom, and institutional contexts. This model, according to Seedhouse, enables us to link the micro with the macro, and to see the specificity and diversity of instances of L2 classroom discourse at the micro level, as well as the commonalties between them at the macro level. Based on data from different L2 classroom contexts, he further demonstrated how the CA approach illuminates reflexivity of the interactional organization of classroom discourse, as managed by participants, and pedagogical focus. He cautioned, however, that the direct application of conversational structures to L2 classroom discourse structures may result in unintended interactional consequences that work against pedagogical efforts. For example, the application of preference organization in conversation (i.e. avoidance of direct and unmitigated negative evaluations) to the treatment of learners' errors may reinforce the perception that making errors is embarrassing and undesirable.

This brief review of the history of classroom discourse research shows that there has been considerable progress made in the field over the fifty years since its inception. From a relatively simplistic and reductionist view of classroom processes, research on classroom discourse has moved to a more holistic understanding of classroom processes as a constituent of the larger society. Accordingly, it has moved from decontextualized micro-level analyses from an 'etic' perspective, to an integration of micro and macro levels from an 'emic' perspective that draws on conceptual frameworks and research methodologies from a number of disciplines. In the ensuing discussion, I shall elaborate on this by outlining the major issues addressed, future developments, and the challenges faced by the field.

Major issues in classroom discourse research

Information-processing approach to classroom discourse research

Much of the early research on classroom discourse (conducted in the 1970s and 1980s) was guided by an information-processing theory of learning based on an input-output model that perceived learning as a process that takes place inside the head of the individual (see Ortega, this volume). The majority of the studies focused on the analysis of language input, interaction, and language output from an etic perspective, and a minimalist approach was adopted with regard to the role of context (for reviews of classroom discourse research, see Allwright 1988; Chaudron 1988; van Lier 1988; Allwright and Bailey 1991).

Studies of teachers' language input undertaken at that time were motivated by the belief that teachers' language use had a direct impact on learners' language output. One strand of research was teachers' comprehensible input. A number of studies found that linguistic modifications made by teachers were similar to those used by native speakers (NS) of the target language when talking to non-native speakers (NNS), referred to as 'foreigner talk'. Early studies focused on the linguistic features of teachers' modified speech (Gaies 1977; Chaudron 1982). Subsequent studies, however, pointed out that it was the linguistic modifications made by teachers in light of learners' responses that facilitated language learning. The research focus therefore shifted to the study of the modification of interactional structures as a result of the negotiation of meaning between the teacher and the learners, and the modification devices used by NSs in NS-NNS conversations, such as confirmation, clarification and comprehension checks (Long 1983; Varonis and Gass 1985).

Another strand of research on language input was the study of teachers' questions and their corrective feedback. *Referential* questions (analogous to Barnes' [1969] *genuine* questions) were found to elicit linguistically more complex learner responses than *display* questions (analogous to Barnes' *pseudo* questions) (Long and Sato 1983). Modifications of questions by teachers (both comprehension-oriented and response-oriented), and the impact of these modifications on students' responses were also investigated (Tsui 1995). The function of teacher feedback was reconceptualized from evaluation of learners' response to provision of information for learners to confirm or disconfirm their hypotheses about the target language. The notion of *error* was also reconceptualized from a developmental perspective (Allwright and Bailey 1991). More recent research has emphasized the importance of form-focused corrective

Amy B. M. Tsui

feedback and reformulations. The latter, which rephrase learners' utterances by correcting the errors without changing the meaning, are considered to facilitate learning (see papers collected in Doughty and Williams 1998). The research findings of the studies, however, have been inconclusive (Lightbown 2000).

A third strand of research was on the language output produced by learners. The lack of evidence that comprehensible input actually produced higher quality learner output led to the shift in focus from teachers' comprehensible input to learners' language output. Swain (1985) proposed the *Output Hypothesis*, which states that pushing learners to produce comprehensible as well as grammatically accurate output is equally, if not more, important for language acquisition. According to Swain, attention to output forces learners to process language at a deeper level and to notice the gaps in their interlanguage (i.e. an emerging linguistic system developed by learners in the process of learning L2/FL). Subsequently, a number of studies argued that when communication failure occurs or when learners are required to complete structured tasks involving information gaps, the process of negotiation of meaning connects input with output and enhances attention to linguistic form. As such, it is considered parti- cularly effective for language acquisition (see the *Interaction Hypothesis* proposed by Long 1996; see also papers collected in Doughty and Williams 1998). However, the findings of stu- dies on the relationship between negotiation of meaning and language acquisition have also been somewhat inconclusive.

In addition to the quality of language output, studies of learners' output also include lear- ners' turn-taking behaviour and the extent to which they participate orally in different class- room settings. Studies were conducted on learners who took more turns and those who took fewer turns, and their learning effectiveness (Seliger 1983). Subsequently, factors which impinge on learners' interactional behaviour, such as cultural background, learning arrangements (such as teacher-fronted versus pair or group work) and task types were also taken into consideration (see, for example, Doughty and Pica 1986; Plough and Gass 1993).

Sociocultural perspectives of classroom discourse research

In the 1990s, the shift in the research paradigm in general education from information pro- cessing to sociocultural theories of learning began to make an impact on L2 research (see papers collected in *Modern Language Journal*, vol. 78, 1994). This shift has led to a recon- ceptualization of language, context, and learning in profound ways. Sociocultural theories (SCT) of learning conceptualize the relationship between the learner and the social world as dialectical and mediated by cultural artefacts, among which language is primary. Learners are not just passive recipients of language input and teachers are not just providers of input. Rather, the learners, the teacher, and the sociocultural context in which the discourse takes place are constitutive of what is being learned (see Thorne and Tasker, this volume). Seen from this perspective, classroom discourse studies based on the input-output model present an impoverished and reductionist view of L2 learning (see papers collected in Lantolf and Appel 1994; and in Lantolf 2000).

Since the 1990s, an increasing number of studies have begun to examine classroom discourse more holistically from sociocultural perspectives of learning. Classroom discourse has been reconceptualized as a major semiotic resource that mediates learning in the classroom. Simi- larly, curriculum materials, pedagogical activities and tasks have been reconceptualized as semiotic resources rather than ways of packaging target language input (Tsui 2007). Key concepts in SCT have been used as interpretive frameworks for analyzing classroom discourse data, including the Vygotskian concepts of mediated learning, Zone of Proximal Development

(ZPD) and scaffolding (Bruner 1983). Several studies adopted the notion of scaffolded instruction in the learners' ZPD and concluded that scaffolding facilitates learning only if the teacher is sensitive to the learners' level of linguistic competence and the specific features of their interlanguage. The studies also pointed out that scaffolding can be mutual rather than unidirectional (i.e. from expert to novice), and that peer scaffolding can be highly effective, even among very young FL learners (Lantolf and Appel 1994). Adopting the notion of mediated learning, Swain (2000) extended the notion of *output* as external speech. She argued that external speech in collaborative dialogues is a powerful mediational tool for language learning because it not only encourages learners to reflect on what is said in language-related episodes, while still being oriented to making meaning, but also helps learners to monitor their own language use, to notice the gaps in their interlanguage, and to set goals for themselves.

Activity Theory, developed on Vygotsky's conception of mediated action as the unit of analysis for understanding human mental processes (Vygotsky 1978; Leont'ev 1978), has also been drawn on by a number of classroom discourse studies (see, for example, Lantolf and Appel 1994). According to Leont'ev (1978), goal-oriented human action is part of a larger activity and is shaped by the broader sociocultural system in which the activity is situated. The individual's participation in these socially meaningful activities is mediated by the cultural tools that he or she appropriates. In the course of the interaction, the cultural tools, the nature of the activity, and the modes of participation are transformed. The same activity may be realized by different actions mediated by different tools; conversely, the same action may be driven by different motives, hence realizing different activities (see also Engeström 1999). According to this perspective of learning, the same learning task may be operationalized as different learning activities with different goal-oriented actions by different learners, and by the same learner in different contexts (see also Thorne and Tasker, this volume). From this theoretical perspective, the discourse that emerges in task completion plays an important part in shaping the way learners orient themselves to the task and to each other. Hence, it is the agency of learners in terms of the way they orient themselves to the task, not the task per se, that determines the way the task will be performed and the learning that will take place. Tasks should therefore be understood as emergent interactions and not as the packaging of language input. An example of a classroom discourse study that draws on Activity Theory is Nassaji and Wells (2000), in which spoken discourse is seen as a mediating tool through which the goal of an activity system is achieved, and units of discourse are identified according to their role in advancing the goal of an activity system in the classroom.

Also working within the sociocultural paradigm, a number of researchers have adopted an ecological perspective of language learning. For example, van Lier (2000) argued for the totality of the relationships between the learner and all other elements or participants in the context with which he or she interacted. He proposed *affordance* as an alternative conception of *input* and pointed out that the environment makes available opportunities for learners to engage in meaning-making activities with others (a *semiotic budget*), and what is perceived as relevant and acted on by the learner becomes an affordance. In other words, input has been reconceptualized as the linguistic affordances perceived and used by the learner for linguistic action. Input is therefore not something standing outside the learner waiting to be acquired, but rather the interaction between the learner and the environment.

Classroom discourse research has also begun to draw on social theories of learning which are sociocultural in orientation (Lave and Wenger 1991; Wenger 1998). For example, Donato (2004) distinguished the notion of *interaction* used in the second language acquisition (SLA) literature from the notion of *collaboration* used in social theory of learning. The latter entails mutual engagement of participants in a joint enterprise that is socially meaningful to them. He drew attention to the relational dimension of collaboration, which takes time to develop, and argued that the analysis of discourse generated by isolated task completion by group members new to group work does not capture the reality of how learning is co-constructed in collaborative work. Drawing on the notions of *community of practice* and *legitimate peripheral participation* (Lave and Wenger 1991), Donato maintained that the value of collaboration lies in helping novices to move from peripheral to full participation as competent members in their communities of practice. Also drawing on the notion of learning as moving from peripheral to fuller participation, Young and Miller (2004) examined students' changing participation in discursive practice in writing conferences.

The notion that the classroom is a community of practice and that learners construct identities as they engage in the processes of classroom discourse, has also begun to receive attention in recent years (see Norton, this volume). For example, Duff (2002) investigated the co-construction of cultural identity in classrooms where learners were linguistically and socio-culturally heterogeneous. Richards (2006) argues that in classroom talk, similar to other forms of talk, it is through the moment-to-moment development of interaction that the membership categories, and hence the identities of the participants, are constructed. He shows that classroom discourse features are reflective of the negotiation of different types of identity between the teacher and the students, as well as among students themselves.

Finally, the emphasis on a holistic view of classroom discourse has drawn researchers' attention to a relatively neglected, but by no means less important, aspect of classroom discourse: what is referred to as 'what happens in the margins of instructional conversations' by Bannink and van Dam (2006: 284). This includes silences, disruptions, laughter, and time-out, as well as the non-verbal, prosodic and paralinguistic features of talk. Bannink and van Dam argue that these features are important because they affect what is taught and what is learnt, and can lead to empowerment or disempowerment of learners. They argue that classroom discourse should take into account the multimodal participation of all parties, with their multiple agendas and roles. Furthermore, they maintain that the discursive contexts and interactional conditions that mediate learning should be articulated for teacher education purposes. The challenge is, as they point out, how the context-sensitive and situated nature of interactions among multiple participants in the classroom can be adequately captured, and how these events can be made analytically transparent.

Critical approaches to classroom discourse analysis

A holistic approach to classroom discourse analysis involves situating the classroom in the larger context of society and seeing classroom processes as shaped by pedagogical concerns as well as by broader social, economic, political, and cultural forces. Kumaravadivelu (1999) proposed a critical approach to classroom discourse analysis based on poststructuralist (e.g. Foucault 1972) and postcolonialist (e.g. Said 1978) perspectives of discourse. He maintained that analyses of classroom discourse should capture not only its sociolinguistic dimension but also its sociocultural and sociopolitical dimensions. He suggested critical ethnography as the research tool to unravel the 'hidden meanings and underlying connections' in classroom discourse 'through posing questions relating to ideology, power, knowledge, class, race and gender' (1978: 476). An example of recent work adopting this approach is Menard-Warwick (2008), who looks at the issue of gender and social positioning in an ESL course for adult immigrants. By examining linguistic and interactional structures, she shows the tension between the identities that the female immigrant learners claimed for themselves as competent members of the community and the gendered social identities that are assigned to them by their teacher. She argues that teachers should listen for and support learners' reflexive positioning, in order to facilitate their reconstruction of L2 identities and voices (see also Richards 2006).

Another example of a study that has given voice to students is Fisher and Larkin (2008), which investigates student and teacher perceptions of talk in school through questionnaire surveys with over 180 primary pupils and through focus group interviews with over sixty of these, as well as interviews with eight teachers. The findings show that the pupils had very different views from their teachers with regard to what they perceived was expected of them and what constituted good talk. While all teachers mentioned *confidence* as being an important aspect of pupil talk, the pupils saw the teacher being in control of the expected amount, manner, and topic of talk, and the need for them to conform to these expectations. Fisher and Larkin observe that because of the unequal power relationship in the classroom, teachers should reassess their expectations of the rules of participation and value the skills and knowledge that young children bring to school. Whether classroom discourse processes empower or disempower learners, and whether learners' voices are heard and respected, are central concerns in critical classroom discourse analysis. To date, these concerns have been much neglected, not least because of the asymmetrical power relationship between the teacher and the students in the classroom.

Future developments

Since the 1990s, research on classroom discourse has advanced the field in several respects. First, as we have seen, there has been an emphasis on context, an aspect which was minimalized in the 1970s and 1980s. Moreover, instead of focusing on specific aspects of classroom interaction, research has taken a more holistic view of classroom interaction, integrating micro and macro analyses and attending to multiple dimensions of context and multiple levels of discourse in the classroom. Critical classroom discourse analysis will continue to receive attention, and issues such as power, identity, culture, and gender, as (co)constructed in the classroom, and the impact these issues have on learner (dis)empowerment and opportunities for learning will continue to receive attention (see Norton, this volume).

Second, the theoretical frameworks drawn from neighbouring disciplines to illuminate the complexity of classroom discourse data will continue to widen. For example, Lantolf (2000) advocates a pluralistic approach to SLA, and the papers collected in that edited volume brought together the work of Vygotsky and Bakhtin, social philosophers such as Bourdieu and Habermas, cognitive psychologists such as Rommeveit, and psychologists such as Gibson, Bateson, and Bronfrenbrenner. Van Lier (2000) proposed that the input-output model should be replaced by an ecological perspective. This was echoed by Kramsch (2002), who considered an ecological approach to language learning a powerful way of capturing the symbiotic relationship between the language user and the environment (see also van Lier 2004). This approach is considered to reconcile the tension between language acquisition and language socialization, and offers a new way of bringing together theoretical frames from other disciplines to enhance our understanding of the complexities of classroom discourse. In the collection of chapters in Kramsch (2002), concepts in sociology, such as Goffman's frame analysis and participatory structures (Goffman 1974, 1981), have been adopted to analyze the multiple discourse units and levels recursively embedded in classroom discourse, and the variety of speaker and addressee roles. Marton and Tsui (2004), building on the theory of variation in learning in phenomenography, have explored how classroom discourse in a variety of classrooms, including L2, can shape learners' awareness of the critical features of the object of learning and how dimensions of its critical features can be varied to bring about learning. Efforts to unravel the cultural, institutional, and interactional dimensions of the contexts in which classroom discourse are situated, in order to gain a deeper understanding of its mediating role in learning, will continue.

Third, classroom discourse studies will increasingly adopt eclectic research methodologies. For example, Young (2009) has adopted analytic tools from three different theoretical frameworks, namely systemic functional linguistics, social theory of learning and ethnomethodology, to analyze discursive practices of learners and instructors. Markee (2008) has also demonstrated how conversational analysis tools can be used to analyze classroom discourse data from an SLA perspective (see also Nassaji and Wells 2000).

Finally, the teachers' and the learners' voices in the analysis of classroom discourse data is still under-explored. This is an important area of inquiry not only because both teachers and learners should be aware of the implications of the classroom discourse that they are co-constructing, but also because both voices provide an emic perspective on the data. In particular, as Cazden points out, classroom discourse should be the object of focal attention for students, as well as teachers, because 'all students' public words become part of the curriculum for their peers' (2001: 169).

Challenges in classroom discourse research

Classroom discourse research has made significant progress in illuminating our understanding of the complex interplay between factors that impinge on what appear to be simple classroom interchanges. Research in the 1970s and 1980s placed classroom discourse data at the centre of inquiry and studies were typically 'data-heavy but theory-light' (Donato 2004: 299). However, the last decade has seen more attention being given to theoretical motivation. The appropriation of theoretical frameworks from neighbouring disciplines has enriched our understanding of classroom discourse, and the adoption of their research methods has introduced more rigour into the investigations. These achievements notwithstanding, the field is faced with a number of challenges. I shall only attempt to outline a few obvious ones in this concluding section.

First, as the field draws on theoretical concepts from a variety of disciplines, it is important to ensure that these concepts are explicitly and rigorously defined, with full awareness of their theoretical assumptions, irrespective of whether they have been adopted wholesale, extended or redefined. There does seem to be a potential danger that the same terminology may be used with different theoretical assumptions in the discussions. For example, the term *community* has been used by different researchers in different ways, and the term *community of practice* has been adopted without regard to the way it was originally defined by Lave and Wenger (1991) and Wenger (1998) (see papers collected in Zuengler and Mori 2002). There is also a tendency to adopt uncritically some of the key notions in other disciplines. For example, the notion of scaffolding might be accepted uncritically as assistance that necessarily leads to more effective learning. As research on learning has shown, scaffolded instruction may not facilitate learning; in fact over-scaffolding may even inhibit learning. Another example is the notion of collaboration, which has been taken as the corollary of interaction. As Donato (2004) points out, not all forms of classroom interaction are collaborative and conducive to the development of discourse competence.

Second, as the field adopts an eclectic approach to research methodologies, there could be a tendency to adopt methodologies without understanding their origins and theory-method relationships. In this regard, the special issue of Zuengler and Mori (2002), which was devoted to methodological approaches in the micro-analysis of classroom discourse, was necessary and timely. It presented a collection of papers containing exemplars and critiques of three influential and well-defined methodologies, within which classroom discourse analysis had been conducted: ethnography of communication; conversation analysis; and systemic functional linguistics (which emerged respectively from anthropology, sociology, and linguistics). More discussion of this kind is necessary to move the field forward.

Third, the analysis of classroom discourse as situated in its sociohistorical context typically involves an eclectic approach in data collection from different sources over a period of time. A rigorous analysis of data requires an iterative process of data interpretation and theory generation, which is extremely time-consuming. It is often difficult to present a full account of the research processes within the word limit of a journal article (see, for example, the exemplars of research methodologies presented in Zuengler and Mori 2002), and an abbreviated report often fails to do justice to the complex processes involved in data collection and interpretation. This is probably one of the reasons why, as Donato (2004) points out, research studies from a sociocultural perspective are rich in theoretical concepts but thin on data.

Finally, similar to all educational research, most classroom discourse studies are motivated by the ultimate goal of improving student learning. Yet, as we have seen in this review, classroom processes are highly complex, and the large number of mediating variables makes it difficult to substantiate claims made about the relationship between language learning and the data analyzed. This is also why the findings of research studies relating classroom discourse to SLA have so far been inconclusive. Nevertheless, this has not stopped researchers from exploring this area. The conflicting findings of the effect of form-focused corrective feedback, such as focused recasts, on learners' output have led researchers to investigate other effective strategies. For example, Ellis *et al.* (2001) proposed that pre-emptive rather than corrective focus on form by the learner was more likely to result in learner uptake. Similarly, the inconclusive relationship between negotiation of meaning and language acquisition has led to more recent studies on the relationship between the two. Foster and Ohta (2005) find that with supportive peer assistance, learners engaged in output modification and form-focused negotiation even when they were not required to fill information gaps or repair communication breakdowns. The challenge is for teachers to interpret judiciously the findings of these studies in the specific contexts in which they operate.

Summary

In this chapter I have reviewed the emergence of classroom discourse analysis as a field of study in the 1960s and how it has developed in the last fifty years. We have seen that the shift from a prescriptive to a descriptive approach to classroom discourse research in the 1980s was an important phase in its development in that it resulted in a number of studies which revealed the complexities of classroom processes. The shift from information-processing to sociocultural theories of learning in the 1990s was also an important landmark in that more recent studies have taken a more holistic view of classroom processes. This has led to the adoption of an eclectic approach to research methodologies and theoretical frameworks, which have illuminated and will continue to shed light on our understanding of the dialectical relationship between classroom discourse, discourse participants, and context.

Related topics

discourse analysis; identity; institutional discourse; second language acquisition; sociocultural and cultural-historical theories of language development; systemic functional linguistics

Further reading

Marton, F. and Tsui, A. B. M. (with contributions from Chik, P., Ko, P. Y., Lo, M. L., Mok, I., Ng, F. P., Pang, M. F., Pong, W. Y. and Runnesson, U.) (2004) *Classroom Discourse and the Space of Learning*, Mahwah, NJ: Lawrence Erlbaum Associates. (This is the first volume that attempts to apply the theory of variation in phenomenography to investigage how classroom discourse can be either expansive or restrictive in bringing about learning.)

Seedhouse, P. (2004) *The Interactional Architecture of Second Language Classroom: A Conversational Analysis Perspective*, Oxford: Blackwell. (This volume draws heavily on the methodological tools of ethnomethodogy in the analysis of the organization of classroom discourse in relation to pedagogical focus across a range of L2 classrooms.)

van Lier, L. (2004) *The Ecology and Semiotics of Language Learning: A Sociocultural Perspective*, Boston: Kluwer Academic. (In this volume van Lier provides an overview of an ecological world view and how it could provide a coherent framework for making sense of language learning and language teaching processes at both micro and macro levels.)

Young, R. (2009) *Discursive Practice in Language Learning and Teaching*, Malden, MA/Oxford: Wiley-Blackwell. (The volume draws on ethnomethodology, social theory of learning as participation, and systemic linguistics in the elucidation of a discourse inside and outside the classroom.)

References

Allwright, D. (1988) *Observation in the Language Classroom*, London: Longman.

Allwright, D. and Bailey, K. M. (1991) *Focus on the Language Classroom*, New York: Cambridge University Press.

Bailey, K. M. and Nunan, D. (eds) (1996) *Voices from the Language Classroom*, New York: Cambridge University Press.

Bannink, A. and van Dam, J. (2006) 'A dynamic discourse approach to classroom research', *Linguistics and Education* 17: 283–301.

Barnes, D. (1969) 'Language in the secondary classroom', in D. Barnes, J. Britton and H. Rosen (eds) *Language, the Learner and the School*, Harmondsworth: Penguin.

Bellack, A., Kliebard, H., Hyman, R. and Smith, F. (1966) *The Language of the Classroom*, New York: Teachers' College Press.

Bruner, J. S. (1983) *Child's Talk: Learning to Use Language*, New York: Norton.

Cazden, C. (2001) *Classroom Discourse: The Language of Teaching and Learning*, 2nd edn, Portsmouth, NH: Heinemann.

Chaudron, C. (1982) 'Vocabulary elaboration in teachers' speech to L2 learners', *Studies in Second Language Acquisition* 4: 170–80.

——(1988) *Second Language Classrooms*, New York: Cambridge University Press.

Donato, R. (2004) 'Aspects of collaboration in pedagogical discourse', *Annual Review of Applied Linguistics* 24: 284–302.

Doughty, C. and Pica, T. (1986) '"Information gap" tasks: do they facilitate second language acquisition?', *TESOL Quarterly* 20: 305–25.

Doughty, C. and Williams, J. (eds) (1998) *Focus on Form in Classroom Second Language Acquisition*, Cambridge: Cambridge University Press.

Duff, P. A. (2002) 'The discursive co-construction of knowledge, identity, and difference: an ethnography of communication in the high school mainstream', *Applied Linguistics* 23(3): 289–322.

Ellis, R., Basturkmen, H. and Loewen, S. (2001) 'Preempting focus on form in the ESL classroom', *TESOL Quarterly* 35(3): 407–32.

Engeström, Y. (1999) 'Activity theory and individual and social transformation', in Y. Engeström, R. Miettinen and R.-L. Punamäki (eds) *Perspectives on Activity Theory*, New York: Cambridge University Press.

Fanselow, J. (1977) 'Beyond Rashomon: conceptualizing and describing the teaching act', *TESOL Quarterly* 11(1): 17–39.

Fisher, R. and Larkin, S. (2008) 'Pedagogy or ideological struggle? An examination of pupils' and teachers' expectations for talk in the classroom', *Language and Education* 22(1): 1–16.

Flanders, N. A. (1960) *Interaction Analysis in the Classroom: A Manual for Observers*, Ann Arbor: University of Michigan Press.

Foster, P. and Ohta, A. S. (2005) 'Negotiation for meaning and peer assistance in second language classrooms', *Applied Linguistics* 26(3): 402–30.

Foucault, M. (1972) *The Archaeology of Knowledge and the Discourse on Language*, New York: Pantheon Books.

Gaies, S. (1977) 'The nature of linguistic input in formal second language learning: linguistic and communicative strategies in ESL teachers' classroom language', in H. D. Brown, C. A. Yorio and R. H. Crymes (eds) *On TESOL '77*, Washington, DC: TESOL.

Goffman, E. (1974) *Frame Analysis: An Essay on the Organization of Experience*, New York: Harper and Row.

——(1981) *Forms of Talk*, Oxford: Blackwell.

Halliday, M. A. K. (1961) 'Categories of the theory of grammar', *WORD* 17(3): 241–92.

Hammersley, M. and Atkinson, P. (1995) *Ethnography: Principles in Practice*, 2nd edn, London: Routledge.

Johnson, K. (1995) *Understanding Communication in Second Language Classrooms*, New York: Cambridge University Press.

Kramsch, C. (2002) 'Introduction: "How can we tell the dancer from the dance?"', in C. Kramsch (ed.) *Language Acquisition and Language Socialization: Ecological Perspectives*, London: Continuum.

Kumaravadivelu, B. (1999) 'Critical classroom discourse analysis', *TESOL Quarterly* 33: 453–84.

Lantolf, J. P. (2000) 'Introducing sociocultural theory', in J. P. Lantolf (ed.) *Sociocultural Theory and Second Language Learning*, Oxford: Oxford University Press.

Lantolf, J. P. (ed.) (1994) *Modern Language Journal*.

Lantolf, J. P. and Appel, G. (eds) (1994) *Vygotskian Approaches to Second Language Research*, Norwood, NJ: Ablex.

Lave, J. and Wenger, E. (1991) *Situated Learning: Legitimate Peripheral Participation*, New York: Cambridge University Press.

Leont'ev, A. N. (1978) *Activity, Consciousness, and Personality*, Englewood Cliffs, NJ: Prentice Hall.

Lightbown, P. M. (2000) 'Anniversary article: classroom SLA research and second language teaching', *Applied Linguistics* 21(4): 431–62.

Long, M. (1983) 'Native-speaker/non-native speaker conversation and the negotiation of comprehensible input', *Applied Linguistics* 4: 126–41.

——(1996) 'The role of the linguistic environment in second language acquisition', in W. C. Ritchie and T. K. Bhatia (eds) *Handbook of Second Language Acquisition*, San Diego, CA: Academic Press.

Long, M. H. and Sato, C. (1983) 'Classroom foreigner talk discourse: forms and functions of teachers' questions', in H. W. Seliger and M. H. Long (eds) *Classroom-oriented Research in Second Language Acquisition*, Rowley, MA: Newbury House.

Markee, N. (2008) 'Towards a learning behaviour tracking methodology for CA-for-SLA', *Applied Linguistics* 29(3): 404–27.

Marton, F. and Tsui, A. B. M. (2004) *Classroom Discourse and the Space of Learning*, Mahwah, NJ: Lawrence Erlbaum Associates.

Menard-Warwick, J. (2008) '"Because she made beds every day": social positioning, classroom discourse, and language learning', *Applied Linguistics* 29(2): 267–89.

Moskowitz, G. (1967) 'The FLint system: an observational tool for the foreign language class', in A. Simon and E. G. Boyer (eds) *Mirrors for Behaviour: An Anthology of Classroom Observation Instruments*, Philadelphia, PA: Center for the Study of Teaching, Temple University.

Nassaji, H. and Wells, G. (2000) 'What's the use of "triadic dialogue"? An investigation of teacher-student interaction', *Applied Linguistics* 21(3): 376–406.

Plough, I. and Gass, S. (1993) 'Interlocutor and task familiarity: effects on interactional structure', in G. Crookes and S. Gass (eds) *Tasks and Language Learning: Integrating Theory and Practice*, Clevedon: Multilingual Matters.

Richards, K. (2006) '"Being the teacher": identity and classroom conversation', *Applied Linguistics* 27(1): 51–77.

Rosenshine, B. (1970) 'Interaction analysis: a tardy comment', *Phi Delta Kappan* 51: 445–6.

Said, E. W. (1978) *Orientalism*, New York: Pantheon Books.

Seedhouse, P. (2004) *The Interactional Architecture of Second Language Classroom: A Conversational Analysis Perspective*, Oxford: Blackwell.

Seliger, H. W. (1983) 'Learner interaction in the classroom and its effect on language acquisition', in H. W. Seliger and M. H. Long (eds) *Classroom-oriented Research in Second Language Acquisition*, Rowley, MA: Newbury House.

Sinclair, J. and Coulthard, R. M. (1975) *Towards an Analysis of Discourse: The English Used by Teachers and Pupils*, London: Oxford University Press.

Swain, M. (1985) 'Communicative competence: some roles of comprehensible input and comprehensible output in its development', in S. M. Gass and C. G. Madden (eds) *Input in Second Language Acquisition*, Rowley, MA: Newbury House.

——(2000) 'The output hypothesis and beyond: mediating acquisition through collaborative dialogue', in J. P. Lantolf (ed.) *Sociocultural Theory and Second Language Learning*, Oxford: Oxford University Press.

Tsui, A. B. M. (1995) *Introducing Classroom Interaction*, London: Penguin.

——(1996) 'Reticence and anxiety in second language learning', in K. Bailey and D. Nunan (eds) *Voices from the Language Classroom*, New York: Cambridge University Press.

——(2007) 'Classroom discourse as a semiotic resource for EFL learning', *The Language Teacher* 31(7): 13–16.

van Lier, L. (1988) *The Classroom and the Language Learner*, London: Longman.

——(2000) 'From input to affordance: social-interactive learning from an ecological perspective', in J. P. Lantolf (ed.) *Sociocultural Theory and Second Language Learning*, Oxford: Oxford University Press.

——(2004) *The Ecology and Semiotics of Language Learning: A Sociocultural Perspective*, Boston: Kluwer Academic.

Varonis, E. M. and Gass, S. (1985) 'Nonnative/nonnative conversations: a model for negotiation of meaning', *Applied Linguistics* 6: 71–90.

Vygotsky, L. S. (1978) *Mind in Society: The Development of Higher Psychological Processes* Cambridge, MA: Harvard University Press.

Walsh, S. (2006) *Investigating Classroom Discourse*, London and New York: Routledge.

Wenger, E. (1998) *Communities of Practice: Learning, Meaning and Identity*, Cambridge: Cambridge University Press.

Young, R. (2009) *Discursive Practice in Language Learning and Teaching*, Malden, MA/Oxford: Wiley-Blackwell.

Young, R. and Miller, E. (2004) 'Learning as changing participation: discourse roles ESL writing conferences', *The Modern Language Journal* 88: 519–35.

Zuengler, J. and Mori, J. (eds) (2002) (special issue) *Applied Linguistics*, 23(3).

20

Language socialization

Agnes Weiyun He

Introduction

Language socialization is a research tradition that is rooted in linguistic anthropology and that considers language not as a formal code, a medium of communication or a repository of meaning, but as a semiotic resource for 'invoking social and moral sentiments, collective and personal identities tied to place and situation, and bodies of knowledge and belief' (Ochs and Schieffelin 2008: 8). In this view, all communicative forms, including lexico-grammar, prosody, speech styles and genres, turn-taking structures and sequences, language and dialectal choices, bear a symbiotic relation to culture and context.

As initially formulated by Ochs and Schieffelin (Ochs 1990, 1996; Ochs and Schieffelin 1984; Schieffelin and Ochs 1986a, 1986b, 1996), language socialization is concerned with: (1) how novices (e.g. children, second/foreign/heritage language learners, new members of given communities and workplaces) are socialized to be competent members in the target culture through language use; and (2) how novices are socialized to use language. This approach focuses on the language used by and to novices and the relations between this language use and the larger cultural contexts of communication – local theories and epistemologies concerning social order, local ideologies and practices concerning socializing the novices (e.g. rearing children, teaching students, apprenticing newcomers), relationships between the novice and the expert, the specific activities and tasks at hand, and so forth. Most work in language socialization has focused on analyzing the organization of communicative practices through which novices acquire socio-cultural knowledge. Methodologically, it examines audio-/video-recorded, carefully transcribed, recurrent socialization activities and relates the grammatical, discursive, and non-verbal details of interaction to the construction of social and cultural ideologies that define a community.

By its very conceptualization, language socialization is centrally concerned with human development and growth in areas where language and culture intersect. In other words, it views language education not just as a physical site, but more importantly as a set of practices. It asks questions such as how learning takes place in and through language, regardless of the setting. Although earlier work in language socialization has focused on non-school settings such as traditional cultures, non-American cultures, and everyday encounters (e.g. Goodwin

1990; Heath, 1983; Ochs 1988; Schieffelin 1990; Watson-Gegeo and Gegeo 1986), subsequent research guided by language socialization has also directed its attention to formal educational settings such as second/foreign/heritage/bilingual language teaching and learning in the classroom (Atkinson 2002; Bayley and Schecter 2003; Crago 1992; Duff 2007; He 2000, 2001, 2004; Kanagy 1999; Lo 2004; Ohta 1999; Poole 1992; Schecter and Bayley 2004; Watson-Gegeo and Nielsen 2003; Zuengler and Cole 2005).

After a discussion of the notion of indexicality, something that constitutes language as a context-bound, interactively accomplished phenomenon (Duranti and Goodwin 1992; Ochs 1990), this chapter will provide a brief overview of how a language socialization perspective can illuminate some central concerns in applied linguistics (cf. Duff and Hornberger 2008). It will then critically evaluate two types of inadequacies in existing language socialization-oriented applied linguistics research, namely, the focus on a single setting and the conceptualization of language socialization as linear. Finally, this chapter will delineate the challenges facing language socialization research, using the socialization of Chinese as a heritage language as an example.

The notion of indexicality

Within the framework of language socialization, indexicality is conceived of as a property of speech through which socio-cultural contexts (e.g. identities, activities) are constituted by particular stances and acts which in turn are indexed through linguistic forms (Ochs 1990, 1992, 1993). That is to say, the indexical relationship between linguistic forms and socio-cultural contexts is often achieved indirectly, instead of directly (i.e. one or more linguistic forms indexing some contextual dimension). According to language socialization,

> [a] feature of the communicative event is evoked indirectly through the indexing of some *other* feature of the communicative event. … the feature of the communicative event directly indexed is conventionally linked to and helps to constitute some second feature of the communicative event, such that the indexing of one evokes or indexes the other.
>
> *(Ochs 1990: 295)*

Further, it is not random that some features of the communicative event bear a direct or indirect relationship to linguistic forms. Major socio-cultural dimensions include social identities of the participants, relationships among participants, affective dispositions of participants (feelings, moods, and attitudes of participants toward some proposition), epistemological dispositions of participants (beliefs or knowledge vis-à-vis some proposition, e.g. the source of their knowledge or the degree of certainty of their knowledge), social/speech acts and activities, and genre.

The advantages of this perspective is illustrated in He (2000), for example, which documents a three-phased directive pattern in the teacher-student interaction in Chinese language classes, namely, Orientation → Evaluation → Directive. Specifically, the teacher first orients the students to some state of affairs which in turn renders the students' behavior problematic, then formulates negative consequences which may result from the students' problematic behavior, and only then does she issue a directive to correct the behavior. Thus, rather than simply issuing directives, the teacher weaves cultural values (e.g. appreciating parents' efforts and conforming to the group) in the prefaces so as to warrant the directives for desirable behavior.

Moralized directives as described in He (2000) index both an affective disposition and social identity. They directly index affective dispositions of being moral and authoritative and indirectly index the social identity of the speaker – that of a parent or a teacher, as in the Chinese culture parent/teacher roles are largely defined in terms of or constituted by moral and author-itative dispositions. Confucian teachings, which have provided the dominant educational and social ethos for the major part of Chinese history, are primarily concerned with moral conduct as the basis of social harmony. It is thus the teacher's and the parents' prerogative as well as responsibility to socialize the students/children into the various virtues (known as *li*) that regulate all human conduct.

Although 'teacher' is a universal social role, the communicative practices of teachers vary considerably across cultures and societies. In other words, there is not a one-to-one mapping relationship between three-phased moralized directives (language forms) and the social identity of the teacher (cultural context). Instead, the relation of moralized directives to the identity of the Chinese teacher is constituted and mediated by the relation of language forms to stances (e.g. moral and authoritative), activities and other social constructs. As such, students in these classes come to understand teacher-related meanings in part through coming to understand certain recurrently displayed stances (e.g. upholding moral values such as filial piety).

The language socialization approach to indexicality provides a systematic account of how language relates to cultural context. With language socialization, we can examine how differ-ent displays of and reactions to certain acts and stances (e.g. moralizing) construct different identities and relationships. It also allows us to examine the construction of multiple yet compatible/congruent identities, blended and blurred identities in multilingual, multicultural, immigrant contexts.

Language socialization and applied linguistics

Language socialization considers language learning and teaching as a social, cultural, and interactional process which inherently involves both the learner/novice and the teacher/expert. This perspective has appealed to applied linguistics for several reasons. First, it interfaces with some of the primary concerns of language acquisition research, such as the impact of the acculturation of the learner on his/her second language acquisition (Schumann 1978). Second, its ethnographic orientation and the importance it attaches to context shows strong affinity with various socio-cultural approaches to language learning (e.g. Atkinson 2002; Bayley and Preston 1996; Block 2003; Kramsch 2002; Li 1994; Lantolf 2006; Lantolf and Thorne 2007; Norton 2000; Rampton 1995, 1997, 1999). Third, its focus on communicative practices resonates with the more inter-actionally and ethnomethodologically oriented approaches to second/foreign language acqui-sition (Hatch 1978; He 2004; Markee 2000, 2008; Pica 1994; Pica *et al.* 1987; Young, 2009; Young and He 1998; Young and Miller 2004). And, last but not least, its emphasis on develop-mental cultural competence and its theory of indexicality contribute directly to the understanding of the learner's language use throughout the developmental stages (Kasper 2001).

Not only has language socialization been appealing, but it has also been challenging to the field of applied linguistics. It reconceptualizes language development in a number of ways. It redefines what it means to know a language, advances an indexical (rather than correlational) view concerning language and culture, enables us to see the acquisition of language forms in a culturally accountable way, and takes ordinary interaction to be the primary site for learning and socialization.

What it means to know a language

Language socialization considers language practice as a set of indexicals participating in a network of semiotic systems and treats language acquisition and socialization as an integrated process. Linguistic meanings and meaning makings are therefore necessarily embedded in cultural systems of understanding. An account of linguistic behavior (speaking and listening) must then draw on accounts of culture. Accordingly, the knowledge of a language includes a set of norms, preferences and expectations relating linguistic structures to context, which language users draw on in producing and interpreting language (Ochs 1988).

For example, the acquisition of modal elements in language is a particularly interesting area developmentally. Epistemic modals (e.g. *must* in 'Everything that goes up must come down') provide learners with a resource for developing the capacity to infer, predict, generalize, and hypothesize; and deontic modals (e.g. *should* in 'When playing with your friends, you should always take turns') provide a resource for learner's exploration and understanding of social obligations, responsibilities, constraints, and cultural and moral values. Rather than focusing on the timing and frequency of isolated instances of production, a language socialization approach would argue that (1) it is not context-free frequency but rather the understanding of the degree of situational relevance and cultural meaningfulness that indexes the learner's competence; and (2) learners' acquisition and use of modal language is as integral part of a more general socialization process. Lo (2004), for instance, demonstrates how expressions of epistemic stance relate to moral evaluations by looking at cases in which teachers in a Korean language class claim to read their students' mind with a high degree of certainty. Lo argues that Korean language learners are socialized to portray their access to the thoughts and sensations of other individuals differently depending upon who these individuals are. If the individuals are perceived as morally worthy, then the access is portrayed as distant; if they are perceived as morally suspect, then the access is presented as self-evident.

How culture/context relates to language

From a language socialization perspective, language learners' acquisition of linguistic forms requires a developmental process of delineating and organizing contextual dimensions in culturally sensible ways. Indexical knowledge, as Ochs (1996) argues, is at the core of linguistic and cultural competence and is the locus where language acquisition and socialization interface. A language socialization model accounts for learners' grammatical development in terms of the indexical meanings of grammatical forms. The underlying assumption is that, 'in every community, grammatical forms are inextricably tied to, and hence index, culturally organized situations of use and that the indexical meanings of grammatical forms influence children's [and learners' in general] production and understanding of these forms' (Ochs and Schieffelin 1995: 74). In this model, learners are viewed as tuned into certain indexical meanings of grammatical forms that link those forms to, for example, the social identities of interlocutors and the types of social events. This model relates learner's use and understanding of grammatical forms to complex yet orderly and recurrent dispositions, preferences, beliefs and bodies of knowledge that organize how information is linguistically packaged and how speech acts are performed within and across socially recognized situations (Garret and Baquedano-Lopez 2002; Kulick and Schieffelin 2004).

What constitutes evidence of learning

While acquisition research has largely focused on frequency in output as evidence of learning, language socialization research has looked for culturally meaningful practices across settings and situations (Ochs and Schieffelin 1995). Within a socio-cultural perspective, language socialization views language acquisition 'as increasing competence in both the formal and functional potential of language. By functional, I mean the multiplicity of relations between language and context, including that in which language creates context' (Ochs 1988: 13). Over developmental time, language learners acquire repertoires of language forms associated with contextual dimensions (e.g. role relationships, acts, events).

In the case of acquisition of modal expressions mentioned above, as directives masked with modals of low obligation are used by persons of power and authority (e.g. teachers, parents or any elderly person), a learner who has acquired the meaning of the modal verb 'can/may' may in fact not be using the form in his/her speech to the teacher in the same manner the teacher does to the students, because it would be pragmatically and culturally inappropriate. Hence frequency in output alone will lead to a misguided interpretation of the student's acquisition of modals (He 2010). From a language socialization perspective, we need to ask the following questions: (i) In what contexts is the modal form used by the learner? (ii) What is the impact, if any, of the sequential organization of interaction on the learner's (non-)use of modals? (iii) What is the impact, if any, of the local activity on the learner's (non-)use of modals? (iv) What stances are exhibited by the (non-)use of modals? and (v) How are these stances associated with social roles, identities, responsibilities, and obligations in the local community?

Two avenues for further growth

We have seen an increasingly large body of empirical studies documenting the various formal and functional aspects of language socialization that are concerned with different subgroups of learners (Duff and Hornberger 2008). These studies largely focus on one language proficiency level of the subjects at one life stage in one specific life circumstance. They have shown that successful language socialization depends on the role of school systems, social institutions, and historical experiences of particular language communities, as well as language ideologies, proficiency assessment that is suitable for specific types of learners (second, foreign or heritage language), and adequate literacy development. They have also indicated that a range of variables may influence language socialization, including social prestige of the language, number of speakers, affinity to native country, vitality of language programs, learners' social and ethnic positionings, degree of family bond, and discourse and interactional practices (Baker 2006; Bayley and Schecter 2003; Creese and Martin 2006; Fishman 2001; Gibbons and Ramirez 2004; He 2006; He and Xiao 2008; Shin 2005; Zentella 1997). However, given that language socialization and language development are not limited to any specific point in time or to any given period of time (He 2006; Markee 2008; Wortham 2005), language competencies, choices, and ideologies change over the language learner's lifespan, reflecting changing motivations, social networks, opportunities, and other variables. Consequently, future research needs to examine the different stages as well as different domains of language development.

In addition to expansion of research along the temporal dimension, language socialization studies can also benefit from an extended focus from the individual language learner to other co-participants as well. It will be important to realize that expert guidance in language socialization may be multiple, conflicting and contested. The language learner is engaged in multiple speech events in multiple settings for multiple purposes. The learning of heritage languages, as shown in the next section for example, takes place through the learner's interactions with multiple participants including language instructors, parents, grandparents, siblings, and peers, each of whom positions the learner in unique speech and social roles and each of whose reactions and responses to the heritage language learner helps to shape the path of his/her language development. Future language socialization research needs to highlight the co-constructed, multi-directional, interactive nature of socialization activities (He 2006; Talmy 2008).

Toward a temporal-spatial specification: a case in point

To illustrate the potential of, as well as challenges facing, language socialization research suggested in the previous section, I describe here a profile of a composite heritage language learner and provide a gist of a multi-site, longitudinal study of this learner's language socialization process.

Jason Chen is a sophomore in a Chinese as a heritage language (CHL) class in a university. He speaks Cantonese and understands Mandarin, but cannot read or write in Chinese. He was born in China and emigrated to the US when he was three years old. At that time, he spoke Cantonese at home with his parents, grandmother, and aunt. He had some knowledge of English from television and from the children he played with who spoke a mixture of English, Vietnamese, Cantonese, Fujianese, Chaozhou dialect, and Mandarin. When Jason first started school, his English was weak. But very soon, he was speaking English fluently and became one of the highest achieving students in his class. Since a time he no longer recalls, he has been speaking English to his parents and his aunt at home too; the only person he still speaks Cantonese to is his grandmother, with whom he keeps a minimum level of communication. His parents once sent him to a weekend Chinese language school, where he was taught Mandarin. He went for a year but felt 'the teacher was just totally boring' and he 'didn't learn anything'. His best friends include Brad, his roommate, who is from a Jewish cultural background. He is also seriously dating a Mandarin-speaking girl. When asked why he is taking CHL, Jason said, 'I am Chinese. I feel stupid not knowing the language. Plus I'd like to do business in China, some day.'

In order to unravel the complexities of Jason's language development, efforts were made to reconstruct his life, by collecting data from a wide range of subjects in settings and situations that Jason has experienced at various stages of his life from kindergarten to university. (The data segments below are thus drawn from different corpora involving different participants.) The end result is a composite 'Jason', representing a model of his life experiences with respect to his language development (see He, in press). The objective is to examine the developmental stages and diverse spaces of the prototype learner to gain insight into how CHL socialization takes place as the learner moves across time and space. The approach adopted here enables one to go beyond the learner's language use in different domains and settings but also to include the temporal aspect of the analysis, examining how the learner's behavior changes according to his different developmental stages by defining time as an additional co-ordinate.

As mentioned previously, before entering school, Jason's exposure to English was limited. At the beginning of his formal schooling, he was usually only seen but not heard. He rarely responded to the teacher or other students verbally, as can be seen in (1).

(1) Kindergarten classroom (field notes)

MRS B:	My friends, let's get ready. It's center time.
	((*Jason doesn't move.*))
MRS B:	Jason, which center do you wanna go?
	((*Jason doesn't respond. Mrs B takes his hand and brings him to the art center next to an easel.*))
MRS B:	You like to paint? I know you are a good artist.
	((*Jason looks at the easel and then at other kids who are at the number center working with numbers 0 through 9. Jason joins the number center. Mrs B leaves.*))

Jason's parents were concerned with Jason's lack of English language competence on the one hand and were doing their best to talk to him in English in spite of their own limited command of the language. But on the other hand, they also wanted Jason to keep speaking Chinese and to develop literacy in Chinese. As a result, the parents increased their use of English at home and at the same time sent Jason to a weekend Chinese language school in their community. (2) is an example of what happens in the classroom of the language school. In cases of data in Chinese, the first line is the Chinese original, the second line is phonetic annotation of Chinese, the third line is grammatical gloss, and the fourth line is English translation.

(2) Chinese language school (audio- and video-recorded data)

((in the context of '孔融让梨' – Kong Rong yields pears)).

TEACHER: 要把-应该 把 玩具让:: 给 弟弟 妹妹
           Yao ba yinggai ba wanju rang gei didi meimei
           should BA ought BA toy yield DIR younger brother younger sister
           Should-Ought to yie::ld the toys to younger brothers and sisters
           (.2)

TEACHER: 谦::让:(.) 懂 吗? 谦让 就 是 这 个 意思
           Qian rang dong ma qianrang jiu shi zhe ge yisi
           Yield understand Q yield just be this CL meaning
           Yield   (.) Understand? This is what yield means.

JASON: 让 给 他? 我们 share 就 可以 了。
           Rang gei ta? Women share jiu keyi le
           yield DIR he we share just ok CRS
           Yield to him? We can share.

TEACHER: Share (.) 噢:: share 是 不 错
           Share ao share shi bu cuo
           Share PRT share be NEG wrong
           Share (.) uh:: share is not wrong
           (.4)

TEACHER: 可是能 让 更好 =
           Keshi neng rang geng hao
           But able yield even better
           But being able to YIELD will be EVEN better.

JASON: = Oh:: no::: Do I really have to?

TEACHER: 不是-不是说 非-不是 说 ‹必须得 让›
           Bushi bushi shuo fei- bushi shuo bixu dei rang
           NEG NEG say have to- NEG say must must yield
           I'm not saying you have to-not saying that you MUST yield
           能 让 (.) 最:好啊
           Neng rang zui hao a
           Able yield best PRT
           Being able to yield is THE BEST ok

Here, the teacher is leading a discussion of the Chinese cultural preference of 'yielding' in the context of a widely circulated folk story of 'Kong Rong Yields Pears', which apparently requires more of a child than the American notion of 'sharing', which Jason has brought to the Chinese class from his daytime regular school. That the two cultural norms could not be reconciled with each other most likely played a role in Jason's eventual dropping out of Chinese language school.

From 4th grade onward, Jason was consistently one of the top students. He became a very confident and successful student at school. His 6th grade school report card reads, 'Jason is a superior student who excels across all subject areas … ' However, he was speaking less and less at home. (3) is illustrative of the kind of interaction he had at home at that stage.

(3) 6th grade: at dinner table (audio-recorded data)

(This interaction took place when Jason's Mandarin-speaking paternal grandmother was visiting around Chinese New Year.)

GRANDMA: 吃，来，吃，来
chi, lai, chi, lai
eat come eat come
eat, come, eat, come
((*Grandma pushes Jason to dinner table*))

GRANDMA: 那么瘦！多吃多吃不吃怎么胖
name shou Duo chi duo chi bu chi zenme pang
so skinny much eat much eat NEG eat Q fat
So skinny! Eat a lot eat a lot if you don't eat how can you gain weight
只长个儿不长肉
zhi zhang ge'r bu zhang rou
only grow height NEG grow flesh
[You] only gain height but not weight.
啊哟：：你看看他们拿来这么多吃的
ayo::: ni kan kan tamen na lai zhe me duo chi de
PRT you see they bring DIR this much eat NOM
ayo::: you see they brought this much food
想吃什么？
xiang chi she me
want eat Q
What do you want to eat?

MOTHER: 姥姥跟你说话呢
laolao gen ni shuohua ne
grandma PREP you speak PRT
Grandma is talking to you
这孩子 = 哎别拿了够了够 =
zhe haizi =
this child
This kid = ai don't bring anything more enough enough

JASON: = I'm not hungry.

Jason keeps his speech at the dinner table to a minimum, and when he has to speak, he does so in English. The attrition of home language and the consequent alienation from family that accompany English language acquisition (Wong Fillmore 1991) are evident here.

During high school, Jason was perceived differently by different people in his life, as can be seen in (4). At this point, he was speaking English almost exclusively. His aunt and grandmother no longer lived with them. His parents were doing better in their business and they were also speaking much more, and better English themselves.

(4) High school: others' perceptions of Jason (interview data)

- GUIDANCE COUNSELOR: He is the kind of student we all dream to have.
- SCHOOLMATE: Oh that Chinese guy? Or is he Vietnamese or some other kind of Asian? He is okay. Never bothers me. But what is he doing here? I think people like him should go back to China or wherever they came from.
- NEIGHBOR: Nice young man! He will have a great future. I wish my son more like him. You know, my son only play with people like him, you know, only Chinese. Too narrow, you know. You live in America, you want to be American, you know.
- An elderly at temple: '这孩子不错。他父母人很好，可他从来也不叫我奶奶。都美国化了。 (He is a good kid. His parents are very nice people, but he never calls me 'Grandma'. He is Americanized.)
- MOTHER: He study not bad. Has good grades. He like computer. Play computer game all the time. Never stop. Spend a lot money too. He like brand. Waste money!
- SISTER: He talks to me but he really doesn't talk to anyone else [in the family] that much. He's real busy'n stuff.

By the time Jason entered the university, he decided that he would like to seriously learn Chinese. Due to his language background and language proficiency, it was not immediately clear which track of the elementary Chinese language class Jason should be placed in – the foreign language track or the heritage language track. In (5), an instructor was interviewing Jason for the purpose of his placement.

(5) University: with CHL instructor (audio-recorded data)

PROFESSOR: Ok if I- I speak Mandarin, do you follow me well?

JASON: I mean (.) >I underSTAND Mandarin.< At home my mom'n my aunt the- they sometimes speak Mandarin b't (.) not all that well. .hhh Most of the time everybody (.) jus speak Canto[nese.

PROFESSOR: [Ok, =

JASON: =I like Mandarin. Sounds better than other dialects. >Don't know why jus feels that way.< I mean if I want to find a jo:b like (.) in China I wanna be in big (cities/places) like < Beijing > or something =

PROFESSOR: =Uhuh,
(.2)

JASON: I don't wanna be (.) like (.) you know (.) where THEY came from.

One might think that to learn one's heritage language is to (re)establish similarities with members of one's heritage culture and/or to (re)establish differences from members of mainstream American culture. However, as can be seen in (5), to learn CHL appears to be not merely to inherit one's heritage language and maintain one's heritage cultural identity but also to transform the heritage language (in terms of changes in dialect, script, accent, discourse norms, etc.) and re-create one's identity. When Jason walks into the CHL classroom, he brings with him linguistic and behavioral patterns that were formed when he was six or twelve and that remain active or that await to be reactivated; he brings with him richly textured experiences interacting with his Cantonese- and Mandarin-speaking family members, his English-, Vietnamese-, Cantonese-, Fujianese-, Chaozhou dialect-, and Mandarin-speaking neighbors, his English-speaking but multi-ethnic peers and teachers, his English- and Mandarin-speaking girlfriend; he brings with him ways of speaking and being that mirror those of these diverse groups of people; he brings with him memories of his past experience learning CHL as well as expectations and anticipations about the verbal and non-verbal behavior of his present CHL teacher and CHL classmates; he also brings with him dreams of working in China some day and ideas of what being a Chinese-American means. In a nutshell, Jason embodies elements that are both hetero-temporal and hetero-spatial. He has learned and is still learning to cope with, to understand, to accept or reject, to model or modify the language and cultural behaviors of every community he has encountered throughout his life. Learning CHL will enable him to inherit some of the 'Chineseness' from his family and his neighborhood but will also enable him to become a very different kind of Chinese-American from his family and his neighbors.

Most interestingly, whereas Jason may consider himself a beginning learner of the Chinese language, his best friend Brad, who is from a non-Chinese family background and who is learning Chinese as a foreign language, sees him differently, as in (6).

(6) University: best friend Brad (who is taking CFL) (audio recorded data)

JASON:	When's your oral?
BRAD:	Friday, (.) I think, (.) .hhh oh no actually I don think she's told us yet. I'm gonna fail hhahaha =
JASON:	=no you won't,
BRAD:	C'mon (hhh I'm gonna) say 'wo: (.) jue::de (.2) fa:yin (.) he::n nan'((I think pronunciation is hard)) hhahhhaha
JASON:	Oh yea you can do it, you just did it hhuhuhuh
BRAD:	Easy for YOU ((it's)) your (.) lan[guage
JASON:	[ne::: my mom-I don=
BRAD:	=but s[till
JASON:	[I guess.

Here, regardless of Jason's minimal level of proficiency in Chinese, Jason is perceived by Brad as 'owning' the language ('Easy for YOU ((it's)) your (.) language'). After a brief and unsuccessful protest of such a characterization, Jason acquiesced.

Earlier, I have discussed the central role of identity formation and transformation in the development and maintenance of heritage languages. Most often, the connection between language and identity is tacit and requires inferences. Segment (7), however, caught an extremely rare moment when language and identity was explicitly marked and linked.

(7) University: with math TA (audio- and video-recorded data)

((*Jason is seeking help in TA's office. TA is a native of China who has arrived in the USA not long ago for graduate school. 'ABC' stands for 'American-born Chinese'.*))

TA:	This-this is the rule, the equation. What I tell you (.2) you mus must follow. The right way.

	((*Jason is still confused*))
TA:	Are you Chinese?
	((*Jason stares at TA*))
TA:	I tell you in Chinese.
	(.2)
JASON:	uh: my Chinese isn't that good=
TA:	=So you are ABC. No problem. I tell you again …

What is noteworthy in (7) is that Jason does not seem to be prepared for any explicit discussion of his ethnic identity. When the TA first inquires about his ethnicity, Jason gives a blank answer (both verbally and visually). When the TA assumes that he is an American-born Chinese, Jason does not correct the TA's mistake (Jason was in fact born in China). This is a revealing moment where Jason is compelled to confront the issue of identity and yet he appears ambivalent and ill-equipped to handle the matter.

I argued earlier that heritage language socialization concerns and transforms all parties involved. As the years went by, Jason's parents were speaking more and better English. His father does not speak much in general. By the time Jason is in college, his mother has become quite comfortable talking to him in English, as seen in (8).

(8) *University: with mother (audio recorded data)*

JASON:	I'm also (.2) taking uh Chinese history.
	(.4)
JASON:	It's hard.
MOTHER:	Hard? You study hard (.) it's easy.
JASON:	Ma you don't get it.
	((*pause*))
MOTHER:	Why- why Chinese history? Economy major need Chinese history? I study my major I never study history=
JASON:	=Ma you never get it. *ni bu dong la::* ((*You don't understand this*)) I'm taking it cus I want to. Nobody asks me to.

Two items are worth particular mention. First, at this stage, Jason is, on of his own initiative, trying to learn as much Chinese language and history as possible, to an extent that is surprising and perplexing to his mother. Second, in interaction with his mother, now it is Jason who code-switches to Chinese from English, while his mother uses English consistently.

The above shows that, in the complex process of heritage language socialization, Jason's language and identity resources develop, stabilize, shrink or expand as his social networks, attitudes, allegiances and affinities evolve over time. Instead of a linear growth (or attrition) pattern suggested in most existing language acquisition/attrition literature, Jason's case illustrates a language learning trajectory that is sometimes a plateau, sometimes exponential. Hence in the long process of acquiring, challenging, rejecting, resisting, learning, embracing Chinese from birth to college, Jason is not learning a 'target' language X as a 'native speaker' of language Y. His motivation to (re-)learn Chinese is neither strictly 'instrumental' nor 'integrative'. Instead, Jason's journey in Chinese can be characterized by expanded practices and participation in everyday life, extended identity options (Norton, this volume) and continual intercultural adjustments (Kramsch, this volume).

The case of Jason thus epitomizes language socialization's position that language development is grounded in the learner's participation in social practice and continuous adaptation to the unfolding, multiple activities and identities that constitute the social and communicative worlds which s/he inhabits. This perspective also compels us to take a more dialectical, dialogical and ecological perspective on language and cultural development, in the sense that the process will be viewed as reciprocal. Language learners are not merely passive, uniform recipients of socialization. As the learner's allegiances and competencies evolve, the language choices and competencies of their parents, siblings, neighbors and friends will also change, consequently and/or concurrently. In other words, it is important to keep in mind that the language learner contributes to the socialization process of the very people who socialize him/her to use the language. Language learning has the potential to transform all parties involved in the socialization process.

Summary

Language socialization is concerned with the symbiotic process of language and cultural development. Originating from linguistic anthropology, it is becoming an influential research perspective in applied linguistics in general and in language acquisition studies in particular. Its main thesis is that novices across the lifespan are socialized into using language and socialized through language in socio-culturally recognized and organized practices. More recently, language socialization research has expanded from primary language socialization during childhood to the fields of bilingualism, multilingualism and second or heritage language acquisition in linguistically and socio-culturally heterogeneous settings characterized by two or more languages and cultures.

Language socialization provides a culturally enriched, theoretically grounded, and empirically accountable perspective on issues and concerns central to applied linguistics. Along with parallel socio-cultural approaches to language acquisition (Ortega, this volume), language socialization has in a sense precipitated a social turn (Block 2003) in applied linguistics. With a broader temporal and spatial specification, research inspired and guided by language socialization will be poised to further illuminate the nature as well as the trajectory of language and cultural development across the lifespan and even across generations in multiple, inter-related spaces for all participants.

Appendix A: Transcription Symbols

CAPS	emphasis, signaled by pitch or volume
.	falling intonation
,	falling-rising intonation
°	quiet speech
[ ]	overlapped talk
-	cut-off
=	latched talk
:	prolonged sound or syllable
(0.0)	silences roughly in seconds and tenths of seconds
(.)	short, untimed pauses of one tenth of a second or less
( )	undecipherable or doubtful hearing
(( ))	additional observation
< >	slow speech
> <	fast speech

Appendix B: Grammatical Gloss

COMP	directional or resultative complement of verb
CONJ	conjunction
COP	copula
DUR	durative aspect marker
EMP	emphatic marker
LOC	locative marker
MSR	measure
NEG	negative marker
PERT	perfective aspect marker
POS	possesive
PRT	sentence, vocative or nominal subordinative particle
PTP	pre-transitive preposition
Q	question marker

Related topics

culture; identity; second language acquisition

Further reading

Agha, A. and Wortham, S. (2005) 'Discourse across speech events: intertextuality and inter-discursivity in social life', *Journal of Linguistic Anthropology* 15(1). (This special issue highlights the urgent need to examine language and cultural practices on multiple timescales.)

Duff, P. and Hornberger, N. H. (eds) (2008) *Encyclopedia of Language and Education*, vol. 8: *Language Socialization*, New York: Springer. (This volume presents the most current comprehensive review of the field.)

Kramsch, C. (ed.) (2002) *Language Acquisition and Language Socialization: Ecological Perspectives*, New York: Continuum. (This volume presents various socio-cultural, ecological perspectives on language development in a discussion format.)

Ochs, E. and Schieffelin, B. B. (1995) 'The impact of language socialization on grammatical development', in P. Fletcher and B. MacWhinney (eds) *The Handbook of Child Language*, Cambridge, MA: Blackwell. (This chapter delineates how language socialization engages and interfaces with language acquisition.)

Watson-Gegeo, K. A. (2004) 'Mind, language, and epistemology: toward a language socialization paradigm for SLA', *The Modern Language Journal* 88(3). (This article specifies a language socialization take on SLA.)

References

Atkinson, D. (2002) 'Toward a sociocognitive approach to SLA', *The Modern Language Journal* 86: 525–45.

Baker, C. (2006) *Foundations of Bilingual Education and Bilingualism*, Clevedon: Multilingual Matters.

Bayley, R. (1996) 'Competing constraints on variation in the speech of adult Chinese learners of English', in R. Bayley and D. R. Preston (eds) *Second Language Acquisition and Linguistic Variation*, Philadelphia: John Benjamins.

Bayley, R. and Preston, D. R. (eds) (1996) *Second Language Acquisition and Linguistic Variation*, Philadelphia: John Benjamins.

Bayley, R. and Schecter, S. (eds) (2003) *Language Socialization in Bilingual and Multilingual Societies*, Clevedon: Multilingual Matters.

Block, D. (2003) *The Social Turn in Second Language Acquisition*, Washington, DC: Georgetown University Press.

Byon, A. (2003) 'Language socialization and Korean as a heritage language: a study of Hawaiian classrooms', *Language, Culture and Curriculum* 16(3): 269–83.

Crago, B. M. (1992) 'Communicative interaction and second language acquisition: an Inuit example', *TESOL Quarterly* 26: 487–505.

Creese, A. and Martin, P. (2006) (eds) 'Interaction in complementary school contexts', special issue, *Language and Education* 20(1).

Drew, P. and Heritage, J. (eds) (1992) *Talk at Work: Interaction in Institutional Settings*, New York: Cambridge University Press.

Duff, P. (2007) 'Second language socialization as sociocultural theory: insights and issues', *Language Teaching* 40: 309–19.

Duff, P. and Hornberger, N. H. (eds) (n.d.) *Encyclopedia of Language and Education*, vol. 8: *Language Socialization*, New York: Springer.

Duranti, A. and Goodwin, C. (1992) *Rethinking Context: Language as an Interactive Phenomenon*, New York: Cambridge University Press.

Fishman, J. A. (2001) '300-plus years of heritage language education in the United States', in J. K. Peyton, D. A. Ranard and S. McGinnis (eds) *Heritage Languages in America: Preserving A National Resource*, McHenry, IL: CAL.

Garret, P. B. and Baquedano-Lopez, P. (2002) 'Language socialization: reproduction and continuity, transformation and change', *Annual Review of Anthropology* 31: 339–62.

Gibbons, J. and Ramirez, E. (2004) *Maintaining a Minority Language: A Case Study of Hispanic Teenagers*, Clevedon: Multilingual Matters.

Goodwin, M. H. (1990) *He-Said-She-Said*, Bloomington: Indiana University Press.

Hatch, E. (1978) 'Discourse analysis and second language acquisition', in E. Hatch (ed.) *Second Language Acquisition: A Book of Readings*, Rowley, MA: Newbury House.

He, A. W. (2000) 'Grammatical and sequential organization of teachers' directives', *Linguistics and Education* 11(2): 119–40.

——(2001) 'The language of ambiguity: practices in Chinese heritage language classes', *Discourse Studies* 3(1): 75–96.

——(2003) 'Novices and their speech roles in Chinese heritage language classes', in R. Baley and S. Schecter (eds) *Language Socialization in Bilingual and Multilingual Societies*, Clevedon: Multilingual Matters.

——(2004) 'Identity construction in Chinese heritage language classes', *Pragmatics* 14(2–3): 199–216.

——(2005) 'Discipline, directives, and deletions: grammar and interaction in Chinese heritage language classes', in C. Holten and J. Frodesen (eds) *The Power of Context in Language Teaching and Learning: A Festschrift for Marianne Celce-Murcia*, Boston: Thomson Heinle.

——(2006) 'Toward an identity theory of the development of Chinese as a heritage language', *Heritage Language Journal* 4(1): 1–28.

——(2009a) 'Sequences, scripts, and subject pronouns in the construction of Chinese heritage identity', in A. Reyes and A. Lo (eds) *Beyond Yellow English: Toward a Linguistic Anthropology of Asian Pacific America*, New York: Oxford University Press.

——(2009b, July) 'Heritage language across the life span', Lecture Presented at the 3rd National Heritage Language Summer Research Institute, Urbana Champaign, Illinois.

——(2009c) 'Conversational repair: where modality and morality converge', in Y. Xiao (ed.) *21st North American Conference on Chinese Linguistics Conference Proceedings*, Smithfield, RI: Bryant University.

——(2010) The heart of heritage: socio-cultural dimensions of heritage language learning, *Annual Review of Applied Linguistics* 30, 66–82.

——(in press) 'Heritage language socialization', in A. Duranti, E. Ochs and B. Schieffelin (eds) *The Handbook of Language Socialization*, Oxford: Blackwell.

He, A. W. and Xiao, Y. (eds) (2008) *Chinese as a Heritage Language: Fostering Rooted World Citizenry*, Honolulu: University of Hawaii Press.

Heath, S. B. (1983) *Ways with Words: Language, Life and Work in Communities and Classrooms*, New York: Cambridge University Press.

Kanagy, R. (1999) 'Interactional routines as a mechanism for L2 acquisition and socialization in an immersion context', *Journal of Pragmatics* 31: 1467–92.

Kasper, G. (2001) 'Four perspectives on L2 pragmatics development', *Applied Linguistics* 22: 502–30.

Kulick, D. and Schieffelin, B. B. (2004) 'Language socialization', in A. Duranti (ed.) *A Companion to Linguistic Anthropology*, Oxford: Blackwell.

Lantolf, J. P. (2006) 'Sociocultural theory and L2: state of the art', *Studies in Second Language Acquisition* 28: 67–109.

Lantolf, J. P. and Thorne, S. L. (2007) *Sociocultural Theory and the Genesis of Second Language Development*, Oxford: Oxford University Press.

Lemke, J. (2002) 'Language development and identity: multiple timescales in the social ecology of learning', in C. Kramsch (ed.) *Language Acquisition and Language Socialization: Ecological Perspectives*, New York: Continuum.

Li, W. (1994) *Three Generations, Two Languages, One Family*, Clevedon: Multilingual Matters.

Lo, A. (2004) 'Evidentiality and morality in a Korean heritage language school', *Pragmatics*, 14(2/3): 235–56. Reprinted in A. Reyes and A. Lo (eds) (2009) *Beyond Yellow English: Toward a Linguistic Anthropology of Asian Pacific America*, New York: Oxford University Press.

Markee, N. (2000) *Conversation Analysis*, Mahwah, NJ: Lawrence Erlbaum Associates.

——(2008) 'Towards a learning behavior tracking methodology for CA-for-SLA', *Applied Linguistics*, 29(3): 404–27.

Norton, B. (2000) *Identity and Language Learning: Gender, Ethnicity, and Educational Change*, Harlow: Longman.

Ochs, E. (1988) *Culture and Language Development*, Cambridge: Cambridge University Press.

——(1990) 'Indexicality and socialization', in J. W. Stigler, R. Shweder and G. Herdt (eds) *Cultural Psychology: Essays on Comparative Human Development*, Cambridge: Cambridge University Press.

——(1992) 'Indexing gender', in A. Duranti and C. Goodwin (eds) *Rethinking Context: Language as an Interactive Phenomenon*, New York: Cambridge University Press.

——(1993) 'Constructing social identity', *Research on Language and Social Interaction* 26: 287–306.

——(1996) 'Linguistic resources for socializing humanity', in J. J. Gumperz and S. C. Levinson (eds) *Rethinking Linguistic Relativity*, Cambridge: Cambridge University Press.

Ochs, E. and Schieffelin, B. B. (1984) 'Language acquisition and socialization: three developmental stories', in R. Schweder and R. LeVine (eds) *Culture Theory: Essays on Mind, Self and Emotion*, Cambridge: Cambridge University Press.

——(1995) 'The impact of language socialization on grammatical development', in P. Fletcher and B. MacWhinney (eds) *The Handbook of Child Language*, Cambridge, MA: Blackwell.

——(2008) 'Language socialization: an historical overview', in P. Duff and N. Hornberger (eds) *Encyclopedia of Language and Education*, vol. 8: *Language Socialization*, New York: Springer.

Ohta, A. S. (1999) 'Interactional routines and the socialization of interactional style in adult learners of Japanese', *Journal of Pragmatics* 31: 1493–1512.

Park, E. (2008) 'Intergenerational transmission of cultural values in Korean American families: an analysis of the verb suffix–ta', *Heritage Language Journal* 6(2). Available at: www.heritagelanguages.org

Pica, T. (1994) 'Research on negotiation: what does it reveal about second-language learning conditions, processes, and outcomes?', *Language Learning*, 44: 493–527.

Pica, T., Young, R. and Doughty, C. (1987) 'The impact of interaction on comprehension', *TESOL Quarterly* 21: 737–58.

Poole, D. (1992) 'Language socialization in the second language classroom', *Language Learning* 42: 593–616.

Rampton, B. (1995) *Crossing: Language and Ethnicity Among Adolescents*, New York: Longman.

——(1997) 'A sociolinguistic perspective on L2 communicative strategies', in G. Kasper and E. Kellerman (eds) *Communication Strategies: Psycholinguistic and Sociolinguistic Perspectives*, London: Longman.

——(1999) 'Dichotomies, differences and ritual in second language learning and teaching', *Applied Linguistics* 20(3): 316–40.

Reyes, A. and Lo, A. (eds) (2009) *Beyond Yellow English: Toward a Linguistic Anthropology of Asian Pacific America*, New York: Oxford University Press.

Schecter, S. E. and Bayley, R. (2004) 'Language socialization in theory and practice', *International Journal of Qualitative Studies in Education* 17, 605–25.

Schieffelin, B. B. (1990) *The Give and Take of Everyday Life*, New York: Cambridge University Press.

Schieffelin, B. B. and Ochs, E. (1986b) 'Language socialization', *Annual Review of Anthropology* 15: 163–91.

——(1996) 'The microgenesis of competence', in D. Slobin, J. Gerhardt, A. Kyratzis, and J. Guo (eds) *Social Interaction, Social Context, and Language*, Mahwah, NJ: Lawrence Erlbaum Associates.

Schieffelin, B. B. and Ochs, E. (eds) (1986a) *Language Socialization Across Cultures*, New York: Cambridge University Press.

Schumann, J. H. (1978) 'The acculturation model for second language acquisition', in R. Gingras (ed.) *Second Language Acquisition and Foreign Language Teaching*, Arlington, VA: Center for Applied Linguistics.

Shin, S. J. (2005) *Developing in Two Languages: Korean Children in America*, Clevedon: Multilingual Matters.

Talmy, S. (2008) 'The cultural productions of the ESL student at Tradewinds High: contingency, multidirecionality, and identity in L2 socialization', *Applied Linguistics* 29(4): 619–44.

Watson-Gegeo, K. A. and Gegeo, D. W. (1986) 'Calling-out and repeating routines in Kwara'ae children's language socialization', in B. B. Schieffelin and E. Ochs (eds) *Language Socialization Across Cultures*, Cambridge: Cambridge University Press.

Watson-Gegeo, K. A. and Nielsen, S. (2003) 'Language socialization in SLA', in C. J. Doughty and M. H. Long (eds) *The Handbook of Second Language Acquisition*, Malden, MA: Blackwell.

Wong Fillmore, L. (1991) 'When learning a second language means losing the first', *Early Childhood Research Quarterly* 6: 323–46.

Wortham, S. (2005) 'Socialization beyond the speech event', *Journal of Linguistic Anthropology* 15(1): 95–112.

Young, R. F. (2009) *Discursive Practice in Language Learning and Teaching*, Malden MA and Oxford: Wiley-Blackwell.

Young, R. F. and He, A. W. (eds) (1998) *Talking and Testing: Discourse Approaches to the Assessment of Oral Proficiency*, Amsterdam and Philadelphia: John Benjamins.

Young, R. F. and Miller, E. R. (2004) 'Learning as changing participation: discourse roles in ESL writing conferences', *The Modern Language Journal* 88(4): 519–35.

Zentella, A. (1997) *Growing up Bilingual*, Oxford: Blackwell.

Zuengler, J. and Cole, K. M. (2005) 'Language socialization and L2 learning', in E. Hinkel (ed.) *Handbook of Research in Second Language Teaching and Learning*, Mahwah, NJ: Lawrence Erlbaum Associates.

Part III

Language, culture and identity

21
Language and culture

Claire Kramsch

History of the relationship of language and culture in applied linguistics

Until the 1970s: separate areas of inquiry

Language and culture have not been seen by everyone as inseparable as they might be seen today by an applied linguist. Indeed, the study of language was since its inception the domain of linguists, not anthropologists, and language teaching was about the teaching of linguistic forms, not foreign cultures. There is no better illustration of this than the Cornell model of teaching foreign languages. At Cornell University in the United States, after World War II, the study of foreign languages was taken out of departments of foreign language and literature and clustered together under the purview of linguists who had supported the war effort and taught languages according to the new audiolingual or Army method (Stern 1983). The prestige of linguistics and the new technology of the language laboratory encouraged an emphasis on language as skill, not as cultural understanding.

The foundation of the English Language Institute at the University of Michigan in 1941 and of the School of Applied Linguistics at the University of Edinburgh in 1957 are generally seen as the beginning of the field of applied linguistics. At that time, the study of language was distinct from the study of both literature (big C Culture) and anthropology (little c culture). On the one hand, linguists and grammarians, following the path set by Saussure, studied language as a closed system of signs shared by all members of a community of ideal native speakers. On the other hand, cultural anthropologists like Lévi-Strauss studied culture as a closed system of relational structures shared by homogeneous social groups in exotic primitive societies. Oddly enough, the legacy of scholars who were both anthropologists and linguists, like Wilhelm von Humboldt, Bronislaw Malinowski, Edward Sapir, and Benjamin Whorf did not initially influence the emerging field of applied linguistics. For example, even though attention was paid early on to the social context of second language acquisition (SLA) and to acculturation factors in SLA, the Sapir-Whorf hypothesis, that posited the constructivist relation of language and thought and the mutual dependency of linguistic forms and cultural worldviews (for a review, see Kramsch 2004), was not taken seriously among psycholinguists, many of whom had studied under Noam Chomsky (see, for example, Pinker 1994: ch. 3).

Claire Kramsch

Culture was to make its way into applied linguistics through the study of language as discourse. The fact that applied linguistics was an applied science confronted its researchers with the need to take into account the social and historical context of language in use. Culture was another name for context, i.e. the constraints imposed on individual language users by the forces of tradition, convention, fashion, and ideology. Culture in applied linguistics came to mean 'membership in a discourse community that shares a common social space and history, and common imaginings' (Kramsch 1998: 10). Such a membership had to be seen as heterogeneous, often contested and subject to change, even in seemingly homogeneous societies. Thus, beyond the standard linguistic system, culture made it necessary to study linguistic and stylistic variation, socially and historically situated discourse communities, different ways of exercising symbolic power, and struggles for cultural recognition and legitimation.

Because applied linguistics emerged at a time of national ideologies and ethnic consciousness, culture was at first essentialized as the patrimony of national or ethnic groups. In the early twentieth century, the structure of language as a symbolic system (Saussure) had been mapped on the structure of culture as the principle of organization of primitive societies (Lévi-Strauss). After World War II, applied linguists tended at first to equate one standard national linguistic system and one national culture. Nowadays, with the global spread of information technologies and global migrations, culture has lost much of its national moorings. It lives in the communicative practices of native and non-native speakers. In the teaching of foreign languages, and even more so in the teaching of English as an international language, culture has become the contextual foil of language practices in everyday life.

1970s–90s: little c culture of everyday life enters the communicative picture

The social turn in applied linguistics (e.g. for SLA, see Block 2003) brought to the fore a vigorous interest in the cultural component of language study, based on a variety of research domains that have to do with the little c culture of language use in everyday life: discourse and conversation analysis, cross-cultural pragmatics, intercultural communication and intercultural learning.

Discourse analysis was hailed in the 1970s as the golden road to understanding language in use. Culture was to be found not in institutional monuments and artifacts, nor in artistic products, but in the meaning that speakers and listeners, writers and readers gave them through the discourse of verbal exchanges, newspaper articles or political speeches. To understand culture, one had to understand both the universal and the culture-specific constraints on language use in discourse: for example, how social actors initiate and end conversations, how they manage or avoid topics, how they structure an argument and organize information, how they negotiate meaning, how they relate text to context (e.g. Gumperz 1982; Scollon and Scollon [1995] 2001; Widdowson 2007).

The field of conversation analysis (CA) emerged in the 1970s from the work of ethnomethodologist Harold Garfinkel and sociologist Erving Goffman. It attracted scholars like Emanuel Schegloff, who, having moved from literary studies at Harvard to sociology at UC Berkeley in the late 1960s, was searching for the very site of construction of the social world. Sacks, Schegloff and Jefferson found it in the systematics of turn-taking in daily conversations (Sacks *et al.* 1974). Their detailed analysis of the mechanics of turns-at-talk opened up vistas on how culture gets produced and reproduced through language. Since then, conversation analysis has experienced spectacular growth to the point that for some it has become synonymous with discourse analysis. While CA has been traditionally more focused on the here-and-now sociological aspects of turns-at-talk, conversational sequences and the organization of repairs than on the historical or ideological dimensions of conversation, some conversation analysts have combined ethnography and conversation analysis in the study of culture in talk (Moerman 1988), that is, in Elinor Ochs' phrase, of how one 'becomes a speaker of culture' (Ochs 2002).

Another related field that studies culture in action is pragmatics, especially cross-cultural pragmatics (e.g. Blum-Kulka *et al.* 1989; Kasper 2001). Cross-cultural pragmatics studies the realization of speech acts like requests and apologies in different cultural contexts (Blum-Kulka *et al.* 1989), as well as the cultural variations of the Gricean cooperative principle in conversation (Matsumoto 1989) and of politeness strategies (Lakoff 1990). Cross-cultural or intercultural discourse studies are associated with linguists like Jochen Rehbein (1985) and Juliane House (House *et al.* 2003) in Germany; Michael Clyne (1994) in Australia; Srikant Sarangi and Celia Roberts in the UK (Sarangi and Coulthard 2000); Ron and Suzanne Scollon (Scollon and Scollon [1995] 2001) in the USA (see essential readings in Kiesling and Paulston 2005). This field of research studies the exchanges between interlocutors from various cultural backgrounds, mostly in professional or institutional contexts, very often with unequal speaking rights. It has helped professionals in the legal, medical or service industry deal with the pitfalls of communication across cultural and national contexts. It has helped foreign language teachers design authentic communicative tasks and activities in preparation for using language in real contexts of everyday life. Cross-cultural discourse studies have benefited from research done in cognitive semantics, and specifically the exploration of semantic universals across different languages (Wierzbicka 1992). Since the 1980s, cognitive linguistics has helped us understand how culture relies on shared idealized cognitive models of reality and conceptual metaphors that enable members of a cultural community to make sense of the world around them (Lakoff 1987).

Intercultural communication (IC) has become since the 1980s a broad field of research (for a review see Kramsch 2002b). In applied linguistics, it is related mostly to language education and professional language use. In language education, the concept of intercultural competence was defined in Europe by Byram and Zarate (1997) on the basis of research in cultural studies and cultural anthropology. It has been elaborated as intercultural communicative competence by Byram (1997, 2003), Byram and Fleming (1998) and Guilherme (2000). In the professional world, the major contribution of applied linguistics to IC has been the work of Scollon and Scollon ([1995] 2001).

The field of intercultural education manifests itself differently in Europe and in the USA. In Europe, two strands of intercultural education are noteworthy. First, a German strand of applied linguistics (*Sprachlehr- und lernforschung*) that focuses on interpreting the culturally foreign Other. This strand of research on the intercultural is the work of German and Austrian scholars in educational linguistics. It is associated with literature scholars like Lothar Bredella and Werner Delanoy (Bredella and Delanoy 1999) and applied linguists like Christine Schwerdtfeger (see Duxa *et al.* 2005). Drawing on phenomenological and hermeneutic strands of European continental philosophy, it deals with the cultural identity of language learners, cultural stereotypes and the dialectic of Self and Other. It considers its goals as promoting tolerance, empathy, personal transformation and cross-cultural understanding.

Intercultural learning is a second strand of research developed in Europe through the work of such educational researchers as Ingrid Gogolin (1994), Adelheid Hu (1999), Barbara Schmenk (2004) and Jörg Roche (2001) in Germany, Michael Byram (1997) in the UK, Karen Risager (2007) in Denmark, and Hans-Jürgen Krumm in Austria (see Barkowski and Faistauer 2002). It is represented in the electronic journal *Zeitschrift für interkulturellen Fremdsprachenunterricht* edited by Britta Hufeisen and Manfred Prokop (Lorey *et al.* 2007). The

Claire Kramsch

adjective 'intercultural' has been applied to competences, speakers, learning, pedagogy, stances. Coupled with 'communicative', as in 'intercultural communicative pedagogy', it is firmly aimed at facilitating concrete practical encounters within the EU and at improving cooperation across European borders. Intercultural learning, originally anchored in the field of British cultural studies and German social studies, has been the object of public controversy between education researchers like Adelheid Hu, whose primary concern is the schooling of immigrant children and their integration in the host society, and linguistic discourse analysts like Juliane House and Willis Edmondson, whose main concern is adult second language acquisition and use (see Edmondson and House 1998; Hu 1999). Recently, the growing heterogeneity of national cultures and the increasing mobility of people across national borders are challenging simplistic dichotomies of Self and Other and are inviting us to re-think the relation of language and culture in language education.

In the USA, intercultural competence has often been associated with communication studies, and cross-cultural psychology, which do not give much attention to language per se. When the European concept gained interest among American language educators, it lost the strong moral and political dimension it had in European educational circles (Byram 2003; Neuner 2003; Zarate 2003) and was given an individualistic and instrumental dimension. If in Europe intercultural competence strives to promote tolerance and citizenship, in the USA it focuses more on participation and collaboration around common tasks for the empowerment of the individual (e.g. Pavlenko and Lantolf 2000; Pavlenko and Blackledge 2004; Lantolf and Thorne 2007). In Australia, intercultural learning has become the major pedagogic objective for foreign language educators (Lo Bianco *et al.* 1999), with the more cosmopolitan goal of preparing citizens of the world who can act as a bridge between East and West.

Finally, the 1990s saw the growth of computer technology to mediate and foster communication across cultures. Through hypermedia and multimodal technology, it has facilitated access to the visual and verbal culture of distant others (e.g. Kramsch and Andersen 1999; Warschauer and Kern 2000). Telecollaboration has encouraged verbal exchanges across social and cultural contexts (Kern *et al.* 2004; Ware and Kramsch 2005; Belz and Thorne 2006). However, while the focus on discourse in the 1980s coincided with a constructivist view of culture as historically contingent and relative to one's perspective on events, and was steering the field in post-structuralist directions, the binary structure of the computer and its use as a procedural tool for the transmission of information have encouraged a structuralist approach to studying language and culture based on objective, measurable phenomena.

Indeed, there is a noticeable tension between interest in culture and interest in discourse, between structuralist and emerging post-structuralist/constructivist views of language and culture. Is language a reflection/representation of culture, or does language in discourse actually construct what we call culture? As the Scollons describe in the second edition of their best-seller *Intercultural Communication* (2001), they originally had in mind to write a book about interdiscursive communication, but the publisher felt that the term 'intercultural' would appeal to a larger readership. The term 'discourse' implies a relational, decentered, multiperspectival, variable approach to culture that offers less certainties to businessmen, politicians and language teachers, who prefer to see in 'culture' something stable, predictable and controllable. It has been left to critical discourse analysts and applied linguists like Alastair Pennycook (2001), Norman Fairclough (1992) and Ruth Wodak (1994), and to post-structuralist sociolinguists like Jan Blommaert (2005) to draw attention to the decentered, historically contingent, and conflictual nature of discourse across cultures.

2000 to the present: culture as portable historicity and subjectivity, constructed in and through discourse

Some anthropologists are moving away from studying culture to studying historicities and subjectivities. The spectacular ascendancy of linguistic anthropology following in the footsteps of Dell Hymes and John Gumperz has transformed the nature of what used to be called 'culture'. As linguistic anthropologist William Hanks (1996) demonstrates, language as symbolic practice constructs the genres, identities, and subjectivities of our daily existence. Through the pervasive indexicality of discourse and the citationality of speech acts, present utterances are permeated with prior discourses that irrupt into the present and bring about both the historical continuity and the discontinuities of culture.

Several developments have made a discourse approach to culture more desirable in recent years. The increased importance given to symbolic forms of power – global information networks, round-the-clock media, mass marketing and the communication culture of fast capitalism, has increased the gap between the realities on the ground and the discourses that give meaning to these realities. Economic globalization has exacerbated the clash between the discourse of a global market and the discourse of local traditions and beliefs (Coupland 2010). Given the widespread migrations and the divergence of interests around the globe, intercultural communication can no longer be seen as the dispassionate, rational negotiation of meaning between two interlocutors who come from two different national cultures. It has to be seen as a complex system of emergent multilingual meanings with non-linear and unpredictable outcomes, where interlocutors occupy various subject positions on various timescales and with various forms of dominance and control (Lemke 2000; Pennycook 2007; Larsen-Freeman and Cameron 2008). Some have proposed 'language ecology' as a metaphor for this complexity approach to the study of language as cultural context (van Lier 2004; Kramsch 2002a; Kramsch and Whiteside 2008). Blommaert (2005) has suggested the notion of 'layered simultaneity' to capture the fact that actions and events occur at any given time on various temporal and spatial scales, often causing miscommunication. Indeed, in the era of globalization linguistic and literacy resources that would be functional in one place become dysfunctional when transplanted to other places, as in the case, for example, of a Congolese woman in Belgium accused of shoplifting who was asked by the police to write her version of the events. Her literacy practices were perfectly appropriate in Africa but failed to achieve their effect with the Belgian bureaucracy (ibid.: 82).

The Internet and the networking culture on-line, with its blogs, electronic chatrooms and network sites like Facebook and Twitter, present a challenge to institutional authority and to established cultures. They offer an a-historical world of connections and relations that replace quality with quantity, time with space, reality with hyperreality (e.g. Poster 1990; Mitchell 2003). Virtual worlds like Second Life provide imagined spaces and self-designed avatars that can reconstruct actual cultures without the constraints imposed by history, biology and biography. The construction of these virtual worlds is heavily dependent on symbolic systems and the impact of symbolic form on the emotions and beliefs of computer users. This is an area of applied linguistics that is in dire need of research, as it is increasingly affecting our sense of who we are and who we have been, as well as our understanding of our surrounding culture.

Main current issues

In applied linguistic research

In the last two decades applied linguistics has been concerned about its identity as an interdisciplinary field of research at the intersection of theory and practice. Most of the current

Claire Kramsch

issues which applied linguistic research has to grapple with come from the applied and inter-disciplinary nature of the field, and the problems this presents for the study of language and culture: (1) description vs prescription, (2) description vs prediction, (3) linguistic vs educational concerns, (4) structuralist vs post-structuralist approaches to research, and (5) who gets to frame real-world problems: the practitioner or the researcher? I take each one in turn.

The first issue that confronts an applied field like applied linguistics has to do with the expectation that the findings of researchers will lead to immediate prescriptions for the practice. Businessmen expect from applied linguists prescriptions on how to behave when negotiating deals with partners from other cultures, medical personnel expect to learn how to improve their bedside manners by tailoring their care to their patients' 'culture', court translators expect to learn how to interpret and convey the intentions of their clients beyond the words uttered. The reason the US State Department is currently recruiting anthropologists to join the battlefields in Iraq and Afghanistan is precisely because the US military needs to 'know' the culture of the enemy and hopes to get from these researchers guidelines on how to behave in order to befriend (or capture) local nationals. The issue of description vs prescription lies at the core of any applied field. It raises questions of ethical responsibility that emerge also in the second issue, hotly debated in applied linguistics – the role of culture in language tests.

The cultural bias of language tests has long been a serious concern of applied linguists. While language tests are supposed to predict future verbal behavior in a variety of social contexts, very often their cultural content seems to want to predict cultural assimilation, not merely linguistic ability. Shohamy (2001) demonstrates conclusively how language tests have been used to discriminate against ethnic groups in immigration situations. McNamara (2005) shows how tests that purport to test linguistic abilities, in fact, like the biblical shibboleth, often test cultural allegiance and loyalty. Language tests raise the thorny issue of the relation of language and thought and how much cultural knowledge gate-keepers are entitled to require of potential immigrants to industrialized societies. The problem is equally acute in the other real-world problem which applied linguists are called upon to adjudicate, namely achievement tests in educational systems. Testing researchers have shown how standard achievement tests (SATs) are skewed in favor of test takers who are from the same culture as the test designers (Freedle 2003). Current efforts in Europe to test for intercultural competence (Hu and Byram 2009) are fraught with dangers of oversimplifying 'culture' and the notion of 'tolerance toward other cultures'.

Some applied linguists even argue that we should do away with the notion of intercultural learning altogether – a superfluous concept, in their view (Edmondson and House 1998). Doesn't communicative competence already include the ability to negotiate differences in assumptions, worldviews and discourse styles that we call 'culture'? Why should we specifically teach understanding and tolerance of other cultures when communicative language teaching already entails expressing, interpreting and negotiating meanings that might be very different from one culture to the other? The debate that went on in the first years of the twenty-first century was a confrontation between discourse analysts and educationists in Germany around the notion of culture: culture as discourse vs culture as moral universe. The first can be explained and negotiated rationally, the second requires mature judgment and a certain dose of humility to not only accept cultural difference but to acknowledge the power differential among cultures, and, ultimately, the fact that all culture is political.

Many applied linguists, especially those who help immigrants deal with ethnic prejudice and discrimination and facilitate their adjustment in the host country, would agree that applied linguists are called to play a political role. In courtrooms and classrooms, in hospital wards and health services, in boardrooms and at press conferences, applied linguists are confronted with political problems in the real world where the language-culture nexus comes into play. There is currently some debate as to whether to consider this nexus from a structuralist or a post-structuralist perspective. Post-structuralist thinkers like Weedon (1987) and Cameron (2000) see culture as constructed in and through discourse and emerging locally from verbal interactions in historically contingent contexts. Post-structuralism precludes any essentialization of cultures. Rather than focus on the multiple, changing and even conflictual nature of structures in the social world – males vs females, powerful vs powerless, native vs non-native, it turns its attention away from the structures themselves and focuses instead on the conditions of possibility of certain structures rather than others emerging at certain points in time. For example, using Blommaert's example (see above), applied linguists in the post-structuralist vein ask not: how could the Congolese shoplifter write a better letter to persuade the Belgian authorities of her innocence, but: what conditions of colonization, globalization, ethnic prejudice led this woman to move to Belgium in the first place and be accused of shoplifting? The first question leads directly to social welfare and domestic political activism. The second does not lead to a concrete solution to the problem at hand but addresses the more complex and no less political issue of language, culture, and globalization (e.g. Coupland 2010).

The question, then, lies in the nature of the 'real-world' problems that applied linguists are meant to solve. How should these problems be framed? And who gets to frame them: the practitioners and politicians or the researchers? A case in point is the current rift between foreign/second language acquisition research and research on developmental bilingualism in applied linguistics. The first is usually seen as dealing with the development of mature adolescents and young adults learning a foreign/second language in instructional settings. The second is seen as focusing on children learning two languages at birth, or growing up in families that speak two languages or belong to two different cultures, or children of immigrants who don't speak the language of their ancestors but are familiar with their culture and now learn their heritage language in school. But the distinction is not as clear as it seems at first blush. Many foreign language learners can be found in elementary or middle schools, at a time when they are not yet fully socialized in their first language. Many bilinguals are mature adolescents learning their heritage language in instructional settings. Foreign language learners sometimes already know another foreign language, have grown up in various cultures, and undergo an equally powerful emotional experience learning the foreign language as bilinguals do learning the language of their ancestors. But in English-dominant countries where learning a foreign language is seen as an elite activity reserved for the privileged few, fighting for one's rights as a 'bilingual' is considered a more urgent matter of social integration and equal opportunity than choosing to acquire an additional language to enrich one's education. Moreover, foreign languages are framed in terms of foreign policy, while bilingual education and heritage languages are framed in terms of civil rights. Two different political cultures indeed. Some applied linguists are currently questioning the traditional definition of the real-world problems at hand in these two cases (Kramsch 2005, 2009).

In applied linguistic practice

In the field of language education, whether they are native or non-native speakers of the language they teach, language teachers are typically worried that they are not qualified to teach 'culture'. Their persisting question: 'We don't know what culture is nor do we know how to teach it', when so much has been written about it, shows that 'culture' is still taken to be a body of knowledge outside the linguistic system and that teachers might not know how to define their own culture, let alone a foreign one. Fearful of teaching stereotypes and anxious not to bring politics into the language classroom, language teachers don't all agree that they should teach 'meaning' beyond the meanings captured by grammars and dictionaries. They don't feel legitimized to teach the living, idiosyncratic cultural meanings given to words by living speakers who might or might not be native speakers. In the old days when 'culture' was synonymous with literature and the arts, language teachers had no qualms about assessing a student's ability to interpret a poem or a painting in the language class. Today the democratization and popularization of culture and its fragmentation into various sub- and hybrid cultures make teachers feel inadequate to the task of knowing, let alone interpreting, foreign cultures. In our days of multiple choice tests, many teachers have lost the ability to evaluate the validity of arguments explaining cultural events on the basis of historical, literary, social or political knowledge. Ultimately, they fear not being able to control the transmission of cultural knowledge, if it cannot be standardized or normativized. The link that applied linguistics establishes between discourse and culture invites language teachers to reflect on how their own discourse and culture have shaped their identity as individuals and as teachers.

In public life, applied linguists' understanding of the relation between discourse and cultural identity has served to improve relations between staff and customers at hospitals and factories in Australia, and to improve health services, industrial relations and medical examinations in the UK (Sarangi and Coulthard 2000). The challenge is how to improve interaction between doctors and patients, lawyers and clients, corporate managers and consumers in a variety of cultural contexts, while furthering the interests of the company. These interests might be channeled by economic or political forces that critical applied linguists are sensitive to.

In the same manner as the notion of culture has often become politicized in the struggle for the recognition of ethnic identity and minority rights, it has become commodified in the economic sphere by narrow-cast marketing strategies that strive to target an ever more differentiated range of consumers based on their individual tastes and their cultural affiliations. The link between language and culture is not lost on marketing strategists like Frank Luntz (2006), who consults for political campaign managers and CEOs and sells them the linguistic and cultural 'hidden persuaders' that will make people vote for their candidate or buy their product. Applied linguists are concerned about this technologization of culture, especially in the interactions between global funding agencies and local NGOs in developing countries. The clashes between the neo-liberal discourse of development and the local discourse of economic survival are starting to be documented (Coupland 2010, Kramsch and Boner 2010). They offer as yet the best example of the usefulness of a discourse approach to intercultural communication in our era of globalization.

Finally, the role of technology has to be mentioned in the creation of a cyberculture that is increasingly shaping both language and culture and transforming social life. As the computer transforms the very time/space axes of our existence and redefines the real, it has generated feelings of empowerment, of liberation from cultural conventions and constraints; it has opened up dreams of connectivity and ubiquity of an a-cultural, a-historical kind. But at the same time, it has ushered in feelings of uncommon vulnerability, uncertainty and uncontrollability. In such periods, ideologies (explicit, highly organized meaning systems, both political and religious), symbols and rituals tend to shape people's actions more than conscious, rational decision making (Swidler 1986). Applied linguists are turning their attention to these ideologies and rituals (Rampton 2009) as well as to the proliferation of parody, simulation, and humor that deals with the contradictions of social life (Yurchak and Boyer 2008). In the teaching of foreign languages, the relentless pressure to use networked computers and multimedia technology to teach both the language and the culture in attractive ways is calling for more research on the part of applied linguists into the effects of technology on the very nature of the language and the culture they teach.

Future trajectory and new debates

In applied linguistic research and practice the link between any given language and any given culture has become controversial. It is evoked by various interest groups for economic or political gain. Computer technology promises to do away with cultural boundaries altogether, but it only exacerbates the desire to create new communities of practice that will, in time, establish their own cultures of inclusion and exclusion, their own gate-keeping conventions for the use of symbolic systems.

In research

Culture might slowly lose its power to explain human behavior in a multilingual/multicultural world where people are born in one culture, grow up in another, and end up living and work-ing in a third. In the multimedia environments of the computer, language itself may change its value and use. More important than a person's 'language' and 'culture' might be the socio-economic, historical or ideological subject positions that people take and that get expressed through the multiple symbolic systems they choose to use, be they verbal, visual, musical or virtual, to represent and act upon the world and others in multiple ecological dimensions. Culture in action is less a question of stable values, identities or ideologies that cause people to act in certain ways, than a repertoire of strategies for action that individuals activate differently depending on whether they lead 'settled' or 'unsettled' lives (Swidler 1986).

The debate between structuralist and post-structuralist views on language and culture is sure to continue in the future. Post-structuralism is a challenge for applied linguistics because it seems to blur the distinction between the social sciences, with their positivistic, objective, evidence-based methods of inquiry, and the human sciences with their hermeneutic, subjective interpretation-based modes of analysis. Given the increasing prestige accorded to the physical and natural sciences over the humanities, any attempt to make the interpretation of culture dependent on the subject position of the researcher brings the applied linguist, as Clifford Geertz would say, 'rather closer to what a critic does to illumine a poem than what an astronomer does to account for a star' (1983: 10).

As always, the applied linguist studying the language-and-culture nexus has to weigh scien-tific validity against scientific reliability, or attempt to redefine altogether the very bases of its scientific endeavor.

In practice

For language teachers, the question of culture will become more acute: Which culture to teach in a multilingual world of diasporas, forced migrations and global communication technolo-gies? In the USA as in Europe, there is right now a push to de-institutionalize the teaching of foreign languages and cultures: sending the students abroad, pairing them up with native speakers, and telecollaboration over the Internet have all transformed language study into skill training for the real world of the job market. This instrumentalization of FL education is of great concern to educators in Europe (see Doff *et al.* 2008) as well as in the USA (see MLA Ad Hoc Committee on Foreign Languages 2007). In the USA, the struggle for attention between the proponents of bilingual education and education in minority languages on the

313

Claire Kramsch

one hand, and the proponents of foreign language education on the other will continue. Both face serious challenges. While a xenophobic ideology threatens bilingual and minority education, a nationalistic ideology threatens to reduce foreign language study to a weapon in the fight for US economic superiority and national security. In both cases, the dispassionate research of applied linguists needs to go beyond the culture wars taking place in American academia.

The global spread of English and of the neo-liberal ideology with which it is often associated risks fostering a kind of 'multilingualism lite' in which other languages are seen as exotic variations on the common neo-liberal culture of the English-dominant world. It is significant that translation, language awareness and metadiscursive reflection are making a comeback in a field still very much dominated by communicative language teaching and its utilitarian view of human communication. Both in the research and in the practice of applied linguistics, we can look forward to a greater awareness of and importance given to borders of all kinds, as well as to the historicities and the subjectivities of those who live on both sides of these borders.

Summary

Culture, defined as membership in a discourse community that shares a common social space and history, and common imaginings, entered the field of applied linguistics through the study of language in its sociocultural context, i.e. discourse. Discourse, as verbal communicative practices and habits of thought, embodies a community's identity and moral values, its understanding of history and its aspirations for the future. Cross-cultural pragmatics, intercultural communication, and intercultural learning are some of the areas of applied linguistics that study the link between language and culture. The field right now is grappling with the tension between structuralist and post-structuralist approaches to culture, and with the revolution brought about by computer technology in our experience of time and space, and our sense of reality. In the future, the attention of applied linguists will shift from stable, national cultures to portable historicities and subjectivities that people carry in their minds as so many potential strategies for action.

Related topics

critical discourse analysis; identity; language and teacher education; language learning; language socialization; sociocultural theory; technology and language learning

Further reading

Bourdieu, P. (1991) *Language and Symbolic Power*, J. Thompson (ed.), G. Raymond and M. Adamson (trans.) Cambridge, MA: Harvard University Press. (Canonical reading for understanding the symbolic nature of culture and its social reproduction.)

Gumperz, J. J. and Levinson, S. C. (eds) (1996) *Rethinking Linguistic Relativity*, Cambridge: Cambridge University Press. (A collection of papers that represent the latest thinking on the relation of language and thought.)

Hanks, W. F. (1996) *Language and Communicative Practices*, Boulder, CO: Westview Press, esp. part 2, 'Language the nexus of context'. (A comprehensive conceptualization of language as symbolic, social and cultural practice by one of the leading linguistic anthropologists.)

Kramsch, C. (1993) *Context and Culture in Language Teaching*, Oxford: Oxford University Press. (A readable presentation of the relation of discourse and culture for foreign language teachers.)

Poster, M. (1995) *The Second Media Age*, New York: Blackwell. (A thought-provoking study of the interrelations between the technology-shaped contexts of urban life and the kind of communication that these contexts make possible.)

References

Barkowski, H. and Faistauer, R. (eds) (2002) *Sachen Deutsch als Fremdsprache: Festschrift für Hans-Jürgen Krumm*, Hohengehren, Germany: Schneider Verlag.

Belz, J. A. and Thorne, S. L. (eds) (2006) *Internet-mediated Intercultural Foreign Language Education and the Intercultural Speaker*, Boston, MA: Heinle and Heinle.

Block, D. (2003) *The Social Turn in Second Language Acquisition*, Edinburgh: Edinburgh University Press.

Blommaert, J. (2005) *Discourse: A Critical Introduction*, Cambridge: Cambridge University Press.

Blum-Kulka, S., Kasper, G. and House, J. (eds) (1989) *Cross-cultural Pragmatics: Requests and Apologies*, vol. XXXI in the series Advances in Discourse Processes, R. O. Freedle (ed.), Norwood, NJ: Ablex.

Bredella, L. and Delanoy, W. (eds) (1999) *Interkultureller Fremdsprachenunterricht*, Tübingen: Gunter Narr.

Byram, M. (1997). *Teaching and Assessing Intercultural Communicative Competence*, Clevedon: Multilingual Matters.

Byram, M. (ed.) (2003) *Intercultural Competence*, Strasbourg: Council of Europe.

Byram, M. and Zarate, G. (eds) (1997) *The Sociocultural and Intercultural Dimension of Language Learning and Teaching*, Strasbourg: Council of Europe.

Byram, M. and Fleming, M. (eds) (1998) *Language Learning in Intercultural Perspective*, Cambridge: Cambridge University Press.

Cameron, D. (2000) *Good to Talk? Living and Working in a Communication Culture*, London: Sage.

Clyne, M. (1994) *Inter-cultural Communication at Work: Cultural Values in Discourse*, Cambridge: Cambridge University Press.

Coupland, N. (ed.) (2010). *The Handbook of Language and Globalization*, Oxford and Malden, MA: Wiley-Blackwell.

Doff, S., Hüllen, W. and Klippel, F. (eds) (2008) *Visions of Language in Education*, Munich: Langenscheidt.

Duxa, S., Hu, A. and Schmenk, B. (eds) (2005) *Grenzen überschreiten. Menschen, Sprachen, Kulturen: Festschrift für Inge Christine Schwerdtfeger*, Tübingen: Gunter Narr.

Edmondson, W. and House, J. (1998) 'Interkulturelles lernen: ein überflüssiger Begriff', *Zeitschrift für Fremdsprachenforschung* 9(2): 161–88.

Fairclough, N. (1992) *Discourse and Social Change*, Cambridge: Polity Press.

Freedle, R. O. (2003) 'Correcting the SAT's ethnic and social-class bias: a method for reestimating SAT scores', *Harvard Educational Review*, 73(1): 1–43.

Geertz, C. (1983) *Local Knowledge: Further Essays in Interpretive Anthropology*, New York: Basic Books.

Gogolin, I. (1994) *Der monolinguale Habitus der multilingualen Schule*, Münster: Waxman Verlag.

Guilherme, M. (2000) 'Intercultural competence', in M. Byram (ed.) *Routledge Encyclopedia of Language Learning and Teaching*, London: Routledge.

Gumperz, J. J. (1982) *Discourse Strategies*, Cambridge: Cambridge University Press.

House, J., Kasper, G. and Ross, S. (eds) (2003) *Misunderstanding in Social Life*, London: Longman.

Hu, A. (1999) 'Interkulturelles Lernen. Eine Auseinandersetzung mit der Kritik an einem umstrittenen Konzept', *Zeitschrift für Fremdsprachenforschung* 10(2): 277–303.

Hu, A. and Byram, M. (eds) (2009) *Interkulturelle Kompetenz und fremdsprachliches Lernen: Modelle, Empirie, Evaluation / Intercultural Competence and Foreign Language Learning: Models, Empiricism, Assessment*, Tübingen: Narr Francke Attempto Verlag.

Kasper, G. (2001) 'Four perspectives on L2 pragmatic development', *Applied Linguistics* 22(4): 502–38.

Kern, R., Ware, P. and Warschauer, M. (2004) 'Crossing frontiers: new directions in online pedagogy and research', *Annual Review of Applied Linguistics* 24: 243–60.

Kiesling, S. F. and Bratt Paulston, C. (eds) (2005) *Intercultural Discourse and Communication: The Essential Readings*, Oxford: Blackwell.

Kramsch, C. (1998) *Language and Culture*, Oxford Introductions to Language Studies, Oxford: Oxford University Press.

——(2002a) 'Introduction. How can we tell the dancer from the dance?', in C. Kramsch (ed.) *Language Acquisition and Language Socialization: Ecological Perspectives*, London: Continuum.

——(2002b) 'In search of the intercultural', *Journal of Sociolinguistics* 6(2): 275–85 (review article).

——(2004) 'Language, thought, and culture', in A. Davies and C. Elder (eds) *Handbook of Applied Linguistics*, Oxford and Malden, MA: Wiley-Blackwell.

——(2005) 'Post 9/11: 'Foreign languages between knowledge and power', *Applied Linguistics* 26(4): 545–67.

——(2009) *The Multilingual Subject*, Oxford: Oxford University Press.

Kramsch, C. and Andersen, R. (1999) 'Teaching text and context through multimedia', *Language Learning and Technology* 2(2): 31–42.

Kramsch, C. and Boner, E. (2010) 'Shadows of discourse: intercultural communication in global contexts', in N. Coupland (ed.) *The Handbook of Language and Globalization*, Oxford and Malden, MA: Wiley-Blackwell.

Kramsch, C. and Whiteside, A. (2008) 'Language ecology in multilingual settings. Towards a theory of symbolic competence', *Applied Linguistics* 29(4): 645–71.

Lakoff, G. (1987) *Women, Fire, and Dangerous Things: What Categories Reveal about the Mind*, Chicago: University of Chicago Press.

Lakoff, R. (1990) *Talking Power: The Politics of Language in our Lives*, New York: Basic Books.

Lantolf, J. and Thorne, S. (2007) *Sociocultural Theory and the Genesis of Second Language Development*, Oxford: Oxford University Press.

Larsen-Freeman, D. and Cameron, L. (2008) *Complex Systems and Applied Linguistics*, Oxford: Oxford University Press.

Lemke, J. (2000) 'Across the scales of time: artifacts, activities and meanings in ecosocial systems', *Mind, Culture, and Activity* 7(4): 273–90.

Lo Bianco, J., Liddicoat, A. and Crozet, C. (1999) *Striving for the Third Place: Intercultural Competence Through Language Education*, Melbourne: Language Australia.

Lorey, C., Plews, J. L. and Rieger, C. L. (eds) (2007) *Interkulturelle Kompetenzen im Fremdsprachenunterricht: Intercultural Literacies and German in the Classroom, Festschrift für Manfred Prokop*, Tübingen: Gunter Narr.

Luntz, F. (2006) *Words that Work*, New York: Hyperion.

Matsumoto, Y. (1989) 'Politeness and conversational universals: observations from Japanese', *Multilingua* 8(2–3): 207–21.

McNamara, T. (2005) '21st century shibboleth: language tests, identity and intergroup conflict', *Language Policy* 4(4): 351–70.

Mitchell, W. J. (2003) *Me++: The Cyborg Self and the Networked City*, Cambridge, MA: MIT Press.

MLA Ad Hoc Committee on Foreign Languages (2007) 'Foreign languages and higher education: new structures for a changed world', *Profession 2007*, 234–45.

Moerman, M. (1988) *Talking Culture: Ethnography and Conversation Analysis*, Philadelphia: University of Pennsylvania Press.

Neuner, G. (2003) 'Sociocultural interim worlds in foreign language teaching and learning', in M. Byram (ed.) *Intercultural Competence*, Strasbourg: Council of Europe.

Ochs, E. (2002) 'Becoming a speaker of culture', in C. Kramsch (ed.) *Language Acquisition and Language Socialization: Ecological Perspectives*, London: Continuum.

Pavlenko, A. and Blackledge, A. (eds) (2004) *Negotiation of Identities in Multilingual Contexts*, Clevedon: Multilingual Matters.

Pavlenko, A. and Lantolf, J. (2000) 'Second language learning as participation and the (re)construction of selves', in J. P. Lantolf (ed.) *Sociocultural Theory and Second Language Learning*, Oxford: Oxford University Press.

Pennycook, A. (2001) *Critical Applied Linguistics*, Mahwah, NJ: Lawrence Erlbaum Associates.

——(2007) *Global Englishes and Transcultural Flows*, London: Routledge.

Pinker, S. (1994) *The Language Instinct: How the Mind Creates Language*, New York: Harper.

Poster, M. (1990) *The Mode of Information: Poststructuralism and Social Context*, Chicago: University of Chicago Press.

Rampton, B. (2009) 'Interaction ritual and not just artful performance in crossing and stylization', *Language in Society* 38: 149–76.

Rehbein, J. (ed.) (1985) *Interkulturelle Kommunikation*, Tübingen: Gunter Narr.

Risager, K. (2007) *Language and Culture Pedagogy: From a National to a Transnational Paradigm*, Clevedon: Multilingual Matters.

Roche, J. (2001) *Interkulturelle Sprachdidaktik: Eine Einführung*, Tübingen: Gunter Narr.

Sacks, H., Schegloff, E. A. and Jefferson, G. (1974) 'A simplest systematics for the organization of turn taking in conversation', *Language* 50(4): 696–735.

Sarangi, S. and Coulthard, M. (eds) (2000) *Discourse and Social Life*, London: Pearson.

Schmenk, B. (2004) 'Interkulturelles Lernen *versus* Autonomie?', in W. Börner and K. Vogel (eds) *Emotion und Kognition im Fremdsprachenunterricht*, Tübingen: Gunter Narr.

Scollon, R. and Scollon, S. ([1995] 2001) *Intercultural Communication*, 2nd edn, Oxford: Blackwell.

Shohamy, E. (2001) *The Power of Tests. A Critical Perspective on the Uses of Language Tests*, London: Longman.

Stern, H. H. (1983) *Fundamental Concepts of Language Teaching*, Oxford: Oxford University Press.

Swidler, A. (1986) 'Culture in action: symbols and strategies', *American Sociological Review* 51(2): 273–86.

van Lier, L. (2004) *The Ecology and Semiotics of Language Learning: A Sociocultural Perspective*, Dordrecht: Kluwer Academic.

Ware, P. and Kramsch, C. (2005) 'Toward an intercultural stance: teaching German and English through telecollaboration', *Modern Language Journal* 89(2): 190–205.

Warschauer, M. and Kern, R. (eds) (2000) *Network-based Language Teaching: Concepts and Practice*, Cambridge: Cambridge University Press.

Weedon, C. (1987) *Feminist Practice and Poststructuralist Theory*, Oxford: Blackwell.

Widdowson, H. G. (2007) *Discourse Analysis*, Oxford: Oxford University Press.

Wierzbicka, A. (1992) *Semantics, Culture, and Cognition: Universal Human Concepts in Culture-specific Configurations*, Oxford: Oxford University Press.

Wodak, R. (1994) 'Critical discourse analysis', in J. Blommaert (ed.) *Handbook of Pragmatics*, The Hague: Mouton

Yurchak, A. and Boyer, D. (2008) 'Postsocialist studies, cultures of parody and American *Stiob*', *Anthropology News* November: 9–10.

Zarate, G. (2003) 'Identities and plurilingualism: preconditions for the recognition of intercultural competences', in M. Byram (ed.) *Intercultural Competence*, Strasbourg: Council of Europe.

22
Identity

Bonny Norton

A history of the area

Interest in identity in the field of applied linguistics, more broadly, and language education, more specifically, is best understood in the context of a shift from a predominantly psycho-linguistic approach to second language acquisition (SLA) to include a greater focus on sociological and anthropological dimensions of language learning, particularly with reference to socio-cultural, post-structural, and critical theory (Block 2003; Morgan 2007, Norton and Toohey 2001; Ricento 2005; Zuengler and Miller 2006). This chapter will focus on this extensive body of literature, in which researchers are interested not only in linguistic input and output in SLA, but in the relationship between the language learner and the larger social world. It will thus pay particular attention to research that has examined the diverse social, historical, and cultural contexts in which language learning takes place, and how learners negotiate and sometimes resist the diverse opportunities those contexts offer them.

In the 1970s and 1980s, language education scholars interested in identity tended to draw distinctions between social identity and cultural identity. While 'social identity' was seen to reference the relationship between the individual language learner and the larger social world, as mediated through institutions such as families, schools, workplaces, social services, and law courts (e.g. Gumperz 1982), 'cultural identity' referenced the relationship between an individual and members of a particular ethnic group (such as Mexican and Japanese) who share a common history, a common language, and similar ways of understanding the world (e.g. Valdes 1986). However, as Atkinson (1999) has noted, past theories of cultural identity tended to essentialize and oversimplify identity in problematic ways. In more recent years, the difference between social and cultural identity is seen to be theoretically more fluid, and the inter-sections between social and cultural identities are considered more significant than their differences (Duff and Uchida 1997). In this research, identity is seen as socioculturally con-structed, and scholars draw on both institutional and community practices to understand the conditions under which language learners speak, read, and write the target language (see Kramsch, this volume).

The diverse research covered in journal special issues of *Linguistics and Education* (Martin-Jones and Heller 1996), the *TESOL Quarterly* (Norton 1997), and *Language and Education*

(Sarangi and Baynham 1996), anticipated the wide range of research on identity, characteristic of the early years of the twenty-first century. Many monographs on the topic have also been published over the past decade (Block 2007; Clarke 2008; Day 2002; Heller 2007; Kanno 2008; Kramsch 2009; Miller 2003; Nelson 2009; Norton 2000; Potowski 2007; Stein 2008; Toohey 2000); and the establishment in 2002 of the award-winning *Journal of Language, Identity, and Education*, edited by Ricento and Wiley, has published an exciting array of research on language, identity and education.

Main issues

Theories of language

One of the main issues in language education research on identity concerns post-Saussurean theories of language, which achieved much prominence in the late twentieth century, and are associated, amongst others, with the work of Bakhtin (1981), Bourdieu (1991), Hall (1997) and Weedon (1997). These theories build on, but are distinct from, structuralist theories of language, associated predominantly with the work of Saussure (1966). For structuralists, the linguistic system guarantees the meaning of signs (the word and its meaning) and each linguistic community has its own set of signifying practices that give value to the signs in a language. Post-structuralists have critiqued these theories of language on the grounds that structuralism cannot account for struggles over the social meanings that can be attributed to signs in a given language. The signs /success/, /education/, /time/, for example, can have different meanings for different people within the same linguistic community. While structuralists conceive of signs as having idealized meanings, and linguistic communities as being relatively homogeneous and consensual, post-structuralists take the position that the signifying practices of a society are sites of struggle, and that linguistic communities are heterogeneous arenas characterized by conflicting claims to truth and power. Thus language is not conceived of as a neutral medium of communication, but is understood with reference to its social meaning in a frequently inequitable world.

In post-structuralist theories of language, there is much interest in the way power is implicated in relationships between individuals, communities, and nations (Janks 2010). Identity researchers often draw on Foucault (1980) and Bourdieu (1991) to better understand how power operates within society, constraining or enabling human action. Foucault (1980) argues, for example, that power is often invisible in that it frequently naturalizes events and practices in ways that come to be seen as 'normal' to members of a community. Bourdieu (1991), who is particularly interested in language and symbolic power, notes further that the value ascribed to speech cannot be understood apart from the person who speaks, and the person who speaks cannot be understood apart from larger networks of social relationships. Every time we speak, we are negotiating a sense of self in relation to the larger social world, and reorganizing that relationship across time and space. Our gender, race, class, ethnicity, sexual orientation, among other characteristics, are all implicated in this negotiation of identity.

The research of feminist post-structuralists such as Weedon (1997) has been particularly influential in helping applied linguists theorize identity, or what feminist post-structuralists call subjectivity. Three defining characteristics of subjectivity that are of particular interest to language educators are the multiple, non-unitary nature of the subject; subjectivity as a site of struggle; and subjectivity as changing over time. In post-structuralist theory, subjectivity and language are theorized as mutually constitutive. As Weedon (1997) notes, it is through language that a person negotiates a sense of self within and across a range of sites at different points in time, and it is through language that a person gains access to – or is denied access to – powerful social networks that give learners the opportunity to speak. From a language educator's perspective, the conceptualization of subjectivity as multiple and changing is consistent with the view that pedagogical practices can be transformative. While some identity positions may limit and constrain opportunities for learners to speak, read, or write, other identity positions may offer enhanced sets of possibilities for social interaction and human agency.

Identity categories and social change

While much research on identity explores the multiple and intersecting dimensions of language learners' identities, there is a growing body of research that seeks to investigate the ways in which particular relations of race, gender, class, and sexual orientation may impact the language learning process. Innovative research that addresses these issues does not regard such identity categories as 'variables', but rather as sets of relationships that are socially and historically constructed within particular relations of power. Ibrahim's (1999) research with a group of French-speaking continental African students in a Franco-Ontarian high school in Canada explores the impact on language learning of 'becoming black'. He argues that the students' linguistic styles, and in particular their use of Black Stylized English, was a direct outcome of being imagined and constructed as Black by hegemonic discourses and groups. His findings support the view held by Kubota (2004) that a colour-blind conception of multiculturalism does not do justice to the challenges faced by language learners of diverse races and ethnicities.

Similarly, the work of scholars such as Cameron (2006), Pavlenko (2004), and Sunderland (2004) is particularly insightful with regard to intersections of gender and language (see Baxter, this volume). Their conception of gender, which extends beyond female-male divides, is understood to be a system of social relationships and discursive practices that may lead to systemic inequality among particular groups of learners, including women, older people, disabled people, and minorities. Pavlenko, for example, argues for the need to understand the intersections between gender and other forms of oppression, noting that both girls and boys who are silenced in the language classroom are more likely those who are economically marginalized. A number of these issues are taken up in Norton and Pavlenko (2004), who document research from diverse regions of the world that addresses the relationship between gender and language learning with respect to the dominance of the English language internationally.

In a similar spirit, King (2008), Moffatt and Norton (2008), and Nelson (2009) explore the extent to which sexual orientation might be an important identity category in the language classroom. Of central interest is the way in which a teacher can create a supportive environment for learners who might be gay, lesbian, or transgendered. Nelson contrasts a pedagogy of inquiry, which asks how linguistic and cultural practices naturalize certain sexual identities, most notably heterosexuality, with a pedagogy of inclusion, which aims to introduce images as well as experiences of gays and lesbians into curriculum materials. Nelson's approach can fruitfully be applied to other issues of marginalization, helping learners to question normative practices in the target culture into which they have entered.

Interest in identity categories and language learning is gaining momentum. Special issues of the *TESOL Quarterly* on 'Gender and Language Education' (Davis and Skilton-Sylvester 2004) and 'Race and TESOL' (Kubota and Lin 2006) include insightful debates on gender, race, and language learning, while recent monographs by May (2008), Heller (2007), and Rampton (2006) ensure that issues of language, ethnicity, and class remain on the radar in the field. However, while taking race, class, gender, and other structural issues into account in their analysis, language educators argue that there is a need to leave conceptual room for the actions and investments of human agents (Menard-Warwick 2006).

Identity and language teaching

The relevance of identity research for classroom teaching is also of much interest to language educators in different parts of the world. As Lee's (2008) research in a Canadian post-secondary institution suggests, while many language teachers strive to enhance the range of possibilities available to their students, there is often a disjuncture between the pedagogy as conceptualized by the teacher and the practices adopted in the classroom. Despite the best intentions, classroom practices can recreate subordinate student identities, thereby limiting students' access not only to language learning opportunities, but to other more powerful identities. Lee's findings are consistent with those of Ramanathan (2005), whose research in India found that teachers' language practices can reinforce existing inequities among diverse learners of English. Her research suggests that pedagogical language practices that are ritualized and allow for little meaning-making on the part of students may limit the learner's access to more powerful identities. To promote meaning-making in the learning process, Wallace (2003) has worked with adult language learners in the United Kingdom on critical reading courses in which she uses text-focussed activities to address how meaning and power are encoded in texts. Wallace contrasts her approach with dominant English foreign language methodologies that can be seen as 'domesticating' for learners, teaching them only how to fit in with dominant cultures rather than to question and reshape the conditions of their lives.

Other research projects, which have taken place in diverse regions of the world, are illustrative of the ways in which particular pedagogical practices in language classrooms can offer students opportunities for an expanded range of identities. In Mexico, Clemente and Higgins (2008) drew on their longitudinal study of pre-service English teachers in Oaxaca to raise questions about the dominant role that English plays in the globalized political economy, and to illustrate the ways in which non-native English teachers sought to appropriate and 'perform' English without sacrificing local identities. In South Africa, Stein (2008) explored the way in which English language classrooms in under-resourced township schools became transformative sites in which textual, cultural, and linguistic forms were re-appropriated and 're-sourced', with a view to validating those practices that had been marginalized and undervalued by the apartheid system. In a similar spirit, scholars have investigated the extent to which multimodal pedagogies that include drawing, photography, and drama can be incorporated more systematically into the English curriculum in Uganda, enhancing identity options for language learners (Kendrick *et al.* 2006).

In many transformative classrooms that have been discussed in language education literature, language teachers' conceptions of 'language' and thus 'language teaching' are broad in scope (Norton and Toohey 2004). The teachers conceive of language not only as a linguistic system, but as a social practice in which experiences are organized and identities negotiated. There is recognition that if learners are not invested in the language practices of the classroom, learning outcomes are limited, and educational inequities perpetuated. Further, such teachers take great care to offer learners multiple identity positions from which to engage in the language practices of the classroom, the school, and the community.

New debates and future directions

Identity and investment

One of the new debates in language education research on identity concerns the construct of 'investment', developed in my work to complement constructs of motivation in the field of SLA (Norton 2000; Norton Peirce 1995). In my research with immigrant women in Canada, I observed that existing theories of motivation in the field of SLA were not consistent with my findings, and that theories of motivation did not pay sufficient attention to unequal relations of power between language learners and target language speakers. Most theories at the time assumed motivation was a character trait of the individual language learner and that learners who failed to learn the target language were not sufficiently committed to the learning process (see, for example, Schumann 1986). My research found that high levels of motivation did not necessarily translate into good language learning, and that unequal relations of power between language learners and target language speakers was a common theme in the data.

The construct of investment, inspired by the work of Bourdieu (1991), signals the socially and historically constructed relationship of learners to the target language and their often ambivalent desire to learn and practise it. If learners 'invest' in the target language, they do so with the understanding that they will acquire a wider range of symbolic and material resources, which will in turn increase the value of their cultural capital. Unlike notions of instrumental motivation, which often conceive of the language learner as having a unitary, fixed, and ahistorical 'personality', the construct of investment conceives of the language learner as having a complex identity, changing across time and space, and reproduced in social interaction. Thus while motivation can be seen as a primarily psychological construct (Dornyei 2001), investment must be seen within a sociological framework, and seeks to make a meaningful connection between a learner's desire and commitment to learn a language, and their changing identity.

The construct of investment thus provides for a different set of questions associated with a learner's commitment to learning the target language. In addition to asking, for example, 'To what extent is the learner motivated to learn the target language?' the researcher asks, 'What is the learner's investment in the target language practices of this classroom or community?' A learner may be a highly motivated language learner, but may nevertheless have little investment in the language practices of a given classroom or community, which may, for example, be racist, sexist, elitist, or homophobic. Thus despite being highly motivated, a learner could be excluded from the language practices of a classroom, and in time characterized as a 'poor' or unmotivated language learner.

The construct of investment has sparked considerable interest in the field of language education and applied linguistics (see, for example, Cummins 2006; Haneda 2005; McKay and Wong 1996; Pittaway 2004; Potowski 2007; Skilton-Sylvester 2002), including a special issue on the topic in the *Journal of Asian Pacific Communication* (Arkoudis and Davison 2008). Indeed, Cummins (2006), who has drawn on the construct of investment to develop the notion of 'identity texts', has argued that investment has emerged as a 'significant explanatory construct' (2006: 59) in the second language learning literature. As the following projects illustrate, the contexts in which the construct is used varies considerably: McKay and Wong (1996) have drawn on the construct to explain the English language development of four Mandarin-speaking students in grade 7 and 8 in a California school, noting that the needs, desires, and negotiations of students are integral to their investment in the target language. Skilton-Sylvester (2002), drawing on her research with four Cambodian women in adult ESL classes in the

USA, has argued that traditional views of adult motivation and participation do not adequately address the complex lives of adult learners, and that an understanding of a woman's domestic and professional identities is necessary to explain their investment in particular adult ESL programmes. Haneda (2005) has drawn on the construct of investment to understand the engagement of two university students in an advanced Japanese literacy course, concluding that their multimembership in differing communities may have shaped the way they invested in writing in Japanese. Potowski (2007) uses the construct of investment to explain students' use of Spanish in a dual Spanish/English immersion programme in the USA, noting that even if a language programme is well run, a learner's investment in the target language must be consistent with the goals of the programme if language learning is to meet expectations.

Identity and imagined communities

An extension of debates on identity and investment are the imagined communities (Anderson 1991) that language learners aspire to when they learn a new language. In Norton (2001), I drew on my research with two adult immigrant language learners to argue that while the learners were initially actively engaged in classroom practices, the realm of their desired community extended beyond the four walls of the classroom. This imagined community was not accessible to their respective teachers, who, unwittingly, alienated the two language learners, who then withdrew from the language classroom. I have drawn on the work of Lave and Wenger (1991) and Wenger (1998) to argue that in many second language classrooms, all of the members of the classroom community, apart from the teacher, are newcomers to the language practices of that community. The question that arises then is: What community practices do these learners seek to learn? What, indeed, constitutes 'the community' for them?

In many language classrooms, the community may be, to some extent, a reconstruction of past communities and historically constituted relationships, but also a community of the imagination – a desired community that offers possibilities for an enhanced range of identity options in the future. Such imagined communities can be highly varied, from the imagined community of the more public professional to that of the more local homemaker. Learners have different investments in particular members of the target language community, and the people in whom learners have the greatest investment may be the very people who represent or provide access to the imagined community of a given learner. Of particular interest to the language educator is the extent to which such investments are productive for learner engagement in both the classroom and the wider target language community. In essence, an imagined community assumes an imagined identity, and a learner's investment in the target language must be understood within this context.

Such issues have been taken up more extensively in publications such as Pavlenko and Norton (2007) and in a co-edited special issue of the *Journal of Language, Identity, and Education* on 'Imagined Communities and Educational Possibilities' (Kanno and Norton 2003) in which a number of scholars have explored the imagined communities of learners in diverse regions of the world – some of whom have subsequently followed up this initial research in more recent publications. In the Japanese context, for example, Kanno (2008) examines the relationship between school education and inequality of access to bilingualism in five different Japanese schools promoting bilingual education. Kanno argues that in the schools she researched, different visions of children's imagined communities called for different forms of bilingual education, exacerbating existing inequities between students with unequal access to resources.

In Canada, Dagenais and her colleagues (2008) have investigated the linguistic landscape in the vicinity of two elementary schools in Vancouver and Montreal, illustrating the ways in which the children imagined the language of their neighbourhoods, and constructed their identities in relation to them. Dagenais *et al.* describe the innovative ways in which researchers and students drew on multimodal resources such as digital photography to document the linguistic landscape of these neighbourhoods, and the way children in both cities were encouraged to exchange letters, posters, photographs, and videos. Dagenais *et al.* argue that documenting the imagined communities of neighbourhoods, as depicted and understood by children, can provide much information on the children's understanding of their community, an important consideration for language educators.

Identity and resistance

Debates on language, identity, and resistance have also become a compelling and fruitful area of research in applied linguistics. While larger structural constraints and classroom practices might position learners in undesirable ways, researchers have found that learners, with human agency, can resist these positions in innovative and unexpected ways. In exploring what he calls the subversive identities of language learners, Canagarajah (2004a), for example, addresses the intriguing question of how language learners can maintain membership of their vernacular communities and cultures while still learning a second language or dialect. He draws on his research with two very different groups, one in the USA and the other in Sri Lanka, to argue that language learners are sometimes ambivalent about the learning of a second language or dialect, and that they may resort to clandestine literacy practices to create 'pedagogical safe houses' in the language classroom. In both contexts, the clandestine literacy activities of the students are seen to be forms of resistance to unfavourable identities imposed on the learners. At the same time, however, these safe houses serve as sites of identity construction, allowing students to negotiate the often contradictory tensions they encounter as members of diverse communities.

Another example of identity and resistance is found in the work of McKinney and van Pletzen (2004). Working with relatively privileged students at a historically white and Afrikaans university in South Africa, McKinney and van Pletzen introduced critical reading into their first year English studies course using two curriculum units on South African literature. In exploring representations of the apartheid past, McKinney and van Pletzen encountered significant resistance from students to the ways in which they felt uncomfortably positioned by the curriculum materials on offer. McKinney and van Pletzen attempted to create discursive spaces in which both they and the students could explore the many private and political processes through which identities are constructed. In doing so, they re-conceptualized students' resistance more productively as a meaning-making activity which offers powerful teaching moments.

The research of Talmy (2008) provides a final example of new debates on identity and resistance. Talmy investigated the multiple ways in which English language learners in a Hawai'i high school resisted being positioned as 'ESL students' in their dedicated ESL classes. While the school-sanctioned ESL student was expected to bring required materials to class, read assigned fiction, do bookwork, meet assigned dates, follow instructions, and work for the full class session, resistant ESL students engaged in a wide variety of oppositional activities, including leaving materials 'at home', talking with friends, and playing cards. Talmy found that ESL teachers needed to change their pedagogical practices in response to the resistance of their students, necessitating a significant shift in teacher identity.

Future directions

With regard to future directions on identity and applied linguistics, one area that is receiving increasing attention is that of the language teacher and the language teacher educator (see Clarke 2008; Hawkins and Norton 2009; Pennycook 2004; Varghese *et al.* 2005). In a compelling narrative, Pennycook (2004) reflects on his experience of observing a teacher in a TESOL practicum in Sydney, Australia. His experience reminds us that a great deal of language teaching does not take place in well-funded institutes of education, but in community programmes, places of worship, and immigrant centres, where funds are limited and time at a premium. Of central interest in his narrative is a consideration of the way in which teacher educators can intervene in the process of practicum observation to bring about educational and social change. To this end, Pennycook argues that 'critical moments' in the practicum can be used to raise larger questions of power and authority in the wider society, and provide an opportunity for critical discussion and reflection.

A second area that has much potential for future research on applied linguistics and identity concerns growing interest in globalization and language learning (see, for example, Block and Cameron 2002; Blommaert 2008; Garciá *et al.* 2006; Lin and Martin 2005; Morgan and Ramanathan 2005; Pennycook 2007; Prinsloo and Baynham 2008; Rassool 2007). Morgan and Ramanathan (2005) argue persuasively that the field of language education needs to consider ways in which English language teaching can be decolonized, proposing that there is a need to decenter the authority that Western interests have in the language teaching industry. In particular, applied linguists need to find ways to restore agency to professionals in periphery communities (Kumaravadivelu 2003) and to give due recognition to local vernacular modes of learning and teaching (Canagarajah 2004b; Tembe and Norton 2008). In this regard, special issues of a number of journals are significant, including: the *TESOL Quarterly* on 'Language in Development' (Markee 2002) and 'Language Policies and TESOL' (Ramanathan and Morgan 2007); and two recent issues of the AILA *Review of the International Association of Applied Linguistics* on 'Africa and Applied Linguistics' (Makoni and Meinhof 2003) and 'World Applied Linguistics' (Gass and Makoni 2004).

The influence of new technology

Much emerging research on identity addresses the impact of literacy practices on relationships beyond the classroom, much of which is mediated through technology (Andema 2009; Kramsch and Thorne 2002; Lam 2000; Snyder and Prinsloo 2007; Warschauer 2003; Warriner 2007; White 2007). Lam (2000) for example, who studied the Internet correspondence of a Chinese immigrant teenager in the USA who entered into transnational communication with a group of peers, demonstrates how this experience in what she calls 'textual identity' related to the student's developing identity in the use of English. In another context, White (2007) has investigated innovation in distance language teaching in the Australian context, arguing that attention to issues of identity can enhance our understanding of educational innovation. The research of Kramsch and Thorne (2002) indicates, however, that not all transnational Internet communication leads to positive identity outcomes. In their study of the synchronous and asynchronous communication between American learners of French in the USA and French learners of English in France, they found that students had little understanding of the larger cultural framework within which each party was operating, leading to problematic digital exchanges.

Significantly, as scholars such as Andema (2009), Snyder and Prinsloo (2007) and Warschauer (2003) note, much of the digital research in applied linguistics has focused on research in wealthier regions of the world, and there is a great need for research in poorly resourced communities to impact global debates on digital literacy. With reference to the Ugandan context, for example, Mutonyi and Norton (2007) note that as digital technology becomes a globalization tool, Ugandan curriculum developers need to interrogate the ways in which local digital practices may diverge from global expectations. To address this concern, Prinsloo (2005) notes that digital innovations need to be studied as 'placed resources', suggesting that any given technology, when transplanted, takes on new meanings. The extent to which the resource offers opportunities for users, and the ways in which it is used, has important implications for shifts in the identities of both students and teachers.

Summary

This chapter traced the genesis of research on identity and language education from the 1970s to the present day, focusing on some of the major theoretical influences on identity research. A central argument made is that changes in identity research index a shift from a predominantly psycholinguistic to sociolinguistic model of SLA. The main issues identified included the ways in which language is theorized; what identity categories are considered particularly salient in language learning; and the impact of identity research on classroom practice. New debates address the relationship between identity, investment, and imagined communities, with increasing interest in identity and resistance. Research on identity suggests that the extent to which a learner speaks or is silent, and writes, reads, or resists has much to do with the extent to which the learner is valued in any given institution or community. In this regard, social processes marked by inequities of gender, race, class, ethnicity, and sexual orientation may serve to position learners in ways that silence and exclude. At the same time, however, learners may resist marginalization through both covert and overt acts of resistance. Of central interest to researchers of identity is that the very articulation of power, identity, and resistance is expressed in and through language. Language is thus more than a system of signs; it is social practice in which experiences are organized and identities negotiated. Exciting areas of future research include the changing identities of language teachers, and the impact of globalization and technological change on identities of language learners and teachers.

Related topics

culture; ethnicity; gender; language learning and language education; migration; SLA

Further reading

Block, D. (2007) *Second Language Identities*, London and New York: Continuum. (In this monograph, David Block insightfully traces research interest in second language identities from the 1960s to the present. He draws on a wide range of social theory, and brings a fresh analysis to seminal studies of adult migrants, foreign language learners, and study-abroad students.)

Norton, B. (2000) *Identity and Language Learning: Gender, Ethnicity, and Educational Change*, Harlow: Pearson Longman. (Drawing on a longitudinal study of immigrant women in Canada, Bonny Norton draws on post-structuralist theory to argue for a conception of learner identity as multiple, a site of struggle, and subject to change. She also develops the construct of 'investment' to better understand the relationship of language learners to the target language.)

Norton, B. and Toohey, K. (eds) (2004) *Critical Pedagogies and Language Learning*, Cambridge: Cambridge University Press. (Identity is a central theme in this collection of articles by leading researchers in language education. Diverse authors address a wide range of contemporary topics on language learning and teaching, including critical multiculturalism, gender, multimodal pedagogies, popular culture, and action research.)

Pavlenko, A. and Blackledge, A. (eds) (2003) *Negotiation of Identities in Multilingual Contexts*, Clevedon: Multilingual Matters. (The authors in this collection provide insight into the ways in which identities are negotiated in diverse multilingual settings. They analyse the discourses of education, autobiography, politics, and youth culture, demonstrating the ways in which languages may be sites of resistance, empowerment, or discrimination.)

Toohey, K. (2000) *Learning English at School: Identity, Social Relations and Classroom Practice*, Clevedon: Multilingual Matters. (Drawing on a longitudinal ethnography of young English language learners, Kelleen Toohey investigates the ways in which classroom practices are implicated in the range of identity options available to language learners. She draws on sociocultural and post-structural theory to better understand the classroom community as a site of identity negotiation.)

References

Andema, S. (2009) 'Digital Literacy and Teacher Education in East Africa: The Case of Bondo Primary Teachers' College, Uganda', unpublished M.A. thesis, University of British Columbia, Canada.

Anderson, B. (1991) *Imagined Communities: Reflections on the Origin and Spread of Nationalism*, revised edn, New York: Verso.

Atkinson, D. (1999) 'TESOL and culture', *TESOL Quarterly* 33(4): 625–54.

Arkoudis, S. and Davison, C. (eds) (2008) 'Chinese students: perspectives on their social, cognitive, and linguistic investment in English medium interaction', *Journal of Asian Pacific Communication* 18(1), special issue.

Bakhtin, M. M. (1981) *The Dialogic Imagination: Four Essays by M. M. Bakhtin*, M. Holquist (ed.), C. Emerson and M. Holquist (trans.), Austin: University of Texas Press.

Block, D. (2003) *The Social Turn in Second Language Acquisition*, Edinburgh: Edinburgh University Press.

——(2007) *Second Language Identities*, London: Continuum.

Block, D. and Cameron, D. (eds) (2002) *Globalization and Language Teaching*, New York: Routledge.

Blommaert, J. (2008) *Grassroots Literacy: Writing, Identity, and Voice in Central Africa*, London and New York: Routledge.

Bourdieu, P. ([1982] 1991) *Language and Symbolic Power*, in J. B. Thompson, (ed.), G. Raymond and M. Adamson (trans.), Cambridge: Polity Press.

Cameron, D. (2006) *On Language and Sexual Politics*, New York and London: Routledge.

Canagarajah, A. S. (2004a) 'Subversive identities, pedagogical safe houses, and critical learning', in B. Norton and K. Toohey (eds) *Critical Pedagogies and Language Learning*, New York: Cambridge University Press.

Canagarajah, A. S. (ed.) (2004b) *Reclaiming the Local in Language Policy and Practice*, Mahwah, NJ: Lawrence Erlbaum Associates.

Clarke, M. (2008) *Language Teacher Identities: Co-constructing Discourse and Community*, Clevedon: Multilingual Matters.

Clemente, A. and Higgins, M. (2008) *Performing English with a Postcolonial Accent: Ethnographic Narratives from Mexico*, London: Tufnell Publishing.

Cummins, J. (2006) 'Identity texts: the imaginative construction of self through multiliteracies pedagogy', in O. García, T. Skutnabb-Kangas and M. E. Torres-Guzmán (eds) *Imagining Multilingual Schools: Language in Education and Glocalization*, Clevedon: Multilingual Matters.

Dagenais, D., Moore, D., Lamarre, S., Sabatier, C. and Armand, F. (2008) 'Linguistic landscape and language awareness', in E. Shohamy and D. Gorter (eds) *Linguistic Landscape: Expanding the Scenery*, London: Routledge.

Davis, K. and Skilton-Sylvester, E. (eds) (2004) 'Gender in TESOL', *TESOL Quarterly* 38(3), special issue.

Day, E. M. (2002) *Identity and the Young English Language Learner*, Clevedon: Multilingual Matters.

Dornyei, Z. (2001) *Motivational Strategies in the Language Classroom*, Cambridge: Cambridge University Press.

Duff, P. and Uchida, Y. (1997) 'The negotiation of teachers' sociocultural identities and practices in postsecondary EFL classrooms', *TESOL Quarterly* 31: 451–86.

Foucault, M. (1980) *Power/Knowledge: Selected Interviews and Other Writings, 1972–1977*, in C. Gordon (ed.), New York: Pantheon Books.

Garciá, O., Skutnabb-Kangas, T. and Torres-Guzmán, M. E. (eds) (2006) *Imagining Multilingual Schools: Languages in Education and Glocalization*, Clevedon: Multilingual Matters.

Gass, S. M. and Makoni, S. (eds) (2004) 'World applied linguistics: a celebration of AILA at 40', *AILA Review* 17, special issue.

Gumperz, J. J. (ed.) (1982) *Language and Social Identity*, Cambridge: Cambridge University Press.

Hall, S. (1997) *Representation: Cultural Representations and Signifying Practices*, London: Sage.

Haneda, M. (2005) 'Investing in foreign-language writing: a study of two multicultural learners', *Journal of Language, Identity, and Education* 4(4): 269–90.

Hawkins, M. and Norton, B. (2009) 'Critical language teacher education', in A. Burns and J. Richards (eds) *Cambridge Guide to Second Language Teacher Education*, Cambridge: Cambridge University Press.

Heller, M. (2007) *Linguistic Minorities and Modernity: A Sociolinguistic Ethnography*, 2nd edn, London: Continuum.

Ibrahim, A. E. K. M. (1999) 'Becoming black: rap and hip-hop, race, gender, identity, and the politics of ESL learning', *TESOL Quarterly* 33(3): 349–69.

Janks, H. (2010) *Literacy and Power*, New York and London: Routledge.

Kanno, Y. (2008) *Language and Education in Japan: Unequal Access to Bilingualism*, Basingstoke: Palgrave Macmillan.

Kanno, Y. and Norton, B. (eds) (2003) 'Imagined communities and educational possibilities', *Journal of Language, Identity, and Education* 2(4), special issue.

Kendrick, M., Jones, S., Mutonyi, H. and Norton, B. (2006) 'Multimodality and English education in Ugandan schools', *English Studies in Africa* 49(1): 95–114.

King, B. (2008) '"Being gay guy, that is the advantage": queer Korean language learning and identity construction', *Journal of Language, Identity, and Education* 7(3–4): 230–52.

Kramsch, C. (2009) *The Multilingual Subject*, Oxford: Oxford University Press.

Kramsch, C. and Thorne, S. (2002) 'Foreign language learning as global communicative practice', in D. Block and D. Cameron (eds) *Globalization and Language Teaching*, London: Routledge.

Kubota, R. (2004) 'Critical multiculturalism and second language education', in B. Norton and K. Toohey (eds) *Critical Pedagogies and Language Learning*, New York: Cambridge University Press.

Kubota, R. and Lin, A. (2006) 'Race and TESOL: introduction to concepts and theories', *TESOL Quarterly* 40(3), special issue.

Kumaravadivelu, B. (2003) *Beyond Methods: Macrostrategies for Language Learning*, New Haven, CT: Yale University Press.

Lam, W. S. E. (2000) 'L2 literacy and the design of the self: a case study of a teenager writing on the Internet', *TESOL Quarterly* 34(3): 457–82.

Lave, J. and Wenger, E. (1991) *Situated Learning: Legitimate Peripheral Participation*, Cambridge: Cambridge University Press.

Lee, E. (2008) 'The "other(ing)" costs of ESL: a Canadian case study', *Journal of Asian Pacific Communication* 18(1): 91–108.

Lin, A. and Martin, P. (2005) *Decolonisation, Globalisation: Language-in-education Policy and Practice*, Clevedon: Multilingual Matters.

Luke, A. (2004) 'Two takes on the critical', in B. Norton and K. Toohey (eds) *Critical Pedagogies and Language Learning*, New York: Cambridge University Press.

Makoni, S. and Meinhof, U. (eds) (2003) 'Africa and applied linguistics', *AILA Review* 16, special issue.

Markee, N. (2002) 'Language in development', *TESOL Quarterly* 36(3), special issue.

Martin-Jones, M. and Heller, M. (1996) 'Introduction to the special issue on education in multilingual settings: discourse, identities, and power', *Linguistics and Education* 8: 3–16.

May, S. (2008) *Language and Minority Rights*, London and New York: Routledge.

McKay, S. and Wong, S. C. (1996) 'Multiple discourses, multiple identities: investment and agency in second language learning among Chinese adolescent immigrant students', *Harvard Educational Review* 66(3): 577–608.

McKinney, C. and van Pletzen, E. (2004) '" … This apartheid story … we've finished with it": student responses to the apartheid past in a South African English studies course', *Teaching in Higher Education* 9(2): 159–70.

Menard-Warwick, J. (2006) 'Both a fiction and an existential fact: theorizing identity in second language acquisition and literacy studies', *Linguistics and Education* 16: 253–74.

Miller, J. (2003) *Audible Difference: ESL and Social Identity in Schools*, Clevedon: Multilingual Matters.

Moffatt, L. and Norton, B. (2008) 'Reading gender relations and sexuality: preteens speak out', *Canadian Journal of Education* 31(1): 102–23.

Morgan, B. (2007) 'Poststructuralism and applied linguistics: complementary approaches to identity and culture in ELT', in J. Cummins and C. Davison (eds) *International Handbook of English Language Teaching*, New York: Springer.

Morgan, B. and Ramanathan, V. (2005) 'Critical literacies and language education: global and local perspectives', *Annual Review of Applied Linguistics* 25: 151–69.

Mutonyi, H. and Norton, B. (2007) 'ICT on the margins: lessons for Ugandan education. Digital literacy in global contexts', *Language and Education* 21(3): 264–70, special issue.

Nelson, C. (2009) *Sexual Identities in English Language Education: Classroom Conversations*, New York: Routledge.

Norton, B. (ed.) (1997) 'Language and identity', *TESOL Quarterly* 31(3), special issue.

Norton, B. (2000) *Identity and Language Learning: Gender, Ethnicity and Educational Change*, Harlow: Pearson Education.

——(2001) 'Non-participation, imagined communities, and the language classroom', in M. Breen (ed.) *Learner Contributions to Language Learning: New Directions in Research*, London: Pearson Education.

Norton, B. and Pavlenko, A. (eds) (2004) *Gender and English Language Learners*, Alexandria, VA: Teachers of English to Speakers of Other Languages.

Norton, B. and Toohey, K. (2001) 'Changing perspectives on good language learners', *TESOL Quarterly* 35(2): 307–22.

Norton, B. and Toohey, K. (eds) (2004) *Critical Pedagogies and Language Learning*, New York: Cambridge University Press.

Norton Peirce, B. (1995) 'Social identity, investment, and language learning', *TESOL Quarterly* 29 (1): 9–31.

Pavlenko, A. (2004) 'Gender and sexuality in foreign and second language education: critical and feminist approaches', in B. Norton and K. Toohey (eds) *Critical Pedagogies and Language Learning*, New York: Cambridge University Press.

Pavlenko, A. and Norton, B. (2007) 'Imagined communities, identity, and English language teaching', in J. Cummins and C. Davison (eds) *International Handbook of English Language Teaching*, New York: Springer.

Pennycook, A. (2004) 'Critical moments in a TESOL praxicum', in B. Norton and K. Toohey (eds) *Critical Pedagogies and Language Learning*, New York: Cambridge University Press, pp. 327–45.

——(2007) *Global Englishes and Transcultural Flows*, London and New York: Routledge.

Pittaway, D. (2004) 'Investment and second language acquisition', *Critical Inquiry in Language Studies* 4(1): 203–18.

Potowski, K. (2007) *Language and Identity in a Dual Immersion School*, Clevedon: Multilingual Matters.

Prinsloo, M. (2005) 'The new literacies as placed resources', *Perspectives in Education* 23(4): 87–98.

Prinsloo, M. and Baynham, M. (eds) (2008) *Literacies, Global and Local*, Philadelphia, PA: John Benjamins.

Ramanathan, V. (2005) *The English-vernacular Divide: Postcolonial Language Politics and Practice*, Clevedon: Multilingual Matters.

Ramanathan, V. and Morgan, B. (eds) (2007) 'Language policies and TESOL', *TESOL Quarterly* 41(3), special issue.

Rampton, B. (2006) *Language in Late Modernity: Interaction in an Urban School*, Cambridge: Cambridge University Press.

Rassool, N. (2007) *Global Issues in Language, Education, and Development: Perspectives from Postcolonial Countries*, Clevedon: Multilingual Matters.

Ricento, T. (2005) 'Considerations of identity in L2 learning', in E. Hinkel (ed.) *Handbook of Research on Second Language Teaching And Learning*, Mahwah, NJ: Lawrence Erlbaum Associates.

Sarangi, S. and Baynham, M. (eds) (1996) 'Discursive construction of educational identities', *Language and Education* 10(2 and 3) (special issue).

de Saussure, F. (1966) *Course in General Linguistics*, New York: McGraw-Hill.

Schumann, J. (1986) 'Research on the acculturation model for second language acquisition', *Journal of Multilingual and Multicultural Development* 7(5): 379–92.

Skilton-Sylvester, E. (2002) 'Should I stay or should I go? Investigating Cambodian women's participation and investment in adult ESL programs', *Adult Education Quarterly* 53(1): 9–26.

Snyder, I. and Prinsloo, M. (eds) (2007) 'The digital literacy practices of young people in marginal contexts', *Language and Education: An International Journal* 21(3), special issue.

Stein, P. (2008) *Multimodal Pedagogies in Diverse Classrooms: Representation, Rights and Resources*, London and New York: Routledge.

Sunderland, J. (2004) *Gendered Discourses*, Basingstoke: Palgrave Macmillan.

Talmy, S. (2008) 'The cultural productions of the ESL student at Tradewinds High: contingency, multidirectionality, and identity in L2 socialization', *Applied Linguistics* 29(4): 619–44.

Tembe, J. and Norton, B. (2008) 'Promoting local languages in Ugandan primary schools: the community as stakeholder', *Canadian Modern Language Review* 65(1): 33–60.

Toohey, K. (2000) *Learning English at School: Identity, Social Relations and Classroom Practice*, Clevedon: Multilingual Matters.

Valdes, J. M. (1986) *Culture Bound: Bridging the Cultural Gap in Language Teaching*, Cambridge: Cambridge University Press.

Varghese, M., Morgan, B., Johnston, B. and Johnson, K. (2005) 'Theorizing language teacher identity: three perspectives and beyond', *Journal of Language, Identity, and Education* 4: 21–44.

Wallace, C. (2003) *Critical Reading in Language Education*, Basingstoke: Palgrave Macmillan.

Warriner, D. S. (ed.) (2007) 'Transnational literacies: immigration, language learning, and identity', *Linguistics and Education* 18(3–4): 201–14.

Warschauer, M. (2003) *Technology and Social Inclusion: Rethinking the Digital Divide*, Boston: MIT Press.

Weedon, C. (1997) *Feminist Practice and Poststructuralist Theory*, 2nd edn, Oxford: Blackwell.

Wenger, E. (1998) *Communities of Practice: Learning, Meaning, and Identity*, New York: Cambridge University Press.

White, C. (2007) 'Innovation and identity in distance language learning and teaching', *Innovation in Language Learning and Teaching* 1(1): 97–110.

Zuengler, J. and Miller, E. (2006) 'Cognitive and sociocultural perspectives: two parallel SLA worlds?', *TESOL Quarterly* 40(1): 35–58.

23

Gender

Judith Baxter

Introduction

> As men
> Do walk a mile, women should talk an hour
> After supper. 'Tis their exercise.
>
> *(Beaumont and Fletcher,* Philaster, *1609)*

> Silence, the final frontier – where no woman has gone before.
>
> *(British newspaper headline 2009)*

Folk-linguistic evidence has long portrayed the language of women and men to be different, and, as we can see above, this belief lives on in media texts today. Much of this evidence – in the form of proverbs, sayings, literature, diaries, essays, newspaper headlines, advertising captions and so on – takes a *prescriptive* perspective (how women's language ought to be) rather than a *descriptive* view – how it actually is, thus revealing deeply rooted ideological assumptions about gender.

Language and Gender (also known as 'Gender and Language' or 'Feminist Linguistics') is a relatively new field within sociolinguistics, usually said to be marked by the publication of Lakoff's *Language and Woman's Place* in 1975. The field has since aroused huge interest among applied linguists both on ethnographic and ideological grounds. Ethnographically, linguists were keen to gather authentic data to explore and explain folk-linguistic beliefs that males and females speak and act differently (e.g. Fishman 1978; Spender 1980). Ideologically, language and gender scholars aimed to show that language – both in use and as a form of representation – was a primary means of constructing gender differences, and at times hierarchies and inequalities between men and women. Consequently, two aspects emerged in language and gender research; first, how women and men *talked* (and by extension, wrote), and second, how women/men/boys and girls were *represented* in language – as a code, as discourse, and in actual texts. Today, ethnographic and ideological quests appear more integrated in a concern to explore how people's *identities* are constructed in gendered ways within localised 'communities of practice' (Wenger 2000; also see Norton, this volume), but also in relation to

Judith Baxter

larger gendered discourses (Sunderland 2004). While the feminist agenda has been modified since the 1970s in light of developments in women's status, there is nonetheless a consensus that gender continues to be highly relevant to the way people interact through language, and in the way they are positioned and represented by gendered 'discourses' or 'ways of seeing the world' (2004: 6).

Within its short history, language and gender scholars have repeatedly contested the terms 'gender' and 'sex', which are not regarded as interchangeable. 'Gender' has now stabilised as a term to distinguish people in terms of their socio-cultural behaviour, and to signify masculine and feminine behaviours as scales or continua rather than as a dichotomy (Holmes 2001). While I use the term 'sex' in this chapter to refer to categories distinguished by biological characteristics (i.e. 'male' and 'female'), it should be noted that a number of scholars have contested these categories as 'hetero-normative', and have suggested that 'sex' should also be reconceptualised as a socio-cultural construct (e.g. Butler 1990; Bergvall *et al.* 1996).

History of the area

In this chapter I will focus on the two strands of research that have, in my view, contributed most to the development of the field in recent decades: variationist, and more particularly, 'interactional' research. The latter is characterised by a range of theoretical perspectives: *deficiency, dominance, cultural difference* and *social constructionism*. I shall consider the social constructionist perspective in the next section, as it is arguably 'where we are', and it encompasses a number of current issues and debates.

Variationist studies

Most language and gender research on *use* assumes a 'sex-preferential' perspective – a male/female preference for using different forms of the same language. Classic variationist studies looked for evidence of sex-preferential speech in large-scale English-speaking populations such as New York, Detroit, Norwich, the Wirral, Belfast and Sydney. Traditional variationist studies conceptualise 'sex' as a fixed and universal variable determining people's use of language alongside other equally key categories such as class, age and ethnicity. Landmark studies in this field (e.g. Labov 1966; Trudgill 1974) found that men and women did use different forms, particularly phonologically, and drew the conclusion that within every social class, women use more standard forms than men. So, for example, Trudgill (1974) found that many more women than men in Norwich used the standard (iŋ) rather than the vernacular (in) form at the end of words like *speaking* and *writing*. Indeed, he proposed that women prefer standard forms because they are more status-conscious, while men prefer the vernacular because it has connotations of masculine solidarity such as 'toughness'. However, Milroy (1980) found in her Belfast study that the concept of social networks influenced people's speech in that context more than sex/gender, and indeed that the *differences* between women were often more significant than their similarities.

Later variationist research thus moved to situate gender within specific local contexts such as Gal's (1979) study of gender and bilingualism in the Hungarian town of Oberwart, and Eckert's (1989) study of adolescents in the 'community of practice' of a Detroit high school. Variationist research on gender today can be more aptly described as 'sociolinguistic'. It has tended to move away from large-scale, quantitative, correlational methods towards more local, contextualised and ethnographic approaches that explore gender as intersecting with other social identities such as class and sexuality within particular communities of practice (see Eckert 2008 on 'third wave variationist theory').

Interactional studies

The field of language and gender is most strongly associated today with a range of 'interactional' studies, which focus on the distinctively gendered ways in which people interact in various social and professional contexts. Three early but still highly influential theories (deficit, dominance, difference) all emphasised the notion of a gender *dichotomy*. These theories tended to compare men and women as members of two distinctive and polarised social groups, supporting the popular stereotype that 'men are from Mars and women are from Venus' (Gray 1992; for a critique see Cameron 2007), as we shall now consider.

Deficit theory

Lakoff's (1975) 'deficit' theory posited that from an early age, girls are taught how to use a separate 'woman's language': they are socialised to use language in a 'ladylike' way. She suggested that women's subordinate status in American society in the 1970s was reflected and constructed through a basically deficient version of men's language. This language was more tentative, hesitant, indirect, and therefore a more *powerless* version of men's, trapping them in a perpetual double-bind:

> a girl is damned if she does and damned if she doesn't. If she refuses to talk like a lady, she is ridiculed and subjected to criticism as unfeminine. If she does learn [lady-like language], she is ridiculed as unable to think clearly, unable to take part in a serious discussion: in some sense as less than fully human. These two choices which a woman has – to be less than a woman, or less than a person – are highly painful.
>
> *(Lakoff 1975: 5)*

Lakoff argued that this lady-like language was mainly manifested by a range of *modifiers* (such as hedges and tag questions) that in her opinion diluted the message and signified an unconfident and powerless speaker. Her views were later criticised for a variety of reasons, not least her use of largely 'introspective', anecdotal evidence, and her failure to appreciate the multi-functionality of all language forms. Clearly, being a pioneer carries a penalty!

Dominance theory

Lakoff's (1975) thesis that women constructed their own subordination through their language use was a forerunner of 'dominance' theory. This had two distinct, parallel branches: *language as social interaction*, which considered how gender inequalities were constructed through routine interactions between men and women, and *language as a system* focusing on 'sexism' within the language.

In terms of *language as social interaction*, dominance theorists viewed ordinary conversation as highly instrumental in constructing unequal gender relations. In order to reveal the word-by-word reproduction of patriarchy, early feminist linguists conducted numerous small-scale, interactional studies of largely informal conversations which examined the nature and frequency of talk, silences, questions, interruptions and 'back-channelling' (e.g. the woman's use of responses while the man is talking). For example, a famous study by Fishman (1978) showed that men do most of the talking, while women provide the 'interactional shitwork' of being supportive and encouraging listeners. Complementing this, DeFrancisco (1991) showed that men often respond to the conversation of their female partners with silence rather than with encouraging responses, with the effect that women often 'dried up' or stopped talking. Such research showed that women were not the talkative sex as stereotyped in folk-linguistics: in fact, men talked far more.

In terms of *language as a system*, Spender (1980) argued that language has evolved over the centuries to serve male needs, to represent male interests, and to express male experiences: in short, it is 'man-made'. Spender was concerned with the way that grammars and dictionaries prescribed the use of masculine terms such as *he*, *man* and *mankind* as false generics to denote males *and* females, thus reinforcing an andro-centric (male-centred) view of the world. She noted three further ways in which the language sustains this andro-centric perspective:

- linguistic marking of terms to denote women (e.g. *manageress*, *stewardess*),
- semantic derogation (the way terms for women like *mistress* have become 'derogated' or debased over time; also see Schulz 1990),
- lexical gaps (the lack of a woman-centred lexis to describe certain female experiences in positive ways, such as childlessness or remaining a single woman).

The quest for a more inclusive, 'anti-sexist' language is now firmly established within the institutional practices of schools, universities, publishing, the media, business, government and the public services, at least in the Western world. What is interesting is the extent to which this perceived feminist 'political correctness' continues to be ridiculed in the media, for example by the UK satirical magazine, *Private Eye*. Indeed, even feminist linguists have proposed that this institutionalised mission to change language should be treated with a degree of irony and playfulness (Mills 2003).

However, the problem with dominance research was that it appeared to adopt the very andro-centric perspective that it was criticising (Coates 2004). For example, by proposing that a male speech style (assertive, direct, competitive, goal-orientated) was more socially 'powerful' than a female speech style (supportive, conciliatory, co-operative, process-orientated), dominance theorists were in danger of endorsing the dominant cultural view of female linguistic inferiority, and of recommending an 'assertiveness training' strategy that women should learn to speak and sound more like men (Cameron 1995a).

Cultural difference theory

> Early work on women's language had labelled it 'tentative' or 'powerless'. More recently and in reaction to this, there has been a move to value women's talk more positively, using terms such as 'co-operative'.
>
> *(Coates 1988: 95)*

Coates considered that while dominance theory helped to reveal the apparent tendencies of males and females for different linguistic styles of interaction, it took an unfairly negative view of women's talk. Applying the theories of Gumperz (1982) to gender, Maltz and Borker (1982) argued that women and men constitute different 'sub-cultures' learnt through friendly inter-actions as children in single-sex peer groups. So boys learn how to compete with others for access to 'the floor', to use referential, goal-orientated language, and to say things for impact and effect. Girls alternatively learn how to build relationships of equality and trust, to co-operate with others to get things done, and to express feelings and emotions (Maltz and Borker 1982: 207). These contrasting conversational goals corresponded to differently gendered speech 'styles', whereby 'women speak and hear a language of connection and intimacy, while men speak and hear a language of status and independence' (Tannen 1990: 42). So in Tannen's (ibid.) terms, women learn to use 'rapport talk' while men learn to use 'report talk'. Given these separate conversational goals, Coates (1988) argued that women's talk should be 're-valued' in much more positive ways by feminist linguists as different but *equal*, as complementary to men's, not deficient. While Coates' work offered a vital antidote to the negativity of the deficiency and dominance approaches, she has since been criticised on two grounds: for her failure to recognise the power dimension which produces negative cultural evaluations of female language, and for the ways in which difference theory 'essentialises' male and female language as fixed and monolithic characteristics of a universal condition and incapable of change (Cameron 1995b).

Main current issues

Since the 1990s, language and gender research has firmly distanced itself from gender difference theories, and is, according to Holmes (2007) 'engulfed in a wave of social constructionism' emphasising the *diversity* of gender rather than difference. This 'post-modern turn' can partly be explained by the impact of feminism in the West, which has produced profound improvements in the cultural status of women. But Cameron (2005: 483) cautions that 'difference' and social constructionist approaches are 'better seen as representing tendencies in feminist thought which have historically overlapped and co-existed' rather than as a chronological progression. While social constructionism now seems established as the dominant approach, it has not been uniformly perceived as 'a good thing' for feminist linguistics, as we shall now consider.

Social constructionism and the 'post-modern turn'

> Women and men are different because language positions us differently. In this view, subjectivity – our sense of selves – is something constructed, not pre-given and our gender identities are not fixed. We take up positions in our enactment of discourse practices so our identities are constructed moment by moment.
>
> *(Talbot 2010: 110–11)*

Social constructionist theory (e.g. Bergvall *et al.* 1996; Butler 1990; Crawford 1995; also see Norton, this volume) suggests that males and females are not born, or even simply socialised into a pre-fixed gender identity, but they *become* gendered through their interactions. According to this view, individuals don't *have* gender, they *do* gender through repeated behavioural and linguistic interactions. This post-modern perspective argues that males and females do not have an individual essence, character or 'core' (Crawford 1995); there are no intrinsic male or female characteristics, only ones that are brought into being through repeated bodily or linguistic actions. Any apparent characteristics are the *effects* we produce by way of particular things we do. Thus, according to Butler (1990), people's identities are *performative*. We learn to 'perform' many aspects of our identity, such as being feminine or masculine, through:

> the repeated stylisation of the body, a set of repeated acts within a rigid regulatory frame which congeal over time to produce the appearance of a substance, of a 'natural kind of being'.
>
> *(Butler 1990: 33)*

335

Judith Baxter

In this way, gender has constantly to be reaffirmed and publicly displayed by repeatedly performing particular acts in accordance with the cultural norms or, in post-structuralist terms, dominant discourses, of an institution or social group. Butler (1990) adds that routine conversations are conducted by people 'who are striving to constitute themselves as "proper" men and women'. Language is therefore not just a medium to convey social life and interactions, but an essential, constitutive factor. So particular uses of language become culturally associated with masculinity and femininity; they become symbolically gendered or 'index' a gendered identity (Ochs 1992), rather than being the property or attributes of males and females.

According to the social constructionist perspective, gender can therefore be seen as relational, a process, something that is done, and an important resource for constructing gender roles and identities. If gender (and indeed sex) are cultural constructs only, they can be challenged and resisted. Gender has the potential to be reconceptualised in terms of multiple roles and positions for men and women. There is a range of ways in which people can speak and act, some of which may be stereotypically coded 'masculine' and others 'feminine', but they are potentially available to all. In challenging the monolithic character of beliefs grounded in naive assumptions around the 'essential truth' of gender difference, social constructionism has also contested the category of 'woman'. This category is viewed as highly unstable, in the sense that it is difficult to generalise about what being a woman is. Just as there are many inconsistencies and contradictions *within* any individual woman, there are always differences *between* women, often governed by their age, class, ethnicity, family background, education, and so on (Norton and Pavlenko 2004). Overall, the social constructionist approach suggests that gendered roles and identities are not open to generalisation or easy categorisation. They are not fixed and static but shifting, fragmentary, multiple, frequently contradictory and constantly in the process of being negotiated and reconstituted through linguistic interactions.

Gender and sexuality

One issue arising from social constructionist thinking is the *mutually* constitutive relationship of gender and sexual identities. Like gender, sexuality is perceived as fluid, multi-faceted and a form of desire/identity that is constructed and performed through speech and behaviour, and not simply determined by the sex of people's bodies at birth or by early socialisation. Indeed, whether it is even possible to separate the construct of gender from sexuality has itself become a matter of debate (e.g. Cameron and Kulick 2003). The focus of much recent 'gender and sexuality' research has been upon 'hetero-normativity', the system that naturalises and rewards a particular kind of heterosexuality – complementary, monogamous and reproductive male/female partnerships – as the basis for a stable society. One line of research has examined how the hetero-normative principle is achieved through the linguistic performance of heterosexual identities. In a now classic study, Hall (1995) explored the verbal techniques used by telephone sex workers (both male and female) in California to create a range of fantasy women of varying ethnicities and personalities for the benefit of their male, heterosexual clients. In a second example, Kiesling (2003) looked at the ways in which a group of US college fraternity brothers 'played the straight man' in order to differentiate themselves from men they perceived as 'gay' and thus to further approved, platonic relationships with other men. Such studies support the social constructionist contention that gender and sexual identities can be convincingly enacted by a person of any sex, simply by adhering to stereotypical assumptions about male and female language and behaviour.

Another line of research into gender and sexuality has investigated the linguistic performances of people who identify with sexual minorities. These include not only the familiar modern Western categories of 'gay men' and 'lesbians', but also transgendered and transsexual people who move from one category to another during the course of their lives. These may be people who alternate between differently gendered personae, people who refuse to be defined as either men or women but claim to be something 'intermediate or indeterminate' (Cameron 2005: 490). A social constructionist perspective allows theorists to contest the culturally dominant association of (for example) same-sex preference with gender deviance because it transgresses the traditional gender dichotomy, and to reframe this as an investigation of alternative, hybrid, and exploratory identities and practices. For example, Borba and Ostermann (2007) studied the way southern Brazilian 'travestis' (biological males who wish to look, dress and speak like women), manipulate the Portuguese grammatical gender system in order to sound at times like men and at other times like women. But if once stable constructs of gender and sexuality can be contested in these various ways, what does this mean about their salience as a field?

The salience of gender

> If we truly believed a radical version of the anti-essentialism that has recently become an axiom of the field, then we would put away our pens, our tape recorders and our notebooks, and the field of language and gender would disappear.
>
> *(Holmes and Meyerhoff 2003: 10)*

Is the logical conclusion of a social constructionist perspective really the demise of language and gender? In many ways, feminist linguists *have* successfully accomplished their mission of raising public awareness about gendered language, while simultaneously debating that gender is not nearly as significant as we all once thought. The move away from theories of a 'women's language' or separately gendered speech styles, and towards notions of complex social identities and linguistic diversity has indeed challenged gender as a super-ordinate category. Yet, in recent years there has been an upsurge of textbooks and monographs in the field, increased submissions to sociolinguistics journals and the founding of a new international journal, *Gender and Language* (Equinox 2007), which has responded to a need for 'a room of our own, a separate institution, a separate publication' (McElhinny and Mills 2007: 3). Scholars continue to be enchanted by the relationship between language and gender as it is enacted in a range of contexts such as social networks, business, leadership, education, SLA, law, government, health, entertainment and the media, and in diverse locations around the world. We might reasonably question why this attraction to the field persists, and how this interest can still be justified.

There is a radical division of opinion between those social constructionists who argue from a 'local' perspective that gender can be justified as a category but only on a case-by-case basis, 'from the ground up' before it can be legitimately addressed within research, and those who argue from a more 'global' perspective that there is evidence of a wider 'gender order'. This order is viewed as 'a repressive ideology which continues to ensure that deviation from gender norms (by women or men) entails penalties' (Holmes 2007: 53).

In the 'local' corner, theorists of Conversation Analysis (CA) such as Weatherall (2000) argue that an epistemological construct such as gender needs to be made explicitly salient by research participants in order to be considered relevant to any scholarly analysis. In other words, such participants need to refer to their own or other people's gender specifically (for example, by terms such as 'women', 'ladies', 'mothers-in-law', etc.) within an observed conversation as evidence of their orientation to this category. Thus an ethno-methodological focus is upon 'how in every day talk and text [participants] constitute the world, themselves and other people, as recognisably, take-for-grantedly gendered' (Stokoe 2005: 126). The feminist conversation analyst Kitzinger (2007) has since argued that terms such as 'woman', 'gentleman', etc., do not necessarily mean that a speaker is orienting to gender, and has asked that conversation analysts consider other less obvious ways by which language signifies gender (although it is as yet unclear what those 'less obvious ways' would be!). However, Sidnell (2003: 347) emphasises the 'local' case for justifying gender in his claim that 'many researchers advance anti-essentialist, theoretical conceptions of gender … but at the same time employ the very same categories in their analysis', thus reinforcing Holmes and Meyerhoff's (2003) insight above!

In the 'global' corner, a number of theorists have challenged the CA premise that unless participants signal their orientation to the salience of gender within linguistic interactions there is no evidence that it is relevant. Holmes (2007: 54) argues from a sociolinguistic perspective that 'social and pragmatic meanings may be, and frequently are inferred using contextualisation cues', and that the CA approach doesn't sufficiently take into account 'context embedded practices of various kinds'. In line with Mills (2003), Holmes suggests that there is evidence from a range of social contexts that women are still discriminated against and that this discrimination works at both a local level through people's interactions, but also less visibly at a structural level through institutional and state practices. She cites the example of female disadvantage in the workplace where, for example, women are significantly underrepresented at senior level worldwide despite years of equal opportunity legislation in many countries. Taking an expedient view of the issue, she proposes the need for 'strategic essentialism' in language and gender scholarship, such as continuing to use labels like 'women' and 'men'. This, she suggests, could be 'one tactic for regaining the strength which is inevitably dissipated when the focus is on difference and diversity than what is shared [between women]' (Holmes 2007: 56–7).

Nonetheless, this wistfulness for the lost innocence of the feminist cause, once so conveniently rationalised by the 'big stories' of gender difference or dominance, has been a predominant theme in recent feminist linguistics. Cameron (2005: 500) has warned that 'contemporary feminist researchers have become increasingly remote from the common-sense understandings with which most other people operate'. In an attempt to popularise the 'diversity' perspective, she has written the highly readable *The Myth of Mars and Venus* (Cameron 2007), to try to bridge that gap between highbrow theorising and popular conceptions of language and gender issues, but unfortunately it never made the best-seller lists in the way that John Gray's (1992) original volume did. Other linguists of 'a post-structuralist turn' have theorised the continuing salience of gender in more abstract terms. For example, Ochs (1992) used the social semiotic concept of 'indexing' ('pointing to') to suggest that speakers have a range of 'linguistic resources' available to them in order to signal their gender and other aspects of their cultural identities. Some linguistic resources index gender very directly (such as titles like *Mr/s* or *he/she*), but others index gender less directly, such as a speaker's choice of interactional style. All linguistic resources draw upon cultural expectations of femininity and masculinity, which influence our language preferences for interacting. The value of 'indexing' is that it links a local linguistic analysis of how someone speaks with a global consideration of the powerful role gender stereotypes play in governing the language choices women and men routinely make to adapt to different contexts.

In a similar spirit, Baxter (2003) and others draw on a post-structuralist discourse approach (Foucault 1972: 49; also see Norton, this volume) to suggest that dominant discourses of 'gender differentiation' have become crystallised as routine interactional practices in many contexts. The difference between the concept of 'indexing' and a discourse approach is that the latter is constitutive and not simply indicative: discourses position speakers to speak and act in given ways, but speakers can negotiate their subject positions and offer resistance within these discourses. Accordingly, gender differentiation is a set of dominant cultural practices that position women (and some men) in limiting and disadvantaged ways. However, speakers can renegotiate, review and contest their subject positions and adopt alternative ways of 'doing gender'. Sunderland (2004: 190) suggests that 'traces' of 'damaging gendered discourses' (such as 'masculinisation' or 'compulsory heterosexuality') can be identified both through detailed linguistic and semiotic analysis of texts, but also through longer term, ethnographic observations of interactional practices. It remains a challenge for post-structuralist theorists to identify the 'linguistic traces' of gendered discourses without the need to justify these on the CA basis of participants explicitly 'orienting' to gender within a given stretch of discourse. Indeed, Swann has identified six further 'warrants' for gender which provide useful guidance to scholars adopting more global or post-structuralist perspectives in their research (see Swann 2002, for an overview).

To sum up, a social constructionist approach does not lead logically to the demise of the field if it is extended to consider the construction and representation of gender and sexuality in text and discourse. Here, the notion of relevance, the idea that gender becomes *relevant* in some contexts but less so in others, is an important theme across both local and global perspectives.

Future trajectory and new debates

So what new debates are emerging within language and gender literature, which may shape the future direction of the field? I shall mention three here: the rise of biological essentialism, an extended role for communities of practice, and exploiting the plurality of research methodologies.

The first is the possible challenge posed by a resurgence of biological explanations of gender, spearheaded by the Darwinist science of evolutionary psychology. Cameron (2007: 16) has warned scholars that if they fail to take notice of 'conversations' about biological essentialism, 'the result may be to re-marginalise feminist linguistic scholarship'. She suggests that while social constructionism continues to be 'the big story' within language and gender, there has been a 'massive assault' on this position within other, more scientifically based fields such as neuroscience and psychology. One of the discourses of biological essentialism is that women are 'hard-wired' to have more advanced verbal and linguistic abilities whereas men have more sophisticated spatial and mathematical skills. According to Cameron (2005, 2007), these apparently sex-differentiated abilities are used to endorse a Darwinian (and sexist) narrative on evolution. In contrast to men's 'hunter' role, women's 'gatherer' role in interacting with others is viewed as a primary reason for facilitating the development of language among our early ancestors. While this 'prehistoric division of labour' appears to offer a positive evaluation of women's contribution to the human success story, it has damaging social consequences because 'it helps to reproduce arrangements which from a feminist perspective are unjust and harmful for women' (Cameron 2007: 22). In short, positive evaluations of women's talk perpetuate a restrictive, essentialist, gender difference perspective. Moreover, she considers that this type of Darwinian discourse may well be part of a broader reaction to changing gender relations in affluent Western societies where female success may be perceived as a threat. However, Cameron urges that language and gender scholars should not simply engage in this debate on the level of discourse and social practices; it is important to challenge the factual, scientific evidence and the epistemological bases on which this is produced.

A second new direction in the field is a proposal to extend the well-established concept of 'communities of practice' (CofPs; Wenger 2000) within language and gender research in order to enable an 'articulation between the local, the extra-local and the global' (Eckert and McConnell-Ginet 2007: 28). According to the CofP concept, social practice emphasising the social significance of what people do, goes well beyond simple individual acts or conversations (as studied by conversation analysis) to socially regulated, repeated and interpreted colla-borative doings. The authors argue that scholars should aim to analyse how such 'practices articulate with the wider world and with wider discourses of gender and sexuality' (ibid.). Their proposal is that the CofP concept could be extended to achieve this aim in two ways. The first is *comparatively* by examining different but similar kinds of CofP to move beyond particular and specific insights about a community to more general observations about gender and sexuality. Holmes' (2006) work is cited as an example of how the interactional style of female leadership in business settings varies according to the type of community of practice, and how workplaces, not participants, can be described as 'gendered'. Baxter's (2008) work in the same field supplements the CofP thesis by suggesting that there are at least three competing gendered discourses in most workplaces: male-dominated, gender-differentiated and gender-multiple, but one in particular is likely to predominate within a given community of practice.

The second way of extending the CofP concept is *relationally*, by locating communities of practice in relation to a world beyond – other communities, social networks, institutions and more global, imagined communities. This is illustrated by Besnier's (2007) study of a trans-gender beauty pageant in Tonga, in which he shows that the use of English helps to construct an 'imagined cosmopolitanism'. The study reveals that this marginalised, transgendered com-munity needs to connect with a wider, more mainstream world, which the contestants do by using 'the dominant language of English, the language of globality, modernity, [with its] cos-mopolitan possibilities, despite the fact that most of them are more comfortable in Tongan than in English' (Besnier 2007: 73). Another example of 'imagined communities' might be on-line CofPs that have become important in many people's lives such as emails, chat rooms, blogs, game-playing sites, and so on. Within the field, there is a growing interest in exploring the ways in which gender and sexuality are used to construct a range of experimental identities by means of computer-mediated communication.

While Eckert and McConnell-Ginet (2007: 35) argue that it is unreasonable to expect single researchers always to link their study of specific communities of practice to global or ideolo-gical patterns, they propose that a unified interdisciplinary research community 'can keep its collective eye on those connections'.

On this interdisciplinary note, a third new direction for language and gender concerns the wide range of research methodologies through which the discipline is currently investigated. Surely it must be unusual for such a relatively small field of study to draw upon methods as diverse as sociolinguistics, corpus linguistics, conversation analysis, discursive psychology, cri-tical discourse analysis (CDA) and feminist post-structuralist discourse analysis (FPDA)? Harrington *et al.* (2008: 12) argue that the field can only benefit from this range and creative combination of approaches as each method in its own way helps uncover the gender issues at stake in linguistic interactions. They propose that, rather than asking in competitive spirit which method is most appropriate for language and gender research, theorists should inquire what the affordances and limitations are of each method for a particular context or study. In this sense, research methodologies are not simply instrumental, but are conceptually driven with specific theoretical and epistemological imperatives.

While theorists will continue to debate the superior merits of, say, CA over CDA in any social constructionist discussion of gender (e.g. Schegloff 1997; Wetherell 1998), the future for language and gender may well move towards a combined or interdisciplinary approach to study. Complex subject matter may pragmatically require a more nuanced, multi-faceted approach in order to provide plural perspectives on the linguistic enactment of gender in contexts where speakers are often 'positioned' in different ways. For example, a study of the linguistic reasons why women are under-represented at leadership level may well require the selection of an approach that puts 'women back at the centre of language and gender research' as Holmes (2007: 60) argues. For this reason, Baxter (2010) has drawn on a combination of approaches in her study of gendered leadership using a mix of CA, interactional socio-linguistics and FPDA. Kamada (2010) drew upon a combination of discursive psychology and FPDA in her study of the identities of multi-ethnic girls and boys in Japan. Castañeda-Peña (2008) used CDA with FPDA in his study of the multiple performances of masculinity and femininity in a pre-school English as a Foreign Language lesson in Colombia. This combina-tion of principle, flexibility and pragmatism in the deployment of different theoretical and methodological approaches could well characterise the future of language and gender research.

Summing up

This chapter has traced the short but extraordinary history of language and gender from Lakoff's (1975) basic conception of a unified 'women's language' to today's elaborate theore-tical configurations of a socially constructed gender. The field has been driven by a dual mis-sion both to capture ethnographic evidence to argue that gender makes a difference within many linguistic interactions, and to challenge from a feminist standpoint the gendered inequalities that are routinely enacted through language in many contexts. A powerful issue that currently divides the field is the category of 'woman' and by association 'gender'. Scholars have asked, what counts as gender? How can we claim that gender is relevant to a given stretch of talk? What is one's warrant for using these categories at all? At times, it has seemed that the field was set to destroy itself through the inexorable development of the social construc-tionist argument. But whether gender is pinned down at the local level of talk-in-interaction, or whether it is detected on the global level through 'traces' of gendered discourses, I would agree with Holmes (2007: 60) that 'we need to put women back at the centre of language and gender research'. However, we should not exclude from our sights the linguistic experiences of other minorities who are marginalised or discriminated against because of their gender or sexuality. The availability of a range of new interdisciplinary research methods has made such a quest more possible. It will be an exciting time ahead.

Related topics

critical discourse analysis; culture; discourse analysis; identity; sociolinguistics

Further reading

Baxter, J. (2003) *Positioning Gender in Discourse: A Feminist Methodology*, Basingstoke: Palgrave Macmillan. (This is a useful introduction to social constructionist and post-structuralist approa-ches to language and gender. It introduces feminist post-structuralist discourse analysis (FPDA) by means of a classroom and a business case study.)
Harrington, K., Litosseliti, L., Saunston, H. and Sunderland, J. (eds) (2008) *Gender and Language Research Methodologies*, Basingstoke: Palgrave Macmillan. (This is an excellent collection of essays introducing, applying and evaluating the current range of theoretical and methodological approaches to language and gender.)

Judith Baxter

Litosseliti, L. (2006) *Gender and Language: Theory and Practice*, London: Hodder Arnold. (Probably one of the best introductions to language and gender, it gives a history of theories in the field, and reviews significant studies in three professional contexts: education, the media and the workplace.)
Sunderland, J. (2004) *Gendered Discourses*, Basingstoke: Palgrave Macmillan. (Using a series of case studies, this book examines gendered 'ways of seeing the world' and how our identities may be constructed through different discourses.)

References

Baxter, J. (2003) *Positioning Gender in Discourse: A Feminist Methodology*, Basingstoke: Palgrave Macmillan.
——(2008) 'Is it all tough talking at the top? A feminist post-structuralist analysis of the construction of gendered speaker identities of British business leaders within interview narratives', *Gender and Language* 2(2): 193–218.
——(2010) *The Language of Female Leadership*, Basingstoke: Palgrave Macmillan.
Bergvall, V., Bing, J. M. and Freed, A. F. (1996) *Rethinking Language and Gender Research*, London: Longman.
Besnier, N. (2007) 'Language and gender research at the intersection of the global and the local', *Gender and Language* 1(1): 67–78.
Borba, R. and Ostermann, A. (2007) 'Do bodies matter? Travestis' embodiment of (trans)gender identity through the manipulation of the Brazilian Portuguese grammatical gender system', *Gender and Language* 1(1): 131–47.
Butler, J. (1990) *Gender Trouble: Feminism and the Subversion of Identity*, New York: Routledge.
Cameron, D. (1995a) *Verbal Hygiene*, London: Routledge.
——(1995b) 'Rethinking language and gender studies: some issues for the 1990s', in S. Mills (ed.) *Language and Gender: Interdisciplinary Perspectives*, Harlow: Longman.
——(2005) 'Language, gender and sexuality: current issues and new directions', *Applied Linguistics* 26(4): 482–502.
——(2007a) *The Myth of Mars and Venus*, Oxford: Oxford University Press.
——(2007b) 'Unanswered questions and unquestioned assumptions in the study of language and gender: female verbal superiority', *Gender and Language* 1(1): 15–26.
Cameron, D. and Kulick, D. (2003) *Language and Sexuality*, Cambridge: Cambridge University Press.
Castañeda-Peña, H. (2008) 'Interwoven and competing gendered discourses in a pre-school lesson', in K. Harrington, L. Litosseliti, H. Sauntson and J. Sunderland (eds) *Gender and Language Research Methodologies*, Basingstoke: Palgrave Macmillan.
Coates, J. (1988) 'Gossip revisited: language in all-female groups', in J. Coates and D. Cameron (eds) *Women in their Speech Communities*, London: Longman.
——(2004) *Women, Men and Language*, 2nd edn, London: Longman.
Crawford, M. (1995) *Talking Difference: On Gender and Language*, London: Sage.
DeFrancisco, V. (1991) 'The sounds of silence: how men silence women in marital relations', *Discourse and Society* 2(4): 413–23.
Eckert, P. (1989) *Jocks and Burnouts: Social Categories and Identity in the High School*, New York: Teachers College Press.
——(2008) 'Variation and the indexical field', *Journal of Sociolinguistics* 12: 453–76.
Eckert, P. and McConnell-Ginet, S. (2007) 'Putting communities of practice in their place', *Gender and Language* 1(1): 27–38.
Fishman, P. (1978) 'Interaction: the work women do', *Social Problems* 25(4): 397–406.
Foucault, M. (1972) *The Archeology of Knowledge and the Discourse on Language*, New York: Pantheon.
——(1980) *Power/Knowledge: Selected Interviews and Other Writings 1972–1977*, C. Gordon (ed.), Brighton: Harvester Press.
Gal, S. (1979) *Language Shift: Social Determinants of Linguistic Change in Bilingual Austria*, New York: Academic Press.
Gray, J. (1992) *Men are from Mars and Women from Venus*, New York: HarperCollins.

Gumperz, J. J. (ed.) (1982) *Language and Social Identity*, Cambridge: Cambridge University Press.

Hall, K. (1995) 'Lip-service on the fantasy lines', in K. Hall and M. Bucholtz (eds) *Gender Articulated: Language and the Socially Constructed Self*, New York: Routledge.

Harrington, K., Litosseliti, L., Sauntson, H. and Sunderland, J. (eds) (2008) *Gender and Language Research Methodologies*, Basingstoke: Palgrave Macmillan.

Holmes, J. (2001) *An Introduction to Sociolinguistics*, London: Longman.

——(2006) *Gendered Talk at Work*, Oxford: Blackwell.

——(2007) 'Social constructionism, postmodernism and feminist sociolinguistics', *Gender and Language* 1(1): 51–6.

Holmes, J. and Meyerhoff, M. (2003) *A Handbook of Language and Gender*, Oxford: Blackwell.

Jesperson, O. (1922) *Language: Its Nature, Development and Origin*, London: Allen and Unwin.

Kamada, L. (2010) *Hybrid Identities and Adolescent Girls: Being 'Half' in Japan*, Bristol: Multilingual Matters.

Kiesling, S. (2003) 'Playing the straight man: displaying and maintaining male heterosexuality in discourse', in K. Campbell, R. Podesva, S. J. Roberts and A. Wong (eds) *Language and Sexuality*, Stanford, CA: Stanford University Press.

Kitzinger, C. (2007) 'Is "woman" always relevantly gendered?' *Gender and Language* 1(1): 39–50.

Labov, W. (1966) *The Social Stratification of English in New York City*, Washington, DC: Center for Applied Linguistics.

Lakoff, R. (1975) *Language and Woman's Place*, New York: Harper and Row.

Maltz, D. and Borker, R. (1982) 'A cultural approach to male-female miscommunication', in J. J. Gumperz (ed.) *Language and Social Identity*, Cambridge: Cambridge University Press.

McElhinny, B. and Mills, S. (2007) 'Launching studies of *Gender and Language* in the early 21st century', *Gender and Language* 1(1): 1–13.

Mills, S. (2003) 'Third wave feminism and the analysis of sexism', *Discourse Analysis Online*, refereed interactive e-journal. Available at: www.shu.ac.uk/daol

Milroy, L. (1980) *Language and Social Networks*, Oxford: Blackwell.

Mullany, L. (2007) *Gendered Discourse in Professional Communication*, Basingstoke: Palgrave Macmillan.

Norton, B. and Pavlenko, A. (eds) (2004) *Gender and English Language Learners*, London: TESOL Publications.

Ochs, E. (1992) 'Indexing gender', in A. Duranti and C. Goodwin (eds) *Rethinking Context: Language as an Interactive Phenomenon*, Cambridge: Cambridge University Press.

Schegloff, E. (1997) 'Whose text? Whose context?' *Discourse and Society* 8(2): 165–87.

Sidnell, J. (2003) 'Constructing and managing male exclusivity in talk-in-interaction', in J. Holmes and M. Meyerhoff (eds) *A Handbook of Language and Gender*, Oxford: Blackwell.

Schulz, M. R. (1990) 'The semantic derogation of woman', in D. Cameron (ed.) *The Feminist Critique of Language: A Reader*, London: Routledge.

Spender, D. (1980) *Man Made Language*, London: Pandora.

Stokoe, E. (2005) 'Analysing gender and language', *Journal of Sociolinguistics* 1(1): 118–33.

Sunderland, J. (2004) *Gendered Discourse*, Basingstoke: Palgrave Macmillan.

Swann, J. (2000) 'Gender and language use', in R. Mesthrie, J. Swann, A. Deumert and W. L. Leap (eds) *Introducing Sociolinguistics*, Edinburgh: Edinburgh University Press.

——(2002) 'Yes, but is it gender?', in L. Litosseliti and J. Sunderland (eds) *Gender Identity and Discourse Analysis*, Amsterdam: John Benjamins.

Talbot, M. (2010) *Language and Gender*, 2nd edn, Cambridge: Polity Press.

Tannen, D. (1990) *You Just Don't Understand: Women and Men in Conversation*, London: Virago.

Trudgill, P. (1974) *The Social Differentiation of English in Norwich*, Cambridge: Cambridge University Press.

Weatherall, A. (2000) 'Gender relevance in talk-in-interaction and discourse', *Discourse and Society* 11: 290–2.

Wenger, E. (2000) *Communities of Practice*, New York: Cambridge University Press.

Wetherell, M. (1998) 'Positioning and interpretative repertoires: conversation analysis and post-structuralism in dialogue', *Discourse and Society* 9(3): 387–412.

24

Ethnicity

Roxy Harris

Introduction

The question of ethnicity in applied linguistics is such a sprawling topic and so potentially limitless in its scope that a degree of preliminary circumscription is essential. The present text is limited by:

- the angle of vision of a UK-based academic located in London;
- a concentration on the importance of the Anglo world in the field of applied linguistics and the hegemonic importance of the English language in the field, even in contexts concerning the workings of other languages;
- its focus on an interpretive rather than a comprehensive account.

The following will first attempt to present a framework within which ethnicity and its salience to applied linguistics might be manageably understood; then, second, will support this interpretive perspective with a range of illustrative examples.

Ethnicity and applied linguistics

Curiously, ethnicity has received only muted attention within applied linguistics, judging by the very slight reference to it in major comprehensive surveys of the field (Johnson and Johnson 1999; Kaplan 2002; Davies and Elder 2006; although see Sealey and Carter 2004: 115–24). However, the question of ethnicity within applied linguistics has been a persistent background thread in the field with respect to issues of authority and ownership. In the post-World War II period the rise of what has come to be known as applied linguistics has been developed and led by sources of authority located in what will be called here the white Anglo diaspora (the USA, UK, Canada, Australia, New Zealand, South Africa). With some exceptions, a central focus has been the learning of English by those regarded as ethnic and racial 'others'. In this context those of the white Anglo world have been positioned as the legitimate owners and 'native' speakers of the language; with the predominantly brown and black 'others' located on the subordinate side of a relationship which can readily be depicted as explicitly colonial, postcolonial or imperialist. The teaching and learning of English in these contexts, then, cannot plausibly be separated from complex and often contentious perspectives involving *ethnicity* and *'race'*. Of course, applied linguistics is not concerned solely with the teaching and learning of English. However, the field has been dominated by circumstances in which particularly English but also other European languages have played an influential and often pivotal role. It is here that questions of ethnicity have been important.

The concept of 'ethnicity'

According to Hutchinson and Smith (1996), the widespread use of the specific term *ethnicity* is relatively recent, first appearing in the English language, in their estimation, in the 1950s. One source of its propagation has been the endeavour of Anglo majority societies to demarcate themselves from migrant minorities:

> The English and American (White Anglo-Saxon Protestant) tendency to reserve the term 'nation' for themselves and 'ethnic' for immigrant peoples, as in the frequently used term 'ethnic minorities' ...
>
> *(Hutchinson and Smith 1996: 5)*

However, earlier, in the colonial period, ideas of 'race' as opposed to ethnicity held sway, though the two terms have been persistently intertwined and confused. The *Concise Oxford Dictionary*, for example, defines the term 'ethnic' as 'pertaining to race', and 'ethnicity' as referring to 'a specified racial, linguistic, etc., group (usu. a minority)'. Given the complexities, uncertainties and controversies surrounding ethnicity across a range of disciplines, it is not surprising that applied linguistics has not supplied a lead in offering its own explicit conceptualization. The following section proposes a framework for encapsulating ethnicity which can then be used as an interpretive frame for understanding its operations within applied linguistics. This is also a frame which, it will be suggested, has underpinned the relationship between the Anglo and European world on the one hand, and the global 'others' on the other.

An interpretive frame for conceptualizing ethnicity

Stuart Hall, working within the field of British cultural studies, has been internationally influential for his theoretical work on ethnicities. He has also provided a lucid, concise and comprehensive summary of some key sociological and philosophical understandings of the interrelationships between tradition, modernity, late modernity and culture (Hall 1992). For present purposes it is worth utilizing, from this work, some basic understandings to assist the construction of an interpretive frame embracing three dimensions:

(a) the 'traditional' (or 'pre-modern') frame associated with the colonized 'other';
(b) the 'modern' frame – associated with the Anglo and European nation states, science and industrialization;
(c) the 'late modern' frame – associated with Anglo and European nation states in contemporary globalization operating neo-liberal economies characterized by the rapid global circulation of capital, goods, people and cultural products.

(*Note*: In the present text the term 'late modernity' is preferred to the widely used 'postmodernity'. This is so as to emphasize a perspective that regards tradition, modernity and late modernity as conceptual and interpretive frames in constant interaction, rather than as historical epochs succeeding one and other.)

In this schematic rendering there tend to be a couple of key binary contrasts:

(i)   between tradition and modernity;
(ii) between modernity and late modernity.

In these contrasts it is possible to discern tensions which are consequential for an understanding of ethnicity in applied linguistics.

Tensions between tradition and modernity

In the first set of tensions the encounter between 'Western' modernity and its pre-modern Others took concrete form which saw the latter described and classified by the former, especially in areas of what came to be known as the social sciences; including disciplines such as sociology, anthropology and linguistics. The contrasts in play can be represented, albeit in somewhat simplified graphic form, as follows (Table 24.1).

Table 24.1 Tensions between tradition and modernity

Tradition	Modernity
Rural feudal communities	Industrialized cities
Autocracy	Mass democracy
'Tribes', 'natives'	Citizens of nation states
Kinship, folk customs	Class affiliations, reason and science
Locally marked vernaculars	National standard language
Ritual oratory, oral narrative	Mass schooled literacy

These binary contrasts work fairly well as a representation of colonial relationships, and at first they worked in a different way when mass migration brought formerly colonized people to the metropolitan centres of the Anglo and European world:

> this scheme of oppositions continued to operate when the focus on distant places moved back home to the Anglo and European world. Exotic 'tribes' became 'ethnic minorities', and the preoccupation with difference was translated into debates about whether and how modern institutions like schools might become more hospitable to the diversity of putatively 'non-modern' others in their midst.
>
> *(Harris and Rampton 2003: 4)*

Aspects of how this dimension of language and ethnicity has operated within applied linguistics will be explored later, but first it is necessary to outline the second major set of tensions.

Tensions between modernity and late modernity

In the second set of tensions the kinds of binary contrast outlined above have, under the pressures of contemporary globalization, begun to lose their explanatory power and

Table 24.2 Tensions between modernity and late modernity

Modernity	Late modernity
Nation state	Transnational collectivities (e.g. the EU)
Allegiances to single nation state	Transnational diasporic allegiances
Nation state authority	Lightly regulated global flows of capital, people, goods and services
National public broadcasting and national media	Global digital media
Print literacy	Multimodal literacies
National standard languages	Hybrid linguistic practices

usefulness. Once again this will be illustrated though a simplified diagrammatic representation (Table 24.2).

As suggested earlier, the forces at play in the new global migrations from the subordinate peripheries to the Anglo and European metropolitan centres have also generated linguistic consequences, which are partly summarized in the following observation:

> the emergence of global cities provides an environment where multilingualism and cultural hybridity are treated as natural and normal, and this also presents a challenge to the authority of elite cultural canons and national standard languages.
>
> *(Harris and Rampton 2003: 4)*

Although it is tempting to regard tradition, modernity and late modernity as historical epochs, it is more helpful to employ them as interpretive frames. That is to say, all of these dimensions are still in constant interaction with each other, and none has disappeared from the world. It should also be immediately obvious from the quotations above that questions of language, ethnicity and 'race' are deeply embedded within these characterizations. Before turning directly to the implications for applied linguistics it is worth concentrating for a moment on some of the relevant shifts in conceptualizations of ethnicity specifically, since these shifts have had an impact on applied linguistics. They have underpinned many of the debates, encounters, conflicts and anxieties in the field. It is important, then, to recognize that, in relatively recent times there has been something of a consensus within academic milieus that 'race' is a social and cultural construction rather than a biological-scientific fact. However,

> modernity has been inextricably linked with the setting-up of massive systems of slavery and colonial domination, and as a crucial element in the ideological maintenance of these systems, from the late eighteenth century onwards Anglo and European scholars tried to develop elaborate schemes of racial classification, built on biological and genetic foundations, with Europeans invariably placed at the top at the most advanced evolutionary stage, Africans at the bottom, and a variety of colonized others in between.
>
> *(Harris and Rampton 2003: 4)*

Historically, linguistic scholars, too, have participated in these classificatory practices and it is not difficult to find instances where references to 'primitive' languages are linked to notions of 'primitive' peoples (Jespersen [1922] 1964; Ashcroft 2001). Though scientific theories of race were eventually discredited by the Holocaust and the general destruction of World War II, a home

347

was found for 'race' within a reconstituted notion of ethnicity in which peoples were imagined as being classifiable as sharing a common ancestry, a common language, a common religion and a distinctive physical appearance. But latterly,

> Counterposed to this, the most recent contemporary challenge to this way of imagining race/ethnicity lies in the post-modern shift of interest away from identifying essences and locating them in classification systems, to analysing practices and the social processes of categorisation themselves.
>
> *(Harris and Rampton 2003: 4–5)*

To sum up: international relations in the nineteenth and twentieth centuries up to the end of World War II were significantly affected by relations of 'race' linked to a contest between forces of tradition and forces of modernity. In the post-1945 period, with the emergence of a new set of global relations accompanying movements for decolonization and civil rights, discourses of 'race' gradually gave way to discourses of 'ethnicity'. Eventually, this shift began to signal the advent of a new alignment of binary contrasts; this time between perspectives influenced by forces of modernity and those influenced by forces of late modernity. In this process the conceptualization of ethnicity itself began to be transformed. The following sections will offer an interpretation of the effects of these large-scale shifts within applied linguistics.

Tradition, modernity and ethnicity in applied linguistics

The workings of 'ethnicity' within the field of applied linguistics is a complicated and often relatively opaque matter. This first section traces some of the ways in which differing perspectives on ethnicity, informed by frameworks related to tradition or modernity, have played out in the field.

Ethnicity and the 'birth', development and consolidation of applied linguistics

One comprehensive analysis of the origins, development and consolidation of applied linguistics (Howatt and Widdowson 2004) identifies the Anglo world (America and Britain) as its driving force, defined by 'a common commitment to the teaching of English worldwide' (2004: 303). More precisely, for Britain, 'ELT was given over almost entirely to the teaching of English as a second language to children in secondary schools in the Empire' (2004: 294). At the same time an ethnic focus in applied linguistics in America lay for a long time in the tradition of 'record[ing] the indigenous Amerindian languages which were in danger of becoming extinct' (2004: 303). In both of these relationships the location of power and authority was clear. Authority lay with dominant Anglo institutions and individuals, in their interactions with subordinate racialized ethnic others. In this colonialist idiom, whether or not intentions were benign, interactions were framed by an encounter between perspectives relating to tradition and modernity. On the one hand, centres in the Anglo world sought to bring progress to others who were not white; these others were assumed to be easily characterized within essential tribal/ethnic categories involving languages and language practices which needed to be altered in order to secure modernist progress. On the other hand, subordinated racialized others struggled to secure advancement in a world they did not control, while holding on to as much of their traditional linguistic and cultural practices as they could. However, new configurations of these relationships emerged in the postcolonial period.

Ethnicity and postcolonial language planning

As the colonial era drew to a close in the 1950s and 1960s, new processes of modernity emerged. The construction of new independent nation states out of former colonies, such as the British ones, initiated a new collaboration between local elites and the former colonial powers in the name of modernity, development and progress. These new alliances produced consequences for applied linguistics which have been powerfully theorized and described (Phillipson 1992; Pennycook 1994). Traditional social arrangements based on tribes or ethnic groups were replaced by the project of building modern nation states. Typically, the expansion of the modernist project of schooling entailed the imposition of the former colonial language (English, French, etc.) as the medium of instruction and sole language for literacy, and signifier of all that was forward looking, modern and progressive. The local ethnically linked languages became strongly marked as traditional and outdated links with the past, with 'backwardness', and as now having limited utility. In the new nations the rising discipline of language planning exercised an important function in resolving potentially tricky ethnic problems. Here, these processes will be illustrated with two types of example: (a) the case of Sub-Saharan Africa, and (b) the case of Singapore.

Sub-Saharan Africa

According to one prominent scholar,

> Language policies in African countries (in the post-independence period) are characterized by one or more of the following problems: avoidance, vagueness, arbitrariness, fluctuation, and declaration without implementation.
>
> *(Bamgbose 1991: 111)*

For Bamgbose one consequence of this stance has been that:

> In practically all African countries colonized by Britain, English remains an official or co-official language. Attempts to promote an African language as a national or official language have resulted in failure or limited success.
>
> *(Bamgbose 2003: 422)*

Among the reasons given for such developments, the quest for national unity in the face of allegedly intractable scenarios involving a multiplicity of competing ethnicities and languages has often been advanced. Bamgbose, amongst others, casts doubt on what he clearly regards as unconvincing excuses; nevertheless these behaviours have been apparent all over Africa.

In a country such as Nigeria, for example, the adoption of English in official contexts was presented as a way of averting potentially serious conflict that might arise from the adoption of the languages associated with three major rival ethnic groupings: Yoruba, Igbo and Hausa. Elsewhere, in a different but striking example, the renowned writer Ngugi wa Thiong'o provides a vivid exemplification of the forbidding obstacles placed in the way of an African using his own ethnically specific language – Kenya's Kikuyu language in his case – as a language of literacy, in a context in which the learning of English is normalized and promoted. His experience also demonstrates the penalties awaiting those who persist in fighting for the right to write African languages (wa Thiong'o 1981). Even in post-apartheid South Africa, where the state has made a determined effort to overcome the problem of competing ethnicities, the outcomes have not varied very much; this despite strong language planning interventions in parliament, government, broadcasting and education. In the fading years of apartheid a working group involving linguists explored the post-apartheid language policy options. They discovered that in Sub-Saharan Africa since independence the overwhelming majority of countries had adopted a former colonial language (e.g. English, French, Portuguese) as the medium of instruction for schooling in preference to an indigenous African language (NEPI 1992). Though the ANC government enshrined the language rights of the country's major ethnic groups (e.g. Zulu, Xhosa), in the Constitution and made efforts to extend their scope as the medium of instruction in schools, there was a marked tendency for parents to opt for 'straight for English' practices for their children in schools. Given that Afrikaans and English speakers retained their MOI rights, the realities for the black African population remained closer to those of the populations of other Sub-Saharan countries than might at first appear.

Overall, in an African continent replete with ethnic groups and their associated languages, the ethnicity which has counted has clearly been either an Anglo or European one. Particularly noteworthy are Mazrui's observations on the way that this state of affairs persisted in the funding and support policies of international organizations such as the IMF and World Bank; even when research produced by these institutions has acknowledged the greater efficacy of indigenous language medium of instruction policies (Mazrui 1997).

The case of Singapore

Another, quite different illustration of ethnicity in the postcolonial nation-building process concerns the Speak Mandarin campaign in Singapore (Bokhorst-Heng 1999). Governmental efforts were made to hold in place an essentialist version of a majority ethnicity. The majority ethnicity in Singapore was described as Chinese (more than 75 per cent of the population), with Malays (14 per cent +) and Indians (7 per cent +) the next biggest groups. In this example, two language planning approaches are worth noting. First, the main 'ethnic' languages (Mandarin, Tamil and Malay) were given recognition, but only for purposes 'of identity, of ethnicity and of culture' (Bokhorst-Heng 1999: 240). However, a linguistic homogeneity among the ethnically Chinese majority based on Mandarin was imaginary, given strong allegiances to at least eleven other distinct Chinese dialects. Although the efforts to construct a unified Chinese ethnicity through the Speak Mandarin campaign alongside the encouragement given to Malay and Indian languages corresponded with essentialist ethno-racial ideologies, in practical matters the English language achieved dominance. According to Bokhorst-Heng, the language policy for schooling ensured that English language learning either as a first or second language was compulsory for all ethnic groups. The Singapore case was quite different to that of Sub-Saharan Africa in that it made room for non-Anglo languages in the education system. However, it was similar in promoting English language use as a neutral device for uniting a nation of competing ethnicities, and as a tool for modernization and scientific, technological and economic progress in efforts to 'catch-up' with the Western world.

It could be argued that the English language retained its authority in the newly independent and emerging nation states due to the ideologies and language planning practices of their leading politicians. However, this presents only part of the picture. A parallel struggle concerning ethnic authority and authenticity in language matters was also waged within the applied linguistics academy.

A struggle over authority and authenticity

In the applied linguistics academic literature a contestation has taken place concerning the centres of authority and authenticity with regard to English and the teaching of English. This will be illustrated here by two examples:

(i)   the dispute between Quirk and Kachru;
(ii) the native speaker intervention by Rampton.

The Quirk-Kachru debate

Quirk (1990) expressed alarm at what he saw as the introduction of practices vis-à-vis the teaching of English globally, which disputed the idea that authority and authenticity on matters of English language resided in the Anglo world – especially in Britain. Not only did Kachru's work (Kachru 1982) directly acknowledge the legitimacy of differing ethnically rooted stances and affiliations to English, but Kachru's own origins in the Indian sub-continent meant that the conflicting perspectives between himself and Quirk also carried an underlying ethnic/racial embodiment. Kachru's notion of authentic world Englishes as opposed to a single correct and authentic English was an affront to Quirk's deeply felt reliance on the hegemonic applied linguistics ideology of the authentic and authoritative 'native speaker' – paradigmatically the English speaker with an authentic and authoritative Anglo ethnicity. However, Rampton's (1990) intervention pointed out that both sides in this apparent dispute were operating within a familiar conceptual frame. As he put it:

> a good deal of effort is now being made to show the independent legitimacy of Englishes worldwide, but when these are described as *the other tongue* or *nativized varieties*, the English of the ethnic Anglos is still there in the background as the central reference point.
>
> *(Rampton 1990: 97)*

The native speaker intervention

Rampton's deconstruction of the ideas of the 'native speaker' and of 'mother tongue' cast serious doubt on the underlying ethnic and racial certainties which had hitherto been implied in debates and analyses within applied linguistics. For Rampton:

> ['mother tongue' and 'native speaker' as concepts] spuriously emphasize the biological at the expense of the social ... they [biological factors] are only as important as society chooses to make them. They mix up language as an instrument of communication with language as a symbol of social identification.
>
> *(Rampton 1990: 99)*

Rampton's proposal was that links between people and language are better conceived as matters of *expertise*, *affiliation* and *inheritance* and that each of these are, in practice, to be negotiated. The idea that issues of ethnicity, whether or not they are connected with language, are negotiated rather than given, foreshadowed late modern as opposed to modern frames of thought and analysis (see below). Before considering this, it is important now to briefly look at the new kinds of relations involving applied linguistics and ethnicity that arose when they began to involve not just matters in the 'global periphery' or between the 'periphery' and the 'centre'. The new factor was the migration of significant numbers of people from the periphery to the metropolitan centres in the Anglo and European worlds.

Ethnicity and applied linguistics 'at home': majority-minority relations

Post 1945 there was mass migration from poorer areas of the world to the 'home' environment in the metropolitan centres, i.e. to urban areas in Anglo and European settings. These movements very often involved the movement of people from former colonies to the former colonizing countries, for example to the UK from the Caribbean, especially Jamaica, and from India, Pakistan, and Bangladesh; and to France from the Maghreb countries. In this process a key problematic has been the question of the learning of the national standard language by the immigrants in their new environments. The question of language learning has been used as a proxy for a general discourse of hostility towards the new arrivals centred around their ethnicity and their racial characteristics. This general phenomenon will be illustrated, here, by focusing first on the UK example and then supplementing this with brief references to another Anglo-dominated location (the USA). What links these illustrative cases is that they involve nation states dominated by a degree of majority-minority ethnic tension. The language of the majority is taken to have naturally legitimate proprietorial rights over the geographical space which the nation state occupies; conversely the linguistic rights of ethnic minorities are deemed to be unnecessary or at worst a sign of disloyalty to the nation.

The UK

After 1945 ethnicity and applied linguistics in the UK were dominated by difficult ethnic relations rendered even more tense by their racially charged nature. For generations before the 1950s significant numbers of migrants and their children had arrived in the UK speaking languages like Polish, Chinese, French, Italian, Yiddish, and so on. However, their presence as people needing special English language provision provoked little public interest, debate, state intervention or provision (Bourne 1989). By contrast the peak years (the 1960s and 1970s) saw an enormous public furore occasioned by a significant new pattern of migration of black and brown people from the former British empire. These new immigrants were principally from the Indian subcontinent and the Caribbean. Their arrival was greeted with a high degree of racial hostility, often accompanied by racially motivated violence (Goulbourne 1998). Politicians and media joined the denunciation of the new arrivals in an atmosphere challenging their right to be in the country at all. In this context the immigrants' possession of languages other than English and their children's entry into the schools with these languages were received as a kind of affront. The resultant language policy was guided by explicitly assimilationist principles (Grosvenor 1997). English language proficiency was to be inculcated as rapidly as possible at the expense of other languages which ideally would disappear – bilingual education was not an option – even in areas with a strong concentration of a single language other than English. Dispersal and bussing policies were deployed in order to appease the majority ethnic population by diluting the presence of the black and brown minority ethnic immigrant children in any given sensitive school. The point to note here is that decisions ostensibly concerning language learning were formed as a reaction to perceived volatile ethnic relations between majority and minority communities rather than on the basis of coherent pedagogic principles. Significant sums of government money were made available for additional teachers to work with immigrant minority ethnic children, but only those from the Commonwealth (i.e. the black and brown ones), from the mid-1960s onwards. Yet to date there is no compulsory requirement for these teachers to have any specialist knowledge of, or qualifications in, linguistics or language pedagogy. Funding has also been provided for adult minority ethnic immigrants to learn English. But after 9/11, and especially after the London bombings in 2005, leading politicians have raised the temperature. National unity in the face of terrorist attacks has now been said to require the compulsory learning of English by all minority ethnic individuals, and for the first time a UK citizenship test has been introduced and contains an English language requirement (Cooke and Simpson 2008).

The USA

The relationship between ethnicity and applied linguistics in a US context has a complex past and present. As in the UK, the primary contrast has been between Anglo and other ethnicities. Two cases affected by English-only ideology will illustrate this: the case of African American Vernacular English (AAVE), and that of the Spanish language.

It might appear strange to include the AAVE example in a section which has concentrated so narrowly on the majority-minority ethnic relationships arising from postcolonial migrations into highly industrialized nation states. However, the historical relationship between Anglos and African Americans has been violent and severely unequal. Despite their centuries-long insider status in the USA, the treatment of African Americans in their relationship with Anglos (including segregation and lack of civil rights) has been worse than the worst of the treatment suffered by black and brown ex-colonial immigrants to the UK. The unresolved difficulties in this relationship include linguistic issues. African Americans have always claimed allegiance to English language use. Nevertheless, their particular variant of the language has been continuously located at a troubled interface with the Anglo world. Mention of two types of issue will suffice: (i) the suggestion that their use of AAVE is implicated in their educational underachievement; and (ii) the interrelated dispute over whether AAVE should be formally recognized as a different language from the Standard American English with which the Anglo population is ideologically affiliated. Both of these issues induced clarificatory interventions from the renowned sociolinguist William Labov. In the 1960s AAVE use by the black population was blamed for reading and other perceived educational failures. In response, Labov and colleagues presented detailed sociolinguistic descriptions of the regularity and systematicity of AAVE. The key point for present purposes is that apparently purely linguistic considerations served as a proxy masking more salient social and political factors pertaining to racial and ethnic conflict between Anglo and black Americans.

> The major conclusion of our research is that reading failure is primarily the result of political and cultural conflict within the classroom ... the [linguistic] structural differences cited here are quite specific and easily isolated. If they are not recognized, they can become the symbolic issues around which other conflicts arise.
>
> *(Labov 1972: 35)*

The sociolinguistic scholarship and authority of Labov and others has never managed to resolve the festering ethnically charged tension over the provenance of AAVE, which from time to time has entered a quasi-legal/legislative environment. In the Ann Arbor 'Black English trial' in 1979 in Michigan, Judge Joiner ruled that the language spoken by black school children in the area was a distinctive linguistic code and that they were suffering discrimination in that their predominantly Anglo teachers failed to recognize this. The judgment instructed the school district to train all teachers in the sociolinguistic properties of AAVE and to develop a programme for literacy teaching without pathologizing AAVE. Despite this, almost two decades later an intense controversy erupted when the Oakland School Board in California passed its Ebonics resolution on a similar basis (Baugh 1998). Labov offered written evidence in support of AAVE in both the Ann Arbor and Oakland cases, notwithstanding the affiliation of many African Americans to hegemonic common sense ideologies of linguistic deficit. Nevertheless, the dominant Anglo population in the USA has never been seriously concerned that AAVE has ever posed any kind of threat to the hegemony of Standard English. The opposite has been the case in recent times with respect to the Spanish-speaking populations and Spanish language in the United States.

Turning to the case of the Spanish language, whereas the Anglo vs African American linguistic disputes involved two populations behaving as indigenous actors in the United States, the framing of the Spanish speaking populations has been more akin to the immigrant positioning reported earlier with respect to the UK. The entry of these populations to the United States also took place in the wake of a colonial relationship with the Anglo population. However, over time their presence and accrued power in the United States came to be seen as a crucial challenge to Anglo ethnic pre-eminence. One manifestation of this anxiety has been a strong revitalization of the English-only movement; a movement which instigated legislative initiatives intended to shore up the influence and standing of English in the face of a perceived pressing threat from Spanish. A wealthy Californian computer entrepreneur, Ron Unz, has been widely credited with being the most effective activist on this issue. His funding, influence and enthusiasm helped to stimulate the passing of anti-bilingual education legislation in three states – Proposition 227 in California (1998), Proposition 203 in Arizona (2000) and Question 2 in Massachusetts (2002), (Garcia 2009: 182–65; Crawford 2000; Lo Bianco 2004). This success does not necessarily mean that (a) the influence of Spanish in the United States has significantly declined, (b) that Spanish was ever a serious threat to the dominance of English, or (c) Spanish speakers were the only linguistic minorities targeted by the legislation. The Spanish language case provides a distinctive example of the ways in which matters presented in a linguistic guise conceal deeply felt ethnic motivations. For his part, Ron Unz made his profound racial/ethnic foreboding explicitly clear:

> Californians of European ancestry – 'whites' – became a minority near the end of the 1980s, and this unprecedented ethnic transformation is probably responsible for the rise of a series of ethnically-charged political issues such as immigration, affirmative action, and bilingual education, as seen in Propositions 187, 209, and 227. ... Our political leaders should approach these ethnic issues by reaffirming America's traditional support for immigration, but couple that with a return to the assimilative policies which America has emphasized in the past. Otherwise, whites as a group will inevitably begin to display the same ethnic-minority-group politics as other minority groups, and this could break our nation. We face the choice of either supporting 'the New American Melting Pot' or accepting 'the Coming of White Nationalism'.
>
> *(Unz 1999)*

These two illustrations from the USA close this section on the interfaces between tradition, modernity and ethnicity in applied linguistics. The complex relationships described have embraced interactions on language matters between established powerful nation states and 'tribal'/ethnic groupings; between established powerful Anglo and European nation states and newly emerging nation states in the formerly colonized world; and between Anglo and

European ethnic majorities in their nation states and 'visible' immmigrant ethnic minorities from the economically poorer parts of the world. The next, final, section will look at a relatively newly developing conceptualization – the interfaces between modernity, late modernity and ethnicity in applied linguistics.

Modernity, late modernity and ethnicity in applied linguistics

Hitherto, most of the present discussion (excepting Rampton 1990) has proceeded with a settled notion of the concept of ethnicity itself. In short, for most of its history, when applied linguistics has dealt with ethnicity, it has done so assuming that groupings with specific ethnic labels are essentially different from groupings with other ethnic labels, and that each such grouping is internally homogeneous. The field has been relatively slow in absorbing new conceptualizations of ethnicity drawing on theory from other disciplines relating to contemporary globalization, post/late modernity and emerging global diasporas (Hall *et al.* 1992; Cohen 1997). In these new configurations *ethnicity* becomes *ethnicities*, which are fluid, open and hybrid, and previous certainties about language and nation become destabilized:

> an approach in which ethnicity is regarded as something that people can emphasise strategically in a range of different ways, according to their needs and purposes in particular situations. [And,] in this 'strategic' view, ethnicity is viewed more as a relatively flexible resource that individuals and groups use in the negotiation of social boundaries, aligning themselves with some people and institutions, dissociating from others, and this is sometimes described as a 'roUtes' rather than a 'roOts' conception of ethnicity. Compared with its predecessor, this version gives more credit to free will and active agency.
>
> *(Harris and Rampton 2003: 5)*

In this spirit of active agency, human social actors seek to transcend the social categories into which they are born and which they are expected to eternally inhabit. They are not afraid to participate in ethnic practices which allegedly belong legitimately to others, nor do they shrink from participating in the construction of ethnic practices regarded as new. The visible products of these actions include (a) close interethnic friendship groups, and (b) the commercial marketing of minority ethnically marked cultural products, styles and symbols as commodities. The emphasis in this account has been on a broadly conceived notion of ethnicity, but it is intended that real-world language use and second language learning – the province of applied linguistics – be envisaged as being deeply embedded in these everyday processes. In this new perspective a given ethnicity comes with no guarantees with respect to linguistic and cultural practices, and theories of 'hybridity' and 'new ethnicities' begin to emerge. This approach has been explicit in some work with a sociolinguistic orientation (Rampton 2005; Harris 2006; Rampton 2006; Harris and Rampton 2009), but has been less easy to perceive within applied linguistics per se. Leung *et al.* (1997) and Harris *et al.* (2002) attempted to bring thinking of this kind on ethnicity into applied linguistics, using exemplifications drawn from ethnographically informed research in educational contexts in the UK. Heller (1999) in turn used ethnographic research to demonstrate how modernist language ideologies in Francophone Canada have been unsettled by the ethnicities and cultural practices of migrant youth with global diaspora connections in 'high modernity'. This use of ethnography has played an important role in opening up the study of ethnicity within applied linguistics, although the critical ethnography of authors such as Canagarajah (1999) and Norton (2000) is not necessarily as committed to the late modern perspective on ethnicity; its strategic essentialism on matters of ethnicity primarily focuses on advocacy for social justice. Nevertheless, ethnographic approaches have begun to open the field to the myriad particularities and possibilities of new ethnicities. There are emerging insights revealing ways in which orientations to languages are connected to other aspects of social life and cultural practice – including popular cultural practice. This is evident in the work of Heller (ibid.) and Harris *et al.* (ibid.), but more emphatically in the emerging work of Pennycook (2007) and Alim *et al.* (2009) which draws attention to the global influence of hip hop. How contemporary youth learns English and other languages, and which versions they learn, may owe as much to the popular cultural sphere as to the classroom.

One other slowly emerging dimension of the deconstruction of formerly essential ethnic categories, relates to a renewed emphasis on the importance of social class in the context of ethnicity and language. Classic work by Zentella (1997) has all too rarely been followed. However, Collins and La Santa (2006) and Rampton *et al.* (2008) have more recently re-emphasized that ethnicity in applied linguistics in the late modern era is poorly understood without the inclusion of issues of social class. In the present text, the remit to comment on ethnicity has crowded out the importance of social class. However, to take the example of the British colonies, it was commonplace for black and brown bourgeois minorities to master Standard English with ease as a routine part of a process of schooling (Williams 1969) at the same time as the majority working class and peasantry of the same societies struggled with this, and had unequal access to schooling (Devonish 1986). In addition, the mass migrations in contemporary globalization from peripheries to metropolitan centres have predominantly involved working-class, rural, underemployed or unemployed people. Crises and problems of second language learning in the new global cities involve these same populations as they become an integral element of the urban working classes in their new locations. It is also from these same sources that emergent hybrid linguistic practices and new ethnicities can be detected. This is potentially fertile ground for future research in applied linguistics.

Conclusion

This chapter has attempted to discuss, albeit centred on the Anglo experience, the concept of ethnicity in applied linguistics by exploring how it can be understood within interlocking perspectives of tradition, modernity and late modernity. It has then attempted to exemplify this analysis with a range of illustrative summaries of some of the different ways in which ethnicity has been salient in the field over its history. It is important to close by emphasizing that traditional, modern and late modern modes of thought and practices with respect to ethnicity are constantly in play and in interaction with each other – generating nuances which await description and illumination globally by means of ethnographic approaches.

Related topics

language and migration; language policy and planning; linguistic imperialism; world Englishes

Further reading

Alim, H. S., Ibrahim, A. and Pennycook, P. (eds) (2009) *Global Linguistic Flows*, London: Routledge. (An important publication presenting a range of influential global developments in language and ethnicity outside the classroom, which are highly influential with young people, and linked to popular culture.)

Hall, S., Held, D. and McGrew, T. (eds) (1992) *Modernity and its Futures*, Cambridge: Polity Press/ Open University. (Provides a comprehensive analytic framework of social and cultural theory within which differing manifestations of ethnicity can be better understood.)

Harris, R. and Rampton, B. (eds) (2003) *The Language, Ethnicity and Race Reader*, London: Routledge. (A collection of texts by noted authors presented in a way designed to generate a multi-sided debate about the interrelationship between language and ethnicity.)

Heller, M. (ed.) (2007) *Bilingualism: A Social Approach*, Basingstoke: Palgrave Macmillan. (A volume offering rich insights, on a global canvas, into language and ethnicity seen as historically shaped and socially situated.)

References

Alim, H. S., Ibrahim, A. and Pennycook, A. (eds) (2009) *Global Linguistic Flows*, New York and London: Routledge.

Ashcroft, B. (2001) 'Language and race', *Social Identities* 7(3): 311–28.

Bamgbose, A. (1991) *Language and the Nation*, Edinburgh: Edinburgh University Press.

——(2003) 'A recurring decimal: English in language policy and planning', *World Englishes* 22(4): 419–31.

Baugh, J. (1998) 'Linguistics, education and the law', in S. Mufwene, J. Rickford, G. Bailey and J. Baugh (eds) *African American English*, London: Routledge.

Block, D. (2009) 'Economizing Globalization and Resuscitating Social Class in Identity Research', unpublished MS.

Bokhorst-Heng, W. (1999) 'Singapore's Speak Mandarin campaign', in J. Blommaert (ed.) *Language Ideological Debates*, Berlin and New York: Mouton de Gruyter.

Bourne, J. (1989) *Moving into the Mainstream*, Windsor: NFER-Nelson.

Canagarajah, A. S. (1999) *Resisting Linguistic Imperialism in English Teaching*, Oxford: Oxford University Press.

Cohen, R. (1997) *Global Diasporas*, London: UCL Press.

Collins, J. and La Santa, A. (2006) 'Analyzing class and ethnicity as communicative practices'. Available at: www.kcl.ac.uk/content/1/c6/01/42/29/paper40.pdf

Cooke, M. and Simpson, J. (2008) *ESOL: A Critical Guide*, Oxford: Oxford University Press.

Crawford, J. (2000) *At War with Diversity*, Clevedon: Multilingual Matters.

Davies, A. and Elder, C. (eds) (2006) *The Handbook of Applied Linguistics*, Oxford: Blackwell.

Devonish, H. (1986) *Language and Liberation*, London: Karia Press.

García, O. (2009) *Bilingual Education in the 21st Century: A Global Perspective*, Oxford: Wiley-Blackwell.

Goulbourne, H. (1998) *Race Relations in Britain Since 1945*, Basingstoke: Palgrave Macmillan.

Grosvenor, I. (1997) *Assimilating Identities: Racism and Educational Policy in Post 1945 Britain*, London: Lawrence and Wishart.

Hall, S. (1992) 'The question of cultural identity', in S. Hall, D. Held and T. McGrew (eds) *Modernity and its Futures*, Cambridge: Polity Press.

Hall, S., Held, D. and McGrew, T. (eds) (1992) *Modernity and its Futures*, Cambridge: Polity Press/ Open University.

Harris, R. (2006) *New Ethincites and Language Use*, Basingstoke: Palgrave Macmillan.

Harris, R., Leung, C. and Rampton, B. (2002) 'Globalization, diaspora and language education in England', in D. Block, and D. Cameron (eds) *Globalization and Language Teaching*, London: Routledge.

Harris, R. and Rampton, B. (2009) 'Ethnicities without guarantees', in M. Wetherell (ed.) *Identity in the 21st Century*, Basingstoke: Palgrave Macmillan.

Heller, M. (1999) *Linguistic Minorities and Modernity*, London: Longman.

Howatt, A. P. R. and Widdowson, H. G. (2004) *A History of English Language Teaching*, 2nd edn, Oxford: Oxford University Press.

Hutchinson, J. and Smith, A. D. (eds) (1996) *Ethnicity*, Oxford: Oxford University Press.

Jespersen, O. ([1922] 1964) 'The origin of speech', in *Language: Its Nature, Development and Origin*, London: Allen and Unwin.

Johnson, K. and Johnson, H. (eds) (1999) *Encyclopedic Dictionary of Applied Linguistics*, Oxford: Blackwell.

Kachru, B. B. (ed.) (1982) *The Other Tongue: English across Cultures*, Champaign: University of Illinois Press.

Kaplan, R. B. (ed.) (2002) *The Oxford Handbook of Applied Linguistics*, Oxford: Oxford University Press.

Labov, W. (1972) *Language in the Inner City*, Oxford: Basil Blackwell.

Leung, C., Harris, R. and Rampton, B. (1997) 'The idealised native speaker, reified ethnicities, and classroom realities', *TESOL Quarterly* 31: 543–60.

Lo Bianco, J. (2004) 'Uncle Sam and Mr Unz: language needs, politics, and pressures in the United States', *English Today* 20(3): 16–22.

Mazrui, A. (1997) 'The World Bank, the language question and the future of African education', *Race and Class* 38(3): 35–48.

NEPI (1992) *Language*, Oxford and Cape Town: Oxford University Press.

Norton, B. (2000) *Identity and Language Learning: Gender, Ethnicity and Educational Change*, Harlow: Pearson Education.

Pennycook, A. (1994) *The Cultural Politics of English as an International Language*, London: Longman.

——(2007) *Global Englishes and Transcultural Flows*, London: Routledge.

Phillipson, R. (1992) *Linguistic Imperialism*, Oxford: Oxford University Press.

Quirk, R. (1990) 'Language varieties and standard language', *Language Today* 21: 3–10.

Rampton, B. (2005) *Crossing*, London: Longman.

——(2006) *Language in Late Modernity: Interaction in an Urban School*, Cambridge: Cambridge University Press.

Rampton, B., Harris, R., Collins, J. and Blommaert, J. (2008) 'Language, class and education', in S. May and N. Hornberger (eds) *Encyclopedia of Language and Education*, vol. 1, New York: Springer.

Rampton, M. B. H. (1990) 'Displacing the "native speaker": expertise, affiliation, and inheritance', *ELT Journal* 44(2): 97–101.

Sealey, A. and Carter, B. (2004) *Applied Linguistics as Social Science*, London: Continuum.

Unz, R. (1999) 'California and the end of White America', *Commentary* (November). Available at: www.onenation.org/9911/110199.html (accessed 20 November 2009).

wa Thiong'o, N. (1981) *Decolonising the Mind*, London: Heinemann.

Williams, E. (1969) *Inward Hunger*, London: Andre Deutsch.

Zentella, A. (1997) *Growing Up Bilingual*, Oxford: Blackwell.

25

Sign languages

Bencie Woll and Rachel Sutton-Spence

Introduction

This chapter explores applied linguistics in relation to sign languages – the term used to refer to the class of natural human languages which have arisen spontaneously within Deaf communities. These languages are produced and perceived in the visual modality, and are unrelated to the spoken languages which surround them. Despite surface differences from spoken language, they share at a deeper level the linguistic structure of all human language, and are used in parallel social and communicative contexts. They are unwritten languages that occupy minority positions within societies where other languages are dominant.

The chapter takes as its starting point that the driving thrust of applied linguistics is to identify and solve problems (both practical and policy-orientated) within a language situation independent of the modality of the language or languages considered.

The chapter will begin with a brief but comprehensive introduction to the linguistic study of sign languages and the status of different sign languages within their surrounding majority spoken language communities. The section includes a concise description of phonology, morphology, syntax, pragmatics and discourse. We primarily describe sign languages in Europe and North America, but consideration will be given to sign languages in other parts of the world, and to a comparison of urban and village sign languages, and of new and old sign languages. A discussion of current research priorities in applied linguistics of sign language, including lexicography and sign language corpus linguistics, follows. This leads into a consideration of sign languages within a bilingual context, which will cover such topics as access to spoken/written language and literacy, interpreting and translation, and workplace communication in mixed Deaf/hearing settings.

The remainder of the chapter discusses a range of issues pertinent to applied linguistics, grouped around three themes: sign language teaching and learning, sign language politics, and social and technological change. Description of sign language teaching and learning includes L1 and L2 acquisition, curriculum design, learner assessment, and classroom practices. Our exploration of applied linguistics of sign language in relation to language and politics covers sign language planning, language choice, linguistic correctness, identity and language. The final section will look ahead to the potential impact of change on sign language and the Deaf community, including language variation and change, and new technology.

The linguistic structure of signed languages

Structure and modality

In the last fifty years, there has been substantial research on nearly a hundred different sign languages (see the Hamburg sign language bibliographic Website, www.sign-lang.uni-hamburg. de/bibWeb, for a comprehensive listing of sign language research), determining that the sign languages of Deaf communities (lower case 'deaf' is used to refer to deafness in audiological terms; upper case 'Deaf' refers to social, cultural and linguistic identity) throughout the world are complex natural human languages, distinct from gesture and also from spoken languages. Early modern research on sign languages emphasised the underlying structural similarities of spoken and sign languages, but more recent research has moved towards recognition that there are systematic typological differences. These arise mainly from the interaction of language form with modality. Phonological and morphological structures differ because sign languages have greater correspondence between form and meaning (iconicity or visual motivation) than spoken languages do. Sign languages also exploit space for grammatical purposes, creating syntactic structures exhibiting extensive simultaneity, while spoken languages prefer linearity and affixation processes. Other differences arise from the properties of the articulators (sign languages use two primary articulators – the hands – as well as non-manual articulators, including the torso, head and face, eyes and mouth) and the differing properties of the visual and auditory perceptual systems. In the light of this, linguistic theory needs to take greater account of modality (Meier *et al.* 2003). A further step in our understanding of sign languages has been to recognise the interrelationship of language and gesture, for example, the presence of slots in discourse structure where signers can switch to gesturing, such as when they want to show the roles of characters in a story. Cognitive models are increasingly used to account for the visual motivation behind the structure and form of sign languages, irrespective of the level of language analysis (Taub 2001).

Although the social histories of sign languages differ from each other in many respects, there is greater typological similarity among sign languages than among spoken languages. Their relative youth (Kegl *et al.* 1999) and their possible creole status (Fischer 1978) may account for some of this, but visual motivation as an organising factor in the lexicon and syntax may also be significant. The linear syntax of spoken languages and their independence from visual motivation may allow greater differences than spatial, visually motivated syntax (Woll 1984 and Taub 2001).

Many superficial differences in sign grammars stem from the influence of the grammar of surrounding spoken languages, either through natural processes of borrowing (see below) or the use in schools of artificial communication systems such as 'Signed English' or 'Signed Dutch'. However, the basic similarities in structure of sign languages are sufficient for us to treat them together in a brief review here.

Phonology, morphology and syntax

Since Stokoe's pioneering work on American Sign Language (1960), linguists have seen signs as consisting of simultaneous combinations of handshape configuration, a location where the sign is articulated and movement – either a path through signing space or an internal movement of the joints in the hand. Each is understood to be a part of the phonology, because changing one of these parameters can create a minimal pair. Thus, in British Sign Language (BSL) AFTERNOON and ORDER differ only in handshape; AFTERNOON and NAME differ only in location; and AFTERNOON and TWO-HUNDRED differ only in movement. There have been considerable modifications to Stokoe's framework since 1960, but this model has remained the basic description of sign language phonology.

Sign language morphology tends to manifest itself in simultaneous combinations of meaningful handshapes, locations and movements. In derivational morphology, for example, handshape can change to reflect numbers – for example, N-weeks, N-o'clock and N-years-old are articulated with conventionalised location and movement while the handshape indicates the number. Signs referring to objects and actions may also differ only in movement, so the verbs LOCK, OPEN-A-NEWSPAPER, and EAT are made with a single, large movement, compared to the nouns KEY, NEWSPAPER, and FOOD, which have short, repeated movements. Inflectional morphology is also shown by changes in movement and location. Thus, degree is shown through size, speed, onset speed and length of hold in a movement, with, for example, LUCKY having a smaller, smoother movement than VERY-LUCKY. The movement changes conveying temporal aspect are frequently visually motivated, so that repeated actions or events are shown through repetition of the sign; duration of an event is paralleled by duration of the sign (signs for shorter events being articulated for less time than signs for longer events); and when an event is interrupted suddenly, the movement of the sign is interrupted. Some verbs show number and person by movement through signing space. The direction of movement of a verb such as GIVE indicates who gave to whom and to how many. Signs can also change handshape to indicate how the direct object is handled. So I-HAND-OVER-A-SINGLE-FLOWER-TO-EACH-OF-SEVERAL-OF-YOU has the same movement as I-HAND-OVER-AN-ICECREAM-TO-EACH-OF-SEVERAL-OF-YOU but a different handshape.

Sign language has relatively free word order, driven extensively by external factors such as the pragmatics of the signers' communicative aims and what they believe their audience to know, as well as what has already been said. Creating a clear, visually motivated image of the discourse will also influence order, with the ground signed before the figure, and the patient or goal signed before the agent, in order to allow the agent to have something to act upon in a visual sense. For example, WALL PAINT (put paint on a wall) and PAINT PICTURE (create a picture by painting) may be preferred orders.

Educators have often compared sign languages unfavourably to spoken (European) languages, noting that sign languages frequently 'lack' certain features seen in European spoken languages, such as tense, gender, or determiners. In fact, sign languages share many features with other language groups, especially other head-marking languages such as Navajo, Mayan and Abkhaz, rather than dependent-marking languages such as many in the Romance, Germanic and Sino-Tibetan families (Slobin 2005). For example, sign languages share features with the languages of Micronesia (Nichols 1992), including adjectives operating as intransitive verbs, distinctions between inclusive and exclusive pronouns, and lack of a copula. Verbs in languages of this type (both signed and spoken) often use classifiers (based on shape or animacy, for example), show direct object incorporation, have rich inflection including aspect, and show little opposition of active and passive voice.

Different types of visually motivated signs

While signed and spoken languages share many grammatical features, the visual-spatial modality provides structural possibilities unavailable to spoken languages.

Spoken languages can incorporate auditory features of referents into the language (as in onomatopoeia) but there are few opportunities for this since humans perceive the world largely visually. Signs often represent the visual form of a referent, how it moves, or where it is located, although it should be noted that not all signs are visually motivated (for example, WANT, WHO and SISTER in BSL).

Whether or not a sign is visually motivated, all signs exhibit a conventionalised relationship between the form and the referent. A sign can be visually motivated but the particular image selection of the referent for linguistic encoding is arbitrary. For example, the BSL sign TEA reflects the action of 'drinking from a teacup', while the ASL sign reflects the act of 'dipping a teabag in a cup'.

Signed languages can convey spatial relations directly. The linguistic conventions used in such spatial mapping specify the position of objects in a highly geometric and non-arbitrary fashion by situating certain sign forms (e.g. classifiers) in space such that they maintain the topographic relations of the world-space being described (Emmorey et al. 1995). Within these structures, the handshapes in verbs of motion and location in topographic sentences represent object features or classes (how objects are handled, their size and shape, or their function). These have been termed 'classifiers' (Supalla 1986; Engberg-Pedersen 1993), although recently the use of this term has come into question (see Schembri 2003).

Both spoken and signed languages articulate lexical items sequentially. Spoken languages can give some linguistic information simultaneously (as in, for example, tone languages), and prosody adds further grammatical and affective information to the lexemes uttered. Essentially, though, humans have only one vocal apparatus so spoken languages must use sequential structures. The availability of two hands (and head and face) enables sign languages to use simultaneously articulated structures (see Vermeerbergen et al. 2007). Two hands can be used to represent the relative locations of two referents in space, and their spatial and temporal relationships. In representing, for example, a person reaching for a book while holding a pen, English conjoins clauses using 'while' or 'as' to indicate two events happening simultaneously. In sign languages 'holding a pen' can be signed with one hand, while 'reaching for the book' can be signed with the other. English uses prepositions such as 'next to' or 'behind' to represent relative locations, whereas sign languages can simply place the two signs in the relative locations of the two referents.

It should be noted, however, that simultaneity is an option exercised differently by different sign languages. In a comparison of sentences generated from the same picture materials in Irish Sign Language (ISL) and BSL, ISL signers used simultaneous signs in 20 per cent of their utterances and BSL signers used them in 80 per cent (Saeed et al. 2000).

Sign languages within a bilingual context

Case studies of 'non-Western' Deaf communities

Deafness is statistically uncommon, with about 1 in 1,000 children born Deaf in developed countries. The bulk of research on sign languages has been on the sign languages of North America and Europe, where small numbers of relatively well-educated Deaf people are spread across nations but socialise within local and national Deaf communities and share a common national sign language. However, there are also small isolated, often rural, communities around the world where higher rates of genetic deafness create 'Deaf villages' which develop their own sign languages. These include Grand Cayman Island (Washabaugh 1981), the Urubu-Kaapor of Brazil (Ferreira-Brito 1985), the Yucatan Maya (Johnson 1994), the Enga of

New Guinea (Kendon 1980), the people of Desa Kolok on the island of Bali (Branson *et al.* 1996) and the Al-Sayyid Bedouin in Israel (Kisch 2007, 2008). (Also see Kusters 2010, for a comprehensive review of research on 'shared sign languages'.)

In the community in Bali called Desa Kolok by Branson and colleagues, 2 per cent of the 2,000 village residents are Deaf, and marriage between hearing and Deaf villagers is the norm. Deaf members of the community have equal status in decision-making at local community level although few are reported to participate. Those who do, use family members to interpret, since not all village members are fluent in sign language. In earlier times, village Deaf children received no formal education, although there has been a school for hearing children for over fifty years. Recent moves to offer specialist Deaf education have resulted in the placing of Deaf children in a school located outside the village, and this has begun to alter the linguistic and social dynamics of the community.

Al-Sayyid Bedouin Sign Language is used in a Bedouin tribe of around 3,000 people with approximately 5 per cent Deaf. Deaf children have had better access to education in the past than hearing children, since they attended a Deaf school where Hebrew was taught. The Deaf children therefore developed a degree of literacy in the majority language, which is a key to employability, and they are fully economically integrated. While all hearing members of the community have some knowledge of the tribe's sign language, only hearing people in families with a high percentage of Deaf members are fully fluent.

Encounters between Deaf and hearing communities

Even when Deaf and hearing people can sign or where there are interpreters available, there are still instances of conflict and misunderstanding arising between the two groups. Much of the time these arise from their very different experiences of life within society. Deaf communities share life experiences and culture, but these are embedded within the hearing world. When hearing people do not appreciate Deaf values and the importance of certain behaviours, friction and even hostility can occur.

Perhaps the area where such conflict is greatest is in the area of language. Young *et al.* (1998) studied the use of BSL in the workplace (in psychiatric units for Deaf people and in a school for Deaf children), exploring the role of signers as not only service users but also as service providers. The signing skills of Deaf staff were far superior to those of their hearing colleagues. These skills were especially important for communicating with mentally ill Deaf people or with Deaf children. Despite this, the Deaf staff had lower-grade jobs than the hearing staff although the delivery of services depended on Deaf staff and their cultural and linguistic skills. They thus had low status, but high value.

Since only a signed linguistic environment provided Deaf staff with full access to information at work, hearing staff were required to sign at all times when a Deaf person was present or might be present. Deaf and hearing people differed in the way they viewed this policy. For Deaf staff, signing promoted involvement, making Deaf people feel confident, valued and respected, and with a sense of well-being; signing promoted the development of personal and social relationships between Deaf and hearing people; signing also enabled Deaf staff to fulfil their professional roles and responsibilities. In contrast, hearing staff reported that signing caused lack of confidence, and they felt that the pressure to sign was sometimes too great. When they were tired, distracted, or under pressure, they reverted to English. A clear signing policy, good training and a supportive environment encouraged hearing people to sign. This increased recognition of the role of sign language within the workplace for the benefit of both employees and service users, is a positive step.

Bencie Woll and Rachel Sutton-Spence

Bimodal bilingualism

Until recently, studies of bilingualism considered only individuals and communities in which two spoken languages are used. With the development of research on sign languages, it has become clear that bilingualism can be bimodal as well as unimodal. Unimodal bilingualism occurs when either two spoken or two sign languages are used (e.g. Irish and British Sign Language); bimodal bilingualism occurs when the two languages exist in different modalities: one signed and one spoken/written. Recognition of bimodal bilingualism has led to a re-evaluation of models of bilingualism.

Bimodal bilingualism differs from unimodal bilingualism with respect to the temporal sequencing of languages. Hearing people with Deaf parents (in America sometimes called CODAs – children of Deaf adults) can acquire a sign language as a first language. As adults, they have full access to at least two languages: a visual-manual one (signed language) and an auditory-vocal one (spoken language). Emmorey *et al.* (2005) have explored how bimodal bilingualism works in CODAs, showing code blending in the production of words and signs where these reflect a common conceptual source. Code blending reflects the simultaneous use of sign and word in a single utterance, which is not possible for unimodal bilinguals, who must sequence the language items in production.

Deaf bimodal bilinguals may not use voice but still produce code-blends as well as code-mixes (some researchers prefer the term 'cross-modal' to indicate that bilingualism in, for example, BSL and English can be represented in types of code-blends other than speech accompanied by signing). Cross-modal bilingualism is the norm in those countries where Deaf children receive education and use sign language. Mastery of both the sign language of the Deaf community and the spoken/written language of the hearing community is the goal of Deaf bilingual education, since the bedrock of formal education is literacy.

Recording signs

Sign languages are essentially unwritten and no sign language has a written literature. Written forms of some sign languages are being actively promoted, for example, ASL, Brazilian Sign Language and Nicaraguan Sign Language (see www.signwriting.org) but it will be many years, if at all, before these written forms of sign language attain the status and function of written forms of spoken language. Since written language is central to so much of applied linguistics, it is worth considering the implications for teaching and learning, change and standardisation, as well as for dictionary-making and issues of electronic storage of examples of language use.

Sign languages are increasingly recorded and transmitted using digital video technology (Krentz 2006), but the impact of this is different from the impact of writing. Wilcox (2003) has observed that seeing the actual signer (whom many will recognise and whose personality will be known) is not the same as an anonymous written record. This has great implications for the creation of linguistic corpora and language surveys, where anonymity can never be guaranteed. It also has implications for such apparently mundane issues as blind marking in examinations – there can be no anonymous candidates in a sign language examination.

Dictionaries and standardisation

Sign language dictionaries are usually created to collect and preserve the lexicon of the language (such dictionaries have existed for several centuries; for example, Bulwer 1644; Pelissier

1856) or to allow others to learn the language. However, most 'dictionaries' are more accurately 'bilingual word lists' using a written language and illustrations of signs. They are not created for fluent users of the language to consult in order to check the meaning, pronunciation or origin of the sign. Signs are rarely defined using the sign language and are more often defined through the written language. Some specialist bilingual dictionaries offer translations of words and signs used in specific trades or scholarly areas (for example, see www. artsigns.ac.uk).

Recent advances in technology have allowed construction of sign language dictionaries based on signed corpora. Even the largest sign dictionary databases are only of several hundred thousand signs – minimal compared to most spoken language databases for corpus work – but they are proving effective, and corpus-based dictionaries are now available, for example, in German and New Zealand Sign Languages (McKee and Kennedy 2006). Corpora also allow researchers to identify sign frequencies, so that teaching materials can be better designed.

Signs that are in dictionaries are more likely to be accorded high status, be considered 'standard' and be in more widespread use than those that are omitted. Sign language dictionaries have relatively little direct impact on native signers because they rarely use them, but second language learners of sign languages who use these dictionaries often become educators or interpreters and may ultimately have considerable power within the sign language community.

There are similarities between the functions of dictionaries created for minority spoken languages and sign languages. For example, the Jicarilla Apache dictionary (Axelrod *et al.* 2003) was designed to document the endangered language, be a reference dictionary for less fluent speakers, be a teaching tool, standardise the language, and 'celebrate' the language. Dictionaries of minority languages often provide 'a clear and powerful symbolic function of recognition and empowerment of the language' (Lucas 2002: 323) but they can also threaten the language if the making of the dictionary is not carefully controlled (Armstrong 2003).

As an example, van Herreweghe and Vermeerbergen (2004) describe some of the impact of codification on Flemish Sign Language (VGT). Increased official recognition of VGT led to increased demand for educational materials, dictionaries and grammar books. Between 1980 and 1995 a committee of Deaf people worked to standardise VGT across Flanders, creating signs where there were apparent lexical gaps and choosing the most widely used variant to be the standard form. Deaf adults rarely used the new codified form, but its lexicon influenced interpreters. When Deaf schools were replaced by the integration of Deaf children in mainstream schools, reducing their access to each other and especially to Deaf children or teachers from Deaf families, non-native signer interpreters became language role models.

As well as the use of dictionaries as a tool to create language change, many sign languages have undergone language planning designed to create changes in grammar, sometimes through the efforts of Deaf people, but more often because hearing people, especially educators, have sought to improve what they saw as defective systems. The great sign language enthusiasts of the eighteenth and nineteenth centuries, such as the Abbé de L'Epée in France, and Thomas and Edward Gallaudet in America (who were not Deaf) created new morphological markers to match the structure of the spoken languages of their countries. The changes have not been as long-lasting as the planners expected. Those who have invented new signs or sign systems (new manual alphabets or entirely new communication systems such as the Paget Gorman Sign System or Seeing Essential English [SEE]) have found them for the most part rejected by Deaf communities.

Dialect variation in many sign languages is common, and signers from different regions often use different lexical items to refer to the same concept. BSL research in the late 1980s showed that although there were regionally specific signs for many concepts, there was frequently one lexical item that was recognised and used across all regions (Woll 1991). At the time of that study, most Deaf adults had been educated at schools for Deaf children (either residential or day schools) but by 2000 most children were educated in mainstream schools. The implications of this change for BSL have been considerable, as children no longer have the same ready-made circle of signing friends and their sign language role models are now often non-native signers.

Learning sign language as L1

Since the vast majority of Deaf children are born to hearing parents, their exposure to language is very different from that of hearing children learning a spoken language. The typical experience for Deaf children is late and impoverished exposure to a first language (Harris 2001; Spencer 1993). If parents communicate only through spoken language, the child may have greatly reduced access to the linguistic signal; where parents begin to learn a sign language when deafness is diagnosed, they often have only limited sign language skills. The 95 per cent of Deaf children born to hearing parents are therefore often contrasted with the minority of Deaf and hearing children who grow up with Deaf parents and usually have good sign language models from birth.

There is general agreement that sign language acquisition parallels that of spoken language (Newport and Meier 1985; Schick 2003; Mayberry and Squires 2006) when young children (Deaf or hearing) are exposed to sign language by their Deaf parents.

Visual motivation in signs does not appear to help young children learning a sign language as an L1. Studies of children acquiring ASL have reported that less than a third of their first signs are closely linked to iconic properties of the referent. Children's first signs are more likely to be associated with the same sets of semantic categories evident in children's early speech, for example signs for people, animals and food (Anderson and Reilly 2002) irrespective of their iconicity. In a study of first language acquisition of BSL from age 1;10–3;0, Morgan et al. (2008) reported that from 1;10 onwards the majority of signs that were being acquired by the child were non-iconic. Children who acquire a sign language as their first language are unaware of the visual motivation behind a sign such as MILK (which represents the action of milking a cow by hand). The recognition of iconicity depends on increasing world knowledge, and there is evidence that children may return to the language forms they have learned previously, reanalyse them and identify iconicity (Morgan 2005).

Sign language and education

Use of sign languages in education varies greatly around the world and even within countries. An enduring controversy in Deaf education from the early nineteenth century onwards has polarised educators. The dominant approach to communication for Deaf children from the late nineteenth to late twentieth century saw no role for sign language in the education of Deaf children, and the use of sign language in the classroom was actively suppressed. Nevertheless, until the 1980s Deaf children were usually educated in Deaf schools and sign language was transmitted from child to child.

Since the 1980s sign languages have been more accepted in schools, but simultaneously there has been a strong move towards mainstreaming Deaf children. This has produced

improvements in educational achievement but has had serious social and linguistic consequences because of the loss of a natural signing community. Some Deaf children informally
learn sign language once they arrive at primary schools but are neither formally taught the
language, nor are exposed to it as a language of instruction. Their access to sign language may
be via school staff (teachers, classroom aides and communication support workers) and other
pupils, who may vary greatly in their signing competence. Deaf teachers provide the best
sign language role models to children but their numbers vary greatly around the world. For
example, in the USA over 20 per cent of teachers of the Deaf are Deaf signers, while in England
fewer than 5 per cent of teachers are Deaf signers, and in Mexico there are none in the
public sector. In contrast, in Scandinavian countries almost all Deaf children receive bilingual
education.

Studies consistently show superior sign language skills in Deaf children from Deaf families
compared with Deaf children from hearing families (Paul and Quigley 2000), as well as
persistent inadequacies in the language environment provided by education systems that report
using sign language (Ramsey 1997; Greenberg and Kusché 1987). Herman and Roy
(2006) found that many Deaf children do not achieve age-appropriate levels of BSL, and
the majority of Deaf children also do not achieve age-appropriate levels of spoken/written
language.

The extensive dialect differences within many sign languages are generally school-based in
origin. The considerable regional variation in Britain can be attributed to the over forty
schools that were independently established and administered in the nineteenth century.
Schermer (2004) describes five regional dialects of Sign Language of the Netherlands (SLN)
based on the five Deaf schools. Vanhecke and de Weerdt (2004) have described the regional
variation of VGT as based on five main regions of Flanders, each with its own school. Significantly, ISL has very little regional variation because there were only two main Deaf schools
in Ireland, both in Dublin. ASL also has surprisingly little regional variation, given the size of
the country and its Deaf population, possibly because of the centralising effects of Gallaudet
University and the original Hartford Asylum, where initially all training of teachers of the
Deaf took place.

Education in many countries has also had a profound effect on national sign languages
because Deaf educators took on methods of teaching and methods of communication used in
other countries. LSF (French Sign Language) has had the greatest impact; its influence can be
seen clearly in ISL (Burns 1998), ASL (Lane 1984), Russian Sign Language (Mathur and
Rathmann 1998) and on some dialects of BSL influenced by ISL. Other sign languages have
also had this sort of influential role. For example, Portuguese signers use the Swedish Sign
Language manual alphabet, because a Swedish educator helped to found a Deaf school in
Portugal. ISL, originally heavily influenced by LSF, has also had its own considerable impact
on sign languages around the world. Irish nuns and Christian Brothers have taught in Catholic
schools for Deaf children in countries including India, South Africa and Australia, and the
influence of ISL is noticeable in the sign languages in these countries (Aarons and Akach
1998).

The impact of external language pressures on the world's sign languages has been immense.
Woodward (1996) has described how Modern Thai SL has been greatly influenced by American
signs through the education system, although the original sign languages in Thailand have no
influence from ASL. The sign languages in Vietnam all show strong influences from LSF,
which was introduced into the first school for Deaf children in Vietnam in 1886. Schermer
(2004) noted that the Gröningen dialect of SLN was influenced by LSF after a Dutch visit to
the Paris Deaf school in 1784.

ASL, itself originally influenced by LSF, has had an increasing impact on sign languages around the world. Gallaudet University attracts foreign Deaf students who take ASL back to their own countries. The USA has been especially generous in providing teacher training in many Third World countries. Andrew Foster, a Deaf African-American, led a movement for the establishment of schools in African countries where ASL was introduced as the language of tuition (Lane *et al*. 1996). In Nigeria today, ASL, taught in schools, is mixing with the indigenous sign languages (Schmaling 2003).

Learning sign languages as L2

There have been substantial changes in attitudes of the general public to sign language since the 1980s, particularly in the representation of sign languages in the media, and there has been an enormous increase in the number of hearing people learning sign language. There are now significantly more hearing people with some knowledge of their national sign language than members of the Deaf community. Several European countries are planning to offer sign languages as L2 within the general school population (France announced in July 2009 that it would introduce LSF into the Baccalaureate system). In many American universities, ASL is included as part of the modern language requirement for undergraduates (Lamb and Wilcox 1988). The increased interest in learning sign language has implications for teacher training and language resources.

Interpreters

Until the 1970s, in most countries the 'go-between' between hearing and Deaf people was usually a hearing member of a Deaf person's family or a 'missioner' – a church or voluntary worker with the Deaf. Deaf people used the missioner as an interpreter and also frequently as an ally, adviser and advocate. As connections between Deaf communities and the church weakened, this task was taken on by social workers for the Deaf (Brennan and Brown 1997). (The BSL sign SOCIAL-WORKER is derived from the old sign MINISTER because of their similar role in Deaf life.) Social workers for the Deaf and missioners for the Deaf often came from Deaf families and lived and socialised with members of the Deaf community. Professional BSL/English interpreting began in the early 1980s, as a step towards empowerment of Deaf people. These interpreters had undergone formal linguistic and interpreting training and did not make decisions for Deaf people or advise them, but merely relayed information between the two languages, comparable to spoken language interpreters. Pollitt (2000) notes that many Deaf people (especially older Deaf people) see interpreters using this professional approach as 'cold' or 'unhelpful' and unacceptably 'impersonal'.

A shortage of interpreters is also a serious problem, since interpreters enable access to communication with the hearing world. Laws requiring sign language provision in public settings (such as on television or for health and legal settings) do not take into account the shortage of qualified, experienced interpreters. One proposed solution to the shortage is the use of computer-generated signing avatars, although these are still in early stages of development, and need much further work.

Problems have also arisen from the way that interpreters are trained. With interpreter training moving from the community into university settings, many members of the Deaf community feel that interpreters (now often from hearing families) no longer have in-depth knowledge of the Deaf communities with whom they work. Subtle language nuances, contextual information, complex social relationships and specific language skills of a Deaf client are only learned through long-term, committed relationships with a community, such as missioners and social workers had. Interpreters may cover much wider areas of the country and have far less daily interaction with their clients. Interpreters are now beginning to recognise the need to adapt other models of interpreting to the specific needs of the Deaf community today, with calls for a more flexible approach, incorporating ideas from both the 'traditional' and the 'professional' approaches.

Deaf interpreters often work as 'relay' interpreters in situations where a Deaf person (for example, in court) may not understand the signing of a hearing interpreter, who in turn may not understand the Deaf person. In such situations a Deaf relay interpreter may be called upon to act as an interface between the interpreter and the Deaf client (Brennan and Brown 1997). Increasingly, Deaf interpreters also work in the media, providing sign language translations of pre-recorded programmes or pre-prepared live programmes.

Conclusions

The twenty years between 1980 and 2000 saw substantial social and technological change for the Deaf community that might have impacted on sign language. In Britain, for example, there was no BSL on television until after 1980. Thirty years later, there are several hours of sign language broadcast daily (mostly in the form of sign language interpretation of mainstream programming) and an ever-increasing amount of signed video on the Internet, including on sites such as YouTube. This greater national (and international) media exposure may have an impact on dialect variation and on access of signers to foreign sign languages. Dialect levelling can already be seen, and is currently under further investigation as part of a number of sign language corpus projects (e.g. Schembri *et al.* 2009).

In 1980, the Deaf club was the focus of the Deaf community, and it could be assumed that a person who identified as part of the community would attend the Deaf club on a regular basis. Today, many Deaf clubs have an increasingly ageing membership and an overall decreasing membership.

Where next in the study of Deaf people and signed languages? One pressing need is a review and re-examination of the experiences and achievements of Deaf children. Changes in technology and new research into language development and the learning of literacy and numeracy skills need to feed into such a policy review.

The history of sign languages, like that of many minority languages, cannot be separated from a study of their relationship with the majority language communities which surround them. At the beginning of the twenty-first century, there are two contrasting futures: on the one hand, there are pressures, such as the decrease in opportunities for Deaf children to use sign language with their peers as a result of the shift to mainstream education, and the possible decrease in the Deaf population as a result of medical intervention and advances in genetics; on the other hand, increased interest and demand from the hearing community for courses in sign language, increased use of sign language in public contexts such as television, baby sign courses, and increased pride of the Deaf community in their distinctive language and culture. It is to be hoped and expected that sign languages will continue to be living languages.

Related topics

bilingual education; identity; language and culture; language emergence; language policy and planning; lexicography; linguistic imperialism; multilingualism; sociolinguistics

Bencie Woll and Rachel Sutton-Spence

Further reading

Erting, C. J., Johnson, R. E., Smith, D. L. and Snider, B. D. (eds) (1994) *The Deaf Way: Perspectives From the International Conference on Deaf Culture, 1989*, Washington, DC: Gallaudet University Press. (This is a comprehensive collection of papers on sign languages and deaf culture, drawing on a wide selection of sign languages around the world.)

Meier, R., Cormier, K. and Quinto-Pozos, D. (eds) (2003) *Modality and Structure in Signed and Spoken Languages*, Cambridge: Cambridge University Press. (This is a useful reference highlighting the importance of the visual modality in the structure of signed languages.)

Monaghan, L., Schmaling, C. Nakamura, K. and Turner, G. (eds) (2003) *Many Ways to be Deaf: International Variation in Deaf Communities*, Washington, DC: Gallaudet University Press. (A useful overview of some language and cultural issues in languages around the world.)

Sutton-Spence, R. and Woll, B. (1999) *The Linguistics of British Sign Language: An Introduction*, Cambridge: Cambridge University Press. (This provides a general overview of the structure and social and cultural contexts of British Sign Language.)

Young, A., Ackerman, J. and Kyle, J. (1998) *Looking On*, Bristol: Policy Press. (This book is a clear exposition of some of the tensions and positive outcomes that occur through use of sign language in the workplace.)

References

Aarons, D. and Akach, P. (1998) 'South African Sign Language – one language or many? A sociolinguistic question', *Stellenbosch Papers in Linguistics* 31: 1–28.

Anderson, D. and Reilly, J. (2002) 'The MacArthur communicative development inventory: normative data for American Sign Language', *Journal of Deaf Studies and Deaf Education* 7(2): 83–119.

Armstrong, D. (2003) 'Introduction to special issue on dictionaries and lexicography, Part II: the development of national sign language dictionaries', *Sign Language Studies* 3: 378.

Axelrod, M., Gomez, J. and Lachler, J. (2003) 'The roles of literacy and collaboration in documenting Native American Languages: a report from the Jicarilla Apache dictionary project', *Sign Language Studies* 3(3): 296–321.

Branson, J., Miller, D., Marsaja, I. G. and Negara, I. W. (1996) 'Everyone here speaks sign language, too: a deaf village in Bali, Indonesia', in C. Lucas (ed.) *Multicultural Aspects of Sociolinguistics in Deaf Communities,* Washington, DC: Gallaudet University Press.

Brennan, M. and Brown, R. (1997) *Equality before the Law: Deaf People's Access to Justice*, Durham: Deaf Studies Research Unit.

Bulwer, J. (1644) *Chirologia; or the Natural Language of the Hand*, London: R Whitaker.

Burns, S. (1998) 'Irish Sign Language: Ireland's second minority language', in C. Lucas (ed.) *Pinky Extension and Eye Gaze: Language Use in Deaf Communities*, Washington, DC: Gallaudet University Press.

Emmorey, K., Borinstein, H. B. and Thompson, R. (2005) 'Bimodal bilingualism: code blending between ASL and spoken English', in J. Cohen, K. T. McAlister, K. Rolstad and J. MacSwan (eds) *Proceedings of the 4th International Symposium on Bilingualism*, Somerville, MA: Cascadilla Press.

Emmorey, K., Corina, D. and Bellugi, U. (1995) 'Differential processing of topographic and referential functions of space', in K. Emmorey and J. Reilly (eds) *Language, Gesture and Space*, Hillsdale, NJ: Lawrence Erlbaum Associates.

Engberg-Pedersen, E. (1993) *Space in Danish Sign Language*, Hamburg: Signum Press.

Ferreira-Brito, L. (1985) 'A comparative study of signs for time and space in São Paulo and Urubu-Kaapor Sign Language', in W. Stokoe and V. Volterra (eds) *SLR '83. Proceedings of the 3rd International Symposium on Sign Language Research. Rome, June 22–26 1983*, Rome and Silver Spring, MD: CNR/Linstok Press.

Fischer, S. D. (1978) 'Sign language and creoles', in P. Siple (ed.) *Understanding Language Through Sign Language Research*, New York: Academic Press.

Greenberg, M. and Kusché, C. (1987) 'Cognitive, personal, and social development of deaf children and adolescents', in M. C. Wang, M. C. Reynolds and H. J. Walberg (eds) *Handbook of Special Education: Research and Practice*, vol. 3: *Low Incidence Conditions*, New York: Pergamon.

Harris, M. (2001) 'It's all a matter of timing: sign visibility and sign reference in deaf and hearing mothers of 18-month-old children', *Journal of Deaf Studies and Deaf Education* 6(3): 177–85.

Herman, R. and Roy, P. (2006) 'Evidence from the extended use of the BSL receptive skills test', *Deafness and Education International* 8(1): 33–47.

Johnson, R. E. (1994) 'Sign language and the concept of deafness in a traditional Yucatec Mayan village', in C. J. Erting, R. E. Johnson, D. L. Smith and B. D. Snider (eds) *The Deaf Way: Perspectives from the International Conference on Deaf Culture, 1989*. Washington, DC: Gallaudet University Press.

Kegl, J. A., Senghas, A. and Coppola, M. (1999) 'Creation through contact: sign language emergence and sign language change in Nicaragua', in M. DeGraff (ed.) *Comparative Grammatical Change: The Intersection of Language Acquisition, Creole Genesis, and Diachronic Syntax*, Cambridge, MA: MIT Press.

Kendon, A. (1980) 'A description of a deaf-mute sign language from the Enga Province of Papua New Guinea with some comparative discussion: Parts I, II, III', *Semiotica* 32: 1–34; 81–117, 245–313.

Kisch, S. (2007) 'Disablement, gender and deafhood among the Negev Arab-Bedouin', *Disability Studies Quarterly* 27: 4. Available at: www.dsqsds.org/article/view/45/45 (accessed December 2009).

——(2008) '"Deaf discourse": the social construction of deafness in a Bedouin community', *Medical Anthropology* 27(3): 283–313.

Krentz, C. (2006) 'The camera as printing press: how film has influenced ASL literature', in H. Dirksen Bauman, J. Nelson and H. Rose (eds) *Signing the Body Poetic*, Berkeley: University of California Press.

Kusters, A. (2010) 'Deaf Utopias? Reviewing the sociocultural literature on the world's "Martha's Vineyard Situations"', *Journal of Deaf Studies and Deaf Education* 15(1): 3–16.

Lamb, L. and Wilcox, P. (1988) 'Acceptance of American Sign Language at the University of New Mexico: the history of a process', *Sign Language Studies* 17(59): 213–20.

Lane, H. (1984) *When the Mind Hears: A History of the Deaf*, New York: Random House.

Lane, H., Hoffmeister, R. and Bahan, B. (1996) *A Journey into the Deaf World*, San Diego, CA: Dawn Sign Press.

Lucas, C. (2002) 'The role of variation in lexicography', *Sign Language Studies* 3: 322–40.

Mathur, G. and Rathmann, C. (1998) 'Why not "GIVE-US": an articulatory constraint in signed languages', in V. Dively, M. Metzger, S. Taub and A.-M. Baer (eds) *Signed Languages: Discoveries from International Research*, Washington, DC: Gallaudet University Press.

Mayberry, R. I. and Squires, B. (2006). 'Sign language acquisition', in E. Lieven (ed.) Language Acquisition, *Encyclopedia of Language and Linguistics*, vol. 11, 2nd edn, Oxford: Elsevier.

McKee, D. and Kennedy, G. (2006) 'The distribution of signs in New Zealand Sign Language', *Sign Language Studies* 6(4): 372–90.

Meier, R., Cormier, K. and Quinto-Pozos, D. (2003) *Modality and Structure in Signed and Spoken Languages*, Cambridge: Cambridge University Press.

Morgan, G. (2005) 'The development of narrative skills in British Sign Language', in B. Schick, M. Marschark and P. Spencer (eds) *Advances in the Sign Language Development of Deaf and Hard-of-Hearing Children*, Oxford: Oxford University Press.

Morgan, G., Herman, R., Barrière, I. and Woll, B. (2008) 'The onset and mastery of spatial language in children acquiring British Sign Language', *Cognitive Development* 23: 1–19.

Newport, E. L. and Meier, R. P. (1985) 'The acquisition of American Sign Language', in D. I. Slobin (ed.) *The Crosslinguistic Study of Language Acquisition*, vol. 1: *The Data*, Hillsdale, NJ: Lawrence Erlbaum Associates.

Nichols, J. (1992) *Linguistic Diversity in Space and Time*, Chicago: University of Chicago Press.

Paul, P. V. and Quigley, S. P. (2000) *Language and Deafness*, 3rd edn, San Diego, CA: Singular Publishing Group.

Pelissier, M. (1856) *Des Sourds-Muets*, Paris: Paul Dupont.

Pollitt, K. (2000) 'On babies, bathwater and approaches to interpreting', *Deaf Worlds* 16: 60–4.

Ramsey, C. (1997) *Deaf Children in Public Schools: Placement, Context and Consequences*, Washington, DC: Gallaudet University Press.

Saeed, J., Sutton-Spence, R. and Leeson, L. (2000) 'Constituent structure in declarative sentences in Irish Sign Language and British Sign Language: a preliminary examination'. Poster Presented at the 7th International Conference on Theoretical Issues in Sign Language Research, 23–27 July 2000, Amsterdam.

Schembri, A. (2003) 'Rethinking "classifiers" in signed languages', in K. Emmorey (ed.) *Perspectives on Classifier Constructions in Sign Languages*, Mahwah, NJ: Lawrence Erlbaum Associates.

Schembri, A., McKee, D., McKee, R., Pivac, S., Johnston, T. and Goswell, D. (2009) 'Phonological variation and change in Australian and New Zealand Sign Languages: the location variable', *Language Variation and Change* 21: 193–231.

Schermer, G. (2004) 'Lexical variation in sign language of the Netherlands', in M. van Herreweghe and M. Vermeerbergen (eds) *To the Lexicon and Beyond: Sociolinguistics in European Deaf Communities*, Washington, DC: Gallaudet University Press.

Schick, B. (2003) 'The development of ASL and manually-coded English systems', in M. Marschark and P. E. Spencer (eds) *Oxford Handbook of Deaf Studies, Language, and Education*, New York: Oxford University Press.

Schmaling, C. (2003) 'A for apple: the impact of Western education and ASL on the deaf community in Kano State, Northern Nigeria', in L. Monaghan, C. Schmaling, K. Nakamura and G. Turner (eds) *Many Ways to be Deaf: International Variation in Deaf Communities*, Washington, DC: Gallaudet University Press.

Slobin, D. (2005) 'Issues of linguistic typology in the study of sign language development of deaf children', in B. Schick, M. Marschark and P. Spencer (eds) *Sign Language Development of Deaf and Hard-of-hearing Children: Where Have We Been, and Where Are We Going?* Oxford: Oxford University Press.

Spencer, P. E. (1993) 'The expressive communication of hearing mothers and deaf infants', *American Annals of the Deaf* 138: 275–83.

Stokoe, W. C. ([1960] 1978) *Sign Language Structure: The First Linguistic Analysis Of American Sign Language*, Silver Spring, MD:Linstok Press.

Supalla, T. (1986) 'The classifier system in American Sign Language', in C. Craig (ed.) *Noun Classes and Categorization (Typological Sudies in Language 7)*, Amsterdam: John Benjamins.

Taub, S. (2001) *Language from the Body: Iconicity and Metaphor in American Sign Language*, Cambridge: Cambridge University Press.

van Herreweghe, M. and Vermeerbergen, M. (2004) 'Flemish sign language: some risks of codification', in M. van Herreweghe and M. Vermeerbergen (eds) *To the Lexicon and Beyond. Sociolinguistics in European Deaf Communities*, Washington, DC: Gallaudet University Press.

Vanhecke, E. and De Weerdt, K. (2004) 'Regional variation in Flemish Sign Language', in M. van Herreweghe and M. Vermeerbergen (eds) *To the Lexicon and Beyond. Sociolinguistics in European Deaf Communities*, Washington, DC: Gallaudet University Press.

Vermeerbergen, M., Leeson, L. and Crasborn, O. (eds) (2007) *Simultaneity in Signed Languages*, Amsterdam and Philadelphia: John Benjamins.

Washabaugh, W. (1981) 'The Deaf of Grand Cayman, British West Indies', *Sign Language Studies* 31: 117–33.

Wilcox, S. (2003) 'The multimedia dictionary of American Sign Language: learning lessons about language, technology and business', *Sign Language Studies* 3: 379–92.

Woll, B. (1984) 'Comparing sign languages', in F. Loncke, P. Boyes-Braem and Y. Lebrun (eds) *Recent Research on European Sign Languages*, Lisse: Swets and Zeitlinger.

——(1991) *Variation and Recent Change in British Sign Language*. Project final report to Economic and Social Research Council.

Woodward, J. (1996) 'Modern standard Thai Sign Language, influence from ASL, and its relationship to original Thai sign varieties', *Sign Language Studies* 25: 225–52.

Young, A., Ackerman, J. and Kyle, J. (1998) *Looking On*, Bristol: Policy Press.

26

World Englishes

Andy Kirkpatrick and David Deterding

Introduction

This chapter begins by contextualizing the development of World Englishes as a relatively new field of study. First, in showing that there are many Englishes, not just one, the work of Braj Kachru is reviewed and the importance of his contributions are summarized. Next, debates concerning the motivations for language change in New Englishes are reviewed and examples of a few innovative linguistic features in those varieties are provided. Then we consider the developmental stages in the emergence of New Englishes. Finally, we discuss recent developments, including the role of English as a Lingua Franca (ELF) and the influence of new technology.

Models of World Englishes

There have been many models that represent the nature of Englishes around the world. These are summarized in McArthur (1998), where McArthur's own 'Circle of World Englishes' is also described (1998: 97). Perhaps the most influential model is Kachru's Three Circles of English. It also uses a circle analogy, placing each country in one of three circles as follows (with examples added in italicized brackets):

> The current sociolinguistic profile of English may be viewed in terms of three concentric circles ... The Inner Circle refers to the traditional cultural and linguistic bases of English [*e.g. Britain, USA, Australia*]. The Outer Circle represents the institutionalized non-native varieties (ESL) in the regions that have passed through extended periods of colonization [*e.g. Singapore, India, Nigeria*] ... The Expanding Circle includes the regions where the *performance* varieties of the language are used essentially in EFL contexts [*e.g. China, Japan, Egypt*].
>
> *(Kachru 1992c: 356–7)*

The terms ESL (English as a Second Language) and EFL (English as a Foreign Language) in this extract refer to the traditional classification which Kachru challenged. His great contribution to the field lay in recognizing the development of many different varieties of English, so the language should not be seen in terms of a single monolithic standard. Instead, as there are a multitude of different Englishes, variation is the norm. And just as there are many varieties of British English, there are also many New Englishes, which in turn have sub-varieties, so, for example, Indian English consists of a range of varieties.

Some scholars have criticized aspects of the Three Circles model, particularly: it is histori-cally and geographically based; it deals with countries rather than societies or individuals; and it fails to accommodate some places (such as Denmark and Argentina) that seem to be moving from Expanding-Circle to Outer-Circle status even though they have no colonial links with England or the United States (Jenkins 2009: 20–1). Furthermore, Kachru's model does not allow for the possibility of the increasing number of speakers with English as their first language in places such as Singapore and India.

However, as Bolton (2005) has noted, Kachru's Three Circles model was formulated in response to the single-standard orthodoxy of the time, and 'the strength of the World Englishes paradigm has lain and continues to lie in its consistent pluralism and inclusivity' (2005: 78).

Here, we survey linguistic studies of World Englishes and provide examples of features from a range of Englishes. Then we consider the stages through which New Englishes progress as they develop into mature varieties.

Linguistic motivations

A fundamental principle in the study of World Englishes is that variation and change are natural and inevitable (Kirkpatrick 2007a). As a consequence, linguistic features which differ from Standard English are not necessarily errors but may instead represent components of a New English.

Linguistic variation is, of course, nothing new, and Inner-Circle Englishes as well as New Englishes are characterized by variation, not just in pronunciation and vocabulary, but gram-mar as well. For example, historically, all Englishes had a rich set of present tense inflections on verbs. Now, however, the dialects of England generally have substantially reduced inflec-tions, and they are not the same in all varieties. In modern Standard English, for present tense verbs, there is only the -s ending for the third person singular. The dialect of East Anglia, however, generally has no present tense inflections at all, so 'he make them' and 'farmers make them' are grammatical in this variety (though Britain (2007: 87) suggests it may be moving towards the standard in this respect). In contrast, Yorkshire English has an additional present tense inflection, with 'thou hast' for second person singular. Furthermore, the Northern subject rule, originating from Scotland, but attested over several centuries in many vernaculars of the North and North Midlands (McCafferty 2003), requires the use of -s on verbs with plural subjects unless the verb is adjacent to a pronoun (Ihalainen 1994: 228). Following this rule, 'Birds flies', 'They fly' and 'They fly and swoops' are all grammatical.

Variation in present tense marking is also seen in American dialects. 'Folks sings' is gram-matical in the English of the American South (Bailey 1997: 259–60), and the following extract of African American Vernacular English shows variation in the use of -s on verbs:

What's her, what's her name that cooks them? She a real young girl. She bring 'em in every morning. An' they, an' they sells 'em, an' they sells them for that girl there in that store.

(Cukor-Avila 2003: 98)

Given such variation in Inner Circle Englishes, it is not surprising to find similar variation in New Englishes, as well as ELF. In Kortmann *et al.* (2004), half of the forty-six varieties of English surveyed frequently do not mark the third person singular -*s*.

Is it possible to explain which varieties of English are characterized by features such as this? Let us consider motivations for change.

Mesthrie and Bhatt (2008) compare a selection of New Englishes and identify grammatical features which occur in many varieties but not in Standard English. They propose that New Englishes can be classified as either 'deleters' or 'preservers' (2008: 90–2). Deleters are varieties whose speakers commonly leave out grammatical elements, while preservers are those in which deletion is less common, with Singapore English offered as an example of a deleting variety and Black South African English as a preserver. Their explanation for this distinction between deleters and preservers is influence from other languages, as it is 'usually dependent on the characteristic syntax of the substrate languages' (2008: 90).

However, while Kortmann (2010) agrees that language contact and thus geography are important factors influencing language change and development, he argues that variety type is a better predictor of morphosyntactic change. He concludes that whether it is a high- or low-contact Inner-Circle variety, an indigenized Outer-Circle variety, a pidgin or a creole is a better predictor of its morphosyntactic features than the part of the world where it is spoken.

Although language contact has always been a key stimulus for linguistic change, not just with New Englishes but also in the historical development of English in Britain through contact with Scandinavian languages and French (Crystal 2004), a surprising number of shared features have been identified, both in New Englishes and in ELF. In fact, the large number of non-standard forms which are shared by many new varieties has led some scholars to propose that a number of vernacular universals (VUs) exist, as these cannot be solely due to influence from the speakers' first languages (see Filpulla *et al.* 2009 for a review).

> Assuming that language contacts are a factor to be reckoned with when dealing with VUs, the question is: what exactly is the relationship between language contact phenomena and vernacular universals, and to what extent can we distinguish them from each other?
>
> *(Filpulla et al. 2009: 8)*

In the next section, we provide a sample of linguistic features from a range of New Englishes.

Linguistic features: some examples

Many features of New Englishes have been extensively described (e.g. Kortmann *et al.* 2004; Schneider *et al.* 2004). Here, we will not attempt a comprehensive description of their characteristics. Instead, we discuss a small selection of features, focusing particularly on a few that are shared widely among New Englishes. In addition, we consider which of these features also occur in Inner-Circle varieties, and the extent to which they might be influencing the evolution of English.

We start with some phonological features that seem to occur in a range of New Englishes: avoidance of dental fricatives, reduction of final consonant clusters, and use of syllable-based rhythm. Then we consider some grammatical features: absence of past tense marking, and regularization of the count/noncount distinction on nouns. Finally, we discuss some discourse issues: use of the invariant *is it* tag and topic fronting.

Of course, there are also many features that are special to one or more varieties, such as the borrowed word *kiasu* ('fear of losing out') in Singapore (Deterding 2007: 75) or the conflation of /v/ and /w/ in India (Kachru 2005: 49) and Pakistan (Mahboob and Ahmar 2004). In this way, each New English represents a mixture of global features and its own idiosyncratic innovations.

Dental fricatives

One of the most common features of New Englishes is the tendency to avoid using /θ/ and /ð/. However, the sounds that are used in place of these dental fricatives vary. For example, in place of initial /θ/ in a word such as *three*, [t] tends to occur in places such as Singapore (Deterding 2007: 13–16), the Philippines (Tayao 2004), Brunei (Mossop 1996), Ghana (Huber 2004), the Bahamas (Childs and Wolfram 2004) and India (Kachru 2005: 44–6), while [f] occurs in Hong Kong English (Deterding *et al.* 2008), and Gut (2004) reports that, in Nigerian English, Hausa speakers tend to use [s] but Yoruba and Igbo speakers use [t]. The avoidance of dental fricatives also occurs in some Inner-Circle Englishes. In place of /θ/, many speakers in London use [f], while those in Ireland and also New York may use [t] (Wells 1982: 328, 428, 515). However, although it is true that avoidance of dental fricatives is found in Inner-Circle varieties, this phenomenon is almost certainly currently more widespread in New Englishes.

Jenkins (2000: 159) excludes dental fricatives from her Lingua Franca Core (LFC), the features that she suggests are vital for the intelligibility of English as an international language. In fact, they are the only consonants from the full inventory of consonants found in Inner-Circle Englishes that are excluded from the LFC. One might hypothesize that, in the future, the absence of dental fricatives may become increasingly accepted in Standard Englishes. The majority of speakers of English around the world nowadays probably do not customarily use dental fricatives, even if most Inner-Circle speakers do currently use them.

Final consonant clusters

Word-final consonant clusters are commonly simplified in New Englishes, often involving the omission of the final consonant, especially if it is a plosive. For example, in Singapore English, *first, world, ask* and *think* may all be pronounced with the final consonant omitted even when the next word begins with a vowel (Deterding 2007: 18).

Sometimes, this process is reinforced by the phonological shape of words that are borrowed from English into the local language. For instance, Standard Malay has borrowed many words from English in which a final plosive is dropped if the word ends with a consonant cluster. Examples include *lif* ('lift'), *pos* ('post'), *hos* ('host'), *kos* ('cost'), *arkitek* ('architect'), *saintis* ('scientist'), *setem* ('stamp') and *kem* ('camp') (Collins 2002), and it is not surprising that this final consonant is also often omitted when the same words are pronounced in English. Indeed final consonant cluster reduction is common in Malaysian English (Baskaran 2004a) and also Brunei English (Mossop 1996).

Final consonant cluster reduction is similarly reported for many other New Englishes, including those of Hong Kong (Deterding *et al.* 2008), Nigeria (Gut 2004), Ghana (Huber 2004) and East Africa (Schmied 2004).

The omission of plosives from the end of word-final consonant clusters is also frequent in Inner-Circle varieties. Cruttenden (2008: 303–4) offers a long list of phrases in RP (the variety of British English that is usually adopted as the standard) from which /t/ or /d/ at the end of the first word is omitted, including *next day, raced back, last chance, first light, old man* and *loved flowers*, and Guy (1980) shows that the phenomenon is particularly common among speakers of vernacular Black English in the USA. Perhaps the biggest difference is that in New Englishes the omission of the final consonant tends to persist even when the next word begins with a vowel, an environment in which the consonant is more likely to be used for linking in Inner-Circle varieties.

Schreier (2005: 27) suggests that consonant cluster reduction may be a universal property of all varieties of spoken English, and furthermore that this natural tendency towards simplification characterizes the historical development of English. It seems, then, that New Englishes may be leading the way in reducing the complexity of final consonant clusters in English.

Rhythm

While stress-based rhythm is often claimed to be the basis of English speech timing in most Inner-Circle varieties, use of syllable-based rhythm is widely reported for New Englishes. Although nowadays few people adhere to the view of Abercrombie (1967: 97) that all languages can be neatly classified as either stress-timed or syllable-timed, and indeed some scholars have questioned the entire existence of this fundamental rhythmic dichotomy (Cauldwell 2002), it is often still asserted that languages may be placed along a continuum of stress-/syllable-timing (Dauer 1983). Indeed, measurements that compare the duration of the vowels in neighbouring syllables confirm that a clear acoustic difference can be shown between the rhythm of Singapore and British English (Low *et al.* 2000).

In addition to Singapore English, other new varieties that have been observed to have a syllable-based rhythm include those of the Philippines (Tayao 2004), India (Kachru 2005: 46), Nigeria (Gut 2006), East Africa (Schmied 2004), and Jamaica (Trudgill and Hannah 2008: 117).

However, British English can also sometimes have variable rhythm. For example, Crystal (1995a) observes that syllable-based rhythm can be found in a range of speech styles, including baby talk, sarcastic utterances, many types of popular music, and some television commercials, and Crystal (2003: 171) speculates that this kind of rhythm might one day become the norm for all varieties of English. It seems, then, that this is another candidate for a feature where New Englishes may be leading the way for the future evolution of English.

Absence of tense marking

As discussed above, absence of the present tense *-s* inflection is reported in many Englishes. In addition, many speakers of New Englishes see no need to mark the past tense of verbs once the time frame of an event has been established. For Singapore English, Deterding (2007: 46) suggests that use of the present tense in narrating an event is particularly common when dealing with something that may still be true. For example, in the following extract, the speaker switches to the present tense, even though the story is located in the past, possibly because she believes that the funfair is still running at the time she is speaking:

> then later on in the evening … er went to the UK funfair … at Jurong East … mmm … it was, it was interesting, but very expensive … erm the fun, the entrance fee is cheap, it's only two dollars … I guess that's cheap enough, but then the … the games and the rides are all very expensive.

Another factor that may influence the use of tenses in Singapore English is the nature of the verb, as Ho and Platt (1993: 86) show that past tense marking is most common for punctual verbs (i.e. verbs such as *hit*, *speak*, or *give* that describe an action rather than a situation, such as *like*, *know* or *want*).

Similarly, in the English of Brunei, the simple present form of the verb is often used in narrating an event. Cane (1996: 210–11) gives the following examples:

It was quite a new experience for us since it's our first experience overseas.

This song reminds me of the old days when I'm with the group 'The Mixtures'.

Could absence of tense marking for narrating an event become widely accepted as part of standard English? In fact, the historic present is already sometimes used for narrating past events in order to create a sense of immediacy. Carter and McCarthy (2006: 625) give the following example from their corpus of spoken British English, where the speaker is talking about a laser show:

In the beginning there was darkness, and we hear this scraping sound, and you see this little coloured pattern, the coloured pattern gets bigger and bigger.

So, in fact use of the present tense when narrating a story is actually already a common strategy in many varieties of English, both Inner-Circle and new varieties.

Count/noncount nouns

Some distinctions between count and noncount nouns in Inner-Circle Englishes are rather idiosyncratic. For example, *furniture* and *luggage* are treated as mass nouns, but there really does not seem to be any logical reason why we should not count items of furniture or pieces of luggage. And indeed, not surprisingly such words tend to be treated as countable in many New Englishes. For example, we find *furnitures*, *stuffs*, *clothings* and *fictions* in Singapore English (Deterding 2007: 42–3), and Mesthrie and Bhatt (2008: 53) observe that nearly every study of English varieties in Africa and Asia reports examples like *furnitures*, *equipments*, *staffs*, *fruits*, and *accommodations*.

Does this occur in Inner-Circle Englishes? We might note that *mail* is usually noncount, but *email* now is generally used as a countable noun, and this seems to be a modern development (if only because email has only been around for a short while). The widespread occurrence of *furnitures* and similar words therefore seems a classic case where New Englishes may be hastening the process of regularizing the language.

Invariant tags

Invariant tags, particularly *is it* and *isn't it*, are reported in Singapore English (Deterding 2007: 56), such as with the following extract from a blog:

he think I want to listen to his story is it?

Similarly, for Nigerian English, Alo and Mesthrie (2004: 817) offer the following example:

You like that, isn't it?

Comparable use of invariant tags is found in Malaysia (Baskaran 2004b), Hong Kong (Cheng and Warren 2001), India (Kachru 2005: 49) and Pakistan (Mahboob 2004).

But invariant tags also occur in various Inner-Circle Englishes, including that of Wales (Trudgill and Hannah 2008: 38), and the occurrence of *innit* is almost a defining characteristic of the style of English originating in London and sometimes termed Estuary English (Crystal 1995b: 327). Similarly, Anderwald (2004: 191) notes that it is a typical feature of adolescent London speech. Clearly, use of invariant tags is a common simplification strategy that is being adopted in a wide range of different places.

Topic prominence

In many New Englishes, the topic tends to be placed clearly out at the front of the sentence. For example, in Singapore English, the recording in Deterding (2007: 63) includes the following utterances:

So the whole process I need to break down for the different operators.

Australia, I've been to Sydney and Perth.

For Indian English, Bhatt (2004: 1023) offers:

Those people, I telephoned yesterday only.

and Sailaja (2009: 54) gives:

This book, I will return tomorrow.

Sometimes, topic fronting is followed by a resumptive pronoun, as in the following example (Deterding 2007: 65):

Then, er, two of my sisters, they're already married.

Similarly, in East African English, Bokamba (1992: 131) notes the following example:

The boys they like to play outside even if it is cold.

Examples of topic fronting are also noted for Ghanaian English (Huber and Dako 2004) and Indian South African English (Mesthrie 2004: 988).

What about Inner-Circle varieties? Carter and McCarthy (2006: 192) suggest that fronting is common in spoken language, and they give the following examples (2006: 193):

That leather coat, it looks really nice on you.

The white house on the corner, is that where she lives?

So perhaps the use of fronted topics, often with a resumptive pronoun, is actually a universal feature of all Englishes. Furthermore, maybe the frequency of topic fronting in Inner-Circle

Englishes was underestimated when traditional grammars were based so much on formal, written texts. Now that grammars are increasingly being based on corpora of informal, spoken data, it is possible that future descriptions of Inner-Circle English will reflect the common occurrence of this feature.

While topic fronting is not an example of simplification like the previous features discussed here, it seems to be a natural process in human language, and perhaps its widespread occurrence in New Englishes may have a substantial influence on the discourse structures that become increasingly favoured and accepted as mainstream in World Englishes.

General trends in linguistic features

As we have seen, one characteristic of many shared features is that they tend to simplify and/ or regularize English. For example, many speakers find dental fricatives hard to pronounce, so their avoidance makes things easier; and use of plurals for logically plural nouns makes the grammar more regular. Simplifying and regularizing innovations are ones that have a good chance of becoming adopted as standard when a language evolves, and we suggest that New Englishes may be leading the way in this respect.

In Figure 26.1, showing a sign written in Singapore, *close* is used rather than the standard *closed*. At first glance, one is tempted to classify this as an error, as a suffix has not been added to the verb *close* to convert it into an adjective. But we might note that *open* can function perfectly well as both a verb and an adjective, and 'we are open' would be fine. So why not 'we are close'?

In fact, we can regard this use of *close* rather than *closed* as illustrating both simplification (it is easier to say, as the word-final consonant cluster is avoided) and also regularization (it is consistent with the use of *open*). And this is just the kind of change that we might expect to find adopted in Standard English one day. Perhaps this Singaporean signwriter is ahead of their time. And maybe many of the trends that have been noted for New Englishes indicate the future direction of Global English.

In an analogy with the recent evolution of global hip-hop, Pennycook (2007) similarly argues that New Englishes are at the forefront of the current evolution of the language. He

Figure 26.1 Sign on the door of a shop in Singapore
Source: Picture by Ludwig Tan.

observes that hip-hop originated in the inner cities of the United States, but as it has evolved and matured in recent years, indigenized varieties have emerged that no longer make constant reference to American hip-hop, and these new varieties serve to maintain the pace of development of the genre throughout the world. It seems likely that New Englishes are following a similar path, accelerating the development of English quite independently of the traditional roots of the language in Inner-Circle countries.

Stages in the development of New Englishes

So far we have summarized some linguistic features in New Englishes. We now consider the stages that a variety of English goes through on its way to becoming accepted as the standard variety in a society. Kachru (1992b: 56) suggested that New Englishes pass through three stages. The first is marked by non-acceptance of the emerging variety, with locals preferring the colonial or relevant Inner-Circle variety. The second stage sees local and imported varieties existing side-by-side. Finally, the local variety becomes accepted as the standard.

Schneider (2003, 2007) has refined and extended this in his model of the evolution of Englishes, agreeing with Mufwene (2001) that post-colonial varieties of English often follow the same basic developmental path, slowly establishing their own identities through a series of stages till they become independent varieties in their own right. He identifies five stages in the developmental cycle (Schneider 2007: 56):

- Foundation: English first arrives in the area.
- Exonormative Stabilization: standards are provided by the colonial variety. British English originally provided the norms in many colonies.
- Nativization: bilingual and multilingual speakers create a new local variety of English which is influenced by the linguistic systems and cultural norms of the speakers' first languages. During this stage, the new variety is usually considered deficient, so norms are still provided by the colonial variety, especially in the classroom.
- Endonormative Stabilization: the new variety becomes socially accepted and provides the classroom model. In Kachru's terms, this is when Outer-Circle varieties become 'norm providing' rather than 'norm dependent'.
- Differentiation: the new variety itself develops sub-varieties.

While more research is needed on the development of individual varieties, Schneider's model appears fundamentally sound. However, the extent to which the local educated variety is accepted as the classroom model remains the topic of debate, with many Asian countries still insisting on an Inner-Circle variety as the preferred model. It would appear, therefore, that varieties of English can reach Schneider's final stage of differentiation *linguistically*, but *sociolinguistically* they remain at an earlier stage when language planners are not prepared to accept local varieties as classroom models.

In discussing the development of New Englishes, a distinction is often made between the spoken and the written codes, and it is sometimes suggested that, while spoken codes allow significant variation, the written code is more uniform. This, however, is only partly true. Literature written in New Englishes and the expression of popular culture are just two examples where creativity and variation are given full play, and there are many Asian and African writers who now use local varieties of English to represent their cultures. The Pakistani novelist Sidhwa writes:

> We have to stretch the language to adapt it to alien thoughts and values which have no precedent of expression in English, subject the language to a pressure that distorts, or if you like, enlarges its scope and changes its shape ...
>
> *(Sidhwa 1996: 240)*

An excellent example of this is Ken Saro-Wiwa's (1985) novel *Sozaboy: A Novel in Rotten English*. The author's note explains that *Sozaboy* (soldier boy) was the result of his fascination with how English could be adapted to reflect the language of Nigerians.

The way a New English is transplanted and adapted by its new users is nicely captured in Indian English, which is characterized by its bookishness and use of metaphor:

> Years ago, a slender sapling from a foreign field was grafted by 'pale hands' on the mighty and many-branched Indian banyan tree. It has kept growing vigorously and is now an organic part of its parent tree, it has spread its own probing roots into the brown soil below. Its young leaves rustle energetically in the strong winds that blow from the western horizon, but the sunshine that warms it and the rain that cools it are from Indian skies; and it continues to draw its vital sap from 'this earth, this realm,' this India.
>
> *(Naik and Narayan 2004: 253)*

Recent developments

Today, English acts as a lingua franca throughout the world, and recent debate concerns the validity of ELF as an object of linguistic study and also its relationship to World Englishes (Kirkpatrick 2008).

A lingua franca can be defined as 'a language that is used for communication between different groups of people, each speaking a different language' (Richards *et al.* 1985: 214). While it is true that this describes the function rather than a specific variety, recent research into ELF has shown a remarkable number of features shared by ELF speakers and New Englishes. This is quite surprising, as one would expect substantial variation, depending on the first languages of the speakers, and the degree of shared features justifies research into the linguistic nature of ELF.

ELF is now the most common use of English in the world (Jenkins 2007), so a study of its linguistic features and the ways it allows people to achieve successful intercultural communication offers insights about international communication and also guidelines for English language teaching. Thus, the work of scholars such as Barbara Seidlhofer (2001, 2004) and her team at the University of Vienna who have collected the VOICE corpus of ELF (VOICE n.d.) and Anna Mauranen and her team at the universities of Helsinki and Tampere who have assembled a corpus of academic ELF (ELFA n.d.) not only sheds light on the linguistic features of ELF but also offers important observations on how language is actually used in intercultural communication.

Although ELF shares some grammatical and phonological features with New Englishes (Deterding and Kirkpatrick 2006), ELF speakers generally avoid the use of local lexis and idioms (Kirkpatrick 2007b). This is a key distinction between World Englishes and ELF, as one fundamental role of World Englishes lies in their ability to reflect local phenomena and cultural values, often through the use of borrowings from local languages. In contrast, this is avoided in ELF communication, where the fundamental role is to facilitate cross-cultural communication.

The debate about the place of ELF in World Englishes is one reflection of the continuing debate about the role of linguistic imperialism (Phillipson 1992, 2009) in the spread of English as an international language. We do not deal with this in depth here, as it is the subject of a separate chapter (Canagarajah and Ben Said, this volume). However, we propose that the world has moved beyond the post-colonial stage and has now entered a post-Anglophone stage (Clayton 2006). Taking the situation in Cambodia as an example, Clayton shows that English is essential for most jobs with foreign agencies, and even French-run non-governmental organizations (NGOs) now require English. This post-Anglophone role of English is reflected in the following quote from a Cambodian ministry official: 'You know, when we use English, we don't think about the United States or England. We only think about the need to communicate' (2006: 233).

ELF clearly has a major role to play in the modern world, and the choice of English is often seen as natural. For example, the ten countries comprising the Association of Southeast Asian Nations (ASEAN) agreed to adopt English as the sole working language of ASEAN when they signed the ASEAN Charter in February 2009.

While the choice of English may seem natural and the demand for it ever increasing, one key question is the extent to which the need for English will lead to equality or perpetuate further inequality (Pennycook 2010). Graddol (2006), however, envisages that it is those who only have English who may be disadvantaged in future.

The influence of new technology

New technology has had a big influence on the development of worldwide varieties of English. For example, words for parts of the car differ quite substantially between Britain and America (e.g. windscreen/windshield; bonnet/hood; boot/trunk), but words for parts of the computer tend not to vary so much (e.g. keyboard; mouse; hard disk). One reason for this is that communication across the Atlantic was rather easier in the 1980s, when computers were developed, than in the earlier part of the twentieth century, when cars were first produced.

In the modern world, we similarly find that facilities for communicating over a long distance, for recording data, and for sharing information via the Internet are having a profound impact on the evolution of World Englishes, as new words and ways of expressing oneself that arise in one society can easily spread elsewhere. However, at the same time, each variety of English can develop its own idiosyncratic forms of expression, and new media such as email, electronic discussion forums, and blogging can facilitate the establishment of these local features within a society. New technology therefore helps maintain a balance between global and local features in the development of World Englishes (Pennycook 2007).

To illustrate this mixture of global and local in one variety of World English, let us consider an extract from a blog written by a student in Brunei (Hiro 2009):

> Well. ... will be busy working, doing assignments and (the hell) presentation. Gila~-sometimes they think we are super people ka? So much to do ... we have a life too you know!! Lol. X3 Ja. [To the people who read this blog and think I'm crazy now ... yes I am.The stress levels are building up. XD.] And to everyone who gave me full support when I was down.Thanks so much.U now who u all are!

In this extract, there are various features common in worldwide blogs, including abbreviations ('u' for *you*; 'lol' for *laughing out loud*), but there are also a few local words (*gila*, Malay for 'crazy'; *ka*, the Malay question particle). This mixture of global and local innovations characterizes new modes of electronic communication in many different societies (Crystal 2008).

One other aspect of new technology relevant for research into World Englishes is electronic corpora. In particular the International Corpus of English (ICE 2009; Nelson *et al.* 2002) has components from a range of places including Hong Kong, East Africa, India, the Philippines, and Singapore; and the VOICE and ELFA corpora referred to earlier offer researchers the opportunity to investigate English usage in Continental Europe.

Summary

In this chapter, we outlined how the insights of Braj Kachru and other scholars into New Englishes have created fresh fields of study under the term World Englishes, and furthermore, we now see Englishes occurring as a plural term. We showed that variation is normal and inevitable both within and between varieties of English and considered some of the motivations for this. At the same time, we noted the remarkable number of linguistic features shared by New Englishes and how this phenomenon has given rise to a theory of vernacular universals. We also suggested that New Englishes go though comparable stages of development, and argued that English in its role as a lingua franca should be studied as part of the World Englishes paradigm. Finally, we noted that emerging technologies enable new varieties to combine global and local features.

Related topics

culture; language policy and planning; language testing; linguistic imperialism; multilingualism; sociolinguistics

Further reading

Jenkins, J. (2009) *World Englishes: A Resource Book for Students*, 2nd edn, London: Routledge. (A useful introduction to the issues.)

Kachru, B. B., Kachru, Y. and Nelson, C. (2009) *Handbook of World Englishes*, Malden, MA: Blackwell. (A comprehensive survey of the field.)

Kirkpatrick, A. (2007) *World Englishes: Implications for International Communication and English Language Teaching*, Cambridge: Cambridge University Press. (An accessible introduction with a focus on variation and implications for ELT with an accompanying CD illustrating a selection of varieties.)

Kirkpatrick, A. (ed.) (2010) *Handbook of World Englishes*, London: Routledge. (An overall survey of the field with a focus on applications.)

References

Abercrombie, D. (1967) *Elements of General Phonetics*, Edinburgh: Edinburgh University Press.

Alo, M. A. and Mesthrie, R. (2004) 'Nigerian English: morphology and syntax', in B. Kortmann, K. Burridge, R. Mesthrie, E. W. Schneider and C. Upton (eds) *A Handbook of Varieties of English*, vol. 2: *Morphology and Syntax*, Berlin: Mouton de Gruyter.

Anderwald, L. (2004) 'English in the southeast of England: morphology and syntax', in B. Kortmann, K. Burridge, R. Mesthrie, E. W. Schneider and C. Upton (eds) *A Handbook of Varieties of English*, vol. 2: *Morphology and Syntax*, Berlin: Mouton de Gruyter.

Bailey, G. (1997) 'When did Southern American English begin?', in E. W. Schneider (ed.) *Englishes Around the World: Studies in Honour of Manfred Görlach*, Amsterdam: John Benjamins.

Baskaran, L. (2004a) 'Malaysian English: phonology', in E. W. Schneider, K. Burridge, B. Kortmann, R. Mesthrie and C. Upton (eds) *A Handbook of Varieties of English*, vol. 1: *Phonology*, Berlin: Mouton de Gruyter.

——(2004b) 'Malaysian English: morphology and syntax', in B. Kortmann, K. Burridge, R. Mesthrie, E. W. Schneider and C. Upton (eds) *A Handbook of Varieties of English*, vol. 2: *Morphology and Syntax*, Berlin: Mouton de Gruyter.

Bhatt, R. M. (2004) 'Indian English: syntax', in B. Kortmann, K. Burridge, R. Mesthrie, E. W. Schneider and C. Upton (eds) *A Handbook of Varieties of English*, vol. 2: *Morphology and Syntax*, Berlin: Mouton de Gruyter.

Bokamba, E. G. (1992) 'The Africanization of English', in B. B. Kachru (ed.) *The Other Tongue: English Across Cultures*, 2nd edn, Urbana and Chicago: University of Illinois Press.

Bolton, K. (2005) 'Where WE stands: approaches, issues and debate in World Englishes', *World Englishes* 24(1): 69–83.

Britain, D. (2007) 'Grammatical variation in England', in D. Britain (ed.) *Language in the British Isles*, Cambridge: Cambridge University Press.

Cane, G. (1996) 'Syntactic simplification and creativity in spoken Brunei English', in P. W. Martin, C. Ożóg and G. Poedjosoedarmo (eds) *Language Use and Language Change in Brunei Darussalam*, Athens, OH: Ohio University Center for International Studies.

Carter, R. and McCarthy, M. (2006) *Cambridge Grammar of English: A Comprehensive Guide*, Cambridge: Cambridge University Press.

Cauldwell, R. (2002) 'The functional irrhythmicality of spontaneous speech: a discourse view of speech rhythms', *Apples: Applied Language Studies* 2(1). Available at: www.solki.jyu.fi/apples/ (accessed 7 April 2009).

Cheng, M. and Warren, M. (2001) 'She knows more about Hong Kong than you do, isn't it: tags in Hong Kong conversational English', *Journal of Pragmatics* 33: 1419–39.

Childs, B. and Wolfram, W. (2004) 'Bahamian English: phonology', in E. W. Schneider, K. Burridge, B. Kortmann, R. Mesthrie and C. Upton (eds) *A Handbook of Varieties of English*, vol. 1: *Phonology*, Berlin: Mouton de Gruyter.

Clayton, T. (2006) *Language Choice in a Nation Under Transition: English Language Spread in Cambodia*, Boston, MA: Springer.

Collins (2002) *Bilingual Dictionary: English–Malay, Malay–English*, Selangor, Malaysia: Harper-Collins.

Cruttenden, A. (2008) *Gimson's Pronunciation of English*, 7th edn, London: Hodder Education.

Crystal, D. (1995a) 'Documenting rhythmical change', in J. Windsor Lewis (ed.) *Studies in General and English Phonetics: Essays in Honour of Professor J. D. O'Connor*, London: Routledge.

——(1995b) *The Cambridge Encyclopedia of the English Language*, Cambridge: Cambridge University Press.

——(2003) *English as a Global Language*, 2nd edn, Cambridge: Cambridge University Press.

——(2004) *The Stories of English*, London: Allen Lane.

——(2008) *Txting: The gr8 db8*, Oxford: Oxford University Press.

Cukor-Avila, P. (2003) 'The complex grammatical history of African-American and white vernaculars in the South', in S. J. Nagle and S. L. Sanders (eds) *English in the Southern United States*, Cambridge: Cambridge University Press.

Dauer, R. M. (1983) 'Stress-timing and syllable-timing reanalyzed', *Journal of Phonetics* 11: 51–62.

Deterding, D. (2007) *Singapore English*, Edinburgh: Edinburgh University Press.

Deterding, D. and Kirkpatrick, A. (2006) 'Intelligibility and an emerging ASEAN English lingua franca', *World Englishes* 25(3): 391–409.

Deterding, D., Wong, J. and Kirkpatrick, A. (2008) 'The pronunciation of Hong Kong English', *English World-Wide* 29: 148–75.

ELFA (n.d.) 'Welcome to the ELFA Corpus project homepage', Available at: http://uta.fi/laitokset/kielet/engf/research/elfa/index.htm (accessed 23 June 2009).

Filpulla, M., Klemola, F. and Paulasto, H. (eds) (2009) *Vernacular Universals and Language Contacts: Evidence from Varieties of English and Beyond*, London: Routledge.

Graddol, D. (2006) *English Next*, London: The British Council.

Gut, U. (2004) 'Nigerian English: phonology', in E. W. Schneider, K. Burridge, B. Kortmann, R. Mesthrie and C. Upton (eds) *A Handbook of Varieties of English*, vol. 1: *Phonology*, Berlin: Mouton de Gruyter.

——(2006) 'Nigerian English prosody', *English World-Wide* 26: 153–77.

Guy, G. R. (1980) 'Variation in the group and the individual: the case of final stop deletion', in W. Labov (ed.) *Locating Language in Time and Space*, New York: Academic Press.

Hiro (2009) 'Random curiosity: contains anything that comes across my mind' (blog of 15 March 2009). Available at: http://randomcuriosityalongthesidelines.blogspot.com/ (accessed 12 April 2009).

Ho, M. L. and Platt, J. (1993) *Dynamics of a Contact Continuum: Singapore English*, Oxford: Clarendon Press.

Huber, M. (2004) 'Ghanaian English: phonology', in E. W. Schneider, K. Burridge, B. Kortmann, R. Mesthrie and C. Upton (eds) *A Handbook of Varieties of English*, vol. 1: *Phonology*, Berlin: Mouton de Gruyter.

Huber, M. and Dako, K. (2004) 'Ghanaian English: morphology and syntax', in B. Kortmann, K. Burridge, R. Mesthrie, E. W. Schneider and C. Upton (eds) *A Handbook of Varieties of English*, vol. 2: *Morphology and Syntax*, Berlin: Mouton de Gruyter.

ICE (2009) 'International corpus of English'. Available at: www.ucl.ac.uk/english-usage/ice/index. htm (accessed 13 April 2009).

Ihalainen, O. (1994) 'The dialects of England since 1776', in R. Burchfield (ed.) *Cambridge History of the English Language*, vol. 5: *English in Britain and Overseas. Origins and Development*, Cambridge: Cambridge University Press.

Jenkins, J. (2000) *Phonology of English as an International Language*, Oxford: Oxford University Press.

——(2007) *English as a Lingua Franca: Attitude and Identity*, Oxford: Oxford University Press.

——(2009) *World Englishes: A Resource Book for Students*, 2nd edn, London: Routledge.

Kachru, B. B. (1992b) 'Models for non-native Englishes', in B. B. Kachru (ed.) *The Other Tongue: English across Cultures*, 2nd edn, Urbana and Chicago: University of Illinois Press.

——(1992c) 'Teaching world Englishes', in B. B. Kachru (ed.) *The Other Tongue: English across Cultures*, 2nd edn, Urbana and Chicago: University of Illinois Press.

——(2005) *Asian Englishes: Beyond the Canon*, Hong Kong: Hong Kong University Press.

Kachru, B. B. (ed.) (1992a) *The Other Tongue: English across Cultures*, 2nd edn, Urbana and Chicago: University of Illinois Press.

Kirkpatrick, A. (2007a) *World Englishes: Implications for International Communication and English Language Teaching*, Cambridge: Cambridge University Press.

——(2007b) 'The communicative strategies of ASEAN speakers of English as a lingua franca', in D. Prescott (ed.) *English in Southeast Asia: Literacies, Literatures and Varieties*, Newcastle upon Tyne: Cambridge Scholars Publishing.

——(2008) 'English as the official working language of the Association of Southeast Asian Nations (ASEAN): features and strategies', *English Today* 24(2): 37–44.

Kirkpatrick, A. (ed.) (2010) *Handbook of World Englishes*, London: Routledge.

Kortmann, B. (2010) 'Variation across Englishes: syntax', in A. Kirkpatrick (ed.) *Handbook of World Englishes*, London: Routledge.

Kortmann, B., Burridge, K., Mesthrie, R., Schneider, E. W. and Upton, C. (eds) (2004) *A Handbook of Varieties of English*, vol. 2: *Morphology and Syntax*, Berlin: Mouton de Gruyter.

Low, E. L., Grabe, E. and Nolan, F. (2000) 'Quantitative characterizations of speech rhythm: syllable-timing in Singapore English', *Journal of Phonetics* 29: 217–30.

McArthur, T. (1998) *The English Languages*, Cambridge: Cambridge University Press.

——(2002) *The Oxford Guide to World Englishes*, Oxford: Oxford University Press.

McCafferty, K. (2003) 'The Northern subject rule in Ulster: how Scots, how English?' *Language Variation and Change* 15: 105–39.

Mahboob, A. (2004) 'Pakistani English: morphology and syntax', in B. Kortmann, K. Burridge, R. Mesthrie, E. W. Schneider and C. Upton (eds) *A Handbook of Varieties of English*, vol. 2: *Morphology and Syntax*, Berlin: Mouton de Gruyter.

Mahboob, A. and Ahmar, N. H. (2004) 'Pakistani English: phonology', in E. W. Schneider, K. Burridge, B. Kortmann, R. Mesthrie and C. Upton (eds) *A Handbook of Varieties of English*, vol. 1: *Phonology*, Berlin: Mouton de Gruyter.

Martin, P. W., Ożóg, C. and Poedjosoedarmo, G. (eds) (1996) *Language Use and Language Change in Brunei Darussalam*, Athens, OH: Ohio University Center for International Studies.

Mesthrie, R. (2004) 'Indian South African English: morphology and syntax', in B. Kortmann, K. Burridge, R. Mesthrie, E. W. Schneider and C. Upton (eds) *A Handbook of Varieties of English*, vol. 2: *Morphology and Syntax*, Berlin: Mouton de Gruyter.

Mesthrie, R. and Bhatt, R. M. (2008) *World Englishes: The Study of New Linguistic Varieties*, Cambridge: Cambridge University Press.

Mossop, J. (1996) 'Some phonological features of Brunei English', in P. W. Martin, C. Ożóg and G. Poedjosoedarmo (eds) *Language Use and Language Change in Brunei Darussalam*, Athens, OH: Ohio University Center for International Studies.

Mufwene, S. (2001) *The Ecology of Language Evolution*, Cambridge: Cambridge University Press.

Naik, M. K. and Narayan, S. A. (2004) *Indian English Literature 1980–2000: A Critical Survey*, New Delhi: Pencraft International.

Nelson, G., Wallis, S. and Aarts, B. (2002) *Exploring Natural Language: Working with the British Component of the International Corpus of English*, Amsterdam: John Benjamins.

Pennycook, A. (2007) *Global Englishes and Transcultural Flows*, London: Routledge.

——(2010) 'The future of Englishes: one, many or none?', in A. Kirkpatrick (ed.) *Handbook of World Englishes*, London: Routledge.

Phillipson, R. (1992) *Linguistic Imperialism*, Oxford: Oxford University Press.

——(2009) *Linguistic Imperialism Continued*, London: Routledge.

Richards, J. C., Platt, J. and Platt, H. (1985) *Longman Dictionary of Language Teaching and Applied Linguistics*, Harlow: Longman.

Sailaja, P. (2009) *Indian English*, Edinburgh: Edinburgh University Press.

Saro-Wiwa, K. (1985) *Sozaboy: A Novel in Rotten English*, Port Harcourt, Nigeria: Saros International.

Schmied, J. (2004) 'East African English (Kenya, Uganda, Tanzania): phonology', in E. W. Schneider, K. Burridge, B. Kortmann, R. Mesthrie and C. Upton (eds) *A Handbook of Varieties of English*, vol. 1: *Phonology*, Berlin: Mouton de Gruyter.

Schneider, E. W. (2003) 'The dynamics of new Englishes: from identity construction to dialect rebirth', *Language* 79: 233–81.

——(2007) *Postcolonial Englishes: Varieties Around the World*, Cambridge: Cambridge University Press.

Schneider, E. W., Burridge, K., Kortmann, B., Mesthrie, R. and Upton, C. (eds) (2004) *A Handbook of Varieties of English*, vol. 1: *Phonology*, Berlin: Mouton de Gruyter.

Schreier, D. (2005) *Consonant Change in English Worldwide*, Basingstoke: Palgrave Macmillan.

Seidlhofer, B. (2001) 'Closing a conceptual gap: the case for a description of English as a lingua franca', *International Journal of Applied Linguistics* 11: 133–58

——(2004) 'Research perspectives in teaching English as a lingua franca', *Annual Review of Applied Linguistics* 24: 209–39.

Sidhwa, B. (1996) 'Creative processes in Pakistani English fiction', in R. Baumgardner (ed.) *South Asian English: Structure, Use and Users*, Chicago: University of Illinois Press.

Tayao, M. L. G. (2004) 'Philippine English: phonology', in E. W. Schneider, K. Burridge, B. Kortmann, R. Mesthrie and C. Upton (eds) *A Handbook of Varieties of English*, vol. 1: *Phonology*, Berlin: Mouton de Gruyter.

Trudgill, P. and Hannah, J. (2008) *International English: A Guide to Varieties of Standard English*, 5th edn, London: Hodder Education.

VOICE (n.d.) 'The Vienna-Oxford international corpus of English'. Available at: www.univie.ac.at/voice/page/index.php (accessed 13 April 2009).

Wells, J. C. (1982) *Accents of English*, Cambridge: Cambridge University Press.

27

Linguistic imperialism

Suresh Canagarajah and Selim Ben Said

Introduction

Linguistic imperialism (LI) refers to the imposition of a language on other languages and communities. As in other cases of imperialism, this is an exercise of power at the transnational level with geopolitical implications. Though imperialism through economic, cultural, political, and military means has been discussed widely, the realization that language can serve imperialistic purposes has begun to be theorized in its own right only recently. Scholars engaged in this area of research are open to the possibility that language doesn't have to serve a subsidiary role to other material and political factors in the exercise of power; language can play a more central role in enabling the hegemony of a community. For example, some might argue that after decolonization, it is the English language that primarily sustains the power of the United States and Britain in many parts of the world today, facilitating other forms of cultural, educational, and political hegemony (see wa Thiong'o 1986).

In this chapter, we first provide a historical orientation to the study of LI. Next, we review some theoretical constructs that help us understand the manifestations of LI. We illustrate these constructs in relation to educational contexts. We then move on to the controversies and debates surrounding the study of LI. Finally, we explore some new social and theoretical developments that complicate language-based hegemony. We outline the ways in which these new developments call for further study and theorization. This chapter primarily explores LI as it finds expression through the English language.

History

The term LI was first introduced in scholarly circles by Robert Phillipson. He initially used the term to refer exclusively to the global status and role of English and applied the term primarily to English language teaching. For Phillipson, LI is a situation in which 'the dominance of English is asserted and maintained by the establishment and continuous reconstitution of structural and cultural inequalities between English and other languages' (1992: 47). Several terms in this definition need unpacking. LI is not a stable condition. As social conditions change, the dominance of English is asserted through new means. LI will take new forms and realizations in different contexts. Phillipson also sees this dominance as a conscious process, exerted by agents and institutions. He would argue against the notion that the power of English is an impersonal effect of historical conditions. The dominance of English is sustained by both cultural and structural means. In other words, LI is attributable not only to attitudes, assumptions, and values of speakers of English. Geopolitical, social, and educational structures play an important role as well.

Though English is the foremost language that displays imperialistic tendencies worldwide in present times, the notion of LI is not restricted to English. LI can be explored in relation to other languages in other historical periods and regions. Latin hegemony in the Roman Empire around the first to the fourth century, Arabic hegemony over Europe around the eighth to the thirteenth century, and Japanese hegemony in the East Asian region in late nineteenth and early twentieth century are examples of LI by other languages. However, there is a good case to be made that LI by English is different in degree and kind. Though English was first spread in many countries in South Asia, Africa, and the Caribbean by the British empire, English received a new lease on life after decolonization when the United States gained ascendance after the Second World War. The types of economic, cultural, and political power the USA wields in the world today further the currency and status of English. In some ways, the power of English is not dependent on a specific country anymore. It is sustained by transnational processes and institutions. English enables the contemporary forms of financial, production, media, and educational relations across borders. English-based cultural institutions, such as mass media, cinema, and music, also enjoy global status. These sources have spread English far beyond the former British Empire. English expands its reach today through technological, infrastructural, and material resources that other imperialistic languages didn't enjoy in previous periods in history. Given these reasons, we can understand why scholars like Crystal (2004) believe that the global power of English is here to stay.

Central constructs

It is important to define the terms that come up in discussions related to LI before we discuss its manifestations.

Ideologies are ideas, assumptions, attitudes, and values that explain the unequal status of individuals and communities in society. Ideologies are not always conscious. They could be unconsciously internalized through one's social practices and historical experiences. Moreover, ideologies don't always serve a repressive and distorting function. While ideologies can make inequalities appear natural and acceptable, they can also illuminate them to facilitate social change. When ideologies find expression in language, we call them *discourses*. Discourses are genres of thinking and communicating that have social and political functions. Though languages may be treated as a neutral system at the abstract grammatical level, when they play social and ideological functions at the level of communicative practice, they acquire the properties of discourses. *Hegemony* is exercised when the ideologies and discourses of a powerful community are internalized by other social groups, to the extent that they willingly participate in the leadership of that community. For example, the discourse that English is a superior language with the capacity to express complex philosophical, scientific, and technical information gains ideological implications when multilingual communities believe this discourse and learn English at the cost of proficiency in their own languages. When they internalize this discourse and buy into the forms of knowledge, values, and identities that come with English, they become unwitting participants in the power enjoyed by English and Anglophone countries.

We have to consider suitable labels for distinguishing between countries that have unequal relationships based on their language identity. Phillipson (1992) used the terms *center* and *periphery*, borrowing them from political economists of the world systems perspective (Frank 1969; Wallerstein 1991). The terminology has the advantage of connecting language inequality to other forms of economic and political inequalities. However, many now see these terms as reductive and failing to capture the new geopolitical relationships based on a more complex international flow of resources and production. Also, linguistic and material forms of inequality are not isomorphic. For example, Anglophone countries are not always dominant in all domains of finance, production, and technology. Another set of terms refers more specifically to the historical spread, functional differences, and unequal statuses of English in different countries. Kachru (1986) introduced the terms *expanding circle* (where English is used as a foreign language for contact purposes with outsiders – i.e. Vietnam or Angola, which were not former British colonies), *outer circle* (where English is a second language with its own well-established varieties since colonial times – i.e. India, Nigeria), and the *inner circle* (where ownership of English and native speakerhood have been traditionally claimed – i.e. the UK, the USA, Canada, Australia). Kachru classified these communities as norm-dependent, norm-developing, and norm-providing, respectively, to indicate their relative status in relation to grammatial standards. However, the developments in recent forms of globalization have raised doubts about the validity of these distinctions, as we will demonstrate below. Though terms like center/periphery and inner/outer/expanding circles are inadequate, we will use the former set to refer to geopolitical distinctions and the latter set for linguistic distinctions, as we don't have good alternatives at present.

We now turn to constructs directly related to LI.

Linguicism

Linguicism refers to 'Ideologies, structures, and practices which are used to legitimate, effectuate, and reproduce an unequal division of power and resources (both material and immaterial) between groups which are defined on the basis of language' (Phillipson 1992: 47, see also Skutnabb-Kangas and Phillipson 1995, 1996; Phillipson 2000). The term is analogous to racism and sexism, and refers to a discriminatory attitude towards language that is played out in social practices and sustained by social institutions. For example, the lack of policy emphasis and funding for teaching languages other than English in the USA can be considered an institutionalized form of linguicism (see Horner and Trimbur 2002). Policies such as the No Child Left Behind Act don't treat proficiency in other languages as a resource (Harper *et al.* 2007, 2008).

Linguicism leads to the promotion of certain languages and language varieties and the stigmatization of others, as the prestigious language becomes the norm by which other languages derive their status. As argued by van Dijk (2000: 73), linguicism has repercussions for the way people use languages and may lead to an inability to use one's own languages or to an exclusion from certain communicative events. Linguicism may be at play in gatekeeping situations where only one language or variety is recognized while others are excluded. Also, attitudes regarding the knowledgeableness, friendliness, and superior status of people based on the language they speak is a psychological manifestation of linguicism. The implications of linguicism for LI – and for the LI of English in particular – is that English is equated with prestige, while failure to use English or even using other languages may connote lack of status. Oda (2000) demonstrates that those who are not proficient in English are treated as lower in status in Japanese universities. In addition, in English teaching, varieties deemed more 'native-like' are promoted as more prestigious for learners while other 'localized' varieties are stigmatized and suppressed (see Heller and Martin-Jones 2001). For example, in many post-colonial countries like Sri Lanka, Hong Kong, and India, schools insist on teaching British or American English. The varieties used in everyday life, such as Sri Lankan, Chinese, or Indian English are censored from classroom use.

Native speakerism

The discourse of native speakerism is made of the following assumptions: that 'native' speakers are the authorities on the language and enjoy superior competence; that those who use it as an additional language have to treat 'native' speaker competence as the target; and that 'native' speakers are the best qualified to teach that language. Among those who justify the inherent superiority of 'native' speakers, one can mention Prator (1968) and Quirk (1990). They treat the varieties spoken by multilingual speakers as interlanguages attempting to approximate the 'native' speaker norm. However, other scholars argue against native speakerism (see Valdes 1986; Kachru 1991; Braine 1999; Canagarajah 1999a). They point out that the superiority of the 'native' speaker is linguistically anachronistic as it goes against the relativistic tradition in linguistics that postulates that there are no status differences between languages in purely linguistic terms (though there are extra-linguistic reasons for such inequality). Furthermore, languages in situations of contact will always undergo modes of appropriation and, eventually, localization. Language change or diversification cannot be stopped by attempts at purification. Contextually relevant variants of the language have to be used in different situations of communication. In this sense, the English varieties of multilingual speakers are not deficient, but different. Similarly, the treatment of 'native' speaker teachers as superior ignores the view that language learning is a creative cognitive and social process that has its own trajectory, and is not fully dependent on the teacher (much less the teacher's accent).

In fact, many scholars consider the term 'native' speaker itself is questionable. The term doesn't suit the language reality in many communities. With the existence of localized varieties of English developed in postcolonial communities, many multilinguals would consider themselves 'native' speakers of these Englishes. Some in postcolonial communities acquire English simultaneously with one or more local languages to develop multilingual competence. These speakers would consider themselves first language speakers of English as well as of one or more local languages. They would be hard pressed to identify themselves as a 'native' speaker of any single language. The competence of these multilingual speakers needs to be defined in more complex terms. Rather than treating their competence in relation to purported 'native' speakers, or measuring their competence in English in isolation from other languages, Vivian Cook (1999) argues that we should treat multilinguals as endowed with a *multicompetence* that is qualitatively different from the competence of monolingual speakers of English. Cook theorizes the ways in which a multilingual speaker simultaneously works with diverse languages even as he/she communicates in only one of them. Furthermore, this competence is more than the sum of its parts, going beyond the resources provided by the individual languages. Such developments call for new ways of classifying language identities. Rampton (1990) has argued for categorizing linguistic identities not in terms of birth, but in terms of a more diverse set of categories such as expertise, affiliation, and inheritance. We don't have good alternatives to make distinctions between the types of speakers relevant for this chapter. Therefore we use the term 'native' within quotation marks. For 'non-native' speakers, we use the term 'multilingual' speakers.

Monolingualism

Another discourse that facilitates LI is monolingualism. This discourse has implications for many subfields in applied linguistics. In second language acquisition, processes of learning treat monolingual acquisition as the model; in language planning, multilingualism is treated as a problem for social progress; in sociolinguistics, identities and communities are defined in terms of homogeneity (see Blommaert and Verschueren 1998; Canagarajah 2007). To focus more closely on teaching, according to this discourse English is best taught monolingually (Phillipson 1992: 185–93). This discourse takes as its model the pedagogical norms used in countries where English is the primary language, and assumes that speaking English to the exclusion of other languages (including the mother tongue) is the best way to optimize the learning of this language in second language contexts. Other languages are considered to negatively interfere with the acquisition and internalization of English. This discourse gains strength in the light of a reaction against grammar translation methods, a shift in emphasis in language pedagogy from writing to speaking, and a belief in 'natural' L2 language acquisition. 'English only' is institutionalized in many states of the USA, such as Arizona, where other languages are not permitted to be used in classrooms. In colonized countries, local people may themselves desire to be taught in the English language in order to reach a better economic status or because this language represents a valued cultural and economic capital (Bourdieu 1986). As a consequence, the monolingualist discourse is internalized by the local population and motivates them to 'mimicry' (Memmi 2003) aimed at emulating the colonizer.

However, there are several factors that make the monolingualist discourse a fallacy. Phillipson (1992) argues that 'when the mother tongue is banned from the classroom, the teaching leads to the alienation of the learners, deprives them of their cultural identity, and leads to acculturation rather than increased intercultural communicative competence' (1992: 193). Rather than acculturating to English one-sidedly, multilinguals should be encouraged to develop a multicultural identity, with English as one more resource in their linguistic repertoire. Furthermore, the use of first language (L1) can help students bridge home knowledge and school knowledge more effectively (see Faltis and Hudelson 1994). Tove Skutnabb-Kangas (Skutnabb-Kangas and Phillipson 1995) goes to the extent of arguing that the provision of mother tongue in the educational process (including the L2 classes) is a fundamental 'linguistic human right' of the minority language groups. Other scholars argue for the positive functions of first languages in the acquisition of English. Asserting that 'relations of power and their affective consequences are integral to language acquisition', Auerbach has pointed out that the use of students' first language can increase their openness to learning English by reducing the degree of language and culture shock (1993: 16). If Auerbach's justification is socio-political, Cummins' (1991) is cognitive. His *linguistic interdependence principle* explains that proficiency in L1 can enable better proficiency in L2 by activating a common underlying proficiency that enables cognitive/academic and literacy-related skills to transfer across languages. Despite these research findings, the monolingualist discourse continues to hold sway.

Controversies and debates

Ambiguities and ironies in the spread of English

The hegemony of English is not always clear and straightforward. Pennycook's *Cultural Politics of English as an International Language* (1994) grapples with the paradoxes and ironies in the status and functions of English in the periphery. He goes beyond the dichotomies and stereotypes in this historiography to acknowledge greater tension in the roles of English and the vernacular. He captures what he calls the 'critical ambivalences' in which English is caught up, embodying conflicting attitudes and values (1994: 74). Surveying the role of English in the colonial period under the discourses of Orientalism (i.e. made up of 'policies in favor of education in local languages for both the colonized and the colonizers') and Anglicism (i.e. made up of 'policies in favor of education in English'), Pennycook explores the complex ways in which both policies existed side by side to serve the interests of the colonial agenda in the periphery (1994: 74–5). He thereby corrects the stereotypical view that Anglicism blatantly triumphed over Orientalism (a position which other scholars, including Phillipson 1992, seem to adopt). Pennycook theorizes the complementary relation of Orientalism and Anglicism thus:

> First, both Anglicism and Orientalism operated alongside each other; second, Orientalism was as much a part of colonialism as was Anglicism; third, English was withheld as much as it was promoted; fourth, colonized people demanded access to English; and finally, the power of English was not so much in its widespread imposition but in its operating as the eye of the colonial panopticon.
>
> *(Pennycook 1994: 103)*

Pennycook's treatment of the postcolonial status of English, especially in Singapore and Malaysia, goes beyond stereotypes to show the manner in which Anglicism thrives in the local communities at a period of intense nationalism. He surveys discourses such as pragmatism, meritocratism, and internationalism that motivate local people to still 'desire' English. Some features of this positive valuation of English sit side by side with oppositional perspectives. However, Pennycook sees such mixed attitudes of local people as still facilitating the hegemony of English as they fail to develop a critical attitude towards language.

Linguistic resistance and appropriation

Canagarajah (1999b) takes Pennycook's analysis further to show how local people appropriate English to suit their interests and values. This activity constitutes a form of resistance. The resistance perspective differs from the assumptions informing LI. LI holds that subjects are passive and lack agency to manage their linguistic and ideological conflicts to their advantage; that the sole function of language is to spread and sustain the interests of the dominant groups; that languages are monolithic, abstract structures that come with a homogeneous set of ideologies that serve the interests of a single community. Canagarajah considers this a deterministic perspective on power and labels it *reproduction orientation*. This perspective has had considerable influence in linguistics, discourse analysis, social sciences, and education (see Bourdieu and Passeron 1977). The alternative response of engaging creatively with languages assumes a different set of values: namely, that subjects have the agency to think critically and work out ideological alternatives that favor their empowerment; that although language may suppress people, it also has the liberatory potential of facilitating critical thinking, and enabling subjects to rise above domination; that each language is heterogeneous enough to accommodate diverse interests that may be tapped by marginalized groups to serve their own purposes. The *resistance perspective* provides for the possibility that the powerless may negotiate, alter, and oppose political structures in their everyday life through many untheorized ways.

Canagarajah goes on to suggest that the new varieties of English in postcolonial contexts might be a way for local communities to bring in their own values, discourses, and interests into the English language. Therefore, these new varieties have ideological implications. They democratize the language by accommodating values from diverse communities, indicating ownership over the language by those outside the center. However, Tove Skutnabb-Kangas (2004) argues that the appropriation of English doesn't address the prospect of language death for many indigenous languages. Even though local speakers may appropriate English in creative and critical terms, many also ignore proficiency in their own languages in favor of English. She argues that resistance theory should not look at English in isolation, but in relation to other languages in the local ecology.

Linguistic accommodation and multilingualism

Bisong (1995) has brought out the complexity of a multilingual repertoire within which English is accommodated by outer circle members. Focusing on Nigeria, he argues that for local people who are proficient in diverse languages, and enjoy a culture of plurilingualism, learning and using one more language – English in this case – doesn't pose any problems. English became accommodated into their repertoire of codes spoken in the local context during colonization. In fact, multilinguals may develop 'third positions' in culture, ideology, and worldview, that go beyond essentialized identities (see Kramsch and Lam 1999). Third positions are hybrid linguistic or cultural systems that merge competing languages and cultures. These speakers sidestep the deterministic discourse informing LI – i.e. that the speakers of English are conditioned by English to fall prey to its ideology and also lose proficiency in their vernacular codes and cultures. However, a complicating issue is that not all languages are always equal in social life. Local people have to negotiate the power of English with alertness and critical agency. Phillipson (2003) also brings out the paradoxical case in the European Union that in the name of multilingualism, it is English that is gaining more power at the cost of other languages. He argues that the claim of egalitarian multilingualism turns out to be deceptive, because people find the power wielded by English too tempting. As a result, English is on the ascendance in Europe. Also, House points out that 'the lip-service paid to the ideal of a multiplicity of languages' is not matched in reality, and that translating documents into the different languages found in Europe is an expensive and burdensome enterprise (2003: 561).

Future directions

We now discuss the recent geopolitical and communicative developments which complicate the premise of LI.

Transnational flows

The shift from modernist globalization to postmodern globalization ushers in new relations for languages and communities. The modernist globalization that accompanied colonization was motivated by the desire of the dominant Western European communities to spread their values everywhere. It was believed that the values of Enlightenment progress were relevant for all communities (see Mignolo 2000). This movement set up a geopolitical relationship that was centrifugal and hierarchical, involving a unilateral flow of power from the center to the periphery. In addition to shaping social life, this mode of globalization had its effects on language relationships. In many cases, the modernist project involved suppressing or obliterating any traces of local culture or language. In some cases, a hierarchical relationship was set up between the center and the periphery, with the local treating the global as the norm and modeling itself after it. English was imposed on other languages and communities in a similar fashion during colonization.

There are technological, social, and geopolitical factors that account for the shift from modernist globalization (King 1997; Jameson and Miyoshi 1998). In fact, the very success of modernist globalization laid the groundwork for a revision in the patterns of globalization. As all the communities were gradually integrated into a tightly networked system, the local was not suppressed, but received increased visibility. The local propagated itself beyond its narrow bounds through more advanced forms of travel, production relations, business enterprises, and media communication. According to Stuart Hall (1997), these changes forced dominant communities to drop the idea of suppressing the local and attempt to work with it to carry out their interests. For Hall, these altered relationships between the local and the global characterize postmodern globalization.

To understand postmodern globalization, Arjun Appadurai (1996) offers a model of 'transcultural flows'. He tries to capture the new reality of geopolitical relationships not following the unilateral flow from center to periphery. The relationship is more multilateral and fluid. He theorizes these new relationships in relation to the following domains:

ethnoscapes   flow of persons
mediascapes   flow of information
technoscapes   flow of technology
financescapes   flow of finance
ideoscapes   flow of ideology/ideas

English plays a key role in enabling these global flows today. English also gets affected by these flows, undergoing differences in its structure and ethos as it performs these new social functions. Among other things, postmodern globalization has generated the condition for English to work with other languages and carry out the functions of a transnational community. Through the type of fluid interaction we see between languages in various domains, English is also getting more hybridized than ever before. The new geopolitical relationship between languages Canagarajah (2007) calls 'linguascapes' (consistent with the terminology Appadurai coins for the other transcultural flows). The implication of these new linguascapes is that English is becoming deterritorialized. It is losing its identity as belonging to certain traditional 'homes' (the UK or USA, for example). More importantly, it is losing its identity as a language belonging to the inner circle.

We need more research on other features of these transnational flows. There is a burgeoning study of hip-hop and the way it flows across borders and speech communities. Researchers also show how participants in this art form from countries as diverse as Nigeria, Japan, and Sri Lanka mix their own languages and English creatively in their music (see Ibrahim 1999; Mitchell 2001; Pennycook 2003b, 2003c, 2007). This music then travels back to the center, carrying new idioms and values. An interesting feature is that the valued form of English in this music is Black English, not the 'Queen's English'.

Internet

A powerful medium for transnational flows is the new digital technology and the emergent conventions of communication on the Internet. They have created new resources for multilinguals to engage with each other and to negotiate their differences in English. Through such process of negotiation, some users can go on to create new hybrid discourses. For example,

Lam (2004) documents the socialization of two bilingual immigrant Chinese girls in a chat room in which participants develop a hybrid language variety that distinguishes them from both their English-only peers and their Cantonese-only peers. Similarly, Bloch (2004) shows how Chinese learners of English drew on the Chinese rhetorical tradition when communicating in a Usenet group in English, thereby creating a hybrid form of English for that particular context. These discourses resemble the textual strategies of appropriation that we discussed earlier.

English as a lingua franca (ELF)

The English that is used in multilingual contexts in postmodern globalization needs to be distinguished from the varieties spoken by inner circle speakers. ELF is defined as a culture-neutral variety that is commonly owned by multilinguals (Seidlhofer 2002; House 2003; Jenkins 2006a). It is assumed that while speakers may use their own local varieties in their intra-community contexts (whether Britain or India), everyone will switch to ELF in international contexts. Seidlhofer (2002) uses corpus data from her VOICE (Vienna-Oxford International Corpus of English) project to describe the grammar of ELF (www.univie.ac.at/voice/page/index.php). She and Jenkins (2006b) are also interested in developing pedagogical tools by identifying the lingua franca core, whether in grammatical, phonological, or semantic senses. Rather than teaching 'native' forms of English, they find it more profitable to teach the lingua franca core that perhaps wouldn't raise the same animosity or identity conflicts for local people.

More specifically, House (2003: 560) defines ELF as a language not for identification but for communication. English for identification means using a language for purposes of affiliation but also for 'affective' and 'identificatory' ends. The use of English for communication, on the other hand, does not represent a threat to multilingualism nor to the identities of users as English. For House, English in this case is perceived as an auxiliary language and does not have implications for values or identities. It is used for 'transactional' or 'instrumental' purposes only. For such reasons, House argues that English is a commonly owned language and cannot be perceived as hegemonizing any more. However, it is difficult to separate communication and identification in ELF. Any language, whatever the status of the speaker or their objectives in using the language, can raise issues of identification and representation in relative degrees.

Globalization from below

Another development that complicates LI is that different social groups are making efforts at the local level to acquire/use English to suit their own interests and identities, by mixing it with local languages. Blommaert (2005) shows that while the state in Tanzania forms policies favoring Swahili, the poor and marginalized see the need for English. However, they appropriate English in their own fashion, as they don't have access to the educated varieties. The codemixed forms of English that youth use in hip-hop and that salespeople use for attracting buyers are treated by Blommaert as the local interpenetration of the global. In this fashion, local people develop hybrid codes and identities to reconcile their conflicting language allegiances. In the context of schools, students and teachers have been developing similar strategies to manage local values and identities in the face of competing policy discourses. In classrooms in Eritrea (Wright 2001), India (Annamalai 2005), South Africa (Probyn 2005), Tanzania (Brock-Utne 2005), Kenya (Bunyi 2005), Brunei (Martin 2005), and Hong Kong

(Luk 2005), to mention just a few, local languages are mixed with English in many subtle ways to negotiate desired values, identities, and interests. Therefore, many scholars are challenging the stigmatized status given to mixed varieties of English, proposing that they be given a place in education and other institutional contexts and acknowledged in scholarly literature (see Pennycook 2003a; Blommaert 2006; Canagarajah 2009). Blommaert (2006) calls these emergent varieties of English an example of 'globalization from below', which he considers a different form of resistance to the power of English. These varieties show a class-based resistance. While the model of World Englishes describes the educated and middle-class varieties of indigenized English, and boosts the status of the local elite, the mixed varieties represent the interests and values of the less educated (see for further discussion of this point, Parakrama 1995; Canagarajah 2009).

Spread and decline of the English language

In the context of the new geopolitical relationships, new technology, and new communicative media, more diverse languages are gaining prominence. Graddol (2006) cites impressive statistics to suggest the decline of English in various social domains. For example, the number of Internet users for whom English is a first language is quickly declining. English is being overtaken by the Chinese language in terms of number of speakers. A similar decline of English is projected in the domain of news media. Other world languages are adopted more by the mainstream press. The dominance of international news by English language providers such as Associated Press, Reuters, the BBC or CNN is being increasingly challenged by networks in other languages. Recent trends diversify both the viewpoints available in international news in English, and the languages in which global news is provided. Stations like Al-Jazeera and Al-Arabiya provide an independent source of news about events in the Middle East. They have turned to Arabic as an important medium for world news. The Spanish-language rival to CNN, Telesur, which began broadcasting from Caracas in 2005, enjoys popularity in Latin American countries. Graddol also cites other evidence to demonstrate the decline of English vis-à-vis other world languages. He observes that in many Asian countries, Europe and the USA, Mandarin has emerged as the coveted language. He argues that 'An estimated 30 million people are already studying Mandarin worldwide and the Chinese government expects this to rise to around 100 million in the next few years' (2006: 63). Will these developments make a dent in the linguistic imperialism of English?

Conclusion

It is clear from our review that social conditions have changed a lot since colonial times when English was imposed on other communities. To some extent, the values and relationships that English helped internalize among communities still have some power over multilingual people in the periphery. However, LI doesn't take the form it did then. It takes new forms through postmodern globalization, and new technologies and media. The new forms of globalization and social relationships in postmodern times have created favorable conditions for negotiability for other communities and languages. In certain domains (as suggested by Graddol), some other languages have gained more prominence, at times changing English from within, constructing hybrid codes and discourses. Such developments don't mean that we live in a more democratic linguistic environment now. Issues of power are still relevant. However, it is in the nature of power to be contested. Other languages and communities will always resist, modify, and reconfigure the power of English. The struggle for power between languages will go on indefinitely, taking new forms and ramifications. The notion of LI reminds us that we must not ignore the role of power in language relationships. It alerts communities and policy makers to negotiate the relationship between languages in creative and critical ways.

Related topics

language policy and planning; multilingualism; world Englishes

Further reading

Canagarajah, A. S. (ed.) (2005) *Reclaiming the Local in Language Policy and Practice*, Mahwah, NJ: Lawrence Erlbaum Associates. (The authors adopt a multilingual orientation to show how they negotiate the power of English in domains as diverse as teaching, planning, literacy practices, community relations, and identity.)

Edge, J. (ed.) (2006) *(Re-)Locating TESOL in an Age of Empire*, London: Palgrave Macmillan. (This book explores the subtle ways in which English language teaching furthers imperialistic agendas in contemporary times, such as missionary activity and the war on terrorism.)

Pennycook, A. (2007) *Global Englishes and Transcultural Flows*, London: Routledge. (The author focuses on popular culture, especially hip-hop, to show how English gains new norms and identities through its transnational spread and reproduction.)

Prendergast, C. (2008) *Buying into English: Language and Investment in the New Capitalist World*, Pittsburgh, PA: University of Pittsburgh Press. (Studying post-communist Czechoslovakia, the author analyzes the ways in which English has acquired the status of a marketable commodity.)

References

Annamalai, E. (2005) 'Nation building in a globalized world: language choice and education in India', in A. Lin and P. Martin (eds) *Decolonisation, Globalisation: Language-in-Education Policy and Practice*, Clevedon: Multilingual Matters.

Appadurai, A. (1996) *Modernity at Large: Cultural Dimensions of Globalization*, Minneapolis: University of Minnesota Press.

Auerbach, E. (1993) 'Reexamining English only in the ESL classroom', *TESOL Quarterly* 27: 1–19.

Bisong, J. (1995) 'Language choice and cultural imperialism: a Nigerian perspective', *ELT Journal* 49(2): 122–32.

Bloch, J. (2004) 'Second language cyber rhetoric: a study of Chinese L2 writers in an online Usenet group', *Language Learning and Technology* 8(3): 66–82.

Blommaert, J. (2005) *Discourse: A Critical Introduction*, Cambridge: Cambridge University Press.

Blommaert, J. and Verschueren, J. (1998) *Debating Diversity: Analysing the Discourse of Tolerance*, London: Routledge.

Bourdieu, P. (1986) 'The forms of capital', in J. G. Richardson (ed.) *Handbook of Theory and Research for the Sociology of Education*, New York: Greenwood Press.

Bourdieu, P. and Passeron, J.-C. (1977) *Reproduction in Education, Society and Culture*, London: Sage.

Braine, G. (1999) *Non-native Educators in English Language Teaching*, Mahwah, NJ: Lawrence Erlbaum Associates.

Brock-Utne, B. (ed.) (2005) *Language-in-Education Policies and Practices in Africa With a Special Focus on Tanzania and South Africa: Insight from Research in Progress*, Clevedon: Multilingual Matters.

Bunyi, G. (ed.) (2005) *Language Classroom Practices in Kenya*, Clevedon: Multilingual Matters.

Canagarajah, A. S. (1999a) *Interrogating the 'Native Speaker Fallacy': Non-Linguistic Roots, Non-Pedagogical Results*, Mahwah, NJ: Lawrence Erlbaum Associates.

——(1999b) *Resisting Linguistic Imperialism in English Teaching*, Oxford: Oxford University Press.

——(2007) 'From Babel to Pentecost: postmodern glottoscapes and the globalization of English', in L. Anglada, M. Barrios and J. Williams (eds) *Towards the Knowledge Society: Making EFL Education Relevant*, Argentina: British Council.

——(2009) 'The plurilingual tradition and English language in south Asia', *AILA Review* 22: 5–22.

Cook, V. (1999) 'Going beyond the native speaker in language teaching', *TESOL Quarterly* 33: 185–209.

Crystal, D. (2004) *The Language Revolution*, Cambridge: Polity Press.

Cummins, J. (1991) 'Interdependence of first- and second-language proficiency in bilingual children', in E. Bialystok (ed.) *Language Processing in Bilingual Children*, Cambridge: Cambridge University Press.

Faltis, C. and Hudelson, S. (1994) 'Learning English as an additional language in K-12 schools', *TESOL Quarterly* 28(3): 457–68.

Frank, A. G. (1969) *Latin America: Underdevelopment or Revolution*, New York: Monthly Review Press.

Graddol, D. (2006) *English Next: Why Global English May Mean the End of 'English as a Foreign Language'*, British Council. Available at: www.britishcouncil.org/files/documents/learning-research-english-next.pdf (accessed 1 January 2010).

Hall, S. (ed.) (1997) *The Local and the Global: Globalization and Ethnicity*, Minneapolis: University of Minnesota Press.

Harper, C., Platt, E., Naranjo, C. and Boynton, S. (2007) 'Marching in unison: Florida ESL teachers and No Child Left Behind', *TESOL Quarterly* 41(3): 642–51.

Harper, C., de Jong, E. J. and Platt, E. (2008) 'Marginalizing English as a second language teacher expertise: the exclusionary consequence of No Child Left Behind', *Language Policy* 7(3): 267–84.

Heller, M. and Martin-Jones, M. (2001) 'Voices of authority: education and linguistic difference', in M. Heller and M. Martin-Jones (eds) *Contemporary Studies in Linguistics and Education*, London: Ablex.

Horner, B. and Trimbur, J. (2002) 'English only and U.S. college composition', *College Composition and Communication* 53: 594–630.

House, J. (2003) 'English as a lingua franca: a threat to multilingualism?', *Journal of Sociolinguistics* 7: 556–78.

Ibrahim, A. E. K. M. (1999) 'Becoming black: rap and hip-hop, race, gender, identity, and the politics of ESL learning', *TESOL Quarterly* 33: 349–70.

Jameson, F. and Miyoshi, M. (eds) (1998) *The Cultures of Globalization*, Durham, NC: Duke University Press.

Jenkins, J. (2006a) 'Current perspectives on teaching World Englishes and English as a lingua franca', *TESOL Quarterly* 40(1): 157–81.

——(2006b) 'The spread of English as an international language: a testing time for testers', *ELT Journal* 60(1): 51–60.

Kachru, B. B. (1986) *The Alchemy of English: The Spread, Functions and Models of Non-native Englishes*, Oxford: Pergamon.

——(1991) 'Liberation linguistics and the Quirk concern', *English Today* 25: 3–13.

King, A. D. (1997) *Culture, Globalization and the World System: Contemporary Conditions for the Representation of Identity*, Minneapolis: University of Minnesota Press.

Kramsch, K. and Lam, W. S. E. (1999) 'Textual identities: the importance of being non-native', in G. Braine (ed.) *Non-Native Educators in English Language Teaching*, Mahwah, NJ: Lawrence Erlbaum Associates.

Lam, W. S. E. (2004) 'Second language socialization in a bilingual chatroom: global and local considerations', *Language Learning and Technology* 8(3): 44–65.

Luk, J. C. M. (2005) 'Voicing the "self" through an "other" language: exploring communicative language teaching for global communication', in A. S. Canagarajah (ed.) *Reclaiming the Local in Language Policy and Practice*, Mahwah, NJ: Lawrence Erlbaum Associates.

Martin, P. W. (2005) 'Talking knowledge into being in an upriver primary school in Brunei', in A. S. Canagarajah (ed.) *Local Knowledge, Globalization and Language Teaching*, Mahwah, NJ: Lawrence Erlbaum.

Memmi, A. (2003) *The Colonizer and the Colonized*, London: Earthscan.

Mignolo, W. (2000) *Local Histories/Global Designs: Coloniality, Subaltern Knowledges, and Border Thinking*, Princeton, NJ: Princeton University Press.

Mitchell, T. (2001) *Global Noise: Rap and Hip-hop Outside the USA*, Middletown, CT: Wesleyan University Press.

wa Thiong'o, N. (1986) *Decolonizing the Mind: The Politics of Language in African Literature*, London: James Currey.

Oda, M. (2000) 'Linguicism in action: language and power in academic institutions', in R. Phillipson (ed.) *Rights to Language: Equity, Power, and Education*, Mahwah, NJ: Lawrence Erlbaum Associates.

Parakrama, A. (1995) *De-hegemonizing Language Standards: Learning from (Post)Colonial Englishes about 'English'*, Basingstoke: Palgrave Macmillan.

Pennycook, A. (1994) *The Cultural Politics of English as an International Language*, London: Longman.

——(2003a) 'Beyond homogeny and heterogeny: English as a global and worldly language', in C. Mair (ed.) *The Cultural Politics of English*, Amsterdam: Rodopi.

——(2003b) 'Global Englishes, rip slyme and performativity', *Journal of Sociolinguistics* 7(4): 513–33.

——(2003c) 'Global noise and global Englishes', *Cultural Studies Review* 9: 192–200.

——(2007) *Global Englishes and Transcultural Flows*, London: Routledge.

Phillipson, R. (1992) *Linguistic Imperialism*, Oxford: Oxford University Press.

——(ed.) (2000) *Rights to Language: Equity, Power, and Education*, Mahwah, NJ: Lawrence Erlbaum Associates.

——(2003) *English Only Europe? Challenging Language Policy*, London: Routledge.

Prator, C. H. (1968) 'The British heresy in TEFL', in J. A. Fishman, C. A. Ferguson, and J. Das Gupta (eds) *Language Problems of Developing Nations*, New York: Wiley.

Probyn, M. J. (2005) 'Learning science through two languages in South Africa', in J. Cohen, K. T. McAlister, K. Rostlad and J. Macswan (eds) *Proceedings of the 4th International Symposium on Bilingualism*, Somerville, MA: Cascadilla Press.

Quirk, R. (1990) 'Language varieties and standard language', *English Today* 21: 3–10.

Rampton, B. (1990) 'Displacing the "native speaker": expertise, affiliation, and inheritance', *ELT Journal* 44(2): 97–101.

Seidlhofer, B. (2002) *The Shape of Things to Come? Some Basic Questions about English as a Lingua Franca*, Frankfurt: Peter Lang.

Selfe, C. and Selfe, R. J. (1994) 'The politics of the interface: power and its exercise in the electronic contact zone', *College Composition and Communication* 45(4): 480–504.

Skutnabb-Kangas, T. (2004) 'Do not cut my tongue: let me live and die with my language: a comment on English and other languages in relation to linguistic human rights', *Journal of Language, Identity, and Education* 3(2): 127–34.

Skutnabb-Kangas, T. and Phillipson, R. (1995) 'Linguistic human rights, past and present', in T. Skutnabb-Kangas and R. Phillipson (eds) *Linguistic Human Rights: Overcoming Linguistic Discrimination*, Berlin and New York: Mouton de Gruyter.

——(1996) 'Linguicide and linguicism', in G. Hans, P. H. Nelde, Z. Stary and W. Wölck (eds) *Kontaktlinguistic/Contact Linguistics/Linguistique de contact*, vol. 1, Berlin and New York: Mouton de Gruyter.

Valdes, J. M. (1986) *Culture Bound: Bridging the Cultural Gap in Language Teaching*, Cambridge: Cambridge University Press.

van Dijk, T. A. (2000) 'Discourse and access', in R. Phillipson (ed.) *Rights to Language: Equity, Power, and Education*, Mahwah, NJ: Lawrence Erlbaum Associates.

Wallerstein, I. (1991) *Geopolitics and Geoculture*, Cambridge: Cambridge University Press.

Wright, M. W. (2001) 'More than just chanting: multilingual literacies, ideology and teaching methodologies in rural Eritrea', in B. V. Street (ed.) *Literacy and Development: Ethnographic Perspectives*, London: Routledge.

28

Multilingualism

Jasone Cenoz and Durk Gorter

Introduction

Multilingualism can be understood as an individual or a social phenomenon. It can refer to the acquisition, knowledge or use of several languages by individuals or by language communities in a specific geographical area. What is the relationship between multilingualism and applied linguistics? Research in applied linguistics deals with real-world problems related to language. As Auer and Li (2007) point out, multilingualism is not a problem in itself but a traditional monolingual view has seen multilingualism as a problem. In this chapter we consider that multilingualism is a powerful resource for individuals and societies. Multilingualism is not a new phenomenon because there has always been contact between speakers of different languages related to commerce, wars, or immigration. Multilingual individuals, such as Cardinal Giuseppe Caspar Mezzofanti (1774–1849) who spoke almost forty languages, are admired, and speaking languages has traditionally been associated with a high level of education. Nowadays, globalization has spread the use of English all over the world to a greater extent than any other language in the past, and English is increasingly used as a lingua franca, along with many other languages. At the same time, in many parts of the world there is a growing interest in maintaining and developing other languages such as Quechua or Aymara in South America or Basque, Welsh or Frisian in Europe. As Franceschini (2009) points out, the study of multilingualism, a term which is increasingly used to address different forms of language acquisition and language use, has had an important development in the last two decades.

Multilingualism is related to many areas of applied linguistics and therefore to many other chapters in this volume. This chapter will focus on different aspects of multilingualism, including cognitive issues such as the outcomes of multilingualism, language processing in multilinguals, multilingualism and age, and the acquisition of additional languages. It also includes socioeducational issues such as language planning and education, multilingual identities, multilingual practices, multilingualism in the linguistic landscape and multimodality.

Perspectives on multilingualism

The term 'multilingualism' is increasingly used in applied linguistics but not always in the same way. The different ways 'multilingualism' is used are linked at least to three sources of variability: the individual versus social dimension, the number of languages involved and the level of proficiency in the different languages.

Multilingualism has an individual and a social dimension. This broad scope is recognized in some definitions such as that of the European Commission: 'the ability of societies, institutions, groups and individuals to engage, on a regular basis, with more than one language in their day-to-day lives' (European Commission 2007: 6). The term 'plurilingualism' is used in some cases to refer to individual multilingualism but the most common term is multilingualism, both for the individual and social dimensions. Individual and societal multilingualism are widespread in the world because the number of existing languages is much larger than the number of independent states. Individuals and whole communities need to speak more than one language for different reasons. In some cases, they are speakers of an autochthonous minority language such as Navajo in the USA, Maori in New Zealand or Welsh in the UK, and need to learn the dominant state language. In other cases, multilingualism is related to immigration because immigrants speak their first language(s) as well as the language(s) of their host countries. In some cases, languages are learned because they are spread internationally and it is considered that they open doors for better economic and social opportunities. This is the case of English nowadays, which is the most widely spread language and is very common as a school subject and as a language of instruction in schools and universities all over the world.

Regarding the number of languages involved, the term multilingualism implies 'multiple' languages and it usually refers to two or more languages. The term 'bilingualism' means the capacity to use 'two languages' (Greek prefix 'bi' = two) and is widely spread because many studies have focused on two languages. As a result of this tradition 'bilingualism' is also sometimes used instead of 'multilingualism' to include more languages. Nowadays, there is a stronger trend to use multilingualism when two or more languages are involved and sometimes a term like 'bi-/multilingualism' is used (see Skutnabb-Kangas and McCarthy 2008). In this chapter, in accordance with the definition given by the European Commission 'multilingualism' will be used as a cover term including bilingualism as a variation of multilingualism. The term 'bilingualism' will be used when referring specifically to two languages.

The term 'second language acquisition' (SLA) includes the word 'second' that clearly refers to a second language and not to a third or fourth, but it is used by some researchers as a cover term for the acquisition of languages other than the first (see Ortega, this volume). This is the way Saville-Troike uses the term: 'The additional language is called a second language (L2), even though it may actually be the third, fourth or tenth to be acquired' (2006: 2). This use can sometimes be problematic because it does not take into account the specific characteristics of the 'acquisition of additional languages'. In this chapter we will make a distinction between 'second language acquisition' to refer to the 'second' language and the term 'acquisition of additional languages' for all the other languages (third, fourth, fifth, etc.).

Apart from the terminological distinctions, an important question when discussing multilingualism is what we understand by being multilingual. As Baker (2006) points out, there are many different interacting and overlapping dimensions that make the definition 'elusive and ultimately impossible' (2006: 16). One of the most important dimensions is proficiency in the different languages. The idea of 'native control of two languages' suggested by Bloomfield (1933) when referring to bilingualism is extremely demanding and very uncommon when more than two languages are involved. As we have already seen, the definition given by the European Commission does not establish a specific level of proficiency in each of the languages to be multilingual but refers to the use of the languages on a regular basis. Edwards (2004) highlights the need to relate the specific ability to use the languages to the context in which the languages are used. To be 'communicatively competent' in one language involves a number of different components, such as linguistic, sociolinguistic, pragmatic, discourse, and strategic competence. Furthermore these dimensions interact with other dimensions such as formal versus informal contexts, oral versus written language or productive versus receptive multilingualism. The idea of balanced multilingualism at the level of an 'educated ideal native speaker' in several languages is utopian. As it has been pointed out, the term bi-/multi-lingualism 'does not always imply an equally high level of proficiency in all the relevant languages' (Skutnabb-Kangas and McCarthy 2008: 5).

An interesting dimension of multilingualism is the distinction between productive and receptive abilities. Receptive multilingualism is based on language distance and it 'refers to the constellation in which interlocutors use their respective mother tongue while speaking to each other' (Zeevaert and ten Thije 2007: 1). Receptive multilingualism has a strong tradition in Scandinavia where speakers of languages such as Swedish, Danish or Norwegian use their respective first languages when communicating with each other because they can understand the languages used by their interlocutors. Receptive multilingualism is not a new phenomenon, but it has become one of the areas of research in the study of multilingualism and has the support of the European Commision (see ten Thije and Zeevaert 2007). The Euro-Com centre (www.eurocomcenter.de) aims at 'EuroComprehension' on the basis that within Romance, Germanic and Slavonic languages it is possible to develop receptive competence. In order to teach transfer-based deduction strategies to enable receptive multilingualism, Euro-Com offers on-line courses for acquiring receptive competence in different languages. When reading a text in one of the on-line courses, a specific word can be related to other languages. For example, the word *seguridad* in Spanish in the sentence below is related to French *sécurité* and English *security* and also to Spanish *seguro* (sure) French *sûr*, Italian *sicuro*, Catalan *segur*, Portuguese *seguro*, Romanian *sigur* and to words with the same suffix *-dad* in Spanish and other Romance languages (www.kom.tu-darmstadt.de/eurocom):

Por razones de *seguridad* y para evitar posibles problemas …

An important distinction at the social and educational levels is that between additive and subtractive multilingualism. In the case of additive multilingualism a language is added to the linguistic repertoire of the speaker while the first language continues to be developed. In contrast, subtractive multilingualism refers to situations in which a new language is learned and replaces the first language. An example of additive multilingualism can be immersion programmes aimed at speakers of the majority language in different parts of the world. In these programmes, a second language such as French for English L1 speakers in Canada, Catalan for Spanish L1 speakers in Catalonia or Welsh for English L1 speakers in Wales is used as a language of instruction at no cost for the first language. Subtractive multilingualism is often associated with situations of immigration. A typical example would be that of Spanish speakers in the USA when they receive education only through the medium of English without having the opportunity to develop their home language.

The study of multilingualism has been approached from different perspectives such as psycholinguistics, sociolinguistics and education. Different aspects of multilingualism receive more or less attention depending on the discipline. In psycholinguistics the basic topics are the cognitive outcomes of bilingualism, the study of the way different linguistic systems co-exist and interact or the way different languages are acquired simultaneously or consecutively (see also Li 2008). Sociolinguistic studies on multilingualism have focused on the use of different languages and their interaction in specific contexts, the relationship between language use and identity, and the status and vitality of different languages as related to power relationships. Research on education has focused on the use of minority languages as languages of instruction, the development of multiliteracy and the learning of second and additional languages in school contexts (see Cenoz 2009). In this chapter we will focus mainly on psycholinguistic and sociolinguistic dimensions but will also include some developments in education.

Main research areas in multilingualism

In this section we focus on some of the issues that have been researched in the study of multilingualism. These issues are not only relevant for multilingualism because they involve many other areas of applied linguistics such as language learning, language in education and language in society.

The outcomes of bilingualism and multilingualism

Up to the 1960s multilingualism was generally associated with negative results in cognitive ability (see Baker 2006, for a review). Multilingual schoolchildren scored lower than monolinguals, particularly in verbal intelligence, but these tests often had serious methodological problems. As Baker (2006) points out, the definition and measurement of intelligence is complex and simple tests that only measured some aspects of intelligence were used and very often in the bilinguals' weaker language. The multilingual children tested in these studies were in subtractive contexts because their first language was regarded as inferior in society, it was not developed at school and multilingual children often came from lower socioeconomic backgrounds.

This idea of associating multilingualism with detrimental effects in cognitive ability changed in the following decades. A very influential study was published by Peal and Lambert in 1962. This study proved that bilingual children scored higher on several verbal and non-verbal tests of cognitive ability. Although some methodological aspects of this study have been criticized, it triggered off a large number of methodologically stronger studies on the effects of bilingualism. In contrast to the studies conducted between the 1920s and the 1960s, studies carried out in recent decades have generally associated bilingualism with cognitive advantages in metalinguistic awareness and third language acquisition.

Metalinguistic awareness refers to the ability to reflect on language and to manipulate it. Bilinguals have advantages over monolinguals in some dimensions of metalinguistic awareness that demand high levels of control of attention (Bialystok 2001; see also Jessner 2006). Bialystok et al. (2004) also found that lifelong bilingualism could possibly slow down the process of cognitive decline (see also de Bot and van der Hoeven, this volume).

Bilingualism and multilingualism have been associated with possible advantages in the acquisition of additional languages (see Cenoz 2009 for a review). The basic idea is that monolinguals and multilinguals are not on equal footing when facing the task of acquiring an additional language. Multilinguals already have access to at least two linguistic systems with their lexicons, syntax, phonetics, pragmatic and discourse properties. Moreover, with the exception of early bi-/multilinguals, multilingual learners already have the experience of acquiring a second or third language and have developed strategies that can influence the acquisition of additional languages. Communication practices are also different when comparing monolinguals and multilinguals because the latter need to switch between languages according to the situation or the interlocutor. The positive effect of bilingualism on the acquisition of additional languages is not so obvious in the case of immigrants when the first language is not taught and valued at school or in society. In these cases, learners can be in situations of subtractive multilingualism without the opportunity to develop their first language at school and to benefit from the enhanced metalinguistic skills associated with multilingualism. Furthermore, in many cases immigrant children come from weaker socioeconomic and socioeducational backgrounds which are usually associated with poorer achievement.

Language processing in multilinguals

When trying to identify the characteristics of language processing in multilinguals the area that has received most attention has been the organization of the multilingual lexicon (see also Barcroft *et al.*, this volume). Are words from different languages activated at the same time or is there a mechanism to block access to the languages that are not used? Studies on multilingual lexical access seem to indicate that the languages that are not used are not blocked and that there is competition between words in different languages (see, for example, Dijkstra 2007; van Heuven *et al.* 2008). However, not all languages have an equal chance of being selected. Other factors that can affect activation are phonological similarity, active use of the languages, task demands or input/output modality (see also de Bot 2004).

Singleton (2003) analyzes the separation and integration of the operations of the mental lexicon and concludes that there is a 'high degree of connectivity and dynamic interplay between the L1 mental lexicon and additional mental lexicons' (Singleton 2003: 169). This connectivity is clearly seen in studies on cross-linguistic influence. These studies have tried to identify the conditions in which multilingual speakers transfer terms from the other languages they know. Speakers tend to transfer words from languages that are typologically closer (for example from French to Spanish or from German to Dutch rather than from Japanese to French). However, as Ringbom (2007) points out, there is a large number of factors that can determine cross-linguistic influence from the first language or from other languages known by the speaker. In fact, the level of proficiency in the source and the target language, the level of formality, the order of acquisition of the language or the specific context of the interaction can influence the amount of transfer. Other researchers refer to the 'foreign language effect', that is, the use of languages other than the L1 as a source language of cross-linguistic influence (see, for example, De Angelis 2007).

Multilingualism and age

The effect of age on second language acquisition is a controversial area that has received much attention in SLA research (Singleton and Ryan 2004; DeKeyser and Larson-Hall 2005). Research studies conducted in naturalistic language environments tend to support the idea of 'the earlier the better', meaning that an earlier contact with the target languages results in higher levels of proficiency in the language. The study of the age factor in multilingualism is a complex issue because there is a great diversity in the process of acquiring several languages and a large number of individual differences are involved. The distinction between naturalistic and more formal contexts of language acquisition is one of these factors, and most research supporting sensitive periods has taken place in naturalistic contexts where extensive natural exposure to the language is combined with formal learning. Research studies conducted in formal contexts of acquisition in which exposure to the target languages is limited to the classroom have reported advantages on the part of older learners (Muñoz 2006; Cenoz 2009).

Neuroimaging techniques are giving the opportunity to analyze different aspects of bilingual processing with more accuracy and from different angles (see also Ahlsén, this volume). However as Paradis (2005) points out, it is necessary to be cautious when interpreting the results of neuroimaging studies because in many cases they are not theoretically grounded. It is also important to take into account that the results of psycholinguistic studies using very limited stimuli do not necessarily reflect the use of languages in real communication.

Multilingualism, language planning and education

Language planning is understood as a type of intervention into the corpus of a language, its status and acquisition (see also Wee, this volume). The institution of education can be regarded as a crucial tool of language planning (see also Gogolin, this volume). Schools can have an important influence on language learning but also on the status and values associated with different languages. In fact, schools have been regarded as spaces where 'specific languages and specific linguistic practices come to be inculcated with legitimacy and authority' (Martin-Jones 2007: 172).

Some European minority languages such as Basque, Catalan or Welsh are good examples of the effect of language planning (Cenoz and Gorter 2008a). These languages were neglected, or even forbidden to be used in educational contexts, but over the last decades rather elaborate systems have developed for the teaching of the minority language from the earliest stages of education until university and adult education. Nowadays, not only home or first language (L1) speakers of a minority language have it as the language of instruction but also speakers of the majority language learn through the minority language at school. In some schools, such as those in the Basque Country, there is a shift from bilingualism to multilingualism and English is being increasingly used as an additional language of instruction. Nowadays, Basque, the minority language, is the main language of instruction and English is an additional language of instruction in some schools.

Multilingual education not only implies the teaching of two or more languages but also that education aims at multilingualism and multiliteracy as an outcome. There are different types of bilingual and multilingual education depending not only on school variables (teachers, curriculum, etc.) but also on the sociolinguistic context in which the schools are located and the language policy of that society (see Cenoz 2009). The values associated with different languages and their prestige in society is closely related to multilingual education. For example, the strong language policy to protect Basque in the Basque Country is not only aimed at schools but also at the use of Basque in government agencies, town halls, private companies or in the linguistic landscape. This situation is completely different from that of immigrant languages in the Basque Country or elsewhere. Immigrant languages such as Turkish, Punjabi or Ukranian, are usually excluded from the school curriculum in Western Europe and schoolchildren can only attend complementary schools or extra classes outside the school timetable (Blackledge and Creese 2009).

Multilingual identities and multilingual practices

Some trends in the study of multilingualism suggest a more sociolinguistic perspective. This perspective can be also considered 'ecological' because it analyzes languages in their context as related to each other, to speakers and to the social structures of society (Creese and Martin 2003; Blackledge 2008). This approach, based on anthropological, social and cultural studies, critically examines communicative practices and explains them as related to the ideologies developed in a specific social, political and historical context. Some of these studies have taken place in education; they have analyzed discourse practices critically and identified the socio-political implications of the use of different languages in the curriculum and in the school context (see, for example, Heller and Martin-Jones 2001; Creese and Martin 2003; Heller 2007). As Lo Bianco (2008: 47) points out, multilingual education is linked to the socio-political context in which it is located. Research in social psychology has traditionally associated language practices in education and other contexts with identity, but this fixed relationship has been challenged. A poststructuralist view considers identities as multiple and dynamic and subject to negotiation (see Pavlenko and Blackledge 2004; Norton, this volume).

New trends in the study of multilingualism

In this section we will focus on two new areas of development in research on multilingualism: the acquisition of additional languages and the linguistic landscape.

The acquisition of additional languages

One area of recent development in research is the acquisition and use of three or more languages. Even though the acquisition of additional languages is common in many parts of the world, its study has received very little attention until recently. There is now a growing body of research into multilingualism and the acquisition of additional languages which is reflected in a number of recent publications in this area, a specific journal (the *International Journal of Multilingualism*), international conferences and an increasing number of publications on the topic. This research responds to the need to identify the specific characteristics that distinguish third language acquisition and multilingualism from second language acquisition and bilingualism, and covers psycholinguistic, sociolinguistic and educational issues.

The early acquisition of three languages from birth is not common but can sometimes be found when parents are native speakers of different languages that are not spoken in the community and they use the strategy of one parent–one language. The child is exposed to a third language by other carers. Studies on early trilingualism have focused on code-mixing and code-switching (see, for example, Maneva 2004), language choice and interactional strategies (see, for example, Quay 2008). Some studies on early trilingualism point in the direction that multilingual children follow the same route in language acquisition as monolingual children. For example, Barnes (2006) analyzed the questions produced in English by a trilingual child (Basque, English and Spanish) and observed that the acquisition of different types of questions was similar to the process described in the case of monolingual and bilingual children.

Other situations involving the acquisition of three or more languages are linked to foreign language learning at school and multilingual education. As we have already seen, research has focused mainly on psycholinguistic aspects of language processing when more than two languages are involved. Research on the acquisition of additional languages has been influenced by proposals that bilinguals and multilinguals should be regarded as different from monolinguals and that their whole linguistic repertoire should be taken into account (Cook 1995; Grosjean 2008). In fact, multilinguals seldom have balanced proficiency in the different languages because language acquisition and language use are dynamic processes and they depend on many factors including language use. Some theoretical proposals on the acquisition of several languages such as the 'Dynamic Model of Multilingualism' (Herdina and Jessner 2002) adopt a holistic view and emphasize the fact that multilingual competence is dynamic rather than static. A more sociolinguistic and educational approach that can benefit from this holistic approach to multilingualism focuses on literacy practices in the different languages, both in school settings and outside of school (see also Martin-Jones 2007).

Linguistic landscape

The study of the linguistic landscape in its own right is a relatively recent development in applied linguistics and sociolinguistics, although there is a long tradition of the analysis of the meaning of signs in semiotics. The study of the linguistic landscape, also called the 'multilingual cityscape' can be a way to increase our understanding of different aspects of multilingualism (Gorter 2006). The linguistic landscape refers to signs of different types (billboards, road signs, commercial signs, graffiti, etc.) that can be found in the public space.

Studies on the linguistic landscape conducted in various settings show the cultural and linguistic diversity in the use of different languages. For example, Ben Rafael *et al*. (2006) compared Jewish, Palestinian Israeli and non-Israeli Palestinian settings in Israel. They reported on the use of Hebrew, Arabic and English in Jewish and non-Israeli Palestinian locations. The use of different languages on the signs is also reported in other studies conducted in Bangkok (Huebner 2006, 2009), Tokyo (Backhaus 2007) and Taiwan (Curtin 2009). Apart from multilingualism, another trend observed in these studies is the spread of English in the linguistic landscape. In some cases, the use of English in commercial signs could be interpreted as informative when it is aimed at foreign visitors in non-English speaking countries, but at the same time it is clear that English has a strong symbolic function for the local population. The use of English has been associated with values such as international orientation, future orientation, success, sophistication or fun orientation (see Piller 2001).

The linguistic landscape is closely linked to language policy. Cenoz and Gorter (2006) compared two European bilingual cities, Donostia-San Sebastian in the Basque Country (Spain) and Ljouwert-Leeuwarden in Friesland (the Netherlands). The official languages are Basque and Spanish in the Basque Country and Frisian and Dutch in Friesland. Basque and Frisian are minority languages but the institutional support for Basque is much stronger than for Frisian and the linguistic landscape is one of the areas where Basque is promoted to a larger extent than Frisian. Cenoz and Gorter (2006) found that this policy had an important impact on the linguistic landscape, and Basque was a common language in the linguistic landscape while Frisian was exceptional. In both cities, English was also present in many commercial signs.

The study of the linguistic landscape can contribute to the study of multilingualism in different ways. Language signs are indicators of the languages used in a specific setting and their status, and they can also be an additional source of input in language acquisition (Cenoz and Gorter 2008b). Another future possibility of research is the analysis of the linguistic landscape inside schools as related to language teaching and school multilingualism.

Multimodality in the study of multilingualism

In the previous sections we have focused on some of the main trends in research on multilingualism from a psycholinguistic and sociolinguistic perspective and some of the new trends in the study of multilingualism. Research on multilingualism has gone in many other directions in recent years. An interesting direction is the study of multilingualism and emotions (see, for example, Pavlenko and Dewaele 2004; Pavlenko 2005, 2006) or more insider 'emic' perspectives in the study of multilingualism (see, for example, Todeva and Cenoz 2009).

Another development has evolved in educational research in the study of literacy as social practice. The term 'multiliteracies' was coined by the New London Group (1996) to refer to cultural and linguistic diversity and to the use of new technologies and visual texts in school and out-of-school literacies. A basic characteristic of this approach to literacy is multimodality (see also Cope and Kalantzis 2000; Kalantzis and Cope 2008; van Leeuwen, this volume). The development of multimedia technology, communication channels and media has encouraged multimodal literacy which is based on the affordances provided by gesture, sound, visuals and other semiotic symbols including language but not limited to language. For example, texts used in chatting or texting messages include different colours, different types of fonts and icons next to the actual language (see also Crystal 2008). In many cases, these texts are not linear because they include Internet links that the reader is supposed to click so as to navigate between different screens. The traditional borders between speech and writing, and between languages, are also blurred. Multilinguals usually establish soft boundaries between languages in oral communication because they can use their languages as a resource, but nowadays that practice is very extensive and has developed even further in written languages. In a multimodal approach to literacy, full communication is not possible through the means of language only. Shohamy (2006: 172) considers that multilingual competence is derived from hybrids of different languages and the use of multiple codes, including not only printed texts but also visuals and a variety of symbols. This new form of communication has created new literacy practices that are dynamic and multilingual (Kress and Street 2006; Magnan 2008).

Summary

The study of multilingualism both from an individual and social perspective has blossomed in recent years. Research on the influence of bilingualism on the cognitive development and the acquisition of additional languages shows the benefits of being bilingual and multilingual. From a cognitive perspective, new technical developments have contributed to the study of language processing in multilinguals, particularly at the lexical level. From a social perspective, the sociopolitical implications of multilingualism both in educational settings and in society in general have been analyzed. Nowadays, there are new trends in the study of multilingualism such as the acquisition of additional languages, the linguistic landscape and multimodality.

Related topics

bilingual education; identity; language and aging; language policy and planning; lexis; multimodalility; SLA

Further reading

Aronin, L. and Hufeisen, B. (eds) (2009) *The Exploration of Multilingualism*, Amsterdam: John Benjamins. (This volume focuses on the specific characteristics of third language acquisition and multilingualism. The perspective is mainly psycholinguistic.)
Baker, C. (2006) *Foundations of Bilingual Education and Bilingualism*, 4th edn, Clevedon: Multilingual Matters. (This volume is probably the most comprehensive overview of the characteristics, types and outcomes of bilingualism and bilingual education.)
Cenoz, J. (2009) *Towards Multilingual Education*, Bristol: Multilingual Matters. (This volume discusses multilingual education in the Basque Country from an international perspective and covers issues such as the different types of multilingual schools, the age factor, multilingual identities and the outcomes of multilingualism.)

Gorter, D. (ed.) (2006) *Linguistic Landscape: A New Approach to Multilingualism*, Bristol: Multilingual Matters (also published in *International Journal of Multilingualism*, 3(1)). (This is a collection of articles that looks at the use of languages in signs in the public space and shows the spread of English and multilingualism and the importance of language policy in the promotion of minority languages.)

Li, Wei and Moyer, M. (eds) (2008) *Blackwell Guide to Research Methods in Bilingualism and Multilingualism*, London: Blackwell. (This edited volume addresses methodological issues in the study of bilingualism and multilingualism. It discusses research topics, key concepts and approaches, and the methods and tools for collecting and analysing data.)

References

Auer, P. and Li, W. (2007) 'Introduction: multilingualism as a problem? Monolingualism as a problem?', in P. Auer and W. Li (eds) *Handbook of Multilingualism and Multilingual Communication*, Berlin: Mouton de Gruyter.

Backhaus, P. (2007) *Linguistic Landscapes. A Comparative Study of Urban Multilingualism in Tokyo*, Clevedon: Multilingual Matters.

Baker, C. (2006) *Foundations of Bilingual Education and Bilingualism*, Clevedon: Multilingual Matters.

Barnes, J. (2006) *Early Trilingualism: A Focus on Questions*, Clevedon: Multilingual Matters.

Ben-Rafael, E., Shohamy, E., Amara, M. H. and Trumper-Hecht, N. (2006) 'Linguistic landscape as symbolic construction of the public space: the case of Israel', *International Journal of Multilingualism* 3(1): 7–30.

Bialystok, E. (2001) *Bilingualism in Development: Language, Literacy and Cognition*, Cambridge: Cambridge University Press.

Bialystok, E., Craik, F. I., Klein, R. and Viswanathan, M. (2004) 'Bilingualism, aging, and cognitive control: evidence from the Simon task', *Psychology and Aging* 19(2): 290–303.

Blackledge, A. J. (2008) 'Language ecology and language ideology', in A. Creese and P. Martin (eds) *The Encyclopedia of Language and Education*, vol. 9: *Ecology of Language*, Berlin and New York: Springer.

Blackledge, A. and Creese, A. (2009) *Multilingualism: A Critical Perspective*, London: Continuum.

Bloomfield, L. (1933) *Language*, New York: Holt.

Cenoz, J. (2009) *Towards Multilingual Education*, Bristol: Multilingual Matters.

Cenoz, J. and Gorter, D. (2006) 'Linguistic landscape and minority languages', *International Journal of Multilingualism* 3: 67–80.

——(eds) (2008a) 'Applied linguistics and the use of minority languages in education', Association Internationale de Linguistique Appliquée, special issue, *AILA Review* 21.

——(2008b) 'The linguistic landscape as an additional source of input in second language acquisition', *International Review of Applied Linguistics* 46: 267–87.

Creese, A. and Martin, P. (eds) (2003) *Multilingual Classroom Ecologies*, Clevedon: Multilingual Matters.

Cook, V. (1995) 'Multi-competence and the learning of many languages', *Language, Culture and Curriculum* 8: 93–8.

Cope, B. and Kalantzis, M. (eds) (2000) *Multiliteracies: Literacy Learning and the Design of Social Futures*, London and New York: Routledge.

Crystal, D. (2008) *Txtng*, Oxford: Oxford University Press.

Curtin, M. L. (2009) 'Languages on display: indexical signs, identities and the linguistic landscape in Taipei', in E. Shohamy and D. Gorter (eds) *Linguistic Landscape: Expanding the Scenery*, New York: Routledge.

De Angelis, G. (2007) *Third or Additional Language Learning*, Clevedon: Multilingual Matters.

de Bot, K. (2004) 'The multilingual lexicon: modelling selection and control', *International Journal of Multilingualism* 1(1): 17–32.

DeKeyser, R. and Larson-Hall, J. (2005) 'What does the critical period really mean?', in J. F. Kroll and A. M. B. de Groot (eds) *Handbook of Bilingualism: Psycholinguistic Approaches*, Oxford: Oxford University Press.

Dijkstra, A. (2007) 'The multilingual lexicon', in G. Gaskell (ed.) *Handbook of Psycholinguistics*, Oxford: Oxford University Press.

Edwards, J. (2004) 'Foundations of bilingualism', in T. K. Bhatia and W. C. Ritchie (eds) *Handbook of Bilingualism*, London: Blackwell.

European Commission (2007) 'Final report. High level group on multilingualism'. Available at: http://ec.europa.eu/education/policies/lang/doc/multireport_en.pdf

Franceschini, R. (2009) 'The genesis and development of research in multilingualism: perspectives for future research', in L. Aronin and B. Hufeisen (eds) *The Exploration of Multilingualism*, Amsterdam: John Benjamins.

Gorter, D. (ed.) (2006) 'Linguistic landscape: a new approach to multilingualism', special issue, *International Journal of Multilingualism* 3(1).

Grosjean, F. (2008) *Studying Bilinguals*, Oxford: Oxford University Press.

Heller, M. (ed.) (2007) *Bilingualism: A Social Approach*, Basingstoke: Palgrave Macmillan.

Heller, M. and Martin-Jones, M. (eds) (2001) *Voices of Authority: Education and Linguistic Difference*, Westport, CT: Ablex.

Herdina, P. and Jessner, U. (2002) *A Dynamic Model of Multilingualism*, Clevedon: Multilingual Matters.

Huebner, T. (2006) 'Bangkok's linguistic landscapes: environmental print, code mixing, and language change', *International Journal of Multilingualism* 3: 31–51.

——(2009) 'Framework for the linguistic analysis of linguistic landscapes', in E. Shohamy and D. Gorter (eds) *Linguistic Landscape: Expanding the Scenery*, New York: Routledge.

Jessner, U. (2006) *Linguistic Awareness in Multilinguals: English as a Third Language*, Edinburgh: Edinburgh University Press.

Kalantzis, M. and Cope, B. (2008) 'Language education and multiliteracies', in S. May and N. H. Hornberger (eds) *Encyclopedia of Language and Education*, vol 1: *Language Policy and Political Issues in Education*, New York: Springer.

Kress, G. and Street, B. (2006) 'Multi-modality and literacy practices', in K. Pahl and J. Rowsell (eds) *Travel Notes from the New Literacy Studies: Instances of Practice*, Clevedon: Multilingual Matters.

Li, W. (2008) 'Research perspectives on bilingualism and bilingual education', in A. King and N. H. Hornberger (eds) *Encyclopedia of Language and Education*, vol. 10: *Research Methods in Language and Education*, Berlin: Springer.

Lo Bianco, J. (2008) 'Bilingual education and socio-political issues', in J. Cummins and N. H. Hornberger (eds) *Encyclopedia of Language and Education*, vol. 5: *Bilingual Education*, New York: Springer.

Magnan, S. (ed.) (2008) *Mediating on-line Discourse*, Amsterdam: John Benjamins.

Maneva, B. (2004) 'Maman, je suis polyglotte!: a case study of multilingual language acquisition from 0–5 years', *International Journal of Multilingualism* 1: 109–22.

Martin-Jones, M. (2007) 'Bilingualism, education and the regulation of access to language resources', in M. Heller (ed.) *Bilingualism: A Social Approach*, Basingstoke: Palgrave Macmillan.

Muñoz, C. (ed.) (2006) *Age and the Rate of Foreign Language Learning*, Clevedon: Multilingual Matters.

New London Group (1996) 'A pedagogy of multiliteracies: designing social futures', *Harvard Educational Review* 66: 60–92.

Paradis, M. (2005) 'Introduction to part IV: aspects and implications of bilingualism', in J. F. Kroll and A. M. B. de Groot (eds) *Handbook of Bilingualism: Psycholinguistic Approaches*, Oxford: Oxford University Press.

Pavlenko, A. (2005) *Emotions and Multilingualism*, Cambridge: Cambridge University Press.

Pavlenko, A. (ed.) (2006) *Bilingual Minds: Emotional Experience, Expression, and Representation*, Clevedon: Multilingual Matters.

Pavlenko, A. and Blackledge, A. (2004) 'New theoretical approaches to the study of negotiation of identities in multilingual contexts', in A. Pavlenko and A. Blackledge (eds) *Negotiation of Identities in Multilingual Contexts*, Clevedon: Multilingual Matters.

Pavlenko, A. and Dewaele, J. M. (eds) (2004) 'Languages and emotions: a crosslinguistic perspective', special issue, *Journal of Multilingual and Multicultural Development* 25(2–3).

Peal, E. and Lambert, W. E. (1962) 'The relationship of bilingualism to intelligence', *Psychological Monographs* 76: 1–23.

Piller, I. (2001) 'Identity constructions in multilingual advertising', *Language in Society* 30: 153–86.

Quay, S. (2008) 'Dinner conversations with a trilingual two-year-old: language socialization in a multilingual context', *First Language* 28: 5–33.

Ringbom, H. (2007) *Cross-linguistic Similarity in Foreign Language Learning*, Clevedon: Multilingual Matters.

Saville-Troike, M. (2006) *Introducing Second Language Acquisition*, Cambridge: Cambridge University Press.

Shohamy, E. (2006) 'Imagined multilingual schools: how come we don't deliver?', in O. García, T. Skutnabb-Kangas and M. E. Torres-Guzmán (eds) *Imagining Multilingual Schools: Language in Education and Globalization*, Clevedon: Multilingual Matters.

Singleton, D. (2003) 'Perspectives on the multilingual lexicon: a critical synthesis', in J. Cenoz, U. Jessner and B. Hufeisen, *The Multilingual Lexicon*, Dordrecht: Kluwer Academic, pp. 167–76.

Singleton, D. and Ryan, L. (2004) *Language Acquisition: The Age Factor*, Clevedon: Multilingual Matters.

Skutnabb-Kangas, T. and McCarthy, T. L. (2008) 'Key concepts in bilingual education: ideological, historical, epistemological, and empirical foundations', in J. Cummins and N. H. Hornberger (eds) *Encyclopedia of Language and Education*, vol. 5: *Bilingual Education*, Berlin: Springer.

ten Thije, J. D. and Zeevaert, L. (eds) (2007) *Receptive Multilingualism*, Amsterdam: John Benjamins.

Todeva, E. and Cenoz, J. (eds) (2009) *The Multiple Realities of Multilingualism*, Berlin: Mouton de Gruyter.

van Heuven, W. J. B., Schriefers, H., Dijkstra, T. and Hagoort, P. (2008) 'Language conflict in the bilingual brain', *Cerebral Cortex* 18: 2706–16.

Zeevaert, L. and ten Thije, J. D. (2007) 'Introduction', in J. D. ten Thije and L. Zeevaert (eds) *Receptive Multilingualism*, Amsterdam: John Benjamins.

29

Language and migration

Mike Baynham

Introduction

> Migrations are acts of settlement and of habitation in a world where the divide between origin and destination is no longer a divide of Otherness, a world in which borders no longer separate human realities.
>
> *(Sassen 1999: 6)*

The multilingual landscapes of the twenty-first century are a product of continuing transnational and translocal mobility and exchange of people, information and products across physical and virtual boundaries. Knowledge of local and global/international languages is necessary in order to gain access to a society of information, for the exchange of material goods and to be able to communicate with the people in our immediate social space and beyond (Castells 2000). Languages themselves migrate or are re-made through migration. Within this context of linguistic hyper- or super-diversity (Vertovec 2006), language plays a key role in the constitution of public and private institutions, but is also crucial for the actors who come into contact with these institutions (Heller 2003) wishing thereby to gain access to material and symbolic resources.

In the context of these multilingual landscapes of mobility and exchange, both transnational and translocal, public discourses, particularly in the media, increasingly view migration through the lenses of nationalist and racist rhetoric (Reisigl and Wodak 2001), creating atmospheres of social panic in which immigrants and refugees are seen as threatening the stable borders of national identities. Applied linguistic research aims to increase our understanding of the linguistic dimensions of migration and the subtle ways that language ideologies and practices contribute to social processes of 'othering' and exclusion in crucial institutional contexts. This applied linguistic research investigates such processes 'from the inside and from the perspective of language', while remaining attuned to large-scale social processes (political, policy-oriented and institutional), providing analyses capable of offering an 'emic' perspective and of illustrating the subjective construction of these movements of human beings, rather than their objectivist 'othering' in nationalist or racist mainstream discourses.

Applied linguistic research into language and migration is thus based on two simple, inter-related, but far-reaching propositions: (i) that for migrants in a new society, access to the crucial material and symbolic resources that enable survival and integration is mediated through repeated face-to-face interactions with institutions; (ii) that these face-to-face interactions are significantly shaped by changing policy environments and institutional arrangements as well as sometimes volatile national political and media attitudes towards diversity, integration, citizenship, and accompanying ideologies concerning who should have access to what resources and how. These face-to-face institutional encounters are typically realized through different sets of language practices: monolingual where migrants struggle with using the majority language; multilingual and mediated by formal or informal interpreting involving code-switching and mixes of various languages; and lingua franca where both sides use a lingua franca (frequently English). It is these face-to-face encounters, typically characterized by asymmetries of power between participants, which are the empirical focus of the applied linguistic study of language and migration, along with representations of them in media, political and popular discourses.

An applied linguistic research agenda on language and migration seeks to understand how language practices in domains such as health, education, the law and work are shaped both by the dynamics of face-to-face encounters and the constraints of the political, policy and institutional environment: what linguistic factors enable and constrain access for migrants to health services and education, what languages and forms of communication get used, when, why and where, and what are the consequences for the migrant? Institutions can organize and deploy multilingual resources by using different modes (oral and written modes) and modalities (visual, with mediators or interpreters, using written language). Not all such multilingual practice is the same, and the way it gets organized (or not) in a given institution has consequences for migrants seeking access to services and resources.

Development of the field of language and migration studies

Language and migration research in applied linguistics has been influenced by understandings of migration in terms of the dynamics of globalization and the new economy. Emerging sociolinguistic agendas, rather than focusing on the sociolinguistic description of settled communities, a concept memorably critiqued by Mary Louise Pratt (Pratt 1987: 56), have developed in the context of globalization a sociolinguistics of movement and flows and also what Pratt terms 'contact zones':

> Imagine, then, a linguistics that decentred community, that placed as its centre the operation of language *across* lines of social differentiation, a linguistics that focused on modes and zones of contact between dominant and dominated groups, between persons of different and multiple identities, speakers of different languages, that focused on how such speakers constitute each other relationally and in difference, how they enact differences in language.
>
> *(Pratt 1987: 60)*

Of course, the notion of migration and movement has always been associated, even if inexplicitly, with the study of the sociolinguistics of settled communities: language varieties are formed historically by population movements and flows. So language and migration studies involve a re-centring of population movement and flows in a globalized world as a key theme in sociolinguistics. This is rather analogous to earlier insights which established bi/multilingualism rather than monolingualism as the default sociolinguistic reality. Under-pinning the emergence of multilingual environments, however, are processes of population movement, acutely so in the context of the accelerating time-space compression which theorists such as Giddens (1990) and Harvey (1989) have identified as characteristic of mod-ernity and late modernity. So in one sense the renewed focus on movement and flow in socio-linguistics is a re-introduction of the diachronic dimension of time and history into the synchronic linguistic description. (For a fuller discussion of these issues see Collins *et al.* 2009.)

Another influence on language and migration studies has been work on institutional dis-course (Sarangi and Slembrouck 1996). Migration trajectories have been characterized as repeated series of institutional encounters, mediated through talk, which can gatekeep access to resources, forming powerful means of exclusion and othering. Such research points to deeply embedded inequalities in power/knowledge, played out in daily encounters with tea-chers, social workers, migration lawyers and others. The work of Maryns (2005, 2006) on the asylum hearing is a case in point of such research, as is work on legal processes and migration, for example Haviland (2003) on the impact of language ideologies on court cases involving Latino migrant workers, and the work of Trinch (2003) on Latina narratives in the disclosure of domestic violence.

As suggested above, the default sociolinguistic context for language and migration studies is multilingualism, even in contexts where powerful social forces equate migration with giving up a language in favour of the language of the country of settlement. This is not of course to deny the significance of such linguistic ideological issues, currently brought to the fore in debates around citizenship (cf. Milani 2008; Cooke and Simpson 2009). Indeed, as we shall see below, another applied linguistic strength, the analysis of media and policy discourse, can be brought to bear to investigate the discursive constructions of migration in the media and public policy.

So if the influences in language and migration studies have been largely sociolinguistic, how can we characterize the applied linguistic agendas that have emerged? Many of them, such as language learning and teaching, interpreting and translation, doctor-patient encounters, job interviews and other institutional encounters, are not exactly new in themselves, while emer-ging themes, such as the impact of new policies on citizenship and exclusion, also claim the attention of applied linguists (Milani 2006, 2008; Cooke and Simpson 2009). What is new is the bringing together of these disparate topics into a coherent theme, that permits their interlinking and articulation as part of general processes of migration and population flow.

To give one example: classroom-based language learning has been a major topic of applied linguistics. Underpinning all language learning is an assumption of actual or potential mobi-lity, particularly so in migration contexts. Yet classroom-based research is curiously insulated from the other contexts and domains of social life. Researchers gain ever deeper insights into what constitutes classroom discourse and language learning, while ignoring for analytical purposes the location of the classroom in an educational institution, an educational institution in a state or national education system, the national education system and its policies in the globalized markets of knowledge and resources. Conventional categories of applied linguistic research have the effect of dislocating research efforts. Another example: Schumann's classic study of the migrant worker Alberto (1978) focuses on the emergence of a restricted, 'pidginized' variety of English and correlates this with various social and motivational factors. Yet what do we know about the other domains and arenas of Alberto's life as a migrant in California: what is the linguistic economy of his workplace, what are his preferred ways of socializing, how does he maintain contact with friends and family in his home country, are there significant others who translate and mediate for him on occasions? Schumann shines a bright analytical light on structural linguistic issues, leaving these other aspects of language use in context in the penumbra. Other studies at about this time, such as the pan-European Ecology of Adult Language Acquisition project, attempted to address this, but instead of gathering data systematically across a range of contexts, relied mainly on interview and role play (Perdue 1993). This was perhaps in large part to do with the technical limitations of the time on recording equipment. The present day researcher has many more sophisticated and less obtrusive options for recording interaction.

Language and migration provides a powerful integrating theme for applied linguistic research, bringing together fields of research (such as language teaching, interpreting and translation, doctor-patient encounters, job interviews) which have typically been treated separately and developed in a piecemeal way. In this chapter, having identified such a framework for applied linguistic research into language and migration, I go on to present some examples of such research and identify directions for future work.

A framework for applied linguistic research into language and migration

As has been suggested above, this is an emergent field of inquiry, so there is room for some programmatic statement of scope. An applied linguistic research agenda on language and migration might therefore have the following dimensions:

- investigations of the linguistic ideological influences on migration policies at global, regional (i.e. the EU), national and local levels;
- investigations of the discursive construction of migration processes and migrants in the media and in art production;
- mapping the linguistic aspects of migration trajectories and the opening up of diasporic spaces;
- analysis of the dominant and popular discourses on migration as well as the investigation of migration processes 'from the inside', for example through narrative and life history;
- analysis of key 'sites of institutional encounter', related to work, education, social welfare, health, law, both ethnographically and using tools for the analysis of spoken language interaction (including mediated interaction of different kinds), and document analysis drawn from linguistic ethnography, CA, CDA and literacy studies;
- concern with the social processes leading through categorization to exclusion and the operation of power in institutional encounters;
- concern with the role of new media in reshaping diasporic space through the compression of time-space.

While retaining its linguistic focus, such a research agenda would be alert to the work on migration in fields such as sociology, anthropology, cultural geography and political economy as theoretical sources for the description of large-scale phenomena that shape and influence migration flows and diasporic settlements. To be sure, specific research projects would focus on more than one of these dimensions: it would be hard to consider language educational issues without bringing in larger scale concerns such as national policy and the global linguistic economy. The following section reviews research that is ongoing in relation to these themes, pointing out directions for future work.

Public policy and language ideology

Language issues, particularly those concerning migration, have rarely had an explicit place in public policy at national level, with notable exceptions such as Australia (cf. Lo Bianco and

Wickert 2001), though moments of perceived crisis may trigger this focus on language. Post-war assimilationism gave way in the 1970s and 1980s to policies which emphasized to varying degrees cultural and linguistic diversity and inclusion. The 1987 Australian National Policy on Languages, for example, emphasized both 'English for all', support for linguistic diversity and the provision of services such as interpreting and translation in the languages of migration (for a historical overview of this aspect see Ozolins 2001). However, progressive refocusing of national policy in the neo-liberal political context in Australia (as elsewhere) through the 1990s shifted the emphasis away from linguistic diversity onto the mobilization of human capital through literacy and the acquisition of fluency in English at the expense of diasporic linguistic diversity, apart from those languages which could be linked with economic benefits.

There has been, however, in the last decade a profound shift away from policies informed primarily by diversity and inclusion to those which highlight citizenship and settlement in the context of social cohesion. As Cooke and Simpson point out, referring to the UK:

> The relationship between national security, immigration, integration, social cohesion and language is becoming progressively tighter. In most government reports and in very much political and media discourse, a great deal of attention is paid to English as the greatest shared resource and the need for everyone to speak it to integrate fully in their communities.
>
> *(Cooke and Simpson 2008: 10)*

Arising out of this has been a strand of research which examines the linguistic ideologies which inform policies such as language testing for citizenship (Piller 2001; Hansen-Thomas 2007; Blackledge 2008; Milani 2008). Piller looks at the interrelationship of ideologies of national and linguistic identity in Germany and their impact on ideologies of citizenship (Piller 2001: 259) using the case of the introduction of language tests for naturalization in the early 2000s. Her arguments show how at policy level the linguistic issues posed by migration and diaspora challenge basic political and moral assumptions of the nation-state. Milani (2008) similarly addresses the impact of language testing on the citizenship process in Sweden, examining debates around the proposed introduction of language testing for citizenship, showing how arguments are mobilized that language testing is a way of diminishing dis-crimination, while implicitly, Milani argues, testing contributes to social differentiation and exclusion. In relation to the UK, Blackledge (2008) shows how debates on language testing and citizenship create discursive links between speaking 'other' languages and lack of fluency in English and threats to social stability, underachievement in school, ghettoization: threats, as Rings and Ife put it, 'to democracy, citizenship and nationhood' (Rings and Ife 2008: 9).

This strand of research draws on the notion of linguistic or language ideology (Schieffelin *et al.* 1998; Blommaert 1999; Irvine and Gal 2000) using tools of linguistic analysis to uncover the web of explicit and tacit assumptions about the role of language in the construction and maintenance of the social order. Anxieties concerning migration are, it seems, a special case which triggers explicit formulation of language-related policy, making explicit what have pre-viously perhaps been tacit though widely held assumptions linking national language(s) with the nation-state.

Language, migration and media discourse

Another strand of the language and migration research agenda concerns the discursive con-struction of representations of migrants and migration processes in the media and other forms of public discourse. An early example of this approach is van Dijk (1991). The language ideology work on citizenship described above also draws on media texts as one of its data sources. Typical research approaches to media texts employ critical discourse analysis (CDA), as for example van Leeuwen and Wodak (1999), Wodak and van Dijk (2000), and Reisigl and Wodak (2001), although more recently combinations of CDA and corpus linguistics have been advocated (for example, Baker *et al.* 2008; Gabrielatos and Baker 2008). In a relatively large-scale study (reported in Baker *et al.* 2008; KhosraviNik 2008), media texts are sampled from periods when issues of migration and asylum reached a high profile in the media (similar perhaps to the trigger moments of public anxiety discussed above), for example the NATO invasion of Kosovo in 1999; September 2001, with the 9/11 terrorist attacks, but also attention on asylum seekers in the UK and 'boat people' in Australia.

The researchers (Baker *et al.* 2008: 295) propose a sequence of research interventions combining CDA and corpus linguistics. Corpus linguistics is able to track the distribution of lexical items and collocates (i.e. 'looming' + 'influx' below) in such media texts as, for example:

> BRITAIN was warned last night it faces a massive benefits bill to pay for the looming influx of immigrants, including gypsies, from eastern Europe.
>
> *(Daily Express, 9 February 2004, cited in Baker et al. 2008: 286)*

CDA, with its focus on text structure, is able to track the discursive patterns of othering that occur in reporting of immigrants and asylum seekers, through identifying textual and inter-textual chains of linguistic strategies such as referring and predicating, argumentation, discourse representation, intensification/mitigation and linking the micro textual detail (which can tell us that there is something negative about the collocation of 'looming' + 'influx') to ideological macro structures of exclusion.

Insider perspectives on migration (migration narratives)

While language ideology and discourse analysis have been used to investigate the representations of migrants and migration in public discourse, narrative and live history methods have been used to investigate 'from the inside' the discursive construction of the experience of migration (de Fina 2003; Baynham and de Fina 2005; McElhinny *et al.* 2007). Themes in this research include issues of migration and space-time orientation in narrative (cf. Baynham 2003; de Fina 2003) and identity (cf. chapters in de Fina *et al.* 2006), migration and agency (Baynham 2005; Relaño Pastor and de Fina 2005). The Filipino Canadian Life History Group at the University of Toronto (McElhinny *et al.* 2007), for example, investigates the life stories of Filipino professionals settled in Canada, uncovering issues of agency and life choice, constructions of fate and fatality in migration narratives. Relaño Pastor and de Fina (2005) investigate the narratives of Mexican migrant women in California, focusing on narratives of engagement with school, healthcare and work, place, displacement and identity. Their research illustrates the interaction between the different dimensions of the language and migration research agenda identified above: language ideology and policy is clearly seen as constructing the life experiences of the narrators, as are their encounters with the institutions of work, schooling and healthcare; constructions of migration 'from the inside' are overwhelmingly narratives of encounters with the institutions of the 'receiving' country. The sharpness of these encounters is best demonstrated in the narratives that make up the institutional encounters themselves, as Maryns (2005, 2006) demonstrates.

Migration doesn't always involve migration across national borders, as the research of McCormick (2005) on forced migration due to the internal restrictions on black people in apartheid South Africa demonstrates. Here, forcible segregation pulled apart and relocated existing communities in ways that are painfully remembered in the oral history interviews that documented this displacement. The linguistic consequences of internal migration in China is a theme in Dong and Blommaert (2009). Liebscher and Dailey-O'Cain (2005) document through narrative the West–East migration movements in the post-1989 reunified Germany. Narratives also document migratory mobility in geopolitical units larger than the nation-state, such as in the expanded European Union, in the work of Galasinska and Koslowska (2009). Changes to EU legislation, leading to increased internal mobility, have emphasized narratives of short-term migration and return. Meinhof (2009) draws on life history narrative to examine the flows and movements in the migration patterns of Malagasy musicians both within Madagascar and between Madagascar and Europe.

Key themes in this research are the discursive construction of the complex orientations and reorientations that are involved in migration processes, the spatial and temporal dislocations involved. These narratives can be of disempowerment but also of agency and empowerment, of finding a voice as well as losing it. We see clearly the ways that large-scale political and social phenomena shape the interactional worlds of the migrant narrators, of the significance of institutional encounters in opening up or closing down opportunities, which will be addressed in more detail in later sections. While contributing substantively to understanding of migration processes, this research has also contributed to the development of narrative theory, most notably in the way that migration narratives foreground and problematize space in narrative, echoing de Certeau's claim that 'every story is a travel story – a spatial practice' (1988: 115).

Diasporic spaces

Influences from writers such as de Certeau (1988), Harvey (1989), from cultural geography and indeed the tradition of neighbourhood studies in urban sociolinguistics, have placed a research emphasis on how urban spaces are appropriated and made over by migration and diaspora. This can involve the successive making over and appropriation of neighbourhood spaces by successive migrations, as Gregory and Williams (2000: ch. 1) show in their ethnography of literacy lives in the Spitalfields area of east London. They describe a neighbourhood that has been appropriated and made over by successive migrations: Huguenots in the seventeenth and eighteenth centuries, Irish in the early nineteenth century, Jewish in the nineteenth and early twentieth centuries, and in the mid-twentieth century, post-Second World War, a migration from what is now Bangladesh. A caption to a photograph of a mosque illustrates this layering of occupancy and appropriation:

> The London Jamme Masjid on the corner of Fournier Street and Brick Lane. Built in 1743 as a Huguenot church, it became a Methodist chapel in the early 1800s and the Machzike Hadas Synagogue in 1898. In 1975 it opened as the largest mosque in the East End.

> *(Gregory and Williams 2000: 31)*

In a study of the streetscapes of multilingual neighbourhoods in Ghent as part of a larger multi-sited ethnography of language contact in urban neighbourhoods, Blommaert, Slembrouck and Collins (Blommaert *et al.* 2005; Collins and Slembrouck 2007) have examined the constitutive indexical role of multilingual shop signs in creating these interpretative spaces or 'linguistic landscapes' (cf. Shohamy and Gorter 2009), involving novel cultural syntheses and blends (businesses that might combine real estate, insurance, accounting and loans, with more generalized cultural brokering). In a sociolinguistic environment characterized more by Pratt's contact zones than by discrete speech communities, these signs attract different readerships and interpretations, ranging from the local Belgian, who might read this signage as evidence of an ethnic neighbourhood takeover, buying up houses and property, to the locally settled bilingual who sees in the linguistic choices a creative adaption to settlement processes, to the educated visitor from back home who can see traces of sociolinguistic diversity (urban/rural) in the language chosen and variable literacy, bespeaking different amounts of cultural capital, in both languages.

These diasporic spaces have also been explored by Keating (2009) in her study of the literacy practices of immigrant Portuguese women in London, one who migrated in the late 1960s/early 1970s, the other in the late 1980s. Keating contrasts the migration trajectories of Dina, towards hospital work, union activism and community involvement in London and that of Zelia towards work as a legal interpreter based in a driving school business, which mirrored those found by Blommaert *et al.* in Ghent: 'The driving school was a family-based hybrid setting serving as school, travel agency and community advice centre' (Keating 2009: 241). It is from this base that Zelia engages in her work of cultural brokering and interpreting. Vigouroux (2009) in her study of an Internet café in Cape Town as a focal site for the communicative practices of Congolese migrants, identifies a similar multifunctional space, investigating the impact of interacting time-spaces of different scale on the semiotic artefacts and language practices which are characteristic of the Internet café and its various topographical spaces as well as the indexical relationships produced through these interactions.

Jie Dong's fieldwork in China (Dong and Blommaert 2009) shows how a centre/periphery metropolitan/urban/rural dynamic is played out in service encounters in Beijing, where the capacity to speak Putonghua has a high value attached. Jie Dong interviews Xiao Xu, a street seller of breakfast dumplings:

> there are several layers to Xiao Xu's multi-identities displayed in the conversation: when he speaks about the shrimps from his hometown he switches to a marked provincial accent which indexes his identity of coming from that particular place. ... During his metapragmatic talk about his Putonghua, he shifts to near-Putonghua accent which enacts his identity of high social mobility and hence an elite identity. But this identity is not stable: ... identity does not easily travel across spaces, and therefore he is in a process of seeking ratification of his identity in a new and up-scale space.
>
> *(Dong and Blommaert 2009: 56–7)*

There are complex indexical relations between social spaces and linguistic forms.

Work and enterprise

A number of the diasporic spaces described in the preceding section involved some kind of work: the delivery of services in small business contexts, Xiao Xu selling breakfast dumplings on a Beijing street, Zelia in her driving school, in the multifunctional enterprises of Ghent and Cape Town. This introduces another significant theme in language and migration research, that of work and enterprise. Martin-Jones (2000) takes up the notion of 'enterprising women' in an ethnographic study of the multilingual literacy practices of Gujerati women in Leicester, women for whom the process of migration has opened up possibilities that they have grasped. The Portuguese women in London that Keating studied were also enterprising women in this sense. Dina, the other subject of Keating (2009), has another employment trajectory, in the unionized public sector workforce. Current work by Vigouroux on Congolese migrants in Cape Town examines linguistic differentiation in the informal economy.

Research into diasporic spaces has tended to see the linguistic dimension of these spaces in terms of multilingual literacy practices, or oral communicative practices such as language choice, code switching or shifting. Dina's case raises the issue of the linguistic demands of the mainstream public sector workplace, in particular issues of access via the dominant language and gatekeeping. The research of Roberts and Campbell (Roberts and Campbell 2005; Campbell and Roberts 2007) examines employment interviews as gatekeeping devices for migrant applicants, whose education and work experience has been largely out of the UK, identifying a 'linguistic penalty' for migrant applicants, weighing against them if their education, training and work experience has been in their country of origin. Campbell and Roberts (2007) additionally show how the interview requires an artful presentation of worker and personal identities expressed in narratives told in response to interviewer questions. Failure to succeed in interviews for jobs for which their training and work experience would fit them leads such applicants on a downward spiral of de-professionalization.

In recent work (e.g. 2011) Beatriz Lorente has described the role of the Phillipines as a sending country of migrant labour in trying to form the migrant workforce prior to migration, pointing out that the major focus in language and migration research to date has been on issues arising in the country of destination.

Health

Applied linguistic research in the area of health relevant to migration has focused overwhelmingly on issues of intercultural communication (for an overview see Candlin and Candlin 2003) and mediation through interpreting, formal and informal, and cultural brokering (Valdes and Angelelli 2003). The most characteristic research focus, unsurprisingly, has been on the medical consultation, with Davidson (2000) discussing his research into Spanish-English medical interpreting in a Californian public hospital emphasizing the role of the interpreter as institutional gatekeeper as well as active partner with the physician in the diagnostic process. Micro-analysis of interpreted interactions show how the voice of the patient often disappears from the interaction due to selective interpreting and the interpreter's alignment with and recruitment into the communicative purposes of the physician. As such, the interpreted medical consultation is a very salient example of the gatekeeping institutional encounters referred to above (Sarangi and Roberts 1999). The role of interpreter can be understood both in terms of the distinction between discourse role and social role of Sarangi and Slembrouck (1996) and the potential of the interpreter to align with the communicative purposes of different participants. From an interactional perspective, the apparently marginal and neutral figure of the interpreter can thus be seen as a powerful broker of access to medical treatment. Applied linguistic issues raised here concern the professionalization of interpreters, the reliance on informal interpreting and cultural brokering, the interactional dynamics of the interpreted interaction, and the stance of the interpreter (Inghilleri 2005).

Another strategy for medical encounters is to try and optimize the communication possibilities between doctors and patients in contexts where interpreting is not available and communication is in the dominant language. The PLEDGE (Patients with Limited English and Doctors in General Practice) project of Roberts et al. (2004) is an example of this, with a focus on oral interaction The research identifies contrasting interactional frameworks between patients speaking local varieties of English and Standard English and patients from non-English speaking backgrounds, with implications for the sensitization of the healthcare professional in differences in conversational interaction in intercultural settings. Collins and Slembrouck (2006) supply a linguistic ethnography of an inner city health clinic where, in contrast, such issues are addressed by the planning and implementation of a manual for doctors designed to facilitate communication. The researchers describe a variety of organizational responses to migrant multilingualism in the health clinic, ranging from reliance on informal interpreting, with a family member or friend accompanying the patient, to the use of professional interpreters, including phone interpreting, multilingual leaflets and the manual, called in Dutch 'Ijsbreker' with connotations both of 'breaking the ice' and successful communication (Collins and Slembrouck 2006: 254). The manual is presented in Dutch, Russian, Slovakian and Albanian and is constructed round a flow chart which models the stages of the medical consultation. For a variety of reasons, the manual turns out rather predictably to be a somewhat inflexible approach to the communication problems of intercultural cross-linguistic medical encounters, influenced as it is, Slembrouck and Collins suggest, by an anxiety about the uncertainties of the oral interpreting situation and the dynamics of intercultural communication more generally on the part of the professionals involved, exemplified in the quote used as the title of the paper 'You don't know what they translate'.

Education and training

Historically, this has been the most sustained area of focus for applied linguistic work on the language needs of migrants. Within it we can distinguish (i) education and training provision for adult migrants, either on arrival or ongoing (see Cooke and Simpson 2008), the latter including workplace language training with a history going back to workplace language training in the 1970s (Roberts *et al.* 1992), recent work reported in Sandwall (2010 forthcoming); and (ii) the language issues involved in the education of the children of migrants, both in mainstream schooling (for an overview see Baker 2003) and in complementary schooling (Blackledge and Creese 2009). Issues in relation to (i) include language learning and access to it through policy (Cooke and Simpson 2008; Baynham and Simpson forthcoming), particularly the current impact of citizenship on ESOL pedagogy (Cooke 2006; Griswold forthcoming); issues of adult language learning pedagogy (for example, Baynham 2006); the learning trajectories of ESOL learners (de Costa 2010); and indeed the learning identities of bilingual learners (Kanno and Norton 2003; Relaño Pastor and de Fina 2005). Issues in relation to (ii) include the impact of policy, linguistic barriers to access to curriculum achievement in the dominant language, and also opportunities to maintain and develop bilingual skills. Linking to our emphasis on institutional encounters, such encounters would include sustained engagement with education and training, but also occasions both where access to these is gatekept by interviews and selection processes and where significant others, such as parents in relation to their children's schooling, become involved (or not) in interactions with teachers and other school representatives. While the typical interaction in the healthcare context is focused on the medical consultation, interactions with school are more diffuse and textually mediated.

In relation to the education of children from migrant communities, important studies look across from home to school and back again. Both using an ethnographic approach, Gregory and Williams examine the home-school environments of Bangladeshi children in east London, UK (Gregory and Williams 2000), and Cruickshank the language situation of teenage students of Lebanese background in Sydney, Australia (Cruickshank 2006). Such studies reflect a more holistic perspective on research into language, migration and settlement, emphasizing the interaction between different domains typically investigated separately. Increased attention is currently being paid to the role and functions of complementary schooling in supporting the bilingualism and cultural identity of children from migrant families (Blackledge and Creese 2009).

At the policy level, the education and training of adult migrants is increasingly linked to a human capital agenda, with language training for work and economic benefit predominating, although current anxieties about integration and social cohesion, strengthening the border and boundaries of the nation-state, is also, as suggested above, a powerful influence.

Transnationalism and virtual space

As suggested at the beginning of this chapter, migration has arguably always been a transnational project of trajectories and flows, but this has been increasingly highlighted by rapid change in both the speed and possibility of travel and the exponential increase in virtual means for creating connectedness between people separated by distance, shrinking and compressing space-time and enabling migrants to be in virtual and face-to-face contact with family and networks back home in regular, sometimes instantaneous ways. As Low and Lawrence-Zuñiga (2003) put it: 'This process of cultural globalization creates new translocal spaces and forms of public culture embedded in the imaginings of people that dissolves notions of state-based territoriality' (2003: 25). Developments on the Web have enabled the accelerated creation and sharing of transnational virtual spaces, in ways that go well beyond the traditional boundaries of nation-states. The impact of this on language and migration is increasingly coming into the research agenda, for example in the theme issue of *Linguistics and Education* on transnational literacies, edited by Warriner (2007). Young people from Colombia, India and Israel in McGinnis *et al.* (2007) use blogs and Facebook to create transnational, multilingual identities. Similarly, American Chinese teenagers in Lam (2004) use a bilingual on-line chatroom, an environment where global, transnational uses of English intersect with the local, as an opportunity for language socialization. Lam (2006) and Warschauer (2009) point out how the translocal varieties produced in these contexts often involve multilingual mixes and blends, with switches to Arabic or Chinese incorporated using English orthography.

Such changes, combined with the speed and availability of means of transport, suggest a blurring of the sharp distinction between 'being here' and 'being there', when the migrant may be able to simultaneously maintain a virtual presence in his/her country of origin through electronic means, giving an added sharpness to the point made by Sassen in the epigraph to this chapter. Its consequences for the emergence of linguistic varieties is just beginning to be investigated.

Future directions

What is perhaps certain is that issues of language and migration, however conceived, are not set to disappear from the applied linguistics agenda. However, how we conceive of migration is liable to develop and change. On the one hand we are unlikely to see a lessening of the desire of states for control of their borders in a period of uncertainty, and there are disturbing signs of the stratification of labour markets mapping on to particular kinds of language competence, powerfully expressed in recent contributions by Piller and Lorente, in another kind of policy-driven transnationalism, driven by the push-pull of economic activity and necessity. Lorente has powerfully investigated this impact on the Filipino migrant domestic workforce, both from the perspective of the 'sending' as well as the 'receiving' countries. On the other hand, changes in the electronic communication landscape will contribute to shape virtual spaces and their affordances that will work against the strengthening of national and ideological boundaries, tensions with which are currently in evidence in struggles over restrictions over Google in China and various kinds of Internet connectedness in the Gulf states. It is possible that we are working with an oversimplified and restricted notion of the migration process itself, which must be expanded to include other types of more short-term migration/mobility such as seasonal working, serial migration, migration 'sans papiers', return migration, migration associated with the collapse of the nation-state (as documented by Vigouroux [2009] in relation to the Congo), and the consequent needs of refugees and asylum seekers. There is a tendency for such changes and disruptions to problematize language in some way, and if applied linguists are alert to these problematizations, applied linguistic insights and expertise can be drawn into the search for viable solutions. Finally, there is a tendency to emphasize through sociological pessimism the negative aspects of migration and related linguistic issues. While recognizing the powerful exploitative forces at work in the economically driven push-pull of international migration flows, we have also to learn to see it in a more upbeat and positive light, as offering opportunities for agency, change and enterprise, the linguistic imagination and hybridity produced potentially contributing to new forms of language and social activity, which could not have been envisaged if everyone had stayed at home.

Related topics

institutional discourse; language policy and planning; multilingualism; translation and interpreting

Further reading

Baynham, M. and de Fina, A. (eds) (2005) *Dislocations/Relocations: Narratives of Displacement*, Manchester: St Jerome Publishing. (Papers from a series of seminars held in the early 2000s on migration narratives.)
Collins, J., Slembrouck, S. and Baynham, M. (eds) (2009) *Globalization and Language in Contact*, London: Continuum. (Papers from the first AILA Language and Migration network seminars.)
de Fina, A. (2003) *Identity in Narrative: A Study of Immigrant Discourse*, Amsterdam: Benjamins. (A monograph on migration narratives of Mexican migrants to the USA.)
Maryns, K. (2006) *The Asylum Speaker: Language in the Belgian Asylum Procedure*, Manchester: St Jerome Publishing. (Linguistic ethnographic analysis of the asylum process in Belgium.)

References

Baker, C. (2003) 'Education as a site of language contact', *Annual Review of Applied Linguistics: Language Contact and Change* 23: 95–112.
Baker, P., Gabrielatos, C., KhosraviNik, M., Krzyzanowski, M., McEnery, T. and Wodak, R. (2008) 'A useful methodological synergy? Combining critical discourse analysis and corpus linguistics to examine discourses of refugees and asylum seekers in the UK press', *Discourse and Society* 19(3): 273–306.
Baynham, M. (2003) 'Narrative in space and time: beyond "backdrop" accounts of narrative orientation', *Narrative Inquiry* 13(2): 347–66.
——(2005) 'Network and agency in the migration stories of Moroccan women', in M. Baynham and A. de Fina (eds) *Dislocations/Relocations: Narratives of Displacement*, Manchester: St Jerome Publishing.
——(2006) 'Agency and contingency in the language learning of refugees and asylum seekers', *Linguistics and Education* 17(1): 24–39.

Baynham, M. and de Fina, A. (eds.) (2005) *Dislocations/Relocations: Narratives of Displacement*, Manchester: St Jerome Publishing.

Baynham, M. and Simpson, J. (forthcoming) 'Onwards and upwards: space, placement, and liminality in adult ESOL classes', *TESOL Quarterly* 44(3): 420–40.

Blackledge, A. (2008) 'Liberalism, discrimination and the law: language testing for citizenship in Britain', in G. Rings and A. Ife (eds) *Neo-colonial Mentalities in Contemporary Europe? Language and Discourse in the Construction of Identities*, Cambridge: Cambridge Scholars Publishing.

Blackledge, A. and Creese, A. (2009) '"Because tumi Bangali": inventing and disinventing the national in multilingual communities in the UK', *Ethnicities* 9(4): 451–76.

Blommaert, J. (ed.) (1999) *Language Ideological Debates*, Berlin: Mouton de Gruyter.

Blommaert, J., Collins, J. and Slembrouck, S. (2005) 'Spaces of multilingualism', *Language and Communication* 25(3): 197–216.

Campbell, S. and Roberts, C. (2007) 'Migration, ethnicity and competing discourses in the job interview: synthesizing the institutional and personal', *Discourse and Society* 18(3): 243–71.

Candlin, C. and Candlin, S. (2003) 'Healthcare communication: a problematic site for applied linguistics research', *Annual Review of Applied Linguistics* 23: 134–54.

Castells, M. (2000) *End of Millennium*, Malden, MA: Blackwell.

Collins, J. and Slembrouck, S. (2006) '"You don't know what they translate": language contacts, institutional procedure and literacy practice in neighbourhood health clinics in urban Flanders', *Journal of Linguistic Anthropology* 16(2): 249–68.

——(2007) 'Reading shop windows in globalised neighbourhoods: multingual literacy practices and indexicality', *Journal of Literacy Research* 39(3): 335–59.

Collins, J., Slembrouck, S. and Baynham, M. (eds.) (2009) *Globalization and Language in Contact*, London: Continuum.

Cooke, M. (2006) '"When I wake up I dream of electricity": the lives, aspirations and "needs" of Adult ESOL learners', *Linguistics and Education* 17(1): 56–73.

Cooke, M. and Simpson, J. (2008) *ESOL: A Critical Guide*, Oxford: Oxford University Press.

Cooke, M. and Simpson, J. (2009) 'Challenging agendas in ESOL: skills, employability and social cohesion', *Language Issues* 20(1): 19–31.

Cruickshank, K. (2006) *Teenagers, Literacy and School: Researching in Multilingual Contexts*, London: Routledge.

Davidson, B. (2000) 'The interpreter as institutional gatekeeper: the social-linguistic role of interpreters in Spanish-English medical discourse', *Journal of Sociolinguistics* 4(3): 379–405.

de Certeau, M. (1988) *The Practice of Everyday Life*, Berkeley: University of California Press.

de Costa, P. (2010) 'From refugee to reformer: a Bourdieusian take on a Hmong learner's trajectory', *TESOL Quarterly* 44(3): 517–41.

de Fina, A. (2003) *Identity in Narrative: A Study of Immigrant Discourse*, Amsterdam: John Benjamins.

de Fina, A., Schiffrin, D. and Bamberg, M. (2006) *Discourse and Identity*, Cambridge: Cambridge University Press.

Dong, J. and Blommaert, J. (2009) 'Space, scale and accents: constructing migrant identity in Beijing', in J. Collins, S. Slembrouck and M. Baynham (eds) *Globalization and Language in Contact*, London: Continuum.

Gabrielatos, C. and Baker, P. (2008) 'Fleeing, sneaking, flooding: a corpus analysis of discursive constructions of refugees and asylum seekers in the U.K. press: 1996–2005', *Journal of English Linguistics* 36(1): 5–38.

Galasinska, A. and Koslowska, O. (2009) 'Either and "both": the changing concept of living space among Polish post-communist migrants to the United Kingdom', in J. Collins, S. Slembrouck, and M. Baynham (eds) *Globalization and Language in Contact*, London: Continuum.

Goldstein, T. (1996) *Two Languages at Work: Bilingual Life on the Production Floor*, New York: Mouton de Gruyter.

Gregory, E. and Williams, A. (2000) *City Literacies*, London: Routledge.

Griswold, O. (2010) 'Narrating America in adult ESL/citizenship classes', *TESOL Quarterly* 44(3): 488–516.

Hansen-Thomas, H. (2007) 'Language ideology, citizenship and identity: the case of modern Germany', *Journal of Language and Politics* 6(7): 249–64.

Harvey, D. (1989) *The Condition of Postmodernity: An Enquiry into the Origins of Cultural Change*, Oxford: Blackwell.

Haviland, J. (2003) 'Ideologies of language: some reflections on language and U.S. law', *American Anthropologist* 105(4): 764–74.

Heller, M. (2003) Globalization, the new economy and the commodification of language and identity, *Journal of Sociolinguistics* 7(4): 473–92.

Inghilleri, M. (ed.) (2005) 'Special issue on Bourdieu and the sociology of translating and interpreting', *The Translator* 11(2).

Irvine, J. T. and Gal, S. (2000) 'Language ideology and linguistic differentiation', in P. V. Kroskrity (ed.) *Regimes of Language: Ideologies, Politics and Identities*, Santa Fe, NM: School of American Research.

Kanno, Y. and Norton, B. (eds) (2003) 'Imagined communities and educational possibilities: introduction', *Journal of Language, Identity, and Education* 2(4), 241–9.

Keating, C. (2009) 'Changing participation in changing practice: uses of language and literacy among Portuguese migrant women in the United Kingdom', in J. Collins, S. Slembrouck and M. Baynham (eds) *Globalization and Language in Contact*, London: Continuum.

KhosraviNik, M. (2008) 'British newspapers and the representation of refugees, asylum seekers and immigrants between 1996 and 2006', Centre for Language in Social Life, working papers, Lancaster University.

——(2010) 'The representation of refugees, asylum seekers and immigrants in British newspapers: a critical discourse analysis', *Journal of Language and Politics* 9(1): 1–28.

Lam, W. S. E. (2004) 'Second language socialization in a bilingual chatroom: global and local considerations', *Language Learning and Technology* 8(3): 44–65.

——(2006) 'Re-envisioning language, literacy and the immigrant subject', *New Mediascapes, Pedagogies: An International Journal* 1(3): 171–95.

Liebscher, G. and Dailey-O'Cain, J. (2005) 'West Germans moving east: place, political space, and positioning in conversational narratives', in M. Baynham and A. de Fina (eds) *Dislocations/Relocations: Narratives of Displacement*, Manchester: St Jerome Publishing.

Lo Bianco, J. and Wickert, R. (eds) (2001) *Australian Policy Activism in Language and Literacy*, Melbourne: Language Australia.

Lorente, B. P. (2011) 'The making of workers of the world: language and the labor brokerage state', in A. Duchene and M. Heller (eds) *Pride and Profit: Language in Late Capitalism* (pp. 183–206), London and New York: Routledge.

Low, S. and Lawrence-Zuñiga, D. (2003) *The Anthropology of Space and Place: Locating Culture*, Oxford: Blackwell.

McCormick, K. (2005) 'Working with Webs: narrative constructions of forced removal and relocation', in M. Baynham and A. de Fina (eds) *Dislocations/Relocations: Narratives of Displacement*, Manchester: St Jerome Publishing.

McElhinny, B., Yeung, S., Damasco, V., DeOcampo, A., Febria, M., Collantes, C. and Salonga, J. (2007) '"Talk about luck": coherence, contingency, character and class in the life stories of Filipino Canadians in Toronto', in A. Lo and A. Reyes (eds) *Beyond Yellow English: Toward a Linguistic Anthropology of Asian Pacific America*, Oxford: Oxford University Press.

McGinnis, T., Goodstein-Stolzenberg, A. and Costa-Saliani, E. (2007) '"Indnpride": online spaces of transnational youth as sites of creative and sophisticated literacy and identity work', *Linguistics and Education* 18(3–4): 283–304.

Martin-Jones, M. (2000) 'Enterprising women: multilingual literacies in the constructing of new identities', in M. Martin-Jones and K. Jones (eds) *Multilingual Literacies*, Amsterdam: John Benjamins.

Maryns, K. (2005) 'Displacement in asylum seekers' narratives', in M. Baynham and A. de Fina (eds) *Dislocations/Relocations: Narratives of Displacement*, Manchester: St Jerome Publishing.

——(2006) *The Asylum Speaker: Language in the Belgian Asylum Procedure*, Manchester: St Jerome Publishing.

Meinhof, U. (2009) 'Transnational flows, networks and "transcultural capital": reflections on researching migrant networks through linguistic ethnography', in J. Collins, S. Slembrouck and M. Baynham (eds) *Globalization and Language in Contact*, London: Continuum.

Milani, T. M. (2008) 'Language testing and citizenship: a language ideological debate in Sweden', *Language in Society* 37(1): 27–59.

Milani, T. M. (2006) 'Discourse and power in a multilingual world', *Journal of Sociolinguistics* 10(3): 402–6.

Norton, B. (2000) *Identity and Language Learning*, London: Longman.

Ozolins, U. (2001) 'Inventiveness and regression: interpreting/translating and the vicissitudes of Australian language policy', in J. Lo Bianco and R. Wickert (eds) *Australian Policy Activism in Language and Literacy*, Melbourne: Language Australia.

Perdue, C. (ed.) (1993) *Adult Language Acquisition: Cross-linguistic, Perspectives*, vols. I and II, Cambridge: Cambridge University Press.

Piller, I. (2001) 'Naturalization language testing and its basis in ideologies of national identity and citizenship', *International Journal of Bilingualism* 5(3): 259–78.

Pratt, M. L. (1987) 'Arts of the contact zone', in N. Fabb, D. Attridge, A. Durant and C. MacCabe (eds) *The Linguistics of Writing: Arguments Between Linguistics and Literature*, Manchester: Manchester University Press.

Reisigl, M. and Wodak, R. (2001) *Discourse and Discrimination: Rhetorics of Racism and Anti-semitism*, London: Routledge.

Relaño Pastor, M. and de Fina, A. (2005) 'Contesting social place: narratives of language conflict', in M. Baynham and A. de Fina (eds) *Dislocations/Relocations: Narratives of Displacement*, Manchester: St Jerome Publishing.

Rings, G. and Ife, A. (eds) (2008) *Neo-colonial Mentalities in Contemporary Europe? Language and Discourse in the Construction of Identities*, Cambridge: Cambridge Scholars Publishing.

Roberts, C. and Campbell, S. (2005) 'Fitting stories into boxes: rhetorical and textual constraints on candidates' performances in British job interviews', *Journal of Applied Linguistics* 2(1): 45–73.

Roberts, C., Davies, E. and Jupp, T. (1992) *Language and Discrimination*, London: Longman.

Roberts, C., Moss, B., Wass, V., Sarangi, S. and Jones, R. (2005) 'Misunderstandings: a qualitative study of primary care consultations in multilingual settings, and educational implications', *Medical Education* 39(5): 465–75.

Roberts, C., Sarangi, S. and Moss, B. (2004) 'Presentation of self and symptoms in primary care consultations involving patients from non-English speaking backgrounds', *Communication and Medicine* 1(2): 159–69.

Sandwall, K. (2010) '"I learn more at school": ecological perspectives on work placement for second language learning', *TESOL Quarterly*, 44(3): 542–74.

Sarangi, S. and Roberts, C. (1999) *Talk, Work, and Institutional Order: Discourse in Medical, Mediation and Management Settings*, Berlin: Mouton de Gruyter.

Sarangi, S. and Slembrouck, S. (1996) *Language, Bureaucracy and Social Control*, London: Longman.

Sassen, S. (1999) *Guests and Aliens*, New York: New Press.

Schieffelin, B., Woolard, K. and Kroskrity, P. (eds) (1998) *Language Ideologies: Practice and Theory*, New York: Cambridge University Press.

Schumann, J. (1978) *The Pidginization Process: A Model for Second Language Acquisition*, Rowley, MA: Newbury House.

Shohamy, E. and Gorter, D. (2009) *Linguistic Landscape: Expanding the Scenery*, Abingdon: Routledge.

Trinch, S. (2003) *Latinas Narratives of Domestic Abuse: Discrepant Versions of Violence*, Amsterdam: John Benjamins.

Valdes, G. and Angelelli, C. (2003) 'Interpreters, interpreting and the study of bilingualism', *Annual Review of Applied Linguistics* 23: 58–78.

van Dijk, T. A. (1991) *Racism and the Press: Critical Studies in Racism and Migration*, London: Routledge.

van Leeuwen, T. and Wodak, R. (1999) 'Legitimizing immigration control: a discourse-historical analysis', *Discourse Studies* 1(1): 83–118.

Vertovec, S. (2006) 'The emergence of super-diversity in Britain', Working Paper 25, Centre on Migration, Policy and Society, University of Oxford.

Vigouroux, C. (2009) 'A relational understanding of language practice: interacting timespaces in a single ethnographic site', in J. Collins, S. Slembrouck and M. Baynham (eds) *Globalization and Language in Contact*, London: Continuum.

Warriner, D. S. (ed.) (2007) 'Transnational literacies: immigration, language learning, and identity', *Linguistics and Education* 18(3–4): 201–338.

Warschauer, M. (2009) 'Digital literacy studies', in M. Baynham and M. Prinsloo (eds) *The Future of Literacy Studies*, Basingstoke: Palgrave Macmillan.

Wodak, R. and van Dijk, T. (eds) (2000) *Racism at the Top: Parliamentary Discourses on Ethnic Issues in Six European States*, Klagenfurt, Austria: Drava.

Part IV

Perspectives on language in use

30

Discourse analysis

Guy Cook

Introduction

Applied linguistics (AL) interest in discourse analysis (DA) originated in an awareness of the inability of formal linguistics to account for how participants in communication achieve meaning. As such DA has been a major impetus in ending an early narrow conception of AL as a subsidiary discipline which merely applies insights from linguistics to language-related problems (Widdowson 1984: 21–8), and moving it towards the broader independent enterprise it is today. Although there are many diverse approaches to discourse in AL, there are also common principles and themes. Discourse can be defined as a stretch of language in use, of any length and in any mode, which achieves meaning and coherence for those involved. Discourse *analysis* can be defined as the use and development of theories and methods which elucidate how this meaning and coherence is achieved.

This quest makes DA inevitably concerned not only with language, but with all elements and processes which contribute to communication. Consequently, AL discourse analysts have espoused and also developed a wide range of approaches to language beyond linguistics. These have included pragmatics, schema theory, conversation analysis, ethnography, semiotics, multimodal analysis, literary theory, rhetoric, genre analysis, and social theory. This widening purview has led to encounters with many different disciplines and definitions of discourse. One major influence, which changed the direction of DA in AL, has been social theory, especially the ideas of Foucault, for whom discourses (used in the plural) are conceived as distinct ways of using language which express institutionalised values and ideology, delimiting and defining what can be said and how: for example, sexist discourse, medical discourse, legal discourse, etc. Rather than simply adding yet another dimension to understanding, for many AL discourse analysts this approach fundamentally changed the original conception of DA in AL as merely an extension of linguistic analysis. Yet while this Foucauldian tradition emphasises the key importance of language use in ideology, it has not in practice paid close attention to linguistic detail in the same way as the AL tradition. While DA in AL has absorbed this Foucauldian tradition, and subsequently other social theoretical approaches such as that of Bourdieu, it has often used these social theories to supplement rather than replace close linguistic and textual analysis. It has thus merged two traditions, one from linguistics, the other from social and critical theory, using the two in a complementary manner. At its best, the AL DA tradition thus currently combines the strengths of linguistics and non-linguistic perspectives, making it the most powerful and rigorous tool for the analysis of language in use. Consequently, it has a great deal to offer to social theory and sociology on the one hand, and to linguistics on the other.

With this power and breadth, however, comes a problem of scope. AL DA embraces all aspects of language in use, eclectically deploying insights from a variety of traditions to arrive at a rounded and rich interpretation of language in use. It is in this sense open to criticism for being a 'study of everything', concerned with such a wide variety of phenomena that it has no distinct identity of its own. It is certainly true and frequently remarked that the terms 'discourse' and 'discourse analysis' are very variously defined and often loosely used. Many approaches to DA proceed down their own paths without mentioning or even showing awareness of others. Nor is it clear in many cases whether particular DA studies belong to AL or some other discipline. The broadening of scope has thus made it harder to define and describe DA than when it first emerged in the 1970s. Recent years have, however, seen some successful attempts to provide inclusive structured overviews of the field (Gee 1999; Johnstone 2002; Paltridge 2006; Widdowson 2007; Bhatia *et al.* 2008; Slembrouck 2009).

An issue for this chapter is how to distinguish DA from the other approaches to language use included elsewhere in this volume. The study of ESP, EAP, institutions, medical communication, the media, and classrooms all involve the practice of DA, while conversation analysis, corpus linguistics, critical discourse analysis, linguistic ethnography, multimodal analysis, and stylistics are all among its tools. Each such area of study is in its own field or in its own way concerned with the achievement of meaning in actual communication, making each a constituent of DA as much as of AL. As such, each could validly appear in the contents of a 'handbook of discourse analysis' as easily as in a 'handbook of applied linguistics'. For both DA and AL, like the areas listed above, distinguish themselves from formal linguistics by their resolute focus upon attested language use in actual social contexts, and their lack of concern with invented or decontextualised models of language as an idealised abstraction. How then is DA to be distinguished from AL on the one hand, or from the many branches of study which address specific aspects of language use on the other? And how can a summary of DA do more than briefly allude to several other areas of AL, with a vague implication that these approaches, taken together but not separately, constitute DA? How can the description of DA here be more than a composite, giving summaries of approaches which are dealt with more fully elsewhere? These are difficult problems for the contemporary discourse analyst – not only within the covers of this handbook, but in the study of language in general. They were not perhaps so problematic in the past, for reasons which will become apparent. I shall return to the problem at the end of this chapter, having in the meantime done exactly what I have just cast doubt upon: summarised a number of different developments as constituent of an overarching DA.

Early AL DA

In the 1950s DA was understood in theoretical structural linguistics as the potential extension of language analysis beyond the level of single sentences to discover distributional principles between sentences as well as within them (Harris 1952). In descriptive linguistics in the Firthian tradition, it was concerned with describing stages of interaction as communicative acts in context (Mitchell 1957). Both enterprises acknowledged the impossibility of accounting for structure above sentence level without reference to non-linguistic factors, although for theoretical linguists this was seen as a reason *not* to include DA in their enquiries (Harris 1952). For those linguists who did pursue DA (or the closely related field of text linguistics) elaborate attempts to construct 'text grammars' (e.g. van Dijk 1972; Werlich 1976) in which sentences would combine in accordance with quasi-linguistic rules proved limited in explanatory power. More successful was work on inter-sentential cohesion in a functionalist linguistic paradigm (Halliday and Hasan 1976) which did reveal structures above sentence level in texts. Yet while important and influential in extending the scope of linguistic description, analyses of cohesion could not fully account for coherence – the perceived quality of meaning and unity which characterises actual linguistic communication – as it is possible for a sentence sequence to be coherent without cohesion, or cohesive without apparent coherence. (*Casualties are high. The president has resigned.* vs *Charles has a spoon. He drives it.*). More generally however, Halliday's concerns with language function (e.g. 1973) and the use of language as a social semiotic (e.g. 1978), were key influences from linguistics which helped move DA in AL beyond an interest in merely extending linguistic analysis. Another such influence was Hymes' (1972a) depiction of communicative competence as involving social and psychological factors beyond what is linguistically possible.

In response to theoretical stimuli, the 1970s and 1980s saw a number of major works on DA emerging from an AL perspective (Widdowson 1973; Sinclair and Coulthard 1975; Brown and Yule 1983; Stubbs 1983; Coulthard 1985) or useful to it (van Dijk 1977; de Beaugrande and Dressler 1981). In keeping with the dominant concern of AL with language teaching at that time, there were also a number of treatments of DA in relation to language teaching and learning (Widdowson 1979: 89–153, 1984: 37–137; Riley 1987; Cook 1989; McCarthy 1991; Hatch 1992). DA was and remains fundamental to the guiding principle of communicative language teaching and its later developments such as task-based language teaching, namely that successful language learning involves much more than acquiring a static formal knowledge of the new language, but must also entail an ability to achieve meaning in communication. A good deal of DA has thus emerged from, or in conjunction with, the investigation of effective language teaching and learning – and I shall refer to this as the language learning approach to DA. The leading figure of this movement, whose own early work (1973) predates more general approaches to DA in descriptive linguistics, was H. G. Widdowson.

At this point in its history, DA was fairly readily defined as an extension of formal linguistics, or a refutation of it, depending on one's point of view. However, as AL has moved away from a conception of itself as an extension of linguistics, and acquired a more complex disciplinary identity, encountering other definitions of discourse in the process, this definition has become problematic. There are many varieties of DA, none of which is in itself coterminous with DA as a whole, yet there is also no 'pure' version of DA which is not one of these varieties, or an amalgam of several.

Text, context, and discourse

Much early DA work in AL saw text (the linguistic element in communication) as essentially distinct from context (the non-linguistic elements) and discourse as the two in interaction to create meaning. Context itself was further treated as having a series of components, with different approaches to DA tending to emphasise the role of one or another. Thus, context variously included consideration of such factors as:

- the situation or immediate environment of communication;
- the participants and their intentions, knowledge, beliefs, attitudes, affiliations and feelings, as well as their roles, relations, and status;
- the cultural and ideological norms and assumptions against which a given communication occurs;
- language which precedes or follows that under analysis, sometimes referred to as 'co-text' (Halliday *et al.* 1964);
- other texts evoked for the participants and affecting their interpretation – sometimes referred to as 'intertext' (Kristeva 1986);
- non-linguistic meaningful communicative behaviour, i.e. paralanguage, such as voice quality, gestures, and facial expressions (in face-to-face spoken interaction), and choice of typeface and letter sizes (in writing);
- use of other modes of communication accompanying the use of language, such as music and pictures;
- the physical medium of communication, such as speech, writing, print, telephone, computer.

This binary opposition of text and context, however, and the itemisation of contextual components, has come to be seen as problematic. If context and text are separate, then the status of text itself becomes precarious. If considered as linguistic forms, temporarily and artificially separated from context for the purposes of analysis, text ceases to have any actual existence, and seems at odds with the aim of DA to deal with the realities of language in use rather than linguistic abstractions. While the consideration of linguistic forms may be an idealisation which is useful in linguistics, it may be less so for DA, as in actual communication language is inextricably bound to all other elements in communication. There is no use of language which does not also have a situation, participants, co-text, paralanguage, etc. Much recent DA work, sometimes evoking the earlier theories of Bakhtin in its support (e.g. Bakhtin 1986; Volosinov 1988), has thus preferred a less dichotomous view, and eschewed consideration of isolated elements, whether linguistic or non-linguistic, preferring instead a more holistic approach, which regards discourse as irreducible, rather than as a simple addition of context and text. In this sense contemporary DA often positions itself in opposition to the tradition of idealisations and binary distinctions (langue vs parole, form vs meaning, competence vs. performance) which have characterised linguistics from Saussure to Chomsky.

Early DA did, however, often work with this binary text/context distinction. This was understandable. For the applied linguists of that time, trained as they were in more traditional linguistics, DA was indeed experienced as the addition of a new dimension (i.e. context) to their existing object of study (i.e. text). Better to understand this new dimension, DA turned to a variety of approaches to communication from outside linguistics. This gave rise to a number of traditions of DA within AL to which we shall now turn. Though many of these traditions have their origins in the 1960s and 1970s, they continue to be developed and refined today.

Pragmatics

Interest in the role of context led initially to the classic texts of pragmatics (Austin 1962; Searle 1969, 1975; Grice 1975) and attention to how discourse is structured by what speakers are trying to do with their words, and how their intentions are recognised by their interlocutors. Explication of pragmatic principles became and has remained standard fare in introductions to DA, which typically explain to students the basic tenets of speech act theory, the cooperative principle, and politeness principles. This is despite the fact that early classic pragmatics deals only with brief invented examples without reference to many significant aspects of context.

Despite this limitation, pragmatics was put to good to use in discourse analysis of real-world extended communication. In a landmark work analysing the discourse of primary school lessons, Sinclair and Coulthard (1975) used the pragmatic notion of the act as a fundamental unit of analysis, showing how acts combine to form higher units (which they called moves, exchanges and transactions) in an attempt to formulate rules analogous to those in structural grammars. The approach, known as the Birmingham School of Discourse Analysis (Birch 1982), provided an important impetus to further work (e.g. Coulthard and Montgomery 1981), but remained tightly focused upon language in isolation from other modes of communication, and, working from transcriptions after the event, tended to treat discourse as a product rather than a process.

Schema theory

Another approach to context derived from psychology and artificial intelligence were the related notions of schemata (Bartlett 1932) and scripts (Schank and Abelson 1977). These are posited mental constructs of expected sequences of events or combinations of elements which discourse participants use to interpret what is said or written (Cook 1994: 9–23; Semino 2002). Schema theory is a powerful tool in DA as it can help to explain both high level aspects of understanding such as coherence, and low level linguistic phenomena such as article choice. For example, the sequence *The taxi was late. The driver couldn't find our house.* appears coherent and uses the definite article appropriately because a 'taxi schema' specifies that taxis have drivers and pick people up from houses. However, the sequence *The taxi was late. The sailor couldn't find our house.* appears incoherent and its definite article inappropriate, as taxis are not expected to be driven by sailors. In the binary conception of discourse as text + context a schema can be classed as context, as it is a kind of knowledge, derived from experience of the world, in whose light each new text is interpreted. The relation of text and schema is, however, dynamic, with schemata being deployed to interpret texts, but also being changed by them (Cook 1994).

Both pragmatics and schema theory have remained salient in many approaches to DA. But their focus is very much on understanding as a product, explained after the event, rather than a process. Their representations of how communication works can seem removed from the actual development of discourse as it appears for participants.

Conversation analysis

One powerful influence on DA from outside linguistics which did, however, focus studiously on process and participant perspectives rather than product and analytic constructs was conversation analysis (CA) (Liddicoat 2007). Developed from the late 1960s onwards following seminal work by Garfinkel (1967) and Sacks *et al.* (1974), CA's primary interest is in the social act (Seedhouse 2004: 3) and it 'is only marginally interested in language as such' (Hutchby and Wooffit 1998: 14). Working from the premise, consistently denied in Chomskyan linguistics, that talk in interaction, including casual conversation, is fundamentally ordered, CA made use of newly available recording technology to transcribe and closely analyse actually occurring conversation, seeking to understand how participants 'make sense of, find their way about in, and act on the circumstances in which they find themselves' (Heritage 1984: 4) and through this close analysis to understand the patterns of social life (Bhatia *et al.* 2008: 4) as realised in talk. Its enterprise differs fundamentally from linguistics in that order, patterns and principles are sought not in the language being used itself, nor through the top-down deployment of explanatory theories, but in the common-sense conventional ways in which participants themselves orient to, and locally manage what is happening. In this sense CA was a branch of ethnomethodology and is determinedly and uncompromisingly *emic* (taking the participants' perspective) rather than *etic* (taking the outsider's/theorists' perspective). The idea is to establish patterns of behaviour, and to attribute significance to everything that happens, whether it follows expectations or departs from them. To give a simple example, one greeting being answered by another is an expected norm (e.g. Speaker A: *Good morning.* Speaker B: *Good morning.*). If there is no such reciprocation from Speaker B, that absence is significant.

Although initially concerned with conversation, later CA work has moved on to study talk in a variety of contexts, for instance workplace interaction (e.g. Nevile 2008), classroom interaction (Seedhouse 2004; see Tsui, this volume), and computer mediated interaction. Yet while it has been an important impetus in the development of DA, and is still widely used within it, CA when strictly defined is different in kind from DA. This is not only for the superficial reason that its subject matter is talk in interaction rather than language use in general. There is a more fundamental reason too. Unlike DA, it confines itself, in the interests of methodological rigour, to the analysis of the immediate mechanisms of talk, avoiding speculation about the mental states these mechanisms reflect and create, or the larger social realities and histories which they both constitute and reflect.

Ethnography, language ecology, linguistic ethnography

Another source of insight for DA has been ethnography (Hammersley and Atkinson 2007). Like CA, it is firmly committed to seeking significance in the details and apparent disorder of everyday communication, and understanding participants' own perspectives on the meaning and dynamics of what is happening. It too rejects the idealisations and generalisations of formal linguistics. Its scope, however, is much broader than CA, or indeed of DA. Ethnography seeks an understanding of culture through an analysis of all details of everyday life in a given context, and does not therefore confine itself to spoken face-to-face interaction as CA does, or to communication involving language as DA does. Yet though broader in scope and method, it is in harmony with the overall aim of DA, and has much to offer to it. One particular ethnographic notion from which DA can benefit is that of the irreducibility of experience – that there are aspects of any act of communication that are particular to it and cannot be generalised. Another is the ethnographer's preoccupation with the relationship between researcher and participants, and how findings may be skewed by the former's identity and preconceptions. This is of particular value to DA, where the inevitable subjective involvement of the discourse analyst in anything s/he reads or hears poses a similar problem to that encountered by ethnographers.

Ethnography has, however, been criticised for being too locked into the particular to be able to make significant large-scale generalisations (Hammersley 1992: 85–95), and from a DA point of view it is not concerned enough with the details of language use. There is, therefore, a potential for two-way interaction in which linguistic and ethnographic analysis contribute to each other as DA. Early attempts to effect such a union can be found in Hymes' ethnography of communication (1972b) and Gumperz's interactional sociolinguistics (1986). A more recent attempt to synthesise the two, and to strengthen the power of both, is to be found in the linguistic ethnography (LE) movement (Rampton *et al.* 2004; Creese 2008; see Maybin and Tusting, this volume). Arguing that close linguistic analysis is always a sound entry point into cultural understanding, linguistic ethnographers draw upon a number of precedent influences, such as new literacy studies (Street 1984; Barton *et al.* 2000), interactional sociolinguistics (Gumperz 1986), and critical discourse analysis (see below), as well as the mainstream applied linguistics language learning approach to DA (see above). LE seeks simultaneously to 'tie ethnography down' and 'to open linguistics up' making it highly relevant resource for DA, if not in many ways – and problematically for definitions of both – synonymous with it.

Closely related to linguistic ethnography, though with a difference of emphasis, is language ecology (van Lier 2000, 2004; Kramsch 2002; Kramsch and Whiteside 2008). Often applying its insights to the field of language teaching and learning, it seeks to relate language use to its physical and social environment, and the affordances this environment provides. It sees language as a historically contingent phenomenon negotiated in daily interactions, and pays particular attention to the dynamic relation of language and cultural change, historical expansion, displacement (e.g. by migration), continuity, and transformation. A similar approach is taken by Blommaert (2005) who argues for a more sociolinguistically and historically informed DA suited to an analysis of the contemporary globalised contexts.

Semiotics, paralanguage and multimodality

Despite their very different origins and approaches, the approaches described so far have worked with brief invented dialogues or transcripts of recorded actually occurring talk. None, however, makes more than a limited and unsystematic reference to communicative channels other than language. There is some reference to pupils' raised hands effecting the act of bidding in Sinclair and Coulthard 1975; there is laughter and timing built into CA transcription systems; there are notes about significant non-linguistic elements of communication in linguistic ethnography. They are nevertheless all essentially transcript-based methodologies, in which the words are central and other aspects of communication added as optional supplements, despite the fact that such elements are an integral and indispensible aspect of how meaning and coherence are achieved.

Consequently, if DA is to fulfil its goal of accounting for how people make sense of language use in real contexts and in real time, it must take stock of much more than the bare words which are spoken and treat other communicative phenomena as more than just an occasional explanatory gloss on their meaning. In talk, a host of paralinguistic phenomena not only carry meaning in parallel to the words (as the term 'paralanguage' suggests), but can be essential to understanding of the words, or even contradict them. (An interpersonal claim such as *I like you a lot* is unlikely to be believed if the accompanying 'body language' communicates the opposite.) Nor can paralanguage be ignored in DA as it is never absent or insignificant. The notion of language without paralanguage is indeed one of the idealisations of linguistics against which DA defines itself. Every spoken utterance has a volume, speed, pitch and intonation in addition to its linguistic form, propositional content and pragmatic force, and these paralinguistic elements convey key information about the speaker's identity, attitude, and commitment. This is so even in telephone conversations when participants do not see each other. When participants do see each other, there are in addition a host of paralinguistic visual phenomena such as gesture, facial expressions, eye movements and contact (or lack of it) and a rich semiotics of such factors as dress, proximity, position, and touch. Discourse analysts have long shown awareness of the need to incorporate such phenomena into their analyses, but also of the difficulty of doing so systematically. The issue of how paralanguage can be transcribed and analysed raises considerable problems as paralinguistic phenomena are of their nature graded, irreducible and often ambiguous, and transcriptions of them necessarily a selection and an interpretation (Ochs 1979; Cook 1995; Norris 2004; Swann 2010). Technology is also a factor here. Early spoken-discourse analysts had only tape recorders, and this accounts in part for their disproportionate devotion to the transcript as the object of analysis, despite the fact that it freezes interaction, making living speech into a written document and excluding most paralanguage from consideration. More recent computer technology, however, allows complex on-screen cross-reference between transcripts, sound recordings and video, and work relating these elements (e.g. Hosoda 2006; Carter and Adolphs 2008; Rizza 2009; Stokoe forthcoming) is an expanding and important enterprise in contemporary DA.

The exploitation of paralanguage in spoken communication is an instance of multimodality as it involves visual, non-linguistic sound, and other sensory stimuli. Closely related to the increased attention to paralanguage in discourse analysis of talk, therefore, are recent advances in the analysis of multimodal communication in general, and the growing awareness that language cannot for DA purposes be analysed in isolation from other communicative elements (Kress and van Leeuwen 2001; Scollon and Wong-Scollon 2003; Norris 2004; Adolphs and Carter 2007; Kress 2010; see van Leeuwen, this volume). Yet while the complex interactions of language and paralanguage in speech are ancient and universal aspects of human communication (Finnegan 2002), and in this sense the phenomenon is nothing new, the term 'multimodality' is mostly associated with written communication. Multimodal analysis concerns itself largely with the multiple dimensions of meaning made possible by modern printing, computer and mobile technologies, paying attention to the significance of the presentation of the written words themselves (Walker 2001), in different fonts, colours, sizes, arrangements, animations, etc., and to the many communicative modes with which they co-occur, such as still and moving pictures, music, diagrams, tables, etc. Particular attention has been paid to multimodality in the media (e.g. O'Keefe 2006; Talbot 2007), in advertising (Myers 1999; Cook 2001; Johnson 2008), in educational resources, and in computer mediated communication (e. g. Herring 2004). The 'mediated discourse analysis' initiated by Scollon (1998, 2001; Scollon and Wong-Scollon 2003) concentrates on the 'sites of engagement', actions, practices and objects with which language use always occurs.

Multimodal meaning, whether in speech or writing, should then be an essential element of any DA, as it plays a major part in human linguistic communication. Yet while there is now general consensus that this is so, there is still little agreement as to quite how multimodality can be captured and related to linguistic communication for DA purposes. Multimodal elements in communication, because they are graded rather than discrete signs, cannot be simply reduced to linguistic terms as they were in early semiotics (Barthes 1977; Kress and van Leeuwen 1996). They signify by being more or less rather than either/or. Eye contact may be constant or instantaneous or anything in-between, a colour brighter or dimmer along a continuum. Two words on the other hand, such as *bat* and *pat*, are distinguished by a binary contrast (Saussure 1974) – even though in use they may also have graded paralinguistic features such as pitch or volume too. It is perhaps, however, precisely the uncertainty, and the sense of things yet to be done and discovered, combined with the self-evident importance of multimodality in contemporary discourse, which makes the field so exciting and the work on it so stimulating.

Larger structures

Despite their differences, all of the approaches discussed so far have an important element in common. Though they may aim for, and obtain, far reaching conclusions about communication, culture and society, they take as a starting point a fine-grained analysis of language in use, assembling evidence of what happens in instances of communication, before making generalisations. Other approaches, however, take the opposite approach, beginning with larger structures and working top-down from these – though they may also deploy detailed analysis to validate these posited structures.

Genre analysis

One such approach is genre analysis, which seeks to understand any communicative event as an instance of a genre, defined as 'a class of communicative events which share some set of communicative purposes' (Swales 1990: 58). Examples of genres are such events as *academic articles, news bulletins, advertisements, prayers, operas, menus*. Genre analysis then seeks, through fine-grained analysis, to identify the conventions which characterise these different genres:

> These purposes ... constitute the rationale for the genre. This rationale shapes the schematic structure of the discourse and influences and constrains choice of content and style. ... In addition to purpose, exemplars of a genre exhibit various patterns of similarity in terms of structure, style, content and intended audience.
>
> *(Swales 1990: 58)*

Genre analysis was developed by Swales and colleagues in connection with the teaching of English for Specific Purposes and is thus closely linked to the language learning approach to DA. Another school of genre analysis has drawn upon systemic functional linguistics (Martin 1985, 1992; see Young, this volume), relating it to the Hallidayan notion of register and drawing heavily on Halliday's functional grammar. In both manifestations genre analysis has both an identity of its own and has drawn upon other traditions including CDA, corpus linguistics, multimodal analysis, etc. for the purposes of the micro analysis necessary to discover, categorise and validate posited genres. Here again then we face the problem of disentangling different approaches to discourse analysis, establishing what if anything they have to make them distinct and independent from each other or from DA as a whole.

Critical discourse analysis (CDA)

An extremely influential approach to DA, which like genre analysis begins with larger concepts and structures, is Critical Discourse Analysis (CDA) (Fairclough 1989; van Dijk 1993; Fairclough and Wodak 1997; see O'Halloran, this volume). Drawing on the Foucauldian notion of discourses as institutionalised ways of using language, CDA is concerned with ideology, power relations and social injustices, and how these are represented and reproduced through language. Its political allegiances are explicit, and it claims that discourse analysis cannot avoid taking a political stance. Within this overall framework various approaches have different emphases. They may focus primarily upon discourse practices and ideologies, or seek to link discourse and social structures, or to situate specific discourses such as those of racism within a broader historical perspective. While CDA has attracted widespread support it has also been subjected to criticism for bias and partiality (Widdowson 1995, 1998), lack of rigour and circularity (Stubbs 1998), and confusion and inconsistency in its cognitive and linguistic theoretical bases (Stubbs 1998; O'Halloran 2003) or methodology (Hammersley 1997).

Back to detail and forward to generalisation: corpus linguistics

As approaches to DA have developed and accumulated, and as factors deemed relevant to analysis have multiplied, there has been a tendency to move away from the close attention to linguistic detail which characterised DA's early days. In addition, the desire for thick description has led actual analyses to focus of necessity upon one or a few communicative events at a time. There are frequently attempts to relate specific instances to general trends in language use, but these have tended to be speculative rather than systematic. The advent of corpus analysis, however (see Adolphs and Lin, this volume) has enabled DA partially to redress these shortcomings, and to add a quantitative dimension to research. With its power to place any particular instance of language in the context of its use across a wide range of comparable texts or the language as a whole, corpus comparisons have enabled discourse analysts to talk with confidence about the typicality of any text under consideration. Corpus analysis has thus given a major boost to DA in recent years (Baker 2006), with some of the most impressive work being done in corpus stylistics, i.e. in the discourse analysis of literary texts (Stubbs 2002: 123–44, 2005; O'Halloran 2007a, 2007b; see Semino, this volume). This fertile link of DA with stylistics has indeed a long history – and literary stylistics, which links literary language to its effect, can be regarded as a form of DA.

The greater attention to textual features enabled by corpus linguistics and the benefits it has brought to DA should not, however, be taken to mean that a corpus analysis and a discourse analysis are the same thing. Corpus linguistics, like other forms of linguistic analysis before it, is an invaluable tool for DA. Yet in its quest for understanding of how participants in communication achieve meaning, DA cannot limit itself to textual analysis alone, any more than it can limit itself to the cultural and psychological context of language use without attention to actual text. In any act of communication there is someone talking, someone they are talking to, and something they say – sender, receiver and text – and a full discourse analysis must describe analyse and relate each corner of this 'triangle of communication' (Widdowson 1975: 47–70, 91–99; Cook 2004: 4–5; Widdowson 2004). A good deal of DA has emphasised one corner at the expense of the other two, but the full range of approaches described in this chapter provides a formidable resource for the contemporary discourse analyst, who can select and eclectically combine techniques to gain a rich and nuanced understanding of what happens when human beings communicate through language.

Final word

The question touched upon earlier, however remains, and becomes more acute as the resources available multiply: whether discourse analysis still has any identity separate from the many traditions on which it has drawn. While it may be commendable to draw eclectically upon the strengths of many research traditions to gain a rich insight into communication, there is a valid case for saying that there is no longer a single theory or method of analysis which can be clearly labelled as discourse analysis. It has become a superordinate term for a wide range of traditions for the analysis of language in use, so general and all-inclusive that it is hardly worth using. Perhaps the term discourse analysis has had its day. It is now so built into the fabric of applied linguistics that any analysis of language in use is discourse analysis of some kind.

Related topics

corpus linguistics; critical discourse analysis; linguistic ethnography; multimodality; stylistics

Further reading

Blommaert, J. (2005) *Discourse: A Critical Introduction*, Cambridge: Cambridge University Press. (A version of DA suited to the analysis of identity and power relations in contemporary globalised contexts.)

Cook, G. (1989) *Discourse*, Oxford: Oxford University Press. (An introduction to the basic principles of early DA and its relevance to language teachers.)

Gee, J. P. (1999) *An Introduction to Discourse Analysis: Theory and Method*, London: Routledge. (A view of DA as process and interaction.)

Paltridge, B. (2006) *Discourse Analysis: An Introduction*, London: Continuum. (A clear, balanced and comprehensive introduction to the field.)

Widdowson, H. G. (2007) *Discourse Analysis*, Oxford: Oxford University Press. (A brief and accessible overview of key concepts in DA.)

References

Adolphs, S. and Carter, R. (2007) 'Beyond the word: new challenges in analysing corpora of spoken English', *European Journal of English Studies* 11(2): 133–46.

Austin, J. L. (1962) *How To Do Things with Words*, Oxford: Clarendon Press.

Baker, P. (2006) *Using Corpora in Discourse Analysis*, London: Continuum.

Bakhtin, M. M. (1986) *Speech Genres and other Late Essays*, V. McGee (trans.), Austin: University of Texas.

Barthes, R. (1977) 'The rhetoric of the image', in R. Barthes (ed.), S. Heath (trans.), *Image, Music, Text*, London: Fontana.

Bartlett, F. C. (1932) *Remembering*, Cambridge: Cambridge University Press.

Barton, D., Hamilton, M. and Ivanic, R. (2000) *Situated Literacies: Reading and Writing in Context*, London: Routledge.

Bhatia, V. K., Flowerdew, J. and Jones, R. (eds) (2008) *Advances in Discourse Studies*, London: Routledge.

Birch, D. (1982) 'The Birmingham school of discourse analysis and communicative approaches to language teaching', *RELC Journal* 13(2): 98–110.

Blommaert, J. (2005) *Discourse: A Critical Introduction*, Cambridge: Cambridge University Press.

Brown, G. and Yule, G. (1983) *Discourse Analysis*, Cambridge: Cambridge University Press.

Carter, R. and Adolphs, S. (2008) 'Linking the verbal and visual: new directions for corpus linguistics', *Language and Computers* 64: 275–91.

Cook, G. (1989) *Discourse*, Oxford: Oxford University Press.

——(1994) *Discourse and Literature: The Interplay of Form and Mind*, Oxford: Oxford University Press.

——(1995) 'Theoretical issues: transcribing the untranscribable', in G. Leech, G. Myers and J. Thomas (eds) *Spoken English on Computer: Transcription, Mark-up and Applications*, London: Longman.

——(2001) *The Discourse of Advertising*, London: Routledge.

——(2004) *Genetically Modified Language*, London: Routledge

Coulthard, M. (1985) *Introduction to Discourse Analysis*, London: Longman.

Coulthard, M. and Montgomery, M. (eds) (1981) *Studies in Discourse Analysis*, London: Routledge and Kegan Paul.

Creese, A. (2008) 'Linguistic ethnography', in K. A. King and N. H. Hornberger (eds) *Encyclopedia of Language and Education*, 2nd edn, vol. 10: *Research Methods in Language and Education*, New York: Springer.

de Beaugrande, R. and Dressler, W. (1981) *Introduction to Text Linguistics*, London: Longman.

Fairclough, N. (1989) *Language and Power*, London: Longman.

Fairclough, N. and Wodak, R. (1997) 'Critical discourse analysis', in T. A. van Dijk (ed.) *Discourse as Social Interaction*, London: Sage.

Finnegan, R. (2002) *Communicating: The Multiple Modes of Human Interconnection*, London and New York: Routledge.

Garfinkel, H. (1967) *Studies in Ethnomethodology*, Englewood Cliffs, NJ: Prentice Hall.

Gee, J. P. (1999) *An Introduction to Discourse Analysis: Theory and Method*, London: Routledge.

Grice, H. P. (1975) 'Logic and conversation', in P. Cole and J. L. Morgan (eds) *Syntax and Semantics*, vol. 3: *Speech Acts*, New York: Academic Press.

Gumperz, J. J. (1986). 'Interactional sociolinguistics in the study of schooling', in J. Cook-Gumperz (ed.) *The Social Construction of Literacy*, Cambridge: Cambridge University Press.

Halliday, M. A. K. (1973) *Explorations in the Function of Language*, London: Edward Arnold.

——(1978) *Language as a Social Semiotic*, London: Arnold.

Halliday, M. A. K. and Hasan, R. (1976) *Cohesion in English*, London: Longman.

Halliday, M. A. K., McIntosh, A. and Strevens, P. (1964) *The Linguistic Sciences and Language Teaching*, London: Longman.

Hammersley, M. (1992) *What's Wrong with Ethnography?*, London: Routledge.

——(1997) 'On the foundations of critical discourse analysis', *Language and Communication* 17(3): 237–48.

Hammersley, M. and Atkinson, P. (2007) *Ethnography: Principles in Practice*, London: Routledge.

Harris, Z. (1952) 'Discourse analysis', *Language* 28: 1–30.

Hatch, E. (1992) *Discourse and Language Education*, Cambridge: Cambridge University Press.

Heritage, J. (1984) *Garfinkel and Ethnomethodology*, Cambridge and New York: Polity Press.

Herring, S. C. (2004) 'Computer-mediated discourse analysis: an approach to researching online behavior', in S. A. Barab, R. Kling and J. H. Gray (eds) *Designing for Virtual Communities in the Service of Learning*, New York: Cambridge University Press.

Hosoda, Y. (2006) 'Repair and relevance of differential language expertise in second language conversations', *Applied Linguistics* 27(1): 25–51.

Hutchby, I. and Wooffitt, R. (1998) *Conversation Analysis*, Cambridge: Polity Press.

Hymes, D. (1972a) 'On communicative competence', in J. B. Pride and J. Holmes (eds) *Sociolinguistics: Selected Readings*, Harmondsworth: Penguin.

——(1972b) 'Models of the interaction of language and social life', in J. J. Gumperz and D. Hymes (eds) *Directions in Sociolinguistics: The Ethnography of Communication*, Oxford: Blackwell.

Johnson, F. L. (2008) *Imaging in Advertising: Verbal and Visual Codes of Commerce*, London: Routledge.

Johnstone, B. (2002) *Discourse Analysis*, Oxford: Blackwell.

Kramsch, C. and Whiteside, A. (2008) 'Language ecology in multilingual settings: towards a theory of symbolic competence', *Applied Linguistics* 29(4): 645–72.

Kramsch, C. (ed.) (2002) *Language Acquisition and Language Socialization: Ecological Perspectives*, London: Continuum.

Kress, G. (2010) *Multimodality: A Social Semiotic Approach to Contemporary Communication*, London: Routledge.

Kress, G. and van Leeuwen, T. (1996) *Reading Images: The Grammar of Visual Design*, London: Routledge.

——(2001) *Multimodal Discourse: The Modes and Media of Contemporary Communication*, London: Edward Arnold.

Kristeva, J. (1986) 'Word, dialogue and novel', in T. Moi (ed.) *The Kristeva Reader*, Oxford: Blackwell, pp. 34–61.

Liddicoat, A. J. (2007) *An Introduction to Conversation Analysis*, London: Continuum.

Martin, J. R. (1985) *Factual Writing: Exploring and Challenging Social Reality*, Oxford: Oxford University Press.

——(1992) *English Text: System and Structure*, Philadelphia, PA and Amsterdam: John Benjamins.

McCarthy, M. (1991) *Discourse Analysis for Language Teachers*, Cambridge: Cambridge University Press.

Mitchell, T. F. (1957) 'The language of buying and selling in Cyrenaica: a situational statement', *Principles of Firthian Linguistics*, *Hesperis* 44: 31–71. Reprinted in T. F. Mitchell (ed.) *Principles of Firthian Linguistics*, London: Longman.

Myers, G. (1999) *Ad Worlds: Brands, Media, Audience*, London: Arnold.

Nevile, M. (2008) 'Being out of order: overlapping talk as evidence of trouble in airplane pilots' work', in V. K. Bhatia, J. Flowerdew and R. Jones (eds) *Advances in Discourse Studies*, London: Routledge.

Norris, S. (2004) *Analyzing Multimodal Interaction: A Methodological Framework*, London: Routledge.

Ochs, E. (1979) 'Transcription as theory', in E. Ochs and B. B. Schieffelin (eds) *Developmental Pragmatics*, New York: Academic Press.

O'Halloran, K. A. (2003) *Critical Discourse Analysis and Language Cognition*, Edinburgh: Edinburgh University Press.

——(2007a) 'Corpus-assisted literary evaluation', *Corpora* 2(1): 33–63.

——(2007b) 'The subconscious in James Joyce's "Eveline": a corpus stylistic analysis which chews on the "Fish hook"', *Language and Literature* 16(3): 227–44.

O'Keefe, A. (2006) *Investigating Media Discourse*, London: Routledge.

Paltridge, B. (2006) *Discourse Analysis: An Introduction*, London: Continuum.

Rampton, B., Tusting, K., Maybin, J., Barwell, R., Creese, A. and Lytra, V. (2004) 'UK linguistic ethnography: a discussion paper'. Available at: www.lancs.ac.uk/fss/organisations/lingethn/docum ents/discussion_paper_jan_05.pdf (accessed 13 January 2010).

Riley, P. (1987) *Discourse and Learning*, London: Longman.

Rizza, C. (2009) 'Semantically redundant language: a case study', *Applied Linguistics* 30(2): 276–94.

Sacks, H., Schegloff, E. A. and Jefferson, G. (1974) 'A simplest systematics for the organization of turn-taking for conversation', *Language* 50(4): 696–735.

de Saussure, F. (1974) *Course in General Linguistics*, W. Baskin (trans.), London: Fontana/Collins.

Schank, R. C. and Abelson, R. P. (1977) *Scripts, Plans, Goals and Understanding: An Inquiry into Human Knowledge*, Hillsdale, NJ: Lawrence Erlbaum Associates.

Scollon, R. (1998) *Mediated Discourse as Social Interaction: A Study of News Discourse*, London: Longman.

——(2001) *Mediated Discourse: The Nexus of Practice*, London: Routledge.

Scollon, R. and Wong-Scollon, S. (2003) *Discourses in Place: Language in the Material World*, London: Routledge.

Searle, J. R. (1969) *Speech Acts: An Essay in the Philosophy of Language*, Cambridge: Cambridge University Press.

——(1975) 'A taxonomy of illocutionary acts', in K. Gunderson (ed.) *Language, Mind and Knowledge*, Minneapolis: University of Minnesota Press.

Seedhouse, P. (2004) *The Interactional Architecture of the Language Classroom: A Conversation Analysis Perspective*, Malden, MA: Blackwell.

Semino, E. (2002) 'A cognitive stylistic approach to mind style in narrative fiction', in E. Semino, and J. Culpeper (eds) *Cognitive Stylistics: Language and Cognition in Text Analysis*, Amsterdam: John Benjamins.

Sinclair, J. and Coulthard, M. (1975) *Towards an Analysis of Discourse: The English used by Teachers and Pupils*, London: Oxford University Press.

Slembrouck, S. (2009) 'Discourse analysis', in K. Malmkjær (ed.) *The Routledge Linguistics Encyclopaedia*, London: Routledge, pp. 133–7.

Stokoe, E. (forthcoming) *Talking Relationships: Analyzing Speed-dating Conversations*, Cambridge: Cambridge University Press.

Street, B. (1984) *Literacy in Theory and Practice*, Cambridge: Cambridge University Press.

Stubbs, M. (1983) *Discourse Analysis*, Oxford: Blackwell.

——(2002) *Words and Phrases*, Oxford: Blackwell.

——(2005) 'Conrad in the computer: examples of quantitative stylistic methods', *Language and Literature* 14(1): 5–24. Reprinted in R. Carter and P. Stockwell (eds) (2008) *The Language and Literature Reader*, London: Routledge.

——(1998) 'Whorf's children: critical comments on critical discourse analysis', in A. Ryan and A. Wray (eds) *Evolving Models of Language: British Studies in Applied Linguistics 12*, Clevedon: BAAL/Multilingual Matters.

Swales, J. (1990) *Genre Analysis*, Cambridge: Cambridge University Press.

——(2010) 'Transcribing spoken interaction', in S. Hunston and D. Oakey (eds) *Introducing Applied Linguistics: Key Concepts and Skills*, London: Routledge.

Swann, J. (2010) 'Transcribing spoken interaction', in S. Hunston and D. Oakey (eds.) *Introducing Applied Linguistics: Key Concepts and Skills*, London: Routledge.

Talbot, M. (2007) *Media Discourse: Representation and Interaction*, Edinburgh: Edinburgh University Press.

van Dijk, T. (1972) *Some Aspects of Text Grammars*, The Hague: Mouton.

——(1977) *Text and Context*, London: Longman.

——(1993) 'Principles of critical discourse analysis', *Discourse and Society* 4(2): 249–83.

van Lier, L. (2000) 'From input to affordance: social-interactive learning in an ecological perspective', in J. P. Lantolf (ed.), *Sociocultural Theory and Language Learning*, Oxford: Oxford University Press.

——(2004) *The Ecology and Semiotics of Language Learning: A Sociocultural Perspective*, Dordrecht: Kluwer Academic.

Vološinov, V. N. (1988) *Marxism and the Philosophy of Language*, L. Matejka and R. Titunik (trans.), Cambridge, MA: Harvard University Press.

Walker, S. (2001) *Typography and Language in Everyday Life: Prescriptions and Practices*, Harlow: Longman Pearson.

Werlich, E. (1976) *A Text Grammar of English*, Heidelberg: Quelle und Meyer.

Widdowson, H. G. (1973) 'An Applied Linguistic Approach to Discourse Analysis', unpublished Ph.D. Thesis, Department of Linguistics, University of Edinburgh.

——(1975) *Stylistics and the Teaching of Literature*, London: Longman.

——(1979) *Explorations in Applied Linguistics*, Oxford: Oxford University Press.

——(1984) *Explorations in Applied Linguistics 2*, Oxford: Oxford University Press.

——(1995) 'Review of Fairclough's discourse and social change', *Applied Linguistics* 16(4): 510–16.

——(1998) 'The theory and practice of critical discourse analysis', *Applied Linguistics* 19(1): 136–51.

——(2004) *Text, Context, Pretext: Critical Issues in Discourse Analysis*, Oxford: Blackwell.

——(2007) *Discourse Analysis*, Oxford: Oxford University Press.

31

Critical discourse analysis

Kieran O'Halloran

Introduction

Critical discourse analysis (CDA) investigates how language use may be affirming and indeed reproducing the perspectives, values and ways of talking of the powerful, which may not be in the interests of the less powerful. The relationship between language, power and ideology is a crucial focal point. CDA consists of an interdisciplinary set of approaches which attempt to describe, interpret and explain this relationship. Among its principal architects are Paul Chilton, Norman Fairclough, Teun van Dijk and Ruth Wodak.

In this chapter, I shall set out what 'critical', 'discourse' and 'analysis' mean in CDA, outline a number of key approaches within it, and then demonstrate a critical discourse analysis.

Critical

In CDA, 'critical' is usually taken to mean studying and taking issue with how dominance and inequality are reproduced through language use:

> Analysis, description and theory formation play a role especially in as far as they allow better understanding and critique of social inequality, based on gender, ethnicity, class, origin, religion, language, sexual orientation and other criteria that define differences between people. Their ultimate goal is not only scientific, but also social and political, namely *change*. In that case, social discourse analysis takes the form of a *critical* discourse analysis.
>
> *(van Dijk 1997: 22–3)*

CDA is critical of how unequal language use can do ideological work. *Ideologies* are representations of aspects of the world which contribute to establishing and maintaining relations of power, domination and exploitation. When language use reflects inequality (e.g. 'man and wife' as opposed to 'husband and wife'), CDA argues that sustained use of such unequal representations does ideological work because it tacitly affirms inequitable social processes. A key assumption in this argument is that there is a 'dialectical' or 'bi-directional' relationship between social processes and language use. With such a focus on the ideological effects of unequal language use, CDA is especially drawn to texts where the marginal and relatively powerless are (mis)represented by the powerful. The take on 'critical' as described has its roots in the twentieth century in the work of the social theorist and philosopher, Jürgen Habermas, and further back to Frankfurt school theorists such as Max Horkheimer. Furthermore, given the significance of the dialecticalism between language use and social processes in its ontology, CDA has a more thorough-going social-historical perspective on context than many other types of discourse analysis (see Cook, this volume):

> A fully 'critical' account of discourse would … require a theorization and description of both the social processes and structures which give rise to the production of a text, and of the social structures and processes within which individuals or groups as social historical subjects create meanings in their interaction with texts.
>
> *(Wodak 2001: 2–3)*

Of course, one does not need to have the appellation of 'critical discourse analyst' to be critical of how language use can be bound up with (ab)use of power. However, where a critical discourse analysis differs from 'lay' critique is in its 'systematic approaches to inherent meanings', its reliance on 'scientific procedures' and the necessity as it sees it to include the 'self-reflection of the researchers themselves' (Fairclough and Wodak 1997: 279). Another feature which distinguishes CDA from other branches of discourse analysis is that CDA is 'committed', with analysts often being actively involved in challenging the phenomena they study. Indeed, for critical discourse analysts, there can only ever be committed discourse analysis and so their political persuasion (usually left-liberal) is often evident in their reflection and interpretation. CDA is, in the words of one of its major proponents, 'discourse analysis "with an attitude"' (van Dijk 2001: 96).

Discourse

Usually in CDA, the concept of discourse has two different but related senses (Fairclough 2003: 3–4). The first is 'language in use'. Let me refer to this type as discourse 1. The discourse 1 of a conversation refers to the meanings made in interaction with those features of context which are deemed relevant, e.g. tone of voice of participants, facial movements, hand-gestures. If the conversation is recorded, its 'text' would be the transcription of the conversation. Discourse 1 refers to meanings made in reading too, that is, those meanings we derive from the text in line with the knowledge we possess, the amount of effort we invest, our values, how we have been educated and socialised, our gender, etc.

A second meaning of discourse in CDA is associated with the work of the French social theorist/philosopher, Michel Foucault. Foucault (1972) describes discourses as ways of talking about the world which are tightly connected to ways of seeing and comprehending it. For Foucault, discourses place limits on the possibilities of articulation (and by extension, what to do or not to do) with respect to the area of concern of a particular institution, political programme, etc. For example, different religions promote their own discourses which frame explanation of natural behaviour. Roman Catholicism now approves of 'the big bang' theory of the universe's birth (scientific discourse) but that its genesis was by divine means (religious discourse). Let me refer to this second meaning as discourse 2. Importantly, for Foucault and for CDA, it is the powerful who ultimately control discourse 2 and have the means to regenerate it (e.g. newspaper moguls). (See also the definition of discourse in Cook, this volume.)

Analysis

Probably the most widely used analytical framework in CDA is Fairclough's (see, for example, Fairclough 2001). It consists of three stages: description, interpretation and explanation. In the first stage, *description*, the text should be described as rigorously and as comprehensively as possible relative to the analytical focus. A key descriptive tool used in CDA is *systemic functional linguistics* (SFL) (see Young, this volume).

Systematicity in the description stage is important since this helps ground *interpretation* of how the text might lead to different discourses 1 for different readers in different *discourse practices* or the situations of language use, e.g. a political speech, a chat between strangers at a bus stop, a debate on Twitter. The focus in the interpretation stage is concerned with conjecturing the cognition of readers/listeners, how they might mentally interact with the text. Fairclough refers to this as 'processing analysis' (see Figure 31.1). Critique in the interpretation stage means pointing to a *misrepresentation* or a *cognitive problem* (Chouliaraki and Fairclough 1999: 33). This might mean that some significant information is absent from a particular text, which leads to the reader either being misled or not being fully apprised of the most relevant facts. This stage also seeks to show how wider social and cultural contexts and power relations within them (discourse 2) might shape the interpretation (discourse 1) of a text.

In *explanation*, CDA critically explains connections between texts and discourse(s) 2 circulating in the wider social and cultural context, the 'sociocultural practice'. Critique here

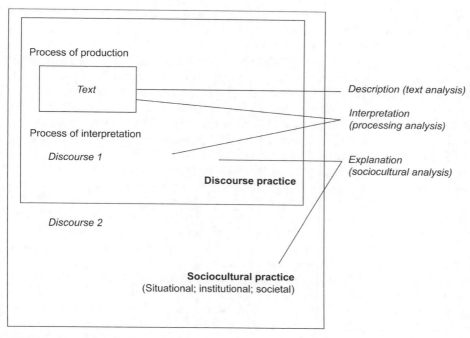

Figure 31.1 The scope and foci of critical discourse analysis
Source: Adapted from Fairclough 1995a: 98.

involves showing how the 'ideological function of the misrepresentation or unmet need' helps 'in sustaining existing social arrangements' (Chouliaraki and Fairclough 1999: 33).

Approaches

CDA is multidisciplinary, encompassing a number of different but related approaches which may be combined in description, interpretation and explanation. Some salient approaches are featured below.

Critical linguistics aims to reveal the biases, or the 'angles of representation', in seemingly 'transparent' language use (Fowler 1991; Fowler *et al.* 1979; Kress and Hodge 1979) and to show how these biases can mystify the actual nature of the events in reporting. One key focus of critical linguistics is how agency for an action is represented. Trew (1979), regarded as a classic in CDA, highlights in a report from the British newspaper, *The Times*, how responsibility for a police action in Rhodesia in 1975 is downplayed. To do so, Trew uses systemic functional categories, that is, categories which track the relationship between grammar and meaning in a clause. Here is an extract from *The Times* and Trew's analysis:

Eleven Africans were shot dead and 15 wounded when Rhodesian police opened fire on a rioting crowd of about 2,000.

-	shoot dead	eleven Africans	(when) Rhodesian police opened fire on a rioting crowd of about 2,000
ACTOR	PROCESS PASSIVE	GOAL	CIRCUMSTANCE

The functional analysis helps to reveal the following: because of the use of the passive voice, there is an absence of explicit connection between the Actor (or the doer in the clause) and the process 'shoot dead'. As a result, agency for the shooting has to be inferred from the Circumstance, i.e. information which supplements 'eleven Africans', the Goal (or the 'done to' in the clause) and 'shoot dead', the process. From this functional analysis, Trew argues that in *The Times* 'the effects of the linguistic facts pointed out are a tendency to shift the focus away from those who did the shooting and onto the victims' (Trew 1979: 99).

Another linguistic concept that critical linguists are vigilant of is *nominalisation*, the representation of a process by a noun form rather than by a verb. Using nominalisation, information about an Actor in a clause, and thus responsibility for an action, can be removed. For example, the sentence 'the shooting of 11 demonstrators yesterday caused widespread outrage' includes the nominalisation 'shooting' and not the agent of the shooting. Given what I have outlined, it should be clear that critical linguistics describes texts so as to perform critical discourse 1 analysis, i.e. make an interpretation that significant information is absent from a reader's discourse 1. Synergy between SFL and CDA is still current (e.g. Coffin and O'Halloran 2006; White 2004; Young and Harrison 2004).

The critical linguistic work completed at the University of East Anglia in the 1970s, for example Fowler *et al.* (1979) and Kress and Hodge (1979), is often referenced as a precursor of CDA. While the social theoretical base of CDA has become much more complex and varied than the non-Foucauldian critical linguistics of the 1970s, the perspective in critical linguistics on how language can be used to mystify responsibility for social action is still a fixture of CDA. This is not to say there are no problems with this approach. Critical linguistics makes a number of tacit assumptions about the relationship between mystification and cognition which are connected to cognitive paradigms of the 1970s. These implicit premises are problematised by contemporary cognitive paradigms. O'Halloran (2003) underwrites mystification analysis in CDA by basing it in a synthesis of contemporary cognitive paradigms.

Socio-cognitive analysis focuses on the dialectical relationships between social structure, discourse 2 and cognition in discourse 1. The extent to which cognitive theory is employed in socio-cognitive analysis fluctuates. Fairclough (2001), for example, uses a limited number of cognitive concepts, e.g. member's resources – the socio-politicised knowledge people bring to texts and from which they make inferences in reading. Consider Fairclough's (2001: 44–5) socio-cognitive analysis of the following newspaper text at the time of the Falklands/Malvinas conflict:

> The wife of the new Commanding Officer of the 2nd Parachute Battalion spoke last night of her fears for her husband's safety.
>
> As she played in the sunshine with her four children, Jenny Keeble said she hoped her husband would not have to go into battle again.
>
> She said: 'I pray he and his men have done enough. But if they do go on I know that he is a man who will do his job to the best of his ability and I am certain he and the 2nd Parachute Battalion will succeed … '
>
> *(Daily Mail, 1 June 1982)*

For Fairclough, the text positions the reader to infer Jenny Keeble is a 'good wife or an admirable person' (this evaluation is not made explicit in the text). This is because the text positions the reader to draw on a member's resource of sexist discourse 2 (should they possess this). And should the reader not oppose the reading position being set up, Fairclough argues that this inference leads to a sexist reading (discourse 1). Moreover, because of its assumption of a dialectical relationship between language use/cognition and social structure, CDA would hold that such a reading can do ideological work in reproducing inequitable discourse 2 and social structure. It should be highlighted that van Dijk has been more consistently explicit than Fairclough or Wodak that discussion of the relationship between discourse and social structure should take place with due consideration to an individual's cognition (e.g. van Dijk 1998). As such, van Dijk offers a more thorough-going theoretical base for socio-cognitive analysis (e.g. van Dijk 2001).

The *discourse-historical approach* is associated with Ruth Wodak. It places importance on the contextualising and historicising of texts. To foster critical analysis, this approach systematically synthesises available background information in the analysis and interpretation of a written or spoken text. Wodak has advanced a detailed, concentrically circular, model of context:

> The smallest circle is the discourse unit itself and the micro-analysis of the text. The next circle consists of the speakers and audience, of the interactants with their various personality features, biographies and social roles. The next context level involves the 'objective setting', the location in times and space, the description of the situation. Then, the next circle signifies the institution in which the event takes place. And we could naturally expand to the society in which the institution is integrated, its function in society and its history. … The interaction of all these context levels would then lead to an analysis of discourse as social practice.
>
> *(Wodak 1996: 21)*

Much of the discourse-historical approach was cultivated in an interdisciplinary study of post-war anti-Semitism in Austria (Wodak *et al.* 2009). Anti-Semitism and racist prejudice generally are often tacit, which can make it problematic for the writer/speaker to be indicted for bigotry. Via motion between different levels of context, the discourse-historical approach facilitates revelation of implicitly prejudiced discourse 1. Furthermore, this movement fosters the identification of the codes and allusions which reproduce prejudiced discourse 2. More generally speaking, the discourse-historical approach seeks to comprehend how discourse 2 helps to generate and reinforce ideas such as 'race', 'nation' and 'ethnicity' (Wodak and Reisgl 2001: 385).

Fairclough's *socio-cultural change* approach trains its focus generally on how socio-cultural change, the globalisation of capitalism and modification in discourse are related. He observes how the border shift between public and private discourse in the late twentieth/early twenty-first century is revealed in texts where subjects are positioned in a more informal, chatty manner (e.g. in advertising). For this shift in discourse 2, he uses the term *conversationalisation*. As public institutions have come more and more within the purview of the ideology of consumer capitalism, Fairclough notes how the texts of public institutions (e.g. university Websites) have become more and more conversational, this being more conducive to the sales-pitch discourse of late twentieth/early twenty-first century life (e.g. Fairclough 1995b).

For Fairclough, then, texts are barometers of changes in contemporary capitalism, or what is also referred to as 'late modernity'. He contends that 'late modernity' is reflected in textual hybridity – the mixing together of different genres, styles and discourses:

> Late modernity entails a radical unsettling of the boundaries of social life – between economy and culture, between global and local, and so forth – one aspect of which is an unsettling of the boundaries between different domains of social use of language.
>
> *(Chouliaraki and Fairclough 1999: 83)*

In tracing textual hybridity as a reflex of late modernity, Fairclough more expressly employs SFL than Wodak or van Dijk (see, for example, Fairclough 2003). Emblematic of his work is an interest in traversing social theory, which tends not to analyse texts in a detailed linguistic fashion, and work in text/discourse analysis, which has not traditionally sought to engage with social theoretical issues. Fairclough's engagement with critical realism, the social theoretical approach of Roy Bhaskar, is one such instance (e.g. Fairclough *et al.* 2002).

I finish this section by mentioning briefly some other approaches within CDA. Feminist critical discourse analysis aims to analyse the relationships between gender, language use and power (see, for example, Lazar 2005; Litosseliti 2006). Sexism and the construction of gender identity, as well as the appreciation of gender as a dynamic construct, are key foci. Other work within CDA takes account of the relationship between text and image (or what is known as multimodal studies, see van Leeuwen, this volume) e.g. Lassen *et al.* (2006), Kress and van Leeuven (2006) (which also draws upon SFL).

Aside from van Dijk, there are other scholars working in CDA who saliently draw on/adapt cognitive theory, particularly the conceptual metaphor theory associated with the work of George Lakoff (e.g. Lakoff 1987; Lakoff and Johnson 1980); see, for example, Chilton (1985), Charteris-Black (2004), Goatly (2007), Koller (2004), Wodak (2006). Hart and Lukeš (2007) is an anthology which draws together different uses of cognitive theory in CDA. Evolutionary psychology is also drawn upon in more recent CDA (Chilton 2004; 2005; Goatly 2007; O'Halloran 2005). Chilton (2004) is a key work in CDA which draws on both cognitive theory and evolutionary theory.

A counterpoint perspective to CDA is 'positive discourse analysis' (e.g. Bartlett 2009; Martin 2004). The focus here is on understanding and promoting discourse which inspires and uplifts (e.g. writing by Mandela and Tutu) as well as discourse which is effective in mediation, diplomacy and promoting reconciliation, peace and happiness. Toolan (1997) calls for a different kind of positive discourse analysis in arguing that it is not enough in CDA to criticise manipulative representations in texts; CDA should also be explicit about showing what non-manipulative texts would look like. Finally, influenced largely by the pioneering work of Michael Stubbs, there is a host of new scholarship in CDA which uses methods of analysis from corpus linguistics (see 'Empirically-driven CDA' below).

A critical discourse analysis

Let me demonstrate a critical discourse analysis by looking at a short news text which appeared in the British popular tabloid, the *Mirror* on 13 August 2007; I have numbered all sentences:

1   *Air protesters target travellers*
2   Police are on a war footing at the UK's biggest airport as they wait for 2,000 protesters determined to cause chaos for three million travellers.
3   The organisers of a week-long Camp for Climate Action are hell-bent on bringing Heathrow to a halt in 'mass direct action' that could cost tens of millions of pounds.
4   Last night 150 people turned up at a camp on the site of the proposed third runway, the first of 100 camps expected to be set up around the airport.
5   An 800-strong police force already on terror alert at Heathrow will be joined by up to 1,800 extra officers.
6   Leaked memos sent to airport managers by Heathrow owner BAA reveal what is expected during the campaign, which starts tomorrow.
7   One said: 'The means in which campaigners are aiming to achieve their protests will vary … Blocking roads and railways into Heathrow is a common practice and this was used last year at the 2006 Drax Climate Camp and at G8 protests in Rostock, Germany.'
8   BAA last week won a High Court injunction banning members of the protest group Plane Stupid from the airport.
9   But it did not include the Camp for Climate Action.
10   BAA expects demonstrators to pose as passengers to infiltrate the four terminals where it is feared they will set up fake ticket booths so innocent travellers miss flights.
11   Police are bracing themselves for 'life-threatening acts' such as climbing perimeter fences, blocking runways and disrupting nearby roads, including the M25.
12   Protesters are also expected to try to storm and occupy offices belonging to airport-related firms and take direct action to disrupt the supply of food for passengers.
13   Huge banners will be dropped in awkward spots around Heathrow to cause traffic chaos and maximum embarrassment.
14   Also expected are disruption to meetings and seminars.
15   Bosses of major airport firms have been warned to expect 'custard pie attacks' and protests at their homes.
16   BAA has told workers: 'Remain calm, do not physically touch or engage in discussion with protesters.'
17   Do not follow a protester into a dangerous situation.
18   BAA warned that three million people could face disruption during the campaign, which starts tomorrow and runs for a week.

19 Managing Director Mark Bullock said: 'BAA has always respected people's democratic right to protest lawfully.'

20 'However, we do not believe our passengers and staff should be harassed or obstructed by any unlawful direct action.'

21 The Camp for Climate Action is an umbrella organisation bringing together environmental protest groups.

22 It is demonstrating against the fifth terminal already being built and the proposed third runway.

23 68,000 is the number of people employed by Heathrow, including 4,500 BAA staff.

24 It contributes £5bn to UK economy.

25 There are 1.54 Tonnes of CO_2 emissions as a result of a return flight to New York, according to climatecare.org.

(Stephen Moyes; © Mirror Syndication International)

When examining a text for bias, it is worth reflecting on how political and cultural attitudes, for instance, can affect what we regard as bias. Just because we view aspects of a text as objectionable (politically, culturally, etc.), this does not necessarily mean the text is inherently biased. It is important, then, to try to separate out our political/cultural, etc. attitudes, and how they can direct what we regard as bias, from bias which is in a text irrespective of these attitudes. This is where employing linguistic analysis can help, by allowing us to describe a text's meanings systematically. In so doing, it enables us to establish the inherent bias of a text in a rigorous way while reducing the chance of identifying bits of a text as biased because they refer to things we find undesirable.

One must, however, take care with the term 'bias'. This is because all texts carry bias in one way or another. There is no neutral text; bias is a matter of degree. For this reason, many critical discourse analysts often prefer instead to employ an expression used above – 'angle of representation' – in case by 'bias' the impression is given that they are subscribing to the possibility of a neutral text. However, as long as it is understood that there is no such thing as a neutral text, my use of 'bias' in this chapter is synonymous with 'angle of representation'.

In the Approaches section above, under 'Critical linguistics', you saw reference to a process, 'shoot dead'. This process is known as a material process in SFL; material processes relate to the world of matter. There are other processes in SFL (see Halliday and Matthiessen 2004) which are useful in appreciating a text's angle of representation. Let me flag two of them, since they will be useful in critical analysis of the *Mirror* text: mental processes and verbal processes. These are concerned respectively with the workings of the mind (e.g. know, believe) and communication (e.g. speak, inform). To indicate how grammatical subjects, objects, etc. can function differently in a clause, SFL assigns various participant roles around different process types. Material processes are accompanied by Actor (who or what is the 'doing' participant) and Goal (who or what is the 'done to' participant). In mental processes, the participant performing the mental behaviour is termed a Senser. So 'She' is a Senser in 'She believed in God'; 'God', i.e. what is being 'sensed', is termed a Phenomenon. In the verbal process, 'She shouted out "help"', 'She' is termed a Sayer and what is being communicated, 'help', is referred to as Verbiage.

Description

An SFL description of the *Mirror* text's angle of representation – of its material, mental and verbal processes and associated participant roles – can be found in the appendix. Let me summarise the results of this analysis: when protesters are described, it is mostly via material processes in which they (or their campaign) are realised as Actor (twenty-six times) and act on people or things, e.g. in sentence 1:

Air protesters	target	travellers
ACTOR	PROCESS	GOAL

On only three occasions, protesters are realised as Goal, e.g. in sentence 16:

Do not touch	protestors
PROCESS	GOAL

Protesters are not realised as Sayer or Senser.

In contrast, non-protesters are represented not only as Actor (twelve times), e.g. in sentence 8:

High Court injunction	banning	members of the protest group Plane Stupid
ACTOR	PROCESS	GOAL

but as Senser (eight times), e.g. in sentence 10:

BAA	expects	demonstrators to pose as passengers ... miss flights
SENSER	PROCESS	PHENOMENON

and Sayer (six times), e.g. in sentence 18:

BAA	warned	that three million people could face disruption ... week
SAYER	PROCESS	VERBIAGE

The distribution of the participant roles of Actor, Senser and Sayer is more equal for non-protesters than protesters.

I will move on to an interpretation of these quantitative patterns shortly. Before doing so, I describe another aspect of the text's make-up – its *stance*. This is how a text indicates how certain the author is about what is being conveyed, that is whether it is certain, probable or possible. The first three sentences, as well as sentences 7 and 13, signal with a stance of certainty what the protesters intend to/will do, e.g. sentence 2:

Police are on a war footing at the UK's biggest airport as they wait for 2,000 protesters determined to cause chaos for three million travellers.

In contrast, there are six sentences which signal a stance of probability about protesters' action via the verb 'expect', e.g. sentence 10:

BAA expects demonstrators to pose as passengers to infiltrate the four terminals …

and two sentences which signal a stance of possibility using 'could', e.g. sentence 18:

BAA warned that three million people could face disruption during the campaign, which starts tomorrow and runs for a week.

Now that we have a reasonably sound description of the text, we are in a good place to interpret and explain it.

Interpretation

Having a quantitative perspective on participant roles is useful because it enables us to see inconsistencies in their realisation. There is no space given to the protesters as Sayer to warn, for example, of the ecological effects of increased airplane travel. Neither is there space given over to protesters as Senser to signal reflection on these effects, nor to signal what protesters believe, and what they hope to achieve, i.e. to prevent huge CO_2 emissions which a new runway and new terminal are likely to bring through increased air traffic. Given that the dominant pattern in the angle of representation is Actor Process Goal, readers may just view the protestors in terms of the damage they allegedly wish to achieve (cognitive problem 1).

'Life-threatening acts' (sentence 11) is a noun phrase. Since this is nominal, and not clausal, there is no Actor or Goal. In turn, this leads to an ambiguity: 'life-threatening' could be referring to passengers whose lives are potentially threatened. But it might actually just be referring to protesters who threaten only their own lives and are therefore of little danger to the public. The ambiguity of 'life-threatening acts' means it may sound more alarmist to the reader than what actually occurred (cognitive problem 2).

'Embarrassment' (sentence 13) is also nominal rather than clausal, so we do not know who the alleged target of the embarrassment is. As such, 'embarrassment' can be seen as strategically vague (cognitive problem 3).

'Disruption' (sentence 18) is a nominalisation and so again one can read this as strategic vagueness. Is disruption a serious delay to a flight, a delay in supply of food to passengers or merely a restriction on shopping in an airport mall? (cognitive problem 4).

Lastly, compare sentence 2 with sentence 18. Sentence 2, which immediately follows the headline 'Air protesters target travellers' suggests through its strong stance that the protesters are intensely set on affecting passengers. The sensationalist lexis of 'war-footing' and 'chaos' reinforces this. But much later in the news article, in sentence 18, we find that the information in sentence 2 is only based on a BAA prediction. There is no longer the strong stance (as evidenced by use of 'could'), and the sensationalist chaos has been toned down to 'disruption'. There is, then, a tension, if not a contradiction, between sentences 2 and 18 (cognitive problem 5).

Explanation

The text does ideological work by promoting the advantage to a country's economy of an airport (e.g. sentence 24), and implicitly over detrimental effects to the environment. Climate change/global warming has been exacerbated by the globalisation of capitalism, in which the leisure/holiday industry forms an important part. This form of econo-politics brings benefits to many people, but in its augmenting of the exercising of consumer rights (in this case the right to purchase air tickets), it inadvertently marginalises a discourse 2 of social duty (in this case, not to travel by plane so as to reduce CO_2 emissions). The discourse of consumer rights (e.g. 'I have a right to purchase air travel which shouldn't be disrupted') could well be cued by the text since the dominant angle of representation pattern of the text is how protesters will negatively affect passengers. As a result of this dominant pattern, the chances of a discourse 2 of social duty being cued in relation to reducing CO_2 emissions is not so high. While sentence 25 hints at this discourse, is it likely to be effective in cueing it? There does not seem to be a reason why only a return flight to New York is focused on when Heathrow airport is a hub for so many global destinations; this sentence is largely irrelevant anyway since it is not grounded in predictions of CO_2 yield as a result of the extra runway or fifth terminal. It is also the last sentence and so, one might argue, its salience is diminished since impact in hard news texts is usually in headlines and opening paragraphs.

Empirically driven CDA

As I said earlier with reference to the description stage, it is important to be as rigorous and comprehensive as possible (although for reasons of space the above analysis lacks an ideal level of comprehensiveness). This is because when critical discourse analysts have not used linguistic analysis rigorously, consistently or as comprehensively as possible given their particular focus, they have been vulnerable to the following: charges that their analyses of texts are subjective because they are influenced by their own political commitments and thus that they 'cherry-pick' facets of text to focus on which fit a pre-figured interpretation. This is a critique of CDA made in Widdowson (2004). (See also criticisms by Billig (2003); Blommaert (2005); Hammersley (1997); Stubbs (1997); Toolan (1997) as well as those referred to in Cook, this volume).

When there is empirically based investigation which can illuminate audience response or the aspects of a text that the audience is likely to notice, CDA is in a better place to defend its analyses against accusations of: (i) arbitrariness of analysis; (ii) circularity from analysis to interpretation and back to analysis. See, for example, Murata (2007) who uses reader-response data in her critical discourse analysis and Bartlett (2004) who combines ethnographic data with SFL. Wodak's discourse-historical approach has often involved ethnographic investigation (see Maybin and Tusting, this volume) of how subjects engage with texts which, in turn, helps to reduce analyst subjectivity in textual interpretation. Moreover, the recent use of large reference corpora (see Adolphs and Lin, this volume) in CDA for purposes of comparison with the text(s) under investigation helps to reduce arbitrariness, and thus analyst subjectivity, in the choice of salient textual features (for examples of corpus-based CDA, see Baker *et al.* (2008); Charteris-Black (2004); Hidalgo Tenorio (2009); Koller and Davidson (2008); Krishnamurthy (1996); Mautner (2009); O'Halloran (2007, 2009); Stubbs (1996, 2001). Indeed, the linkage between the qualitative text analysis of CDA and the statistically based quantitative analysis of corpus linguistics is proving not only to enhance rigour but also insight in the description, interpretation and explanation of language use. Having said this, ultimately the most comprehensive and satisfactory CDA, like any form of discourse analysis, cannot limit itself to text/corpus analysis; it would also need to include a detailed qualitative and quantitative empirical investigation of text production and/or its reception in particular discourse practices.

Appendix

Table 31.1 SFL description of *The Mirror* text's angle of representation

Non-protesters as Actor	Material processes	Goal
1. Air protesters	target	travellers
2. 2,000 protesters	to cause	chaos
3. The organisers…Action	bringing to a halt	Heathrow
4. 150 people	turned up	
4. [Protesters]	to be set up	100 camps
6. The campaign	starts	
7. Campaigners	are aiming to achieve	their protests
7. The means…protests	will vary	
7. [Protesters]	blocking	roads and railways
7. [Protesters]	was used	blocking roads and railways
10. Demonstrators	to pose	
10. Demonstrators	to infiltrate	the four terminals
10. They [Demonstrators]	will set up	fake ticket booths
11. [Demonstrators]	climbing	
11. [Demonstrators]	blocking	runways
11. [Demonstrators]	disrupting	nearby roads
12. Protesters	to try to storm/to occupy	offices belonging…firms
12. [Protesters]	take	direct action
12. [Protesters]	to disrupt	the supply of food
13. [Protesters]	will be dropped	huge banners
13. [Huge banners]	to cause	traffic chaos; maximum embarrassment
18. campaign	starts	
18. campaign	runs	
20. any unlawful action	should be harassed/ obstructed	our passengers and staff
21. The Camp for Climate Action	bringing together	environmental protest groups
22. The Camp for Climate Action	is demonstrating against	the fifth terminal…runway

Protesters as Goal	Material processes	Actor
16. protesters	not touch	
16. protesters	not engage	
17. a protester	not follow	

Non-protesters as Actor	Material processes	Goal
2. Police	wait	
5. by up to 1,800 extra officers	will be joined	An 800-strong police force…
6. Heathrow owner BAA	sent	leaked memos
8. BAA	won	a High Court injunction
8. High Court injunction	banning	members of…Plane Stupid
10. Innocent travellers	miss	flights

Table 31.1 (continued)

Non-protesters as Actor	Material processes	Goal
11. Police	are bracing	themselves
18. three million people	could face	disruption
19. BAA	has respected	people's...lawfully
19. people	to protest	
22.	being built	fifth terminal
23. Heathrow	employed	68,000 people
24. Heathrow	contributes	£5bn

Non-protesters as Senser	Mental processes	Phenomenon (or projected clause)
4. [BAA]	expected	100 camps to be set up
6. [BAA]	is expected	[to happen] during the campaign
10. BAA	expects	Demonstrators...four terminals
10. [BAA]	is feared	[demonstrators] will set up...miss flights
12. [BAA and Police]	are expected	to try to storm ... passengers.
14. [BAA and Police]	are expected	disruption to meetings and seminars
15. Bosses of major airport firms	to expect	'custard pie attacks'...homes
20. BAA	do not believe	our passengers...direct action

Non-protesters as Sayer	Verbal processes	Verbiage
6. leaked memos...BAA	reveal	what is expected during the campaign
7. One [Leaked memo]	said	'The means...Rostock, Germany'
15. [BAA]	have been warned	to expect...homes.
16-17. BAA	has told	'Remain calm...situation.'
18. BAA	warned	that three million people could...a week.
19. Managing Director Mark Bullock	said	'BAA has always...lawfully'

Related topics

corpus linguistics; discourse analysis; linguistic ethnography; multimodality; stylistics; systemic functional linguistics

Further reading

Chilton, P. (2004) *Analysing Political Discourse*, London: Routledge. (An important cognitive perspective in CDA.)

Fairclough, N. (2001) *Language and Power*, 2nd edn, Harlow: Longman. (A key work in CDA which contains the most commonly used framework for analysis.)

O'Halloran, K. A. (2003) *Critical Discourse Analysis and Language Cognition*, London: Routledge. (Questions cognitive assumptions within critical linguistics.)

Widdowson, H. G. (2004) *Text, Context, Pretext: Critical Issues in Discourse Analysis*, Oxford: Blackwell. (Contains lucid and illuminating critical engagements with analyses in CDA.)

Wodak, R., de Cillia, R., Reisigl, M. and Liebhart, K. (2009) *The Discursive Construction of National Identity*, 2nd edn, Edinburgh: Edinburgh University Press. (An intellectually rich and significant milestone work in CDA.)

References

Baker, P., Gabrielatos, C., KhosraviNik, M., Krzyzanowski, M., McEnery, T. and Wodak, R. (2008) 'A useful methodological synergy? Combining critical discourse analysis and corpus linguistics to examine discourses of refugees and asylum seekers in the UK press', *Discourse and Society* 19(3): 273–306.

Bartlett, T. (2004) 'Mapping distinction: towards a systemic representation of power in language', in L. Young and C. Harrison (eds) *Systemic Functional Linguistics and Critical Discourse Analysis: Studies in Social Change*, London: Continuum.

——(2009) 'Towards intervention in positive discourse analysis', in C. Coffin, T. Lillis and K. A. O'Halloran (eds) *Applied Linguistics Methods: A Reader*, London: Routledge.

Billig, M. (2003) 'Critical discourse analysis and the rhetoric of critique', in G. Weiss and R. Wodak (eds) *Critical Discourse Analysis: Theory and Interdisciplinarity*, Basingstoke: Palgrave Macmillan.

Blommaert, J. (2005) *Discourse: A Critical Introduction*, Cambridge: Cambridge University Press.

Charteris-Black, J. (2004) *Corpus Approaches to Critical Metaphor Analysis*, Basingstoke: Palgrave Macmillan.

Chilton, P. (1985) 'Words, discourse and metaphors: the meanings of deter, deterrent and deterrence', in P. Chilton (ed.) *Language and the Nuclear Arms Debate*, London: Pinter.

——(2004) *Analysing Political Discourse*, London: Routledge.

——(2005) 'Missing links in mainstream CDA: modules, blends and the critical instinct', in R. Wodak and P. Chilton (eds) *A New Agenda in (Critical) Discourse Analysis*, Amsterdam: John Benjamins.

Chouliaraki, L. and Fairclough, N. (1999) *Discourse in Late Modernity: Rethinking Critical Discourse Analysis*, Edinburgh: Edinburgh University Press.

Coffin, C. and O'Halloran, K. A. (2006) 'The role of appraisal and corpora in detecting covert evaluation', *Functions of Language* 13(1): 77–110.

Fairclough, N. (1995a) *Critical Discourse Analysis: The Critical Study of Language*, London: Longman.

——(1995b) *Media Discourse*, London: Edward Arnold.

——(2001) *Language and Power*, 2nd edn, Harlow: Longman.

——(2003) *Analysing Discourse: Textual Analysis for Social Research*, London: Routledge.

Fairclough, N., Jessop, R. and Sayer, A. (2002) 'Critical realism and semiosis', *Journal of Critical Realism* 5(1): 2–10.

Fairclough, N. and Wodak, R. (1997) 'Critical discourse analysis', in T. A. van Dijk (ed.) *Discourse as Social Interaction*, London: Sage.

Foucault, M. (1972) *The Order of Things*, London: Tavistock.

Fowler, R. (1991) *Language in the News: Discourse and Ideology in the Press*, London: Routledge.

Fowler, R., Hodge, R., Kress, G. and Trew, T. (1979) *Language and Control*, London: Routledge/Kegan Paul.

Goatly, A. (2007) *Washing the Brain: Metaphor and Hidden Ideology*, Amsterdam: John Benjamins.

Halliday, M. A. K. and Matthiessen, C. M. I. M. (2004) *An Introduction to Functional Grammar*, 3rd edn, London: Hodder Arnold.

Hammersley, M. (1997) 'On the foundations of critical discourse analysis', *Language and Communication* 17(3): 237–48.

Hart, C. and Lukeš, D. (eds) (2007) *Cognitive Linguistics in Critical Discourse Studies*, Cambridge: Cambridge Scholars Press.

Hidalgo Tenorio, E. (2009) 'The metaphorical construction of Ireland', in K. Ahrens (ed.) *Politics, Gender and Conceptual Metaphors*, Basingstoke and New York: Palgrave Macmillan.

Koller, V. (2004) *Metaphor and Gender in Business Media Discourse: A Critical Cognitive Study*, Basingstoke: Palgrave Macmillan.

Koller, V. and Davidson, P. (2008) 'Social exclusion as conceptual and grammatical metaphor: a cross-genre study of British policy-making', *Discourse and Society* 19(3): 307–31.

Kress, G. and Hodge, R. (1979) *Language as Ideology*, London: Routledge.

Kress, G. and van Leeuwen, T. (eds) (2006) *Reading Images: The Grammar of Visual Design*, 2nd edn, London: Routledge.

Krishnamurthy, R. (1996) 'Ethnic, racial and tribal: the language of racism?', in C. Caldas-Coulthard and C. Coulthard (eds) *Texts and Practices: Readings in Critical Discourse Analysis*, London: Routledge.

Lakoff, G. (1987) *Women, Fire, and Dangerous Things: What Categories Reveal about the Mind*, Chicago: University of Chicago Press.

Lakoff, G. and Johnson, M. (1980) *Metaphors We Live By*, Chicago: University of Chicago Press.

Lassen, I., Strunck, J. and Verstergaard, T. (eds) (2006) *Mediating Ideology in Text and Image*, Amsterdam: John Benjamins.

Lazar, M. (ed.) (2005) *Feminist Critical Discourse Analysis: Gender, Power and Ideology in Discourse*, Basingstoke: Palgrave Macmillan.

Litosseliti, L. (2006) *Gender and Language: Theory and Practice*, London: Hodder Arnold.

Martin, J. (2004) 'Positive discourse analysis: power, solidarity and change', *Revista Canaria de Estudios Ingleses* 49: 179–200.

Mautner, G. (2009) 'Checks and balances: how corpus linguistics can contribute to CDA', in R. Wodak and M. Meyer (eds) *Methods of Critical Discourse Analysis*, 2nd edn, London: Sage.

Murata, K. (2007) 'Unanswered questions: cultural assumptions in text interpretation', *International Journal of Applied Linguistics* 17(1): 38–59.

O'Halloran, K. A. (2003) *Critical Discourse Analysis and Language Cognition*, Edinburgh: Edinburgh University Press.

——(2005) 'Mystification and social agent absences: a critical discourse analysis using evolutionary psychology', *Journal of Pragmatics* 37(12): 1945–64.

——(2007) 'Critical discourse analysis and the corpus-informed interpretation of metaphor at the register level', *Applied Linguistics* 28(1): 1–24.

——(2009) 'Inferencing and cultural reproduction: a corpus-based critical discourse analysis', *Text and Talk* 29(1): 21–51.

Stubbs, M. (1996) *Text and Corpus Analysis: Computer-assisted Studies of Language and Culture*, Oxford: Blackwell.

——(1997) 'Whorf's children: critical comments on critical discourse analysis' in A. Ryan and A. Wray (eds) *Evolving Models of Language: British Studies in Applied Linguistics* 12, Clevedon: BAAL/Multilingual Matters.

——(2001) *Words and Phrases: Corpus Studies of Lexical Semantics*, Oxford: Blackwell.

Toolan, M. J. (1997), 'What is critical discourse analysis and why are people saying such terrible things about it?', *Language and Literature* 6(2): 83–103.

Trew, T. (1979), 'Theory and ideology at work', in R. Fowler, R. Hodge, G. Kress, and T. Trew, *Language and Control*, London: Routledge/Kegan Paul.

van Dijk, T. A. (1991) *Racism and the Press: Critical Studies in Racism and Migration*, London: Routledge.

——(1997) 'The study of discourse', in T. A. van Dijk (ed.) *Discourse as Structure and Process*, London: Sage.

——(1998) *Ideology: A Multidisciplinary Approach*, London: Sage.

——(2001) 'Multidisciplinary CDA: a plea for diversity', in R. Wodak and M. Meyer (eds) *Methods of Critical Discourse Analysis*, London: Sage.

White, P. R. R. (2004) 'Subjectivity, evaluation and point of view in media discourse', in C. Coffin, A. Hewings and K. A. O'Halloran (eds) *Applying English Grammar: Functional and Corpus Approaches*, London: Hodder Arnold.

Widdowson, H. G. (2004) *Text, Context, Pretext: Critical Issues in Discourse Analysis*, Oxford: Blackwell.

Wodak, R. (1996) *Disorders of Discourse*, London: Longman.

——(2001) 'What CDA is about: a summary of its history, important concepts and its developments', in R. Wodak, and M. Meyer (eds) *Methods of Critical Discourse Analysis*, London: Sage.

——(2006) 'Mediation between discourse and society: assessing cognitive approaches in CDA', *Discourse Studies* 8(1): 179–90.

Wodak, R., de Cillia, R., Reisigl, M. and Liebhart, K. (2009) *The Discursive Construction of National Identity*, 2nd edn, Edinburgh: Edinburgh University Press.

Wodak, R. and Reisgl, M. (2001) 'Discourse and racism', in D. Schiffren, D. Tannen and H. E. Hamilton (eds) *The Handbook of Discourse Analysis*, Oxford: Blackwell.

Young, L. and Harrison, C. (eds) (2004) *Systemic Functional Linguistics and Critical Discourse Analysis: Studies in Social Change*, London: Continuum.

32

Neurolinguistics

Elisabeth Ahlsén

Introduction: what is neurolinguistics?

The broad definition of neurolinguistics is that it is the study of language in relation to the brain. This makes it truly interdisciplinary, involving, for example, neuroscience, psychology, linguistics, speech pathology and biology. It also involves the use of a multitude of research methods, such as experimental research, neuroimaging, simulation of brain processes and video recording of spoken interaction. Traditionally, the study of people with brain damage, especially acquired brain damage, which causes a language disorder, has dominated the field. Neurolinguistics can, however, also be about how the brain and human language and communication developed during evolution and how they develop in children and adults; it can also be about making computer simulations of linguistic processing by the brain; and it can be about localizing activity in parts of the brain involved in language processing by using neuroimaging methods. Neurolinguists can be focused on any of these aspects or on combinations of them. This overview will begin with some of the historical developments of neurolinguistics; it will then give examples of how research in different areas of neurolinguistics is pursued. Methods in neurolinguistics will be described and research dealing with different aspects of linguistics – phonology, morphology, syntax, semantics, pragmatics, multilingualism and reading and writing processes – will be presented. Finally, current trends and future trajectories in neurolinguistics are outlined.

A historical overview

Although the term 'neurolinguistics' was not introduced until the late 1970s, in a series of volumes called *Studies in Neurolinguistics* edited by Whitaker *et al.* (1976–9), the interest in studying language in relation to the brain dates far back, probably even as far as Egypt over 5,000 years ago, when trepanation, i.e. drilling holes in the skull bone, was practised as a way to release evil spirits that made people 'quiet from sadness'. Many observations of brain damage and language problems were made, often as case studies. In ancient Greece, Plato thought of the brain as controlling thought and action, whereas Aristotle thought of the heart as the site of the human soul and the brain as regulating temperature by controlling cooling fluids. In general, there was for a long time a focus on the liquid in the ventricles (holes) of the brain, perhaps also because it was noticed early that consciousness was lost when there was a deep brain lesion affecting the ventricles. It also seemed natural to connect a dynamic flow with the flow of thoughts. Language was therefore, for example, seen as placed in the fourth ventricle, and a loss of speech could be connected to phlegm making the flow of liquid in the fourth ventricle slow down. In the seventeenth century, there was a strong wish to connect the soul, and thereby thought and language, to a unitary centre in the brain. Candidate structures were the pineal gland, which is central in the brain and which Descartes saw as the centre of the soul, and the corpus callosum, which is also central and connects the two hemispheres of the brain and was suggested by Willis. There was a long conflict between the view supported by the church, that the human soul had to be one, and thus have one organ as its site, and researchers who tried to locate different abilities or faculties in different areas of the brain. Already in the Roman era, the importance of the cortex, i.e. the surface layer of the two hemispheres, was recognized. In the nineteenth century, there was a renewed interest in localizing brain functions in different cortical areas, starting with Gall, who outlined the location of twenty-six human faculties, which he identified from a study of biographies, in a map of the surface on the cortex (Gall and Spurzheim 1810–19). His method of crainoscopy, i.e. studying the size of different areas of the skull to identify faculties, later fell into disrepute. He did, however, have supporters in the French Anthropological Society, who set out to prove that Gall's assumptions about speech and memory for words being placed in the frontal lobe. Thus, Bouillaud and Auburtin tried to demonstrate that this was true, for example, by referring to cases that could support the claim. Paul Broca, who is often claimed to be the father of neurolinguistics, also demonstrated to the Society the brain of his patient Leborgne, usually referred to as Tan (because that was all he said) in 1861. He had predicted that the brain would have a lesion in the left frontal lobe and this turned out to be true, when the brain was dissected as a demonstration to the Society. He also identified the area for speech production as situated in the left frontal lobe in 1865. Shortly thereafter, Carl Wernicke discovered another cortical area, more posterior in the temporal and to some extent parietal lobes, which was connected to the ability to understand language; he started to sketch a model of language processing by the brain, which covered perception and production by repetition of words. This model was later extended by Lichtheim, who added a not clearly localized 'concept center' for the understanding and generation of speech. The findings by Broca and Wernicke relating descriptions and demonstrations of brain damage to certain areas of the cortex related to speech production and speech comprehension respectively (Broca 1861, 1865; Wernicke 1874) are often considered the starting point of what today is called neurolinguistics. Following their descriptions, localism and associationism, i.e. trying to find specific areas in the brain for specific language functions and trying to make models based also on the connections between such areas and the role of these connections, continued. In parallel, there was also a more 'holistic' and evolutionary development started by J. H. Jackson in 1874 and emphasizing the interplay between evolutionary primary and deep (subcortical) brain structures and more recently developed cortical areas in language functions (i.e. more automatized versus more consciously planned language). There were also, during the nineteenth and twentieth centuries, theories inspired by, for example, gestalt psychology searching for an underlying important cognitive ability, such as intelligence, abstraction or the ability to use symbols, as the crucial ability being damaged in aphasia (e.g. Marie, Glodstein, Head). In 1965, the model designed by Wernicke and Lichtheim was revived by Geschwind in his book *Disconnection Syndromes in Animals and Man* and became the basis of the most widely used classification of aphasic syndromes (see below).

Elisabeth Ahlsén

Some classical frameworks in neurolinguistics

Three main classical influencing frameworks in neurolinguistics are

- The classical view building on Broca, Wernicke, Geschwind and co-workers from the Boston Aphasia Research Center (e.g. Goodglass and Kaplan 1973), which mainly identifies cortical centres and connections between centres, where lesions can cause different types of aphasia.
- The view of Alexander Luria (e.g. 1976) where dynamic functional systems consisting of several sub-functions in different brain areas handle language functions and can be disrupted or reorganized by lesions in these areas.
- The more evolution-based, hierarchical (sometimes called more holistic) view of language processes 'repeating evolution' by activation from the older and deeper parts of the brain to the later developed and more specialized cortical areas. This view was proposed by John Hughlings Jackson (1932) and further developed by Jason Brown (1977, 1988) in his theory of 'microgenesis'.

Although none of the three frameworks provides the whole truth about brain and language, they have framed the thinking of researchers in neurolinguistics, who have used the terminology and models they developed. Today, there are no comprehensive frameworks to take their place and it is probably fair to say that they all contribute parts of our available information, but that we now have many more findings that have to be clarified and which can only partly be explained using the three frameworks. Many researchers, however, still build on parts or combinations of them.

Although many of the classical views and frameworks listed above are still to some extent adequate, current theories as well as data point to far more complex interactions between many different parts of the brain in language processing. There is less focus on the left hemisphere than before, although it is still considered crucial for the sequencing and rhythm of syntax and phonology. The right hemisphere, with its possibly more holistic and spatial focus, including parts of semantic and pragmatic processing, as well as subcortical structures, such as the limbic system, the thalamus and the cerebellum, have come much more into focus. This is connected to neuroimaging findings of activation and to the increased interest in emotion and volition raised by evolutionary studies. It is also connected to the development in linguistics, with its increased interest in semantics and especially pragmatics and with the focus on embodiment, which means that multimodal communication is included. Due to these developments, the delimitation of what is neurolinguistics has changed in terms of what parts of the brain and what parts of language and communication should be studied. Patterns and circuits of activation related to different language processing tasks are the main target of most neurolinguistic studies using measurement and imaging of brain activation. The role of different systems of transmittor substances affecting the activation patterns of cells and cell assemblies is, on a more micro level, also intensively studied.

Research areas in neurolinguistics

After this general introduction, it is time to turn to some of the main research areas in neurolinguistics.

Brain damage and language disorders

This has been by far the most central area with a long tradition of aphasiology studying different aspects of language after brain lesions with different localizations and using this to design, inspire, confirm, challenge and further develop psycholinguistic models of linguistic processing. A further aim has been to use models and findings in developing more refined methods for investigating and treating various types or aspects of aphasia. Different approaches have been used, depending on the focus of the studies. One tradition, mainly originating from British studies, is to use psycholinguistic models and only indirectly refer to brain localizations (clinical neuropsychology, e.g. Kay *et al.* 1992). Another tradition is to build on a traditional neurolinguistic model and try to extend parts of it to directly relate areas of the brain to specific linguistic symptoms of people with aphasia. By using this approach, neurolinguistics has developed more extended typologies of aphasia syndromes, specific process modelling of linguistic production and perception of spoken and written language, and further linkage of brain areas to specific functions involved in sub-processes of language functions.

Localization of language function

Currently, the most common ways of studying the relationship between specific brain areas and language functions are brain activation studies using neuroimaging techniques. The expansion of possibilities to study brain activation during language processing during the last twenty years has been revolutionary for neurolinguistics. It provides the possibility of testing hypotheses by performing reliable group experiments involving linguistic tasks with registrations of brain activity in subjects without brain damage. This has led to a number of creative approaches, which are continuously coming up with new findings and hypotheses. There has not, however, been a corresponding updating of frameworks for description and explanation, so the current state of the art is characterized by a number of findings about language and brain activation, but no comprehensive and coherent theory or framework.

The evolution of language and brain

Part of the fascination with many of the studies of brain activation performed today stems from the finding of mirror neurons in macaques, which was made by Rizzolatti and coworkers in 1996 using single cell electrodes for registration. Mirror neurons are single neurons activated both by action and perception, for example both by performing and by watching the hand movement of grasping an object. Findings of 'mirroring functions' of brain areas as located by functional magnetic resonance imaging have given rise to new ideas about action-perception relations, also in language. The fact that Broca's area developed on top of the area where mirror neurons were found in macaques has given rise to hypotheses about the evolution of language from grasping movements via gestures to language production in 'verb-object' constructions (Arbib 2005). This has also lead to a renewed interest in the motor theory of speech perception (Lieberman 1998).

There are a number of related areas that are also studied by neurolinguists, e.g. the development of language and brain in children, and artificial intelligence simulation of language and communication. Two areas that will be presented below are reading and writing disorders, especially dyslexia, and multilingualism.

In all of the above areas, different views of what language is in relation to cognitive functions are set against each other. How much of our linguistic ability is hard-wired and congenital versus how much is learned from external stimuli? To what extent is language a separate ability emanating from a mutation and present only in humans, versus how much is it the result of more gradual evolution and to some extent present also in other primates? The first alternatives in these two questions have been proposed by Chomsky (1992), Pinker (1994) and others, who claim that 'linguistic ability' (which in their terminology stands for syntax, morphology and phonology) is specific, unique to humans and to a large extent pre-wired. Other, more functionalist oriented researchers, such as Bates (Bates *et al.* 1998) and Tomasello (2008) claim that external stimuli and imitation are crucial and that more general cognitive abilities provide the prerequisites for language development. This is the view associated with research on embodied cognition and communication.

Methods and technology in neurolinguistic research

Methods for measuring and visualizing brain activity

As mentioned in the introduction, many and vastly different methods can be used for the study of brain and language. In early case studies, disturbance of some aspect of language processing was related to areas of the brain which could be identified only by post mortem dissection. Later, computed tomography (CT), a radiographic method showing X-ray attenuation and thus density variations in brain tissue, and magnetic resonance imaging (MRI), measurement of magnetic activity of hydrogen, made it possible to get a 'picture' of the brain lesion. Today, most studies in neurolinguistics are based on dynamic measurement of brain activation. Such methods are functional MRI (fMRI) and positron emission tomography (PET). In fMRI, magnetic resonance imaging detects changes in regional blood-oxygen levels (Blood Oxygen Level Dependent signal – BOLD), associated with neural activity and thus identifies dynamic activation patterns, for example, when performing a language task. PET traces injected radioactive positron isotopes tagged with water molecules or glucose. Neural patterns of activation can then be identified from emitted gamma rays. SPECT (single photon emission tomography) measures cerebral blood flow (rCBF) from a single gamma ray. Dynamic measurements are also made by using electroencephalography (EEG), showing the electrical activity (brain waves) from brain cells by fixing electrodes to the scalp. EEG measurements can be used with repeated stimuli, where the resulting recurring potential can be identified by an average change over numerous events. This technique is called event related potentials (ERP) and has proven very useful in neurolinguistic studies. Magnetoencephalography (MEG) measures electrical activity related to neural transmission. It is a fairly direct type of measurement, which does not require averaging and can, thus, be used in single case studies.

Using TMS (transcranial magnetic stimulation) by applying magnetic impulses to a specific region, it is also possible to disturb the function of this region and in this way simulate brain damage and study the temporary effects of this.

Methods for simulating language functions and language loss using ANN

There are two main types of modelling: symbol processing (based on traditional box-and-arrow models) and artificial neural network (ANN) modelling. Hybrid models also exist. ANN modelling is, for example, described by Franklin (1999) and Murre and Goebel (1996). Basically, an ANN model builds on simplified principles from real neural networks and consists of layers of nodes with interconnections. The nodes function as model 'neurons' which fire if the sum of activation hitting them exceeds a threshold value. Activations can be modified and the network can learn by matching a repeated input to a desired output. It is possible to model lesions in the network by, for example, removing nodes or distorting the flow of activation between the nodes. If different linguistic 'layers' are modelled, it is thus possible to simulate the symptoms of a particular person with an acquired language disorder, by adapting the network to the behaviour of that person.

Methods for studying linguistic behaviour in neurolinguistics

The methods used for studying linguistic behaviour in neurolinguistics overlaps with methods used in psycholinguistics, pragmatics and conversation analysis (see also Field, this volume; Cook, this volume). There is a heavy emphasis on off-line and especially on-line experimental designs and testing, supplemented by questionnaires and interviews and, in the pragmatic tradition, video recording or keystroke logging and analysis of naturalistic communication. The main characteristic of neurolinguistics is the clear and explicit link to the brain, in one of two ways: (i) by studying people with brain damage, and (ii) by measuring brain activation more or less directly, e.g. by imaging techniques or by measuring reaction times and relating them to processing models.

Methods and technologies in clinical and other applications

Neurolinguistics has a strong tradition of direct links to treatment of language disorders after acquired brain injury (aphasia). Many studies are performed by clinicians and studies of treatment effects are common. The main traditional neurolinguistic frameworks of the Boston group and Luria are still widely applied in diagnosing aphasia by identifying aphasia types or syndromes, for example by using the Boston Diagnostic Aphasia Examination (BDAE) (Goodglass and Kaplan 1973) or Luria's neuropsychological investigation (Christensen 1974). Psycholinguistic process models of the symbol manipulation type are used as a basis for interpreting disruptions of linguistic processing in the PALPA (Psycholinguistic Assessment of Language Processing in Aphasia) (Kay *et al.* 1992). Pragmatics-based studies of conversation phenomena, the use of gestures and other strategies, including repair, have inspired many speech and language therapists and have promoted the introduction of training of conversation strategies for patients, medical staff and family members. There is, however, a considerable time lag between neurolinguistic research and clinical application of its results in most cases, due to the fairly time-consuming development of clinically useful methods. The most recent trends in research are therefore not always directly reflected in therapy.

Neurolinguistics and aspects of language

A closer look at some neurolinguistic studies of particular phenomena or systems of language will hopefully give a more concrete picture of what neurolinguists can typically do. This will be illustrated by selected examples. (The different aspects of language per se are described in chapters of this volume on phonetics and phonology, grammar, lexis and discourse and also on multimodality and multilingualism.)

Phonology

In phonology, a recurring question is whether there is a particular basic processing unit and what that unit might be. Candidates have been phonemes (the smallest meaning-distinguishing units between words), phonological features, such as voicing, place or manner of articulation. The syllable is another candidate which has proven very useful in the study of language disorders. For example, the sonority of a syllable rises to the peak of the syllable – a vowel – and then recedes. Sonority is important for patients with phonological problems and this affects which consonant in a consonant cluster is preserved and which is omitted. It also causes vowel-insertions between the consonants in a cluster, which then makes more, but less complex, syllables. By referring to sonority it is thus possible to explain why certain phonological structures appear in phonological errors and others do not.

Grammar

In the study of grammar of people with language disorders, mainly agrammatism (i.e. a limited 'telegram style' grammar, with omissions and substitutions of grammatical morphemes), different hypotheses about grammatical processing have been proposed. One is the mapping hypothesis, which claims that it is the mapping between the semantic roles (such as agent and patient) of a sentence and parts of speech that is disturbed. A consequence of this hypothesis would be that other strategies are overused, for example, that the first noun represents the agent or that the noun that represents the semantically most likely agent is assigned the agent role, in comprehension. A second hypothesis, the adaptation hypothesis, assumes that agrammatism is an adaptation to a restricted time for processing which does not allow for complex or elaborated sentence structures. This leads to the use of a restricted register with short and simple structures that can be processed fast. According to a third hypothesis, the trace deletion hypothesis, traces of moved elements in syntactic tree structures (according to Chomskyan theories of syntax) are deleted in agrammatism, leaving certain structures remaining. In the framework of embodied communication and mirror neuron-based hypotheses, grammar, which relates to Broca's area, is in focus when relating basic actions, especially a grasping hand movement, to verb-object structures in grammar through an evolutionary process where actions and gestures develop into language (cf. Arbib 2005).

In descriptions of agrammatism, the relatively limited *grammatical morphology* has been the target of many studies. Cross-linguistic comparisons of agrammatic speech have led to a description of agrammatic morphology as not only loss, but also substitution of grammatical morphemes, especially free morphemes (more than prefixes and suffixes) and problems also with main verbs.

Lexical semantics

Since word finding and object naming problems, so-called anomia, is a cardinal feature of aphasia and semantically based word substitutions often occur, lexical semantic theories have come into use in trying to describe and explain what happens in the word processing of people with these symptoms. Descriptions have used semantic features as potential units to be modified, for example *gender* in the case of substituting *girl* for *boy*. Semantic networks have also been used. In the example, *girl* and *boy* would be close to each other in such a network and have many connections to other words in common. A third way of describing lexical semantic disorders in aphasia is to use prototype theory, where a typical exemplar is central in a prototype field with less typical items more in the periphery of the field. A typical dog could, for example, be a terrier with more exotic dog types like Great Danes and Chihuahuas more peripherally represented. The words for more prototypical items would be easier to find. For example, it has been shown that word training for more peripheral items results in better naming of more central items, whereas the opposite course of action does not show these results for more periheral items (Kiran *et al.* 2005). Although many studies of naming have focused on nouns, comparisons with naming of actions by verbs have attracted increasing interest, and the question of how verbs and nouns are encoded and retrieved is the focus of many studies. Here, of course, the role of the verb for the grammatical structure of sentences is central, although many utterances in fact consist of nouns only (cf. Allwood 2001). Activation of pre-motor areas involved in programming movements of different body parts has been shown in relation to the words for actions involving the same body parts (Pulvermüller 2005). Motor areas are, thus, suggested to be involved in the acquisition and retrieval of motion verbs. In fact, motor areas as well as sensory areas (the sensory-motor region) are now assumed, at least by some researchers (e.g. Gallese and Lakoff 2005), to be responsible for a great part or even all of lexical semantics. This assumption is one of the extensions of mirror neuron-based theories. So-called category specific anomias have also attracted some attention in neurolinguistics. These can, for example, be anomias selectively affecting only nouns or verbs or only words for natural items or artefacts. Is the encoding of the different types of words relying more on certain types of features, e.g. types of visual forms or motor actions, etc., or is there some other category specific to semantic encoding and organization of the 'mental lexicon'? These types of questions are being asked in this research.

Semantics, pragmatics and multimodal communication

It is now fairly generally accepted that semantics and pragmatics are interdependent aspects which are difficult to treat separately. An example of this is the use and meaning of deictic expressions, such as *here, now, I*, etc., which all depend on context for their interpretation of meaning. Also, the meaning of most words as well as constructions of several words is most often fully specified only in relation to the particular context. An important aspect of pragmatics is the study of communication in informal conversation and in other everyday life situations by using video recording and analyzing features of interaction and multimodal communication, including also gesture and other actions. The question of how interrelated and interdependent the production of words and gestures are is controversial and related to the question of gesture use as a possible compensatory strategy for people with aphasia. It seems clear that compensatory gesturing occurs and is successful in some patients (Ahlsén 1990; Feyereisen 1991; Lott 1999) and this causes some difficulty for theories claiming very strong interdependence (e.g. McNeill 2000). The close relation of gestures to speech and the possibility that gestures are sometimes more 'robust' in relation to aphasia can both be supported by the embodiment and mirror neuron-based approach to the evolution of language.

Reading and writing

One of the research areas in neurolinguistics is the relation between speech and writing, both concerning comprehension and production. Similar symptoms have often been assumed for writing as for speech in people with aphasia. Difficulties in executing writing for many people with aphasia, accompanied by apraxia (a disorder affecting the execution of intended movements and actions) and/or right sided hemiplegia affecting the right hand, have made studies of the often slow and strenuous writing of people with aphasia rare. Since partly different areas of the brain are used for sub-processes of speech and writing, and since different time constraints apply to the two modes of communication, it is not surprising that there are actually differences. In studies of text writing by people with aphasia, both based on the produced texts and the on-line production process (as shown by time logging of keystrokes) some differences in relation to their speech output can be noted. The texts produced by many people with aphasia were good, involving correct sentences, an adequate and often well-structured

Elisabeth Ahlsén

beginning, plot and end and, surprisingly, spelling and grammar errors (in relation to what was expected on the basis of their speech). An analysis of the logged keystrokes showed that the text production had been extremely slow and time-consuming and that almost every word had been changed, often several times (Ahlsén 2006; Behrns *et al.* 2008).

In the study of acquired *dyslexias* and in the application of the same perspective to developmental dyslexias and other reading difficulties, two main routes of processing, whole word reading versus grapheme-phoneme conversion, have mostly been assumed (the dual route model of reading) (Coltheart *et al.* 1993), although ANN alternatives have also been suggested. Two main types of reading disorder in relation to brain damage are, according to this model, surface dyslexia, which involves problems 'sounding out words', i.e. new and long words that are difficult to read, and phonological dyslexia, which involves problems using whole word reading, seen in the inability to read irregular words and sometimes in semantic errors. Deep dyslexia is a third form which combines features from both of the other types, giving rise to, for example, visual and semantic errors in reading. The causes of dyslexia in children are not entirely known, although dyslexia is often associated with a language disorder which also affects speech. The FOX P2 gene is one suggestion of a critical factor. The different types of dyslexia found with acquired brain damage also occur in developmental dyslexia.

Multilingualism

Another question in neurolinguistics which attracts attention is how the different languages are organized or processed by the brains of multilingual people. There have been many suggestions of different areas of the brain being active for the two languages and this seems to some extent to be the case. The interpretation is, however, not generally agreed on. The right hemisphere seems to be more active when a person uses a second or third language than when the first language is used. Paradis (2004) provides a likely explanation for this in that much more effort is spent on pragmatic strategies when using a language that one is less proficient in. Cases of bilingual people with different retrieval patterns for the two languages have attracted some interest, for example, that only one of the languages is recovered; one language is recovered first, then fades away when the second is recovered and the two languages recover to different degrees and with different speed. However, the most common pattern of recovery is parallel for the two languages. Code switching between languages is another area of interest which is compared to the switching between different registers/genres/activity languages that people use in one language. As multilingualism and code switching are becoming increasingly dominant for many people, this area will continue to be important.

Current trends and developments

One important trend in neurolinguistic research is the development and use of more varied and refined ways of measuring brain activity in relation to language and communication. Further development of methods such as fMRI, PET, SPECT, MEG and TMS is taking place, but many other methods have also been introduced that can reflect new aspects and give more refined information.

Another trend in neurolinguistics is the development and use of more varied and refined ways of measuring and analyzing behaviour, for example, multimodal registration of interaction patterns. The development and use of dynamic measures, such as eye movement recordings, automatic recognition and tracing of faces, speakers, magnitude of body movements, head movements, arm movements, etc., as well as phonetic analysis of voice and prosody features, identity, interaction patterns, attitudes and emotions, information structure, etc., can give us a much more multifaceted and complete picture of linguistic communicative behaviour.

In combination, the strong and speedy development of analysis techniques and methods in both neuroscience and language and communication studies provides substantial possibilities for interdisciplinary studies in neurolinguistics in the near future, but challenges arise when it comes to combining new methods from the two fields and relating them to theoretical frameworks.

The further development of simulation of brain and language using artificial neural networks (ANN) is a third line of development, which is promising for neurolinguistics and can be linked to the other two. Network models of many different types exist and have been used, for example, to simulate children's acquisition of grammatical forms and syndromes in aphasia. A challenge for this area is to develop network models further and exploit them to pursue simulation based on mirror neuron theories of interactive communication. The widening scope of neurolinguistics will provide more phenomena to simulate. How to link different 'levels' of processing – basic units and means of processing, thereby linking neurophysiology to different aspects of neurolinguistics – is a task for ANN modelling.

Future trajectories

Widening the scope of neurolinguistics

Some of the most active research areas in neurolinguistics are studies of the role of emotions, multimodality, body movements and actions, all examples of the widening of scope and topics for neurolinguistic research. As described above and seen in the increasing number of methods and phenomena of analysis, the focus of what is included in neurolinguistics has widened considerably. Pragmatics, multimodality, action-movement-language and context are in focus and many new findings enhance the need for new and more developed models of interpretation (see Ahlsén 2008).

The evolutionary trend and the embodiment trend – the study of mirror functions (imitation and simulation) as a basis for language and communication represent a very strong current development. This also involves a revival of the motor theory of speech perception (Galantucci and Fowler 2006). The link between evolution, ontogeny/acquisition and loss of language is being further explored. If mirroring and imitation are basic functions behind linguistic communication, is there a possible relation of impairment and autism (Frith et al. 2000; Frith and Wolpert 2004)? If the grasping hand movement is assumed to be central for the development of grammar, what is the relation between aphasia and apraxia (cf. Goldenberg 2003; Ahlsén 2008)?

Some examples that illustrate this trend are the following recent studies and claims:

- A paper by Corballis adopting the idea that gestures, via pantomime and conventionalization, developed into spoken language, claiming that the addition of voice and vocal features was the cause of left hemisphere dominance and stating that grammaticalization was part of this conventionalization, caused by the evolution of episodic memory and 'mental time travel' (Corballis 2010).
- A paper arguing for maps of coordinated actions rather than continuous maps of the body as the pattern behind our motor repertoires (Fernadino and Iacoboni 2010).
- A paper arguing that linguistic areas, through top-down mechanisms, stimulate a semantic content-specific reactivation of modal simulations (Ghio and Tettamanti 2010).

- A paper discussing data from measurements of voice parameters and arm kinematics, in terms of the possibility that gestures and words are integrated so that social intention to interact with the interlocutor is transferred from gesture to word (Barbieri *et al.* 2009).

Summary

Neurolinguistics is a research area which is in a phase of considerable dynamic development and expansion. This is due to new theories, methods and techniques in linguistics and neuro-science, based on mirroring functions, embodiment, pragmatics, neuroimaging and simulation techniques. These developments make possible the study of many new aspects of the brain and of language processing. More and more findings are being gathered, and the challenge of combining frameworks from different disciplines and developing theories is enormous. No doubt it is also inspiring and essential in the quest for answers to some of the most intriguing questions we have regarding a better understanding of language functions and language disorders.

Related topics

clinical linguistics; cognitive linguistics; discourse analysis; multimodality; psycholinguistics

Further reading

Ahlsén, E. (2006) *Introduction to Neurolinguistics*, Amsterdam: John Benjamins. (A basic introduction to the field of neurolinguistics which gives a good overview for beginners.)
Ingram, J. (2007) *Neurolinguistics: An Introduction to Spoken Language Processing and its Disorders*, Cambridge: Cambridge University Press. (Ingram provides an introduction to neurolinguistics with an overview of language processing and disorders.)
Stemmer, B. and Whitaker, H. (2008) *Handbook of the Neuroscience of Language*, New York: Academic Press. (Stemmer and Whitaker's updated version of the earlier *Handbook of Neurolinguistics* is a comprehensive work covering most aspects of current neurolinguistics.)

References

Ahlsén, E. (1990) 'Body communication and speech in a Wernicke's aphasic: a longitudinal study', *Journal of Communication Disorders* 24: 1–12.
——(2006) 'Comparing corpora of spoken and written narrations produced by persons with aphasia', in J. Toivanen and P. J. Henrichsen (eds) *Current Trends in Research on Spoken Language in the Nordic Countries*, Oulu: Oulu University Press.
——(2008) 'Embodied communication: aphasia, apraxia and the possible role of mirroring and imitation', *Clinical Linguistics and Phonetics* 22(4–5): 1–5.
Allwood, J. (2001) 'Capturing differences between social activities in spoken language', in I. Kenesei and R. M. Harnish (eds) *Perspectives on Semantics, Pragmatics and Discourse*, Amsterdam: John Benjamins.
Arbib, M. A. (2005) 'From monkey-like action recognition to human language: an evolutionary framework for neurolinguistics', *Brain and Behavioral Sciences* 28: 105–24.
Barbieri, F., Buonocore, A., Dalla Volta, R. and Gentilucci, M. (2009) 'How symbolic gestures and words interact with each other', *Brain and Language* 110(1): 1–11.
Bates, E., Elman, J., Johnson, M., Karmiloff-Smith, A., Parisi, D. and Plunkett, K. (1998) 'Innateness and emergentism', in W. Bechtel and G. Graham (eds) *A Companion to Cognitive Science*, Oxford: Basil Blackwell.
Behrns, I., Ahlsén, E. and Wengelin, Å. (2008) 'Aphasia and the process of revision in writing a text', *Clinical Linguistics and Phonetics* 22: 95–110.
Broca, P. (1861) 'Perte de la parole', *Bulletin de la Sociéte d'Anthropologie de Paris* 2: 219–37.
——(1865) 'Remarques sur la siège de la faculté du langage articulé', *Bulletin de la Société d'Anthropologie de Paris* 6: 330–57.

Brown, J. (1977) *Mind, Brain and Consciousness*, New York: Academic Press.

——(1988) *Life of the Mind*, Hillsdale, NJ: Lawrence Erlbaum Associates.

Chomsky, N. (1992) 'A minimalist program for linguistic theory', MIT Working Papers in Linguistics, 1, Cambridge, MA: MIT Press.

Christensen, A.-L. (1974) *Luria's Neuropsychological Investigation*, Copenhagen: Munksgaard.

Coltheart, M., Curtis, B., Atkins, P. and Haller, M. (1993) 'Models of reading aloud: dual-route and parallel-distributed-processing approaches', *Psychological Review* 100: 589–608.

Corballis, M. (2010) 'Mirror neurons and the evolution of language', *Brain and Language* 112(1): 25–35.

Fernandino, L. and Iacoboni, M. (2010) 'Are cortical motor maps based on body parts or coordinated actions? Implications for embodied semantic', *Brain and Language* 112(1): 44–53.

Feyereisen, P. (1991) 'Communicative behaviour in aphasia', *Aphasiology* 5: 323–33.

Franklin, S. (1999) *Artificial Minds*, Cambridge, MA: MIT Press.

Frith, C., Blakemore, S. and Wolpert, D. (2000) 'Abnormalities in the awareness and control of action', *Philosophical Transactions of the Royal Society B, Biological Sciences* 355: 1771–88.

Frith, C. and Wolpert, D. (2004) *The Neuroscience of Social Interaction*, Oxford: Oxford University Press.

Galantucci, B. and Fowler, C. (2006) 'The motor theory of speech perception reviewed', *Psychonomic Bulletin and Review* 13(3): 361–77.

Gall, F. and Spurzheim, G. (1810–19) *Anatomie et physiologie du système nerveus en général et du cerveau en particulier*, Paris: Schoel.

Gallese, V. and Lakoff, G. (2005) 'The brain's concepts: the role of the sensory-motor system in conceptual knowledge', *Cognitive Neuropsychology* 21: 455–79.

Geschwind, N. (1965) 'Disconnection syndromes in animals and man', *Brain* 88: 237–94 and 585–644.

Ghio, M. and Tettamanti, M. (2010) 'Semantic domain-specific functional integration for action-related vs. abstract concepts', *Brain and Language* 112(3): 223–32.

Goldenberg, G. (2003) 'Language shares neural prerequisites with non-verbal capacities', *Behavioral Brain Science* 26: 679–80.

Goodglass, H. and Kaplan, E. (1973) *The Boston Diagnostic Aphasia Examination*, Philadelphia: Lea and Febiger.

Jackson, J. H. (1932) *Selected Writings*, in J. Taylor (ed.), London: Hodder & Stoughton.

Kay, J., Lesser, R. and Coltheart, M. (1992) *PALPA: Psycholinguistic Assessments of Language Processing in Aphasia*, Hove: Lawrence Erlbaum Associates.

Kiran, S., Ntourou, K., Eubanks, M. and Shamapant, S. (2005) 'Typicality of inanimate category exemplars in aphasia: further evidence for the semantic complexity effect', *Brain and Language* 95: 178–80.

Lieberman, P. (1998) *Eve Spoke: Human Language and Human Evolution*, London: W. W. Norton.

Lott, P. (1999) *Gesture and Aphasia*, Bern: Peter Lang.

Luria, A. R. (1976) *Basic Problems in Neurolinguistics*, The Hague: Mouton.

McNeill, D. (ed.) (2000) *Language and Gesture*, Cambridge: Cambridge University Press.

Murre, J. and Goebel, R. (1996) 'Connectionist modeling', in T. Dijkstra and K. de Smedt (eds) *Computational Psycholinguistics*, London: Taylor & Francis.

Paradis, M. (2004) *A Neurolinguistic Theory of Bilingualism*, Amsterdam: John Benjamins.

Pinker, S. (1994) *The Language Instinct: How the Mind Creates Language*, New York: William Morrow.

Pulvermüller, F. (2005) 'Brain mechanisms linking language and action', *Nature* 6: 576–82.

Rizzolatti, G. and Arbib, M. A. (1998) 'Language within our grasp', *Trends in the Neurosciences* 21: 188–94.

Rizzolatti, G. and Craighero, L. (2004) 'The mirror neuron system', *Annual Review of Neuroscience* 27: 169–92.

Rizzolatti, G., Faciga, L., Gallese, V. and Fogassi, L. (1996) 'Premotor cortex and the recognition of motor actions', *Cognitive Brain Research* 3: 131–41.

Tomasello, M. (2008) *Origins of Human Communication*, Cambridge, MA: MIT Press.

Wernicke, C. (1874) *Der aphasische Symptomencomplex*, Breslau: Cohn and Weigert.

Whitaker, H. and coeditors (1976–79) *Studies in Neurolinguistics*, New York: Academic Press.

33

Psycholinguistics

John Field

Introduction

Psycholinguistics as a field of study

Psycholinguistics is the study of how the mind equips human beings to handle language. Its central concern is with the cognitive processes that underlie the storage, use and acquisition of language, and their correlates in observable neural activity in the brain. In addition, psycholinguists use their understanding of the mind to shed light on certain long-standing questions concerning language as a phenomenon. They include how language evolved, whether and why it is restricted to the human race, what the precise relationship is between language and thought and whether language shares functions with general cognition or operates independently of it.

Psycholinguistics is a relatively new area of study, though interest in the mind-language relationship has a long history. Over the centuries, there has been frequent discussion of language acquisition and of the origins of language – notably in the writings of Aristotle and in the Enlightenment debate between rationalist followers of Descartes, who believed that much human knowledge was innate, and empiricists such as Hume and Locke, who asserted that it was entirely acquired. A parallel interest in the psychology of adult language developed during the nineteenth century, with initiatives such as Broca's work on the location of language in the brain and Galton's on word association.

However, in the first half of the twentieth century, progress in all areas of cognitive science was discouraged by the dominant *behaviourist* view that the human mind is unknowable. The term 'psycholinguistics' was probably first coined in the 1930s but the field did not emerge as a discipline in its own right until the mid-1950s, when George Miller mapped out possible areas of inquiry in a series of essays (reprinted as Miller 1968). About the same time, researchers at Haskins Laboratories began their pioneering work into the perception of phonemes. A further landmark was Chomsky's 1959 rebuttal of the behaviourist assumptions of Skinner's book *Verbal Behavior*. Chomsky concluded that language is a genetically acquired faculty; this *nativist* stance triggered a new, and more scientific, interest in first language acquisition, and began a controversy that continues to the present day.

Much early inquiry into how adults assemble and understand language was closely allied to linguistic theory, on the assumption that Chomsky's early transformational-generative grammar (1965) represented *psychological reality* – i.e. provided a model of the operations of the mind as well as a linguistic account of grammatical structure. Attempts were made to investigate the *Derivational Theory of Complexity*, which hypothesised a correlation between the number of transformations that a given sentence demanded in TG theory and the difficulty of processing the sentence. There was particular interest in passive and negative structures. The findings were mainly negative or inconclusive, and at this point the paths of linguistics and psycholinguistics began to diverge.

Today, psycholinguistics is a multi-disciplinary field, drawing upon cognitive psychology, theoretical linguistics, speech science, phonetics, computer modelling, neurolinguistics, clinical linguistics, discourse analysis and pragmatics. One can identify two distinct traditions. The dominant one applies principles and research methods from cognitive science, and is strongly evidence-led. Typically, researchers study small-scale effects with a view to building a composite account of the language operation under investigation. Research methods include observation of natural language, controlled experiments that tap in to a specific process, concurrent and retrospective verbal reports and the imaging of the brains of individuals performing a particular language function The second tradition continues to assume that the accounts of language proposed by linguists correspond closely to the way in which the mind actually performs. Researchers employ a theoretical framework, often a Chomskyan one, in order to interpret samples of language. Because their concern is with competence rather than performance, they often rely upon indirect methods, such as grammaticality judgements, for eliciting information.

What both traditions share is a concern with cognition – with the types of mental process, some highly automatic, some more intentional, that language users employ. It is this that separates psycholinguistics from cognitive linguistics, whose roots lie in semantic theory rather than cognitive psychology. Similarly, while psycholinguists do not ignore personal variables such as affect or contextual variables such as interlocutor relationships, they tend to leave research in these areas to social psychologists and discourse analysts, who have very different research traditions.

Research assumptions

Much psycholinguistic research is normative, tracing shared patterns of behaviour in language users, but there is no implicit assumption that all users behave identically. Individuals clearly vary in their vocabulary range and in their powers of self-expression. Their performance also varies from situation to situation according to interlocutor, to level of formality, to genre of discourse and to transient factors such as tiredness, level of noise or the effects of alcohol.

That said, behind these local differences, there are patterns of physical and mental behaviour that reflect the demands of the language task being undertaken. Thus, all readers have to move their eyes across a page or screen and have to link groups of graphic symbols to stored mental representations. While the performance of an individual is indeed affected by contextual and personal factors, the chief concern of psycholinguistics is with the fundamental processes that enable us to communicate at all. Here, account may need to be taken of the language or the writing system being employed. The processes adopted by a reader of a logographic script such as the Chinese one obviously differ in important respects from those adopted by a reader of an alphabetic script. The study of the mental operations underlying language use thus has to allow for cross-linguistic comparison.

The present chapter

It will be clear from this brief profile that psycholinguistics is a very diverse field, though interfaces between its various areas and a common interest in cognition provide it with a degree of coherence. The present account focuses upon the three main areas identified at the outset, namely language storage, use and acquisition. They clearly fall within applied linguistics viewed as the study of language in performance, but they are also relevant to those who associate applied linguistics more closely with language learning, since they provide insights into the cognitive challenges that attend the use of a second language (L2). Space does not permit discussion of the wider 'What is language?' issues.

Language storage and retrieval

Memory and the nature of knowledge

An early model of the role of human memory in language use (Atkinson and Shiffrin 1968) represented it as consisting of three stores: a sensory store in which a reader or listener very briefly retains a trace of the linguistic input; a temporary store in which spoken/written input is analysed or output is assembled; and a more permanent store holding both linguistic and world knowledge. Current models refer to the short-term store as *working memory* (WM) and the durable one as *long term memory* (LTM). The former holds not only the words of the current utterance but also linguistic information retrieved temporarily from LTM for the purpose of assembling or analysing them. In the most well-known account of memory (Baddeley 1990), a *central executive* (functioning not unlike a control tower in an airport) directs operations. It also determines the level of *attention* within WM that a language user needs to accord (a higher level, for example, for a listener in conditions of noise or a speaker giving a formal speech); and how attention is to be distributed if there are twin demands upon it (for example, when listening and writing notes in a lecture).

The chief characteristic of WM is its limited capacity. Language users overcome this constraint by developing form-meaning connections which are *automatic* (Shiffrin and Schneider 1977) and thus make minimal demands upon attention. In addition, WM contains an *articulatory/phonological loop* (Gathercole and Baddeley 1993) which enables a language user to rehearse a piece of language so that it can be held in the mind for longer without decaying.

Psycholinguistic accounts of storage explore the nature of the linguistic knowledge in LTM which enables the language user to command phonology, to retrieve lexical items and to produce utterances that are grammatically correct. Alongside the question of representation (the precise form in which this information is stored), one also needs to consider how language users manage to access the information when they have need of it. This demands highly automatic processes, of which the user is largely unaware.

A recent shift in thinking has led many commentators to favour an *exemplar* view of how linguistic knowledge is stored. It challenges traditional notions of language as rule-governed behaviour or as reliant upon 'ideal' templates of words or phonemes. Instead, the premise is that linguistic knowledge is constructed on the basis of traces of multiple encounters with the features in question, which have been stored in LTM (Bybee and Hopper 2001). Thus, if one hears an [a:] that diverges markedly from one's own value or a dialectal variant of a syntactic pattern, one does not compare it to a standard version or to an internalised rule, but to the memory of a similar form heard in the past. Exemplar models lead to a view of language acquisition (whether in L1 or L2) as *emergent*, in the sense that it is a process driven by accumulating random samples of language in use and generalising across them.

Phonology

The exemplar view has particular relevance when considering phonological representation. Speech scientists have long struggled to account for the variability of the phoneme, which has no simple one-to-one relationship with acoustic cues in the input and varies greatly according to the phonemes that adjoin it. One way of dealing with the issue is to conclude that the syllable rather than the phoneme forms the smallest unit of analysis for the listener or speaker; and that we are only capable of separating words into phonemes because literacy and rhyming games have taught us how to. In contrast, the exemplar position rejects the long-standing assumption that there are idealised phonological representations in the mind against which variants can be matched. By assuming instead that language users store many different versions of a single phoneme (Bybee 2001), one accounts for the way in which listeners adjust gradually to an unfamiliar variety through multiple encounters with speakers of that variety. Each speaker leaves a trace, enabling the listener to build up an increasingly detailed record of how this particular group realises phonemes or words.

Lexis

Lexical representation forms a major area of psycholinguistic enquiry (see Aitchison 2003). A language user is said to possess a vocabulary store in the mind: a *mental lexicon*. Content words are stored there in the form of lexical entries, which contain sufficient information about each word to enable its use in speech or writing. There is a degree of controversy as to whether productive derivational affixes such as *un*-have their own entries or whether a word like *unhappy* is stored as a whole.

Levelt (1989) represents a lexical entry as consisting of two parts, one relating to form and one to meaning. The first includes mental representations of the phonological and orthographic forms of an item together with inflectional information. The second (the *lemma*) represents the range of possible senses associated with the item. It also includes information on syntactic structure (for example, the valency of a verb).

Producing and receiving language make different demands upon the lexicon. The point of departure for a speaker or writer is a meaning which he/she needs to map on to the most appropriate form; while that of a listener or reader consists of a form (auditory or visual) that has to be mapped on to a meaning. Early research on lexical retrieval focused on speech production and sought evidence in *slips of the tongue* (Fromkin 1980). The rationale was that, by comparing an incorrectly selected word with the target, one might identify the characteristics of the word that were driving the search. Semantic links between chosen word and target were to be expected, but it was noted that speakers also seem to be guided by formal information about the word being sought, including its number of syllables, its first syllable, its stressed syllable and its rhythm. Producers of language thus seem to possess an awareness that a sought word exists and certain prior intimations as to the form it takes.

In terms of reception, current accounts of how words are identified by a listener or reader do not assume a simple one-to-one match between input and word. *Competition models* (Rastle 2007: 72) postulate that a listener or reader balances cues at many levels in order to achieve word recognition: a reader might take account of letters, digraphs, sub-letter features, letter order, syllables and whole word forms. Potential word matches are accorded different levels of confidence, according to how closely they fit the evidence on the page and according to criteria such as frequency – until one of these candidates wins out over the others. The term *activation* is often used to describe this process.

Lexical retrieval in both production and reception is assisted by the way in which entries are stored in the mind. Current models envisage them as linked by a complex network of inter-connections. A word such as CHAIR has links to others in the lexical set of furniture. But, for listeners, it also has links to words such as CARE that resemble it phonologically and, for readers, links to words such as CHAIN which resemble it orthographically. Other associations are based upon frequency of co-occurrence (CHAIR-TABLE, CHAIR-MEETING) and upon sense relations such as synonymy, antonymy and hyponymy. The connections between words differ in strength, with CHAIR-TABLE much stronger than CHAIR-BED. *Connectionist* computer programs have simulated the way in which strengths of connection are said to evolve. They do so by means of a mechanism which strengthens a connection that occurs frequently and allows infrequent ones to atrophy.

Listeners and readers are assisted by a process of *spreading activation*. On encountering a word such as *doctor*, they automatically activate closely linked words such as *nurse* or *patient*, and thus recognise them more readily if and when they occur. Researchers investigate lexical connections of this kind by means of a method known as *priming*, which measures how much faster words are identified when preceded by a word that appears to be associated with them.

A further important line of lexical research addresses the question of how language users succeed in classifying real-world objects by reference to categories such as BIRD or FURNI-TURE. Rosch (1975) premised that users base their categories upon a highly typical example (in the case of BIRD, a robin). They ascertain whether a newly encountered object fits the category by considering how closely it resembles this ideal. Rosch's *Prototype Theory* has been much challenged. Recent commentators have preferred an exemplar view, with the category constituted by the user's ability to recall many different instances of items that belong to it.

Grammar

The fact that speech is assembled successfully under tight pressures of time raises questions about the traditional notion of a syntax based upon applying elaborate rules which license permissible combinations of words and exclude others. An alternative, psycholinguistic account (Wray 2002) holds that our capacity to produce speech rapidly is dependent upon frequently occurring groups of words being stored in the mind as pre-assembled chunks. Thus, one does not have to assemble afresh a sequence such as *I wish I knew …* or *What would you say if …* each time one utters it, but can draw on a unit which is, in effect, part of the lexicon. Similarly, one can recognise it as a fixed formulaic utterance when it occurs in connected speech, without having to parse its parts.

Language use

We now turn to the *processes* that are employed when a language user engages in speaking, writing, reading and listening. Psycholinguistic models of these skills are heavily influenced by an *information processing* approach, which tracks a given piece of information through a number of stages, at each of which it is transformed. A listener, for example, might be represented as constantly reshaping the form of the message being received: proceeding from acoustic input to a phonological representation and then from phonemes to syllables and on to words, to clauses and to an 'idea unit'.

The progression can be shown in flow-chart form, but it does not tell the whole tale. Evidence suggests that, in producing or analysing language, the human mind is capable of operating at several different levels in parallel. The listener is capable of detecting an emerging syntactic pattern while at the same time extracting word meanings, identifying words and detecting phonemes. In addition, a language user is more flexible than a sequential model might suggest. If a disparity is noted, he/she can loop back at any point to reverse a decision. This kind of regression is especially seen in writers, who sometimes change part of a text while actually producing it, as well as in a final editing phase.

As already remarked, the productive and receptive skills follow opposite directions of processing. The former take a meaning to be expressed and map it on to a form of words, while the latter take a form of words and map it on to a meaning. All four skills draw heavily on non-linguistic as well as linguistic knowledge, but they do so at different stages of the operation. Thus, what is often broadly termed 'context' (world knowledge, knowledge of the individual being communicated with, perception of the user's own goals) affects the initial planning in speaking and writing but contributes to interpreting the signal in the case of listening and reading.

An important distinction can also be made in repect of modality. Writers normally have time to plan their ideas and to polish the words that give expression to them. Similarly, readers can vary their speed and the level of attention that they bring to their task. By contrast, most speech (especially in interactional situations) has to be assembled under pressures of time, while a listener has little control over the speech rate of the interlocutor and thus over the pace at which the input is received.

Speaking

As noted, the planning of speech takes place under enormous pressures of time. A degree of thinking ahead occurs while the speaker is actually articulating, but brief pauses of 0.2 to 1.0 seconds are necessary for planning the form of the next utterance. *Juncture pauses* of this type occur mainly at syntactic boundaries; the clause seems to form an important unit of planning. By contrast, *hesitation pauses* (filled and unfilled) can occur anywhere within an utterance and even within words. They might result from a failure to retrieve a word or from a failure of planning: i.e. a plan that is revised, is not adequately formulated or is lost during articulation.

Early speech production research examined slips of the tongue involving syntax and morphology. The evidence suggested that a syntactic frame is prepared by a speaker and that lexical items are then slotted into it (hence an error like *He found a wife for his job*). Morphological markings are added at quite a late stage (hence *She come backs tomorrow*).

Drawing upon this and other evidence, a number of researchers have proposed models that represent the stages through which a speaker proceeds when assembling an utterance. The most comprehensive and authoritative account is offered by Levelt (1989). Levelt's original 1989 model features four major stages (conceptualisation, formulation, articulation and self-monitoring); however, an updated version (1999) subdivides the second and third of them as follows:

Conceptualisation:	generating an idea or set of ideas for expression and planning how to express them;
Grammatical encoding:	constructing a syntactic frame for the next utterance and identifying the lexical items to be slotted into it;
Phonological encoding:	converting the abstract plan into a string of words in phonological form;

Phonetic encoding:	adjusting the phonological sequence to make articulation easier; linking each of the syllables to a set of neural instructions to the articulators; storing the instructions temporarily in the mind;
Articulation:	producing the utterance;
Self-monitoring:	focusing attention on the message just before or while it is uttered in order to check for accuracy, clarity and appropriateness.

Writing

The path adopted by a writer follows that of a speaker in terms of conceptualising an idea, converting it to linguistic form and checking the accuracy, clarity and appropriacy of the end-product. Accounts of writing (e.g. Kellogg 1996) have therefore tended to follow Levelt's model of speaking quite closely. However, there are major differences in the greater opportunity allowed for planning and self-monitoring, the substitution of orthography for phonology and the fact that neural signals are sent to the fingers, not the articulators. To this, one can add that the product of writing is typically expected to be more precise, concise and polished than that of speaking – emphasising the importance of the planning and monitoring phases.

Unsurprisingly, there has been much discussion of the role of planning. An influential model by Hayes and Flower (1980) defines the environment within which the writer operates and takes account of rhetorical considerations relating to the writer's own goals as well as to target readership, topic and genre. Scardamalia and Bereiter (1987) distinguish the *knowledge telling* of less skilled writers, a largely linear approach to the generation, linking and presentation of ideas, from the *knowledge transforming* of more skilled ones, based on planning, structuring and revision. The same commentators (Bereiter and Scardamalia 1987) analyse the challenges that children face in holding writing plans in their minds while carrying out the mechanics of forming letters.

There has also been research interest in the *execution* stage of writing (equivalent to Levelt's 'articulation'). Early studies of slips of the pen and keyboard (Hotopf 1983) demonstrated that writers give reduced attention to function words and that incorrect keyboard sequences of letters (THE → *teh*) can become highly automatic and difficult to reverse. Evidence suggested that the writer's plan for the text that is currently being produced is held in the mind in some kind of phonological form (explaining why the intention to write '20A' might result in *28*).

Listening

In accounts of the receptive skills, a distinction is usually made between a perceptual phase in which the input is analysed into linguistic units and a conceptual phrase when a meaning-based representation is constructed. The former, often referred to as *decoding*, requires the detection of lexical and syntactic forms in the input. Like a reader, a listener weighs multiple cues when establishing the identity of a word: matching phoneme, syllable and contextual information against a stored record of the different forms that the word can take.

Matters are complicated in listening by the fact that pauses between words in connected speech are irregular and infrequent. The listener thus has to engage in a process of *lexical segmentation*, determining where word boundaries are most likely to fall. The decisions made are often supported by prosodic features of the language being heard: among them, lexical stress and syllable structure. The main segmentation strategy in English appears to exploit the fact that 90 per cent of content words in running speech begin with a stressed syllable – making it relatively fail-safe to assume that each stressed syllable initiates a new word (Cutler 1990).

A further headache for listening researchers lies in the highly variable nature of the signal. It is not simply phonemes that vary. Words are subject to great variation because of the pressures of the intonation group, which affect their duration and the precision with which they are articulated. They also vary in the extent to which they are assimilated to the word that follows them. It has to be assumed that the oral forms of words are represented in the listener's lexicon in a way that allows considerable deviation from the citation form – or, again, that users store separate examples of the many variations they have encountered.

In addition, speakers differ enormously in terms of voice pitch, speech rate, hesitancy, prosody and accent. Traditional accounts envisaged listeners as *normalising* to these features: editing them out in order to focus on the message being conveyed. However, recent research (Johnson and Mullenix 1997) suggests that they may actually be processed alongside the message and retained in memory.

Accounts of how listeners handle syntax (a process known as *parsing*) have to come to terms with evidence that listeners start analysing what they hear at a delay behind the speaker of about the length of a syllable (Marslen-Wilson and Tyler 1980), rather than waiting until the end of a clause. They rely upon probability, word order, intonation and factors such as animacy in order to anticipate the syntactic structure of a piece of incoming speech before it is complete (van Gompel and Pickering 2007). It seems that listening, even in one's first language, is a highly tentative process, with hypotheses constantly being formed and revised. For an accessible account, see Field 2008.

Reading

Eye tracking equipment has taught researchers a great deal about the physical process of reading (Rayner and Pollatsek 1989). The reader's eye moves across the page in short sweeps known as *saccades*. It rests on most content words, though around 60 per cent of function words are read peripherally. In many alphabetic languages, a *fixation point* occurs every 7 to 9 characters. Fixation by a skilled reader lasts on average for about a quarter of a second, but is extended where there are longer or unfamiliar words. Readers regress from time to time: with skilled readers this tends be to check understanding; with less skilled readers it is often to check the accuracy of word identification. An important consideration is that a major component of reading skill is the ability to adjust one's reading style (length of saccade and length of fixation) to the type of text being read and to the reader's own goals.

As with listening, it is necessary for readers to hold decoded words in their minds until the end of a clause or sentence is reached and a syntactic pattern can be imposed on them. There is evidence that the words are stored in some kind of phonological form (Perfetti 1985) – hence the fact that readers sometimes report a 'voice in the head'. This may be a relic of how reading is acquired, but it seems more likely that it serves to separate recall of the earlier part of a sentence from the visual processing of the current word.

An understanding of reading processes is especially useful for shedding light on controversies over how to teach the skill. There has long been disagreement between those who argue for the importance of *phonics* based upon sound–spelling relationships and those who argue that a *whole-word* approach is more suitable to a language like English with a relatively opaque orthography. However, a *dual-route* model of reading (Coltheart 2005), based upon evidence from dyslexia, indicates that in decoding words a reader has need of both routes – a faster (lexical) one that identifies whole words and a slower (sub-lexical) one that applies *grapheme-phoneme correspondence* (GPC) rules to achieve word recognition. An adult reader still requires the latter route in order to deal with unfamiliar names, to match words never seen before in print to words known orally or to work out how to pronounce words only encountered in writing.

A second controversy was triggered by Goodman's (1967) claim that good readers employ context and co-text to predict what is to come, in order to avoid having to decode every word they encounter. This led to a *whole language* approach in which early readers were encouraged to read for pleasure, guessing the meaning of text that they could not decode. Goodman's assertion has been widely discredited (see Gough and Wren 1999). It is by no means as easy to predict upcoming words as he suggested. In addition, a skilled reader is capable of decoding words highly automatically and matching them to their meanings; there is thus no benefit in falling back upon prediction, which (unlike decoding) makes major demands upon working memory. In fact, it is weak readers who use context in this way, because they find word recognition too demanding. Competent readers do indeed make use of context, but do so in order to enrich their interpretation of what they have read, understand the writer's intentions, etc.

Meaning construction

The output of decoding in both listening and reading is said to be an abstract and decontextualised 'idea unit'. Two further phases of processing are then necessary. In the first, the listener or reader invokes world knowledge, knowledge of the speaker or writer and knowledge of the immediate situation, in order to achieve a semantically enriched interpretation of the raw proposition. It may be necessary to employ *inference* (Brown and Yule 1983), recognising connections that have only been made implicitly. Understanding a sequence like *Bill lay on the floor. A knife lay by the body.* requires the reader to infer that Bill is dead and that the knife may have been a murder weapon.

In a further phase, a listener/reader has to make decisions concerning the information derived from the input. If it is trivial, it can be allowed to decay. If not, it is added to the mental representation of the discourse so far. This entails recognising a logical link between each new item of information and the one that immediately preceded it. It also entails monitoring to ensure that the new item is consistent with what has been heard or read already, or whether any misunderstanding has occurred.

Finally, in constructing a wider discourse representation, macro-information has to be distinguished from micro-information and a hierarchical model has to be built of the overall line of argument. Skilled comprehenders build more complex representations because they are more able to determine when to initiate a new conceptual structure and when not (Gernsbacher 1990). Weak comprehenders operate linearly, repeatedly starting new structures instead of elaborating existing ones.

Language acquisition

Nativist theory

The agenda in language acquisition studies was set by Noam Chomsky's assertion (1965) that language is an innately acquired faculty. Chomsky's arguments were based upon aspects of acquisition which are difficult to account for unless genetic transmission gives the child a head start. They include: the short period of time within which a child achieves grammatical competence; the lack of correction or explicit teaching by adults; the 'poverty of the stimulus' available to the child in the form of natural speech with its hesitations, false starts and syntactic errors; and the fact that all normally developing children acquire full competence, regardless of differences in their intellectual capacity.

Any nativist account has to deal with the fact that human beings acquire not simply language but a specific tongue. Chomsky's current theory (Chomsky and Lasnik 1993) posits that the innate *universal grammar* (UG) which enables the acquisition of a first language has two components. The first is a set of *principles,* which enable the infant to recognise features that are common to most or all of the world's languages. The second is a set of binary *parameters*, which can be set to accord with the language to which the child is exposed. Thus, an infant exposed to a language such as Italian, where a subject pronoun can be omitted, adopts the so-called *pro-drop* setting; while one exposed to English recognises a situation where such a pronoun is obligatorily employed in all circumstances and sets the parameter against pro-drop.

Often associated with nativist accounts is the notion that there is a *critical period* for the acquisition of a first language, possibly determined by the way in which UG functions. It originated in a theory that the two hemispheres of the brain might be 'plastic' at birth, with the left hemisphere gradually becoming the dominant one for language during the first five years of life. The evidence was that children who suffered left hemisphere brain damage before the age of five were more likely to end up as right hemisphere dominant. In fact, this finding was not corroborated by recent studies; and inconsistency was introduced when commentators extended the cut-off point to adolescence. There is considerable evidence (Skuse 1993) that children who are denied exposure to language early in life acquire vocabulary but master syntax only imperfectly. However, in such cases, it is often difficult to rule out the possible effects of neglect, delayed cognitive development and even brain damage from abuse.

Alternative theories

A number of alternatives to the nativist view emphasise the role of the linguistic environment to which the child is exposed. Some of them can be broadly defined as cognitive. They include the view of Jean Piaget (Piatelli-Palmerini 1980) that language acquisition is driven by cognitive development as the child succeeds in making sense of the world around it. On this analysis, a sense of *object permanence* (the continued existence of objects when they are out of sight) might be a prerequisite for an utterance such as *cup gone.* Other cognitive accounts assume that the human mind is structured in a way that permits it to trace patterns in real-world phenomena, including speech, without the need for a special language-related device. It is possible (Deacon 1997) that language took advantage of cognitive operations that served other purposes and that the brain then gradually evolved to accommodate it.

Much quoted in recent years as signalling a return to empiricism (even behaviourism) have been simulations of language acquisition based upon computer modelling. A connectionist computer program employed a learning mechanism that strengthened past tense connections that were correct (e.g. SEE linked to past form SAW) and weakened those that were not (SEE linked to the rule-governed form SEED). The program was shown to be capable of 'acquiring' accurate past tense links (Rumelhart and McClelland 1986). No abstract rule was employed; performance was purely based upon generalisation across examples and upon identifying cases that did not fit the norm. However, the extent to which programs such as this can be said to reproduce the real-life acquisition of inflections is open to challenge. They rely upon standardised input from programmers; the input focuses on only one inflection type; and the learning process requires many passes before the links are established.

Child language development

Chomsky's theories triggered a wave of research into first language acquisition, much of it focusing on empirical data and neutral on whether language is innate. Many studies, some experimental, some longitudinal, have investigated the syntax, morphology, lexis, and phonology of the developing child. A consistent finding has been that the rate and timing of language development vary greatly from one infant to another. Instead of age, *mean length of utterance* (Brown 1973) is often used as an indicator of development, since there is an obvious correlation between how many words (or morphemes) an infant can produce and the complexity of the syntactic patterns (SVO, SVOA, etc.) that the infant can command.

A further mark of the child's growing mastery of syntax is the range of verbs used and the complexity of the valencies associated with them (PUT, for example, requires the specification of both the object and the location where it is put). Other indicators are found in the emergence of features that are lacking or inconsistent in early speech. They include sentence subjects, correct form of the subject pronoun, the verb *to be* (both copula and auxiliary), and function words generally. Progress can also be traced in the acquisition of syntactic patterns such as the correct ordering of questions and negatives, where there is evidence of a common developmental path.

In morphology, thinking has been shaped by Berko's early (1958) demonstration that infants appear to move from holistic forms of words (e.g. *dogs* acquired as a single unit) to generalised rules that enable them to attach the relevant inflection to an unfamiliar word (*WUG+s*). The process follows a pattern of *U-shaped development* in which infants first show signs of (e.g.) having acquired an irregular past tense form (*made*), then resort temporarily to the overgeneralised use of a regular inflection (*maked*) before reverting again to the correct form. Contradictory evidence has led some researchers to question how widespread and consistent this phenomenon is. Another early research question, inspired by nativist theories, was whether inflections are acquired by a child in a fixed order. The early work of Brown (1973) is sometimes quoted as demonstrating such an order, but the 'bound morphemes' investigated were very mixed, and the sequence was by no means clear-cut.

Research into the acquisition of lexis has suggested that an early vocabulary of 50–100 words in which nouns predominate, is followed by a *vocabulary spurt* (Clark 1993) where there is a sudden and rapid increase in the number of words, including verbs, that are acquired each day. The spurt is believed to coincide with a *naming insight*, a recognition by the child of the symbolic nature of language. However, not all children follow the standard pattern; some appear to acquire vocabulary more steadily, perhaps because they are oriented towards syntactic as well as lexical features.

A second area of lexical acquisition research explores the way in which infants succeed in associating meanings with words. One line of enquiry concerns the way in which categories such as DOG or FURNITURE are formed. A much-quoted theory (see 'Lexical storage' above) proposed that a child identifies a *prototype*, a highly typical member of a category, and then determines whether a newly encountered creature or object belongs to the category by its 'closeness of fit' to the prototype. More recently, an exemplar account has been favoured, with (taking DOG as an example) the child storing in the mind traces of many different instances of creatures that have had the label DOG attached to them (Hintzman 1986). Membership of the group is then determined not by a single prototypical breed but by a whole range of dogs that can be called up in memory.

Attention has also been given to the various possible meanings that could in theory be attached to a word. How does the child determine that the word DOG refers to the whole creature rather than (say) its tail or the fact that it is eating a bone? Markman (1990), Clark (1987) and other commentators have identified a number of assumptions which a child appears to bring to the acquisition of lexis. They include: that a noun refers to a whole object rather than part of it; that there is a one-to-one match between a word and a type of object; and that the first word encountered in a given area is likely to be at *basic level* (not a superordinate such as ANIMAL or a subordinate such as SPANIEL).

In phonological development, the child faces the important challenges of establishing articulatory settings and of co-ordinating the movement of the articulators from one setting to another. Certain phonemes are acquired earlier than others, with plosives and nasals preceding fricatives. The child compensates for an incomplete phonological repertoire by substituting a mastered phoneme for a more problematic one (Smith 1973). This seems to reflect difficulties of production rather than of perception, since children have proved capable of distinguishing the difference between their own realisation of a word and an adult's. There is evidence (Werker and Tees 1984) that children can distinguish between a wide range of speech sounds at a very early age, but that their phoneme categories gradually become more restricted to conform to the contrasts made by the target language.

Child directed speech

Chomsky's assertions that adult speech is 'degenerate' and that adults do not correct children's language have been subjected to considerable scrutiny. The way in which adults address children appears to be informed by an instinct for how much the child comprehends rather than attempting to emulate the child's own speech, and is finely attuned to the child's development. *Child directed speech* (once referred to as *motherese* or *baby talk*) has been found to be largely correct grammatically and to contain a number of features (for example, stress and intonation patterns) which potentially assist the acquisition process. Adults also employ features such as tag questions that draw the child into communication. The view that adults correct content rather than language has been confirmed, but there is extensive evidence in adult-child discourse of back-channelling and confirmation checks that recast the child's productions in a correct form. A caveat here is that most studies of interaction relate to Western societies; there has been discussion on the extent to which CDS is culturally determined.

Future trends

Psycholinguists rely increasingly upon brain imaging to confirm and refine assumptions about language storage and use that are derived from experimental studies. The use of neurolinguistic data is sure to expand as the technology becomes more widely available. Modern scanning techniques such as fMRI permit, not just a one-off snapshot of the parts of the brain engaged in a particular linguistic process, but a sequence of images of how the brain reacts over time. Similarly, electrodes attached to the scalp can be used to track small variations in electrical activity in the brain known as *event related potentials*. Especially promising is the recent use of this technology with pre-linguistic infants, to investigate the extent to which they respond to different features of phonetic and lexical input.

The eye-tracking equipment employed in reading studies is now being put to other uses, such as tracking a language user's gaze across pictures to establish how rapidly semantic relationships are processed. A parallel trend in writing is the development of computer programs that log both the keystrokes and the timing of writers. In studies of speech perception, increasing use is being made of synthetic speech, which can be manipulated to heighten particular features, to reduce audibility or to change speech rate.

A number of unresolved issues identified in this chapter are likely to feature prominently over the next few years. They include competition in lexical retrieval; the part played by formulaic language in the assembly of speech; the role of phonology in reading and writing; and how listeners normalise to voices and accents. Exemplar accounts of language storage and acquisition will be widely discussed, as will the emergentist view of language which they foster. The notion of the grammar rule is likely to be further questioned and conventional views of lexical and phonological categories may be overturned.

Final remarks

Psycholinguistics is a fast-growing field of study which has contributed enormously over the past fifty years to our understanding of language as a phenomenon. However, there are two causes for regret in relation to its present status. The first is the fragmented nature of the field, even within academic institutions: psycholinguists can be found in departments of psychology, applied linguistics, education, clinical linguistics and speech science, often with limited cross-departmental links. The second is the failure of psycholinguists to disseminate their findings adequately to a wider audience (including within applied linguistics). There is a tendency for cognitive psychologists to present their results in jargon-heavy prose, intended solely for the eyes of close colleagues, and not to transmit important insights to others who might benefit from them. The result is that psycholinguistics is sometimes regarded by the applied linguistics community as esoteric or unnecessarily complex. Psycholinguists need to do more to build contacts with those who share their preoccupation with language in use.

Related topics

clinical linguistics; the emergence of language as a complex adaptive system; neurolinguistics; second language acquisition; sign language

Further reading

Aitchison, J. (2003) *Words in the Mind*, 3rd edn, Oxford: Blackwell. (An accessible overview of lexical storage and retrieval.)

Clark, E. V. (2003) *First Language Acquisition*, Cambridge: Cambridge University Press. (Comprehensive outline of findings by a leading name in the field.)

Field, J. (2004) *Psycholinguistics: The Key Concepts*, Abingdon: Routledge. (Reference work aimed at applied linguists, providing concise outlines of terms and concepts in the field.)

Gaskell, M. G. (ed.) (2007) *The Oxford Handbook of Psycholinguistics*, Oxford: Oxford University Press. (Comprehensive set of papers by specialists, each reviewing current thinking in one area.)

Oakhill, J. and Garnham, A. (1988) *Becoming a Skilled Reader*, Oxford: Blackwell. (Extensive review of both decoding and comprehension in reading.)

Whitney, P. (1998) *The Psychology of Language*, Boston: Houghton Mifflin. (Introductory book, strong on detail and user-friendly for non-psychologists.)

References

Aitchison, J. (2003) *Words in the Mind*, 3rd edn, Oxford: Blackwell.

Atkinson, R. C. and Shiffrin, R. M. (1968) 'Human memory: a proposed system and its control processes', in K. W. Spence and J. T. Spence (eds) *The Psychology of Learning and Motivation*, vol. 2, London: Academic Press.

Baddeley, A. D. (1990) *Human Memory*, Hove: Lawrence Erlbaum Associates.

Bereiter, C. and Scardamalia, M. (1987) *The Psychology of Written Composition*, Hillsdale, NJ: Lawrence Erlbaum Associates.

Berko, J. (1958) 'The child's learning of English morphology', *Word* 14: 150–77.

Brown, G. and Yule, G. (1983) *Discourse Analysis*, Cambridge: Cambridge University Press.

Brown, R. (1973) *A First Language: The Early Stages*, Cambridge, MA: Harvard University Press.

Bybee, J. (2001) *Phonology and Language Use*, Cambridge: Cambridge University Press.

Bybee, J. L. and Hopper, P. (eds) (2001) *Frequency and the Emergence of Language Structure*, Amsterdam: John Benjamins.

Chomsky, N. (1959) 'Review of Skinner's "Verbal Behavior"', *Language* 35: 26–58.

——(1965) *Aspects of the Theory of Syntax*, Cambridge, MA: MIT Press.

Chomsky, N. and Lasnik, H. (1993) 'The theory of principles and parameters', in J. Jacobs, W. von Stechow, W. Sternfeld and T. Vennemann (eds) *Syntax: An International Handbook of Contemporary Research*, vol. 1. Berlin: Walter de Gruyter.

Clark, E. V. (1987) 'The principle of contrast: a constraint on language acquisition', in B. MacWhinney (ed.) *Mechanisms of Language Acquisition*, Hillsdale, NJ: Lawrence Erlbaum Associates.

——(1993) *The Lexicon in Acquisition*, Cambridge: Cambridge University Press.

Coltheart, M. (2005) 'Modeling reading: the dual-route approach', in M. J. Snowling and C. Hulme (eds) *The Science of Reading: A Handbook*, Malden, MA: Blackwell.

Cutler, A. (1990) 'Exploiting prosodic possibilities', in G. Altmann (ed.) *Cognitive Models of Speech Processing: Psycholinguistic and Computational Perspectives*, Cambridge, MA: MIT.

Deacon, T. (1997) *The Symbolic Species*, London: Penguin.

Field, J. (2008) *Listening in the Language Classroom*, Cambridge: Cambridge University Press.

Fromkin, V. (ed.) (1980) *Errors in Linguistic Performance: Slips of the Tongue, Ear, Pen and Hand*, New York: Academic Press.

Gathercole, S. and Baddeley, A. (1993) *Working Memory and Language*, Hove: Lawrence Erlbaum Associates.

Gernsbacher, M. A. (1990) *Language Comprehension as Structure Building*, Hillsdale, NJ: Lawrence Erlbaum Associates.

Goodman, K. S. (1967) 'Reading: a psycholinguistic guessing game', *Journal of the Reading Specialist* 6: 126–35.

Gough, P. B. and Wren, S. (1999) 'Constructing meaning: the role of decoding', in J. Oakhill and R. Beard (eds) *Reading Development and the Teaching of Reading*, Oxford: Blackwell.

Hayes, J. R. and Flower, L. S. (1980) 'Identifying the organization of writing processes', in L. W. Gregg and E. R. Steinberg (eds) *Cognitive Processes in Writing*, Hillsdale, NJ: Lawrence Erlbaum Associates.

Hintzman, D. L. (1986) 'Schema abstraction in a multiple-trace memory model', *Psychological Review* 93: 411–28.

Hotopf, W. N. (1983) 'Lexical slips of the pen and tongue: what they tell us about language production', in B. Butterworth (ed.) *Language Production*, vol. II: *Development, Writing and Other Language Processes*, London: Academic Press.

Johnson, K. and Mullenix, J. W. (1997) *'Talker Variability in Speech Processing'*, San Diego, CA: Academic Press.

Kellogg, R. T. (1996): 'A model of working memory in writing', in C. M. Levy and S. Ransdell, *The Science of Writing*, Mahwah, NJ: Lawrence Erlbaum Associates.

Levelt, W. J. M. (1989) *Speaking*, Cambridge, MA: MIT Press.

——(1999) 'Language production: a blueprint of the speaker', in C. Brown and P. Hagoort (eds) *Neurocognition of Language*, Oxford: Oxford University Press.

Markman, E. M. (1990) 'Constraints children place on word meanings', *Cognitive Science* 14: 57–77.

Marslen-Wilson, W. and Tyler, L. K. (1980) 'The temporal structure of spoken language understanding', *Cognition* 88: 1–71.

Miller, G. (1968) *The Psychology of Communication: Seven Essays*, London: Penguin.

Perfetti, C. (1985) *Reading Ability*, New York: Oxford University Press.

Piatelli-Palmarini, M. (1980) *Language and Learning: The Debate between Chomsky and Piaget*, Cambridge, MA: Harvard University Press.

Rastle, K. (2007) 'Visual word recognition', in M. G. Gaskell (ed.) *The Oxford Handbook of Psycholinguistics*, Oxford: Oxford University Press.

Rayner, K. and Pollatsek, A. (1989) *The Psychology of Reading*, Englewood Cliffs, NJ: Prentice Hall.

Rosch, E. (1975) 'Cognitive representations of semantic categories', *Journal of Experimental Psychology: General* 104: 192–233.

Rumelhart, D. E. and McClelland, J. L. (1986) 'On learning the past tense of English verbs', in D. E. Rumelhart, J. L. McClelland and the PDP Research Group (eds) *Parallel Distributed Processing*, vol. 1, Cambridge, MA: MIT.

Scardamalia, M. and Bereiter, C. (1987) 'Knowledge telling and knowledge transforming in written composition', in S. Rosenberg (ed.) *Advances in Applied Psycholinguistics*, vol. 2, Cambridge: Cambridge University Press.

Shiffrin, R. M. and Schneider, W. (1977) 'Controlled and automatic human information processing: II', *Psychological Review* 84: 127–90.

Skuse, D. H. (1993) 'Extreme deprivation in early childhood', in D. Bishop and K. Mogford (eds) *Language Development in Exceptional Circumstances*, Hove: Psychology Press.

Smith, N. V. (1973) *The Acquisition of Phonology: A Case Study*, Cambridge: Cambridge University Press.

van Gompel, R. P. G. and Pickering, M. J. (2007) 'Syntactic parsing', in M. G. Gaskell (ed.) *The Oxford Handbook of Psycholinguistics*, Oxford: Oxford University Press.

Werker, J. F. and Tees, R. C. (1984) 'Cross-language speech perception: evidence for perceptual reorganization during the first year of life', *Infant Behavior and Development* 7: 49–63.

Wray, A. (2002) *Formulaic Language and the Lexicon*, Cambridge: Cambridge University Press.

34

Sociocultural and cultural-historical theories of language development

Steven L. Thorne and Thomas Tasker

Introduction

This chapter describes closely related theories of human development that are rooted in the writings of the early twentieth-century Russian psychologist, L. S. Vygotsky. Within this approach, learning and development are seen to occur from the outside in; that is, in contrast to theories that presume the environment to be a mere trigger for genomic expression, or which posit linear stage development that is largely a function of biological maturation, Vygotskian sociocultural theory argues that human mental development is fundamentally constructed through engagement with cultural practices, artifacts, and milieus. In this way, sociocultural/cultural-historical approaches emphasize the dialectical relationship between ontogenesis (an individual's development across the life span) and the social and material conditions of everyday life, including those comprising formal instructional settings.

This chapter begins with a discussion of contemporary theories associated with Vygotsky's ideas and the core constructs and perspectives that are central to them, namely mediation, internalization, the relationship between biology and culture, and the Zone of Proximal Development. This is followed by a discussion of the contemporary application of sociocultural theories to second language learning and educationally related research and pedagogy.

Sociocultural and cultural-historical theories

The use of the plural marker with the term sociocultural 'theories' has to do with the different labels applied to developmental research directly associated with, or significantly influenced by, the Vygotskian lineage. The term 'sociocultural theory' (SCT) is often used in applied linguistics research, which follows from the early work of James Wertsch, who sought to differentiate Vygotskian theory as it was coming to be developed in the West from what he perceived as some problematic elements within the Russian tradition (see Wertsch *et al.* 1995). Researchers in education, computer science and informatics, workplace studies, cognitive science, and other fields, often produce research under the title cultural-historical activity theory (or CHAT), with references to A. R. Luria and specifically A. N. Leont'ev, both of whom were contemporaries of Vygotsky and who continued and elaborated Vygotsky's research after his death. In practice, the terms SCT and CHAT have been used interchangeably and even in collocated form ('sociocultural/cultural-historical'), since they refer to a common intellectual tradition and core set of principles. However, the use of CHAT tends to refer specifically to the post-Vygotskian framework initiated by A. N. Leont'ev (e.g. 1978, 1981).

One of the more prominent researchers within the Vygotskian tradition, Yrjö Engeström (2001), helps to clarify the relationship between sociocultural/cultural-historical theories by describing their historical development over three generations. The first generation centers on Vygotsky and his concept of mediation via 'auxiliary means', arguing that cultural tools enable, and are necessary for, specifically human forms of cognitive and material functions. The second generation begins with A. N. Leont'ev (e.g. 1981), who accepted the importance of cultural mediation but emphasized participation in practical life *activity* as the principle that dialectically relates external forms of social life to individual and collective psychology. Activity in this sense refers to social relations and rules of conduct that are governed by cultural, political, and economic institutions (Ratner 2002). Engeström describes the third generation's on-going task as that of developing conceptual tools to address dialogue, a multiplicity of perspectives, and the interrelations between defined systems of culturally organized activity (2001). As part of this effort, what has become known as CHAT has continued to develop as a network of contemporary conceptual and methodological influences that incorporate insights from hybridity scholarship, actor network theory, distributed cognition, and social practice theory, among others.

For the remainder of this chapter, reference to the broad tradition of sociocultural and cultural-historical approaches will be designated by SCT, while the use of CHAT will refer specifically to cultural-historical activity theory as outlined by post-Vygotskian theorists such as Leont'ev and Engeström.

Background: the sociogenesis of mind, sociocultural theories, and method

The intellectual roots of sociocultural theories of human development extend back to eighteenth- and nineteenth-century German philosophy (particularly Hegel), the sociological and economic writings of Marx and Engels (specifically *Theses on Feuerbach* and *The German Ideology*) and most directly to the research of Vygotsky and his colleagues Luria and Leont'ev (see Valsiner and van der Veer 2000). Despite the fact that Vygotsky suffered an early and untimely death in 1934 at only 38 years of age, he had a tremendously productive career that was deeply influenced by the fact that he came of age during the Russian Revolution. In his work, Vygotsky attempted to formulate 'a psychology grounded in Marxism' (Wertsch 1995: 7), which emphasized locating individual development within material, social, and historical conditions. Wertsch (1985: 199) has suggested that Vygotsky's developmental research was inspired by three essential principles of Marxist theory: (1) the idea that human consciousness is fundamentally social, rather than biological, in origin; (2) that human activity is mediated by material artifacts (e.g. computers, hammers) and psychological and symbolic tools/signs (e.g. language, literacy, numeracy, concepts); and (3) that units of analysis for understanding human activity and development should be holistic in nature.

These Marxian influences, coupled with Vygotsky's insights into method and theory, created a new ontology of human development, one that shifts away from long entrenched dualisms of individual-social and biology-culture and toward a dialectical understanding of biology and culture as unified processes that interweave with one another. In an attempt to overcome the mind-body-society dichotomies that dominated psychology and philosophy early in the twentieth century (and still today), Vygotsky proposed four mutually influencing 'genetic' (or historical time frame) domains in application to the study of human development. The first is the phylogenesis of humans as a species, which focuses on the approximately two-million-year co-evolution of human biology in relation to the appearance of language, material tools, and increasingly complex symbolic and cultural practices. Two examples of the co-evolutionary interplay of biology and culture include the evolution of the human hand and oppositional thumb (providing greater manual dexterity), which is isomorphic with the archaeological record showing an increasing complexity of material artifacts and implements, and the enlargement of the frontal cortex of the human brain in tandem with the emergence of language and complex communication (see Cole 1996; Deacon 1997; Tomasello 1999; Evans and Levinson 2009).

The second time frame is the sociocultural domain, which focuses on the multi-generational development of human cultures over historical time, with the implication that humans are born into an existing environment that provides powerful conceptual and material resources for communication, thinking, problem solving, and acting on the world through the use of symbolic tools and material implements. Tomasello (1999: 37) coined the term 'ratchet effect' to describe the preservation and creative modification of both material and symbolic forms of culture from generation to generation.

The third domain examines the ontogenesis of individuals over the life span. Here Vygotsky recognized two lines of development: biological maturation through chronological aging, and the internalization of cultural forms of cognition and behavior beginning in infancy and continuing across the life span. Ontogenesis can be described as the merger point or nexus of the phylogenetic and sociocultural domains during which the individual develops out of the interaction between biological and cultural inheritances (Lantolf and Thorne 2006: 45).

The fourth domain is labeled microgenesis, which describes the particular mental functions, abilities, and processes that develop over shorter periods of time. The latter two domains are the most relevant and utilized time frames for applied linguistics and second language (L2) research, though studies focusing on the phylogenetic domain (Tomasello 1999) and the sociocultural domain (Scribner and Cole 1981; Cole 1996) have been highly productive in illuminating the relationships between human cultures and the universal and heterogeneous qualities of higher-order, which is to say socioculturally informed and internalized, mental functions.

The principle contructs of sociocultural/cultural-historical theories

Internalization, mediation, and regulation

In relation to psychological theory in the early twentieth century, Vygotsky (1981) stated that the challenge to psychology was to 'show how the individual response emerges from the forms of collective life [and] in contrast to Piaget, we hypothesize that development does not proceed toward socialization, but toward the conversion of social relations into mental functions' (1981: 165). Drawing from earlier theorists such as Janet (see Valsiner and van der Veer 2000), Vygotsky termed this process of internalization the 'genetic law of cultural development' and described it as follows:

> Any function in the child's cultural development appears twice, or on two planes. First it appears on the social plane, and then on the psychological plane. First it appears between people as an interpsychological category, and then within the child as an intrapsychological category. This is equally true with regard to voluntary attention, logical memory, the formation of concepts, and the development of volition.

(Vygotsky 1981: 163)

As this quotation makes clear, higher order cognitive functions, which in addition to those mentioned above include planning, categorization, interpretive strategies, and forms of rationality, are internalized and made available as cognitive resources. This process of creative appropriation occurs through participation in informal social interaction and formal schooling, and more generally through exposure to, and use of, semiotic systems such as languages, textual (and now digital) literacies, numeracy and mathematics, and other historically accumulated cultural practices. In this sense, internalization describes the developmental process whereby humans gain the capacity to perform complex cognitive and physical-motor functions with progressively decreasing reliance on overt external assistance, or mediation.

In practical terms, human-created tools and artifacts such as language, explicit and implicit rules for appropriate conduct, and alarm clocks (to take a few diverse examples) mediate everyday cognition and interaction in the world, and subsequently, afford humans the capacity to better control their biological and behavioral activity (Frawley 1997). SCT researchers describe a developmentally sequenced shift in the locus of control of human activity as object-, other-, and self-regulation. Object-regulation describes instances when artifacts in the environment afford or make possible cognition/activity, such as the use of a dictionary to look up unknown words while reading or writing, the use of PowerPoint or an outline when making an oral presentation, or pen and paper for making a to-do list or working out mathematical problems. Other-regulation describes mediation by people and could include explicit or implicit feedback on grammatical form, editorial comments on a manuscript, or guidance from an expert. Self-regulation, as the label implies, refers to individuals for whom object- or other-regulation is unnecessary because originally external forms of mediation have been internalized and are therefore no longer needed for the execution or completion of a task. In this way, development can be described as the process of gaining greater voluntary control over one's capacity to think and act either by becoming more proficient in the use of meditational resources, or through a lessening of reliance on external meditational means.

Culture, language, cognition, and biology

'Culture' in the sense intended by Vygotsky and subsequent sociocultural theorists includes, but extends far beyond, 'high culture' phenomena such as literature, architecture, works of art, and the like. In a more significant way, culture refers to the historical accretion of all of human life, including the everyday rituals of interpersonal communication, family structure, institutional and group identities, creation and use of material artifacts and technologies, approaches to problem solving, literacy and numeracy practices, and most fundamentally, to the lexicalization and grammaticalization patterns specific to language (or languages).

Thus, the sociocultural tradition argues that human mental functioning is fundamentally a mediated process that is organized by cultural tools and activities, the primary of which involve language. The key that links thinking to social and communicative activity resides in the double function of the linguistic sign, which simultaneously points in two directions – outwardly, 'as a unit of social interaction (i.e. a unit of *behavior*)', and inwardly, 'as a unit of thinking (i.e. as a unit of *mind*)' (Prawat 1999: 268, italics in original). The inward or self-directed use of language as a symbolic tool for cognitive regulation is called 'private speech' (see McCafferty 1992; Lantolf 2003). Private speech is defined as an individual's use of language for purposes of maintaining or regaining self-regulation, i.e. to aid in focusing attention, problem solving, orienting oneself to a task, and to facilitate internalization of novel or difficult information (e.g. language forms) (Frawley 1997; Ohta 2001). The use of initially social forms of talk to regulate one's mental activity illustrates the interpenetration between an individual's psychology and the sociocultural world. In this sense, language is argued to serve as the primary tool through which humans construe the world (discussed below), and through the process of learning a language and using it for cognitive regulation, biologically endowed capacities for perception and cognition are reshaped into culturally and conceptually specific forms of perception and thinking (Lantolf and Thorne 2007).

From within the sociocultural tradition, Vološinov describes the relationship between signs/language and consciousness as follows:

> Consciousness takes shape and being in the material of signs created by an organized group in the process of its social intercourse. The individual consciousness is nurtured on signs; it derives growth from them; it reflects their logic and laws. The logic of consciousness is the logic of ideological communication, of the semiotic interaction of a social group.
>
> *(Vološinov 1973: 13)*

This view of language-as-culture and language as a building block for consciousness and perception is supported by current linguistic, anthropological, and neuroscience research associated with the Sapir-Whorf hypothesis of linguistic relativity (e.g. Whorf 1956; Gumperz and Levinson 1996; Slobin 1996; Gentner and Goldin-Meadow 2003). Linguistic relativity is the notion that the organization of language and its conventions carries forward historically developed systems of meaning – what can be termed more simply as culture – into the here-and-now of activity in the present (for a review, see Lucy 1996). Indeed, the diversity of obligatory semantic distinctions that characterize all languages has been demonstrated to correspond to habitual and speech-community specific forms of thought in the areas of spatial cognition (Bowerman and Choi 2003; Levinson 2003a) and categorization (Lakoff 1987). Levinson (2003b) sums up the cognition-language-culture connections of this position as follows:

> (1) languages vary in their semantics just as they do in their form, (2) semantic differences are bound to engender cognitive differences, (3) these cognitive correlates of semantic differences can be empirically found on a widespread basis.
>
> *(Levinson 2003b: 41–2)*

Sociocultural theory places great emphasis on the linguistic means people employ in the service of everyday activity, whether oriented toward multiparty communication or to regulate one's own cognitive activity. This has resulted in affinities between sociocultural theories of development and systemic functional linguistics (see Wells 1999), as well as a proposal to selectively recover key insights from early research on semiotics and communication (as outlined by Peirce, Wittgenstein, Garfinkel, and others), and to bring these traditions into contact with contemporary scholarship drawing upon corpus-informed theories of language structure and usage-based models of language acquisition (e.g. Hopper 1998; Tomasello 2003; Thorne and Lantolf 2007). Language in the sense defined by sociocultural theory is not concerned with rule-governed, a priori, or prescriptivist conceptions of grammar, but instead focuses on communicative resources, such as semiosis and gesture, that are formed and reformed in the very activity in which they are used – in situated and goal-directed communicative and cognitive activity.

This view of language is very much aligned with recent research emerging from cognitive-functional linguistics and usage-based approaches to language development, which emphasize that language structure emerges from, rather than precedes, language use (see Hopper 1998). A principle contributor to usage-based approaches is the evolutionary anthropologist and linguist Michael Tomasello, who describes the integration of child language learning with the more general cognitive and social skills of intention-reading and pattern recognition. He notes that these skills are 'evolutionarily fairly old, probably possessed in some form by all primates' (2003: 4), and hence, like other Vygotskian developmental psychologists, such as Luria (1976) and Cole (1996), Tomasello acknowledges the contribution of evolutionarily developed cognitive adaptations that make language learning possible. However, in sharp contrast to proponents of biologically driven models of language acquisition, Tomasello's empirical research supports a dual inheritance theory: humans inherit both genes *and* sociocultural environments. Tomasello argues that 'children begin to acquire language when they do because the learning process depends crucially on the more fundamental skills of joint attention, intention-reading, and cultural learning – which emerge near the end of the first year of life' (2003: 21). From this perspective, language learning occurs through the imitative process of cultural learning, and the biological capacity supporting language learning is not specific to language per se, but involves the broader ability to share attentional frames and to culturally attune to, and to imitate, the intentional actions, gesture and gaze orientations, and conceptual perspectives exhibited by people in one's environment. Tomasello emphasizes that homo sapiens has evolved the capacity for cultural learning in particular, which is supported by more general (non-language specific) cognitive skills such as schematization, categorization, pattern finding, and analogy-making. Usage-based models of language acquisition have been recently incorporated into sociocultural theorizations of second language development, notably by Lantolf and Thorne (2006) and Thorne and Lantolf (2007), and more broadly, have come to inform a variety of cognitive and computational approaches to second language and applied linguistics research (e.g. N. Ellis 2008; Zykik 2009).

The zone of proximal development and dynamic assessment

Among Vygotsky's numerous contributions to developmental psychology, the zone of proximal development (ZPD) has had arguably the greatest impact (Chaiklin 2003; related to L2 research, see Kinginger 2002). According to Chaiklin's (2003) exhaustive search of Vygotsky's available published works, there are a total of eight that mention the ZPD. Though the ZPD concept is often assumed to have originated with Vygtosky, Vygotsky himself credits American psychologists, particularly Meumann and McCarthy, with establishing the 'double-level approach' of attempting to understand not only what a child can do at a given point in time, but also what his or her future potential might be.

The most frequently referenced definition of the ZPD is 'the distance between the actual developmental level as determined by independent problem solving and the level of potential development as determined through problem solving under adult guidance or in collaboration with more capable peers' (Vygotsky 1978: 86). With greater specificity, Vygotsky describes the ZPD as follows:

> The [ZPD] defines those functions that have not yet matured but are in the process of maturation, functions that will mature tomorrow but are currently in an embryonic state. These functions could be termed 'buds' or 'flowers' of development rather than the 'fruits' of development. The actual developmental level characterizes mental development retrospectively, while the [ZPD] characterizes mental development prospectively. ... the [ZPD] permits us to delineate the child's immediate future and his dynamic developmental state,

allowing not only for what already has been achieved developmentally but also for what is in the course of maturing.

(Vygotsky 1978: 86–7)

Thus, the defining aspect of the ZPD concept is that, in contrast to traditional assessment measures that indicate the level of development that has been already attained, the ZPD is forward-looking through its assertion that mediated performance, and importantly the discovery of the qualities of assistance necessary for an individual to perform particular competencies, are indicative of the readiness for independent functioning in the future. Vygotsky was particularly interested in the effects of formal schooling on cognitive development.

One of Vygotsky's most important findings is that learning collaboratively with others, particularly in instructional settings, precedes and shapes development. The relationship between learning and development is not directly causal, but intentionally designed learning environments (e.g. instructed L2 settings) can stimulate qualitative developmental changes. In this sense, the ZPD is not only a model of the developmental process, but also a conceptual tool that educators can use to understand aspects of students' emerging capacities that are in early stages of maturation. When used proactively, teachers using the ZPD as a diagnostic have the potential to create conditions for learning that may give rise to specific forms of development in the future. This point leads to a topic discussed later in this chapter – assessment practices rooted in the ZPD.

Within applied linguistics and language educational research, the diverse adoptions and adaptations of the ZPD concept may not always align with doctrinal interpretations of Vygotskian theory (see Chaiklin 2003; Donato 2004). The ZPD concept has proliferated to the point that it now encompasses research and pedagogical innovation that includes parent–child interaction, teacher–student interaction, and peer interaction dynamics. The ZPD has been applied primarily in regard to individual development, but it has also been proposed as a model of whole class teaching (Guk and Kellogg 2007). It is clear that the ZPD concept is divergently understood, and this is the case not only for casual adopters, but also is evident among researchers working primarily or exclusively within cultural-historical psychology itself.

In a review of research in applied linguistics and second language research, Kinginger (2002) has identified three uses of the ZPD, each of which differ from, or significantly extend, Vygotsky's core emphasis on the learner and emerging capacities: (1) a 'skills' interpretation, (2) a 'scaffolding' interpretation, and (3) a 'metalinguistic' interpretation. Within what she considers to be the most problematic category, the 'skills' interpretation, Kinginger identifies uses of the ZPD concept that illustrate:

> a process of reduction and simplification such that [use of the ZPD] can serve to justify extant institutionalized practices and reinforce traditional views of the language classroom as a locus of skill acquisition in the service of standardized education. Stripped of its original meanings, the ZPD is inserted into a conventional descriptive scheme and provides no new object for reflection on theory or practice.

(Kinginger 2002: 253)

For its part, the 'scaffolding interpretation' involves an interesting reciprocal formulation of the ZPD, where ostensibly the focus is on the learner, but in actual fact, and certainly as an entailment of the scaffolding metaphor, power is located primarily in the teacher or expert who is providing the 'scaffold' or assistance. In most descriptions of scaffolding, the adult (or teacher) 'controls' the elements that are beyond the child's capacity, allowing the child to focus on 'only those elements that are within his range of competence' (Wood *et al.* 1976). It is this element of scaffolding that has been explicitly linked to the ZPD (see Rogoff and Wertsch 1984; Bruner 1986), and in some cases, seems to have erroneously become synonymous with it (see Stone 1993, for a discussion). In summarizing the 'skills' and 'scaffolding' variants of the ZPD, Kinginger (2002) notes that in the skills case, the ZPD concept is uncritically appropriated and used to describe what are essentially transmission models of teaching (see Moll 1989), and while the scaffolding interpretation productively acknowledges contingently provided assistance, as the name would suggest, there is an implicit shift in focus from development (ZPD) to instruction (scaffolding).

Kinginger describes a third, and in her (and our) assessment, a highly productive extension of the ZPD which emphasizes metalinguistic functions of language use and learner discussion about their own language production. In this vein, Swain and colleagues (Swain 2000; Swain *et al.* 2009) describe 'collaborative dialogue' and 'languaging' as uses of language that help to problem solve, share and build knowledge, and complete thoughts. Swain *et al.* (2009: 5) define languaging as 'a form of verbalization used to mediate the solution(s) to complex problems and tasks' and the use of language to shape knowledge and experience. The metalinguistic function of language is critical to the learning processes as it externalizes current thinking and ideas, which in turn become objects for individual and collaborative reflection and transformative action.

Within applied linguistics, there have been a number of elaborations and proposals for the broadening of the ZPD concept. Wells (1999) has suggested that the ZPD need not be characterized as a fixed or stable attribute of an individual or environment, but rather as an unpredictable nexus of people and tools in joint activity, which together create conditions for transformation and development. In a number of publications, Mercer (2000, 2002) describes what he terms the Intermental Development Zone (IDZ), which draws elements from both the ZPD and scaffolding. The IDZ is defined as a 'contextualizing framework for joint activity, whose effectiveness is likely to depend on how well a teacher can create and maintain connections between the curriculum-based goals of activity and a learner's existing knowledge, capabilities, and motivations' (Mercer 2002: 143). In an insightful revision of the ZPD, Negueruela (2008) has proposed the Zone of Potential Development (ZPOD) as a ZPD-informed approach that is more attuned to second language acquisition and adult L2 learning. Negueruela argues that development follows diverse trajectories. Thus, by replacing 'proximal' with 'potential', he removes the telos of a 'proximal' next stage of development, and acknowledges situational contingency and the necessity of a learner's agency in realizing his or her developmental path. In particular, Negueruela stresses the importance of concepts as 'psychological mediators' and the importance of 'devising pedagogical sequences that allow learners to create their own conceptualizations through guided imitation' (2008: 2001).

The ZPD has also come to inform a proposal for the dialectical union of assessment and learning called Dynamic Assessment (DA). DA is a procedure that unifies the goals of assessing a learner's developmental potential through structured sets of interactions that also are meant to foster learning. DA methods of assessment involve mediating an examinee's performance by providing a scaled continuum of learner-contingent prompts, leading questions, and more direct assistance during the assessment intervention itself. Its primary goal is to fuse assessment procedures with interactive opportunities for learning, and in so doing, to produce a more nuanced understanding of an examinee's current level of development and future potential. Though further discussion is beyond the scope of this chapter, Lantolf and Poehner (2004) provide an in-depth description of DA use in education broadly, and also suggest guidelines for its use in second- and foreign-language contexts. Additionally, Poehner (2008) describes DA in use with learners of French as a foreign language and extends its principles to formative assessment and foreign language classroom practice.

SCT and CHAT: applied research and pedagogy

Vygotsky was inspired by Marxist notions of social justice and spent much of his career committed to research and pedagogical interventions that he hoped would positively influence public education, a project that was nascent in Russia (and the world) at that time and which he hoped would serve a socially progressive function (Prawat 2000).

In principle, SCT investigations aim to afford analyses that will lead to the development of material and symbolic-conceptual tools necessary to enact positive interventions. Though SCT is also used descriptively and analytically as a diagnostic framework, its essence is to take a situation or condition and transform it in an effort to create something qualitatively new. In this sense, SCT, and in particular CHAT, have been used equally as research frameworks and heuristics supporting innovation in a wide array of contexts, including education (Engeström 1987; Prior 1998; Daniels 2001; Sawchuk *et al.* 2007), human-computer interaction (Kaptelinin and Nardi 2006) and uses of new media (Thorne 2003, 2009), and second- and foreign language learning (Kramsch 2000; Lantolf 2000; Thorne 2000, 2005; Swain and Lapkin 2002; Robbins 2003; van Lier 2004).

To conclude with specific examples of SCT-informed applied linguistics research, two contexts and approaches will be briefly reviewed: concept-based teaching and the use of CHAT in teacher professional development and school restructuring projects.

Concept-based teaching, also referred to as Systemic-Theoretical Instruction (STI), is an approach that is closely associated with the work of Gal'perin (1992). In this approach pedagogical materials are conceived of as cognitive tools. Gal'perin emphasized the importance of orienting students to the conceptual structuring of complex domains of knowledge and/or action, or the 'orienting basis' for action, which he argued must precede guided practice (Arievitch and Stetsenko 2000: 86). Gal'perin's model proposes that without a conceptually coherent orientation, learning is not optimized and instead occurs on a hit-or-miss basis. Within foreign language education, Negueruela (2003, 2008: 203) outlines four essential principles and processes of this model: (1) the minimal unit of L2 instruction is the concept; (2) concepts must be materialized – for example, in the form of diagrams and flow charts, so as to help learners understand the semantic, structural and functional properties of the target concepts; (3) learners verbalize the processes and linguistic choices represented in concept-based materializations; and (4) the concepts and/or categories of meaning represented by the materializations must be systematically connected to other relevant concepts. Areas of L2 grammar instruction that have been addressed using concept-based instruction include the organization of tense, aspect, and mood in a university-level Spanish foreign language course (Negueruela 2003, 2008); the formation of the passive voice by L2 learners of German (Kabanova 1985); the grammatical concept of voice in L2 French (Swain *et al.* 2009); and deontic and directive language use for advanced learners of English in preparation for taking on instructional roles as teaching assistants (Thorne *et al.* 2008).

A CHAT-informed approach called Developmental Work Research (DWR) (Engeström 1999, 2007) has been used to assist people in addressing the contradictions and problems they face in the workplace. DWR methodology involves creating a space for participants and interventionist-researchers to explore the past and current practices of the group. The participants are then introduced to CHAT as a conceptual tool that they can use to identify, make sense of, and potentially use to overcome the workplace contradictions they face. Engeström

(2007) states that DWR methodology aligns with Vygotsky's (1978) 'method of double stimulation' in that the participants are presented with a problem or contradiction that they themselves have identified (the first stimulus), and then are guided by mediational means introduced by the researcher (the second stimulus) with the goal of developing new understandings and potential solutions.

Daniels *et al.* (2007) explored the professional development of educators engaged in forging a partnership between schools and agencies with the goal of promoting creativity. In a series of meetings and workshops, the participants explored the divergent goals of the groups involved and eventually developed the tools they needed to form a productive partnership. In related research, V. Ellis (2008) has applied DWR methodology to investigate the trajectory of teacher professional development. Ellis examined the transformation of school–university activity systems through a program aimed at remediating relationships between pre-service and mentor teachers. Implementing collaborative planning led to changes in the way some of the mentor teachers conceptualized professional learning and increased the opportunities for dialogue with novice teachers. In these studies, DWR methodology with CHAT provided the means for educators to explore novel solutions to entrenched contradictions in the workplace that resulted in new understandings of professional practice and new systems of professional activity.

Summary

This chapter has described the intellectual foundation of sociocultural/cultural-historical perspectives on human development and their relevance to applied linguistics research and pedagogy. At the core of this approach is mediation, the principle that humans do not act directly on the world – rather their cognitive and material activities are mediated by cultural tools, artifacts and technologies. The concept of internalization describes the processes through which interpersonal and person–environment interactions form, and transform, one's internal mental functions. This developmental process occurs within the ZPD, which is defined as the difference between the level of development already obtained and that which may only be possible, and visible, in joint activity. In this sense, the ZPD is a model of developmental processes, and through related methods such as dynamic assessment, can provide insight into students' emerging capacities that are in early stages of maturation.

Because of its emphasis on praxis, SCT is both a powerful analytic research framework and also an approach with deep roots in emancipatory traditions of activist engagement. In other words, SCT, and particularly CHAT, encourage engaged critical analysis that supports the development of material and symbolic tools necessary to enact positive change. In this sense, the value of the theory resides not just in the analytical lens it provides for understanding human development, but in its capacity to directly impact that development.

Related topics

language and culture; language emergence; language learning and language education; SLA

Further reading

Lantolf, J. P. (ed.) (2000) *Sociocultural Theory and Second Language Learning*, Oxford: Oxford University Press. (Lantolf includes a diverse range of chapters by leading scholars in second language acquisition and pedagogy, addressing primarily L2 classroom research focused on issues of mediation, the ZPD, identity, teacher development, and the relation of SCT to other theories of language, learning, and social practice.)

Lantolf, J. P. and Thorne, S. L. (2006) *Sociocultural Theory and the Genesis of Second Language Development*, Oxford: Oxford University Press. (Lantolf and Thorne present a close exegesis of fundamental tenets of SCT and CHAT and provide a comprehensive review of existing L2 research and pedagogical projects.)

Lantolf, J. P. and Poehner, M. E. (2008). *Sociocultural Theory and the Teaching of Second Languages*, London: Equinox. (Lantolf and Poehner, focusing exclusively on issues of L2 teaching and pedagogy, have published an edited volume that includes chapters addressing concept-based teaching, dynamic assessment, and instructional initiatives framed by the ZPD and related constructs.)

Lantolf, J. P. and Beckett, T. (2009) 'Sociocultural theory and second language acquisition', *Language Teaching* 42(4): 459–75. (Lantolf and Beckett (2009: 1) provide a 'research timeline' of L2 SCT studies that includes synopses of forty-eight 'notable publications, all of which in some way implicate the basic claim ... that all mental activity is symbolically mediated'.)

van Lier, L. (2004) *The Ecology and Semiotics of Language Learning: A Sociocultural Perspective*, Boston: Kluwer Academic. (Van Lier insightfully combines Vygotskian theory with detailed discussions of semiotics and ecological approaches to language and L2 development.)

References

Arievitch, I. and Stetsenko, A. (2000) 'The quality of cultural tools and cognitive development: Gal'perin's perspective and its implications', *Human Development* 43: 69–92.

Bowerman, M. and Choi, S. (2003) 'Space under construction: language-specific spatial categorization in first language acquisition', in D. Gentner and S. Goldin-Meadow (eds) *Language in Mind*, Cambridge, MA: MIT Press.

Bruner, J. S. (1986) *Actual Minds, Possible Worlds*, Cambridge, MA: Harvard University Press.

Chaiklin, S. (2003) 'The zone of proximal development in Vygotsky's analysis of learning and instruction', in A. Kozulin, B. Gidnis, V. S. Ageyev and S. Miller (eds) *Vygotsky's Educational Theory in Cultural Context*, Cambridge: Cambridge University Press.

Cole, M. (1996) *Cultural Psychology: A Once and Future Discipline*, Cambridge, MA: Belknap Press.

Daniels, H. (2001) *Vygotsky and Pedagogy*, London: RoutledgeFalmer.

Daniels, H., Leadbetter, J., Soares, A. and MacNab, N. (2007) 'Learning in and for cross-school working', *Oxford Review of Education* 33: 125–42.

Deacon, T. (1997) *The Symbolic Species: The Co-evolution of Language and the Brain*, New York: W. W. Norton & Company.

Donato, R. (2004) 'Aspects of collaboration in pedagogical discourse', *Annual Review of Applied Linguistics* 24: 284–302.

Ellis, N. C. (2008) 'Usage-based and form-focused language acquisition: the associative learning of constructions, learned-attention, and the limited L2 endstate', in P. Robinson and N. C. Ellis (eds) *Handbook of Cognitive Linguistics and Second Language Acquisition*, London: Routledge.

Ellis, V. (2008) 'Exploring the contradictions in learning to teach: the potential of Developmental Work Research', *Changing English: Studies in Culture and Education* 16(1): 53–63.

Engeström, Y. (1987) *Learning by Expanding: An Activity Theoretical Approach to Developmental Research*, Helsinki: Orienta-Konsultit.

——(1999) 'Innovative learning in work teams: analysing cycles of knowledge creation in practice', in Y. Engeström, R. Miettinen and R.-L. Punamäki (eds) *Perspectives on Activity Theory*, Cambridge: Cambridge University Press.

——(2001) 'Expansive learning at work: toward an activity theoretical reconceptualization', *Journal of Education and Work* 14: 133–56.

——(2007) 'Putting Vygotsky to work: the change laboratory as an application of double stimulation', in H. Wells, M. Cole and J. V. Wertsch (eds) *The Cambridge Companion to Vygotsky*, New York: Cambridge University Press.

Evans, N. and Levinson, S. C. (2009) 'The myth of language universals: language diversity and its importance for cognitive science', *Behavioral and Brain Sciences* 32(5): 429–92.

Frawley, W. (1997) *Vygotsky and Cognitive Science. Language and the Unification of the Social and Computational Mind*, Cambridge, MA: Harvard University Press.

Gal'perin, P. (1992) 'Linguistic consciousness and some questions of the relationships between language and thought', *Journal of Russian and East European Psychology* 30(4): 28–49.

Gentner, D. and Goldin-Meadow, S. (eds) (2003) *Language in Mind*, Cambridge, MA: MIT Press.

Guk, I. and Kellogg, D. (2007) 'The ZPD and whole class teaching: teacher-led and student-led interactional mediation of tasks', *Language Teaching Research* 11(3): 281–99.

Gumperz, J. J. and Levinson, S. C. (1996) *Rethinking Linguistic Relativity*, Cambridge: Cambridge University Press.

Hopper, P. (1998) 'Emergent grammar', in M. Tomasello (ed.) *The New Psychology of Language: Cognitive and Functional Approaches to Language Study*, London: Lawrence Erlbaum Associates.

Kabanova, O. Ya. (1985) 'The teaching of foreign languages', *Instructional Science* 14: 1–47.

Kaptelinin, V. and Nardi, B. (2006) *Acting with Technology: Activity Theory and Interaction Design*, Cambridge, MA: MIT Press.

Kinginger, C. (2002) 'Defining the zone of proximal development in US foreign language education', *Applied Linguistics* 23: 240–61.

Kramsch, C. (2000) 'Social discursive constructions of self in L2 learning', in J. P. Lantolf (ed.) *Sociocultural Theory and Second Language Learning*, Oxford: Oxford University Press.

Lakoff, G. (1987) *Women, Fire, and Dangerous Things: What Categories Reveal about the Mind*, Chicago: University of Chicago Press.

Lantolf, J. P. (2000) 'Second language learning as a mediated process', *Language Teaching* 33: 79–96.

——(2003) 'Intrapersonal communication and internalization in the second language classroom', in A. Kozulin, V. S. Ageev, S. Miller and B. Gindis (eds) *Vygotsky's Theory of Education in Cultural Context*, Cambridge: Cambridge University Press.

Lantolf, J. P. and Poehner, M. E. (2004) 'Dynamic assessment: bringing the past into the future', *Journal of Applied Linguistics* 1: 49–74.

Lantolf, J. and Thorne, S. L. (2006) *Sociocultural Theory and the Genesis of Second Language Development*, Oxford: Oxford University Press.

——(2007) 'Sociocultural theory and second language acquisition', in B. van Patten and J. Williams (eds) *Explaining Second Language Acquisition*, Cambridge: Cambridge University Press.

Leont'ev, A. N. (1978) *Activity, Consciousness, and Personality*, Englewood Cliffs, NJ: Prentice Hall.

——(1981) 'The problem of activity in psychology', in J. V. Wertsch (ed.) *The Concept of Activity in Soviet Psychology*, Armonk, NY: M. E. Sharpe.

Levinson, S. (2003a) *Space in Language and Cognition*, New York: Cambridge.

——(2003b) 'Language and mind', in D. Gentner and S. Goldin-Meadow (eds) *Language in Mind*, Cambridge, MA: MIT Press.

Lucy, J. A. (1996) 'The scope of linguistic relativity: an analysis and review of empirical research', in J. J. Gumperz and S. C. Levinson (eds) *Rethinking Linguistic Relativity*, New York: Cambridge University Press.

Luria, A. R. (1976) *Cognitive Development: Its Cultural and Social Foundations*, Cambridge, MA: Harvard University Press.

McCafferty, S. (1992) 'The use of private speech by adult second language learners: a cross-cultural study', *Modern Language Journal* 78: 179–89.

Mercer, N. (2000) *Words and Minds: How We Use Language to Think Together*, London: Routledge.

——(2002) 'Developing dialogues', in G. Wells and G. Claxton (eds) *Learning for Life in the 21st Century: Sociocultural Perspectives on the Future of Education*, Oxford: Blackwell.

Moll, L. (1989) 'Teaching second language students: a Vygotskian perspective', in D. M. Johnson and D. H. Oren (eds) *Richness in Writing: Empowering ESL Students*, New York: Longman.

Negueruela, E. (2003) 'A Sociocultural Approach to the Teaching and Learning of Second Languages: Systemic-theoretical Instruction and L2 Development', Ph.D. Dissertation, Pennsylvania State University.

——(2008) 'Revolutionary pedagogies: learning that leads (to) second language development', in J. P. Lantolf and M. E. Poehner (eds) *Sociocultural Theory and the Teaching of Second Languages*, London: Equinox.

Ohta, A. S. (2001) *Second Language Acquisition Processes in the Classroom: Learning Japanese*, Mahwah, NJ: Lawrence Erlbaum Associates.

Poehner, M. E. (2008) *Dynamic Assessment: A Vygotskian Approach to Understanding and Promoting Second Language Development*, Berlin: Springer.

Prawat, R. (1999) 'Social constructivism and the process-content distinction as viewed by Vygotsky and the Pragmatists', *Mind, Culture, and Activity*, 6: 255–73.

——(2000) 'Dewey meets the "Mozart of psychology" in Moscow: the untold story', *American Education Research Journal* 37: 663–96.

Prior, P. A. (1998). *Writing/Disciplinarity: A Sociohistorical Account of Literate Activity in the Academy*, Mahwah, NJ: Lawrence Erlbaum Associates.

Ratner, C. (2002) *Cultural Psychology: Theory and Method*, New York: Kluwer Academic/Plenum Publishers.

Robbins, D. (2003) *Vygotsky's and A. A. Leontiev's Semiotics and Psycholinguistics: Applications for Education, Second Language Acquisition, and Theories of Language*, Westport, CT: Praeger.

Rogoff, B. and Wertsch, J. V. (eds) (1984) *Children's Learning in the 'Zone of Proximal Development'*, San Francisco: Jossey-Bass.

Sawchuk, P., Duarte, N. and Elhammoumi, M. (2007) *Critical Perspectives on Activity*, New York: Cambridge.

Scribner, S. and Cole, M. (1981) *The Psychology of Literacy*, Cambridge, MA: Harvard University Press.

Slobin, D. (1996) 'From "thought and language" to "thinking for speaking"', in J. J. Gumperz and S. C. Levinson (eds) *Rethinking Linguistic Relativity*, Cambridge: Cambridge University Press.

Stone, C. A. (1993) 'What's missing in the metaphor of scaffolding?', in E. A. Forman, N. Minick and C. A. Stone (eds) *Contexts of Learning: Sociocultural Dynamics of Children's Development*, New York: Oxford University Press.

Swain, M. (2000) 'The output hypothesis and beyond: mediating acquisition through collaborative dialogue', in J. P. Lantolf (ed.) *Sociocultural Theory and Second Language Acquisition*, Oxford: Oxford University Press.

Swain, M. and Lapkin, S. (2002) 'Talking it through: two French immersion learners' response to reformulation', *International Journal of Educational Research* 37: 285–304.

Swain, M., Lapkin, S., Knouzzi, I., Suzuki, W. and Brooks, L. (2009) 'Languaging: university students learn the grammatical concept of voice in French', *The Modern Language Journal* 93: 5–27.

Thorne, S. L. (2000) 'Second language acquisition and the truths about relativity', in J. P. Lantolf (ed.) *Sociocultural Theory and Second Language Acquisition*, Oxford: Oxford University Press.

——(2003) 'Artifacts and cultures-of-use in intercultural communication', *Language Learning and Technology* 7(2): 38–67.

——(2005) 'Epistemology, politics, and ethics in sociocultural theory', *The Modern Language Journal* 89: 393–409.

——(2009) '"Community", semiotic flows, and mediated contribution to activity', *Language Teaching* 42(1): 81–94.

Thorne, S. L. and Lantolf, J. P. (2007) 'A linguistics of communicative activity', in S. Makoni and A. Pennycook (eds.) *Disinventing and Reconstituting Languages*, Clevedon: Multilingual Matters.

Thorne, S. L., Reinhardt, J. and Golombek, P. (2008) 'Mediation as objectification in the development of professional discourse: a corpus-informed curricular innovation', in J. P. Lantolf and M. E. Poehner (eds) *Sociocultural Theory and the Teaching of Second Languages*, London: Equinox.

Tomasello, M. (1999) *The Cultural Origins of Human Cognition*, Cambridge, MA: Harvard University Press.

——(2003) *Constructing Language: A Usage-based Theory of Language Acquisition*, Cambridge, MA: Harvard University Press.

Valsiner, J. and van der Veer, R. (2000) *The Social Mind: Construction of the Idea*, Cambridge: Cambridge University Press.

van der Veer, R. and Valsiner, J. (1993) *Understanding Vygotsky: A Quest for Synthesis*, Cambridge, MA and Oxford: Blackwell.

van Lier, L. (2004) *The Ecology and Semiotics of Language Learning: A Sociocultural Perspective*, Boston, MA: Kluwer Academic.

Vološinov, V. N. (1973) *Marxism and the Philosophy of Language*, New York: Seminar Press.

Vygotsky, L. S. (1978) *Mind in Society: The Development of Higher Psychological Processes*, in M. Cole, V. John-Steiner, S. Scribner and E. Souberman (eds), Cambridge, MA: Harvard University Press.

——(1981) 'The genesis of higher mental functions', in J. V. Wertsch (ed.) *The Concept of Activity in Soviet Psychology*, Armonk, NY: M. E. Sharpe.

Wells, G. (1999) *Dialogic Inquiry: Toward a Sociocultural Practice and Theory of Education*, New York: Cambridge University Press.

Wertsch, J. V. (1985) *Vygotsky and the Social Formation of Mind*, Cambridge, MA: Harvard University Press.
——(1995) 'The need for action in sociocultural research', in J. V. Wertsch, P. del Río and A. Alvarez (eds) *Sociocultural Studies of Mind*, New York: Cambridge University Press.
Wertsch, J. V. del Río, P. and Alvarez, A. (eds) (1995) *Sociocultural Studies of Mind*, Cambridge: Cambridge University Press.
Whorf, B. (1956) 'The relation of habitual thought and behavior to language', in J. B. Carroll (ed.) *Language, Thought and Reality: Selected Writings of Benjamin Lee Whorf*, Cambridge, MA: MIT Press.
Wood, D., Bruner, J. and Ross, G. (1976) 'The role of tutoring in problem-solving', *Journal of Child Psychology and Psychiatry* 17: 89–100.
Zykik, E. (2009) 'The role of input revisited: nativist versus usage-based models', *L2 Journal* 1(1): 42–61.

35

Sociolinguistics

Carmen Llamas

Introduction

Sociolinguistics as a field is extremely wide-ranging and includes a multitude of models, methods and theoretical frameworks. Dealing, as it does, with language use in social contexts, research in the area of sociolinguistics concerns itself primarily with how language is actually used by speakers: how it varies, how it changes, how meaning is signalled and interpreted in social interaction. As such, as well as allowing a better understanding of the structure of language and of the structure of society, sociolinguistic findings also have immediate and significant applied value.

Surveys which document the facts of linguistic variation over geographical space, and studies which describe structured variation in the speech of a socially stratified sample of speakers provide much-needed knowledge and points of reference for all manner of people who are responsible for taking language-related decisions in the real world. For the forensic phonetician in a court of law assessing a case involving disputed utterances or speaker identification, being in possession of detailed knowledge of regional and social varieties of a language will clearly be necessary. For the speech and language therapist responsible for assessing the needs and problems of the late developing child, understanding the nature of and processes involved in the emergence of structured variation will undoubtedly be advantageous. And for the language planner developing the policies involved in maintaining a minority language and raising its status in the community, knowledge of the relevant language attitudes and the functions of code-switching in the multilingual community will have obvious benefits. Countless other contexts involving real-life language-related issues and problems are aided by knowledge and insights gained through research that is undertaken within the sociolinguistic field of enquiry. By providing a level of understanding of how language is used to signal who we are and how we fit into the world, sociolinguistic research is immediately relevant to questions involving language users in real world contexts. Indeed, it could be argued that sociolinguists have a particular responsibility to take an ethically involved position and to use the knowledge they gain to influence the direction of government language policies, educational practices and so on (see, for example, Wolfram 1998).

Within the field, it is naturally occurring speech data, rather than intuitions about how language is structured, which constitute the basis for much of what can be described as sociolinguistic research. Variation in language use, which is inherent and ubiquitous, is centrally important in sociolinguistics. The structured variability in language, which is systematic and socially conditioned, is not dismissed as free or random, nor (being difficult to model elegantly) of little consequence to mainstream linguistic theory. Analysis of this structured variation, and of the linguistic and social constraints on it, allow us to better understand how and why language changes. And knowledge of how and why language varies across time, space, place, topic, audience, style and so on is of direct benefit to those who make language-related decisions.

For some, variationist sociolinguistics/sociophonetics – associated with the work of William Labov – lies at the heart of sociolinguistics as a discipline, and the statistical correlation of structured variation in production patterns with global social variables such as socio-economic class and gender is considered the core area of research in the field. Indeed, Cameron (1990: 82) argues that 'the rise and rise of the quantitative paradigm' has led to the marginalisation of other methods and models which can sit comfortably underneath the umbrella term of sociolinguistics to the extent that:

> for most people in the field (and especially most *linguists* in the field) 'sociolinguistics' does indeed mean primarily if not exclusively 'Labovian quantitative sociolinguistics'.

Others take a broader view, and for them the field of sociolinguistics subsumes both variationist sociolinguistics and interactional sociolinguistics, as well as fields such as the sociology of language and linguistic anthropology, among others.

Interactional sociolinguistics is linked to the names of the sociologist Erving Goffman, and the anthropological linguist John Gumperz. Much of the early work (for example, Gumperz 1982) was concerned with the mechanisms of miscommunication in intercultural interaction, as interaction depends not only on the content of what is said, but also on the processes of evaluation and perception of signalling mechanisms. In broad terms, research in interactional sociolinguistics examines meaning-making processes in contextualised language use and ways in which speakers signal and interpret meaning in social interaction. Work in the area is primarily done through an ethnographic research design which examines the local complexities of particular contexts. This allows a detailed view of a specific use of language rather than a generalisation about broad linguistic tendencies. Discourse and conversational analysis techniques are used in this type of research, and detailed transcriptions are produced which may involve non-verbal aspects of the interaction, such as gestures or spatial alignment of speakers, as well as details of pausing, overlap, etc. Use of these contextualisation cues can mark different types of speech events and different alignments between interactants. All such features may have an influence on how meaning is made and perceived. The field encompasses a broad variety of contexts (for example, clinical interaction, courtroom interaction, workplace settings) and focuses (for example, politeness, discourse strategies, reported speech), and more detail on this side of sociolinguistics can be obtained through various chapters in this volume, for example those on Medical Communication, Language and Ageing, Linguistic Ethnography, Institutional Discourse, Classroom Discourse, among others.

Less detail on variationist sociolinguistics is provided in other chapters in the volume, so for this reason we focus our attention in this chapter on the variationist side of the sociolinguistic coin. We begin by briefly outlining the history of the discipline of variationist sociolinguistics and consider some of the more prominent research methods associated with the field. Discussion of some of the main current issues will then be outlined before consideration is given to future directions and areas of developing interest.

Background

Variationist sociolinguistics, as we would recognise it today, really begins with the seminal work of William Labov in his Martha's Vineyard (MV) (1963) and his Lower East Side, New York (LES, NY) (1966) studies. Many of the techniques and methods pioneered in these early studies are still used today, and insights gained from this research have formed part of the foundations of the majority of variationist work since.

Prior to Labov's early work in the USA, the belief that sound change was too slow to observe was widely held (see, for example, Hockett 1958) and earlier works on urban varieties of American English maintained that variation was random and singularly without pattern (Hubbell 1950). Labov's early studies were not only able to reveal the structured heterogeneity in language, but were able to demonstrate that by using the apparent time construct (that is, by hypothesising that the individual's phonological system remains stable throughout adulthood) and comparing the speech of older and younger speakers, evidence strongly suggestive of linguistic change in progress could be found. Also, by examining the social characteristics of the informants, speaker-based explanations for why language may vary and change could be offered. Labov's earlier MV study, which explored the relationship between the use of linguistic forms (in this case the centralisation of the first elements of the diphthongs /ay/ and /aw/) with orientation to local place and practices, has come to be hugely influential. However, it was his later LES, NY project in which global categories, such as socio-economic class and sex, were correlated with linguistic variables in a broad demographic survey study, which had the initial and immediate influence on the developing field. Studies which replicated the methodological procedures used in the LES, NY study were undertaken throughout the late 1960s and 1970s (see, for example, Wolfram 1969; Cedergren 1973; Trudgill 1974; among others) and many of the concepts and techniques became established and are still used as standard today.

This early work in sociolinguistics saw the development of the tool of the linguistic variable – a linguistic unit with two or more variants involved in covariation with other social and/ or linguistic variation – which allowed variation in speech production to be correlated with social variables. By using the linguistic variable and the principle of accountability (Labov 1982) which states that the analyst must account for all occurrences of a variant of a variable and all non-occurrences, the new techniques allowed examination of the *frequency* of usage of a particular form, rather than simply indicating its presence/absence, which had been standard practice in traditional dialectological surveys. The new techniques allowed quantification and statistical testing of production patterns and enabled the correlation of linguistic variation with social variation, primarily in the form of socio-economic class differences, but also sex, age and ethnic background.

As well as patterns of inter-speaker difference, these early studies also investigated intra-speaker variation, and manipulations of the elicitation task adjusted the attention paid to speech which in turn affected the frequency of the use of forms. The direction of the shift in frequency was thought to reveal much about the prestige/stigma carried by linguistic forms and also, therefore, the norms of the speech community, as well as indicating some of the social characteristics of the speakers at the vanguard of change. For example, in Labov's LES, NY findings, use of coda /r/ increases steadily and consistently as the socio-economic grouping of speakers moves from working class to middle class (nine socio-economic groups were used in the study, ranked from lower working class, 0, to upper middle class, 9). Usage of coda /r/ also increases steadily and consistently as the formality of the speech style increases (five speech styles were placed on a continuum of formality ranging from casual speech in which

Carmen Llamas

the least attention was paid to speech to the reading of minimal pairs in which the most attention was paid). Thus, as the attention to speech increases, the speakers produce a level of use of coda /r/ which approaches that used by the socio-economic cohort directly above them in the previous speech style, producing a pattern of very tightly structured variation (see below, Figure 35.1).

One exception to the very consistent and sharp stratification in this pattern is found in the speech of the lower middle-class cohort (SEC 6–8) who tend to overshoot the target when the style shifts to word list and minimal pair reading. This demonstrates a crossover pattern which, according to Labov (1972), is indicative of hypercorrection possibly due to the linguistic insecurity of this particular socio-economic cohort, thus revealing one of the potential causes of linguistic change.

As this pattern is consistent, the evaluative norms of the speech community are thought to be revealed in the overt prestige given to the form (in this case, that carried by coda /r/). Studies of this kind almost invariably establish a regular and replicable pattern of stratification in which the use of localised or non-standard forms correlates inversely with socio-economic class. Additionally, localised or non-standard forms are found to be more frequently

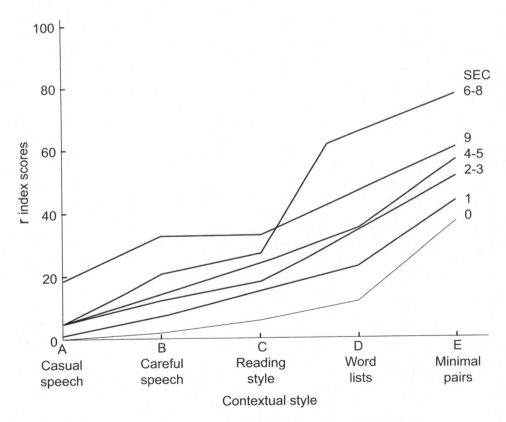

Figure 35.1 Rhoticity across socio-economic class (SEC) in various speech styles
Source: Adapted from Labov 1966.

used by male speakers as opposed to female speakers of the same socio-economic group in studies of this kind. The uniformity of these patterns across the class hierarchy and the direction of style shifting suggest a consensual view of the assignment of overt prestige to forms associated with the standard variety and speech associated with higher socio-economic classes.

Eckert (2005) has described the methodological developments in quantitative socio-linguistics in terms of a series of waves. Although these waves are not necessarily chronological and all approaches are in use today, the differences in approach allow for a useful demarcation of the progress of the field. The first wave comprises the broad demographic surveys, such as Labov's LES, NY study outlined above, which typically look for statistically significant corre-lations of global social categories, such as socio-economic class and sex, with variants of lin-guistic variables. Early studies such as Labov (1966) and Trudgill (1974), and more recent studies (for example, Docherty *et al.* 1997) which follow a first wave approach use pre-determined social categories and tend to view variables as markers of these global categories. With the second wave of studies, the level of abstraction between the social context and the social structures used to represent the situation is lessened, however, and the local dynamics which may give meaning to the broad global categories and the evaluation of linguistic forms become the focus of interest. This type of research more closely replicates Labov's earlier MV study which analysed the use of centralised diphthongs in the context of the local speakers' orientation to the island of Martha's Vineyard (an island off the coast of Massa-chusetts) in the face of resistance to but dependence on the incursions of the summer residents from the mainland. The variable use of the centralised forms of the diphthongs was interpreted in terms of the social meaning of the phonetic forms as being representa-tive of an authentic member of that particular speech community – a 'Vineyarder' in other words – in opposition to the holidaying mainlanders. Labov's account, therefore, locates the meaning of linguistic variation not in abstract global social categories of class and sex but within concrete forms of social participation and engagement located in the context of wider social interaction.

Through second wave studies, more detail of the potential social meaning of linguistic features, as well as the mechanisms and processes involved in language change, became accessible. By using ethnography, the relevance of the local setting such as the neighbourhood (see, for example, the Milroys' study of Belfast [Milroy 1987]) or the peer group (for example, Cheshire's [1982] Reading study) became observable. The social network model, as used by the Milroys, measures the strength of the speakers' social networks, calculated by classifying whe-ther networks are 'dense' or 'loose' and whether they are 'uniplex' or 'multiplex'. Dense and multiplex networks tend to act as norm-enforcing mechanisms and are implicated in the maintenance of traditional linguistic forms, whereas those speakers with looser networks are able to act as innovators of change and diffuse new forms into the community. Though social class and gender are implicated in the make-up of these differing network models, the relations between people are crucial and the groupings used by the analysts have a reality for the speakers which is absent in first wave studies.

This attention to analysis of the pre-existing social group has been refined further in work by Eckert, among others, who models the individual's connection to the group through use of the communities of practice construct. A community of practice is an aggregate of people who come together to engage in practices, or ways of doing things, on a regular basis. This can mean any manner of things from a sports team to a profession. Practices involve the devel-opment and negotiation of shared orientations to the world around the members of the community, and use of language constitutes one of these practices.

Eckert's (2000) ethnographic work in a suburban Detroit high school examines the nature of socio-economic class stratification among adolescents – the life stage believed to be at the forefront of sound change. Using the communities of practice model, Eckert investigated the adolescents' orientation to the categories of *Jocks* and *Burnouts* through which class is articulated (the Jocks constitute a middle-class culture, while the Burnouts represent the working class, broadly speaking). Correlations of linguistic use with social category affiliation were found to be more significant than correlations with parents' socio-economic status. And the Burnouts were found to make greater use of the changes associated with the Northern Cities Shift in the USA (a rotation of the low and mid vowels), than the Jocks. Thus the variables can be seen as indexing locally defined categories which link to demographics, and we are able to see connections between the big picture of the correlation of broad global categories with linguistic variation and local dynamics.

First and second wave studies are similar in that the approach to linguistic meaning they adopt is as a reflection of social meaning. With both approaches the speakers are presented as members of social categories and groups, whether pre-existing or not, and the social meaning attached to linguistic forms reflects the speakers who use them. These groups are still abstract organising structures to some extent, however, and the social meaning of linguistic forms remains analyst-imposed. The third wave of sociolinguistic studies shifts focus to consider more closely the use and meaning of stylistic variation. How speakers combine linguistic features to produce distinctive ways of speaking is examined in third wave studies rather than how they adjust frequencies of individual variables through manipulations made to the degree of perceived formality, for example.

Third wave studies (for example, Zhang 2008) examine social practice in order to account for the relationship between language and the social world, as the meaning of language is emergent in context as part of the process of social differentiation. If we think again of the opposed categories of Jocks and Burnouts, for example, the social meaning of variation attaches to the categories indirectly via the practices and ideologies that constitute the categories. Third wave studies are concerned with stylistic practice and stance. The Burnouts, for example, in keeping with their anti-school stance, make more use of a variable such as negative concord. And the 'burned-out Burnout' girls, those whose stance is seriously anti-authority and anti-establishment, lead the school in their use of negative concord (Eckert 2000). Another example can be found in Podesva's (2007) analysis of the speech of homosexual men across multiple contexts. He demonstrates how phonetic detail is used to construct social meaning through analysis of the duration and intensity of /t/ release and the phonetic properties of falsetto voice quality. Different personae are adopted in the differing contexts and the variation in production is interpreted in light of the characteristics the speakers are intending to convey, for example intelligence and preciseness in keeping with the medical context that one speaker is in versus prissiness in keeping with the 'bitchy diva' persona performed by the same speaker in the social barbecue context with friends.

Third wave studies, then, focus on stylistic practice and style as persona construction. Linguistic variation indexes stances and social characteristics, and third wave studies look to the meanings that motivate particular variable usage rather than assigning the social meaning of linguistic variation to the speakers who use the forms under investigation.

Methods

Although we can discern differences in approach as outlined in the first, second and third waves of studies, the methods used in sociolinguistics are many and varied and they don't necessarily coincide neatly with the demarcated waves. Rather, field methods can overlap and vary depending on the theoretical underpinnings and the larger objectives of the individual study.

In terms of data collection, different speaker sampling methods are used according to the approach taken to how the individual connects to the group and the nature of the social variables in the study. Few studies use random sampling techniques wherein a sampling frame, such as an electoral register, is used to select informants in a random and unbiased way from a population in which everyone theoretically has the same chance of being selected (see Houck 1968 for an example). Instead, most studies use judgement or quota sampling so informants are selected to fulfil predetermined social criteria. Individuals can then be combined into cohorts by virtue of their social characteristics with linguistic behaviour expressed generally as mean cohort scores only (as in first wave studies – see, for example, Trudgill 1974), or pre-existing groups of individuals can be examined (as in second and third wave studies – see, for example, Moore 2010) with both individual and group mean results examined.

As well as speaker sampling, speech sampling is also approached differently depending on the model of intra-speaker variation utilised. The attention to speech model (as noted in discussion of Labov's LES, NY study) adjusts the formality of the speech produced by manipulating the attention the speaker pays to speech through tasks such as reading, interview and casual conversation. The speech in which the least amount of attention is paid to production, the vernacular, is what is of interest primarily to the analyst. Manipulations of task, by and large, result in an increase in use of forms carrying overt prestige – those associated with standard varieties – as the amount of attention to speech is increased. However, the adjustment in attention to speech does not automatically initiate a shift to a more standard form, as speakers are able to increase their use of forms carrying covert prestige, or those associated with local or stigmatised varieties, as they become more aware of their production.

How much attention is drawn to speech is not the only factor that speakers respond to, and another influential model, the audience design model (see further Bell 1984), holds that speakers adjust their speech – converging or diverging – depending on the perceived identities of their interlocutors and of unseen audience members. Examples of style shifting towards the audience can be seen in Coupland's (1984) study of a Cardiff travel agent and her capacity to approximate the rates of non-standard forms used by her clients, and Rickford and McNair-Knox's (1994) examination of the shifting of an African-American teenager across different interviews and different topics. The speaker design model takes the view that speakers are not simply reactive, but they are also continually constructing and performing personae through proactive exploitation of the linguistic repertoire at their disposal.

As noted earlier, rather than indicating whether a linguistic feature is present or absent in speech, the tool of the linguistic variable allows the examination of the frequency of usage of a particular form. The linguistic variable can demonstrate how an utterance can be propositionally the same, but socially different, indexing social information about the geographical origins or social characteristics of the speaker, which is interpreted by the listener alongside the propositional meaning of the utterance. For phonological variables, this analysis is usually at the level of the segment, but we can look at much more fine-grained phonetic detail in the utterance, such as formant values, duration, etc., and find structured patterns across socially stratified samples of speakers which, while highly systematic, may actually be very difficult to perceive auditorily. Similarly, we can examine the pitch, rhythm, voice quality, intonational contour and other suprasegmental features which can also provide information on the speaker's social characteristics as well as emotional intent, pragmatic meaning and negotiation of conversation. Through quantification and statistical testing the correlation of linguistic variation with social variation is possible. Due to questions of linguistic equivalence, the tool of the linguistic variable is less readily applicable to morpho-syntactic, lexical or discoursal levels, and it is perhaps for this reason that the majority of variationist sociolinguistic work to date has concentrated on phonological or systematic phonetic variation and change. A good body of work does exist on the morpho-syntactic level, however (for example, analysis of negative concord, *was/were* variation, copula deletion and so on; see, for example, Tagliamonte 1998), and an amount of work exists on the discoursal level (for example, work on discourse markers, sentence tags, minimal responses etc.; see, for example, Macaulay 2002), but the approach to such analyses, which take function into account alongside form, is becoming increasingly more qualitative than quantitative. Work on lexical variation is less common still from the point of view of a variationist perspective.

Other techniques exist for the analysis of attitudes, perceptions and evaluations of varieties as a whole. For example, perceptual dialectological studies use mapping techniques to elicit how language varieties are delimited geographically and evaluated by informants (see Preston's [1989] work on US varieties); and the technique of accessing implicit attitudes, the matched-guise technique (for example, Lambert 1967) where recordings of speakers using different languages or varieties are presented to listeners who evaluate them on a number of social and personal dimensions concerned with authority and social attractiveness, for example, using semantic differential scales.

Which data elicitation and analysis techniques are used depends upon the larger objectives of the individual study, and these objectives and theoretical underpinnings depend on the current issues and research questions the study aims to explore.

Current issues

Language change

Although consideration of the processes involved in language change is not a new issue in the field (see early discussion by Weinreich *et al.* 1968), this topic is so germane to sociolinguistic enquiry that it remains as current an issue as it ever was. Although certain types of individuals have been identified as being likely to act as innovators or early adopters of changes, for example, adolescents, language missionaries, etc., why a particular change begins in a particular language at a particular time, but not in other languages with the same feature, or in the same language at other times – the actuation problem in other words – is still not well understood. Instead, discussion of language change generally centres on the processes and causes involved once a change is quite far advanced.

In the context of British English, many recent studies have investigated the process of levelling of localised forms in urban varieties (see, for example, Kerswill 2003; Britain 2010). Levelling is a process during which localised or traditional forms are eradicated in favour of forms with a wider geographical spread. However, unlike in findings from early studies in which variation predominantly aligned with a standard/non-standard opposition, the spreading forms need not necessarily be forms associated with the standard variety, and the majority of the current changes in British English are best viewed as aligning with a local/supra-local continuum (an example can be seen in Watt and Milroy's [1999] work on the Tyneside vowel system in the northeast of England). Investigation of regional dialect levelling in British English combines with research into the processes of diffusion of non-standard consonantal features, such as TH-fronting, labiodental (r), among other forms, which are spreading rapidly throughout the British Isles, mostly from a southeastern epicentre (see, for example, Williams and Kerswill 1999; Torgersen *et al.* 2006).

Regarding North American English, much analysis has been devoted to chain shifts – the co-ordinated movement of vowels to maintain phonological contrast following the spread of one vowel's area of dispersion into that of another's (see further Docherty and Watt 2001). In particular, the Northern Cities Shift, as mentioned earlier, which constitutes a rotation of the low and mid vowels in urban varieties of the north and central USA, has been the subject of much examination (for example, Gordon 2000). As well as the processes involved in language change, much discussion and debate concerns which speakers participate in on-going changes and which speakers resist or reject them.

Certain factors have been identified as facilitating or accelerating the spread of change. The social and geographical mobility that people experience in the modern world, at least from a Western perspective, are often looked to as major causes of change. These can entail large scale social changes such as urbanisation, counter-urbanisation, globalisation and so on. Such processes are thought to have effects on how we live our lives and therefore on how language varies and changes (see also Baynham, this volume, on language and migration). The processes of accommodation and maintenance/divergence are implicated in mobility, and it is thought that small instances of accommodation in face-to-face contact can lead to long term change. However, the automaticity of accommodation has been the subject of recent experimental work (see, for example, Kraljic et al. 2008), and the extent of speaker agency involved in such processes is a topic for which much finer understanding is necessary (see further Deumert 2003; Watt 2009).

Other potential sources of influence on how language changes are education and the media, the first of which is believed to have a standardising influence, while the latter is thought potentially to be instrumental in the spread of non-standard forms. Beyond the peer influence which exerts pressure at school by virtue of the fact of it being where adolescents meet, the standardising influence of the experience of education appears uncontested. However, there is much debate about whether and to what extent the media, particularly television, can effect change. Because linguistic variation, and therefore potentially change, is thought to be primarily affected by face-to-face interaction, a role for television in language change has been customarily denied as no face-to-face interaction is present in the act of passively watching television (Trudgill 1986). The extent of the influence of television has been argued to lie in its potential to increase awareness of linguistic variation and innovations (Milroy and Milroy 1985) and may possibly, through engendering favourable attitudes, have a 'softening-up' effect which can influence the speed of change (Trudgill 1988: 44). However, recent research on the spread of ostensibly southern English features (TH-fronting, L-vocalisation, etc.) into the speech of young, non-mobile, working-class speakers in Glasgow suggests that there is a role for exposure to and engagement with television in that subtle phonetic alterations are found to take place after watching television (see further Stuart-Smith 2007a). The precise nature of television as a factor remains somewhat unclear, however, and there is much variation at the level of the individual speaker/viewer.

Language variation

As all change in language is the product of variation, the external, social sources of variation have always been a major interest in sociolinguistics, and remain central to work in the field.

Among the social sources of language variation, the global categories of gender, socio-economic class, age, ethnicity, region, among others, have been examined in relation to ways in which they correlate with variation in speech production since the beginnings of research in the field, and they remain current issues. Understanding of the nature of these social variables has become increasingly sophisticated and, importantly, awareness of how these variables interact and how they interact with other socio-psychological correlates or factors associated with the local setting advances continually. Most of these broad social categories are dealt with in other chapters (for example Baxter, this volume, on gender; de Bot and van der Hoeven, this volume, on language and ageing; Harris, this volume, on ethnicity), so detailed discussion will not be presented here.

Variation across region remains an area of investigation, though the ambitious geographical coverage of dialectological surveys is no longer attempted. However, rather than approaching geographical location uncritically as a given entity, a considerable amount of recent work has concerned itself with how place is constructed and how space is perceived. These more complex notions of space and place deal with the ways in which 'distance' between places is social and psychological, not merely geographical (see, for example, Britain's [2005] work on the Fens), and also how place as a construct can be viewed differently by inhabitants of the same community (see work on Middlesbrough by Llamas [2007], for example).

Social meaning of variability

Although it is widely accepted that social variables such as gender, ethnicity, socio-economic class, region, etc. are important influences on speech, as Johnstone and Bean (1997: 236) point out, such factors do not determine how people speak. Rather, the individual is able to exploit the rich resource of structured variation in order to achieve communicative goals and project personae which are emergent in context. As well as the investigation of the social meaning of variation of varieties as a whole (as undertaken through perceptual dialectology and implicit attitudinal tests), the social meaning of particular linguistic forms and how such meanings can become attached to ways of speaking is an area of much current interest. Furthermore, exploration of the ideological aspects of linguistic differentiation and the identity work done via the socio-indexicality inherent in language are increasingly becoming fundamental parts of variationist studies (see, for example, Dyer 2002).

How language forms index speakers' social identities can be viewed as being ranked into different orders of generality (see further Silverstein 2003). First-order indexicality involves an association or correlation of a linguistic form with some socially meaningful category. These correlations may be observed by analysts and the associations are often assumed in sociolinguistic work, but they may not be noticed by speakers. As such, first-order indexicals are analogous to what Labov (1972: 178–80) terms 'indicators' in his taxonomy of the kinds of social meaning linguistic forms can carry. Second-order indexicality occurs when speakers use first-order correlations to 'do social work' which can be interpretive or performative (Johnstone et al. 2006: 83). This can involve overt or covert awareness of basic first-order indexicality, and ideology can become visible in style shifting in careful speech and so on. Features that begin to be noticed by speakers and that begin to have social meaning associated with them – concerning, for example, region or class – can be seen as corresponding to 'markers' in Labov's categorisation. How variable linguistic behaviour is linked to the negotiation and performance of identities is considered through such indexicality and is a major area of current research.

New methods and debates

As the field matures, the methods used in sociolinguistic research are becoming increasingly sophisticated. New technologies allow for ever more advanced methods of data analysis, data collection, statistical testing and so on. Similarly, approaches to both linguistic variables and social variables are ever more nuanced and comprehensive, as fine-grained variation is uncovered and examined.

Acoustic phonetic analysis has been used for investigation of vowel variables for a considerable amount of time, with the frequencies of the first and second formants of vowels customarily measured from their midpoints in order to position them in a two-dimensional vowel space plotted on an x–y scattergram. This enables the capture of fine-grained differences between different speakers and contexts and allows for examination of, for example, mergers in progress.

However, acoustic analysis is increasingly being used to examine fine-grained variation in consonantal features, which is found to correlate with the social characteristics of the speakers beyond those attributable to physiological differences of vocal tract length and so on. For example, acoustic analysis of [s] in Glasgow English has been carried out (Stuart-Smith 2007b) and investigation of realisations of voiceless stops have been undertaken (see, for example, Docherty and Foulkes 1999, Jones and Llamas 2008), among other variables.

Statistical analysis is also advancing as along with the Varbrul program (Rand and Sankoff 1990), which has been used routinely by sociolinguists to identify variable patterns, more use of regression analysis, cluster analysis and analysis of variance is to be found. Furthermore, recent advances in mixed effects models which distinguish between fixed effects and random effects (see the Rbrul program, Johnson 2009) overcome some of the limitations of Varbrul (for example, Varbrul's restriction to use with categorical data, which is inappropriate for many phonetic variants positioned along a multi-dimensional continuum).

Although sociolinguistic research has, for the most part, concerned itself with production patterns and the extent to which linguistic variation can be seen to correlate with social variables, much greater emphasis is being placed on examining the nature of the socio-indexical meaning that attaches to linguistic forms, as noted, and the processes involved in the development of such associations. With the study of the influence of perception and memory on language variation and change (see current interest in the episodic memory-based Exemplar Theory), as well as the relations between speech perception and other modalities (for example, visual perception), this looks set to develop further. And understanding speakers' perceptions and evaluations of linguistic features is becoming more of a priority in recent and on-going sociolinguistic research.

As social meaning is attached to linguistic forms, it stands to reason that listeners will make judgements about speakers based on the linguistic information they receive. What is perhaps more surprising in recent studies is that sociolinguistic expectations may influence speech perception. For example, in experiments by Niedzielski (1999) the decisions of listeners to choose exemplars from a set of synthesised vowels that were most appropriate to the variety they had heard differed according to whether they had been exposed to voice samples they were told were either Canadian or Michigan English. It is anticipated that work will continue in this area.

Current research seeks to connect the production and perception of variability in a systematic way, by using a triangulation of methods which analyse structured variation in production patterns in conjunction with evidence from perceptual experiments examining which forms cue which type of social category or meaning in the local setting. Additionally, these production and perception data can be combined with cognitive and affective attitudinal information from speakers with regard to their orientations towards relevant social categories and oppositional identities collected either through ethnographic observation or through targeted elicitation. More defensible interpretations of the motivating factors underlying speakers' variable linguistic behaviour can be obtained from such an approach (an example can be seen in Llamas 2010).

More insight into what linguistic forms signal for the speakers who use them will allow us to better understand how variation in language reflects and is caused by social change more generally, and also the extent to which speakers have agency in and awareness of exploiting their linguistic repertoires for socio-indexical purposes. Furthermore, by approaching social categories as multi-layered and more nuanced than the global categorisations of first wave studies, a more detailed and sophisticated understanding of the social world of speakers, their identities and orientations is achieved, which allows us to better understand the social meaning of the language variation they exploit.

Summary

Writing in the early 1970s, Labov (1972: xiii) stated that he had resisted the term 'socio-linguistics' for many years since 'it implies that there can be a successful linguistic theory or practice which is not social'. The field has come a long way in its short history and the impact it has had on mainstream linguistic theory is increasingly felt. Additionally, sociolinguistics borrows from and in turn offers insights for other fields such as sociology, social theory, anthropology, education, social psychology and more. Through the various approaches, methods and models used in sociolinguistics, our understanding of how language reflects and creates how the individual fits into the world has increased enormously.

Understanding and identifying which features listeners use to index which social information is of clear value in advancing theories of language change, but it is also of immediate and obvious benefit in applied contexts. Similarly, understanding attitudinal and evaluative responses to linguistic variation is important for assessing the structured heterogeneity in language, but it also relates to more concrete concerns in the real world, such as the likelihood that a jury will convict, or success in the job market. Findings from sociolinguistics have implications for speech and language therapy, forensic phonetics and linguistics, speech technology, and education, to name but a few fields. The messy variation, which is everywhere in language use, is not simply noise, but it signals, in minute ways, who we are, how we feel and how we respond to the world around us. The implications of understanding this are as wide-ranging as they are disparate.

Related topics

ethnicity; gender; language and ageing; language and migration

Further reading

Chambers, J. K. (2003) *Sociolinguistic Theory: Linguistic Variation and its Social Significance*, 2nd edn, Oxford: Blackwell. (This book offers a comprehensive overview of key concepts and theories in variationist sociolinguistics.)

Coupland, N. and Jaworski, A. (eds) (2009) *The New Sociolinguistics Reader*, Basingstoke: Palgrave Macmillan. (This volume provides a collection of key readings in the field.)

Llamas, C., Mullany, L. and Stockwell, P. (eds) (2007) *The Routledge Companion to Sociolinguistics*, London: Routledge. (This volume offers a broad overview of the field in terms of theories and methods.)

Meyerhoff, M. (2006) *Introducing Sociolinguistics*, London and New York: Routledge. (This book is a useful introduction to the field.)

Milroy, L. and Gordon, M. (2003) *Sociolinguistics: Method and Interpretation*, Oxford: Blackwell. (This book is an invaluable guide to the methodological side of the field.)

References

Bell, A. (1984) 'Language style as audience design', *Language in Society* 13(2): 145–204.

Britain, D. (2005) 'Innovation diffusion, "Estuary English" and local dialect differentiation: the survival of Fenland Englishes', *Linguistics* 43(5): 995–1022.

——(2010) 'Supralocal regional dialect levelling', in C. Llamas and D. Watt (eds) *Language and Identities*, Edinburgh: Edinburgh University Press.

Cameron, D. (1990) 'Demythologizing sociolinguistics: why language does not reflect society', in J. E. Joseph and T. J. Taylor (eds) *Ideologies of Language*, London and New York: Routledge.

Cedergren, H. (1973) 'The Interplay of Social and Linguistic Factors in Panama', Ph.D. dissertation, Cornell University.

Cheshire, J. (1982) *Variation in an English Dialect: A Sociolinguistic Study*, Cambridge: Cambridge University Press.

Coupland, N. (1984) 'Accommodation at work: some phonological data and their applications', *International Journal of the Sociology of Language* 46: 49–70.

Deumert, A. (2003) 'Bringing the speakers back in? Epistemological reflections on speaker-oriented explanations of language change', *Language Sciences* 25: 15–76.

Docherty, G. J. and Foulkes, P. (1999) 'Derby and Newcastle: instrumental phonetics and variationist studies', in P. Foulkes and G. J. Docherty (eds) *Urban Voices: Accent Studies in the British Isles*, London: Hodder Arnold.

Docherty, G. J., Foulkes, P., Milroy, J., Milroy, L. and Walshaw, D. (1997) 'Descriptive adequacy in phonology: a variationist perspective', *Journal of Linguistics* 33: 275–31.

Docherty, G. J. and Watt, D. (2001) 'Chain shifts', in R. Mesthrie (ed.) *The Concise Encyclopedia of Sociolinguistics*, Amsterdam: Pergamon (Elsevier Science).

Dyer, J. (2002) '"We all speak the same round here": dialect levelling in a Scottish English community', *Journal of Sociolinguistics* 6(2): 99–116.

Eckert, P. (2000) *Linguistic Variation as Social Practice: The Linguistic Construction of Identity in Belten High*, Oxford: Blackwell.

——(2005) 'Variation, convention and social meaning', Paper Presented at the Annual Meeting of the Linguistic Society of America. Oakland, CA.

Gordon, M. J. (2000) 'Small-town values and big-city vowels: a study of the Northern Cities Shift in Michigan', *American Speech* 84(1): 1–39.

Gumperz, J. J. (1982) *Discourse Strategies*, Cambridge: Cambridge University Press.

Hockett, C. F. (1958) *A Course in Modern Linguistics*, New York: Macmillan.

Houck, C. L. (1968) 'Methodology of an urban speech survey', in *Leeds Studies in English*, Leeds: University of Leeds.

Hubbell, A. F. (1950) *The Pronunciation of English in New York City*, New York: Columbia University Press.

Johnson, D. (2009) 'Getting off the GoldVarb standard: introducing Rbrul for mixed-effects variable rule analysis', *Language and Linguistics Compass* 3(1): 359–83.

Johnstone, B., Andrus, J. and Danielson, A. E. (2006) 'Mobility, indexicality, and the enregisterment of "Pittsburghese"', *Journal of English Linguistics* 34(2): 77–104.

Johnstone, B. and Bean, M. (1997) 'Self-expression and linguistic variation', *Language in Society* 26: 221–46.

Jones, M. and Llamas, C. (2008) 'Fricated realisations of /t/ in Dublin and Middlesborough English: an acoustic analysis of plosive frication and surface fricative contrasts', *English Language and Linguistics* 12(3): 419–43.

Kerswill, P. (2003) 'Dialect levelling and geographical diffusion in British English', in D. Britain and J. Cheshire (eds) *Social Dialectology: In Honour of Peter Trudgill*, Amsterdam: Benjamins.

Kraljic, T., Brennan, S. E. and Samuel, A. G. (2008) 'Accommodating variation: dialects, idiolects, and speech processing', *Cognition* 107(1): 51–81.

Labov, W. (1963) 'The social motivation of a sound change', *Word* 19: 273–309.

——(1966) *The Social Stratification of English in New York City*, Washington, DC: Center for Applied Linguistics.

——(1972) *Sociolinguistic Patterns*, Philadelphia, PA: University of Philadelphia Press.

——(1982) 'Building on empirical foundations', in W. P. Lehmann and Y. Malkiel (eds) *Perspectives on Historical Linguistics*, Amsterdam and Philadelphia: Benjamins.

Lambert, W. E. (1967) 'A social psychology of bilingualism', *Journal of Social Issues* 23: 91–108.

Llamas, C. (2007) '"A place between places": language and identities in a border town', *Language in Society* 36(4): 579–604.

——(2010) 'Convergence and divergence across a national border', in C. Llamas and D. Watt (eds) *Language and Identities*, Edinburgh: Edinburgh University Press.

Macaulay, R. K. S. (2002) 'You know, it depends', *Journal of Pragmatics* 34(6): 749–67.

Milroy, J. and Milroy, L. (1985) *Authority in Language*, London: Routledge.

Milroy, L. (1987) *Language and Social Networks*, 2nd edn, Oxford: Blackwell.

Moore, E. (2010) 'Communities of practice and peripherality', in C. Llamas and D. Watt (eds) *Language and Identities*, Edinburgh: Edinburgh University Press, pp. 123–33.

Niedzielski, N. (1999) 'The effect of social information on the perception of sociolinguistic variables', *Journal of Language and Social Psychology* 18(1): 62–85.

Podesva, R. J. (2007) 'Phonation type as a stylistic variable: the use of falsetto in constructing a persona', *Journal of Sociolinguistics* 11(4): 478–504.

Preston, D. R. (1989) *Perceptual Dialectology: Nonlinguists' Views of Areal Linguistics*, Dordrecht: Foris.

Rand, D. and Sankoff, D. (1990) *Goldvarb 2.1: A Variable Rule Application for the Macintosh*, Montreal: Centre de Recherches Mathématiques, University of Montreal.

Rickford, J. R. and McNair-Knox, F. (1994) 'Addressee- and topic-influenced styleshift: a quantitative sociolinguistic study', in D. Biber and E. Finegan (eds) *Sociolinguistic Perspectives on Register*, Oxford: Oxford University Press.

Silverstein, M. (2003) 'Indexical order and the dialectics of social life', *Language and Communication* 23: 193–229.

Stuart-Smith, J. (2007a) 'The influence of the media on language', in C. Llamas, L. Mullany and P. Stockwell (eds) *The Routledge Companion to Sociolinguistics*, London: Routledge.

——(2007b) 'Empirical evidence for gendered speech production: /s/ in Glaswegian', in J. Cole and J. Hualde (eds) *Change in Phonology, Laboratory Phonology 9*, Berlin: Mouton de Gruyter.

Tagliamonte, S. (1998) '"Was/were" variation across the generations: view from the city of York', *Language Variation and Change* 10(2): 153–92.

Torgersen, E., Kerswill, P. and Fox, S. (2006) 'Ethnicity as a source of changes in the London vowel system', in F. Hinskens (ed.) *Language Variation – European Perspectives: Selected Papers from the Third International Conference on Language Variation in Europe (ICLaVE3)*, Amsterdam: Benjamins.

Trudgill, P. (1974) *The Social Differentiation of English in Norwich*, Cambridge: Cambridge University Press.

——(1986) *Dialects in Contact*, Oxford: Blackwell.

——(1988) 'Norwich revisited: recent linguistic changes in an English urban dialect', *English World-Wide* 9: 33–49.

Watt, D. (2009) 'Rethinking the role of speaker agency', Keynote Paper Presented at *UK Language Variation and Change 5*, University of Newcastle.

Watt, D. and Milroy, L. (1999) 'Patterns of variation and change in three Tyneside vowels: is this dialect levelling?', in P. Foulkes and G. J. Docherty (eds) *Urban Voices: Accent Studies in the British Isles*, London: Hodder Arnold.

Weinreich, U., Labov, W. and Herzog, M. I. (1968) 'A theory of language change', in W. P. Lehmann and Y. Malkiel (eds) *Directions for Historical Linguistics: A Symposium*, Austin: University of Texas Press.

Williams, A. and Kerswill, P. (1999) 'Dialect levelling: change and continuity in Milton Keynes, Reading and Hull', in P. Foulkes and G. J. Docherty (eds) *Urban Voices: Accent Studies in the British Isles*, London: Hodder Arnold.

Wolfram, W. (1969) *A Sociolinguistic Description of Detroit Negro Speech*, Washington, DC: Centre for Applied Linguistics.

——(1998) 'Language ideology and dialect: understanding the Oaklands Ebonics controversy', *Journal of English Linguistics* 26(2): 108–21.

Zhang, Q. (2008) 'Rhotacization and the "Beijing smooth operator": the social meaning of a linguistic variable', *Journal of Sociolinguistics* 12: 201–22.

36

Linguistic ethnography

Janet Maybin and Karin Tusting

Introduction

'Linguistic ethnography' combines ethnographic and linguistic methodologies to study language use in a range of social settings. The term describes a broad area of shared interests rather than a distinctly bounded field. It refers to a body of research by scholars with overlapping interests and connections who share an orientation towards using ethnographic approaches to address linguistic and social questions. This chapter will explore the disciplinary antecedents of linguistic ethnography, and of linguistic anthropology in the USA, and review more recent developments in these closely related areas of work. It will move on to describe work which can be located under the broad umbrella of the term, identifying current productive tensions in the field, and exploring possible developments and emerging areas.

History

Linguistic anthropology

The term 'linguistic anthropology' was first used in the 1880s in north America when Franz Boas and his students Alfred Kroeber and Edward Sapir established linguistics as an important tool for the analysis of culture (e.g. Boas 1940). During this period, linguistic anthropologists were principally focused on documenting and describing the indigenous languages of the fast disappearing North American aboriginal societies, and their encoding of different world views (linguistic relativity). Duranti (1997, 2003) offers a useful and comprehensive overview of the historical development of linguistic anthropology. He claims that this focus on American Indian languages can be seen as the first of three paradigms co-existing in the field.

Duranti identifies the second wave or paradigm, which emerged in the 1960s and 1970s, as a more socially constituted linguistic anthropology, part of the reaction against the formalism of structural linguistics and Chomskian cognitivism. Defined by Hymes as 'the study of language within the context of anthropology' (1964: xxiii), linguistic anthropology, as conceived in the mid-twentieth century, foregrounds language use rather than the language system (although knowledge of the system is still important for the analyst), emphasising the situated and culturally constituted experience of language users in diverse communities.

Hymes proposed an approach he called the 'ethnography of speaking'. He developed the well-known mnemonic 'SPEAKING' (1974: 53–62) to list the eight dimensions of language in use that research should address, to specify what speakers needed to know in order to function in a particular context (their 'communicative competence'). This was expanded into the 'ethnography of communication' through Hymes' collaboration with Gumperz, a sociolinguist who used ethnographic methods to study language contact and multilingualism (Duranti 1997). Hymes' mapping out of this methodological approach emphasises the shift of focus from the language system to its situated use. His insistence on the need to analyse language use in relation to participants' perspectives, in 'contexts of situation', has been a seminal reference point for the work of scholars in this area, who have since developed more interactional conceptions of the relationship between language and context and a more dynamic understanding of culture itself (see, for example, Gumperz 1982; Duranti and Goodwin 1992; Street 1993; Kramsch, this volume).

Duranti recounts the strengthening of this second paradigm from the 1970s onwards, particularly through linguistic anthropological work on language performance (e.g. Bauman 1986; Bauman and Briggs 1990) and on primary and secondary language socialisation (e.g. Ochs and Schieffelin 1984; He, this volume). It was additionally consolidated, he suggests, in work on indexicality which drew on semiotics (e.g. Silverstein 1976; Silverstein and Urban 1996) and in research on 'participation' (Philips 1983; Goodwin 1990). This last strand of work draws on Goffman's notion of participation framework, the configuration of participation statuses (author, animator, principal, hearer, over-hearer and bystander) which are activated in talk by the use of a particular linguistic form (Goffman 1981). It is also influenced by Bakhtin's work on reported speech (Vološinov [1929] 1973; Bakhtin [1935] 1981).

The third theoretical and methodological paradigm identified by Duranti arose through a combination of intellectual developments. The growing influence of social constructionism in the 1980s and 1990s, coupled with increasing interest across the social sciences in post-structuralist social theories, highlighted how authoritative knowledge, different subjectivities and power relationships are encoded within various levels of discursive practice. In linguistic anthropology, this stimulated the development of an approach which is distinctly different from the ethnography of communication of the 1960s and 1970s. It is concerned with issues such as construction of meanings, texts, narratives, and language ideologies; multiple voices and identities; and relationships between the micro-level of interaction and the macro-levels of culture and society. Within this paradigm, language is viewed as an interactional achievement, saturated with indexical, ideological values. Researchers working within this third paradigm use linguistic practices to 'document and analyse the reproduction and transformation of persons, institutions and communities across space and time' (Duranti 2003: 333). Data is collected via sociohistorical analysis and audiovisual documentation of human encounters. The research focus is on social constructs such as hierarchy, prestige and taste, and social processes such as formation of self, speech community and nationhood. Duranti suggests that linguistic anthropology provides a culturally delicate approach, particularly attractive to postmodernist sensibilities, for examining the constitutive role of language in establishing gender, ethnic and class identities (e.g. Gal 2001; Trechter and Bucholtz 2001; Rampton 2006; Baxter, this volume; Harris, this volume; Norton, this volume).

One distinctive area of work within the latter two paradigms in US linguistic anthropology is research in educational contexts. Wortham (2008) argues that the focus of linguistic anthropology on 'how language use both presupposes and creates social relations in cultural contexts' (2008: 38) has particular relevance for understanding how social, linguistic and cultural processes are dynamically configured in educational practices. In particular, linguistic anthropologists have used Silverstein's work on language ideology and metapragmatics (e.g. Silverstein and Urban 1996) to examine how societal beliefs about language as a symbol of nationalism, a marker of difference, or a tool of assimilation are reproduced and sometimes challenged by individuals within schools (see, for example, Wortham and Rymes 2003).

Linguistic ethnography

While work in linguistic ethnography, primarily in Britain and other parts of Europe, has also been strongly influenced by Hymes' legacy (Rampton 2007), and has developed in close connection with US work in the two latter paradigms Duranti describes, it is theoretically inflected by a different tradition. With some exceptions, language and linguistics have not been an important interest in British anthropology. The links between language, culture and society have been explored instead within applied linguistics. For example, while the British anthropologist Malinowski's notion of 'context of situation' was an important influence on Hymes' work in North America, in Britain itself Malinowski's interest in meaning and functionalism was taken up and developed not within anthropology, but in the rather different disciplinary trajectory of Firthian linguistics (e.g. Firth 1957; Hasan 1985). More recently, a number of scholars and researchers have developed a strand of related work which has been termed 'linguistic ethnography' (Rampton *et al.* 2004; Creese 2008).

Linguistic ethnographers tend to draw not on anthropology for their disciplinary framework, but on linguistics and sociolinguistics, broadly conceived to include the ethnography of communication. In methodological terms, 'the commitment within ethnography to particularity and participation, holistic accounts of social practice and openness to reinterpretations over time', is combined with 'a more formalist framework from linguistics, with its powerfully precise procedures and terminology for describing patterns within communication' (Rampton *et al.* 2004). This combination is seen, on the one hand, as having the capacity to 'tie ethnography down' through pushing for more precise, falsifiable analyses of local language processes. On the other hand, it can also 'open linguistics up' through stressing the importance of reflexive sensitivity in the production of linguistic claims, foregrounding issues of context and highlighting the primacy of direct field experience in establishing interpretative validity.

'Ethnography' in this context does not necessarily imply the sort of immersion in a distant, culturally strange context which has been typical of anthropological work. Researchers are more likely to follow the methodological approach outlined by the British sociologist Hammersley (e.g. 1994). Hammersley defines ethnography as social research gathering empirical data from real world contexts, often focusing on relatively small-scale social groups, via a range of unstructured methods including participant observation. He suggests that data analysis should focus on interpreting the meanings and functions of human actions. Analysis often takes the form of verbal descriptions and explanations, with quantification and statistical analysis playing, at most, a minor role. The essence of ethnographic analysis, for Hammersley (2007), is a tension between trying to understand participants' perspectives (the emic perspective), while also viewing them and their behaviour through a more distant analytic framework constructed by the researcher (the etic perspective). In the case of linguistic ethnographers, this analytic framework is grounded in a socially inflected linguistics.

In the UK context, a number of distinct lines of research have fed into linguistic ethnography (Rampton 2007). In interactional sociolinguistics, linguists used Gumperz's synthesis of dialectology, pragmatics, conversation analysis, ethnography and Goffmanian interaction analysis to address issues of language, ethnicity and inequality. Researchers in New Literacy Studies drew on Hymes' ethnography of communication, mediated through reconceptualisations of literacy from Heath and Street, to research literacy practices in everyday life. Both of these will be presented in more detail below.

Three other lines of research, while not involving ethnographic methodology, have influenced theoretical directions in current work. Marxist-oriented critical discourse analysis drew attention to the relevance of social theorists such as Foucault, Habermas and Hall for questions about language in society, and advocated critical language study. Neo-Vygotskian sociocultural research provided important insights into processes of knowledge construction in classroom dialogue. And the frame of interpretative linguistics, applied to English language teaching in the 1980s, provided both an early critique of autonomous linguistics and a developing recognition of the dependence of knowledge production on the social positioning of researcher and researched. Interpretative approaches in linguistic ethnography have also been influenced by the 'turn to discourse' in the social sciences, informed particularly by Bourdieu's practice theory, Bakhtin and Vološinov's dialogism and Foucault's work on discourse, knowledge and power (e.g. Foucault 1980). More recent work in linguistic ethnography, as in the third linguistic anthropology paradigm described in the previous section, includes work focusing on the construction of meanings, texts, narratives, identities and ideologies.

Areas of focus

We will now describe in more detail a range of areas which combine linguistics with ethnography. As we have already acknowledged, the distinction between 'linguistic anthropology' and 'linguistic ethnography' is not clear-cut. We have selected research which has been of particular interest to applied linguists involved in developing linguistic ethnography, although some of this work (e.g. Heller; Eckert; Hornberger and Chick) could be located in either tradition.

Linguistic ethnography in educational settings

Education has been one key site for linguistic ethnographic research. Researchers in educational settings have focused in particular on three overlapping areas of inquiry. First, they have studied how language in classrooms provides indications of societal patterns and beliefs about language. Second, they have sought to produce more contextually sensitive accounts of language and learning, informed by ethnographic study of students' language experience in and outside of school. Third, they have focused on student voice.

An example of the first area of work is Heller (1999), who analyses the tensions between a Canadian French monolingual school's promotion of standard Parisian French and the varying language proficiencies, cultural experience and educational aspirations of its students from different language and cultural backgrounds. Heller uses ethnographic data on language choice and turn-taking in classroom dialogue to trace how the school constructs particular kinds of language use as 'legitimate' (Bourdieu 1990). She argues that bilingual education is not only about learning or maintaining a language, but also about constructing the value of different languages and defining who has the right to use them in which circumstances. In a similar way, Jaffe (1999) explores the school as a site of struggle in the revitalisation of the Corsican language.

Studies from a range of international contexts in Heller and Martin-Jones (2001) draw on Bourdieu's social theory, together with ethnographic research in schools, to trace how relationships of power and inequality in society (often related to colonial histories) are reproduced and sustained through activities and relationships in classrooms. Hornberger and Chick analyse societal pressures and local contingencies in Peru and South Africa, where teachers and students use a former colonial language (Spanish or English) to produce ritualised, vacuous 'safetalk'. Martin-Jones and Saxena describe how bilingual teaching assistants in multilingual primary schools in north England are marginalised from the main action of the classroom by monolingual English-speaking class teachers. (See also Creese 2005 on teacher talk in multilingual classrooms.)

A number of studies have focused on the re-creation of ideological social categories in young people's talk and interaction. Rampton (1995), using recordings of informal talk from teenagers of Indian, Pakistani and Anglo descent in secondary schools and youth clubs, analyses how they challenge dominant notions of ethnicity through strategic use of each other's languages, a process he terms 'language crossing'. Rampton combines ethnography with Gumperzian sociolinguistics and Goffman's work on interaction. Eckert (2000) combines ethnography with a quantitative analysis of sociolinguistic variation to study the recreation and configuration of class identities among US high school students. She demonstrates how students orienting towards the subcultural categories of 'Jock' and 'Burnout' used distinctly different kinds of voice pitch, accent and dialect. She argues that these teenagers were re-creating the class divisions of their parents' world through their different combinations of speech, clothing and activity style (Jock = middle class and Burnout = working class), but that they also appropriated and recombined specific aspects of existing styles in a unique personal bricolage. Other work combining ethnography with variationist sociolinguistics includes Alim (2004) on style shifting by black youth, and Mendoza-Denton (2007) on identification in Latina youth gangs.

In relation to the second area of enquiry, interaction between in-school and out-of-school cultures (e.g. Pahl 2007) has been a key area of interest for researchers aiming to provide sensitive accounts of language and learning in culturally diverse classrooms. Early research in the ethnography of communication tradition often highlighted mismatches between home and school language use for students from minority ethnolinguistic groups, and the resulting misunderstandings and inequities (e.g. Michaels 1981; Philips 1983). From this perspective, reading and writing in school are viewed as intrinsically social rather than individual processes. A focus on literacy events can foreground how teachers and students act and react in complex and ambiguous ways, influenced by and shaping social identity, power relations and broader cultural processes (Bloome *et al.* 2005).

Recently, researchers have addressed how information about students' language experience outside school could inform the educational curriculum, for instance through creating a 'third space' where teachers and students can bring everyday and school knowledge together in cooperative dialogue and problem-solving (Gutierrez *et al.* 2000); through drawing on sibling teaching in home/school partnerships (Gregory and Williams 2000); or through building on multilingual children's experience in complementary schools (Creese *et al.* 2008). Educational researchers have combined linguistic ethnography with a neo-Vygotskian framework to explore ways of bringing in 'funds of knowledge' from outside school, to build bridges between communities and classrooms (e.g. Moll *et al.* 1992).

A third area of work focuses more specifically on student voice. Rampton's fine-grained analysis of the heteroglossic 'language crossing' (1995) and use of 'posh and Cockney' (2006) in teenagers' talk involves both linguistic and interactive conceptions of voice, with a focus on double voicing (Bakhtin [1935] 1981) and styling. His more recent study also includes an analysis of student references to popular culture, used in classroom talk to exclude teachers and undermine their authority, which contributes to a more general disintegration of the traditional structure of classroom discourse. Linguistic ethnographers have also been interested in the effects of students 'voicing' popular culture in student/student interaction. Lytra (2007) traces how Turkish minority students in an Athens school use references to mainstream popular culture in off-task talk to claim a shared bicultural identity with Greek peers. From another perspective, the voicing of popular texts by students has been seen as a potentially valuable educational resource, producing hybrid learning practices which enable teachers and students to fuse authoritative and inwardly persuasive discourses (Kamberelis 2001). Finally, Maybin (2006) uses a Bakhtinian analysis of voicing in 10–11-year-olds' talk across the school day to illustrate how they try out and convey judgments about people, relationships and events and negotiate entry into institutional practices, through the orchestration of reproduced voices in talk among themselves.

Linguistic ethnography in the workplace and community

Relationships between local language use and broader patterns of inequality have also been addressed beyond the school context. One key site for this has been research in workplaces. An early precursor to this work came from the pioneering Industrial Language Training Service (ILTS) in the 1970s. This organisation aimed to improve communication in multilingual workplaces, both by responding to the English language needs of migrant workers, and by heightening awareness of language issues for their co-workers (Roberts *et al.* 1992). The ILTS worked with the American linguistic anthropologist Gumperz to produce a BBC film and accompanying book, *Crosstalk* (Gumperz *et al.* 1979), which explored common workplace miscommunications. By identifying systematic cultural and linguistic differences underlying misunderstandings, the programme challenged negative stereotypical assumptions. While not identifying itself as 'linguistic ethnography', the sociolinguistic research carried out by the ILTS shared many of the characteristics outlined above, analysing communication in real settings within frameworks from anthropology and conversation analysis (Gumperz 1978, 1982). More recently, a range of ethnographic research has focused specifically on workplace literacy practices and changing social processes (Hull 1997; Belfiore *et al.* 2004; Farrell 2006; Tusting 2010).

Sociolinguistic and linguistic anthropological perspectives have also been brought together to explore complex urban social settings shaped by flows of migration. Blommaert, Collins, and Slembrouck have described patterns of interaction in neighbourhoods in Ghent characterised by 'densely layered patterns of multilingualism' (Blommaert *et al.* 2005a; Collins and Slembrouck 2006). They argue that semiotic and material processes offer a sensitive indicator of globalisation processes 'on the ground'. For instance, they show how interactional regimes in different centres in the area shape differing expectations about patterns of behaviour. This work is characteristic of linguistic ethnography: drawing on detailed, fine-grained sociolinguistic fieldwork to give insight into much broader social processes, paying particular attention to issues of inequality and the workings of power (Blommaert *et al.* 2005b).

Ethnographically grounded studies of language competence have been carried out in many multilingual settings. Collins and Slembrouck (2005) include research from Belgium, the Netherlands, Italy and South Africa, exploring the production of space through language practices shaped by language ideologies. This work interrogates and challenges established sociolinguistic concepts, as globalisation processes force us to 'reshuffle' existing ideas – one good example of ethnography 'opening linguistics up'. (See also chapters by Harris, this volume, and Baynham, this volume.)

New literacy studies

Literacy studies is another area in which linguistic ethnography has moved beyond the educational setting. There are various approaches to studying literacy in applied linguistics (see Warriner, this volume, for a fuller discussion). In its insistence on seeing literacy as a social practice and using an ethnographic approach, the approach known as the 'new literacy studies' (e.g. Barton 2007) has been closely associated with the development of linguistic ethnography in the UK.

This approach is often traced back to works by Street, Heath, and Scribner and Cole. Scribner and Cole (1981) studied the literacy practices of the Vai in Liberia. By drawing on observations and interviews, they were able to explain conflicting results from psychological testing, by showing that different literacies were associated with different domains of life. This raised questions about unitary conceptions of literacy as a single skill. In her long-term ethnographic and sociolinguistic work in US Appalachian communities, Heath (1983) explored continuities and disjunctures between home and school literacy practices, giving new insight into patterns of educational inequalities. Street (1984) studied writing practices in a village in Iran. By using anthropological methods, approaching reading and writing as practices rather than as skills, he developed an 'ideological' understanding of literacy as being rooted in and shaped by the practices of people's lives, in contrast to the dominant 'autonomous' model which saw literacy purely as a cognitive ability. This view of literacy as ideologically shaped language practice, and the intrinsically social view of language it entailed, challenged – and continues to challenge – dominant skills-focused approaches.

Ethnographic methods have been employed to study literacy practices in many sites, including minority language communities (Martin-Jones and Jones 2000), across different cultures (Gregory and Williams 2000), and in local and community settings (Barton and Hamilton 1998; Barton *et al.* 2007). Ethnographically informed literacies research is pushing forward our understandings of reading and writing practices in a social world in which textually mediated organisation is increasingly significant (Smith 1990). In turn, literacies research is developing theory and practice in linguistic ethnography (see, for example, Lillis 2008).

Productive tensions

The broad focus of interest of linguistic ethnography has enabled a wide range of questions to be addressed, developing new approaches to the study of language and culture and new combinations of theoretical paradigms. However, the very eclecticism of the approach generates some productive tensions.

Realist and constructionist epistemologies

Linguistic ethnography seeks to address questions about language, society, and the relationship between the two. Many of the studies cited above have been exploring social questions, such as the impact of globalisation on multilingual communities, or how class and ethnicity affect learning in schools. Exploring these questions is challenging, because it entails bringing together phenomena at different 'levels of reality': local interaction and social processes. As is clear from the examples above, linguistic ethnography is, by definition, seeking to explain phenomena at these different levels.

The challenges of bringing together linguistic and social theoretical frameworks of explanation are formidable. Social interaction can be directly observed. But social inequalities, class structures and ethnic identities cannot simply be 'read off' linguistic data. Broader patterns of language use can be inferred from social interactions – but does this mean that they 'exist', in any meaningful sense, or are they just an analytic construct? Similarly, to explore class, ethnicity, or globalisation requires theories about broader forces in the social world. But do such things really 'exist', or are they merely theoretical constructs we use to talk about data? Researchers need to think through the complexities of these relationships, and the mechanisms by means of which these different levels of reality can influence one another. The underlying understanding of how reality works and how we can know about it, that is, the ontological and epistemological framings of the research, shape how these relationships and mechanisms are understood.

Such questions have been framed in linguistic ethnography in terms of a tension between social constructionist and realist perspectives. Interactional sociolinguistics (along with some other approaches to linguistic analysis, e.g. ethnomethodologically-influenced conversation analysis) has tended to stress that social reality is produced in interaction, and to shy away from explanatory categories which are not observable in the way participants orient to one another. Others (e.g. Sealey and Carter 2004) have argued that applied linguistics could benefit from the insights of 'realist' philosophers. They claim that real structures and processes exist beyond immediate social interactions, independently of our descriptions of and orientations towards them, and that these can therefore be studied as entities in themselves by social scientists, albeit indirectly.

The validity of the statements made by linguistic ethnographic work rests on understandings of the interrelationship between language and social processes that often remain implicit. Making these ontological assumptions explicit, and working through the possibilities and limitations that follow from them, can only strengthen the field.

The role and focus of the researcher

The researcher's role in producing truth claims in ethnographic work needs serious consideration. The tension identified by Hammersley (2007) between participants' and analysts' perspectives makes ethnographic work distinctly different from a grounded approach, which would claim that theory generation should be based solely on data collected in the field. An ethnographic approach involves not only the accumulation of data generated by various qualitative methods employed to capture insider or emic understandings of social phenomena. It also requires that these understandings be re-visioned and re-articulated within the conceptual frameworks of social sciences disciplines which inform the researcher's outsider or etic orientations (Heath and Street 2008). There is thus a tension between the goal of making truth claims on the basis of the data (which may include recordings, transcripts, fieldnotes, photographs, etc.), and the recognition of the role of the researcher's positioning, interpretative capacities and theoretical framings in shaping research findings.

In addition, tensions persist between the detailed micro-level analysis of interaction (which, it could be argued, provides direct evidence of participant behaviour and orientations) and the desire to identify longer term evolving patterns which constitute identities, institutions and communities. Understandably, many researchers tend to focus on manageable chunks of data: a few minutes of interaction, rather than continuous stretches over days and weeks. While patterns of language use can be productively identified and compared across these chunks of data, it is more difficult to map long-term processes of situated meaning-making.

There is also a tension between the fine-grained analysis of texts (spoken, written or visual) and the interpretation of the sociohistorical context. Unlike conversation analysts, who limit their accounts of context solely to that which can be grounded in references made by speakers, ethnographers use their knowledge of the wider cultural context to interpret specific instances of dialogue, guided by theoretical concepts and observational insights. A number of mediational concepts have been developed which help to bridge between text and context (see Lillis 2008, in relation to academic writing). For instance, the concept of indexicality (e.g. Silverstein 1976; Bauman and Briggs 1990; Blommaert 2005) refers to how particular uses of language point to different dimensions of context, from past, present or future, at a local or more general scale. The term 'style' (Eckert 2000; Rampton 2006) links linguistic choices to other dimensions of behaviour and to social constructs and processes. Concepts like these create a synergy between linguistic and ethnographic analyses, describing the mutual shaping of language and social life to provide insights into, for example, identity, ideology, or institutional processes.

Emerging areas of focus

Online and digital research

New technologies offer intriguing possibilities for exploring changing language practices. A precursor in this field is Cherny (1999), who draws on linguistics and ethnography in her participant observation study of the register of chat in online text-based gaming communities or multi-user domains (MUDs).

As well as offering new tools for carrying out research, online ethnography raises new questions about the constitution of social groups, the nature and significance of context, and approaches to participant observation. Androutsopoulos' (2008) 'discourse-centred online ethnography' combines systematic observation of postings on various Internet sites with interviews with individuals about their practices. Ethnographically influenced in his approach to real-life data, and his attempts to map the field holistically, engage with people over a period of time, and take a responsive approach to interviewing, his approach is positioned further towards the 'observation' end of the participant-observation spectrum than Cherny's.

Davies (2006) illustrates a more participatory approach in her insider account of new literacy practices associated with the photosharing Website Flickr, as does her account with Merchant of academic blogging, drawing on their own experiences (Davies and Merchant 2007). Research in virtual worlds, such as Gillen's (2009) 'virtual literacy ethnography' of the Schome Park project in Second Life, offers possibilities for a different approach. Gillen drew on a mixture of methods to collect data about the diverse literacy practices young people developed in this virtual world, keeping ethnographic field notes, and recording many examples of the different forms of written communication participants engaged in. Participation as an avatar in the virtual world enabled her to approach the 'hanging around' often associated with 'real-life' (non-virtual) participant-observation.

Multimodality research

Another area where technologies have provided new methodological possibilities is in the use of digital video technology to capture multimodal dimensions of communication. In Britain, multimodal analysis has been influenced by Hallidayan functional linguistics. Researchers have looked at the affordances of different modes (e.g. speech, writing, image, body movement, gesture or gaze) in terms of their limitations and potential for meaning-making in particular communicative contexts, and how these are brought together to create ensembles of meaning.

Combining observations and detailed video analysis with social theory, researchers have studied how modal configurations contribute to meaning and learning in classrooms, and to the construction of particular disciplinary subjects (Kress *et al.* 2001, 2004).

Other examples include Goodwin (2006), who analyses video data of pre-adolescent girls' interactions in North American school playgrounds. She draws on ethnographic observations and informal interviews, together with an expanded version of conversation analysis, to explore the articulation of body language and movement with talk. She describes how disagreement, insult, comparisons and stories are used to construct hierarchy, opposition, alliance and friendship in ways which challenge popular dualistic thinking about gendered behaviour. Finally, Flewitt (2005) uses video ethnography to track the integration of different modes in three-year-olds' communication at home and in the nursery.

Future trajectory and new debates

Linguistic ethnography as a field of study is still at an early stage of development, although its antecedents stretch back to the nineteenth century. As this chapter has demonstrated, the term has been used for a range of work which combines linguistics and ethnography in different ways, researching educational, work and community settings. This research addresses broad and complex social questions in areas as diverse as learning, inequality, globalisation, and identity construction, often with a strong orientation towards intervention (e.g. Roberts *et al.* 2000; Ivanič *et al.* 2009), and always drawing attention to the complex interdependencies of language use and social process (Blommaert 2006). Researchers in this developing area have formed the Linguistic Ethnography Forum (www.uklef.net), a Special Interest Group of the British Association for Applied Linguistics, which organises events and makes linguistic ethnographic resources more widely available. A number of training programmes, for instance the Lancaster Literacy Research Centre summer school series and the ESRC Development Initiatives 'Ethnography, Language and Communication Researcher' (www.rdi-elc.org.uk), and 'Researching Multilingualism, Multilingualism in the Research Process' have provided opportunities to refine methodological tools and extend linguistic ethnographic work in new constituencies.

The various tensions identified above underlie not only linguistic ethnography but also much social science research, and are unlikely to be easily resolved. Other challenges include the difficulty of obtaining funding for linguistic ethnographic research, which is expensive in researchers' time and tends to focus in depth rather than offer policy-friendly generalisations. Nevertheless, awareness and ongoing discussion of theoretical and methodological challenges are driving expansion of the field. New mediational concepts continue to be developed, and existing ones refined, as new researchers come into this area of work, enriching it with their intellectual histories and positionalities. New technologies open up possibilities both for researching changing practices, and for developing new techniques for data collection, analysis and communication of research. The definition of 'linguistic' is being challenged by work which insists on the multimodality and complex contextuality of communicative practices. And the methodological capacity of ethnography is being enhanced by linguistic procedures and terminology which facilitate a more precise understanding of how culture and social life are mediated through language.

Related topics

ethnicity; gender; identity; language and culture; language and migration; language socialization; literacy; multimodality; sociolinguistics

Further reading

Creese, A. (2008) 'Linguistic ethnography', in K. A. King and N. H. Hornberger (eds) *Encyclopedia of Language and Education*, 2nd edn, vol. 10: *Research Methods in Language and Education*, New York: Springer. (An introduction and overview.)

Duranti, A. (1997) *Linguistic Anthropology*, Cambridge: Cambridge University Press. (An authoritative overview of the field of linguistic anthropology.)

Duranti, A. (ed.) (2009) *Linguistic Anthropology: A Reader*, 2nd edn, Malden, MA: Wiley-Blackwell. (A comprehensive collection of readings in linguistic anthropology.)

Rampton, B. (2006) *Language in Late Modernity: Interaction in an Urban School*, Cambridge: Cambridge University Press. (A thorough and complex example of contemporary linguistic ethnography, combining detailed language analysis with theoretically informed social analysis to address class and ethnicity in young people's lives.)

Rampton, B., Maybin, J. and Tusting, K. (eds) (2007) *Journal of Sociolinguistics* 11(5). (A special issue on linguistic ethnography, which includes articles reflecting on different aspects of the field.)

References

Alim, H. S. (2004) 'You know my steez: an ethnographic and sociolinguistic study of style shifting in a Black American speech community', *Publications of the American Dialect Society* 89, Durham, NC: Duke University Press.

Androutsopoulos, J. (2008) 'Potentials and limitations of discourse-centered online ethnography', *Language@Internet* 5: 8. Available at: www.languageatInternet.de/articles/2008/1610/index_html (accessed 2 October 2009).

Bakhtin, M. ([1935] 1981) 'Discourse in the novel', in M. Holquist (ed.) *The Dialogic Imagination: Four Essays by M. M. Bakhtin*, C. Emerson and M. Holquist (trans.), Austin: University of Texas Press, pp. 259–422.

Barton, D. (2007) *Literacy: An Introduction to the Ecology of Written Language*, 2nd edn, Oxford: Blackwell.

Barton, D. and Hamilton, M. (1998) *Local Literacies: Reading and Writing in One Community*, London and New York: Routledge.

Barton, D., Ivanič, R., Appleby, Y., Hodge, R. and Tusting, K. (2007) *Literacy, Lives and Learning*, London and New York: Routledge.

Bauman, R. (1986) *Story, Performance and Event*, Cambridge: Cambridge University Press.

Bauman, R. and Briggs, C. (1990) 'Poetics and performance as critical perspectives on language and social life', *Annual Review of Anthropology* 19: 59–88.

Belfiore, M. E., Defoe, T. A., Folinsbee, S., Hunter, J. and Jackson, N. (2004) *Reading Work: Literacies in the New Workplace*, Mahwah, NJ: Lawrence Erlbaum Associates.

Blommaert, J. (2005) *Discourse: A Critical Introduction*, Cambridge: Cambridge University Press.

——(2006) 'Ethnography as counter-hegemony: remarks on epistemology and method', Working Papers in Urban Language and Literacies no. 34, London: Kings College. Available at: www.kcl.ac.uk/content/1/c6/01/42/29/paper34.pdf (accessed 2 October 2009).

Blommaert, J., Collins, J. and Slembrouck, S. (2005a) 'Polycentricity and interactional regimes in "global neighbourhoods"', *Ethnography* 6: 205–35.

——(2005b) 'Spaces of multilingualism', *Language and Communication* 25(3): 197–216.

Bloome, D., Carter, S. P., Christian, B. M., Otto, S. and Shuart-Faris, N. (2005) *Discourse Analysis and the Study of Classroom Language and Literacy Events: A Microethnographic Perspective*, London: Lawrence Erlbaum Associates.

Boas, F. (1940) *Race, Language and Culture*, New York: The Free Press.

Bourdieu, P. (1990) *The Logic of Practice*, Cambridge: Polity Press.

Cherny, L. (1999) *Conversation and Community: Chat in a Virtual World*, Stanford, CA: CSLI Publications.

Collins, J. and Slembrouck, S. (2006) 'You don't know what they translate: language contact, institutional procedure, and literacy practice in neighborhood health clinics in urban Flanders', *Journal of Linguistic Anthropology* 16(2): 249–68.

——(eds) (2005) 'Multilingualism and diasporic populations: spatializing practices, institutional processes, and social hierarchies', special issue, *Language and Communication* 25(3): 189–334.

Creese, A. (2005) *Teacher Collaboration and Talk in Multilingual Classrooms*, Clevedon: Multilingual Matters.

——(2008) 'Linguistic ethnography', in K. A. King and N. H. Hornberger (eds) *Encyclopedia of Language and Education*, 2nd edn, vol. 10: *Research Methods in Language and Education*, New York: Springer.

Creese, A., Baraç, T., Bhatt, A., Blackledge, A., Hamid, S., Wei, L., Lytra, V., Martin, P., Wu, C. and Yagcioglu-Ali, D. (2008) 'Investigating multilingualism in complementary schools in four communities (RES–000–023–1180): final report', Birmingham: Birmingham University.

Davies, J. (2006) 'Affinities and beyond! Developing ways of seeing in online spaces', *e-learning* 3. Available at: www.wwwords.co.uk/pdf/freetoview.asp?j=elea&vol=3&issue=2&year=2006&article= 8_davies_elea_3_2_Web, (accessed 2 October 2009).

Davies, J. and Merchant, G. (2007) 'Looking from the inside out: academic blogging as new literacy', in C. Lankshear and M. Knobel (eds) *A New Literacies Sampler*, New York: Peter Lang.

Duranti, A. (1997) *Linguistic Anthropology*, Cambridge: Cambridge University Press.

——(2003) 'Language as culture in US anthropology: three paradigms', *Current Anthropology* 44: 323–47.

Duranti, A. and Goodwin, C. (1992) *Rethinking Context: Language as an Interactive Phenomenon*, Cambridge: Cambridge University Press.

Eckert, P. (2000) *Linguistic Variation as Social Practice*, Oxford: Blackwell.

Farrell, L. (2006) *Making Knowledge Common: Literacy and Knowledge at Work*, New York: Peter Lang.

Firth, J. R. (1957) 'Ethnographic analysis and language with reference to Malinowski's views', in R. Firth (ed.) *Man and Culture: An Evaluation of the Work of Malinowski*, London, Boston and Henley: Routledge. Also in F. R. Palmer (ed.) (1968) *Selected Papers of J. R. Firth 1952–59*, London: Longman.

Flewitt, R. (2005) 'Is every child's voice heard? Researching the different ways three year-old children communicate and make meaning at home and in a pre-school playgroup', *Early Years* 25(3): 207–22.

Foucault, M. (1980) *Power/Knowledge: Selected Interviews and Other Writings 1972–1977*, in C. Gordon (ed.), London: Harvester Press.

Gal, S. (2001) 'Language, gender, and power: an anthropological review', in A. Duranti (ed.) *Linguistic Anthropology: A Reader*, Malden, MA: Blackwell.

Gillen, J. (2009) 'Literacy practices in Schome Park: a virtual literacy ethnography', *Journal of Research in Reading* 32(1): 57–74.

Goffman, E. (1981) 'Footing', in *Forms of Talk*, Oxford: Basil Blackwell.

Goodwin, M. H. (1990) *He-Said-She-Said: Talk as Social Organization Among Black Children*, Bloomington: Indiana University Press.

——(2006) *The Hidden Life of Girls: Games of Stance, Status and Exclusion*, Oxford: Blackwell.

Gregory, E. and Williams, A. (2000) *City Literacies: Learning to Read Across Generations and Cultures*, London: Routledge.

Gumperz, J. J. (1978), 'The conversational analysis of interethnic communication', in E. L. Ross (ed.) *Interethnic Communication*, Athens, GA: University of Georgia Press.

——(1982) *Discourse Strategies*, New York: Cambridge University Press.

Gumperz, J., Roberts, C. and Jupp, T. C. (1979) *Crosstalk: A Study of Cross-cultural Communication. Background Material and Notes to Accompany the BBC Film*, Southall: NCILT.

Gutierrez, K. D., Baquedano-Lopez, P. and Tejeda, C. (2000) 'Rethinking diversity: hybridity and hybrid language practices in the third space', *Mind, Culture and Activity* 6(4): 286–303.

Hammersley, M. (2007) 'Reflections on linguistic ethnography', *Journal of Sociolinguistics* 11(5): 689–95.

Hammersley, M. and Atkinson, M. (1994) *Ethnography: Principles in Practice*, 2nd Rev. edn, London: Routledge.

Hasan, R. (1985) 'Meaning, context, text: fifty years after Malinowski', in J. D. Benson and W. S. Greaves (eds) *Systemic Perspectives on Discourse*, vol. 15: *Advances in Discourse Processes*, Norwood, NJ: Ablex.

Heath, S. B. (1983) *Ways with Words*, New York: Cambridge University Press.

Heath, S. B. and Street, B. V. (2008) *Ethnography: Approaches to Language and Literacy Research*, New York and London: Teachers College Press/Routledge.

Heller, M. (1999) *Linguistic Minorities and Modernity: A Sociolinguistic Ethnography*, London: Longman.

Heller, M. and Martin-Jones, M. (eds) (2001) *Voices of Authority: Education and Linguistic Difference*, London: Ablex.

Hull, G. (1997) *Changing Work, Changing Workers: Critical Perspectives on Language, Literacy and Skills*, Albany, NY: State University of New York Press.

Hymes, D. (1964) 'General introduction', in D. Hymes (ed.) *Language in Culture and Society: A Reader in Linguistics and Anthropology*, New York: Harper and Row.

——(1974) *Foundations in Sociolinguistics: An Ethnographic Approach*, Philadelphia: University of Pennsylvania Press.

Ivanič, R., Edwards, R., Barton, D., Fowler, Z., Mannion, G., Miller, K., Satchwell, C. and Smith, J. (2009) *Improving Learning in College: Rethinking Literacies Across the Curriculum*, London and New York: Routledge.

Jaffe, A. (1999) *Ideologies in Action: Language Politics on Corsica*, Berlin: Mouton, Walter de Gruyter.

Kamberelis, G. (2001) 'Producing heteroglossic classroom (micro)cultures through hybrid discourse practice', *Linguistics and Education* 12(1): 85–125.

Kress, G., Jewitt, C., Bourne, G., Franks, A., Jones, K. and Reid, E. (2004) *English in Urban Classrooms: A Multimodal Perspective on Teaching and Learning*, London: Routledge.

Kress, G., Jewitt, C., Ogborn, J. and Tsatsarelis, T. (2001) *Multimodal Teaching and Learning: The Rhetorics of The Science Classroom*, London: Continuum.

Lillis, T. (2008) 'Ethnography as method, methodology and "deep theorising": closing the gap between text and context in academic writing research', *Written Communication* 25(3): 353–88.

Lytra, V. (2007) *Play Frames and Social Identities*, Amsterdam: John Benjamins.

Martin-Jones, M. and Jones, K. (eds) (2000) *Multilingual Literacies: Reading and Writing Different Worlds*, Amsterdam: John Benjamins.

Maybin, J. (2006) *Children's Voices: Talk, Knowledge and Identity*, Basingstoke: Palgrave Macmillan.

Mendoza-Denton, N. (2007) *Homegirls: Language and Cultural Practices Among Latina Youth Gangs*, Maldon, MA: Blackwell.

Michaels, S. (1981) '"Sharing time": children's narrative styles and differential access to literacy', *Language in Society* 10: 423–42.

Moll, L., Amanti, C., Neff, D. and Gonzalez, N. (1992) 'Funds of knowledge for teaching: using a qualitative approach to connect homes and classrooms', *Theory into Practice* 31(2): 132–41.

Ochs, E. and Schieffelin, B. (1984) 'Language acquisition and socialization: three developmental stories and their implications', in R. Schweder and R. Levine (eds) *Culture Theory: Mind, Self and Emotion*, Cambridge: Cambridge University Press.

Pahl, K. (2007) 'Timescales and ethnography: understanding a child's meaning-making across three sites: a home, a classroom and an adult literacy class', *Ethnography and Education* 2(2): 175–90.

Philips, S. U. (1983) *The Invisible Culture*, New York: Longman.

Rampton, B. (1995) *Crossing: Language and Ethnicity Among Adolescents*, London: Longman.

——(2006) *Language in Late Modernity: Interaction in an Urban School*, Cambridge: Cambridge University Press.

——(2007) 'Neo-Hymesian linguistic ethnography in the United Kingdom', *Journal of Sociolinguistics* 11(5): 584–607.

Rampton, B., Tusting, K., Maybin, J., Barwell, R., Creese, A. and Lytra, V. (2004) 'UK Linguistic ethnography: a discussion paper'. Available at: www.ling-ethnog.org.uk/documents/papers/ramptonetal2004.pdf (accessed 7 June 2009).

Roberts, C., Jupp, T. and Davies, E. (1992) *Language and Discrimination: A Study of Communication in Multi-ethnic Workplaces*, London and New York: Longman.

Roberts, C., Sarangi, S., Southgate, L., Wakeford, R. and Vass, W. (2000) 'Oral examination: equal opportunities, ethnicity and fairness in the MRCGP', *British Medical Journal* 320: 370–4.

Scribner, S. and Cole, M. (1981) *The Psychology of Literacy*, Cambridge, MA: Harvard University Press.

Sealey, A. and Carter, B. (2004) *Applied Linguistics as Social Science: Advances in Applied Linguistics*, London: Continuum.

Silverstein, M. (1976) 'Shifters, linguistic categories, and cultural description', in K. Basso and H. Selby (eds) *Meaning in Anthropology*, Albuquerque: University of New Mexico Press.

Silverstein, M. and Urban, G. (eds) (1996) *The Natural History of Discourse*, Chicago: University of Chicago Press.

Smith, D. (1990) 'Textually mediated social organization', in *Texts, Facts and Femininity: Exploring the Relations of Ruling*, London: Taylor & Francis.

Street, B. (1984) *Literacy in Theory and Practice*, Cambridge: Cambridge University Press.

——(1993) 'Culture is a verb: anthropological aspects of language and cultural process', in D. Graddol, L. Thompson and M. Byram (eds) *Language and Culture: British Studies in Applied Linguistics 7*, Clevedon: Multilingual Matters.

Trechter, S. and Bucholtz, M. (2001) 'White noise: bringing language into whiteness studies', *Journal of Linguistic Anthropology* 11(1): 3–21.

Tusting, K. (2010) 'Eruptions of interruptions: managing tensions between writing and other tasks in a textualized childcare workplace', in D. Barton and U. Papen (eds) *Anthropology of Writing: Understanding Textually Mediated Worlds*, London and New York: Continuum.

Vološinov, V. N. ([1929] 1973) *Marxism and the Philosophy of Language*, L. Matejka and I. R. Titunik (trans.), Cambridge, MA: Harvard University Press.

Wortham, S. (2008) 'Linguistic anthropology of education', *Annual Review of Anthropology* 37: 37–51.

Wortham, S. and Rymes, B. (2003) (eds) *Linguistic Anthropology of Education*, Westport, CT: Praeger.

37

Literacy

Doris S. Warriner

Introduction

While defining the scope and purview of applied linguistics, Cook (2003) noted that applied linguists investigate 'problems' (educational and social) in which language is implicated, and he divided the different kinds of 'problems' that are systematically examined in the field into three broad categories: language and education; language, work and law; and language, information and effect (2003: 7–8). While Cook's account depicts central concerns of the field, it does not represent some of the more recent shifts that have moved away from an emphasis on so-called 'problems' and towards an understanding that all language and literacy practices are situated within particular social, historical, political contexts and are therefore potential resources which might be differentially valued and supported depending on situation, place, audience, and goals.

The purpose of this chapter is to explore questions such as *what does literacy have to do with applied linguistics?* And *what does a view of literacy as a social-cultural-historical practice contribute to the field?* I argue it is important to consider 'the relation of knowledge about language to decision-making in the real world' (Cook 2003: 5) through a 'theoretical and empirical investigation of real-world problems in which language is a central issue' (Brumfit 1995: 27). I further argue that it is necessary to understand the dynamic ways that literacy and literacies (including multilingual literacies and digital literacies) influence processes and practices that are of growing concern in current and emerging applied linguistics research. Although language teaching and learning remain dominant areas of inquiry, the field has branched out into new areas, and this branching out has required new methodologies and theories.

According to Widdowson (2003: 14), applied linguistics 'does not impose a way of thinking but points out things which might be worth thinking about'. With this in mind, I consider the position of literacy studies within the field of applied linguistics by revisiting their shared concerns, shared priorities, and shared questions. Before getting to that, however, it is necessary to provide a brief account of how particular views of literacy emerged, the context in which they emerged, and the lasting consequences of new theories and approaches to the study of literacy and literacies.

History

For many decades, and across a wide range of contexts, the term literacy has been commonly used to capture a very specific kind of phenomenon: the skills involved in reading and writing, or decoding and producing texts. In this framework, the term 'literate' indicates an ability to read or write letters or symbols in a way that allows meaning-making and comprehension to ensue. The definition emphasizes the importance of learning phonics (sound-symbol relationships), individual literacy levels, individual achievement, and the role of cognitive processes. The assumption is that increased levels of literacy result in greater social participation; it is taken for granted that those who can read and write will ultimately have more and better opportunities – academically, economically, socially, and politically. In this view, great attention is given to what the individual learner is able to do and little attention is given to issues of social context, cultural influences, ideological factors, or relations of power. Unfortunately, this remains the dominant view of literacy in both developed and under-developed contexts, around the world.

While most still agree that such common-sense understandings provide a useful starting point for discussions of what it means to 'be literate' or 'have literacy', most literacy scholars now argue that a more accurate understanding and depiction of literacy would include but go beyond these conventional understandings of the term. In the 1980s, researchers (e.g. Collins 1986; Heath 1983; Street 1984) began to problematize the many assumptions that had been made about what 'counts' as literacy, for whom, and in what contexts. They advocated an expanded view of literacy that would recognize the many factors that influence reading and writing as well as the fact that many different kinds of literacies are taught, learned, valued and privileged depending on purpose, situation, actors involved, and contexts (social, cultural and ideological). Increasingly, literacy scholars began to ask critical questions about what kinds of literacy practices are promoted/required in what contexts and for what purposes. Literacy, in other words, came to be viewed as a social practice located in and influenced by a wide range of factors rather than a set of skills possessed by individuals and yielded in neutral ways.

Noteworthy critiques of those 'common sense' assumptions that drove limited views of literacy moved the field in new and important directions. Taking on the claims of Walter Ong (that there is a great divide between orality and literacy, and that literacy is far superior to orality), Street argued that 'Ong's account of "literate society" turns out on examination to be an account of the particular literate practices of a subculture within his own society, specifically the academic subculture of which he himself is a part' (1995: 150). Rather than focus on the distinctions and disconnects between the two (which Street argues have been manufactured and overstated), it is far more accurate (and productive) to consider the *interactions* between orality and literacy. This represents a fundamental shift in how we view literacy, and orality, that continues to be evident in current literacy research. As Street points out, it is not necessary to 'deny the significance of technical aspects of reading and writing, such as decoding, sound/shape correspondence and reading "difficulties"'; but it is important to recognize the many ways in which those aspects are 'embedded in particular social practices' (1995: 151).

But such myths about literacy are persistent and consequential, as Collins so eloquently states:

> The central claims of the [literacy] thesis are that writing is a technology and transforms human thinking, relations to language, and representations of tradition, a technology that also enables a coordination of social action in unprecedented precision and scale, thus enabling the development of unique social and institutional complexity.
>
> *(Collins and Blot 2003: 17)*

Writing against this rationale, Collins, Street, Gee and many others have persuasively argued that it is critical that literacy scholarship not only recognize and name the myths but also identify what/whose agendas such myths serve. Describing the disconnect between the claims evident in the literacy myth and what actually happens to real people, Gee identifies how literacy myths have throughout history served the political goals of a small but powerful minority, usually to increase their power and control:

> The most striking continuity in the history of literacy is the way in which literacy has been used, in age after age, to solidify the social hierarchy, empower elites, and ensure that people lower on the hierarchy accept the values, norms, and beliefs of the elites, even when it is not in their self-interest or group interest to do so.
>
> *(Gee 1996: 36)*

Arguing against these myths (and the cognitive consequences of literacy that they assume), a number of literacy scholars have analyzed the social, material, and ideological consequences of literacy in order to show empirically how different things are in reality and on the ground (e.g. Bartlett 2007; Farrell 2009; Luke 2004; Martin-Jones *et al.* 2009; Street and Lefstein 2007; Warriner 2007b; Warschauer 2009).

Advances in the study of literacy and literacies

The idea that literacy should be considered a social-cultural-historical practice emerged in the 1980s out of work that took an anthropological perspective and utilized ethnographic approaches in the study of literacy across cultural contexts (e.g. Collins 1986, 1988; Heath 1983; Scribner and Cole 1981; Street 1984). This work collectively challenged the assumptions that had been made in decades of research by cultural anthropologists and literacy scholars, including the notion that literacy was best defined as a neutral set of skills (e.g. those involved with decoding, comprehending, and writing texts) that are not only distinct from orality and associated with modernity but, also, the property of individuals (rather than communities, societies, or institutional-level actors). According to Scribner and Cole (1981), a careful examination of the letter-writing practices of the Vai in Liberia revealed that literacy is best understood as a set of 'socially organized practices which made use of a symbolic system as well as a technology for producing and disseminating it' (Baynham and Prinsloo 2009: 3). This view of literacy as more than the process of decoding texts by attaching sounds to symbols was affirmed by Brian Street during his work in Iran. Street (1984) found that the literacy practices that existed in an Iranian village not only varied but also reflected a range of different religious, economic, and educational goals and priorities. In other words, one's access to certain literacy practices was greatly influenced by one's access to the community of practice that engaged in those practices; and what is valued in one context is not necessary of value in another.

Building on this argument that the *contexts, purposes, audiences, ideologies, and sponsors* of literacy are as important to examine as the actual processes involved in reading and writing, a group of New Literacy Studies scholars (e.g. Collins 1986, 1988; Gee 1996; Heath 1983; New London Group 1996; Street 1984, 1995) began asking questions that explicitly focused on the contexts in which literacy was defined, taught, and learned. In contrast to what was called *autonomous* or *universalist* approaches to literacy (as described above), New Literacy Studies scholars (and those they influenced) adopted a more *ideological* perspective on literacy. In part influenced by the 'social turn' occurring in the social sciences more generally, and in part influenced by the findings of the ethnographic work described above, literacy scholarship moved from viewing literacy as a neutral set of skills possessed by an individual to the idea that questions about literacy are always also questions about the social, cultural, material, institutional, and ideological contexts of literacy.

As part of a larger attempt to re-envision literacy as a socially situated, ideologically influenced set of practices, New Literacy Studies scholars questioned the often-made juxtapositions and assumed contrasts made between literacy and orality often referred to as the 'great divide' (Goody 1977; Ong 1982). In addition, they examined how participation is defined in particular communities of practice, the role of language and literacy in levels of participation, and the educational, social and material consequences of exclusion from certain communities of practices. In this framework, different questions emerged as the guideposts, including: What 'counts' as literacy?; Who is doing the defining?; Who benefits from such definitions?; What practices are excluded from those definitions of what 'counts'?; and What are the ideological or political agendas of this definitional/ideological work?

Two theoretical (and methodological) contributions came out of this early work – the notion of *literacy event* (Heath 1983) and the notion of *literacy practice* (Street 1984) – and both constructs continue to influence the ways in which we investigate literacy today. A literacy event is any event that involves reading or writing, or any 'occasion in which written language is intergral to the nature of participants' interactions and their interpretive processes and strategies' (Heath 1983: 319). Building on Heath's work and his own anthropological work in Iran, Street distinguished *literacy events* from *literacy practices*. Looking back on decades of his work and others', he defined literacy practices as 'social practices and conceptions of reading and writing' as well as 'the social models of literacy that participants bring to bear upon those events and that give meaning to them', or the 'particular ways of thinking about and doing reading and writing in cultural contexts' (Street 2000: 20–2). By emphasizing *conceptions, social models, ways of thinking about literacy*, and the *cultural dimensions* of those experiences, the notion of literacy practices continues to shape the issues and questions that drive the field today.

Such approaches influenced the investigation of literacy as a social practice in a number of ways. First, a great deal of literacy studies scholarship continues to adopt an anthropological lens and utilize ethnographic methods while exploring (across cultures, contexts, situations, and interactions) what gives meaning to particular literacy events and links those events with the practices identified and documented. This work contributes to our understanding of the nuances, complexities and historical influences that give rise to particular literacy practices and events in particular moments and spaces (Collins and Blot 2003). In addition, current work continues to critique the dichotomous views of orality and literacy that were dominant in the field for so many years. Finally, most recent work on literacy shares an understanding that all views of literacy are constructs of the viewer/researcher (and not necessarily an accurate portrayal of reality across cultures). It has become clear that a decontextualized model of learning or development does not adequately account for culturally diverse ways of acquiring knowledge, language, or literacy.

Current issues and ongoing debates

From all the new literacy scholarship that has been conducted across a range of different cultural contexts (including in a range of informal learning contexts), some very large but important research agendas have emerged, including how language and literacy mediate both learning and identity simultaneously, and how new technologies might influence learning, literacy, and identity. One particularly interesting but challenging aspect of the New Literacy Studies research agenda has been the explicit attention paid to questions about how to cultivate a long and broad view of learning that focuses on questions such as 'how can we construct pedagogy and curriculum that support students to construct and hold on to enduring literate identities and to become powerful speakers, readers, and writers while they are in school and beyond?' (Hull and Schultz 2002: 50). The growing interest in how literacy events and practices are embedded within sociocultural contexts continues to take researchers outside of formal educational contexts to identify and document literacy events, literacy practices, and the relationship between events or practices and the trajectories of individuals and their communities (e.g. Barton 2001; Black 2007, 2009; Gee 1996; Hull and Nelson 2005; Lam 2000, 2006, 2009; Schultz 2001; Schultz and Hull 2002, Warriner 2004, 2007a, 2007b, Yi 2007, 2008). By going outside schools and classrooms, literacy scholars have gained insights about the range and variation of literacy practices in use, the function of those practices, and the beliefs or views held by members of communities engaged in them.

The systematic but qualitative investigation of out-of-school literacies prompted educational researchers and practitioners alike to reconceptualize what might be possible in more formal educational contexts (e.g. schools) while opening up new ground conceptually. Within the area now known as the New Literacy Studies, researchers have built on the contributions of this early work by asking questions such as: What is the value of ethnographic methods for understanding literacy as a social practice that is both situated in specific local contexts and influenced by global and transnational processes? For understanding biliteracy and multi-literacy? For understanding the role of power in access to education, social goods (e.g. credentials), material resources?

As Schultz and Hull note, literacy scholars examine not just processes of decoding and meaning making but also 'its social, cultural, historical, economic, and politics contexts both in school and out' (2002: 23). In addition, it is very common to see a microanalysis of language and literacy combined with a macroanalysis of discourse and power. Influenced by these theoretical frames and methodological approaches, broad questions emerged about the relationship between in-school and out-of-school literacies. For instance, we now routinely ask questions such as: When there are so many different types of literacy practices, why is it that school literacy has come to be seen as the defining form of reading and writing? (Hull and Schultz 2002: 27). In addition, the language and theoretical constructs used by literacy studies scholars have been used in a variety of ways to identify and analyze the many close connections that exist between literacy practices and social identities.

Building on the findings and insights gleaned from this work, the study of literacy as a social practice has started to 'return to questions of schooling' (Baynham 2004; Baynham and Prinsloo 2009) in critical and productive ways. In addition, key contributions in the field ask very fundamental questions about the relationship between literacy as a social practice (Barton 2001); the ideological influences on the ways in which we think, talk, and write about literacy (Street 2004); and the very consequential 'material consequences of literacy' (Luke 2004) for both individuals and communities. In the work described here, it is clear that researchers in the field of New Literacy Studies are now looking across a range of sites and groups in order to understand the many different kinds of factors (e.g. cognitive, interactional, ideological, cultural, and institutional) that might influence how learners engage with and think about literacy practices in their different life worlds (in and out of the formal education system).

Inspired by the social turn in literacy studies and reflecting the literacy-as-social-cultural-historical-practice perspective, a number of different research agendas have emerged within the field in recent years, including academic literacies (e.g. Canagarajah 2004; Curry and Lillis 2004); adolescent literacies (Lam 2000; 2009; Lam and Rosario-Ramos 2009; Yi 2008, 2009); multilingual literacies (e.g. Martin-Jones and Jones 2000; Martin-Jones *et al.* 2009; Warriner 2007a, 2007b); and transnational literacies (Bartlett 2007; Black 2007, 2009; Lam 2006, 2009; Warriner 2007a, 2007b; Yi 2007, 2008, 2009). By simultaneously foregrounding an explicit interest in the situated and sociocultural nature of the varied literacy practices involved in language learning processes and re-prioritizing questions of schooling in relation to what's going on outside the classroom, work from the field of literacy studies continues to influence the research agendas of applied linguists from around the world.

In addition, insights from Bartlett and Holland (2002) and Bartlett (2007, 2008) have illuminated the relationship between the different worlds that might be occupied by individuals and communities (e.g. life worlds and literacy worlds, or linguistic worlds) and their understandings of what literacy is and does in specific contexts and situations (Bartlett 2008). In local efforts to preserve or modify conventional notions of literacy, power – or more precisely, asymmetrical relations of power – comes to influence how literacy is defined, by whom, for what purposes, and with what kinds of consequences. Bartlett and Holland's (2002) efforts to theorize 'the space of literacy practices' has yielded important conceptual and empirical insights while highlighting the complicated ways that culture is always and everywhere a dynamic, emergent, situated set of practices.

Current work on literacy as a social practice also focuses on the many ways that literacy practices might be influenced by local contexts while providing opportunities for transcending the limitations of that context. Influenced by the insights and recommendations of Brandt and Clinton (2002), Hull and Schultz (2002), and Bartlett and Holland (2002), many posit that looking beyond the particulars of local contexts illuminates the specific nature of situated social practice. In addition, current work endeavors to address how time and space influence the processes, events, and practices involved with reading and writing in a twenty-first century world. While many literacy scholars have continued to use a literacy-as-social-practice lens to investigate questions about reading and writing (and multimodal practices), these views are now accompanied by an interest in theorizing the role of time and space in such processes, while *also* returning to questions of schooling. For more than a decade, the field has worked to address the processes, relationships, and influences involved with reading and writing across formal and informal learning contexts in ways that build on but extend the insights of earlier work. As Hull and Schultz (2002) mentioned, certain questions about literacy remain central, including:

> How can we construct a pedagogy and curriculum that support students to construct and hold on to *enduring literate identities* and to become powerful speakers, readers, and writers while they are in school and beyond?
>
> How are *time and space* organized in adolescents' lives while they are in school in such a way as to allow them to develop identities as writers? Is the personal writing students engage in connected to a particular *time* in their lives? If so, will these students hold on to the knowledge that writing was important to them at one time and return to it later on?
>
> How can educators re-conceptualize classroom practices to account for the writing students engage in *outside of school*, and how can practitioners teach in such a way that adolescents acquire and hold onto literate identities past their time in classrooms?
>
> *(Hull and Schultz 2002: 50)*

As part of this effort to understand and learn from what learners are doing outside of school contexts, there has been growing interest in the language learning and literacy development of bilingual or multilingual learners (immigrants and refugees). Martin-Jones (Martin-Jones and Jones 2000) has identified a couple of common threads in the research on multilingual literacies. First, because *multilingual literacies* are, by definition, multiple and complex, research on this topic requires a unique set of conceptual and methodological approaches. Recognizing that 'there are multiple paths to the acquisition of the spoken and written languages within the group repertoire and people have varying degrees of expertise in these languages and literacies' (2000: 6) is an important first step. Another emphasis is on the 'the multiple ways in which people draw on and combine the codes in their communicative repertoire when they speak and write' such that the contrasts themselves become meaning-making resources (2000: 7).

Extending the insights and priorities of the aforementioned scholars, recent work on transnational literacies (see, for example, Warriner 2007a) actively works to break down often-invoked binaries and bridge previously unconnected intellectual inquiries by coupling the examination of transnationalism with the investigation of specific and local literacy practices. Moving beyond a purely theoretical discussion of 'the-local-vs.-the-global' to a more nuanced account of the specific ways that individual actors experience transnationalism 'day-in-day-out', this work compliments the insights of both the transnational literature and our understanding of literacy as a social-historical-political practice. Bartlett (2007), for instance, examines how a Dominican transmigrant student's bilingual literacies and educational trajectory might be shaped by social interactions across classroom contexts and how these processes and practices might simultaneously create and break down the boundaries between different moments in time. Other work (e.g. Richardson Bruna 2007; Sánchez 2007) illuminates how the sustained transnational movement between the USA and Mexico provides particular linguistic and cultural resources for US immigrant children as well as the creative use of multimodal literacy practices by immigrant youth in the construction and performance of identity in local contexts. This work draws needed attention to informal literacy practices that are often relegated to our 'peripheral vision' but, also, 'provides an interactional ethnographic account of the informal literacy practices newcomer Mexican youth employ to reflect and reproduce their transnational identities' (Richardson Bruna 2007: 53). In my ethnographic work (Warriner 2007b), I have described how the 'ideological consequences of literacy' are realized both locally and globally through the widespread use of standardized assessment policies and practices that devalue meaningful and effective approaches to language teaching and learning. The analysis of data collected from an adult ESL program demonstrates that testing, as a bureaucratic mechanism, receives, sorts, arranges, and classifies students in ways that foster identities desired by the new global economy. Together, such work has implications for how we might reconceptualize theories of language learning and language teaching in communities across the developed world, particularly when economic conditions are driven by rapid technological advancements, the continued movement of goods and people across borders, and growing distinctions between the rich and poor.

New directions in literacy studies

The recent 'spatial turn' (Leander and Sheehy 2004) in literacy research has helped provide a set of theories and methods for examining how digital technologies (including information and communication technologies) influence our notions of what counts as literacy, how/whether/when individuals learn to participate in particular (online) communities of practice, and the material consequences (Luke 2004) of the opportunities and constraints provided by digital technologies. Also called the 'social semiotic multimodal perspective on learning', this work helps literacy studies as a field reconsider and envision a new set of conceptual and methodological tools as well as a new set of guiding questions. Greater attention is now being given to issues such as the relationship between modes of representation and issues of content; how learners and learning might be influenced by differences in mode; whether 'learning' happens differently or in the same way when we engage with the world primarily through image rather than through speech or writing; and what is accomplished (e.g. aesthetically, materially, or symbolically) when images supplement or replace writing.

Within this growing body of research, a growing number of studies have contributed important insights about the situated ways that digital literacy practices intersect with and support the language learning efforts of recently arrived immigrants in the US context. Whether analyzing how teenagers use the Internet to position themselves in particular ways in and through writing (Lam 2000; McGinnis *et al.* 2007), how fanfiction promotes language learning and literacy development by engaging adolescents in meaningful activities (Black 2007, 2009), or the 'biliterate composing practices' of high school students from immigrant families (Yi 2007, 2008, 2009), this work continues to raise questions about how literacy is defined, by whom, and with what consequences of learning and identity for immigrant youth. Such research has also opened up spaces for identifying, documenting, and analyzing how new immigrants combine multiple semiotic resources in order to learn English, maintain connections with people and practices from their 'homeland', and establish new sets of practices valued in the communities of practice they wish to join. This recent work on the digitial literacy practices of immigrant youth contributes valuable insights and raises important questions about the intersections between second language learning processes, social identities, and multilingual literacies. It also gives much-needed attention to the dynamic and complicated intersections between learning, language, and literacy for individuals often overlooked in the field of literacy studies. As such, this work illustrates effectively and powerfully the many common interests and concerns that literacy studies and applied linguistics have. Future research on the digital literacy practices of multilingual, multinational individuals and communities living in a variety of contexts promises to yield exciting and consequential findings that are certain to influence many different subfields of applied linguistics.

Similarly, a collection of chapters by scholars 'actively involved in shaping the field of literacy studies' (Baynham and Prinsloo 2009) – entitled *The Future of Literacy Studies* – demonstrates that literacy studies scholarship is now concerned with identifying, documenting and analyzing the kinds of literacies, multilingual literacies, and digital literacies that are associated with new technologies, forces of globalization and individual or community efforts to maintain affiliations with multiple communities of practice. Contributions highlight not only the value of a social practice lens (Barton 2009; Kell 2009; Street 2009; Warriner 2009) but also the advances made in digital literacy studies (Warschauer 2009), the aesthetic turn in our investigations of new media (Hull and Nelson 2009), the implications of these advances for teaching and learning in formal educational contexts (Ivanič 2009; Snyder 2009), and the economic consequences of valuing new literacies in workplace settings (Farrell 2009). This volume demonstrates powerfully the many ways that:

> literacy goings-on are always and already embedded in particular forms of activity; that one cannot define literacy or its uses in a vacuum; that reading and writing are studied in the context of social (cultural, historical, political and economic) practices of which they are a part and which operate in particular social spaces.
>
> *(Baynham and Prinsloo 2009: 2)*

Summary

Literacy occupies a central role in processes that interest applied linguists the most, including language learning and language. The field of applied linguistics benefits from examining the socially situated but ideologically and institutionally influenced ways in which literacy is defined, conceptualized, and examined. Similarly, the study of literacy as a social practice is enhanced when the theories and tools of applied linguistics are applied. Increasingly, applied linguists are paying attention to the social, cultural, ideological, and material dimensions of literacy events and practices, and many are focused on 'the education of children, the rights of the disadvantaged, the changing balance of cultures and languages, the effects of technology on communication' (Cook 2003: 78). In such ways, it is clear that a systematic examination of literacy practices supports many of the current and emerging research agendas in the field of applied linguistics.

Moving from a dichotomous distinction between orality and literacy to the notion that, like all social practices, literacies are situated and multiple, literacy studies scholarship has become a field of inquiry that intersects with a number of other intellectual pursuits, including the pursuits of applied linguistics but also those of the social sciences more generally. Situated at the boundaries between different fields of inquiry, literacy studies scholarship remains both a conceptual undertaking and a systematic examination of empirical data. Sometimes focused on what is going on outside of formal educational contexts, and sometimes returning to questions of schooling and pedagogy (Baynham 2004), literacy studies scholarship remains focused on the pursuit of literacy as a set of social-cultural-historical practices that are simultaneously local and global. Whether we are examining reading, writing, digitial literacies, or multilingual literacies, literacy studies scholars are increasingly aware of need to also examine the role of time and space – within and across contexts, within and across communities, and within and across practices.

Related topics

identity; language and migration; language socialization; multilingualism; multimodality

Further reading

Barton, D. and Hamilton, M. (1998) *Local Literacies: Reading and Writing in One Community*, New York: Routledge. (A detailed ethnographic study of one community in Britain; demonstrates how ethnography might be utilized to capture what happens in 'everyday reading and writing'.)

Barton, D., Hamilton, M. and Ivanic, R. (2000) *Situated Literacies: Reading and Writing in Context*, New York: Routledge. (An edited volume that brings together scholars that have greatly influenced literacy studies; addresses the material consequences of literacy, the relationship between text and practices, the concepts of time and space, and the functions of literacies.)

Baynham, M. and Prinsloo, M. (2009) *The Future of Literacy Studies*, New York: Palgrave Macmillan. (Provides recent accounts of theoretical and methodological advances in literacy studies; recommends examining the nature of 'transcontextual flows' and digital literacies in the future study of literacy and literacy practices.)

Gee, J. P (1996) *Social Linguistics and Literacies: Ideology in Discourses*. Bristol, PA: Taylor & Francis. (Provides useful historical context on current debates and discussions on literacy; describes and illustrates a sociocultural approach to literacy.)

Heath, S. B. (1983) *Ways with Words: Language, Life and Work in Communities and Classrooms*, New York: Cambridge University Press. (Reports on an ethnographic study of the language and literacy practices of families living in three communities in the Piedmont Carolinas; introduces the notion of 'literacy event' and demonstrates the value of using this as a unit of analysis.)

Street, B. (1995) *Social Literacies: Critical Approaches to Literacy in Development, Ethnography and Education*, New York: Longman. (Introduces Street's anthropological, social, and critical approach to the study of literacy practices; debunks the myth of the 'great divide' between orality and literacy; describes the uses of literacy and anthropology in Iran.)

References

Bartlett, L. (2007) 'Bilingual literacies, social identification, and educational trajectories', *Linguistics and Education* 18: 215–31.

——(2008) 'Literacy's verb: exploring what literacy is and what literacy does', *International Journal of Economic Development* 28(6): 737–53.

Bartlett, L. and Holland, D. (2002) 'Theorizing the space of literacy practices', *Ways of Knowing Journal* 2(1): 10–22.

Barton, D. (2001) 'Directions for literacy research: analysing language and social practices in a textually mediated world', *Language and Education* 15(2–3): 92–104.

——(2009) 'Understanding textual practices in a changing world', in M. Baynham and M. Prinsloo (eds) *The Future of Literacy Studies*, New York: Palgrave Macmillan.

Baynham, M. (2004) 'Ethnographies of literacy: an introduction', *Language and Education* 18(4): 285–90.

Baynham, M. and Prinsloo, M. (2009) 'Introduction: the future of literacy studies', in M. Baynham and M. Prinsloo (eds) *The Future of Literacy Studies*, New York: Palgrave Macmillan.

Black, R. (2007) 'Digital design: English language learners and reader reviews in online fiction', in M. Knobel and C. Lankshear (eds) *A New Literacies Sampler*, New York: Peter Lang.

——(2009) 'Online fan fiction, global identities, and imagination', *Research in the Teaching of English* 43(4): 397–425.

Brandt, D. (2009) 'Writing over reading: new directions in mass literacy', in M. Baynham and M. Prinsloo (eds) *The Future of Literacy Studies*, New York: Palgrave Macmillan.

Brandt, D. and Clinton, K. (2002) 'Limits of the local: expanding perspectives on literacy as social practice', *Journal of Literacy Research* 34(3): 337–56.

Brumfit, C. J. (1995) 'Teacher professionalism and research', in G. Cook and B. Seidlhofer (eds) *Principals and Practice in Applied Linguistics*, Oxford: Oxford University Press.

Canagarajah, S. (2004) 'Multilingual writers and the struggle for voice in academic discourse', in A. Pavlenko and A. Blackledge (eds) *Negotiation of Identities in Multilingual Contexts*, Buffalo, NY: Multilingual Matters.

Collins, J. (1986) 'Differentiated instruction in reading groups', in J. Cook-Gumperz (ed.) *The Social Construction of Literacy*, New York: Cambridge University Press.

——(1988) 'Language and class in minority education', *Anthropology and Education Quarterly* 19(4): 299–326.

Collins, J. and Blot, R. (2003) *Literacy and Literacies: Texts, Power, and Identity*, New York: Cambridge University Press.

Cook, G. (2003) *Applied Linguistics*, New York: Oxford University Press.

Curry, M. J. and Lillis, T. (2004) 'Multilingual scholars and the imperative to publish in English: negotiating interests, demands, and rewards', *TESOL Quarterly* 38(4): 663–88.

Farrell, L. (2009) 'Texting the future: work, literacies, and economies', in M. Baynham and M. Prinsloo (eds) *The Future of Literacy Studies*, New York: Palgrave Macmillan.

Gee, J. P. ([1990] 1996) *Social Linguistics and Literacies: Ideology in Discourse*, 2nd edn, Bristol, PA: Taylor & Francis.

González, N. and Arnot-Hopffer, E. (2003) 'Voices of the children: language and literacy ideologies in a dual language immersion program', in S. Wortham and B. Rymes (eds) *Linguistic Anthropology of Education*, Westport, CT: Praeger.

Goody, J. (1977) *Domestication of the Savage Mind*, Cambridge: Cambridge University Press.

Goody, J. and Watt, I. (1963) 'The consequences of literacy', in J. Goody and I. Watt (eds) *Literacy in Traditional Societies*, Cambridge: Cambridge University Press.

Heath, S. B. (1983) *Ways with Words: Language, Life and Work in Communities and Classrooms*, Cambridge: Cambridge University Press.

Hornberger, N. H. (1989) 'Continua of biliteracy', *Review of Educational Research* 59(3): 271–96.

——(2003) 'Multilingual language policies and the continua of biliteracy: an ecological approach', in N. H. Hornberger (ed.) *Continua of Biliteracy: An Ecological Framework for Educational Policy, Research, and Practice in Multilingual Settings,* Clevedon: Multilingual Matters.

Hull, G. and Nelson, M. (2005) 'Locating the semiotic power of multimodality', *Written Communication* 22(2): 224–61.

——(2009) 'Literacy, media, and morality: making the case for an aesthetic turn', in M. Baynham and M. Prinsloo (eds) *The Future of Literacy Studies,* New York: Palgrave Macmillan.

Hull, G. and Schultz, K. (2002) 'Connecting schools with out-of-school worlds: insights from recent research on literacy in non-school settings', in G. Hull and K. Schultz (eds) *School's Out: Bridging Out-of-school Literacies with Classroom Practice,* New York: Teachers College Press.

Ivanič, R. (2009) 'Bringing literacy studies into research on learning across the curriculum', in M. Baynham and M. Prinsloo (eds) *The Future of Literacy Studies,* New York: Palgrave Macmillan.

Kell, C. (2009) 'Literacy practices, text/s and meaning making across time and space', in M. Baynham and M. Prinsloo (eds) *The Future of Literacy Studies,* New York: Palgrave Macmillan.

Lam, W. S. E. (2000) 'Literacy and the design of the self: a case study of a teenager writing on the Internet', *TESOL Quarterly* 34: 457–82.

——(2006) 'Re-envisioning language, literacy, and the immigrant subject in new mediascapes', *Pedagogies: An International Journal* 1(3): 171–95.

——(2009) 'Multiliteracies on instant messaging in negotiating local, translocal, and transnational affiliations: a case of an adolescent immigrant', *Reading Research Quarterly* 44(4): 377–97.

Lam, W. S. E. and Rosario-Ramos, E. (2009) 'Multilingual literacies in transnational digitally-mediated contexts: an exploratory study of immigrant teens in the U.S.', *Language and Education* 23(2): 171–90.

Leander, K. M. and Sheehy, M. (eds) (2004) *Spatializing Literacy Research and Practice* (New Literacies and Digital Epistemologies, vol. 15), New York: Peter Lang.

Luke, A. (2004) 'On the material consequences of literacy', *Language and Education* 18(4): 331–5.

McCarty, T. L. (2005) 'Introduction: the continuing power of the "great divide"', in *Language, Literacy, and Power in Schooling*, Mahwah, NJ: Lawrence Erlbaum Associates.

McGinnis, T., Goodstein-Stolzenberg, A. and Costa Saliani, E. (2007) '"indnpride": online spaces of transnational youth as sites of creative and sophisticated literacy and identity work', *Linguistics and Education* 18(3–4): 283–304.

Martin-Jones, M., Hughes, B. and Williams, A. (2009) 'Bilingual literacy in and on working lives on the land: case studies of young Welsh speakers in North Wales', *International Journal of the Sociology of Language* 195(1): 39–62.

Martin-Jones, M. and Jones, K. (2000) 'Introduction: multilingual literacies', in M. Martin-Jones and K. Jones (eds) *Multilingual Literacies,* Philadelphia: John Benjamins.

Martinez-Roldan, C. M. and Franquiz, M. (2009) 'Latino/a youth literacies: hidden funds of knowledge', in *Handbook of Adolescent Literacy,* New York: Guilford Press.

New London Group (1996) 'A pedagogy of multiliteracies: designing social futures', *Harvard Educational Review* 66(1): 60–92.

Ong, W. J. 1982. *Orality and Literacy: The Technologizing of the Word,* London: Methuen.

Orellana, M. F. and Reynolds, J. F. (2008) 'Cultural modeling: levering bilingual skills for school paraphrasing tasks', *Reading Research Quarterly* 43(1): 48–65.

Orellana, M. F., Reynolds, J. F., Dorner, L. and Meza, M. (2003) '"In other words": translating or "para-phrasing" as a family literacy practice in immigrant households', *Reading Research Quarterly* 38(1): 12–34.

Pahl, K and Rowsell, J. (eds) (2006) *Travel Notes from the New Literacy Studies: Instances of Practice,* Clevedon: Multilingual Matters.

Prinsloo, M. and Baynham, M. (eds) (2008) *Literacies, Global and Local,* Amsterdam: John Benjamins.

Reyes, I. and Azuara, P. (2008) 'Emergent biliteracy in young Mexican immigrant children', *Reading Research Quarterly* 43(4): 374–98.

Reyes, I. and Moll, L. (2008) 'Bilingual and biliterate practices at home and school', in B. Spolsky and F. Hult (eds) *The Handbook of Educational Linguistics,* Malden, MA: Blackwell.

Richardson Bruna, K. (2007) 'Traveling tags: the informal literacies of Mexican newcomers in and out of the classroom', *Linguistics and Education* 18(3–4): 232–57.

Rubenstein-Avila, E. (2007) 'From the Dominican Republic to Drew High: what counts as literacy for Yanira Lara?', *Reading Research Quarterly* 42(4): 568–89.

Sánchez, P. (2007) 'Cultural authenticity and transnational Latina youth: constructing a meta-narrative across borders', *Linguistics and Education* 18(3–4): 258–82.

Schultz, K. (2001) 'Looking across space and time: reconceptualizing literacy learning in and out of school', *Research in the Teaching of English* 36(3): 356–90.

Schultz, K. and Hull, G. (2002) 'Locating literacy theory in out-of-school contexts', in G. Hull and K. Schultz (eds) *School's Out: Bridging Out-of-school Literacies with Classroom Practice,* New York: Teachers College Press.

Scribner, S. and Cole, M. (1981) *The Psychology of Literacy,* Cambridge, MA: Harvard University Press.

Snyder, I. (2009) 'Shuffling towards the future: the enduring dominance of book culture in literacy education', in M. Baynham and M. Prinsloo (eds) *The Future of Literacy Studies,* New York: Palgrave Macmillan.

Street, B. (1984) *Literacy in Theory and Practice,* Cambridge: Cambridge University Press.

——(1995) *Social Literacies: Critical Approaches to Literacy in Development, Ethnography and Education,* New York: Longman.

——(2000) 'Literacy events and literacy practices: theory and practice in the new literacy studies', in M. Martin-Jones and K. Jones (eds) *Multilingual Literacies,* Philadelphia, PA: John Benjamins.

——(2004) 'Futures of the ethnography of literacy?', *Language and Education* 18(4): 326–30.

——(2009) 'The future of "social literacies"', in M. Baynham and M. Prinsloo (eds) *The Future of Literacy Studies,* New York: Palgrave Macmillan.

Street, B. and Lefstein, A. (2007) *Literacy: An Advanced Resource Book,* Applied Linguistics Series, New York: Routledge.

Vasudevan, L. (2006) 'Looking for angels: knowing adolescents by engaging with their multimodal literacy practices', *Journal of Adolescent and Adult Literacy* 50(4): 252–8.

Warriner, D. S. (2004) 'Multiple literacies and identities: the experiences of two women refugees', *Women's Studies Quarterly* 32(1–2): 179–95.

——(2007a) 'Introduction: transnational literacies: immigration, language learning and identity', *Linguistics and Education* 18(3–4): 201–14.

——(2007b) '"It's just the nature of the beast": re-imagining the literacies of schooling', *Linguistics and Education* 18(3–4): 305–24.

——(2009) 'Transnational literacies: examining global flows through the lens of social practice', in M. Baynham and M. Prinsloo (eds) *The Future of Literacy Studies,* New York: Palgrave Macmillan.

Warschauer, M. (2009) 'Digital literacy studies: progress and prospects', in M. Baynham and M. Prinsloo (eds) *The Future of Literacy Studies,* New York: Palgrave Macmillan.

Watahomigie, J. and McCarty, T. L. (1996) 'Literacy for what? Hualapai literacy and language maintenance', in N. H. Hornberger (ed.) *Indigenous Literacies in the Americas: Language Planning from the Bottom Up,* Berlin: Mouton de Gruyter.

Widdowson, H. G. (2003) *Defining Issues in English Langauge Teaching,* Oxford: Oxford University Press.

Yi, Y. (2007) 'Engaging literacy: a biliterate student's composing practices beyond school', *Journal of Second Language Writing* 16: 23–39.

——(2008) 'Relay writing in an online adolescent online community', *Journal of Adolescent and Adult Literacy* 51: 670–80.

——(2009) 'Adolescent literacy and identity construction among 1.5 generation students: from a transnational perspective', *Journal of Asian Pacific Communication* 19(1): 100–29.

——(2010) 'Identity matters: theories that help explore adolescent multilingual writers and their identities', in M. Cox, J. Jordan, C. Ortmeier-Hooper and G. Schwartz (eds) *Inventing Identities in Second Language,* Urbana Champaign, IL: National Council of Teachers of English.

38

Stylistics

Elena Semino

Introduction: stylistics and style

In its broadest sense, stylistics is concerned with the description and interpretation of distinctive linguistic choices and patterns in texts. 'Style' in language is generally defined as the result of patterns of choice at different linguistic levels that may be characteristic of a text, the oeuvre of an author, a genre, etc. The notion of style is thus fundamentally comparative: different styles in language arise from the possibility of speaking or writing in different ways, and the style of any text or group of texts can only be described in contrast with that of a different text or group of texts, or in contrast with dominant patterns in the relevant language as a whole.

This view of style in language as depending on both choice and difference raises two issues. The first issue is whether only some types of linguistic choices are relevant to style, or whether all choices result in stylistic differences. The former view relies on a distinction between 'form' on the one hand and 'meaning' or 'content' on the other, so that it is possible to express the same meaning via different formal choices. Within this view, selecting the noun 'steed' as opposed to 'horse' in a narrative is a stylistic choice, as both nouns can refer to the same equine participant in a story. In contrast, selecting 'zebra' as opposed to 'horse' is not a stylistic choice, as the nouns evoke different animals, and involve differences in the content of the story rather than its style. In contrast, the opposing view emphasises that any variation in form has implications for meaning (e.g. 'steed' and 'horse' have different connotations and may evoke different equine images), so that no distinction can be made between choices of content and choice of form. Hence, all linguistic choices have implications for both style and meaning. These different views of the relationship between choice and style are sometimes referred to as, respectively, 'dualism' and 'monism' (see Wales 2001). Leech and Short (1981: 10–40) attempt to resolve this opposition by distinguishing between two notions of style, namely: a broader notion of style as 'linguistic choice in general', and a more restricted notion of style within which '[s]tylistic choice is limited to those aspects of linguistic choice which concern *alternative ways of rendering the same subject matter*' (Leech and Short 1981: 31, italics in original). Even within this more restricted definition, however, stylistic choices are meaningful in that they contribute to the reader's or listener's interpretation of the text.

The second issue that arises from defining style in terms of choice and difference relates to how difference, or distinctiveness, can be determined. In an early and influential discussion of this issue, Enkvist (1973: 21–6) argued that the style of a text can only be accounted for by comparing the text with a larger group of texts that functions as a contextually relevant 'norm':

> The norm may be chosen from a wide field. One portion of a text may be matched against other portions or the whole of the same text. One text may be compared to other texts. Or the text may be set against an imaginary norm that only exists in a critic's mind.
>
> *(Enkvist 1973: 26)*

Enkvist suggests that the comparison will lead to the identification of 'style markers', namely '[f]eatures whose densities are significantly different in the text and in the norm' (1973: 25). I will return below to the different methods that have been developed in stylistics for identifying what Enkvist calls 'style markers'.

A history of stylistics

While it is difficult to establish clear boundaries for what counts as 'stylistics', the term is primarily associated with a line of research that can be traced back to the studies of style in language conducted in continental Europe by Bally (1909) and Spitzer (1948) in the first half of the twentieth century. The second half of the twentieth century saw the rise of an Anglo-American tradition, initially under the influence of Russian and Prague Formalism and Practical Criticism, and subsequently benefiting from advances in linguistics more generally. Stylistics is now an international and diverse field of study. This chapter is, however, limited to work published in English since the 1960s.

An initial distinction needs to be made between what have been called 'general stylistics' and 'literary stylistics' (see Wales 2001). General stylistics is concerned with the relationship between language and context of use, and involves the study of the styles associated with different genres. It is closely related to other areas of linguistics that are concerned with language variation, such as sociolinguistics (e.g. Coupland 2007). Literary stylistics is primarily concerned with the relationship between the language of literary texts and their meanings and effects, broadly conceived.

General stylistics

The terms 'style' and 'stylistics' feature in the titles of two landmark studies which were published in the late 1960s and early 1970s, while linguistics was becoming established as the new 'science of language': Crystal and Davy's (1969) *Investigating English Style* and Enkvist's (1973) *Linguistic Stylistics*. Enkvist's approach to the study of style was briefly mentioned above. Crystal and Davy (1969) similarly see the goal of stylistics as the systematic study of how and why language varies depending on the context of use. They outline a method of linguistic analysis involving five 'levels' of language (phonetic/graphetic, phonological/graphological, grammatical, lexical, semantic), and describe extra-linguistic situations in terms of several different 'dimensions of situational constraint' (including, for example, dialect, time, speech vs writing, type of activity, social relations, etc.). This approach is applied to the identification of what Crystal and Davy call 'stylistically significant' or 'stylistically distinctive' features in a range of different types of language use, including informal conversation, newspaper reporting, and the language of religion (see also Leech 1966 for an early study of the language of advertising). Crystal and Davy (1969: 12–13) also explicitly discuss the issue of 'objectivity' in stylistic analysis, which, as shown in more detail below, has vexed the field since its origins. They suggest that the initial selection of the linguistic features that might be stylistically significant can only be based on the analyst's intuitions, which are 'informed' but inevitably subjective. The subsequent analysis of these features, which involves both classification and explanation, is in contrast described as 'objective', as it is based on the application of relevant theoretical frameworks and on a systematic understanding of patterns of variation in language use.

Studies such as Enkvist's and Crystal and Davy's were not immediately followed by further work in general stylistics. In the late 1980s, Carter, for example, points out that 'no single study has emerged in the 1970s or 1980s which builds systematically on work on non-literary style and language variation by Crystal and Davy (1969)' (Carter 1989: 13). Since the early 1990s, however, some important work in general stylistics has been conducted, thanks to theoretical and methodological developments in linguistics more generally. First, the rise of pragmatics and (critical) discourse analysis has made it possible to explain more systematically why particular patterns of choice are made in particular contexts of use. Carter and Nash (1990) point out the political and ideological implications of style: they argue that writers fashion their texts in order to facilitate particular 'ways of seeing (and believing)', and to suppress others. Hence, the analysis of style requires an understanding of asymmetries in power relations between writers and readers, and can reveal the ways in which dominant ideologies are textually constructed, maintained and reinforced (see also Toolan 1992; Simpson 1993).

Second, the application of the methods of corpus linguistics to text analysis has made it possible to place the selection and description of stylistically significant features on a firmer empirical footing. For example, a text or group of texts can be automatically compared with another text or (usually larger) body of texts in terms of the frequencies of words or multi-word strings, grammatical categories and semantic fields (see Adolphs's [2006] notion of 'inter-textual' electronic analysis). This provides lists of potential style markers (in Enkvist's sense) independently of the analyst's decisions, although the further interpretation and analysis of such lists inevitably relies on the analyst's intuitions and knowledge of the data. In addition, individual texts or groups of texts can be investigated electronically via concordances (lists of particular expressions obtained automatically) and collocations (statistically significant patterns of co-occurrence in the use of words) (see Adolphs's [2006] notion of 'intra-textual' electronic analysis). Stubbs (1996), for example, combines an 'inter-textual' and an 'intra-textual' computer-aided approach in order to compare Baden-Powell's last messages to the Boy Scouts and the Girl Guides. He shows the sexist implications of the different uses of 'happy' and 'happiness' in the two texts, by analysing concordances of these two words in both texts and in two larger corpora of English.

Language corpora can also be used to investigate variation across text-types, both synchronically and diachronically. Biber (1988), for example, uses multivariate analysis to arrive at a systematic account of the clusters of linguistic features that characterise different modes of speaking and writing in a large corpus of English. In addition, it is possible to enrich corpora by adding further information, either manually or electronically. This process, known as annotation, enables analysts to carry out computer-aided analyses of textual phenomena that cannot be studied by searching for particular words or groups of words. For example, Semino and Short (2004) annotated a corpus for different categories of speech, writing and thought presentation (e.g. direct speech, free indirect thought), and then used the corpus to investigate the forms, functions and patterning of different modes of presentation in fictional and non-fictional narratives.

Literary stylistics

Literary stylistics is concerned more specifically with the relationship between form and meaning in literary texts. In introducing a book on the linguistic analysis of poetry, prose fiction and drama, Short (1996) defines stylistic analysis as follows:

> stylistic analysis is a method of linking linguistic form, *via* reader inference, to interpretation in a detailed way and thereby providing as much explicit evidence as possible for and against particular interpretations of texts.
>
> *(Short 1996: 27)*

This approach to stylistic analysis first developed in Britain in the 1960s under the influence of practical criticism, Russian formalism, and the Prague Linguistic Circle. Practical criticism, which was developed at Cambridge University in the 1930s, advocated close attention to the language and structure of texts, in contrast with a concern for the social, cultural and historical context that was prevalent in literary criticism more generally (e.g. Richards 1929). The group of scholars known as the Russian Formalists operated in Moscow and St Petersburg in the early twentieth century, and similarly regarded texts as the main object of study. They were particularly concerned with the formal and functional features that distinguish literary from 'non-literary' language. They argued that the function of art generally, and of verbal art in particular, is to deautomatise or defamiliarise our routine perceptions of experience and reality. According to Shklovsky, this is achieved by 'mak[ing] objects "unfamiliar"', 'mak[ing] forms difficult', and 'increas[ing] the difficulty and length of perception because the process of perception is an aesthetic end in itself and must be prolonged' (Shklovsky 1965: 12). The Prague Linguistic Circle was influenced by the Russian Formalists, especially via the work of Roman Jakobson, who moved from Moscow to Prague in the 1920s. The members of this group combined the insights of the Russian Formalists with greater attention for language. Mukařovský (1964) argued that poetry is characterised by the systematic deviation from the norms of 'standard' language, which foregrounds the language itself and leads to defamiliarising effects. Jakobson's (1960) multi-functional approach to communication includes what he calls the 'poetic' function, which involves a focus on the text for its own sake, and manifests itself in the presence of linguistic patterns, or parallelism.

Jakobson is often credited with having launched the linguistic approach to literature that characterises literary stylistics by stating that:

> a linguist deaf to the poetic function of language and a literary scholar indifferent to linguistic problems and unconversant with linguistic methods are equally flagrant anachronisms.
>
> *(Jakobson 1960: 377)*

The early applications of linguistic analysis to literary texts by Jakobson himself (e.g. Jakobson and Lévi-Strauss 1962) involved painstaking inventories of linguistic choices (phonetic, grammatical and lexical), with no consideration for degrees of salience and interpretative significance. This reflected a deliberate attempt to separate description from evaluation in the linguistic study of literature. In contrast, other linguists strove to connect linguistic description with the interpretative issues that are the traditional concerns of literary criticism. Leech (1969), for example, developed some of the central notions from the formalist tradition into powerful tools for the stylistic analysis of poetry. He suggests that foregrounding effects can be achieved both via deviation (unexpected irregularity) and parallelism (unexpected regularity), and argues that the patterning of foregrounding devices is central to the overall significance of (poetic) texts.

The rise and development of literary stylistics since the 1960s can best be explained with reference to the growth of linguistics generally, as stylisticians have tended to exploit relevant advances in linguistics for the purposes of literary text analysis. As the concerns of linguists broadened from sentential to textual, pragmatic and discoursal phenomena, stylistic analysis came to be applied not just to poetry, but also to prose fiction (e.g. Leech and Short 1981; Fowler 1986) and drama (e.g. Herman 1995; Culpeper *et al.* 1998). In addition, stylistics has been influenced by advances in narratology (notably on the study of plot and point of view), and by some aspects of literary theory (e.g. reader response criticism). These multiple influences and interactions have led to a proliferation of labels for different branches of stylistics, such as 'affective stylistics' (Fish 1970), 'pragmastylistics' (Hickey 1989), 'discourse stylistics' (Carter and Simpson 1989), 'critical stylistics' (Weber 1992), 'feminist stylistics' (Mills 1995) 'cognitive stylistics' (Semino and Culpeper 2002), 'corpus stylistics' (Semino and Short 2004), and so on (see also Weber 1996). The rest of this section focuses on a selection of key studies in literary stylistics since the 1960s, which give an overview of the historical development of the field, and of its variety.

The rise of Chomsky's generative grammar in the 1960s and 1970s was reflected in a series of studies that described the styles of particular texts or authors in terms of the application of particular sets of syntactic rules or transformations. Thorne (1965), for example, treats each of a series of poems as a sample of a different language, which can be accounted for by constructing a specific grammar. In present-day stylistics, the influence of the Chomskyan tradition in stylistics is limited to some influential work on poetic metre, which is treated as a separate module operating independently of phonology and syntax (Fabb and Halle 2008). Since the 1970s, Halliday's systemic-functional approach to language, and grammar in particular (e.g. Halliday 1978), has had a more long-lasting influence on stylistics. Halliday himself applied his approach to transitivity to a literary text in a seminal analysis of William Golding's *The Inheritors* (Halliday 1971). Halliday showed how different patterns of choices in the system of transitivity are used to contrast the world view of the novel's protagonist, Lok (a member of 'the people' – a group of early humans usually described by the critics as Neanderthals), with that of the members of a more advanced group (referred to as 'the new people' in the novel, and usually identified as homo sapiens). The part of the novel that reflects Lok's point of view is characterised by a high frequency of intransitive structures and inanimate entities functioning as grammatical subjects. So, for example, the sentence 'The stick began to grow shorter at both ends' is used to describe Lok's perception of an action that readers are likely to identify as someone drawing a bow. Similarly, Lok's perception of the noise caused by an arrow hitting a tree is conveyed by the following description 'The dead tree by Lok's ear acquired a voice. "Clop!"' These patterns, Halliday concludes, suggest that Lok has a poor understanding of agency and cause-effect relationships. This limited understanding in turn explains the demise of his group when faced with 'the new people', who appear to have a more sophisticated understanding of the world.

Halliday's model of language is part of the analytical frameworks adopted in some landmark later works in stylistics (e.g. Leech and Short 1981; Fowler 1986). More specifically, Halliday's analysis of *The Inheritors* has inspired further studies of the role of transitivity in conveying unusual world views, or 'mind styles' (Fowler 1977). Both Leech and Short (1981: 202–7) and Fowler (1986: 133–4), for example, discuss the section of William Faulkner's *The Sound and the Fury* that is narrated by Benjy, a cognitively impaired 33-year-old man. Both studies point out the lexical and grammatical simplicity of Benjy's narrative, as well as some transitivity patterns that, as in Lok's case, suggest a limited understanding of human actions and intentions: a high frequency of intransitive structures, and a tendency to use transitive verbs without direct objects (e.g. the verb 'hit' is used intransitively to describe the actions of people who, readers are likely to infer, are engaged in a game of golf).

The analysis of transitivity patterns also plays a central role in those applications of stylistics that are concerned with the relationship between linguistic patterns in literary texts on the one hand, and power relations, discrimination and ideologies on the other. Indeed, Halliday's systemic-functional grammar has also often been adopted within critical discourse analysis, which has influenced, and overlaps with, some influential work in literary stylistics. Burton (1982) for example, applies an adapted version of Halliday's model of transitivity to an extract from Sylvia Plath's semi-autobiographical novel *The Bell Jar*, in which the narrator/protagonist undergoes electroshock treatment aimed at alleviating her depression. Burton's analysis of the realisation of participants and processes in the extract shows how the other two characters in the scene (a female nurse and a male doctor) are consistently presented as in control, and as acting on the protagonist or the equipment in the treatment room. In contrast, the protagonist does not act to affect others or her environment, but is solely affected by others' actions. Burton argues that Plath's linguistic choices 'disenable' the protagonist, and thus result in a representation of the female protagonist as passive and helpless. This representation is consistent with dominant tendencies in the representation of women, both in fiction and elsewhere, which are potentially detrimental to women's self-image. Burton's goal is to provide an example of what, in her view, stylistics should aim to achieve:

> stylistic analysis is *not* just a question of discussing 'effects' in language and text, but a powerful method for understanding the ways in which all sorts of 'realities' are constructed through language.
>
> *(Burton 1982: 230)*

In Burton's view, therefore, stylistics both cannot and should not be politically neutral, but should contribute to the promotion of human rights, especially in relation to sexism (see also Weber 1992; Mills 1995).

The study of fictional interactions, in both prose fiction and drama, began in the 1980s following the rise of pragmatics and conversation analysis. In spite of the differences between real-life conversations and fictional conversations (see, for example, Short 1996: 172–86), stylisticians have shown how the theories and analytical frameworks developed by linguists interested in interaction can explain the ways in which readers or audiences perceive characters and infer 'meanings between the lines' in interpreting fictional interactions. Widdowson (1982), for example, argues that Othello's tendency to confuse first- and third-person pronominal references in Shakespeare's play reflects his inability to distinguish semblance from reality, and makes him vulnerable to Iago's strategic manipulation of language. Short (1989a) discusses characterisation and the creation of absurdist effects in drama by means of an analytical framework that includes notions such as speech acts, presupposition, and conversational implicature (see also Herman 1995; Culpeper *et al.* 1998; Black 2006). The notions of 'face', politeness and impoliteness have also been applied to the analysis of fictional interactions, especially in order to explain the attribution of goals to characters, and the perception of their mutual relationships (e.g. Leech 1992; Culpeper 1998). A recent development in this area is the study of interactions in films, which requires the development of a multimodal form of stylistic analysis (e.g. McIntyre 2007).

Since the earliest developments of the stylistics tradition described in this section, stylisticians have been interested in the pedagogical applications of stylistic analysis, both in mother-tongue and second/foreign-language contexts (see Widdowson 1975, 1992; Short 1989b; Watson and Zyngier 2007). The use of stylistics in the classroom is seen as a way of bringing together the teaching of language with the teaching of literature, and as an alternative to the more traditional literary critical approach that tends to dominate literature classrooms around the world.

Literary stylistics in the twenty-first century: directions and challenges

Two main approaches to stylistics have been particularly productive in the first few years of the twenty-first century: corpus-based or computer-aided stylistics, and cognitive stylistics. Both approaches have their roots in earlier work in stylistics, but both have gained considerable impetus from recent developments in, respectively, corpus linguistics and cognitive science.

Corpus-based or computer-aided stylistics

Quantification, broadly conceived, is relevant to both general and literary stylistics. The claim that the style of a particular text or groups of texts is distinctive in some way ideally involves evidence that some linguistic features are more (or less) frequent in those texts than elsewhere. Similarly, the claim that particular linguistic choices are foregrounded in a text requires evidence that those linguistic choices are indeed deviant or unusual as compared with language use generally. Manual quantification has often been used in stylistics analysis (e.g. Leech and Short 1981: 74ff.), and there is a long tradition of statistical approaches to literary style (e.g. Milic 1967). In the last two decades, however, the increasing availability, flexibility and user-friendliness of language corpora and computer-aided methods has increasingly been exploited in literary (as well as general) stylistics. More specifically, computer-aided methods have been used in order to investigate the language of individual texts and the oeuvres of particular authors (for overviews of the area, see Adolphs 2006; Archer 2007).

Louw (1997), for example, investigates the 'semantic prosody' of a particular word (the adverb 'utterly') in the Bank of English corpus in order to account for the use and potential effects of that word in a poem by Philip Larkin. Hoover (1999) uses a corpus of British and American novels in order to carry out a systematic quantitative analysis of the language of Golding's *The Inheritors*, thus building on and extending Halliday's (1971) earlier 'manual' analysis of the novel. Culpeper (2002) employs the automatic analysis of 'key words' in order to investigate the linguistic features that characterise the language of the main characters in Shakespeare's *Romeo and Juliet*. Following in a venerable tradition of computer-aided approaches to authorial style (e.g. Burrows 1987), Mahlberg (2007) shows how the automatic retrieval of multi-word sequences or 'clusters' can reveal some distinctive aspects of Dickens's style and characterisation techniques. Hoover (2002) demonstrates a corpus-based technique for attributing novels to authors by considering the distribution of the most frequent words and word clusters.

It needs to be acknowledged that corpus-based and computer-aided methods have inevitable limitations, both in terms of *what* can be investigated and *how*. Hence, these methods cannot replace the more traditional, intensive, approach to stylistic analysis, nor do away with the role of the analyst's intuitions (which are, for example, involved in the interpretation of the output of software tools). Nonetheless, these methods are an invaluable addition to the methodologies available to stylisticians, as they enable scholars to test out empirically their intuitions about texts, and to study patterns that could not be realistically investigated manually.

Cognitive stylistics

The second area of study I mentioned earlier, cognitive stylistics, also has its roots in earlier work within literary stylistics. Although stylistic analysis is primarily focused on texts, its concern for interpretative effects inevitably involves readers. Traditionally, however, stylisticians have used general notions such as inference, but without adopting particular models of cognition or text processing. Between the end of the twentieth century and the beginning of the twenty-first century, some linguistic approaches to literary text analysis began to draw more explicitly and systematically from work in psychology and cognitive science. Cook (1994), for example, exploits and extends schema theory in order to propose a theory of literariness that reformulates the central tenets of the formalist approach to literary language. Semino (1997) adapts Cook's approach in a study of how text worlds are imagined by readers of poetry in their interactions with texts. Culpeper (2001) combines some insights from social psychology with well-established techniques in the stylistic analysis of drama in order to develop a model of characterisation in plays. Werth (1999) and Emmott (1997) consider both linguistic choices and mental representations in order to account for how readers imagine the worlds of narrative texts (see also Gavins 2007). Other cognitively oriented approaches to literature have built on relevance theory (e.g. Pilkington 2000) and some relevant advances in brain science (Tsur 1992).

Since the 1990s, a large body of work has been influenced by the growth of cognitive linguistics, and particularly conceptual metaphor theory (Lakoff and Johnson 1980). This work has been subsumed under the labels 'cognitive stylistics' (Semino and Culpeper 2002) or 'cognitive poetics' (Stockwell 2002). In a series of influential studies, Freeman (1993, 1995) has applied conceptual metaphor theory to the analysis of Shakespeare's plays, and argued that the dominant source domains in each play account for each text's thematic unity, characterisation, and plot development, as well as for the interpretations that have been proposed by critics. Similarly, Popova (2002) investigates the dominant metaphorical patterns in Henry James's *The Figure in the Carpet*, and suggests that the findings of her analysis can explain the literary critical debate over the interpretation of the novel. Blending theory (Fauconnier and Turner 2002) has also been applied to the analysis of literary texts, in order to account for phenomena as diverse as rhyming patterns (Sweetser 2006) and point of view (Dancygier 2005).

It could be argued that cognitively oriented approaches to the language of literature represent the fastest-growing area within stylistics at the end of the first decade of the twenty-first century. In the collection *Contemporary Stylistics* (Lambrou and Stockwell 2007), for example, at least half of the chapters explicitly involve a 'cognitive' element. This is in fact consistent with the rise of cognitive approaches to narratology, both in Europe and the USA (e.g. Herman 2003; Palmer 2004). On the other hand, however, cognitive stylistics/poetics is rather controversial, and has been at the centre of several debates. Its practitioners (especially those working within the tradition of cognitive linguistics) have been accused of overstating the validity and implications of their analyses, ignoring the ideological dimension of text production and reception, and of simply introducing a new set of unnecessary descriptive terms for familiar phenomena (e.g. Hall 2002; Weber 2004). While it is debatable whether all of these criticisms are equally justified, they do point at some important challenges for practitioners of cognitive stylistics/poetics. The first challenge is to attempt to clarify the different ways in which the term 'cognitive' is used when analysing the language of literature; the second challenge is to do greater justice to phenomena that rightly preoccupy literary scholars of various persuasions, such as the emotional aspects of interpretation and the social, cultural and ideological dimensions of literary communication; the third challenge is to take into account the findings of recent groundbreaking work in neuroscience, and its implications for the role of fiction and literature in human development and experience (e.g. Ramachandran 2004: 40–59); a further challenge is to strive to provide greater empirical evidence for their work by generating hypotheses that can be tested in experiments involving real readers.

With respect to the last point above, it should be mentioned that stylistics has, over the decades, intersected with an area of study that has come to be known as the Empirical Study of Literature (e.g. Zwaan 1993). More specifically, some stylisticians have tested out the validity of their linguistic analyses via informant-based work. For example, van Peer (1986) conducted a series of experiments aimed at verifying the validity of the predictions he made about the sections within a series of poems that readers would perceive to be foregrounded (see also the papers in *Language and Literature*, 16(2), 2007). His findings broadly confirmed his hypotheses, and showed more specifically that greater consensus about foregrounding effects was reached in relation to stretches of text that contained several foregrounding devices. Further work of this kind has led to considerable insights into literary reading, but further research will be needed in future to test out the robustness of more recent approaches within stylistics (e.g. see Emmott *et al.* 2006). Some recent developments suggest that future work will not be limited to relatively artificial reading experiments, but will involve the study of a range of 'natural' reading practices, such as reading groups and mass reading events (see papers in *Language and Literature*, 18(3), 2009).

Long-standing debates and future challenges

The strengthening of the connection between stylistics and the study of 'real' readers would have the advantage of avoiding the repetition of debates between stylisticians and other literary scholars that have re-occurred cyclically since the 1960s (see, for example, Fowler 1971; Fish 1980; Mackay 1996; Toolan 1996; Short *et al.* 1998). Within such debates, stylisticians have mainly been accused of claiming a degree of objectivity in their work that does not properly apply, both in relation to the selection of linguistic features for analysis and to the interpretative implications of the findings of their analyses. While some mutual stereotyping tends to occur in such debates, it is probably fair to acknowledge that the confident tone of some work in stylistics may be mistaken for the belief that linguistic analysis enables one to arrive at the 'true' or 'best' interpretation of a text. Most stylisticians seem to agree that they do not aim for some general (and indeed suspect) notion of objectivity, but rather that their goal is to produce textual analyses that are explicit, rigorous, systematic and replicable (e.g. Wales 2001: 373; Simpson 2004: 4). Nonetheless, stylisticians fundamentally differ from some of their critics due to their belief that language matters, namely that the linguistic choices made in texts affect readers' interpretations, so that stylistic analysis can be used to explain how particular interpretations came about. Simpson puts it as follows:

> While linguistic features do not of themselves constitute a text's 'meaning', an account of linguistic features nonetheless serves to ground a stylistic interpretation and to help explain why, for the analyst, certain types of meaning are possible.

(Simpson 2004: 2)

As mentioned above, new computer-aided methods in text analysis can, in some cases, be used to select distinctive linguistic features independently of the analyst's intuitions. Similarly, a greater consideration for real readers' interpretations can make stylistic analysis less vulnerable to the accusation that the analysis is arbitrarily used to prove the validity and superiority of the analyst's own interpretation of a text.

Another long-standing debate which is likely to re-occur in future concerns the status of 'literature' or 'literary language' as opposed to other bodies of texts or uses of language. As mentioned earlier, within the formalist tradition, 'poetic language' was defined in terms of both formal characteristics (deviation, parallelism) and function (defamiliarisation, a focus on the text for its own sake). Such definitions were subsequently found to be inadequate when considering the variety of the texts that are called 'literary', and the creativity of the texts that are called 'non-literary', but they remained influential when the issue was reformulated in different terms. As mentioned earlier, Cook (1994) restates the formalists' insights in terms of subsequent developments in linguistics and artificial intelligence when he defines literary discourse in terms of what he calls 'discourse deviation' – the phenomenon whereby linguistic deviation and patterns result in the refreshment of the readers' pre-existing schemata. In other words, Cook defines literary discourse in terms of a particular kind of interaction between textual features and readers' background knowledge that is likely to result in some change in the readers' pre-existing assumptions. Carter and Nash (1990) define 'literariness' as a bundle of properties that include textual phenomena (e.g. linguistic patterns across a whole text), the communicative situation (e.g. a spatial and temporal detachment between the producer and the receivers of a text), and particular goals and dispositions in both writers and readers (e.g. the intention to defamiliarise the reader's world view).

Stylisticians do not always state explicitly their position in relation to the status of literary language. When they do, it is usually to point out that no clear-cut distinction can be made between the language of literature and the language associated with other types of activities, and that texts come to be regarded as 'literary' for a variety of complex historical, cultural and ideological reasons (e.g. Carter 2004). The debate as to what, if anything, makes literary texts 'special' is likely to continue, however.

Summary

Stylistics is the study of the relationship between language choice, contexts and effects. 'General' stylistics is concerned with the description and explanation of language variation across different genres and contexts of use. 'Literary' stylistics is concerned with how linguistic choices and patterns in texts contribute to particular interpretations. Stylistics has developed in close connection with other areas of linguistics, and currently shares with other branches of linguistics a concern for ideology and cognition. It is also benefiting from developments in corpus linguistics. Literary stylistics remains controversial due to its position at the interface between linguistics and literary criticism.

Related topics

cognitive linguistics; corpus linguistics; critical discourse analysis; systemic functional linguistics

Further reading

Lambrou, M. and Stockwell, P. (eds) (2007) *Contemporary Stylistics*, London: Routledge. (A collection of papers by new scholars in the field, written in an accessible style.)

Leech, G. N. and Short, M. H. (2007) *Style in Fiction*, 2nd edn, London: Longman. (The second edition of one of the landmarks volumes in stylistics, with two new chapters.)

Toolan, M. (1998) *Language in Literature: An Introduction to Stylistics*, London: Hodder Arnold. (An accessible introduction to stylistics.)

Verdonk, P. (2002) *Stylistics*, Oxford: Oxford University Press. (A concise and accessible introduction to stylistics.)

Weber, J.-J. (ed.) (1996) *The Stylistics Reader: From Roman Jakobson to the Present*, London: Hodder Arnold. (A collection of classic papers on stylistics.)

References

Adolphs, S. (2006) *Introducing Electronic Text Analysis: A Practical Guide for Language and Literary Studies*, Abingdon and New York: Routledge.

Archer, D. (2007) 'Computer-assisted literary stylistics', in M. Lambrou and P. Stockwell (eds) *Contemporary Stylistics*, London: Routledge.

Bally, C. (1909) *Traité de stylistique française*, Heidelberg: Carl Winters.

Biber, D. (1988) *Variation Across Speech and Writing*, Cambridge: Cambridge University Press.

Black, E. (2006) *Pragmatic Stylistics*, Edinburgh: Edinburgh University Press.

Burrows, J. (1987) *Computation into Criticism: A Study of Jane Austen's Novels, and An Experiment in Method*, Oxford: Oxford University Press.

Burton, D. (1982) 'Through glass darkly: through dark glasses', in R. Carter (ed.) *Language and Literature*, London: Allen and Unwin.

Carter, R. A. (1989) 'Directions in the teaching and study of English Stylistics', in M. Short (ed) *Reading, Analysing and Teaching Literature*. London: Longman.

Carter, R. (2004). *Language and Creativity: The Art of Common Talk*, London: Routledge.

Carter, R. and Nash, W. (1990) *Seeing Through Language*, Oxford: Blackwell.

Carter, R. and Simpson, P. (eds) (1989) *Language, Discourse and Literature*, London: Unwin Hyman.

Cook, G. (1994) *Discourse and Literature: The Interplay of Form and Mind*, Oxford: Oxford University Press.

Coupland, N. (2007) *Style: Language Variation and Identity*, Cambridge: Cambridge University Press.

Crystal, D. and Davy, D. (1969) *Investigating English Style*, London: Longman.

Culpeper, J. (1998) '(Im)politeness in drama', in J. Culpeper, M. Short, and P. Verdonk (eds) *Studying Drama: From Text to Context*, London: Routledge.

——(2001) *Language and Characterisation: People in Plays and Other Texts*, London: Longman.

——(2002) 'Computers, language and characterisation: an analysis of six characters in Romeo and Juliet', in U. Melander-Marttala, C. Ostman and M. Kytö (eds) *Conversation in Life and in Literature: Papers from the ASLA Symposium, Association Suedoise de Linguistique Appliquee* (ASLA), 15. Universitetstryckeriet: Uppsala.

Culpeper, J., Short, M. and Verdonk, P. (eds) (1998) *Exploring the Language of Drama: From Text to Context*, London: Routledge.

Dancygier, B. (2005) 'Blending and narrative viewpoint: Jonathan Raban's travels through mental spaces', *Language and Literature* 14: 99–127.

Emmott, C. (1997) *Narrative Comprehension: A Discourse Perspective*, Oxford: Oxford University Press.

Emmott, C., Sanford, A. J. and Morrow, L. I. (2006) 'Capturing the attention of readers? Stylistic and psychological perspectives on the use and effect of text fragmentation in narratives', *Journal of Literary Semantics* 35: 1–30.

Enkvist, N. E. (1973) *Linguistic Stylistics*, The Hague: Mouton.

Fabb, N. and Halle, M. (2008) *Metre in Poetry: A New Theory*, Cambridge: Cambridge University Press.

Fauconnier, G. and Turner, M. (2002) *The Way We Think: Conceptual Blending and the Mind's Hidden Complexities*, New York: Basic Books.

Fish, S. (1970) 'Literature in the reader: affective stylistics', *New Literary History* 2: 123–62.

——(1980) *Is there a Text in this Class?*, Cambridge, MA: Harvard University Press.

Fowler, R. (1971) *The Languages of Literature*, London: Routledge.

——(1977) *Linguistics and the Novel*, London: Methuen.

——(1986) *Linguistic Criticism*, Oxford: Oxford University Press.

Freeman, D. C. (1993) '"According to my bond": *King Lear* and recognition', *Language and Literature* 2: 1–18.

——(1995) '"Catch[ing] the nearest way": *Macbeth* and cognitive metaphor', *Journal of Pragmatics* 24: 689–708.

Gavins, J. (2007) *Text World Theory: An Introduction*, Edinburgh: Edinburgh University Press.

Hall, G. (2002) 'The year's work in stylistics: 2002', *Language and Literature* 12: 353–70.

Halliday, M. A. K. (1971) 'Linguistic function and literary style: an inquiry into the language of William Golding's *The Inheritors*', in S. Chatman (ed.) *Literary Style: A Symposium*, Oxford: Oxford University Press.

——(1978) *Language as Social Semiotic: The Social Interpretation of Language and Meaning*, London: Edward Arnold.

Herman, V. (1995) *Dramatic Discourse*, London: Routledge.

Herman, D. (ed.) (2003) *Narrative Theory and the Cognitive Sciences*, Stanford, CA: Center for the Study of Language and Information.

Hickey, L. (ed.) (1989) *The Pragmatics of Style*, London: Routledge.

Hoover, D. L. (1999) *Language and Style in The Inheritors*, Lanham, MD: University Press of America.

——(2002) 'Frequent word sequences and statistical analysis', *Literary and Linguistic Computing* 17: 157–80.

Jakobson, R. (1960) 'Closing statement: linguistics and poetics', in T. A. Sebeok (ed.) *Style in Language*, Cambridge, MA: MIT Press.

Jakobson, R. and Lévi-Strauss, C. (1962) '"Les chats" de Baudelaire', *L'Homme* 2: 5–21.

Lakoff, G. and Johnson, M. (1980) *Metaphors We Live By*, Chicago: University of Chicago Press.

Lambrou, M. and Stockwell, P. (eds) (2007) *Contemporary Stylistics*, London: Routledge.

Leech, G. N. (1966). *English in Advertising: A Linguistic Study of Advertising in Great Britain*, London: Longman.

——(1969) *A Linguistic Guide to English Poetry*, London: Longman.

——(1992) 'Pragmatic principles in Shaw's "You never can tell"', in M. Toolan (ed.) *Language, Text and Context*, London: Routledge.

Leech, G. N. and Short, M. H. (1981) *Style in Fiction*, London: Longman.

Louw, B. (1997) 'The role of corpora in critical literary appreciation', in A. Wichmann, S. Fligelstone, A. McEnery and G. Knowles (eds) *Teaching and Language Corpora*, London: Longman.

McIntyre, D. (2007) 'Integrating multimodal analysis and the stylistics of drama: a multimodal perspective on Ian McKellen's *Richard III*', *Language and Literature* 17: 309–34.

Mackay, R. (1996) 'Mything the point: a critique of objective stylistics', *Language and Communication* 16: 81–93.

Mahlberg, M. (2007) 'A corpus stylistic perspective on Dickens's *Great Expectations*', in M. Lambrou and P. Stockwell (eds) *Contemporary Stylistics*, London: Routledge.

Milic, L. T. (1967) *A Quantitative Approach to the Style of Jonathan Swift*, Berlin: Mouton de Gruyter.

Mills, S. (1995) *Feminist Stylistics*, London: Routledge.

Mukařovský, J. (1964) 'Standard language and poetic language', in P. L. Garvin (ed.) *A Prague School Reader on Aesthetics, Literary Structure and Style*, Washington, DC: Georgetown University Press.

Palmer, A. (2004) *Fictional Minds*, Lincoln, NE and London: University of Nebraska Press.

Pilkington, A. (2000) *Poetic Effects: A Relevance Theory Perspective*, Amsterdam: John Benjamins.

Popova, Y. (2002) 'The figure in the carpet: discovery or re-cognition', in E. Semino and J. Culpeper (eds) *Cognitive Stylistics: Language and Cognition in Text Analysis*, Amsterdam: John Benjamins.

Ramachandran, V. S. (2004) *A Brief Tour of Human Consciousness: From Impostor Poodles to Purple Numbers*, New York: Profile Books.

Richards, I. A. (1929) *Practical Criticism*, London: Kegan Paul.

Semino, E. (1997) *Language and World Creation in Poems and Other Texts*, London: Longman.

Semino, E. and Culpeper, J. (eds) (2002) *Cognitive Stylistics: Language and Cognition in Text Analysis*, Amsterdam: John Benjamins.

Semino, E. and Short, M. (2004) *Corpus Stylistics: Speech, Writing and Thought Presentation in a Corpus of English Writing*, London: Routledge.

Shklovsky, V. (1965) 'Art as technique', in L. Lemon and M. J. Reis (eds) *Russian Formalist Criticism*, Lincoln: University of Nebraska Press.

Short, M. (1989a) 'Discourse analysis and the analysis of drama', in R. Carter and P. Simpson (eds) *Language, Discourse and Literature*, London: Unwin Hyman.

——(1996) *Exploring the Language of Poems, Plays and Prose*, London: Longman.

Short, M. (ed.) (1989b) *Reading, Analysing and Teaching Literature*, London: Longman.

Short, M., Freeman, D. C., van Peer, W. and Simpson, P. (1998) 'Stylistics, criticism and myth representation again: squaring the circle with Ray Mackay's subjective solution to all problems', *Language and Literature* 7: 39–50.

Simpson, P. (1993) *Language, Ideology and Point of View*, London: Routledge.

——(2004) *Stylistics: A Resource Book for Students*, London: Routledge.

Spitzer, L. (1948) *Linguistics and Literary History*, Princeton, NJ: Princeton University Press.

Stockwell, P. (2002) *Cognitive Poetics: An Introduction*, London: Routledge.

Stubbs, M. (1996) *Text and Corpus Analysis: Computer-assisted Studies of Language and Culture*, Oxford: Blackwell.

Sweetser, E. (2006) 'Whose rhyme is whose reason? Sound and sense in *Cyrano de Bergerac*', *Language and Literature* 15: 29–54.

Thorne, J. P. (1965) 'Stylistics and generative grammars', *Journal of Linguistics* 1: 49–59.

Toolan, M. (1996) 'Stylistics and its discontents; or, getting off the Fish "hook"', in J.-J. Weber (ed.) *The Stylistics Reader: From Roman Jakobson to the Present*, London: Hodder Arnold.

Toolan, M. (ed.) (1992) *Language, Text and Context*, London: Routledge.

Tsur, R. (1992) *Toward a Theory of Cognitive Poetics*, Amsterdam: Elsevier.

van Peer, W. (1986) *Stylistics and Psychology*, London: Croom Helm.

Wales, K. (2001) *A Dictionary of Stylistics*, 2nd edn, London: Longman.

Watson, G. and Zyngier, S. (eds) (2007) *Literature and Stylistics for Language Learners: Theory and Practice*, Basingstoke: Palgrave Macmillan.

Weber, J.-J. (1992) *Critical Analysis of Fiction*, Amsterdam: Rodopi.

——(2004) 'A new paradigm for literary studies, or: the teething troubles of cognitive poetics', *Style* 38(4): 515–23.

Werth, P. (1999) *Text Worlds: Representing Conceptual Space in Discourse*, London: Longman.

Widdowson, H. G. (1975) *Stylistics and the Teaching of Literature*, London: Longman.

——(1982) 'Othello in person', in R. Carter (ed.) *Language and Literature: An Introductory Reader in Stylistics*. London: Allen and Unwin.

——(1992) *Practical Stylistics*, Oxford: Oxford University Press.

Zwaan, R. A. (1993) *Aspects of Literary Comprehension*, Amsterdam: John Benjamins.

Part V
Descriptions of language for applied linguistics

39

Grammar

Michael Swan

Introduction

This chapter deals with grammar in the narrower sense; that is to say, it refers not to all linguistic systems, but specifically to syntax and morphology. Narrow or not, this is a vast subject, relevant to very many topics which come under the heading of 'applied linguistics'. I have shaped what follows partly in order to avoid excessive overlap with other chapters in this volume, and have therefore said relatively little about some matters which are dealt with in detail elsewhere. I begin by discussing briefly what grammar is, why languages need it and how they use it. This is followed by a word on the remarkable proliferation of grammatical models in present-day linguistic theory, and a note on the relationship, such as it is, between these models and applications of linguistics. I then look briefly at applied linguistics at its most ambitious: the period when it was believed that investigating the nature of language would inform us about the world; and at later offshoots of this line of thought. A short note on the language-mind-brain relationship is followed by two more extensive sections, on grammar in mother tongue education and foreign language teaching, respectively.

What is grammar?

Not all meanings can be conveyed by simply stringing words together in an unstructured way. For one thing, unsupported vocabulary cannot specify the direction of causal and other relationships. Putting together the words *man*, *dog* and *bite*, or *floorboards*, *water* and *under*, for instance, leaves important questions unanswered. A second limitation is to do with modality: no string of words on its own can indicate whether it is intended as a statement, a question, an expression of uncertainty, a negation or some other type of communication. And finally, words are mostly labels for classes of things, qualities, processes and so on, whereas we most often talk about particular members of these classes. So in order to construct references to particulars, we need to group words: while the words *my*, *old* and *dog*, for example, taken separately, can each refer to millions of entities, the phrase *my old dog* pins down one specific individual. In more complex communications, grouping may not be transparent, so that we need ways of showing what goes with what.

Languages solve these problems essentially by the devices that we call 'syntax' and 'morphology', supplementing purely lexical information by establishing ordering and movement conventions, changing the forms of words, and using function words (like English *may* or *not*). These devices – grammar – make it possible to distinguish, for example, *dog bites man* from *man bites dog* or (the Latin equivalents) *canis hominem mordet* from *canem homo mordet*. They permit the expression of modality, distinguishing for instance *floorboards are under water* from *are floorboards under water*, *floorboards may be under water* and *floorboards are not under water*. And they facilitate grouping, showing where necessary which words go together (*small man bites big dog* as against *big man bites small dog*).

Simple in principle, grammar generates considerable complexity in practice. Given a way of grouping words, you can group groups of words, and group groups of groups of words, and so on upwards. Grammatical mechanisms also give rise to, and operate differentially on, distinct word classes. And ordering and movement conventions can be applied in complicated ways to whole assemblies of language. In addition, once grammar is in place it turns out to be useful for many purposes beyond those identified above. The world's languages put time relations, number distinctions, evidentiality, social relationships and any number of other meanings into their grammars – notions that *can* be handled by vocabulary, but for which grammar seems to be a convenient vehicle. All of this is somewhat analogous to the elaboration that characterizes computer programs, so simple in their basic mechanism – sequences of 0 and 1 – and so complex and multi-functional in their applications.

The conventional syntax-morphology distinction – like that between grammar and lexis – is not always clear-cut, and varies somewhat in scope from one language to another. Also, languages seem to balance off their use of the different devices to a certain extent, with some relying largely on morphology while others put a heavier load on syntax. There is an old belief that all languages are pretty well equally complex, with simplicity in one area being counterbalanced by complexity in another. There is, however, no good evidence for this, and it may be that some languages just are simpler than others. Certainly there are languages in which morphology, in particular, reaches baroque levels of complication – gender-marking in the West African language Fula (McWhorter 2001: 188–9) is a striking example. However that may be, some aspects of complexity seem to be limited in all languages in the interests of processing efficiency, so as to facilitate production and comprehension (Hawkins 2004).

Models of grammar: a bewildering variety

Grammarians attempt to establish categories of linguistic elements and operations which can capture accurately and economically the nature of particular languages. They may also wish to go further, setting up theoretical models at a level of abstraction which will accommodate the multifarious structural features of all possible human languages, and thus illuminate the nature of language in general. In addition, some linguists are concerned to show how the structure of language enables children to perform the astonishing feat of learning their mother tongues. Because the grammatical systems of languages are so complex, and differ so greatly, there is room for substantial disagreement about what kind of generalized model can best account for the facts. It is in fact remarkable how much controversy there is about the analysis of a phenomenon, language, for which we have so much data – at least as much as many physical scientists have for the subjects of their investigations. A glance at the index of a linguistics encyclopaedia will direct the reader to a daunting range of different 'grammars': transformational, phrase structure, dependency, word, functional, systemic, construction, cognitive and dozens of others. (For accounts of some of these, see the chapters on generative grammar, systemic functional linguistics, and cognitive linguistics in this volume.)

These differences partly reflect researchers' choice of focus. Linguistic structures can be investigated primarily in terms of their internal characteristics, or on the basis of the functions they perform. This formal-functional divide can also bring with it important differences of opinion. Formally oriented grammarians tend to account for shared features of languages – universals – in the belief that these reflect features of the language faculty in the human mind. Proponents of this view may postulate innate knowledge of what defines the range of possible grammars – so-called 'Universal Grammar' (UG) – on the grounds that we allegedly know things about our language for which the input provides inadequate evidence (the 'poverty of the stimulus' argument). A commonly used example concerns 'island constraints'. In an English complex sentence, a word like *who* or *what* can be used in a main clause to question an element in a dependent clause in some structures, but not others. For example:

You said that this nut goes on the wing mirror.
 → *What did you say that this nut goes on?*
John thinks this nut goes on the wing mirror.
 → *What does John think this nut goes on?*
You asked Paul whether this nut goes on the wing mirror.
 → **What did you ask Paul whether this nut goes on?*

It is not a straightforward matter to establish a reliable innate rule which will account for the complex range of such constraints, generating correct structures like the first two examples above and disallowing incorrect structures, and which will work for the equivalent constraints in all languages (since UG, if it exists, is necessarily language-independent). Models which assume innate knowledge of grammar therefore tend to operate at a very high and, in the view of some critics, implausible level of abstraction and complexity. The difficulty of the enterprise is strikingly demonstrated by the remarkable changes of course of one prominent approach – Chomskyan generative grammar – over the last half century, with one key idea after another (e.g. transformations, government and binding, principles and parameters) being modified out of recognition or finally abandoned.

Functionally oriented grammarians, in contrast, regard language universals primarily as reflecting the structural features that languages need to have in order to do what they do. Language acquisition and use, for many grammarians of this persuasion, can be accounted for on the basis of general principles of cognition rather than any wired-in knowledge unique to language. 'Usage-based associative learning' models attribute to the child learner a powerful unconscious capacity to detect regularities in the input, and to abstract patterns at increasing levels of generality (N. Ellis 2003, and this volume). Knowledge of constraints like those illustrated above, in this view, is perhaps explicable simply on the grounds that sentences like the incorrect ones have never occurred in the input, and have therefore never been registered as possible by the child's inbuilt monitor. While most grammatical models have little to say about how the proposed structures and operations might be instantiated in the brain, associative learning or 'connectionist' models incorporate hypotheses, in principle testable, concerning the possible functioning of neural networks.

Grammar and the world: models and applications

For a model of language to support investigation of a real-world problem, two things are necessary. The model must give reliable linguistic information, and it must do so in terms

Michael Swan

which can be applied effectively to the problem in question, as Crystal (2001) makes clear in relation to a case in clinical linguistics:

> In the field of grammar, it is easy to spot such morphological errors as *mouses* or *tooked*; far less easy to work out what is going on when there are problems with sentence structure. One six-year-old boy was able to say such sentences as *That car is red* and *My car is in the garage*, but could not be persuaded to say *That's a red car* or *My red car*. Asked 'Is that a red car or a yellow car?' he would become non-fluent and produce such strings as *A car – a red*, losing control of the clause structure as a whole. The problem turned out to be a difficulty in simultaneously using a developed noun phrase within a clause: as long as the noun phrase consisted solely of a determiner + noun, there was no problem. But asked to insert an adjective (or any other extra element), and the whole sentence structure broke down. To appreciate the nature of this difficulty requires the analyst not only to make an appropriate syntactic analysis but also to appreciate the implications of a syntactic hierarchy for mental processing. Both syntactic and psycholinguistic perspectives are essential.
>
> *(Crystal 2001: 675)*

It is clear from Crystal's example that, while a reasonably fine-grained analysis is valuable for the clinical linguist, it needs to stay relatively close to the surface of the language. A more abstract analysis – perhaps of greater value to a generative grammarian – might be more difficult to apply and less directly illuminating. (For further discussion in the area of clinical linguistics, see Perkins and Howard, this volume.) This is likely to be the case for many other applications of grammatical models to real-world problems, such as forensic linguistics (Rock, this volume), stylistics (Semino, this volume) or language teaching (see discussion below). Computational linguistics, in contrast, is an area where more complex models may be indispensable. Attempts to create analogues to the human language faculty, for such purposes as machine translation or machine reading, depend crucially on parsing algorithms, which can perhaps only operate successfully on the basis of relatively sophisticated grammatical analyses.

Grammar as a window on the world

Languages are used to convey messages about the world, so it seems reasonable to suppose that their structure must in one way or another reflect that of the world, at least as this is perceived by human beings. Given that we analyze our experience in terms of situations and events, and that we identify participants in these, it is not surprising that language structure distinguishes ways of referring to situations and events (prototypically verbs), from ways of identifying participants (prototypically nouns). Cognitive grammarians, indeed (e.g. Langacker 2008), see language structure as reflecting in quite detailed respects, albeit at an abstracted and metaphorical level, our conceptual and perceptual engagement with the physical world.

For classical Western philosophers like Aristotle and Plato, the relationship between language and the world was such that linguistic structure could in fact be taken as a key to the organization of reality: the categories into which Aristotle analyzed the physical world coincided with the grammatical categories of the Greek language (Allan 2007: 44). Grammar was, so to speak, a window on the world. The structure of language and the structure of logic were also seen as being closely linked, so that a proper understanding of Greek and Latin grammar was taken to provide a basis for sound argument (Allan 2007: chs 3, 4). These ideas continued through later history. The 'speculative' grammarians of the late Middle Ages saw grammatical structure as mirroring the structure of God's creation – Latin *speculum* means 'mirror' – (Allan 2007: 155–7), while the rationalist philosophers of the seventeenth and eighteenth centuries saw grammar as reflecting the structure of the human mind, as do present-day generative grammarians. Leibniz believed that a tidied-up language, in which meanings could be expressed without ambiguity, would allow for precise and conclusive logical argument, a view echoed 300 years later by Bertrand Russell (Russell 2004: 540, 1919: 172).

A variant of the belief that language is a window on the world is found in the notion of linguistic relativity. In this view, any language gives us information not about an objective outside world, but about the subjective reality perceived by its speakers – indeed, it shapes that reality through the kinds of meaning encoded in its grammar. Indo-European languages, to take one example, typically use the verbal system to express certain kinds of time relation, whereas native American or Australian languages may not conceptualize time in the grammar at all. On the other hand, the choice of verb forms in some languages (e.g. Bulgarian, Turkish, some native American languages) may indicate evidentiality, showing, for instance, whether a speaker was an eyewitness to what he/she is reporting. The view that differences of this kind may entail different perspectives on external reality goes back to philosophers such as von Humboldt in the early nineteenth century, and was pursued energetically by American anthropological linguists, notably Sapir and Whorf (see, for example, Sapir 1921), 100 years later. For some recent discussions in this field, see Gentner and Goldin-Meadow (2003).

Grammar, the mind and the brain

Many grammarians claim that the characteristics of language structure must tell us something about the mental organ responsible for it. While there is considerable controversy in this area, it certainly seems highly possible that the organization of language can provide clues to the structure and operation of the mind and brain. A much-debated question concerns modularity: does the human mind have a special module, or modules, for handling language, distinct from the faculties involved in other aspects of cognition? There is evidence that language learning, storage and use are at least partly independent of other cognitive functions. For example, there seems to be a 'critical period' related specifically to language acquisition: after a certain age, most people do not achieve native-like command of all aspects of a new language. And in some recorded cases where young children have been deprived of linguistic input and only started learning their mother tongue when older, their output has remained defective and ungrammatical. Confirmatory evidence for modularity comes from brain-damaged patients. Strokes or accidents sometimes cause people to lose some or all of their ability to use language, while leaving their other mental faculties apparently unimpaired. Conversely, it is possible for people with severe mental handicap to exhibit normal or even exceptional linguistic competence.

Knowledge of how language works can feed into investigations of the mind and brain, while information can also flow in the other direction, with the results of brain research confirming or extending our understanding of linguistic structure (Perkins and Howard, this volume). Studies of brain-damaged patients have long since demonstrated associations between specific parts of the brain and particular aspects of language behaviour, with lesions in one or other area being found to correlate with problems of comprehension, fluent production, control of syntactic and lexical categories, or handling of meaning. Our knowledge of such associations has been greatly extended and refined by modern functional neuro-imaging techniques, which make it possible to monitor changes in blood flow and electrical activity during language use, and thus to link patterns of excitation in specific areas with different categories of linguistic activity. However, the data that are being collected are complex and difficult to analyze, and while knowledge is growing very rapidly, much more work will be necessary before a clear picture emerges. For the moment, we still understand little about the physical correlates of our mental and linguistic representations of the world. (For detailed discussion, see Ahlsén, this volume.)

Grammar in society; standardization and education

For most people, perhaps, linguistics and everyday life intersect primarily in the area of education. Most societies have one language that is the principal vehicle of cultural transmission. This may be a high-status classical or foreign language (like Sumerian in ancient Mesopotamia, Latin in the European Middle Ages, Classical Arabic in the Islamic world, or the former colonial languages in some African countries); it may be one of several languages that are spoken in a country (like English in the United States); or it may be the single language of a mainly monolingual culture (like Icelandic or Hungarian). Whatever the situation, the study of that language necessarily features centrally in school curricula. Education and language study can indeed sometimes become almost synonymous. A large part of the mediaeval European educational syllabus, the 'trivium', was made up of grammar (correct language use), dialectic (language for valid argument) and rhetoric (language for effective public communication). Although the link between language, logic and the world later became less generally accepted, classical languages enjoyed continuing prestige in European education up to comparatively recently. Indeed, the study of their grammar is still often seen as having a special if ill-defined value as a training for the mind, and they may continue to feature in some educational curricula out of inertia long after outliving their original purpose, as Latin does in some British schools.

Even where a single local language is spoken and carries the culture of the community, different regional or social groups are likely to speak different varieties, and these differences may cause communication problems. This creates a need for language standardization, which is typically met by the emergence or designation of one variety as the national standard; this variety then becomes the main vehicle of administration, legislation, business, education and publishing. The favoured variety may simply be the dialect spoken by that section of the population which, through historical accident, has come to be socially and politically dominant, as in Britain and many other countries. Or it may be a deliberate creation, codified out of a need to facilitate communication in a country where no single standard has arisen, as happened for instance in Norway after it gained independence from Denmark (Foley 1997: 405). (See also Wee, this volume.)

The prestige and utility of a standard variety generates social and institutional pressure to master its conventions. Non-standard speakers must learn a new dialect in order to achieve literacy and operate effectively in society. Educational systems may use language as a social filter, putting such a premium on linguistic correctness that higher education and many career paths are effectively closed to those who fail to master the prestige variety, whatever their strengths in other areas. Grammar often has a starring role in this connection. Grammatical correctness, after all, has a powerful symbolic value: getting your language right implies that you can obey rules and respect authority. All of this can mean that a substantial part of an educational curriculum may be given up to study of the standard language. Even those who already speak this variety can have to work hard to master the written code: this is in a sense a foreign language for everyone, and may not be at all easy to learn. In French, to take a somewhat bizarre instance, the spelling of the written language preserves a number of grammatical distinctions which have long since disappeared from speech because of changes in pronunciation; so that French-speaking schoolchildren actually have to develop an explicit knowledge of older French grammar in order to be able to spell correctly. Without this knowledge, they cannot know whether to write, for instance, [aʃte] as *acheter, acheté, achetés, achetée, achetées, achetai, achetais, achetait* or *achetaient* – various forms of the verb for 'to buy' which are pronounced identically by most younger speakers of standard European French.

Unfortunately, elevating one variety of a language to standard status easily entails the devaluation of others, which may be stigmatized as 'incorrect' forms of speech, used by ignorant or uneducated people who have 'not learnt correct grammar', or who 'cannot be troubled to get things right'. This attitude is common in Britain, although all dialects of English have their own history, going back to the distinct forms of speech of the various early mediaeval Germanic and Scandinavian invaders, and although all well-preserved dialects have their own rich and systematic grammars, however much these may diverge from that of their standard counterpart. Interestingly, this is generally easier to accept for 'remote' dialects. Someone from Oxfordshire who says 'I wants them papers what I give you yesterday' may well be criticized for 'failing' to produce standard grammar. In contrast, a Scot who says 'He'll can tell us the morn' ('He'll be able to tell us tomorrow') is more easily seen as speaking an independent variety with its own rule system. In fact, though, the Oxfordshire speaker, just like the Scot, is using forms which are historically rooted and regular and correct in his or her dialect, however much they may upset the standard speaker next door.

Standard languages often acquire a body of prescriptive rules which are devised by individuals in the belief that their languages need regulating, tidying up or protecting against change, and which are frequently codified in 'usage guides'. Where one form is prescribed at the expense of another, the favoured alternative is often the more formal, written variant, or the older form: people in literate societies tend to give more prestige to the written language than to speech, and to regard language change as evidence of falling standards (Aitchison 2001). Many English prescriptive rules were laid down by eighteenth- and nineteenth-century grammarians, often because they believed that English grammar should imitate Latin, a language with higher prestige. Typical examples are the old condemnation of 'split infinitives' like *to boldly go* (a Latin infinitive is a single word, so cannot be split), or the lingering superstition that a preposition is a bad word to end a sentence with (Latin clauses do not end in prepositions, and anyway, it was felt, a *pre*position should logically *pre*cede). Logic is often invoked to condemn sentences like *It's me* or *John and me saw a good film* (both typical of informal standard British English): a nominative (subject) form is said to be 'logically' required in both cases. However, the choice between *I* and *me* depends in complex ways on syntactic environment and level of formality, and is not determined by a simple rule of the kind that works for pronouns in, say, Latin, Russian or German. Grammatical case systems actually vary considerably across languages, and many languages organize themselves in ways that cut right across typical European subject-object categories. To condemn *John and me saw* on the 'logical' grounds that 'subjects are nominative' is rather like insisting that penguins should get up in the air because 'birds fly'.

As Pinker points out (1994: 374), many prescriptive rules are so psychologically unnatural that only those with access to the right kind of education can learn to observe them. Once acquired they can serve as shibboleths, differentiating the elite from the rest ('I'm better than you because I get my pronouns right.'). To admit that these rules are mistaken or unimportant would mean abandoning such easy claims to superiority, as well as accepting that the effort expended on learning the rules was wasted. Not surprisingly, therefore, prescriptive rules have long lives.

It is unfortunate that a good deal of time is lost, in some educational systems, by insistence on a command of the standard variety at a level of correctness which goes far beyond any practical value that standardization may have. Uncertainty as to the effectiveness of explicit language instruction can also contribute to inefficiency, as educational philosophy swings from one extreme ('Kids today can't write a correct sentence – bring back grammar!') to the other ('This grammar teaching isn't doing a bit of good – kids today can't write a correct sentence!'). At the time of writing, it seems that the British National Literacy Strategy, brought in in 1998 to improve literacy through explicit grammar instruction, is about to be abandoned as we move into the second phase of the cycle.

However this may be, efficient grammar instruction, up to a point, is surely important in education. If knowledge of a standard language, spoken or written, is advantageous, it is clearly desirable that children be given accurate information at least about those more important aspects of its grammar which they find difficult to get right, in the hope that this may feed into more accurate linguistic performance. Well-informed grammar teaching can have other advantages. It can counteract the devaluation of non-standard dialects and their speakers by providing a more accurate view of language variation. It can perhaps help to illuminate the ways in which public attitudes can be deliberately manipulated by language (Cook 2003), as did the study of rhetoric in the Middle Ages. And, of course, the study of the workings of the mother tongue has general educational value in the same way as, for instance, the study of biology. Perhaps more so. After all, as Walter has put it (2008): while children are taught about photosynthesis, no child is called on to photosynthesize, but all children use language.

Grammar in foreign language teaching

Foreign languages have always had an important place in many educational systems, for both cultural and practical reasons. And with the steady growth in international communication, travel and emigration, more and more people now need to learn other languages – especially world languages such as English, Mandarin, Arabic or Spanish. However, foreign language study is time-consuming, expensive and difficult. Any language contains grammatical features which are hard to master after early childhood, whether because of their structural complexity, as with Russian noun morphology, or because they signal abstract meanings which are not easily grasped if the mother tongue does not encode equivalent concepts, as with article systems in Western European languages. Teaching professionals are therefore faced with questions of principle to which there are no very clear answers. How much grammatical correctness should be expected of learners? How much is feasible: *can* foreign-language learners become as native-speaker-like as is considered desirable? What type of grammatical model is appropriate? What kinds of input and practice activity will enable learners to internalize the grammatical systems of the foreign language most effectively? Opinions in these areas have varied very widely, and continue to do so. The learning and teaching of grammar, in Larsen-Freeman's words, is 'the vortex around which many controversies in language teaching have swirled' (2003: 9).

The choice of a grammatical model is perhaps partly a non-question. Granted, theoretical perspectives on first-language acquisition may have some apparent relevance for foreign-language pedagogy. Views about whether 'Universal Grammar' remains available for the learning of new languages can impact on the question of what is, or is not, regarded as teachable and learnable (White 2003; Slabakova 2009). Usage-based models, which see grammatical knowledge as emerging by abstraction from patterns detected in the input (N. Ellis 2003 and this volume), can be invoked in support of 'lexical' approaches. In general, however, foreign language teaching does not seem to depend on specific theoretical models, and attempts to import, say, transformational grammar, cognitive grammar or construction grammar wholesale into the classroom have not been shown to work well. Theoretical grammarians seek relatively abstract generalizations which can be applied to languages and language as a whole. Day-to-day teaching, on the other hand, is directed at people who already have an implicit knowledge of how language works in general, and who are more concerned with language-specific details than with ways in which these details fit into higher-level abstractions.

The most useful kind of grammatical model as a starting-point for teaching, therefore, is arguably descriptive rather than theoretical – the close-to-the-surface picture offered for instance for English by Quirk *et al.* (1985), Huddleston and Pullum (2002), or by the smaller grammars which teachers and students generally use. In this area, pedagogy owes a very considerable debt to linguistic research, past and present. Much of what we know about English grammar was established by early twentieth-century scholars from Jespersen (1909) onwards. More recent work in discourse analysis and related fields has greatly enriched our understanding of grammar above the sentence level. Although language corpora are not new – Jespersen and his contemporaries based their work on substantial written corpora, and even spoken corpora are over half a century old – their exploitation has been transformed out of recognition by our current ability to compile and analyze massive electronic databases of authentic language in use (see Adolphs and Lin, this volume). This makes it possible not only to verify and refine our traditional grammatical descriptions, but also to detect previously unobserved regularities and ongoing changes. Corpus analysis also allows us – in what amounts to a knowledge explosion – to investigate in detail the frontier between grammar and lexis, amassing far more complete and reliable information about the structural behaviour and external relations of individual words and word families than was previously available. In addition, technological developments have made it easier for structural descriptions to cover the whole range of spoken, written and signed language and to explore the significant ways in which these differ (see, for example, Biber *et al.* 1999; Carter and McCarthy 2006; Woll and Sutton-Spence, this volume).

There are, however, crucial differences between descriptive and pedagogic grammars. Most importantly, a pedagogic grammatical description of a language is necessarily fragmentary. Time constraints do not allow language learners to learn, or their teachers to teach, anything approaching the whole of a language. The findings of descriptive grammarians, discourse analysts, corpus researchers or others cannot therefore be fed directly into teaching programmes: they only provide menus, from which course designers must select those high-priority elements that can be taught in the time available. While a descriptive grammar will aim at complete coverage, a pedagogic grammar will consequently miss out or simplify material of lesser practical importance. Further, a pedagogic grammar does not describe a language from a neutral standpoint. Ideally, it provides information which learners do not already possess, glossing over or leaving out what they already know by courtesy of their mother tongue. This may be a great deal. No learners need to be told that a new language has nouns and verbs. For Mandarin speakers, English SVO word order is unproblematic. French-speaking learners take it for granted that English relative clauses follow their nouns, and that they do not contain resumptive pronouns (whereas Japanese learners do need to be told where to put relative clauses, and Farsi-speaking learners do need to learn that, for instance, *That's the man that he sold me the bike* is not grammatical in English). German-speaking students of Italian (unlike Polish learners) need relatively little information about article usage. The very

Michael Swan

boundaries between grammar and vocabulary may be drawn differently for different learners. English *because*-clauses constitute a grammatical topic for students whose mother tongue does not handle clause structure on the European model; however, speakers of most European languages only need to learn that *because* corresponds to *perchè, parce que, weil, fordi, jer* or whatever. English prepositions are vocabulary for Swedish speakers, whose language also has prepositions; for Finnish speakers, whose language expresses the relevant notions mostly by noun-endings, prepositions are a difficult grammatical category. For these and other reasons (Swan 1994) a pedagogic grammar for a given group of learners may look very different indeed from an academic descriptive grammar.

Methodological questions in this area are especially intractable, and find few reliable answers. (For a detailed survey of past and present views on methodology, see Thornbury, this volume.) Does grammar teaching have any effect on learning? Most teachers probably think so, but how can we be sure? If students' grammar improves, is this because of the teaching, or would it have improved anyway as a result of unconscious acquisition processes acting on the input? If grammar teaching does work, how should it be approached? In particular – the key question – how useful is explicit instruction? When students learnt to read and write classical languages, this question was less crucial. In the time necessary to write a Latin sentence, a rule like 'use the subjunctive in indirect questions' could easily be recalled, and the appropriate form of the relevant verb retrieved from a memorized paradigm. Spontaneous speech is a very different matter: structures have to be chosen and forms retrieved far too quickly for conscious control to be exercised. This being so, is systematic explicit attention to structure a valuable starting-point nonetheless, on the basis that one can get from declarative to procedural knowledge of language 'by engaging in the target behaviour ... while temporarily leaning on declarative crutches' (DeKeyser 1998: 49), with a progressive reduction of conscious attention to form (Johnson 2001: 195)? Or is the grammar of a language best learnt incidentally in the context of communicative activity, as many current SLA theorists believe? Or is it pointless to pose the question in such general terms – does the answer depend mainly on the nature of the grammatical feature in question, the personality of the learner, the learning context, or other factors? While a great deal of valuable research has addressed this problem over the last half century or so, we are still a long way from a solution.

Successive approaches to language teaching are often described in terms of pendulum swings between one type of stance and its opposite. Although the metaphor is over-simple (especially in implying that there is no progress), it does have some validity. As a formal code, used to convey meaningful messages, a language necessarily has a dual character. Reflecting this, teaching philosophies oscillate between the two poles of form and meaning, control and freedom, imitation and expression, knowledge and skill, learning and using. At any one time, theorists and researchers claim that they have, at last, got the balance right, unlike the previous generation who, it is now clear, were excessively committed to a formal or functional view of the matter. The role of grammar in all of this – central, marginal or non-existent – depends largely on the current position of the pendulum.

At the time of writing there is a modest rehabilitation of grammar instruction in second language acquisition (SLA) theory, and a partial rejection of the earlier claim of Krashen (1981) and others that explicit grammatical teaching is irrelevant to the acquisition of linguistic competence (see Norris and Ortega 2000; R. Ellis 2006). Theoretically informed attitudes to language teaching are, however, still coloured by the heavily communicative bias of the last thirty years, and are situated well down towards the meaning-freedom-expression-skill-using end of the pendulum swing. Language proficiency is often measured in 'can-do' terms (as in the specifications for the Council of Europe's *Common European Framework* 2001); with the danger that doing things with language may assume more importance than systematically learning the language needed to do the relevant things. Skills and strategies can receive more attention in teaching programmes than grammar, pronunciation and vocabulary. Grammar and pragmatics are often yoked together, to their mutual disadvantage (Swan 2007). Naturalistic 'real-world' activities are widely favoured, in the belief that classroom experience should approximate as closely as feasible to mother-tongue acquisition and use. 'Learner-centred', 'meaning-based', 'holistic', 'discourse', 'discovery', 'process', 'interaction', 'negotiation' and 'strategy' are good things to say. 'Teacher-dominated', 'form-based', 'discrete', 'sentence-level', 'transmission model', 'product', 'memorization', 'repetition' and 'drill' are not so good. The view that 'now, at last, we have got the balance right' surfaces in the common claim that language teaching has moved into a 'postmethod' era (e.g. Kumaravadivelu 2006). As Bell (2003) makes clear, however, postmethod thinking is not at all methodologically neutral. Kumaravadivelu's list of 'macrostrategies' (2006: 201) for language teaching has a powerful communicative orientation: while it refers to such things as negotiated interaction, learner autonomy, intuitive heuristics, social relevance and the raising of cultural consciousness, it has nothing whatever of substance to say about language and how to teach it.

Current orthodoxies, like earlier attitudes, are heavily dependent on hypotheses, often promoted with more assurance than they merit. To cite one among many: some researchers assert that linguistic regularities can only be effectively learnt during genuine communication while learners are carrying out 'real-world' tasks: interlanguage restructuring (it is claimed) is triggered by incidental 'focus on form' and conscious 'noticing' during communicative activity, for instance while resolving communication breakdowns (see, for example, contributions to Doughty and Williams 1998). For criticism of this and some other currently influential hypotheses, see Swan (2005).

Fashionable research interests can easily bias language-teaching content and methodology. This has sometimes been the case recently, for instance, with discourse grammar, pragmatics, the emergence of grammar from lexis, and formulaic language. Some specialists in corpus linguistics have stepped outside their territory to make powerful pedagogic recommendations regarding the use of corpora and 'real' corpus-attested language in teaching materials and practice (for a critical discussion, see Carter 1998; Cook 1998; Widdowson 2003). The specific research context can also create bias. Many scholars in the field have gained the bulk of their experience in 'English as a second language' (ESL) situations, working with university-level learners studying in English-speaking countries. Such learners typically have rich language input outside the classroom, and having studied English for many years at school, they may know far more than they can use effectively. This can naturally encourage a focus on language use, and away from systematic study of the linguistic basics. Unfortunately, theoretically sanctioned approaches such as task-based teaching (Willis 1996; R. Ellis 2003), while suitable for students of this kind, may be far less suitable for many of the world's language learners, who are working under very much tighter time constraints in very different situations. The ESL bias also means that researchers work mostly with multilingual groups; this may explain a baffling feature of present-day mainstream SLA theory: the almost complete neglect of learners' mother tongues, as if these had no relevance to their learning of new languages. (Butzkamm and Caldwell 2009; Cook 2010). It is also worth bearing in mind that experiential-learning models designed for teaching English (a language with few inflections) may not work well for languages which require beginning students to master parts of complex morphological systems.

Despite decades of research and theorizing, we still know little about the acquisition of second-language grammar, and pendulum swings will continue. One thing that could perhaps reduce their amplitude is a more realistic conception of what we are about. Teachers often seem to assume – consciously or unconsciously – that learners should aim at a close approximation to native-speaker competence. This is quite unrealistic: language learning and teaching are difficult, only a relatively small part of a language can be learnt in the time generally available, and limited success is all that can be hoped for. More general recognition of this fact might reduce the recurrent tendency to reject a viable language-teaching approach in the disillusioned belief that it has 'failed', only to replace it with something else that may work no better. In this connection the current interest in English as a lingua franca, and the associated questioning of native-speaker norms as an appropriate target for learners (see, for example, Kirkpatrick and Deterding, this volume), is an extremely constructive development.

Summary and conclusion

Grammatical analysis may not, as classical philosophers believed, give us information about the world. Nor, probably, does it give us a direct insight into the nature of cognition. None the less, the cluster of mechanisms that we call 'grammar' is central to language, and it is language that enables us to conceptualize and theorize about our world, to progressively expand our knowledge, and to consolidate and pass on our discoveries through cultural transmission. This being so, the better we understand grammar – what it is, how it operates in language and languages, how it is acquired, how it is instantiated in the brain – the better our grasp is likely to be of the many human activities and concerns in which language is implicated: from foreign-language teaching at the most practical extreme, through the many other matters that engage the attention of applied linguists, to the very nature of consciousness itself.

Related topics

Many articles in this volume deal with matters discussed or touched on above: in particular those on: clinical linguistics; cognitive linguistics; corpus linguistics; forensic linguistics; generative grammar; key concepts in language learning and education; language emergence; language teaching methodology; neurolinguistics; second language acquisition; sign languages; sociolinguistics; stylistics; systemic functional linguistics; and world Englishes.

Further reading

Aitchison, J. (2001) *Language Change: Progress or Decay?*, Cambridge: Cambridge University Press. (Interesting, well-documented and extremely readable study of attitudes to correctness.)

Dąbrowska, E. (2004) *Language, Mind and Brain*, Edinburgh: Edinburgh University Press. (Brings evidence from a wide range of languages to bear on the question of psychological and neurological constraints on theories of grammar.)

Johnson, K. (2008) *An Introduction to Foreign Language Learning and Teaching*, 2nd edn, Harlow: Pearson Longman. (Excellent survey of the field.)

Moravcsik, E. (2006) *An Introduction to Syntactic Theory*, London: Continuum. (Includes an interesting and accessible comparison of different models.)

Swan, M. (2005) *Grammar*, Oxford: Oxford University Press. (More extensive discussion of some of the topics covered in this article.)

References

Aitchison, J. (2001) *Language Change: Progress or Decay?*, Cambridge: Cambridge University Press.

Allan, K. (2007) *The Western Classical Tradition in Linguistics*, London: Equinox.

Bell, D. M. (2003) 'Method and postmethod: are they really so incompatible?', *TESOL Quarterly* 37(2): 325–36.

Biber, D., Johanssen, S., Leech, G., Conrad, S. and Finegan, E. (1999) *Longman Grammar of Spoken and Written English*, Harlow: Pearson Longman.

Butzkamm, W. and Caldwell, J. (2009) *The Bilingual Reform*, Tübingen: Gunter Narr.

Carter, R. (1998) 'Orders of reality: CANCODE, communication and culture', *ELT Journal* 52(1): 43–56.

Carter, R. and McCarthy, M. (2006) *Cambridge Grammar of English*, Cambridge: Cambridge University Press.

Cook, G. (1998) 'The uses of reality: a reply to Ronald Carter', *ELT Journal* 52(1): 57–63.

——(2003) *Applied Linguistics*, Oxford: Oxford University Press.

——(2010) *Translation*, Oxford: Oxford University Press.

Council of Europe (2001) *Common European Framework of Reference for Languages: Learning, Teaching, Assessment*, Cambridge: Cambridge University Press.

Crystal, D. (2001) 'Clinical linguistics', in M. Aronoff and J. Rees-Miller (eds) *The Handbook of Linguistics*, Oxford: Blackwell.

DeKeyser, R. (1998) 'Beyond focus on form: cognitive perspectives on learning and practicing second language grammar', in C. Doughty and J. Williams (eds) *Focus on Form in Classroom Second Language Acquisition*, Cambridge: Cambridge University Press.

Doughty, C. and Williams, J. (eds) (1998) *Focus on Form in Classroom Second Language Acquisition*, Cambridge: Cambridge University Press.

Ellis, N. (2003) 'Constructions, chunking and connectionism: the emergence of second language structure', in C. J. Doughty and M. H. Long (eds) *The Handbook of Second Language Acquisition*, Oxford: Blackwell.

Ellis, R. (2003) *Task-based Language Teaching and Learning*, Oxford: Oxford University Press.

——(2006) 'Current issues in the teaching of grammar: an SLA perspective', *TESOL Quarterly* 40: 83–107.

Foley, W. (1997) *Anthropological Linguistics*, Oxford: Blackwell.

Gentner, D. and Goldin-Meadow, S. (eds) (2003) *Language in Mind*, Cambridge, MA: MIT Press.

Hawkins, J. (2004) *Efficiency and Complexity in Grammars*, Oxford: Oxford University Press.

Huddleston, R. and Pullum, G. (2002) *The Cambridge Grammar of the English Language*, Cambridge: Cambridge University Press.

Jespersen, O. (1909) *A Modern English Grammar on Historical Principles*, Heidelberg: Winter.

Johnson, K. (2001) *An Introduction to Foreign Language Learning and Teaching*, Harlow: Pearson Longman.

Krashen, S. (1981) *Second Language Acquisition and Second Language Learning*, Oxford: Pergamon.

Kumaravadivelu, B. (2006) *Understanding Language Teaching: From Method to Postmethod*, Cambridge: Cambridge University Press.

Langacker, R. (2008) *Cognitive Grammar: A Basic Introduction*, New York: Oxford University Press.

Larsen-Freeman, D. (2003) *Teaching Language: From Grammar to Grammaring*, Boston: Thomson Heinle.

McWhorter, J. (2001) *The Power of Babel: A Natural History of Language*, London: Heinemann.

Norris, J. and Ortega, L. (2000) 'Effectiveness of L2 instruction: a research synthesis and quantitative meta-analysis', *Language Learning* 50(3): 417–528.

Pinker, S. (1994) *The Language Instinct: How the Mind Creates Language*, London: Allen Lane/the Penguin Press.

Quirk, R., Greenbaum, S., Leech, J. and Svartvik, J. (1985) *A Comprehensive Grammar of the English Language*, Harlow: Pearson Longman.

Russell, B. (1919) *Introduction to Mathematical Philosophy*, London: Allen and Unwin.

——([1946] 2004) *History of Western Philosophy*, London: Routledge.

Sapir, E. (1921) *Language: An Introduction to the Study of Speech*, New York: Harcourt, Brace.

Slabakova, R. (2009) 'L2 fundamentals', in R. Slabakova (ed.) 'The fundamental difference hypothesis twenty years later', *Studies in Second Language Acquisition*, special issue, 31(2): 155–73.

Swan, M. (1994) 'Design criteria for pedagogic language rules', in M. Bygate, A. Tonkyn, and E. Williams (eds) *Grammar and the Language Teacher*, Hemel Hempstead: Prentice Hall.

——(2005) 'Legislation by hypothesis: the case of task-based instruction', *Applied Linguistics* 26(3): 376–401.

——(2007) 'Grammar, meaning and pragmatics: sorting out the muddle', *TESL-EJ* 11(2): A-3. Available at: http://tesl-ej.org

Walter, C. (2008) Conference presentation, IATEFL Poland, Łódź.

White, L. (2003) 'On the nature of interlanguage representation: universal grammar in the second language', in C. J. Doughty and M. H. Long (eds) *The Handbook of Second Language Acquisition*, Oxford: Blackwell.

Widdowson, H. G. (2003) *Defining Issues in English Language Teaching*, Oxford: Oxford University Press.

Willis, J. (1996) *A Framework for Task-based Learning*, Harlow: Pearson Longman.

40

Lexis

Joe Barcroft, Gretchen Sunderman and Norbert Schmitt

A history of the area

The term *lexis*, from the ancient Greek for 'word', refers to all the words in a language, the entire vocabulary of a language. Plato and Aristotle spoke of lexis in terms of how the words of a language can be used effectively. Plato focused on different types of diction and distinguished between *mimesis*, speech involving imitation, and *diegisis*, or simple narration not involving such imitation (see, for example, Gennette 1979). In his discussion of style in *Rhetoric*, Aristotle distinguished between *lexis graphikê* and *lexis agonistikê*, the former referring to 'the most precise style ... to be used in compositions designed for a careful reading' and the latter, which consisted of two aspects (*êthikê* and *pathêtikê*), referring to 'the style of plays written for a full performance on the stage as opposed to those designed for reading' (Sonkowsky 1959: 260). In *Categories*, Aristotle also worked to describe numerous properties of words, including semantic properties of words ('A man and an ox are both "animal"'), words that are synonymous, homonymous, and so forth (see Aristotle 350 BCE).

Many of the important contributions of early Indian linguists, such as Pāṇini, Patañjali, and Bhartrihari, concerned basic properties of words, including the notion of what is invariant (*sphota*) and what is variant (*nāda*) in words and other types of linguistic form. Such work also had an impact on Saussure, a professor of Sanskrit himself, and the development of structural linguistics. Consider, for example, the relationship between the notions of *sphota* and *nāda* and Saussure's distinction between the 'signifier', or the (spoken or written) form of a word, and the 'signified', the mental concept of the word (Saussure 1916).

In the history of modern linguistics, since approximately the middle of the twentieth century, the treatment of lexis has evolved substantially by acknowledging to a greater degree the important and central role of words and lexicalized phrases in the mental representation of linguistic knowledge and in linguistic processing. Within generative linguistics, individual words and the syntactic constraints that they project have come to play an increasingly important role. For example, lexical structure needed to be 'represented categorically at every syntactic level' (Chomsky 1986) in generative-transformational grammar (e.g. the verb 'throw' requires a noun phrase, as in *She threw the ball*, as opposed to the ungrammatical **She threw*). In cognitive linguistics, words and lexicalized chunks play a central role. As a final example, in construction grammar, words and lexical phrases have taken center stage completely because words and lexicalized phrases, as well as syntactic frames in which lexical items can be inserted (e.g. *X causes Y to* …), are viewed as form that can be attached to different types of meaning, blurring previously held distinctions between the domains of lexis and syntax. Linguists and psycholinguists who study lexis are in a unique position because they focus on the place in linguistic analysis and language processing where form (phonological or otherwise) meets meaning at the most basic level.

Key concepts

What is a word?

We often distinguish between what it means to know a word and how we access that information. The mental lexicon is the storage repository for words and the information we know about those words; it is our internal dictionary. Much like a dictionary entry, the mental representation of a word contains information about the spelling, pronunciation, grammatical category, and meaning of the word. But what exactly counts as a word? If we think of a word like *builders*, there are at least three meaningful parts to the word, or morphemes. The free morpheme *build* (a verb) is then combined with a derivational bound morpheme *-er,* and thus changes the word to a noun, *builder.* An inflectional plural morpheme *-s* is then added to finally arrive at *builders.* However, although orthographically an *-s* is added, phonologically the sound is /z/, an allomorph for plural morpheme *-s*. At the most basic level, we know that *builders* are people who build things.

Formal properties of words

Words are a type of linguistic form, but the nature of that form and the physical source that we use to create that form can vary. In spoken languages, we use our vocal tract to produce units of sound, or phonemes, by contrasting features such as +/-voicing (e.g. *ban/pan*). In signed languages, we use hands to produce visual elements that function like phonemes by contrasting features related to location, movement, and hand shape. For example, location distinguishes between the words 'mother' (thumb on the chin) and 'father' (thumb on the forehead) in American Sign Language. In addition to these sources of lexical form, writing systems and tactile forms of communication, such as Braille, allow us to produce and perceive words using alternative means of distinguishing between different lexical forms (graphemic for writing and tactile for Braille).

Semantic properties of words

A basic characteristic of vocabulary is that meaning and form do not always have a one-to-one correspondence. Consider the following items:

- die
- expire
- pass away
- bite the dust
- kick the bucket.
- give up the ghost

The six examples all have the meaning 'to die'. However, several of the items contain more than one word. In some languages, and especially in English, meanings can be represented by multiple words operating as single units. To accommodate the fact that both single and multi-word units can realize meaning, we use the terms *lexeme*, *lexical unit*, and *lexical item*. These interchangeable terms are all defined as 'an item that functions as a single meaning unit, regardless of the number of words it contains'. Thus, all of the above examples are lexemes with similar meanings.

Cases where several forms map onto the same meaning are referred to as *synonymy*. Synonymy is common in languages, but so is the converse, where a single form has several meanings. This can be called either *polysemy* or *homonymy*. The distinction usually revolves around whether the different meaning senses are related or not. *Chip* is usually considered polysemous, in that a *chip* of wood, a computer *chip*, a potato *chip*, and a poker *chip* all have the same underlying concept of being small, thin, and flat(ish). A financial *bank*, a river *bank*, and the *banking* of an airplane when it turns are usually thought of as homonyms, as the meaning senses are totally unrelated.

Often a general area of meaning is covered by a certain set of related words, and is referred to as a *semantic field* or *semantic category*. 'Food' is an example, and the names of various fruits, grains, meats, etc. make up the *lexical set* of words describing this semantic field. In some cases, the meaning of the words in the lexical set is defined by their relationships to the other words in the set. This particularly true with gradable adjectives, as *warm* does not refer to an absolute temperature, but is cooler than *hot* but warmer than *lukewarm*. For instance, 25°C would be considered a warm summer day in Britain, but would be positively cool in a Saudi Arabian summer!

Lexical characteristics of words

What happens in our minds when we see the string of letters making up the word *builders*? Lexical access is the term used to refer to the process of retrieving those words from the lexicon, our mental store of words. Many factors can speed up or slow down the retrieval process. For example, word frequency (how often a particular item appears in a corpus of language data) is highly related to how easily a word can be recognized (see, for example, English Lexicon Project, Washington University in St Louis, http://elexicon.wustl.edu/, a free database that contains lexical characteristics, along with reaction time and accuracy measures from two different experiments, visual lexical decision and naming, studies of 40,481 words and 40,481 nonwords, Balota *et al.* 2007). Based on the data that can be retrieved from the Website, the word *builders* has a frequency of 2,006 and it takes on average 677ms (with 94 per cent accuracy) to recognize it is a word in a lexical decision task. Compare this with a low frequency eight-letter word like *flautist*. *Flautist* requires an average of 1,000ms (with 38 per cent accuracy) to recognize; its word frequency is 24. The frequency effect is quite robust in the process of word recognition.

Frequency is only one of many lexical characteristics that can affect lexical access. The number of derivations a word has (word family size) can also affect speed of processing. Another is the number of orthographic neighbors a word has. An orthographic neighbor is any word differing by a single letter from the target word, respecting length and letter position (Coltheart *et al.* 1977). The ability to recognize a word can be affected by the number of neighbors it has. For example, based on the ELP database, the three-letter word *ink* has a frequency of 5,593, whereas the three-letter word *mad* has a higher frequency of 17,811. Based on frequency alone, we would assume that *mad* would be recognized faster than *ink*. However, the word *mad* comes from a popular neighborhood (*bad*, *sad*, *mat*, *map*, etc.). Its orthographic neighbor count is 17, compared to *ink*'s three. Indeed, *ink*, on average, is recognized slightly faster than *mad*, possibly due to the competition the word *mad* must overcome to be recognized. Interested readers should consult the ELP database, which contains many other lexical characteristics of words that may affect processing.

Formulaic language

Formulaic language is now recognized as an important component of language learning and use. Normal discourse, both written and spoken, contains large (but not yet fully determined) percentages of formulaic language. Erman and Warren (2000) calculated that 52–58 per cent of the L1 English language they analyzed was formulaic, and Foster (2001) came up with a figure of 32 per cent using different procedures and criteria. If much discourse is made up of formulaic language, then this implies that proficient language users know a large number of formulaic expressions. Pawley and Syder (1983: 213) suggest that the number of 'sentence-length expressions familiar to the ordinary, mature English speaker probably amounts, at least, to several hundreds of thousands'. Jackendoff (1995) concludes from a small corpus study of spoken language in a TV quiz show that people may know at least as many formulaic sequences as single words. Mel'cuk (1995: 169) believes that phrasemes are more numerous than words by a ratio of at least 10 to 1.

Formulaic language is not a homogeneous phenomenon, but is rather quite varied. Formulaic sequences can be long (*You can lead a horse to water, but you can't make him drink*) or short (*Oh no!*), or anything in between. They are commonly used for different purposes. They can be used to express a message or idea (*The early bird gets the worm* = do not procrastinate), functions ([*I'm*] *just looking* [*thanks*] = declining an offer of assistance from a shopkeeper), social solidarity, and to transact specific information in a precise and understandable way. They realize many other purposes as well, as formulaic sequences can be used for most things society requires of communication through language. These sequences can be totally fixed (*Ladies and gentlemen*) or have a number of 'slots' which can be filled with appropriate words or strings of words (*[someone/thing, usually with authority] made it plain that [something as yet unrealized was intended or desired]*). Formulaic language also includes the multitude of collocations which exist in language (*blue sky, hard work*).

This variety of formulaic language realizes a number of different communicative purposes in language use, including:

Functional use: There are recurring situations in the social world that require language to deal with them. These are often described as *functions,* and include such speech acts as apologizing, making requests, giving directions, and complaining. These functions typically have conventionalized language attached to them, such as *I'm (very) sorry to hear about* – to express sympathy and *I'd be happy/glad to* – to comply with a request (Nattinger and DeCarrico 1992). Because members of a speech community know these expressions, they serve a quick and reliable way to achieve the related speech act.

Social interaction (phatic communion): People commonly engage in 'light' conversation for pleasure or to pass the time of day, where the purpose is not really information exchange or to get someone to do something. Rather, the purpose is social solidarity, and people rely on non-threatening phrases to keep the conversation flowing, including comments about the weather (*Nice weather today*; *Cold isn't it*), agreeing with your interlocutor (*Oh, I see what you mean*; *OK, I've got it*), providing backchannels and positive feedback to another speaker (*Did you really? How interesting*). Research has shown that such phrases are a key element of informal spoken discourse (McCarthy and Carter 1997).

Discourse organization: Formulaic phrases are a common way to signpost the organization of both written (*in other words, in conclusion*) and spoken discourse (*on the other hand, as I was saying*).

Precise information transfer (technical vocabulary): These are words which have a single and precise meaning in a particular field (*scalpel* is a specific type of knife used in medicine). But this phenomenon is not restricted to individual words. Indeed, fields often have phraseology to transact information in a way which minimizes any possible misunderstanding. For example, in aviation language, the phrase *Taxi into position and hold* clearly and concisely conveys the instructions to move onto the runway and prepare for departure, but to wait for final clearance for takeoff.

The use of formulaic language also helps speakers be fluent. It is a well-known tenet of psychology that people have cognitive limitations in how quickly they can process language. However, Pawley and Syder (1983) suggested that these limitations can be compensated for by using formulaic language, which is already memorized and stored as single wholes and are, as such, instantly available for use without the cognitive load of having to assemble them on-line as one speaks. There is now converging evidence that formulaic language is indeed processed more quickly than non-formulaic language, at least by native-speakers (Underwood *et al.* 2004; Jiang and Nekrasova 2007; Schmitt 2008).

Regional variation in words and lexical phrases

Examples of regional variation at the lexical level abound in languages all over the world. Sometimes the variants may be similar forms, and the number of variants may be limited. In Spanish, for example, 'tomato' is *jitomate* in Mexican Spanish and *tomate* in most of the rest of the Spanish-speaking world. These two variants are clearly related in form. Other variants may have completely distinct forms. 'Popcorn' in Spanish might be expressed as *palomitas (de maíz)* (Spain, Mexico), *cabritas (de maíz)* (Chile), *canguil* (Ecuador), or *cancha* (Peru). Regional lexical variation is also extensive across numerous semantic fields. For example, the concept of 'cool' (meaning good or interesting in English) might translate as *padre* in Mexico, *guay* in Spain, *chévere* in Colombia or Ecuador, *bacán* in Perú, and so forth. Lexical phrases also have variants. For example, an idiomatic expression such as *estoy en el quinto cielo* (literally 'I am in the fifth heaven') might be used to express 'I'm in seventh heaven' in Spain but not in Mexico.

In English, regional lexical variants are also widespread. Some fairly well-known British/ American English lexical variants include *football/soccer, lorry/truck, lift/elevator, flat/apartment* and *biscuit/cookie*, but we also find other perhaps less well-known variants, such as *bonnet/ (car) hood, paraffin/kerosene, silencer/muffler, dummy/pacifier* and *flyover/overpass*. Variants on multiword phrases are not uncommon either: *to faff around/to goof off; to be chuffed/to be psyched;* and *to put your skates on/to get a move on*. Of course, regional English lexical variants are in not limited to British/American varieties either. To provide one example, consider the British/ South African/American English variants *trainers* or *pumps/takkies/sneakers* or *tennis shoes*.

Critical discussion of selected current issues

In this section we opt to provide an overview of the development of theory and research and focus on two of the many lines of research related to lexis: second language (L2) vocabulary and instruction and the bilingual mental lexicon. We do so based on space limitations and acknowledge that there are numerous other topics related to lexis that we could have selected.

L2 vocabulary learning and instruction

Vocabulary learning and vocabulary knowledge are central to both L1 and L2 language learning. Words are the building blocks of language, and linguists increasingly point to the inextricable role of words and lexical phrases in the projection and construction of syntax. Vocabulary is also indispensable when it comes to successful communication. Compared to the impact of accented speech or minor syntactic violations (e.g. subject-verb or gender agreement), the impact of lexical errors can be a much greater impediment to successful communication. Consider, as one example, an L2 speaker who wishes to say, in Italian, *Io voglio i gamberetti* ('I want the shrimp'.) With a syntactic error like *Io volere i gamberetti,* literally meaning 'I to want the shrimp' (and sounding something like 'Me want shrimp' in Italian), the speaker most likely would receive their desired dish. With a lexical error, however, such as *Io voglio le gallete* ('I want the crackers'), the speaker is likely to receive something else.

Vocabulary size and amount of comprehension

One area of L2 vocabulary research has focused on vocabulary size and the relationship between vocabulary size and varying degrees of text comprehension or spoken discourse comprehension. For text comprehension, whereas Laufer (1989) found that knowing only 95 per cent of words in an English text was sufficient to understand the text adequately, more recently, Hu and Nation (2000) found the figure to be a bit higher, with 98 per cent of the words needing to be known. For spoken discourse, Bonk (2000) found no specific threshold was needed for successful listening comprehension, but after including running words and making other considerations, Schmitt (2008) calculated a figure of 95 per cent for adequate listening comprehension in light of the results reported by Bonk.

'Receptive versus productive' vocabulary knowledge and methods of testing

Somewhat related to the issue of vocabulary size is the question of how one chooses to test vocabulary. When testing via translation, should one provide the learners with the L1 word and ask him or her to produce the L2 word, or vice versa? Traditionally, a distinction has been made between 'receptive' and 'productive' vocabulary knowledge in the study of L2 vocabulary, the former being much larger than the latter. Some have maintained that the receptive/productive distinction may correspond to different systems. Melka (1997: 101–2), however, considered the possibility of a single lexical store being accessed in different ways: 'It is certainly not clear whether [reception] and [production] ought be considered as two separate systems dependent on each other, or rather as one unique system (one lexical store) used in two different ways, receptively or productively.'

If the 'receptive-productive' distinction concerns a single store being accessed in different ways, this has important implications for L2 vocabulary testing. Performance on a more receptive vocabulary test may be higher simply because the testee is provided with a greater amount of the target word form and, in essence, has less to 'fill in' regarding the form of the word in question. Imagine, for example, that the word for 'circle' in some (imaginary) L2 is *glinalor* but the learner has retained only *gl-n–*. An L1-to-L2 translation test would demonstrate that the learner has not reached complete knowledge of the target word form whereas a more receptively oriented test, such as L2-to-L1 translation, would provide the entire word form for the learner, making it easier to 'fill in' what is missing in word form knowledge.

Word-based determinants of learnability

Studies on word-based determinants of learnability have isolated specific properties of L2 words that make them more or less difficult to learn. Ellis and Beaton (1995), for example, found the learnability of L2 words to be affected by word-based factors such as word length and degree of phonological similarity between L1 and L2 words. Longer words and L2 words that were less phonologically similar to L1 words were more difficult. In another study, Laufer (1997) demonstrated that 'deceptive transparency' can make it more difficult to learn L2 words. *Deceptive transparency* refers to when a learner incorrectly thinks s/he knows the meaning of an expression because they know words with in it, such as if a learner of L2 English were to understand the expression 'break the ice' in its literal sense instead of in its idiomatic sense.

Incidental and intentional vocabulary learning

As attention to the importance of vocabulary increased within the field of SLA, one issue and area of debate that began to emerge during the 1980s and 1990s was that of incidental versus intentional vocabulary learning and its pedagogical counterpart, indirect versus direct (explicit) vocabulary instruction. *Incidental vocabulary learning* refers to learning new words from context without intending to do so, such as when picking up new words during free reading or during a conversation without intending to do so. *Intentional vocabulary learning*, on the other hand, refers to situations in which learners actively and consciously try to learn new words, such as when looking at word-picture pairs on a screen and attempting to learn them or completing activities in a workbook in an effort to learn a set of target L2 words.

Indirect vocabulary instruction refers to instructional activities designed to promote incidental vocabulary learning, known as indirect vocabulary instruction, such as when an instructor asks learners to read for meaning or complete an information-exchange task without asking the learners to attempt to learn new words provided in the text or materials for the task. *Direct vocabulary instruction* refers to activities designed to teach new vocabulary explicitly, such as using a picture file, a word-definition matching task, or picture-labeling task to teach learners new words. Note also that the *incidental-intentional* distinction should not be viewed as a dichotomous concept only, nor should the *indirect-direct* distinction in instruction (Haynes 1998, as cited in Wesche and Paribakht 1999).

On the whole, studies have indicated relatively low amounts of new word gain or 'pick up' of new words in contexts of purely incidental L2 vocabulary learning (see, for example, Horst *et al.* 1998). However, other studies, such as that of Horst (2005) in which learners picked up over half of the target words after extensive reading, have demonstrated larger gains. Increasing the number of exposures to target words in a text is one way of increasing the amount of word gain. Rott (1999) demonstrated that six exposures led to improved learning as compared to four or two exposures. Other studies have used higher numbers of repetitions but have failed to ensure complete (incidental) learning of target words. Waring and Takaki (2003), for example, found that eight exposures led to only a 50 per cent chance of the learners being able to accurately match the word to its meaning a few months later.

Other studies (e.g. Hulstijn 1992) have demonstrated that L2 vocabulary learning during reading improves if learners are simply instructed to attempt to learn target words and told that they will be tested on them, pointing to the strong impact of maintaining an intentional orientation toward L2 vocabulary learning. Other research on intentional L2 vocabulary learning has isolated variables that lead to improved vocabulary learning in this context.

Prince (1996) compared translation-based L2 vocabulary learning with presenting L2 vocabulary in the context of sentences and found translation-based learning to be more effective. Allowing learners opportunities to attempt to retrieve target words on their own also has been found to increase learning (e.g. Royer 1973). Also, varying talker, speaking style, and speaking rate during intentional L2 vocabulary learning has been found to substantially improve intentional L2 vocabulary learning (Barcroft and Sommers 2005; Sommers and Barcroft 2007).

Vocabulary attrition

Vocabulary acquisition is not a tidy linear affair, with only incremental advancement and no backsliding. All teachers recognize that learners forget material as well. This forgetting (attrition) is a natural fact of learning. We should view partial vocabulary knowledge as being in a state of flux, with both learning and forgetting occurring until the word is mastered and 'fixed' in memory. For example, Schmitt (1998) found that advanced L2 university students improved their knowledge of the meaning senses of target words about 2.5 times more than that knowledge was forgotten (over the course of one year), but this means there was some backsliding as well.

Of course attrition can also occur even if vocabulary is relatively well known, such as when one does not use a second language for a long time, or one stops a course of language study. Studies into attrition have produced mixed results, largely due to the use of different methods of measuring vocabulary retention (e.g. Bahrick 1984; Weltens and Grendel 1993; Hansen et al. 2002). In general though, lexical knowledge seems to be more prone to attrition than other linguistic aspects, such as phonology or grammar. This is logical because vocabulary is made up of individual units rather than a series of rules, although we have seen that lexis is much more patterned than previously thought. It appears that receptive knowledge does not attrite dramatically, and when it does, it is usually peripheral words, such as low-frequency noncognates, which are affected (Weltens and Grendel 1993). On the other hand, productive mastery is more likely to be lost (Cohen 1989; Olshtain 1989), although see Schmitt (1998) for contrary results. There is some evidence that the rate of attrition is connected to proficiency level, with learners with larger vocabularies retaining more residual knowledge of their vocabulary (Hansen et al. 2002). Weltens et al. (1989) found that most of the attrition for the participants in their study occurred within the first two years and then leveled off. Overall, once vocabulary is learned, it does not seem to ever completely disappear, as Bahrick (1984) found residual vocabulary knowledge in his informants even after fifty years of language disuse. It is therefore probably best to think of attrition in terms of loss of lexical access, rather than in terms of a complete elimination of lexical knowledge.

The developing bilingual mental lexicon

Second language vocabulary acquisition is a complicated and often error-ridden process. It is no surprise that second language learners make frequent lexical errors. In fact, most every language learner can likely recall some type of humorous error that has happened. For example, in Spanish the false cognate *embarazadola* (meaning 'pregnant') sometimes gets substituted for *avergonzadola* (meaning 'embarrassed'), resulting in, as one could imagine, quite amusing sentences. Why do errors like this happen? More importantly, what do these errors tell us about the underlying architecture of the developing bilingual lexicon?

To answer these questions, we turn to one of the most well-known developmental models of the lexicon, the Revised Hierarchical Model (RHM: Kroll and Stewart 1994). This model directly addresses the connections between lexical and conceptual links and how they change as an L2 learner becomes more proficient in the L2. We limit ourselves to discussing this one model and this one specific claim of the model in particular because its applications to vocabulary learning are salient. In the section below, we first present and describe the RHM. We then provide an illustrative example of an empirical test of the model that uses a translation recognition task, a psycholinguistic task that has recently been quite popular in investigating the developmental claims of the RHM.

The revised hierarchical model

One of the central claims of the RHM is that second language learners, in beginning stages of language learning, rely on an L1 translation strategy. In other words, when L2 learners are trying to link a new lexical form to its corresponding concept, they will initially use the L1 lexical link to access the concept. This translation strategy is depicted in the model below (see Figure 40.1). First, the model contains two separate lexicons for L1 and L2 words and one common conceptual store.

The L1 lexicon is represented as larger and containing more words than the L2 lexicon. Second, the arrows in the model represent the lexical and conceptual links assumed to be active in bilingual memory. There are both lexical, word-to-word links, and conceptual, word-to-concept links, in this model. Third, the relative strength of these links, as represented by the thickness of the arrows, is assumed to be a function of language dominance. For a beginning learner, the associations between L1 words and concepts will be very strong, whereas the associations between L2 words and concepts will be weaker. Similarly, the model suggests that lexical associations from L2 to L1 will be strong, whereas the L1 to L2 lexical links will be

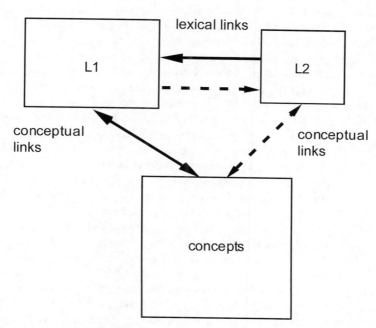

Figure 40.1 Revised hierarchical model
Source: Adapted from Kroll and Stewart 1994.

579

weaker. Last, what is striking about this model is that it captures the asymmetry in the interlanguage connections between the lexical representation and the conceptual information in the developing lexicon. As proficiency in the L2 increases, the interlanguage connections change and shift from lexical processing to semantic processing. In other words, L2 learners move away from the L1 translation strategy.

One study that is directly related to the idea that L2 learners move away from a translation strategy with increasing skill in the L2 is Talamas *et al.* (1999). In their study, Talamas *et al.* described evidence from the classroom setting in which learners in a basic level language class made errors based on lexical form relations. For example, beginning Spanish learners would confuse words like *mujer* (meaning woman) for *mejor* (meaning best), or *cuida* (meaning to take care of) with *ciudad* (meaning city). Learners, in what they describe as a more enriched or advanced classroom setting, did not seem to make those types of errors, and instead made more semantic-based errors. Using this idea that less proficient learners were tricked more by form-related similarities, Talamas *et al.* created experimental stimuli that would reflect the nature of L2 vocabulary errors to test this developmental prediction of the RHM.

Talamas *et al.* (1999) compared the performance of more and less proficient bilinguals on a translation recognition task (de Groot 1992). In a translation recognition task, a word is presented briefly on a computer screen in one of the participant's two languages and is then followed by a word in the other language. The task was to decide as quickly and as accurately as possible whether the second word was the correct translation of the first. In the Talamas *et al.* study, the critical focus concerned those trials on which the two words were not translation equivalents (i.e. the *no* trials). On half of the *no* trials, the two words were related by virtue of word form similarity (e.g. man-*hambre* where *hambre* means hunger and looks like the correct translation *hombre*) or meaning (e.g. man-*mujer* where *mujer* means woman). Thus, the experimental stimuli reflected the types of errors that were occurring in the classroom. The logic of the task was that if a learner had a difficult time (i.e. took longer in terms of reaction time in milliseconds or was more inaccurate) rejecting these tricky 'no' pairs compared to unrelated 'no' pairs, then the type of relationship (either form or meaning) was to blame.

Talamas *et al.* tested English-dominant individuals who differed in their level of proficiency in Spanish. They found that the two types of related trials produced different results for the more and less proficient bilinguals. For less proficient bilinguals, there was significant interference for form-related pairs (man-*hambre*), but little effect for semantically related pairs (man-*mujer*). For more proficient bilinguals, the pattern was reversed; form-related pairs produced inconsistent effects in performance but semantically related pairs produced significant interference. The overall pattern of results mirrors the anecdotal classroom evidence and provides support for the hypothesis that early in second language learning, lexical form relations between L2 and L1 provide the basis of interlanguage connection (see Sunderman and Kroll 2006 for additional evidence also using a translation recognition task).

Thus, the RHM provides valuable insights into answering why L2 learners make the types of errors they do. Over the years, scholars have challenged aspects of the architecture and the various claims of the RHM. For example, some have called into question the degree to which the semantics are shared across languages (e.g. de Groot 1993; Pavlenko 1999). Others have questioned whether the lexicons are integrated (e.g. Brysbaert 1998; van Heuven *et al.* 1998). However, the RHM remains a valuable model for those interested in research on the underlying representations of form and meaning in L2 vocabulary acquisition. Readers interested in learning more about additional claims and research on the RHM, as well as other models of the bilingual lexicon, should consult Kroll and Sunderman 2003.

Chapter summary

This chapter highlighted key points in the history of linguistic research on lexis and clarified key concepts related to what words are, including the various formal and semantic properties of words and the lexical characteristics of words such as word frequency and orthographic neighborhoods. The chapter also emphasized and exemplified the important role of formulaic language in language learning and language use and the abundant amount of regional variation that exists in language at the lexical level. In light of the large number of research areas related to lexis, we selected two areas of research, L2 vocabulary learning and the bilingual mental lexicon, as our foci for the final two sections of the chapter. Among the issues discussed in these sections were the incidental-intentional distinction in L2 vocabulary learning and the development of concept mediation over time within the bilingual mental lexicon.

Related topics

cognitive linguistics; corpus linguistics; generative grammar

Further reading

Goulden, R., Nation, P. and Read, J. (1990) 'How large can a receptive vocabulary be?', *Applied Linguistics* 11(4): 341–63. (An early study into the vocabulary size of English native speakers.)
Kroll, J. F. and Sunderman, G. (2003) 'Cognitive processes in second language learners and bilinguals: the development of lexical and conceptual representations', in C. J. Doughty and M. H. Long (eds) *The Handbook of Second Language Acquisition*, Cambridge, MA: Blackwell. (This chapter presents a comprehensive overview of empirical research on the bilingual lexicon.)
Laufer, B. (1997) 'What's in a word that makes it hard or easy? Intralexicalfactors affecting the difficulty of vocabulary acquisition', in N. Schmitt and M. McCarthy (eds) *Vocabulary: Description, Acquisition, and Pedagogy*, Cambridge: Cambridge University Press. (An overview of some of the word properties which make lexical items relatively easier or more difficult to learn.)
Nation, I. S. P. (2006) 'How large a vocabulary is needed for reading and listening?', *Canadian Modern Language Review* 63(1): 59–82. (A key article outlining current thinking on the vocabulary size requirements for using English.)
Read, J. (2000) *Assessing Vocabulary*, Cambridge: Cambridge University Press. (The standard book on vocabulary measurement.)
Wray, A. (2002) *Formulaic Language and the Lexicon*, Cambridge: Cambridge University Press. (Still the most comprehensive overview of formulaic language.)

References

Aristotle (350 BCE) *Categories*, E. M. Edghill (trans.) Available at: http://classics.mit.edu/Aristotle/categories.html
Bahrick, H. P. (1984) 'Fifty years of language attrition: implications for programmatic research', *Modern Language Journal* 68: 105–18.
Balota, D. A., Yap, M. J., Cortese, M. J., Hutchison, K. A., Kessler, B., Loftis, B., Neely, J. H., Nelson, D. L., Simpson, G. B. and Treiman, R. (2007) 'The English lexicon project', *Behavior Research Methods* 39: 445–59.
Barcroft, J. and Sommers, M. S. (2005) 'Effects of acoustic variability on second language vocabulary learning', *Studies in Second Language Acquisition* 27: 387–414.
Bonk, W. (2000) 'Second language lexical knowledge and listening comprehension', *International Journal of Listening* 14: 14–31.
Brysbaert, M. (1998) 'Word recognition in bilinguals: evidence against the existence of two separate lexicons', *Psychologica Belgica* 38: 163–75.
Chomsky, N. (1986) *Knowledge of Language: Its Nature, Origin and Use*, New York: Praeger.

Cohen, A. D. (1989) 'Attrition in the productive lexicon of two Portuguese third language speakers', *Studies in Second Language Acquisition* 11: 135–49.

Coltheart, M., Davelaar, E., Jonasson, J. T. and Besner, D. (1977) 'Access to the internal lexicon', in S. Dornic (ed.) *Attention and Performance VI*, New York: Academic Press.

de Groot, A. M. B. (1992) 'Determinants of word translation', *Journal of Experimental Psychology: Learning, Memory, and Cognition* 18: 1001–18.

——(1993) 'Word-type effects in bilingual processing tasks: support for a mixed-representational system' in R. Schreuder and B. Weltens (eds.) *The Bilingual Lexicon*, Vol. 6: *Studies in Bilingualism*, Amsterdam: John Benjamins.

Ellis, N. and Beaton, A. (1995) 'Psycholinguistic determinants of foreign language vocabulary learning', in B. Harley (ed.) *Lexical Issues in Language Learning*, Ann Arbor, MI: John Benjamins.

Erman, B. and Warren, B. (2000) 'The idiom principle and the open choice principle', *Text* 20(1): 29–62.

Foster, P. (2001) 'Rules and routines: a consideration of their role in the task-based language production of native and non-native speakers', in M. Bygate, P. Skehan and M. Swain (eds) *Researching Pedagogic Tasks: Second Language Learning, Teaching, and Testing*, Harlow: Longman.

Gennette, G. (1979) *Narrative Discourse: An Essay in Method*, J. E. Lewin (trans.), Ithaca, NY: Cornell University Press.

Hansen, L., Umeda, Y. and McKinney, M. (2002) 'Savings in the relearning of second language vocabulary: the effects of time and proficiency', *Language Learning* 52: 653–78.

Horst, M. (2005) 'Learning L2 vocabulary through extensive reading: a measurement study', *Canadian Modern Language Review* 61: 355–82.

Horst, M., Cobb, T. and Meara, P. (1998) 'Beyond clockwork orange: acquiring second language vocabulary through reading', *Reading in a Foreign Language* 11(2): 207–23.

Hu, M. and Nation, I. S. P. (2000) 'Vocabulary density and reading comprehension', *Reading in a Foreign Language* 23: 403–30.

Hulstijn, J. (1992) 'Retention of inferred and given word meanings: experiments in incidental learning', in P. J. L. Arnaud and H. Be'joint (eds) *Vocabulary and Applied Linguistics,* London: Macmillan.

Jackendoff, R. (1995) 'The boundaries of the lexicon', in M. Everaert, E.- van der Linden, A. Schenk and R. Schreuder (eds) *Idioms: Structural and Psychological Perspectives*, Hillsdale, NJ: Lawrence Erlbaum Associates.

Jiang, N. and Nekrasova, T. M. (2007) 'The processing of formulaic sequences by second language speakers', *Modern Language Journal* 91(3): 433–45.

Kroll, J. F. and Stewart, E. (1994) 'Category interference in translation and picture naming: evidence for asymmetric connections between bilingual memory representations', *Journal of Memory and Language* 33: 149–74.

Kroll, J. F. and Sunderman, G. (2003) 'Cognitive processes in second language learners and bilinguals: the development of lexical and conceptual representations', in C. J. Doughty and M. H. Long (eds) *The Handbook of Second Language Acquisition*, Cambridge, MA: Blackwell.

Laufer, B. (1989) 'What percentage of text-lexis is essential for comprehension?', in C. Lauren and M. Nordman (eds) *Special Language: From Humans to Thinking Machines*, Clevedon: Multilingual Matters.

——(1997) 'The lexical plight in second language reading: words you don't know, words you think you know, and words you can't guess', in J. Coady and T. Huckin (eds) *Second Language Vocabulary Acquisition*, Amsterdam: John Benjamins.

McCarthy, M. and Carter, R. (1997) 'Written and spoken vocabulary', in N. Schmitt and M. McCarthy (eds) *Vocabulary: Description, Acquisition, and Pedagogy*, Cambridge: Cambridge University Press.

Mel'cuk, I. A. (1995) 'Phrasemes in language and phraseology in linguistics', in M. Everaert, E.-J. van der Linden, A. Schenk and R. Schreuder (eds) *Idioms: Structural and Psychological Perspectives*, Hillsdale, NJ: Lawrence Erlbaum Associates.

Melka, F. (1997) 'Receptive vs. productive aspects of vocabulary', in N. Schmitt and M. McCarthy (eds) *Vocabulary: Description, Acquisition, and Pedagogy,* Cambridge: Cambridge University Press.

Nattinger, J. R. and DeCarrico, J. S. (1992) *Lexical Phrases and Language Teaching*, Oxford: Oxford University Press.

Olshtain, E. (1989) 'Is second language attrition the reversal of second language acquisition?', *Studies in Second Language Acquisition* 11: 151–65.

Pavlenko, A. (1999) 'New approaches to concepts in bilingual memory', *Bilingualism: Language and Cognition* 2: 209–30.

Pawley, A. and Syder, F. H. (1983) 'Two puzzles for linguistic theory: nativelike selection and nativelike fluency', in J. C. Richards and R. W. Schmidt (eds) *Language and Communication*, London: Longman.

Prince, P. (1996) 'Second language vocabulary learning: the role of context versus translations as a function of proficiency', *The Modern Language Journal* 80: 478–93.

Rott, S. (1999) 'The effect of exposure frequency on intermediate second language learners' incidental vocabulary acquisition through reading', *Studies in Second Language Acquisition* 21(1): 589–619.

Royer, J. M. (1973) 'Memory effects for test-like events during acquisition of foreign language vocabulary', *Psychological Reports* 32: 195–8.

de Saussure, F. (1916) *Course in General Linguistics*, R. Harris (trans.), Peru, IL: Open Court Publishing.

Schmitt, N. (1998) 'Tracking the incidental acquisition of second language vocabulary: a longitudinal study', *Language Learning* 48: 281–317.

——(2008) 'Instructed second language vocabulary learning', *Language Teaching Research* 12(3): 329–63.

Sommers, M. and Barcroft, J. (2007) 'An integrated account of the effects of acoustic variability in L1 and L2: evidence from amplitude, fundamental frequency, and speaking rate variability', *Applied Psycholinguistics* 28(2): 231–49.

Sonkowsky, R. P. (1959) 'An aspect of delivery in ancient rhetorical theory', *Transactions and Proceedings of the American Philological Association* 90: 256–74.

Sunderman, G. and Kroll, J. F. (2006) 'First language activation during second language first language activation during second language lexical processing: an investigation of lexical form, meaning, and grammatical class', *Studies in Second Language Acquisition* 28: 387–422.

Talamas, A., Kroll, J. F. and Dufour, R. (1999) 'Form related errors in second language learning: a preliminary stage in the acquisition of L2 vocabulary', *Bilingualism: Language and Cognition* 2: 45–58.

Underwood, G., Schmitt, N. and Galpin, A. (2004) 'The eyes have it: an eye-movement study into the processing of formulaic sequences', in N. Schmitt (ed.) *Formulaic Sequences*, Amsterdam: John Benjamins.

van Heuven, W. J. B., Dijkstra, T. and Grainger, J. (1998) 'Orthographic neighborhood effects in bilingual word recognition', *Journal of Memory and Language* 39: 458–83.

Waring, R. and Takaki, M. (2003) 'At what rate do learners learn and retain new vocabulary from reading a graded reader?', *Reading in a Foreign Language*, 15: 130–63.

Weltens, B. and Grendel, M. (1993) 'Attrition of vocabulary knowledge', in R. Schreuder and B. Weltens (eds) *The Bilingual Lexicon*, Amsterdam: John Benjamins.

Weltens, B., van Els, T. J. M. and Schils, E. (1989) 'The long-term retention of French by Dutch students', *Studies in Second Language Acquisition* 11: 205–16.

Wesche, M. and Paribakht, T. S. (1999) 'Introduction', *Studies in Second Language Acquisition*, 21: 175–80.

Zimmerman, C. (1997) 'Historical trends in second language vocabulary instruction', in J. Coady and T. Huckin (eds) *Second Language Vocabulary Acquisition*, Amsterdam: John Benjamins.

41

Phonetics and phonology

Helen Fraser

Introduction

Phonetics and phonology are among the branches of linguistics with least impact on applied linguistics. This is unfortunate, as they have a great deal to offer research and teaching in the many applications that investigate the production, understanding or representation of speech, especially second language teaching, which will be the focus of this chapter.

One reason for their lack of impact might be that they are often perceived as highly complicated topics, dominated by theoretical issues of limited relevance to practical applications. It is useful in this regard to invoke a distinction between 'complicated' and 'complex'. A simple system has few parts, related by a small enough number of rules as to be easily understood by the average person. A complicated system is quantitatively different, with many more parts, related by more numerous, more inter-related rules. A complex system is qualitatively different, with larger, less clearly defined parts, connected by a smaller number of general, context-dependent principles (Ellis, this volume).

Working effectively with either kind of system requires recognition of which kind it is. However, since their products can seem superficially similar, it is possible to confuse them, with unfortunate results (Westley *et al.* 2006). The argument of this chapter is that speech is a complex system, but most current theories of phonetics and phonology model it as a complicated system. While this is appropriate for some applications, for others, a theoretical framework which recognises the complex nature of speech is needed.

One problem is that understanding speech as a complex system means revising basic ideas in ways that challenge not just existing academic theories, but apparently obvious facts about speech. The intention here, however, is not to contradict existing ideas, but to place them in a wider context, with the aim of encouraging cross-fertilisation between branches of theoretical and applied research that have had too little contact in recent decades.

The chapter begins by reviewing some well-known observations, and equally well-known misconceptions, about speech. It then provides a simple analogy as a basis for understanding and comparing different views about speech, and goes on to use the analogy in an interpretive overview of the historical development of phonetics and phonology in relation to applied linguistics. Discussion then turns to how the knowledge acquired by phonetics and phonology can be framed in a way that allows fruitful, two-way interaction with various branches of applied linguistics, especially sociocognitive theories of second language teaching.

Foundational observations about speech

It is useful to start by weaving together several pretheoretical observations about speech. First is the extraordinary skill with which ordinary people use speech. Speech is a highly intricate, continuous signal (Ladefoged 2005). Much more than just a linguistic message, it incorporates interlocking systems of meaning conveying subtle distinctions of attitude, personal and social identity, emotional and physical state, and more (Laver 1994). Despite this, it is produced and perceived with great rapidity and accuracy, even in the face of severe distortion (Erard 2007).

The second, converse, observation is the extraordinary limitation on speech perception and production. The skills just mentioned depend greatly on context, without which they are severely reduced (Warren 1999). For example, a conversation that is perfectly comprehensible to participants may be difficult to understand when replayed from a decontextualised recording (Fraser 2003, Fraser 2010b). The third, related, observation is the extraordinary lack of insight people have into the nature of speech. Though in interpreting speech they clearly take note of many details, their ability to identify these details accurately is extremely poor (Fraser 2009b).

This pattern, of high-level skill within a meaningful context, coupled with limited ability to accurately describe the basis of that skill, is typical of complex cognitive systems (Frith 2008; Macdonald 2008). One effect is that many tasks people assume will be easy, turn out to be much more difficult than expected. For example, students generally find the idea of transcribing speech with phoneme symbols easy to grasp, and may be keen to learn a representation of speech that avoids the difficulties of spelling. Actually using such as system, however, is surprisingly hard (Scarborough *et al.* 1998). It is interesting to consider the response to this difficulty. Many attribute it to a failing on their own part: 'I'm hopeless at phonetics.' Only rarely is the question raised: 'Why would something so hard be expected to be easy?' Answering this question points to a widespread misconception about the nature of speech.

The fundamental misconception about speech

Even those who know no theories of phonetics and phonology have an informal theory about speech: that, despite some obvious irregularities, such as 'silent-k' in *knee*, speech consists of a sequence of discrete sounds, much like the letters in a printed text. This informal theory is incorrect – a product of literacy education that teaches that each letter represents a 'sound', and words are formed by 'sounding out' letters. Such teaching is a necessary step in literacy acquisition (Byrne 1998), but it is not how reading actually works. Indeed, to continue the 'sounding out' process beyond the earliest stages is to have a serious reading disability. Skilled literacy depends on contextualised, meaning-based processing (Just and Carpenter 1987).

The problem is that, even after it is understood that reading is not really 'sounding out', there remains the residual sense that speech itself is a sequence of 'sounds'. This inaccurate belief can be called a 'literacy bias', a bias towards interpreting the continuous flow of speech as a sequence of sounds equivalent to those represented in one's writing system. This bias is deeply ingrained, and rarely challenged unless formal study of linguistics is undertaken.

The reason phonemic transcription is hard is because phonemes are not, as the literacy bias would have it, objective bits of speech, but products of abstract theoretical analysis, open to debate. Even when a set of symbols is agreed, choosing the right symbols in particular cases raises many further questions (Wells 2003). It is natural, in teaching applied linguistics, to simplify for students by choosing an appropriate system and providing consistent answers to such questions. Unfortunately, glossing over the complexity can give those who learn phonemes the impression they have overcome the literacy bias, when really they have only replaced a simplistic 'spelling bias' with a more sophisticated 'phoneme bias' – the belief that speech is a sequence not of letters but of phonemes.

The phoneme bias, too, is incorrect, as shown by the false expectations it gives rise to. For example, it suggests using phoneme-based pronunciation guides to help poor spellers. These are certainly useful in particular contexts, but they are hard even for good spellers to interpret, and harder still for poor spellers (Fraser 1997).

More importantly, the phoneme bias encourages teaching second language pronunciation by teaching phonemes, an approach known to have many limitations. Before considering these limitations, however, it is necessary to fully understand the literacy bias, too often glossed over in both theory and practice.

The nature of speech

The problem with the literacy bias is that it makes it hard to appreciate that speech is really a continuous stream of sound. At first it can seem strange that something appearing so clearly to be a sequence of discrete units is really continuous, but actually it is quite common. The rainbow offers a simple example. English speakers think of it as a sequence of seven discrete colours. In reality, however, it is a continuous gradation of colour. This can be easily pointed out by observing that each basic colour actually covers a range of colour variants, which merge into a continuum. It is the same with speech, though it is much harder to notice the variants in speech. Few English speakers, for example, notice that the phoneme /s/ has quite different variants in the words *sue* and *sea*. A phoneme is not 'a sound' but a category of sounds – just as *blue* is not 'a colour' but a category of colours (Schmid and Ungerer, this volume). Using a computer speech editor, it is easy to demonstrate that phonemes in speech have internal variation and indistinct boundaries, making a continuous flow (Shockey 2003; Fraser 2004).

Both colour and speech, then, can be viewed on several distinct levels of analysis: the continuous flow of reality, basic categories, category variants, and others. This gives an easy way to understand the distinction between phonetics and phonology: phonetics aims to study what speech is 'really like', while phonology studies how people 'think about' speech, often viewed in terms of systems of mental representations, though as we will see, this view has its limitations.

There is a crucial difference between speech and colour, however: with speech, people have very limited awareness of levels other than the basic categories. We will return to consider the reason for this, but for now the analogy can highlight its practical implications. Recognition that the rainbow is really a continuous gradation of colour opens the possibility there could be other ways of dividing it into basic colours – and indeed different cultures do divide the colour spectrum into different sets of colours (Hardin and Maffi 1997). This means the translation of terms like 'green' and 'blue' can refer to quite different colours in different languages, creating problems for second language learners.

It is the same with speech. Of course it is true that, unlike the rainbow, whose reality remains the same for all cultures, the phonetic reality of speech is different in each language. More important, however, is the fact that languages provide different ways for their speakers to divide the continuous flow of sound into 'basic sounds'. This is why people hear a foreign language, not in terms of its different phonetic reality, but in terms of the basic sounds of their own language – a well-known phenomenon known as perceptual assimilation (Bohn and

Munro 2007). The key problem for second language learners, then, is similar for colours and speech: a problem of recategorisation. However, in the case of speech, the problem is much greater. Due to the lack of awareness just discussed, teaching second language pronunciation is like teaching colours would be if learners were so strongly focused on their own basic colours, they could barely notice other levels. Clearly, the first step would be for the teacher to help learners gain awareness of relevant variants.

In such a situation it would clearly be a major problem if teachers themselves were unaware of the other levels. That is why it is so essential for teachers to know enough phonetics and phonology to understand the effect of the literacy bias on themselves and their students, and recognise the task of second language acquisition for what it is. Unfortunately, many do not. To see why, it is useful to briefly review some relevant aspects the history of phonetics and phonology.

A brief interpretive history of phonetics and phonology

The scientific study of speech goes back many centuries (Asher and Henderson 1981), but perhaps its most important milestone is development of the concept of phoneme.

Around the turn of the twentieth century, though a great deal of knowledge had been accumulated, especially about the articulation of speech sounds and the sound systems of Indo-European languages, various problems of analysis had arisen for which, interestingly, several scholars converged upon a similar solution (Anderson 1985). This exploited the notion of contrast, now very familiar in the study of semantics. It is well known that the meaning of a word (its 'signified') cannot be defined purely in terms of its physical reality, but requires reference to the system of other meanings with which it contrasts (Saussure [1916] 1983). In just the same way the sound of a word (its 'signifier') cannot be defined purely in terms of phonetic reality, but requires reference to the system of other signifiers with which it contrasts. Thus, to define the signifier of English *sue*, it is not enough just to describe the sound. It is necessary to understand the system of contrasts that distinguishes the large category of sounds that count as *sue* from the large category of similar sounds that count as other words.

This is the basis of the definition of 'phoneme': a unit of sound serving to contrast word meanings in a particular language. It is important to note that the relevant contrasts are between whole signifiers, the carriers of word meanings, which contrast in 'minimal pairs'. However, it is hard to talk about the sound of whole signifiers. Early phonologists naturally and unarguedly did so in terms of units of sound similar in size to the letters of their writing system, already well established as the units of phonetic analysis. Of course, this was no simplistic spelling bias. Saussure and others railed against the inaccurate equation of phonemes and letters. Nevertheless, it is important to recognise that, crucial and lastingly important as the definition of the phoneme is, its roots lie in the literacy bias (Linell 1988).

The phoneme idea was soon put to use in a practical task new to linguistics, when Sapir, Whorf and other anthropologists undertook the analysis of previously undescribed languages (Sapir 1949; Carroll 1956). To discover their phonemes, it was necessary not just to describe their sounds, but to investigate the system of minimal pairs in each language. It was found that, in any language, every phoneme has a range of variants ('allophones'), which, though clearly evident to analysts, were unnoticed by native speakers. The key to providing a writing system was to represent each phoneme with a single letter, ignoring allophonic variation, which only confuses native speakers (Pike 1947).

In this work, linguists were strongly and explicitly committed to the role of meaning, culture and context in the practical description of languages. Although they continued to use the

Helen Fraser

simple phoneme-allophone model, they did so flexibly, in recognition that all sound systems 'leak': there is never a fixed set of phonemes, each with its fixed set of allophones, but always exceptions and special cases. This can be understood readily by reference to the rainbow analogy introduced earlier. While it is easy to see that basic colours have variants, trying to formally associate every variant with a basic colour would create many uncertainties: is turquoise blue or green? What about aqua? Maybe the boundary between green and blue should be redefined? Similar but far more complex questions arise in defining the relationship between phonemes and allophones. Debating them is useful for developing understanding of the system as a whole, but it is clear they have no universal, factual answers. Insisting on a single fixed analysis would surely reduce, rather than increase, understanding.

This, in simple terms, is what happened with the advent of strict behaviourism, and its refusal to admit 'unobservable' entities such as meaning into analysis (Anderson 1985). Flexible phoneme-allophone analysis was formalised into a 'method', which insisted allophones be identified 'bottom up', then organised into a system of phonemes by procedures which made no reference to 'higher' level morphemes or words (Bloomfield [1933] 1984). Unsurprisingly, this did not work well, and though practical language analysis continued, a good deal of attention was diverted to theoretical problems arising from the method. One was coarticulation, specifying how allophones merge into a continuous stream of speech. Another was non-biuniqueness, where a single allophone appears to associate with different phonemes in different contexts. When viewed from the perspective of the colour analogy, the reason for these problems is clear: the variants are not separate 'bits of reality' put together into larger units, but abstractions derived from analysis of the larger units.

However, this was not the solution offered by Chomsky's generative grammar, in the next major theoretical shift, called the cognitive revolution, though a better term would be computational revolution, since its major innovation was modelling the human mind as a computer, as a means of explaining mental processes without recourse to unobservable entities like concepts. Meaning was restored to respectability by formalising it on its own level of 'mental representation'. This allowed non-biuniqueness to be explained via the operation of 'top-down' processes in the subconscious computation of mental representations. Coarticulation was handled by representing the phonetic level not as unitary allophones but as collections of 'features', able to influence one another through computational rules.

These innovations made the model very complicated, so much so that it predicted it should be impossible for children to learn language in a mere five years. Since this clearly conflicted with observable facts, it was necessary to postulate a 'Language Acquisition Device', to jump-start the acquisition process. This had the effect of directing a good deal of attention to discovery of the Universal Grammar embodied in the LAD, and away from the 'performance' of real language. Generative theory also predicted it should be impossible for adults to learn new phonological contrasts. Since this was less clearly in conflict with the facts, it was accepted as the Critical Age Hypothesis, and little attention given to teaching. Second language speech was studied mainly as a test-bed for theories of Universal Grammar (Archibald 1995).

The computer model did, however, have the advantage of insisting assumptions and hypotheses be explicitly tested, and by this means a great deal of new knowledge was generated. Interestingly, the same two issues that had caused problems for behaviourist theory continued to dominate generative theory. Developments in speech technology made it impossible to ignore the fact that speech is genuinely continuous (Perkell and Klatt 1986), and psycholinguistic evidence showed meaning influences phonological processing to a much greater degree, and in far more complex ways, than first recognised (Nusbaum and Goodman 1994; Field, this volume).

588

Incorporating findings such as these made the theory more and more complicated. The original model was overhauled in various 'post-generative' developments (Gussenhoven and Jacobs 2005), most of which require in-depth study of the history of the discipline for their understanding. This of course is the situation from which this chapter started: highly complicated theory dominated by self-referential issues of limited relevance to most branches of applied linguistics.

Phonetics, phonology and applied linguistics

With the intention of highlighting issues to be taken up in later discussion, the previous section has given the impression that twentieth-century speech research was wholly dominated by abstract theoretical debate. This is certainly not the case. Many researchers used generative theory flexibly, as a practical framework for the scientific investigation of speech and speech processing, and many advances in knowledge of the nature of speech and sound systems of wide range of languages were achieved (Ladefoged and Maddieson 1996; Hardcastle et al. 2010), though it is fair to say that every area of research uncovered greater complexity than predicted by the theory.

Some of these advances came through basic research applied to practical tasks, others in the direct pursuit of practical applications. Topics include, but are by no means limited to: speech pathology (Ball and Lowry 2001); the description of accents (Collins and Mees 2003); forensic phonetics (Rose 2002); and social variation in speech (Jannedy and Hay 2006). In some cases, knowledge gained from applied research has fed back fruitfully into theory (Pennington 2006) with Laboratory Phonology providing a particularly valuable contribution (Pierrehumbert et al. 1993). There was also considerable research on second language speech, stemming from interest in disproving the simplistic Critical Age Hypothesis, but broadening to a strong programme investigating many aspects of the acquisition of second language pronunciation (Strange 1995; Bohn and Munro 2007).

What is notable about these applications is that they generally do not require direct communication about speech with ordinary people, especially speakers from different language and literacy backgrounds. Even second language speech research uses methods more akin to training a computer system than teaching a human being (Fraser 2009a). Viewing speech as a subconscious computational system is useful in getting a bird's eye perspective on what is involved in acquiring new phonological systems. Actually teaching pronunciation, however, requires understanding speech as conscious processing by a human agent. For this, the generative framework has proven of less value.

For many years, communicative language teaching tried to 'go it alone' with regard to pronunciation, relying on implicit learning, and phonetics and phonology were largely dropped from teacher education. However, it is rare for adults to learn pronunciation well without explicit instruction, and these decades are now widely agreed to be a dark period in the history of language teaching (Celce-Murcia et al. 1996).

Eventually a revival occurred, led by teachers determined to help their students with this essential aspect of language. Courses and textbooks were designed to give teachers relevant background in phonetics and phonology (Roach 1991; Yavas 1994; Yallop 1995), and a growing community of teacher-researchers developed methods and materials for classroom use (Morley 1994; Underhill 1994; Gilbert 2005). Several studies provided empirical evidence of the value of an explicit pronunciation programme (Derwing et al. 1998; Couper 2006), with an important finding being the need to focus not only on phonemes but also on suprasegmental aspects of stress, syllable structure and intonation (Hahn 2004; Gilbert 2010).

Most of our knowledge of 'what works' in teaching second language pronunciation, as opposed to training second language contrasts, comes from this work (Kenworthy 1987; Morley 1991; Venkatagiri and Levis 2007; Henderson 2010), and there is much in it that supports and extends the view of speech as a complex system. However, there has been relatively little recognition of its theoretical implications. Indeed, there still tends to be relatively low interest in theory, with many teachers explicitly stating a preference to focus on practical outcomes, and choose teaching materials in an eclectic manner. This practical orientation has served well, with enormous strides in pronunciation teaching since the 'dark ages' of the 1960s and 1970s. Nevertheless, greater improvement is both necessary and possible, and the key is greater understanding of relevant aspects of phonetics and phonology.

The problem is that most textbooks, though they do an excellent job of simplifying complicated material to make it accessible to teachers, almost all concentrate almost exclusively on describing English phonology, with many blurring the distinction between phonetics and phonology in a way that entrenches, rather than overcoming, the literacy bias. In short, they simplify for teachers at the expense of missing the crucial information that allows teachers to simplify for learners. The result is that pronunciation lessons often involve teachers unconfidently passing on information they themselves understand imperfectly (Macdonald 2002).

Understanding the problem

While it is natural to speak of the seven colours as being 'parts' of the rainbow, it is clearly incorrect to think a rainbow is created by putting together separate bands of colour. The idea that words are created by putting together separate phonemes is equally incorrect. Unfortunately, the literacy bias makes this incorrect idea seem not just right, but self-evident. Questioning it evokes puzzlement: 'How else would it be possible to make words?'

But is it really necessary to identify phonemes in order to recognise words? Looking to experience, rather than to theory, suggests not. Recognising words is easy. Identifying phonemes is hard – even when the words in which they appear are known. Contrary to popular opinion, even experts cannot make a sensible transcription of an unknown language.

This leaves the question of how people do recognise words in continuous speech. Without the literacy bias, however, this question has a rather obvious answer: the same way they recognise anything else. Through embodied experience in meaningful social contexts, people learn to conceptualise the continuous reality of speech as a sequence of signifiers, then project their signifier-concepts onto continuous speech (Berko-Gleason 2005). In fact, the harder question is how and why they could recognise meaningless units like phonemes, allophones or features.

Looking, again, to experience, shows that meaningless units are learned after meaningful units, through informal analysis of signifiers which produces, first, the basic units referred to with everyday metalanguage (Gombert 1992; Vihman 1996), and later, through formal analysis, units referred to with the technical metalanguage of linguistics. All these units are derived from, not constitutive of, the primary units, meaningful words and phrases (Fraser 2010a).

The relationship between the levels of analysis, then, is the same for speech as for the rainbow. First, people learn to recognise the rainbow as a whole, the meaningful aspect of reality picked out through social experience. Then they analyse it into basic colours, colour variants, and more technical descriptions.

Speech is far more complex than a rainbow, but the overall relationship among the levels is the same: people must learn words before they can learn spelling, spelling before phonemes, phonemes before allophones, and allophones before all the technical units of scientific phonetics and phonology. The crucial difference is that, with speech, a 'strange inversion' occurs, whereby, as they learn each new level, people come to believe its units are real, when in fact they are merely more abstract ways of conceptualising the same continuous reality that lies behind them all.

This is the real literacy bias: not the belief that speech is a sequence of letters, but the belief that speech is a sequence of any kind of meaningless units, put together to create meaningful words and phrases. An enormous quantity of evidence shows exactly the opposite is true: using small units of speech involves recognising and producing large meaningful chunks of speech (Field, this volume). This is why the suprasegmental structure of speech is so vitally important – but syllables, feet and other suprasegmental units are not made up of phonemes, as often thought. Rather phonemes are derived from the larger units (Gillon 2007; Fraser 2010a).

Of course, once the literacy bias is understood, it is quite acceptable to model speech in any of many different ways, depending on the purpose. In particular, structural-generative models have shown themselves very useful for describing speech 'at a distance'. But a theory of phonology is not, contra Chomsky, a theory of pronunciation. Teaching, especially of learners from very different language and literacy backgrounds, requires a sound practical theory of the literacy bias to allow effective communication between teacher and learner. It is well agreed that generative theory is too complicated for this purpose. Unfortunately, merely simplifying it is not enough. It is necessary to understand the source of the complication.

The right tool for the job

The rainbow analogy shows that, despite their apparent opposition, generative theory really addresses the same problem as the behaviourists. The difference is like replacing the question, 'How are colour variants transformed into basic colours to allow recognition of the rainbow without recourse to meaning?' with 'How are cyan-yellow-magenta pixels converted to primary colours to allow recognition of the rainbow using only formalised meaning?' It is not a new question, merely a more complicated restatement of the old one.

The problems of generative theory are not caused by Chomsky's innovations. They are inherent in any theory that takes too seriously the idea that meaningful words are created by combining meaningless symbols – the literacy bias. What generative theory has done is push the literacy bias to its logical extreme. As we have seen, it is scientific research in the generative framework that has most clearly demonstrated the continuous nature of speech, and the essential role of meaning and context in speech processing. Indeed, the foundational observations with which this chapter began are largely the product of research in the generative tradition.

But generative theory ultimately cannot explain its own discoveries. Computation is essentially about meaningless discrete symbols. The paradox is, the theory that has provided the greatest evidence against the literacy bias itself remains trapped in the literacy bias (Port 2007; Ladd 2009), a kind of *reductio ad absurdum* of the belief that meaningful words and phrases can be created from meaningless sublexical parts, and a clear demonstration of the dangers of treating a complex system as a complicated one.

This is still, emphatically, not to discount the value of generative theory, merely to emphasise that, like any theory, it is just a theory, useful for some purposes and not for others. Specifically, it is inadequate for language teaching, for which a theory is needed that gives practical understanding of the difficulties faced by learners, and how to give the help they most need – especially one that gives an adequate treatment of the relationship between segmental and suprasegmental levels of analysis (Fraser 2011). Fortunately, an entirely suitable candidate is already available, requiring only minor modification.

Speech as a complex system

Complex systems have been a focus of a great deal of research across many disciplines (Ellis, this volume), and have been defined in a range of ways. Here, we focus just on the aspects most relevant to the present discussion. What makes speech a complex, as opposed to complicated, system is the fact that it is organised in the service, not of meaningless bits of sound, but of meaningful words and phrases, intended for symbolic communication between embodied, socially situated agents. This view is compatible with current thinking across a range of sociocognitive theories of language, many of whose key insights are highly relevant to pronunciation teaching. In extending such theories as the basis of a practical theory of pronunciation teaching, however, several dangers need to be navigated.

One danger is the drift to abstraction. Applied linguistics has now developed theories at least as abstract as generative grammar. Explaining the complexity of language and culture in meticulous but distant detail has many uses. However, it does not always answer the question, 'What should I do next with my class?' Another danger is a tendency to drift from 'there are no ultimate rules' to 'there are no rules', which risks a return to the dark ages of learning by induction and teaching by intuition. While it is true there are no hard and fast rules for language teaching (Thornbury, this volume), for pronunciation, at least, explicit teaching is necessary. Since teachers are the conduit between researchers and learners, it is incumbent on theorists to give teachers a framework and principles they can use to decide quickly, confidently and accurately what their students need next, and provide it in accessible form.

A further danger is letting the literacy bias creep in the back door. This happens commonly in discussing categorisation. Many theories recognise that learning to pronounce a new language involves learning new phonological categories. But 'categorisation' is used in two distinct senses. Often it is explicitly or implicitly assumed that what is required is recategorisation of phonetic units, such as allophones, in terms of new phonological units, such as phonemes. This process is better called classification, and is of little relevance to pronunciation teaching. Even if it is agreed that such classification takes place at low levels of consciousness, the fact that it is inaccessible to awareness makes knowing about it of little use to teachers.

The relevant process is the kind involved in categorising a continuous aspect of reality, such as a rainbow, in terms of meaningful units, such as basic colours, perhaps better termed conceptualisation. Though very hard to explain with a computer model of mind, this process is extremely well understood in everyday life (Bandura 1976), and especially in education (Ramsden 2003). It lies at the heart of sociocognitive theories of language and culture learning (Thorne and Tasker, this volume), and such theories are indeed entirely suitable for extension to the domain of pronunciation – so long as the dangers above are navigated appropriately. Perhaps the most useful approach is to remain as grounded as possible in the original insights of Saussure and Sapir, but update them as necessary with equally important insights from twentieth-century phonetics and phonology.

Saussure was quite clear that it was not only the signified, or meaning of a word, that must be recognised as a concept (Taylor 2002). The signifier, or sound of a word must also be seen, not merely as a piece of 'phonetic reality', but as a conceptualisation of that reality, defined in relation to the system of contrasts with other signifiers in the language. Indeed, the terms 'emic' and 'etic', now used broadly to refer to the distinction between the level of discrete, meaningful, culturally relevant units, as opposed to the level of continuous uninterpreted reality, derived originally from phonetics and phonology (Pike 1947).

Everything that is true of the signified, is also true of the signifier, including the principle of linguistic relativity (Bohn 2000), with the crucial difference being the lack of awareness associated with the signifier. This lack is readily understandable when it is remembered that the role of the signifier is precisely to direct attention away from itself and towards the signified. However, it not only makes learning second language pronunciation difficult, but also makes studying phonetics particularly challenging, as it is very difficult to focus on the signifier without being distracted by the signified, and even harder to focus on the continuous reality of speech without being distracted by presuppositions about its phonological analysis.

On this view, the key to successful pronunciation teaching is recognition that teaching pronunciation is just like teaching anything else, except that far more attention needs to be paid to ensuring learners understand the basic concepts used in the lessons. In practice, this means engaging in ongoing metalinguistic dialogue, which in turn requires the recognition that metalanguage is not merely technical terminology, but a form of language like any other, to be used in the service of effective metalinguistic communication (Fraser in press).

Conclusion

The notion of a clear divide between 'theoretical' and 'applied' linguistics is long outdated. The terms are now used more often to refer more often to the distinction between computational and sociocognitive theories than in their proper senses. Most other branches of linguistics have by now developed a range of strong alternative theories, allowing choice of computational, sociocognitive or other approaches, according to the task in hand. It is time phonetics and phonology created a practical theory appropriate to today's teaching applications.

Achieving this requires not just transfer of information in one or both directions, but genuine dialogue and shared experience. Applied linguists need to learn more phonetics and phonology, and phoneticians and phonologists need to spend more time in the language classroom, locus of a continuous stream of fascinating data desperately seeking theoretical interpretation.

Related topics

cognitive linguistics; language and culture; language emergence; language teacher education; psycholinguistics; sociocultural theory

Further reading

Bohn, O.-S. and Munro, M. J. (eds) (2007) *Language Experience in Second Language Speech Learning*, Amsterdam and Philadelphia: John Benjamins. (A key collection of recent papers covering many aspects of the phonetics, phonology and psycholinguistics of second language speech.)

Celce-Murcia, M., Brinton, D. M., Goodwin, J. M. and Griner, B. (2010) *Teaching Pronunciation: A Course Book and Reference Guide*, Cambridge: Cambridge University Press. (A thorough text specifically designed for teachers, covering many aspects of pronunciation teaching.)

Ladefoged, P. (2005) *Vowels and Consonants: An Introduction to the Sounds of Language*, 2nd edn, Oxford: Blackwell. (An accessible introduction to many important aspects of phonetics and phonology by the world's pre-eminent phonetician; despite the impression given by the title it does cover suprasegmentals.)

Sapir, E. (1949) *Language: An Introduction to the Study of Speech*, London: Harvest Books. (A classic text setting phonetics and phonology in the context of the broader study of language and culture.)

Shockey, L. (2003) *Sound Patterns of Spoken English*, Oxford: Blackwell. (A thorough treatment of the phonetics of spontaneous connected speech, emphasising the differences between how people think about speech and what speech is really like.)

Helen Fraser

References

Anderson, S. R. (1985) *Phonology in the Twentieth Century: Theories of Rules and Theories of Representation*, Chicago: University of Chicago Press.

Archibald, J. (ed.) (1995) *Phonological Acquisition and Phonological Theory*, Hillsdale, NJ: Lawrence Erlbaum Associates.

Asher, R. E. and Henderson, J. A. (eds) (1981) *Towards a History of Phonetics*, Edinburgh: Edinburgh University Press.

Ball, M. J. and Lowry, O. (2001) *Methods in Clinical Phonetics*, London: Whurr.

Bandura, A. (1976) *Social Learning Theory*, Englewood Cliffs, NJ: Prentice Hall.

Berko-Gleason, J. (2005) *The Development of Language*, 6th edn, Boston: Pearson Education.

Bloomfield, L. ([1933] 1984) *Language*, Chicago: University of Chicago Press.

Bohn, O.-S. (2000) 'Linguistic relativity in speech perception: an overview of the influence of language experience on the perception of speech sounds from infancy to adulthood', in S. Niemeier and R. Dirven (eds.) *Evidence for Linguistic Relativity*, Amsterdam and Philadelphia: John Benjamins.

Bohn, O.-S. and Munro, M. J. (eds) (2007) *Language Experience in Second Language Speech Learning*, Amsterdam and Philadelphia: John Benjamins.

Byrne, B. (1998) *The Foundation of Literacy: The Child's Acquisition of the Alphabetic Principle*, Hove: Psychology Press.

Carroll, J. B. (ed.) (1956) *Language, Thought, and Reality: Selected Writings of Benjamin Lee Whorf*, Cambridge, MA: MIT Press.

Celce-Murcia, M., Brinton, D. M. and Goodwin, J. M. (1996) *Teaching Pronunciation: A Reference for Teachers of English to Speakers of Other Languages*, Cambridge: Cambridge University Press.

Collins, B. and Mees, I. M. (2003) *Practical Phonetics and Phonology: A Resource Book for Students*, London: Routledge.

Couper, G. (2006) 'The short and long-term effects of pronunciation instruction', *Prospect* 21: 44–64.

Derwing, T., Munro, M. and Wiebe, G. (1998) 'Evidence in favour of a broad framework for pronunciation instruction', *Language Learning* 48: 393–410.

Erard, M. (2007) *Um: Slips, Stumbles and Verbal Blunders, and What They Mean*, New York: Random House.

Fraser, H. (1997) 'Dictionary pronunciation guides for English', *International Journal of Lexicography* 10: 181–208.

——(2003) 'Issues in transcription: factors affecting the reliability of transcripts as evidence in legal cases', *International Journal of Speech Language and the Law* 10: 203–26.

——(2004) *Teaching Pronunciation: A Guide for Teachers of English as a Second Language (CD-ROM)*, Canberra: Commonwealth of Australia, Department of Education Training and Youth Affairs. Available at: http://helenfraser.com.au

——(2009a) 'Pronunciation as categorization: the role of contrast in teaching English /r/ and /l/', in A. Mahboob and C. Lipovsky (eds) *Studies in Applied Linguistics and Language Learning*, Newcastle upon Tyne: Cambridge Scholars Publishing.

——(2009b) 'The role of "educated native speakers" in providing language analysis for the determination of the origin of asylum seekers', *International Journal of Speech Language and the Law* 16: 113–38.

——(2010a) 'Cognitive phonology as a tool for teaching pronunciation', in S. de Knop, F. Boers and T. de Rycker (eds) *Fostering Language Teaching Efficiency Through Cognitive Linguistics*, Berlin: Mouton de Gruyter.

——(2010b) 'Transcripts in the legal system', in I. Freckelton and H. Selby (eds) *Expert Evidence*, Sydney, NSW: Thomson Reuters.

——(2011) 'Speaking of speech: developing metalanguage for effective communication about pronunciation between English language teachers and learners', in A. Henderson (ed.) *Proceedings of the International Conference on English Pronunciation: Issues and Practices*, Chambéry: Université de Savoie.

Frith, C. (2008) *Making up the Mind: How the Brain Creates the Mental World*, Oxford: Blackwell.

Gilbert, J. (2005) *Clear Speech from the Start: Basic Pronunciation and Listening Comprehension in North American English*, 2nd edn, Cambridge: Cambridge University Press.

594

——(2010) 'Pronunciation as orphan: what can be done', *Speak Out!* 43: 3–7.

Gillon, G. (2007) *Phonological Awareness: From Research to Practice*, New York: Guilford Press.

Gombert, J.-E. (1992) *Metalinguistic Development*, Hemel Hempstead: Harvester Wheatsheaf.

Gussenhoven, C. and Jacobs, H. (2005) *Understanding Phonology*, 2nd edn, London: Hodder Arnold.

Hahn, L. (2004) 'Primary stress and intelligibility: research to motivate the teaching of supraseg-mentals', *TESOL Quarterly* 38: 201–23.

Hardcastle, W. J., Laver, J. and Gibbon, F. E. (eds) (2010) *The Handbook of Phonetic Sciences*, 2nd edn, Oxford: Wiley-Blackwell.

Hardin, C. L. and Maffi, L. (eds) (1997) *Color Categories in Thought and Language*, Cambridge: Cambridge University Press.

Henderson, A. (ed.) (2010) *Proceedings of the International Conference on English Pronunciation: Issues and Practices*, Chambéry: Université de Savoie.

Jannedy, S. and Hay, J. (eds) (2006) 'Modelling sociophonetic variation', special issue, *Journal of Phonetics* 34(4).

Just, M. and Carpenter, P. A. (1987) *The Psychology of Reading and Language Comprehension*, Boston: Allyn and Bacon.

Kenworthy, J. (1987) *Teaching English Pronunciation*, London: Longman.

Ladd, D. R. (2009) 'Phonetics in phonology', in J. Goldsmith, J. Riggle and A. Yu (eds) *Handbook of Phonological Theory*, Oxford: Blackwell.

Ladefoged, P. (2005) *Vowels and Consonants: An Introduction to the Sounds of Language*, 2nd edn, Oxford: Blackwell.

Ladefoged, P. and Maddieson, I. (1996) *The Sounds of the World's Languages*, Oxford: Basil Blackwell.

Laver, J. (1994) *Principles of Phonetics*, Cambridge: Cambridge University Press.

Linell, P. (1988) 'The impact of literacy on the conception of language: the case of linguistics', in R. Saljö (ed.) *The Written World: Studies in Literate Thought and Action*, Berlin: Springer.

Macdonald, M. (2008) *Your Brain: The Missing Manual*, Sebastopol, CA: O'Reilly.

Macdonald, S. (2002) 'Pronunciation: views and practices of reluctant teachers', *Prospect* 17: 3–15.

Morley, J. (1991) 'The pronunciation component in teaching English to speakers of other lan-guages', *TESOL Quarterly* 25: 481–520.

——(ed.) (1994) *Pronunciation Pedagogy and Theory: New Views, New Directions*, Alexandria, VA: TESOL.

Nusbaum, H. and Goodman, J. (1994) 'Learning to hear speech as spoken language', in J. Goodman and H. Nusbaum (eds) *The Development of Speech Perception*, Cambridge, MA: MIT Press.

Pennington, M. C. (ed.) (2006) *Phonology in Context*, New York: Palgrave Macmillan.

Perkell, J. and Klatt, D. (eds) (1986) *Invariance and Variability in Speech Processes*, Hillsdale, NJ: Lawrence Erlbaum Associates.

Pierrehumbert, J., Beckman, M. E. and Ladd, D. R. (1993) 'Conceptual foundations of phonology as a laboratory science', in N. Burton-Roberts, P. Carr and G. Docherty (eds) *Phonological Knowledge: Its Nature and Status*, Cambridge: Cambridge University Press.

Pike, K. L. (1947) *Phonemics: A Technique for Reducing Languages to Writing*, Ann Arbor: University of Michigan Press.

Port, R. (2007) 'The graphical basis of phones and phonemes', in O.-S. Bohn and M. J. Munro (eds) *Second Language Speech Learning: The Role of Language Experience in Speech Perception and Production*, Amsterdam: John Benjamins.

Ramsden, P. (2003) *Learning to Teach in Higher Education*, 2nd edn, Abingdon: Routledge.

Roach, P. (1991) *English Phonetics and Phonology: A Practical Course*, 2nd edn., Cambridge: Cambridge University Press.

Rose, P. (2002) *Forensic Speaker Identification*, London: Taylor and Francis.

Sapir, E. (1949) *Language: An Introduction to the Study of Speech*, London: Harvest Books.

de Saussure, F. ([1916] 1983) *Course in General Linguistics*, London: Duckworth.

Scarborough, H. S., Ehri, L. C., Olson, R. K. and Fowler, A. E. (1998) 'The fate of phonemic awareness beyond the elementary school years', *Scientific Studies of Reading* 2: 115–42.

Shockey, L. (2003) *Sound Patterns of Spoken English*, Oxford: Blackwell.

Strange, W. (ed.) (1995) *Speech Perception and Linguistic Experience: Issues in Cross-language Research*, Baltimore: York Press.

Taylor, J. R. (2002) *Cognitive Grammar*, Oxford: Oxford University Press.

Underhill, A. (1994) *Sound Foundations: Living Phonology*, Oxford: Heinemann.

Venkatagiri, H. S. and Levis, J. (2007) 'Metaphonological knowledge and comprehensibility: an exploratory study', *Language Awareness* 16: 263–77.

Vihman, M. (1996) *Phonological Development*, Oxford: Basil Blackwell.

Warren, R. (1999) *Auditory Perception: A New Analysis and Synthesis*, 2nd edn, Cambridge: Cambridge University Press.

Wells, J. C. (2003) 'Phonetic research by written questionnaire', International Congress of Phonetic Sciences, Barcelona.

Westley, F., Zimmerman, B. and Patton, M. (2006) *Getting to Maybe: How the World is Changed*, New York: Random House.

Yallop, C. (1995) *English Phonology*, Sydney, NSW: National Centre for English Language Teaching and Research.

Yavas, M. (ed.) (1994) *First and Second Language Phonology*, San Diego, CA: Singular Publishing Group.

42

Corpus linguistics

Svenja Adolphs and Phoebe M. S. Lin

Introduction

Corpus linguistics most commonly refers to the study of machine-readable spoken and written language samples that have been assembled in a principled way for the purpose of linguistics research. At the heart of empirically based linguistics and data-driven description of language, corpus linguistics is concerned with language use in real contexts. Therefore, it is often contrasted with Chomskyan linguistics, which emphasises language competence and often involves made-up examples as the basis of its exploration of language. Access to ever larger spoken and written corpora has already revolutionised the description of language in use; however, the impact of corpus linguistics has reached far beyond the disciplines that are purely concerned with linguistic descriptions of language. As an approach, corpus linguistics continues to gain recognition and popularity, with an increasing number of researchers across different disciplines exploring innovative ways of using corpus-based research as part of their methods toolkit.

This chapter provides a brief overview of some of the different types of corpora available and some of the methods used within the area of corpus linguistics, including the generation of frequency lists, concordance outputs and keyword analyses. It then moves on to a discussion of selected current issues in corpus linguistics. We focus here on three issues which we believe are marked by the persistent attention they have received in the field, as well as by their prominent status among researchers and end-users. The issues we will introduce include an area of language description (phraseology and corpus research), an area of application (English language teaching and corpus research), and an area of resource development (the Web as corpus). The chapter will conclude with a discussion of the impact which technological developments may have on the discipline. All the corpus resources mentioned in this chapter can be found after the 'Further reading' section.

Corpus as data

Corpora are designed to represent a particular language variety. Common distinctions are made between *specialised* and *general* corpora, where the former includes texts that belong to

597

a particular type, e.g. academic prose, while the latter includes many different types of texts, often assembled with the aim to serve as reference resources for linguistic research or to produce reference materials such as dictionaries. Other types of corpora include *historical* and *monitor* corpora, *parallel* corpora and *learner* corpora. Historical corpora include texts from different periods of time and allow for the study of language change when compared with corpora from other periods. Monitor corpora can be used for a similar purpose, but tend to focus on current changes in the language. New texts from the same variety are added to the existing corpus at regular intervals, thus contributing to a constantly growing text database. Parallel corpora include texts in at least two languages that have either been directly translated, or produced in different languages for the same purpose. Such corpora are often used in translation studies. Learner corpora contain collections of texts produced by learners of a language. They allow the researcher to identify patterns in a particular variety of learner English, and to compare the language of the learner to that of other users of a language.

In terms of the history of corpus design, a distinction is often made between the early corpora developed in the 1950s, 1960s and 1970s and the larger corpora developed from the late 1980s onwards. Early corpora include the London-Lund Corpus of Spoken English (LLC), the Brown Corpus based on American written English, and the Lancaster-Oslo/Bergen Corpus based on written British English. The parallel design of the latter two corpora allowed for a corpus-based comparison between British and American English. Early corpora were often limited in size to a one million word threshold, which is partly a reflection of the technological possibilities at the time.

Two of the most substantial corpus projects developed in the 1980s and 1990s are the Collins and Birmingham University International Language Database (COBUILD) and the British National Corpus. Both offer a valuable resource for the study of everyday spoken and written English. The COBUILD corpus, which is also referred to as the Bank of English, was developed in the 1990s as a monitor corpus. This means that new texts are constantly added to this database: the size of the corpus stood at 450 million words. One of the main aims of this project has been to provide a textual database for the compilation of dictionaries and lexicography research. The corpus contains samples of mainly British written language, as well as transcribed speech from interviews, broadcast, and conversation. The British National Corpus (BNC) was compiled in the late 1980s and early 1990s, and is a 100 million word corpus of modern British English, consisting of 90 per cent written and 10 per cent spoken texts (including speeches, meetings, lectures, and some casual conversation). Apart from these two major corpora, many publishing houses have developed their own corpora which serve as a resource for authors, mainly in the area of lexicography. Examples are the Cambridge International Corpus (CIC), the Longman Corpus Network and the Oxford English Corpus. Another large corpus project is the International Corpus of English (ICE), which was initiated in 1990 as a resource for comparing different varieties of English. At the time of writing, the ICE consists of 22 one-million-word corpora, each representing a regional variety of English. More recently, two substantial American English corpora have been developed: the American National Corpus (ANC) and the Corpus of Contemporary American English (COCA). By 2009 the ANC contained 22 million words of written and spoken texts in American English produced since 1990. The COCA consists of more than 400 million words of American English, with 21 per cent spoken and 79 per cent written material. With 20 million words added each year, the COCA can also be used as a monitor corpus to capture language change.

The corpora above mainly focus on the collection of general English in use. As such they contrast with specialised corpora which range from those that represent the language of a particular group of people, such as the Bergen Corpus of London Teenage Language (COLT), to those that represent a particular mode of discourse. Some of the major developments of specialised corpora have taken place in the domain of academic discourse and include, for example, the Michigan Corpus of Academic Spoken English (MICASE), and its British counterpart, the British Academic Spoken English corpus (BASE).

Another category of corpora captures the language use of language learners. The analysis of learner corpora makes it possible to track developmental aspects of learner language, as well as to highlight particular areas of difficulty for the learner. At the same time, learner corpora can be used as a basis for better descriptions of different varieties that emerge from communication between speakers who communicate in a language other than their first language. The design criteria for learner corpora have a slightly different focus to native speaker corpora in that particular emphasis has to be placed on the level of consistency of the resource in terms of the language background of the speakers, including their level of proficiency and first language. Examples of learner corpora include the Cambridge Learner Corpus the Longman Learners' Corpus and the International Corpus of Learner English (ICLE). Examples of corpora which are used as the basis for exploring the use of English as a lingua franca include the Vienna-Oxford International Corpus of English (VOICE) and the English as a Lingua Franca in Academic Settings (ELFA) corpus.

Many of the corpora outlined above come with their own concordancing interface, often available via the Internet. The next section will consider in more detail the various tools and methods which may be used to explore the language captured in spoken and written corpora.

Metadata

Apart from the process of assembling written and spoken language samples in a principled way into a corpus, it is also important to collect and document further information about the collected discourse itself. Metadata, or 'data about data', is the conventional method used to do this. Burnard (2005) states that 'without metadata the investigator has nothing but disconnected words of unknowable provenance or authenticity'. Thus, metadata are critical to a corpus to help achieve the standards for *representativeness*, and of *balance* and *homogeneity* (see Sinclair 2005).

Burnard (2005) uses the term *metadata* as an umbrella term which includes editorial, analytic, descriptive and administrative categories:

- Editorial metadata: providing information about the relationship between corpus components and their original source.
- Analytic metadata: providing information about the way in which corpus components have been interpreted and analysed.
- Descriptive metadata: providing classificatory information derived from internal or external properties of the corpus components.
- Administrative metadata: providing documentary information about the corpus itself, such as its title, its availability, its revision status, etc.

Metadata are particularly important when the corpus is shared and reused by others in a research community, and they also assist in the preservation of electronic texts. Metadata can be kept in a separate database or included as a 'header' at the start of each document (usually encoded though mark-up language). A separate database with this information makes it easier to compare different types of documents and has the distinct advantage that it can be further extended by other users of the same data. The documentation of the design rationale, as well as the various editorial processes that an individual text has been subjected to during the collection and archiving stages, facilitates replicability of research and validation of results.

Corpus linguistics: tools and methods

A number of user-friendly software packages are available which facilitate the manipulation and analysis of corpus data. Common functionalities include the generation of frequency counts according to specified criteria, comparisons of frequency information in different texts, different formats of concordance outputs, including the Key Word In Context (KWIC) concordance, and the extraction of multiword units or clusters of items in a text. Many of these programs can be downloaded from the Internet or used directly via an interactive Website (see, for example, the Compleat Lexical Tutor, BNCWeb and BYU-BNC). Other programs are distributed commercially, often by publishing houses, and can be purchased for a fee.

Word lists

The frequency of a word or a phrase in different contexts is an important part of its description. Various word lists that are based to some degree on word frequency in a corpus exist especially in the English language teaching (ELT) context, such as the Academic Word List (Coxhead 2000) and the Academic Formulas List (Simpson-Vlach and Ellis 2010). Word lists are a good starting point for subsequent searches of individual items at concordance level and can be useful in the comparison of different corpora. Word lists can be generated to account for individual items or for recurrent sequences of two or more items. Lemmatised frequency lists group together words from the same lemma. For example, the words 'say', 'said', 'saying', 'says' are all part of the lemma SAY. Lemmatisation can be done manually using an alphabetical frequency list, or in an automated way which is often based to some degree on lists of predefined lemmas. Different forms of the same lemma tend to vary significantly in terms of their overall frequency, with one particular form tending to be more frequent than others in the lemma. Previous research has shown that there often are variations in meaning between different variants of the lemma (Stubbs 1996; Tognini-Bonelli 2001). Lemmatised lists also have a place in more applied contexts, including ELT where it can be beneficial to teach all forms of one lemma together while giving priority to the most frequently used form.

The kind of basic information that can be gathered from a frequency list is illustrated with reference to Table 42.1, which shows the ten most frequent items in the spoken Limerick Corpus of Irish English (LCIE) and in the written component of the British National Corpus (O'Keeffe *et al.* 2011). LCIE is a corpus of naturally occurring contemporary spoken Irish

Table 42.1 Ten most frequent words in the BNC (written) and LCIE (spoken)

	BNC	LCIE
1	the	the
2	of	I
3	and	and
4	a	you
5	in	to
6	to	it
7	is	a
8	was	that
9	it	of
10	for	yeah

English (for more details see Farr *et al.* 2004). A comparison of the ten most frequent words in a spoken and a written corpus highlights some of the key differences between the two modes of discourse. Both contain mainly grammatical items, which is expected in terms of the general distribution of different items in the English language. However, the spoken corpus list also includes the personal pronouns 'I' and 'You' which shows the interactive nature of the discourse that makes up this corpus. In addition, the vocalisation 'Yeah' occurs amongst the most frequent items in the spoken data reflecting the pervasive occurrence of listener response tokens in conversation. These three items are at the heart of spoken interaction and the frequency list helps to identify those defining items.

Table 42.2 shows the ten most frequent two-word, three-word and four-word n-grams in LCIE. This type of frequency output highlights the phrasal nature of language. Although the kinds of sequences generated in this way do not necessarily reflect the underlying phraseology of language fully, the output is strongly suggestive of common phrases of which the sequences in Table 42.2 form a part. However, a mere frequency-based list of continuous sequences is limited in its explanatory power when it comes to the study of phraseology. Research in the area of computational linguistics has introduced new techniques for extracting meaningful units from corpora, both on the basis of frequency information (see, for example, Danielsson 2003) and on the basis of part-of-speech tagged corpora which include further annotation of semantic fields (Rayson 2003).

Keywords and key sequences

Keywords are as words which occur either with a significantly higher frequency (positive keywords) or with a significantly lower frequency (negative keywords) in a text or collection of texts, when they are compared to a reference corpus (Scott 1997). Keywords are identified on the basis of statistical comparisons of word frequency lists derived from the target corpus and the reference corpus. Each item in the target corpus is compared with its equivalent in the reference corpus, and the statistical significance of difference is calculated using chi-square or log-likelihood statistics (see Dunning 1993). Both of these statistics compare actual observed frequencies between two items with their expected frequencies, assuming random distribution. If the difference between observed and expected frequency is large then it is likely that the relationship between the two items is not random. The procedure thus generates words that are characteristic, as well as those that are uncharacteristic in a given target corpus. The choice of the

Table 42.2 Ten most frequent 2-word, 3-word and 4-word units in LCIE results per million words

Frequency rank	2-word units		3-word units		4-word units	
1	you know	4406	I don't know	1212	you know what I	230
2	in the	3435	do you know	769	know what I mean	215
3	of the	2354	a lot of	522	do you know what	208
4	do you	2332	you know what	379	I don't know what	134
5	I don't	2200	do you want	373	do you want to	121
6	I think	2003	I don't think	338	are you going to	103
7	It was	1939	you know the	323	you know the way	103
8	I was	1891	you have to	308	I don't know I	91
9	going to	1849	going to be	307	thank you very much	91
10	on the	1801	yeah yeah yeah	297	the end of the	85

reference corpus used as the basis for such a comparison is crucial in this context, as it affects the output of keywords. For example, in a comparison of a transcript of medical consultation with a reference corpus that consists solely of written texts, the characteristics of spoken versus written language may interfere with the analysis of keywords in the medical consultation genre.

We can generate keyword lists as well as lists of key sequences. The list below contains key sequences resulting from a comparison of health communication used as part of a UK telephone health advice service with the CANCODE, a five-million-word corpus of casual conversation in British English. The sequences are the ten most significant positive key sequences in the Nottingham Health Communication Corpus featuring health communication in the British context (see Adolphs et al. 2004; Adolphs 2006).

1 NHS Direct
2 NHS
3 Just bear with
4 Call you back
5 Bear with me
6 Date of birth
7 Your date of
8 You're calling from
9 Manage their services
10 However anybody with

As can be expected, quite a few of the recurrent sequences in this list form part of the responses that typically mark the beginning of telephone interactions with the health advice service NHS Direct. Other sequences relate to the gathering of basic information about the caller. The most significant negative key sequence, i.e. the one that occurs with a significantly lower frequency in the Health Communication Corpus, in comparison to the corpus of casual conversation, is 'I don't know'. This highlights the professional nature of this encounter where the emphasis is on providing knowledge and advice. 'I don't know' is a common hedge and politeness marker in casual conversation and does not fit with the more asymmetrical medical exchanges by telephone.

The concordance output

An example of a Key Word in Context (KWIC) concordance of the word 'corpus' using the BNCWeb is shown in Figure 42.1. Corpus users can normally specify the number of words to the left and to the right of the search word that are displayed as part of the output. If a corpus is tagged for part-of-speech (POS), then users may also carry out a concordance search based on word class or grammatical structure.

There are many ways of examining and interpreting concordance data. A concordance output can be useful in providing a representation of language data which allows the user to notice patterns relating to the way in which a lexical item or a sequence is used in context. Sinclair (1996) argues that a new unit of meaning emerges from the analysis of concordance data that extends beyond the single word and takes into account the properties and patterns that are revealed by concordance analysis. Such units, as Sinclair points out, are going to be 'largely phrasal' (1996: 82). In order to describe the nature of individual units of meaning, Sinclair (1996) suggests four parameters: collocation, colligation, semantic preference and semantic prosody. Collocation refers to the habitual co-occurrence of words and will be discussed in more detail below. Colligation is the co-occurrence of grammatical choices. Grammatical

Your query "[word="corpus"%c]" returned 773 hits in 201 different texts (98,313,429 words [4,048 texts]; frequency: 7.86 instances per million words) (displayed in random order)

No	Filename	Hits 1 to 10	Page 1 / 78	
1	J0V 2050	a heading and extensive bibliographic information wherever a new item in the	**corpus**	began. The package would also recognize footnotes (perhaps nested to
2	HGR 1504	. Clear (1990) suggests that perhaps the size of a	**corpus**	is more significant than its composition although the two parameters are inter-dependent
3	A03 129	lower courts. However, the Supreme Court subsequently annulled the habeas	**corpus**	on grounds of procedural irregularites . Dr. Zúñiga was warned that the
4	HU9 1148	held in Belgium at Liege — the city where the Feast of	**Corpus**	Christi originated. However, because of political circumstances it was held
5	A68 1367	imagined as a wet blanket. In those days the Fellows of	**Corpus**	were rather proud of the briskness of their conversation. Instead Ramsey
6	B77 2169	one scholar of native American languages calls the manuscripts 'the largest	**corpus**	of texts' of them and 'a remarkable resource'.
7	CMH 935	of this approach is the work on the effects of cutting the	**corpus**	callosum in humans (Gazzaniga 1985). Some thirty years ago
8	CFF 333	pay for him to study at the latter's old college of	**Corpus**	Christi at Oxford. Here his most influential teacher was John Reynolds
9	CG6 151	the linguist studying children's language, children have access to a	**corpus**	or sample of language in the utterances they hear. This appears
10	EES 1839	were. Evidently, the general collocation dictionary derived from the LOB	**corpus**	can make a significant contribution to the recognition of domain-specific documents

Figure 42.1 A KWIC concordance of the word 'corpus' using the BNCWeb
Source: Extracted from the British National Corpus Online service, managed by Oxford University Computing Services on behalf of the BNC Consortium.

patterning around a particular word accounts for the 'variation' of a phrase, which 'gives the phrase its essential flexibility, so that it can fit into the surrounding co-text' (Sinclair 1996: 83). Many of the so-called 'fixed phrases' are therefore only fixed if we consider the lexico-grammatical 'core'. If we extend the units of meaning, however, to patterns in the co-text, the expressions become more variable. One of the examples Sinclair provides is the phrase 'true feelings' which, in the Bank of English, exhibits the following patterns:

At N-3 position and beyond: 'will never reveal', 'prevents me from expressing', 'careful about expressing', 'less open about showing', 'guilty about expressing'

At N-2 position: 'communicate', 'show', 'reveal', 'share', 'pour out', 'give vent to', 'indicate' and 'make public'

At N-1 position: possessives such as 'our'

The collocates of 'true feelings' show clear patterns in terms of semantic prosody, semantic preference and colligation. The semantic preference of a lexical item or expression is a semantic abstraction of its prominent collocates. In his discussion of the expression 'the naked eye', Sinclair (1996) finds that most of the verbs and adjectives preceding this expression are related to the concept of 'vision'. The verbs 'see' and 'seen' together occur 25 times within four words to the left of the expression in a sample of 151 examples of 'the naked eye' that he studies. Sinclair (1996) uses, as his fourth parameter in the description of the units of meaning, the concept of *semantic prosody*. First discussed by Sinclair (1987) and Louw (1993), semantic prosodies are associations that arise from the collocates of a lexical item and are not easily detected using introspection. Semantic prosodies have mainly been described in terms of their positive or negative polarity (Sinclair 1991a; Stubbs 1995) but also in terms of their association with 'tentativeness/indirectness/face saving' (McCarthy 1998: 22). Carter and McCarthy (1999) find, for example, that there is a consistently negative semantic prosody associated with the *get*-passive in the corpus data they examine (e.g. 'get arrested', 'get sued' and 'get nicked').

Current issues in corpus linguistics

Phraseology

John Sinclair's (1991a) contributions relating to lexical patterning have been highly influential in the field (see Stubbs 2009). One of the most notable aspects of his work is his research on the prevalence of phraseology or multiword units. The idea that everyday language is full of highly recurrent sequences of words challenges the traditional perception of language processing in the brain and the belief that language production (and reception) relies on a completely rule-based system. Corpus evidence, which highlights the prevalence of highly recurrent chunks or multiword units, suggests that we have a large store of conventional, preferred expressions that we use regularly to express meaning. Therefore, Sinclair (1991a) suggests that highly recurrent chunks are fundamental to the organisation and the production of language, and proposes that language production is the result of the alternation between the idiom principle and the open-choice principle. The idiom principle posits that 'a language user has available to him or her a large number of semi-preconstructed phrases that constitute single choices, even though they might appear to be analyzable into segments' (1991a: 110). The open-choice principle is also known as the slot-and-filler model, for it sees a text as constituted by a series of slots to be filled by lexis which satisfies certain grammatical constraints. According to Sinclair (1991a), for normal texts the idiom principle is the first (i.e. the default) mode to be applied. The switch to the open-choice principle occurs only when there is good reason for the switch to occur. This explains why multiword units are so prevalent. According to a study by Erman and Warren (2000), multiword units account for slightly over half of English speech and writing. Altenberg (1998: 102), who adopts an alternative definition of phraseology, estimates that 'over 80 percent of the words in the [London-Lund] corpus form part of a recurrent word-combination in one way or another'.

A related major contribution to the field relates to the study of word sense and relations where J. R. Firth's (1957: 11) idea that 'you shall know a word by the company it keeps' has found support from corpus evidence. A simple example to illustrate the dynamics of word meanings as a result of collocation is shown in the concordance of the word 'stand' (Table 42.3 below), taken from the BNCWeb. We know that the basic meaning of the word 'stand' is to rise to or to maintain an upright position. But when 'stand' collocates with other words, it takes up a metaphorical meaning.

The term *multiword unit* is often used in this context as an umbrella term for sequences of interrelated words which are retrieved from memory as single lexical units. They occur with varying degrees of fixedness, including formulae (e.g. *have a nice day*), metaphors (e.g. *kick the bucket*) and collocations (e.g. *rancid butter*) (Moon 1998; Wray 2002). The description and conceptualisation of multiword units are a key concern in many different areas of language study ranging from psycholinguistics to Natural Language Processing (NLP). There are many different ways of identifying multiword units. These include intuitive identification, the use of discourse analytical techniques, and automatic extraction from electronic texts (see

Table 42.3 Concordance of the word 'stand', taken from the BNCWeb

up for huge amounts of emotional strain, knowing that their clients	stand	to lose more than their liberty. Since almost all those on
, all modes of thought and life. Certainly Lady Lisa might	stand	as the embodiment of the old fancy, the symbol of the
, or obeyed it only in so far as he took a	stand	against conservative taste. He did not take sides against Abstraction,
any view. Reynolds was a notable conversationalist, well able to	stand	up to his friends, who included Samuel Johnson and Edmund Burke
approach, it must be admitted. In Rome a visitor can	stand	in front of a Baroque church, but a few minutes later
the progress of this mad love – to which he did not	stand	all that close at the time, brother as he was –
to revel in his own discomfiture here, in his desperate last	stand	for freedom – he clearly enjoys the sensation of falling in love,
of them were particularly concerned with 'glamour'. What does	stand	out is that everyone believes that the profession, its standards and
number of higher clergy in Ulster and many of its lay intellectuals	stand	a long way off from protestant–loyalist politics and are in
will do now, he wrote. It must be impossible to	stand	up against it, he wrote, impossible to draw breath before

Wray 2002, 2008). The classification into different types of multiword units tends to be linked to particular characteristics. Formulae, for example, are marked by their pragmatic function (see Aijmer 1996) while collocations are marked by their frequency of co-occurrence in discourse. Multiword units are closely linked to the particular genre in which they occur (see, for example, Biber and Conrad 1999; Biber *et al.* 2003; Oakey 2002; Schmitt 2004; Simpson 2004; Biber 2006, 2009 for discussions of multiword units in academic speech and writing).

Corpora and English language teaching

While corpus linguistics has enabled better descriptions of language in use, its real impact lies in the enhancement of applications based on those descriptions. A key area to highlight in this context is that of English language teaching, where the latest findings from corpus research have led to real innovations in material design and classroom practice. There are two main areas in which corpora can benefit language teaching and learning: first, by incorporating the latest corpus-based findings into language syllabuses, teaching materials and dictionaries; second, by encouraging teachers and learners to examine language patterns in corpus as part of their (independent) learning activities in and outside classrooms (see Gavioli and Aston 2001).

Corpus linguists and language teaching researchers are often found collaborating in these two areas and there are now publications on the subject. Some of these (e.g. Meunier and Granger 2008) provide further corpus-based descriptions of aspects of language which target the needs of specific groups of language learners, e.g. ESP/EAP learners or learners of the same L1 background. Others (e.g. Hunston 2002; Sinclair 2003) aim to equip teachers and learners with the skills of concordancing and extracting useful information from concordance lines. Other publications (e.g. Tribble and Jones 1997; O'Keeffe *et al.* 2007) include practical suggestions on the various ways in which corpus research can be introduced into the language classroom to enrich the experience of language learners.

Despite the growing interest in the pedagogical applications of corpus linguistics, there have been a number of debates relating to the place of corpus linguistics in language teaching (see Sinclair 1991b; Widdowson 1991; Seidlhofer 2003). Widdowson (1991), for instance, argues that the fact that a language pattern is particularly frequent in a corpus does not necessarily mean that it should take priority in the language teaching syllabus. Further discussion centres around the issue of authenticity and whether it is beneficial to present learners with authentic, real language in use (see McCarthy and Carter 1995; Carter and McCarthy 1996; Prodromou 1996a, 1996b, 1998). According to Prodromou (1996b), it is a 'fallacy' to assume that real language is spontaneously interesting and useful to foreign language learners. He argues that train timetables, advertisements, letters published in British newspapers and consumer leaflets are only real to members of the speech community that these texts target. When such data are used as teaching material in a foreign language classroom, they mean very little to the language learners because they lack the same reality for this specific audience. Prodromou (1996a) suggests that an 'authentic' discourse has its 'here and nowness', and when the discourse is presented in a context that is detached from the 'here and now' it automatically loses its authenticity. Similarly, Widdowson (2000) argues that the language presented in a corpus is decontextualised and only partially real. If the decontextualised language in a corpus is to be presented to learners as language in use, it has to be recontextualised. Yet, the reconstituted context is not always the same as the original context of the texts (see Prodromou 2008).

Despite these arguments, corpus data are increasingly becoming an accepted and desirable basis for the development of English language teaching materials, and most major dictionaries and grammars now advertise the fact that they are based on 'real' language from a corpus.

The Web as corpus

Today, corpus size has long exceeded the one million word standard set by the Brown Corpus in the 1960s. The Cambridge International Corpus (CIC), which collects spoken and written texts of American English, British English and learner English, is currently one of the biggest corpora of English, with over a billion words. However, with the advent of the world-wide-Web we now have access to language data which far exceeds even the most substantial corpus.

Kilgarriff and Grefenstette (2003) suggest that checking spelling and usage of a word by typing it into an Internet search engine is a practical example of how the World Wide Web is already being used as a language corpus on a daily basis by a large number of people. They give the example of 'speculater' and 'speculator'. A search engine reveals that these two spellings generate, respectively, 67 hits and 82,000 hits on the Web. Therefore, based on the higher frequency of occurrence of 'speculator', one may conclude that this is the preferred spelling.

However, for the Web to provide more than free, instant suggestions on spellings, corpus linguists have developed Web-based interfaces that allow researchers to use the Web as a compatible resource for linguistic research. WebCorp, for example, allows users greater control over the type of texts to be searched. They can specify the register, textual domain, topic range, date of modification and so on. These facilities support investigations into both synchronic and diachronic changes in language (see Renouf 2003; Renouf *et al.* 2007). Another advantage of using WebCorp over general Internet search engines in lexical research is that the former offers basic statistical information, including the collocational profile of search items and the option to disambiguate polysemous items (Renouf 1993). The WebCorp interface can also be used to generate frequency lists of Websites specified by the user. It is clearly a valuable resource to use in its own right, but it can also be used to complement research on finite corpora in terms of the up-to-date evidence of language in use that it offers.

While the World Wide Web is a very large repository of naturally occurring language, further research is needed as to the type of language that is being used on the Web, what it represents, and how balanced it is in the context of a particular research question. Given the ubiquity of Internet-based and Internet-stored discourse, this endeavour becomes particularly urgent.

The impact of new technologies on corpus linguistics: an example

One of the main impacts of new technology on the area of corpus linguistics is no doubt the use of the Web as a corpus. In addition, there have been significant advances in spoken corpus linguistics which have been afforded by the alignment of different modalities with a transcript. This development started with the alignment of audio recordings with transcripts, and has recently been extended to include video data as well. It has long been pointed out by corpus linguists working with spoken data that the lack of audio and video leads to problems in the analysis of this kind of corpus data. De Cock (1998), for example, in a discussion of the sequence 'you know', argues that it is virtually impossible to decide whether 'you know' has a literal or a formulaic meaning on the basis of the orthographic transcript alone. Similarly, Lin and Adolphs (2009) observe that it is not possible to determine the functions of some instances of 'I don't know why' in context unless one can refer to their prosody. Similar concerns arise from a corpus-based analysis of multimodal written texts, i.e. those containing images and graphics.

Gesture, prosody and kinesics all add meaning to utterances and discourse as a whole, and recent research in the area of spoken corpus analysis has started to explore the potential impact of drawing on multimodal corpus resources for our descriptions of spoken language (see, for example, Knight *et al.* 2009). In addition to offering a more comprehensive resource for describing discourse, multimodal corpora also allow us to reflect on and evaluate some of the methods for analysing textual renderings of spoken discourse established so far. The representation and analysis of 'textual' concordance data thus becomes limited and limiting in a way that can now be avoided by using one of the tools and interfaces developed for aligning and searching text, audio and video data, such as ELAN or Transana.

Summary

In this chapter we have provided a brief overview of some of the key methods and current issues in corpus linguistics. This has included an overview of different types of corpora, as well as an introduction to analytical methods. Key issues that have been highlighted in this chapter relate to the use of corpus linguistics in phraseology research, English language teaching and the use of the Web as corpus. We have also discussed the role of new technologies in the development of multimodal corpus resources. As a discipline, corpus linguistics is gathering pace with the development of ever larger data-sets and with an increasingly sophisticated suite of tools that can be used to analyse these data and represent the outputs. One of the main challenges for the future will be to fully explore the implications of these advances, not only for language description in its own right, but also crucially for other disciplines, and the impact that this work may have in applied contexts.

Related topics

critical discourse analysis; discourse; English for academic purposes; ESP and business communication; language learning and language education; lexicography; lexis; medical communication; SLA; technology and language learning; the media; translation and interpreting; world Englishes

Further reading

Anderson, W. and Corbett, J. (2009) *Exploring English with Online Corpora*, Basingstoke: Palgrave Macmillan. (This volume offers an introduction to how online corpora can be used in the teaching and learning of English.)
Baker, P., Hardie, A. and McEnery, A. (2006) *A Glossary of Corpus Linguistics*, Edinburgh: Edinburgh University Press. (This book provides a comprehensive overview of key concepts and relevant references in corpus linguistics.)
Hoffmann, S., Evert, S., Smith, N., Lee, D. and Prytz, Y. B. (2008) *Corpus Linguistics with BNCWeb: A Practical Guide*, Frankfurt: Peter Lang. (This book offers a practical, hands-on introduction to corpus linguistic methods using the BNCWeb corpus interface.)
Sinclair, J. (2004) *Trust the Text: Language, Corpus and Discourse*, London: Routledge. (This volume is a collection of some of Sinclair's most influential papers in the area of corpus linguistics and lexico-grammar.)

Resources mentioned in the chapter

Language corpora

American National Corpus: www.americannationalcorpus.org/
Bank of English: www.titania.bham.ac.uk/
Bergen Corpus of London Teenage Language (COLT, now a constituent of the BNC): www.hit.uib.no/colt/

British Academic Spoken English (BASE) corpus: http://www2.warwick.ac.uk/fac/soc/al/research/collect/base/; www.reading.ac.uk/AcaDepts/ll/base_corpus/

British National Corpus (BNC): www.natcorp.ox.ac.uk/

Brown Corpus: http://khnt.hit.uib.no/icame/manuals/brown/index.htm

Cambridge and Nottingham Corpus of Discourses in English (CANCODE, now a constituent of the CIC): see McCarthy (1998)

Cambridge International Corpus (CIC): www.cambridge.org/elt/corpus/

Corpus of Contemporary American English: www.americancorpus.org/

English as a Lingua Franca in Academic Settings (ELFA) Corpus: www.uta.fi/laitokset/kielet/engf/research/elfa/

Health Communication Corpus: see Adolphs *et al.* (2004)

International Corpus of English (ICE): http://ice-corpora.net/ice/

International Corpus of Learner English (ICLE): see Granger *et al.* (2009)

Lancaster-Oslo-Bergen Corpus (LOB): see Johansson *et al.* (1978; 1986)

Limerick Corpus of Irish-English (LCIE) http://www.ul.ie/~lcie/homepage.htm

London Lund Corpus of Spoken English (LLC): http://khnt.hit.uib.no/icame/manuals/londlund/index.htm

Longman Corpus Network: www.pearsonlongman.com/dictionaries/corpus/index.html

Michigan Corpus of Academic Spoken English (MICASE): http://micase.elicorpora.info/

Oxford English Corpus: www.askoxford.com/oec/

Vienna-Oxford International Corpus of English (VOICE): www.univie.ac.at/voice/page/index.php

Corpus tools/interfaces

BYU-BNC: http://corpus.byu.edu/bnc/

BNCWeb: http://corpora.lancs.ac.uk/BNCWeb/home.html

Compleat Lexical Tutor: www.lextutor.ca/

ELAN: www.lat-mpi.eu/tools/elan

Transana: www.transana.org/

WebCorp: www.Webcorp.org.uk/

References

Adolphs, S. (2006) *Introducing Electronic Text Analysis: A Practical Guide for Language and Literary Studies*, Abingdon and New York: Routledge.

Adolphs, S., Brown, B., Carter, R., Crawford, P. and Sahota, O. (2004) 'Applying corpus linguistics in a health care context', *Journal of Applied Linguistics* 1(1): 9–28.

Aijmer, K. (1996) *Conversational Routines in English*, London and New York: Longman.

Altenberg, B. (1998) 'On the phraseology of spoken English: the evidence of recurrent word-combinations', in A. P. Cowie (ed.) *Phraseology: Theory, Analysis and Applications*, Oxford: Clarendon Press.

Biber, D. (2006) *University Language: A Corpus-based Study of Spoken and Written Registers*, Amsterdam: John Benjamins.

——(2009) 'A corpus-driven approach to formulaic language in English: multi-word patterns in speech and writing', *International Journal of Corpus Linguistics* 14(3): 275–311.

Biber, D. and Conrad, S. (1999) 'Lexical bundles in conversation and academic prose', in H. Hasselgard and S. Oksefjell (eds) *Out of Corpora: Studies in Honour of Stig Johansson*, Amsterdam: Rodopi.

Biber, D., Conrad, S. and Cortes, V. (2003) 'Lexical bundles in speech and writing: an initial taxonomy', in A. Wilson, P. Rayson and T. McEnery (eds) *Corpus Linguistics by the Lune: A Festschrift for Geoffrey Leech*, Frankfurt: Peter Lang.

Biber, D., Johansson, S., Leech, G., Conrad, S. and Finegan, E. (1999) *Longman Grammar of Spoken and Written English*, Harlow: Pearson Longman.

Burnard, L. (2005) 'Metadata for corpus work', in M. Wynne (ed.) *Developing Linguistic Corpora: A Guide to Good Practice*, Oxford: Oxbow Books.

Carter, R. and McCarthy, M. (1996) 'Correspondence', *ELT Journal* 50(4): 369–71.

——(1999) 'The English get-passive in spoken discourse: description and implications for an interpersonal grammar', *English Language and Linguistics* 3(1): 41–58.

Coxhead, A. (2000) 'A new academic word list', *TESOL Quarterly* 34(2): 213–38.

Danielsson, P. (2003) 'Automatic extraction of meaningful units from corpora: a corpus-driven approach using the word stroke', *International Journal of Corpus Linguistics* 8(1): 109–27.

De Cock, S. (1998) 'A recurrent word combination approach to the study of formulae in the speech of native and non-native speakers of English', *International Journal of Corpus Linguistics* 3(1): 59–80.

Dunning, T. (1993) 'Accurate methods for the statistics of surprise and coincidence', *Computational Linguistics* 19(1): 61–74.

Erman, B. and Warren, B. (2000) 'The idiom principle and the open choice principle', *Text* 20(1): 29–62.

Farr, F., Murphy, B. and O'Keeffe, A. (2004) 'The Limerick corpus of Irish English: design, description and application, *Teanga* 21: 5–30.

Firth, J. R. (1957) 'A synopsis of linguistic theory, 1930–55', in *Studies in Linguistic Analysis*, Oxford: Blackwell.

Gavioli, L. and Aston, G. (2001) 'Enriching reality: language corpora in language pedagogy', *ELT Journal* 55(3): 238–46.

Granger, S., Dagneaux, E., Meunier, F. and Paquot, M. (2009) *International Corpus of Learner English, version 2*, Louvain: Presses Universitaires de Louvain.

Hunston, S. (2002) *Corpora in Applied Linguistics*, Cambridge: Cambridge University Press.

Johansson, S., Leech, G. and Goodluck, H. (1978) *Manual of Information to Accompany the Lancaster-Oslo/Bergen Corpus of British English, for Use with Digital Computers*, Oslo: University of Oslo.

Johansson, S., Atwell, E., Garside, R. and Leech, G. (1986) *The Tagged LOB Corpus: User's Manual*, Bergen: Norwegian Computing Centre for the Humanities.

Kilgarriff, A. and Grefenstette, G. (2003) 'Introduction to the special issue on the Web as corpus', *Computational Linguistics* 29(3): 333–48.

Knight, D., Evans, D., Carter, R., and Adolphs, S. (2009) 'HeadTalk, HandTalk and the corpus: towards a framework for multi-modal, multi-media corpus development', *Corpora* 4(1): 1–32.

Lin, P. M. S. and Adolphs, S. (2009), 'Sound evidence: phraseological units in spoken corpora', in A. Barfield and H. Gyllstad (eds) *Researching Collocations in Another Language: Multiple Interpretations*, Basingstoke: Palgrave Macmillan.

Louw, B. (1993) 'Irony in the text or insincerity in the writer? The diagnostic potential of semantic prosodies', in M. Baker, G. Francis and E. Tognini-Bonelli (eds) *Text and Technology: In Honour of John Sinclair*, Amsterdam: John Benjamins.

McCarthy, M. (1998) *Spoken Language and Applied Linguistics*, Cambridge: Cambridge University Press.

McCarthy, M. and Carter, R. (1995) 'Spoken grammar: what is it and how can we teach it?', *ELT Journal* 49(3): 207–18.

Meunier, F. and Granger, S. (eds) (2008) *Phraseology in Foreign Language Learning and Teaching*, Amsterdam: John Benjamins.

Moon, R. (1998) 'Frequencies and forms of phrasal lexemes in English', in A. P. Cowie (ed.) *Phraseology: Theory, Analysis and Applications*, Oxford: Clarendon Press.

O'Keeffe, A., McCarthy, M. and Carter, R. (2007) *From Corpus to Classroom: Language Use and Language Teaching*, Cambridge: Cambridge University Press.

O'Keeffe, A., Clancy, B., and Adolphs, S. (2011) *Introducing Pragmatics in Use*, London: Routledge.

Oakey, D. (2002) 'Formulaic language in English academic writing', in R. Reppen, S. Fitzmaurice and D. Biber (ed.) *Using Corpora to Explore Linguistic Variation*, Philadelphia, PA: John Benjamins.

Prodromou, L. (1996a) 'Correspondence', *ELT Journal* 50(4): 371–3.

——(1996b) 'Correspondence', *ELT Journal* 50(1): 88–9.

——(1998) 'Correspondence', *ELT Journal* 52(3): 266–7.

——(2008) *English as a Lingua Franca: A Corpus-based Analysis*, London: Continuum.

Rayson, P. (2003) 'Matrix: A Statistical Method and Software Tool for Linguistic Analysis Through Corpus Comparison', unpublished thesis, Lancaster University.

Renouf, A. (1993) *Making Sense of Text: Automated Approaches to Meaning Extraction*, Proceedings of the 17th International Online Information Meeting, 7–9 December 1993.

——(2003) 'WebCorp: providing a renewable data source for corpus linguists', in S. Granger and S. Petch-Tyson (eds) *Extending the Scope of Corpus-based Research: New Applications, New Challenges*, Amsterdam: Rodopi.

Renouf, A., Kehoe, A. and Banerjee, J. (2007) 'WebCorp: an integrated system for Web text search', in M. Hundt, N. Nesselhauf and C. Biewer (eds) *Corpus Linguistics and the Web*, Amsterdam: Rodopi.

Schmitt, N. (ed.) (2004) *Formulaic Sequences*, Amsterdam: John Benjamins.

Scott, M. (1997) 'PC analysis of key words – and key key words', *System* 25(2): 233–45.

Seidlhofer, B. (ed.) (2003) *Controversies in Applied Linguistics*, Oxford: Oxford University Press.

Simpson, R. (2004) 'Stylistic features of academic speech: the role of formulaic expressions', in U. Connor and T. A. Upton (eds) *Discourse in the Professions: Perspectives from Corpus Linguistics*, Amsterdam: John Benjamins.

Simpson-Vlach, R. and Ellis, N. C. (2010) 'An academic formulas list: new methods in phraseology research', *Applied Linguistics* [advance access published online 12 January 2010]: 1–26.

Sinclair, J. McH. (1991a) *Corpus, Concordance and Collocation*, Oxford: Oxford University Press.

——(1991b) 'Shared knowledge', in J. E. Alatis (ed.) *Linguistics and Language Pedagogy: The State of the Art*, Washington, DC: Georgetown University Press.

——(1996) 'The search for units of meaning', *Textus* 9(1): 75–106.

——(2003) *Reading Concordances*, Harlow: Longman.

——(2004) *Trust the Text: Language, Corpus and Discourse*, London: Routledge.

——(2005) 'Corpus and text: basic principles', in M. Wynne (ed.) *Developing Linguistic Corpora: A Guide to Good Practice*, Oxford: Oxbow Books.

Sinclair, J. McH. (ed.) (1987) *Looking Up: An Account of the COBUILD Project in Lexical Computing and the Development of the Collins COBUILD English Language Dictionary*, London: Harper-Collins.

Stubbs, M. (1995) 'Collocations and semantic profiles: on the cause of the trouble with quantitative methods', *Functions of Language* 2(1): 1–33.

——(1996) *Text and Corpus Analysis: Computer-assisted Studies of Language and Culture*, Oxford: Blackwell.

——(2009) 'Memorial article: John Sinclair (1933–2007): the search for units of meaning: Sinclair on empirical semantics', *Applied Linguistics* 30(1): 115–37.

Tognini-Bonelli, E. (2001) *Corpus Linguistics at Work*, Amsterdam: John Benjamins.

Tribble, C. and Jones, G. (1997) *Concordances in the Classroom: A Resource Guide for Teachers*, 2nd edn, Harlow: Longman.

Widdowson, H. G. (1991) 'The description and prescription of language', in J. E. Alatis (ed.) *Linguistics and Language Pedagogy: the State of the Art*, Washington, DC: Georgetown University Press.

——(2000) 'On the limitations of linguistics applied', *Applied Linguistics* 21: 3–25.

Wray, A. (2002) *Formulaic Language and the Lexicon*, Cambridge: Cambridge University Press.

——(2008) *Formulaic Language: Pushing the Boundaries*, Oxford: Oxford University Press.

43

Cognitive linguistics

Hans-Jörg Schmid and Friedrich Ungerer

Introduction

Like many other notions in linguistics, the term *cognitive linguistics* is used in a number of ways. What may be special about this notion, however, is that two competing and in many respects incompatible approaches to the study of language go by the same name. While these two approaches share the idea that linguists should consider psychological aspects of speakers' knowledge about language (cf. the Latin *cognoscere* '(get to) know') rather than merely describe linguistic behaviour, they differ with regard to how they explain the nature and sources of this knowledge. The first view, very much associated with Chomsky and known as *generative grammar* (cf. Wakabayashi, this volume), sees knowledge about language – i.e. *linguistic competence* – as a very special human ability which is not, or only remotely, related to other cognitive faculties such as perception, attention or memory. The second view of cognitive linguistics takes a completely different perspective and emphasizes the experiential nature of linguistic competence. It is this approach, and its vision of explaining the cognitive foundations of linguistic structure and usage, that this chapter will be concerned with. In this account, knowledge about linguistic structures is explained with recourse to our knowledge about the world, and it is assumed that language both reflects and contributes to shaping this knowledge. Introduced by linguists such as Fillmore, Lakoff, Langacker and Talmy in key publications in the 1980s, this notion of cognitive linguistics is today represented, for example, by the International Cognitive Linguistics Association (ICLA) and in the papers published in the journal *Cognitive Linguistics*.

History and key issues

Categorization, prototype theory and basic levels

An important starting-point of cognitive-linguistic thinking – which actually predates the term *cognitive linguistics* itself, which was not used before the early 1980s – was the empirical research into the nature of conceptual categories carried out by the anthropologists Berlin and Kay (1969) and the psychologist Rosch (1973, 1978). Studying the denotational ranges of basic colour terms like *red, blue* and *yellow* in a large number of languages, Berlin and Kay found that there was a surprising degree of agreement on what informants from different linguistic and cultural backgrounds considered as the best examples of *red, blue*, etc. For the border areas, e.g. the range of colours from dark red to purple or from a turquoise-like blue to green, there was much less agreement. Berlin and Kay referred to the areas on the colour spectrum which represented the best examples of basic colours as *focal colours*, and Kay and McDaniel (1978) later demonstrated that physiological aspects of the visual apparatus were responsible for the observed inter-subjective and cross-cultural commonalities. This is an interesting and very straightforward example of how properties of linguistic units, in this case the meanings of basic colour terms, are influenced by other cognitive abilities, here perception.

Berlin and Kay's work was taken up by Rosch and extended to other types of categories including geometrical shapes (SQUARE, TRIANGLE) as well as everyday concepts such as FURNITURE, VEHICLE, WEAPON and others. What Rosch found was that just like in the case of colour categories, the members of these object categories could be rated on a goodness-of-example scale by informants in psychological tests. For example, informants agreed that cars and trucks were very good examples of the category VEHICLE, but rated skis, skateboards and elevators as very poor ones. Rosch introduced the term *prototype* for the best examples of categories and argued that they served as cognitive reference points for the storage and retrieval of categories. This idea was complemented by the notion of *fuzzy boundaries* between categories (cf. Labov 1973), referring to the observation that conceptual categories such as CUP, MUG and BOWL are not separated by strict category boundaries, but seem to fade into each other, with objects possibly being named as *cup* by some informants and as *mug* by others. In short, rather than being subject to a checklist of necessary and sufficient features as suggested by structuralist semantics (and Aristotelian philosophy), conceptual categories are internally structured in terms of prototypes, good and less good members, as well as fuzzy boundaries to 'neighbouring' categories. This idea is one of the cornerstones of what is known as *prototype theory of categorization* and, since these categories are labelled by words and have conceptual content, as *prototype semantics*. Prototypes can be shown to differ from less typical members of categories with regard to the number (and nature) of attributes associated with them. For example, while cars and trucks are associated with crucial attributes of the concept VEHICLE such as 'used to transport people and things', skis and skateboards can indeed be used as a means of transport but are much more strongly linked with attributes like 'sports' or 'fun'.

Although the idea of prototype theory first came up in connection with superordinate categories such as FURNITURE, VEHICLE and WEAPON, it soon emerged that the notion of prototype is even more helpful when it comes to explaining *basic level categories* or *concepts* (BED and TABLE, CAR and TRUCK, GUN and KNIFE rather than FURNITURE, VEHICLE and WEAPON, etc). It is here that we find words which are short, morphologically simple, acquired early in ontogenetic development and introduced into discourse in unmarked contexts. As shown by Rosch *et al.* (1976), the members of basic level categories have a similar shape which lends itself to perception, and possibly representation, as a holistic gestalt. In addition, we interact with similar motor movements with members of basic level categories; for example, we sit down on all types of chairs. Superordinate categories, on the other hand, rely on a different principle, also often subsumed under the label *prototype theory*, the principle of family resemblances. As Rosch and Mervis (1975) showed, the seemingly different members of superordinate categories such as FURNITURE or VEHICLE, rather than depending on large numbers of category-wide attributes as basic-level categories do, are held together by clusters of overlapping attributes, just like the members of one family will usually not all resemble each other but have certain sets of characteristics in common. Indeed, the notion of family resemblances had been invoked much earlier to explain the internal conceptual coherence of the category GAME by the philosopher Wittgenstein (1958).

Frames, cognitive models and conceptual metaphors

Conceptual categories are not only linked in memory with attributes associated with the category members, but also embedded in a huge conceptual network of more or less firmly stored knowledge structures. One type of these structures is known as *frames* and defined as 'cognitive structures […] knowledge of which is presupposed for the concepts encoded by the words' (Fillmore and Atkins 1992: 75). A classic and very influential example from the pre-cognitive-linguistic era is the so-called *commercial transaction frame* (Fillmore 1977) presupposed by verbs such as *buy*, *sell*, *pay* or *cost*. The frame is described in terms of the frame components BUYER, SELLER, MONEY and GOODS, and it is assumed that even though the verbs do not require all of these components to occur on the syntactic surface (cf. examples 1 and 2), mention of any of the verbs will invariably activate the whole frame.

1   *The book* [GOODS] *cost ten pounds* [MONEY].
2   *Mary* [BUYER] *bought an expensive book* [GOODS].

In addition, depending on the verb chosen, certain components of the frame are highlighted to various degrees. For example, while the verb *cost* draws attention to the GOODS and the MONEY which fill the subject and object slots in the sentence (example 1), the verb *buy* highlights the BUYER (subject) and the GOODS (object) (example 2). Obviously, this has to do with putting a certain perspective on a scene and deploying attention to certain aspects, a cognitive ability reflected in other areas of language we will look at later.

While frames are conceived of as somehow delimitable knowledge structures, other types of cognitive models are less restricted. Lakoff, for instance, in his treatment of *idealized cognitive models* (1987), takes up Fillmore's discussion of the noun *bachelor* and argues that this concept only makes sense within an idealized cognitive model of a society whose members share certain expectations as to the institution of marriage. Ungerer and Schmid (2006: 49), who opt for a deliberately comprehensive definition of cognitive models as 'stored representations that belong to a certain field', provide the example ON THE BEACH, which 'includes' closely interrelated person and object categories such as PEOPLE, SAND, SHELLS, BUCKET as well as action and event categories, for example SWIM, SUNBATHE, BUILDING A SANDCASTLE and others. While it may be criticized that these descriptions of cognitive models are totally subjective, open-ended and apparently of a somewhat unscientific ad-hoc nature, it may well be the case that this is exactly how our minds work. The psychological reality of these knowledge structures can be tested with priming experiments and other tests and gleaned from language use, for example when speakers use definite noun phrases with anaphoric reference to components of frames that are not explicitly mentioned but still activated, cf. the NP *the sea* in example 3:

3   *We spent some time on the beach yesterday. The sea was very rough.*

Cognitive models are not individual, purely subjective knowledge structures, but presumably shared to a large extent by the members of a culture and therefore also seen as *cultural models*. It goes without saying that frames and cognitive as well as cultural models are also based on our experience of the world around us.

Hans-Jörg Schmid and Friedrich Ungerer

One particularly fruitful early field in cognitive linguistics which relies on the idea of cognitive models (or *domains*) is the conceptual theory of metaphor, introduced in the pioneering book by Lakoff and Johnson ([1980] 2003). In a nutshell, this theory claims that conventionalized metaphorical expressions such as examples 4 or 5 are by no means dead metaphors but surface manifestations of deeply entrenched underlying mappings of one domain, the *source domain*, onto another, the *target domain*:

4   *He got all* steamed up.
5   *I almost* exploded.

In these two examples the cognitive model of a hot fluid in a container is mapped onto the concept of anger, yielding a conceptual metaphor dubbed ANGER IS A HOT FLUID IN A CONTAINER. Other examples of conceptual metaphors discussed by Lakoff and Johnson include AN ARGUMENT IS A JOURNEY (cf. 6 and 7), IDEAS ARE OBJECTS (cf. 8 and 9) or COMPANIES ARE PLANTS (cf. 10 and 11):

6   *We have* arrived at *a disturbing conclusion.*
7   *Do you* follow *my argument?*
8   *We* dropped *the idea.*
9   *They* canvassed *a new idea.*
10 *The company has several* branches.
11 *We've been* growing *continuously over the past years.*

From an experiential point of view, it is important to emphasize that conceptual metaphors typically use a more tangible and concrete domain as a source, which is mapped onto a more abstract domain in need of conceptual structure.

Figure and ground, prominence and salience

Another experiential aspect related to the cognitive abilities of perception and attention is the gestalt psychological principle of figure and ground. This principle suggests that when viewing a given scene we will invariably single out certain elements as prominent figures while relegating others to the less prominent ground. For example, looking up into the dark sky at night, we inadvertently select the moon as a salient figure which stands out from the black ground behind it. Arguably, a reflection of this perceptual principle can be identified in the structures of linguistic utterances describing such a scene: while example 12 sounds fairly natural, as it highlights the salient figure in the more prominent syntactic slot of subject, a complementary utterance like example 13, although an equally true depiction of the scene, would be decidedly weird, or at least marked:

12 *The moon is in the sky.*
13 *The sky is around the moon.*

Perceptual stimuli which are likely to be selected as figures tend to be smaller, more movable, geometrically simpler, more dependent and more prominent (once perceived) than typical ground entities (Talmy 2000: 315); in addition, figures tend to be more relevant, and thus both perceptually and conceptually more salient, for the language user, and this is all reflected in degrees of prominence awarded to the linguistic material referring to these salient entities in actual utterances.

A large part of the early research into figure-ground phenomena focused on prepositions (Brugman 1981; cf. Lakoff 1987: 416ff.). Central to these and later studies on prepositions is the notion of *image-schema*, defined as

> relatively simple structures that constantly recur in our everyday bodily experience: containers, paths, links, forces, balance, and in various orientations and relations: up-down, front-back, part-whole, center-periphery, etc. These structures […] are directly meaningful, first, because they are directly and repeatedly experienced because of the nature of the body and its mode of functioning in our environment.

> *(Lakoff 1987: 267–8)*

It is common practice to refer to the figure in these schemata as *trajector* and to the ground as *landmark*. Probably the most powerful aspect of these schematic structures is the potential of schematic mental imagery for specific context-sensitive elaborations. This explains, for instance, the wide range of semantic variation for the preposition *over* illustrated in examples 14 to 18:

14 *They have a horseshoe over their door.*
15 *The dog jumped over the fence.*
16 *Carl cycled over the bridge.*
17 *The village clouded over.*
18 *The wall fell over.*

Example 14 describes a stative configuration of a trajector above a landmark, which is considered as representing the fundamental image schema associated with *over* in a recent treatment by Tyler and Evans (2003: 66). Examples 15 and 16 represent dynamic scenes in which the trajector moves through a stage that corresponds to the central schema, with the trajector being in contact with the landmark in 16. In 17, the trajector is encoded in the verb *clouded* and covers the landmark, while in 18, trajector and landmark coincide but perform a movement similar to the trajector in 15.

Yet image schemas can also be metaphorically extended and then account for the motivation behind figurative, non-spatial or non-visual experiences. For example, Tyler and Evans (2003: 85–9) trace the meaning 'excess' encoded by *over* in example 20 to more concrete meanings like the one exemplified in 19, and the 'completion' sense in 22 to uses of type 21:

19 *The arrow flew over the target and landed in the woods.*
20 *Many students wrote over the word limit.*
21 *The cat's jump is over.*
22 *The film/game/match is over.*

Image schemas and their elaborations and metaphorical extensions thus contribute to accounting for meaning relation in the complex polysemy networks associated with linguistic elements such as *in*, *over*, *out* or *up*, which function, among other things, as prepositions, particles and prefixes in English. Unlike in conventional dictionary entries, which simply list meanings of lexemes, the motivations and links between the wide range of senses become plausible – an effect on the internal conceptual coherence of these 'radial categories', which is sometimes considered a further amendment to the prototype theory of meaning introduced in the section on categorization above.

More recent developments

Prototype theory, basic levels and entrenchment

Though by no means uncontroversial, prototype theory has gained a firm place in linguistic theorizing. A substantial part of the recent discussion of the prototype model of categorization has revolved around the issues of the theoretical status and cognitive reality of prototypes. This has to do with the question as to whether the results of goodness-of-example ratings are basically just a superficial effect of the rating task (e.g. with low ratings for an ostrich as a bird), or whether they reflect a marginal membership of the subcategory OSTRICH within the category BIRD. Croft and Cruse (2004: 79–81) insist on the importance of the distinction, stressing that while OSTRICH may indeed be a poor example of the category BIRD, it is still undoubtedly a fully fledged member. Taylor (2003), like Ungerer and Schmid (2006: 55–6), makes a distinction between folk and expert models of categories and claims that everyday models corresponding to discrete, hard-and-fast expert categories can still show prototypicality effects and fuzzy boundaries. Taylor also transfers the notion of prototypicality to technical categories in linguistics, for example in the area of phonology and morphology.

The notion of basic level has recently come to be viewed as just one manifestation of the more general cognitive process (and product) of *entrenchment* (Langacker 1987: 100, 2008a: 16–17; Geeraerts *et al.* 1994; Schmid 2007). For example, when telling a story of a dog chasing a cat, the terms that will first come to mind are precisely these basic-level terms, *dog* and *cat*, rather than superordinates such as *mammal* or subordinates like *retriever* and *ginger cat*. Observations of this type are interpreted as evidence of the higher degree of entrenchment of basic-level terms vis-à-vis words on other levels of categorization. It is assumed that the entrenchment of linguistic units is facilitated by repeated use, which, due to increasing auto-matization and routinization of access and retrieval, reduces the cognitive effort required for processing. Entrenchment is also linked with an increasing conventionality of linguistic units in the speech community (Langacker 2008a: 21) and diachronic changes such as grammaticali-zation, which can be explained as a gradual shift from syntactic structures constructed afresh each time they are used towards the storage of entrenched and conventionalized patterns and routines (cf. Bybee 2006). For instance, complex prepositions such as *with regard to, on behalf of* or *in terms of* presumably undergo entrenchment and conventionalization processes similar to those already completed by coalesced prepositions or conjunctions like *notwithstanding* or *nevertheless*.

From specific frames to universal event-frames

As has been shown above, frames were originally envisaged as linguistically relevant knowl-edge structures pertaining to fairly restricted conceptual domains, which are abstracted from similar actual situations. If the mind indeed distils such frames from recurrent experiences that are perceived as being comparable in their overall structure, it does not seem unlikely that frames can be stored on several levels, or layers, of specificity. A highly schematic, i.e. unspe-cific, type of knowledge structure has been postulated by Leonard Talmy in his highly influ-ential work on event-frames (Talmy 1991, 2000). Talmy defines event-frames as sets 'of conceptual elements and interrelationships that […] are evoked together or co-evoke each other' (2000, vol. 1: 259). Being related to very fundamental experiences of concrete physical events such as moving objects or people causing objects to move, event-frames are very likely universal. While this does not mean that all languages use the same means of encoding certain types of event-frames, Talmy actually manages to show for one type, the so-called *motion event-frame*, that there are two basic ways of mapping the components of the frame to linguistic elements to be found in the languages of the world. The two patterns of encoding are illustrated with equivalent English and Spanish examples in Figure 43.1 taken from Ungerer and Schmid (2006: 235; based on Talmy 1991):

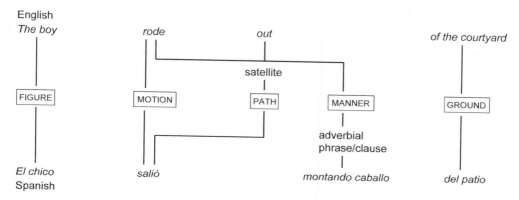

Figure 43.1 Illustration of the encoding of motion event-frame components in English and Spanish
Source: Ungerer and Schmid 2006: 235; based on Talmy 1991.

As the figure shows, the motion event-frame consists of five components (plus the optional CAUSE, not represented in the example sentences): FIGURE, GROUND, MOTION and PATH are the essential core components, MANNER (and CAUSE) have a less central status. While the mappings of frame components onto syntactic slots are identical for FIGURE (surfaces as subject), MOTION (verb) and GROUND (adverbial), the crucial difference concerns the encoding of PATH and MANNER. In English, information about the PATH is typically encoded in particles ('satellites', here *out*) accompanying the verbal form proper (*rode*), while in Spanish it is conflated with the motion component in the verb (*salió*, 'exited'). On the other hand, the MANNER component is lexicalized in the verb in English (*rode*), but must be added by means of an optional adverbial in Spanish (*montando caballo*, lit. 'mounted on horse'). Talmy (2000, vol. 2: 117–18, 221–30) refers to the two types of encoding, or 'lexicalization', patterns as mainly *satellite-framed* (e.g. English, German, Russian, Finno-Ugric, Chinese) and *verb-framed* (e.g. the Romance and Semitic languages, Japanese, Tamil, Bantu).

From an applied linguistic perspective, the problems that arise from these systematic contrasts for translation are particularly interesting (cf. Slobin 1999). Starting from English to Spanish, although it is no problem to render the MANNER component encoded in the English verb *rode* by means of an adverbial such as *montando caballo* in Spanish, this clearly has an extra effect: the manner of the action is much more prominent in the translated Spanish than in the original English version, as it is encoded by a fully fledged clause constituent consisting of two 'heavy' words. Whether the Spanish translation is really conceptually equivalent to the English is therefore doubtful. Conversely, translators from Spanish to English often face the problem that translations which sound natural in English are strictly speaking not true to the original version in the respect that they bring in a MANNER component that is not expressed in the Spanish original. While this would not be too difficult for *El chico salió del patio*, which could quite naturally be rendered as *The boy went out of the yard*, Slobin (1999: 212) shows that 'English translators actually *add* manner to the Spanish originals in almost a quarter of their translations' (ibid., emphasis in original). Spanish translators, on the other hand, omit information about the manner of motion events in about 50 per cent of their translations.

Conceptual metaphor, metonymy and blending

Ever since it was launched by Lakoff and Johnson (1980), conceptual metaphor theory has aroused massive interest among cognitive linguists. While the paradigm has essentially remained intact, some theoretical developments, many of which are summarized in the afterword to the second edition of *Metaphors We Live By* (Lakoff and Johnson 2003), can be observed. These include the idea that the major part of the metaphorical system has a bodily basis and that this embodied nature of metaphor and the connections between concrete bodily and abstract experience is even reflected in the structure and workings of the brain (Lakoff and Johnson 1999; Gallese and Lakoff 2005). To readers of this *Handbook of Applied Linguistics*, it may be of particular interest that conceptual metaphor theory has spawned a huge number of applications on a wide range of registers, among them advertising, political, media, medical, religious and sports discourse (cf., for example, Cameron and Deignan 2006; Lakoff 2004; Musolff 2006; Nerlich 2010). As a further recent development, metaphor theorists have begun to search for methods of identifying metaphors in large corpora in a more or less automatic way (cf. Charteris-Black 2004; Deignan 2005; Stefanowitsch and Gries 2007).

Although Lakoff and Johnson did mention metonymy in *Metaphors We Live By* as a second basic type of figurative language, which is based on contiguity rather than similarity, it was not until much later that cognitive linguists started to see the fundamental role of this linguistic phenomenon for conceptualization. Triggered to a large extent by an important paper by Zoltan Kövecses and Günter Radden (1998) and the volume edited by Klaus-Uwe Panther and Günter Radden soon afterwards (1999), linguistic effects of metonymic conceptualizations such as PART FOR WHOLE, CAUSE FOR EFFECT or AGENT FOR ACTION have been found in many areas of language. For example, the conversion of *tutor* from noun to verb illustrated in example 23 can be interpreted as being cognitively motivated by the conceptual metonymy AGENT FOR ACTION. In the field of pragmatics, the functioning of indirect speech acts such as example 24 has been explained with recourse to the metonymy ABILITY FOR ACTION (Panther and Thornburg 1999). That metonymy is a highly productive process in the lexicon creating new meanings for existing lexemes (cf. example 25) is of course hardly a new insight, but has thus been placed in a wider cognitive context:

23 *She has tutored many students.* [AGENT FOR ACTION]
24 *Can you step aside, please.* [ABILITY FOR ACTION]
25a *wear glasses* 'spectacles' [SUBSTANCE FOR OBJECT]
  b *have another bottle* 'content of a bottle' [CONTAINER FOR CONTENT]
  c *she married money* 'a rich man' [POSSESSED FOR POSSESSOR]

As pointed out in the section on frames and cognitive models above, the conceptual theory of metaphor (and metonymy) is mainly interested in highly conventionalized metaphorical expressions and tries to unveil their conceptual underpinnings. A cognitive-linguistic theory that focuses on the online combinatorial processes involved in the interpretation of novel and original figurative expressions is known as *conceptual blending* or *conceptual integration theory*. This approach, introduced by Fauconnier and Turner (1998; cf. also Fauconnier and Turner

2002), works with the notion of *mental spaces*, that is, 'small conceptual packets constructed as we think and talk, for purposes of local understanding and action', which 'operate in working memory but are built up partly by activating structures available from long-term memory' (Fauconnier and Turner 2002: 40, 102). Conceptual blending theory tries to account for all kinds of conceptual combinations, not only metaphors and metonymies. For example, a reader not familiar with the recent coinage *fridgegoogling* ('using the names of the things in your fridge as input for a Google search in order to find a useful recipe') will, according to the model, construct two mental spaces triggered by the familiar constituents *fridge* and *google*. These spaces presumably include information retrieved from long-term memory such as 'cool', 'used to store food', 'located in the kitchen' and 'cook' for *fridge* and 'computer', 'search the Internet' and 'look for information' for *google*. Given a facilitating context such as example 26, the reader then tries to project what seems to be relevant information from these two input spaces and to integrate this information in the 'blended space' in such a way that a sensible conceptual structure can emerge:

26   *We couldn't think of anything nice to cook for dinner last night, but when we switched on the computer and did some fridgegoogling we came across an excellent recipe for chicken cassava.*

Information likely to be projected from the *fridge* space includes 'food' and 'cook', and from the *google* space 'search the Internet' and 'look for information'. Once these pieces of information are brought together by means of basic cognitive relations such as 'identity' (what is searched for in Google is identical to the food found in the fridge) or 'cause-effect' ('the reason for the googling is the aim of preparing food in the fridge'), a sensible and relevant interpretation can be arrived at.

Figure and ground, cognitive grammar and construction grammar

The basic principle of figure and ground lies at the heart of the most detailed and comprehensive cognitive-linguistic theory of grammar known as cognitive grammar. Introduced by Langacker in the 1980s (cf. Langacker 1987, 1991), this approach explains, for example, the structural properties and conceptual impact of basic sentence patterns as manifestations of the allocation of different degrees of prominence. In simple SVO-sentences, the subject is regarded as syntactic figure or trajector and the object as syntactic ground or landmark. From this perspective, syntactic surface structures are the effect of cognitive processes such as profiling, perspectivizing and focusing, which are subsumed by Langacker under the label *construal* (cf. Langacker 2008a: 55–89). To take a very simple example, in 27 *Dylan* is profiled as syntactic figure and *Patrick* as syntactic ground. Encoding the identical content from a truth-conditional point of view, 28 reverses the perspective and allocates complementary degrees of prominence to the two participants:

27   *Dylan resembles Patrick.*
28   *Patrick resembles Dylan.*

Cognitive grammar departs from more formal models of grammar, especially the generative one, in other fundamental respects. Knowledge of grammar is not modelled as a set of rules and high-level generalizations based on the linguist's introspection. Instead, grammar is conceived as a huge network of symbolic units consisting of semantic and phonological poles, which in a way are reminiscent of the pairing of *signifier* and *signified* in Saussure's classic model of the linguistic sign. These symbolic units vary in terms of specificity and size from simple lexemes or even derivational morphemes (e.g. suffixes such as *-er*, *-ize* and *-able*) to schematic clause-level constructions (as illustrated in examples 27 and 28), thus bridging the gap between what has traditionally been strictly separated as (idiosyncratic) lexicon and (rule-based) grammar. What is also important is that the knowledge of symbolic units including syntactic structures is claimed to be derivable from the actual use of linguistic structures: it is usage-based.

These basic assumptions are also shared by a range of recent cognitive-linguistic models commonly subsumed under the label of *construction grammar*. Protagonists and milestone publications include Fillmore and Kay (e.g. Fillmore *et al*. 1988), Goldberg (1995, 2006) and Croft (2001). As stressed for instance by Goldberg (2006), form-meaning pairings can be observed on all meaning-bearing linguistic levels, from single morphemes, lexemes and idioms to abstract argument-structure constructions, such as the caused-motion construction, the resultative construction or the ditransitive, or better 'cause-receive', construction exemplified in examples 29, 30 and 31. Even more significant, constructions acquire a constructional meaning, which does not necessarily depend on the meaning of the lexical items involved. This is particularly impressive on the syntactic level of argument structure. A well-known case is Goldberg's *sneeze* example rendered in 32. Here, the overall semantic impact is one of caused-motion, even though, taken by itself, the meaning of the intransitive verb *sneeze* as such would not be interpreted as expressing caused motion:

29   *Joanna kicked the ball to Sally.* [Subject – Verb – Object – Adverbial]
      'someone causing someone else to move'
30   *Joanna wiped her mouth clean.* [Subject – Verb – Object – Object complement]
      'someone causing something to change state'
31   *Joanna sent a text message to Sally.* [Subject – Verb – ind. Object – dir. Object]
      'someone causing someone else to receive something'
32   *Fred sneezed the tissue off the table.*

(Goldberg 1995: 152)

A very productive area of construction grammar relies on the (semi-)automatic retrieval and advanced statistical analysis of attested uses of constructions from large computer corpora to study degrees of attraction between schematic constructions and lexical elements filling slots in them (cf. Gries and Stefanowitsch 2004; Stefanowitsch and Gries 2003). For example, it has been shown, perhaps not surprisingly, that the verb attracted most strongly by the cause-receive construction is *give*, followed by *tell*, *send*, *offer* and *show*. Known as *collostruction analysis* (a blend from 'collocation' and 'construction'), representatives of this framework have recently stepped up efforts to bring together quantitative corpus data with results from psychological tests to produce converging evidence from several sources using different methods (Gries *et al*. 2005).

If collostruction analysis is applied to corpora of carer-child talk, it can also be used to support a usage-based language acquisition theory, which, to some extent at least, promises to mediate between the behavourist emphasis on imitative learning and Chomsky's insistence on an innate language function based on universal grammar. Following Goldberg (2006), for example, the extremely frequent and early use of general purpose verbs like *go*, *put* or *give* by carers encourages the child to use these verbs as item-specific constructions because they reflect basic patterns of experience and can also be applied to a fairly wide range of arguments without overgeneralization. The more these specific constructions are entrenched, the more generalizations in terms of argument-structure constructions are facilitated, and this can be taken as a general pattern of grammatical development, as investigated in numerous studies by Tomasello and Lieven (e.g. Lieven and Tomasello 2008; Tomasello 2000, 2003).

Cognitive linguistics and language teaching

Although the implications of cognitive linguistics for language teaching have attracted a great deal of attention in the last few years, Langacker's remark (2008b) that his own article has been 'long on theory and short on practical recommendations' applies to many contributions of recently published collections in this field (e.g. Achard and Niemeier 2004; Boers and Lindstromberg 2008; de Knop and de Rycker 2008; Robinson and Ellis 2008). Against this background, the following summary is restricted to selected aspects whose regular use in the second-language classroom is feasible.

The usage-based account of first-language acquisition provides support for a number of well-established teaching principles and methods: Even where rule-based competence is the goal, as in grammar, it is best derived inductively from practice and explanation of item-specific constructions. Lexical items, in turn, should be mainly selected from basic-level categorization, where frequent and therefore deeply entrenched lexical concepts are readily available in prototypical examples and simple morphology (e.g. *girl, boy, pen, paper, book*), and they should be presented in combination with general purpose verbs (e.g. *go, put, give*) and basic evaluative adjectives (*good, bad, big, small*) in frequent collostructions.

Another key notion suggested by cognitive-linguistic thinking is the notion of 'anchoring'. New lexical items and item-specific structures are not only to be represented in suitable situational contexts. Equally, if not more, important is their embedding in mind maps – the frames, scripts, scenarios or, more generally, cognitive models through which lexical concepts are motivated. Care should be taken that, at least in the initial stages of language learning, these mind maps are based on a grid of part-whole, container-contained or path relationships, namely links that have been identified above as being based on our bodily experiences. Concepts like KITCHEN, BEDROOM, BATHROOM, ROOF and CHIMNEY would be shown as parts of houses; HOUSE, GARAGE, GARDEN, SHOP and CHURCH as parts of villages and VILLAGE, TOWN and CITY as contained in a country, etc. (Ungerer 2001). Later, the cognitive explanation should be extended to the motivation of figurative language, especially where metonymic and metaphorical extensions of basic conceptual models can be explained both verbally and visually (Boers and Lindstromberg 2008). An area particularly suitable for the anchoring approach is the acquisition of prepositions and phrasal verbs, where meaning extension can be related to the figure-ground (or trajector-landmark) contrast discussed above (Dirven 2001; Tyler and Evans 2003).

Anchoring can also take the form of 'grounding', especially where a deictic perspective is involved, as in the teaching of articles (Achard 2008) and tense (Niemeier and Reif 2008) as well as modals; their root meaning can be explained and visually represented as the impact of external authority-based force or internal will-powered force on the path pursued by an individual, while the choice of present and past forms of modals is accounted for by the proximal-distal metaphor (Tyler 2008: 470–6). In a wider sense, anchoring also applies to clause patterns, which need no longer be taught as formal configurations, but should be seen as semantic constructions 'anchored' in human experience (as shown above for the caused-motion construction) or as event frames, as originally suggested by Talmy and developed into a teachable system by Radden and Dirven (2007).

Finally, focusing on our perceptual access to the world, the principle of gestalt perception could be used to facilitate learning, for example in the area of noun grammar, where it is common to distinguish between count nouns and uncountable nouns, although countability is not easily defined in a grammatical context (nor is its cognitive explanation as boundedness/unboundedness). Starting from holistic gestalts like 'person', 'group' and 'collection of things' would make it easier for many students to grasp the use of grammatical number and concord.

In the domain of verb grammar, 'signal' grammar, such as recommending the use of the simple form for habitual concepts indicated by adverbs denoting high frequency and of the progressive form sparked off by simultaneity indicators (e.g. *at this moment, at present*), can be understood holistically. In general, the possibilities of the gestalt approach, especially for young learners, do not seem to be exhausted yet, and this is just one area in which the application of cognitive-linguistic ideas to language teaching requires further research and invites practical recommendations.

Related topics

generative grammar; grammar; psycholinguistics

Further reading

Croft, W. and Cruse, D. A. (2004) *Cognitive Linguistics*, Cambridge and New York: Cambridge University Press. (A textbook with a very strong focus on the construction grammar approach.)

Geeraerts, D. and Cuyckens, H. (eds) (2007) *The Oxford Handbook of Cognitive Linguistics*, Oxford: Oxford University Press. (A comprehensive overview of cognitive linguistics in fifty chapters. Useful as a reference work and as a source of detailed accounts of selected areas.)

Kövecses, Z. (2002) *Metaphor: A Practical Introduction*, Oxford: Oxford University Press. (Accessible and richly illustrated introduction to the conceptual theory of metaphor and metonymy; includes a chapter on conceptual blending.)

Langacker, R. W. (2008) *Cognitive Grammar: A Basic Introduction*, Oxford: Oxford University Press. (Labelled a *basic introduction*, this textbook gives a very good state-of-the-art account of Langacker's cognitive grammar, but is still quite demanding.)

Ungerer, F. and Schmid, H.-J. (2006) *An Introduction to Cognitive Linguistics*, 2nd edn, Harlow: Pearson Longman. (Accessible introduction covering all major areas of cognitive linguistics.)

References

Achard, M. (2008) 'Teaching construal: cognitive pedagogical grammar', in P. Robinson and N. C. Ellis (eds), *Handbook of Cognitive Linguistics and Second Language Acquisition*, London: Routledge.

Achard, M. and Niemeier, S. (eds) (2004) *Cognitive Linguistics, Second Language Acquisition and Foreign Language Teaching*, Berlin: Mouton de Gruyter.

Berlin, B. and Kay, P. (1969) *Basic Color Terms: Their Universality and Evolution*, Berkeley and Los Angeles: University of California Press.

Boers, F. and Lindstromberg, S. (eds) (2008) *Cognitive Linguistic Approaches to Teaching Vocabulary and Phraseology*, Berlin: Mouton de Gruyter.

Brugman, C. M. (1981) *The Story of Over*, Trier: LAUT.

Bybee, J. (2006) 'From usage to grammar: the mind's response to repetition', *Language* 82: 711–33.

Cameron, L. and Deignan, A. (2006) 'The emergence of metaphor in discourse', *Applied Linguistics* 27(4): 671–90.

Charteris-Black, J. (2004) *Corpus Approaches to Critical Metaphor Analysis*, Basingstoke: Palgrave Macmillan.

Croft, W. (2001) *Radical Construction Grammar: Syntactic Theory in Typological Perspective*, Oxford: Oxford University Press.

Croft, W. and Cruse, D. A. (2004) *Cognitive linguistics*, Cambridge and New York: Cambridge University Press.

de Knop, S. and de Rycker, T. (eds) (2008) *Cognitive Approaches to Pedagogical Grammar: A Volume in Honour of René Dirven*, Berlin: Mouton de Gruyter.

Deignan, A. (2005) *Metaphor and Corpus Linguistics*, Amsterdam and Philadelphia: John Benjamins.

Dirven, R. (2001) 'English phrasal verbs: theory and didactic application', in M. Pütz, S. Niemeier and R. Dirven (eds) *Applied Cognitive Linguistics II: Language Pedagogy*, Berlin: Mouton de Gruyter.

Fauconnier, G. and Turner, M. (1998) 'Conceptual integration networks', *Cognitive Science* 22(2): 133–87.

——(2002) *The Way We Think: Conceptual Blending and the Mind's Hidden Complexities*, New York: Basic Books.

Fillmore, C. C. (1977) 'Topics in lexical semantics', in R. W. Cole (ed.) *Current Issues in Linguistic Theory*, Bloomington and London: Indiana University Press.

Fillmore, C. C. and Atkins, B. T. (1992) 'Toward a frame-based lexicon: the semantics of RISK and its neighbors', in A. Lehrer and E. Kittay (eds) *Frames, Fields, and Contrasts*, Hillsdale, NJ: Lawrence Erlbaum Associates.

Fillmore, C. C., Kay, P. and O'Connor, M. C. (1988) 'Regularity and idiomaticity in grammatical constructions: the case of let alone', *Language* 64: 501–38.

Gallese, V. and Lakoff, G. (2005) 'The brain's concepts: the role of the sensory-motor system in conceptual knowledge', *Cognitive Neuropsychology* 21: 455–79.

Geeraerts, D. and Cuyckens, H. (eds) (2007) *The Oxford Handbook of Cognitive Linguistics*, Oxford: Oxford University Press.

Geeraerts, D., Grondelaers, S. and Bakema, P. (1994) *The Structure of Lexical Variation: A Descriptive Framework for Cognitive Lexicology*, Berlin: Mouton de Gruyter.

Goldberg, A. E. (1995) *Constructions: A Construction Grammar Approach to Argument Structure*, Chicago: University of Chicago Press.

——(2006) *Constructions at Work: The Nature of Generalization in Language*, Oxford: Oxford University Press.

Gries, S. T., Hampe, B. and Schönefeld, D. (2005) 'Converging evidence: bringing together experimental and corpus data on the associations of verbs and constructions', *Cognitive Linguistics* 16: 635–76.

Gries, S. T. and Stefanowitsch, A. (2004) 'Extending collostructional analysis: a corpus-based perspective on "alternations"', *International Journal of Corpus Linguistics* 9: 97–129.

Kay, P. and McDaniel, C. K. (1978) 'The linguistic significance of the meanings of basic color terms', *Language* 54: 610–46.

Kövecses, Z. and Radden, G. (1998) 'Metonymy: developing a cognitive linguistic view', *Cognitive Linguistics* 9: 37–77.

Labov, W. (1973) 'The boundaries of words and their meaning', in C.-J. N. Bailey and R. W. Shuy (eds) *New Ways of Analyzing Variation in English*, Washington, DC: Georgetown University Press.

Lakoff, G. (1987) *Women, Fire, and Dangerous Things: What Categories Reveal about the Mind*, Chicago and London: University of Chicago Press.

——(2004) *Don't Think of a White Elephant: Know Your Values and Frame the Debate*, White River Junction, VT: Chelsea Green Publishing.

Lakoff, G. and Johnson, M. ([1980] 2003) *Metaphors We Live By* (2nd edn with a new afterword), Chicago and London: University of Chicago Press.

——(1999) *Philosophy in the Flesh: The Embodied Mind and its Challenge to Western Thought*, New York: Basic Books.

Langacker, R. W. (1987) *Foundations of Cognitive Grammar*, vol. 1: *Theoretical Prerequisites*, Stanford, CA: Stanford University Press.

——(1991) *Foundations of Cognitive Grammar*, vol. 2: *Descriptive Application*, Stanford, CA: Stanford University Press.

——(2008a) *Cognitive Grammar: A Basic Introduction*, Oxford: Oxford University Press.

——(2008b) 'The relevance of cognitive grammar for language pedagogy', in S. de Knop and T. de Rycker (eds) *Cognitive Approaches to Pedagogical Grammar: A Volume in Honour of René Dirven*, Berlin: Mouton de Gruyter.

Lieven, E. and Tomasello, M. (2008) 'Children's first language acquisition from a usage-based perspective', in P. Robinson and N. C. Ellis (eds) *Handbook of Cognitive Linguistics and Second Language Acquisition*, London: Routledge.

Musolff, A. (2006) 'Metaphor scenarios in public discourse', *Metaphor and Symbol* 2(1): 23–38.

Nerlich, B. (2010) 'Breakthroughs and disasters: the politics and ethics of metaphor use in the media', in H.-J. Schmid and S. Handl (eds) *Cognitive Foundations of Linguistic Usage Patterns*, Berlin and New York: Mouton de Gruyter.

Niemeier, S. and Reif, M. (2008) 'Making progress simpler? Applying cognitive grammar to tense-aspect teaching in the German EFL classroom', in S. de Knop and T. de Rycker (eds) *Cognitive*

Hans-Jörg Schmid and Friedrich Ungerer

Approaches to Pedagogical Grammar: A Volume in Honour of René Dirven, Berlin: Mouton de Gruyter.

Panther, K.-U. and Radden, G. (eds) (1999) *Metonymy in Language and Thought*, Amsterdam and Philadelphia: John Benjamins.

Panther, K.-U. and Thornburg, L. (1999) 'The potentiality for actuality metonymy in English and Hungarian', in K.-U. Panther and G. Radden (eds) *Metonymy in Language and Thought*, Amsterdam and Philadelphia: John Benjamins.

Pütz, M., Niemeier, S. and Diven, R. (eds) (2001) *Applied Cognitive Linguistics II: Language Pedagogy*, Berlin: Mouton de Gruyter.

Radden, G. and Dirven, R. (2007) *Cognitive English Grammar*, Amsterdam and Philadelphia: John Benjamins.

Robinson, P. and Ellis, N. C. (2008) *Handbook of Cognitive Linguistics and Second Language Acquisition*, London: Routledge.

Rosch, E. (1973) 'On the internal structure of perceptual and semantic categories', in T. E. Moore (ed.) *Cognitive Development and the Acquisition of Language*, New York, San Francisco and London: Academic Press.

——(1978) 'Principles of categorization', in E. Rosch and B. B. Lloyd (eds) *Cognition and Categorization*, Hillsdale, NJ: Lawrence Erlbaum Associates.

Rosch, E. and Mervis, C. B. (1975) 'Family resemblances: studies in the internal structure of categories', *Cognitive Psychology* 7: 573–605.

Rosch, E., Mervis, C. B., Gray, W. D., Johnson, D. M. and Boyes-Braem, P. (1976) 'Basic objects in natural categories', *Cognitive Psychology* 8: 382–439.

Schmid, H.-J. (2007) 'Entrenchment, salience, and basic levels', in D. Geeraerts and M. Cuyckens (eds) *The Oxford Handbook of Cognitive Linguistics*. Oxford: Oxford University Press.

Slobin, D. I. (1999) 'Two ways to travel: verbs of motion in English and Spanish', in M. Shibatani and S. A. Thompson (eds) *Grammatical Constructions: Their Form and Meaning*, Oxford: Oxford University Press.

Stefanowitsch, A. and Gries, S. T. (2003) 'Collostructions: investigating the interaction of words and constructions'. *International Journal of Corpus Linguistics* 8(2): 209–43.

——(eds) (2007) *Corpus-based Approaches to Metaphor and Metonymy*, Berlin: Mouton de Gruyter.

Talmy, L. (1991) 'Path to realization: a typology of event conflation', *Proceedings of the Seventeenth Annual Meeting of the Berkeley Linguistics Society*, Berkeley, CA: Berkeley Linguistic Society.

——(2000) *Toward a Cognitive Semantics*, 2 vols, Cambridge, MA and London: MIT Press.

Taylor, J. (2003) *Linguistic Categorization*, 3rd edn, Oxford: Oxford University Press.

Tomasello, M. (2000) 'First steps in a usage-based theory of first language acquisition', *Cognitive Linguistics* 11: 61–82.

——(2003) *Constructing a Language: A Usage-based Theory of Language Acquisition*, Cambridge, MA: Harvard University Press.

Tyler, A. (2008) 'Cognitive linguistics and second language instruction', in P. Robinson and N. C. Ellis (eds), *Handbook of Cognitive Linguistics and Second Language Acquisition*, London: Routledge.

Tyler, A. and Evans, V. (2003) *The Semantics of English Prepositions*, Cambridge: Cambridge University Press.

Ungerer, F. (2001) 'Basicness and conceptual hierarchies in foreign language learning: a corpus-based study', in M. Pütz, S. Niemeier and R. Diven (eds) *Applied Cognitive Linguistics II: Language Pedagogy*, Berlin: Mouton de Gruyter.

Ungerer, F. and Schmid, H.-J. (2006) *An Introduction to Cognitive Linguistics*, 2nd edn, Harlow: Pearson Longman.

Wittgenstein, L. (1958) *Philosophical Investigations*, 2nd edn, G. E. M. Anscombe (trans.), Oxford: Blackwell.

44

Systemic functional linguistics

Lynne Young

Introduction

To fully understand a particular theory about language and communication it is useful to examine the roots of the theory before going on to discuss the main conceptual base of the theory itself. Also consistent in introducing a theory is contrasting it with other prominent approach(es) to language that surface at the same or similar time frames. Such a perspective offers core contextual information. For that reason I begin by briefly discussing the roots of Systemic Functional Linguistics (SFL) in the Prague School of Linguistics and in the work of J. R. Firth, followed by a short explanation of how SFL differs from the Chomskian tradition of the early 1980s just after Halliday's central book, *Language as Social Semiotic: The Social Interpretation of Language and Meaning*, appeared (1978).

Roots of SFL

Systemic Functional Linguistics (SFL) has particularly strong connections to the Prague School of Linguistics founded in the 1920s in Czechoslovakia. Four central tenets of this school provide the roots for early and current SFL and especially the work of Halliday:

1   The view of language as a network of relations which has to do with the fact that different features and aspects of language are related to each other and therefore do not exist in isolation.
2   The view of language as a system composed of sub-systems which consist of levels or strata. In other words, every language has different levels and at each level different aspects of language are prominent. For example, at the lexicogrammatical stratum, the focus of study is on the structure of the language and the lexical or vocabulary choices. At the semantic or meaning level, the focus is on the ways in which these grammatical patterns realize different meanings related to content, attitude, etc.
3   The emphasis is on the functional nature of language, how language reveals the different meanings of language, and the different purposes it serves.
4   The view that form derives from function, emphasizing that the form or the structure of a language, is rooted in the meanings that people want to convey as they speak or write to each other.

Vachek (1964, 1966), one of the leading Prague linguists, wrote that the structural concepts of the Prague School, originating with Russian linguists such as Jakobson and Trubetzkoy (Young 1990), were based on the idea that no element in a language could be studied in isolation. Rather, each element had to be examined in relation to all others co-existing with it. Menshikova (Vachek 1964), another Prague linguist, reiterates this point viewing language as a system of interrelated linguistic values as opposed to the sum total of minute, unconnected phenomena. This relational view is further maintained by Trinka and others who defined structuralism, as it applied to the Prague School as a 'trend which is concerned with analyzing relations between the segments of language, conceived as a hierarchically arranged whole' (Vachek 1964).

Not only relational considerations were emphasized, but that of the different levels or strata in the consideration of language, a theoretical concept that figures largely also in Halliday and other systemicists today. The Prague School focused on the functional nature of language, examining how language performs certain functions 'serving the needs and wants of the mutual understanding of individual members of the given language community' (Vachek 1972: 14). Vachek and other Prague linguists were then the first to attempt to build functional theories into the linguistic description of language to centre the discussion of language around these.

The Prague framework built on these conceptual views is further expanded in the work of J. R. Firth, the first professor of general linguistics and founder of the London School of Linguistics. Halliday was one of his early students and followed Firth, who maintained that language is a network of systems revealing again the focus on the relational nature of language. Firth further insisted that meaning is central in linguistic explanation, and that language expresses central functions in a variety of situational contexts.

Particularly central to Firth's work was his focus on language as a system of networks, a system of meanings, which has remained a core concept in current SFL theory. Firth's interest in the uses to which people put language led to his early theorizing about the role of functions in contexts of use. For Firth, function was tied to context in the sense that systems of options become available in different situations. Although there were earlier concerns with context and how this influenced language choices, he was the first to incorporate contextual influences into linguistic considerations, a position Halliday has also taken and expanded on.

Early systemic functional linguistics and generative grammar

Having looked briefly at the roots of SFL, a different way to contextualize the theory is to contrast it with early generative grammar, which was emerging as a major paradigm around the same time as Halliday's *Language as Social Semiotic* (1978). In this volume, Halliday outlines his views of language as functionally organized and as accounting for language use in different contexts. This is one of the core early works of Halliday's in which he sets out his view of language as a social phenomenon.

The two theories raise different questions, one about how the mind of an individual in the abstract sense works, and the other, on how people carry out their daily lives in interaction with each other in a variety of social settings.

Considering uses and contexts derives from the view that language, a social phenomenon (Halliday 1994), leads to social rather than psychological explanations of language; further, the social view involves examination of the functional nature of language as it occurs in different situational constructs. Since the functions of language are influenced by different situations, there has been extensive study of context and register in SFL.

Chomsky (1980: 27), on the other hand, wrote that the 'Generative Grammar of a language provides the systematic definition of a *sentence*. Grammatical sentences are those generated by the grammar.' The object of study is an idealized language divorced from context. He maintained early on that he did not see any proof that the study of language function contributed to the study of language form, a point in direct contrast to the SFL model. Linguistics for Chomsky consisted of a psychological view focusing on the faculty of mind: it adopts, in other words, an intraorganism approach, looking within organisms rather than outward between organisms focusing on mental representations as a set of abstract properties.

For Chomsky, to know a language is to be in a mental state; the state consists of a system of rules, representations, and principles generating mental representations, which produce the grammar, a system of rules for the representations of sound and meaning. In contrast, for systemicists, knowing a language means being able to select the appropriate resources to accomplish various tasks, from the set of resources available in each situation needed to carry out different purposes.

In terms of language development, Chomsky adopts the nativist's view, maintaining that humans possess a specific language learning faculty distinct from other learning faculties. This provides the infant with a ready-made blueprint for the structure of language. Learning the mother tongue means fitting patterns into the framework with which a child comes equipped.

In what is known as the environmentalist view, a child learns and uses language in different environments which influence their learning and use of that language, a Hallidayan perspective. Halliday and other systemicists further maintain that language learning is not distinct from other kinds of learning; rather, it depends on the same sort of mental faculties involved in all aspects of a child's learning. The specific properties of a language that are learned originate in the environment, consistent with the view of language as a social construct.

The focal point for systemicists is that language is seen as a resource, not a set of rules. Further, SFL is designed to show the ways in which language serves and realizes certain social functions using different resources that each situation engenders. For this reason SFL is an inter-organism approach. Because of the need to function in different settings, the set of resources varies from situation to situation, which necessitates a theory about context (Martin 1992).

The orientation of functional grammar, then, is social rather than biological as it is in early generative grammar.

An in-depth look at SFL

SFL is a perspective for describing language both externally as a social and cultural phenomenon and internally as a formal system for expressing meanings. It does so through a theory designed not only to explain how people interact with each other through language, but to provide a methodology for the analysis of many types of discourse. Theoretically, SFL views language as organized functionally; these functions (technically referred to as metafunctions) underlie and generate the structures of language. The functional focus allows researchers to examine any text – verbal or visual – and be able to analyse it and explain why texts mean what and how they do so. SFL researchers view language as a system of choices, which allows them to explain choices made in a particular instance of language use, such as giving a talk in a seminar classroom. The emphasis in SFL, then, on functions and systems of choice is responsible for the name of the approach: systemic functional linguistics. Systemicists study what language *does*, not what it *is*; showing what it does better illustrates what it is. Language is a form of activity, a form of meaningful human behaviour. The focus is on how language performs a variety of tasks in a situation and is influenced by and in turn influences the settings in which it is being used; inherent in this perspective of language is that language both realizes and creates the culture of which it is a part. This view of the instrumental nature of language underlies the theory; language is the way it is because of the uses it has evolved to serve. Language results, then, from an ongoing act of choices that occurs in and is fashioned by different social and cultural situations. Inherent in the theory is the view that language acts as a bridge between the cultural meanings that exist in society and the grammar of the code.

For Halliday (1994), the concept of function has two meanings. First, function equals use; and second, it is a fundamental property of language, basic to the evolution of the semantic or meaning system: every natural language can be interpreted in terms of a functional theory. In terms of the meanings we exchange, there are three general functions or *metafunctions* of language, which are simultaneously expressed in instances of language use. Butt *et al.* (2000: 5) explain that language is used to: talk about what is happening at any given moment, what will happen at some future time and what has been happening (the *ideational* metafunction, and more specifically the *experiential* sub-function of the ideational metafunction); interact through language expressing a point of view or an opinion on the present or future happening (the *interpersonal* metafunction); and make the output of the previous two functions into a coherent whole (the *textual* metafunction).

These functions of language are built into the language code, allowing users to combine different functions into each utterance. When people speak they not only share some experience but also express their stance towards it, their opinion of it and attitude towards it; and they also seek to relate the experience to what has gone before; they seek to make their interaction cohere to what has already been said, not only in this language event but also in previous ones. The grammar of a language is there to connect the selections in meaning derived from the metafunctions of language and realize them in a unified structural form (Halliday 1978). Each utterance then simultaneously expresses three metafunctions, making the language code tri-functionally organized.

Looking further at the metafunctions and their structural realization, the ideational metafunction has two sub-categories: the experiential and the logical; the experiential function is responsible, as suggested above, for expressing the happenings, the content – real or unreal – of experiences, and can be initially understood through questions such as, who is doing what to whom, where and when. At a more delicate level researchers examine different types of meanings that are achieved through what is called the transitivity system, a structural term to account for how processes, participants and circumstances, which make up the experiential sub-function, are realized. It permits a speaker or writer to express the ways in which the world of experience is represented and is conveyed through different process types: material or action, mental and relational, and the different participants and circumstances involved in each (Halliday 1994: 107).

For example, in a statement such as 'Tom killed the intruder', a researcher would identify the process realized by the verbal group 'killed' as a material or action process, with two participants, one realizing the actor – the being who carries out the action – and realized by one of the nominal groups that precedes the verbal one, and the second nominal group which realizes the participant role receiving the action, known as the goal. So, experientially there is an action process, involving an actor and a goal. The logical sub-system deals mainly with ways in which clauses are connected to each other. First, they are connected through 'a system that describes the type of interdependency between clauses'. Second, 'the logico-semantic system describes the type of meaning relationship between linked clauses' (Eggins 2004: 258–9).

To illustrate the combined metafunctional realizations, another related statement can be added to our original one: 'But, unfortunately after he did so he did not call the police.' Here the relationship of expansion – one that adds information to the original – is evident through the choice of the word 'but' realizing the logical sub-function.

The interpersonal metafunction accounts for a different set of meanings which focus on speakers' and listeners' interactions with each other and with the material being conveyed in terms of attitudes and stances expressed in the discourse. The realizations of these meanings occur in terms of mood choices: statement, question, command; and modality realized by modal operators (Eggins 2004: 172) such as 'might', 'could', 'should'. They are also realized by adjuncts like 'probably', 'usually' or different sentence adjuncts which relate to the whole of the sentence; examples include 'frankly', 'unfortunately'.

In addition to the interpersonal realizations above there has been recent work on appraisal theory, which is an extension of SFL's interpersonal metafunction. It has many sub-categories, only three of which will be mentioned briefly here (adapted from Eggins and Slade 1997: 125). *Appreciation* covers the ways in which speakers or writers express their likes and dislikes and personal evaluations of people and events through either lexical choices or whole clauses. The focus is on evaluation of an item or idea. The second form of appraisal, labelled *affect*, expresses emotions and feelings. Affective appraisals are typically expressed through adjectives, which express attitudes towards some event, person or object. The last sub-category, *judgment*, accounts for people's judgments in terms of social values and ethics.

But, to return to the two statements above, there is a very clear indication of the speaker's attitude or stance expressed through the adjunct 'unfortunately', which expresses a particular judgment.

The last metafunction, the textual, serves to ensure that the utterance achieves relevance in a context. Resources for doing so include cohesive features such as ellipsis, reference, repetition, conjunction, collocation and thematic development, which connect different parts of texts to each other structurally or lexically. Coherence, also a part of the textual metafunction, accounts for how speakers and writers create coherent texts, texts that 'hang' together through exophoric reference, reference outside the text to the immediate context or to the broader cultural one.

And so, once again we return to the two statements above to identify the role of the textual metafunction. 'Tom killed the intruder. But unfortunately he did not call the police.' Cohesively, there are three features that show how the statements are connected to each other and to the situation. First, the use of what is called 'anaphoric reference', is realized by the word 'he' which connects the second statement to the previous nominal group realized by 'Tom' in the first sentence. Second, the logical factor realized by the connector 'but' also plays a role in cohesion, indicating to the listeners or readers the contrast posited here. And finally, coherence is achieved through the judgment expressed by 'unfortunately', based on cultural assumptions that one is supposed to call the police after a killing.

As briefly illustrated above, each of the metafunctional strands is realized in quite distinctive structures of the clause complex. Ideational content is realized by nominal and verbal groups as well as conjunctions. Interpersonally, the content is presented through a sentence adjunct above. Textual realizations are achieved through lexical and grammatical choice of reference.

SFL, concerned with how users exchange meanings in different socially situated contexts, is a theory of meanings represented as sets of choices. System networks identify those choices and are designed to show how language is made up of sets of interrelated options. The systems represent the choices available in a given situation from which language users make selections appropriate to the context of situation. A system network reflects, in other words, a theory of language as choice where language expresses meanings by choosing between alternatives. Eggins (2004: 198) provides a clear and simple system involving dinner choices:

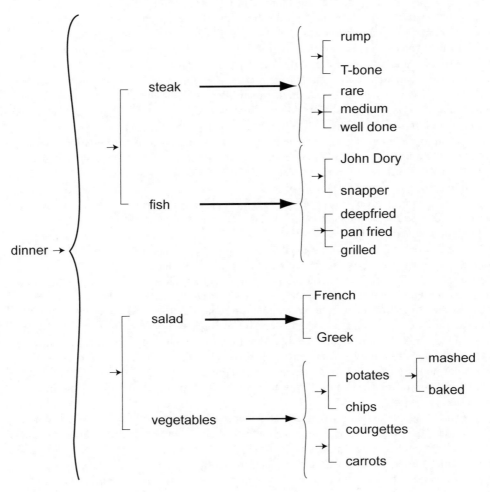

Figure 44.1 A system network
Source: Eggins 2004: 198.

Each point in the network specifies two things about the possibility of choices:

1 The environment consisting of choices that have already been made; that is, every time a choice is made it is not made in isolation but in the context of other choices that have previously been selected.
2 It is a set of possibilities of which one has to be chosen. Both of these points taken together constitute a system such as the one by Eggins above.

First, there is the environment of the choices – dinner. There are two sets of simultaneous choices to be made: in the steak or fish category and in the salad or vegetable one indicated by the curlicued line. Once these choices have been made in each set there are further choices. If fish is selected, then the curlicued line again offers choices about the type of fish and how it is to be prepared; a choice from each set has to be simultaneously made before one can make further choices. The same applies to the choice of steak. In terms of the salad, the choice is simple, between French or Greek; if a vegetable is selected then there are again two simultaneous sets of choices – potatoes or chips and courgettes or carrots; if potatoes, a further choice again is between types of potatoes.

Of particular importance to note is how systems reflect increased delicacy or detail in choices in the progression from left to right. Systems and system networks are designed to indicate the categories of the choices and the more specific choices that arise after initial selections have been made.

Systems are further designed to show how meanings are presented as sets of choices from which speakers and writers choose; distinct sets of resources are available in different situations; that is, they do not occur in vacuums but in the situational and linguistic contexts.

Contexts of situation and register

In SFL as described by Halliday (1978), the semiotic structure of the situation in which language occurs is formed out of three sociosematic variables of *field, tenor* and *mode*. These components of a situation are viewed as part of a social semiotic system of meanings that together constitute a culture. They both derive from and in turn influence the social and cultural structures of different types of context.

SFL rooted in a social view of language necessitates a focus on how people communicate and interact with each other using language 'to get on with life', as Martin suggests. The interplay of the dialectical relationship between language and society becomes clearer in the discussion of these features that follows.

Each context is described in term of these three situational constructs:

1   Field accounts for what is happening discursively – the role that language plays in a particular happening or event. It accounts for the experience or the content that receives focus in the situation. One way to understand field is to ask, what activity is taking place?
2   Tenor accounts for the types of interactions between the addressers and the addressees and between the addressers and the content, the position that speakers and writers adopt both in terms of information being conveyed as well as interactions shared with audiences. In examining the nature of tenor, the following questions help to identify the realizations in the code (Butt *et al.* 2000: 18): what is the relationship between the interactants? Is there a social distance between them? Is the relationship between them equal or not?
3   Mode concerns the nature of language itself, whether it is spoken or written or spontaneous or planned language; further, whether the information is presented in a newspaper, or on television, in a lecture or a recipe.

Functional variation or register produces determines different metafunctional choices; but the context is in turn influenced by the language choices, creating a bi-directional influence between language and contexts of situation.

The field of discourse is realized through the experiential sub-function of the ideational metafunction, in processes, participants and circumstances in language. The tenor, accounting for the role relationships between interactants, is expressed through interpersonal meanings through mood, attitudinal and modality choices as well as in appraisals. Mode accounts for whether the interaction is spoken or written, and influences textual selections through cohesion, coherence and thematic patterns.

Halliday (1994) suggests that each type of meaning is related in a predictable, systematic way to each situational variable. The status of the three constructs derives from the fact that they are linked to the three types of meaning language is structured to make: the experiential (the ideational), the textual and the interpersonal. When a set of texts share the same context of situation to a greater or lesser extent, they will share the same experiential, interpersonal and textual meanings since they belong to the same register (Butt *et al.* 2000).

Register delineates different functional varieties that every society has, ranging from a recipe to a lecture, a novel to a specific set of instructions; each is a particular discursive realization in different situations, a realization in terms of choices available in that situation.

The situational contexts themselves arise and are determined by the broader context of culture in which they are found. Cultural contexts are those that account for and 'allow' specific situations to exist; the latter being determined by what is culturally acceptable. For example, in some cultures like those in Western societies, letters to advice columnists exist, whereas in some Asian cultures this is not so. Cultures determine the nature of the situational contexts that can and do exist in particular societies.

Context of culture/genres

The analysis of any text within the functional model of language then, involves not only a clausal explanation of lexicogrammatical patterns realizing semantic metafunctional choices, but also an explanation of how the text is influenced by the immediate situation in terms of field, tenor and mode.

Further, SFL description focuses on the staged structure of the discourse as a whole to show 'how ... we use language to live; it tries to describe the ways in which we mobilize language' (Martin 2009: 13). Genres and generic analysis are designed to focus on the overall purpose of the text, the ways in which we get things done through language. Generic considerations broaden findings available in the SFL framework by making explicit the purposeful activity which a text accomplishes.

> Genres develop as ways of dealing linguistically with recurrent configurations of register variables. In other words, as certain contextual combinations become stable, ways of interacting within those contexts also become habitualized and, eventually institutionalized as genres. There come to be preferred, typical ways of negotiating such contexts.
>
> *(Eggins 2004: 58)*

Eggins also suggests that genres tell us the cultural purpose of texts, which are realized by register configurations. The schematic structure of a text then is the generic structure and gives it its generic identity (ibid.).

To further understand the distinction between register and genre, Couture suggests that:

> While registers impose explicitness constraints at the level of vocabulary and syntax, genres impose additional explicitness constraints at the discourse level. They define conventional patterns of linguistic structure for the complete discourse, and they are intertextual – that is, they are defined by their capacity to evoke other texts. ... Rhetoricians traditionally associate genre with a complete, unified textual structure. Unlike

register, genre can only be realized in completed texts or texts that can be projected as complete.

(Couture 1986: 82)

The staging of a particular genre will differ from other genres because the overall purpose differs, so if we examine narratives, we might expect the generic structure to include at least the following stages: orientation, complication, evaluation, resolution. If we were examining, on the other hand, a lecture, the stages would be very different and might include: introduction, explanation(s), exemplifications, conclusion. Genres, then, can be defined as a 'recurrent configuration of meanings and a culture as a system of genres' (Martin 2009: 13).

Genre analysis together with register analysis provides the contextual information for a lexicogrammatical and semantic analysis, providing a complete framework for discourse analysis.

Whatever genre we are involved in, and whatever the register of the situation, our use of language will also be influenced by our ideological positions: the values we hold (consciously or unconsciously) the perspectives acquired through our particular path through the culture.

(Eggins 2004: 10)

Applications and extensions of SFL

Having discussed SFL in terms of its roots and the theory itself, it is important to sketch, however briefly, two closely related applications of SFL to highlight how the examination of discourse from a functional perspective can contribute to analysis and even more importantly to social action and the resolution of real-world problems – in areas such as education, translation, speech pathology, etc.

SFL has never been simply a theory of language; it has always been designed to be applied to an understanding of how people make and exchange meanings in a broad range of contexts. The aim of the functional grammar of Halliday 'has been to construct a grammar for purposes of text analysis: one that would make it possible to say sensible and useful things about the text, spoken or written' (Halliday 1994: xv) and one might extend this easily to include visuals – still and moving.

SFL is meant to answer questions such as why a text means what it does and why it is valued (Halliday 1994: xxix). By so doing it offers the researcher a theory that provides a set of methodological tools for discourse analysis. Two approaches influenced by SFL have become particularly prominent. The first is critical discourse analysis (CDA) and the second, social and visual semiotics, or what is now also known as multimodality. Iedema explains the origins of these different but related analytical directions:

On the one hand, there is the critical theoretical work inspired by Fairclough's 'reworking' of Foucault and Bakhtin (Fairclough 1992; Fairclough and Wodak 1997). On the other hand, there is the work of Kress and Van Leeuwen (1996) [and] Van Leeuwen (1999) which is becoming increasingly definitive of approaches to text analysis and meaning making, and where the discourse analytical term 'multimodality' originates.

(Iedema 2003: 82)

The set of methodological tools provided by SFL is central in the work of both CDA and multimodality. Linguists interested in the relationships between language and ideology began extending discourse analysis to include and to cover more critical considerations. Kress (1995) has suggested that linguistics itself needed to be moved into the domain of social and political relevance and that it provide a social critique by documenting linguistic structures of inequality. SFL is ideally suited to explain why certain selections are made and others not, and how inequalities are expressed discursively.

Discourse analysists, particularly those trained as systemicists, began in the late 1970s and early 1980s to look more critically at uses of language and the meanings that get exchanged in different situations, focusing on how positions and interrelationships among interactants have been encoded and how this is accomplished linguistically. One of the strengths of SFL realized early on in the work of critical linguists from the University of East Anglia such as Kress, Hodge, Trew and Fowler was, as Martin was to comment much later (2000), to ground concerns about power and ideology in the detailed analyses of texts as they unfold clause by clause and in real contexts of language. In Martin's terms (2000), SFL provides a technical language to talk about language. This is one of the main reasons for the close connection to and reliance on SFL in much of the work of linguists such as Fowler and Kress (Fowler *et al.* 1979). The connection between SFL and CDA is also evident in the seminal work of Fairclough, *Language and Power* ([1989] 2001), in which he sets out methods of analysis again extending the SFL metafunctional approach to the critical study of discourse. The influence of SFL is equally evident in applications in the research of Lemke (1995, 2002).

More currently, in the collection by Young and Harrison, *Systemic Functional Linguistics and Critical Discourse Analysis: Studies in Social Change* (2004), the connection between the two areas of research was made more explicit than it had perhaps been before. As suggested in the introduction, many researchers

> have focused to differing degrees on SFL elements in their frameworks and analyses. Early researchers examined the connections between language and the social structure though SFL analysis of metafunctional components. ... As CDA matured as a field of study, however some analysis developed in areas of CDA outside of SFL; nevertheless, all researchers in CDA acknowledge that SFL is centrally important to the critical study of situated language events.
>
> *(Young and Harrison 2004: 2–3)*

Since SFL from the beginning was designed for text analysis, it is not surprising that is has been so prominent in CDA studies (see, for example, Fairclough 1989, 1992, 1993, 2001, 2004; Lemke 1995, 1998; Martin 2000; Wodak and Meyer 2001). In this volume, the relationship between SFL and CDA is treated in detail in the chapter on CDA (O'Halloran, this volume).

The second extension of SFL, into visual semiotics/multimodality, also has its origins in early Hallidayan theory that maintains that language is only one of many semiotic resources for making meaning. Recently, non-verbal semiotic resources have been taken up by current research into other semiotic resources because meaning-making in most situations rarely involves only one mode of communication; much more frequent is the interplay of visual and verbal modes in current discursive events. And as Kress and Van Leeuwen (1996) suggest, in order to fully understand the meanings that each mode contributes to the totality of meanings in any given situation we need to examine the role of each mode and the contributions each makes to the totality of meaning.

One of the most concise and complete answers to how to do this and to establish the questions about the connection between SFL, discourse analysis, and multimodality has been supplied recently by O'Toole (2006). He is particularly well placed to discuss this since he is perhaps the first to apply SFL to visual analysis, showing how the metafunctional approach to language could be adapted to the study of art. He carried out the earliest complete analysis based on the metafunctional approach of Halliday in his work *The Language of Displayed Art* (1994), showing how the metafunctional considerations of verbal texts could be adapted and extended to non-verbal discourse.

He has more recently (2006) suggested that multimodality, discourse analysis and CDA all share a commitment to close SFL analysis of the text itself and to understanding it in its socio-political context. The core of his argument is that Halliday's theory about metafunctions and systems for language can be adapted, with changes appropriate for different modalities, as a basis for the analysis of visual texts. As with language texts, he maintains, it is not the labelling of particular components of the visual text as such, but the recognition of areas of semantic/semiotic convergence and divergence between the realizations of the functions that provides a focus for interpretation. A current adaptation for visual analysis of O'Toole's original presentation, along with Kress and van Leeuwen, and Lemke can be found in Young and Fitzgerald (2006: 172–3, 177).

Multimodality, then, is a term to make explicit semiotic complexity, a complexity that is revealed in the exchange of meanings across semiotic boundaries such as image and verbal texts (Iedema 2003: 39). Research in this area has also been carried out by Lemke (2002) in his work on traversals, in which he studies how meanings are made across semiotic boundaries on the Internet and other settings. In addition, the work of Kress and van Leeuwen (2006) has become central to the study of multimodal meanings through extensions of SFL. Van Leeuwen's (2005) examination of social semiotics indicates clearly how to apply SFL to visual means of communication. Recent work of O'Halloran also illustrates applications of SFL in the multimodal world through her examination of mathematics taught at the tertiary level ([2005] 2008).

Once again the chapter in this volume by van Leeuwen covers these connections more thoroughly. This brief discussion of CDA and multimodality is intended to make explicit the connections among CDA, SFL and multimodality to illustrate the role SFL has played in the research of these two discursive fields.

Summary

We have examined the major features of SFL, situated its origins and then compared it to the other major paradigm of language study that was also prominent when Halliday's early work appeared. The in-depth examination of SFL covered the major metafunctions that form the organizational basis of language and how each metafunction is realized by different structural resources or choices realized through systems.

Looking at language from a functional perspective means that we can begin to understand how language selections in a given situation are made, which allows us to suggest why they were made and why others were not, and how a set of choices contributes to the meaning of a particular text.

In addition, the original conceptualizing of Halliday in his early writing on SFL suggested that language should be viewed as a social semiotic, as a system of meaning-making in different social contexts, and that the theory could be applied to non-verbal resources as much as verbal ones. This conceptualizing also led to descriptions of how meanings are made, and why some meanings were selected over others in different situations. These questions led to others, such as who is advantaged by certain selections and who is disadvantaged by them. This led to further questions about issues of language and power and the relationships between the two in public discourse expressed visually and verbally in the media, in politics and in everyday uses of language.

These are natural extensions of questions about language that originate in a social view in which researchers ask and answer questions about how we use language to survive in daily, familiar situations as well as in the new and broader contexts of current life.

Related topics

critical discourse analysis; multimodality

Further reading

Butt, D., Fahey, R., Feez, S., Spinks, S. and Yallop, C. (2000) *Using Functional Grammar: An Explorer's Guide*, Sydney, Australia: National Centre for English Language Teaching and research, Macquarie University. (A very accessible introduction to SFL.)

Eggins, S. (2004) *An Introduction to Systemic Functional Linguistics*, London: Frances Pinter. (A thorough presentation of SFL.)

Martin, J. R. (2000) 'Close reading: functional linguistics as a tool for critical discourse analysis', in L. Unsworth (ed.) *Researching Language in Schools and Communities: Functional Linguistic Perspectives*, London: Cassell. (A chapter which illustrates the ways in which SFL can be applied to CDA questions.)

Young, L. and Fitzgerald, B. (2006) *The Power of Language: How Discourse Influences Society*, London: Equinox. (A book designed to connect SFL and CDA; intended to provide practice in critical discourse analysis based on SFL.)

References

Butt, D., Fahey, R., Feez, S., Spinks, S. and Yallop, C. (2000) *Using Functional Grammar: An Explorer's Guide*, Sydney, Australia: National Centre for English Language Teaching and Research, Macquarie University.

Chomsky, N. (1980) 'Rules and representations', *The Behavioural and Brain Sciences*, 3: 1–61.

Couture, B. (ed.) (1986) 'Effective ideation in written text: a functional approach to clarity and exigence', *Functional Approaches to Writing: Research Perspectives*, London: Frances Pinter.

Eggins, S and Slade, D. (1997) *Analysing Casual Conversation*, London: Continuum.

Eggins, S. (2004) *An Introduction to Systemic Functional Linguistics*, London: Frances Pinter.

Fairclough, N. and Wodak, R. (1997) 'Critical discourse analysis', in T. van Dijk (ed.) *Discourse as Social Interaction. Discourse Studies: A Multidisciplinary Introduction*, Vol. 2, London: Sage.

Fairclough, N. ([1989] 2001) *Language and Power*, London: Longman.

——(1992) *Discourse and Social Change*, Cambridge: Polity Press.

——(1993) 'Critical discourse analysis and the marketization of public discourse', *Discourse and Society*, 4(2): 133–68.

——(2004) 'Critical discourse analysis in researching language in the new capitalism: over-determination, transdisciplinarity, and textual analysis', in L. Young and C. Harrison (eds) *Systemic Functional Linguistics and Critical Discourse Analysis: Studies in Social Change*. New York and London: Continuum.

Fowler, R., Hodge, R., Kress, G. and Trew, T. (eds) (1979) *Language and Control*, London: Routledge/Kegan Paul.

Halliday, M. A. K. ([1978] 1979) *Language as Social Semiotic: The Social Interpretation of Language and Meaning*, London: Edward Arnold.

——(1994) *An Introduction to Functional Grammar*, 2nd edn, London: Edward Arnold.

Iedema, R. (2003) 'Multimodality, resemiotization: extending the analysis of discourse as multi-semiotic practice', *Visual Communication*, 2(1): 29–57.

Kress, G. (1995) 'The social production of language: history and structures of domination', in P. Fries and M. Gregory, *Discourse in Society: Systemic Functional Perspectives. Meaning and Choice in Language: Studies for Michael Halliday*, Norwood, NJ: Ablex.

Kress, G. and van Leeuwen, T. ([1996] 2006) *Reading Images*, London: Routledge.

Lemke, J. (1995) *Textual Politics: Discourse and Social Dynamics*, London: Taylor & Francis.

——(1998) 'Multiplying meaning: visual and verbal semiotics in scientific text', in J. R. Martin and R. Veel (eds) *Reading Science: Critical and Functional Perspectives on Discourses of Science*, London: Routledge.

——(2002) 'Travels in hypermodality', *Visual Communications*, 1(3): 299–325.

Martin, J. R. (1992) *English Text: System and Structure*, Amsterdam: John Benjamins.

——(2000) 'Close reading: functional linguistics as a tool for critical discourse analysis in researching language', in L. Unsworth (ed.) *Schools and Communities: Functional Linguistic Perspectives*, London: Cassell.

——(2009) 'Genre and language learning: a social semiotic perspective', *Linguistics and Education*, 20: 10–21.

Martin, J. R., Matthiessen, C. M. I. M and Painter, C. (1997) *Working With Functional Grammar*, London: Edward Arnold.

Mensikova, A. (1972) 'Sentence patterns in the theory and practice of teaching French as a foreign language', in V. Fried (ed.) *The Prague School of Linguistics and Language Teaching*, London: Oxford University Press.

O'Halloran, K. ([2005] 2008) *Mathematical Discourse: Language Symbolism and Visual Images*, London and New York: Continuum.

O'Toole, M. (1994) *The Language of Displayed Art*, London: Leicester University Press.

——(2006) From an email sent on 9 October 2006 to Sysfling-L@listserv.uam.es

Trinka, B. (1964) 'Prague school of linguistics', in J. Vachek (ed.) *A Prague School Reader in Linguistics*, 2nd edn, Bloomington: Indiana University Press.

Vachek, J. ([1964] 1982) *A Prague School Reader in Linguistics*, Bloomington: Indiana University Press.

——(1966) *The Linguistic School of Prague: An Introduction to its Theory and Practice*, Bloomington: Indiana University Press.

——(1972) 'The linguistic theory of the Prague school', in V. Fried (ed.) *The Prague School of Linguistics and Language Teaching*, London: Oxford University Press.

van Leeuwen, T. (1999) *Speech, Sound, Music*, London: Macmillan.

——(2005) *Introducing Social Semiotics*, London: Routledge.

van Leeuwen, T. and Jewitt, C. (eds) (2001) *Handbook of Visual Analysis*, London: Sage.

Wodak, R. (1996) *Disorders of Discourse*, London: Longman.

Wodak, R. and M. Meyer (eds) (2001) *Methods of Critical Discourse Analysis*, London: Sage.

Young, L. (1990) *Language as Behaviour, Language as Code: A Study of Academic English*, Amsterdam: John Benjamins.

Young, L. and Fitzgerald, B. (2006) *The Power of Language: How Discourse Influences Society*, London: Equinox.

Young, L. and Harrison, C. (eds) (2004) *Systemic Functional Linguistics and Critical Discourse Analysis: Studies in Social Change*, London: Continuum.

45

Generative grammar

Shigenori Wakabayashi

Introduction

One of the major contributions of generative grammar to our understanding of human language has been to foreground facts about language that previously went unrecognized, or were considered unimportant, such as the fact that *who* and *he* can refer to the same person in (1a), but not in (1b), and that every native speaker of English knows this without ever having been taught it:

(1a)   Who said he didn't vote?
(1b)   Who did he say didn't vote?

Another fact that every native speaker of English knows without instruction is that *he* and *John* can be the same person in (2a), whereas in (2b) they must be different people:

(2a)   When he arrived, John was wearing a fur coat.
(2b)   He was wearing a fur coat when John arrived.

In (1) and (2) the linear ordering of the relevant constituents, *who … he, he … John*, is the same in both pairs of sentences. The difference in meaning derives from structural differences in the organization of the sentences that are not immediately obvious from their surface forms. It has been one of the strengths of generative grammar to highlight the abstract organizational properties of sentences that give rise to such differences, which play a major role in our ordinary use of language.

Those who undertake applied linguistics research have often misunderstood the goals, scope and limits of generative grammar. It is the aim of this chapter to try to clarify what generative grammar is, and how it offers insights into some important areas of applied linguistic research. It will be made clear that generative grammar provides a reliable base for research in applied linguistics.

General background: assumptions in generative linguistics

Context free grammar

Generative grammar adopts certain approaches to language. First, it deals with sentences independent of discourse and context, despite the fact that we typically use our language in context. In fact, it is usually impossible to understand the intention of a speaker without any reference to the context. Consider the 'meaning' of the following sentence:

(3)   Mike occasionally drinks tea around this time of the day.

This sentence can be interpreted in a number of ways: e.g. an answer to a question uttered by a person who is looking for Mike; or a complaint uttered by Mike's brother who works for their family business with Mike (Mike always disappears around late afternoon, which is the busiest time for their business); or something else. However, this does not mean sentences have to be studied in context. Why are such interpretations possible in the first place? The answer is because the sentence (3) is grammatical and meaningful. This is not a trivial matter. Consider the following sentences:

(4a)   Occasionally Mike drinks tea around this time of the day.
(4b)   Mike drinks tea around this time of the day occasionally.
(4c)   *Mike drinks occasionally tea around this time of day
(4d)   *Mike drinks tea around this time occasionally of day

(3, 4a, b) are 'good', while (4c, d) are 'bad' whatever the contexts are, despite the fact that all the words are identical in (3) and (4) and that it is easy to work out what (4c, d) mean.

Furthermore, even when a sentence is not 'meaningful', it can be grammatical. The famous contrast between 'colorless green ideas sleep furiously' and '*furiously sleep ideas green colorless' tells us this fact (Chomsky 1957: 15). The former is meaningless yet sounds English (i.e. grammatical), but the latter does not follow the form of English. Speakers of a language can distinguish grammatical sentences in their language from those that are not, independent of what they mean.

This leads us to conclude that certain context-free rules distinguish grammatical sentences from ungrammatical ones. What makes this possible should be the knowledge of English as represented in a native speaker's brain. 'What is knowledge of language?' is one of the questions that generative linguists try to answer.

Productivity, the poverty of stimulus, and the purpose of generative grammar

Human languages are unique in many respects. One of their most striking characteristics is productivity. Every day we use sentences that we have never encountered. The innovation of generative grammar in Chomsky (1955, 1957) was its emphasis on trying to develop an explicit theory of how language learners can, on the basis of encountering finite examples of language, come to understand and produce novel combinations in a potentially infinite number of sentences. This system not only allows for the production of grammatical sentences but also disallows ungrammatical sentences.

Every human being acquires a mother tongue. The acquisition of the system despite limited input is known as the issue of the poverty of the stimulus (or the logical problem of language acquisition, or Plato's problem). Now consider the following sentences:

(5a) Jack dislikes himself.
(5b) Jack admires a picture of himself.
(5c) *Himself dislikes Jack.

In (5a, b), the referent of *himself* is *Jack*, while it is not so in (5c), which is in fact ungrammatical. The reason for the difference appears to be the differences in word order: *Jack* precedes *himself* in (5a, b) but *himself* precedes *Jack* in (5c). If this is correct, all sentences in which *himself* comes before *Jack* should be ungrammatical, but this is not the case, as shown in (6):

(6) That picture of himself surprised Jack.

How do we know that *himself* can refer to *Jack* in (6) but not in (5c)? It is unlikely that we have received any instruction from someone around us. In fact, it is very unlikely that we gained the rule by external means. Instead, the source must, logically speaking, come from inside ourselves. That is, we know this contrast because the rule exists tacitly in our mind. This tacit knowledge is likely to be derived from the psychological device used for first language acquisition (L1A). If such a system exists, it should be used in L1A regardless of the language to be acquired. In other words, this device – the Language Acquisition Device (for grammar), or Universal Grammar (UG) – is universal. In fact, Chomsky considered human languages (e.g. English, Japanese, Hindu, etc.) to be variations of one human language UG. The main inquiry of generative grammar is to describe what UG is.

Modularity, I-language (competence) and E-language (performance)

In generative grammar, linguistic knowledge is considered to be independent of other cognitive systems. This is supported by physiological data (see Obler and Gjerlow 1999), especially by the existence of developmental and pathological cases where linguistic knowledge is dissociated from other cognitive capacities. On the one hand there are people whose linguistic abilities are normal or even enhanced, while their non-linguistic capacities are impaired, such as the polyglot savant Christopher, described by Smith and Tsimpli (1995). On the other hand, there are people whose linguistic knowledge is deviant but other cognitive abilities are normal (e.g. people suffering from aphasia).

As illustrated above, the grammaticality of a sentence is usually independent of its meaning. This implies that the grammar consists of a 'syntactic module' which is independent of meaning (the 'semantic module'). Traditionally, linguistics is divided into subfields, including phonology, morphology, syntax, semantics, and pragmatics, each of which can be considered to constitute a module, with the rules of each field existing independently of the others. Modules are connected with one another through interfaces.

When a speaker produces non-target-like linguistic output, the causes are likely to lie in this 'connecting' system. Positing a multi-layered system makes it possible to investigate the cause of deviance. Hence, it is possible to suggest that, for example, second language learners' syntactic knowledge is native-like but their morphophonological system is not (Hazneder and Schwartz 1997; Prévost and White 2000).

In generative grammar, what is directly observable is referred to as E-language (performance: *E* stands for External). Linguistic knowledge (I-language, i.e. competence: *I* stands for Internal) is the object of research (Chomsky 1965, 1986, 1995). In order to investigate I-language, we need to use E-language data (cf. chapters in this volume on clinical linguistics and on neurolinguistics).

The development of generative grammar

Changes of theoretical frameworks

There have been several radical changes in the framework of generative grammar: the Standard Theory in Chomsky (1955, 1957), the Extended Standard Theory (Chomsky 1965), the Principles and Parameters framework (Chomsky 1981, 1986a) and the Minimalist Program (Chomsky 1995, 1999). I will briefly illustrate the main changes below, following Lasnik (2005).

The earliest model in Chomsky (1955) offered a phrase structure grammar, where the structure of a sentence can be depicted in tree diagrams, which consist of sets of strings. An important assumption in this model, as well as subsequently, is that any sentence has more than one structure, each at a different level: the structure that reflects almost completely the way the sentence is pronounced, as well as an additional abstract structure, and intermediate structures between the two. In the Extended Standard Model (Chomsky 1965), by inserting items from the lexicon into the structure, a 'deep structure' is constructed, and then transformations apply. When all transformations have been applied, the 'surface structure' is constructed. Chomsky (1973) introduced the notion of a 'trace', which an item leaves behind when it moves. This allows the deep structure to be represented in the surface structure and indicates where an item should be interpreted. So, semantic interpretation does not have to be associated with deep structure. Later, it was assumed that additional transformations take place between surface structure and logical form (cf. May 1977). All transformations were subsequently reduced to only one operation (move α), as illustrated in (7) (Figure 45.1):

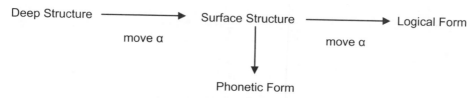

Figure 45.1 Derivation in Government and Binding Theory

The theory associated with the schema in Figure 45.1 is called Government and Binding Theory or the Principles and Parameters framework. In this theory, it was assumed that all natural languages have common abstract rules, called Principles, and vary along a limited number of choices among values (mostly binary) associated with parameters. In later versions of Principles and Parameters, parameters are considered to be associated with functional categories, such as C(omplementizer), I(nflection) or T(ense), and D(eterminer), and the differences in the syntax of different languages are attributed to formal features associated with these categories (e.g. Chomsky 1993).

In the mid-1990s, a new framework called the Minimalist Program was proposed (Chomsky 1995), where the concepts of deep and surface structure were abandoned. Instead, all operations are based on the demands at the interfaces where 'sounds' and 'meaning' are interpreted. The schema of this model is shown in Figure 45.2.

Constructing a syntactic object starts from the Lexicon, where all lexical items are taken into a lexical array called Numeration. A structure is constructed by Merge, which merges one object with another, and other operations, such as Agree, take place where necessary.

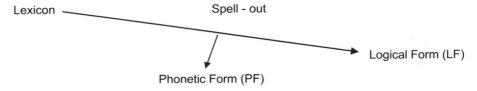

Figure 45.2 Derivation in the Minimalist Program

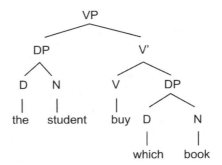

Figure 45.3 VP Structure

Now let us look at a syntactic computation in the Minimalist Program. In the construction of (7), at some point of the derivation, the structure in Figure 45.3 is constructed:

(7)   Which book will the student buy?

At this point, the argument structure is constructed, and the syntactic object has propositional content. Then, T(ense) merges with this object (Figure 45.4):

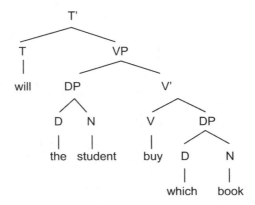

Figure 45.4 T' Structure

English T has a feature (EPP: Extended Projection Principle), which requires its specifier position to be filled by a DP. So, the DP closest to this position is attracted and moved into the position. A copy is left at the original position and deleted, as shown by strikethrough (Figure 45.5):

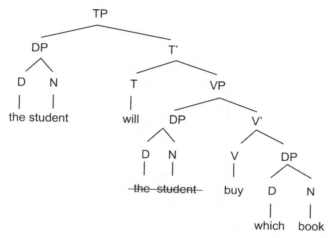

Figure 45.5 TP Structure

Then, C merges with TP, and the affix feature [+Q] attracts and moves the tense feature associated with T. The auxiliary *will* is moved as a whole to C (Figure 45.6).

C has a [+wh] and an EPP feature, which attracts and moves an element that also has a [+wh] feature. Hence, the DP *which book* is moved to the specifier position of CP (Figure 45.7).

At this point, the syntactic operations needed for presentation to the 'sound' module are completed, and hence the aspects of the structure relevant for phonology are 'spelled out' to the PF interface. No further syntactic operation is required for semantic interpretation either; hence the structure is also sent to the LF interface. (When a sentence requires some operations after spell-out, they take place after spell-out but before the syntactic object is interpreted at LF.)

Research strategy behind generative grammar

Certain research strategies have been adopted in different frameworks within generative grammar. From the beginning, unlike traditional grammars, generative grammar tried to explain why certain structures are *not* allowed in a grammar as well as why others are allowed (Smith 2005). Before the Principles and Parameters approach, researchers were mainly interested in finding new 'facts' of this kind, by investigating natural languages intensively and deeply, to find relevant evidence for discussing the human mind (Reibel and Schane 1969). If a rule is too abstract to be learned from input, it is inferred to be present innately as part of UG.

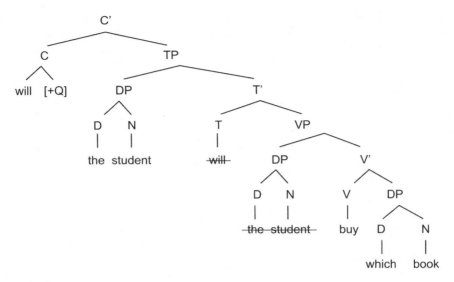

Figure 45.6 C' Structure

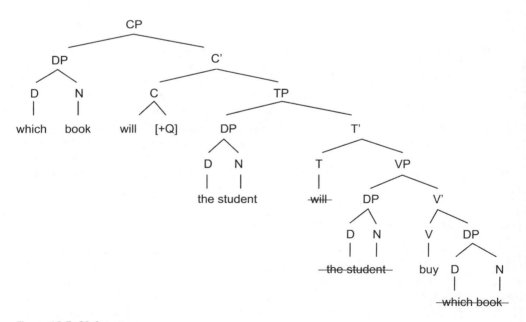

Figure 45.7 CP Structure

Given the new tools (i.e. phrase structure rules and transformation rules), researchers argued for a number of new rules. As the theory developed, it became clear that these rules were inadequately constrained, resulting in the transition from phrase structure and transformations to Principles and Parameters (Newmeyer 1986).

The Principles and Parameters (Chomsky 1981, 1986a) provided researchers with a theoretical framework to account for similarities and differences among languages. Given this framework, generative linguists try to account for the differences among adult languages (e.g. Haegeman 1997), historical changes (e.g. Roberts 1993), L1A, and SLA. Principles include, for example, X-bar theory (all phrase structure constituents in human language have an identical structure); the Subjacency Condition (see below); Principle of Structure Dependency (all syntactic operations are governed by the structure of the syntactic object), and so on. If these are innately given, they will reduce the burden on children in L1A because they do not have to entertain those logical possibilities that violate these principles. Parameters are offered to capture variation among languages. For example, the 'wh-parameter' says that wh-phrases have to move to the specifier position of CP between deep and surface structures in some languages (e.g. English), while they may stay in the original position in other languages (e.g. Japanese). This difference is determined by parametric values: English has the value [+ wh-movement] and Japanese has the value [-wh-movement]. Other parameters include the Bounding Node Parameter (see below), the Null Subject Parameter (whether a sentential subject without sound [i.e. null subject] is allowed or not), and so on. Parameters tell us not only that languages may vary in accordance with their values but also that no other possibilities are allowed. For example, the wh-parameter says that there is no language that allows (or requires) wh-phrases to move somewhere other than the specifier position of CP.

A large number of phenomena were described and explained in the Principles and Parameters framework. Subsequently, Chomsky (1995) advanced a new approach, the Minimalist Program, where cross-linguistic differences are attributed to formal features associated with functional categories.

Generative grammar and applied linguistics

Theoretical linguistics and applied linguistics

Although generative grammar is mainly considered a theoretical enterprise, studies in the area that describe the linguistic competence of speakers other than adult native speakers are of relevance to this volume. Such studies rely on performance data collected through recordings in natural settings or through experimental tasks (see below). Moreover, although the main goal is to describe and explain learners'/acquirers' linguistic knowledge (and ultimately the human mind), these studies may serve as a foundation for establishing how to help learners develop their linguistic knowledge. Of all the possible areas of applied linguistics to which generative grammar relates (e.g. clinical linguistics, neurolinguistics, psycholinguistics), I focus on studies of child grammar and L2 grammar (i.e. *interlanguage*) here.

Generative approaches to L1A

For its whole history, a central line of inquiry for generative grammar has been how a first language (L1) is acquired. Researchers who study child language have shown that child grammar develops very quickly and rather uniformly (e.g. Brown 1973). The Principles and Parameters perspective promoted a large number of theory-based studies of child grammar and provided a theoretical framework to describe it in terms of what is given innately and what must be acquired. Since Hyams' (1983) study on the acquisition of overt sentential subjects by child learners of English, a large number of such studies have been carried out.

In the 1990s two competing hypotheses were offered. Radford (1990) proposed a unified account for the differences between child and adult English: children's grammars lack functional categories, which makes their utterances different from those of adults. For example, the lack of I(NFL) (= T in Figures 45.4–7 above) results in the absence of tense or agreement morphemes on verbs, modals, *do*-support, copula *be*, progressive *be*, perfective *have*, infinitival *to* and in the use of default case forms. Functional categories are assumed to 'mature' biologically in the same way as wisdom teeth do. Because the sentential structure extends (from VP to TP, and from TP to CP) in accordance with children's knowledge of language, this hypothesis is called the structure-building hypothesis. Hyams (1994) (and Hyams and Wexler 1993, among others) argued against Radford, suggesting that functional categories are projected from the beginning of L1A but their relevant features must mature. They considered the structure [CP [TP [VP ...]]] to be present in child grammar from the beginning. This is called the structural continuity hypothesis.

Under both hypotheses, children proceed by acquiring the properties associated with functional categories. This fits well with the view that the parametric differences among languages are attributable to the features associated with functional categories.

Applying generative grammar to SLA

The advent of the Principles and Parameters framework brought about a large body of research adopting a generative approach to SLA. This framework offered an explicit description and explanation of cross-linguistic differences between natural languages. The theoretical assumptions of generative grammar – for example, the claim that knowledge of language constitutes a modular system (Towell and Hawkins 1994) – are also appropriate for SLA research. In fact, early studies in SLA research suggested that the nature of SLA is similar to L1A, involving processes of rule construction based not only on input but also on learners' innate knowledge (Corder 1967), with differences in input or environment being unlikely to alter the path by which second language learners (L2ers) progress in advancing their knowledge of a second language (see, for example, Larsen-Freeman and Long 1991).

However, a number of researchers considered L1A and SLA to be fundamentally different: UG works as a language acquisition device in the former case, but not in the latter. Bley-Vroman (1989, 1990) pointed out a number of differences between L1A and SLA and insisted that they should be seen as fundamentally different (see also Bley-Vroman 2009). Clahsen and Muysken (1986) found that non-target-like sentence types produced by children acquiring German as their L1 and those produced by L2ers were different, and attributed this difference to different systems underlying the acquisition processes. Namely, L1A is guided by UG while SLA is not. DuPlessis *et al.* (1987) proposed a UG-based account for the development of these non-target-like productions by L2ers.

The 'UG or not UG' question was intensely debated during the 1980s. One property used to address this debate involved the availability of a constraint on wh-movement in SLA by L2ers whose L1s do not have wh-movement. The movement of wh-phrases is constrained by structure, rather than by the linear distance between the position where the wh-phrase is base generated and the surface position where it is pronounced (Ross 1967). In (8), the linear distance between the wh-word (*what*) and its trace is longer in (8a) than in (8b), but only (8a) is grammatical:

(8a)   What did Tom believe that John said that Mike hoped that Jack bought t?

(8b)   *What did Tom reject the claim that he wrote t ?

        cf. Tom rejected the claim that he wrote this document.

To explain such cases, the Subjacency Condition (Chomsky 1973) was proposed, according to which a wh-word cannot move beyond two 'bounding nodes' at once. What constitutes a 'bounding node' differs across languages: IP and NP are bounding nodes in English, whereas CP and NP are bounding nodes in French.

    Let us see how the Subjacency Condition excludes the sentence (8b) above. First of all, wh-phrases move cyclically via the specifier positions of CPs such that none of the movements in (8a), shown in Figure 45.8, violates the Subjacency condition. On the other hand, the second wh-movement in Figure 45.9 goes beyond two bounding nodes. Bounding nodes are identified by '|'.

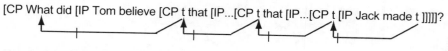

[CP What did [IP Tom believe [CP t that [IP...[CP t that [IP...[CP t [IP Jack made t]]]]]?

Figure 45.8 wh-movement in (8a)

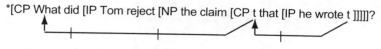

*[CP What did [IP Tom reject [NP the claim [CP t that [IP he wrote t]]]]]?

Figure 45.9 wh-movement in (8b)

Whether L2ers know this constraint was used to examine whether UG operates in SLA (see Belikova and White (2009) for a recent overview). The logic behind it is as follows: Some languages have wh-movement while others do not. When wh-phrases do not move, the constraints related to wh-movement are irrelevant. Suppose a learner's L1 is this type but the target language has wh-movement. If UG, including the Subjacency Condition, operates in SLA, such a learner should have access to the constraint. Hence, he or she should reject sentences like (8b). In contrast, if UG does not operate and acquisition proceeds solely based on the L1 grammar and/or general problem solving mechanisms, then learners should be unaware of such a constraint and accept those sentences. A number of studies were carried out following this logic. The results were inconclusive to a large extent as to whether UG operates in SLA.

    Martohardjono's (1993) findings were much more compelling than those reported earlier. She adopted Chomsky's (1986b) theory and suggested that some ungrammatical sentences are worse than others. Compare the sentences in (9) with (8b):

(9a) *What did the picture of t surprise you?

       cf. The picture of my brother's house surprised me.

(9b) *What did Mike meet the man who was wearing t?

       cf. Mike met the man who was wearing a red jacket.

Even though these three sentences are all ungrammatical, native speakers of English judge (9a, b) much worse than (8b). If this difference were observed among L2ers' judgments, this would strongly suggest that learners' intuitions come from the same kind of knowledge that native speakers have, that is, a grammar of English constructed on the basis of UG. The crucial point is that this difference cannot be learned from input because none of these sentences (or similar structures) would be included in input as they are ungrammatical. Martohardjono (1993) carried out an experiment with three groups of L2ers and a native-speaker control group. All learner groups' results, including those whose L1 does not have wh-movement, showed differences among sentence types similar to those in the native speakers' responses. Hence, it is plausible that UG constrains L2ers' grammar.

Another interesting finding related to wh-movement in the discussion of UG operation is that L2ers may produce a kind of wh-question that is not found in adult speakers' production but resembles the non-adult-like performance observed in children's production. Wakabayashi and Okawara (2003) used the same experimental procedure as Crain and Thornton (1998) and found that Japanese learners of English produce sentences similar to children's non-adult-like production as in (10). This again strongly supports the argument that children's grammars and L2ers' grammars are based on the same innate system:

(10)   What do you think what is in the bag?

Hence, we have strong evidence that UG operates in SLA. However, some may argue as follows: if UG operates in SLA, L2ers should be able to acquire native-like competence (because UG makes children native-speakers of a language) (e.g. Akiyama 2002). This argument is flawed: the availability of UG is a necessary condition for L1A (and probably for SLA) but is not a sufficient condition. In other words, without UG, a language cannot be acquired, but UG alone does not guarantee the success of language acquisition.

Topics in generative approaches to SLA: brief historical review

As mentioned above, the central issue in the 1980s was whether UG is available or not in SLA. For example, papers in Eubank (1991) argued for and against UG operation in SLA. In that volume, several researchers provide data that show L2ers' grammars to be much more restricted than the range of logically plausible grammars; in particular, they fall within the range of natural languages (e.g. Thomas 1991).

To explain L2ers' performance, several UG-based models/hypotheses have been offered since the mid-1990s. The Full Transfer/Full Access Model (Schwartz and Sprouse 1994) proposes that learners' L1 knowledge serves as the initial state for a developing grammar in SLA and the interlanguage grammar changes through parameter resetting under the sanction of UG. The Minimal Trees Model (Vainikka and Young-Scholten 1994) suggests that the initial grammar in SLA lacks functional categories and that L1 transfer is limited to the headedness of VP. Functional categories are added in the course of development, triggered by free morphemes associated with these categories. Another model similarly assumes that the initial grammar lacks functional categories and functional categories are acquired in the course of development, but when a functional category comes to be used, its behaviour in L1A may appear as well (i.e. transfer gradually emerges in the course of development) (Hawkins 2001; Wakabayashi 1997, 2002). There are a few more models: the initial grammar has the L1 settings and parameter resetting cannot take place (Hawkins and Chan 1997; Tsimpli and Roussou 1991); the initial grammar has full CP structure but lacks some features (Eubank

1994); the initial grammar has full CP and relevant features are present from the beginning exactly as in L1A (Epstein *et al.* 1996).

Since the late 1990s, researchers have focused especially on learners' difficulties in the consistent use of certain syntactic operations and certain grammatical morphemes, and two types of explanations have been offered. One is the Failed Functional Features Hypothesis (Hawkins and Chan 1997; Tsimpli and Roussou 1991), the current version of which is called the Intepretability Hypothesis (Hawkins and Hattori 2006; Tsimpli and Dimitrakopoulou 2007), according to which L2ers are unable to acquire certain kinds of formal features if they are not instantiated in their L1. The other suggests that formal features are acquirable but that learners have difficulties in mapping the syntactic object onto phonological structure. This is called the Missing Surface Inflection Hypothesis (Hazneder and Schwartz 1997; Prévost and White 2000).

L2ers' difficulty in the use of morphemes has evoked a number of explanations for their behaviour and of the underlying system. The Interface Hypothesis (Tsimpli and Sorace 2006; Sorace 2007) suggests that L2ers' linguistic knowledge is a native-like system within each module; their non-native behaviour is due to problems lying at the interfaces between modules and at the interface between linguistic knowledge and other knowledge systems. The Fluctuation Hypothesis (Ionin *et al.* 2004) suggests that L2ers have difficulty in associating certain features with a relevant functional category, but because their L2 grammars are restricted by UG, L2ers do not 'invent' any non-UG features; rather, they 'fluctuate' in selecting one among a few UG-based features. The Feature Assembly Hypothesis (Lardiere 2008) suggests that L2ers have to re-assemble formal features to different functional categories in the process of language acquisition when their first and second languages have features assembled in a different way. Wakabayashi (1997, 2002) suggests that development in the use of target-like (and non-target-like) morphosyntax in SLA arises through improved consistency in the inclusion of relevant features in the lexicon. All of these hypotheses assume (in accordance with the Minimalist Program) that the computational system is uniform in all natural languages, including interlanguage grammars, and that this system is given innately.

The shift from the Principles and Parameters perspective to the Minimalist Program forces L2 researchers to reconsider the relationship between parameters and features in the context of SLA, as well as the nature of formal features. Although the argument is highly technical, such a level of abstraction and technicality is inevitable given the complexity of SLA and the goal of describing and explaining the knowledge underlying L2ers' behaviour.

Experimental data and generative grammar

In the studies of L1A and SLA, studies of I-language are carried out with E-language data. Researchers often rely on production data in a natural setting. However, such data are not adequate when we want to investigate whether learners have knowledge that certain structures are not allowed in language. Production data can tell us what forms a speaker produces, but cannot tell us what forms they do *not* produce: It is impossible to tell whether they do not produce a type of sentence even though they would consider it 'possible'; or whether they do not do so because their linguistic system disallows such sentences.

In order to investigate whether L2ers' knowledge goes beyond the input to which they are exposed, a grammaticality judgment task (where learners judge whether or not a given sentence is acceptable, or indicate how good it sounds) is a useful way to collect relevant data. However, it is also true that meta-linguistic knowledge may be brought to bear on such tasks, making them less reliable as indicators of underlying linguistic competence. Hence, researchers recently have begun to make greater use of psycholinguistic tools, such as the measurement of reaction time, to avoid the effects of non-linguistic knowledge.

For example, the third person singular -s in English is notoriously difficult for L2ers to use consistently. In, for example, Japanese junior and senior high schools, the rule underlying this morpheme is explicitly taught in a traditional grammatical instruction and frequently appears in textbooks. However, students still make errors in using it. Hence, this is a case of what Chomsky (1986a) refers to as "Orwell's problem", i.e. why a property is difficult to acquire even when evidence for it in the input is plentiful.

In order to investigate causes for this problem, Wakabayashi (1997) used reading time measurement in a task of self-paced reading with moving-windows, and found that intermediate Japanese learners of English are sensitive to [person] disagreement but insensitive to [number] disagreement in the overuse of the third person singular -s. That is, learners are sensitive to the ungrammaticality in sentences such as (11a) but not necessarily to (11b):

(11a)   You speaks English.
(11b)   The students speaks English.

Similar findings were obtained in an experiment where Event Related Potentials (ERP) were measured (Wakabayashi *et al.* 2007). Hence, it is plausible that the [number] feature is likely to be the cause. This feature is obligatorily associated with noun phrases in English but not with noun phrases in Japanese, while the [person] feature is inherently associated with noun phrases in all languages.

Note that the experimental methods used in these studies made it possible to investigate the difference between learners' knowledge of [person] and [number]. When data were collected for the sentence types in Wakabayashi (1997) in a pencil-and-paper grammaticality judgment task, participants answered 100 per cent correctly even though their general proficiency was lower than that of the participants in the reading time measurement in Wakabayashi (1997). Hence, without psycholinguistic experimental methods, the difference between features could not be found.

The important point is that we need to describe speakers' grammars and/or L2ers' interlanguage grammars, as well as those of their processing mechanisms, no matter what experimental methods are used. The descriptions of the sentence structures in the experimental materials are based on their analysis in generative grammar, and it would be impossible to discuss the results or even the predictions of learners' behaviour without them.

Summary

Every day we use new sentences. Our knowledge of language is the system that makes it possible for us to produce and interpret sentences that we have never come across in our life. This system is constrained in a certain way, as illustrated by the examples with reflexive pronouns and wh-phrases earlier in this chapter. The sentences we produce and interpret are not merely strings of words, but they have structures.

As shown in the examples throughout this chapter, learners' behaviour shows that their use of language reflects what is (far) beyond memorization of chunks; rather, what they have is a system which generates target-like and non-target-like linguistic behaviours and which is sanctioned by the constraints common to all human languages, that is, Universal Grammar.

In applied linguistics, it is certainly a main issue to investigate what learners' knowledge of language is, how it is acquired and how it is used. With regard to native speakers' knowledge of syntax (and other aspects of language), generative grammar has tried to answer these questions (Chomsky 1986a). As described in the first part of this chapter, there have been a few radical changes of the theoretical paradigm in generative grammar, but the purpose of the research has been retained throughout its history: now we have reliable tools to examine what is going on in learners' minds, and insights obtained through generative grammar will surely continue to play important roles in applied linguistics, especially studies of first and second language acquisition.

There are a number of interesting questions waiting for us to investigate, including whether, how, and what kinds of instruction influence learners' linguistic knowledge; whether and how learners' linguistic knowledge is influenced by environmental factors; and whether and how learners' non-linguistic psychological factors affect their use of linguistic knowledge. Investigation of these questions is possible only when learners' linguistic knowledge is described in a reliable theoretical framework. In this sense, generative grammar will play an important role in these interdisciplinary areas, as a framework for applied linguistics in the future.

Related topics

grammar; psycholiguistics

Further reading

Hawkins, R. (2001) *Second Language Syntax: A Generative Introduction*, Oxford: Blackwell. (An accessible introduction to UG-based SLA.)
Lardiere, D. (2009) 'Some thoughts on the contrastive analysis of features in second language acquisition', *Second Language Research* 25, 173–227. (This paper, with commentaries from leading experts in the same volume of the journal, discusses issues in generative approaches to SLA.)
Slabakova, R., Montrul, S. A. and Prévost, R. (eds) (2009) *Inquiries in Linguistic Development: In honor of Lydia White*, Amsterdam: John Benjamins. (A collection of papers by leading figures in generative approaches to SLA.)
Towell, R. and Hawkins, R. (1994) *Approaches to Second Language Acquisition*, Clevedon: Multilingual Matters. (This book compares UG-based approaches to SLA with other approaches to SLA.)
White, L. (2003) *Second Language Acquisition and Universal Grammar*, Cambridge: Cambridge University Press. (This book discusses developments in generative approaches to SLA since 1990.)

References

Akiyama, Y. (2002) 'Japanese adult learners' development of the locality condition of English reflexives', *Studies in Second Language Acquisition* 24, 27–54.
Belikova, A. and White, L. (2009) 'Evidence for the fundamental difference hypothesis or not? Island constraints revisited', *Studies in Second Language Acquisition* 31, 1–24.
Bley-Vroman, R. (1989) 'What is the logical problem of foreign language learning?' in S. Gass and J. Schachter (eds) *Linguistic Perspectives on Second Language Learning*, Cambridge: Cambridge University Press.
——(1990) 'The logical problem of foreign language learning', *Linguistic Analysis* 20, 3–49.
——(2009) 'The evolving context of the fundamental difference hypothesis', *Studies in Second Language Acquisition* 31, 175–98.
Brown, R. (1973) *A First Language: The Early Stages*, London: George Allen and Unwin.
Chomsky, N. (1955) *The Logical Structure of Linguistic Theory*, manuscript, Harvard University (Published in part by New York: Plenum, 1975; Chicago: University of Chicago Press, 1985).
——(1957) *Syntactic Structures*, The Hague: Mouton.

——(1965) *Aspects of the Theory of Syntax*, Cambridge, MA: MIT Press.
——(1973) 'Conditions on transformations', in S. Anderson and P. Kiprasky (eds) *A Festschrift for Morris Halle*, New York: Holt, Rinehart and Winston.
——(1981) *Lectures on Government and Binding*, Dordrecht: Foris.
——(1986a) *Knowledge of Language: Its Nature, Origin, and Use*, New York: Praeger.
——(1986b) *Barriers*, Cambridge, MA: MIT Press.
——(1993) 'A minimalist program for linguistic theory', in K. Hale and S. J. Keyser (eds) *The View from Building 20: Essays in Linguistics in Honor of Syvain Bromberger*, Cambridge, MA: MIT Press.
——(1995) *The Minimalist Program*, Cambridge, MA: MIT Press.
——(1999) 'Derivation by phase', MIT Occasional Papers in Linguistics 18 (also published in M. Kenstowicz (ed.) *Hen Hale: A Life in Language*, Cambridge, MA: MIT Press).
Clahsen, H. and Muysken, P. (1986), 'The availability of universal grammar to adult and child learners: a study of the acquisition of German word order', *Second Language Research* 2, 93–119.
Corder, S. P. (1967) 'The significance of learners' errors', *International Review of Applied Linguistics* 5, 161–9.
Crain, S. and Thornton, R. (1998) *Investigations in Universal Grammar: A Guide to Experiments on the Acquisition of Syntax and Semantics*, Cambridge, MA: MIT Press.
duPlessis, J., Solin, D, Travis, L. and White, L. (1987) 'UG or not UG, that is the question: a reply to Clahsen and Muysken', *Second Language Research* 3, 56–75.
Epstein, S. D., Flynn, S. and Martohardjono, G. (1996) 'Second language acquisition: theoretical and experimental issues in contemporary research', *Behavioral and Brain Science* 19, 677–758.
Eubank, L. (1994) 'Optionality and the "initial state" in L2 development', in T. Hoesktra and B. D. Schwartz (eds) *Language Acquisition Studies in Generative Grammar*, Amsterdam: John Benjamins.
Eubank, L. (ed.) (1991) *Point Counterpoint: Universal Grammar in the Second Language*, Amsterdam: John Benjamins.
Haegeman, L. (ed.) (1997) *The New Comparative Syntax*, Harlow: Longman.
Hawkins, R. (2001) *Second Language Syntax: A Generative Introduction*, Oxford: Blackwell.
Hawkins, R. and Chan, C. Y. (1997) 'The partial availability of Universal Grammar in second language acquisition: the "failed functional features hypothesis"', *Second Language Research* 13, 187–226.
Hawkins, R. and Hattori, H. (2006) 'Interpretation of multiple wh-questions by Japanese speakers: a missing uninterpretable feature account', *Second Language Research* 22, 269–301.
Hazneder, D. and Schwartz, B. D. (1997) 'Are there optional infinitives in child L2 acquisition?', in E. Hughes, M. Hughes and A. Greenhill (eds) *Proceedings of the 21st Annual Boston University Conference on Language Development*, Somerville, MA: Cascadilla Press.
Hyams, N. (1983) 'The Acquisition of Parameterized Grammars', Ph.D. thesis, City University of New York.
——(1994) 'V2, null arguments and COMP projections', in T. Hoekstra and B. D. Schwartz (eds) *Language Acquisition: Studies in Generative Grammar*, Amsterdam: John Benjamins.
Hyams, N. and Wexler, K. (1993) 'On the grammatical basis of null subjects in child language', *Linguistic Inquiry* 24, 421–59.
Ionin, T., Ko, H. and Wexler, K. (2004) 'Article semantics in L2-acquisition: the role of specificity', *Language Acquisition* 12, 3–69.
Lardiere, D. (2008) 'Feature assembly in second language acquistion', in J. M. Liceras, H. Zobl and H. Goodluck (eds) *The Role of Formal Features in Second Language Acquisition*, New York: Lawrence Erlbaum Associates.
Larsen-Freeman, D. and Long, M. H. (1991) *An Introduction to Second Language Acquisition Research*, London: Longman.
Lasnik, H. (2005) 'Grammar, levels, and biology', in J. McGilvray (ed.) *The Cambridge Companion to Chomsky*, Cambridge: Cambridge University Press.
Martohardjono, G. (1993) 'Wh-movement in the Acquisition of a Second Language: A Cross-linguistic Study of 3 Languages With and Without Overt Movement', Ph.D. thesis, Cornell University.
May, R. C. (1977) 'The Grammar of Quantification', Ph.D. Dissertation, Massachusetts Institute of Technology. Published 1990 (New York: Garland).
Newmeyer, F. J. (1986) *Linguistic Theory in America*, 2nd edn, Orlando, FL: Academic Press.
Obler, L. K. and Gjerlow, K. (1999) *Language and the Brain*, Cambridge: Cambridge University Press.

Prévost, P. and White, L. (2000) 'Missing surface inflection or impairment in second language acquisition? Evidence from tense and agreement', *Second Language Research* 16: 103–33.

Radford, A. (1990). *Syntactic Theory and the Acquisition of English Syntax: The Nature of Early Child Grammars of English*, Oxford: Blackwell.

Reibel, D. A. and Schane, S. A. (1969) 'Preface', in D. A. Reibel, and S. A. Schane (eds) *Modern Studies in English: Readings in Transformational Grammar*, Englewood Cliffs, NJ: Prentice Hall.

Roberts, I. (1993) *Verbs and Diachronic Syntax*, Dordrecht: Kluwer Academic.

Ross, J. R. (1967) 'Constraints on Variables in Syntax', Ph.D. thesis, MIT. Published (1986) as *Infinite Syntax!* Norwood, NJ: Ablex.

Schwartz, B. and Sprouse, R. (1994) 'Word order and nominative case in nonnative language acquisition: a longitudinal study of (L1 Turkish) German interlanguage', in T. Hoesktra and B. D. Schwartz (eds) *Language Acquisition: Studies in Generative Grammar*, Amsterdam: John Benjamins.

Selinker, L. (1972) 'Interlanguage', *International Review of Applied Linguistics* 10, 209–31.

Smith, N. (2005) 'Chomsky's science of language', in J. McGilvray (ed.) *The Cambridge Companion to Chomsky*, Cambridge: Cambridge University Press.

Smith, N. and Tsimpli, I. M. (1995) *The Mind of a Savant*, Oxford: Basil Blackwell.

Sorace, A. (2007) 'Optionality at the syntax-discourse interface in near-native L2 speakers', *Second Language* 6, 3–15.

Thomas, M. (1991) 'Do second language learners have "rogue" grammars of anaphora?' in L. Eubank (ed.) *Point Counterpoint: Universal Grammar in the Second Language*, Amsterdam: John Benjamins.

Tsimpli, I.-M. and Dimitrakopoulou, M. (2007) 'The interpretability hypothesis: evidence from wh-interrotagives in second language acquisition', *Second Language Research* 23, 215–42.

Tsimpli, I.-M. and Roussou, A. (1991) 'Parameter resetting in L2?' *UCL Working Papers in Linguistics* 3, 149–69.

Tsimpli, I. M. and Sorace, A. (2006) 'Differentiating interfaces: L2 performance in syntax-semantics and syntax-discourse phenomena', *BUCLD Proceedings* 30: 653–64.

Vainikka, A. and Young-Scholten, M. (1994) '"Direct access to X"-theory: evidence from Korean and Turkish adults learning German', in T. Hoekstra and B. D. Schwartz (eds) *Language Acquisition: Studies in Generative Grammar*, Amsterdam: John Benjamins.

Wakabayashi, S. (1997) 'The Acquisition of Functional Categories by Learners of English', Ph.D. thesis, University of Cambridge.

——(2002) 'Why free morphemes are acquired earlier than bound morphemes: a minimalist account', in M. Swanson, D. McMurray and K. Lane (eds) *The Proceedings of PAC3 at JALT2001: A Language Odyssey*, Japan Association of Applied Linguistics.

Wakabayashi, S., Bannai, M., Fukuda, K. and Asaoka, S. (2007) 'Japanese speakers' sensitivity to third person singular -s in English based on ERP data', *Second Language* 6, 19–46.

Wakabayashi, S. and Okawara, I. (2003) 'Japanese learners' errors on long distance wh-questions', in S. Wakabayashi (ed.) *Generative Approaches to the Acquisition of English by Native Speakers of Japanese*, Berlin: Mouton de Gruyter.

White, L. (1991) 'Second language competence versus second language performance: UG or processing strategies?' in L. Eubank (ed.) *Point Counterpoint: Universal Grammar in the Second Language*, Amsterdam: John Benjamins.

46

The emergence of language as a complex adaptive system

Nick C. Ellis

History: the mysterious process

Saussure (1916) characterized the units of language as linguistic signs, the signifiers of linguistic form and their associated signified functions, concepts or meanings. In Saussure's view linguistic signs arise from the dynamic interactions of thought and sound – from patterns of usage:

> what happens is neither a transformation of thought into matter, nor a transformation of sound into ideas. What takes place is a somewhat mysterious process by which 'thought-sound' evolves divisions, and a language takes place with its linguistic units in between these two amorphous masses.
>
> *(Saussure 1916: 110–11)*

Thus began structuralist linguistics, the study of language as a relational structure, whose elemental constructions derive their forms and functions from their distributions in texts and discourse. This approach had a significant impact upon applied linguistics too. Fries, the founder of the English Language Institute at the University of Michigan, distinguished between lexical and structural meaning, with structural meaning concerning the patterns relating a particular arrangement of form classes to particular structural meanings. In this view, language acquisition is the learning of an inventory of patterns, as arrangements of words, with their associated structural meanings. Fries' (1952) *The Structure of English* presented an analysis of these patterns, and Roberts' (1956) *Patterns of English* was a textbook presentation of this system for classroom use. Harris (1955), founder of the first US linguistics department at the University of Pennsylvania, developed rigorous discovery procedures for phonemes and morphemes based on the distributional properties of these units. For Harris, form and information (grammar and semantics) were inseparable. He proposed that each human language is a self-organizing system in which both the syntactic and semantic properties of a word are established purely in relation to other words, and that the patterns of a language are learned through exposure to usage in social participation (Harris 1982, 1991). Structuralism, the dominant approach in linguistics for the earlier part of the twentieth century, was overtaken in the 1960s in the US by generative approaches. Harris' student, Chomsky (1965, 1981), abandoned structure-specific rules and developed the Principles-and-Parameters approach, the general grammatical rules and principles of that is assumed to an innate Universal Grammar. Grammar became top-down and rule-governed, rather than bottom-up and emergent. It was modularized, encapsulated, and divorced from performance, lexis, social usage, and the rest of cognition. The analysis of linguistic structures as functional patterns and their 'somewhat mysterious' emergence from usage was no longer pursued within generative linguistics.

Language and cognition, however, are mutually inextricable; they determine each other. Language has come to represent the world as we know it; it is grounded in our perceptual experience. Language is used to organize, process, and communicate information, from one person to another, from one embodied mind to another. Learning language involves determining linguistic structures from usage and this, like learning about all other aspects of the world, involves the full scope of cognition: the remembering of utterances and episodes, the categorization of experience, the determination of patterns among and between stimuli, the generalization of conceptual schema and prototypes from exemplars, and the use of cognitive models, metaphors, analogies, and images in thinking. Language is used to focus the listener's attention to the world; it can foreground different elements in the theater of consciousness to potentially relate many different stories and perspectives about the same scene. What is attended is learned, and so attention affects the acquisition of language itself. The functions of language in discourse determine its usage and learning. Language usage, language change, language acquisition, and language structure are similarly inseparable. There is nothing that so well characterizes human social action as language. Cognition, consciousness, experience, embodiment, brain, self, and human interaction, society, culture, and history are all inextricably intertwined in rich, complex, and dynamic ways.

Despite this complexity and despite its lack of overt government, instead of anarchy and chaos, patterning pervades the complex system of language. The patterns are not pre-ordained by God, by genes, by school curriculum, or by other human policy, but instead they are emergent from the interactions of the agents involved – synchronic patterns of linguistic organization at different scales (phonology, lexis, syntax, semantics, pragmatics, discourse genre, etc.), dynamic patterns of usage, diachronic patterns of language change (linguistic cycles of grammaticization, pidginization, creolization, etc.), ontogenetic developmental patterns in child language acquisition, global geopolitical patterns of language growth and decline, dominance and loss, need and education, etc.

Various disciplines within cognitive science (including cognitive psychology, child language studies, cognitive linguistics, corpus linguistics, and connectionism) focus upon their own local patterns of interest to try to understand the processes by which they come about. But above and beyond these particular investigations, other approaches (under banners such as emergentism, complex adaptive systems, and dynamic systems theory) recognize that there are general principles which characterize the emergence of patterns in complex systems whatever their content or scale. In what follows in this chapter I will first consider some of the specific disciplines focusing upon the patterning of information and its creation in human mind, brain, culture and society, before I then introduce the study of emergence itself. The chapter concludes with a view of language as a complex adaptive system (CAS).

Local perspectives on the mysterious process

An overview of the ways in which relevant disciplines are studying the origins of patterns in language can be conveniently organized by first focusing upon Saussure's linguistic sign.

However convenient, this does not imply that the structure of language is primary; far from it – we should look to meaning and social communication for that.

Usage-based theories of language acquisition hold that we learn language incidentally while engaging in communication (Barlow and Kemmer 2000; Hopper 1998), the 'interpersonal communicative and cognitive processes that everywhere and always shape language' (Slobin 1997). Within these approaches, the modern parallel to the sign as a basic unit of language representation is the *construction*. Constructions are the fundamental units of language acquisition and reflect the most direct embodiment of learners' communicative intentions. Some of the basic tenets of usage-based approaches to language and its acquisition, many of them explicitly addressed by Saussure (1916), are:

- Language is intrinsically linked to human cognition and processes of perception, attention, learning, categorization, schematization, and memory.
- Language is intrinsically symbolic, constituted by a structured inventory of constructions as conventionalized form-meaning pairings used for communicative purposes.
- Adult language knowledge consists of a continuum of linguistic constructions of different levels of complexity and abstraction. Constructions can comprise concrete and particular items (as in words and idioms), more abstract classes of items (as in word classes and abstract constructions), or complex combinations of concrete and abstract pieces of language (as mixed constructions). Consequently, no rigid separation is postulated to exist between lexis and grammar.
- Constructions may be simultaneously represented and stored in multiple forms, at various levels of abstraction (e.g. concrete item: table + s = tables and [Noun] + (morpheme +s) = plural things).
- Linguistic constructions can thus be meaningful linguistic symbols in their own right, existing independently of particular lexical items. Nevertheless, constructions and the particular lexical tokens that occupy them attract each other, and grammar and lexis are inseparable.
- Language structure emerges ontogenetically from usage in particular contexts. Development is slow and gradual, moving from an initial heavy reliance on concrete items to more abstract linguistic schemata. This process is crucially dependent on the type and token frequencies with which particular constructions appear in the input. Storage of wholes depends on token frequency; the development of abstract linguistic schema depends on type frequency.

Particular approaches to language and cognition within the language sciences, psychology, and cognitive science concentrate upon different facets of patterning. The linguistic approaches analyze the units of language, the psychological approaches their learning and usage:

Functional analyses of language catalogue the inventory of constructions, investigating the ways in which constructions are symbolic, their defining properties of morphological, syntactic, and lexical form being associated with particular semantic, pragmatic, and discourse functions (Croft 2001; Croft and Cruse 2004; Halliday 1994; Taylor 2002).

Corpus linguistic analyses of large collections of language show how there are recurrent patterns of words, collocations, phrases, and constructions, that syntax and semantics are inextricably linked, and that grammar cannot be described without lexis, nor lexis without grammar (Biber *et al.* 1998, 1999, Hoey 2005; McEnery and Wilson 1996; Sinclair 1991, 2004).

Construction grammar and phraseological analyses of language show that much of communication makes use of fixed expressions memorized as formulaic chunks, that language is rich in collocational and colligational restrictions and semantic prosodies, and that the phrase is the basic level of language representation where form and meaning come together with greatest reliability (Ellis 1996, 2008b; Fillmore 1988; Goldberg 1995, 2003; Granger and Meunier 2008; Pawley and Syder 1983; Sinclair 1991, 2004; Wray 2002).

Child language acquisition researchers gather dense longitudinal corpora in order to chart the emergence of creative linguistic competence in children's analyses of the utterances in their usage history and their abstraction of regularities within them (Goldberg 2006; Tomasello 1998, 2003).

Psycholinguistic theories of the mental representation of language show that fluent language users are sensitive to the relative probabilities of occurrence of different constructions in the language input and to the contingencies of their mappings to meaning (Ellis 2002a; Gaskell 2007; Gernsbacher 1994).

Psychological analyses of perception and attention investigate the ways in which human embodiment and our perceptuo-motor systems govern our representation of the world and the ways that language can guide our attention to these representations (Barsalou 1999, 2008; Mandler 2004; Talmy 1988, 2000a, 2000b).

Associative learning theory analyses how the learning of stimulus-outcome contingencies is affected by: factors relating to the form such as frequency and salience; factors relating to the interpretation such as significance in the comprehension of the overall utterance, proto-typicality, generality, redundancy, and surprise value; factors relating to the contingency of form and function; and factors relating to learner attention, such as automaticity, transfer, overshadowing, and blocking. Selective attention, salience, expectation, and surprise are key elements in the analysis of all learning, animal and human alike (Shanks 1995). These principles pervade language acquisition too (Ellis 2002a, 2003, 2006, 2008c).

Learning theory recognizes three major experiential factors that affect cognition: frequency, recency, and context (e.g. Anderson 2000; Bartlett [1932] 1967; Ebbinghaus 1885). Learning, memory and perception are all affected by frequency of usage: the more times we experience something, the stronger our memory for it, and the more fluently it is accessed. The more recently we have experienced something, the stronger our memory for it, and the more fluently it is accessed. The more times we experience conjunctions of features, the more they become associated in our minds and the more these subsequently affect perception and categorization; so a stimulus becomes associated to a context and we become more likely to perceive it in that context. The power law of learning (Anderson 1982; Ellis and Schmidt 1998; Newell 1990) describes the relationships between practice and performance in the acquisition of a wide range of cognitive skills – the greater the practice, the greater the performance, although effects of practice are largest at early stages of leaning, thereafter diminishing and eventually reaching asymptote. The power function relating probability of recall (or recall latency) and recency is known as the forgetting curve (Baddeley 1997; Ebbinghaus 1885). These three factors pervade the acquisition, form, access, and processing of constructions (Ellis and Cadierno 2009).

Cognitive theories of categorization and generalization analyze how schematic constructions are inferred inductively by the learner in acquisition (Barsalou 2008; Harnad 1987; Lakoff 1987; Schank and Abelson 1977; Taylor 1998). Prototypes, exemplars which are most typical of a category, are those which are similar to many members of that category and not similar to members of other categories. The operationalization of this criterion predicts human categorization performance – people more quickly classify as *birds* sparrows (or other average sized, average colored, average beaked, average featured specimens) than they do birds with less common features or feature combinations like geese or albatrosses (Rosch and Mervis 1975;

Rosch *et al.* 1976). Prototypes are judged faster and more accurately, even if they themselves have never been seen before – someone who has never seen a sparrow, yet who has experienced the rest of birds, will still be fast and accurate in judging it to be a bird (Posner and Keele 1970). Such effects make it very clear that although people don't go around consciously counting features, they nevertheless have very accurate knowledge of the underlying frequency distributions and their central tendencies. The prototype emerges from the conspiracy of memorized exemplars (Rogers and McClelland 2008).

Connectionist, competition model, and *rational* analyses of language demonstrate the ways in which generalizations emerge from the conspiracy of memorized instances, the ways in which different cues and their cue reliabilities compete for activation, and the ways in which these representations provide the best model of language that is available from the learner's sample of experience, one that is optimized in its organization for usage (Anderson 1989; Anderson and Schooler 2000; Bates and MacWhinney 1987; Chater and Manning 2006; Christiansen and Chater 2001; Ellis 2006; Elman *et al.* 1996; MacWhinney 1987, 1997).

Probabilistic and frequency-based theories of language analyze how frequency and repetition affect and ultimately bring about form in language and how probabilistic knowledge drives language comprehension and production (Bod *et al.* 2003; Bybee and Hopper 2001; Ellis 2002a, 2000b; Jurafsky 2002; Jurafsky and Martin 2000). Distributional analyses of language also show the importance of Zipf's law at all levels in determining the structure and network characteristics of linguistic systems and the effects of these properties on learning (Ferrer i Cancho and Solé 2001).

Sociocultural theory analyzes how language learning takes place in a social context, involving action, reaction, collaborative interaction, intersubjectivity, and mutually assisted performance, and how individual language learning is an emergent, holistic property of a dynamic system comprising many dialectic influences, both social, individual, and contextual, involving the learner in a conscious tension between the conflicting forces of their current interlanguage productions and the evidence of feedback, either linguistic, pragmatic, or metalinguistic, that allows socially scaffolded development (Ellis 2008b; Kramsch 2002; Lantolf and Pavlenko 1995; Lantolf and Thorne 2006; Vygotsky 1980, 1986). Current child language acquisition research emphasizes how language learning is 'socially gated' (Kuhl 2007) in the same way that the Interaction Approach (Gass 1997) to second language acquisition shows how interaction is not simply language usage, but negotiation, with participants' attention being focused on resolving a communication problem and thus 'connecting input, internal learner capacities, particularly selective attention, and output in productive ways' (Long 1996).

The scientific study of consciousness, its neural correlates, and its involvement in learning and memory (Baars 1997; Koch 2004) show there are different forms of language learning, broadly, the implicit tallying and chunking that take place during usage (Ellis 2002a, 2002b) and explicit learning in the classroom, sometimes a consequence of communication breakdown (Ellis 1994, 2005: sections 3–4). Implicit learning from usage occurs largely within modality and involves the priming or chunking of representations or routines within a module, with abstract schema and constructions emerging from the conspiracy of memorized instances. It is the means of tuning our zombie agents, the menagerie of specialized sensori-motor processors that carry out routine operations in the absence of direct conscious sensation or control. It is largely automatized. It operates in parallel. In contrast, conscious processing is spread wide over the brain and unifies otherwise disparate areas in a synchronized focus of activity. Conscious activity affords much more scope for focused long-range association and influence than does implicit learning. It brings about a whole new level of potential associations. It operates serially.

Consciousness too is dynamic; it is perhaps the prototype example of an emergent phenomenon: the stream of consciousness is one of ever-changing states, each cued by prior state and perceptual context, the units of consciousness being identifiable as patterns of brain synchrony in time. The dynamics of language learning are inextricably linked to the dynamics of consciousness, in neural activity and in the social world as well.

As these diverse research efforts illustrate, language usage involves agents and their processes at many levels, and we need to try to understand language emergence as a function of interactions within and between them. This is a tall order. Hence, Saussure's 'mysterious process' and his observations that

> to speak of a 'linguistic law' in general is like trying to lay hands on a ghost ... Synchronic laws are general, but not imperative. [They] are imposed upon speakers by the constraints of common usage ... In short, when one speaks of a synchronic law, one is speaking of an arrangement, or a principle of regularity.
>
> *(Saussure 1916: 90–1)*

Nevertheless, a century of subsequent work within the disciplines introduced above has put substantial flesh on the bone, as you will see if you follow up on the readings. And more recently, work within emergentism, CAS, and dynamic systems theory (DST) has started to describe a number of scale-free, domain-general processes which characterize the emergence of pattern across the physical, natural, and social world. Next, I consider language in this light.

Common mysteries of emergence

Emergentism and complexity theory (Ellis 1998; Ellis and Larsen-Freeman 2006a; Elman *et al.* 1996; Larsen-Freeman 1997; Larsen-Freeman and Cameron 2008; MacWhinney 1999) analyze how complex patterns emerge from the interactions of many agents, how each emergent level cannot come into being except by involving the levels that lie below it, and how at each higher level there are new and emergent kinds of relatedness not found below: 'More is different' (Anderson 1972). Emergentism and complexity theory align well with DST which considers how cognitive, social and environmental factors are in continuous interactions, where flux and individual variation abound, and where cause-effect relationships are non-linear, multivariate and interactive in time (de Bot *et al.* 2007; Ellis 2008a; Ellis and Larsen-Freeman 2006a, 2006b; Port and van Gelder 1995; Spencer *et al.* 2009; Spivey 2006; van Geert 1991).

> Emergentists believe that simple learning mechanisms, operating in and across the human systems for perception, motor-action and cognition as they are exposed to language data as part of a communicatively-rich human social environment by an organism eager to exploit the functionality of language, suffice to drive the emergence of complex language representations.
>
> *(Ellis 1998: 657)*

Language cannot be understood in neurological or physical terms alone, nevertheless, neurobiology and physics play essential roles in the complex interrelations; equally from the top down, though language cannot be understood purely in experiential terms, nevertheless, conscious experience is an essential part too.

Language considered as a CAS of dynamic usage and its experience involves the following key features:

- The system consists of multiple agents (the speakers in the speech community) interacting with one another.
- The system is adaptive, that is, speakers' behavior is based on their past interactions, and current and past interactions together feed forward into future behavior.
- A speaker's behavior is the consequence of competing factors ranging from perceptual mechanics to social motivations.
- The structures of language emerge from interrelated patterns of experience, social interaction, and cognitive processes.

The advantage of viewing language in these ways is that it provides a unified account of seemingly unrelated linguistic phenomena (Holland 1995, 1998; Beckner *et al.* 2009). These phenomena include: variation at all levels of linguistic organization; the probabilistic nature of linguistic behavior; continuous change within agents and across speech communities; the emergence of grammatical regularities from the interaction of agents in language use; and stage-like transitions due to underlying non-linear processes.

Characteristics of language as a CAS

The following are seven major characteristics of language as a CAS, which are consistent with studies in language change, language use, language acquisition, and with the computer modeling of these aspects which is a core component of CAS research (Beckner *et al.* 2009).

Distributed control, and collective emergence

Language exists both in individuals (as idiolect) as well as in the community of users (as communal language). Language is emergent at these two distinctive but inter-dependent levels: an idiolect is emergent from an individual's language use through social interactions with other individuals in the communal language, while a communal language is emergent as the result of the interaction of the idiolects. Distinction and connection between these two levels is a common feature in CASs. Patterns at the collective level (such as bird flocks, fish schools, or economies) cannot be attributed to global coordination among individuals; the global pattern is emergent, resulting from long-term local interactions between individuals.

Intrinsic diversity

In a CAS, there is no ideal representing agent for the system. Just as in an economy, there is no ideal representative consumer, similarly, there is no ideal speaker-hearer for language use, language representation, or language development. Each idiolect is the product of the individual's unique exposure and experiences of language use (Bybee 2006). Sociolinguistics studies have revealed the large degree of orderly heterogeneity among idiolects (Weinreich *et al.* 1968), not only in their language use, but also in their internal organization and representation (Dąbrowska 1997). Mindfulness of intrinsic diversity is helpful for theory construction.

Perpetual dynamics

Both communal language and idiolects are in constant change and reorganization. Languages are in constant flux, and language change is ubiquitous (Hopper 1987). At the individual level, every instance of language use changes an idiolect's internal organization (Bybee 2006). As we define language primarily through dynamical rules, rather than by forces designed to pull it to a static equilibrium, it shares, along with almost all complex systems, a fundamentally far-from-equilibrium nature (Holland 1995).

Adaptation through amplification and competition of factors

CASs generally consist of multiple interacting elements, which may amplify and/or compete with one another's effects. Structure in complex systems tends to arise via positive feedback, in which certain factors perpetuate themselves, in conjunction with negative feedback, in which some constraint is imposed (for instance, due to limited space or resources) (Camazine et al. 2001; Steels 2006). Likewise in language, all factors interact and feed into one another.

Non-linearity and phase transitions

In complex systems, small quantitative changes in certain parameters often lead to phase transitions, i.e. qualitative differences. Elman (2005) points out that multiple small phenotypic differences between humans and other primates (such as in degree of sociability, shared attention, memory capacity, rapid sequencing ability, vocal tract control, etc.) may in combination result in profound consequences, allowing means of communication of a totally different nature. Also, in a dynamic system, even when there is no parametric change, at a certain point in a continuous dynamic, system behavior can change dramatically and go through a phase transition. For example, constant heating of water leads to a transition from liquid to gas, without having any parametric change. In language development, such phase transitions are often observed, for example developmental 'lexical spurts' which often lead to rapid grammatical development (Bates and Goodman 1997).

Sensitivity to and dependence on network structure

Network studies of complex systems have shown that real-world networks are not random, as was initially assumed (Barabási 2002; Barabási and Albert 1999; Watts and Strogatz 1998), and that the internal structure and connectivity of the system can have a profound impact upon system dynamics (Newman et al. 2006). Similarly, linguistic interactions are not via random contacts; they are constrained by social networks. The social structure of language use and interaction has a crucial effect in the process of language change (Milroy 1980) and language variation (Eckert 2000), and the social structure of early humans must also have played important roles in language origin and evolution.

Change is local

Complexity arises in systems via incremental changes, based on locally available resources, rather than via top-down direction or deliberate movement toward some goal (see, for example, Dawkins 1985). Similarly, in a complex systems framework, language is viewed as an extension of numerous domain-general cognitive capacities such as shared attention, imitation, sequential learning, chunking, and categorization (Bybee 1998; Ellis 1996). Language is emergent from ongoing human social interactions, and its structure is fundamentally molded by the pre-existing cognitive abilities, processing idiosyncrasies and limitations, and general and specific conceptual circuitry of the human brain. Because this has been true in every generation of language users from its very origin, in some formulations language is said to be a form of cultural adaptation to the human mind, rather than the result of the brain adapting to process natural language grammar (Christiansen and Chater 2008; Deacon 1997; Schoenemann 2005). These perspectives have consequences for an understanding of how language is processed in the brain. Specifically, language will depend heavily on brain areas fundamentally linked to various types of conceptual understanding, the processing of social interactions, and pattern recognition and memory. It also predicts that so-called 'language areas' should have more general, pre-linguistic processing functions even in modern humans, and further, that the homologous areas of our closest primate relatives should also process information in ways that makes them predictable substrates for incipient language. Further, it predicts that the complexity of communication is to some important extent a function of social complexity. Given that social complexity is in turn correlated with brain size across primates, brain size evolution in early humans should give us some general clues about the evolution of language (Schoenemann 2006). Recognizing language as a CAS allows us to understand change at all levels.

Future directions: dynamic structure

As the diverse research cited in this chapter illustrates, understanding the emergence of language requires the full range of techniques of cognitive, social and natural science. But more than that, it requires the overarching frameworks of emergentism, CAS, and DST.

A common counterpoint within linguistics is the contrast between Saussure and Vygotsky, between structuralist approaches to language and those that emphasize the processes of language use in social interaction, between thin and thick descriptions (Geertz 1973). Vygotsky's ([1935] 1986) *Thinking and Speaking* addresses that same mystery as Saussure's, and makes equal resort to metaphor, for example: 'A thought may be compared to a cloud shedding a shower of words' (1986: 150), and

> Consciousness is reflected in the word like the sun is reflected in a droplet of water. The word is a microcosm of consciousness, related to consciousness like a living cell is related to an organism, like an atom is related to the cosmos. The meaningful word is a microcosm of human consciousness.
>
> *(Vygotsky 1986: 285)*

While we remember Saussure more for his analysis of linguistic signs, we remember Vygotsky more for his emphasis on process and context:

> A word acquires its sense from the context in which it appears; in different contexts, it changes its sense. Meaning remains stable throughout the changes of sense. The dictionary meaning of a word is no more than a stone in the edifice of sense, no more than a potentiality that finds diversified realisation in speech.
>
> *(Vygotsky 1986: 245)*

> The relation of thought to word is not a thing but a process, a continual movement back and forth from thought to word and from word to thought. In that process the relation of thought to word undergoes changes which themselves may be regarded as development in the functional sense. Thought is not merely expressed in words; it comes into existence through them. Every thought tends to connect something with something else, to establish a relationship between things. Every thought moves, grows and develops, fulfils a function,

solves a problem. This flow of thought occurs as an inner movement through a series of planes.

(Vygotsky 1986: 218)

The relation between thought and word is a living process; thought is born through words. A word devoid of thought is a dead thing, and a thought unembodied in words remains a shadow. The connection between them, however, is not a preformed and constant one. It emerges in the course of development, and itself evolves.

(Vygotsky 1986: 255)

Language emerges in both the Saussurian sign and the Vygotskian process.

Related topics

cognitive linguistics; corpus linguistics; language learning and language education; psycholinguistics; SLA

Further reading

Collins, L. and Ellis, N. C. (2009) 'Input and second language construction learning: frequency, form, and function', special issue, *Modern Language Journal*, 93(2). (SLA has always emphasized input. This special issue presents new ways of analyzing its latent properties.)
Ellis, N. C. and Larsen-Freeman, D. (eds) (2006) 'Language emergence: Implications for applied linguistics', special issue, *Applied Linguistics*, 27(4). (A special issue considering implications of emergentism for applied linguistics.)
——(2009) 'Language as a complex adaptive system', special issue, *Language Learning*, 59(Suppl. 1). (A special issue gathering experts from various language domains who share the CAS perspective.)
Ellis, N. C. and Cadierno, T. (2009) 'Constructing a second language', *Annual Review of Cognitive Linguistics* 7. (A special issue of new research over the bridge.)
Elman, J. L., Bates, E. A., Johnson, M. H., Karmiloff-Smith, A., Parisi, D. and Plunkett, K. (1996) *Rethinking Innateness: A Connectionist Perspective on Development*, Cambridge, MA: MIT Press. (A paradigm-shifting work.)
Robinson, P. and Ellis, N. C. (eds) (2008) *Handbook of Cognitive Linguistics and Second Language Acquisition*, London: Routledge. (A bridge.)

References

Anderson, J. R. (1982) 'Acquisition of cognitive skill', *Psychological Review* 89(4): 369–406.
——(1989) 'A rational analysis of human memory', in H. L. Roediger and F. I. M. Craik (eds) *Varieties of Memory and Consciousness: Essays in Honour of Endel Tulving*, Hillsdale, NJ: Lawrence Erlbaum Associates.
——(2000) *Cognitive Psychology and Its Implications*, 5th edn, New York: Worth Publications.
Anderson, J. R. and Schooler, L. J. (2000) 'The adaptive nature of memory', in E. Tulving and F. I. M. Craik (eds) *The Oxford Handbook of Memory*, London: Oxford University Press.
Anderson, P. W. (1972) 'More is different', *Science* 177: 393–6.
Baars, B. J. (1997) *In the Theater of Consciousness: The Workspace of the Mind*, Oxford: Oxford University Press.
Baddeley, A. D. (1997) *Human Memory: Theory and Practice*, revised edn, Hove: Psychology Press.
Barabási, A-L. (2002) *Linked: The New Science of Networks*, Cambridge, MA: Perseus Books.
Barabási, A.-L. and Albert, R. (1999) 'Emergence of scaling in random networks', *Science* 286: 509–11.
Barlow, M. and Kemmer, S. (eds) (2000) *Usage Based Models of Language*, Stanford, CA: CSLI Publications.

Barsalou, L. W. (1999) 'Perceptual symbol systems', *Behavioral and Brain Sciences* 22: 577–660.
——(2008) 'Grounded cognition', *Annual Review of Psychology* 59: 617–45.
Bartlett, F. C. ([1932] 1967) *Remembering: A Study in Experimental and Social Psychology*, Cambridge: Cambridge University Press.
Bates, E. and Goodman, J. C. (1997) 'On the inseparability of grammar and the lexicon: evidence from acquisition, aphasia and real-time processing', *Language and Cognitive Processes* 12: 507–86.
Bates, E. and MacWhinney, B. (1987) 'Competition, variation, and language learning', in B. MacWhinney (ed.) *Mechanisms of Language Acquisition*, Hillsdale, NJ: Lawrence Erlbaum Associates.
Beckner, C., Blythe, R., Bybee, J., Christiansen, M. H., Croft, W., Ellis, N. C., *et al.* (2009) 'Language is a complex adaptive system', position paper, *Language Learning* 59(Suppl. 1): 1–26.
Biber, D., Conrad, S. and Reppen, R. (1998) *Corpus Linguistics: Investigating Language Structure and Use*, New York: Cambridge University Press.
Biber, D., Johansson, S., Leech, G., Conrad, S. and Finegan, E. (1999) *Longman Grammar of Spoken and Written English*, Harlow: Pearson Education.
Bod, R., Hay, J. and Jannedy, S. (eds) (2003) *Probabilistic Linguistics*, Cambridge, MA: MIT Press.
Bybee, J. (1998) 'A functionalist approach to grammar and its evolution', *Evolution of Communication* 2: 249–78.
——(2006) 'From usage to grammar: the mind's response to repetition', *Language* 82: 711–33.
Bybee, J. and Hopper, P. (eds) (2001) *Frequency and the Emergence of Linguistic Structure*, Amsterdam: John Benjamins.
Camazine, S., Deneubourg, J-L., Franks, N. R., Sneyd, J., Theraulaz, G. and Bonabeau, E. (2001) *Self-organization in Biological Systems*, Princeton, NJ: Princeton University Press.
Chater, N. and Manning, C. (2006) 'Probabilistic models of language processing and acquisition', *Trends in Cognitive Science* 10: 335–44.
Chomsky, N. (1965) *Aspects of the Theory of Syntax*, Cambridge, MA: MIT Press.
——(1981) *Lectures on Government and Binding*, Dordrecht: Foris.
Christiansen, M. H. and Chater, N. (2008) 'Language as shaped by the brain', *Behavioral and Brain Sciences* [target article for multiple peer commentary] 31: 489–509.
Christiansen, M. H. and Chater, N. (eds) (2001) *Connectionist Psycholinguistics*, Westport, CT: Ablex.
Collins, L. and Ellis, N. C. (2009) 'Input and second language construction learning: frequency, form, and function', *Modern Language Journal* 93(2): whole issue.
Croft, W. (2001) *Radical Construction Grammar: Syntactic Theory in Typological Perspective*, Oxford: Oxford University Press.
Croft, W. and Cruse, A. (2004) *Cognitive Linguistics*, Cambridge: Cambridge University Press.
Dąbrowska, E. (1997) 'The LAD goes to school: a cautionary tale for nativists', *Linguistics* 35: 735–66.
Dawkins, R. (1985) *The Blind Watchmaker*, New York: Norton.
de Bot, K., Lowie, W. and Verspoor, M. (2007) 'A dynamic systems theory to second language acquisition', *Bilingualism: Language and Cognition* 10: 7–21.
Deacon, T. W. (1997) *The Symbolic Species: The Co-evolution of Language and the Brain*, New York: W. W. Norton.
Ebbinghaus, H. (1885) *Memory: A Contribution to Experimental Psychology*, New York: Teachers College, Columbia University.
Eckert, P. (2000) *Linguistic Variation as Social Practice: The Linguistic Construction of Identity in Belten High*, Oxford: Blackwell.
Ellis, N. C. (1996) 'Sequencing in SLA: phonological memory, chunking, and points of order', *Studies in Second Language Acquisition* 18(1): 91–126.
——(1998) 'Emergentism, connectionism and language learning', *Language Learning* 48(4): 631–64.
——(2002a) 'Frequency effects in language processing: a review with implications for theories of implicit and explicit language acquisition', *Studies in Second Language Acquisition* 24(2): 143–88.
——(2002b) 'Reflections on frequency effects in language processing', *Studies in Second Language Acquisition* 24(2): 297–339.
——(2003) 'Constructions, chunking, and connectionism: the emergence of second language structure', in C. J. Doughty and M. H. Long (eds) *The Handbook of Second Language Acquisition*, Oxford: Blackwell.
——(2005) 'At the interface: dynamic interactions of explicit and implicit language knowledge', *Studies in Second Language Acquisition* 27: 305–52.

——(2006) 'Language acquisition as rational contingency learning', *Applied Linguistics* 27(1): 1–24.

——(2008a) 'The dynamics of language use, language change, and first and second language acquisition', *Modern Language Journal* 41(3): 232–49.

——(2008b) 'The psycholinguistics of the interaction hypothesis', in A. Mackey and C. Polio (eds) *Multiple Perspectives on Interaction in SLA: Second Language Research in Honor of Susan M. Gass*, New York: Routledge.

——(2008c) 'Usage-based and form-focused language acquisition: the associative learning of constructions, learned-attention, and the limited L2 endstate', in P. Robinson and N. C. Ellis (eds) *Handbook of Cognitive Linguistics and Second Language Acquisition*, London: Routledge.

Ellis, N. C. (ed.) (1994) *Implicit and Explicit Learning of Languages*, San Diego, CA: Academic Press.

Ellis, N. C. and Cadierno, T. (2009) 'Constructing a second language', *Annual Review of Cognitive Linguistics* 7 (special section).

Ellis, N. C. and Larsen-Freeman, D. (2006a) 'Language emergence: implications for applied linguistics', *Applied Linguistics* 27(4): whole issue.

——(2006b) 'Language emergence: implications for applied linguistics (introduction to the special issue)', *Applied Linguistics* 27(4): 558–89.

Ellis, N. C. and Schmidt, R. (1998) 'Rules or associations in the acquisition of morphology? The frequency by regularity interaction in human and PDP learning of morphosyntax', *Language and Cognitive Processes* 13(2–3): 307–36.

Elman, J. L. (2005) 'Connectionist views of cognitive development: where next?', *Trends in Cognitive Science* 9: 111–17.

Elman, J. L., Bates, E. A., Johnson, M. H., Karmiloff-Smith, A., Parisi, D. and Plunkett, K. (1996) *Rethinking Innateness: A Connectionist Perspective on Development*, Cambridge, MA: MIT Press.

Ferrer i Cancho, R. and Solé, R. V. (2001) 'The small world of human language', *Proceedings of the Royal Society of London*, B. 268: 2261–5.

Fillmore, C. (1988) 'The mechanisms of construction grammar', *Berkeley Linguistics Society* 14: 35–55.

Fries, C. C. (1952) *The Structure of English*, New York: Harcourt, Brace and Co.

Gaskell, G. (ed.) (2007) *Oxford Handbook of Psycholinguistics*, Oxford: Oxford University Press.

Gass, S. (1997) *Input, Interaction, and the Development of Second Languages*, Mahwah, NJ: Lawrence Erlbaum Associates.

Geertz, C. (1973) 'Thick description: toward an interpretive theory of culture', in C. Geertz (ed.) *The Interpretation of Cultures: Selected Essays*, New York: Basic Books.

Gernsbacher, M. A. (1994) *A Handbook of Psycholinguistics*, San Diego, CA: Academic Press.

Goldberg, A. E. (1995) *Constructions: A Construction Grammar Approach to Argument Structure*, Chicago: University of Chicago Press.

——(2003) 'Constructions: a new theoretical approach to language', *Trends in Cognitive Science* 7: 219–24.

——(2006) *Constructions at Work: The Nature of Generalization in Language*, Oxford: Oxford University Press.

Granger, S. and Meunier, F. (eds) (2008) *Phraseology: An Interdisciplinary Perspective*, Amsterdam: John Benjamins.

Halliday, M. A. K. (1994) *An Introduction to Functional Grammar*, 2nd edn, London: Edward Arnold.

Harnad, S. (ed.) (1987) *Categorical Perception: The Groundwork of Cognition*, New York: Cambridge University Press.

Harris, Z. (1955) 'From phoneme to morpheme', *Language* 31: 190–222.

——(1982) *A Grammar of English on Mathematical Principles*, New York: John Wiley and Sons.

——(1991) *A Theory of Language and Information: A Mathematical Approach*, Oxford: Oxford University Press.

Hoey, M. P. (2005) *Lexical Priming: A New Theory of Words and Language*, London: Routledge.

Holland, J. H. (1995) *Hidden Order: How Adaption Builds Complexity*, Reading, MA: Addison-Wesley.

——(1998) *Emergence: From Chaos to Order*, Oxford: Oxford University Press.

Hopper, P. J. (1987) 'Emergent grammar', *Berkeley Linguistics Society* 13: 139–57.

——(1998) 'Emergent grammar', in M. Tomasello (ed.) *The New Psychology of Language: Cognitive and Functional Approaches to Language Structure*, Mahwah, NJ: Lawrence Erlbaum Associates.

Jurafsky, D. (2002) 'Probabilistic modeling in psycholinguistics: linguistic comprehension and production', in R. Bod, J. Hay and S. Jannedy (eds) *Probabilistic Linguistics*, Cambridge, MA: MIT Press.

Jurafsky, D. and Martin, J. H. (2000) *Speech and Language Processing: An Introduction to Natural Language Processing, Speech Recognition, and Computational Linguistics*, Englewood Cliffs, NJ: Prentice Hall.

Koch, C. (2004) *The Quest for Consciousness: A Neurobiological Approach*, Englewood, CO: Roberts and Company.

Kramsch, C. (ed.) (2002) *Language Acquisition and Language Socialization: Ecological Perspectives*, London: Continuum.

Kuhl, P. K. (2007) 'Is speech-learning gated by the "social brain"?', *Developmental Science* 10: 110–20.

Lakoff, G. (1987) *Women, Fire, and Dangerous Things: What Categories Reveal About the Mind*, Chicago: University of Chicago Press.

Lantolf, J. and Pavlenko, A. (1995) 'Sociocultural theory and second language acquisition', *Annual Review of Applied Linguistics* 15: 38–53.

Lantolf, J. and Thorne, S. (2006) *Sociocultural Theory and the Genesis of Second Language Development*, Oxford: Oxford University Press.

Larsen-Freeman, D. (1997) 'Chaos/complexity science and second language acquisition', *Applied Linguistics* 18: 141–65.

Larsen-Freeman, D. and Cameron, L. (2008) *Complex Systems and Applied Linguistics*, Oxford: Oxford University Press.

Long, M. H. (1996) 'The role of linguistic environment in second language acquisition', in W. C. Ritchie and T. K. Bhatia (eds) *Handbook of Second Language Acquisitiom*, San Diego, CA: Academic Press.

McEnery, T. and Wilson, A. (1996) *Corpus Linguistics*, Edinburgh: Edinburgh University Press.

MacWhinney, B. (1987) 'The competition model', in B. MacWhinney (ed) *Mechanisms of Language Acquisition*, Hillsdale, NJ: Lawrence Erlbaum Associates.

——(1997) 'Second language acquisition and the competition model', in A. M. B. de Groot and J. F. Kroll (eds) *Tutorials in Bilingualism: Psycholinguistic Perspectives*, Mahwah, NJ: Lawrence Erlbaum Associates.

MacWhinney, B. (ed.) (1999) *The Emergence of Language*, Hillsdale, NJ: Lawrence Erlbaum Associates.

Mandler, J. (2004) *The Foundations of Mind: Origins of Conceptual Thought*, Oxford: Oxford University Press.

Milroy, J. (1980) *Language and Social Networks*, Oxford: Blackwell.

Newell, A. (1990) *Unified Theories of Cognition*, Cambridge, MA: Harvard University Press.

Newman, M. E. J., Barabási, A-L. and Watts, D. J. (eds) (2006) *The Structure and Dynamics of Networks*, Princeton, NJ and Oxford: Princeton University Press.

Pawley, A. and Syder, F. H. (1983) 'Two puzzles for linguistic theory: nativelike selection and nativelike fluency', in J. C. Richards and R. W. Schmidt (eds) *Language and Communication*, London: Longman.

Port, R. F. and van Gelder, T. (1995) *Mind as Motion: Explorations in the Dynamics of Cognition*, Cambridge, MA: MIT Press.

Posner, M. I. and Keele, S. W. (1970) 'Retention of abstract ideas', *Journal of Experimental Psychology* 83: 304–8.

Roberts, P. (1956) *Patterns of English*, New York: Harcourt, Brace and World.

Robinson, P. and Ellis, N. C. (eds) (2008) *A Handbook of Cognitive Linguistics and Second Language Acquisition*, London: Routledge.

Rogers, T. T. and McClelland, J. L. (2008) 'Precis of semantic cognition: a parallel distributed processing approach', *Behavioral and Brain Sciences* 31: 689–749.

Rosch, E. and Mervis, C. B. (1975) 'Cognitive representations of semantic categories', *Journal of Experimental Psychology: General* 104: 192–233.

Rosch, E., Mervis, C. B., Gray, W. D., Johnson, D. M. and Boyes-Braem, P. (1976) 'Basic objects in natural categories', *Cognitive Psychology* 8: 382–439.

de Saussure, F. (1916) *Cours de linguistique générale*, London: Duckworth.

Schank, R. C. and Abelson, R. P. (1977) *Scripts, Plans, Goals, and Understanding: An Inquiry into Human Knowledge Structures*, Hillsdale, NJ: Lawrence Erlbaum Associates.

Schoenemann, P. T. (2005) 'Conceptual complexity and the brain: understanding language origins', in W. S.-Y. Wang and J. W. Minett (eds) *Language Acquisition, Change and Emergence: Essays in Evolutionary Linguistics*, Hong Kong: City University of Hong Kong Press.

——(2006) 'Evolution of the size and functional areas of the human brain', *Annual Review of Anthropology* 35: 379–406.

Shanks, D. R. (1995) *The Psychology of Associative Learning*, New York: Cambridge University Press.

Sinclair, J. (1991) *Corpus, Concordance, Collocation*, Oxford: Oxford University Press.

——(2004) *Trust the Text: Language, Corpus and Discourse*, London: Routledge.

Slobin, D. I. (1997) 'The origins of grammaticizable notions: beyond the individual mind', in D. I. Slobin (ed.) *The Crosslinguistic Study of Language Acquisition*, Mahwah, NJ: Lawrence Erlbaum Associates.

Spencer, J. P., Thomas, M. S. C. and McClelland, J. L. (eds) (2009) *Toward a Unified Theory of Development: Connectionism and Dynamic Systems Theory Re-considered*, New York: Oxford.

Spivey, M. (2006) *The Continuity of Mind*, Oxford: Oxford University Press.

Steels, L. (2006) 'How to do experiments in artificial language evolution and why', *Proceedings of the 6th International Conference on the Evolution of Language*.

Talmy, L. (1988) 'The relation of grammar to cognition', in B. Rudzka-Ostyn (ed.) *Topics in Cognitive Linguistics*, Amsterdam: John Benjamins.

——(2000a) *Toward a Cognitive Semantics: Concept Structuring Systems*, Cambridge MA: MIT Press.

——(2000b) *Toward a Cognitive Semantics: Typology and Process in Concept Structuring*, Cambridge, MA: MIT Press.

Taylor, J. R. (1998) 'Syntactic constructions as prototype categories', in M. Tomasello (ed.) *The New Psychology of Language: Cognitive and Functional Approaches to Language Structure*, Mahwah, NJ: Lawrence Erlbaum Associates.

——(2002) *Cognitive Grammar*, Oxford: Oxford University Press.

The Five Graces Group (Beckner, C., Blythe, R., Bybee, J., Christiansen, M. H., Croft, W., Ellis, N. C., Holland, J., Ke, J., Larsen-Freeman, D. and Schoenemann, T.) (2009) 'Language is a complex adaptive system', position paper, *Language Learning* 59(Suppl. 1).

Tomasello, M. (2003) *Constructing a Language*, Cambridge, MA: Harvard University Press.

Tomasello, M. (ed.) (1998) *The New Psychology of Language: Cognitive and Functional Approaches to Language Structure*, Mahwah, NJ: Lawrence Erlbaum Associates.

van Geert, P. (1991) 'A dynamic systems model of cognitive and language growth', *Psychological Review* 98: 3–53.

Vygotsky, L. S. ([1935] 1986) *Thought and Language*, Cambridge, MA: MIT Press.

——(1980) *Mind in Society: The Development of Higher Mental Processes*, Cambridge, MA: Harvard University Press.

Watts, D. J. and Strogatz, S. H. (1998) 'Collective dynamics of "small-world" networks', *Nature* 393: 440–2.

Weinreich, U., Labov, W. and Herzog, M. I. (1968) 'Empirical foundations for a theory of language change', in W. P. Lehmann and Y. Malkiel (eds) *Directions for Historical Linguistics*, Austin: University of Texas Press.

Wray, A. (2002) *Formulaic Language and the Lexicon*, Cambridge: Cambridge University Press.

47

Multimodality

Theo van Leeuwen

Multimodality

The term 'multimodality' dates from the 1920s. It was a technical term in the then relatively new field of the psychology of perception, denoting the effect different sensory perceptions have on each other. An example of this is the so-called McGurk effect: if people are shown a video of someone articulating a particular syllable, e.g. /ga/, while hearing another syllable, e.g. /ba/, they perceive neither /ga/, nor /ba/, but /da/ (Stork 1997: 239). In other words, perception is multimodal. It integrates information received by different senses.

More recently, linguists and discourse analysts have taken up the term, broadening it to denote the integrated use of different communicative resources, such as language, image, sound and music in multimodal texts and communicative events. As soon as they had begun to study texts and communicative events rather than isolated sentences, they realized what they should have known all along: that communication is multimodal; that spoken language cannot be adequately understood without taking non-verbal communication into account; and that many forms of contemporary written language cannot be adequately understood unless we look, not just at language, but also at images, layout, typography and colour. In the past twenty or so years this led to the development of multimodality as a field of study investigating the common as well as the distinct properties of the different modes in the multimodal mix and the way they integrate in multimodal texts and communicative events.

It is not difficult to see why such a field of study should have developed. From the 1920s onwards, public communication had become increasingly multimodal. Film had changed acting, enlarging subtle aspects of non-verbal communication, and so influencing how people talk and move and smile the world over. Later, television had made non-verbal communication a decisive factor in politics, most famously in the televised debate between Nixon and Kennedy. Writing, too, had become multimodal, as illustrations and layout elements such as boxes and sidebars broke up and reshaped the pages of books and magazines. Like scholars in other fields of study, linguists took notice. In the course of the twentieth century, several schools of linguistics engaged with communicative modes other than language. The first was the Prague School, which, in the 1930s and 1940s, extended linguistics into the visual arts and the non-verbal aspects of theatre, and which included studies of folklore, and collaborations with avant-garde artists (see, for example, Matejka and Titunik 1976). Paris School structuralist semiotics of the 1960s also used concepts and methods from linguistics to understand communicative modes other than language. Largely inspired by the work of Roland Barthes, it mostly focused on analyses of popular culture and the mass media, rather than on folklore or avant-garde art (e.g. Barthes 1967, 1977, 1983). In roughly the same period, American linguists began to take an interest in the multimodal analysis of spoken language and non-verbal communication. Birdwhistell (e.g. 1973) developed an intricate set of tools for analyzing body motion, and Pittenger *et al.* (1960) published a highly detailed and groundbreaking multimodal analysis of the first five minutes of a psychiatric interview. In the late 1960s, conversation analysis replaced the 16mm film sound camera with the cassette recorder as the research tool of choice, which diminished attention to non-verbal communication, although some scholars in this tradition have, more recently, re-introduced it (Ochs 1979; Goodwin 2001). A fourth school emerged in the 1990s. Inspired by the linguistics of M. A. K. Halliday (1978, 1985), it was this school which adopted and broadened the term 'multimodality', and introduced it into applied linguistics, and especially into the study of language and literacy in education. More recently a further approach, mediated discourse analysis, inspired by the work of Ron and Suzie Scollon (2003, 2004), returned to American micro-analysis of social interaction, but in a new way, linking it to the wider social and political context, and adding a new emphasis on technological mediation (see, for example, Jones 2009).

By now, multimodality has its own bi-annual conference and a range of edited books (e.g. O'Halloran 2004; Ventola *et al.* 2004; Levine and Scollon 2004; Norris and Jones 2005; Unsworth 2008; Jewitt 2009), and it is regularly included in handbooks and encyclopedias of linguistics, discourse analysis, visual communication and so on. Although it encompasses a number of distinct theoretical and methodological approaches, it has nevertheless remained a united field of study, with productive dialogue and mutual influence between the different 'schools' (cf. Jewitt 2009, for a more extensive overview of the different approaches in the field).

Educational applications

The New London Group (Gunther Kress, James Gee, Allan Luke, Mary Kalantzis and others) stimulated an interest in applying multimodal analysis to education (New London Group 1996). This led to three kinds of studies: studies of the development of multimodal literacy in young children, often connected to a call for integrating multimodal literacy into the curriculum; studies of multimodal learning resources, including textbooks, toys, CD-ROMs, and the Internet; and studies of multimodal classroom interaction. Below, I will briefly deal with all three.

Gunther Kress' *Before Writing* (1997) initiated the study of the development of multimodal literacy, investigating how very young children use the affordances of whatever materials are at hand, or whatever techniques they have mastered, on the basis of 'interest', of what is of crucial importance to them at the given moment. In one of his key examples, a three-year-old child draws a car as a series of circles ('wheels'). Having mastered the drawing of circles, the child now uses circles as a means of expressing what, to him, is a crucial characteristic of cars. As a semiotic resource, the circle has many possible meanings, but the one the child selects is motivated by his interest of the moment, his interest in thinking about cars. Thus, learning to draw and learning to understand the world around him go hand in hand. But, Kress said,

> As children are drawn into culture, 'what is to hand' becomes more and more that which the culture values and therefore makes readily available. The child's active, transformative

practice remains, but it is more and more applied to materials which are already culturally formed. In this way children become the agents of their own cultural and social making.

(Kress 1997: 13)

Kress' work has inspired many other studies of the way young children use a range of materials and techniques to create representations of the world around them (e.g. Ormerod and Ivanovic 2002).

Closely related is the study of the affordances and learning potentials of different communicative modes. In *Literacy in the New Media Age* (2003: 52–7), Kress studied the use of different modes by junior high school students learning about blood circulation. One used language, writing a kind of travel diary, with a red blood cell as its protagonist, making a voyage through the body. Another drew a concept map, with boxes representing the heart, the arteries, the lungs, and so on, and arrows representing the movement of blood from one 'box' to another. The linearity of the story, Kress said, was an apt signifier for the blood moving from organ to organ, and language allowed the expression of causality, but the use of many different words for the idea of movement ('leave', 'come', 'squeeze', 'drop off', 'enter', etc.), while stylistically desirable, diminished the generality scientific discourse normally requires. The diagrammatic elements of the concept map (boxes and arrows), on the other hand, did provide scientific generality, but as the arrows in the student's concept map radiated from the central 'blood' box, the concept of 'circularity' was less clearly expressed, and the idea of causality remained unexpressed, as drawings do not, or not yet, lend themselves to the expression of causality. Each mode, Kress concluded, has its own epistemological affordances and limitations, and understanding these is fundamental for creating effective multimodal representations.

This applies not only to student work, but also to textbooks and other learning resources, which have all become increasingly multimodal in recent years. Jewitt (2006) studied how children use computer games to learn science, struggling to match the rules of the game with their everyday experience of the phenomena the game recontextualizes. When learning to understand 'bouncing' through a game called *Playground*, for instance, children can choose a behaviour (a particular kind of bounce, represented by pictures of a spring, a ball, etc.) and attach it to an object, a bullet, which can then bounce off bars. But this is confusing. Can bullets be bouncy? And isn't the 'behaviour' of 'bouncing' the property of the bars the bullets bounce against rather than of the bullets? Everyday experience can seem at odds with the constraints of the computer program. Nevertheless, games of this kind do allow children to explore the rules of mechanics systematically, interactively, and multimodally, practically without any verbal input. Jewitt's transcriptions of the conversations children engage in as they are working with the program threw light on the active nature of this kind of learning. 'I want there to be little bars where if you hit it, it goes another way and another way', said one of the children, and then proceeded to do exactly that. Many other studies of this kind, too, combine analysis of the meaning potential of multimodal resources with ethnographic accounts of their use in concrete situations, thus documenting the learning process as an active 'transformative practice', to use Kress' term again.

Studies of classroom interaction, finally, have also moved from the traditional emphasis on linguistic exchange structures to strong contextualization and detailed attendance to non-verbal communication and setting, e.g. to the way classrooms are arranged, to what is hung on the walls, the technological resources available, and so on. Kress *et al.* (2005), for instance, described one classroom as realizing a 'transmission' pedagogy, with individual student tables lined up in rows; another as realizing a 'participatory/authoritarian' pedagogy: tables were put together to create teams of four or five students facing each other ('participation'), yet these groups of tables were angled to allow the teacher total visual control from the front of the classroom, and the arrangement constrained the postures of the students, at least if they wanted to see the teacher and follow the lesson ('authoritarian').

In all this work, multimodality is seen as a key way towards better learning, with different modes enabling the representation of different aspects of, and perspectives on, the objects of learning, and they stress that the learning potential of different modes needs to be better understood by teachers, and that multimodal literacy needs to be more fully integrated into the curriculum, in ways based on what we can learn from studying the spontaneous learning of very young children, and from studying other forms of informal learning, such as playing with toys or computer games.

Multimodality and (critical) discourse analysis

Multimodal analysis has also been applied to the critical analysis of media discourses (e.g. Kress and van Leeuwen 1998; Knox 2007; Machin 2007). In *Global Media Discourse* (2007), Machin and van Leeuwen analyzed how, in the Internet image bank Getty Creative Images, photographic images can be searched for the concepts they express, rather than for the people, places and events they record and document. The visual expression of concepts by means of staged photographs, has of course long existed in advertising, but now, Machin and van Leeuwen show, it also extends to the editorial content of newspapers and magazines, where we traditionally expect 'records of reality'. Conceptual images of this kind are produced to fit into multimodal designs, using restricted colour palettes that will easily harmonize with page layout and leaving space for words, and they are generic rather than specific, using a range of decontextualizing devices, and a restricted vocabulary of attributes to indicate the identity of people and places (e.g. hard hat and rolled-up blueprint means 'architect'; 'laptop' means office; nondescript skyscraper means 'city'). Such generic images are deliberately designed to be used in multiple contexts, and hence sold over and over, and cheaply so. Finally, Machin and van Leeuwen explored the kinds of concepts that can be expressed with this new visual 'language' (as Getty Images explicitly calls itself [Machin and van Leeuwen 2007: 151]), and found that the positive values of contemporary corporate discourse dominate: *freedom, creativity, innovation, determination, concentration, spirituality, well-being,* and so on.

van Leeuwen (2008) developed a framework for analyzing how the identity of 'social actors' can be signified verbally, visually, and with the 'Playmobil' toy system. Social actors can, for instance, be represented as individuals or as 'types', and individually or collectively, and they can be 'functionalized', categorized by what they *do* (e.g. their profession or some other kind of activity) or classified, categorized by what they are deemed to *be* (e.g. gender, class, ethnicity, nationality). His analysis demonstrated that many identity categories can be expressed verbally as well as visually. But not every category can be expressed in every mode, and the ways in which the same categories are expressed in different modes make a difference and add further meanings and values. Individual identity, for instance, is linguistically expressed by names, visually by pictures that have to be detailed enough to show individual characteristics, and in which these details should not be overwhelmed by attributes with group identity connotations (e.g. hair styles or hats, turbans, scarves, etc.). Playmobil, finally, does not allow the expression of individual identity at all. Its minimalistic characters offer children a range of social roles and types, a microcosm of the social world, differentiated by skin colour, hair style, and dress.

van Leeuwen stresses the importance of analysing the expression of identity in images in relation to racist discourse:

> Visually communicated racism can be much more easily denied, much more easily dismissed as 'in the eye of the beholder' than verbal racism [...] It is for this reason that a consideration of images should have pride of place in any inquiry into racist discourse. If images seem to just show 'what is', we need to show that that may not always be so. If images seem to just *allude* to things and never 'say them explicitly', we need to make these allusions explicit.
>
> *(van Leeuwen 2000: 335)*

The critical multimodal analysis of speech and non-verbal communication in media discourse, on the other hand, remains underdeveloped, despite Norman Fairclough's call for including it in the critical analysis of political discourse:

> Communicative style is a matter of language in the broadest sense – certainly verbal language (words), but also all other aspects of the complex bodily performance that constitutes political style (gestures, facial expressions, how people hold themselves and move, dress and hairstyle, and so forth) A successful leader's communicative style is not simply what makes him attractive to voters in a general way, it conveys certain values which can powerfully enhance the political message.
>
> *(Fairclough 2000: 4)*

Multimodality and everyday interaction

Ron and Suzie Scollon (e.g. 2003, 2004) pioneered a new approach to the multimodal analysis of everyday situated interactions. Many of their studies departed from a simple everyday action such as having a cup of coffee (Scollon 2001), making a physical object (e.g. a paper coffee cup, and the printed messages on it) the centre of a set of converging lines of inquiry – interaction analysis, down to the micro-level of conversational and non-verbal rhythms; semiotic analysis of the setting of the interaction; and critical analysis of the broader social, cultural and political setting (for instance, contemporary corporate social responsibility practices).

Sigrid Norris (2005) analyzed one of her ethnographic interviews in this vein, including in her analysis not just the interview itself, but also the activity in which the interviewee was engaged while talking to her (ironing clothes), the soap opera that was running on television in the background, the game played by her daughter on the floor of the room, and at a larger scale, the interviewee's life story and the discourses she invoked to represent it – discourses about women as professionals and housewives, about mothering, about the power relations between men and women, and so on. Thus, the interview became one of the strands in a complex multimodal texture that wove several practices together – conversing, ironing, playing, watching television, as well as larger scale practices and their attendant identities – being the subject of an interview, mothering, being a housewife – all this in different densities, and with shifting foregroundings and backgroundings of the various strands of the multimodal texture. The results of the analysis then led to theoretical reflections on issues of social theory such as agency, identity and habitus. Norris makes the complexities of analyses of this kind visible by means of different techniques of transcription (cf. also Norris 2002), including elements of traditional conversation analysis as well as photographs on which lines spoken by the characters, complete with intonation transcription, and relevant television or computer screen images that would otherwise be invisible, are superimposed.

Describing modes

Multimodal analysis has two main concerns: investigating the similarities and differences between different semiotic modes; and studying how different semiotic modes are integrated into multimodal texts and communicative events. Both require attending to the semiotic resources and their communicative potential, as well as to the way they are taken up in concrete settings. In other words, multimodal analysis is concerned with structure as well as agency, and needs to pay close attention to their mutual influence on each other. Below I will deal with the first of these two concerns.

A key question for linguists turning to the study of non-linguistic modes is the question of whether, or to which degree, non-linguistic modes are like language, and to what degree they can be studied with the concepts and methods of linguistic analysis. Christian Metz (1974a, 1974b), investigating the 'language of cinema', came to a negative conclusion: cinema does not have equivalents to the key units of language, to phonemes, words, clauses, and so on. Kress and van Leeuwen ([1996] 2006) came to a different conclusion. They agreed that there is no point in making formal comparisons, in asking whether a shot in a film is like a word, or like a sentence. The forms of visual communication are radically different from those of language. But this does not mean that both cannot fulfil the same communicative functions, and, at some level, express the same meanings. Kress and van Leeuwen therefore combined functional concepts and methods from the linguistic theory of Halliday (1978, 1985) with formal concepts and methods from the art theory of Arnheim (1969, 1974, 1982) and others. They assumed that, like language, visual communication can realize Halliday's 'metafunctions' – the 'ideational' function of constructing representations of the world; the 'interpersonal' function of constituting interactions; and the 'textual' function of bringing combined representations-embedded-in-interactions together into the kind of larger wholes we recognize as coherent texts or communicative events. And they assumed that, like the grammar of language, the 'grammar' of visual communication can be described as a system of functional-semantic choices. But they took care to point out that not all meanings that can be realized verbally can be also realized visually, and vice versa, and that, even when two modes can realize the same meaning, each will add its own overtones and resonances.

To take a relatively simple example, both language and image can realize 'social distance', but they do so in different ways. In language social distance can be realized through degrees in formality of style and mode of address, or through pronoun systems, with one form for the second person indicating 'far' distance – respect, deference and so on (e.g. French *vous*), another 'close' distance – intimacy, familiarity, equality, etc. (e.g. French *tu*). In images, social distance is realized by means of 'size of frame'. The close shot, showing only head and shoulders, realizes close social distance, the long shot, showing people at full length, far social distance, and the medium shot something in between (Figure 47.1 represents this as a Hallidayan 'system network').

This, in turn, relates closely to the way Edward Hall (e.g. 1966) has described the distances we keep from each other in everyday interaction. Normally, only people with whom we have a personal relationship may come close enough to allow easy touching, while we 'keep our distance' from others, for instance, but just where each 'zone' begins and ends will differ from culture to culture. In other words, within a given culture, a single social system of 'social distance' regulates interpersonal relations, but this can be expressed in different modes – through

Theo van Leeuwen

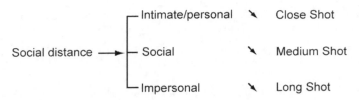

Figure 47.1 Social distance (system network)

language, through proxemic behaviour, through images, and so on. At the same time, linguistically expressed 'close distance' does not mean quite the same thing as visually expressed 'close distance', and visual and verbal realizations can combine in different ways. Formality is not quite the same as social distance, for instance, you can use informal language, yet keep your distance, or vice versa.

In their book *Reading Images* ([1996] 2006), Kress and van Leeuwen presented a range of system networks detailing the 'ideational', 'interpersonal' and 'textual' meanings that can be realized by images. Their account of visual 'ideation' broke with earlier traditions which saw only the symbolic or 'connotative' meanings of the people, places and things in images as semiotic, but not the way these combined into larger compositional wholes, which tended to be discussed only from a formal aesthetic point of view. Kress and van Leeuwen, however, argued that, just as linguistic grammar connects nominal groups and verbal groups into clauses, so visual 'grammar' can connect, for instance, 'volumes' and 'vectors' (the terms come from Arnheim 1982) into larger compositional syntagms. A vector is a line, usually oblique, formed by some element of the image, e.g. an arrow or an outstretched arm, and pointing at another element. This structure (element a → element b) serves to represent actions in which one element acts upon another, or moves towards another, or transforms into another. In a concept map of blood circulation, for instance, the arrows between the boxes represent the movement of blood from one part of the body to another.

Different multimodal theories may differ as to which linguistic concepts and methods they see as relevant for multimodal analysis. For Kress and van Leeuwen, visual syntagms can combine together or be embedded into each other in a number of different ways. For O'Toole (1994), on the other hand, analyzing visual art should take place at clearly defined ranks that are analogous to the ranks in linguistic analysis (word, word group, clause, clause complex) – the rank of the 'work' as a whole; the rank of the 'episode' (defined as a configuration of figures involved in a common action or situation); the rank of the 'figures'; and the rank of the 'parts of the figures'. At each rank there are specific systems related to each of the three metafunctions. The 'figure', for instance, will ideationally have specific 'attributes', interpersonally a certain degree of 'prominence', and textually certain 'stylistic features'.

Kress and van Leeuwen's (2001) distinction between 'modes' and 'media' should also be mentioned. Modes are meaning-making resources of the kind I have just discussed. They can be described as a set of 'systems' for the expression of ideational, interpersonal and textual meanings that are relatively abstract, that is, not tied to a particular material means of expression – language, for instance, can be materialized as speech or as writing, and close shots can be materialized in still as well as in moving images, in photographs as well as in paintings, and so on. Media, on the other hand, are the concrete and material substances or physical actions in and through which modes can be realized, and they add meanings and emotive resonances of their own. To put it another way, modes are resources for *designing* semiotic artifacts or events, e.g. for composing a piece of music or writing a play; media are resources for *materializing* them, e.g. for performing the music or the play – and as we know, a good performance can add meanings and values that the composer or playwright may not even have foreseen. In some cases, e.g. everyday speech, or improvised music, the distinction will not be felt by the speakers or musicians, but it can still have analytical value for multimodal analysis.

van Leeuwen (2009) has studied the voice as 'medium', discussing the meanings and values that can be communicated by the timbral qualities of actors' or singers' voices. A voice can be rough, for instance, and this can be used, by an actor or singer, to express a range of things that all relate to what that voice literally is – rough. Roughness can mean 'wear and tear', for instance, indicating, perhaps, that a character has had a hard life, or it can indicate harshness, suggesting that an actor is voicing the 'unvarnished truth'. In the course of the history of the sound film, iconic actors such as Marilyn Monroe, Lauren Bacall, Marlon Brando and James Stewart, have created unique voice qualities that are now recognized the world over, all on the basis of the affordances of specific aspects of vocal timbre and delivery. Today, these voices have become a repertoire for actors to draw on. As Michel Chion has said, in film:

> The voice is ceasing to be identified with a specific face. It appears much less stable, identified. […] Compare two roughly contemporaneous Dustin Hoffman movies. In Barry Levinson's *Rain Man*, he has a metallic and nasal voice and in Stephen Frears' *Hero* it is coarser. If you listen to both films without the picture, it is quite difficult to identify both voices as coming from the same actor.
>
> *(Chion 1999: 174)*

After Kress and van Leeuwen and O'Toole wrote their 'grammars' of visual communication, a number of other 'grammars' of non-linguistic modes have been written, sometimes in outline, sometimes in detail – colour (Kress and van Leeuwen 2002; van Leeuwen 2010), typography (van Leeuwen 2006), gesture and movement (Kress *et al.* 2001, 2005; Martinec 2000; 2001) voice and music (van Leeuwen 1999), and space (Stenglin 2009), to name just a few. They have been used, not just in the educational studies already mentioned, but also in analyzing furniture, museum exhibitions, buildings, films, hypermedia, computer games, and more, as can be gleaned from the edited collections I have already cited. But describing semiotic resources by themselves, or analyzing the work of the modes separately, does not begin to show what happens when they are put together and integrated in multimodal texts and communicative events, and this is what I will turn to in the next section.

Word and image

In the 1960s, Roland Barthes distinguished between three types of image-text relation. In the first two, 'illustration' and 'anchorage', image and text convey essentially the same content, though, of course, in different ways, but the order in which they are read and understood creates a subtle difference. In the case of 'illustration', the text is primary, and the image interprets it in a particular context and for a particular audience. In the Middle Ages, Barthes said, 'illustration' was the dominant text-image relation. The most highly valued images illustrated the key stories and key concepts of the time – stories from the Bible and ancient mythology, and theological concepts. In the case of 'anchorage', images are not understood with reference to a text but seen as naturalistic representations of the world. Therefore, they do not come already impregnated with cultural meaning, but are potentially open to a variety of readings, so that they need linguistic interpretation, linguistic closure, both in terms of their denotation, of who or what they represent, and in terms of their connotation, of their more abstract, conceptual significance. 'Anchorage', Barthes said, began to take over as the dominant form of image-text relation in the Renaissance, when science and exploration encouraged images that could document the world, so making it amenable to scientific labelling, classification and interpretation. In the case of 'relay', Barthes' third category, there is no redundancy between text and image. Text and image do not 'say the same thing' but convey different, complementary content. In the case of 'dialogue scenes' in films and comic strips, for instance, the image shows the speakers while what they say is conveyed linguistically. Text and image therefore depend on each other to convey the whole of the content, a relation which, today, is becoming increasingly significant.

Martinec and Salway (2005) have provided the most detailed Barthes-inspired account of the semantics of text-image relations. The core of their approach was a distinction between the relative status of text and image and their logico-semantic relationship. When image and text are equal in status, they said, the whole of the image connects to the whole of the text. An image may, for instance, show a group of people walking to a courthouse while the text says 'Janklow walks up to the courthouse with his legal team'. Image and text can be equal in both 'independent' ('anchorage' and 'illustration') and 'complementary' ('relay') image-text relations. If a newspaper article about the actions of a politician is illustrated by a photographic portrait of that politician, then that image relates only to part of the text, only to the politician, not to his or her actions. The status of the image can therefore be likened to that of a subordinate clause in a sentence.

Martinec and Salway's account of the logico-semantic relationships was based on Halliday's theory of conjunction (1985). They first of all distinguished different types of 'elaboration', instances where the text 'rephrases' the image in some way (as in Barthes' anchorage), or the image the text (as in Barthes' 'illustration'). In the case of 'exposition' image and text are at the same level of generality; in the case of 'exemplification' either the text is more general than the image, or the image more general than the text, as in a skull-and-crossbone icon accompanied by the words 'high voltage'. 'Extension' is then the addition of new, related information (as in Barthes' 'relay'). The captions of paintings in art books, for instance, may 'extend' the image by adding details that cannot be seen, such as the year in which the painting was created, and the museum that owns it. They also introduced the possibility of 'enhancement', where the text may add a 'circumstantial' element to the image, or vice versa – for instance the location or timing of an event, or its reason or result. And finally they included the relation of 'projection' – the relation between the image of a speaker and his or her words (this may also include the relation between a 'thinker' and his or her thoughts, as indicated by thought bubbles in comic strips).

Martinec and Salway's approach took its cues from the linguistics of conjunction and complex clause construction. But it is also possible to approach text-image relations from the other, visual, end, using theories of visual composition to explain the relation between text and image. These two approaches do not contradict each other. People are perfectly capable of understanding multimodal texts at two or more levels simultaneously. Kress and van Leeuwen ([1996] 2006) have suggested that the spatial 'zones' of pictures, pages and screens (left and right; top and bottom; centre and margins) interrelate textual elements, regardless of whether they are visual (e.g. images) or textual (e.g. text boxes), by providing them with specific 'information values'. To start with left and right, if there is polarization (some kind of difference or contrast) between an element placed on the left and an element placed on the right, then the left element will be understood as the Given, as a departure point for the message that is, or should be, already familiar to the reader or viewer, while the right element will be understood as the New, the element that contains the information the message is trying to get across. This left-right information flow clearly corresponds to the left-right mode of writing and reading in Western culture, and is indeed reversed in cultures that write from right to left.

When there is vertical polarization, polarization between an element placed in the upper and an element placed in the lower section of a picture, page or screen, the top element is the Ideal, the idealized or generalized essence of the message, and the bottom element the Real, contrasting with the Ideal in presenting factual details, or documentary evidence, or practical consequences. In single-page magazine advertisements, for instance, the Ideal usually depicts the 'promise' of the product, the glamour or success it will bring to consumers, or of the sensual satisfaction it will give them, while the Real shows the product itself and provides factual information about it.

The Centre, finally, is another key compositional zone. Instead of polarizing the elements of the composition, the Centre unifies them, providing the Margins that surround it with a common meaning or purpose. In a Rank Xerox company brochure, for instance, the Centre represented a happy, indeed overjoyous, Rank Xerox employee, and the words that surrounded him suggested the various ways in which Xerox makes its employees happy by 'recognizing and rewarding' their efforts.

Such compositional schemas are multimodal for two reasons. They can apply to any kind of spatial configuration, whatever its mode – image, text, museum display, stage design, architectural facade – and they can integrate different kinds of element (e.g. text and image) into a multimodal whole. But it is a different kind of integration from that described by Martinec and Salway. The connections it establishes between elements are visual rather than verbal, informational rather than semantic, and geared towards hierarchies of importance and attention rather than to internal, logical coherence. Again, verbal integration and visual integration have their own logics, their own epistemologies.

Rhythm

Kress and van Leeuwen's account of visual composition describes a spatially based form of integrating different modes. Its time-based counterpart is rhythm (van Leeuwen 2005).

Rhythm provides cohesion, bundling speech, action and music together, and segmenting the resulting multimodal whole into the communicative moves that propel it forward. And rhythm is also the physical substratum, the *sine qua non* of all human action. Everything we do has to be rhythmical and in all our interactions we synchronize with others as finely as musical instruments in an orchestra. Without rhythm we fall over and trip each other up.

Analyzing multimodality in films brings out how it is now the rhythm of speech, now the rhythm of action, now the rhythm of music, which provides the framework with which the signs of other semiotic modes are aligned. Figure 47.2 analyzes a short excerpt from Hitchcock's *North by Northwest* in which the rhythm is carried by the dialogue. The rhythmic accents that provide the 'beat' are in italics. The rhythmic phrases are enclosed in brackets and the 'nuclear accent', the key moment of each phrase, is capitalized as well as italicized. Double brackets enclose larger rhythmic units which are also, and at the same time, larger narrative moves. Note the increase in tempo and tension at the start of the second of these units, where Eve says 'Wait a minute.' Elements other than speech – the edits of the film, the gestures of Thornhill and Eve – find their place within the temporal order of the speech rhythm. The cuts (indicated by a vertical line across all the rows) coincide with stressed syllables, the gestures with the boundaries between rhythmic phrases. Even when there is no speech, towards the end of the excerpt, the timing of the cuts still follows the rhythm initiated by the preceding speech.

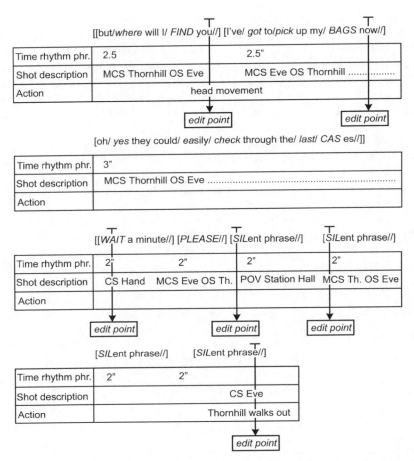

[[but/*where* will I/ *FIND* you//] [I've/ *got* to/*pick* up my/ *BAGS* now//]

Time rhythm phr.	2.5	2.5"
Shot description	MCS Thornhill OS Eve	MCS Eve OS Thornhill ....
Action	head movement	

edit point   edit point

[oh/ *yes* they could/ *easily*/ *check* through the/ *last*/ *CAS* es//]]

Time rhythm phr.	3"
Shot description	MCS Thornhill OS Eve ....
Action	

[[*WAIT* a minute//] [*PLEASE*//] [*SIL*ent phrase//]   [*SIL*ent phrase//]

Time rhythm phr.	2"	2"	2"	2"
Shot description	CS Hand MCS Eve OS Th.		POV Station Hall	MCS Th. OS Eve
Action				

edit point   edit point   edit point

[*SIL*ent phrase//]   [*SIL*ent phrase//]

Time rhythm phr.	2"	2"
Shot description		CS Eve
Action		Thornhill walks out

edit point

Figure 47.2 Rhythmic analysis of an excerpt from *North by Northwest* (Alfred Hitchcock 1959)

Rhythm not only integrates the different modes but also frames and delineates the communicative moves of the unfolding text, here the moves of the narrative. The excerpt immediately precedes the famous scene in which Thornhill (Cary Grant) is attacked by a cropduster plane. Eve Kendall (Eva Marie Saint) has just told Thornhill when and where to meet a mysterious man called Kaplan. What Eva knows, and what Thornhill does not know, is that the meeting is a trap and that Thornhill will be attacked. After some perfunctory lines of dialogue, during which the audience is left to wonder whether Eve will intervene, there is a change of pace. Tension rises. At the last minute Eve seems to have second thoughts. 'Wait a minute', she says, 'Please.' A tense silence hangs between them. But the moment passes, and Thornhill leaves to board his train.

Figure 47.3 shows a brief scene from an anonymous travel documentary called *Latin American Rhapsody*. The shots of mothers and babies have neither continuity of action, nor continuity of commentary or dialogue. It is the musical rhythm which provides cohesion here – edits and gestures are aligned to the musical accents and the boundaries of musical phrases, underlining the expository structure of the short scene, which forms a mini-catalogue of ethnic variety in Latin America.

In sum, the different modes in the multimodal texture – actors' movements, dialogue, music – are integrated in a time-based structure, just like the parts of the different instruments in an

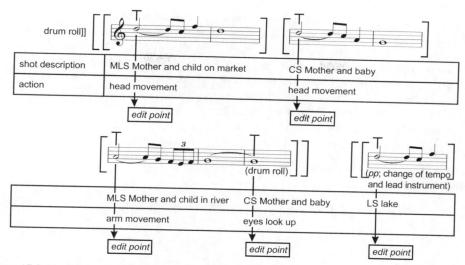

Figure 47.3 Rhythmic structure of *Latin American Rhapsody*

orchestral composition. Any one of them can carry the main 'beat', or the more incidental percussive accents, and the role division between the modes can shift as the text unfolds. What unites them is an element they all possess: rhythm.

Future developments

Multimodality analysis is a relatively new enterprise. There is much room for further development of the approaches discussed in this chapter, and for new applications. It is nevertheless possible to list a few desirables for the future development of multimodality as a branch of applied linguistics. I will focus on three: the need for self-reflexivity; the need for attending to cultural diversity; and the need for engaging with technology.

To start with self-reflexivity: as my examples have shown, multimodality is a multi-disciplinary field. It needs to draw on different disciplines, for instance, in the case of the visual mode, on functional linguistics as well as on art and design theory. To be effective, it needs to combine different methods, for instance discourse analysis and ethnography. And to be able to not just describe, but also explain multimodal practices, it requires detailed cultural-historical contextualization, both in the study of semiotic resources, and in the study of their uses in specific institutional settings. But there has perhaps not been enough discussion of just how these various disciplines should interact – what each can and cannot achieve, and how they are best combined. The eagerness of multimodal analysts to rush into new territories and explore new data, is understandable, but needs to be balanced by moments of critical self-reflection.

As for the need to focus on cultural diversity, to date multimodality has predominantly looked at 'Western' modes and 'Western' ways of using them. But just as linguistics has been immensely enriched by the study of languages which express radically different meaning systems in radically different ways, multimodality would also be much enriched by engaging with cultural diversity, and by mining the rich resources of anthropological literature.

Finally, there is a need to engage with technology. In the past, technology has often been seen as a means for recording and/or distributing communicative artefacts and events which does not affect them semiotically. However, today's multimodal technologies – ubiquitous writing softwares such as Word, Excel, PowerPoint, etc., and Internet-based social media – are themselves semiotic resources which build in constraints and affordances that deeply influence, not only what can be 'said' and how in these media, but also how the different semiotic modes they include can combine. A multimodal approach to studying technologically mediated communication, combining close attention to their built-in resources and structuring devices, as well as to the way these are used in different settings, would have much to contribute to our understanding of contemporary mediated communication.

With so much work still to be done, multimodality is certain to play an important role in helping to build the applied linguistics of the future and enabling it to face the tasks ahead.

Related topics

critical discourse analysis; discourse analysis; linguistic ethnography; media; systemic functional linguistics

Further reading:

Jewitt, C. (ed.) (2009) *The Routledge Handbook of Multimodality*, London, Routledge. (A representative and up-to-date collection of approaches to and applications of multimodal analysis.)

Kress, G. (2010) *Multimodality*, London, Routledge. (This book brings together Kress' influential work on the development of multimodal literacy in young children, on multimodality in education, and on the social semiotics which underlies this work.)

Kress, G. and van Leeuwen, T. (2006) *Reading Images: The Grammar of Visual Design*, 2nd edn, London, Routledge. (An extended and widely used Halliday-inspired account of the 'language' of visual communication.)

Norris, S. and Jones, R. (eds) (2005) *Discourse in Action: Introducing Mediated Discourse Analysis*, London, Routledge. (Many of the papers in this book build on Ron and Suzie Scollon's approach to the multimodal analysis of face-to-face interaction.)

van Leeuwen, T. (2005) *Introducing Social Semiotics*, London, Routledge. (The third part of this book deals extensively with the ways different modes can be integrated into multimodal texts.)

References

Arnheim, R. (1969) *Visual Thinking*, Berkeley and Los Angeles: University of California Press.

——(1974) *Art and Visual Perception*, Berkeley and Los Angeles: University of California Press.

——(1982) *The Power of the Centre*, Berkeley and Los Angeles: University of California Press.

Barthes, R. (1967) *Elements of Semiology*, S. Heath (trans.) London: Jonathan Cape.

——(1977) *Image, Music, Text*, S. Heath (trans.) London: Fontana.

——(1983) *The System of Fashion*, New York: Hill and Wang.

Birdwhistell, R. (1973) *Kinesics in Context: Essays on Body Motion Communication* Harmondsworth: Penguin.

Chion, M. (1999) *The Voice in Cinema*, New York: Columbia University Press.

Fairclough, N. (2000) *New Labour, New Language?* London: Routledge.

Goodwin, C. (2001) 'Practices of seeing visual analysis: an ethnomethodological approach', in T. van Leeuwen and C. Jewitt (eds) *Handbook of Visual Analysis*, London: Sage.

Hall, E. (1966) *The Hidden Dimension*, New York: Doubleday.

Halliday, M. A. K. (1978) *Language as Social Semiotic: The Social Interpretation of Language and Meaning*, London: Edward Arnold.

——(1985) *An Introduction to Functional Grammar*, London: Edward Arnold.

Jewitt, C. (2006) *Technology, Literacy and Learning: A Multimodal Approach*, London: Routledge.

Jewitt, C. (ed.) (2009) *The Routledge Handbook of Multimodality*. London: Routledge.

Jones, R. (2009) 'Technology and sites of display', in C. Jewitt (ed.) *The Routledge Handbook of Multimodal Analysis*, London: Routledge.

Knox, J. (2007) 'Visual-verbal communication on online newspaper home pages', *Visual Communication* 6(1): 19–55.

Kress, G. (1997) *Before Writing: Rethinking the Paths to Literacy*, London: Routledge.

——(2003) *Literacy in the New Media Age*, London, Routledge.

Kress, G., Jewitt, C., Bourne, J., Franks, A., Hardcastle, J., Jones, K. and Reid, E. (2005) *English in Urban Classrooms: A Multimodal Perspective on Teaching and Learning*, London: Routledge.

Kress, G., Jewitt, C., Ogborn, J. and Tsatsarelis, C. (2001) *Multimodal Teaching and Learning: The Rhetorics of the Science Classroom*, London: Continuum.

Kress, G. and van Leeuwen, T. (1998) 'Front pages: the (critical) analysis of newspaper layout', in A. Bell and P. Garrett (eds) *Approaches to Media Discourse*, Oxford: Blackwell.

——(2001) *Multimodal Discourse: The Modes and Media of Contemporary Communication*, London: Arnold.

——(2002) 'Colour as a semiotic mode: notes for a grammar of colour', *Visual Communication* 1(3): 343–68.

——([1996] 2006) *Reading Images: The Grammar of Visual Design*, 2nd edn, London: Routledge.

Levine, P. and Scollon, R. (eds) (2004) *Discourse and Technology: Multimodal Discourse Analysis*, Washington, DC: Georgetown University Press.

Lupton, E. (2004) *Thinking with Type: A Critical Guide for Designers, Writers, Editors and Students*, New York: Princeton Architectural Press.

Martinec, R. (2000) 'Types of processes in action', *Semiotica* 130(3–4): 243–68.

——(2001) 'Interpersonal resources in action', *Semiotica* 135(1–4): 117–45.

Martinec, R. and Salway, A. (2005) 'A system for image-text relations in new (and old) media', *Visual Communication* 4(3): 337–72.

Matejka, L. and Titunik, I. R. (eds) (1976) *Semiotics of Art: Prague School Contributions*, Cambridge: MA, MIT press.

Metz, C. (1974a) *Film Language*, New York: Oxford University Press.

——(1974b) *Language and Cinema*, The Hague: Mouton.

New London Group (1996) 'A pedagogy of multiliteracies: designing social futures', *Harvard Educational Review* 66: 60–92.

Norris, S. (2002) 'The implication of visual research for discourse analysis: transcription beyond language', *Visual Communication* 1(1): 97–121.

——(2005) 'Habitus, social identity, the perception of male dominations – and agency?', in S. Norris and R. Jones (eds) *Discourse in Action: Introducing Mediated Discourse Analysis*, London: Routledge.

Norris, S. and Jones, R. (eds) (2005) *Discourse in Action: Introducing Mediated Discourse Analysis*, London: Routledge.

Ochs, E. (1979) 'Transcription as theory', in E. Ochs and B. B. Schiefflin (eds) *Developmental Pragmatics*, New York: Academic Press.

O'Halloran, K. (ed.) (2004) *Multimodal Discourse Analysis: Systemic-Functional Perspectives*, London: Continuum.

Ormerod, F. and Ivanovic, R. (2002) 'Materiality in children's meaning-making practices', *Visual Communication* 1(1): 65–92.

O'Toole, M. (1994) *The Language of Displayed Art*, Leicester: Leicester University Press.

Pittenger, R. E., Hockett, C. F. and Danehy, J. J. (1960) *The First Five Minutes*, Ithaca, NY: Cornell University Press.

Scollon, R. (2001) *Mediated Discourse: The Nexus of Practice*, London: Routledge.

Scollon, R. and Scollon, S. (2003) *Discourses in Place-Language in the Material World*, London: Routledge.

——(2004) *Nexus Analysis: Discourse and the Emerging Internet*, London: Routledge.

Stenglin, M. (2009) 'Space odyssey: towards a social semiotic model of 3D space', *Visual Communication* 8(1): 35–64.

Stork, D. G. (ed.) (1997) *HAL's Legacy*, Cambridge, MA: MIT Press.

Unsworth, L. (ed.) (2008) *Multimodal Semiotics*, London: Continuum.

van Leeuwen, T. (1999) *Speech, Music, Sound*, London: Macmillan.

——(2000) 'Visual racism' in M. Reisigl and R. Wodak (eds) *The Semiotics of Racism: Approaches in Critical Discourse Analysis*, Vienna: Passagen Verlag.

——(2005) *Introducing Social Semiotics*, London: Routledge.

——(2006) 'Towards a semiotics of typography', *Information Design Journal* 14(2): 139–55.

——(2008) *Discourse and Social Practice: New Tools for Critical Discourse Analysis*, New York: Oxford University Press.

——(2009) 'Parametric systems: the case of voice quality', in C. Jewitt (ed.) *The Routledge Handbook of Multimodal Analysis*, London: Routledge.

——(2010) *The Language of Colour: An Introduction*, London: Routledge.

van Leeuwen, T. and Caldas-Coulthard, C. (2004) 'The semiotics of kinetic design', in D. Banks (ed.) *Text and Texture: Systemic Functional Viewpoints on the Nature and Structure of Texts*, Paris: L'Harmattan.

Ventola, E., Charles, C. and Kaltenbacher, M. (eds) (2004) *Perspectives on Multimodality*, London: Continuum.

Index

Aarons, D. and Akach, P. 367
Abad Florescano, A. 265
Abberton, E, and Fourcin, A. 114
Abbs, B. et al. 189
Abdous, M. et al. 201
Abercrombie, D. 377
Abrahamsson, N. and Hyltenstam, K. 176
Achard, M. and Niemeier, S. 621
acoustic analysis 511
acquisition: acquisition research, language
    socialization and 290–91; additional
    languages, multilingualism and 407–8, 409;
    alternative theories of language acquisition
    481; child language acquisition 657;
    language, psycholinguistics and 480–83; of
    linguistic forms 290; modal expressions,
    acquisition of 290–91; sign languages 366;
    see also SLA (Second Language
    Acquisition)
activity theory 279
additive bilingualism 235
additive multilingualism 403
Ädel, A. 249
A'Dhahab, S.M. 220
Adolphs, S. xi, 543, 547, 597–610
Adolphs, S. and Carter, R. 438
Adolphs, S. and Lin, P.M.S. 7, 75, 164, 201,
    440, 455, 565
Adolphs, S. et al. 602
affective disposition 288–89
Agar, M. 84–86
ageing, language and 124–34; bilingualism,
    executive control functions and 128–29;
    bilingualism in ageing 127–30, 133–34;
    cognitive advantages of bilingualism in
    ageing 127–30; cognitive processes, potential
    for change in 130; CR (Cognitive Reserve)
    127, 128; debates in 131–32, 134; dynamic
    systems perspective 126; dynamic systems
    theory 126, 134; elderspeak 130–31;
    electronic media 133, 134;

electrophysiological techniques 132;
historical perspective 124–25; identity,
language and ageing 130–31; influence of
new technology 132–33; labour migration
and 126–27; *Le langage des déments*
(Irigaray, L.) 124; *Language, Society and the
Elderly* (Coupland, N. et al.) 131; life-span
developmental psychology 124–25; main
issues, critical discussion of 125–27; MMSE
(Mini Mental State Examination) 129;
multilingualism and 129, 405–6;
neuroimaging 132–33, 134; synaptic
pruning 130
Ageing and Society (Coupland, J.) 131
Agnihotri, R.K. 233
Ahlsén, E. xi, 5, 112, 406, 460–71, 562
Aijmer, K. 605
Aitchison, J. 475, 563
Akbari, R. 194, 220
Akiyama, Y. 648
Alderson, J.C. 265
Alderson, J.C. et al. 266
Aldridge, M. 147
Alemán, A.M.M. and Wartman, K.L. 201
Alexander, N. 229
Alim, H.S. 519
Alim, H.S. et al. 356
Allan, K. 560, 561
Allen, I.E. and Seaman, J. 206
Allison, D. and Carey, J. 221
Allwood, J. 467
Allwright, D. 163, 189, 194, 195, 275, 276, 277
Allwright, D. and Bailey, K. 276, 277
Allwright, D. and Hanks, J. 194
Alo, M.A. and Mesthrie, R. 378
Altenberg, B. 604
alternative medicine 99–100
American National Corpus (ANC) 598
American Sign Language: lexis 572; sign
    languages 360
Amunts, K. et al. 130

Heath, S.B. and Street, B.V. 522
Heffer, C. 145, 147
Hegel, G.W.F. 488
hegemony, linguistic imperialism and 389
Heller, M. 15, 17, 20, 88, 89, 319, 321, 355, 356, 407, 413, 518
Heller, M. and Martin-Jones, M. 391, 407, 518
Hellermann, J. 175
Henderson, A. 590
Herdina, P. and Jessner, U. 126, 407
Heritage, J. 73, 76, 435
Heritage, J. and Maynard, D.W. 84, 88, 102
Heritage, J. and Sefi, S.W. 85
Heritage, J. and Stivers, T. 97
Heritage, J. et al. 102, 104, 105
heritage speakers 161
Herman, R. and Roy, P. 367
Herman, V. 545, 546, 548
Hermans, T. 41
Herring, S.C. 201, 203, 204, 438
Hervey, S. and Higgins, I. 40
Heugh, K. 233
Hewings, M. and Nickerson, C. 28
Heydon, G. 85, 144
Hickey, L. 545
Hidalgo Tenorio, E. 455
Hillegas, M.B. 259
Hindmarsh, J. et al. 89, 91
Hinkel, E. 249
Hinton, Leanne 16
Hintzman, D.L. 482
historical corpora 598
historical dictionaries 54
historical-structural approach to LPP 14
historicity, culture as portable 309
Hitchcock, A. 677, 678
Ho, M.L. and Platt, J. 377
Hobbs, P. 141, 147
Hobsbawm, Eric J. 229, 230
Hobson, A.J. et al. 221
Hockett, C.F. 503
Hodge, R. 69, 634
Hodson, S. and Jardine, B. 115
Hoey, M. 58, 656
Hoffman, D. 675
Hogan-Brun, G. and Wolff, S. 232
Holec, H. 187
Holland, J.H. 660, 661
Holland, V.M. and Fisher, F.P. 201
Holliday, A. 161, 193
Holmberg, B. et al. 206
Holmes, J. 250, 332, 335, 337, 338, 340, 341
Holmes, J. and Meyerhoff, M. 337, 338
homonymy 573
Hoover, D.L. 547
Hopper, P.J. 491, 492, 656, 660
Hopper, R. and Drummond, K. 73

Horace 40
Horkheimer, M. 446
Hornberger, H. and Chick, J.K. 518, 519
Hornberger, N.H. 525, 526
Hornberger, N.H. and Corson, D. 233
Hornby, A.S. 54, 56, 188
Hornby, A.S. et al. 56
Horner, B. and Trimbur, J. 390
Horst, M. et al. 577
Horton, D. and Wohl, R.R. 67, 68
Hosoda, Y. 438
hospital consultations 99–100
Hotopf, W.N. 478
Houck, C.L. 507
House, J. 40, 47, 394, 396
House, J. et al. 307
Houston, Whitney 76
Howard, R. and Brown, G. 252
Howard, S.J. xiii–xiv, 3, 111–23
Howard, S.J. and Heselwood, B.C. 115
Howatt, A.P.R. and Widdowson, H.G. 215, 348
Hsu, J. et al. 102
Hu, A. 307, 308
Hu, M. and Nation, I.S.P. 576
Hubbard, P. and Siskin, C.B, 201
Hubbell, A.F. 503
Huber, M. 376
Huber, M. and Dako, K. 379
Huddleston, R. and Pullum, G. 565
Huebner, T. 408
Hufeisen, B. and Prokop, M. 307
Hull, G. 89, 520
Hull, G. and Nelson, M. 533, 536
Hull, G. and Schultz, K. 533, 534
Hulstijn, J. 577
humanist approaches 187–88
Humboldt, Wilhelm von 305
Hume, David 472
Humphris, G.M. and Kaney, S. 104
Hung, E. and Wakabayashi, J. 49
Hunston, S. 605
Hunt, M. et al. 217
Hussein, Violet 140
Hutchby, I. 72, 73, 205
Hutchby, I. and Wooffitt, R. 72, 73, 435
Hutchinson, J. and Smith, A.D. 345
Hutchinson, T. and Waters, A. 244, 246
Hyams, N. 646
Hyams, N. and Wexler, K. 646
Hyland, K. 28, 243, 246, 247, 248, 250, 252–53
Hyland, K. and Anan, E. 218
Hyland, K. and Milton, J. 249
Hyland, K. and Tse, P. 250
Hyltenstamm, K. and Stroud, C. 127
Hymes, D. 157, 188, 436, 515, 516, 517
Hymes, D. and Gumperz, J. 309
Hymes, influence of 517

Talamas, A. et al. 580
Talbot, M. 335, 438
TALIS (Teaching and Learning International Survey) 223
TalkBank 113
Tallal, P. and Piercy, M. 117
Talmy, L. 611, 614, 616, 617, 621, 657
Talmy, S. 291, 324
Tannen, D. 335
target domains in cognitive linguistics 614
Tarone, E. 172, 174
Tarone, E. et al. 180, 239
task demands in business communication 29–30
Tasker, T. xvi, 6, 487–500
Taub, S. 360
Tayao, M.L.G. 376, 377
Taylor, C. 18
Taylor, J.R. 592, 616, 656, 657
TBI (Traumatic Brain Injury) 117–18
TBLT (Task-Based Language Teaching) 189
teachers: communicative practices of 289; language learning and education 161–63; teacher cognition 218
teaching: goals and objectives in 191, 192; language and 164, 167; language learning and education 161–63; materials, EAP and 252; novice teachers 222; roles of teachers, learners and instructional materials 191, 192; situational language teaching 188; subject teachers, cooperation with 246; teacher training, EAP and 252; see also foreign language teaching; LTE (Language Teacher Education); methodology in language teaching
technology: advances in translating and interpreting 48; change in sign languages and 369; engagement with, multimodality and 679–80; identity 325–26; impact on corpus linguistics 606–7; influence of new technology on ageing, language and 132–33; influence of World Englishes 383–84; influences of new technology in medical communication 102; innovation in institutional discourse 89, 91; institutional discourse, technical jargon 87; language learning and education 166–67; language testing 268–70; language testing, technical aspects 266–67; in neurolinguistics research 464–65; role in language and culture 312–13; technical vocabulary 575
technology and language learning 200–212; blended learning 206; blogs 203, 205–6; chat 203, 205; communicative motivation 203; community participation 208–10, 211; computer-mediated games 209; *Cultura* Project 202, 207; cultural interactions 201,

203, 204, 205, 206, 208, 209, 210, 211; digital technology 200–201; discussion forums 208–9; distance learning 206; electronically mediated communication (EMC) 202–6, 211; *Facebook* 202; focused role-play tasks 209–10; genre in EMC 203–4, 211; instructional applications 206, 211; intercultural competence, development of 207–8; massively multiplayer online games (MMOG) 209; mediation in EMC 204–6, 211; 'medium' metaphor 201–2; metaphors of 201–2; multimedia environments 209; multimedia language courses 206; *MySpace* 202; non-instructional applications 206, 211; online discourse 204; online intercultural encounters 206–10; projects 202; register in EMC 204, 205; *Second Life* 202, 209; *Skype* 202; 'tool' metaphor 201, 202; 'tutor' metaphor 201, 202; virtual reality games 209; wikis 203
Tedick, D. 216, 219
television: media discourse 70; multimodality 668
Tembe, J. and Norton, B. 325
temporal-spatial specification 292–98
ten Have, P. 72
Ten Thije, J.D. and Zeevaert, L. 403
TESOL Quarterly 318–19, 320–21, 325
TESOL (Teaching English to Speakers of Other Languages) 215, 217, 218, 223
test delivery 269
test design 268
test development 268–69
test validation 260–62, 263; see also language testing
text: context and discourse in discourse analysis 433–34; and image, relationship between 450, 675–76; text-task relationships in business communication 26–27; textual metafunctions 628
textbooks: and teaching materials, corpora and 250; textbook knowledge 194
theoretical directions in linguistic ethnography 518
theoretical frameworks in generative grammar 641–43
theoretical lexicography 53
theoretical linguistics: applied linguistics, generative grammar and 645; phonetics, phonology and 593
theoretical strands in translating and interpreting 41
theories of language, identity and 319–20
Thinking and Speaking (Vygotsky, L.) 662
Thomas, M. 648
Thompson, P. 249, 251
Thornborrow, J. 72, 85, 144

Warren, R. 585
Warriner, D.S. xvii, 6, 325, 423, 529–40
Warschauer, M. 325, 423, 531, 536
Warschauer, M. and Grimes, D. 201
Warschauer, M. and Kern, R. 202, 308
Washabaugh, W. 362
Waters, A. 222
Watson, G. and Zyngier, S. 547
Watson-Gegeo, K.A. and Gegeo, D.W. 288
Watson-Gegeo, K.A. and Nielsen, S. 288
Watt, D. 509
Watt, D. and Milroy, L. 508
Watt, I. xvii, 3, 96–110
Watts, D.J. and Strogatz, S.H. 661
Watts, J.H. 102
wave studies 505–6
Weatherall, A. 337
WebCorp 606
Weber, J.-J. 545, 546, 548
Weber, Max 83, 86
Wedell, E.G. 70
Wee, L. xvii, 11–23, 19, 406, 562
Weedon, C. 311, 319
Weinreich, U. et al. 508, 660
Weir, C.J. 266
Weir, C.J. and O'Sullivan, B. 261, 262
Weir's socio-cognitive framework 261–62
Weismer, G. et al. 115
Wells, G. 491, 494
Wells, J.C. 585
Weltens, B. and Grendel, M. 578
Weltens, B. et al. 578
Wenger, E. 279, 282, 323, 331, 340
Werker, J.F. and Tees, R.C. 483
Werlich, E. 433
Wernicke, Carl 461, 462
Werth, P. 548
Wertsch, J. et al. 487
Wertsch, J.V. 488
Wesche, M. and Paribakht, T.S. 577
West, C. 84, 85
West, M. 54
West, M.P. and Endicott, J.G. 55
West, R. 245, 246
Westerfield, K. 28
Westley, F. et al. 584
Wetherell, M. 340
Whale, J. 70
Whalen, M.R. and Zimmerman, D.H. 73
Whitaker, H. et al. 460
White, C. 206, 325
White, L. 173, 564
White, P. 68, 70
White, P.R.R. 448
Whitehill, T.L. and Lee, A. 114
whole language movement 189
Whorf, B. 305, 491

Widdowson, H.G. 3, 6, 25. 27, 157, 188, 306, 431, 432, 433, 439, 440, 455, 529, 546, 547, 567, 605
Wierzbicka, A. 307
wikis 203
Wilcox, S. 364
Wiley, T.G. 14, 15
Wilkins, D.A. 158, 188
Wilkinson, R. 114
Williams, A. 356
WIlliams, A. and Kerswill, P. 508
Williams, R. et al. 31
Willis, J. 159, 189, 461
Willis, J. and Willis, D. 189
Winitz, H. 187
Wittgenstein, Ludwig 54, 491, 613
WM (Working Memory) 474
Wodak, R. 89, 308, 445, 446, 449, 450
Wodak, R. and Reisigl, M. 450
Wolfram, W. 501, 503
Woll, B. xviii, 359–72
Woll, B. and Sutton-Spence, R. 5, 565
Wong Fillmore, L. 294
Wood, D. et al. 494
Woodbury,H. 145
Woods, D. 162, 216
Woodward, J. 367
Woolls, D. 140
Word Routes (Cambridge University Press) 64
WordNet 64
words: lexical characteristics of 573–74; lexis and 572; mental lexicon, words and 572; word and image 675–77; word-based determinants of learnability 577; word grammar 558; word lists 600–601; word sketches 59–60
World Englishes 373–84; absence of tense marking 377–78; count/noncount nouns 378; dental fricatives 376; development of New Englishes, stages in 381–82; ELF (English as a Lingua Franca) 373, 375, 382, 383, 384; final consonant clusters 376–77; invariant tags 378–79; linguistic features, examples of 375–81; linguistic features, general trends in 380–81; linguistic motivations 374–75; models of 373–74; recent developments 382–83; rhythm 377; technology, influence of 383–84; tense marking, absence of 377–78; topic prominence 379–80
Wortham, S. 291, 516
Wortham, S. and Rymes, B. 517
Wray, A. 476, 604, 605, 657
Wright, E.B. et al. 98, 102
Wright, M.W. 396
Wright, S. 11
Wright, T. and Bolitho, R. 222
writing: multimodality 668; neurolinguistics 467–68; psycholinguistics 478; studies in media discourse, written vs spoken 69–72